studies in jazz

Institute of Jazz Studies
Rutgers—The State University of New Jersey
General Editors: Dan Morgenstern and Edward Berger

ELLINGTONIA

*The Recorded Music of
Duke Ellington and His Sidemen*

Fifth Edition

Compiled by

W. E. Timner

Studies in Jazz, No. 54

The Scarecrow Press, Inc.
Lanham, Maryland • Toronto • Plymouth, UK
2007

SCARECROW PRESS, INC.

Published in the United States of America
by Scarecrow Press, Inc.
A wholly owned subsidiary of The Rowman & Littlefield Publishing Group, Inc.
4501 Forbes Boulevard, Suite 200, Lanham, Maryland 20706
www.scarecrowpress.com

Estover Road
Plymouth PL6 7PY
United Kingdom

British Library Cataloguing in Publication Information Available

Library of Congress Cataloging-in-Publication Data

Timner, W. E., 1930–
  Ellingtonia : the recorded music of Duke Ellington and his sidemen / compiled by W.E. Timner. —
5th ed.
     p. cm. — (Studies in jazz ; no. 54)
  Includes index.
  ISBN-13: 978-0-8108-5889-3 (hardcover : alk. paper)
  ISBN-13: 978-0-8108-6028-5 (pbk. : alk. paper)
  ISBN-10: 0-8108-5889-4 (hardcover : alk. paper)
  ISBN-10: 0-8108-6028-7 (pbk. : alk. paper)
  1. Ellington, Duke, 1899–1974—Discography. I. Title.

ML156.5.E45T5 2007
016.78165092—dc22   2007030240

CONTENTS

EDITOR'S FOREWORD

It was eleven years ago that, in my foreword to the fourth edition of W. E. Timner's masterpiece, I apologetically quoted myself from the 1988 introduction to the effect that "the universe of Duke Ellington's recorded music is a constantly expanding one."

And now, 33 years after Ellington's death, that still holds true and is, as the author points out in his introduction, the rationale for his fifth expanded and refined edition that we take great pride in presenting to the also constantly expanding constituency of Ellingtonians worldwide.

It was 60 years ago that this Ellingtonian-to-be acquired his first sample of the master's work, the OKeh (blue label) of "Black And Tan Fantasy" backed with "What Can A Poor Fellow Do?" Duke was the first jazz artist I collected, and in those days of 78's, each newly acquired disc became a close friend, every note was savored over and over again. Nowadays, boxed sets of CDs present the listener with not just a meal but a marathon banquet, if consumed all at once.

But what is important is that the music is out there, and this book is a marvelous guide to the incredibly rich lode that is the living legend of the man who some very knowledgeable people call the greatest of American composers—no modifiers attached.

Mr. Timner has made *ELLINGTONIA* more user-friendly, more inclusive and more accurate than ever before, doing the kind of meticulous and dedicated work that requires great patience and diligence, and the scholars, students, players and collectors who will make good use of it owe him a great debt of gratitude. Though he claims that his work is not a discography, I am not alone in having found it perhaps more useful (and reliable) than that genre of research tools. It is, however, one of a kind in the ever-growing field of jazz literature, and to know it and use it is to learn to love it. As Duke might have put it, *it is* beyond categorization, just like the music itself.

Dan Morgenstern

INTRODUCTION

This book—like its predecessors—is dedicated to all collectors and lovers of the music of Duke Ellington. This compilation contains the recorded music of Duke Ellington and his sidemen as far as known to date, comprising studio recordings, movie soundtracks, concerts, dance dates, radio broadcasts, telecasts and private recordings, released as well as not (yet) released.

Also included are recordings by the Ellington sidemen made under their own names and with other bands, while they have been associated with the Ellington organization. However, sometimes the "Ellingtonians" have joined up with other big bands for recording dates without any solo responsibilities. It would have gone beyond the scope of this book to also include these sessions. On the other hand, included are recordings of some of the "Ellingtonians" who have left the Ellington orchestra temporarily, like Johnny Hodges, Cootie Williams and Lawrence Brown, for they have always been "True Blue Ellingtonians."

The amount of new material, which was released since the printing of the fourth edition of *ELLINGTONIA* (1996), plus changes to the existing material due to ongoing research, have tempted me to once again take up the challenge of rewriting this tome. It gave me the opportunity to add a few features and make some changes, which will make the book more user friendly. Again I have resisted the temptation to write a discography, because this would have expanded into several volumes, defeating the purpose of this book, to serve as a one-volume handy reference source for my fellow collectors. And besides, there are a few fine discographies available on the market.

In this edition all of the studio facilities the band used for its recordings could be listed. Most of the time the recordings were made at the recording studios of the label the band was under contract with. In later years, when Ellington was not under contract for a specific label, he rented studio time at locations of his choice and at his own expense to make his so-called stockpile recordings. Also listed in the new section "On the Air" are the radio and TV stations which broadcast the band's music, as far as they could be identified.

Some critics suggested to leave out the un-issued live recordings, which would bloat the volume, without contributing much otherwise. Admittedly, some of these recordings are barely adequate as far as the sound quality is concerned, however, there are some that are brilliant. (By the same token, wouldn't under such criteria the inclusion of some of the early acoustic recordings become questionable?) However, these live recordings, often done by dedicated amateurs, give us something that the studio is unable to transmit: The working band on the road and in concert. Often one can sense the wear and tear of a string of grueling one-nighters, but more often than not the band gets elevated by the enthusiastic response of the audience. Without the live recordings we would hardly have any documentation of and idea about Ellington's output during his last years, because the studio sessions became quite scarce from 1972 on. All of the live recordings listed in the book are accessible to the dedicated collector, which is reason enough for their inclusion.

The reader will notice a large number of footnotes mentioning that particular songs are derivatives of others. In the early years of the recording business, Jazz was an unregulated art form, shared by its performers, and melodies were freely borrowed and varied. Musicians traveled and carried the music as they remembered it, with them. This might explain some of Duke Ellington's early works, like for example *Creole Love Call* and *Mood Indigo*, and his many usages of *Tiger Rag*, issued under other titles, and for which he took composer credits. Ellington recomposed and rearranged the tunes so radically that they became his own creations. As we all know, Ellington also borrowed heavily from himself and in doing so, revived and expanded on his own past achievements.

A change was made to the *Chronological Section* by deleting takes which can be considered irretrievably lost. However, to maintain the completeness of the book, titles which have been recorded, but remained un-issued, were kept in and are shown in brackets. Due to the extended indices, the section *Attendance List* became superfluous.

My very special thanks go to Sjef Hoefsmit, Steven Lasker and Jerry Valburn who assisted me with fresh material and valuable advice.

At this point I would also like to pay tribute to the late Benny H. Aasland, whose *Wax Works of Duke Ellington* (1954) was the first Duke Ellington discography, which inspired many of us fledgling collectors. Benny was also the founder of the *Duke Ellington Music Society (DEMS),* which is still very much alive and issues its quarterly bulletins.

I am also grateful to the authors and editors who gave permission to use their books and publications as reference works:

The Wax Works of Duke Ellington (1954, 1978, 1979), Benny H. Aasland, Järfälla, Sweden.
Bulletins, Duke Ellington Music Society (DEMS), Meerle, Belgium.
Jazz Records 1942-1980, vol. 6, Duke Ellington, Ole J. Nielsen; Jazz Media ApS, Copenhagen, Denmark.
Jazz and Ragtime Records (1897-1942), sixth ed., Brian Rust; Malcolm Shaw, editor.
    Highlands Ranch, CO: Mainspring Press, 2002.
Duke Ellington—Day by Day and Film by Film, Dr. Klaus Stratemann; Jazz Media AsP, Copenhagen,
    Denmark.
The New DESOR, 1999, Luciano Massagli and Giovanni M. Volonté, Milan, Italy.
Duke Ellington's Music for the Theatre, © 2001 John Franceschina; by permission of
    McFarland & Company, Inc., Box 611, Jefferson, NC 28640. www.mcfarlandpub.com.

I recommend any of the above publications to those who have a serious interest in expanding their knowledge about the work of Duke Ellington.

This book does not claim to be the last word on this subject, but it will most probably be mine.

W. E. Timner
Toronto, Ontario

Guide for Users

LIST OF ORCHESTRAS

This section consists of three parts

a) The band names under which the original recordings of Duke Ellington have been released.

b) The names of orchestras and bands (other than his own) or persons, Duke Ellington recorded with.

c) The names of orchestras and bands or persons, the Ellington sidemen (the "Ellingtonians") recorded with.

KEY TO ABBREVIATIONS

a) PERSONNEL: To save space, the names of all performers mentioned in this book have been reduced to four letters or less. A dash (/) between two names means that only either one of the two musicians attended the session.

b) LABELS: Also here abbreviations were used to save space.

c) INSTRUMENTS ETC: The same as for b) applies.

d) OTHERS: The same as for b) applies.

CHRONOLOGICAL SECTION

This part contains all known recordings by Duke Ellington in chronological sequence. The headings for each session are as given on the original labels. Each session or performance has been listed individually, with location and band personnel, when known. Broadcasts/telecasts are indicated in brackets next to the venue. Sessions or events of which only either date, location, number of titles or other particulars are known, have been listed with whatever specifics at hand. Recordings for which a confirmed date is not known, are listed in the time slot where they are assumed to belong. As a rule, only such titles and events are listed, which were in fact recorded. With the advent of the portable tape recorder and later the cassette recorder, the number of private recordings of mainly public events increased significantly. (Hence the reader will find events—mostly concerts and dance dates—which look incomplete.) Often the quality of these recordings is poor, however, they are valuable for the collector regardless and are therefore listed together with the professional recordings.

All recordings have been listed under date lines. If two or more events took place on one and the same date, the date line has not been repeated, however, changes in location or personnel of the subsequent event are mentioned.

There is a bit of discographical confusion about some of the live performances as issued on LP, cassette and CD. Sometimes the material is identified as originating from one single event, but in fact are compiled from several occasions. In the case of early broadcasts it may be the case that they were transcribed from several prerecordings. This book lists the titles under the date on which they were actually recorded, unless mentioned otherwise. If the date of broadcast or telecast differs from the recording date, explanation is given in a footnote for the particular session. More specific information with regards to network, station and program can be found in the section "On the Air," where all known broadcasts and telecasts are listed chronologically.

When Duke Ellington relinquished his piano chair to somebody else during a recording session or concert, the entire event is listed notwithstanding.

Because of the ever growing volume of this book, I have conceded to include only the takes which are known to have survived in the form of a test pressing, acetate or tape. Notwithstanding these restrictions and in keeping up with the principle of giving a complete record of Duke Ellington's body of work, sessions or titles of which no known recording exists, are shown in an abbreviated form and the titles in brackets.

As in the previous editions, only the labels under which the original recordings have been released, are shown. However, when the original release on a non-commercial label was later issued on a commercial label, only the commercial label is mentioned, because this would be the one the average collector would have access to. In any case, master numbers are given, when known.

The letters in brackets following the recording date, indicate the kind of recording:

> P = Public performance (in front of a live audience).
> S = Studio recording (recording studio or studio-like environment).
> T = Movie soundtrack (includes rehearsed TV taping sessions).

The book does not differentiate between rehearsed (recording sessions) and unrehearsed (radio transcriptions) studio sessions, because this would have set double standards and confused the issue. Radio transcriptions can be recognized by their different numbering system or the lack of it.

The song titles are spelled as they have appeared on the record label of the original release. Variant spellings used on recording sheets or reissues as well as alternate titles, are mentioned in footnotes. It is apparent that sometimes Ellington had his own ways with words, but who are we to question these little idiosyncrasies of the maestro.

THE ELLINGTONIANS

Who is an "Ellingtonian"? He or she is a person who stayed with the Ellington organization for any length of time and has made a significant contribution to the style and/or general performance of the band. By this definition, some big name guests do not qualify. It also leaves no room for transient personnel hired occasionally to fill a vacant seat in the band when one of the regulars was out of action, or to enhance the band's volume for a special arrangement or event.

We even have to make a destinction between the "Ellingtonians." There are those who can be considered natural or born "Ellingtonians," like Johnny Hodges or Cootie Williams, for example. They continued to be "Ellingtonians" even during their prolonged absences from the Ellington organization. I have followed the tracks they and others falling into the same category have made throughout their respective careers, until they have rejoined the Ellington band. In the case of Hodges, all recordings are listed which he made during his time away from the Ellington band, whereas in other cases only the recordings of typical band numbers—mostly Ellington and Strayhorn compositions—are included.

Then there are those whom we can consider "Ellingtonians" only during their active engagement with the Ellington band. However, I have made some exceptions to the rule in cases of outstanding performances by men like Rex Stewart, Barney Bigard and Ben Webster, for example, although they have not rejoined the Ellington organization.

As a rule, all outside activities of the regular members of the Ellington band while they were serving in the band have been listed. In doing so, it becomes quite obvious that many of the "Ellingtonians" did a lot of moonlighting and it is interesting to see and hear how they fared in different environments and without the safety net of the Ellington orchestra behind them.

During the early days of the band, men like Charlie Irvis worked for and recorded with a multitude of bands and it can be argued whether or not it is of any value to give a complete account of all these outside activities. However, I have tried to be as consistent as possible in this respect, and it is up to the reader to draw his or her own line.

Then there are the vocalists. I tend to believe that many of my fellow collectors will agree with me that Mr. Ellington had a rather peculiar taste as far as the band's vocalists were concerned, and there were only a few exceptions to the rule. I have to admit, however, that this is to a certain extent a matter of personal taste, and I have therefore applied the same rules for the vocalists as for the instrumentalists of the band.

In this section only the actually issued titles and takes are listed, with the exception of a few taped interviews, which are circulating among collectors. The initials of the "Ellingtonians" in the personnel line-ups are italicized to make them better visible.

INDEX OF TITLES

This part is an alphabetical listing of all song titles mentioned in both the Chronological and Ellingtonians sections of the book, with their recording dates. Also included are compositions by Duke Ellington which have never been recorded, particularly his music for the stage, most of which was never performed. Posthumously produced musicals or other stage works, based on Duke Ellington's music in which his songs were used as incidental music have not been included.

The number of alternate takes of a particular tune recorded in any one session are given in brackets before the recording date. Repeat performances or encores of one and the same title, for example in concert performances, are listed individually.

All entries referring to the section "The Ellingtonians" are italicized, which will make it easier for the reader to trace the titles in either one of the two chronologies.

INDEX OF MUSICIANS

Here all musicians mentioned in the book are listed in alphabetical order under their correct and full names. Nicknames are given in quotation marks. The abbreviated form of their names as used throughout the book is repeated in brackets. Following the names are the instruments played by the respective person on the recordings listed in the book. Finally, the page numbers will allow the reader to trace the musicians in either one of the chronologies. This section replaces the "Attendance List" contained in the previous editions.

GENERAL INDEX

This section contains all names of persons who are mentioned in the book but are not included in the "Index of Musicians," plus the names of bands and orchestras other than Duke Ellington and his sidemen under their own names. Also included are titles of motion pictures and shows as well as other events of importance or of general interest.

INDEX OF CITIES AND VENUES

This index was badly needed. To keep things as simple and concise as possible, the two related categories have been lumped together.

ON THE AIR

Although Duke Ellington never accomplished getting his own sponsored network series, he achieved a high degree of exposure, both on radio and television. The airshots from the Cotton Club brought his music in its early stages to the general public and stimulated record sales. By 1933—after he had left the Cotton Club and went touring—radio stations across America broadcast his live performances, without sponsorship. Later in his career, longer tenures at various other venues, like for example the Hurricane Club, were also broadcast on a regular basis. Otherwise, his work aired on radio and television consisted mainly of concerts, interviews and guest appearances, the cumulative effect of which, however, was of great commercial value. As is evident from the listing, Duke Ellington stayed on the air throughout his career and these performances constitute an integral and important part of his body of work. The information given is kept as concise as possible, and the cross-referencing with the "Chronological Section" will make it easy to use. I am aware that this section is probably not complete, however, it is a beginning and it should give future compilers who pick up after me, something to base their research on.

ADDENDA

The material listed in this section is not included in any of the foregoing sections.

LIST OF ORCHESTRAS

a) The original recordings of Duke Ellington have been released and listed under the following band names:

Cat Anderson & His Orchestra
Ivie Anderson & Her Boys From Dixie
Barney Bigard & His Jazzopaters
Barney Bigard & His Orchestra
Broadway Revellers
Frank Brown & His Tooters
Bunta's Storyville Jazz Band
Chicago Footwarmers
Coronets
Dixie Jazz Band
Duke's Big Four
Duke Ellington
Duke Ellington and ... (various persons/bands)
Duke Ellington & Billy Strayhorn
Duke Ellington & Friends
Duke Ellington & Herb Jeffries
Duke Ellington & His Award Winners
Duke Ellington & His Cotton Club Orchestra
Duke Ellington & His Famous Orchestra
Duke Ellington & His Group
Duke Ellington & His Jazz Group
Duke Ellington & His Kentucky Club Orchestra
Duke Ellington & His Memphis Men
Duke Ellington & His Men
Duke Ellington & His Octet
Duke Ellington & His Orchestra
Duke Ellington & His Orchestra with ... (various artists)
Duke Ellington & His Quartet
Duke Ellington & His Rhythm
Duke Ellington & His Septet
Duke Ellington & His Sextet
Duke Ellington & His Trio
Duke Ellington & His Washingtonians
Duke Ellington & Jimmy Blanton
Duke Ellington & Jimmy Grissom
Duke Ellington & Jimmy Woode
Duke Ellington & John Lamb
Duke Ellington & John Lamb with Tony Watkins
Duke Ellington & Paul Gonsalves
Duke Ellington & Ray Brown
Duke Ellington & Sam Woodyard
Duke Ellington & Tony Watkins
Ellingtonians
Duke Ellington Players
Duke Ellington's All Stars
Duke Ellington's Hot Five
Duke Ellington's Jazz Violins
Duke Ellington's Octet
Duke Ellington's Orchestra

Duke Ellington's Quartet
Duke Ellington's Quintet
Duke Ellington's Septet
Duke Ellington's Sextet
Duke Ellington's Spacemen
Duke Ellington's Trio
Duke Ellington's Washingtonians
Duke Ellington's Wonder Orchestra
Ellington Trio
Ellington Twins
Duke Ellington with ... (various persons/bands)
Duke Ellington with Rhythm Accompaniment
Georgia Syncopators
Milt Grayson
Sonny Greer & His Memphis Men
Harlem Footwarmers
Harlem Hot Chocolates
Harlem Music Masters
Johnny Hodges & His Orchestra
Hot Five
Earl Jackson & His Musical Champions
Lonnie Johnson's Harlem Footwarmers
Jungle Band
Louisiana Rhythmakers
Lulu Belle's Boy Friends
Memphis Bell Hops
Memphis Hot Shots
Irving Mills & His Hotsy Totsy Gang
Mills Ten Blackberries
New York Syncopators
Oscar Pettiford, His Cello & Quartet
Philadelphia Melodians
Cliff Roberts' Dance Orchestra
Six Jolly Jesters
Dick Sparling & His Orchestra
Rex Stewart & His 52nd Street Stompers
Rex Stewart & His Orchestra
Billy Strayhorn's Group
Billy Strayhorn Trio
Sunny & The D C'ns
Ten Blackberries/Black Berries
Ten Blackbirds/Black Birds
Ten Red Dandies
Traymore Orchestra
Joe Turner & His Memphis Men
Washingtonians
Whoopee Makers
Cootie Williams & His Rug Cutters
Chick Winters Orchestra

b) Duke Ellington (& His Orchestra/Group) also recorded with the following soloists/orchestras:

Eadie Adams
Larry Adler
Gussy Alexander
Steve Allen
All Star Band
All Star Orchestra
Louis Armstrong (& His All Stars)
Alice Babs
Mildred Bailey
Dick Baker
Baltimore Symphony Orchestra
Paul Baron Orchestra
Count Basie & His Orchestra
Beatrice Benjamin
Tony Bennett
Jay Blackton Orchestra
Ray Bloch Orchestra

Boston Pops Orchestra
Teresa Brewer
Aaron Bridgers
Lou Bring & His Orchestra
Florence Bristol
Buffalo Philharmonic Orchestra
California Youth Symphony Orchestra
Ray Charles
Cincinnati Symphony Orchestra
Cleveland Pops Orchestra
Cleveland Symphony Orchestra
Rosemary Clooney
Marie Cole
Nat King Cole
Ron Collier Orchestra
John Coltrane
Bing Crosby

Vic Damone
Wild Bill Davis & His Real Gone Organ
Detroit Symphony Orchestra
Dollar Brand Trio
Tommy Dorsey (& His Orchestra)
Dorsey Brothers
Ethel Ennis
Percy Faith Orchestra
Bert Farber Orchestra
Leonard Feather's Esquire All-Americans
Ella Fitzgerald
Sarah Forde
Vittorio Gassman
Stan Getz
Norman Granz
Stephane Grappelli
Adelaide Hall
Hamburg Symphony Orchestra
Coleman Hawkins
Woody Herman & His Orchestra
Billie Holiday
Mahalia Jackson
Zaidee Jackson
Jazz Piano Workshop
Alberta Jones
Jack Kane & His Music Makers
Chubby Kemp
Stan Kenton
Brooks Kerr
Frankie Laine
La Scala Symphony Orchestra
Paul Lavalle & The Chamber Music Society of Lower Basin
   Street
Marguerite Lee
Michél Legrand
London Philharmonic Orchestra
Los Angeles Symphony Orchestra
Muzzy Marcellino Trio
Barbara McNair
Jimmy McPhail
Yehudi Menuhin
Metronome All Stars
Miami Beach Symphony Orchestra
Million Dollar Band
Mills Brothers
Warren Mills & His Blue Serenaders

Miami Beach Symphony Orchestra
Million Dollar Band
Mills Brothers
Warren Mills & His Blue Serenaders
Charles Mingus
Johnny Nash
Nashville Symphony Orchestra
National Symphony Orchestra
New Haven Symphony Orchestra
Newport All Stars
New York Philharmonic Orchestra
North Texas State University Lab Band
Patti Page
Paris Symphony Orchestra
Performing Orchestra
Philadelphia Symphony Orchestra
Evelyn Preer
Alberta Prime (Pryme)
Quintones
Johnny Ray
Della Reese
Walter Richardson
Max Roach
Bill Robinson
San Diego Symphony Orchestra
Vic Schoen Orchestra
Scott Music Hall Orchestra
Raymond Scott Orchestra
Joya Sherrill
Dinah Shore
Frank Sinatra
Willie "The Lion" Smith
Snowden's Novelty Orchestra
Rex Stewart's All Stars
Stockholm Symphony Orchestra
Studio Orchestra/Band
Symphony of the Air Orchestra
Don Thompson Quartet
Teri Thornton
Jo. Trent & The D C'ns
John Scott Trotter Orchestra
Uwis Brass Band
Sarah Vaughan
Ozie Ware
Ethel Waters
Paul Whiteman & The Hall of Fame Orchestra

c) The Ellington sidemen recorded under the following band names and with the following bands/orchestras:

Larry Adler with John Kirby & His Orchestra
All Star Band
Cat Anderson
Cat Anderson & His Orchestra
Cat Anderson & The Ellington All Stars
Cat Anderson Sextet
Ivie Anderson
Harold Ashby & His Group
Harold Ashby & Paul Gonsalves
Mildred Bailey & Her Alley Cats
Mildred Bailey & Her Orchestra
Eugenie Baird & The Duke's Boys
Harold Baker & His Quartet
Harold Baker Ensemble
Harold Baker Sextet
Band
Count Basie All Stars
Josephine Beatty with The Red Onion Jazz Babies
Sidney Bechet & His New Orleans Feetwarmers
Louie Bellson
Louie Bellson & The Just Jazz All Stars
Tony Bennett & The Duke Ellington Orchestra
Emmett Berry Sextet
Barney Bigard & His Orchestra
Booker's Jazz Band
Johnny Bothwell's Swingtet

Kitty Brown
Lawrence Brown
Lawrence Brown All Stars
Ruth Brown with Budd Johnson's Orchestra
Willie Bryant with the Tab Smith Septet
Butterbeans & Susie with Eddie Heywood's Jazz Trio
Jackie Cain & Roy Kral
Cab Calloway & His Cab Jivers
Cab Calloway & The Duke Ellington Orchestra
Una Mae Carlisle
Harry Carney
Harry Carney All Stars
Harry Carney & Mercer Ellington
Harry Carney & The Duke's Men
Harry Carney's Big Eight
Cats & Chicks
Buddy Christian's Creole Five
Savannah Churchill with Al Killian & His Orchestra
C Jam All Stars
Nat King Cole & His Trio
Martha Copeland
Wilton Crawley & His Orchestra
Miles Davis Quintet
Wild Bill Davis All Stars
Wild Bill Davis & Johnny Hodges
Ellington All Stars

Duke Ellington All Stars
Mercer Ellington & His Orchestra
Ellington Gang
Ellingtonians
Mercer Ellington Octet with Jacques Butler
Mercer Ellington Septet
Esquire All-American Award Winners
Roy Evans
Herbie Field's Band
Ella Fitzgerald & Her Orchestra
Brick Fleagle & His Orchestra
Sarah Forde & Billy Strayhorn
Slim Gaillard & His Flat Foot Floogie Boys
Andy Gibson & His Orchestra
Tyree Glenn All Stars
Paul Gonsalves All Stars
Paul Gonsalves & Finn Enger
Paul Gonsalves & Friends
Paul Gonsalves & Harold Ashby
Paul Gonsalves & Johnny Hodges
Paul Gonsalves & Roy Eldridge
Paul Gonsalves & Sonny Stitt
Paul Gonsalves Quartet
Paul Gonsalves Sextet
Paul Gonsalves with Willie Cook and Enrique Villegas
Benny Goodman & His Orchestra
Gotham Stompers
Sonny Greer & His Rextet
Sonny Greer & The Duke's Men
Helen Gross with the Kansas City Five
Gulf Coast Seven
Al Hall Quartet
Edmund Hall's Swingtet
Jimmy Hamilton All Stars
Jimmy Hamilton & His Orchestra
Jimmy Hamilton & The Duke's Men
Jimmy Hamilton's Jazz Ensemble
Jimmy Hamilton with the Emitt Slay Trio
Lionel Hampton & His Orchestra
Coleman Hawkins & His Sax Ensemble
Coleman Hawkins Sextet
Rosa Henderson
Rosa Henderson with the Kansas City Five
Woody Herman & His Orchestra
Eddie Heywood & His Orchestra
Eddie Heywood Trio
Al Hibbler
Al Hibbler & His Orchestra
Al Hibbler & The Ellingtonians
Al Hibbler with Johnny Hodges & His Orchestra
Al Hibbler with the Harry Carney All Stars
Earl Hines & Johnny Hodges
Earl Hines & Paul Gonsalves
Earl Hines & The Ellingtonians
Earl Hines Quartet
Earl Hines Sextet
Johnny Hodges
Johnny Hodges All Stars
Johnny Hodges & Earl Hines
Johnny Hodges & Friends
Johnny Hodges & His Band
Johnny Hodges & His Orchestra
Johnny Hodges & The Duke's Men
Johnny Hodges & The Ellington Giants
Johnny Hodges & The Ellingtonians
Johnny Hodges & The Ellington Men
Johnny Hodges & the Harry Carney Sextet
Johnny Hodges & Wild Bill Davis
Johnny Hodges Trio
Johnny Hodges with Billy Strayhorn & The Orchestra
Johnny Hodges with Oliver Nelson & His Orchestra
Johnny Hodges with Orchestra
Johnny Hodges with the Al Waslon Trio
Johnny Hodges with the Claus Ogermann Orchestra
Johnny Hodges with the Lawrence Welk Orchestra
Johnny Hodges with the Stuttgart Light Orchestra

Bob Howard & His Orchestra
Alberta Hunter with Perry Bradford's Mean Four
Ivory Joe Hunter
Chubby Jackson & His Jacksonville Seven
Harry James & His Orchestra
Frankie "Half Pint" Jaxon
Cousin Joe with Leonard Feather's Hiptet
Johnson's Jazzers
Budd Johnson & The Four Brass Giants
Margaret Johnson with Clarence Williams' Blue Five
Margaret Johnson with Clarence Williams' Harmonizers
Jimmy Jones' Big Eight
Quincy Jones & His Orchestra
Kansas City Five
Chubby Kemp & Her All Stars
Billy Kyle's Orchestra
Roberta Lee
John Lewis All Stars
Virginia Liston with Clarence Williams' Blue Five
Mainstream Sextet
Sara Martin
Sara Martin with Clarence Williams' Blue Five
Sara Martin with Clarence Williams' Harmonizers
Viola McCoy
Viloa McCoy with the Kansas City Five
George McClennon's Jazz Devils
Metronome All Stars
Josie Miles
Josie Miles with the Choo Choo Jazzers
Josie Miles with the Jazz Casper
Josie Miles with the Kansas City Five
Lizzie Miles
Irving Mills & His Modernists
Julia Moody
Dwight "Gatemouth" Moore
Monette Moore
Monette Moore with the Choo Choo Jazzers
Thomas Morris & His Seven Hot Babies
Benny Morton Trombone Choir
Jelly-Roll Morton Trio
Gerry Mulligan—Johnny Hodges Quintet
Jimmy Mundy's Orchestra
Musical Stevedores
Ray Nance & Paul Gonsalves
Ray Nance & The Ellingtonians
New Orleans Blue Five
King Oliver & His Dixie Syncopators
Original Jazz Hounds
Alberta Perkins with the Jazz Casper
Oscar Pettiford & His Orchestra
Nat Pierce Orchestra
Netty Potter
Prestige Blues Swingers
Russell Procope's Big Six
Della Reese with Jimmy Hamilton Orchestra
Timme Rosenkrantz & His Barons
Timme Rosenkrantz & His Barrelhouse Barons
Tony Scott & His Orchestra
Tony Scott Quintet
Al Sears & His Orchestra
Joya Sherrill
Six Black Diamonds
Six Hot Babes
Clementine Smith with the Kansas City Five
Laura Smith with Clarence Williams' Harmonizers
Trixie Smith
Elmer Snowden & His Small's Paradise Orchestra
Joe Stafford
Rex Stewart All Stars
Rex Stewart & Cootie Williams
Rex Stewart & His Feetwarmers
Rex Stewart & His Orchestra
Rex Stewart & The Ellington Alumni All Stars
Rex Stewart's Big Eight
Rex Stewart's Big Seven
Billy Strayhorn

Billy Strayhorn All Stars
Billy Strayhorn & Bea Benjamin
Billy Strayhorn & His Orchestra
Billy Strayhorn & The Ellingtonians
Billy Strayhorn Septet
Billy Strayhorn with Dollar Brand & Bea Benjamin
Billy Strayhorn with the Paris String Quartet
Studio Band
Maxine Sullivan
Billy Taylor & His Orchestra
Billy Taylor's Orchestra
Eva Taylor
Eva Taylor with Clarence Williams' Harmonizers
Jack Teagarden's Big Eight
Clark Terry All Stars
Clark Terry Quintet
Clark Terry Septet
Clack Terry's Happy Horns
Texas Blues Destroyers
Lucky Thompson & His Orchestra
T-Bone Walker
Sippie Wallace with Clarence Williams' Harmonizers
Fats Waller & His Buddies

Dinah Washington
Dinah Washington with Eddie Chamblee's Orchestra
Dinah Washington with Jimmy Cobb's Orchestra
Laurel Watson
Ben Webster
Ben Webster All Stars
Ben Webster & Billy Strayhorn
Ben Webster & His Orchestra
Ben Webster Quartet
Ben Webster Quintet
Ben Webster with Strings
Ernie Wilkins & His Orchestra
Clarence Williams' Blue Five
Clarence Williams' Blue Seven
Clarence Williams' Stompers
Cootie Williams & His Orchestra
Cootie Williams Sextet
Nelson Williams & His Orchestra
Sandy Williams' Big Eight
Gerald Wilson & His Orchestra
Teddy Wilson & His Orchestra
Booty Wood All Stars
Jimmy Woode All Stars

KEY TO PERSONNEL

AB	Aaron Bell –b tu	
ABbs	Alice Babs –vcl p	
ABk	Albert Burbank –cl vcl	
ABky	Art Blakey –dr	
ABrd	Aaron Bridgers –p	
ABrn	Art Baron –tb	
ABst	Artie Bernstein –b	
AC	Alfred Cobbs –tb	
ACas	Al Casey –gt	
AChn	Al Cohn –ts	
ACht	Al Chernet –gt	
ACrk	Arthur Clark –ts	
AE	Allen Eager –ts	
AF	Andres Ford –tp	
AFkn	Aretha Franklin –vcl	
AFmr	Art Farmer –tp	
AFcs	Arlene Francis –vcl	
AH	Al Hibbler –vcl	
AHl	Adelaide Hall –vcl	
AHll	Al Hall –b	
AHrs	Arville Harris –cl as	
AHth	Al Heath –dr	
AHtr	Alberta Hunter –vcl	
AJ	Alberta Jones –vcl	
AJck	Ambrose Jackson –tp	
AK	Al Killian –tp	
AL	Al Lucas –b gt	
ALmx	Allen Lomax –vcl	
AM	Aake Malmquist –tp	
AMC	Alva McCain –ts	
AMgn	Al Morgan –b	
AMK	Al McKibbon –b	
AMo	Anita Moore –vcl	
AN	Albert Nicholas –cl as ts	
AO	Anthony Ortega –ts	
AOD	Anita O'Day –vcl	
AP	Alberta Prime –vcl	
APns	Alberta Perkins –vcl	
APor	Al Porcino –tp	
APry	Arthur Prysock –vcl	
APsn	Aake Persson –tb	
AR	Al Rubin –tp	
ARln	Adrian Rollini –ts	
ARly	Aura Rully –vcl	
ARms	Alfredo Remus –b	
ARs	Allen Reuss –gt	
AS	Al Sears –ts	
ASh	Arvell Shaw –b	
AShp	Archie Shepp –ts	
AShw	Artie Shaw –cl	
ASm	Allem Smith –tp	
ASms	Art Simmons –p	
ASrs	Andrew Sisters –vcl	
ASs	Aaron Sachs –cl	
ASt	Al Stoller –dr	
AStr	Arne Styhr –b	
AT	Aaron Thompson –tb	
ATlr	Art Taylor –dr	
AW	Arthur Whetsel –tp	
AWas	Al Waslon –p	
AWkr	Al Walker –dr	
AWms	Al Williams –p	
AWtn	Alec Wyton –org	

BA	Bernard Addison –gt
BAhn	Bob Ahearn –gt
B&CC	Benny & The Crinoline Choir –vcl
B&S	Butterbeans & Susie –vcl
BAr	Bernard Archer –tb
BaW	Barry Wood –vcl
BB	Barney Bigard –cl ts dr

BBab	Babs Barbineau –vcl
BBal	Benny Bailey –tp
BBgn	Bunny Berigan –tp
BBgs	Bunny Briggs –tap vcl
BBjm	Beatrice Benjamin –vcl
BBld	Butch Ballard –dr
BBly	Buster Bailey –cl
BBr	Billy Bauer –gt
BBrn	Bob Brown –ts
BBrs	Billy Byers –tb
BBry	Bill Berry –tp vib
BBsh	Bob Bushnell –b
BBtl	Billy Butler –gt
BBwn	Bob Brown –b
BC	Bing Crosby –vcl
BChr	Buddy Christian –gt bj
BCk	Buddy Clark –b
BClk	Bill Clark –dr
BClt	Buddy Colette –as fl
BCmn	Bill Coleman –tp
BCpr	Buster Cooper –tb
BCrk	Buddy Clark –vcl
BCrs	Bob Cranshaw –b
BCrt	Benny Carter –as tp
BCtl	Buddy Catlett –b
BCtn	Buck Clayton –tp arr
BCx	Baby Cox –vcl
BD	Wild Bill Davis –org p
BDds	Baby Dodds –dr
BDF	Buddy DeFranco –cl
BDhm	Bobby Durham –dr
BDon	Bob Donaldson –dr
BDsn	Bill Dodson –vcl
BDvs	Bobby Davis –tap
BDxn	Ben Dixon –dr
BE	Bass Edwards –bb
BEsh	Bill English –dr
BEvs	Bill Evans –p
BF	Brick Fleagle –gt
BFld	Bernard Flood –tp
BFlr	Bob Fuller –cl as
BFmn	Bud Freeman –ts
BFmr	Betty Farmer –vcl
BFrm	Bob Freedman –ts vcl
BG	Benny Goodman –cl
BGar	Bob Garcia –ts
BGbr	Barry Gailbraith –gt
BGbs	Bob Gibbons –gt
BGhm	Bill Graham –as
BGlw	Bernie Glow –tp
BGmn	Betty Glaman –hrp
BGrc	Buddy Greco –p
BGrd	Bobbie Gordon –vcl
BGrn	Bennie Green –tb vcl
BH	Bob Haggart –b
BHck	Bobby Hackett –tp
BHgs	Billy Higgins –vcl
BHik	Billy Hicks –tp
BHks	Bud Hicks –b
BHol	Billie Holiday –vcl
BHrd	Bob Howard –vcl
BHrs	Bill Harris –tb
BJ	Bruce Johnson –wb
BJms	Benny James –gt
BJsn	Budd Johnson –cl ts
BK	Barney Kessel –gt
BKle	Billy Kyle –p
BKrr	Brooks Kerr –p
BL	Bernie Leighton –p org
BLau	Baby Laurence –tap
BLcn	Bobby Leecan –gt dr
BLcs	Buddy Lucas –hca

BLH	Barrie Lee Hall –tp
BM	Bubber Miley –tp
BMN	Barbara McNair –vcl
BMo	B. Morrow –vcl
BMr	Bill Moore –tp
BMre	Bass Moore –b
BMtn	Benny Morton –tb
BP	Bennie Payne –p vcl
BPl	Budd Powell –p
BPmr	Buster Perrymore –vcl
BPsn	Buddy Pearson –as
BPtn	Bill Pemberton –b
BPtr	Brock Peters –vcl
BPwl	Benny Powell –tb
BR	Betty Roché –vcl
BRbn	Bill Robinson –b
BRch	Buddy Rich –dr
BRd	Bill Richard –p
BRly	Ben Riley –dr
BRnd	Barney Richmond –b
BRoy	Benny Roy –tp
BRsn	Bill Robinson –tap vcl
BRso	Bartelemy Rosso –gt
BS	Billy Strayhorn –p cel dr vcl
BSh	Bud Shank –as fl
BSht	Bobby Short –p vcl
BSm	Billy Smith –vcl
BT	Billy Taylor –b
BTlr	Billy Taylor –p
BW	Ben Webster –ts cl p
BWbr	Bob Wilber –ss cl as
BWd	Booty Wood –tb
BWht	Bob White –p org
BWmn	Britt Woodman –tb
BWn	Bea Wain –vcl
BWsn	Bob Wilson –tb
BY	Bill Yance –b

CA	Cat Anderson –tp
C&A	Coles & Atkins –tap
CAS	Cliff Adams Singers –vcl
CB	Chick Bullock –vcl
CBas	Count Basie –p
CBk	Charles Booker –as
CBke	Ceele Burke –gt
CBlg	Claude Bolling –p
CBlr	Charles Blareau –b
CBrn	Clifford Brown –tp
CBsn	Carl Brisson –vcl
CC	Chester Crumpler –vcl
CCbs	Call Cobbs –p
CCC	Carthage College Choir –vcl
CClb	Chris Columbus –dr
CCle	Cozy Cole –dr
CCnd	Conte Condoli –tp
CCor	Chick Corea –p
CCrs	Chuck Connors –tb
CCS	Central Connecticut State College Singers –vcl
CCsn	Cass Carson –vcl
CCwl	Candy Caldwell –vcl
CCwy	Cab Calloway –vcl
CD	Carlos Diernhammer –p
CF	Cecily Ford –vcl
CG	Catherine Gotthofer –hrp
CGrn	Charlie Green –tb
CGrs	Charlie Grimes –cl ss as
CGst	Claude Gousset –tb
CH	Chauncey Haughton –cl as
ChB	Charlie Barnet –chm
CHdy	Clarence Holiday –gt
ChG	Christian Garros –dr

ChH	Charlie Harris –b		DJ	Dave Jackson –dr		EShp	Ernie Shepard –b vcl
ChJ	Chubby Jackson –b		DjR	Django Reinhardt –gt		EShy	Ed Shaughnessy –dr
ChJn	Christian Jensen –b		DK	Don Kirkpatrick –p		ESly	Emitt Slay –gt
CHks	Claude Hopkins –p		DL	Dorothy Loudon –vcl		ESpn	Edgar Sampson –as bs
CHms	Charlie Holmes –cl ss as ts		DLW	Dave LeWinter –p		ET	Ed Thigpen –dr
ChP	Charlie Parker –as		DM	Dave Matthews –ts		ETlr	Eva Taylor –vcl
ChR	Charlie Rouse –ts		DMtn	Dean Martin –vcl		EV	Enrique Villegas –p
CHrt	Clyde Hart –p		DO	Dillon Ober –dr		EVal	Erkki Valaste –dr
ChS	Charlie Shavers –tp		DP	Dolores Parker –vcl		EVsn	Eddie Vinson –as vcl
CHth	Cliff Heathers –tb		DR	Don Redman –as arr		EW	Ethel Waters –vcl
ChW	Chick Webb –dr		DRiv	Dave Rivera –p		EWlk	Ernie Wilkins –ts
CHwk	Coleman Hawkins –ts		DRse	Della Reese –vcl		EWls	Earl Williams –dr
CI	Charlie Irvis –tb		DRsn	Dick Robertson –vcl		EWms	Elbert Williams –ts cl
CJ	Claude Jones –tb		DS	Davey Schildkraut –as		EWrn	Earle Warren –as
CJck	Cliff Jackson –p		DSev	Doc Severinsen –tp ct		EWtn	Earl Washington –p
CJoe	Cousin Joe –vcl		DSh	Don Shirley –p			
CJon	Charlie Johnson –tb		DShe	Dinah Shore –vcl		FA	Fred Avendorph –dr
CJsn	Charlie Johnson –tp		DT	Dave Tough –dr		FB	Florence Bristol –vcl
CK	Chubby Kemp –vcl		DTho	Dickie Thompson –gt		FBlr	Frank Butler –dr
CKay	Connie Kay –dr		DV	Dick Vance –tp arr		FC	Frank Capp –dr
CKrs	Carl Kress –gt		DW	Dickie Wells –tb		FD	Frank Dunlop –dr
CL	Carl Lynch –b gt		DWls	Dave Wells –bs		FdR	Frank de la Rosa –b
ClR	Clarence Ross –tb		DWsn	Dick Wilson –dr		FE	Finn Enger –acc
CM	Charles Mingus –b		DWtn	Dinah Washington –vcl		FFst	Frank Foster –ts
CN	Calvin Newborn –gt					FG	Fred Guy –bj gt
Cnd	Camero Candido –bgo		EA	Edie Adams –vcl		FGn	François Guin –tb
CP	Cue Porter –as		EAm	Eugene Amaro –as		FGpd	François Galépedes –dr
CPn	Cecil Payne –ts		EAsn	Ed Anderson –tp		FGrn	Freddie Green –gt
CPrt	Carl Pruitt –b		EB	Edgar Brown –b		FJ	Freddie Jenkins –tp
CPry	Charlie Pryme –p		EBfd	Eddie Barefield –tp		FJck	Fletcher Jackson –dr
CR	Connie Russell –vcl		EBkd	Everett Barksdale –gt		FL	Frankie Laine –vcl
CS	Charlie Smith –dr		EBrd	Eugenie Baird –vcl		FLwe	Francis Lowe –ts
CSC	Cyrus St. Clair –bb		EBry	Emmett Berry –tp		FM	Frank Marvin –vcl
CSct	Cecil Scott –bs		EBst	Earl Bostic –as		FP	Flip Phillips –ts
CSds	Charles Saudrais –dr		EBtn	Eileen Barton –vcl		FPC	Fifth Avenue Presbyterian Church
CSrn	Clementine Smith –vcl		EC	Ernie Caceres –bs			Choir –vcl
CSms	Cliff Smalls –p		ECdn	Eddie Condon –gt		FPS	Frank Parker Singers –vcl
CT	Clark Terry –tp flh vcl		EChb	Eddie Chamblee –ts		FR	Frank Rullo –cga
CTd	Clarence Todd –vcl		ECsl	Eduardo Casalla –dr		FRhk	Frank Rehak –tb
CV	Charlie Ventura –as		ED	Eddie Davis –ts		FS	Frank Sinatra –vcl
CW	Cootie Williams –tp tb vcl		EDk	Edward Duke –p		FSkt	Frank Skeete –b
CWls	Clarence Williams –p vcl		EDwl	Edgar Dowell –p		FSt	Fred Stone –tp flh
CWn	Chuck Wayne –gt		EE	Ernest Elliott –cl ts		FW	Francis Williams –tp
CWsn	Claude Williamson –p		EEns	Ethel Ennis –vcl		FWlr	Fats Waller –p gt
			EF	Ella Fitzgerald –vcl		FWne	Frances Wayne –vcl
DB	Dave Burns –tp		EFkl	Ed Finckle –p		FWrs	Four Wanderers –vcl
DBag	Doc Bagby –org		EG	Eric Gale –gt		FWss	Frank Wess –as ts fl
DBbr	Dave Barbour –gt		EGm	Eydie Gormé –vcl		FWts	Freddy Waits –dr
DBck	Dave Black –dr		EH	Earl Hines –p			
DBcl	Danny Barcelona –dr		EHd	Eddie Heywood –p		GA	Georgie Auld –ts
DBks	Duke Brooks –p		EH4	Emmanuel Hall Quartet –vcl		GArv	George Arvanitas –p
DBly	Dave Bailey –dr		EHll	Edmund Hall –cl		GAx	Gussie Alexander –vcl
DBmn	David Bowman –p		EHpr	Ernie Harper –p		GB	Gerard Badini –ts
DBnk	Dany Bank –bs		EHwd	Eddie Heywood, Jr. –p		GBr	George Butcher –p
DBrl	Daniel Bruley –tb		EJ	Elvin Jones –dr		GBrt	Guy Béart –vcl
DBs	Don Byas –ts		EJms	Elmer James –b		GBsh	Garvin Bushell –ss cl
DBst	Denzil Best –dr		EJns	Elayne Jones –tym		GCC	Grace Cathedral Choir –vcl
DBut	Don Butterfield –bb		EJsn	Eddie Johnson –ts		GCh	George Chisholm –tb
DClk	Dick Clark –tp		EK	Earl Knight –p		GChp	Gus Chappel –tb
DD	Dorothy Donegan –p		EKnl	Ed Knill –dr		GD	George Duvivier –b
DDW	Dee Dee Warwick –vcl		EL	Evan Long –vcl		GDrs	George Dorsey –as
DE	Duke Ellington –p ep cel tom vcl		ELck	Eddie Locke –dr		GE	Gene Easton –bs
DF	Don Fagerquist –tp		EM	Ernest Myers –b		GF	George Francis –bj
DFbr	Dick Fullbright –b		EMay	Earl May –b		GG	Goodie Goodwin –vcl
DFks	Don Francks –vcl		EMcC	Ed McConney –dr		GGbs	Gérard Gambus –p
DFre	Don Frye –p		EMls	Ed Mullens –tp		GG4	Golden Gate Quartet –vcl
DFtz	David Fitz –xyl		EMrw	Esther Marrow –vcl		GGrn	Grant Green –gt
DG	Dizzy Gillespie –tp		EN	Eddie Nicholson –dr		GGwn	George Goodwin –b
DGdn	Dexter Gordon –ts		EP	Evelyn Preer –vcl		GHbt	Gregory Herbert –as
DGM	Dwight Gatemouth Moore –vcl		EPtn	Edward Preston –tp		GHdr	Geoffrey Holder –tap
DGrd	Devonne Gardner –vcl		ER	Ernie Royal –tp		GHll	Gene Hull –as
DH	Dick Hyman –org		ERch	Emil Richards –p vib		GJ	George Jean –tb
DHff	Darlene Huff –vcl		ERsn	Eli Robinson –tb		GJns	George Jones –dr
DHmr	Daniel Humair –dr		ES	Elmer Snowden –bj		GJsn	Gus Johnson –dr
DHrs	Doug Harris –ts		ESaf	Eddie Safranski –b		GK	Gene Krupa –dr

GL	Guy Lafitte –ts
GM	Gerry Mulligan –bs
GMbg	Gunnar Medberg –tb
GMC	George McClennon –cl
GMcr	Grachen Moncur –b
GMlr	Gene Miller –dr
GMrw	George Morrow –b
GN	Gertrude Niesen –vcl
GP	Georgie Price –tap
GR	Gilbert Rovére –b
GTH	G.T. Hogan –dr
GTt	Grady Tate –dr
GW	Gerald Wilson –tp arr
GWbb	George Webb –vcl
GWn	George Wein –p
GWrn	Guy Warren –dr
GWtn	George Washington –tb
GWz	Gus Wallez –dr
HA	Hayes Alvis –b
HAsh	Harold Ashby –ts cl
HB	Harold Baker –tp
HBo	Hoyt Bohannon –tb
HBsh	Herb Bushler –b
HBwn	Hillard Brown –dr
HBxt	Helen Baxter –vcl
HC	Harry Carney –bs cl as bcl vcl
HChb	Henderson Chambers –tb
HCol	Honi Coles –tap
HCpr	Harry Cooper –tp
HCro	Harold Cromer –vcl
HE	Harry Edison –tp
HEds	Hank Edmonds –p
HEls	Herb Ellis –gt
HF	Herbie Fields –as ts cl
HFlg	Herb Flemming –tb
HG	Herman Grimes –tp
HGdm	Harry Goodman –b
HGlr	Herb Geller –as
HGms	Henry Grimes –b
HGrs	Helen Gross –vcl
HH	Henry Hicks –tb
HJ	Herb Jeffries –vcl
HJC	Hall Johnson Choir –vcl
HJck	Hayward Jackson –dr
HJms	Harry James –tp
HJns	Herbie Jones –tp arr
HJo	Hank Jones –p
HJon	Harold Johnson –tp
HJs	Harold Jones –tp
HJsn	Hilton Jefferson –as
HK	Harold King –tap
HL	Herbie Lovelle –dr
HLd	Harold Land –ts
HMC	Herman McCoy Choir –vcl
HMG	Howard McGhee –tp
HMn	Harold Minerve –as fl pic cl bs
HP	Herb Pomeroy –tp
HPJ	Half Pint Jaxon –vcl
HR	Harold Randolph –vcl kaz
HRA	Henry "Red" Allen, Jr. –tp
HRch	Henry Richards –bs
HS	Hal Stein –ts
HSct	Hazel Scott –p vcl
HSgr	Hal Singer –ts
HSml	Harry Smiles –ob
HSvr	Horace Silver –p
HWrd	Helen Ward –vcl
HWst	Hal West –dr
IA	Ivie Anderson –vcl
IBH	Ingvar Blicher-Hansen –vcl
IBS	Irving Bunton Singers –vcl
IC	Inez Cavanaugh –vcl
IJ	Illinois Jacquet –ts

IJH	Ivory Joe Hunter –p vcl
IM	Irving Mills –vcl kaz
IMng	Irving Manning –b
JA	Juan Amalbert –cga
JAC	John Alldis Choir –vcl
JAnd	John Anderson –tp tb
JAsh	John Ashworth –ts
JAW	Jo Anne Woodward –vcl
JB	Jimmie Blanton –b
JBck	Joe Beck –gt
JBH	Johnny "Brother" Hodges –dr
JBjm	Joe Benjamin –b
JBlr	Jacques Butler –tp
JBr	John Blair –vcl v
JBrd	Jacki Byard –ep
JBrt	Jimmy Britton –vcl
JBsh	Joe Bushkin –p
JBty	Josephine Beatty –vcl
JBwl	Johnny Bothwell –as
JBwn	Joe Brown –b
JBws	John Blowers –dr
JC	John Collins –gt
JCbb	Jimmy Cobb –dr
JCfd	Jimmy Crawford –dr
JCft	Joe Comfort –b
JCH	J.C. Higginbotham –tb
JChm	Jimmy Cheatham –tb
JChr	June Christy –vcl
JCJ	J.C. Johnson –p
JCl	John Coles –tp
JCld	Jimmy Cleveland –tb
JClk	June Clark –tp
JCmn	Jeff Castleman –b
JCn	Jackie Cain –vcl
JCrg	James Craig –p
JCrr	John Carroll –tp
JCrs	James Cross –vcl
JCS	Joe Cornell-Smelser –acc p
JCte	John Conte –vcl
JCtr	John Coltrane –ts ss
JD	Jerome Darr –gt
JDbg	Joe Darensbourg –cl
JDch	Jimmy Deuchar –tp
JDle	Jimmy Dale –vcl
JDn	Johnny Dunn –ct tp
JDrs	Jimmy Dorsey –ct as
JDs	Joe Davis –chm
JDvs	Jackie Davis –p org
JE	Jean Eldridge –vcl
JF	Jimmy Forrest –ts
JFds	Jackie Fields –as
JFrz	Jake Frazier –tb
JG	Joe Garland –ts cl
JGfn	John Griffin –ts
JGn	Jimmy Green –p
JGrl	Jimmy Gourley –gt
JGrn	Johnny Guarnieri –p
JGrs	John Graas –frh
JGsm	Jimmy Grissom –vcl dr
JGsn	Jimmy Garrison –b
JGze	Johnny Gertze –p
JH	Johnny Hodges –as ss
JHck	John Hendricks –vcl
JHee	John Hardee –ts
JHgh	Jim Hughart –b
JHko	Joe Hrasko –as
JHks	John Hicks –ts
JHll	Jim Hall –gt
JHnt	John Hunt –tp
JHrd	J.C. Heard –dr
JHs	Johnny Hicks –p
JHtn	Jimmy Hamilton –cl ts arr
JJ	Jo Jones –dr
JJJ	J.J. Johnson –tb

JJns	Jimmy Jones –p
JJo	Jonah Jones –tp
JJsn	Jimmie Johnson –dr
JJst	Jimmy Johnston –b
JK	Jerry Kruger –vcl
JKlp	John Kulp –ts cl
JKpr	Jimmy Knepper –tb
JKrb	John Kirby –b
JL	John Lamb –b
JLds	John Lindsay –b
JLnd	Jack Leonard –vcl
JLsb	Jack Lesberg –b
JLvy	John Levy –b
JLws	John Lewis –p
JM	Jack Maisel –dr
JMce	Junior Mance –p
JMdn	Joe Mondragon –b
JMdy	Julia Moody –vcl
JMgn	Johnny Mehegan –p
JMK	James McKeever –p org
JMlm	John Malcolm –tp
JMlr	Jimmy Miller –vcl
JMls	Josie Miles –vcl
JMP	Jimmy McPhail –vcl
JMsl	Joe Marshall –dr
JMtm	James Mtume –cga
JMV	Jack McVea –ts
JMxl	Jimmy Maxwell –tp
JN	Joe Nanton –tb
JNm	Jimmy Nottingham –tp
JNn	Joe Newman –tp
JNsh	Johnny Nash –vcl
JNtn	June Norton –vcl
JO	Jimmy Owens –tp
JP	Julian Priester –tb
JPdr	Jimmy Ponder –gt
JPJ	James P. Johnson –p
JPs	Joe Pass –gt
JPsn	John Pederson –tb
JPte	Johnny Pate –b
JPtn	Janet Putman –hrp
JPts	Jack Pettis –Cm
JR	Junior Raglin –b
JRay	Johnny Ray –vcl
JRd	Jimmy Randolph –vcl
JRM	Jelly-Roll Morton –p
JRo	Jorge Rojas –b
JRsh	Jimmy Rushing –vcl
JRsn	Jerome Richardson –as fl bs
JRss	Jules Ross –ts
JRws	Jimmy Rowles –p
JS	Joya Sherrill –vcl
JSam	Jacky Samson –b
JSbl	Jean Sablon –vcl
JSch	Joe Schmalz –b
JSh	Jackie Sharpe –ts bs
JShl	Jimmy Shirley –gt
JSlr	James Slaughter –dr
JSmn	Joe Shulman –b
JSms	John Simmons –b
JSmt	Jabbo Smith –tp
JSpr	Jimmy Spear –tp
JSrs	John Sanders –tb vtb
JStd	Jo Stafford –vcl
JSth	Joe Smith –ct
JSty	Jess Stacy –p
JSvn	Joe Sullivan –p
JT	Juan Tizol –vtb
JTdn	Jack Teagarden –tb vcl
JTms	Joe Thomas –tp
JTrn	Joe Turner –p vcl
JTrt	Jo. Trent –vcl
JV	Joe Venuto –vib
JVs	Jean Vees –gt
JW	Jimmy Woode –b

JWld   Joe Wilder –tp
JWlm   John Williams –b
JWls   Joe Williams –vcl
JWms   John Williams –dr
JWS   John W. Sublett –vcl

KB   Kenny Burrell –gt
KBts   Keter Betts –b
KBwn   Kitty Brown –vcl
KC   Kenny Clarke –dr
KChr   Keith Christie –tb
KD   Kay Davis –vcl
KDhm   Kenny Dorham –tp
KK   Ken Kersey –p
KMrs   Kathy Myers –vcl
KN   Kenny Napper –b
KO   King Oliver –ct
KOH   Karl Otto Hoff –dr
KP   Keg Purnell –dr
KS   Ken Shroyer –tb

LA   Louis Armstrong –tp vcl
LArm   Lil Armstrong –p
LB   Lawrence Brown –tb
LBcn   Louis Bacon –tp
LBin   Larry Binyon –ts
LBlb   Louis Blackburn –tb
LBsh   Lennie Bush –b
LBsn   Louie Bellson –dr
LC   Lyle Cox –tb
LCdn   Les Condon –tp
LD   Leonard Davis –tp
LDon   Larry Donnel –vcl
LE   Lu Elliott –vcl
LF   Leonard Feather –p
LFts   Luis Fuentés –tb
LG   Lil Greenwood –vcl
LGkn   Leonard Gaskin –b
LGls   Larry Gales –b
LH   Lurlean Hunter –vcl
LHpr   Louis Hooper –p
LHpt   Lionel Hampton –vib dr p vcl
LHrn   Lena Horne –vcl
LHrs   Leroy Harris –bj
LHs   Louis Hayes –dr
LHsn   Luther Henderson –cel p
LJ   Lonnie Johnson –gt
LJck   Lawrence Jackson –dr
LJks   Leslie Johnakins –bs
LJnf   Jena Junoff –vcl
LL   Leroy Lovett –p cel
LLF   Leon LaFell –vcl
LLuc   Larry Lucie –gt
LLvy   Lou Levy –p
LM   Louis Metcalf –tp
LMch   Lloyd Michaels –tp
LMls   Lizzie Miles –vcl
LO   Lloyd Oldham –vcl
LPts   Leon Petties –dr
LR   Luis Russell –p
LRls   Lou Rawls –vcl
LRtl   Leroy Rutledge –tp
LRx   Lawrence Rix –gt
LS   Leslie Spann –gt fl
LSb   Lou Shoobe –b
LSch   Lalo Schifrin –p
LSH   Lyle "Skitch" Henderson –p
LSm   Laura Smith –vcl
LStd   Les Strand –org
LT   Lloyd Trotman –b
LTho   Lucky Thompson –ts
LThs   Leon Thomas –vcl
LTio   Lorenzo Tio –cl
LV   Louise Vant –vcl
LVgr   Leroy Vinnegar –b

LW   Leo Watson –dr vcl
LWC   Lady Will Carr –p
LWre   Leonard Ware –gt
LWsn   Laurel Watson –vcl
LY   Lester Young –ts
LYng   Lee Young –dr

MA   Manny Albas –bt
MB   Mills Brothers –vcl kaz
MBG   Miguel Badia Graells –tb
MBkr   Mickey Baker –gt
MBly   Mildred Bailey –vcl
MBnt   Marie Bryant –vcl
MBrc   Marion Bruce –vcl
MBrn   Milt Bernhart –tb
MBrs   Miller Brothers –vcl
MC   Marian Cox –vcl
MCcs   Michél Camicas –tb
MCld   Martha Copeland –vcl
MCle   Marie Cole –vcl
MD   Miles Davis –tp
MDgs   Mike Douglas –vcl
ME   Mercer Ellington –tp frh
MEtn   Maria Ellington –vcl
MF   Maynard Ferguson –tp
MG   Matthew Gee –tb
MGdr   Michél Goudry –b
MGfn   Merv Griffin –vcl
MGsn   Milt Grayson –vcl
MH   Major Holley –b
MHa   Masanga Harada –b
MHbt   Mort Herbert –b
MHtn   Milt Hinton –b
MJ   Mahalia Jackson –vcl
MJck   Mike Jackson –p
MJo   Margaret Johnson –vcl
MJsn   Money Johnson –tp vcl
MKE   McKinley Easton –bs
ML   Marguerite Lee –vcl
MLgd   Michél Legrand –p vcl
MLgn   Marian Logan –vcl
MLn   Morris Lane –ts
MLne   Marion Horne –vcl
MLow   Mundell Lowe –gt
MLst   Melba Liston –p tb
MLws   Mel Lewis –dr
MM   Marlowe Morris –p
MME   Murray McEachern –tb as
MMG   Michael McGettigan –flh
MMH   Mary McHugh –vcl
MMll   Malcolm Mitchell –gt
MMos   Mike Mostello –tp
MMre   Monette Moore –vcl
MMzw   Mezz Mezzrow –cl
MN   Marty Napoleon –p
MNts   Makaya Ntshoko –dr
MO   Mary Osborne –gt
MotC   Men of the Cathedral Choir –vcl
MR   Max Roach –dr
MRoy   Marshal Royal –as
MS   Mike Simpson –cl fl
MSct   Mabel Scott –vcl
MSh   Mack Shaw –bb
MSll   Martial Solal –p
MSvn   Maxine Sullivan –vcl
MT   Mellotones –vcl
MTil   Martha Tilton –vcl
MTlr   Malcolm Taylor –tb fl
MTns   Margaret Tynes –vcl
MTo   Masahiko Togashi –dr
MTrm   Mel Tormé vcl dr
MW   Mae West –vcl
MWld   Mel Waldron –p
MZC   Mother A.M.E. Zion Cathedral
        Choir –vcl

NA   Nat Adderly –tp
NB   Nell Brookshire –vcl
NBr   Nat Brusiloff –v
NGch   Nicky Gerfach –v
NH   Neal Hefti –tp
NJ   Nat Jones –as cl
NK   Norman Keenan –b
NKC   Nat "King" Cole –p vcl
NL   Nanice Lund –vcl
NLbg   Nils Lindberg –p
NM   Norma Miller –vcl
NO   Norma Oldham –vcl
NP   Nat Pierce –p
NPtr   Nettie Potter –vcl
NS   Nat Shilkret –p
NTrn   Norris Turney –as fl
NW   Nelson Williams –tp
NWn   Nat Wynn –vcl
NWrd   Nat Woodard –tp

OB   Ozie Bailey –vcl
OD   Othella Dallas –vcl
OF   Otto Francker –p org
OH   Otto Hardwick –as ss cl bs
OJ   Oliver Jackson –dr
OJsn   Osie Johnson –dr
OM   Olivette Miller –hrp
ON   Oliver Nelson –as
OP   Oscar Pettiford –b clo
OPsn   Oscar Peterson –p
OS   Omer Simeon –cl
OV   Oscar Valdrambini –tp
OW   Ozie Ware –vcl

PB   Perry Bradford –p vcl
PBbn   Paul Barbarin –dr
PBN   Paris Blue Notes –vcl
PBk   Pat Blake –tp
PBrb   Phil Barboza –tp
PC   Pete Clarke –as cl
PChs   Paul Chambers –b
PCnd   Pete Condoli –tp
PD   Pike Davis –tp
PDtr   Pierre Dutour –tp flh
PF   Panama Francis –dr
PFst   Pops Foster –b
PG   Paul Gonsalves –ts cl gt
PGig   Peter Giger –dr
PGo   Pierre Gossez –cl
PH   Paul Horn –as ts cl
PHoy   Patricia Hoy –vcl
PHth   Percy Heath –b
PhWe   Phil Worde –p
PhWs   Phil Woods –cl as
PI   Pastor'n Iversen –p
PJJ   Philly Joe Jones –dr
PK   Paul Kondziela –b
PKi   Porter Kilbert –as
PL   Peggy Lee –vcl
PM   Percy Marion –ts
PMlt   Pierre Michelot –b
PMsn   Peck Morrison –b
PMtn   Paul Motian –dr
PPge   Patti Page –vcl
PPdy   Pretty Purdy –dr
PPt   Patricia Petremont –vcl
PQu   Paul Quinichette –ts
PR   Prince Robinson –ts cl
PS   Phil Sunkel –tp
PSm   Pat Smythe –p
PSo   Paul Serrano –tp
PW   Paul White –vcl
PWR   Pee Wee Russell –cl
PWrd   Prince Woodyard –org

QJ   Quentin Jackson –tb
Qu   Quintones –vcl
QW   Quentin White –dr

RA   Russ Andrews –ts
RB   Rhythm Boys –vcl
RBnd   Ray Biondi –gt
RBrn   Ray Brown –b
RBwn   Ruth Brown –vcl
RBws   Roy Burrowes –tp
RC   Ralph Collier –cga
RCh   Ray Charles –p vcl
RCks   Robert Cooksey –hca
RCln   Rosemary Clooney –vcl
RClr   Red Callender –b
RCpd   Ray Copeland –tp
RCtr   Ron Carter –b
RD   Richard Davis –b
RE   Roy Eldridge –tp
REdm   Robare Edmonston –b
REsn   Rolf Ericson –tp
REst   Roy East –as
REvs   Roy Evans –vcl
RFck   Roberta Flack –vcl
RFo   Raymond Fol –p
RFrn   Russ Freeman –cel p
RFsn   Ruth Fredricson –vcl
RG   Roscoe Gill –vcl
RGlz   Ricardo Galéazzi –b
RGrb   Rollo Garber –b
RGrn   Roger Guerin –tp
RGth   Rollins Griffith –p
RH   Rick Henderson –as arr
RHln   Red Harlan –tp
RHns   Roy Haynes –dr
RHsn   Rosa Henderson –vcl
RHtn   Ralph Hamilton –gt
RJ   Rudy Jackson –cl as
RJck   Ray Jackson –org
RJns   Reunald Jones –tp
RJo   Rufus Jones –dr
RK   Roy Kral –vcl
RKwy   Roger Kellaway –p
RL   Roland Lobligeois –b
RLay   R. Lay –vcl
RLee   Roberta Lee –vcl
RLNG   Richelle Le Noir Guilmenot –vcl
RLws   Ramsay Lewis –p
RM   Ray Mitchell –vcl
RMtn   Ron Martin –vcl
RN   Ray Nance –tp v vcl
RNrv   Red Norvo –xyl
RO   Ruth Olay –vcl
RP   Russell Procope –as cl
RPl   Richie Powell –p
RPlm   Remo Palmieri –gt
RPly   Rheza Paley –ts
RPts   Reggie Pitts –dr
RPwl   Rudy Powell –as
RR   Red Rodney –tp
RRd   Rufus Reid –b
RRR   Roger "Ram" Ramirez –p
RRsn   Rodney Richardson –b
RRss   Ronnie Ross –bs
RS   Rex Stewart –ct vcl
RSct   Ronnie Scott –ts
RSfd   Russ Stableford –b
RSt   Ronnie Stevenson –dr
RT   Ray Triscari –tp
RW   Rudy Williams –ts
RWls   Richard Williams –tp

SA   Steve Allen –p
SAln   Snags Allen –gt
SAs   Svend Asmussen –v

SB   Sidney Bechet –ss cl
SBkn   Sam Benskin –p
SBlk   Sid Block –b
SBrm   Sonny Berman –tp
SBst   Skeeter Best –gt
SCC   Second Community Church Choir –vcl
SChl   Savannah Churchill –vcl
SCT   Sir Charles Thompson –p
SCtl   Sid Catlett –dr
SF   Sarah Forde –vcl
SG   Sonny Greer –dr vcl
SGld   Slim Gaillard –gt vcl
SGrp   Stephane Grappelli –v
SGrs   Sidney Gross –gt
SGry   Sid Garry –vcl
SGtz   Stan Getz –ts
SH   Shelton Hemphill –tp
SHll   Skip Hall –p
SHsn   Skitch Henderson –p
SJ   Sam Jones –b
SJC   Sant Jordi Choir –vcl
SK   Stan Kenton –p
SL   Steve Little –dr
SLw   Steve Lawrence –vcl
SM   Sue Mitchell –vcl
SMld   Sax Mallard –cl as
SMn   Shelly Manne –dr
SMph   Sylvia Murphy –vcl
SMrt   Stu Martin –dr
Sms   Sentimentalists –vcl
SMsh   Skeets Marsh –dr
SMtn   Sara Martin –vcl
SP   Scat Powell –vcl
SPwl   Specs Powell –dr
SRC   Swedish Radio Choir –vcl
SS   Sunny Smith –vcl
SSct   Scotty Scott –as
SShb   Sahib Shihab –b
SShd   Shep Shepherd –dr
SSm   Stuff Smith –v
SSrs   Swingle Singers –vcl
SSt   Slam Stewart –b vcl
SStt   Sonny Stitt –tp
ST   Sam Taylor –ts
STcy   Stan Tracy –p
StHi   St. Hilda's High School Choir –vcl
StHu   St. Hugh's School Choir –vcl
StMa   St. Marc's Choir –vcl
SUC   St. John's Unity Church Choir –vcl
SV   Sarah Vaughan –vcl
SW   Sid Weiss –b
SWlc   Sippie Wallace –vcl
SWls   Sandy Williams –tb
SWrd   Sam Woodyard –dr
SWsn   Shadow Wilson –dr
SWsp   Shirley Witherspoon –vcl
SWte   Sammy White –vcl
SY   Snookie Young –tp

TB   Teddy Bunn –gt
TBnt   Tony Bennett –vcl
TBrn   Ted Brannon –p
TBrw   Teresa Brewer –vcl
TBW   T-Bone Walker –gt vcl
TC   Thelma Carpenter –vcl
TChs   Teddy Charles –vib
TCoe   Tony Coe –as ts
TD   Tommy Dorsey –tb
TF   Tommy Fulford –p
TFgn   Tommy Flanagan –p
TFlw   Tal Farlow –gt
TG   Tyree Glenn –tb vib
TGfn   Tom Griffin –as
TGrs   Tiny Grimes –gt

TH   Tubby Hayes –as ts vib
TJ   Taft Jordan –tp vcl
TJo   Thad Jones –tp
TK   Theodore Kelly –tb
TM   Tony Miranda –frh
TMac   Tom Macey –cl
TMk   Thelonious Monk –p
TMrs   Thomas Morris –ct
TMtn   Teddy Martin –dr
TN   Ted Nash –ts
TP   Tony Pastor –vcl
TPti   Tony Parenti –cl
TR   Timmie Rogers –vcl
TS   Terry Snyder –dr
TSct   Tony Scott –ts cl
TShn   Terry Shannon –p
TSm   Tab Smith –as
TStd   Tony Studd –tb
TSth   Trixie Smith –vcl
TT   Trish Turner –vcl
TTB   Two Ton Baker –p vcl
TTge   Thurman Teague –b
TTh   Teri Thornton –vcl
TW   Teddy Wilson –p
TWlt   Teddy Wolters –gt
TWrn   Tony Warren –vcl
TWtk   Tony Watkins –vcl
TY   Trummy Young –tb vcl

UG   Urbie Green –tb
UL   Ulysses Livingston –gt
UMC   Una Mae Carlisle –p vcl

VB   Vernon Brown –tb
VBB   Vince Bair Bey –as
VD   Vic Dickinson –tb
VDmn   Vic Damone –vcl
VDvs   Virgil Davis –ts as
VF   Victor Feldman –p
VG   Victor Gaskin –b
VGmn   Vittorio Gassman -recital
VHC   Vox Humana Choir –vcl
VL   Virginia Liston –vcl
VMC   Viola McCoy –vcl
VP   Vince Prudente –tb
VPn   Vess Payne –dr

WB   Wellman Braud –b bb
WBcb   Wilbur Bascomb –tp
WBrd   Will Bradley –tb
WBrt   Willie Bryant –vcl
WBsb   Wilbur Brisbois –tp
WBsp   Walter Bishop, Jr. –p
WC   Willie Cook –tp
WCrl   Wilton Crawley –cl
WCvr   Wayman Carver –cl as ts
WDP   Wilbur DeParis –tb dr
WF   Woolf Freedman –eb
WG   Willie Gardner –org
WGry   Wardell Gray –ts
WH   Woody Herman –cl as vcl
WJ   Wallace Jones –tp
WJn   Walter Johnson –dr
WJns   Willie Jones –p
WJon   Wini Johnson –vcl
WJsn   Will Johnson –bj gt
WK   Wynton Kelly –p
WLS   Willie "The Lion" Smith –p vcl
WM   Wilfred Middlebrooks –b
WMlr   William Miller –dr
WMsl   Wendell Marshall –b
WP   Walter Page –b
WPks   Walter Perkins –dr
WR   Walter Rosenberger –gsp
WRch   Walter Richardson –vcl

WRff	Willie Ruff –frh		XCh	Xavier Chambon –tp		ZE	Ziggy Elman –tp
Wrs	Winners –vcl					ZH	ZiggyHarrell –tp
WS	Willie Smith –as		YA	Yasuo Arawaka –b		ZJ	Zaydee Jackson –vcl
WSct	William Scott –tp		YL	Yvonne Lanauze –vcl		ZS	Zoot Sims –ts
WSlw	Ward Silloway –tb		YM	Yehudi Menuhin –v		ZStn	Zutty Singleton –dr
WW	William White, Jr. –reed						

PSEUDONYMS

Edward Duke	=	Duke Ellington
Goody Goodwyn	=	Irving Mills
Bobbie Gordon	=	Nell Brookshire
Cue Porter	=	Johnny Hodges
Alberta Prime	=	?Alberta Hunter
Sunny Smith	=	Irving Mills
Prince Woodyard	=	Wild Bill Davis
Josephine Beatty	=	Alberta Hunter

KEY TO LABELS

ABC	American Broadcasting Corporation	Crb	Crabapple	Hds	Hindsight	
Aby	Abbey	Crl	Circle	Hit	Hit	
ACh	Air Check	Crn	Crown	HJC	Hot Jazz Club of America	
AdJ	Anthologie du Jazz	CS	Contemporary Sound	HMV	His Master's Voice	
Adn	Aladdin	CT	Capitol Transcriptions	HoF	Hall of Fame	
Aff	Affinity (Charly Records Ltd.)	Ctl	Continental	HRS	Hot Record Society	
AFR	Armed Forces Radio Service	Ctn	Carlton	HS	Hollywood Soundstage	
AH	Ace of Hearts			HW	Hit of the Week	
Ajx	Ajax	DBD	Dance Band Days			
Alt	Alto	Dbt	Debut	IA	International Achievement Conference (souvenir record)	
Apo	Apollo	DC	Discos Continental			
Apx	Apex	DD	Desor Disc	IAC	International Association of Jazz Record Collectors	
ARC	American Record Company	De	Decca			
Arg	Argo	DET	Duke Ellington Treasury Series	Ips	Impulse	
Ari	Ariston	Df	Dynaflow			
Atc	Atlantic	Div	Diva	JA	Jazz Archives	
Att	Attic	DJ	Doctor Jazz	JAn	Jazz Anthology	
Aur	Aurora	Dji	Dooji Records	J&J	Jazz&Jazz	
AV	AVision	Dk	Delmark	JBd	J-Bird Records	
Az	Az	Dnb	Downbeat	Jbl	Jubilee	
		Doc	Document	JBR	Jazz Band Records	
BA	Blue Ace	Dom	Domino	JBS	Jazz/Blues/Soul	
Ban	Banner	Dsn	Design	JC	Jazz Club	
Bb	Bluebird	Duk	Duke Records	JCo	Jazz Connoisseur	
BBA	Big Band Archives	DVD	Digital Video Disc (any label)	JD	Joe Davis	
Bbd	Bellbird	DWD	Date with the Duke	JDr	JazzDoor	
BBI	Blue Bell	Dyn	Dynamic	JG	Jazz Guild	
Bcn	Beacon			JGs	Jazz Giants	
BD	Blu-Disc	Ech	Echo Jazz	JGt	Jazz Greats	
BF	Bear Family Records	Ed	Edison	JHr	Jazz Hour	
BJ	Black Jack	Egm	Egmont	JHt	Jazz Heritage	
BJz	Blu Jazz	EJ	Europa Jazz	JI	Jazz Information	
BL	Black Lion	Em	Em-Arcy	JJ	Just Jazz	
BLb	Blue Label	Emb	Ember	JK	Jazz Kings	
BMG	Buddah Records	EN	ENJA Records	JL	Jazz Live	
BMn	Bertelsmann	Eph	Epitaph	JLg	Jazz Legacy 44	
BMR	Book-of-the-Month Records	Epi	Epic	JLd	Jazzland	
BN	Blue Note	ER	Extreme Rarities	JM	Jazz Moderne	
Bon	Bonsare	Esq	Esquire	JMY	Jazz Music Yesteryear	
Br	Brunswick	Ev	Everest	Jo	Jobel	
BSJ	Basin Street Jazz	Evb	Everybodys	Jok	Joker	
BSt	Blue Star			Joy	Joyce	
Bst	Bandstand	Fab	AB Fable	JP	Jazz Panorama	
Bth	Bethlehem	Fam	Family	JPo	Jazz Portrait	
Btm	Biltmore	Fan	Fantasy	JS	Jazz Selection	
BYG	BYG Records	FD	Flying Dutchman	JSo	Jazz Society	
		FDC	For Discriminate Collectors	JSp	Jazz Supreme	
Cam	Cameo	Ffr	Fanfare	Jt	Jazztone	
Cap	Capitol	FM	Franklin Mint	Jtm	Jazztime	
Car	Caracol	Fox	Foxy	JU	Jazz Up	
Cat	Catalyst	FR	Fairmont Records	JUn	Jazz Unlimited	
CC	Collectors Classics	Frl	Federal	Jwl	Jewel	
Cdn	Camden	Fst	Felsted	Jzy	Jazzy	
Cdy	Candy	4St	4 Star			
Cen	Century	Fvl	Festival	KD	KayDee Records	
Ch	Challenge	Fws	Folkways	Kg	King	
Chs	Chess			KJ	King Jazz	
Clf	Clef	GA	Grand Award	Kn	Keynote	
Clr	Clarion	Gap	Gaps	Koa	Koala	
Cls	Classics	GC	Grinnell College	KoJ	Kings of Jazz	
Cmy	Camay	GdJ	I Giganti del Jazz	Kri	Kristall	
Cnt	Coronet	Gdr	Goodyear			
Co	Columbia (CBS)	GE	Good Era	LL	Laser Light	
Com	Commodore	GNP	GNP Crescendo	Lin	Lincoln	
Con	Contact	Gnt	Gennett	Llt	Limelight	
Cor	Coral	GoJ	Giants of Jazz	LMR	Lefrak-Fuhrman-Moelis Records	
Cos	Cosmopolitan	GS	Guest Star	Lon	London Records	
CP	Columbia Pictures	Gth	Gotham	LSR	Lost Secret Records	
Cpr	Caprice	Gzl	Gazelle	Ly	Lucky	
Cqr	Conqueror					
Cr	Creole	Har	Harmony	M&A	Music & Arts	
		Hcn	Hurricane	Mad	Madly	

Mag	Magic	Plm	Palm	SR	Souvenir Record
Maj	Majestic	Pmt	Paramount	SRT	Standard Radio Transcription
Man	Manor	Pol	Polydor	SSR	Solid State Records
Mar	Marlor Productions	PP	Private Pressing	ST	Swing Treasury
Mas	Master Records	Pr	Prima	Std	Stardust
Max	Max	Prd	Period	STJ	Sarpe Top Jazz
MCA	MCA-Records	Pre	Prestige	Stg	Sterling
Md	Mood	Prt	Privateer	Sts	Status
MdJ	I Maestri del Jazz	PS	Port Songs	Stv	Storyville
Mdv	Moodsville	Pth	Pathé	Svl	Swingville
Mer	Mercer Records	Ptp	Pentape	Sw	Swing
Met	Metro	PVS	P-Vine Special	SwH	Swing House
MFC	Manny Fox Distribution Company				
MGM	Metro-Goldwyn-Meyer	QuD	Queen Disc	Tax	Tax
Mgn	Magnetic			TJC	The Jazz Collection
MHS	Marriott Hot Shoppers, Inc.	Rar	Rarities	TL	Time-Life
Mir	Miracle	RB	Red Baron	ToE	Toshiba EMI
MJ	Musica Jazz	RC	Radio Canada	TOM	The Old Masters
MJR	Master Jazz Recordings	RD	Reader's Digest	Ton	Tono
Mlt	Melotone	RDB	Radio Denmark Broadcast	Tpl	Temple
MM	Music Masters		(Not a label; cassettes	Tpo	Tempo
Mnm	Magnum		available from DEMS.)	Trg	Tring
Mo	Mosaic Records	RDs	Radio Days	Trp	Trip
MoJ	Masters of Jazz	Re	Regal	Trv	Trova
Mon	Montage	Rem	Remington	TTC	TETCO
MP	Marlor Productions	Rho	Rhino	Tx	Timex
MPS	MPS (Germany)	Riv	Riverside		
MR	Moon Records	Rlm	Realm	UA	United Artists Records
Mrt	Meritt	Rlt	Roulette	UJ	Unique Jazz
Mry	Mercury	Rn	Roan Records	Ur	Urania
Msl	Masterseal	Rom	Romeo	UST	United States Treasury Dept.
Mu	Musicraft	Ros	Rosetta	UTD	Up-To-Date
		Roy	Royal		
Nat	Natasha	Rpr	Reprise	VD	V-disc
NC	Non Commercial	RR	Rare Records	VET	Victor Electrical Transcriptions
Ngr	Norgran	Rt	Raretone	Vge	Vogue
NGT	National Guard Transcriptions	RTE	RTE/UNE Musique Europe I	Vi	Victor (RCA)
Ntl	National	RV	R/V Records	Vid	Video (any label)
NTR	Neon Tonic Records	Rx	Radlex	VIn	Varèse International
NW	New World			VJC	Vintage Jazz Classics
		Sag	Saga	VJM	Vintage Jazz Masters
Od	Odeon	Saj	SAJA	Vo	Vocalion
OK	OKeh	Sal	Salle	VoA	Voice of America
Onx	Onyx	Sbm	Sunbeam	Vri	Variety
Ori	Oriole	Sbt	Sunburst	Vrv	Verve
OTR	Old Time Radio	SC	Smithsonian Collection	Vt	Velvet Tone
Ozo	Ozone	Sco	Seeco	Vta	Vista
		Sct	Soundcraft	VY	Video Yesteryear
Pa	Parlophone	SD	Steiner Davis		
Pab	Pablo Records	SE	Special Edition	Wax	Wax
Pau	Pausa	Seq	Sequel	WEA	Warner-Elektra-Atlantic
PBx	Properbox	SES	SESAC	WET	World Electrical Transcriptions
PC	Palm Club	SGL	Sounds Great Live	Wi	Wing
Pck	Pickwick	Sig	Signature	WL	White Label
Pdt	Président	SJ	Savoy Jazz	WRC	World Record Club
Pen	Pennington	Skt	Skata	WT	World Transcriptions
Per	Perfect	Slm	Selmer	WW	West Wind
Phi	Philips	Sn	Session Disc	Wwk	Warwick
Pho	Phontastic	Sna	Sonora	Wyn	Wynne
Pir	Pirate	So	Sony		
Pj	Poljazz	SoJ	Sign of Jazz	"X"	X-Label
Pkn	Pumpkin	SoP	Stars on Parade		
Plk	Polk	Spk	Spokane	ZIM	ZIM Records

KEY TO ABBREVIATIONS

a)   INSTRUMENTS

acc	-	accordion	ct	-	cornet	p	- piano
as	-	alto saxophone	dr	-	drums	pic	- piccolo
b	-	bass	eb	-	electric bass	ss	- soprano saxophone
bb	-	brass bass	ep	-	electric piano	tap	- tap dancing
bcl	-	bass clarinet	fb	-	fender bass	tb	- trombone
bgo	-	bongo	fl	-	flute	tim	- timpani
bj	-	banjo	flh	-	flugelhorn	tom	- tom-tom
bs	-	baritone saxophone	frh	-	French horn	tp	- trumpet
bt	-	bell tree	gsp	-	glockenspiel	ts	- tenor saxophone
c	-	cello	gt	-	guitar	tu	- tuba
cel	-	celesta	har	-	harmonium	v	- violin
cga	-	conga	hca	-	harmonica	vcl	- vocal
chm	-	chimes	hrp	-	harp	vib	- vibraphone
cl	-	clarinet	kaz	-	kazoo	vtb	- valve trombone
clo	-	cello	ob	-	oboe	wb	- washboard
Cm	-	C-melody saxophone	org	-	organ	xyl	- xylophone

The instruments mentioned next to the musicians' names are only those actually played on the recordings listed in this book.
In fact many of the musicians may master a variety of other instruments as well.

b)   OTHER

acc. by	-	accompanied by	ear.	-	early	*sa*	- same as[2]
aka	-	also known as[1]	grp	-	group	spg.	- spring
alt. (tk.)	-	alternate (take)	lt.	-	late	sum.	- summer
aut.	-	autumn	mx	-	matrix	tc	- telecast
bc	-	broadcast	*p*	-	probably	tk.	- take
c	-	circa	pp	-	probable personnel	win.	- winter
cond.	-	conducting	qv	-	quod vide (which see)		

[1]Refers to a tune with an alternate title, which will <u>not</u> appear <u>subsequently</u> in this book.
[2]Refers to a tune listed <u>previously</u> in this book under a different title.

Chronological Section

			26 Jul 1923	(S)

SNOWDEN'S NOVELTY ORCHESTRA
AW, OH, DE ES SG.[2]

.... [3] [Home]

[1]Victor Studios (Recording Laboratory).
[2]Band personnel according to Snowden's personal recollection, who at times has been talking about six men.
[3]The piece was most likely rejected on the spot and the wax master destroyed; no test pressing is known to exist.

No evidence could be traced in the Victor ledgers referring to the alleged recording session by Snowden's Novelty Orchestra on 18 Oct 1923; it can therefore be concluded that the session did not take place.

Nov 1924 (S)
?Plaza Studios
New York City, NY

ALBERTA PRIME[1]
Vcl, acc. by DE, JTrt.

.... BD   T2001-1   It's Gonna Be A Cold, Cold Winter –vAP JTrt[2]

[1]The correct spelling of this artist's name appears to be Pryme.
[2]Complete: "It's Gonna Be A Cold, Cold Winter, So Get Another Place To Stay."

ALBERTA PRIME—SONNY GREER, Piano Accom.
Vcl, acc. by DE, SG.

.... BD   T2002-2   Parlor Social De Luxe –vAP SG

Masters T2003 and T2004 are untraced.

Nov 1924 (P)
?Plaza Studios
New York City, NY

THE WASHINGTONIANS
BM, CI, OH, DE GF SG.

.... BD   T2005-2   Choo Choo[1]
.... BD[2]   T2006-1[3]   Rainy Nights[4]

[1]Complete: "Choo Choo, Gotta Hurry Home."
[2]Pen and possibly other labels as by *Chick Winters Orchestra*.
[3]Contrary to such claims in various publications and sleeve notes, take 2 remains unissued.
[4]"Rainy Days" on some releases. Compare: "Naughty Man" by Fletcher Henderson; master #13953, 7 Nov 1924. Both versions sound like they were arranged by Don Redman.

JO. TRENT & THE D C'NS[1]
Vcl, acc. by OH, DE GF SG.

.... BD   T2007-1   Deacon Jazz –vJTrt

SUNNY & THE D C'NS[1, 2]
OH, DE GF SG.

.... BD   T2008-1   Oh How I Love My Darling –vSG

[1]Often erroneously referred to as the *DEACONS*.
[2]The handbill shows *Sonny Greer and the D C'ns*.

Nov/Dec 1924 (S)
?Plaza Studios
New York City, NY

FLORENCE BRISTOL WITH DUKE ELLINGTON AND OTTO HARDWICK
Vcl, acc. by OH, DE.

.... BD   T2018-2   How Come You Do Me Like You Do –vFB

25 Sep 1925 (S)
Pathé Studios[1]
New York City, NY

DUKE ELLINGTON'S WASHINGTONIANS
PD, CI, PR OH, DE FG BE.

.... Pth   n106250[2]   I'm Gonna Hang Around My Sugar[3]
.... Pth   n106251[2]   Trombone Blues

[1]At East 53rd Street.
[2]The records were dubbed from master cylinders and the take suffixes are not known. The "n" prefix indicates a needle cut, or lateral recording as opposed to a vertical one.
[3]Complete: "I'm Gonna Hang Around My Sugar Till I Gather All The Sugar That She's Got."

26 Mar 1926 (S)
Pathé Studios
New York City, NY

DUKE ELLINGTON'S WASHINGTONIANS
HCpr LRtl, CI, PR OH DR, DE FG BE.

.... Pth   n106729[1]   Georgia Grind
.... Pth   n106730[1]   Parlor Social Stomp   >>>

[1]The records were dubbed from master cylinders and the take suffixes are not known.

				30 Mar 1926 (S)

DUKE ELLINGTON & HIS ORCHESTRA
HCpr LRtl, CI, PR OH DR, DE FG BE SG.

30 Mar 1926 (S)
Gennett Studios[1]
New York City, NY

.... Gnt   X-57-A   Wanna-Go-Back-Again Blues –vSG[2]
.... Gnt   X-58-A   If You Can't Hold The Man You Love –vSG[3]

[1]At 9-11 E. 37th Street.
[2]Complete: "You've Got Those 'Wanna-Go-Back-Again Blues.'"
[3]Complete: "If You Can't Hold The Man You Love, Don't Cry When He's Gone."

DUKE ELLINGTON & HIS WASHINGTONIANS
BM CJsn, JN, PR ?? OH, DE FG MSh SG.

21 Jun 1926 (S)
Gennett Studios
New York City, NY

.... Gnt[1]   X-190   Animal Crackers[2]
.... Gnt[1]   X-191   Li'l Farina

[1]Ch as by *Memphis Bell Hops*.
[2]Complete: "I'm Just Wild About Animal Crackers In My Soup."

ALBERTA JONES ACC. BY THE ELLINGTON TWINS. "LULU BELLE'S BOY FRIENDS."
Vcl, acc. by OH, DE.

14 Oct 1926 (S)
Gennett Studios
New York City, NY

.... Gnt   X-323   Lucky Number Blues –vAJ
.... Gnt   X-324-A   I'm Gonna Put You Right In Jail –vAJ

DUKE ELLINGTON & HIS KENTUCKY CLUB ORCHESTRA
BM LM, JN, ?PR ?? OH, DE FG MSh SG.

29 Nov 1926 (S)
799 Seventh Ave., Room 1[1]
New York City, NY

....   E4108W/4109W   [A Night In Harlem]
.... Vo   E4110W   East St. Louis Toodle-Oo[2]
....   E4112W/4113W   [Who Is She?]
.... Vo   E4114W   Birmingham Breakdown[3]

[1]Brunswick Studios.
[2]Recté: "East St. Louis Todalo"; "... Toadle-O" on the recording sheet; variant spelling "East St. Louis Toddle-O."
[3]*aka* "Birmingham Backdown."

ZAIDEE JACKSON WITH LULU BELLE'S BOY FRIENDS
Vcl, acc. by OH, DE.

Nov/Dec 1926 (S)
?Gennett Studios
New York City, NY

....   [They Call Me Lulu Belle –vZJ]
....   [I'm Tired Of Being A Fool Over You –vZJ]

No hard evidence referring to this alleged Gennett recording session could be traced in the company files and should therefore be treated as doubtful.

GUSSIE ALEXANDER
Vcl, acc. by OH, DE.

1 Dec 1926 (S)
OKeh Studios[1]
New York City, NY

....   74430-A   [I Do It –vGAx]
....   74431-A/-B   [Drifting From You Blues –vGAx]

> OH omitted.[2]

....   80235[3]   [Drifting From You Blues –vGAx]

[1]At 25 W. 45th Street.
[2]The pianist for the following item is not named in the files, but it is presumably DE.
[3]The master number discrepancy is caused by numbers assigned from different series, one acoustic (74430/31), the other electric (80235).

DUKE ELLINGTON & HIS KENTUCKY CLUB ORCHESTRA
BM LM, JN, ?PR ?? OH, DE FG MSh SG.

29 Dec 1926 (S)
799 Seventh Ave., Room 1
New York City, NY

.... Vo   E4321W   Immigration Blues
.... Vo   E4323W   The Creeper[1]
.... Vo   E4324W   The Creeper

[1]This title is a derivative of *Tiger Rag*. Compare: Fletcher Henderson "Rocky Mountain Blues," master #143344, and "Tozo," master #143345, 21 Jan 1927.

10 Jan 1927 (S)
44th St. Studios
New York City, NY

EVELYN PREER
Vcl, acc. by BM, PR OH, v,[1] DE SG.

.... BVE-37527-1/-2/-3 [Make Me Love You –vEP]
.... Tax BVE-37528-1[2] If You Can't Hold The Man You Love –vEP

[1]Unidentified v; it has been suggested that it was ESpn, who played with the band on several occasions during this time.
[2]Contrary to sleeve notes for Vi (F) 731043 and other publications, take 3 remains unissued.

On 21 Jan 1927 Gussy Alexander recorded at the OKeh Studios—likely at 145 W. 45th Street—in NYC another "I Do It" (master #80322-A) and "Drifting From You Blues" (master #80323-A), acc. by piano. The pianist is not named in the files. Without hearing the recordings, which seem to be forever lost, there is no way to establish his/her identity.

3 Feb 1927 (S)
799 Seventh Ave., Room 1
New York City, NY

DUKE ELLINGTON & HIS KENTUCKY CLUB ORCHESTRA
BM LM, JN, ?PR ?? OH, DE FG MSh SG.

.... Vo E4510W New Orleans Low-Down
.... Vo E4511W Song Of The Cotton Field[1]

[1]*aka* "Song From The Cotton Field."

28 Feb 1927 (S)
799 Seventh Ave., Room 1
New York City, NY

DUKE ELLINGTON & HIS KENTUCKY CLUB ORCHESTRA
BM LM, JN, ?PR ?? OH, DE FG MSh SG.

.... E21636/37/38 [East St. Louis Toodle-Oo]
.... Br E21641 Birmingham Breakdown

14 Mar 1927 (S)
799 Seventh Ave., Room 1
New York City, NY

DUKE ELLINGTON & HIS KENTUCKY CLUB ORCHESTRA
BM LM, JN, ?PR ?? OH, DE FG MSh SG.

.... Br E21872 East St. Louis Toodle-Oo

22 Mar 1927 (S)
Columbia Studios[1]
New York City, NY

THE WASHINGTONIANS
BM LM, JN, ?PR ?? OH, DE FG MSh SG.

.... Co 143705-3 East St. Louis Toodle-Oo
.... Co[2] 143706-2 Hop Head[3]
.... Co[2] 143707-2 Down In Our Alley Blues[4]

[1]At 1819 Broadway.
[2]On the original release the two titles were inverted.
[3]*aka* "Surprise."
[4]*aka* "Indian Rubber."

7 Apr 1927 (S)
799 Seventh Ave., Room 2
New York City, NY

THE WASHINGTONIANS
BM LM, JN, ?? ?? OH, DE FG MSh SG.

.... Br[1] E22299/E4874W Black And Tan Fantasy

[1]Br A500166, Plk and Mlt as by *Earl Jackson & His Musical Champions*, Vo as by *Traymore Orchestra*.

30 Apr 1927 (S)
799 Seventh Ave., Room 3
New York City, NY

TRAYMORE ORCHESTRA
JClk LM, JN, ?? ?? OH, DE FG MSh SG.

.... Vo[1] E22809/E4965W Soliloquy

[1]Br as by *The Washingtonians.*

6 Oct 1927 (S)
44th St. Studios
New York City, NY

DUKE ELLINGTON & HIS ORCHESTRA
BM LM, JN, RJ OH HC, DE FG WB SG.

.... BVE-40155-1/-2 [Black And Tan Fantasie[1]]
.... Pir BVE-40156-1 Washington Wobble[2]
.... "X" BVE-40156-2 Washington Wobble

[1]"Black And Tan Fantasie" on the recording sheet and all record labels.
[2]Actually "Washington Wabble."

26 Oct 1927 (S)
Camden Studio 1[1]
Camden, NJ

DUKE ELLINGTON & HIS ORCHESTRA
BM ?LM, JN, RJ OH HC, DE FG WB SG, AHl.

.... Vi BVE-40155-4 Black And Tan Fantasie
.... Vi BVE-40156-5 Washington Wobble
.... Vi BVE-39370-1 Creole Love Call –vAHl[2] >>>

....	Vi	BVE-39371-1	Blues I Love To Sing –vAHI
....	"X"	BVE-39371-2	Blues I Love To Sing –vAHI[3]

[1]Victor Studios.
[2]Compare: "Camp Meeting Blues" by King Oliver; master #81303-2, 16 Oct 1923.
[3]"Blues I Love To Hear" on Pir; "The Blues I Love To Sing" on many reissues.

3 Nov 1927   (S)
OKeh Studios[1]
New York City, NY

DUKE ELLINGTON & HIS ORCHESTRA
JSmt LM, JN, RJ OH HC, DE FG WB SG.

....	OK	W81775-A[2]	What Can A Poor Fellow Do?
....	OK	W81776-B	Black And Tan Fantasy
....	OK	W81776-C	Black And Tan Fantasy

[1]At 11 Union Square West. This applies to all following OKeh recording sessions unless stated otherwise.
[2]The electrical recording procedure was licensed by Western Electric, designated by the prefix "W."

THE CHICAGO FOOTWARMERS
AHI added, otherwise same personnel.

....	OK	W81777-C	Chicago Stomp Down –vAHI

8 Nov 1927   (S)
799 Seventh Ave., Room 1
New York City, NY

MARGUERITE LEE WITH THE ELLINGTON TRIO
Vcl, acc. by v c, DE.

....		E6783W/6784W	[You Will Always Live In Our Memory –vML]

WALTER RICHARDSON WITH THE ELLINGTON TRIO
Vcl, acc. by same as above.

....		E6785W/6786W	[Gone But Not Forgotten –vWRch]

MARGUERITE LEE WITH THE ELLINGTON TRIO
Vcl, acc. by same as above.

....		E6787W/6788W	[She's Gone To Join The Songbirds In Heaven –vML]

19 Dec 1927   (S)
Liederkranz Hall[1]
New York City, NY

DUKE ELLINGTON & HIS ORCHESTRA
BM LM, JN, RJ OH HC, DE FG WB SG.

....	Vi	BVE-41244-1	Harlem River Quiver[2]
....	Vi	BVE-41244-2	Harlem River Quiver
....	"X"	BVE-41244-3	Harlem River Quiver
....	Vi	BVE-41245-2[3]	East St. Louis Toodle-Oo[4, 5]
....	Vi	BVE-41246-1	Blue Bubbles
....	Vi	BVE-41246-2	Blue Bubbles

[1]At 111 E. 58th Street.
[2]*aka* "Brown Berries" and as such on all post-1930, 78-rpm reissues.
[3]"Takes" 1, 3 and 4 on various releases are dubs of take 2, the latter being the only one that was issued.
[4]"East St. Louis Toddleo" on the recording sheet.
[5]This title was coupled on Vi 21703 with BVE-43504-2 and issued as by *Duke Ellington & His Cotton Club Orchestra*.

29 Dec 1927   (S)
799 Seventh Ave., Room 1
New York City, NY

DUKE ELLINGTON & HIS COTTON CLUB ORCHESTRA
BM LM, JN, RJ OH HC, DE FG WB SG.

....	Vo	E6824W	Red Hot Band
....	Vo	E6826W	Doin' The Frog

9 Jan 1928   (S)
Columbia Studios
New York City, NY

THE WASHINGTONIANS
BM LM, JN, BB OH HC, DE FG WB SG.

....	Har	145488-3	Sweet Mamma (Papa's Getting Mad)[1]
....	Har	145489-3	Stack O'Lee Blues
....	Har	145490-3	Bugle Call Rag

[1]"Sweet Mama" on most releases.

19 Jan 1928   (S)
OKeh Studios
New York City, NY

DUKE ELLINGTON & HIS ORCHESTRA
BM LM, JN, BB OH HC, DE FG WB SG.

....	OK[1]	W400030-B	Take It Easy
....	OK[1]	W400031-A	Jubilee Stomp[2]

[1]Pa (E) 144 as by *Duke Ellington's Wonder Orchestra*.   >>>

[2]This title is a derivative of *Tiger Rag.*

LONNIE JOHNSON'S HARLEM FOOTWARMERS
Same personnel.

.... OK   W400032-A   Harlem Twist[1]

[1]*sa* "East St. Louis Toodle-Oo."

21 Mar 1928   (S)
799 Seventh Ave., Room 2
New York City, NY

THE WASHINGTONIANS
AW LM, JN, BB OH HC, DE FG WB SG.

.... Br   E27090/E7510W[1]   Take It Easy
.... Vo[2]   E27091/E7513W   Jubilee Stomp
.... Br[3]   E27093/E7511W   Black Beauty[4]
.... Br   E27094/E7512W   Black Beauty

[1]Contrary to sleeve notes for AH 89, the first take (E27089) remains unissued; AH 89 did use take 2 (E27090).
[2]Vo 15710 as by *Duke Ellington & His Cotton Club Orchestra.*
[3]Copies of Br 4044 processed in Los Angeles for sale west of the Rockies contain this title instead of the intended master E27903 "Don't Mess Around With Me" by the *Hotsy Totsy Gang.* Copies pressed in Muskegon, MI, for sale east of the Rockies play as labeled. All copies of Br 4044, even those with "Black Beauty," credit "Don't Mess Around With Me" by the *Hotsy Totsy Gang.*
[4]*aka* "Firewater."

26 Mar 1928   (S)
44th Street Studios
New York City, NY

DUKE ELLINGTON & HIS COTTON CLUB ORCHESTRA
BM AW LM, JN, BB OH HC, DE FG WB SG.

.... Vi   BVE-43502-2   Black Beauty
.... Vi   BVE-45503-2   Jubilee Stomp
.... Vi   BVE-45504-2   Got Everything But You

28 Mar 1928   (S)
Pathé Studios
New York City, NY

THE WHOOPEE MAKERS
BM LM, JN, BB OH HC, DE FG WB SG.

.... Pth   108079-1   East St. Louis Toodle-Oo

THE WASHINGTONIANS
Same personnel.

.... Cam   2944-A   East St. Louis Toodle-Oo

THE WHOOPEE MAKERS
Same personnel.

.... Pth   108080-1   Jubilee Stomp

THE WASHINGTONIANS
Same personnel.

.... Cam   2945-B   Jubilee Stomp

THE WHOOPEE MAKERS
Same personnel.

.... Pth   108081-?[1]   Take It Easy

[1]This master number is an educated guess and could not be verified as yet.

THE WASHINGTONIANS
Same personnel.

.... Cam   2946-B   Take It Easy

All Lin and Rom of the above as by *The Washingtonians,* all Per as by *The Whoopee Makers.*

25 Jun 1928   (S)
799 Seventh Ave., Room 3
New York City, NY

DUKE ELLINGTON & HIS ORCHESTRA
BM LM, JN, BB JH HC, DE FG WB SG.

....   E27770-A/-B   [What A Life]
.... Br   E27771-A[1]   Yellow Dog Blues[2]
.... Br   E27772-A   Tishomingo Blues
.... Br[3]   E27772-B   Tishomingo Blues

[1]"Takes" B, C and D as used on various releases are dubs of take A; take B remains unissued.
[2]Compare: "Happy Hour (Blues)" by Lloyd Scott & His Orchestra: master #37531-1/2, 10 Jan 1927.
[3]Only a few copies of this take on Canadian Br 3987 are known to exist.

THE HARLEM FOOTWARMERS
BM AW, JN, BB JH HC, DE FG WB SG, IM.

	OK	W400859-B	Diga Diga Doo –vIM
	OK	W400860-C	Doin' The New Lowdown –vIM

DUKE ELLINGTON
Piano solo.

	OK	W401172-B	Black Beauty
	OK	W401173-B	Swampy River

DUKE ELLINGTON & HIS ORCHESTRA
BM AW, JN, BB JH HC, DE LJ FG WB SG, BCx.

	OK	W401175-A	The Mooche –vBCx[1]

[1]Recté "The Mooch."

Master #W401174 is not an Ellington item.

LONNIE JOHNSON'S HARLEM FOOTWARMERS
BCx omitted, otherwise same personnel.

	OK	W401176-B	Move Over

DUKE ELLINGTON & HIS ORCHESTRA
BCx added, otherwise same personnel.

	OK	W401176-A	Hot And Bothered –vBCx[1]

[1]This title is a derivative of *Tiger Rag.*

DUKE ELLINGTON & HIS COTTON CLUB ORCHESTRA
BM AW, JN, BB JH HC, DE FG WB SG.

	Br	E28441-A/-B	Awful Sad

DUKE ELLINGTON & HIS COTTON CLUB ORCHESTRA
BM AW FJ/LM, JN, BB JH HC, DE FG WB SG.

	Br	E28359-A	The Mooche
	Br	E28360-A	Louisiana
		E28361-A/-B	[Memphis Wail]

THE WASHINGTONIANS
BM AW, JN, BB JH HC, DE FG WB SG.

	Cam[1]	108446-1*	The Mooche

[1]Per as by The *Whoopee Makers.*

THE WHOOPEE MAKERS
Same personnel.

	Per[1]	108446-2	The Mooche

[1]Cam, Lin, Rom as by The *Washingtonians.*

THE WASHINGTONIANS
Same personnel.

	Cam[1]	108447-2*	Hot And Bothered
	Cam[1]	108448-1*	Move Over

[1]Per and Pth as by The *Whoopee Makers.*

*Pathé/Perfect numbers 108446, 108447, 108448 were assigned Cameo transfer numbers 3530, 3528, 3529 respectively, about early Dec 1928. The Cameo numbers do not bear take suffixes.

OZIE WARE WITH DUKE ELLINGTON'S HOT FIVE[1]
Vcl, acc. by ?FJ, BB, DE WB SG.

	Vi	BVE-48100-1	Santa Claus, Bring My Man Back To Me –vOW
	Vi	BVE-48101-2	I Done Caught You Blues –vOW

[1]Vi 21777 as by *Ozie Ware Soprano With "Hot Five."*   >>>

DUKE ELLINGTON & HIS COTTON CLUB ORCHESTRA
AW ?FJ, JN, BB JH HC, DE FG WB SG, BCx OW GG.

.... Vi   BVE-47799-2   The Mooche
.... Mrt   BVE-48102-1[1]   I Can't Give You Anything But Love –vBCx GG

> AW omitted.

.... Vi   BVE-48103-1   No, Papa, No
.... Vi   BVE-48103-2   No, Papa, No –vOW

[1]Contrary to liner notes for Hot 'N Sweet CD 151272, take 2 remains unissued; see also footnote for the next session.

			10 Nov 1928 (S)

DUKE ELLINGTON & HIS COTTON CLUB ORCHESTRA   10 Nov 1928   (S)
BM AW FJ, JN, BB JH HC, DE FG WB SG, BCx GG.   44th Street Studios
                                                                             New York City, NY

.... Vi   BVE-48102-4[1]   I Can't Give You Anything But Love –vBCx GG
....   BVE-401-1[2]   [Since You Went Away]

[1]Remake. Releases marked "-2R" are copies of take 4.
[2]This (lost) test record was labeled as by *The Duke Ellington Players*.

Note on the recording sheet: "Orchestra men had worked through the night up until 5:00 a.m. at the Cotton Club and are too tired to play. Mr. Mills suggests that he be given an afternoon date." The above session lasted officially from 9:00 a.m. to 1:10 p.m. Notwithstanding, some or all of the men stayed until 2:00 p.m. to record the last title.

DUKE ELLINGTON & HIS COTTON CLUB ORCHESTRA   15 Nov 1928   (S)
BM AW FJ, JN, BB JH HC, DE FG WB SG, OW GG.   44th St., Studio 1
                                                                             New York City, NY

.... Vi   BVE-48166-2   Bandanna Babies –vOW
.... Vi   BVE-48167-2   Diga Diga Doo –vOW GG[1]
.... Vi   BVE-48168-1   I Must Have That Man –vOW

[1]Variant spellings: "Diga Diga Do"; "Digga Digga Doo."

DUKE ELLINGTON & HIS ORCHESTRA   20 Nov 1928   (S)
p BM AW FJ, JN, BB JH HC, DE FG WB SG.   OKeh Studios
                                                                             New York City, NY

....   W401350-A/-B   [The Blues With A Feelin']
....   W401351-A/-B/-C   [Goin' To Town]
....   W401352-A/-B   [Misty Mornin']

All takes from this session were rejected. Neither personnel nor instrumentation are noted in files.

DUKE ELLINGTON & HIS ORCHESTRA   22 Nov 1928   (S)
BM AW FJ, JN, BB JH HC, DE FG WB SG.   OKeh Studios
                                                                             New York City, NY

.... OK[1]   W401350-D   The Blues With A Feelin'

[1]Vo as by *The Jungle Band*.

THE CHICAGO FOOTWARMERS
Same personnel.

.... OK   W401351-E   Goin' To Town

DUKE ELLINGTON & HIS ORCHESTRA
LJ added, otherwise same personnel.

.... OK[1]   W401352-D   Misty Mornin'

[1]Vo as by *The Jungle Band*.

THE WHOOPEE MAKERS   *c* 30 Nov 1928[1]   (S)
AW FJ, JN, BB JH HC, DE FG WB SG.   Pathé Studios
                                                                             New York City, NY

.... Pth   108532-3[2]   Hottentot[3]
.... Pth   108533-3[2]   Misty Mornin'

[1]Some sources date this session to *c* 12 Dec 1928.
[2]Pathé/Perfect numbers 108532 and 108533 were assigned Cameo transfer numbers 3563 and 3564 respectively. Cameo transfer numbers do not bear take suffixes.
[3]Complete: "Hottentot Tot."

OZIE WARE   *c* 12 Dec 1928   (S)
Vcl, acc. by AW, JN, BB, DE FG SG.   Pathé Studios
                                                                             New York City, NY

.... Cam[1]   3532-B[2]   Hit Me In The Nose Blues –vOW   >>>

> DE, OW.

.... Cam   3533-B   It's All Coming Home To You –vOW

[1]Per as by Ozie Ware acc. by *The Whoopee Makers*.
[2]In this case, master #108671 (no take suffix) is the transfer. Unissued take #3532-A did not receive a transfer number.

20 Dec 1928   (S
Liederkranz Hall
New York City, NY

WARREN MILLS & HIS BLUE SERENADERS
BM AW FJ, JN, BB JH HC, DE FG WB SG, with an unidentified orchestra and chorus,
directed by Matty Malneck.

.... JA   CVE-49007-1   St. Louis Blues –vChorus
.... Vi   CVE-49007-2   St. Louis Blues –vChorus
.... Vi   CVE-49007-3   St. Louis Blues –vChorus
....   CVE-49008-1/-2/-3   [Gems from "Blackbirds Of 1928" –vSG[1]]

[1]Including: I Can't Give You Anything But Love; Doin' The New Lowdown; I Must Have That Man.

8 Jan 1929   (S)
799 Seventh Ave., Room 2
New York City, NY

THE JUNGLE BAND
BM AW FJ, JN, BB JH HC, DE FG WB SG.

.... Br   E28939-A/-B   Doin' The Voom Voom
.... Br   E28940-A   Tiger Rag, part 1
.... Br   E28940-B   Tiger Rag, part 1
.... Br   E28941-A   Tiger Rag, part 2

16 Jan 1929   (S)
44th Street Studios
New York City, NY

DUKE ELLINGTON & HIS COTTON CLUB ORCHESTRA
BM AW FJ, JN, BB JH HC, DE FG WB SG.

.... UTD   BVE-49652-1   Flaming Youth
.... Vi   BVE-49652-2   Flaming Youth
.... Vi   BVE-49653-2   Saturday Night Function
.... Vi   BVE-49654-1   High Life[1]
.... Vi   BVE-49655-1   Doin' The Voom Voom
.... Vi   BVE-49655-2   Doin' The Voom Voom

[1]This title is a derivative of *Tiger Rag*.

18 Feb 1929   (S)
46th Street Studio
New York City, NY

DUKE ELLINGTON'S ORCHESTRA
AW FJ, JN BB JH HC, DE FG WB SG.

.... Vi   BVE-48373-2   Japanese Dream
.... Vi   BVE-48374-1   Harlemania

1 Mar 1929   (S)
799 Seventh Ave. Studios
New York City, NY

THE JUNGLE BAND
CW AW FJ, JN, BB JH HC, DE FG WB SG.

.... Br   E29381-A/-B   Rent Party Blues
.... Br   E29382-A   Paducah
.... Br   E29383-B   Harlem Flat Blues

c 4 Mar 1929   (S)
Pathé Studios
New York City, NY

THE WASHINGTONIANS
CW, BB JH, DE FG WB.

.... Cam   3713-C   Saratoga Swing
.... Cam   3714-A   Who Said "It's Tight Like That"? –vCW

OZIE WARE
Vcl, acc. by same as above.

.... Cam   3715-B   He Just Don't Appeal To Me –vOW

7 Mar 1929   (S)
Liederkranz Hall
New York City, NY

DUKE ELLINGTON & HIS COTTON CLUB ORCHESTRA
CW AW FJ, JN, BB JH HC, DE FG WB SG.

.... Vi   BVE-49767-1[1]   The Dicty Glide[2]
.... Vi   BVE-49767-2   The Dicty Glide
.... Vi   BVE-49768-2   Hot Feet –vCW

> JN omitted.

.... Vi   BVE-49769-1[1]   Sloppy Joe –vSG
.... Vi   BVE-49769-2   Sloppy Joe –vSG   >>>

> JN added.

.... Vi   BVE-49770-2[3]   Stevedore Stomp[4]

[1]Although takes 1 of masters BVE-49767 and BVE-49769 were the first choice master takes, every commercially issued 78 rpm record was pressed from the second takes.
[2]aka "A-Flat Shout."
[3]Take 1 of master BVE-49770 was originally marked "master" and take 2 was marked "hold indefinitely." In fact, take 1 was ordered to be destroyed and take 2 mastered. Contrary to sleeve notes for various LP/CD releases no test or commercial pressing of BVE-49770-1 is known to exist.
[4]aka "Stevedore Jump."

                                                                    4 Apr 1929   (S)
JOE TURNER & HIS MEMPHIS MEN   Columbia Studios
CW AW FJ, JN, BB JH HC, DE FG WB SG.   New York City, NY

.... Co   148170-3   I Must Have That Man
.... Co   148171-1   Freeze And Melt
.... Co   148172-3   Mississippi Moan

                                                                    12 Apr 1929   (S)
DUKE ELLINGTON & HIS COTTON CLUB ORCHESTRA   Liederkranz Hall
CW AW FJ, JN, BB JH HC, hca, DE FG WB SG, IM.   New York City, NY

.... Pir   CVE-51158-1[1]   A Nite At The Cotton Club, part 1 –IM talking[2]
.... Pir   CVE-51159-1[1]   A Nite At The Cotton Club, part 2 –IM talking[3]

[1]Contrary to sleeve notes for Pir and RCA/Vi (F) 741.029, take 2 of part 1 and take 3 of part 2 remain unissued.
[2]Including: Cotton Club Stomp; Misty Mornin'.
[3]Including: Goin' To Town; Freeze And Melt –vGrp.

                                                                    3 May 1929   (S)
DUKE ELLINGTON & HIS COTTON CLUB ORCHESTRA   Liederkranz Hall
CW AW FJ, JN, BB JH HC, DE FG WB SG.   New York City, NY

.... Vi   BVE-51971-2   Cotton Club Stomp
.... Vi   BVE-51972-2   Misty Mornin'
.... Vi   BVE-51973-2   Arabian Lover

> CW, BB JH, DE FG WB SG.

.... Vi   BVE-51974-2   Saratoga Swing

                                                                    28 May 1929   (S)
DUKE ELLINGTON & HIS MEMPHIS MEN   Columbia Studios
AW FJ, JN, BB JH HC, DE FG WB SG.   New York City, NY

.... Co   148640-1   That Rhythm Man

SONNY GREER & HIS MEMPHIS MEN
Same personnel.

.... Co   148641-3   Beggar's Blues
.... Co   148642-1   Saturday Night Function

                                                                    29 Jul 1929   (S)
THE JUNGLE BAND   799 Seventh Ave. Studios
CW AW FJ, JN, BB JH HC, DE FG WB SG.   New York City, NY

.... Br   E30585-B[1]   Black And Blue[2]

> JT added.

.... Br   E30586-A/-B   Jungle Jamboree[3]

[1]Contrary to sleeve notes for BD T1001, take A remains unissued.
[2]Complete: "What Did I Do To Be So Black And Blue."
[3]Actually "That Jungle Jamboree."

                                                                    31 Jul 1929   (S)
DUKE ELLINGTON & HIS ORCHESTRA   44th Street Studios
CW AW FJ, JN/JT, BB JH HC, DE FG WB SG.   New York City, NY

....   BVE-53971-1/-2   [Ain't Misbehavin']

The above waxes were cut, but not processed.

                                                                    2 Aug 1929   (S)
THE HARLEM FOOTWARMERS   OKeh Studios
AW, JN, BB, DE FG WB SG.   New York City, NY

.... OK   W402551-C   Jungle Jamboree
....   W402552-A/-B   [Six Or Seven Times –v??]   >>>

.... OK   W402553-B   Snake Hip Dance

DUKE ELLINGTON & HIS FAMOUS ORCHESTRA
AW, DE.

.... Fam   Black And Tan Fantasy
.... Fam   Black And Tan Fantasy
.... Fam   Black And Tan Fantasy
.... AdJ[3]   X5258   Black And Tan Fantasy

> CW FJ, JN JT, BB JH HC, FG WB SG added.

.... AdJ[3]   X5258   The Duke Steps Out
.... AdJ[3]   X5258   Black Beauty
.... Fam   The Duke Steps Out
.... Fam   Black Beauty
.... Fam   Cotton Club Stomp
.... Fam   Flaming Youth[4]

> HJC a cappella.

.... AdJ[3]   X5259   Same Train –vHJC

> Entire band added.

.... AdJ[3]   X5259   Black And Tan Fantasy

[1]Music for the movie short "Black And Tan."
[2]"Gramercy Studio."
[3]On Gzl as by *Bunta's Storyville Jazz Band*.
[4]Erroneously as "Hot Feet" on most releases.

THE WHOOPEE MAKERS
CW AW FJ, JN, BB JH HC, DE FG WB SG.

.... Pth[1]   4062-A   Doin' The Voom Voom
.... Pth   4063-B   Flaming Youth

[1]Rom as by *The Washingtonians*.

THE WASHINGTONIANS
Same personnel.

.... Cam[1]   4064-B   Saturday Night Function

[1]Ban as by *The Whoopee Makers*, Orl as by *Dixie Jazz Band*.

BILL ROBINSON acc. by IRVING MILLS & HIS HOTSY TOTSY GANG
Vcl & tap, acc. by CW AW, BB JH, DE FG WB SG.

.... Br   E30526-A/-B   Ain't Misbehavin' –vBRsn

> BB, DE omitted, JN added.

.... Br   E30527-A/-B   Doin' The New Lowdown –BRsn talking

THE JUNGLE BAND
CW AW FJ, JN JT, BB JH HC, DE FG WB SG.

.... Br   E30937-A   Jolly Wog
.... Br   E30938-A   Jazz Convulsions
....   E30939-A/-B   [Slow Motion[1]]

[1]*aka* "Jungle Rhythm."

DUKE ELLINGTON'S ORCHESTRA
CW AW, JN JT, BB JH HC, DE FG TB WB SG.

.... Vi   BVE-55845-2   Mississippi[1]

> TB omitted.

.... Vi   BVE-55846-2   The Duke Steps Out

> JH omitted, TB added.

.... Vi   BVE-55847-2   Haunted Nights

> JH added.

.... Vi   BVE-55848-2   Swanee Shuffles[2]

[1]"Mississippi Dry" on English and French 78-rpm releases.
[2]Correctly as "Swanee Shuffle" on English and French 78-rpm releases and some other reissues.

25 Oct 1929   (S)
799 Seventh Ave. Studios
New York City, NY

THE SIX JOLLY JESTERS
FJ, JN, JH, DE FG WB SG.

.... Vo   E31301-A/-B[1]   Six Or Seven Times –vSG FJ ??
.... Vo   E31301-B/-A   Six Or Seven Times –vSG FJ ??

[1]Which one of the releases is take A and which one is take B is still open to debate.

29 Oct 1929   (S)
799 Seventh Ave., Room 3
New York City, NY

THE SIX JOLLY JESTERS
CW FJ, JN, DE TB SG BJ, HR.

.... Vo   E31371-A   Goin' Nuts –vHR

> HR omitted, JH, FG WB added.

.... Vo   E31372-A   Oklahoma Stomp[1]
.... MCA   E31372-B   Oklahoma Stomp
....   E31372 off[2]   Oklahoma Stomp

[1]aka "Oklahoma Stuff"; this title is a derivative of Soda Fountain Rag.
[2]Test extant; "off" is likely an abbreviation for "office master" or "office take."

14 Nov 1929   (S)
Liederkranz Hall
New York City, NY

DUKE ELLINGTON & HIS COTTON CLUB ORCHESTRA
CW AW FJ, JN JT, BB JH HC, DE FG WB SG.

.... Vi   BVE-57542-1   Breakfast Dance[1]
.... Vi   BVE-57543-2   Jazz Lips[2]
.... Vi   BVE-57544-1   March Of The Hoodlums

[1]Originally titled "Ever-Day"; aka "Everyday."
[2]Originally titled "Zonky Blues"; aka "Fish Mouth."

20 Nov 1929   (S)
OKeh Studios
New York City, NY

THE HARLEM FOOTWARMERS
FJ, BB HC, DE FG SG.

.... OK   W403286-B   Lazy Duke

> JH added.

.... OK   W403287-B   Blues Of The Vagabond
.... OK   W403288-B   Syncopated Shuffle

10 Dec 1929   (S)
799 Seventh Ave. Studios
New York City, NY

THE JUNGLE BAND
CW AW FJ, JN JT, BB JH HC, DE FG WB.

.... Br   E31508-A   Sweet Mama[1]

> HC omitted.

.... Br   E31509-A   Wall Street Wail
.... MCA   E31509-B   Wall Street Wail

> HC added.

.... AH   E31510-A   Cincinnati Daddy

[1]No resemblance with "Sweet Mamma."

18 Dec 1929   (S)
799 Seventh Ave. Studios
New York City, NY

BILL ROBINSON WITH IRVING MILLS & HIS HOTSY TOTSY GANG[1]
Vcl & tap, acc. by unlisted personnel.

....   E31728-A/?-B   [Sweet Mama –vBRsn]
....   E31729-A/?-B   [Black Beauty –BRsn, vcl or talking]

[1]This recording session is listed on the artist's card of Bill Robinson, without giving any further details. On account of the titles and the fact that BRsn has recorded previously with DE, using the same pseudonym for the band, there is little doubt that this is an Ellington recording. Both masters, however, were destroyed before 1932, and test pressings are not known to exist.

29 Jan 1930   (S)
1776 Broadway Studios[1]
New York City, NY

TEN BLACK BERRIES
CW AW FJ, JN JT, BB JH HC, DE FG WB SG, SS.

.... Per[2]   9319-1   St. James Infirmary –vSS
.... Ban   9319-2   St. James Infirmary –vSS
.... Ban[3]   9319-3   St. James Infirmary –vSS
.... Ban   9320-1   When You're Smiling –vSS
.... Per[4]   9320-3   When You're Smiling –vSS
.... Ban   9321-1   Rent Party Blues
.... Cam   9321-2   Rent Party Blues   >>>

....	Ban	9321-3	Rent Party Blues
....	Ban	9322-1	Jungle Blues
....	Cam[5]	9322-2	Jungle Blues

[1]ARC Studios.
[2]Apx and Dom as by *Ten Black Birds;* Crn as by *Ten Blackbirds;* Stg as by *Ten Red Dandies;* Roy is unknown.
[3]Simultaneous issues on Cam and Jwl.
[4]Apx as by *Ten Black Birds.*
[5]Simultaneous issues on Orl and Rom.

                                                                                    21 Feb 1930   (S)
                                                                                    799 Seventh Ave. Studios
THE JUNGLE BAND   New York City, NY
CW AW FJ, JN JT, BB JH HC, DE FG WB SG, IM.

....		E32209-A/-B	[Admiration]
....	Br	E32210-A/-B	Maori[1]
....		E32211-A/-B	[Maori]
....		E32212-A/-B	[When You're Smiling –vIM]

[1]Subtitled "A Samoan Dance."

                                                                                    20 Mar 1930   (S)
                                                                                    799 Seventh Ave., Room 3
THE JUNGLE BAND   New York City, NY
CW AW FJ, JN JT, BB JH HC, DE FG WB SG, IM.

....	Br	E32447-A	When You're Smiling –vIM
....	UTD	E32447-B	When You're Smiling –vIM
....	Br	E32448-A	Maori
....	MCA	E32448-B	Maori
....	Br	E32449-A/-B	Admiration[1]

[1]*aka* "Admiration; Hawaiian Idyl."

                                                                                    Mar 1930   (S)
                                                                                    Durium Studios[1]
HARLEM HOT CHOCOLATES   New York City, NY
CW AW FJ, JN JT, BB JH HC, DE FG WB SG, IM.

| .... | HW | 1045-C | Sing, You Sinners –vIM |
| .... | HW | 1046-D | St. James Infirmary –vIM |

[1]McGraw-Hill Building, West 42nd Street and Ninth Avenue.

                                                                                    3 Apr 1930   (S)
                                                                                    Columbia Studios
MILLS TEN BLACKBERRIES   New York City, NY
CW AW FJ, JN JT, BB JH HC, DE FG WB SG.

....	Vt	150165-2	The Mooche
....	Div	150165-3	The Mooche
....	FDC	150166-1	Ragamuffin Romeo
....	VT	150167-2	East St. Louis Toodle-Oo[1]
....	VT	150167-3	East St. Louis Toodle-Oo[1]

[1]Most VT and Div copies as "East St. Louis Toodle-O"; some west coast pressings were erroneously labeled
"East St. Louis Toolle-O."

                                                                                    11 Apr 1930   (S)
                                                                                    44th Street Studios
DUKE ELLINGTON & HIS COTTON CLUB ORCHESTRA   New York City, NY
CW AW, JN JT, BB JH HC, DE FG WB SG, FM.

....	Vi	BVE-59692-2	Double Check Stomp[1]
....	Vi	BVE-59693-2	My Gal Is Good For Nothin' But Love –vFM[2]
....	Vi	BVE-59694-1	I Was Made To Love You –vFM

[1]Originally titled "Check And Double Check."
[2]The copyright claim shows the title as "My Man Is Good For Nothin' But Love."

                                                                                    22 Apr 1930   (S)
                                                                                    799 Seventh Ave., Room 3
THE JUNGLE BAND   New York City, NY
CW AW FJ, JN JT, BB JH HC, DE JCS FG WB SG, DRsn.

....	Br	E32612-A	Double Check Stomp
....	Br	E32613-A	Accordion Joe –vDRsn
....	UTD	E32613-B	Accordion Joe –vDRsn
....	Br	E32614-A	Cotton Club Stomp[1]
....	UTD	E32614-B	Cotton Club Stomp[1]

[1]Totally different from the composition of that name issued previously on Vi or subsequently on other labels. However,
there is a strong resemblance with Eubie Blake's composition *Keep Your Temper.* To add to the confusion, this "Cotton
Club Stomp" was put out on the flip side of "Wall Street Wail" with inverted labels. This mistake has not always been
noted with the result that also on many reissues *Cotton Club Stomp* is labeled as *Wall Street Wail* and vice versa.

4 Jun 1930   (S)
46th Street Studio
New York City, NY

DUKE ELLINGTON & HIS COTTON CLUB ORCHESTRA
CW AW FJ, JN JT, BB JH HC, DE FG WB SG.

....	Vi	BVE-62192-1	Sweet Dreams Of Love
....	Bb	BVE-62192-2	Sweet Dreams Of Love
....	Vi	BVE-62193-2	Jungle Nights In Harlem
....	Vi	BVE-62194-1	Sweet Jazz Of Mine[1]
....	Vi	BVE-62194-2	Sweet Jazz Of Mine
....	Vi	BVE-62195-2	Shout 'Em, Aunt Tillie[2]

[1]This title was released in England as "Sweet Dreams Of Mine."
[2]Originally titled "Shout 'Em Down, Aunt Tillie."

12 Jun 1930   (S)
Columbia Studios
New York City, NY

MILLS TEN BLACKBERRIES
CW AW FJ, JN, BB JH HC, DE FG WB SG.

....	VT	150584-1	Sweet Mama[1]
....	VT	150584-2	Sweet Mama
....	VT	150585-1	Hot And Bothered
....	VT	150586-1	Double Check Stomp
....	VT	150586-2	Double Check Stomp
....	VT	150590-1	Black And Tan Fantasy

[1]"Sweet Papa" on JSo.

Masters #150587/88/89 are not Ellington items.

20 Aug 1930   (S)
Hollywood Recording Studio[1]
Hollywood, CA

DUKE ELLINGTON & HIS ORCHESTRA
CW AW FJ, JN JT, BB JH HC, DE FG WB SG, JMlr EH4.

....	Pir	PBVE-61011-2	Ring Dem Bells –vCW
....	Vi	PBVE-61011-3[2]	Ring Dem Bells –vCW
....	UTD	PBVE-61012-1	Old Man Blues[3]
....	Pir	PBVE-61012-2[4]	Old Man Blues
....	FM	PBVE-61012-3[5]	Old Man Blues
....	Vi	PBVE-61013-1	Three Little Words –vEH4[6]

[1]Victor Studios, at 1016 N. Sycamore Avenue.
[2]Take stamped on Vi 20-1532 is "7R."
[3]Originally titled "Ow Wa! Ow Wa Blues," based on a character from the *Amos 'n' Andy* show.
[4]Misidentified as take 3 on Pir and Vi 741.048.
[5]Misidentified as take 6 on FM.
[6]On the unissued take 3 the vocal is by JMlr.

26 Aug 1930   (S)
Hollywood Recording Studio
Hollywood, CA

DUKE ELLINGTON & HIS ORCHESTRA
CW AW FJ, JN JT, BB JH HC, DE FG WB SG, RB.

....	Vi	PBVE-61013-5	Three Little Words –vRB
....	Vi	PBVE-61011-6	Ring Dem Bells –vCW
....	JA	PBVE-61012-4	Old Man Blues
....	Vi	PBVE-61012-6	Old Man Blues

Aug 1930   (T)[1]
RKO Studios
Hollywood, CA

DUKE ELLINGTON & HIS ORCHESTRA
CW AW FJ, JN JT, BB JH HC, DE FG WB SG, RB.

....			Instrument tuning
....	Pr		When I'm Blue
....	MoJ	403	The Mystery Song
....			When I'm Blue
....	Prt	404	East St. Louis Toodle-Oo
....	Prt	405[2]	[Three Little Words] –vRB
....	Prt	406	Old Man Blues
....	Rn	407[3]	Three Little Words

[1]Music for the motion picture "Check And Double Check."
[2]It is assumed that although DE's orchestra with a vocal trio of bandsmen is seen on screen performing the piece, one actually hears a white studio orchestra backing the Rhythm Boys.
[3]A 15-second fragment, believed to originate from #407, has been used in the motion picture "Laugh And Get Rich."

2 Oct 1930   (S)
24th St., Studio 4
New York City, NY

DUKE ELLINGTON & HIS COTTON CLUB ORCHESTRA
CW AW FJ, JN JT, BB JH HC, DE FG WB SG, DRsn.

....	Vi	BVE-63360-1	Hittin' The Bottle –vDRsn
....	Vi	BVE-63360-2	Hittin' The Bottle –vDRsn
....	Vi	BVE-63361-3	That Lindy Hop –vDRsn >>>

....	Vi	BVE-63362-2	You're Lucky To Me –vDRsn
....	Vi	BVE-63363-1	Memories Of You –vDRsn

                                                                              14 Oct 1930   (S)

THE HARLEM FOOTWARMERS   OKeh Studios[1]
AW, JN, BB, DE FG WB SG.   New York City , NY

....	OK	W404481-A[2]	Mood Indigo
....	OK	W404482-C	Big House Blues
....	OK	W404483-B	Rocky Mountain Blues

[1]From here on the OKeh recordings were most certainly done at the combined Columbia/OKeh Studios, at 1819 Broadway.
[2]First issue OK 8840, pressed from dub matrix #W480023-B.

                           17 Oct 1930   (S)

THE JUNGLE BAND   799 Seventh Ave. Studios
CW AW FJ, JN JT, BB JH HC, DE FG WB SG, DRsn.   New York City, NY

....	Br[1]	E34927-A	Runnin' Wild –vDRsn

> AW, JN, BB, DE FG WB SG.

....	Br[1]	E34928-A	Dreamy Blues[2]

[1]Ban and Per as by *Louisiana Rhythmakers*.
[2]sa "Mood Indigo"; Barney Bigard "borrowed" the idea for the song from his teacher Lorenzo Tio, Jr. and reworked it together with Duke Ellington. The first pressing of Br 4952 was released as "Dreamy Blues," which is believed to be the original title. Later pressings of Br 4952 and all subsequent pressings were issued under the title of *Mood Indigo*. The composer credits were claimed by Ellington and Mills. Bigard was acknowledged as cocomposer only in 1958. Lorenzo Tio was never credited for the music.

                           27 Oct 1930   (S)

THE JUNGLE BAND   799 Seventh Ave. Studios
CW AW FJ, JN JT, BB JH HC, DE FG WB SG, DRsn BP.   New York City, NY

....	Br	E35035-B	Home Again Blues –vDRsn
....	Br	E35036-A	Wang-Wang Blues –vDRsn BP

                           30 Oct 1930   (S)

THE HARLEM MUSIC MASTERS   OKeh Studios
CW AW FJ, JN JT, BB JH HC, DE FG WB SG, IM.   New York City, NY

....	Od[1]	W404519-A	Ring Dem Bells –vCW
....	Od[2]	W404520-A[3]	Three Little Words –vIM

[1]Od (Ar+F) as by *The Harlem Footwarmers*, Pa (US) as by *Frank Brown & His Tooters*; OK (reissue) as by *The Harlem Music Masters*.
[2]Pa (US) as by *Frank Brown & His Tooters*. Pa (E) as by *The Philadelphia Melodians*.
[3]Only take A is presumed to be issued. All reissues are erroneously identified as take C. Pa (E) used the dub matrix #W480028E.

THE HARLEM FOOTWARMERS
IM omitted, otherwise same personnel.

....	OK	W404521-B	Old Man Blues
....	OK	W404522-B	Sweet Chariot –vCW

                           21 Nov 1930   (S)

DUKE ELLINGTON & HIS COTTON CLUB ORCHESTRA   24th St., Studio 1
CW AW FJ, JN JT, BB JH HC, DE FG WB SG, BSm.   New York City, NY

....		BVE-64811-1/-2	[Mood Indigo]
....	Vi	BVE-64812-1	Nine Little Miles From Ten-Ten-Tennessee –vBSm
....	Vi	BVE-64812-2	Nine Little Miles From Ten-Ten-Tennessee –vBSm
....	Vi	BVE-64813-1	I'm So In Love With You –vBsm
....	Vi	BVE-64813-2	I'm So In Love With You –vBSm

                           26 Nov 1930   (S)

DUKE ELLINGTON & HIS COTTON CLUB ORCHESTRA   24th St., Studio 2
CW AW FJ, JN JT, BB JH HC, DE FG WB SG, DRsn SGry.   New York City, NY

....	Tax	BVE-64378-1	What Good Am I Without You? –vDRsn
....	Vi	BVE-64379-1	Blue Again –vSGry
....	Tax	BVE-64380-2	When A Black Man's Blue –vSGry

                           10 Dec 1930   (S)

DUKE ELLINGTON & HIS COTTON CLUB ORCHESTRA   24th St., Studio 2
CW AW FJ, JN JT, BB JH HC, DE FG WB SG, DRsn BP.   New York City, NY

....	Vi	BVE-64811-4	Mood Indigo
....	Vi	BVE-64378-4	What Good Am I Without You? –vDRsn
....	Vi	BVE-64380-4	When A Black Man's Blue –vBP

<u>NEW YORK SYNCOPATORS</u>
CW AW FJ, JN JT, BB JH HC, DE FG WB SG, SGry.

| .... | Od[1] | W404802-A | I Can't Realize You Love Me –vSGry |
| .... | Od[1] | W404803-B | I'm So In Love With You –vSGry |

[1]Clr, Har, VT as by *Memphis Hot Shots*, and bearing transfer nos. W100549-1 and W100550-1 respectively; Pa (US) as by *The Harlem Footwarmers*.

<u>THE HARLEM FOOTWARMERS</u>
SGry omitted, otherwise same personnel.

| .... | OK | W404804-A | Rockin' In Rhythm |

> AW, JN, BB, DE FG WB SG.

| .... | | W404481-D/-E | [Mood Indigo] |

<u>THE WHOOPEE MAKERS</u>
CW AW FJ, JN JT, BB JH HC, DE FG WB SG, CB.

....	Orl	10356-1	Them There Eyes –vCB
....	Orl[1]	10356-2	Them There Eyes –vCB
....	Ro	10356-3	Them There Eyes –vCB
....	Orl	10357-1	Rockin' Chair –vCB
....	Orl	10357-2	Rockin' Chair –vCB
....	Per	10357-3[2]	Rockin' Chair –vCB
....	Ro	10357-4	Rockin' Chair –vCB

[1]Bbd as by *Broadway Revellers*. Crn 91059 and Roy as by *Cliff Roberts' Dance Orchestra;* Dom and Stg are unknown.
[2]Contrary to sleeve notes for BD T1001, take 2 was reissued instead of take 3.

<u>THE GEORGIA SYNCOPATORS</u>
Same personnel.

| .... | Mlt | 10359-3 | I'm So In Love With You –vCB |

Master #10358 is not an Ellington item.

<u>THE JUNGLE BAND</u>
CW AW FJ, JN JT, BB JH HC, DE FG WB SG, BP.

| .... | | E35920[1] | [Rockin' Chair –vBP] |
| .... | | E35921[1] | [Rockin' In Rhythm] |

[1]The above waxes were cut, but not processed. The master numbers have been reassigned to recordings by Grace Johnson on 13 Jan 1931. "The Peanut Vendor" and "Twelfth Street Rag" were scheduled for the same session, but not made.

<u>EARL JACKSON & HIS MUSICAL CHAMPIONS</u>
CW AW FJ, JN, BB JH HC, DE FG WB SG, BP.

| .... | Mlt[1] | E35800-A | Rockin' Chair –vBP |

[1]Aur as by *Dick Sparling & His Orchestra*.

<u>THE JUNGLE BAND</u>
BP omitted, otherwise same personnel.

| .... | Br[1] | E35801-A | Rockin' In Rhythm |

> JT, BP –p added.

| .... | Br[1] | E35802-A | Twelfth Street Rag |

[1]Per, Kri, Mlt as by *Louisiana Rhythmakers*.

<u>DUKE ELLINGTON & HIS COTTON CLUB ORCHESTRA</u>
CW AW FJ, JN JT, BB JH HC, DE FG WB SG, CB.

....	Vi	BVE-67798-2	The River And Me –vCB
....	Vi	BVE-67799-1	Keep A Song In Your Soul –vCB
....	Vi	BVE-67800-1	Sam And Delilah –vCB

<u>DUKE ELLINGTON & HIS ORCHESTRA</u>
CB omitted, otherwise same personnel.

| .... | Vi | BVE-67401-1 | Rockin' In Rhythm |
| .... | Vi | BVE-67401-2 | Rockin' In Rhythm |

EARL JACKSON & HIS MUSICAL CHAMPIONS
CW AW FJ, JN JT, BB JH HC, DE FG WB SG.

.... Mlt   E35938-A   The Peanut Vendor

THE JUNGLE BAND
Same personnel.

.... Br   E35939-A   Creole Rhapsody, part 1
.... Br   E35940-A   Creole Rhapsody, part 2
.... Br   E35940-AA   Creole Rhapsody, part 2

EARL JACKSON & HIS MUSICAL CHAMPIONS
DRsn added, otherwise same personnel.

.... Mlt   E35941-A   Is That Religion? –vDRsn

DUKE ELLINGTON & HIS ORCHESTRA
CW AW FJ, JN JT, BB JH HC, DE FG WB SG.

.... Vi   CRC-68231-2   Creole Rhapsody, part 1
....   CRC-68232-1/-2   [Creole Rhapsody, part 1]
.... Vi   CRC-68233-2   Creole Rhapsody, part 2
.... Vi   CRC-68233-3   Creole Rhapsody, part 2

[1]Victor Studios, at 114 N. 5th Street.

DUKE ELLINGTON & HIS COTTON CLUB ORCHESTRA
CW AW FJ, JN JT, BB JH HC, DE FG WB SG.

.... Vi   BRC-68237-1   Limehouse Blues
.... Vi   BRC-68238-1   Echoes Of The Jungle

DUKE ELLINGTON & HIS ORCHESTRA
CW AW FJ, JN JT, BB JH HC, DE FG WB SG.

.... Vi   BRC-68239-1   It's Glory[1]
.... Vi   BRC-68240-1   The Mystery Song
.... Vi   BRC-68240-2   The Mystery Song

[1]"It's A Glory" on English and French 78-rpm releases; *aka* "M'monia"; "Shim Sham."

DUKE ELLINGTON & HIS ORCHESTRA
CW AW FJ, JN JT, BB JH HC, DE WB SG.

....   C7938-A/-B   [Tootsie Hill[1]]
....   C7939-A/-B   [It Don't Mean A Thing[2]]

[1]Complete: "Tootsie Hill From Louisville."
[2]Complete: "It Don't Mean A Thing If It Ain't Got That Swing."

Although both titles are subtitled "Fox-trot with vocal chorus," no vocalist has been mentioned on the recording sheet. It is assumed that JH (ss) played the parts that were assigned to IA on the 2 Feb 1931 recording. However, it is worth noting that IA had joined the band earlier in the year.

DUKE ELLINGTON & HIS FAMOUS ORCHESTRA
CW AW FJ, JN JT, BB JH HC, DE FG WB SG, IA.

.... Br   B11200-A   Moon Over Dixie –vSG
.... Br   B11204-A   It Don't Mean A Thing –vIA
.... Br   B11205-A   Lazy Rhapsody –vCW[1]
.... Co   B11205-B   Lazy Rhapsody –vCW

[1]Originally titled "Lullaby"; *aka* "Swanee Rhapsody."

DUKE ELLINGTON & HIS ORCHESTRA
CW AW FJ, JN JT, BB JH HC, DE FG WB SG.

.... Vi   LBRC-71811-1[1]   Mood Indigo—Hot And Bothered—Creole Love Call
.... Vi   LBSHQ-71812-2[1] Mood Indigo—Hot And Bothered—Creole Love Call
.... Vi   LBSHQ-71812-3   Mood Indigo—Hot And Bothered—Creole Love Call

[1]The takes are identical; however, the recordings were made from two different microphone placements in the studio, thus giving a stereo image when both records are played simultaneously.

DUKE ELLINGTON & HIS FAMOUS ORCHESTRA
CW AW FJ, JN JT, BB JH HC, DE FG WB SG.

....	Br	B11223-A	Blue Tune
....	Co	B11223-B	Blue Tune
....	Br	B11224-A	Baby, When You Ain't There –vCW

DUKE ELLINGTON & HIS ORCHESTRA
CW AW FJ, JN JT, BB JH HC, DE FG WB SG.

....	Vi	LBRC-71836-2[1]	East St. Louis Toodle-Oo—Lots O'Fingers—Black And Tan Fantasy[2]
....	Evb	LBSHQ-71837-1[1]	East St. Louis Toodle-Oo—Lots O'Fingers—Black And Tan Fantasy
....	Vi	BRC-71838-1	Dinah –vSG CW Band
....	Vi	BRC-71839-1	Bugle Call Rag[3]

[1]The takes are identical; however, the recordings were made from two different microphone placements in the studio, thus giving a stereo image when both records are played simultaneously.
[2]The label shows "East St. Louis Toddle" and "Lot O'Fingers."
[3]Compare: "Sergeant Dunn's Bugle Call Blues" by Johnny Dunn, master #145759-2, 13 Mar 1928.

BING CROSBY WITH DUKE ELLINGTON & HIS FAMOUS ORCHESTRA
Vcl, acc. by CW AW FJ, JN JT, BB JH HC, DE FG WB SG.

....	Br	BX11263-A	St. Louis Blues –vBC
....	Br	BX11263-B	St. Louis Blues –vBC

DUKE ELLINGTON & HIS FAMOUS ORCHESTRA
BC omitted, otherwise same personnel.

....	Br	BX11264-A	Creole Love Call
....		BX11264-B[1]	Creole Love Call
....	Br	B11265-A	Rose Room[2]

[1]Test extant.
[2]Subtitled "In Sunny Roseland."

DUKE ELLINGTON & HIS ORCHESTRA
CW AW FJ, JN LB JT, BB JH OH HC, DE FG WB SG.

....			East St. Louis Toodle-Oo
....			When Its Sleepy-Time Down South –vSG
....			Double Check Stomp

DUKE ELLINGTON & HIS FAMOUS ORCHESTRA
CW AW FJ, JN LB JT, BB JH OH HC, DE FG WB SG.

....	Br	B11839-A	Blue Harlem[1]
....	Br	B11840-A	The Sheik Of Araby

[1]aka "Send Me."

DUKE ELLINGTON & HIS FAMOUS ORCHESTRA
CW AW FJ, JN LB JT, BB JH OH HC, DE FG WB SG.

....	Br	B11850-A	Swampy River
....	Br	B11851-A	Fast And Furious[1]
....	Co	B11852-A	Best Wishes
....	Br	B11852-B	Best Wishes

[1]sa "Lots O'Fingers."

DUKE ELLINGTON & HIS FAMOUS ORCHESTRA
CW AW FJ, JN LB JT, BB JH HC, DE FG WB SG.

....	Co	B11865-A/-B[1]	Slippery Horn

> OH added.

....	Br	B11866-A	Blue Ramble
....	Co	B11866-B	Blue Ramble
....		B11867-A[2]	Clouds In My Heart[3]
....	Co	B11867-B	Clouds In My Heart

[1]The "alternate" take B issued on BD T1001 is identical with the original release on Co and all reissues. Which one of the two takes has in fact been issued is still open to debate. This title is a derivative of *Tiger Rag*.   >>>

[2]Test extant.
[3]*aka* "Harlem Romance"; "Never Again."

				19 Sep 1932 (S)

DUKE ELLINGTON & HIS FAMOUS ORCHESTRA
CW AW FJ, JN LB JT, BB JH OH HC, DE FG WB SG.

....	Co	B12332-A	Blue Mood
....	GAP	B12332-B[1]	Blue Mood
....	Rt	B12232-C[1]	Blue Mood
....	Br	B12233-A	Ducky Wucky
....	Co	B12233-B	Ducky Wucky

[1]CBS/Co (F) 88035 has takes B and C inverted.

19 Sep 1932 (S)
1776 Broadway Studios
New York City, NY

DUKE ELLINGTON & HIS ORCHESTRA
CW AW FJ, JN LB JT, BB JH OH HC, DE FG WB SG.

....	FDC	BS-73557-1	Maori
....		BS-73558-1/-2	[Jive]
....		BS-73559-1/-2	[Sophisticated Lady[1]]
....		BS-73560-1/-2	[Margie –vSG]

[1]Originally titled "My Sophisticated Daddy."

21 Sep 1932 (S)
24th St., Studio 1
New York City, NY

DUKE ELLINGTON & HIS FAMOUS ORCHESTRA
Same personnel.

....	Br	B12343-A	Jazz Cocktail
....	GAP	B12343-B	Jazz Cocktail
....	Br	B12344-A	Lightnin'
....	Co	B12344-B	Lightnin'

1776 Broadway Studios (S)

DUKE ELLINGTON & HIS FAMOUS ORCHESTRA
CW AW FJ, JN LB JT, BB JH OH HC, DE FG WB SG, RM.

....	Br	B12345-A	Stars –vRM
....	Co	B12345-B	Stars –vRM
....	Co	B12346-A	Swing Low
....	Br	B12346-B	Swing Low

A Victor recording session planned for the same date was called off; men were too tired.

22 Sep 1932 (S)
1776 Broadway Studios
New York City, NY

ADELAIDE HALL WITH DUKE ELLINGTON & HIS FAMOUS ORCHESTRA
Vcl, acc. by CW AW FJ, JN LB JT, JH OH HC, DE FG WB SG.

....	BD	B12773-A	I Must Have That Man –vAHl
....	BD	B12773-B	I Must Have That Man –vAHl
....	Co	B12774-A	Baby –vAHl
....	BD	B12774-B	Baby –vAHl

21 Dec 1932 (S)
1776 Broadway Studios
New York City, NY

DUKE ELLINGTON & HIS FAMOUS ORCHESTRA
AHl omitted, IA added, otherwise same personnel.

....	Br	B12775-A	Any Time, Any Day, Anywhere –vIA
....	Ly	B12775-B	Any Time, Any Day, Anywhere –vIA
....	Co	B12776-A	Delta Bound –vIA
....	BD	B12776-B	Delta Bound –vIA

THE MILLS BROTHERS WITH DUKE ELLINGTON & HIS FAMOUS ORCHESTRA
Vcl, acc. by CW AW FJ, JN LB JT, JH OH HC, DE FG WB SG.

....	Br	B12781-A	Diga Diga Doo –vMB
....	Co	B12781-B	Diga Diga Doo –vMB

22 Dec 1932 (S)
1776 Broadway Studios
New York City, NY

Master #B12782 is not an Ellington item.

ETHEL WATERS WITH DUKE ELLINGTON & HIS FAMOUS ORCHESTRA
Vcl, acc. by CW AW FJ, JN LB, JH HC, DE FG WB SG.

....	Br	B12783-A	I Can't Give You Anything But Love –vEW
....	Co	B12783-B	I Can't Give You Anything But Love –vEW
....	Br	B12784-A	Porgy –vEW
....		B12784-B[1]	Porgy –vEW
....		B12784-C[1]	Porgy –vEW

[1]Test extant.

ADELAIDE HALL WITH DUKE ELLINGTON & HIS FAMOUS ORCHESTRA
Vcl, acc. by CW AW, JN LB JT, BB JH OH HC, DE FG WB SG.

7 Jan 1933   (S)
1776 Broadway Studios
New York City, NY

....	Br	B12773-C	I Must Have That Man –vAHl
....	Co	B12773-D	I Must Have That Man –vAHl
....	Br	B12774-C	Baby –vAHl
....	BD	B12774-D	Baby –vAHl

DUKE ELLINGTON & HIS FAMOUS ORCHESTRA
AHl omitted, otherwise same personnel.

| .... | Br | B12855-A | Eerie Moan |
| .... | Ly | B12855-B | Eerie Moan |

DUKE ELLINGTON & HIS ORCHESTRA
CW AW FJ, JN LB JT, BB JH OH HC, DE FG WB SG, IA.

15 Feb 1933[1]   (S)
55 Fifth Avenue Studio
New York City, NY

....	Co	W265049-2	Merry-Go-Round[2]
....	Co	W265049-3	Merry-Go-Round
....	Co	W265050-1	Sophisticated Lady
....	Co	W265050-2	Sophisticated Lady
....	Co	W265051-2	I've Got The World On A String –vIA

[1]This session and the following one were produced exclusively for BMI.
[2]*aka* "King Of Spades"; "Cotton Club Shim Sham"; "142nd Street And Lenox Avenue."

DUKE ELLINGTON & HIS ORCHESTRA
CW AW FJ, JN LB JT, BB JH OH HC, DE FG WB SG.

16 Feb 1933   (S)
55 Fifth Avenue Studio
New York City, NY

| .... | Co | W265052-3 | Down A Carolina Lane |

DUKE ELLINGTON & HIS FAMOUS ORCHESTRA
CW AW FJ, JN LB JT, BB JH HC, DE FG WB SG.

17 Feb 1933   (S)
1776 Broadway Studios
New York City, NY

| .... | Br | B13078-A | Slippery Horn |
| .... | BD | B13078-B | Slippery Horn |

> OH added.

....	Br	B13079-A	Blackbirds Medley, part 1[1]
....	Co	B13079-B	Blackbirds Medley, part 1[1]
....	Br	B13080-A	Blackbirds Medley, part 2[2]
....	Co	B13080-B	Blackbirds Medley, part 2[2]
....	UTD	B13080-C	Blackbirds Medley, part 2[2]
....	Br	B13081-A	Drop Me Off At Harlem[3]
....	Co	B13081-B	Drop Me Off At Harlem

[1]Including: I Can't Give You Anything But Love; Doin' The New Lowdown; I Must Have That Man; Baby.
[2]Including: Dixie; Diga Diga Doo; Porgy; I Can't Give You Anything But Love.
[3]"Drop Me Off In Harlem" on some reissues as well as on some subsequent new releases of this title.

DUKE ELLINGTON & HIS ORCHESTRA
CW AW FJ, JN LB JT, BB JH OH HC, DE FG WB SG.

p 4 Mar 1933   (T)[1]
Paramount Eastern Service Studios
Astoria, Long Island, NY

| .... | Vid | | Sophisticated Lady—Creole Rhapsody |

[1]Music for the movie short "The World At Large" (Paramount Pictorial P3-1).

DUKE ELLINGTON & HIS FAMOUS ORCHESTRA
CW AW FJ, JN LB JT, JG JH HC, DE FG WB SG, IA.

9 May 1933   (S)
1776 Broadway Studios
New York City, NY

| .... | Br | B13306-A | Happy As The Day Is Long –vIA |

> OH added.

| .... | Br | B13307-A | Raisin' The Rent –vIA |
| .... | Br | B13308-A | Get Yourself A New Broom –vIA[1] |

[1]Complete "Get Yourself A New Broom And Sweep The Blues Away."

DUKE ELLINGTON & HIS FAMOUS ORCHESTRA
CW AW FJ, JN LB JT, BB JH OH HC, DE FG WB SG.

16 May 1933   (S)
1776 Broadway Studios
New York City, NY

| .... | Br | B13337-A | Bundle Of Blues[1]   >>> |

....	Co	B13337-B	Bundle Of Blues
....	Br	B13338-A[2]	Sophisticated Lady
....	Br	B13339-A	Stormy Weather

[1]*aka* "Dragon's Blues."
[2]Contrary to sleeve notes for BD T1003, take B remains unissued.

DUKE ELLINGTON & HIS ORCHESTRA
CW AW FJ, JN LB JT, BB JH OH HC, DE BJms/CHdy WB SG, IA.

23 May 1933   (T)[1]
Paramount Eastern Service Studios
Astoria, Long Island, NY

....	Prt		Lightnin'
....	Prt		Rockin' In Rhythm
....	Prt		Stormy Weather −vIA
....	Prt		Bugle Call Rag
....	Prt		Lightnin'

[1]Music for the movie short "Bundle Of Blues" (Paramount Headliner A3-2).

DUKE ELLINGTON & HIS FAMOUS ORCHESTRA
CW AW FJ, JN LB JT, BB JH OH HC, DE FG WB SG.

13 Jul 1933   (S)
Chenil Galleries
London, England

....	De	GB6038-3	Hyde Park[1]
....	De	GB6039-1	Harlem Speaks
....	De	GB6039-2	Harlem Speaks
....	De	GB6040-1	Ain't Misbehavin'
....	De	GB6041-1	Chicago
....	De	GB6041-2	Chicago

[1]*aka* "Ev'ry Tub."

DUKE ELLINGTON
DE, piano and talking, interviewed by Percy Mathison Brooks.

14 Jul 1933   (S)
Unidentified location
London, England

....	BD	538	Souvenir of Duke Ellington's First Visit to England 1933
....	Orl	539	Souvenir of Duke Ellington's First Visit to England 1933

DUKE ELLINGTON & HIS FAMOUS ORCHESTRA
CW AW FJ, JN LB JT, BB JH OH HC, DE FG WB SG, IA.

15 Aug 1933   (S)
1776 Broadway Studios
New York City, NY

....	Br	B13800-A	I'm Satisfied −vIA
....	Br	B13801-A	Jive Stomp
....		B13801-B[1]	Jive Stomp
....	Br	B13802-A	Harlem Speaks
....	Br	B13803-A	In The Shade Of The Old Apple Tree

[1]Test extant.

DUKE ELLINGTON & HIS ORCHESTRA
CW AW FJ LBcn, JN LB JT, BB JH OH HC, DE FG WB SG.

26 Sep 1933   (S)
Victor Studios[1]
Chicago, IL

....	Vi	BS-77025-1	Rude Interlude −vLBcn
....	Vi	BS-77025-2	Rude Interlude −vLBcn
....	Vi	BS-77026-1	Dallas Doings[2]
....	Vi	BS-77026-2	Dallas Doings

[1]At Suite 1143, Merchandise Mart, 222 W. North Bank Street.
[2]*aka* "Blue Eagle Stomp"; this title is a derivative of *Rockin' In Rhythm*.

DUKE ELLINGTON & HIS ORCHESTRA
CW AW FJ LBcn, JN LB, BB JH OH HC, DE FG WB SG.

4 Dec 1933[1]   (S)
Victor Studios
Chicago, IL

....	Vi	BS-77199-1	Dear Old Southland −vLBcn
....	Vi	BS-77199-2	Dear Old Southland −vLBcn
....		BS-77200-1/-2/-3	[Awful Sad]
....	Vi	BS-77201-1	Daybreak Express[2]
....	Vi	BS-77201-2	Daybreak Express

[1]For bookkeeping purposes this session was considered as having taken place on 4 Dec 1933, but was held actually in the early morning of 5 Dec 1933.
[2]This title is a derivative of *Tiger Rag/Milenberg Joys,* originally titled "Sleepy Town Express." Coarranged by Jimmy Hillard.

DUKE ELLINGTON & HIS ORCHESTRA
CW AW FJ LBcn, JN LB, BB HC, DE FG WB SG.

9 Jan 1934   (S)
Victor Studios
Chicago, IL

....	Vi	BS-80144-1	Delta Serenade[1]	>>>

.... Vi   BS-80144-2   Delta Serenade
.... Vi   BS-80145-2   Stompy Jones

[1]*aka* "Oh! Babe."

				10 Jan 1934	(S)

DUKE ELLINGTON & HIS ORCHESTRA   Victor Studios
CW AW FJ LBcn, JN LB JT, BB JH OH HC, DE FG WB SG.   Chicago, IL

.... Vi   BS-80149-1   Solitude
.... Vi   BS-80150-1   Blue Feeling

26 Feb 1934   (T)[1]
Paramount Studios
Hollywood, CA

DUKE ELLINGTON & HIS ORCHESTRA
CW AW FJ, JN LB JT, BB JH OH HC, DE FG WB SG.

....   PBS-79093-1[2]   Ebony Rhapsody
....   PBS-79094-1[2]   Ebony Rhapsody
....   PBS-79105-1[2]   Ebony Rhapsody
....   PBS-79106-1[2]   Ebony Rhapsody

[1]Music for the motion picture "Murder At The Vanities." The version of *Ebony Rhapsody* used in the film soundtrack intercut Ellington's band with the Paramount studio orchestra.
[2]Tests extant. (One collector holds the only three test pressings of one of these instrumental prerecordings.) An overdub made with the voice of Getrude Michael was made on 18 Mar 1934 and rejected. Another overdub with the voice of Barbara van Brunt made on 16 Apr 1934 was used for the soundtrack. Paramount's exploitation disc for *Murder at the Vanities* was mastered onto two 78-rpm sides and assigned master nos. PCS-79193-1 and PCS-79194-1, in late April or early May 1934. Master nos. PBS-79091 and PBS-79092 are untraced.

5 Mar 1934   (T)[1]
Paramount Studios
Hollywood, CA

DUKE ELLINGTON & HIS ORCHESTRA
CW AW FJ, JN LB JT, BB JH OH HC, DE FG WB SG.

....   Here Comes The Bride
....   Here Comes The Bride

[1]Music for the movie short "A Jazz Wedding" (Hollywood on Parade Z3-10).

15 Mar 1934   (T)[1]
Paramount Studios, Sound Stage #1
Hollywood, CA

DUKE ELLINGTON & HIS ORCHESTRA
CW AW FJ, JN LB JT, BB JH OH HC, DE FG WB SG, MW.

.... WET   PCS-79320-1   When A St. Louis Woman Goes Down To New Orleans –vMW[2]
.... FDC   When A St. Louis Woman Goes Down To New Orleans –vMW

[1]Music for the motion picture "Belle Of The Nineties."
[2]*sa* "St. Louis Blues."

16 Mar 1934   (T)[1]
Paramount Studios, Sound Stage #1
Hollywood, CA

DUKE ELLINGTON & HIS ORCHESTRA
CW AW FJ, JN LB JT, BB ??, DE FG WB SG, MW.

.... VET   PCS-79321-1   Memphis Blues –vMW
.... ER   Memphis Blues –vMW

[1]Music for the motion picture "Belle Of The Nineties."

21 Mar 1934   (T)[1]
Paramount Studios, Sound Stage #13
Hollywood, CA

LARRY ADLER
Hca, acc. by tp, tb, BB JH OH HC, DE FG WB SG.

.... UTD   Sophisticated Lady

[1]Music for the motion picture "Many Happy Returns."

24 Mar 1934   (T)[1]
Paramount Studios, Sound Stage #1
Hollywood, CA

DUKE ELLINGTON & HIS ORCHESTRA
CW AW FJ, JN LB JT, BB, DE FG WB SG, MW.

.... Cos   PBS-79181-1   My Old Flame –vMW

[1]Music for the motion picture "Belle Of The Nineties."

26 Mar 1934   (T)[1]
Paramount Studios, Sound Stage #1
Hollywood, CA

DUKE ELLINGTON & HIS ORCHESTRA
JN LB JT, JH, DE FG WB SG, MW.

.... FDC   Hesitation Blues –vMW

[1]Music for the motion picture "Belle Of The Nineties."

DUKE ELLINGTON & HIS ORCHESTRA
CW AW FJ, JN LB JT, BB JH HC, DE FG WB SG, IA.

12 Apr 1934   (S)
Hollywood Recording Studio
Hollywood, CA

....	Vi	PBS-79155-2	Ebony Rhapsody –vIA
....	Vi	PBS-79156-1	Cocktails For Two
....	Vi	PBS-79156-2	Cocktails For Two
....	Vi	PBS-79157-2	Live And Love Tonight

DUKE ELLINGTON & HIS ORCHESTRA
CW AW FJ, JN LB JT, BB JH OH HC, DE FG WB SG.

17 Apr 1934   (S)
Hollywood Recording Studio
Hollywood, CA

| .... | Vi | PBS-79169-2 | I Met My Waterloo |

DUKE ELLINGTON & HIS ORCHESTRA
CW AW FJ, JN LB JT, BB JH HC, DE FG WB SG, har org, MW chorus.

7 May 1934   (T)[1]
Paramount Studios, Sound Stage #1
Hollywood, CA

| .... | WET | PCS-79325 | Troubled Waters –vMW Chorus[2] |
| .... | FDC | | Troubled Waters –vMW Chorus |

[1]Music for the motion picture "Belle Of The Nineties."
[2]Released erroneously under the title "I've Got To Wash Away My Sins Before Morning," which is part of the lyrics of "Troubled Waters."

DUKE ELLINGTON & HIS ORCHESTRA
CW AW FJ, JN LB JT, BB JH HC, DE FG WB SG, MW.

8 May 1934   (T)[1]
Paramount Studios, Sound Stage #1
Hollywood, CA

....			When A St. Louis Woman Goes Down To New Orleans (new intro/rejected)
....			My Old Flame (new ending in ¾ time)
....			I Met My Waterloo (two instrumental choruses/rejected)
....			Troubled Waters –vMW

[1]Music for the motion picture "Belle Of The Nineties."

DUKE ELLINGTON & HIS ORCHESTRA
CW AW, JN LB JT, BB JH HC, DE WB SG, IA.

9 May 1934   (S)
Hollywood Recording Studio
Hollywood, CA

....	Vi	PBS-79211-1[1]	Troubled Waters –vIA
....	Vi	PBS-79211-2	Troubled Waters –vIA
....	Vi	PBS-79212-2	My Old Flame –vIA

[1]First issued as part of the centennial edition; wrongly claimed by RCA/Vi (F) FPM1-7002.

DUKE ELLINGTON & HIS ORCHESTRA
CW AW FJ, JN LB JT, BB JH OH HC, DE FG WB SG.

12 Sep 1934   (S)
1776 Broadway Studios
New York City, NY

....	Br	B15910-A	Solitude
....	Br	B15911-A	Saddest Tale –DE talking
....	Br	B15912-A	Moonglow[1]
....	Br	B15913-A	Sump'n 'Bout Rhythm

[1]This title is a derivative of *Lazy Rhapsody.*

DUKE ELLINGTON & HIS ORCHESTRA
CW AW FJ, JN LB JT, BB JH OH HC, DE FG WB SG, BHol.[3]

c 17-24 Oct 1934[1]   (T)[2]
Paramount Eastern Service Studios
Astoria, Long Island, NY

SYMPHONY IN BLACK

....	Max		- The Laborers
....	Max		- A Triangle –vBHol[4]
....	Max		- A Hymn Of Sorrow
....	Max		- Harlem Rhythm[5]

[1]The soundtrack was done in Oct 1934, while the filming was completed only by Mar 1935.
[2]Music for the movie short "Symphony In Black" (Paramount Headliner A5-3).
[3]DE's band was augmented visually by additional musicians brought in from the Mills Blue Rhythm Band, who did, however, not play a note.
[4]Including: Dance (a derivative of *Ducky Wucky*); Jealousy; Big City Blues (a derivative of *Saddest Tale*).
[5]This title is a derivative of *Merry-Go-Round.*

DUKE ELLINGTON & HIS ORCHESTRA
CW AW RS, JN LB JT, BB JH OH HC, DE FG WB SG, IA.

9 Jan 1935   (S)
Columbia Studios
Chicago, IL

| .... | FDC | C883-2 | Admiration[1] |
| .... | FDC | C884-2 | Farewell Blues   >>> |

> BT added.

.... FDC   C885-3   Let's Have A Jubilee –vlA

> CW RS, JT, HC, DE FG WB SG.

....   C886-1[2]   [Porto Rican Chaos]

[1]Sometimes referred to as "Admiration Stomp."
[2]Contrary to sleeve notes for FDC 1022, CBS/Co (F) 88137 and Cls 659, this take remains unissued; master #B16974-2 was used for all pressings instead.

                                                        5-6 Mar 1935   (S)

DUKE ELLINGTON & HIS ORCHESTRA   1776 Broadway Studios
RS, JN LB JT, JH OH HC, DE FG BT SG.   New York City, NY

.... Br   B16973-1   Margie

> CW added.

.... SE   B16974-1   Moonlight Fiesta[1]
.... FDC   B16974-2[2]   Moonlight Fiesta

[1]sa "Porto Rican Chaos."
[2]This "take" as issued on CBS/Co (F) 88137 is in fact master #M526-1, whereas #B16974-2 was erroneously issued as #C886-1, both on FDC 1022 and CBS/Co (F) 88137.

DUKE ELLINGTON'S SEXTET
RS, JH HC, DE WB BT.

.... Rt   B16975-1   Tough Truckin'
.... Co   B16975-2   Tough Truckin'
.... BD   B16976-1   Indigo Echoes
.... Co   B16976-2   Indigo Echoes

                                                    30 Apr 1935   (S)

DUKE ELLINGTON & HIS ORCHESTRA   1776 Broadway Studios
CW AW RS, JN LB JT, BB JH OH HC, DE FG WB FA.[1]   New York City, NY

.... Br   B17406-1   In A Sentimental Mood[2]
.... Br   B17407-1   Showboat Shuffle[3]
.... Br   B17408-1   Merry-Go-Round
.... Br   B17409-1   Admiration

[1]Sonny Greer recalls that he took a leave of absence for health reasons at the time of this session and Fred Avendorph was called in from Chicago to replace him temporarily. SG was on and off until the next recording session.
[2]Originally titled "In The Middle Of A Kiss"; aka "Paradise."
[3]aka "Mellotude."

                                                      19 Aug 1935   (S)

DUKE ELLINGTON & HIS ORCHESTRA   1776 Broadway Studios
CW AW RS, JN LB JT, BB JH OH BW HC, DE FG BT HA SG, IA.   New York City, NY

.... Br   B17974-1   Cotton –vlA
.... Br   B17975-1   Truckin' –vlA
.... Br   B17976-1   Accent On Youth

                                                      12 Sep 1935   (S)

DUKE ELLINGTON & HIS ORCHESTRA   1776 Broadway Studios
CW AW RS, JN JT, BB JH OH HC, DE FG BT HA SG.   New York City, NY

.... Br   B18072-1   Reminiscing In Tempo, part 1
.... Br   B18073-1   Reminiscing In Tempo, part 2
.... Br   B18074-2   Reminiscing In Tempo, part 3
.... Br   B18075-1   Reminiscing In Tempo, part 4

                                                      3 Jan 1936   (S)

DUKE ELLINGTON & HIS ORCHESTRA   Columbia Studios
CW AW RS, JN LB JT, BB JH OH HC, DE FG BT SG.   Chicago, IL

....   C1195-1   [Cootie's Concerto[1]]
....   C1196-1   [Jumpy]
....   C1197-1   [Barney's Concerto[2]]
....   C1198-1   [Farewell Blues]

[1]aka "Sweetest Gal Goin'."
[2]aka "King's Lament." This title is a derivative of Basin Street Blues.

                                                      20 Jan 1936   (S)

DUKE ELLINGTON & HIS ORCHESTRA   Columbia Studios
CW AW RS, JN LB JT, BB JH OH HC, DE FG BT SG, IA.   Chicago, IL

.... Co   C1199-1   I Don't Know Why I Love You So   >>>

....	Rt	C1199-2	I Don't Know Why I Love You So
....	FDC	C1200-1	Dinah Lou –vlA
....	Rt	C1200-3	Dinah Lou –vlA

27 Feb 1936   (S)
1776 Broadway Studios
New York City, NY

DUKE ELLINGTON & HIS ORCHESTRA
CW AW RS, LB JT, BB JH PC HC, DE FG BT HA SG, IA.

....	Br	B18734-1	Isn't Love The Strangest Thing? –vlA
....	Br	B18735-1	No Greater Love[1]

> PC omitted, JN added.

....	Br	B18736-1	Clarinet Lament[2]
....	Br	B18737-1	Echoes Of Harlem[3]

[1]Complete "There Is No Greater Love."
[2]sa "Barney's Concerto"; "King's Lament."
[3]sa "Cootie's Concerto"; "Sweetest Gal Goin'."

28 Feb 1936   (S)
1776 Broadway Studios
New York City, NY

DUKE ELLINGTON & HIS ORCHESTRA
CW AW RS, JN LB JT, BB JH PC HC, DE FG HA SG, IA.

....	Br	B18738-1	Love Is Like A Cigarette –vlA

> BT added.

....	Br	B18739-1	Kissin' My Baby Goodnight –vlA

> BT omitted.

....	Br	B18740-1	Oh Babe! Maybe Someday –vlA

8 May 1936   (P)
Joseph Urban Room, Congress Hotel (bc)
Chicago, IL

DUKE ELLINGTON &HIS ORCHESTRA
CW AW RS, JN LB JT, BB JH OH HC, DE FG BT HA SG, IA.

....	Stompy Jones
....	In A Sentimental Mood
....	My Old Flame –vlA
....	Cotton –vlA
....	Harlem Speaks

16 May 1936   (P)
Joseph Urban Room, Congress Hotel (bc)
Chicago, IL

DUKE ELLINGTON & HIS ORCHESTRA
CW AW RS, JN LB JT, BB JH OH HC, DE FG BT HA SG, IA.

....	Clarinet Lament
....	Hyde Park
....	My Old Flame –vlA
....	Showboat Shuffle
....	The Scene Changes
....	Oh Babe! Maybe Someday –vlA
....	Echoes Of Harlem

23 May 1936   (P)
Joseph Urban Room, Congress Hotel (bc)
Chicago, IL

DUKE ELLINGTON & HIS ORCHESTRA
CW AW RS, JN LB JT, BB JH OH HC, DE FG ?BT HA SG.

....	East St. Louis Toodle-Oo
....	Stompy Jones
....	Clarinet Lament
....	Showboat Shuffle

17 Jul 1936   (S)
1776 Broadway Studios
New York City, NY

DUKE ELLINGTON & HIS ORCHESTRA
CW AW RS, JN LB JT, BB JH OH HC, DE FG BT HA SG, IA.

....	Br	B19562-2	Shoe Shine Boy –vlA

> OH omitted.

....	Br	B19563-1	It Was A Sad Night In Harlem –vlA

> OH added.

....	Br	B19564-1	Trumpet In Spades[1]
....	Br	B19565-2	Yearning For Love[2]

[1]aka "Rex's Concerto."
[2]aka "Lawrence's Concerto."

DUKE ELLINGTON & HIS ORCHESTRA
CW AW RS, JN LB JT, BB JH OH BW HC,DE FG BT HA SG.

29 Jul 1936   (S)
1776 Broadway Studios
New York City, NY

....	Br	B19626-1	In A Jam
....	Vo	B19627-1	Exposition Swing
....	Co	B19627-2	Exposition Swing
....	Br	B19628-1	Uptown Downbeat[1]

[1] *aka* "Blackout."

REX STEWART & HIS FIFTY-SECOND STREET STOMPERS
RS, LB, JH HC, CBke BT SG.[1]

16 Dec 1936   (S)
Recordings Inc.[2]
Hollywood, CA

....	Vri	B4369-A	Rexatious
....	RV	B4369-B	Rexatious
....	Rlm	B4370-A	Lazy Man's Shuffle
....	Vri	B4370-B	Lazy Man's Shuffle

[1] There is no audible evidence of DE being present at this session.
[2] At 5505 Melrose Avenue.

BARNEY BIGARD & HIS JAZZOPATERS
CW, JT, BB HC, DE BT SG.

19 Dec 1936   (S)
Associated Cinema Studios
Hollywood, CA

....	UTD	L0371-1	Clouds In My Heart[1]
....	Vri	L0371-2	Clouds In My Heart
....	UTD	L0372-1	Frolic Sam
....	Vri	L0372-2	Frolic Sam
....	Vri	L0373-1	Caravan[2]
....	Vri	L0373-2	Caravan

> JT omitted.

....	Vri	L0374-1	Stompy Jones
....	Vri	L0374-2	Stompy Jones

[1] *aka* "Never Again"; "Harlem Romance."
[2] Originally titled "Caravan Of Love."

DUKE ELLINGTON & HIS ORCHESTRA
CW AW RS, JN LB JT, BB JH OH HC, DE FG BT HA SG.

21 Dec 1936   (S)
Associated Cinema Studios
Hollywood, CA

....	FDC	L0375-1	Scattin' At The Cotton Club[1]

> BT omitted.

....	Br	L0376-1	Black Butterfly
....		L0376-2[2]	Black Butterfly

[1] Some releases (FDC, Co) are missing an introduction of 4 bars by either CW or RS; FM is complete.
[2] Test extant.

DUKE ELLINGTON
Piano solo.

....	Mas	L0377-1	Mood Indigo—Solitude—Mood Indigo[1]
....	Mas	L0378-1	In A Sentimental Mood—Sophisticated Lady[1]

[1] On Mas MA102 and reissues the titles are shown either incomplete or in a different sequence: "Mood Indigo—Solitude"
and "Sophisticated Lady—In A Sentimental Mood."

DUKE ELLINGTON & HIS ORCHESTRA
CW AW RS, JN LB JT, BB JH OH HC, DE FG BT HA SG, IA B&CC.

Jan/Feb 1937   (T)[1]
M-G-M Studios
Culver City, CA

....	BJ		All God's Chillun Got Rhythm –vIA
....	Rho		All God's Chillun Got Rhythm[2]

[1] Music for the motion picture "A Day At The Races." The band provided the music for IA's vocal, but is not visible on film.
[2] This one-minute instrumental run-through of the tune was scrapped and has surfaced only recently.

DUKE ELLINGTON & HIS ORCHESTRA
CW AW RS, JN LB JT, BB JH OH HC, DE FG BT HA SG, IA.

18-26 Feb 1937   (T)[1]
Republic Studio
North Hollywood, CA

....	TOM		I've Got To Be A Rug Cutter –vIA RS HC HA
....			It Don't Mean A Thing –vIA

> SWte added.

....			Along Came Pete –vSWte >>>

.... > SWte omitted.
....   Sophisticated Lady
....   Love Is Good For Anything That Ails You

[1]Music for the motion picture "The Hit Parade." The non-Ellington portion was filmed at the Biograph Studios in the Bronx section of New York City, in late Jan 1937.

5 Mar 1937   (S)
Master Records Studios[1]
New York City, NY

DUKE ELLINGTON & HIS FAMOUS ORCHESTRA
CW AW RS, JN LB JT, BB JH OH HC, DE FG BT SG, IA.

.... Mas   M177-1   The New Birmingham Breakdown
.... Rt   M177-2   The New Birmingham Breakdown

> HA added.

.... Mas   M178-1   Scattin' At The Kit Kat[2]
.... Rt   M178-2   Scattin' At The Kit Kat
.... Mas   M179-1   I've Got To Be A Rug Cutter –vlA RS HC HA
.... Rt   M179-2   I've Got To Be A Rug Cutter –vlA RS HC HA

> BT omitted.

.... Mas   M180-1   The New East St. Louis Toodle-Oo
.... Rt   M180-2   The New East St. Louis Toodle-Oo

[1]At 1780 Broadway.
[2]sa "Scattin' At The Cotton Club."

The band made only initially use of the Master Records Studios, which were owned by Duke Ellington's impresario Irving Mills. They were inaugurated on 12 March 1937 for the recordings of the Master and Variety labels and did not last long. In October 1938 Mills withdrew the Master and Variety labels from the market and ceased recording.

8 Mar 1937   (S)
Master Records Studios
New York City, NY

COOTIE WILLIAMS & HIS RUG CUTTERS
CW, JN, JH HC, DE HA SG.

.... Vri   M185-1   I Can't Believe That You're In Love With Me
.... UTD   M185-2   I Can't Believe That You're In Love With Me
.... Vri   M186-1   Downtown Uproar[1]
.... UTD   M186-2   Downtown Uproar
.... Vri   M187-1   Diga Diga Doo[2]
.... Co   M187-2   Diga Diga Doo
.... Co   M188-1   Blue Reverie
.... Vri   M188-2   Blue Reverie
.... Tax   M189-1   The Whispering Tiger[3]
.... FDC   M189-2   The Whispering Tiger

[1]Shouted interjections probably by Jerry Rhea.
[2]Variant spelling "Digga Digga Doo" on some releases.
[3]This title is a derivative of *Tiger Rag*.

18 Mar 1937   (P)
Cotton Club (bc)
New York City, NY

DUKE ELLINGTON & HIS ORCHESTRA
CW AW FJ RS, JN LB JT, BB JH OH HC, DE FG BT HA SG, IA.

.... Crb   The New East St. Louis Toodle-Oo
.... CC   Harlem Speaks

> CW, JT, BB HC, DE ?BT SG.

.... CC   Caravan

> Entire band.

.... CC   One, Two, Button Your Shoe –vlA
.... BJ   Pennies From Heaven –vlA
.... BJ   Mexicali Rose –vlA
.... CC   Sophisticated Lady
.... CC   Rockin' In Rhythm
.... CC   The New East St. Louis Toodle-Oo

9 Apr 1937   (S)
Master Records Studios
New York City, NY

DUKE ELLINGTON & HIS FAMOUS ORCHESTRA
CW AW RS, JN LB JT, BB JH OH HC, DE FG BT/HA SG, IA.

.... Mas   M379-1   There's A Lull In My Life –vlA
.... Rt   M379-2   There's A Lull In My Life –vlA
.... Mas   M380-1   It's Swell Of You –vlA
.... Rt   M380-2   It's Swell Of You –vlA
.... Mas   M381-1   You Can't Run Away From Love Tonight –vlA
.... Rt   M381-2   You Can't Run Away From Love Tonight –vlA

DUKE ELLINGTON & HIS FAMOUS ORCHESTRA
AW RS, JN LB JT, BB JH OH HC, DE FG BT/HA SG.

22 Apr 1937   (S)
Master Records Studios
New York City, NY

.... FDC   M416-1   Azure
.... FDC   M416-2   Azure

> CW added.

.... Mas   M417-1   The Lady Who Couldn't Be Kissed

IVIE ANDERSON & HER BOYS FROM DIXIE
IA added, otherwise same personnel.

.... Vri   M418-1   Old Plantation –vIA
.... Rt   M418-2   Old Plantation –vIA

29 Apr 1937   (S)
Master Records Studios
New York City, NY

BARNEY BIGARD & HIS JAZZOPATERS
RS, JT, BB HC, DE BT SG.

.... BD   M433-1   Solace[1]
.... Vri   M433-2   Solace
.... Vri   M434-1   Four And One-Half Street
.... BD   M434-2   Four And One-Half Street
.... Vri   M435-1   Demi-Tasse[2]
.... BD   M435-2   Demi-Tasse
.... BD   M436-1   Jazz à la Carte[3]
.... Vri   M436-2   Jazz à la Carte

[1]*aka* "Lament For A Lost Love."
[2]*aka* "Evah Day."
[3]*aka* "Sauce For The Goose."

8 May 1937   (P)
CBS Studios (bc)
New York City, NY

DUKE ELLINGTON
Piano solo.

.... JA   Swing Session[1]
.... JA   Solitude—In A Sentimental Mood—Solitude

[1]This title is a derivative of *Soda Fountain Rag*.

14 May 1937   (S)
Master Records Studios
New York City, NY

DUKE ELLINGTON & HIS FAMOUS ORCHESTRA
CW AW RS, JN LB JT, BB JH OH HC, DE FG BT/HA SG.

.... Mas   M470-2[1]   Caravan[2]
.... Mas   M471-1   Azure

[1]Contrary to sleeve notes for various CBS/Co releases, take 1 remains unissued.
[2]Complete: "Caravan Of Love."

20 May 1937   (S)
1776 Broadway Studios
New York City, NY

JOHNNY HODGES & HIS ORCHESTRA
CW, BB JH OH HC, DE FG HA SG, BCrk.

.... Vri   21186-1   Foolin' Myself –vBCrk
.... Rt   21186-2   Foolin' Myself –vBCrk
.... Vri   21187-1   A Sailboat In The Moonlight –vBCrk
.... Rt   21187-2   A Sailboat In The Moonlight –vBCrk

> OH omitted.

....   21188-1[1]   You'll Never Go To Heaven –vBCrk
.... Vri   21188-2   You'll Never Go To Heaven –vBCrk[2]
.... FDC   21189-1   Peckin' –vCW Band[3]
.... Rt   21189-2   Peckin' –vCW Band
.... Rt   21189-3   Peckin' –vCW Band

[1]Test extant.
[2]DE seems to be absent.
[3]This title is a derivative of *Rockin' In Rhythm*.

8 Jun 1937   (S)
Master Records Studios
New York City, NY

DUKE ELLINGTON & HIS FAMOUS ORCHESTRA
CW AW RS, JN LB JT, BB JH OH HC, DE FG BT HA SG.

.... Mas   M519-1   All God's Chillun Got Rhythm
.... Rt   M519-2   All God's Chillun Got Rhythm   >>>

IVIE ANDERSON & HER BOYS FROM DIXIE
IA added, otherwise same personnel.

| .... | Vri | M520-1 | All God's Chillun Got Rhythm –vIA |
| .... | Co | M520-2 | All God's Chillun Got Rhythm –vIA |

DUKE ELLINGTON & HIS FAMOUS ORCHESTRA
Same personnel.

| .... | Mas | M521-1 | Alabamy Home –vIA |
| .... | Rt | M521-2 | Alabamy Home –vIA |

12 Jun 1937   (P)
CBS Studio (bc)
New York City, NY

DUKE ELLINGTON'S SEPTET
CW, JT, BB HC, DE LSb JWms.

| .... | Sct | | Frolic Sam |

16 Jun 1937   (S)
Master Records Studios
New York City, NY

BARNEY BIGARD & HIS JAZZOPATERS
RS, JT, BB HC, DE FG BT SG, SM.

| .... | Vri | M525-1 | Get It Southern Style –vSM |
| .... | BD | M525-2 | Get It Southern Style –vSM |

> ChB added.

| .... | Co | M526-1 | Moonlight Fiesta |
| .... | Vri | M526-2 | Moonlight Fiesta |

> ChB omitted.

....	Vri	M527-1	Sponge Cake And Spinach[1]
....	BD	M527-2	Sponge Cake And Spinach
....	Vri	M528-1	If You're Ever In My Arms Again –vSM
....	BD	M528-2	If You're Ever In My Arms Again –vSM

[1]This title is a derivative of *Swing Session*.

c late June 1937   (T)[1]
Master Records Studios
New York City, NY

DUKE ELLINGTON & HIS ORCHESTRA
CW AW RS, JN LB JT, BB JH OH HC, DE FG BT HA SG, IA.

....	Bb		Oh Babe! Maybe Someday—Daybreak Express (incomplete)[2]
....	Bb		Daybreak Express (rehearsal)
....	Bb		Daybreak Express (incomplete)
....	Bb		Oh Babe! Maybe Someday (incomplete)
....	Bb		Oh Babe! Maybe Someday –vIA (in progress)

[1]Music for the movie short "Record Making With Duke Ellington & His Orchestra" (Paramount Pictorial P7-2).
[2]DE directing.

7 Jul 1937   (S)
Master Records Studios
New York City, NY

REX STEWART & HIS FIFTY-SECOND STREET STOMPERS
RS FJ, JH HC, DE BF HA JM.

| .... | Vri | M549-1 | The Back Room Romp[1] |
| .... | Rlm | M549-2 | The Back Room Romp |

> FJ omitted.

....	Vri	M550-1	Swing Baby Swing[2]
....	Co	M550-2	Swing Baby Swing
....	Vri	M550-1	Sugar Hill Shim Sham[3]
....	Rlm	M551-2	Sugar Hill Shim Sham
....	Vri	M552-1	Tea And Trumpets[4]
....	RV	M552-2[5]	Tea And Trumpets
....	Rlm	M552-3	Tea And Trumpets

[1]Subtitled "A Contrapuntal Stomp."
[2]*aka* "Love In My Heart" and as such on later pressings.
[3]*aka* "You Ain't In Harlem Now."
[4]*aka* "Trumpetology."
[5]Contrary to sleeve notes for Rlm M-52628 and CBS/Co (F) 88210, take 2 was not issued on these records.

20 Sep 1937   (S)
1776 Broadway Studios
New York City, NY

DUKE ELLINGTON & HIS FAMOUS ORCHESTRA
CW AW FJ RS, LB JT, BB JH OH HC, DE FG BT/HA SG.

| .... | Br | M646-1 | Chatter-Box[1] |
| .... | SE | M647-2 | Jubilesta |

> JN added.

| .... | Br | M648-1 | Diminuendo In Blue   >>> |

....	Rt	M648-2	Diminuendo In Blue
....	Br	M649-1	Crescendo In Blue
....	Rt	M649-2	Crescendo In Blue
....	Rt	M650[2]	Harmony In Harlem
....		M650-1[3]	Harmony In Harlem[4]
....	Br	M650-2	Harmony In Harlem
....		M651-1[5]	Dusk In The Desert[6]
....	Br	M651-2	Dusk In The Desert

[1]*aka* "Jumpy"; "Jumpy Chatter-Box."
[2]Edited version on CBS/Co (F) 88210.
[3]Test extant.
[4]*aka* "Have Some," and as such on the test pressing.
[5]Test extant.
[6]*aka* "Jamming And Jiving"; "Dusk On The Desert" on some reissues, and as per copyright recordation.

The recording ledger noted only two trombones on this date, however, listening tests let us believe that JN was added during the session.

COOTIE WILLIAMS & HIS RUG CUTTERS   26 Oct 1937   (S)
CW, JT, BB OH HC, DE BT SG, JK.   1776 Broadway Studios
                                                                                New York City, NY

....	Vo	M669-2	Jubilesta
....	Vo	M670-1	Watchin' –vJK
....	Vo	M671-1	Pigeons And Peppers
....	Vo	M672-1	I Can't Give You Anything But Love

DUKE ELLINGTON & HIS ORCHESTRA   13 Jan 1938   (S)
CW AW FJ RS, JN LB JT, BB JH OH HC, DE FG BT HA SG.   1776 Broadway Studios
                                                                                New York City, NY

....	Br	M713-1	Steppin' Into Swing Society[1]

> OH omitted.

....	Br	M714-1	Prologue To Black And Tan Fantasy

> JH omitted.

....	Br	M715-1	The New Black And Tan Fantasy

[1]*aka* "Sex In A Flat."

BARNEY BIGARD & HIS ORCHESTRA   19 Jan 1938   (S)
RS, JT, BB HC, DE FG BT SG.   1776 Broadway Studios
                                                                                New York City, NY

....	Vo	M724-1	Drummer's Delight
....	Vo	M725-1	If I Thought You Cared[1]
....	BD	M725-2	If I Thought You Cared

[1]*aka* "Imagination."

COOTIE WILLIAMS & HIS RUG CUTTERS
CW, JN, BB JH HC, DE FG BT SG.

....	Co	M726-1	Have A Heart
....	Vo	M726-2	Have A Heart[1]

[1]Late pressings as "Lost In Meditation."

JOHNNY HODGES & HIS ORCHESTRA
CW, LB, JH OH HC, DE FG BT SG, MMH.

....	Vo	M727-2	My Day –vMMH
....	Vo	M728-1	Silv'ry Moon And Golden Sands –vMMH

COOTIE WILLIAMS & HIS RUG CUTTERS
CW, JN, BB JH HC, DE BT SG.

....	Mo	M729[1]	Echoes Of Harlem (rehearsal)
....	Co	M729-1	Echoes Of Harlem
....	Vo	M729-2	Echoes Of Harlem

[1]The source is a 12" rehearsal lacquer.

DUKE ELLINGTON & HIS FAMOUS ORCHESTRA   2 Feb 1938   (S)
CW AW FJ RS, JN LB JT, BB JH HC, DE BT HA SG.   1776 Broadway Studios
                                                                                New York City, NY

....	Br	M751-1	Riding On A Blue Note	
....	Rt	M751-2	Riding On A Blue Note	>>>

> OH added.

....	Br	M752-1	Lost In Meditation[1]
....	Br	M753-1	The Gal From Joe's[2]
....	Co	M753-2	The Gal From Joe's

[1]*sa* "Have A Heart."
[2]*aka* "Aah, Take All Of Me."

<table>
<tr><td></td><td colspan="3" align="right">24 Feb 1938   (S)
1776 Broadway Studios[1]
New York City, NY</td></tr>
</table>

DUKE ELLINGTON & HIS FAMOUS ORCHESTRA
CW WJ FJ, JN LB JT, BB JH OH HC, DE FG BT HA SG, IA.

....	Rt[2]	M770-1	If You Were In My Place –vIA[3]
....	Br	M770-2	If You Were In My Place –vIA
....	Rt	M771-1	Skrontch –vIA[4]
....	Br	M771-2	Skrontch –vIA

[1]Some sources suggest that this one and the following session were recorded at the 1776 Broadway Studios.
[2]Edited edition (as is CBS/Co (F) 88220); the first section up to the 10th bar of JH's solo has been taken from M770-2. The only known intact test pressing is held by Steven Lasker. Contrary to sleeve notes for CBS/Co KG 32064 and equivalents, take 2 has been used for the pressings.
[3]Complete: "If You Were In My Place, What Would You Do?"
[4]Variant spellings "Scronch"; "Scrounch"; complete: "Doin' The Skrontch" (a dance).

p 24 Feb/3 Mar 1938 (S)
1776 Broadway Studios
New York City, NY

DUKE ELLINGTON
Piano solo.

| .... | JP | | I've Got To Be A Rug Cutter –vDE |

> CW –tb added.

| .... | PP | | Untitled Blues In B-Flat |

The above is a 12" acetate that DE recorded for Leonard Feather to take back to his native England.

3 Mar 1938   (S)
1776 Broadway Studios
New York City, NY

DUKE ELLINGTON & HIS FAMOUS ORCHESTRA
CW WJ FJ RS, JN LB HFlg, BB JH OH HC, DE FG BT HA SG, IA.

....	Co	M772-1	I Let A Song Go Out Of My Heart
....	Br	M772-2	I Let A Song Go Out Of My Heart
....	Br	M773-1	Braggin' In Brass[1]
....	Pa	M773-2	Braggin' In Brass
....	Br	M774-1	Carnival In Caroline –vIA

[1]This title is a derivative of *Tiger Rag*.

24 Mar 1938   (P)
Cotton Club (bc)
New York City, NY

DUKE ELLINGTON & HIS ORCHESTRA
CW WJ RS, JN LB JT, BB JH OH HC, DE FG BT HA SG, IA.

....	JA	Harmony In Harlem
....	JA	If You Were In My Place –vIA
....	BF	Mood Indigo
....	BF	East St. Louis Toodle-Oo
....	BF	East St. Louis Toodle-Oo
....	JA	Oh Babe! Maybe Someday –vIA
....	JA[1]	Dinah –vCW HC HA
....	JA	If Dreams Come True –vIA
....	Stv	Skrontch –vIA

[1]Incomplete on JA.

28 Mar 1938   (S)
1776 Broadway Studios
New York City, NY

JOHNNY HODGES & HIS ORCHESTRA
CW, LB, JH HC, DE BT SG, MMH.

....	Vo	M793-1	Jeep's Blues
....	Vo	M794-1	If You Were In My Place –vMMH
....	Vo	M795-1	I Let A Song Go Out Of My Heart –vMMH
....	Vo	M796-2	Rendez-vous With Rhythm[1]

[1]"Rendezvous ..." on some labels.

4 Apr 1938   (S)
1776 Broadway Studios
New York City, NY

COOTIE WILLIAMS & HIS RUG CUTTERS
CW, JN, BB JH OH HC, DE FG BT SG, JK.

....	Vo	M801-1	A Lesson In C –vJK
....	Vo	M802-1	Swingtime In Honolulu –vJK
....	Vo	M803-1	Carnival In Caroline –vJK >>>

.... Vo   M804-1   Ol' Man River –vJK

DUKE ELLINGTON & HIS FAMOUS ORCHESTRA   11 Apr 1938   (S)
CW WJ FJ RS, JN LB JT, BB JH OH HC, DE FG BT SG, IA.   1776 Broadway Studios
                                                               New York City, NY

.... Br   M809-1   Swingtime In Honolulu –vIA

  > RN replaces CW.

.... Br   M810-1   I'm Slappin' Seventh Avenue[1]
.... Br   M811-1   Dinah's In A Jam

       [1]Complete: "I'm Slappin' Seventh Avenue With The Sole Of My Shoe."

DUKE ELLINGTON & HIS ORCHESTRA   17 Apr 1938   (P)
CW WJ RS, JN LB JT, BB JH OH HC, DE FG BT SG, IA.   Cotton Club (bc)
                                                               New York City, NY

.... JA   You Went To My Head –vIA
.... JA   Three Blind Mice
.... Stv   Solitude

  > CW, JN, JH HC, DE BT SG.

.... JA   Downtown Uproar

DUKE ELLINGTON & HIS ORCHESTRA   24 Apr 1938   (P)
RS, JT, BB HC, DE BT SG.   Cotton Club (bc)
                                                               New York City, NY

.... JP   Evah Day[1]

  > CW WJ RS, JN LB JT, BB JH OH HC, DE FG BT SG, IA.

.... JP   Azure
.... JP   Carnival In Caroline –vIA
.... JP   On The Sunny Side Of The Street –vIA
.... JP   Dinah's In A Jam

       [1]sa "Demi-Tasse"; this title is often wrongly referred to as "Ev'ry Day."

DUKE ELLINGTON & HIS ORCHESTRA   29 Apr 1938   (P)
CW WJ RS, JN LB JT, BB JH OH HC, DE FG BT SG.   Cotton Club (bc)
                                                               New York City, NY

.... JUn   Chatter-Box
....   Diminuendo In Blue
....   Caravan
....   Black And Tan Fantasy

DUKE ELLINGTON & HIS ORCHESTRA   1 May 1938   (P)
CW WJ RS, JN LB JT, BB JH OH HC, DE FG BT SG, IA.   Cotton Club (bc)
                                                               New York City, NY

.... JA   Harmony In Harlem
.... JA   At Your Beck And Call –vIA
.... BF   Solitude –vIA
.... JA   The Gal From Joe's
.... JA   Riding On A Blue Note
.... JA   If Dreams Come True

DUKE ELLINGTON & HIS ORCHESTRA   5 May 1938   (P)
CW WJ RS, JN LB JT, BB JH OH HC, DE FG BT SG.   Cotton Club (bc)
                                                               New York City, NY

.... JP   Lost In Meditation

DUKE ELLINGTON & HIS ORCHESTRA   8 May 1938   (P)
CW WJ RS, JN LB JT, BB JH OH HC, DE FG BT SG, IA.   Cotton Club (bc)
                                                               New York City, NY

.... JP   Oh Babe! Maybe Someday –vIA
.... Max   I Let A Song Go Out Of My Heart

DUKE ELLINGTON & HIS ORCHESTRA   15 May 1938   (P)
CW WJ RS, JN LB JT, BB JH OH HC, DE FG BT SG, IA.   Cotton Club (bc)
                                                               New York City, NY

.... JA   Lost In Meditation –vIA

  > RS, JT, BB HC, DE BT SG.

.... JA   Evah Day   >>>

> Entire band.

.... JA   Echoes Of Harlem
.... JA   Birmingham Breakdown
.... JA   Rose Room
.... JA   If Dreams Come True
.... JA   It's The Dreamer In Me

                                                          22 May 1938   (P)
DUKE ELLINGTON & HIS ORCHESTRA   Cotton Club (bc)
CW WJ RS, JN LB JT, BB JH OH HC, DE FG BT SG, IA.   New York City, NY

.... JP   East St. Louis Toodle-Oo
.... JP   Jig Walk[1]
.... JP   In A Sentimental Mood
.... JP   I'm Slappin' Seventh Avenue
.... JP   Lost In Meditation –vIA
.... JP   Alabamy Home –vIA
.... JP   If You Were In My Place

[1]No or hardly any similarity with the original composition of that name.

                                                          29 May 1938   (P)
DUKE ELLINGTON & HIS ORCHESTRA   Cotton Club (bc)
CW WJ RS, JN LB JT, BB JH OH HC, DE FG BT SG.   New York City, NY

.... JA   Prelude In C Sharp Minor
.... JA   Rockin' In Rhythm

                                                          7 Jun 1938   (S)
DUKE ELLINGTON & HIS FAMOUS ORCHESTRA   1776 Broadway Studios
CW WJ RS, JN LB JT, BB JH OH HC, DE FG BT SG, IA.   New York City, NY

.... Br   M835-1[1]   When My Sugar Walks Down The Street –vIA
.... Br   M832-1   You Gave Me The Gate –vIA[2]
.... Br   M833-1   Rose Of The Rio Grande –vIA
.... Sw   M833-2   Rose Of The Rio Grande –vIA
.... Br   M834-1   Pyramid[3]
.... Co   M834-2   Pyramid[3]

[1]This first title to be recorded was initially assigned master #M831, but after realizing that this number was previously allocated, it was changed to M835.
[2]Complete: "You Gave Me The Gate And I'm Swinging."
[3]HC is the only reedman heard on this title.

                                                          20 Jun 1938   (S)
DUKE ELLINGTON & HIS FAMOUS ORCHESTRA   1776 Broadway Studios
CW WJ RS, JN LB JT, BB JH OH HC, DE FG BT SG, IA.   New York City, NY

.... Br   M846-1[1]   The Stevedore's Serenade
.... Br   M847-2[1]   La De Doody Do –vIA
.... Br   M844-1   Watermelon Man –vIA
.... Br   M845-1   A Gypsy Without A Song[2]

[1]The first two titles to be recorded were initially assigned master numbers M842 and M843, but after realizing that these numbers were previously allocated, they were changed to M846 and M847 respectively.
[2]aka "Gypsy Pump"; the arrangement is by Lou Singer.

                                                          22 Jun 1938   (S)
JOHNNY HODGES & HIS ORCHESTRA   1776 Broadway Studios
CW, LB, JH HC, DE BT SG, MMH.   New York City, NY

.... BD   M852-1   You Walked Out Of The Picture –vMMH
.... Vo   M852-2   You Walked Out Of The Picture –vMMH
.... Vo   M853-1   Pyramid
.... Vo   M854-1   Empty Ballroom Blues
.... Rt   M855-1   Lost In Meditation –vMMH
.... Vo   M855-2   Lost In Meditation –vMMH

                                                          1 Aug 1938   (S)
JOHNNY HODGES & HIS ORCHESTRA   1776 Broadway Studios
CW, LB, JH HC, DE BT SG, LLF.   New York City, NY

.... Vo   M872-2   A Blues Serenade –vLLF
.... Vo   M873-1   Love In Swingtime –vLLF
.... Vo   M874-1   Swingin' In The Dell[1]
.... Vo   M875-1   Jitterbug's Lullaby[2]

[1]aka "The Farmer In The Dell."
[2]Sometimes referred to as "Jitterbug's Holiday"; originally titled "Rabbit's Blues."

COOTIE WILLIAMS & HIS RUG CUTTERS
CW, BB JH OH HC, DE BT SG, SP.

2 Aug 1938   (S)
1776 Broadway Studios
New York City, NY

.... Vo   M876-1   Chasin' Chippies
.... Vo   M877-1   Blue Is The Evening –vSP
.... Vo   M878-2   Sharpie –vSP
.... Vo   M879-1   Swing Pan Alley[1]

[1]aka "Pickin' The Blues."

DUKE ELLINGTON & HIS FAMOUS ORCHESTRA
CW WJ RS, JN LB JT, BB JH OH HC, DE FG BT SG, SP.

4 Aug 1938   (S)
1776 Broadway Studios
New York City, NY

.... Br   M880-1   A Blues Serenade
.... Br   M881-1   Love In Swingtime –vSP
.... Br   M882-2   Please Forgive Me

DUKE ELLINGTON & HIS FAMOUS ORCHESTRA
CW WJ RS, JN LB JT, BB JH OH HC, DE FG BT SG.

9 Aug 1938   (S)
1776 Broadway Studios
New York City, NY

.... Br   M883-1   The Lambeth Walk
.... Br   M884-1   Prelude To A Kiss
.... Co   M884-2   Prelude To A Kiss
.... Br   M885-1   Hip Chic
.... Br   M886-1   Buffet Flat[1]

[1]aka "Swing Is Stagnant."

JOHNNY HODGES & HIS ORCHESTRA
CW, LB, JH HC, DE BT SG, MMH.

24 Aug 1938   (S)
1776 Broadway Studios
New York City, NY

.... Vo   M887-1   Prelude To A Kiss –vMMH
.... Vo   M888-1   There's Something About An Old Love –vMMH
.... Vo   M889-1   The Jeep Is Jumpin'
.... Vo   M890-1   Krum Elbow Blues

DUKE ELLINGTON & HIS FAMOUS ORCHESTRA
CW WJ RS, JN LB JT, BB JH OH HC, DE FG BT SG.

2 Sep 1938   (S)
1776 Broadway Studios
New York City, NY

.... RV   M898-1   Twits And Twerps[1]
.... FDC   M898-2   Twits And Twerps
.... Rt   M899-1   Mighty Like The Blues
.... Br   M899-2   Mighty Like The Blues

[1]Originally titled "Stew Burp."

DUKE ELLINGTON & HIS ORCHESTRA
CW WJ RS, JN LB JT, BB JH OH HC, DE FG BT SG.

6 Oct 1938   (P)
Apollo Theater (bc)
New York City, NY

> RS, JT, BB HC, DE BT SG.

.... JUn   Evah Day
.... JUn   Duke Ellington's Greetings to Europe –DE talking

> Entire band.

.... JUn   I Let A Song Go Out Of My Heart
....   Prelude In C Sharp Minor
....   Prelude To A Kiss
....   The Lambeth Walk
....   You Gave Me The Gate
....   Merry-Go-Round

DUKE ELLINGTON & HIS FAMOUS ORCHESTRA
CW WJ RS, JN LB JT, BB JH OH HC, DE FG BT SG.

19 Dec 1938   (S)
1776 Broadway Studios
New York City, NY

.... Br   M947-1   Jazz Potpourri[1]
.... Co   M948-1   T.T. On Toast
.... Co   M948-2   T.T. On Toast
.... Rt   M949-1   Battle Of Swing[2]
.... Br   M949-2   Battle Of Swing

[1]aka "Myrtle Avenue Stomp."
[2]aka "Le Jazz Hot."

JOHNNY HODGES & HIS ORCHESTRA
CW, LB, JH HC, DE BT SG.

....	Vo	M950-2	I'm In Another World[1]
....	Vo	M951-1	Hodge Podge
....	Vo	M952-1	Dancing On The Stars[2]
....	Vo	M953-1	Wanderlust[3]

[1]*aka* "Sexxitta."
[2]Complete: "I'm Riding On The Moon And Dancing On The Stars."
[3]*aka* "Katie Blues."

20 Dec 1938   (S)
1776 Broadway Studios
New York City, NY

COOTIE WILLIAMS & HIS RUG CUTTERS
CW, BB JH OH HC, DE BT SG.

....	Vo	M954-1	Delta Mood
....	Vo	M955-1	The Boys From Harlem[1]
....	Epi	M956-1	Mobile Blues
....	Vo	M956-2	Mobile Blues
....	Vo	M957-1	Gal-Avantin'

[1]*aka* "Cat Rag."

21 Dec 1938   (S)
1776 Broadway Studios
New York City, NY

DUKE ELLINGTON'S SEPTET
CW, LB, JH HC, DE BT SG.

....	PP	Tiger Rag
....	PP	On The Sunny Side Of The Street
....	PP	The Jeep Is Jumpin'

Studios WNEW (bc) (S)

DUKE ELLINGTON & HIS FAMOUS ORCHESTRA
WJ, LB, BB JH OH HC, DE FG BT SG.

....	Co	M958-1	Blue Light
....	Br	M958-2	Blue Light

> CW RS, JN JT added.

....	Br	M959-1	Old King Dooji
....	Br	M960-1	Boy Meets Horn[1]
....	Br	M961-1	Slap Happy
....	Pa	M961-2	Slap Happy

[1]*aka* "Man With The Horn"; *sa* "Twits And Twerps"; "Stew Burp."

22 Dec 1938   (S)
1776 Broadway Studios
New York City, NY

DUKE ELLINGTON & HIS ORCHESTRA
CW WJ RS, JN LB JT, BB JH OH HC, DE FG BT SG, RFsn.

....		Beer Barrel Polka

Feb 1939   (P)
New York City College
New York City, NY

JOHNNY HODGES & HIS ORCHESTRA
CW, LB, JH HC, DE BT SG, JE.

....	Vo	M974-1	Like A Ship In The Night –vJE[1]
....	Vo	M975-1	Mississippi Dreamboat –vJE
....	Vo	M976-1	Swingin' On The Campus
....	Vo	M977-1	Dooji Wooji

[1]This was the first title BS wrote the arrangement for.

27 Feb 1939   (S)
1776 Broadway Studios
New York City, NY

COOTIE WILLIAMS & HIS RUG CUTTERS
CW, BB JH HC, DE BT SG.

....	Vo	M982-1	A Beautiful Romance
....	Vo	M983-1	Boudoir Benny
....	Vo	M984-1	Ain't The Gravy Good? –vCW
....	BD	M984-2	Ain't The Gravy Good? –vCW
....	Vo	M985-1	She's Gone

28 Feb 1939   (S)
1776 Broadway Studios
New York City, NY

DUKE ELLINGTON
Piano solo.

....	FDC	M990-1	Just Good Fun
....	FDC	M991-1	Informal Blues

[1]Studios of the World Broadcasting System.

8 Mar 1939   (S)
711 Fifth Ave. Studios[1]
New York City, NY

DUKE ELLINGTON & HIS ORCHESTRA
CW WJ RS, JN LB JT, BB JH OH HC, DE FG BT SG, IA.

.... JUn		Jazz Potpourri
.... JUn		Lady In Doubt[1]

> RS, JT, BB HC, DE BT SG.

....		Evah Day

> CW, LB, JH HC, DE BT SG.

.... JUn		Jeep's Blues

> Entire band.

.... JUn		Old King Dooji
.... Az		Boy Meets Horn
....		Hold Tight –vIA
....		Pussy Willow
.... JUn		Azure
.... JUn		Harmony In Harlem

[1]*sa* "T.T. On Toast."

REX STEWART & HIS FIFTY-SECOND STREET STOMPERS
LBcn RS, JN, BB, DE BT SG/?JM.

....	Vo	WM994-1	San Juan Hill
....	Vo	WM995-1	So, I'll Come Back For More –vLBcn[1]
....	Vo	WM996-1	Fat Stuff Serenade[2]

[1]"I'll Come Back For More" on some releases.
[2]*aka* "Fat Stuff Swing."

DUKE ELLINGTON & HIS FAMOUS ORCHESTRA
CW WJ RS, JN LB JT, BB JH OH HC, DE FG BT SG.

....	Br	WM997-1	Pussy Willow
....	SC	WM998[1]	Subtle Lament
....	Br	WM998-1[1]	Subtle Lament
....	UTD	WM999	Lady In Blue
....	Co	WM999-1	Lady In Blue
....	Br	WM1000-1	Smorgasbord And Schnapps[2]

[1]The takes have been inverted on SC.
[2]*aka* "Doodle Berry Swing."

JOHNNY HODGES & HIS ORCHESTRA
CW, LB, JH HC, DE BT SG.

....	Vo	WM1001-1	Savoy Strut
....	Co	WM1001-2	Savoy Strut
....	Vo	WM1002-1	Rent Party Blues
....	Vo	WM1003-1	Dance Of The Goons
....	Vo	WM1004-1	Good Gal Blues

DUKE ELLINGTON'S TRIO
JH, DE BT.

....	Co	WM1005-1	Finesse[1]

[1]*aka* "Night Wind."

DUKE ELLINGTON & HIS FAMOUS ORCHESTRA
CW WJ RS, JN LB JT, BB JH OH HC, DE FG BT SG, JE.

....	Br	WM1006-1	Portrait Of The Lion
....	Br	WM1006-2	Portrait Of The Lion

> BS replaces DE.

....	Br	WM1007-1	Something To Live For –vJE[1]

> DE replaces BS.

....	Br	WM1008-1	Solid Old Man

[1]Complete: "I Want Something To Live For." This is the first time the orchestra plays a composition by BS. It is also BS's first record with the band.

<table>
<tr><td></td><td></td><td></td><td>29 Apr 1939   (S)
Grand Hotel
Stockholm, Sweden</td></tr>
</table>

DUKE ELLINGTON
DE interviewed by Manne Berggren.

.... Max   Interview

Konserthuset (bc) (P)

DUKE ELLINGTON & HIS ORCHESTRA
CW WJ RS, JN LB JT, BB JH OH HC, DE FG BT SG, IA.

.... Ari   Serenade To Sweden[1]
.... Dyn   Rockin' In Rhythm
.... Az   In A Red Little Cottage –vIA[2]

[1]*aka* "Moody"; "Kind Of Moody."
[2]English version of the Swedish hit song "I en rod liten stuga."

?28 May 1939[1]   (P)
Loew's State Theater (bc)
New York City, NY

DUKE ELLINGTON & HIS ORCHESTRA
CW WJ RS, JN LB JT, BB JH OH HC, DE FG BT SG.

.... Bst   Pussy Willow

[1]Date of bc; some sources suggest 30/31 Jan 1939 as recording date.

2 Jun 1939   (S)
711 Fifth Ave. Studios
New York City, NY

JOHNNY HODGES & HIS ORCHESTRA
CW, LB, JH HC, DE BT SG.

.... Vo   WM1026-A   Kitchen Mechanic's Day
.... Vo   WM1027-A   My Heart Jumped Over The Moon
.... Vo   WM1028-A   You Can Count On Me
.... Vo   WM1029-A   Hometown Blues

6 Jun 1939   (S)
711 Fifth Ave. Studios
New York City, NY

DUKE ELLINGTON & HIS FAMOUS ORCHESTRA
CW WJ RS, JN LB JT, BB JH OH HC, DE FG BT SG.

.... Br   WM1030-A   Cotton Club Stomp
.... Co   WM1031-A   Doin' The Voom Voom
.... Br   WM1032-A   Way Low
.... Co   WM1033-A   Serenade To Sweden

8 Jun 1939   (S)
711 Fifth Ave. Studios
New York City, NY

THE QUINTONES
Vcl, acc. by RS, JT, BB HC, DE FG BT SG.

.... Vo   WM1034-A   Utt-Da-Zay –vQu
.... Vo   WM1035-A   Chew, Chew, Chew –vQu

BARNEY BIGARD & HIS ORCHESTRA
Qu omitted, otherwise same personnel.

.... Vo   WM1036-A   Barney Goin' Easy
.... OK   WM1037-A   Just Another Dream

12 Jun 1939   (S)
711 Fifth Ave. Studios
New York City, NY

DUKE ELLINGTON & HIS FAMOUS ORCHESTRA
CW WJ RS, JN LB JT, BB JH OH HC, DE FG BT SG, IA.

.... Br   WM1038-A   In A Mizz –vIA
.... Co   WM1039-A   I'm Checkin' Out, Go'om-Bye –vIA[1]
.... Co   WM1040-A   A Lonely Co-Ed –vIA
.... Br   WM1041-A   You Can Count On Me –vIA

[1]*sa* "Barney Goin' Easy."

21 Jun 1939   (S)
711 Fifth Ave. Studios
New York City, NY

COOTIE WILLIAMS & HIS RUG CUTTERS
CW, BB JH HC, DE BT SG.

.... Vo   WM1042-A   Night Song

22 Jun 1939   (S)
711 Fifth Ave. Studios
New York City, NY

COOTIE WILLIAMS & HIS RUG CUTTERS
CW, BB JH HC, BS BT SG.

.... Vo   WM1043-A   Blues A-Poppin'

> DE replaces BS.

.... OK   WM1044-A   Top And Bottom
.... Vo   WM1045-A   Black Beauty

DUKE ELLINGTON & HIS ORCHESTRA
CW WJ RS, JN LB JT, BB JH OH HC, DE FG BT SG, IA.

....	PC		East St. Louis Toodle-Oo
....	PC		Jazz Potpourri
....	PC		Something To Live For
....	PC		Old King Dooji
....	PC		In A Mizz —vlA
....	PC		Rose Of The Rio Grande —vlA
....	PC		Pussy Willow
....	PC		You Can Count On Me —vlA
....	PC		Way Low

26 Jul 1939   (P)
Ritz Carlton Hotel (bc)
Boston, MA

DUKE ELLINGTON & HIS FAMOUS ORCHESTRA
CW WJ RS, JN LB JT, BB JH OH HC, DE FG BT SG.

....	Co	WM1062-A	Bouncing Buoyancy[1]
....	Co	WM1063-A	The Sergeant Was Shy[2]
....	Rt	WM1064-A	Grievin'

[1]*sa* "Exposition Swing."
[2]This title is a derivative of *Bugle Call Rag.*

28 Aug 1939   (S)
711 Fifth Ave. Studios
New York City, NY

JOHNNY HODGES & HIS ORCHESTRA
CW, LB, JH HC, BS BT SG.

....	Vo	WM1072-A	The Rabbit's Jump
....	Vo	WM1073-A	Moon Romance
....	Vo	WM1974-A	Truly Wonderful

> DE replaces BS.

| .... | Vo | WM1075-A | Dream Blues[1] |

[1]*aka* "Cream Blues."

1 Sep 1939   (S)
711 Fifth Ave. Studios
New York City, NY

DUKE ELLINGTON
DE on Georgie Jessel's "Celebrity Program," acc. by a studio orchestra.

| .... | | | Sophisticated Lady—Solitude—I Let A Song Go Out Of My Heart |

20 Sep 1939   (P)
NBC Studios (bc)
New York City, NY

DUKE ELLINGTON & HIS FAMOUS ORCHESTRA
CW WJ RS, JN LB JT, BB JH OH HC, DE FG BT SG.

....	Co	WM1091-A*	Little Posey[2]
....	Co	WM1092-A*	I Never Felt This Way Before
....	Rt	WM1092-B*	I Never Felt This Way Before
....	Co	WM1093-A*	Grievin'
....	Co	WM1094-A*	Tootin' Through The Roof
....	Rt	WM1094-B*	Tootin' Through The Roof

> BS replaces DE.

| .... | Co | WM1095-A* | Weely[3] |

[1]Complete: World Broadcasting Systems Inc., 301 East Eire Street.
[2]*aka* "A Portrait Of Freddy Jenkins."
[3]*aka* "A Portrait Of Billy Strayhorn."

14 Oct 1939   (S)
World's Studio[1]
Chicago, IL

JOHNNY HODGES & HIS ORCHESTRA
CW, LB, JH HC, BS BT SG.

| .... | Vo | WM1096-A* | Skunk Hollow Blues |

> DE replaces BS.

....	Vo	WM1097-A*	I Know What You Do
....	OK	WM1098-A*	Your Love Has Faded

> BS replaces DE.

| .... | Vo | WM1099-A* | Tired Socks |

DUKE ELLINGTON
Piano solo.

| .... | Rt | WM1100-A* | Blues |

*These numbers are transfer numbers. The original master numbers are WC-2802 through WC-2811.

16 Oct 1939   (S)
World's Studio
Chicago, IL

BARNEY BIGARD & HIS ORCHESTRA
RS, BB HC, DE BT SG.

.... Vo   WM1105-A*   Early Mornin'

DUKE ELLINGTON & HIS FAMOUS ORCHESTRA
CW WJ RS, JN LB JT, BB JH OH HC, BS FG BT SG, IA.

.... Co   WM1107-A*   Your Love Has Faded –vIA
.... Co   WM1106-A*   Killin' Myself –vIA

> DE replaces BS.

.... Co   WM1108-A*   Country Gal

*These numbers are transfer numbers. The original master numbers are WC-2812, WC-2813, WC-2814 and WC-2815 respectively.

1939   (P)
Unidentified location(s) (?bc)
U.S.A.

DUKE ELLINGTON & HIS ORCHESTRA
pp CW WJ RS, JN LB JT, BB JH OH HC, DE FG BT SG.

....   Boy Meets Horn
.... Rt   The Sergeant Was Shy

2 Nov 1939[1]   (P)
Club Caprice, Coronado Hotel (bc)
St. Louis, MO

DUKE ELLINGTON & HIS ORCHESTRA
CW WJ RS, JN LB JT, BB JH OH HC, DE FG BT JB SG, IA.

.... JM   Pyramid
.... JM   Pussy Willow
.... JM   I'm Checkin' Out, Go'om-Bye –vIA

[1]The program was probably aired past midnight, since 1 Nov 1939 was closing night at the Club Caprice. On 2 Nov 1939 DE opened at the Blackstone Hotel in Chicago.

22 Nov 1939   (S)
World's Studio
Chicago, IL

BARNEY BIGARD & HIS ORCHESTRA
RS, JT, BB HC, BS JB SG.

.... Vo   WM1117-A   Minuet In Blue
.... Vo   WM1118-A   Lost In Two Flats
.... OK   WM1119-A   Honey Hush

DUKE ELLINGTON & JIMMY BLANTON
DE JB.

.... Co   WM1120-A   Blues
.... Co   WM1121-A   Plucked Again

24 Nov 1939   (S)
CBS Studios, Merchandise Mart (bc)
Chicago, IL

DUKE ELLINGTON & HIS ORCHESTRA
CW WJ RS, JN LB JT, BB JH OH HC, DE FG BT JB SG, IA.

....   Medley[1]
.... VD   JBB-286   I'm Checkin' Out, Go'om-Bye –vIA
.... VD   JBB-286   Tootin' Through The Roof

[1]Including: Mood Indigo; Liza; Black And Tan Fantasy; Ring Dem Bells; It Don't Mean A Thing –vIA; Sophisticated Lady; Solitude; In A Sentimental Mood; Caravan; I Let A Song Go Out Of My Heart.

9 Jan 1940   (P)
Southland Café (bc)
Boston, MA

DUKE ELLINGTON & HIS ORCHESTRA
CW WJ RS, JN LB JT, BB JH OH HC, DE FG BT JB SG, HJ.

.... CC   East St. Louis Toodle-Oo
.... Pir   Me And You –vHJ
.... CC   Grievin'
.... CC   Little Posey
.... Pir   My Last Goodbye –vHJ
.... CC   The Gal From Joe's
.... CC   Tootin' Through The Roof
.... CC   Day In, Day Out
.... CC   Merry-Go-Round

12 Jan 1940   (P)
Southland Café (bc)
Boston, MA

DUKE ELLINGTON & HIS ORCHESTRA
CW WJ RS, JN LB JT, BB JH OH HC, DE FG BT JB SG.

.... Max   The Sergeant Was Shy

DUKE ELLINGTON & HIS ORCHESTRA
CW WJ RS, JN LB JT, BB JH OH BW HC, DE FG JB SG, IA.

2-8 Feb 1940   (P)
State Lake Theater (bc?)
Chicago, IL

....			St. Louis Blues –vCW
....			I Want A Man Like That –vIA
....			Clarinet Lament
....			Serenade To Sweden
....			Boy Meets Horn
....			Pyramid
....			Mood Indigo

DUKE ELLINGTON & HIS FAMOUS ORCHESTRA
CW WJ RS, JN LB JT, BB JH OH BW HC, DE FG JB SG, IA.

14 Feb 1940   (S)
Columbia Studios
Chicago, IL

....	Co	WM1135-A	Solitude –vIA
....	Co	WM1136-A	Stormy Weather –vIA
....	Co	WM1137-A	Mood Indigo –vIA
....	Co	WM1138-A	Sophisticated Lady

BARNEY BIGARD & HIS ORCHESTRA
RS, JT, BB HC, BS JB SG.

....	Epi	WM1139-A	Pelican Drag
....	Epi	WM1140-A	Tapioca

BARNEY BIGARD & HIS ORCHESTRA
RS, JT, BB HC, BS JB SG.

15 Feb 1940   (S)
Columbia Studios
Chicago, IL

....	Vo	WM1141-A	Mardi Gras Madness
....	Vo	WM1142-A	Watch The Birdie

COOTIE WILLIAMS & HIS RUG CUTTERS
CW, BB JH HC, BS JB SG.

....	Vo	WM1143-A	Black Butterfly

> DE replaces BS.

....	Vo	WM1144-A	Dry Long So –vCW
....		WM1144-B[1]	Dry Long So –vCW
....	OK	WM1145-A	Toasted Pickle

> BS replaces DE.

....	Vo	WM1146-A	Give It Up

[1]Test extant.

DUKE ELLINGTON & HIS FAMOUS ORCHESTRA
CW WJ RS, JN LB JT, BB JH OH BW HC, DE FG JB SG, IA HJ.

6 Mar 1940   (S)
Victor Studio A
Chicago, IL

....	Vi	BS-044887-2	You, You Darling –vHJ
....	Vi	BS-044888-1	Jack The Bear[1]
....	Vi	BS-044889-1	Ko-Ko[2]
....	Vi	BS-044889-2	Ko-Ko
....	Vi	BS-044890-1	Morning Glory
....	Vi	BS-044891-1	So Far, So Good –vIA

[1]aka "Take It Away."
[2]aka "Kalina."

DUKE ELLINGTON & HIS FAMOUS ORCHESTRA
CW WJ RS, JN LB JT, BB JH OH BW HC, DE FG JB SG, IA.

15 Mar 1940   (S)
Victor Studio A
Chicago, IL

....	Vi	BS-049015-1	Conga Brava
....	Vi	BS-049016-1	Concerto For Cootie[1]
....	Vi	BS-049017-1	Me And You –vIA[2]

[1]Working title: "Cootie's Concerto."
[2]Originally titled "Lamie Pie."

DUKE ELLINGTON & HIS FAMOUS ORCHESTRA
CW WJ RS, JN LB JT, BB JH OH BW HC, DE FG JB SG.

4 May 1940   (S)
Hollywood Recording Studio
Hollywood, CA

....	Mrt	PBS-049654-1	Bojangles[1]
....	Vi	PBS-049655-1	Cotton Tail[2]
....	Vi	PBS-049656-1	Never No Lament[3] >>>

.... Mrt   PBS-049657-1   Blue Goose

[1]*aka* "A Portrait Of Bill Robinson."
[2]*aka* "Shuckin' And Stiffin'." This title is a derivative of *I Got Rhythm*.
[3]*aka* "Foxy"; originally titled "Zoom-Ha-Laa"; "Zoom-Ha-Ka."

				28 May 1940	(S)
				Victor Studio A	
				Chicago, IL	

DUKE ELLINGTON & HIS FAMOUS ORCHESTRA
CW WJ RS, JN LB JT, BB JH OH BW HC, DE FG JB SG.

.... Vi   BS-053020-1   Dusk
.... Vi   BS-053020-2   Dusk
.... Vi   BS-053021-1[1]   Bojangles
.... Vi   BS-053022-1   A Portrait Of Bert Williams[2]
.... Vi   BS-053023-1[1]   Blue Goose

[1]Remakes.
[2]Originally titled "Bert Williams."

				10 Jun 1940[1]	(S)
				CBS Studios (bc)	
				New York City, NY	

DUKE ELLINGTON & HIS ORCHESTRA
CW WJ RS, JN LB JT, BB JH WW BW HC, DE FG JB SG, IA.

.... MR   East St. Louis Toodle-Oo
.... QuD   Ko-Ko
.... QuD   Blue Goose
.... QuD   So Far, So Good –vIA
.... QuD   Cotton Tail
.... QuD   Concerto For Cootie
.... QuD   Jack The Bear
.... QuD   Boy Meets Horn
.... QuD   The Sergeant Was Shy
.... MR   Never No Lament[2]

[1]Broadcast on 12 Jun 1940.
[2]Announced as "East St. Louis Toodle-Oo."

				12 Jun 1940	(S)
				MBS Studios (bc)	
				New York City, NY	

DUKE ELLINGTON
DE interviewed by Norman Pierce.

....   Interview

> DE piano solo.

....   Never No Lament

				22 Jun 1940	(S)
				24th St., Studio 2	
				New York City, NY	

DUKE ELLINGTON & HIS FAMOUS ORCHESTRA
CW WJ RS, JN LB JT, BB JH OH BW HC, DE FG JB SG, IA.

.... Vi   BS-054606-1   Harlem Air Shaft[1]
.... Vi   BS-054607-1   At A Dixie Roadside Diner –vIA
.... Vi   BS-054608-1   All Too Soon[2]
.... Vi   BS-054609-1   Rumpus In Richmond[3]

[1]Originally titled "Rumpus In Richmond"; *aka* "Once Over Lightly."
[2]Originally titled "I Don't Mind"; *aka* "Slow Tune."
[3]*aka* "Brassiere."

				24 Jul 1940	(S)
				24th St., Studio 2	
				New York City, NY	

DUKE ELLINGTON & HIS FAMOUS ORCHESTRA
CW WJ RS, JN LB JT, BB JH OH BW HC, DE FG JB SG.

.... Vi   BS-054624-1   My Greatest Mistake
.... Vi   BS-054625-1   Sepia Panorama[1]
.... Vi   BS-054625-2   Sepia Panorama

[1]*aka* "Night House."

				29 Jul 1940	(P)
				Eastwood Gardens (bc)	
				Detroit, MI	

DUKE ELLINGTON & HIS ORCHESTRA
CW WJ RS, JN LB JT, BB JH OH BW HC, DE FG JB SG, IA.

....   At A Dixie Roadside Diner
.... JM   Harlem Air Shaft
.... JM   All Too Soon
.... JM   Me And You –vIA
.... JM   Jack The Bear
.... JM   Concerto For Cootie
.... JM   Ko-Ko
.... JM   Orchids For Remembrance

31 Jul 1940[1]   (P)
Eastwood Gardens (bc)
Detroit, MI

DUKE ELLINGTON & HIS ORCHESTRA
CW WJ RS, JN LB JT, BB JH OH BW HC, DE FG JB SG, IA.

.... Evb   Rose Of The Rio Grande –vIA
.... Evb   Warm Valley

[1]Broadcast on 31 Jul 1940.

17 Aug 1940   (P)
Canobie Lake Park (bc)
Salem, NH

DUKE ELLINGTON & HIS ORCHESTRA
CW WJ RS, JN LB JT, BB JH OH BW HC, DE FG JB SG.

.... Evb   Riding On A Blue Note
.... Evb   Boy Meets Horn
.... Evb   Rose Room
.... Evb   Stompy Jones

5 Sep 1940   (S)
Victor Studio A
Chicago, IL

DUKE ELLINGTON & HIS FAMOUS ORCHESTRA
CW WJ RS, JN LB JT, BB JH OH BW HC, DE FG JB SG, IA HJ.

.... Vi   BS-053427-1   There Shall Be No Night –vHJ
.... Vi   BS-053428-1   In A Mellotone[1]
.... Vi   BS-053429-1   Five O'Clock Whistle –vIA
.... Vi   BS-053430-1   Warm Valley

[1]aka "Baby, You And Me." This title is a derivative of Rose Room.

6 Sep 1940   (P)
Panther Room, Hotel Sherman (bc)
Chicago, IL

DUKE ELLINGTON & HIS ORCHESTRA
CW WJ RS, JN LB JT, BB JH OH BW HC, DE FG JB SG, IA.

.... JG   Sepia Panorama
.... JG   Stompy Jones
.... Max   In A Mellotone
.... Max   Chatter-Box
.... Max   Sepia Panorama
.... JG   St. Louis Blues –vIA

7 Sep 1940   (P)
Panther Room, Hotel Sherman (bc)
Chicago, IL

DUKE ELLINGTON & HIS ORCHESTRA
CW WJ RS, JN LB JT, BB JH OH BW HC, DE FG JB SG, IA.

.... JSp   Sepia Panorama
.... JSp   Rumpus In Richmond
.... JSp   You Think Of Everything
.... JSp   My Greatest Mistake
.... JSp   Bojangles
.... JSp   Azure
.... JSp   Five O'Clock Whistle –vIA
.... Max   Concerto For Cootie

10 Sep 1940   (P)
Panther Room, Hotel Sherman (bc)
Chicago, IL

DUKE ELLINGTON & HIS ORCHESTRA
CW WJ RS, JN LB JT, BB JH OH BW HC, DE FG JB SG, IA.

.... JSp   Tootin' Through The Roof
.... JSp   April In Paris
.... JSp   So Far, So Good –vIA
.... JSp   Whispering Grass
.... JSp   The Mystery Song
.... JSp   Warm Valley

12 Sep 1940   (P)
Panther Room, Hotel Sherman (bc)
Chicago, IL

DUKE ELLINGTON & HIS ORCHESTRA
CW WJ RS, JN LB JT, BB JH OH BW HC, DE FG JB SG, HJ.

....   East St. Louis Toodle-Oo
.... JSp   Madame Will Drop Her Shawl
.... JSp   Blue Goose
....   All This And Heaven Too –vHJ
.... Max   Slap Happy
.... JSp   All Too Soon
....   Swing Low
....   Solitude
.... JSp   Rockin' In Rhythm

13 Sep 1940   (P)
Panther Room, Hotel Sherman (bc)
Chicago, IL

DUKE ELLINGTON & HIS ORCHESTRA
CW WJ RS, JN LB JT, BB JH OH BW HC, DE FG JB SG, IA.

....	JSp	Solid Old Man
....	JSp	Maybe –vIA
....	JSp	Oh Babe! Maybe Someday –vIA
....		All Too Soon
....	JSp	Blueberry Hill
....	JSp	Harlem Air Shaft
....		Warm Valley

18 Sep 1940   (P)
Panther Room, Hotel Sherman (bc)
Chicago, IL

DUKE ELLINGTON
Piano solo.

....	JSp	Black Beauty

20 Sep 1940   (P)
Panther Room, Hotel Sherman (bc)
Chicago, IL

DUKE ELLINGTON & HIS ORCHESTRA
CW WJ RS, JN LB JT, BB JH OH BW HC, DE FG JB SG

....	Evb	Jig Walk[1]
....		Warm Valley

[1]No or hardly any similarity with the original composition of that name.

25 Sep 1940   (P)
Panther Room, Hotel Sherman (bc)
Chicago, IL

DUKE ELLINGTON & HIS ORCHESTRA
CW WJ RS, JN LB JT, BB JH OH BW HC, DE FG JB SG.

....	Evb	Little Posey
....	Evb	Warm Valley

27 Sep 1940   (P)
Panther Room, Hotel Sherman (bc)
Chicago, IL

DUKE ELLINGTON & HIS ORCHESTRA
CW WJ RS, JN LB JT, BB JH OH BW HC, DE FG JB SG.

....		Swinging At The Séance
....		Looking For Yesterday
....		Weely

Sep/Oct 1940[1]   (P)
Panther Room, Hotel Sherman (bc)
Chicago, IL

DUKE ELLINGTON & HIS ORCHESTRA
CW WJ RS, JN LB JT, BB JH OH BW HC, DE FG JB SG, IA HJ.

....		Maybe –vIA
....		I Give You My Word
....		So You're The One
....		I Want To Live
....		Madame Will Drop Her Shawl
....		There I Go
....		Harlem Air Shaft
....	JSp	Star Dust –vHJ
....	JSp	Subtle Lament
....	JSp	It's The Same Old Story
....	JSp	Cotton Tail
....	JSp	Lady In Doubt
....	JSp	The Sergeant Was Shy

[1]It is assumed that the above material originates from more than one event. The source is most likely several of the NBC broadcasts listed in the section "On the Air."

1 Oct 1940   (S)
Victor Studio A
Chicago, IL

DUKE ELLINGTON & JIMMY BLANTON
DE JB.

....	Vi	BS-053504-1	Pitter Panther Patter[1]
....	Vi	BS-053504-2	Pitter Panther Patter
....	UTD	BS-053505-1	Body And Soul
....	Vi	BS-053505-2	Body And Soul
....	Vi	BS-053505-3	Body And Soul
....	Vi	BS-053506-1	Sophisticated Lady
....	Vi	BS-053506-2	Sophisticated Lady
....	Vi	BS-053507-1	Mr. J.B. Blues
....	Vi	BS-053507-2	Mr. J.B. Blues

[1]aka "The Panther Patter."

			4 Oct 1940 (P)

DUKE ELLINGTON & HIS ORCHESTRA
CW WJ RS, JN LB JT, BB JH OH BW HC, DE FG JB SG.

4 Oct 1940   (P)
Panther Room, Hotel Sherman (bc)
Chicago, IL

.... QuD   Ring Dem Bells –vCW
.... JSp   In A Mellotone

DUKE ELLINGTON & HIS ORCHESTRA
CW WJ RS, JN LB JT, BB JH OH BW HC, DE FG JB SG, IA.

5 Oct 1940   (P)
Panther Room, Hotel Sherman (bc)
Chicago, IL

.... JSp   The Gal From Joe's
.... JSp   Me And You –vIA
.... JSp   Echoes Of Harlem

DUKE ELLINGTON & HIS FAMOUS ORCHESTRA
CW WJ RS, JN LB JT, BB JH OH BW HC, DE FG JB SG.

17 Oct 1940   (S)
Victor Studio A
Chicago, IL

.... Vi   BS-053552-1   The Flaming Sword[1]
.... Vi   BS-053552-2   The Flaming Sword
.... Vi   BS-053552-3   The Flaming Sword
.... Vi   BS-053430-2[2]   Warm Valley
.... Vi   BS-053430-3   Warm Valley
....   BS-053430-4   Warm Valley

[1]This title is a derivative of *Tiger Rag*.
[2]Remake.

The recording sheet for this session notes that "considerable time was spent rehearsing two other numbers, but Duke felt that the arrangements could be improved upon."

DUKE ELLINGTON & HIS FAMOUS ORCHESTRA
CW WJ RS, JN LB JT, BB JH OH BW HC, DE FG JB SG, HJ.

28 Oct 1940   (S)
Victor Studio A
Chicago, IL

.... Vi   BS-053579-1   Across The Track Blues[1]
.... Vi   BS-053579-2   Across The Track Blues
.... Vi   BS-053580-1   Chloe[2]
.... Vi   BS-053581-1   I Never Felt That Way Before –vHJ
.... Vi   BS-053581-2   I Never Felt That Way Before –vHJ

[1]Originally titled "Pastel."
[2]Subtitled "Song Of The Swamp."

JOHNNY HODGES & HIS ORCHESTRA
CW, LB, JH HC, DE JB SG.

2 Nov 1940   (S)
Victor Studio A
Chicago, IL

.... Bb   BS-053603-1A   Day Dream
.... Bb   BS-053604-1   Good Queen Bess[1]
.... Vi   BS-053604-2   Good Queen Bess
.... Bb   BS-053605-1   That's The Blues Old Man
.... TL   BS-053606-1   Junior Hop
.... Bb   BS-053606-2   Junior Hop

[1]*aka* "Diaesus"; originally titled "Beicers." Bb B-11117 is found in two variant labels: *Queen Bess* and *Good Queen Bess*.

REX STEWART & HIS ORCHESTRA
RS, LB, BW HC, DE JB SG.

.... Bb   BS-053607-1   Without A Song
.... "X"   BS-053607-2   Without a Song
.... Bb   BS-053608-1   My Sunday Gal
.... Bb   BS-053609-1   Mobile Bay
.... "X"   BS-053609-2   Mobile Bay

> BS replaces DE.[1]

.... "X"   BS-053610-1   Linger Awhile
.... Bb   BS-053610-2   Linger Awhile

[1]The piano playing on "Linger Awhile" instigated an ongoing discussion, whether or not BS sat in for DE. Although BS was not mentioned on the recording sheet, this option is well possible, as many instances in future sessions will show.

DUKE ELLLINGTON & HIS ORCHESTRA
WJ RS RN, JN LB JT, BB JH OH BW HC, DE FG JB SG, IA HJ.

7 Nov 1940   (P)
Crystal Ballroom (bc)
Fargo, ND

.... JG   It's Glory
.... Plm   The Mooche
.... JG   The Sheik Of Araby   >>>

....	Plm		Sepia Panorama
....	Plm		Ko-Ko
....	Plm		There Shall Be No Night –vHJ
....	Plm		Pussy Willow
....	Plm		Chatter-Box
....	Plm		Mood Indigo
....	Plm		Harlem Air Shaft
....	Plm		Ferryboat Serenade –vlA
....	Plm		Warm Valley
....	Plm		Stompy Jones
....	Plm		Chloe
....	Plm		Bojangles
....	Plm		On The Air[1]
....	Plm		Rumpus In Richmond
....	Plm		The Sidewalks Of New York[2]
....	Plm		The Flaming Sword
....	Plm		Never No Lament
....	Plm		Caravan
....	Plm		Clarinet Lament
....	Plm		Slap Happy
....	Plm		Sepia Panorama
....	Plm		Boy Meets Horn
....	Plm		'Way Down Yonder in New Orleans –vlA
....	Plm		Oh Babe! Maybe Someday –vlA
....	Plm		Five O'Clock Whistle
....	VJC		Call Of The Canyon
....	VJC		Heaven Can Wait[3]
....	VJC		Unidentified title
....	Plm		Rockin' In Rhythm
....	Plm		Sophisticated Lady
....	Plm		Cotton Tail
....	Plm		Whispering Grass
....	Plm		Conga Brava
....	Plm		I Never Felt That Way Before –vHJ
....	Plm		Across The Track Blues
....	JG		Honeysuckle Rose
....	JG		Wham –vRN
....	Plm		Star Dust
....	Plm		Rose Of The Rio Grande –vlA
....	Plm		St. Louis Blues –vlA
....	JG		Warm Valley
....	JG		God Bless America

[1]"You Took Advantage Of Me" on all LP releases.
[2]*sa* "East Side—West Side."
[3]"All This And Heaven Too" on VJC.

The above dance date has been recorded in situ by Dick Burris and Jack Towers using a portable disc-cutting recorder and microphones.

11 Nov 1940   (S)
Victor Studio A
Chicago, IL

BARNEY BIGARD & HIS ORCHESTRA
RN, JT, BB BW, DE JB SG.

....	Vi	BS-053621-2	Charlie The Chulo
....	Vi	BS-053621	Charlie The Chulo (incomplete)
....	Bb	BS-053621-1	Charlie The Chulo
....	Vi	BS-053622	Lament For Javanette
....	Bb	BS-053622-1A	Lament For Javanette
....	Vi	BS-053623	A Lull At Dawn
....	Vi	BS-053623	A Lull At Dawn
....	Bb	BS-053623-1A	A Lull At Dawn

> BS replaces DE.

....	Vi	BS-053624-1	Ready Eddy
....	Vi	BS-053624	Ready Eddy (incomplete)
....	Vi	BS-053624	Ready Eddy (incomplete)
....	Bb	BS-053624-2	Ready Eddy

28 Dec 1940   (S)
Victor Studio A
Chicago, IL

DUKE ELLINGTON & HIS FAMOUS ORCHESTRA
WJ RS RN, JN LB JT, BB JH OH BW HC, DE FG JB SG, HJ.

| .... | Vi | BS-053780-1 | The Sidewalks Of New York |

> BS replaces DE.

| .... | Vi | BS-053781-1 | Flamingo –vHJ[1]   >>> |

> DE replaces BS.

....	Vi	BS-053782-1	The Girl In My Dreams –vHJ[2]
....	Vi	BS-053782-2	The Girl In My Dreams –vHJ

[1]Originally titled "Flamingos And Moonlight."
[2]Complete: "The Girl In My Dreams Tries To Look Like You."

15 Jan 1941   (S)
Hollywood Recording Studio
Hollywood, CA

DUKE ELLINGTON & HIS ORCHESTRA
WJ RS RN, JN LB JT, BB JH OH BW HC, DE FG JB SG, HJ.

....	FDC	PBS-055250	Take The "A" Train
....	FDC	PBS-055250	I Hear A Rhapsody –vHJ
....	FDC	PBS-055250	Bounce
....	FDC	PBS-055250	It's Sad But True
....	FDC	PBS-055250	Madame Will Drop Her Shawl
....	FDC	PBS-055251	Frenesi
....	FDC	PBS-055251	Until Tonight[1]
....	HJC	PBS-055251	West Indian Stomp
....	FDC	PBS-055251	Love And I
....	FDC	PBS-055251	John Hardy's Wife

[1]aka "Mauve."

The above titles have been recorded for SRT.

16 Jan 1941   (S)
NBC Studios (bc)
Hollywood, CA

DUKE ELLINGTON & JIMMY BLANTON WITH THE JOHN SCOTT TROTTER ORCHESTRA
DE and JB with the John Scott Trotter Orchestra.

....	QuD	Jive Rhapsody
....	QuD	Jumpin' Punkins

28 Jan 1941   (S)
Casa Mañana (bc)
Culver City, CA

DUKE ELLINGTON
DE interviewed by Doug Hatton.

....	Vi	Interview

13 Feb 1941   (P)
Casa Mañana (bc)
Culver City, CA

DUKE ELLINGTON & HIS ORCHESTRA
WJ RS RN, JN LB JT, BB JH OH BW HC, DE FG JB SG, HJ.

....	John Hardy's Wife
....	The Girl In My Dreams –vHJ
....	Clementine
....	A Flower Is A Lovesome Thing

15 Feb 1941   (S)
Hollywood Recording Studio
Hollywood, CA

DUKE ELLINGTON & HIS FAMOUS ORCHESTRA
WJ RS RN, JN LB JT, BB JH OH BW HC, DE FG JB SG.

....	Vi	PBS-055283-1	Take The "A" Train
....	Vi	PBS-055284-1	Jumpin' Punkins
....	Vi	PBS-055284-2	Jumpin' Punkins
....	Vi	PBS-055285-1	John Hardy's Wife
....	Vi	PBS-055286-1	Blue Serge

> BS replaces DE.

....	Vi	PBS-055287-1	After All

16 Feb 1941   (P)
Casa Mañana (bc)
Culver City, CA

DUKE ELLINGTON & HIS ORCHESTRA
WJ RS RN, JN LB JT, BB JH OH BW HC, DE FG JB SG, IA HJ.

....	MR	Take The "A" Train
....	MR	Jumpin' Punkins
....	MR	Flamingo –vHJ

> DE FG JB SG.

....	MR	Jive Rhapsody

> Entire band.

....	MR	After All
....	MR	Chelsea Bridge
....	MR	Love Like This Can't Last –vIA
....	MR	Blue Serge
....	MR	Take The "A" Train

			20 Feb 1941	(P)

DUKE ELLINGTON & HIS ORCHESTRA
WJ RS RN, JN LB JT, BB JH OH BW HC, DE FG JB SG, IA.

20 Feb 1941 (P)
Casa Mañana (bc)
Culver City, CA

....		Blue Serge
....	Bb	Are You Sticking?
....	Bb	Chelsea Bridge
....	Bb	Love Like This Can't Last –vlA
....	Bb	Mist On The Moon[1]
....		Take The "A" Train

[1]*aka* "Atmosphere."

DUKE ELLINGTON & HIS ORCHESTRA
WJ RS RN, JN LB JT, BB JH OH BW HC, DE FG JB SG, HJ.

30 Mar 1941[1] (P)
CBS Studios (bc)
Hollywood, CA

| .... | ACh | Flamingo –vHJ |

[1]Date of broadcast.

DUKE ELLINGTON
Piano solo.

14 May 1941 (S)
Victor Studio 2
New York City, NY

....	Vi	BS-065604-1	Dear Old Southland
....	Vi	BS-065604-2	Dear Old Southland
....	Vi	BS-065605-1	Solitude[1]
....	Vi	BS-065605-2	Solitude

[1]This title was reissued on RCA/Vi 68124-1 with the overdubbed voice of Cleo Lane.

DUKE ELLINGTON & JIMMY BLANTON
DE JB.

29 May 1941 (S)
NBC Studios (bc)
Hollywood, CA

| .... | Spk | Stomp Caprice |

DUKE ELLINGTON & JIMMY BLANTON WITH THE JOHN SCOTT TROTTER ORCHESTRA
DE and JB with the John Scott Trotter Orchestra and chorus.

| .... | Tpl | Frankie And Johnny –vChorus |

DUKE ELLINGTON & HIS ORCHESTRA
WJ RS RN, JN LB JT, BB JH OH BW HC, DE FG JB SG, IA.

May/Jun 1941 (P)
Trianon Ballroom (bc)
Southgate, CA

....		Take The "A" Train
....	Bb	Sepia Panorama
....	Bb	It's Square But It Rocks –vlA
....		Day Dream
....	Bb	In A Mellotone
....		Raincheck

DUKE ELLINGTON & HIS FAMOUS ORCHESTRA
WJ RS RN, JN LB JT, BB JH OH BW HC, DE FG JB SG.

5 Jun 1941 (S)
Hollywood Recording Studio
Hollywood, CA

....	Vi	PBS-061283-1	Bakiff
....	Vi	PBS-061284-1	Are You Sticking?
....	Vi	PBS-061284-2	Are You Sticking?
....	Vi	PBS-061285-1	Just A-Settin' And A-Rockin'[1]
....	Vi	PBS-061286-1	The Giddybug Gallop

[1]*aka* "Leering"; "Swee' Pea." By following the lyrics, the vocal version is often spelled "Just A Sittin' And A-Rockin'."

DUKE ELLINGTON & HERB JEFFRIES
DE, HJ.

9 Jun 1941 (S)
Studios KHJ (bc)
Hollywood, CA

| .... | | The Brown-Skin Gal –vHJ[1] |
| .... | | Chocolate Shake |

[1]Complete: "The Brown-Skin Gal In The Calico Gown."

DUKE ELLINGTON & HIS ORCHESTRA
WJ RS RN, JN LB JT, BB JH OH BW HC, DE FG JB SG, HJ.

12 Jun 1941 (P)
Trianon Ballroom (bc)
Southgate, CA

....	JA	Raincheck
....		Flamingo –vHJ
....	Rar	Just A-Settin' And A-Rockin' >>>

....   The Giddybug Gallop

                                                                                         16 Jun 1941   (P)
DUKE ELLINGTON & HIS ORCHESTRA   Trianon Ballroom (bc)
WJ RS RN, JN LB JT, BB JH OH BW HC, DE FG JB SG, IA.   Southgate, CA

....   Solid Old Man
....   John Hardy's Wife
....   It's Square But It Rocks –vIA

                                                                                         26 Jun 1941   (S)
DUKE ELLINGTON & HIS FAMOUS ORCHESTRA   Hollywood Recording Studio
WJ RS RN, JN LB JT, BB JH OH BW HC, DE FG JB SG, IA.   Hollywood, CA

.... Vi   PBS-061318-1   Chocolate Shake –vIA[1]
.... Vi   PBS-061319-1   I Got It Bad –vIA[2]
.... Vi   PBS-061319-2   I Got It Bad –vIA

[1]Complete "Doin' The Chocolate Shake."
[2]Complete "I Got It Bad And That Ain't Good."

                                                                                         Jun/Jul 1941   (P)
DUKE ELLINGTON & HIS ORCHESTRA   Trianon Ballroom (bc)
WJ RS RN, JN LB JT, BB JH OH BW HC, DE FG JB SG, HJ.   Southgate, CA

....   Flamingo –vHJ

                                                                                         2 Jul 1941   (S)
DUKE ELLINGTON & HIS FAMOUS ORCHESTRA   Hollywood Recording Studio
WJ RS RN, JN LB JT, BB JH OH BW HC, DE FG JB SG, IA HJ.   Hollywood, CA

.... Vi   PBS-061338-1   Clementine
.... Vi   PBS-061339-1   The Brown-Skin Gal –vHJ
.... Vi   PBS-061340-1   Jump For Joy –vHJ
.... Vi   PBS-061340-2   Jump For Joy –vIA
.... Vi   PBS-061341-1   Moon Over Cuba[1]

[1]aka "Porto Rican Gal"; "Lovely Isle Of Porto Rico."

                                                                                         3 Jul 1941   (S)
REX STEWART & HIS ORCHESTRA   Hollywood Recording Studio
RS, LB, BW HC, DE JB SG.   Hollywood, CA

.... Bb   PBS-061342-1   Some Saturday
.... Bb   PBS-061343-1   Subtle Slough
.... HMV   PBS-061344-1[1] Menelik—The Lion Of Judah
.... HMV   PBS-061345-1   Poor Bubber

[1]Wax -2 was cut simultaneously with take -1 from the same performance; i.e. both recordings are identical. Believed to be
different takes, "take -2" was erroneously issued as such both on BD T1003 and the centennial edition.

JOHNNY HODGES & HIS ORCHESTRA
RN, LB, JH HC, DE JB SG.

.... Bb   PBS-061346-1   Squaty Roo[1]
.... Vi   PBS-061347-1   Passion Flower
.... Bb   PBS-061348-1   Things Ain't What They Used To Be
.... Bb   PBS-061349-1   Goin' Out The Back Way[2]

[1]Originally titled "Squateroo."
[2]Originally titled "Out The Back Way."

                                                                                         25 Aug 1941   (S)
DUKE ELLINGTON & HIS ORCHESTRA   CBS Studios (bc)
WJ RS RN, JN LB JT, BB JH OH BW HC, DE FG JB SG, HJ.   Hollywood, CA

....   Take The "A" Train
....   Flamingo –vHJ
....   Jumpin' Punkins

                                                                                         1 Sep 1941   (S)
DUKE ELLINGTON WITH IVIE ANDERSON & HERB JEFFRIES   NBC Studios (bc)
DE, IA HJ JTrn, chorus.   Hollywood, CA

.... Az[1]   DE and Melvyn Douglas talking
.... Az[1]   Medley[2]

[1]Also a non-commercial release on a promotional CD for the radio station KLON, Los Angeles, CA.
[2]Including: The Brown-Skin Gal –vHJ; Jump For Joy –vChorus; I Got It Bad –vIA; Rocks In My Bed –vJTrn; Jump For Joy
–vChorus.

DUKE ELLINGTON & HIS ORCHESTRA
WJ RS RN, JN LB JT, BB JH OH BW HC, DE FG JB SG, IA HJ.

....	Eph	PBS-061661-1	Clementine
....	QuD	PBS-061661-1	Chelsea Bridge
....	Eph	PBS-061661-1	Love Like This Can't Last –vIA
....	Eph	PBS-061661-1	After All
....	Eph	PBS-061661-1	The Girl In My Dreams –vHJ
....	Eph	PBS-061662-1	Jumpin' Punkins
....	Eph	PBS-061662-1	Frankie And Johnny
....	Eph	PBS-061662-1	Flamingo –vHJ
....	QuD	PBS-061662-1	Bakiff

The above titles have been recorded for SRT.

DUKE ELLINGTON & HIS FAMOUS ORCHESTRA
WJ RS RN, JN LB JT, BB JH OH BW HC, DE FG JB SG, IA.

....	Vi	PBS-061684-1	Five O'Clock Drag
....	Vi	PBS-061685-1	Rocks In My Bed –vIA
....	Vi	PBS-061686-1	Bli-Blip –vRN

> BS replaces DE.

....	Vi	PBS-061687-1	Chelsea Bridge

BARNEY BIGARD & HIS ORCHESTRA
RN, JT, BB HC, BS JB SG.

....	Bb	PBS-061688-1	Brown Suede
....	Vi	PBS-061689-1	Noir Bleu

> DE replaces BS.

....	Bb	PBS-061690-1	"C" Blues
....	HMV	PBS-061691-1	June

DUKE ELLINGTON & JIMMY BLANTON WITH THE JOHN SCOTT TROTTER ORCHESTRA
DE and JB with the John Scott Trotter Orchestra.

....	QuD		Take The "A" Train

> JB omitted.

....	VRC		Flamingo

DUKE ELLINGTON & HIS ORCHESTRA
WJ RS RN, JN LB JT, BB JH OH BW HC, DE FG JR SG, IA HJ.

....	ER	5304	Hot Chocolate[2]
....	Stv	5105	I Got It Bad –vIA
....	Vi	4907	Flamingo –vHJ

[1]Music for a series of movie shorts known as "Ellington Soundies"; the above "soundies" originate most probably from one session.
[2]*sa* "Cotton Tail."

DUKE ELLINGTON & HIS ORCHESTRA
WJ RS RN, JN LB JT, BB JH OH BW HC, DE FG JR SG, MBnt PW.

....	Vi	4904	Bli-Blip –vMBnt PW
....	ER	5503	Jam Session[2]

[1]Music for a series of movie shorts known as "Ellington Soundies"; the above "soundies" originate most probably from one session.
[2]*sa* ""C" Blues."

DUKE ELLINGTON & HIS FAMOUS ORCHESTRA
WJ RS RN, JN LB JT, BB JH OH BW HC, BS FG JR SG, HJ.

....	Vi	PBS-061941-1	Raincheck[1]	
....	Vi	PBS-061942-1	What Good Would It Do? –vHJ	

> DE replaces BS.

....	Vi	PBS-061943-1	I Don't Know What Kind Of Blues I Got –vHJ	
....	Vi	PBS-061943-2	I Don't Know What Kind Of Blues I Got –vHJ	>>>

> BS replaces DE.

.... Vi   PBS-061687-2[2]   Chelsea Bridge

[1]"Rain Check" on the recording sheet.
[2]Remake.

3 Dec 1941   (S)
Hollywood Recording Studio
Hollywood, CA

DUKE ELLINGTON & HIS ORCHESTRA
WJ RS RN, JN LB JT, BB JH OH BW HC, DE FG JR SG, HJ.

.... Jso   PBS-061946-1   Stomp Caprice
.... HJC   PBS-061946-1   Bugle Breaks
.... Jok   PBS-061946-1   You And I –vHJ
.... Jok   PBS-061946-1   Have You Changed?[1]
.... Jok   PBS-061946-1   Raincheck
.... Jok   PBS-061947-1   Blue Serge
.... Jok   PBS-061947-1   Moon Mist[2]
.... Jok   PBS-061947-1   I Don't Want To Set The World On Fire –vHJ
.... BA   PBS-061947-1   Easy Street
.... Jok   PBS-061947-1   Perdido

[1]aka "Blue Tears."
[2]sa "Mist On The Moon"; "Atmosphere."

The above titles have been recorded for SRT.

21 Jan 1942   (S)
Victor Studio A
Chicago, IL

DUKE ELLINGTON & HIS FAMOUS ORCHESTRA
WJ RS RN, JN LB JT, BB JH OH BW HC, DE FG JR SG.

.... Vi   BS-070682-1   Perdido
.... Vi   BS-070682-2   Perdido
.... Vi   BS-070683-1   The "C" Jam Blues[1]
               BS-070683-1A[2]   The "C" Jam Blues
.... Vi   BS-070684-1   Moon Mist
.... Vi   BS-070684-2   Moon Mist

[1]aka "Jump Blues"; sa ""C" Blues"; "Jam Session."
[2]A metal of this take survived in the vault of RCA. For reasons unknown it was not included in the centennial edition.

26 Feb 1942   (S)
24th St., Studio 1
New York City, NY

DUKE ELLINGTON & HIS FAMOUS ORCHESTRA
WJ RS RN, JN LB JT, BB JH OH BW HC, DE FG JR SG, IA.

.... Vi   BS-071890-1   What Am I Here For?[1]
.... Vi   BS-071891-1[2]   I Don't Mind –vIA
.... Vi   BS-071891-2   I Don't Mind –vIA
.... Vi   BS-071892-1   Someone[3]

[1]aka "Ethiopian Notion."
[2]First issued as part of the centennial edition; wrongly claimed by Cls 867.
[3]aka "You've Got My Heart."

Apr/May 1942   (P)
Trianon Ballroom (bc)
Southgate, CA

DUKE ELLINGTON & HIS ORCHESTRA
WJ RS RN, JN LB JT, BB JH OH BW HC, DE FG JR SG, IA HJ.

.... RDB   The One I Love Belongs To Somebody Else –vIA
.... RDB   Body And Soul –vHJ[1]
.... RDB   Body And Soul[2]
.... RDB   Take The "A" Train

[1]Incomplete on RDB.
[2]Announced jokingly as "Body And Ben."

2 May 1942   (P)
Trianon Ballroom (bc)
Southgate, CA

DUKE ELLINGTON & HIS ORCHESTRA
WJ RS RN, JN LB JT, BB JH OH BW HC, DE FG JR SG.

....   Take The "A" Train
.... Rar   Swing Shifters Swing
....   Main Stem

p May 1942   (P)
Trianon Ballroom (bc)
Southgate, CA

DUKE ELLINGTON & HIS ORCHESTRA
WJ RS RN, JN LB JT, BB JH OH BW HC, DE FG JR SG.

....   What Am I Here For?
....   Barzallai Lew[1]   >>>

[1]Variant spellings: "Barzallai-Lou"; "Barzililou"; "Brazilali Lou"; "Brazil Lilou." (B.L. is one of the men depicted in the painting "The Spirit of '76.")

			7 May 1942 (P)

DUKE ELLINGTON & HIS ORCHESTRA
WJ RS RN, JN LB JT, BB JH OH BW HC, DE FG JR SG, IA.

7 May 1942 (P)
Trianon Ballroom (bc)
Southgate, CA

....		Take The "A" Train
....		The Strollers
....		I Don't Want To Walk Without You, Baby
....		Just Fiddlin' Around
....		I Don't Mind –vIA
....		John Hardy's Wife
....		Blue Again[1]

[1]sa "Someone"; no resemblance with "Blue Again" as recorded on 26 Nov 1930.

DUKE ELLINGTON & HIS FAMOUS ORCHESTRA
WJ RS RN, JN LB JT, BB JH OH BW HC, BS FG JR SG, HJ.

26 Jun 1942 (S)
Hollywood Recording Studio
Hollywood, CA

....	Vi	PBS-072437-1	My Little Brown Book –vHJ
....	Vi	PBS-072438-1	Main Stem[1]
....	Vi	PBS-072439-1	Johnny Come Lately[2]

[1]The original title for this item on the recording sheet is "Swing Shifters Swing," then changed to "Main Stem." Since both titles were in the band book by this time—see session 2 May 1942—it is assumed that the first entry was made in error. Although this recording has no piano part, it is likely that DE took part in the recording of this important title, which he is the composer of; his name, however, is not mentioned on the recording sheet.
[2]aka "Plane Time."

DUKE ELLINGTON WITH ORCHESTRA
DE with an unidentified orchestra and chorus.

29 Jun 1942 (P)
Hollywood Bowl (bc)
Los Angeles, CA

....		Amapola –vChorus

DUKE ELLINGTON & HIS ORCHESTRA
WJ RS RN, JN LB JT, CH JH OH BW HC, DE FG JR SG.

14 Jul 1942 (P)
El Patio Ballroom, Lakeside Park (bc)
Denver, CO

....	CS	Things Ain't What They Used To Be
....	CS	Ko-Ko
....	CS	Take The "A" Train

DUKE ELLINGTON & HIS ORCHESTRA
WJ RS RN, JN LB JT, CH JH OH BW HC, DE FG JR SG, IA.

15 Jul 1942 (P)
El Patio Ballroom, Lakeside Park (bc)
Denver, CO

....	CS	Take The "A" Train
....	JA	The Strollers
....	CS	Rocks In My Bed –vIA
....	CS	John Hardy's Wife

DUKE ELLINGTON & HIS ORCHESTRA
WJ RS RN, JN LB JT, CH JH OH BW HC, DE FG JR SG.

19 Jul 1942 (P)
Panther Room, Hotel Sherman (bc)
Chicago, IL

....		Bli-Blip –vRN
....		All I Need Is You
....		Perdido

DUKE ELLINGTON & HIS ORCHESTRA
WJ RS RN, JN LB JT, CH JH OH BW HC, DE FG JR SG.

21 Jul 1942 (P)
Panther Room, Hotel Sherman (bc)
Chicago, IL

....		The "C" Jam Blues
....		Take The "A" Train

DUKE ELLINGTON & HIS ORCHESTRA
WJ RS RN, JN LB JT, CH JH OH BW HC, DE FG JR SG.

22 Jul 1942 (P)
Panther Room, Hotel Sherman (bc)
Chicago, IL

....	Az	Just A-Settin-And A-Rockin'
....		Rose Of The Rio Grande
....	Nat	Home[1]
....	BJ	Things Ain't What They Used To Be

[1]It is assumed that this title is not identical with *Home* as recorded on 26 Jul 1923.

DUKE ELLINGTON & HIS ORCHESTRA
WJ RS RN, JN LB JT, CH JH OH BW HC, DE FG JR SG.

24 Jul 1942 (P)
Panther Room, Hotel Sherman (bc)
Chicago, IL

.... JA   Swing Shifters Swing

DUKE ELLINGTON & HIS ORCHESTRA
WJ RS RN, JN LB JT, CH JH OH BW HC, DE FG JR SG, IA.

26 Jul 1942 (P)
Panther Room, Hotel Sherman (bc)
Chicago, IL

....   Blue Again
....   The Sergeant Was Shy
....   I Don't Mind –vIA
....   What Am I Here For?

DUKE ELLINGTON & HIS ORCHESTRA
WJ RS RN, JN LB JT, CH JH OH BW HC, DE FG JR SG.

27 Jul 1942 (P)
Panther Room, Hotel Sherman (bc)
Chicago, IL

....   Bakiff
....   Warm Valley

DUKE ELLINGTON & HIS FAMOUS ORCHESTRA
WJ RS RN, JN LB JT, CH JH OH BW HC, DE FG JR SG, IA.

28 Jul 1942 (S)
Victor Studio A
Chicago, IL

....	Vi	BS-074781-1	Hayfoot, Strawfoot –vIA[1]
....	Bb	BS-074781-2	Hayfoot, Strawfoot –vIA
....	Vi	BS-074782-1	Sentimental Lady[2]
....	Vi	BS-074782-2	Sentimental Lady
....	Vi	BS-074783-1	A Slip Of The Lip –vRN[3]
....		BS-074783-1A[4]	A Slip Of The Lip –vRN
....	Vi	BS-074784-1A	Sherman Shuffle[5]

[1] *aka* "Get Hep."
[2] *sa* "Home" (22 Jul 1942 recording).
[3] Complete: "A Slip Of The Lip Can Sink A Ship."
[4] A metal of this take survived in the vault of RCA; for reasons unknown it was not included in the centennial edition.
[5] *aka* "Fussy Puss."

DUKE ELLINGTON & HIS ORCHESTRA
Same personnel.

Panther Room, Hotel Sherman (bc) (P)

....   John Hardy's Wife
.... Nat   Five O'Clock Drag
.... Nat   Tizol's Stomp[1]
.... Nat   Solitude –vIA
.... Nat   Barzallai Lew

[1] *sa* "Perdido."

DUKE ELLINGTON & HIS ORCHESTRA
WJ RS RN, JN LB JT, CH JH OH BW HC, DE FG JR SG.

7 Aug 1942 (P)
Panther Room, Hotel Sherman (bc)
Chicago, IL

....   Moon Mist

DUKE ELLINGTON & HIS ORCHESTRA
WJ RS RN, JN LB JT, CH JH OH BW HC, DE FG JR SG.

8 Aug 1942 (P)
Panther Room, Hotel Sherman (bc)
Chicago, IL

....   Altitude[1]
....   Sherman Shuffle

[1] *sa* "Main Stem."

DUKE ELLINGTON & HIS ORCHESTRA
WJ RS RN, JN LB JT, CH JH OH BW HC, DE FG JR SG.

11 Aug 1942 (P)
Panther Room, Hotel Sherman (bc)
Chicago, IL

....   Cotton Tail
....   Things Ain't What They Used To Be

DUKE ELLINGTON & HIS ORCHESTRA
WJ RS RN, JN LB JT, CH JH OH BW HC, DE FG JR SG, IA JS.

13 Aug 1942 (P)
Panther Room, Hotel Sherman (bc)
Chicago, IL

....   Manhattan Serenade –vJS
....   At Last
....   Massachusetts –vIA

			Aug 1942 (P)
			Panther Room, Hotel Sherman (bc)
			Chicago, IL

DUKE ELLINGTON & HIS ORCHESTRA
WJ RS RN, JN LB JT, CH JH OH BW HC, DE FG JR SG, IA.

....		Hayfoot, Strawfoot –vIA
....		Unbooted Character
....		Concerto For Cootie

			29 Aug 1942 (P)
			Palace Theater (bc)
			Chicago, IL

DUKE ELLINGTON & HIS ORCHESTRA
WJ RS RN, JN LB JT, CH JH OH BW HC, DE FG JR SG, IA.

....	Tpl	Who Wouldn't Love You?[1]
....	Tpl	Unidentified title[1]
....	Tpl	I Don't Want To Walk Without You, Baby[1]
....	Az	Tangerine

[1]Issued under one title "On Display" on Tpl.

			28 Sep 1942 (T)[1]
			M-G-M Studios
			Culver City, CA

DUKE ELLINGTON & HIS ORCHESTRA
HB WJ RS RN, JN LB JT, CH JH OH BW HC, DE FG JR SG.

| .... | HS | Things Ain't What They Used To Be |
| .... | Rho[2] | Goin' Up |

[1]Music for the motion picture "Cabin In The Sky."
[2]The original release on HS was incomplete.

			29 Sep 1942 (T)[1]
			M-G-M Studios
			Culver City, CA

DUKE ELLINGTON & HIS ORCHESTRA
HB WJ RS RN, JN LB JT, CH JH OH BW HC, DE FG JR SG, JWS, studio orchestra.

| .... | HS | Background music |
| .... | HS | Shine –vJWS |

[1]Music for the motion picture "Cabin In The Sky."

			8 Oct 1942 (T)[1]
			Columbia Studios
			Hollywood, CA

DUKE ELLINGTON & HIS ORCHESTRA
HB WJ RS RN, JN LB JT, CH JH OH BW HC, DE FG JR SG, BR.

| .... | KD | Take The "A" Train –vBR RS RN HC |

[1]Music for the motion picture "Reveille With Beverly."

			9 Oct 1942 (P)
			El Capitan Theater[1] (bc)
			Los Angeles, CA

DUKE ELLINGTON & HIS ORCHESTRA
HB WJ RS RN, JN LB JT, CH JH OH BW HC, DE FG JR SG, BR JBrt.

....		Jubilee Theme
....	Jbl	Hayfoot, Strawfoot –vBR
....	Jbl	Goin' Up

[1]Some sources suggest that the bc originates from the NBC Studios, since the El Capitan Theater was occupied by the Ken Murray show "Blackouts of 1942" every night in this period. However, it should have been possible to set up microphones on the stage at a time when the show was not being performed.

			19 Nov 1942 (P)
			Fort Dix (bc)
			Trenton, NJ

DUKE ELLINGTON & HIS ORCHESTRA
HB WJ RS RN, JN LB JT, CH JH OH BW HC, DE FG JR SG, BR JBrt.

....	Duk	Coca Cola Theme
....	Duk	Perdido
....	Duk	Just As Though You Were Here –vJBrt
....	Duk	Hayfoot, Strawfoot –vBR
....	BJ	Don't Get Around Much Anymore[1]
....	BJ	Goin' Up
....	Duk	Things Ain't What They Used To Be
....	Duk	Take The "A" Train
....	Duk	Coca Cola Theme

[1]sa "Never No Lament."

			17 Dec 1942 (P)
			Biltmore Hotel (bc)
			Providence, RI

DUKE ELLINGTON & HIS ORCHESTRA
HB WJ RS RN, JN LB JT, CH JH OH BW HC, DE FG JR SG, BR JBrt.

....	BJ	What Am I Here For?
....	BJ	Dearly Beloved –vJBrt
....	BJ	Perdido
....	BJ	A Slip Of The Lip –vRN
....	BJ	Mr. Five By Five –vBR

23 Jan 1943   (P)
Carnegie Hall
New York City, NY

DUKE ELLINGTON & HIS ORCHESTRA
HB WJ RS RN, JN LB JT, CH JH OH BW HC, DE FG JR SG, BR.

....		The Star Spangled Banner
....	Pre	Black And Tan Fantasy
....	Pre	Rockin' In Rhythm
....	Std	Moon Mist
....	Std	Jumpin' Punkins
....	Std	A Portrait Of Bert Williams
....	Std	Bojangles[1]
....	Pre	A Portrait Of Florence Mills[2]
		BLACK, BROWN AND BEIGE[3]
....	FDC	- Black[4]
....	FDC	- Brown –vBR
....	FDC	- Beige
....	HoF	Ko-Ko

> BS replaces DE.

....	HoF	Dirge
....	HoF	Stomp[5]

> DE replaces BS.

....	HoF	Are You Sticking?
....	Std	Bakiff
....	HoF	Jack The Bear
....	HoF[6]	Blue Belles Of Harlem
....	HoF	Cotton Tail
....	HoF	Day Dream
....	Std	Boy Meets Horn
....	HoF	Rose Of The Rio Grande
....	HoF	Don't Get Around Much Anymore
....	JS	Goin' Up
....	Std	Mood Indigo

[1]Erroneously as "Portrait #2, A Portrait Of Florence Mills" on Std.
[2]sa "Black Beauty." The opening segment and first part are from the 28 Jan 1943 concert.
[3]Subtitled "A Tone Parallel to the History of the American Negro." The complete suite is structured as follows:

      First movement: Black
        Part 1 – Work Song
        Part 2 – Come Sunday
        Part 3 – Light (or "Montage")

      Second movement: Brown
        Part 1 – West Indian Dance (or "West Indian Influence")
            Emancipation Celebration (or "The Lighter Attitude")
        Part 2 – The Blues (or "Mauve")

      Third movement: Beige
         - A View From Central Park
         - Jazz Waltz
         - Interlude
         - Sugar Hill Penthouse
         - Finale

[4]The opening segment on Pre is from the 28 Jan 1943 concert.
[5]sa "Johnny Come Lately."
[6]On HoF the coda of two bars is missing. On Pre the missing two bars have been taken from the recording of 28 Jan 1943.

28 Jan 1943   (P)
Symphony Hall
Boston, MA

DUKE ELLINGTON & HIS ORCHESTRA
HB WJ RS RN, JN LB JT, CH JH OH BW HC, DE FG JR SG, BR.

....	Pre	The Star Spangled Banner
....		What Am I Here For?
....		On Becoming A Square[1]
....		Day Dream
		BLACK, BROWN AND BEIGE
....	Pre	- Black[2]
....	JA+MJ	- Brown –vBR[3]
....		- Beige
....		Jumpin' Punkins

> BS replaces DE.

....		Dirge
....		Little Light Psalf[4] >>>

        > DE replaces BS.

....	Pre	A Portrait Of Florence Mills[5]
....		Award presentation[6]
....		Bakiff
....		Black And Tan Fantasy
....	Pre[7]	Blue Belles Of Harlem
....		Boy Meets Horn

[1] *sa* "Main Stem"; "Altitude."
[2] Opening segment only; the remaining portion is from the 23 Jan 1943 concert.
[3] On JA only the part known as "The Blues," on MJ only "Emancipation Celebration."
[4] *sa* "Johnny Come Lately"; "Stomp."
[5] Opening segment and first part only from this concert; the remainder is from 23 Jan 1943.
[6] Arthur Fiedler presents an achievement award to DE.
[7] The first two bars of the coda have been edited into the recording of 23 Jan 1943.

                                                            Mar 1943[1]   (P)
                Unidentified location (bc)
                U.S.A.

DUKE ELLINGTON & HIS ORCHESTRA
HB WJ RS RN, JN LB JT, CH JH OH BW HC, DE FG JR SG, BR.

....	Sentimental Lady

[1] Broadcast on 27 Mar 1943. (The band's engagement at the Hurricane Club started on 1 Apr 1943.)

        3 Apr 1943   (P)
        Hurricane Club (bc)
        New York City, NY

DUKE ELLINGTON & HIS ORCHESTRA
HB WJ RS RN, JN LB JT, CH JH SMld BW HC, DE FG JR SG, BR.

....	Az	Take The "A" Train
....	IAC	Hayfoot, Strawfoot –vBR
....	Az	It Can't Be Wrong[1]
....	Az	What Am I Here For?
....	Az	Altitude
....	Az	Could It Be You?
....	Az	Goin' Up
....	Az	Don't Get Around Much Anymore
....	Az	Nevada
....	Az	Things Ain't What They Used To Be

[1] *aka* "Wrong, Can It Be Wrong?"

Although the Hurricane was both club and restaurant, it will in the following be referred to as club only.

        4 Apr 1943   (P)
        Hurricane Club (bc)
        New York City, NY

DUKE ELLINGTON & HIS ORCHESTRA
HB WJ RS RN, JN LB JT, CH JH SMld BW HC, DE FG JR SG, BR.

....	Rar	Take The "A" Train
....	Rar	Don't Get Around Much Anymore
....	IAC	Altitude
....	Rar	I Don't Want Anybody At All –vBR
....	Rar	Johnny Come Lately
....	Rar	Things Ain't What They Used To Be

        Apr 1943   (P)
        Hurricane Club (bc)
        New York City, NY

DUKE ELLINGTON & HIS ORCHESTRA
HB WJ RS RN, JN LB JT, CH JH SMld BW HC, DE FG JR SG, BR.

....	What's The Good Word, Mr. Bluebird? –vBR
....	It Can't Be Wrong
....	Harlem Air Shaft
....	Don't Get Around Much Anymore

        7 Apr 1943   (P)
        Hurricane Club (bc)
        New York City, NY

DUKE ELLINGTON & HIS ORCHESTRA
HB WJ RS RN, JN LB JT, CH JH SMld BW HC, DE FG JR SG, BR.

....	My Gal Sal
....	You'll Never Know –vBR
....	Way Low
....	Hayfoot, Strawfoot –vBR
....	Don't Get Around Much Anymore

        Apr 1943   (P)
        Hurricane Club (bc)
        New York City, NY

DUKE ELLINGTON & HIS ORCHESTRA
HB WJ RS RN, JN LB JT, CH JH SMld BW HC, DE FG JR SG, JBrt.

....	Az	Take The "A" Train
....	Az	What Am I Here For?
....	Az	Barzallai Lew >>>

.... Az   Ring Around The Moon –vJBrt
.... Az   Cotton Tail
.... Az   Don't Get Around Much Anymore

20 Apr 1943   **(P)**
Hurricane Club (bc)
New York City, NY

DUKE ELLINGTON & HIS ORCHESTRA
HB WJ RS RN, JN LB JT, SMld JH SSct BW HC, DE FG JR SG, AH.

....   Johnny Come Lately
....   It Can't Be Wrong –vAH
....   Three Cent Stomp

21 Apr 1943   **(S)**
Radio City (bc)
New York City, NY

DUKE ELLINGTON'S OCTET
HB RN, JN LB, SMld HC, DE JR.

.... Rar   Mood Indigo—Sophisticated Lady
....   It Don't Mean A Thing

24 Apr 1943   **(S)**
Hurricane Club (bc)
New York City, NY

DUKE ELLINGTON & HIS ORCHESTRA
HB WJ RS RN, JN LB JT, SMld JH SSct BW HC, DE FG JR SG.

....   Cabin In The Sky

25 Apr 1943   **(P)**
Hurricane Club (bc)
New York City, NY

DUKE ELLINGTON & HIS ORCHESTRA
HB WJ RS RN, JN LB JT, SMld JH SSct BW HC, DE FG JR SG.

....   Nevada
....   Hayfoot, Strawfoot
....   It Can't Be Wrong
....   It's Been So Long
....   Perdido

1 May 1943   **(P)**
Radio City, Studio 6B (bc)
New York City, NY

DUKE ELLINGTON & HIS ORCHESTRA
HB WJ RS RN, JN LB JT, SMld JH SSct BW HC, DE FG JR SG.

.... JSo   Take The "A" Train
.... JSo   Hayfoot, Strawfoot
.... JSo   Don't Get Around Much Anymore
.... JSo   A Slip Of The Lip –vRN
.... DET   Take The "A" Train
.... DET   Bond promotion

2 May 1943   **(S)**
Studios WJZ (bc)
New York City, NY

DUKE ELLINGTON WITH PAUL LAVALLE
& THE CHAMBER MUSIC SOCIETY OF LOWER BASIN STREET
DE with the orchestra of the Chamber Music Society of Lower Basin Street.

....   Don't Get Around Much Anymore
....   It Don't Mean A Thing

May 1943   **(P)**
Hurricane Club (bc)
New York City, NY

DUKE ELLINGTON & HIS ORCHESTRA
HB WJ RS RN, JN LB JT, SMld JH SSct BW HC, DE FG JR SG, BR.

.... Car   Cabin In The Sky
....   In A Mellotone
....   I Don't Want Anybody At All –vBR
.... Car   Barzallai Lew
....   Don't Get Around Much Anymore

23 May 1943   **(P)**
Hurricane Club (bc)
New York City, NY

DUKE ELLINGTON & HIS ORCHESTRA
HB WJ RS RN, JN LB JT, SMld JH SSct BW HC, DE FG JR SG.

....   As Time Goes By
....   Bakiff

Late May 1943   **(P)**
Hurricane Club (bc)
New York City, NY

DUKE ELLINGTON & HIS ORCHESTRA
TJ HB WJ RN, JN LB JT, JHtn JH NJ BW HC, DE FG JR SG.

.... Duk   Take The "A" Train
.... Duk   Java Jive[1]
.... Duk   Day Dream
.... Duk   Way Low
.... Duk   Perdido   >>>

.... Duk   Don't Get Around Much Anymore

[1]*aka* "I Love Coffee, I Love Tea."

28 May 1943   (P)
Hurricane Club (bc)
New York City, NY

DUKE ELLINGTON & HIS ORCHESTRA
TJ HB WJ RN, JN LB JT, JHtn JH NJ BW HC, DE FG JR SG, JBrt.

.... Dji   Way Low
.... Dji   Around My Heart
.... Dji   Perdido
.... Dji   Ogeechee River Lullaby –vJBrt

29 May 1943   (S)
Studios WNEW (bc)
New York City, NY

DUKE ELLINGTON
DE interviewed by Kathy Craven.

....   Interview

30 May 1943   (P)
NBC Studios (bc)
New York City, NY

DUKE ELLINGTON & HIS ORCHESTRA
TJ HB WJ RN, JN LB JT, JHtn JH NJ BW HC, DE FG JR SG, BR.

....   Take The "A" Train
.... AFR   DE interviewed by Tobe Reed
.... Hds   The Canteen Bounce
.... AFR   Perdido
.... AFR   Interview (ctd.)
.... Hds   Hayfoot, Strawfoot –vBR
.... AFR   Don't Get Around Much Anymore
.... AFR   Interview (ctd.)
.... Hds   A Slip Of The Lip –vRN
.... AFR   Things Ain't What They Used To Be
.... AFR   Interview (ctd.)
.... AFR   Ring Dem Bells

6 Jun 1943   (P)
Hurricane Club (bc)
New York City, NY

DUKE ELLINGTON & HIS ORCHESTRA
TJ HB WJ RN, JN SWls JT, JHtn JH NJ BW HC, DE FG JR SG, BR.

.... Stv   Moon Mist
.... JA   You'll Never Know
....   Oh! Lady Be Good
.... JA   Tonight I Shall Sleep[1]
....   Nevada
....   Subtle Slough
.... Stv   I Don't Know What Kind Of Blues I Got –vBR
.... Stv   Don't Get Around Much Anymore
.... Stv   Moon Mist

[1]Complete: "Tonight I Shall Sleep With A Smile On My Face."

7 Jun 1943   (P)
Hurricane Club (bc)
New York City, NY

DUKE ELLINGTON & HIS ORCHESTRA
TJ HB WJ RN, JN SWls JT, JHtn JH NJ BW HC, DE FG JR SG.

....   Subtle Slough
....   Main Stem

Jun 1943   (S)
Unspecified studio (bc)
New York City, NY

DUKE ELLINGTON & HIS ORCHESTRA
TJ HB WJ RN, JN SWls JT, JHtn JH NJ BW HC, DE FG JR SG, AH.

.... DET   Fanfare
.... DET   Take The "A" Train
.... DET   Don't Get Around Much Anymore
.... DET   Caravan
.... DET   Bond promotion
.... DET   It Can't Be Wrong –vAH
.... DET   Johnny Come Lately
.... DET   Any Bonds Today?[1]

[1]Performed by a studio orchestra.

Jun 1943   (S)
Unspecified studio (bc)
New York City, NY

DUKE ELLINGTON & HIS ORCHESTRA
TJ HB WJ RN, JN SWls JT, JHtn JH NJ BW HC, DE FG JR SG.

.... DET   Fanfare
.... DET   Take The "A" Train
.... DET   Wait For Me, Mary   >>>

```
.............. DET                     Moon Mist
.............. DET                     Bond promotion
.............. DET                     A Slip Of The Lip –vRN
.............. DET                     Things Ain't What They Used To Be
.............. DET                     Any Bonds Today?¹
```

¹Performed by a studio orchestra.

				Jun 1943	(S)

DUKE ELLINGTON & HIS ORCHESTRA
TJ HB WJ RN, JN SWls JT, JHtn JH NJ BW HC, DE FG JR SG, BR.

Jun 1943   (S)
Unspecified studio (bc)
New York City, NY

```
.............. DET                     Fanfare
.............. DET                     Take The "A" Train
.............. DET                     Tonight I Shall Sleep
.............. DET                     Go Away Blues –vBR Band
.............. DET                     Bond promotion
.............. DET                     Creole Love Call¹
.............. DET                     Three Cent Stomp
.............. DET                     Any Bonds Today?²
```

¹Announced as "Creole Love Song."
²Performed by a studio orchestra.

DUKE ELLINGTON & HIS ORCHESTRA
TJ HB WJ RN, JN SWls JT, JHtn JH NJ BW HC, DE FG JR SG.

17+19 Jun 1943   (T)¹
Pathé News Inc.²
New York City, NY

```
.............. Bb                      Mood Indigo
.............. Bb                      Sophisticated Lady
.............. Bb                      It Don't Mean A Thing –vRN TJ
.............. Bb                      Don't Get Around Much Anymore
```

¹Music for the movie short "RKO Jamboree."
²The soundtrack was prerecorded at Pathé News Inc.; the filming took place at the Movietone Studios in Manhattan in the time from 22-27 Jun 1943.

DUKE ELLINGTON & HIS ORCHESTRA
TJ HB WJ RN, JN SWls JT, JHtn JH NJ BW HC, DE FG JR SG.

18 Jun 1943   (P)
Hurricane Club (bc)
New York City, NY

```
..............                         Take The "A" Train
.............. Rar                     Bojangles
.............. Rar                     People Will Say We're In Love
.............. Rar                     Five O'Clock Drag
.............. Rar                     Johnny Come Lately
.............. Rar                     Tonight I Shall Sleep
.............. Rar                     Wait For Me, Mary
.............. Rar                     It's Been So Long
.............. Rar                     Blue Skies
..............                         Don't Get Around Much Anymore
```

DUKE ELLINGTON & BERRY WOOD WITH THE MILLION DOLLAR BAND
DE and BaW, acc. by the "Million Dollar Band."

19 Jun 1943   (S)
NBC Studios (bc)
New York City, NY

```
..............                         Take The "A" Train
..............                         Unidentified title –v DE BaW
..............                         Don't Get Around Much Anymore
```

DUKE ELLINGTON & HIS ORCHESTRA
TJ HB WJ RN, JN SWls JT, JHtn JH NJ BW HC, DE FG JR SG, BR.

20 Jun 1943   (P)
Hurricane Club (bc)
New York City, NY

```
.............. Hcn                     Moon Mist
.............. Hcn                     Black Beauty
.............. Hcn                     Could It Be You?
.............. Hcn                     I Have Faith
.............. Hcn                     Time On My Hands
.............. Hcn                     Tonight I Shall Sleep –vBR
.............. Hcn                     The "C" Jam Blues
.............. Hcn                     Blue Belles Of Harlem
.............. Hcn                     Don't Get Around Much Anymore
.............. Hcn                     Moon Mist
```

DUKE ELLINGTON & FRANK SINATRA
DE and FS talking.

25 Jun 1943   (S)
CBS Studios (bc)
New York City, NY

```
.............. GoJ                     Conversation    >>>
```

> DE piano solo.

.... GoJ   Solitude

> DE, FS.

.... GoJ   Conversation (ctd.)

DUKE ELLINGTON WITH THE RAYMOND SCOTT ORCHESTRA
DE with the Raymond Scott Orchestra.

.... GoJ   Don't Get Around Much Anymore

                                                                                    27 Jun 1943   (P)
DUKE ELLINGTON & HIS ORCHESTRA   Hurricane Club (bc)
TJ HB WJ RN, JN SWls JT, JHtn JH NJ BW HC, DE FG JR SG, AH.   New York City, NY

.... Hcn   Moon Mist
.... Hcn   Close To You
.... Hcn   Baghdad[1]
.... Hcn   Summertime –vAH
.... Hcn   Caravan
.... Hcn   Sunday, Monday And Always
.... Hcn   Tonight I Will Sleep
.... Hcn   Dinah's In A Jam
.... Hcn   Don't Get Around Much Anymore
.... Hcn   Moon Mist

[1]"Bagdad" on Hcn.

                                                                                    30 Jun 1943   (P)
DUKE ELLINGTON & HIS ORCHESTRA   Hurricane Club (bc)
TJ HB WJ RN, JN SWls JT, JHtn JH NJ BW HC, DE FG JR SG.   New York City, NY

....   Blue Skies
....   Altitude

                                                                                    6 Jul 1943   (P)
DUKE ELLINGTON & HIS ORCHESTRA   Studios WMCA (bc)
TJ HB WJ RN, JN SWls JT, JHtn JH NJ BW HC, DE FG JR HWst, BR.   New York City, NY

.... JA   Cotton Tail
....   I Left My Sugar In Salt Lake City –vBR
.... Car   Sweet Georgia Brown
.... JA   Goin' Up

                                                                                    8 Jul 1943   (P)
DUKE ELLINGTON & HIS ORCHESTRA   Hurricane Club (bc)
TJ HB WJ RN, JN SWls JT, JHtn JH NJ BW HC, DE FG JR SG.   New York City, NY

....   Way Low

                                                                                    11 Jul 1943   (S)
DUKE ELLINGTON   BBC Studios (bc)
DE interviewed by Alistair Cooke; intermittent previously recorded music.   New York City, NY

.... JUn   Interview

                                                                                    Hurricane Club (bc) (P)
DUKE ELLINGTON & HIS ORCHESTRA
TJ HB WJ RN, JN SWls JT, JHtn JH NJ BW HC, DE FG JR SG.

.... Hcn   Moon Mist
.... Hcn   Out Of Nowhere
.... Hcn   And Russia Is Her Name
.... Hcn   It Don't Mean A Thing
.... Hcn   Blue Serge
.... Hcn   Blue Belles Of Harlem
.... Hcn   Don't Get Around Much Anymore

                                                                                    14 Jul 1943   (P)
DUKE ELLINGTON & HIS ORCHESTRA   Hurricane Club (bc)
TJ HB WJ RN, JN SWls JT, JHtn JH NJ BW HC, DE FG JR SG.   New York City, NY

....   Barzallai Lew

                                                                                    3 Aug 1943   (P)
DUKE ELLINGTON & HIS ORCHESTRA   Hurricane Club (bc)
TJ HB WJ RN, JN LB JT, JHtn JH NJ BW HC, DE FG JR SG.   New York City, NY

....   Three Cent Stomp

9 Aug 1943   (P)
Hurricane Club (bc)
New York City, NY

DUKE ELLINGTON & HIS ORCHESTRA
TJ HB WJ RN, JN LB JT, JHtn JH NJ BW HC, DE FG JR SG.

....   Take The "A" Train
....   Rumpus In Richmond
....   Creole Love Call
....   Things Ain't What They Used To Be

14 Aug 1943   (P)
Hurricane Club (bc)
New York City, NY

DUKE ELLINGTON & HIS ORCHESTRA
TJ HB WJ RN, JN LB JT, JHtn JH NJ EWms HC, DE FG JR SG, AH.

.... Hcn   Clementine
.... Hcn   Sentimental Lady
.... Hcn   A Slip Of The Lip –vRN
.... Hcn   There Is A Man In My Life

    > DE JR.

.... Hcn   Pitter Panther Patter

    > Entire band.

.... Hcn   Rockin' In Rhythm
.... Hcn   Do Nothin' Till You Hear From Me –vAH[1]
.... Hcn   Main Stem
.... Hcn   Don't Get Around Much Anymore

[1]This title is a derivative of *Concerto For Cootie;* variant spelling: "Do Nothin' 'Til You Hear From Me."

21 Aug 1943   (P)
Hurricane Club (bc)
New York City, NY

DUKE ELLINGTON & HIS ORCHESTRA
TJ HB WJ RN, JN LB BAr, JHtn JH NJ EWms HC, DE FG JR SG.

....   Baby, Please Stop And Think About Me
....   And Russia Is Her Name
....   Don't Get Around Much Anymore

24 Aug 1943   (P)
Hurricane Club (bc)
New York City, NY

DUKE ELLINGTON & HIS ORCHESTRA
TJ HB WJ RN, JN LB BAr, JHtn JH NJ EWms HC, DE FG JR SG.

....   Harlem Air Shaft

26 Aug 1943   (P)
Hurricane Club (bc)
New York City, NY

DUKE ELLINGTON & HIS ORCHESTRA
TJ HB WJ RN, JN LB BAr, JHtn JH NJ EWms HC, DE FG JR SG, BR.

....   What Am I Here For?
.... Car   Baby, Please Stop And Think About Me
....   Rocks In My Bed –vBR
....   Clementine

28 Aug 1943   (P)
Hurricane Club (bc)
New York City, NY

DUKE ELLINGTON & HIS ORCHESTRA
TJ HB WJ RN, JN LB BAr, JHtn JH NJ EWms HC, DE FG JR SG, BR AH.

.... QuD   Take The "A" Train
.... QuD   Way Low
.... QuD   A Slip Of The Lip –vRN
.... QuD   Rockin' In Rhythm
.... QuD   Tonight I Shall Sleep –vAH
.... QuD   Three Cent Stomp
.... Tpl   I Don't Know What Kind Of Blues I Got –vBR
.... QuD   Later Tonight
.... QuD   Don't Get Around Much Anymore

29 Aug 1943   (P)
Hurricane Club (bc)
New York City, NY

DUKE ELLINGTON & HIS ORCHESTRA
TJ HB WJ RN, JN LB BAr, JHtn JH NJ EWms HC, DE FG JR SG, BR AH.

.... QuD   Moon Mist
.... QuD   Do You Know?
.... QuD   Subtle Slough
.... QuD   Do Nothin' Till You Hear From Me –vAH
.... QuD   Graceful Awkwardness[1]
....   Sentimental Lady
.... QuD   Go Away Blues –vBR
.... QuD   Cotton Tail
.... QuD   Tonight I Shall Sleep –vAH   >>>

.... QuD   Don't Get Around Much Anymore

¹Part of "Beige" from *Black, Brown And Beige*.

DUKE ELLINGTON & HIS ORCHESTRA   Aug/Sep 1943   (P)
TJ HB WJ RN, JN LB BAr, JHtn JH NJ EWms HC, DE FG JR SG.   Hurricane Club (bc?)
                                                                 New York City, NY
....   Just Plain Lonesome

DUKE ELLINGTON & HIS ORCHESTRA   Aug/Sep 1943   (P)
TJ HB WJ RN, JN LB BAr, JHtn JH NJ EWms HC, DE FG JR SG.   Hurricane Club (bc)
                                                                 New York City, NY
....   Take The "A" Train
.... WL   Blue Again¹
.... WL   Jump For Joy

¹*sa* "Someone."

DUKE ELLINGTON & HIS ORCHESTRA   1 Sep 1943   (P)
TJ HB WJ RN, JN LB BAr, JHtn JH NJ EWms HC, DE FG JR SG, BR AH.   Hurricane Club (bc)
                                                                 New York City, NY
....   Take The "A" Train
....   Take It From Here
....   Later Tonight
....   Wait For Me, Mary
....   Go Away Blues –vBR
....   Tonight I Shall Sleep –vAH
....   Don't Get Around Much Anymore

DUKE ELLINGTON & HIS ORCHESTRA   3 Sep 1943   (P)
TJ HB WJ RN, JN LB BAr, JHtn JH NJ EWms HC, DE FG JR SG, AH.   Hurricane Club (bc)
                                                                 New York City, NY
....   Barzallai Lew
....   The "C" Jam Blues
....   Do Nothin' Till You Hear From Me –vAH
....   Subtle Slough
....   Take The "A" Train

DUKE ELLINGTON WITH PAUL LAVALLE   5 Sep 1943   (S)
& THE CHAMBER MUSIC SOCIETY OF LOWER BASIN STREET   ABC Studios (bc)
DE with the Orchestra of the Chamber Music Society of Lower Basin Street.   New York City, NY
.... Tpl   Sophisticated Lady

DUKE ELLINGTON & HIS ORCHESTRA   Hurricane Club (bc) (P)
TJ HB WJ RN, JN LB BAr, JHtn JH NJ EWms HC, DE FG JR SG, AH.
....   Moon Mist
....   The "C" Jam Blues
....   It Don't Mean A Thing –vRN TJ
....   Tonight I Shall Sleep
....   Ring Dem Bells –vRN
....   Don't Get Around Much Anymore—Things Ain't What They Used To Be

DUKE ELLINGTON & HIS ORCHESTRA   7 Sep 1943   (P)
TJ HB WJ RN, JN LB BAr, JHtn JH NJ EWms HC, DE FG JR SG, BR.   Hurricane Club (bc)
                                                                 New York City, NY
....   Johnny Come Lately
....   Graceful Awkwardness
....   Go Away Blues –vBR
....   Don't Get Around Much Anymore—Things Ain't What They Used To Be

DUKE ELLINGTON & HIS ORCHESTRA   (bc)
Same personnel.
....   I Don't Want Anybody At All –vBR
....   Blue Skies
....   Don't Get Around Much Anymore—Things Ain't What They Used To Be

DUKE ELLINGTON & HIS ORCHESTRA   9 Sep 1943   (P)
TJ HB WJ RN, JN LB BAr, JHtn JH NJ EWms HC, DE FG JR SG.   Hurricane Club (bc)
                                                                 New York City, NY
....   Way Low   >>>

....	Harlem Air Shaft	
....	Sentimental Lady	

DUKE ELLINGTON & HIS ORCHESTRA
TJ HB WJ RN, JN LB BAr, JHtn JH NJ EWms HC, DE FG JR SG, AH.

10 Sep 1943   (P)
Hurricane Club (bc)
New York City, NY

....	Summertime –vAH
....	Jack The Bear
....	Sentimental Lady
....	In A Mellotone
....	Rockin' In Rhythm

DUKE ELLINGTON & HIS ORCHESTRA
TJ HB WJ RN, JN LB BAr, JHtn JH NJ EWms HC, DE FG JR SG, BR.

11 Sep 1943   (P)
Hurricane Club (bc)
New York City, NY

....		Subtle Slough
....		Go Away Blues –vBR
....		Bojangles
....		West Indian Dance
....		Cotton Tail
....	Tpl	On The Sands Of Time
....		A Slip Of The Lip –vRN
....		Don't Get Around Much Anymore

DUKE ELLINGTON & HIS ORCHESTRA
TJ HB WJ RN, JN LB BAr, JHtn JH NJ EWms HC, DE FG JR SG.

12 Sep 1943   (P)
Hurricane Club (bc)
New York City, NY

| .... | Sunday, Monday And Always |
| .... | Don't Get Around Much Anymore |

DUKE ELLINGTON & HIS ORCHESTRA
Same personnel.

(bc)

....	Johnny Come Lately
....	Later Tonight
....	A Slip Of The Lip –vRN
....	Don't Get Around Much Anymore

DUKE ELLINGTON & HIS ORCHESTRA
TJ HB WJ RN, JN LB BAr, JHtn JH NJ EWms HC, DE FG JR SG.

Sep 1943   (P)
Hurricane Club (bc)
New York City, NY

....	Take The "A" Train
....	Until It Happened To You
....	Jack The Bear
....	On The Sunny Side Of The Street
....	Cotton Tail

DUKE ELLINGTON & HIS ORCHESTRA
TJ HB WJ RN, JN LB BAr, JHtn JH NJ EWms HC, DE FG JR SG, BR AH.

Sep 1943   (P)
Hurricane Club (bc)
New York City, NY

....	Take The "A" Train
....	Do You Know?
....	Go Away Blues –vBR
....	Rockin' In Rhythm
....	Ghost Of Love –vAH
....	What Am I Here For?
....	It Don't Mean A Thing –vRN TJ
....	Sentimental Lady
....	Don't Get Around Much Anymore

DUKE ELLINGTON & HIS ORCHESTRA
TJ HB WJ RN, JN LB BAr, JHtn JH NJ EWms HC, DE FG JR SG, BR.

23 Sep 1943   (P)
Hurricane Club (bc)
New York City, NY

....		'At's In There –vBR
....	Car	Design For Jivin'
....		Jump For Joy –vRN
....		Solid Old Man
....		Sentimental Lady

DUKE ELLINGTON & HIS ORCHESTRA
TJ DG WJ RS, JN LB JT, JHtn JH OH EWms HC, DE FG EM SG, AH.

8 Nov 1943   (S)
Decca Studios
New York City, NY

| .... | Crl | BB37652A C1-1 | Rockin' In Rhythm | >>> |

....	Crl	BB37652A C1-2	Rockin' In Rhythm (incomplete)
....	Crl	BB37652A C1-3	Rockin' In Rhythm (incomplete)
....	Crl	BB37652A C1-4	Rockin' In Rhythm
....	ST	BB37652B C1-1[1]	Rockin' In Rhythm
....	Crl	BB37652B C1-2	Blue Skies
....	Crl	BB37652B C1-3	Blue Skies (incomplete)
....	Crl	BB37652B C1-4	Blue Skies (incomplete)
....	Crl	BB37652C C1-1	Blue Skies (incomplete)
....	Crl	BB37652C C1-2	Boy Meets Horn
....	VD	BB37652C C1-3[1]	Boy Meets Horn
....	Crl	BB37652D C1-1	Do Nothin' Till You Hear From Me –vAH (incomplete)
....	Crl	BB37652D C1-2	Do Nothin' Till You Hear From Me –vAH
....	Crl	BB37652D C1-3[1]	Do Nothin' Till You Hear From Me –vAH
....	Crl	BB37652D C1-4	Summertime (incomplete)
....	ST	BB37652D C1-5[1]	Summertime –vAH
....	Crl	BB37652E C1-1	Sentimental Lady
....	ST	BB37652E C1-2[1]	Sentimental Lady
....	Crl	BB37653E C1-3	Tea For Two (incomplete)
....	Crl	BB37653A C2-1[1]	Tea For Two
....	ST	BB37653A C2-2[1]	The "C" Jam Blues
....	VD	BB37653A C2-3[1]	Hop, Skip And Jump[2]
....	Crl	BB37653B C1-1	Blue Skies (incomplete)
....	ST	BB37653B C1-2[1]	Blue Skies
....	Crl	BB37653B C1-3	Mood Indigo (incomplete)
....	Crl	BB37653B C1-4[1]	Mood Indigo

[1]These masters have been released originally on WT.
[2]aka "Hop-Skip Jump."

DUKE ELLINGTON & HIS ORCHESTRA
TJ HB WJ RS RN, JN LB JT, JHtn JH OH EWms HC, DE FG JR SG, BR.

9 Nov 1943   (S)
Decca Studios
New York City, NY

....	Crl	BB37667A C1-1	Main Stem (incomplete)
....	Crl	BB37667A C1-2	Main Stem
....	VD	BB37667A C1-3[1]	Main Stem
....	Crl	BB37667A C1-4	A Slip Of The Lip –vRN (incomplete)
....	Crl	BB37667A C1-5[1]	A Slip Of The Lip –vRN
....	Crl	BB37667B C1-1	Three Cent Stomp (incomplete)
....	Crl	BB37667B C1-2	Three Cent Stomp
....	ST	BB37667B C1-3[1]	Three Cent Stomp
....	Crl	BB37667C C1-1	I Wonder Why –vBR (incomplete)
....	Crl	BB37667C C1-2	I Wonder Why –vBR
....	Crl	BB37667C C1-3	I Wonder Why –vBR (incomplete)
....	Crl	BB37667C C1-4[1]	I Wonder Why –vBR
....	Tax	BB37667D C1-1[1]	Go Away Blues –vBR
....	Crl	BB37667D C1-2[1]	I Don't Want Anybody At All –vBR
....	ST	BB37667D C1-3[1]	Ain't Misbehavin'
....	VD	BB37668A C1-1[1]	Things Ain't What They Used To Be
....	Crl	BB37668A C1-2	Baby, Please Stop And Think About Me (incomplete)
....	Crl	BB37668A C1-3	Baby, Please Stop And Think About Me
....	Tax	BB37668A C1-4[1]	Baby, Please Stop And Think About Me
....	Crl	BB37668B C1-1[1]	Caravan

[1]These masters have been released originally on WT.

DUKE ELLINGTON
DE interviewed by a disc jockey, commenting on previously recorded music.

11 Nov 1943   (S)
Unidentified studio (bc)[1]
New York City, NY

....			Interview

[1]War Department voice recording.

DUKE ELLINGTON & HIS ORCHESTRA
TJ HB WJ RS RN, JN LB JT, JHtn JH OH EWms HC, DE FG JR SG, BR AH.

27 Nov 1943   (P)
Assembly Hall, Memorial Auditorium (bc)
Buffalo, NY

....	AFR		Coca Cola Theme
....	AFR		Blue Skies
....	AFR		I Wonder Why –vBR
....	AFR		Rockin' In Rhythm
....	AFR		Do Nothin' Till You Hear From Me –vAH
....	AFR		A Slip Of The Lip –vRN
....	UJ		Sentimental Lady
....	AFR		Things Ain't What They Used To Be
....	AFR		Coca Cola Theme

1 Dec 1943   (S)
Decca Studios
New York City, NY

<u>DUKE ELLINGTON & HIS ORCHESTRA</u>
TJ HB WJ RS RN, JN LB JT, JHtn JH OH EWms HC, DE FG JR SG.

....	Crl	N-1055-1	It Don't Mean A Thing –vRN TJ
....	Crl	N-1055-2	It Don't Mean A Thing –vRN TJ
....	ST	N-1055-3[1]	It Don't Mean A Thing –vRN TJ
....	Crl	N-1056-1[1]	Johnny Come Lately
....	Crl	N-1056-2	Johnny Come Lately
....	Crl	N-1057-1	Creole Love Call (incomplete)
....	Crl	N-1057-2	Creole Love Call (incomplete)
....	VD	N-1057-3[1]	Creole Love Call
....	ST	N-1058-1[1]	Somebody Loves Me
....	Crl	N-1059-1[1]	Jack The Bear
....	Crl	N-1060-1	Harlem Air Shaft
....	Crl	N-1060-2	Harlem Air Shaft
....	Crl	N-1060-3[1]	Harlem Air Shaft
....	ST	N-1061-1[1]	Ring Dem Bells –vRN
....	Crl	N-1062-1	Rose Room
....	ST	N-1062-2[1]	Rose Room
....	FDC	N-1063-1[1]	Honeysuckle Rose
....	Tax	N-1064-1[1]	Chopsticks[2]

[1]These masters have been released originally on WT.
[2]The arrangement is by Mary Lou Williams.

8 Dec 1943[1]   (P)
Langley Field AFB (bc)
Hampton, VA

<u>DUKE ELLINGTON & HIS ORCHESTRA</u>
TJ HB WJ RS RN, JN LB JT, JHtn JH OH EWms HC, DE FG JR SG, BR.

....	Duk	Three Cent Stomp
....	Duk	I Wonder Why –vBR
....	Duk	Fanfare
....	Duk	Goin' Up
....	Duk	Boy Meets Horn
....	Duk	Jump For Joy
....	Duk	Take The "A" Train

[1]Broadcast on 9 Dec 1943.

11 Dec 1943   (P)
Carnegie Hall
New York City, NY

<u>DUKE ELLINGTON & HIS ORCHESTRA</u>
TJ HB WJ RS RN, JN LB JT, JHtn JH OH EWms HC, DE FG JR SG, AH.

....	JP	The Star Spangled Banner
....	JP	Take The "A" Train
....	JP	Moon Mist
....	JP	Tea For Two
....	JP	Honeysuckle Rose
....	Emb	Star Dust
....	Emb	The "C" Jam Blues
....	JP	West Indian Dance
....	JP	The Lighter Attitude
....	Stv[1]	New World A-Comin'[2]
....	Emb	Floor Show[3]
....	Emb	Don't Get Around Much Anymore
....	JP	Ring Dem Bells –vRN
....	JP	Medley[4]
....	JP	Jack The Bear
....	JP	Do Nothin' Till You Hear From Me –vAH
....	Emb	Summertime –vAH
....	Emb	Cotton Tail
....	JP	Black And Tan Fantasy
....	Emb	Rockin' In Rhythm
....	Emb	Sentimental Lady
....	Emb	Trumpet In Spades
....	Stv[5]	Things Ain't What They Used To Be

[1]The original release on Emb has been edited; a complete version can be found on CD Stv 103 8341.
[2]aka "Sapph."
[3]sa "Goin' Up."
[4]Including: In A Sentimental Mood; Mood Indigo; Sophisticated Lady; Caravan; Solitude; I Let A Song Go Out Of My Heart.
[5]This closing title has been cut short (3:15) on Emb; it is complete (6:08) on CD Stv 103 8341.

1 Apr 1944   (P)
Hurricane Club (bc)
New York City, NY

<u>DUKE ELLINGTON & HIS ORCHESTRA</u>
TJ HB SH RS RN, JN LB JT, JHtn JH OH EWms HC, DE FG JR SG, AH.

....	Dji	Take The "A" Train >>>

....	Dji	Concerto For Cootie
....	Dji	Johnny Come Lately
....	Dji	My Heart Tells Me –vAH
....	Dji	Blue Skies
....	Dji	Things Ain't What They Used To Be

<table>
<tr><td></td><td></td><td>2 Apr 1944 (P)</td></tr>
</table>

DUKE ELLINGTON   2 Apr 1944   (P)
Piano solo.   Carnegie Hall
                                                          New York City, NY

....		Sophisticated Lady
....	Rar	Dancers In Love[1]

[1]*aka* "Stomp For Beginners"; part of the future *Perfume Suite*.

DUKE ELLINGTON & HIS ORCHESTRA   Hurricane Club (bc) (P)
TJ HB SH RS RN, JN LB JT, JHtn JH OH EWms HC, DE FG JR SG, WJon AH.

....	Take The "A" Train
....	Johnny Come Lately
....	Sentimental Lady
....	Solid Old Man
....	My Ideal –WJon
....	Five O'Clock Drag
....	Honeysuckle Rose
....	No Love, No Nothin' –vAH
....	Boy Meets Horn
....	Things Ain't What They Used To Be

DUKE ELLINGTON & HIS ORCHESTRA   7 Apr 1944   (P)
TJ SH RS RN, JN LB JT, JHtn JH OH EWms HC, DE FG JR SG, AH.   Hurricane Club (bc)
                                                          New York City, NY

....	Take The "A" Train
....	Johnny Come Lately
....	Sentimental Lady
....	Subtle Slough
....	Ring Dem Bells –vRN
....	My Heart Tells Me –vAH
....	My Gal Sal
....	Concerto For Cootie
....	Honeysuckle Rose
....	Sweet Georgia Brown

DUKE ELLINGTON & HIS ORCHESTRA   8 Apr 1944   (P)
TJ SH RS RN, JN LB JT, JHtn JH OH EWms HC, DE FG JR SG.   Hurricane Club (bc)
                                                          New York City, NY

....	Three Cent Stomp
....	Main Stem
....	Sentimental Lady

DUKE ELLINGTON & HIS ORCHESTRA   9 Apr 1944   (P)
TJ SH RS RN, JN LB JT, JHtn JH OH EWms HC, DE FG JR SG.   Hurricane Club (bc)
                                                          New York City, NY

....	Take The "A" Train
....	Concerto For Cootie
....	It Don't Mean A Thing –vRN TJ
....	Things Ain't What They Used To Be

DUKE ELLINGTON & HIS ORCHESTRA   13 Apr 1944   (P)
TJ SH RS RN, JN LB JT, JHtn JH OH EWms HC, DE FG JR SG, AH.   Hurricane Club (bc)
                                                          New York City, NY

....		Take The "A" Train
....	WL	Fickle Fling[1]
....		I'll Get By –vAH
....	WL	Tea For Two
....		Day Dream
....	WL	Three Cent Stomp
....		Concerto For Cootie
....		San Fernando Valley
....		Solid Old Man
....		Things Ain't What They Used To Be

[1]*aka* "Camp Grant Chant."

DUKE ELLINGTON WITH PAUL WHITEMAN & THE HALL OF FAME ORCHESTRA
DE with Paul Whiteman & the Hall of Fame Orchestra and chorus.

16 Apr 1944   (S)
Studios WJZ (bc)
New York City, NY

....   Medley[1]

[1]Including: Mood Indigo; Caravan; Mood Indigo; Solitude*; Don't Get Around Much Anymore –vChorus*; I Got It Bad;
It Don't Mean A Thing; Sophisticated Lady –vChorus*.
*DE can be heard only on these titles.

DUKE ELLINGTON & HIS ORCHESTRA
TJ SH RS RN, JN LB CJ, JHtn JH OH EWms HC, DE FG JR SG, AH.

20 Apr 1944   (P)
Hurricane Club (bc)
New York City, NY

....   Take The "A" Train
....   San Fernando Valley
....   Way Low
....   Suddenly It Jumped
....   Summertime –vAH
....   On The Alamo
....   Things Ain't What They Used To Be

DUKE ELLINGTON & HIS ORCHESTRA
TJ SH RS RN, JN LB CJ, JHtn JH OH EWms HC, DE FG JR SG.

21 Apr 1944   (P)
Hurricane Club (bc)
New York City, NY

....   Boy Meets Horn
....   Jump For Joy
....   Three Cent Stomp

DUKE ELLINGTON & HIS ORCHESTRA
TJ SH RS RN, JN LB CJ, JHtn JH OH EWms HC, DE FG JR SG, AH.

22 Apr 1944   (P)
Hurricane Club (bc)
New York City, NY

....   Take The "A" Train
....   Now I Know
....   Perdido
....   Do Nothin' Till You Hear From Me –vAH
....   Suddenly It Jumped

DUKE ELLINGTON & HIS ORCHESTRA
TJ SH RS RN, JN LB CJ, JHtn JH OH EWms HC, DE FG JR SG.

27 Apr 1944   (P)
Hurricane Club (bc)
New York City, NY

....   Solid Old Man
....   How Blue The Night
....   Ring Dem Bells

DUKE ELLINGTON & HIS ORCHESTRA
TJ SH RS RN, JN LB CJ, JHtn JH OH EWms HC, DE FG JR SG, AH.

28 Apr 1944   (P)
Hurricane Club (bc)
New York City, NY

....   Take The "A" Train
.... WL   Hop, Skip And Jump
.... WL   Jumpin' Frog Jump
....   Do Nothin' Till You Hear From Me –vAH
....   Johnny Come Lately
.... WL   Poinciana
.... WL   On The Alamo
....   Three Cent Stomp
....   Sentimental Lady

DUKE ELLINGTON & HIS ORCHESTRA
TJ SH RS RN, JN LB CJ, JHtn JH OH EWms HC, DE FG JR SG.

5 May 1944   (P)
Hurricane Club (bc)
New York City, NY

....   Indiana[1]
....   How Blue The Night
....   Stomp, Look And Listen
....   Jumpin' Frog Jump
....   Perdido
....   Concerto For Cootie[2]
....   Blue Skies

[1]Complete: "Back Home Again In Indiana."
[2]Announced as "Do Nothin' Till You Hear From Me."

DUKE ELLINGTON & HIS ORCHESTRA
TJ SH RS RN, JN LB CJ, JHtn JH OH EWms HC, DE FG JR SG, AH.

6 May 1944   (P)
Hurricane Club (bc)
New York City, NY

....	Dji	Take The "A" Train
....	MJ	Now I Know
....	MJ	Perdido
....	MJ	Do Nothin' Till You Hear From Me –vAH
....	MJ	My Gal Sal
....	Dji	Sentimental Lady
....	Dji	Take The "A" Train

DUKE ELLINGTON & HIS ORCHESTRA
TJ SH RS RN, JN LB CJ, JHtn JH OH EWms HC, DE FG JR SG, AH.

7 May 1944   (P)
Hurricane Club (bc)
New York City, NY

....	MJ	Jumpin' Punkins
....	MJ	Poinciana
....	MJ	It Don't Mean A Thing –vRN TJ
....		Do Nothin' Till You Hear From Me –vAH
....		Perdido

DUKE ELLINGTON & HIS ORCHESTRA
TJ SH RS RN, JN LB CJ, JHtn JH OH EWms/AS HC, DE FG JR SG, AH.

12 May 1944   (P)
Hurricane Club (bc)
New York City, NY

....		Time Alone Will Tell
....		San Fernando Valley
....		Stomp, Look And Listen
....		Do Nothin' Till You Hear From Me
....		Long Ago And Far Away –vAH
....		Someone
....		Suddenly It Jumped
....		Things Ain't What They Used To Be

DUKE ELLINGTON & HIS ORCHESTRA
TJ SH RS RN, JN LB CJ, JHtn JH OH AS HC, DE FG JR SG.

20 May 1944   (P)
Hurricane Club (bc)
New York City, NY

....		Take The "A" Train
....		Someone
....		Goin' My Way
....		Perdido
....		Since You Went Away
....		How Blue The Night
....		Do Nothin' Till You Hear From Me

DUKE ELLINGTON & HIS ORCHESTRA
TJ SH RS RN, JN LB CJ, JHtn JH OH AS HC, DE FG JR SG, AH.

21 May 1944   (P)
Hurricane Club (bc)
New York City, NY

....		Five O'Clock Drag
....		The "C" Jam Blues
....		How Blue The Night
....	WL	My Honey's Lovin' Arms –vRN[1]
....		I'll Get By –vAH
....		Stomp, Look And Listen
....		Now I Know

> DE JR SG.

....		Pitter Panther Patter

> Entire band.

....	MJ	Blue Skies
....		Do Nothin' Till You Hear From Me –vAH

[1]The arrangement is by Dick Vance.

DUKE ELLINGTON & HIS ORCHESTRA
TJ SH RS RN, JN LB CJ, JHtn JH OH AS HC, DE FG JR SG.

24 May 1944   (P)
Hurricane Club (bc)
New York City, NY

....		Someday I'll Meet You Again
....		And So Little Time
....	MJ	Clementine
....	MJ	Someone
....		Perdido
....		Do Nothin' Till You Hear From Me

DUKE ELLINGTON & HIS ORCHESTRA
TJ SH RS RN, JN LB CJ, JHtn JH OH AS HC, DE FG JR SG, AH.

25 May 1944   (P)
Hurricane Club (bc)
New York City, NY

.... Dji   Take The "A" Train
.... Dji   Someone
.... Dji   G.I. Jive
.... Dji   Three Cent Stomp

    > BS replaces DE.

.... VD   D4TC-200-1   My Little Brown Book –vAH

    > DE replaces BS.

.... Dji   Johnny Come Lately
.... Dji   Blue Skies
.... Dji   Sentimental Lady
.... Dji   Stomp, Look And Listen
.... Dji   Do Nothin' Till You Hear From Me

DUKE ELLINGTON & HIS ORCHESTRA
TJ SH RS RN, JN LB CJ, JHtn JH OH AS HC, DE FG JR SG.

26 May 1944   P)
Hurricane Club (bc)
New York City, NY

.... VD   D4TC-199-1   The Mood To Be Wooed[1]

[1]Original spelling "Mood To Be Woo'd."

DUKE ELLINGTON & HIS ORCHESTRA
TJ SH RS RN, JN LB CJ, JHtn JH OH AS HC, DE FG JR SG, AH.

27 May 1944   (P)
Hurricane Club (bc)
New York City, NY

.... Rar   Someone
.... Car   G.I. Jive
.... Rar   Three Cent Stomp

    > BS replaces DE.

....   My Little Brown Book –vAH

    > DE replaces BS.

.... MJ   Johnny Come Lately
.... MJ   Blue Skies
.... Rar   Sentimental Lady
....   Stomp, Look And Listen
....   Do Nothin' Till You Hear From Me

Although identical in content, the events on 24 and 27 May 1944 took place as listed.

DUKE ELLINGTON & HIS ORCHESTRA
TJ SH RS RN, JN LB CJ, JHtn JH OH AS HC, DE FG JR SG, WJon MEtn.

28 May 1944   (P)
Hurricane Club (bc)
New York City, NY

....   Everything But You –vWJon MEtn[1]
....   Rockin' In Rhythm
....   Suddenly It Jumped
....   The Mood To Be Wooed

[1]Complete: "You Left Me Everything But You."

DUKE ELLINGTON & HIS ORCHESTRA
TJ SH RS RN, JN LB CJ, JHtn JH OH AS HC, DE FG JR SG, AH.

31 May 1944   (P)
Hurricane Club (bc)
New York City, NY

....   Take The "A" Train
....   This Is Love Above All
.... MJ   Midriff
....   My Little Brown Book –vAH
....   Suddenly It Jumped

DUKE ELLINGTON & HIS ORCHESTRA
TJ SH RS RN, JN LB CJ, JHtn JH OH AS HC, DE FG JR SG, AH

1 Jun 1944   (P)
Hurricane Club (bc)
New York City, NY

.... Az   San Fernando Valley
.... Az   Perdido
.... Az   My Little Brown Book –vAH
.... Az   Hop, Skip And Jump
.... Az   Ring Dem Bells –vRN
.... Az   Now I Know
.... Az   The Mood To Be Wooed

DUKE ELLINGTON & HIS ORCHESTRA
TJ SH RS RN, JN LB CJ, JHtn JH OH AS HC, DE FG JR SG, AH.

2 Jun 1944   (P)
Hurricane Club (bc)
New York City, NY

....		Take The "A" Train
....		Dancing In The Dark
....	MJ	Main Stem
....	MJ	My Little Brown Book –vAH
....		Hop, Skip And Jump
....		Ring Dem Bells –vRN
....		The Mood To Be Wooed
....		A Slip Of The Lip –vRN
....		Harlem Air Shaft

DUKE ELLINGTON & HIS ORCHESTRA
TJ SH RS RN, JN LB CJ, JHtn JH OH AS HC, DE FG JR SG.

3 Jun 1944   (P)
Hurricane Club (bc)
New York City, NY

....	Plm	Perdido
....	WL	Irresistible You
....	WL	How Blue The Night
....	Plm	Things Ain't What They Used To Be

DUKE ELLINGTON & HIS ORCHESTRA
TJ SH RS RN, JN LB CJ, JHtn JH OH AS HC, DE FG JR SG.

4 Jun 1944   (P)
Hurricane Club (bc)
New York City, NY

....	Car	Too Much In Love
....		It Don't Mean A Thing –vRN TJ
....	MJ	The Mood To Be Wooed
....	MJ	Things Ain't What They Used To Be

DUKE ELLINGTON & HIS ORCHESTRA
TJ SH RS RN, JN LB CJ, JHtn JH OH AS HC, DE FG JR SG, WJon.

6 Jun 1944   (P)
Hurricane Club (bc)
New York City, NY

....		Everything But You –vWJon
....		Suddenly It Jumped
....		The Mood To Be Wooed
....		Do Nothin' Till You Hear From Me

DUKE ELLINGTON & HIS ORCHESTRA
TJ SH RS RN, JN LB CJ, JHtn JH OH AS HC, DE FG JR SG, AH.

8 Jul 1944   (P)
Naval Training Center (bc)
Bainbridge, MD

....	AFR	Coca Cola Theme
....	SR	G.I. Jive
....	Rar	Amor
....	AFR	Navy promotion and fanfare
....	AFR	My Little Brown Book –vAH
....	Rar	Frankie And Johnny
....	AFR	Sentimental Lady
....	AFR	Coca Cola Theme
....	Rar	It Don't Mean A Thing –vRN TJ
....	AFR	Take The "A" Train
....	AFR	Coca Cola Theme

DUKE ELLINGTON & MILDRED BAILEY
DE and MBly talking.

2 Aug 1944   (S)
CBS Studios (bc)
New York City, NY

....		Conversation

DUKE ELLINGTON WITH THE PAUL BARON ORCHESTRA
DE with the Paul Baron Orchestra.

....	AFR	Dancers In Love

DUKE ELLINGTON & HIS ORCHESTRA
TJ SH CA RS RN, JN LB CJ, JHtn JH OH AS HC, DE FG JR HBwn.

29 Nov 1944   (P)
Apollo Theater (bc)
New York City, NY

....	Evb	Things Ain't What They Used To Be
....		Suddenly It Jumped

DUKE ELLINGTON & HIS ORCHESTRA
TJ SH CA RN, JN LB CJ, JHtn JH OH AS HC, DE FG JR SG, JS KD AH.

1 Dec 1944   (S)
24th St., Studio 2
New York City, NY

....	Vi	D4VB-453-1	I Ain't Got Nothin' But The Blues –vKD AH	>>>

....	Vi	D4VB-454-1	I'm Beginning To See The Light –vJS
....	Vi	D4VB-454-2	I'm Beginning To See The Light –vJS
....	RD	D4VB-455-1	Don't You Know I Care? –vAH[1]
....	Vi	D4VB-455-2	Don't You Know I Care? –vAH
....	Vi	D4VB-456-4	I Didn't Know About You –vJS[2]

[1]Complete: "Don't You Know I Care Or Don't You Care To Know?"
[2]This title is a derivative of *Sentimental Lady*.

DUKE ELLINGTON & HIS ORCHESTRA   11 Dec 1944 (S)
TJ SH CA RN, JN LB CJ, JHtn JH OH AS HC, DE FG JR SG, JS. 24th St., Studio 2
 New York City, NY

BLACK, BROWN AND BEIGE

....	Vi	D4VC-562-3	3 The Blues –vJS
....	Vi	D4VC-563-1	4 Three Dances[1]

[1]Including: West Indian Dance (-3); Emancipation Celebration (-2); Sugar Hill Penthouse (-4). "Emancipation Celebration" is in part a derivative of *Dallas Doings*.

DUKE ELLINGTON & HIS ORCHESTRA   12 Dec 1944 (S)
TJ SH CA RN, JN LB CJ, JHtn JH OH AS HC, DE FG JR SG. 24th St., Studio 2
 New York City, NY

BLACK, BROWN AND BEIGE (ctd.)

....	Vi	D4VC-560-1	1 Work Song
....	Vi	D4VC-561-2	2 Come Sunday

DUKE ELLINGTON WITH STUDIO ORCHESTRA   17 Dec 1944 (S)
DE with an unidentified studio orchestra and chorus. NBC Studios (bc)
 New York City, NY

....	AFR	Medley[1]
....	AFR	Main Stem—The "C" Jam Blues

> GN added.

....	AFR	Do Nothin' Till You Hear From Me –vGN

> GN omitted.

....	AFR	Somebody Loves Me

[1]Including: Sophisticated Lady; Solitude; Caravan; Mood Indigo –vChorus; It Don't Mean A Thing –vChorus.

The recording date of the last two titles of the above MALB program is questionable. According to file cards at the Library of Congress, GN appeared on MALB programs only on 10 Sep 1944 and 27 May 1945. DE and the band were on the road on both dates. Lacking any further information about GN's appearance with DE at any date, the titles should stay listed under the date they were broadcast.

DUKE ELLINGTON & HIS ORCHESTRA   19 Dec 1944 (P)
TJ SH CA RS RN, JN LB CJ, JHtn JH OH AS HC, DE FG JR HBwn, JS KD MEtn AH. Carnegie Hall
 New York City NY

....		The Star Spangled Banner
....	Pre	Blutopia
....	Pre	Midriff
....	Pre	Creole Love Call –vKD
....	Pre	Suddenly It Jumped
....	Rar	Frustration
....	Pre	It Don't Mean A Thing –vRN
....		I Didn't Know About You –vJS
....		Don't You Know I Care? –vJS
....		I Ain't Got Nothin' But The Blues –vJS AH
....		I'm Beginning To See The Light –vJS
....	Pre	Pitter Panther Patter
		THE PERFUME SUITE[1]
....	Pre	- Sonata
....	Pre	- Strange Feeling –vAH
....	Pre	- Dancers In Love[2]
....	Pre	- Coloratura
....	Pre	Things Ain't What They Used To Be
		BLACK, BROWN AND BEIGE
....	Pre	- Work Song
....	Pre	- The Blues –vMEtn
....	Pre	- Three Dances[3]
....	Pre	- Come Sunday
....	Rar	Medley[4]
....	Pre	The Mood To Be Wooed >>>

....	Pre	Blue Cellophane
....	Rar	Air Conditioned Jungle[5]
....	Rar	Frantic Fantasy[6]
....	Pre	Blue Skies
....	Pre	Frankie And Johnny

[1]The parts of the suite represent *Love, Violence, Naïveté, Sophistication* respectively.
[2]DE and his respective bass player only; this applies to all future performances of the suite, unless stated otherwise.
[3]Including: West Indian Dance; Emancipation Celebration; Creamy Brown (*sa* "Sugar Hill Penthouse").
[4]Including: In A Sentimental Mood; Mood Indigo; Sophisticated Lady; Caravan; Solitude; I Let A Song Go Out Of My Heart.
Part of *Solitude* and *I Let A Song Go Out Of My Heart* are missing on Rar.
[5]*aka* "The Air-Minded Jungle."
[6]*aka* "Orion Fantasy."

<table>
<tr><td colspan="3"></td><td>2 Jan 1945</td><td>(S)</td></tr>
<tr><td colspan="3">DUKE ELLINGTON & HIS ORCHESTRA</td><td>Decca Studios</td><td></td></tr>
<tr><td colspan="3">TJ SH CA RS RN, JN LB CJ, JHtn JH OH AS HC, DE FG JR SG, JS.</td><td>New York City, NY</td><td></td></tr>
</table>

....	Crl	N-2994-1	Midriff
....	ST	N-2994-2[1]	Midriff
....	Crl	N-2995-1	I Didn't Know About You –vJS (incomplete)
....	Crl	N-2995-2	I Didn't Know About You –vJS (incomplete)
....	Crl	N-2995-3	I Didn't Know About You –vJS (incomplete)
....	Crl	N-2995-4[1]	I Didn't Know About You –vJS
....	Crl	N-2996-1	I'm Beginning To See The Light –vJS (incomplete)
....	Crl	N-2996-2[1]	I'm Beginning To See The Light –vJS
....	Crl	N-2997-1[1]	The Mood To Be Wooed
....	Crl	N-2998-1	Blue Cellophane (incomplete)
....	Crl	N-2998-2	Blue Cellophane (incomplete)
....	ST	N-2998-3	Blue Cellophane

[1]These masters have been released originally on WT.

<table>
<tr><td colspan="3"></td><td>3 Jan 1945</td><td>(S)</td></tr>
<tr><td colspan="3">DUKE ELLINGTON & HIS ORCHESTRA</td><td>Decca Studios</td><td></td></tr>
<tr><td colspan="3">TJ SH CA RS RN, JN LB CJ, JHtn JH OH AS HC, DE FG JR SG, JS KD AH.</td><td>New York City, NY</td><td></td></tr>
</table>

....	Crl	N-2999-1	Subtle Slough (incomplete)
....	Crl	N-2999-2	Subtle Slough
....	Crl	N-2999-3[1]	Subtle Slough
....	Crl	N-3000-1	Hit Me With A Hot Note –vJS (incomplete)[2]
....	Crl	N-3000-2	Hit Me With A Hot Note –vJS
....	Crl	N-3000-3	Hit Me With A Hot Note –vJS (incomplete)
....	Crl	N-3000-4[1]	Hit Me With A Hot Note –vJS
....	Crl	N-3001-1	Air Conditioned Jungle

> SG omitted.

....	Crl	N-3001-2[1]	Air Conditioned Jungle

> DE JR.

....	Crl	N-3002-1[1]	Pitter Panther Patter

> Entire band.

....	Crl	N-3003-1	Prairie Fantasy[3]
....	Duk	N-3003-2[1]	Prairie Fantasy
....	Crl	N-3004-1	Don't You Know I Care? –vAH
....	Crl	N-3004-2	Don't You Know I Care? –vAH (incomplete)
....	Crl	N-3004-3[1]	Don't You Know I Care? –vAH
....	Crl	N-3005-1	I Ain't Got Nothin' But The Blues –vKD AH
....	Crl	N-3005-2	I Ain't Got Nothin' But The Blues –vKD AH (incomplete)
....	Crl	N-3005-3	I Ain't Got Nothin' But The Blues –vKD AH (incomplete)
....	Crl	N-3005-4	I Ain't Got Nothin' But The Blues –vKD AH (incomplete)
....	Crl	N-3005-5	I Ain't Got Nothin' But The Blues –vKD AH (incomplete)
....	Crl	N-3005-6[1]	I Ain't Got Nothin' But The Blues –vKD AH
....	Crl	N-3006-1	Blutopia
....	Crl	N-3006-2	Blutopia (incomplete)
....	Crl	N-3006-3[1]	Blutopia
....	Crl	N-3007-1	Let The Zoomers Drool (incomplete)
....	Crl	N-3007-2[1]	Let The Zoomers Drool
....	Crl	N-3008-1	You Never Know The Things You Miss
....	Crl	N-3008-2[1]	You Never Know The Things You Miss

[1]These masters have been released originally on WT.
[2]Complete: "Hit Me With A Hot Note And Watch Me Bounce."
[3]*sa* "Frantic Fantasy"; "Orion Fantasy."

DUKE ELLINGTON & HIS ORCHESTRA
TJ SH CA RS RN, JN LB CJ, JHtn JH OH AS HC, DE FG JR SG, JS.

....	Vi	D5VB-12-3	Carnegie Blues[1]
....	Vi	D5VB-13-1	Blue Cellophane
....	Vi	D5VB-14-2	The Mood To Be Wooed
....	Vi	D5VB-15-5	My Heart Sings –vJS[2]

[1]This title is a derivative of *The Blues* from *Black, Brown And Beige.*
[2]Complete: "All Of A Sudden My Heart Sings."

DUKE ELLINGTON & HIS ORCHESTRA
TJ SH CA RS RN, JN LB CJ, JHtn JH OH AS HC, DE FG JR SG, JS.

....	AFR	Take The "A" Train
....	AFR	Suddenly It Jumped
....	AFR	I'm Beginning To See The Light –vJS
....	AFR	It Don't Mean A Thing –vRN TJ

> LHrn added.

....	AFR	I Don't Know About You –vLHrn
....	AFR	I Get A Kick Out Of You –vLHrn

> LHrn omitted.

....	AFR	Midriff
....	AFR	Blue Skies

[1]Broadcast on 26 May 1945.

DUKE ELLINGTON & HIS ORCHESTRA
TJ SH CA RS RN, JN LB CJ, JHtn JH OH AS HC, DE FG JR SG, MEtn.

....		Take The "A" Train
....	GoJ	Blutopia
....	GoJ	Air Conditioned Jungle
....	GoJ	Frustration
....	GoJ	Blue Cellophane
....	GoJ	Suddenly It Jumped
....	GoJ	Coloratura
....	GoJ	It Don't Mean A Thing –vRN TJ
....	Sbm	It Don't Mean A Thing (Begin of broadcast.)
....	FDC	Esquire Jump

> WS added.

....	FDC	Tea For Two

> WS omitted, AOD added.

....	FDC	Wish You Were Waiting For Me –vAOD

> AOD omitted.

....	FDC	Midriff
....	FDC	The Mood To Be Wooed

>BS replaces DE, BHol added.

....	FDC	I Cover The Waterfront –vBHol

> DE ACas JR SCtl.

....	FDC	Honeysuckle Rose

> Entire band, LA, BG added.[1]

....	Sbm	Things Ain't What They Used To Be (End of broadcast.)

> LA, BG omitted, BHol added.

....	MoJ	Lover Man –vBHol

> BHol omitted.

....	GoJ	Frantic Fantasy
		BLACK, BROWN AND BEIGE
....	Dji	- Black
....	Dji	- Mauve –vMEtn[2]
....	Dji	- West Indian Dance
....	Dji	- Creamy Brown[3]
....	Dji	- The Lighter Attitude
....	Dji	- Spiritual Theme[4] >>>

> TJ, JHtn, DE ACas JR SCtl, AOD.

.... GoJ   I Can't Believe That You're In Love With Me –vAOD

> Entire band, ACas SCtl, AOD omitted.

.... GoJ   Frankie And Johnny

[1]Three-way radio hookup from Los Angeles, New Orleans and New York.
[2]*sa* "The Blues."
[3]*sa* "Emancipation Celebration."
[4]*aka* "Come Sunday And Light."

The above comprises only the Ellington portion of the concert.

18 Jan 1945   (P)
NBC Studios (bc)
Hollywood, CA

DUKE ELLINGTON & BING CROSBY
DE and BC talking.

.... Bon   Conversation

DUKE ELLINGTON WITH THE JOHN SCOTT TROTTER ORCHESTRA
DE with the John Scott Trotter Orchestra and chorus.

.... Bon   Frankie And Johnny –vChorus

23 Jan 1945   (P)
Orpheum Auditorium (bc)
Los Angeles, CA

DUKE ELLINGTON & HIS ORCHESTRA
TJ SH CA RS RN, JN LB CJ, JHtn JH OH AS HC, DE FG JR SCtl, JS.

.... AFR   Take The "A" Train
.... AFR   Suddenly It Jumped
.... AFR   I'm Beginning To See The Light –vJS
.... AFR   It Don't Mean A Thing –vRN TJ
.... AFR   I Didn't Know About You

> LHrn added.

.... AFR   I Get A Kick Out Of You –vLHrn

> LHrn omitted.

.... AFR   Midriff
.... AFR   Blue Skies
.... AFR   Take The "A" Train

3 Mar 1945   (P)
Casa Mañana (bc)
Culver City, CA

DUKE ELLINGTON & HIS ORCHESTRA
TJ SH CA RS RN, JN LB CJ, JHtn JH OH AS HC, DE FG JR HBwn, JS KD AH.

.... AFR   Take The "A" Train
.... AFR   I'm Beginning To See The Light –vJS
.... AFR   I Ain't Got Nothin' But The Blues –vKD AH
.... AFR   Blue Skies

19 Mar 1945   (P)
Billy Berg's Vine Street Supper Club (bc)
Hollywood, CA

REX STEWART'S ALL STARS
RS, BWsn, BB, JSvn RGrb ZStn.

.... Duk   Blues Jam
.... Duk   Someday, Sweetheart
.... Duk   Coast Guard promotion
.... Duk   Muskrat Ramble

> DE replaces JSvn.

.... Duk   Mood Indigo

> JSvn replaces DE.

.... Duk   The Sheik Of Araby

25 Mar 1945   (P)
Civic Opera House (bc)
Chicago, IL

DUKE ELLINGTON & HIS ORCHESTRA
TJ SH CA RS RN, JN LB CJ, JHtn JH OH AS HC, DE FG JR SG, JS KD MEtn AH.

....   Blutopia
....   Midriff
....   Creole Love Call –vKD
....   Suddenly It Jumped
....   I Didn't Know About You -vJS
....   My Heart Sings –vJS
....   Air Conditioned Jungle
....   Frantic Fantasy   >>>

		BLACK, BROWN AND BEIGE
....	Joy	- Work Song
....	Joy	- Come Sunday And Light
....	Joy	- The Blues –vMEtn
....	Joy	- Three Dances[1]
....		Things Ain't What They Used To Be
		THE PERFUME SUITE
....	Joy	- Sonata
....	Joy	- Strange Feeling –vAH
....	Joy	- Dancers In Love
....	Joy	- Coloratura

> DE JR SG.

.... Medley[2]

> Entire band.

....	Joy	Take The "A" Train (Begin of broadcast.)
....	Joy	Blue Cellophane
....	Joy	Frustration
....	Joy	I'm Beginning To See The Light –vJS
....	Joy	Down Beat awards presentation
....	Joy	The Mood To Be Wooed
....	Joy	It Don't Mean A Thing –vRN TJ
....	Joy	I Ain't Got Nothin' But The Blues –vKD AH
....	Joy	Blue Skies
....	Joy	Take The "A" Train
....	SD	Frankie And Johnny
....	AFR	Honeysuckle Rose

[1]Including: West Indian Dance; Emancipation Celebration; Sugar Hill Penthouse.
[2]Including: Sophisticated Lady; Solitude; I Let A Song Go Out Of My Heart.

			6 Apr 1945 (P)
			400 Restaurant[1] (bc)
			New York City, NY

DUKE ELLINGTON & HIS ORCHESTRA
TJ SH CA RS RN, JN LB CJ, JHtn JH OH AS HC, DE FG JR SG, KD AH.

....		Hop, Skip And Jump
....		I Miss Your Kiss
....		I Ain't Got Nothin' But The Blues –vKD AH

DUKE ELLINGTON & HIS ORCHESTRA   (bc)
KD AH omitted, JS added, otherwise same personnel.

....	Pho	Frustration
....		Blue Cellophane
....		I'm Beginning To See The Light –vJS
....		I Didn't Know About You

[1]After the Hurricane Club at Broadway and West 51st Street had burned down, it reopened under the name of *400 Restaurant* at the same location.

			7 Apr 1945 (P)
			400 Restaurant (bc)
			New York City, NY

DUKE ELLINGTON & HIS ORCHESTRA
TJ SH CA RS RN, JN LB CJ, JHtn JH OH AS HC, DE FG JR SG, JS KD AH.

....	WL	Take The "A" Train
....	DET	Blutopia
....	DET	Midriff
....	DET	Creole Love Call –vKD
....	DET	Suddenly It Jumped
....	DET	Frustration
....	DET	I'm Beginning To See The Light –vJS
		THE PERFUME SUITE
....	DET	- Sonata
....	DET	- Strange Feeling –vAH
....	DET	- Dancers In Love
....	DET	- Coloratura
....	DET	Air Conditioned Jungle
....	DET	I Ain't Got Nothin' But The Blues –vKD AH
....	DET	Subtle Slough
....	DET	Passion Flower

		11 Apr 1945 (P)
		400 Restaurant (bc)
		New York City, NY

DUKE ELLINGTON & HIS ORCHESTRA
TJ SH CA RS RN, JN LB CJ, JHtn JH OH AS HC, DE FG JR SG, AH.

.... Take The "A" Train >>>

.... Someone
.... Main Stem
.... Don't You Know I Care? –vAH
.... Sentimental Journey
.... I Didn't Know About You

14 Apr 1945   (S)
400 Restaurant (bc)
New York City, NY

DUKE ELLINGTON & HIS ORCHESTRA
TJ SH CA RS RN, JN LB CJ, JHtn JH OH AS HC, DE FG JR SG, KD AH.

.... Ari   Moon Mist

> DE piano solo.

.... Ari   New World A-Comin'

> Entire band.

.... Ari   Nobody Knows The Trouble I've Seen –vAH
.... Ari   Mood Indigo

> DE piano solo.

.... Ari   Chant For F.D. Roosevelt[1]

> Entire band.

.... Ari   Come Sunday
.... Ari   A City Called Heaven –vKD[2]
.... Ari   Creole Love Call –vKD
.... Ari   Moon Mist

[1]Subtitled "American Lullaby."
[2]sa "Poor Pilgrim Of Sorrow."

No audience in attendance.

15 Apr 1945   (S)
Radio City (bc)
New York City, NY

DUKE ELLINGTON
Piano solo.

.... Sophisticated Lady––Solitude

> MTil and chorus added.

.... Nobody Knows The Trouble I've Seen –vMTil Chorus

21 Apr 1945   (P)
400 Restaurant (bc)
New York City, NY

DUKE ELLINGTON & HIS ORCHESTRA
TJ SH CA RS RN, JN LB CJ, JHtn JH OH AS HC, DE FG JR SG, JS KD MEtn.

.... DET   Take The "A" Train
.... WL   The Mood To Be Wooed
.... WL   If You Are But A Dream –vKD
.... WL   Riff Staccato[1]
.... DET   I'm Beginning To See The Light –vJS

BLACK, BROWN AND BEIGE
.... VD   JDB89   - West Indian Dance
.... VD   JDB109   - The Blues –vMEtn
.... VD   JDB89   - Emancipation Celebration
.... VD   JDB89   - Sugar Hill Penthouse

.... WL   Sentimental Lady
.... WL   Stomp, Look And Listen
.... VD   VP1315   Frantic Fantasy
.... VD   VP1316   It Don't Mean A Thing –vRN TJ
.... DET   Sentimental Lady

[1]Complete: "Otto, Make That Riff Staccato"; the arrangement is by Mary Lou Williams.

22 Apr 1945   (S)
Studios WOR (bc)
New York City, NY

DUKE ELLINGTON
DE on the Dick Brown show.

.... Interview

DUKE ELLINGTON & HIS ORCHESTRA
400 Restaurant (bc) (P)
TJ SH CA RS RN, JN LB CJ, JHtn JH OH AS HC, DE FG JR SG, JS KD AH.

.... Duk   Take The "A" Train
.... Duk   After A While
.... Duk   I Ain't Got Nothin' But The Blues –vKD AH
.... Duk   Riff Staccato
.... Duk   I Didn't Know About You –vJS   >>>

.... Duk   Main Stem

| | | | 24 Apr 1945 | (P) |

DUKE ELLINGTON & HIS ORCHESTRA
TJ SH CA RS RN, JN LB CJ, JHtn JH OH AS HC, DE FG JR SG.

24 Apr 1945 (P)
400 Restaurant (bc)
New York City, NY

....   All At Once
....   Candy –vRN

DUKE ELLINGTON & HIS ORCHESTRA
TJ SH CA RS RN, JN LB CJ, JHtn JH OH AS HC, DE FG JR SG, JS.

26 Apr 1945 (S)
24th St., Studio 2
New York City, NY

.... Vi   D5VB-232-1   Kissing Bug –vJS

DUKE ELLINGTON & HIS ORCHESTRA
KD replaces JS, otherwise same personnel.

400 Restaurant (bc) (P)

....   If You Are But A Dream –vKD
....   West Indian Dance

DUKE ELLINGTON & HIS ORCHESTRA
TJ SH CA RS RN, JN LB CJ, JHtn JH OH AS HC, DE FG JR SG.

27 Apr 1945 (P)
400 Restaurant (bc)
New York City, NY

....   Suddenly It Jumped
....   Things Ain't What They Used To Be

DUKE ELLINGTON & HIS ORCHESTRA
TJ SH CA RS RN, JN LB CJ, JHtn JH OH AS HC, DE FG JR SG, JS AH.

28 Apr 1945 (P)
400 Restaurant (bc)
New York City, NY

.... DET   Take The "A" Train
.... DET   Midriff
.... DET   Carnegie Blues
.... UJ   Someone[1]
.... DET   My Little Brown Book –vAH
.... DET   Kissing Bug –vJS
.... DET   Ring Dem Bells –vRN
.... DET   I'm Beginning To See The Light –vJS
.... DET   Work Song
.... DET   Spiritual Theme
.... DET   Candy –vRN
.... DET   Teardrops In The Rain
.... DET   Ac-Cent-Tchu-Ate The Positive –vJS
.... DET   Way Low
.... DET   Take The "A" Train

[1]"I Don't Mind" on UJ.

DUKE ELLINGTON WITH TOMMY DORSEY & HIS ORCHESTRA
DE with Tommy Dorsey & His Orchestra.

29 Apr 1945 (S)
NBC Studios (bc)
New York City, NY

.... AFR   I Didn't Know About You
.... AFR   I'm Beginning To See The Light –vSms

> DE SBlk BRch.

.... AFR   Dancers In Love

DUKE ELLINGTON & HIS ORCHESTRA
TJ SH CA RS RN, JN LB CJ, JHtn JH OH AS HC, DE FG JR SG, JS.

400 Restaurant (bc) (P)

....   Hit Me With A Hot Note –vJS
....   I Should Care
....   Clementine
....   I'm Beginning To See The Light –vJS
....   Things Ain't What They Used To Be

DUKE ELLINGTON & HIS ORCHESTRA
TJ SH CA RS RN, JN LB CJ, JHtn JH OH AS HC, DE FG JR SG, JS.

1 May 1945 (S)
24th St., Studio 2
New York City, NY

.... Vi   D5VB-233-1   Everything But You –vJS
.... Vi   D5VB-234-1   Riff Staccato –vRN

DUKE ELLINGTON & HIS ORCHESTRA
TJ SH CA RS RN, JN LB CJ, JHtn JH OH AS HC, DE FG JR SG, JS KD AH.

4 May 1945 (P)
400 Restaurant (bc)
New York City, NY

.... DET   Take The "A" Train   >>>

....	DET		I Miss Your Kiss
....	DET		He'll Be Home In A Little While –vJS
....	DET		Riff Staccato –vRN
....	DET		I Ain't Got Nothin' But The Blues –vKD AH
....	DET		I'm Beginning To See The Light

5 May 1945   (P)
Adams Theater (bc)
Newark, NJ

DUKE ELLINGTON & HIS ORCHESTRA
TJ SH CA RS RN, JN LB CJ, JHtn JH OH AS HC, DE FG JR SG, JS AH.

....	DET		Take The "A" Train
....	FR		Blutopia
....	DET		Bond promotion
....	WL		Clementine
....	WL		My Heart Sings –vJS
....	WL		Sentimental Journey
....	WL		I Got It Bad –vAH
....	WL		Three Cent Stomp
....	FR		Black And Tan Fantasy
....	DET		Blue Skies (w. bond promotion)
....	DET		Passion Flower
....	DET		Air Conditioned Jungle
....	FR		Frantic Fantasy
....	DET		I'm Beginning To See The Light (w. bond promotion)
....	DET		Main Stem
....	DET		Everything But You –vJS
....	DET		Carnegie Blues
....	DET		Jump For Joy –vRN (w. bond promotion)
....	DET		Things Ain't What They Used To Be

10 May 1945   (S)
24ᵗʰ St., Studio 2
New York City, NY

DUKE ELLINGTON & HIS ORCHESTRA
TJ SH CA RS RN, JN LB CJ, JHtn JH OH AS HC, DE FG JR SG.

| .... | HMV | D5VB-261-1 | Prelude To A Kiss |

11 May 1945   (S)
24ᵗʰ St., Studio 2
New York City, NY

DUKE ELLINGTON & HIS ORCHESTRA
TJ SH CA RS RN, JN LB CJ, JHtn JH OH AS HC, DE FG JR SG, KD.

....	Vi	D5VB-262-1	Caravan
....	HMV	D5VB-263-1	Black And Tan Fantasy
....	HMV	D5VB-264-1	Mood Indigo –vKD

12 May 1945   (S)
Radio City, Studio 6B (bc)
New York City, NY

DUKE ELLINGTON & HIS ORCHESTRA
TJ SH CA RS RN, JN LB CJ, JHtn JH OH AS HC, DE FG BH SG, JS KD MEtn AH.

....	VD	VP1351	Take The "A" Train
....	DET		Carnegie Blues
....	DET		Riff Staccato –vRN
....	DET		Bond promotion
....	DET		All At Once
....	DET		Yesterdays –vKD
....	DET		I Miss Your Kiss
....	JSo		Ac-Cent-Tchu-Ate The Positive –vJS
....	DET		Bond promotion
....	DET		Blue Cellophane
....	DET		Take The "A" Train

> DE piano solo.

| .... | DET | | Take The "A" Train |

> Entire band.

| .... | VD | JDB209 | Prelude To A Kiss |
| .... | DET | | Caravan |

> DE piano solo.

| .... | DET | | Sophisticated Lady |

> Entire band.

....	DET		I Ain't Got Nothin' But The Blues –vKD AH
....	DET		I'm Beginning To See The Light (w. bond promotion)
....	DET		In A Mellotone
....	VD	VP1351	Harlem Air Shaft
....	DET		I Don't Mind –vMEtn
....	DET		Bond promotion
....	DET		The Jeep Is Jumpin'

14 May 1945   (S)
Lotus Club
New York City, NY

DUKE ELLINGTON WITH TOMMY DORSEY & HIS ORCHESTRA
DE with Tommy Dorsey & His Orchestra.

.... Vi   D5VB-758-1   The Minor Goes Muggin'

DUKE ELLINGTON & HIS ORCHESTRA   24th St., Studio 2   (S)
TJ SH CA RS RN, JN LB CJ, JHtn JH OH AS HC, DE FG BH SG, JS KD MEtn.

.... Vi   D5VB-265-1   In A Sentimental Mood
.... HMV   D5VB-266-1   It Don't Mean A Thing –vJS KD MEtn
.... HMV   D5VB-267-1   Sophisticated Lady

TOMMY DORSEY WITH DUKE ELLINGTON & HIS ORCHESTRA
JS KD MEtn omitted, TD added, otherwise same personnel.

.... Vi   D5VB-268-1   Tonight I Shall Sleep

15 May 1945   (S)
24th St., Studio 2
New York City, NY

DUKE ELLINGTON & HIS FAMOUS ORCHESTRA
TJ SH CA RS RN, JN LB CJ, JHtn JH OH AS HC, DE FG SW SG, JS KD MEtn AH.

.... HMV   D5VB-269-1   I Let A Song Go Out Of My Heart –vJS
.... Vi   D5VB-269-2   I Let A Song Go Out Of My Heart –vJS
.... HMV   D5VB-270-1   Solitude –vJS KD MEtn AH

16 May 1945   (S)
24th St., Studio 2
New York City, NY

DUKE ELLINGTON & HIS RHYTHM
DE JR SG.

.... Vi   D5VB-271-1   Frankie And Johnny
.... Vi   D5VB-272-1   Jumpin' Room Only

DUKE ELLINGTON & HIS FAMOUS ORCHESTRA
TJ SH CA RS RN, JN LB CJ, JHtn JH OH AS HC, DE FG JR SG, AH.

.... HMV   D5VB-273-1   Black Beauty
.... Vi   D5VB-274-1   Every Hour On The Hour –vAH[1]

[1]Complete: "Every Hour On The Hour I Fall In Love With You."

19 May 1945   (P)
Paradise Theater (bc)
Detroit, MI

DUKE ELLINGTON & HIS ORCHESTRA
TJ SH CA RS RN, JN LN CJ, JHtn JH OH AS HC, DE FG JR SG, JS KD MEtn AH.

.... DET   Take The "A" Train
.... DET   Teardrops In The Rain
.... DET   Everything But You –vJS
.... DET   Bond promotion
.... JSo   Perdido
.... DET   If You Are But A Dream –vKD

      > DE JR SG.

.... FR   Pitter Panther Patter

      > Entire band.

.... DET   Emancipation Celebration
.... DET   Bond promotion
.... FR   I Should Care
.... DET   Take The "A" Train

      > DE piano solo.

.... DET   Take The "A" Train

      > Entire band.

.... FR   In A Sentimental Mood
.... FR   It Don't Mean A Thing –vJH KD MEtn
.... FR   Solitude –vJS KD MEtn AH
.... DET   I'm Beginning To See The Light (w. bond promotion)
.... FR   Subtle Slough
.... FR   The "C" Jam Blues
.... DET   Don't You Know I Care? –vAH
.... DET   Bond promotion
.... DET   Stomp, Look And Listen
.... DET   Things Ain't What They Used To Be

26 May 1945   (P)
Regal Theater (bc)
Chicago, IL

DUKE ELLINGTON & HIS ORCHESTRA
TJ SH CA RS RN, JN LB CJ, JHtn JH OH AS HC, DE FG JR SG, JS KD AH.

.... DET   Take The "A" Train   >>>

....	DET		Bond promotion
....	DET	VP1754[1]	Sugar Hill Penthouse
....	FR		Suddenly It Jumped
....	DET		Bond promotion
....	FR		Candy –vRN
....	FR		A Friend Of Yours
....	FR		Kissing Bug –vJS
....	VD	VP1397	Hollywood Hangover[2]
....	FR		Laura
....	DET		Bond promotion

> DE piano solo.

| .... | DET | | Take The "A" Train |

> Entire band.

....	VD[3]	VP1687	In The Shade Of The Old Apple Tree
....	VD	VP1752-1753	Frankie And Johnny
....	DET		I'm Beginning To See The Light (w. bond promotion)
....	FR		Midriff
....	DET		I Ain't Got Nothin' But The Blues –vKD AH
....	Pir		My Honey's Lovin' Arms –vRN
....	DET		Rockin' In Rhythm

[1]VD rejected.
[2]The arrangement is by Buck Clayton.
[3]Some of the reissues have been edited.

DUKE ELLINGTON & HIS ORCHESTRA
TJ SH CA RS RN, JN LB CJ, JHtn JH OH AS HC, DE FG JR SG, JS KD AH.

2 Jun 1945   (P)
Percy Jones Hospital Center (bc)
Battle Creek, MI

....	DET	Take The "A" Train
....	FR	The Mood To Be Wooed
....	Car	Jack The Bear
....	DET	Bond promotion
....	DET	The More I See You –vKD
....	Car	Way Low
....	Car	Blues On The Double
....	DET	Bond promotion
....	FR	Summertime –vAH
....	DET	Take The "A" Train

> DE JR SG.

| .... | DET | Take The "A" Train |

> Entire band.

....	FR	Come Sunday
....	FR	Light
....	DET	I'm Beginning To See The Light –vJS (w. bond promotion)
....	Pir	On The Alamo
....	FR	Carnegie Blues
....	DET	Bond promotion
....	FR	Riff Staccato –vRN
....	FR	Blue Skies
....	FR	Things Ain't What They Used to Be

DUKE ELLINGTON & HIS ORCHESTRA
TJ SH CA RS RN, JN LB CJ, JHtn JH OH AS HC, DE FG JR SG, JS KD MEtn AH.

9 Jun 1945   (P)
Paramount Theater (bc)
Toledo, OH

....	Car	Take The "A" Train
....	Car	Blue Is The Night
....	DET	Bond promotion
....	Car	Can't You Read Between The Lines?
....	Car	Hop, Skip And Jump
....	Car	Kissing Bug –vJS
....	Car	Solid Old Man
....	Car	I Ain't Got Nothin' But The Blues –vKD AH
....	DET	Bond promotion
....	Car	I Miss Your Kiss
....	DET	Things Ain't What They Used To Be
....	DET	Things Ain't What They Used To Be
....	Car	Diminuendo In Blue[1]
....	Car	Rocks In My Bed –vMEtn[1]
....	Car	Crescendo In Blue[1]
....	DET	I'm Beginning to See The Light –vJS (w. bond promotion)
....	Car	Teardrops In The Rain >>>

....	FR	My Little Brown Book –vAH
....	DET	Ac-Cent-Tchu-Ate The Positive –vJS
....	DET	Bond promotion
....	Car	The "C" Jam Blues
....	DET	Take The "A" Train

[1]Announced as "The Blues Cluster."

16 Jun 1945 (P)
Franklin Gardens (bc)
Evansville, IN

DUKE ELLINGTON & HIS ORCHESTRA
TJ SH CA RS RN, JN LB CJ, JHtn JH OH AS HC, DE FG JR SG, JS KD.

....	DET	Take The "A" Train
....	Car	Indiana
....	Jso	Blue Serge
....	DET	Bond promotion
....	Car	The Wish I Wish –vJS[1]
....	Car	Jumpin' Punkins
....	Pir	On The Sunny Side Of The Street
....	DET	Bond promotion
....	Car	Cotton Tail

> DE piano solo.

| .... | DET | Take The "A" Train |

> Entire band.

....	DET		Take The "A" Train
....	VD	JDB207-207	New World A-Comin'
....	DET		I'm Beginning To See The Light –vJS (w. bond promotion)
....	Pir		Johnny Come Lately
....	DET		Yesterdays –vKD
....	JSo		Let The Zoomers Drool
....	DET		Bond promotion
....	DET		Boy Meets Horn

[1]Complete: "The Wish I Wish Tonight."

23 Jun 1945 (P)
Palace Theater (bc)
Akron, OH

DUKE ELLINGTON & HIS ORCHESTRA
TH SH CA RS RN, JN LB CJ, JHtn JH OH AS HC, DE FG JR SG, JS KD AH.

....	DET	Take The "A" Train
....	Car	Jump For Joy –vRN
....	FR	All At Once
....	DET	Bond promotion
....	FR	Ko-Ko
....	Car	I Should Care
....	FR	Go Away Blues –vJS
....	Car	Tootin' Through The Roof
....	FR	Every Hour On The Hour –vAH
....	DET	I'm Beginning To See The Light –vJS (w. bond promotion)
....	DET	Take The "A" Train

> DE JR SG.

| .... | DET | Take The "A" Train |

> Entire band.

| .... | FR | Blue Belles Of Harlem |
| .... | Car | Body And Soul (w. bond promotion) |

> BS replaces DE.

| .... | DET | The More I See You –vKD |
| .... | DET | Bond promotion |

> DE replaces BS.

....	Car	What Am I Here For?
....	FR	Warm Valley
....	DET	Bond promotion
....	Car	Stompy Jones
....	DET	Take The "A" Train

27 Jun 1945 (P)
U.S. Coast Guard Training Center (bc)
Atlantic City, NJ

DUKE ELLINGTON & HIS ORCHESTRA
TJ SH CA RS RN, JN LB CJ, JHtn JH OH AS HC, DE FG JR SG, JS KD.

....	Tpl	Take The "A" Train
....	Tpl	Suddenly It Jumped
....	AFR	The More I See You –vKD >>>

....	AFR	Kissing Bug –vJS
....	Tpl	Fanfare
....	Tpl	The Mood To Be Wooed
....	Tpl	The "C" Jam Blues

30 Jun 1945   (P)
Apollo Theater (bc)
New York City, NY

DUKE ELLINGTON & HIS ORCHESTRA
TJ SH CA RS RN, JN LB CJ, JHtn JH OH AS HC, DE FG JR SG, JS KD MEtn AH.

....	DET	Take The "A" Train
....	FR	Caravan
....	FR	Fickle Fling
....	DET	Bond promotion
....	DET	Kissing Bug –vJS
....	FR	Honeysuckle Rose
....	FR	Day Dream
....	FR	One O'Clock Jump
....	DET	Bond promotion

> BS replaces DE.

....	DET	There's No You –vKD

> DE piano solo.

....	DET	Take The "A" Train

> Entire band, BS replaces DE.

....	FR	Chelsea Bridge
....	FR	Something To Live For –vMEtn
....	DET	Clementine (w. bond promotion)
....	FR	My Little Brown Book –vAH

> DE replaces BS.

....	FR	Riff Staccato –vRN
....	FR	Carnegie Blues
....	DET	I'm Beginning To See The Light –vJS (w. bond promotion)
....	Car	Old King Dooji
....	DET	Things Ain't What They Used To Be

Jul 1945   (P)
Apollo Theater (bc)
New York City, NY

DUKE ELLINGTON & HIS ORCHESTRA
TJ SH CA RS RN, JN LB CJ, JHtn JH OH AS HC, DE FG JR SG, JS KD MEtn.

> DE piano solo.

....		Sophisticated Lady[1]
....		I Let A Song Go Out Of My Heart

> Entire band.

....		Solitude
....		It Don't Mean A Thing –vJS KD MEtn RN TJ
....		Take The "A" Train

[1] It is questionable if it is DE at the piano for this title.

6 Jul 1945   (P)
Private residence
New York City, NY

DUKE ELLINGTON
Piano solo.

....		Jumpin' Room Only
....		New World A-Comin'
....		Birthday Greetings (to Timme Rosenkrantz) –DE talking

7 Jul 1945   (P)
Radio City, Studio 6B (bc)
New York City, NY

DUKE ELLINGTON & HIS ORCHESTRA
TJ SH CA RS RN, JN LB CJ, JHtn JH OH AS HC, DE FG JR SG, JS MEtn AH.

....	VD		Take The "A" Train
....	FR		Blue Belles Of Harlem
....	FR		I'm Beginning To See The Light –vJS
....	DET		Bond promotion
....	DET		Can't You Read Between The Lines?
....	VD	VP1492[1]	Diminuendo In Blue[2]
....	FR		Carnegie Blues[2]
....	VD	VP1492[1]	Crescendo In Blue[2]
....	DET		Bond promotion
....	DET		The Mood To Be Wooed

> DE JR SG.

....	DET	Take The "A" Train >>>

> BS piano solo.

.... DET   DE explains the Perfume Suite (over background music)
.... DET   Bond promotion

> Entire band, DE added.

                                           THE PERFUME SUITE
.... VD   VP1478   - Balcony Serenade[3]
.... VD[4]   VP1478   - Strange Feeling –vAH
.... VD   VP1479   - Dancers In Love
.... VD   VP1479   - Coloratura

> BS omitted.

.... FR   Hollywood Hangover
.... DET   I Don't Mind –vMEtn
.... VD   JDB209   Ring Dem Bells –vRN
.... DET   Things Ain't What They Used To Be

[1]Besides the VD number, these titles have also the master #D5TC588.
[2]Announced as "The Trio Of The Blues."
[3]aka "Under The Balcony"; sa "Sonata."
[4]On VD and subsequent reissues the vcl portion has been edited out; also the spoken introduction by DE differs from what is on the original Treasury broadcast, and consequently on the DET label.

14 Jul 1945   (P)
RKO Theater (bc)
Boston, MA

DUKE ELLINGTON & HIS ORCHESTRA
TJ SH CA RS RN, JN LB CJ, JHtn JH OH AS HC, DE FG JR SG, JS KD AH.

.... DET   Take The "A" Train
.... DET   In The Shade Of The Old Apple Tree

> BS replaces DE.

.... DET   Kissing Bug –vJS
.... DET   Bond promotion

> DE replaces BS.

.... DET   Bugle Breaks
.... DET   A Friend Of Yours
.... DET   West Indian Dance
.... DET   Bond promotion

> BS replaces DE.

.... DET   Tonight I Shall Sleep –vAH

> DE replaces BS.

.... DET   Stomp, Look And Listen
.... DET   I'm Beginning To See The Light
.... DET   Take The "A" Train

> BS added.

                                           THE MAGAZINE SUITE
.... Car   - Down Beat Shuffle
.... JSo   - Esquire Swank
.... Car   - Metronome All-Out (w. bond promotion)[1]

> BS omitted.

.... DET   If You Are But A Dream –vKD
.... Car   Blutopia
.... Car   Candy –vRN
.... DET   Bond promotion
.... DET   Main Stem
.... DET   Take The "A" Train

[1]This title is a derivative of part 2 of *Frankie And Johnny* (the extended version).

21 Jul 1945   (S)
Fieldston Ballroom (bc)
Marshfield, MA

DUKE ELLINGTON & HIS ORCHESTRA
TJ SH CA RS RN, JN LB CJ, JHtn JH OH AS HC, DE FG JR SG, JS KD AH.

.... DET   Take The "A" Train
.... DET   In A Mellotone
.... DET   The Wish I Wish –vJS
.... DET   Bond promotion
.... DET   The "C" Jam Blues
.... DET   Ultra Violet
.... DET   There's No You –vKD
.... DET   Emancipation Celebration   >>>

....	DET	Bond promotion
....	DET	Don't Get Around Much Anymore –vAH
....	DET	Let The Zoomers Drool

> DE JR SG.

....	DET	Take The "A" Train

> Entire band.

....	DET	Reminiscing In Tempo
....	DET	Everything But You (w. bond promotion)
....	DET	Ko-Ko
....	DET	The Mood To Be Wooed
....	DET	Tea For Two
....	DET	Bond promotion
....	DET	Blues On The Double
....	DET	Things Ain't What They Used To Be

No audience in attendance.

<table>
<tr><td></td><td></td><td></td><td>24 Jul 1945   (S)</td></tr>
</table>

DUKE ELLINGTON & HIS FAMOUS ORCHESTRA   24th St., Studio 2
TJ SH CA RS RN, JN LB CJ, JHtn JH OH AS HC, DE FG JR AL SG, AH.   New York City, NY

			THE PERFUME SUITE[1]
....	Vi	D5VB-505-1	2 Strange Feeling –vAH
....	Vi	D5VB-506-1	4 Coloratura
....	Vi	D5VB-507-1	1 Balcony Serenade

[1]See also session on 30 Jul 1945.

<table>
<tr><td></td><td></td><td></td><td>28 Jul 1945   (P)</td></tr>
</table>

DUKE ELLINGTON & HIS ORCHESTRA   State Theater (bc)
TJ SH CA RS RN, JN LB CJ, JHtn JH OH AS HC, DE FG JR SG, JS AH.   Hartford, CT

....	DET	Take The "A" Train
....	DET	Teardrops In The Rain
....	DET	Frustration
....	DET	Bond promotion
....	DET	Everything But You –vJS
....	DET	9:20 Special
....	DET	Moon Mist
....	DET	Rockin' In Rhythm
....	DET	Bond promotion
....	DET	Every Hour On The Hour –vAH

> DE JR SG.

....	DET	Take The "A" Train

> Entire band.

....	DET	Medley[1]
....	DET	Bond promotion
....	DET	Trumpet In Spades
....	DET	Just A-Settin' And A-Rockin'
....	DET	Go Away Blues –vJS
....	DET	Bond promotion
....	DET	One O'Clock Jump

[1]Including: In A Sentimental Mood; Black Beauty; Sophisticated Lady; Caravan; Solitude; I Let A Song Go Out Of My Heart.

<table>
<tr><td></td><td></td><td></td><td>30 Jul 1945   (S)</td></tr>
</table>

DUKE ELLINGTON & HIS FAMOUS ORCHESTRA   24th St., Studio 2
TJ SH CA RS RN, JN LB CJ, JHtn JH OH AS HC, DE FG JR SG.   New York City, NY

....	Vi	D5VB-518-1	Time's A-Wastin'[1]
			THE PERFUME SUITE (ctd.)[2]
....	Vi	D5VB-519-1	3 Dancers In Love
....	Vi	D5VB-506-2	4 Coloratura

[1]sa "Things Ain't What They Used To Be."
[2]See also session on 24 Jul 1945.

		THE PERFUME SUITE (summation—original release)
Vi	D5VB-507-1	1 Balcony Serenade
Vi	D5VB-505-1	2 Strange Feeling –vAH
Vi	D5VB-519-1	3 Dancers In Love
Vi	D5VB-506-2	4 Coloratura

DUKE ELLINGTON & HIS ORCHESTRA
TJ SH CA RS RN, JN LB CJ, JHtn JH OH AS HC, DE FG JR SG.

....	Crl	N-3513-1	Teardrops In The Rain
....	Crl	N-3513-2	Teardrops In The Rain (incomplete)
....	Crl	N-3513-3[1]	Teardrops In The Rain
....	Crl	N-3514-1	Metronome All-Out (incomplete)
....	Crl	N-3514-2[1]	Metronome All-Out
....	Crl	N-3515-1[1]	Esquire Swank
....	Crl	N-3516-1	Down Beat Shuffle (incomplete)
....	Crl	N-3616-2	Down Beat Shuffle (incomplete)
....	Crl	N-3516-3	Down Beat Shuffle (incomplete)
....	JSo	N-3516-4[1]	Down Beat Shuffle
....	Crl	N-3517-1	Riff Staccato –vRN (incomplete)
....	Crl	N-3517-2	Riff Staccato –vRN
....	Crl	N-3517-3[1]	Riff Staccato –vRN

[1]These masters have been released originally on WT.

DUKE ELLINGTON & HIS ORCHESTRA
TJ SH CA RS RN, JN LB CJ, JHtn JH OH AS HC, DE FG JR SG.

....	JUn	Black And Tan Fantasy
....	JUn	The Mood To Be Wooed
....	JUn	Frantic Fantasy
....	JUn	The "C" Jam Blues

> AL added.

....	JUn	Air Conditioned Jungle

> AL omitted.

....	JUn	On The Sunny Side Of The Street
....	JUn	Rockin' In Rhythm
....	JUn	Take The "A" Train

[1]This program "Kings of Jazz" was produced for BBC and aired on 28 Dec 1945.

DUKE ELLINGTON & HIS ORCHESTRA
TJ SH CA RS RN, JN LB CJ, JHtn JH OH AS HC, DE FG JR SG, JS KD AH.

....	DET	Take The "A" Train
....	DET	Dancing In The Dark
....	WL	Down Beat Shuffle
....	DET	Bond promotion
....	DET	Tonight I Shall Sleep –vAH
....	WL	Esquire Swank
....	DET	Creole Love Call –vKD
....	DET	I Miss Your Kiss
....	DET	Riff Staccato (w. bond promotion)

> DE piano solo.

....	DET	Take The "A" Train

> Entire band.

....	DET	Passion Flower
....	DET	Frantic Fantasy
....	DET	Air Conditioned Jungle
....	DET	On The Sunny Side Of The Street
....	WL	Metronome All-Out
....	DET	Everything But You –vJS (w. bond promotion)
....	DET	Solid Old Man

DUKE ELLINGTON & HIS ORCHESTRA
TJ SH CA RS RN, JN LB CJ, JHtn JH OH AS HC, DE FG JR SG, JS AH.

....	Crl	N-3533-1	Ultra Blue[1]
....	ST	N-3533-2[2]	Ultra Blue
....	Crl	N-3534-1[2]	Everything But You –vJS
....	Crl	N-3535-1	Frustration (incomplete)
....	Crl	N-3535-2[2]	Frustration
....	IAC	N-3536-1[2]	Hollywood Hangover
....	Crl	N-3537-1	Blues On The Double (incomplete)
....	Crl	N-3537-2	Blues On The Double
....	IAC	N-3537-3[2]	Blues On The Double >>>

....	Crl	N-3538-1[2]	Kissing Bug –vJS
....	Crl	N-3539-1	Every Hour On The Hour –vAH (incomplete)
....	Crl	N-3539-2	Every Hour On The Hour –vAH
....	Crl	N-3539-3[2]	Every Hour On The Hour –vAH

> BS replaces DE.

....	Crl	N-3540-1	Passion Flower (incomplete)
....	Crl	N-3540-2	Passion Flower (incomplete)
....	Crl	N-3540-3	Passion Flower
....	Crl	N-3540-4	Passion Flower (incomplete)
....	FDC	N-3540-5[2]	Passion Flower

> DE replaces BS.

| .... | IAC | N-3541-1[2] | In A Jam |
| .... | Crl | N-3542-1[2] | In The Shade Of The Old Apple Tree |

[1]sa "Ultra Violet."
[2]These masters have been released originally on WT.

DUKE ELLINGTON & HIS ORCHESTRA
TJ SH CA RS RN, JN LB CJ, JHtn JH OH AS HC, DE FG JR SG, JS KD.

11 Aug 1945   (S)
Radio City, Studio 6B (bc)
New York City, NY

....	DET		Take The "A" Train
....	DET		What Am I Here For?
....	DET		Blue Is The Night

> BS piano solo.

| .... | DET | | Background music (w. bond promotion) |

> Entire band, BS replaces DE.

| .... | DET | | The Wish I Wish –vJS |
| .... | DET | | Someone |

> DE replaces BS.

| .... | DET | | Take The "A" Train |
| .... | DET | | Harlem Air Shaft |

> BS replaces DE.

| .... | DET | | Out Of This World –vKD |

> BS piano solo.

| .... | DET | | Background music (w. bond promotion) |

> Entire band, DE replaces BS.

....	DET		Midriff
....	DET		Everything But You –vJS
....	DET		Ring Dem Bells –vRN
....	DET		The Mood To Be Wooed
....	DET		Bond promotion
....	DET		Emancipation Celebration

18 Aug 1945   (P)
Radio City, Studio 6B (bc)
New York City, NY

DUKE ELLINGTON & HIS ORCHESTRA
TJ SH CA RS RN, JN LB CJ, JHtn JH OH AS HC, DE FG JR SG, JS KD MEtn AH.

....	DET		Take The "A" Train
			BLACK, BROWN AND BEIGE
....	WL		- Work Song
....	DET		Bond promotion
....	DET		- The Blues –vMEtn
....	WL		- West Indian Dance
....	DET		Bond promotion
....	WL		- Come Sunday
....	WL		- Light
....	DET		Take The "A" Train
....	DET		Take The "A" Train
....	DET		Subtle Slough
....	DET		Bond promotion
....	DET		Blue Skies
....	DET		I Ain't Got Nothin' But The Blues –vKD AH
....	DET		Riff Staccato –vRN
....	JSo		Bugle Breaks
....	DET		Kissing Bug –vJS
....	DET		Bond promotion
....	DET		Suddenly It Jumped >>>

.... DET   Warm Valley

                                                                                         20 Aug 1945[1]   (P)
ALL STAR BAND   Private residence
BBly HF BW DBs, SSm, DE AL EN.   New York City, NY

.... JA   The Romp

    > BBly omitted, DGdn added.

.... JA   Honeysuckle Rose

    [1]Contradicting the otherwise reliable liner notes for JA-35, some sources suggest that the material originates from
    "Saturday Night Jam Session and Dance" at the Lincoln Center, NYC.

                                                                                         25 Aug 1945   (P)
DUKE ELLINGTON & HIS ORCHESTRA   Fieldston Ballroom (bc)
TJ SH CA RS RN, JN LB CJ, JHtn JH OH AS HC, DE FG JR SG, JS KD MEtn AH.   Marshfield, MA

.... DET   Take The "A" Train
.... DET   Mood Indigo
.... DET   Bond promotion
.... DET   In A Jam
.... DET   Everything But You –vJS

    > DE BS.

.... DET   Pianistically Allied

    > Entire band, BS replaces DE.

.... DET   I Don't Mind –vMEtn

    > DE replaces BS.

.... DET   Bond promotion
.... DET   The Jeep Is Jumpin'
.... DET   Take The "A" Train
.... DET   Take The "A" Train
.... DET   Black And Tan Fantasy
.... DET   I'm Beginning To See The Light –vJS
.... DET   Bond promotion

    > BS replaces DE.

.... DET   After All

    > DE replaces BS.

.... DET   Don't You Know I Care? –vAH
.... DET   Indiana

    > BS replaces DE.

.... DET   The More I See You –vKD

    > DE replaces BS.

.... DET   Bond promotion
.... DET   Let The Zoomers Drool

                                                                                         29 Aug 1945   (S)
DUKE ELLINGTON   BBC Studios (bc)
DE interviewed by Alistair Cooke.   New York City, NY

....   Interview

                                                                                         1 Sep 1945   (P)
DUKE ELLINGTON & HIS ORCHESTRA   Earle Theater (bc)
TJ SH CA RN, JN LB CJ, JHtn JH OH AS HC, DE FG JR SG, KD AH.   Philadelphia, PA

.... DET   Take The "A" Train
.... DET   On The Alamo
.... DET   Bond promotion
.... DET   Sugar Hill Penthouse
.... DET   Stomp, Look And Listen
.... DET   There's No You –vKD
.... DET   Jumpin' Punkins
.... DET   Body And Soul (w. bond promotion)
.... DET   Take The "A" Train
.... DET   Caravan
.... DET   Flamingo –vAH
.... DET   Air Conditioned Jungle
.... DET   Everything But You (w. bond promotion)   >>>

> DE JR SG.

.... DET   Pitter Panther Patter

> Entire band.

.... DET   One O'Clock Jump
.... DET   Moon Mist
.... DET   Bond promotion
.... DET   Jump For Joy –vRN
.... DET   Take The "A" Train

                                                                                                    8 Sep 1945   (S)
                                                                                                    Radio City, Studio 6B (bc)
DUKE ELLINGTON & HIS ORCHESTRA   New York City, NY
TJ SH CA RS RN, JN LB CJ, JHtn JH OH AS HC, DE FG JR SG, JS KD MEtn AH.

.... DET   Take The "A" Train
.... VD   VP1583   Carnegie Blues
.... DET   Bond promotion
.... DET   I Can't Believe That You're In Love With Me
.... DET   The Mood To Be Wooed
.... VD   VP1583   Kissing Bug –vJS

> BS replaces DE.

.... DET   Chelsea Bridge
.... DET   Bond promotion
.... DET   Something To Live For –vMEtn
.... DET   Clementine

> DE piano solo.

.... DET   Take The "A" Train

> Entire band.

.... DET   Way Low
.... DET   Solid Old Man
.... DET   Bond promotion
.... DET   Summertime –vAH
.... DET   Old King Dooji

> BS, KD.

.... DET   If I Loved You –vKD

> Entire band, DE replaces BS.

.... VD   JDB111   Unbooted Character
.... DET   Just A-Settin' And A-Rockin'
.... DET   Bond promotion
.... DET   Hollywood Hangover

                                                                                                    15 Sep 1945   (S)
                                                                                                    Radio City, Studio 6B (bc)
DUKE ELLINGTON & HIS ORCHESTRA   New York City, NY
TJ SH CA RS RN, JN LB CJ, JH OH AS HC, DE FG JR SG, JS KD AH.

.... DET   Take The "A" Train
.... DET   Subtle Slough
.... DET   The "C" Jam Blues
.... DET   Bond promotion
.... DET   Every Hour On The Hour –vAH
.... DET   The Jeep Is Jumpin'
.... DET   Take The "A" Train
.... DET   Creole Love Call –vKD
.... DET   Frankie And Johnny
.... DET   Everything But You –vJS
.... DET   Emancipation Celebration
.... DET   Warm Valley
.... DET   Take The "A" Train

                                                                                                    16 Sep 1945   (P)
                                                                                                    Club Zanzibar (bc)
DUKE ELLINGTON & HIS ORCHESTRA   New York City, NY
TJ SH CA RS RN, JN LB CJ, JHtn JH OH AS HC, DE FG JR SG, KD AH.

....   There's No You –vKD
....   Ko-Ko
....   Flamingo –vAH
....   Rockin' In Rhythm
....   Take The "A" Train

Although the Zanzibar was both club and café, it will in the following be referred to as club only.

17 Sep 1945   (P)
Club Zanzibar (bc)
New York City, NY

DUKE ELLINGTON & HIS ORCHESTRA
TJ SH CA RS RN, JN LB CJ, JHtn JH OH AS HC, DE FG JR SG, JS AH.

....   Midriff
....   Carnegie Blues
....   Everything But You –vJS
....   Teardrops In The Rain
....   The Mood To Be Wooed
....   The "C" Jam Blues
....   I Got It Bad –vAH
> DE JR SG.
....   Pitter Panther Patter
> Entire band.
....   Hollywood Hangover

18 Sep 1945[1]   (P)
Club Zanzibar (bc)
New York City, NY

DUKE ELLINGTON & HIS ORCHESTRA
TJ SH CA RS RN, JN LB CJ, JHtn JH OH AS HC, DE FG JR SG, JS AH.

.... Joy   Take The "A" Train
.... Joy   As Long As I Live
.... Joy   9:20 Special
.... Joy   The Wonder Of You –vJS
.... Joy   Walkin' With My Honey
.... Joy   Three Cent Stomp
.... Joy   Don't Take Your Love From Me –vAH
.... Joy   Court Session

[1]Broadcast on 18 Nov 1945.

20 Sep 1945   (P)
Club Zanzibar (bc)
New York City

DUKE ELLINGTON & HIS ORCHESTRA
TJ SH CA RS RN, JN LB CJ, JHtn JH OH AS HC, DE FG JR SG, JS AH.

....   Take The "A" Train
....   Caravan
....   Teardrops In The Rain
....   My Heart Sings –vJS
....   9:20 Special
....   Frustration
....   Johnny Come Lately
....   Tonight I Shall Sleep –vAH
....   Harlem Air Shaft
....   Take The "A" Train

21 Sep 1945[1]
Club Zanzibar (bc)
New York City, NY

DUKE ELLINGTON & HIS ORCHESTRA
TJ SH CA RS RN, JN LB CJ, JHtn JH OH AS HC, DE FG JR SG, JS AH.

.... Joy   Take The "A" Train[2]
.... Joy   Midriff
.... Joy   A Door Will Open
.... Joy   My Little Brown Book –vAH
.... Joy   Stomp, Look And Listen
.... Joy   Waiting For The Train To Come In
.... Joy   Diminuendo In Blue
.... Joy   Rocks In My Bed –vJS
.... Joy   Crescendo In Blue
.... Joy   Everything But You

[1]Broadcast on 21 Oct 1945.
[2]Incomplete; a longer but also incomplete version can be found on GoJ.

22 Sep 1945   (S)
Radio City, Studio 6B (bc)
New York City, NY

DUKE ELLINGTON & HIS ORCHESTRA
TJ SH CA RS RN, JN LB CJ, JHtn JH OH AS HC, DE FG JR SG, JS KD.

.... DET   Someone
.... DET   Riff Staccato –vRN
.... DET   Homesick—That's All
.... DET   Kissing Bug –vJS
.... DET   Take The "A" Train
.... DET   Take The "A" Train
.... DET   Time's A-Wastin'
.... DET   Bond promotion
.... DET   Three Cent Stomp   >>>

     > BS replaces DE.

.... DET   There's No You –vKD

     > DE replaces BS.

.... DET   Fancy Dan
.... DET   Everything But You –vJS
.... DET   Fickle Fling
.... DET   Bond promotion
.... DET   Blue Serge

23 Sep 1945   **(S)**
NBC Studios (bc)
New York City, NY

DUKE ELLINGTON & TOMMY DORSEY WITH LOU BRING & HIS ORCHESTRA
DE with Lou Bring & His Orchestra.

.... AFR   Conversation between DE and TD
.... AFR   Solitude
.... AFR   Conversation between DE and TD

     > TD added.

.... AFR   The Minor Goes Muggin'

The above are the portions of the program DE participated in.

DUKE ELLINGTON & HIS ORCHESTRA
TJ SH CA RS RN, JN LB CJ, JHtn JH OH AS HC, DE FG JR SG.

                       Club Zanzibar (bc)   **(P)**

....   Take The "A" Train
....   Subtle Slough
....   I'd Do It All Over Again
....   Three Cent Stomp
....   Love Letters
....   Riff Staccato –vRN
....   I'll Buy That Dream
....   Cotton Tail
....   Way Low

24 Sep 1945   **(P)**
Club Zanzibar (bc)
New York City, NY

DUKE ELLINGTON & HIS ORCHESTRA
SH CA RS RN, JN LB CJ, JHtn JH OH AS HC, DE FG JR SG, JS KD AH.

.... DET   Take The "A" Train
.... DET   Stompy Jones
.... DET   Walkin' With My Honey
.... DET   Lily Belle[1]
.... DET   Everything But You –vJS
.... DET   In A Mellotone
.... DET   Solid Old Man
.... DET   I Ain't Got Nothin' But The Blues –vKD AH
.... DET   Blue Skies
.... DET   Suddenly It Jumped
.... DET   Take The "A" Train

[1]Variant spelling: "Lilly Belle."

26 Sep 1945   **(P)**
Club Zanzibar (bc)
New York City, NY

DUKE ELLINGTON & HIS ORCHESTRA
TJ SH CA RS RN, JN LB CJ, JHtn JH OH AS HC, DE FG JR SG, JS.

.... DET   Take The "A" Train
.... DET   Suddenly It Jumped
.... DET   Laura
.... DET   Kissing Bug –vJS
.... DET   Stompy Jones
.... DET   Solid Old Man
.... DET   Carnegie Blues
.... DET   In A Mellotone
.... DET   Fancy Dan
.... DET   Things Ain't What They Used To Be

28 Sep 1945   **(P)**
Club Zanzibar (bc)
New York City, NY

DUKE ELLINGTON & HIS ORCHESTRA
TJ SH CA RS RN, JN LB CJ, JHtn JH OH AS HC, DE FG JR SG, JS.

....   Take The "A" Train
....   Walkin' With My Honey
....   Lily Belle
....   Everything But You –vJS
....   I Can't Believe That You're In Love With Me

DUKE ELLINGTON & HIS ORCHESTRA
TJ SH CA RS RN, JN LB CJ, JHtn JH OH AS HC, DE FG JR SG, JS KD.

....	BMG	Take The "A" Train
....	BMG	Caravan
....	BMG	Three Cent Stomp
....	BMG	Yesterdays –vKD
....	BMG	Things Ain't What They Used To Be
....	BMG	Blues On The Double
....	BMG	Kissing Bug –vJS
....	BMG	Riff Staccato –vRN
....	BMG	Cotton Tail

DUKE ELLINGTON & HIS ORCHESTRA
TJ SH CA RS, JN LB CJ, JHtn JH OH AS HC, DE FG JR SG, JS.

....	Take The "A" Train
....	I'd Do It All Over Again
....	Homesick—That's All
....	Go Away Blues –vJS
....	It Don't Mean A Thing –vTJ

DUKE ELLINGTON & HIS ORCHESTRA
TJ SH CA RS, JN LB CJ, JHtn JH OH AS HC, DE FG JR SG, JS KD AH.

....	DET	Take The "A" Train
....	DET	Main Stem
....	DET	Carnegie Blues
....	DET	I Can't Believe That You're In Love With Me
....	DET	Bond promotion
....	DET	What Am I Here For?
....	DET	Lily Belle
....	DET	Homesick—That's All
....	DET	Go Away Blues –vJS
....	DET	Frantic Fantasy
....	DET	If You Are But A Dream –vKD
....	DET	Bond promotion
....	DET	Jack The Bear
....	DET	Every Hour On The Hour –vAH
....	DET	Cotton Tail
....	DET	Way Low[1]
....	DET	Bond promotion
....	DET	Teardrops In The Rain
....	DET	I Ain't Got Nothin' But The Blues –vKD AH
....	DET	Things Ain't What They Used To Be

[1]Announced as "Lament In A Minor Mood."

DUKE ELLINGTON & HIS ORCHESTRA
TJ SH CA RS, JN LB CJ, JHtn JH OH AS HC, DE FG JR SG, JS AH.

....	Joy	Take The "A" Train
....	Joy	Love Letters
....	Joy	Main Stem
....	Joy	Wishing For The Moon[2]
....	Joy	Riff'n' Drill[3]
....	Joy	Kissing Bug –vJS
....	DET	Suddenly It Jumped
....	DET	Every Hour On The Hour –vAH
....	DET	Cotton Tail
....	DET	Everything But You
....	Joy	Emancipation Celebration
....	Joy	Let The Zoomers Drool

[1]Broadcast on 24 Oct 1945.
[2]"Fishing For The Moon" on Joy.
[3]"Riff 'N' Drill" on Joy; other variant spellings "Riff'n Drill" or "Riff n' Drill."

DUKE ELLINGTON & HIS FAMOUS ORCHESTRA
TJ SH CA RS RN, JN LB CJ, JHtn JH OH AS HC, DE FG JR SCtl, JS

| .... | Vi | D5VB-662-1 | Tell Ya What I'm Gonna Do –vJS |
| .... | Vi | D5VB-663-1 | Come To Baby, Do –vIA |

DUKE ELLINGTON & HIS ORCHESTRA   10 Oct 1945   (P)
TJ SH CA RS, JN LB CJ, JHtn JH OH AS HC, DE FG JR SCtl, JS.   Club Zanzibar (bc)
                                                                           New York City, NY

.... DET   In The Shade Of The Old Apple Tree
.... DET   9:20 Special
.... DET   Tell Ya What I'm Gonna Do –vJS
.... DET   West Indian Dance
.... DET   A Door Will Open
.... MJ   In A Mellotone
.... DET   Everything But You –vJS
.... DET   Solid Old Man
.... DET   Things Ain't What They Used To Be

DUKE ELLINGTON & HIS ORCHESTRA   11 Oct 1945   (P)
TJ SH CA RS, JN LB CJ, JHtn JH OH AS HC, DE FG JR SCtl, JS.   Club Zanzibar (bc)
                                                                           New York City, NY

.... DET   Take The "A" Train
.... DET   Clementine
.... DET   I'll Buy That Dream
.... DET   Come To Baby, Do –vJS
.... DET   Harlem Air Shaft
.... DET   Everything But You

DUKE ELLINGTON & HIS ORCHESTRA   13 Oct 1945   (S)
TJ SH CA RS, JN LB CJ, JHtn JH OH AS HC, DE FG JR SCtl, JS KD AH.   Radio City, Studio 6B (bc)
                                                                           New York City, NY

.... DET   Take The "A" Train
.... JC   Time's A-Wastin'
.... FR   Every Hour On The Hour –vAH
.... DET   Bond promotion
.... FR   Hollywood Hangover
.... JC   Take The "A" Train
.... JC   Autumn Serenade –vJS
.... JC   Hop, Skip And Jump
.... JC   Riding On A Blue Note

    > BS replaces DE.

.... JC   I'll Buy That Dream

    > BS piano solo.

.... DET   Background music (w. bond promotion)

    > Entire band, DE replaces BS.

.... JC   Riff'n' Drill

    > BS replaces DE.

.... DET   Tell Ya What I'm Gonna Do –vJS
.... JC   How Deep Is The Ocean

    > DE replaces BS.

.... DET   Mood Indigo
.... JC   Take The "A" Train
.... JC   Diminuendo In Blue
.... JC   I Got It Bad –vAH
.... JC   Crescendo In Blue
.... DET   Everything But You –vJS (w. bond promotion)
.... JSo   Between The Devil And The Deep Blue Sea

    > BS replaces DE.

.... JC   After All
.... DET   Out Of This World –vKD

    > DE replaces BS.

.... DET   The "C" Jam Blues
.... DET   Take The "A" Train

DUKE ELLINGTON & HIS ORCHESTRA   Oct 1945   (S)
TJ SH CA RS, JN LB CJ, JHtn JH OH AS HC, DE FG JR SG.   Club Zanzibar (bc)
                                                                           New York City, NY

....   Stomp, Look And Listen

DUKE ELLINGTON & HIS ORCHESTRA
TJ SH CA RS, JN LB CJ, JHtn JH OH AS HC, DE FG JR SG, JS.

.... BMG   I'll Buy That Dream
.... BMG   Fickle Fling
.... BMG   Autumn Serenade –vJS
.... BMG   How Deep Is The Ocean

DUKE ELLINGTON & HIS ORCHESTRA
TJ SH CA RS, JN LB CJ, JHtn JH OH AS HC, DE FG JR SG.

.... DET   Take The "A" Train
.... DET   A Door Will Open
.... DET   Lily Belle
.... DET   West Indian Dance
.... DET   Waiting For The Train To Come In
.... DET   Blues On The Double

DUKE ELLINGTON & HIS ORCHESTRA
TJ SH CA RS, JN LB CJ, JHtn JH OH AS HC, DE FG JR SG, JS KD AH.

.... QuD   Take The "A" Train
.... QuD   Ultra Blue
.... QuD   Teardrops In The Rain
.... QuD   Time On My Hands
.... DET   Riff Staccato –vJS
.... DET   Take The "A" Train
.... QuD   Ko-Ko

    > BS, KD.

.... QuD   If I Loved You –vKD

    > Entire band, DE replaces BS.

.... DET   Bond promotion
.... DET   Subtle Slough

    > RP added.

.... QuD   Honeysuckle Rose
.... QuD   Perdido

    > RP omitted.

.... QuD   Air Conditioned Jungle
.... DET   Take The "A" Train
.... DET   Take The "A" Train
.... QuD   Waiting For The Train To Come In
.... QuD   I'd Do it All Over Again
.... DET   Bond promotion
.... QuD   Fancy Dan
.... QuD   Homesick—That's All
.... QuD   Blues On The Double
.... DET   Every Hour On The Hour –vAH

    > BS piano solo.

.... DET   Background music (w. bond promotion)

    > Entire band, DE replaces BS.

.... QuD   Caravan
.... DET   Riff 'n' Drill
.... DET   Things Ain't What They Used To Be

DUKE ELLINGTON & HIS ORCHESTRA
TJ SH CA RS, JN LB CJ, JHtn JH OH AS HC, DE FG JR SG, JS.

.... DET   Take The "A" Train
.... DET   Fancy Dan
.... DET   Walkin' With My Honey
.... DET   Go Away Blues –vJS
.... DET   Homesick—That's All
.... DET   I'd Do It All Over Again

27 Oct 1945   (S)
Radio City, Studio 6B (bc)
New York City, NY

DUKE ELLINGTON & HIS ORCHESTRA
TJ SH CA RS, JN LB CJ, JHtn JH OH AS HC, DE FG JR SG, JS KD AH.

.... DET   Take The "A" Train
.... DET   Johnny Come Lately
.... DET   I Can't Believe That You're In Love With Me

> BS replaces DE.

.... DET   I'll Buy That Dream

> DE replaces BS.

.... DET   Stomp, Look And Listen
.... DET   Take The "A" Train

> BS replaces DE.

.... DET   The Wonder Of You –vJS[1]

> BS piano solo.

.... DET   Background music (w. bond promotion)

> Entire band, DE replaces BS, GG4 added.

.... DET   Joshua Fit The Battle Of Jericho –vGG4
.... DET   The General Jumped At Dawn –vGG4

> GG4 omitted.

.... DET   The Mood To Be Wooed
.... DET   Three Cent Stomp

> BS replaces DE.

.... DET   Yesterday –vKD

> BS piano solo.

.... DET   Background music (w. bond promotion)

> Entire band, DE replaces BS.

.... DET   Do Nothin' Till You Hear From Me –vAH
.... DET   Stompy Jones
.... DET   Time's A-Wastin'

[1]This title is a derivative of *Everything But You*.

28 Oct 1945   (P)
Club Zanzibar (bc)
New York City, NY

DUKE ELLINGTON & HIS ORCHESTRA
TJ SH CA RS, JN LB CJ, JHtn JH OH AS HC, DE FG JR SG, JS AH.

.... GoJ   Things Ain't What They Used To Be
.... GoJ   In A Mellotone
.... GoJ   The Wonder Of You –vJS
.... GoJ   Riff'n' Drill
.... GoJ   The Last Time I Saw You
.... GoJ   How Deep Is The Ocean
.... GoJ   Riff Staccato –vJS
.... GoJ   Every Hour On The Hour –vAH
.... GoJ   Harlem Air Shaft

"Take The "A" Train" on GoJ lp-1020 dates from 21 Oct 1945.

29 Oct 1945   (P)
Club Zanzibar (bc)
New York City, NY

DUKE ELLINGTON & HIS ORCHESTRA
TJ SH CA RS, JN LB CJ, JHtn JH OH AS HC. DE FG JR SG.

....   Take The "A" Train
....   Stompy Jones
....   I'd Do It All Over Again
....   A Door Will Open
....   It Don't Mean A Thing –vTJ
....   Frantic Fantasy
....   Blue Skies
....   Everything But You

Oct/Nov 1945   (P)
Club Zanzibar (bc)
New York City, NY

DUKE ELLINGTON & HIS ORCHESTRA
TJ SH CA RS, JN LB CJ, JHtn JH OH AS HC, DE FG JR SG, KD AH.

.... AFR   Take The "A" Train
.... DET   Jumpin' Punkins
.... DET   A Door Will Open   >>>

....	DET	West Indian Dance
....	DET	I Ain't Got Nothin' But The Blues –vKD AH
....	DET	Jack The Bear

3 Nov 1945 (S)
Radio City, Studio 6B (bc)
New York City, NY

DUKE ELLINGTON & HIS ORCHESTRA
TJ SH CA RS, JN LB CJ, JHtn JH OH AS HC, DE FG JR SG, JS KD AH.

....	DET	Take The "A" Train
....	DET	Clementine
....	DET	The Jeep Is Jumpin'
....	DET	Don't Take Your Love From Me –vAH
....	DET	It Don't Mean A Thing –vTJ

> BS piano solo.

....	DET	Background music (w. bond promotion)

> Entire band.

....	DET	If You Are But A Dream –vKD

> DE replaces BS.

....	DET	Emancipation Celebration

> MT added.

....	DET	Caldonia –vMT

> MT omitted.

....	DET	Ring Dem Bells –vTJ
....	DET	Take The "A" Train
....	DET	A Door Will Open

> BS piano solo.

....	DET	Background music (w. bond promotion)

> Entire band, DE replaces BS.

....	DET	Court Session
....	DET	That's For Me
....	DET	On The Atchison, Topeka And Santa Fe

> BS replaces DE.

....	DET	Every Hour On The Hour –vAH
....	DET	Bond promotion

> DE replaces BS.

....	DET	How Deep Is The Ocean
....	DET	Victory Drive –vJS
....	DET	Autumn Serenade –vJS
....	DET	Take The "A" Train

10 Nov 1945 (S)
Radio City, Studio 6B (bc)
New York City, NY

DUKE ELLINGTON & HIS ORCHESTRA
TJ SH CA RS, JN LB CJ, JHtn JH OH AS HC, DE FG LT SG, JS KD AH.

....	DET	Take The "A" Train
....	DET	Just A-Settin' And A-Rockin'
....	DET	Take The "A" Train
....	DET	9:20 Special

> BS replaces DE.

....	DET	Frustration

> BS piano solo.

....	DET	Background music (w. bond promotion)

> Entire band, DE replaces BS.

....	DET	Jennie[1]
....	DET	Dancing In The Dark –vKD
....	DET	Crosstown
....	DET	Passion Flower

> DE piano solo.

....	DET	Background music (w. bond promotion)

> Entire band.

....	DET	Victory Drive –vJS >>>

> MT added.

.... DET   Get On Board, Little Children –vMT

> MT omitted.

.... GoJ   Take The "A" Train
.... DET   Come Sunday
.... GoJ   Light

> BS piano solo.

.... DET   Background music (w. bond promotion)

> Entire band, DE replaces BS.

.... GoJ   11:60 p.m. –vJS
.... GoJ   Tell It To A Star
.... GoJ   I Ain't Got Nothin' But The Blues –vKD AH
.... GoJ   Cotton Tail
.... DET   Waiting For The Train To Come In
.... DET   The Star Spangled Banner

¹Variant spelling "Jenny."

DUKE ELLINGTON & HIS ORCHESTRA
TJ SH CA RS, WDP LB CJ, JHtn JH OH AS HC, DE FG OP SG, JS.

17 Nov 1945   (S)
Radio City, Studio 6B (bc)
New York City, NY

.... DET   Take The "A" Train
.... DET   Walkin' With My Honey
.... DET   Jack The Bear
.... DET   Autumn Serenade –vJS

> BS piano solo.

.... DET   Background music (w. bond promotion)

> Entire band, DE replaces BS.

.... DET   Tell It To A Star

> MT added.

.... DET   Hey, Diddle Diddle –vMT

> MT omitted.

.... DET   I Can't Begin To Tell You
.... DET   How Deep Is The Ocean
.... DET   The Wonder Of You –vJS
.... DET   Victory Drive –vJS
.... DET   As Long As I Live
.... DET   Take The "A" Train

DUKE ELLINGTON & HIS ORCHESTRA
TJ SH CA RS, WDP LB CJ, JHtn JH OH AS HC, DE FG OP SG, JS.

Nov 1945   (P)
Club Zanzibar (bc)
New York City, NY

.... DET   Take The "A" Train
.... DET   Just A-Settin' And A-Rockin'
.... DET   Clementine
.... DET   The Wonder Of You –vJS
.... Ffr   I'll Buy That Dream
.... DET   Come To Baby, Do –vJS

DUKE ELLINGTON & HIS ORCHESTRA
TJ SH CA RS, WDP LB CJ, JHtn JH OH AS HC, DE FG OP SG, JS KD AH.

24 Nov 1945   (S)
Radio City, Studio 6B (bc)
New York City, NY

.... DET   Take The "A" Train
.... JSo   Way Low
.... JSo   The "C" Jam Blues
.... DET   Kissing Bug –vJS

> BS piano solo.

.... DET   Background music (w. bond promotion)

> Entire band, DE replaces BS.

.... DET   Just A-Settin' And A-Rockin'

> MT added.

.... DET   Caldonia –vMT   >>>

> MT omitted.

.... DET   Fancy Dan
.... DET   I'm Just A Lucky So-And-So –vAH
.... DET   Take The "A" Train
.... DET   Take The "A" Train
.... DET   The Last Time I Saw You
.... DET   On The Atchison, Topeka And Santa Fe

> BS piano solo.

.... DET   Background music (w. bond promotion)

> KD added.

.... DET   If I Loved You –vKD

> Entire band, DE replaces BS.

.... DET   I Can't Begin To Tell You
.... DET   The Wonder Of You –vJS
.... DET   Riff'n' Drill

| | | | 25 Nov 1945 | (S) |

DUKE ELLINGTON & TOMMY DORSEY WITH THE JAY BLACKTON ORCHESTRA NBC Studios (bc)
DE and TD with the Jay Blackton Orchestra and chorus. New York City, NY

> DE piano solo.

.... AFR   Take The "A" Train
.... AFR   Dancers In Love

> TD, JBO added.

.... AFR   Medley –vChorus[1]

[1]Including: Sophisticated Lady; Solitude –vChorus; Caravan; Mood Indigo –vChorus; It Don't Mean A Thing –vChorus.

26 Nov 1945   (S)
DUKE ELLINGTON & HIS FAMOUS ORCHESTRA   24th St., Studio 2
TJ SH CA RS, WDP LB CJ, JHtn JH RP AS HC, DE FG OP SG, JS AH.   New York City, NY

.... Vi   D5VB-949-1   I'm Just A Lucky So-And-So –vAH
.... Vi   D5VB-950-1   Long, Strong And Consecutive –vJS

> BS replaces DE.

.... Vi   D5VB-951-1   The Wonder Of You –vJS

28 Nov 1945   (P)
DUKE ELLINGTON & HIS ORCHESTRA   Club Zanzibar (bc)
TJ SH CA RS, WDP LB CJ, JHtn JH OH AS HC, DE FG OP SG, JS.   New York City, NY

.... DET   Crosstown
.... DET   The Wonder Of You –vJS
.... DET   Cotton Tail
.... DET   I'm Just A Lucky So-And-So
.... DET   Time's A-Wastin'
.... DET   Three Cent Stomp
.... DET   Long, Strong And Executive –vJS
.... DET   Blue Skies
.... DET   Everything But You

Late Nov 1945   (P)
DUKE ELLINGTON & HIS ORCHESTRA   Club Zanzibar (bc)
TJ SH CA RS, WDP LB CJ, JHtn JH OH AS HC, DE FG JR SG.   New York City, NY

.... AFR   Take The "A" Train
.... AFR   I'll Buy That Dream
.... AFR   Tell It To A Star
.... AFR   Stomp, Look And Listen
.... AFR   Autumn Serenade

3 Dec 1945   (P)
DUKE ELLINGTON & HIS ORCHESTRA   Club Zanzibar (bc)
TJ SH CA RS, WDP LB CJ, JHtn JH OH AS HC, DE FG JR SG.   New York City, NY

....   Caravan
....   I Can't Begin To Tell You
....   As Long As I Live

29 Dec 1945 (P)
Queensway Ballroom (bc)
Toronto, ON

DUKE ELLINGTON & HIS ORCHESTRA
TJ SH CA FW, WDP LB CJ, JHtn JH OH AS HC, DE FG OP SG, JS.

....		Take The "A" Train
....		Teardrops In The Rain
....		Creole Love Call
....		The Wonder Of You –vJS
....		The "C" Jam Blues
....		Cotton Tail
....		Magenta Haze
....		Blue Skies

4 Jan 1946 (P)
Carnegie Hall
New York City, NY

DUKE ELLINGTON & HIS ORCHESTRA
TJ SH CA FW, WDP LB CJ, JHtn JH OH AS HC, DE FG OP SG, JS KD AH.

....		The Star Spangled Banner
....	Pre	Caravan
....	Pre	In A Mellotone
....	Pre	Solid Old Man
		BLACK, BROWN AND BEIGE
....	Pre	- Spiritual Theme
....	Pre	- Work Song
....	Pre	- The Blues –vJS
....	Pre	Rugged Romeo
....	Pre	Sono
....	Pre	Air Conditioned Jungle
....		Dancers In Love
....		Coloratura
....		Frankie And Johnny
....	Pre	Take The "A" Train
		A TONAL GROUP
....	Pre	- Meloditty
....	Pre	- Fugue-A-Ditty
....	Pre	- Jam-A-Ditty[1]
....	Pre	Pitter Panther Patter
....	Pre	Diminuendo In Blue
....	Pre	Transblucency –vKD[2]
....	Pre	Crescendo In Blue
....	Pre	Magenta Haze
....	Pre	The Suburbanite
....		My Little Brown Book –vAH
....		Nobody Knows The Trouble I've Seen –vAH
....		Fat And Forty –vAH
....	Pre	I'm Just A Lucky So-And-So –vAH
....	Pre	Riff'n' Drill

[1]Described as "A Quartet Of Jazz Horns."
[2]Subtitled "A Blue Fog You Can Almost See Through"; this title is a derivative of *Blue Light*.

10 Jan 1946 (S)
24th St., Studio 1
New York City, NY

DUKE ELLINGTON & BILLY STRAYHORN
DE BS.

....	Vi	D6VB-1518-1	Tonk[1]
....	Vi	D6VB-1519-1	Drawing Room Blues

[1]*aka* "Sweet William Bauet"; *sa* "Pianistically Allied."

10+11 Jan 1946 (S)
24th St., Studio 1
New York City, NY

LEONARD FEATHER'S ESQUIRE ALL AMERICANS
LA ChS, JHtn JH DBs, DE BS RPlm ChJ SG.

....	Vi	PD6VC-5020-1[1]	Long, Long Journey –vLA

> ChS omitted, NH added.

....	Vi	PD6VC-5021-1	Snafu

> ChS, JHtn JH DBs, RNrv DE BS RPlm ChJ SG.

....	Vi	PD6VC-5022-1	The One That Got Away

> JH DBs, BS RPlm ChJ SG.

....	Vi	PD6VC-5023-1	Gone With The Wind

[1]Contrary to sleeve notes for RCA/Vi (F) PM 42397 there is no take 2 of this title.

METRONOME ALL STARS
HE PCnd NH SBrm, TD BHrs JCH, BDF JH HF FP GA HC, RNrv TW TGrs BBr ChJ DT,
DE directing.

.... Vi   D6VC-5027-2   Metronome All-Out

15 Jan 1946   (S)
24th St., Studio 2
New York City, NY

DUKE ELLINGTON & HIS ORCHESTRA
TJ SH CA FW BFld, WDP LB CJ, JHtn JH OH AS HC, DE FG OP SG.

....   Take The "A" Train
.... Sn   Take The "A" Train
.... Sn   Honeysuckle Rose
.... Sn   Jam-A-Ditty
.... VD   JDB25   Esquire Swank

> FWne added.

.... Sn   I'm Checkin' Out, Go'om-Bye –vFWne

16 Jan 1946   (P)
Ritz Theater (bc)
New York City, NY

DUKE ELLINGTON'S & WOODY HERMAN'S COMBINED ORCHESTRAS
Woody Herman & His Orchestra added, FWne omitted, otherwise same personnel.

.... VD   JDB67   The "C" Jam Blues

The above comprises only the Ellington portion of the concert.

DUKE ELLINGTON & HIS ORCHESTRA
TJ SH CA FW BFld, WDP LB CJ, JHtn JH OH AS HC, DE FG OP SG, KD AH.

.... JHtg   The Star Spangled Banner
.... JHtg   Caravan
.... JHtg   In A Mellotone
....   Solid Old Man

                             BLACK, BROWN AND BEIGE
.... JHtg   - Spiritual Theme
.... JHtg   - Work Song
....   - The Blues –vKD

.... JHtg   Rugged Romeo
.... DET   Sono
.... DET   Air Conditioned Jungle
.... JHtg   Circe
.... JHtg   Dancers In Love
.... JHtg   Coloratura
.... JHtg   Frankie And Johnny
.... JHtg   Take The "A" Train

                             A TONAL GROUP
.... JHtg   - Rhapsoditty[1]
.... JHtg   - Fugue-A-Ditty
.... JHtg   - Jam-A-Ditty

.... JHtg   Magenta Haze
....   Diminuendo In Blue
....   Transblucency –vKD
....   Crescendo In Blue
....   Pitter Panther Patter
.... JHtg   The Suburbanite
....   My Little Brown Book –vAH
....   Every Hour On The Hour –vAH
....   I Ain't Got Nothin' But The Blues –vKD AH
....   Fat And Forty –vAH
....   Blue Skies

[1]*sa "Meloditty."*

20 Jan 1946   (P)
Civic Opera House (bc)*
Chicago, IL

DUKE ELLINGTON & HIS ORCHESTRA
AH omitted, otherwise same personnel.

.... DET   Take The "A" Train
.... DET   Jam-A-Ditty
.... DET   Magenta Haze
.... DET   Diminuendo In Blue
.... DET   Transblucency –vKD
.... DET   Crescendo In Blue
.... JHtg   Pitter Panther Patter
....   The Suburbanite

*The broadcast includes selections from both concerts.

<u>DUKE ELLINGTON & HIS ORCHESTRA</u>
TJ SH CA FW BFld, WDP LB CJ, JHtn JH OH AS HC, DE FG OP SG.

> JCte added.

.... AFR   My Blue Heaven –vJCte

> JCte omitted.

.... AFR   Blue Skies

> JCte added.

.... AFR   In The Eyes Of My Irish Colleen –vJCte

> JCte omitted.

.... AFR   I'm Just A Lucky So-And-So

<u>DUKE ELLINGTON & HIS ORCHESTRA</u>
TJ SH CA FW BFld, JN WDP LB CJ, JHtn JH OH AS HC, DE FG EM SG, KD.

.... Plm   Crosstown

> BS replaces DE.

.... BBA   Passion Flower

> DE replaces BS.

.... QuD   Magenta Haze
.... ST   Everything Goes

> OP replaces EM.

.... QuD   The Eighth Veil
.... BBA   Riff'n' Drill
.... BBA   Blue Abandon
.... QuD   Transblucency –vKD
.... QuD   Embraceable You –vKD
.... BBA   Rugged Romeo
.... BBA   Jennie
.... BBA   Sono
.... BBA   The Jeep Is Jumpin'
.... De   Take The "A" Train
.... De   Take The "A" Train
.... ST   Perdido

> DE OP SG.

.... BBA   Tip Toe Topic

The above titles have been recorded originally for CT.

<u>DUKE ELLINGTON & HIS ORCHESTRA</u>
TJ SH CA FW BFld RN, JN WDP LB CJ, JHtn JH OH AS HC, DE FG OP SG.

.... DET   Jam-A-Ditty
.... DET   Blue Is The Night

> BS replaces DE.

.... DET   Passion Flower

<u>DUKE ELLINGTON & HIS ORCHESTRA</u>
TJ SH CA FW RJns RN, JN WDP LB CJ, JHtn JH RP AS HC, DE FG OP SG, KD AH.

.... DET   Take The "A" Train
.... DET   The Mood To Be Wooed
.... DET   Caravan

> BS piano solo.

.... DET   Background music (w. bond promotion)

> Entire band.

.... DET   Don't Take Your Love From Me –vAH

> DE replaces BS.

.... DET   Take The "A" Train
.... DET   The Blues –vKD

> BS piano solo.

.... DET   Background music (w. bond promotion)   >>>

> Entire band, DE replaces BS.

.... DET   Sono
.... JSo   One O'Clock Jump[1]
.... DET   I'm Just A Lucky So-And-So --vAH
.... DET   Bond promotion
.... DET   Riff Staccato --vRN
.... DET   Just A-Settin' And A-Rockin'

[1]"Half Past Midnight Stomp" on JSo.

No audience in attendance.

                                                        27 Apr 1946   (S)

DUKE ELLINGTON & HIS ORCHESTRA   Municipal Auditorium (bc)
TJ SH FW RJns RN, JN WDP LB CJ, JHtn JH RP AS HC, DE FG OP SG, KD AH.   Worcester, MA

.... DET   Take The "A" Train
.... DET   Stompy Jones
.... DET   Moon Mist

> BS piano solo.

.... DET   Background music (w. bond promotion)

> Entire band.

.... DET   Just A-Settin' And A-Rockin' --vRN
.... DET   I Can't Believe That You're In Love With Me

> DE OP SG.

.... DET   Sophisticated Lady

> BS piano solo.

.... DET   Background music (w. bond promotion)

> Entire band, DE replaces BS.

.... DET   Jennie
.... DET   I'm Just A Lucky So-And-So --vAH
.... DET   Come Sunday
.... DET   Light

> BS piano solo.

.... DET   Background music (w. bond promotion)

> Entire band.

.... DET   We'll Be Together Again --vKD

> DE replaces BS.

.... DET   Hollywood Hangover
.... DET   Subtle Slough

> BS piano solo.

.... DET   Background music (w. bond promotion)

> Entire band, DE replaces BS.

.... DET   Perdido

No audience in attendance.

                                                        4 May 1946   (S)

DUKE ELLINGTON & HIS ORCHESTRA   Webster Hall, Dartmouth College (bc)
TJ SH CA FW RJns RN, JN WDP LB CJ, JHtn JH RP AS HC, DE FG OP SG, KD AH.   Hanover, NH

.... DET   Take The "A" Train
.... DET   Just A-Settin' And A-Rockin' --vRN

> BS piano solo.

.... DET   Background music (w. bond promotion)

> Entire band, DE replaces BS.

.... DET   9:20 Special
.... JSo   I Can't Get Started
.... DET   Flamingo --vAH
.... DET   Fancy Dan
.... WL   Diminuendo In Blue
.... WL   Tranblucency --vKD
.... WL   Crescendo In Blue

> BS piano solo.

.... DET   Background music (w. bond promotion)   >>>

> Entire band, DE replaces BS.

.... DET   Someone
.... DET   Three Cent Stomp

> BS piano solo.

.... DET   Background music (w. bond promotion)

> Entire band, DE replaces BS.

.... DET   I'm Just A Lucky So-And-So –vAH

No audience in attendance.

                                                                                 18 May 1946   (S)

DUKE ELLINGTON & HIS ORCHESTRA   Radio City, Studio 6B (bc)
TJ SH CA FW RJns RN, JN WDP LB CJ, JHtn JH RP AS HC, DE FG OP SG, KD AH.   New York City, NY

.... DET   In A Mellotone
.... DET   I'm Just A Lucky So-And-So –vAH
.... DET   Sono
.... DET   Rugged Romeo
.... DET   Circe
.... DET   Bond promotion
.... DET   Air Conditioned Jungle

> BS, KD.

.... DET   Full Moon And Empty Arms –vKD

> BS piano solo.

.... DET   Background music (w. bond promotion)

> Entire band.

.... DET   Laughing On The Outside[1]

> DE replaces BS.

.... DET   Take The "A" Train

[1]Complete: "Laughing On The Outside, But Crying On The Inside."

The above broadcast was interrupted by three news bulletins which cut off some of the music.

                                                                              25 May 1946   (S)

DUKE ELLINGTON & HIS ORCHESTRA   Radio City, Studio 6B (bc)
TJ SH CA FW RJns RN, JN WDP LB CJ, JHtn JH RP AS HC, DE FG OP SG, AH.   New York City, NY

.... DET   Take The "A" Train
.... DET   Just A-Settin' And A-Rockin' –vRN
.... DET   Crosstown

> BS piano solo.

.... DET   Background music (w. bond promotion)

> Entire band.

.... DET   Summertime –vAH

> DE replaces BS.

.... DET   Teardrops In The Rain
.... DET   Frankie And Johnny

> BS piano solo.

.... DET   Background music (w. bond promotion)

> Entire band, DE replaces BS.

.... DET   Hop, Skip And Jump

                                                              1 Jun 1946   (S)

DUKE ELLINGTON & HIS ORCHESTRA   Rehearsal Hall, Paramount Theater (bc)
TJ SH CA FW RJns RN, JN WDP LB CJ, JHtn JH RP AS HC, DE FG OP SG, KD MC AH.   New York City, NY

.... DET   Take The "A" Train

> BS replaces DE.

.... DET   A Flower Is A Lovesome Thing

> BS piano solo.

.... DET   Background music (w. bond promotion)

> Entire band, DE replaces BS.

.... DET   Main Stem   >>>

.... > BS replaces DE.

.... DET   A Ghost Of A Chance –vMC[1]

.... > BS piano solo.

.... DET   Interview with DE (w. background music)

.... > Entire band, DE replaces BS.

.... DET   In A Jam

.... DET   I'm Just A Lucky So-And-So –vAH

.... DET   Stomp, Look And Listen

.... > BS replaces DE.

.... DET   Come Rain Or Come Shine –vKD

.... > BS piano solo.

.... DET   Background music (w. bond promotion)

.... > Entire band, DE replaces BS.

.... DET   Things Ain't What They Used To Be

[1]Complete: "I Don't Stand A Ghost Of A Chance With You."

No audience in attendance.

DUKE ELLINGTON & HIS ORCHESTRA
TJ SH CA FW RJns RN, JN WDP LB CJ, JHtn JH RP AS HC, DE FG OP SG, KD MC AH.

8 Jun 1946   (S)
Studios WEEU (bc)
Reading, PA

.... DET   Take The "A" Train

.... DET   The Mood To Be Wooed

.... > BS piano solo.

.... DET   Background music (w. bond promotion)

.... > Entire band, DE replaces BS.

.... DET   Johnny Come Lately

.... > BS, KD.

.... DET   They Say It's Wonderful –vKD

.... > Entire band, DE replaces BS.

.... DET   Strange Love

.... DET   Honeysuckle Rose

.... DET   Don't Take Your Love From Me –vAH

.... > BS piano solo.

.... DET   Background music (w. bond promotion)

.... > Entire band, DE replaces BS.

.... DET   Blues On The Double

.... DET   Take The "A" Train

.... DET   Take The "A" Train

.... DET   Come Sunday And Light

.... > BS piano solo.

.... DET   Background music (w. bond promotion)

.... > Entire band.

.... DET   Lover Man –vMC

.... > DE replaces BS.

.... DET   Riff Staccato –vRN

.... DET   Mood Indigo

.... > BS piano solo.

.... DET   Background music (w. bond promotion)

.... > Entire band, DE replaces BS.

.... DET   Riff'n' Drill

DUKE ELLINGTON & HIS ORCHESTRA
TJ SH CA FW RJns RN, JN WDP LB CJ, JHtn JH RP AS HC, DE FG OP SG, KD AH.

6 Jul 1946   (P)
Million Dollar Theater (bc)
Los Angeles, CA

.... DET   Take The "A" Train

.... DET   Caravan

.... DET   Sono   >>>

> BS piano solo.

.... DET   Background music (w. bond promotion)

> Entire band, DE replaces BS.

.... DET   Laughing On The Outside –vAH

> DE piano solo.

.... DET   Take The "A" Train

> Entire band.

.... DET   Take The "A" Train
.... DET   The Blues –vKD
.... DET   Teardrops In The Rain
.... DET   I'm Just A Lucky So-And-So –vAH

> BS piano solo.

.... DET   Background music (w. bond promotion)

> Entire band, DE replaces BS.

.... DET   Metronome All-Out
.... DET   Just A-Settin' And A-Rockin' –vRN
.... DET   One O'Clock Jump

                                                            9 Jul 1946   (S)
DUKE ELLINGTON & HIS ORCHESTRA   Hollywood Recording Studio
TJ SH CA FW HB RN, JN WDP LB CJ, JHtn JH RP AS HC, DE FG OP SG, KD.   Hollywood, CA

.... Vi   D6VB-2093-1   Rockabye River[1]
.... Vi   D6VB-2094-1   Suddenly It Jumped
.... Vi   D6VB-2095-1[2]   Transblucency –vKD
.... Vi   D6VB-2096-1[2]   Just Squeeze Me –vRN[3]

[1]sa "Hop, Skip And Jump."
[2]Contrary to many such claims in sleeve notes and other publications, there are no alternate takes of these titles.
[3]Complete: "Just Sqeeze Me, But Please Don't Tease Me"; sa "Subtle Slough."

                                                            10 Jul 1946   (S)
DUKE ELLINGTON & HIS ORCHESTRA   Hollywood Recording Studio
TJ SH CA FW HB RN, JN WDP LB CJ, JHtn JH RP AS HC, DE FG OP SG, AH.   Hollywood, CA

.... Vi   D6VB-2097-1   A Gathering In A Clearing[1]
.... Vi   D6VB-2098-1   You Don't Love Me No More –vAH
.... Vi   D6VB-2099-1   Pretty Woman –vAH
.... Vi   D6VB-2100-1   Hey, Baby –vRN

[1]aka "Hometown."

                                                            11 Jul 1946   (S)
DUKE ELLINGTON & HIS ORCHESTRA   Capitol Studios
TJ SH CA FW HB RN, JN WDP LB CJ, JHtn JH RP AS HC, DE FG OP SG, KD AH.   Hollywood, CA

.... Plm   Rockabye River
.... BBA   A Gathering In A Clearing
.... ST   You Don't Love Me No More –vAH
.... ST   Pretty Woman –vAH
.... ST   Just Squeeze Me –vRN
.... De   Hey, Baby –vRN
.... BBA   Suddenly It Jumped
.... De   Come Rain Or Come Shine –vKD

The above titles have been recorded originally for Capitol Transcriptions.

                                                            16 Jul 1946   (S)
DUKE ELLINGTON & HIS ORCHESTRA   Capitol Studios
TJ SH CA FW HB RN, JN WDP LB CJ, JHtn JH RP AS HC, DE FG OP SG, MC.   Hollywood, CA

.... ST   Fickle Fling
.... [1]   9:20 Special (incomplete)
.... [1]   9:20 Special (incomplete)
.... [1]   9:20 Special
.... ST   9:20 Special
.... ST   One O'Clock Jump
.... ST   Indiana
.... JSp   A Ghost Of A Chance –vMC
.... JSp   Lover Man –vMC
.... ST   Unbooted Character
.... BBA   The Suburbanite

[1]Acetate extant.

The above titles have been recorded originally for Capitol Transcriptions.

<table>
<tr><td colspan="3"></td><td>17 Jul 1946</td><td>(S)</td></tr>
<tr><td colspan="3"><u>DUKE ELLINGTON & HIS ORCHESTRA</u></td><td>Capitol Studios</td><td></td></tr>
<tr><td colspan="3">TJ SH CA FW HB RN, JN WDP LB CJ, JHtn JH RP AS HC, DE FG OP SG.</td><td>Hollywood, CA</td><td></td></tr>
</table>

....	BBA	Moon Mist
....	BBA	In A Jam
....	ST	On The Alamo
....	ST	I Can't Believe That You're In Love With Me
....	ST	Just You, Just Me
....	ST	Someone
....	ST	Tea For Two
....	ST	Double Ruff

> BS replaces DE.

| .... | BBA | A Flower Is A Lovesome Thing |

> DE replaces BS.

| .... | ST | The Mooche |

The above titles have been recorded originally for Capitol Transcriptions.

<table>
<tr><td colspan="3"></td><td>27 Jul 1946</td><td>(P)</td></tr>
<tr><td colspan="3"><u>DUKE ELLINGTON & HIS ORCHESTRA</u></td><td>Orpheum Theater (bc)</td><td></td></tr>
<tr><td colspan="3">TJ SH CA FW HB RN, WDP LB CJ, JHtn JH RP AS HC, DE FG OP SG, KD AH.</td><td>San Diego, CA</td><td></td></tr>
</table>

....	DET	Take The "A" Train
....	DET	Jump For Joy –vRN
....	DET	A Gathering In A Clearing
....	DET	Bond promotion
....	DET	Come Rain Or Come Shine –vKD
....	DET	Suddenly It Jumped
....	DET	Take The "A" Train
....	DET	Medley[1]
....	DET	Bond promotion
....	DET	Passion Flower
....	DET	Just You, Just Me
....	DET	You Don't Love Me No More –vAH
....	DET	Unbooted Character
....	DET	Bond promotion
....	DET	Cotton Tail

[1]Including: Black And Tan Fantasy; In A Sentimental Mood; Mood Indigo; I'm Beginning To See The Light; Sophisticated Lady; Caravan; Solitude; I Let A Song Go Out Of My Heart/Don't Get Around Much Anymore.

<table>
<tr><td colspan="3"></td><td>3 Aug 1946[1]</td><td>(P)</td></tr>
<tr><td colspan="3"><u>DUKE ELLINGTON & HIS ORCHESTRA</u></td><td>Golden Gate Theater (bc)</td><td></td></tr>
<tr><td colspan="3">TJ SH CA FW HB RN, WDP LB CJ, JHtn JH RP AS HC, DE FG OP SG, KD MC AH.</td><td>San Francisco, CA</td><td></td></tr>
</table>

| .... | DET | Take The "A" Train |
| .... | DET | The Eighth Veil |

> BS piano solo.

| .... | DET | Background music (w. bond promotion) |

> Entire band.

| .... | DET | Lover Man –vMC |

> DE replaces BS.

| .... | DET | Blue Is The Night |
| .... | DET | Just Squeeze Me –vRN |

> BS piano solo.

| .... | DET | Background music (w. bond promotion) |

> Entire band, DE replaces BS.

....	DET	Diminuendo In Blue
....	DET	Transblucency –vKD
....	DET	Crescendo In Blue

> BS piano solo.

| .... | DET | Background music (w. bond promotion) |

> Entire band, DE replaces BS.

| .... | DET | Things Ain't What They Used To Be |
| .... | DET | Take The "A" Train   >>> |

> BS replaces DE.

.... DET   A Flower Is A Lovesome Thing

> BS piano solo.

.... DET   Background music (w. bond promotion)

> Entire band.

.... DET   Hollywood Hangover
.... DET   I Got It Bad –vAH

> DE replaces BS.

.... DET   The Jeep Is Jumpin'

[1]Broadcast on 9 Aug 1946.

                                                                        14 Aug 1946   (T)[1]
                                                                        George Pal Studios
DUKE ELLINGTON & HIS ORCHESTRA   Los Angeles, CA
TJ SH CA FW HB RN, WDP LB CJ, JHtn JH RP AS HC, DE FG OP SG.

....   DE, piano and in conversation with G. Pal's puppets.

> Entire band.

                                     THE PERFUME SUITE
....   - Balcony Serenade

> DE piano solo.

                                     - Strange Feeling

> Entire band.

                                     - Dancers In Love

[1]From the George Pal *Puppetoon* movie short "Date With Duke."

                                                                        Aug 1946   (P)
                                                                        Meadowbrook Gardens Café (bc)
DUKE ELLINGTON & HIS ORCHESTRA   Culver City, CA
TJ SH CA FW HB RN, WDP LB CJ, JHtn JH RP AS HC, DE FG OP SG.

.... AFR   Take The "A" Train
.... AFR   Passion Flower
.... AFR   Teardrops In The Rain
.... AFR   Just Squeeze Me –vRN
.... AFR   Hollywood Hangover

The "Passion Flower" used for the closing is a repeat and therefore not listed again.

                                                                        16 Aug 1946   (P)
                                                                        Meadowbrook Gardens Café (bc)
DUKE ELLINGTON & HIS ORCHESTRA   Culver City, CA
TJ SH CA FW HB RN, WDP LB CJ, JHtn JH RP AS HC, DE FG OP SG, AH.

.... AFR   Take The "A" Train
.... AFR   9:20 Special

> BS replaces DE.

.... AFR   Day Dream

> DE replaces BS.

.... AFR   You Don't Love Me No More –vAH
.... AFR   Metronome All-Out

                                                                        17 Aug 1946   (S)
                                                                        Meadowbrook Gardens Café (bc)
DUKE ELLINGTON & HIS ORCHESTRA   Culver City, CA
TJ SH CA FW HB RN, WDP LB CJ, JHtn JH RP AS HC, DE FG OP SG, KD.

.... DET   Take The "A" Train
.... DET   9:20 Special
.... DET   Day Dream
.... DET   Metronome All-Out
.... DET   Bond promotion

                                     SUITE DITTY[1]
.... DET   - Rhapsoditty
.... DET   - Fugue-A-Ditty
.... DET   - Jam-A-Ditty

> BS piano solo.

.... DET   Background music (w. bond promotion
.... DET   Take The "A" Train   >>>

```
                   > Entire band, DE replaces BS.
...............    DET                     Take The "A" Train
...............    DET                     Just Squeeze Me —vRN
                   > BS piano solo.
...............    DET                     Background music (w. bond promotion)
                   > Entire band, DE replaces BS.
...............    DET                     One O'Clock Jump
                   > BS replaces DE.
...............    DET                     Cynthia's In Love —vKD
                   > DE replaces BS.
...............    DET                     Take The "A" Train
```

¹sa "A Tonal Group."

No audience in attendance.

DUKE ELLINGTON & HIS ORCHESTRA   (P)
KD omitted, otherwise same personnel.

```
...............                            Harlem Air Shaft
...............                            Just Squeeze Me —vRN
...............                            Jumpin' Punkins
...............                            Teardrops In The Rain
...............                            Riff'n' Drill
...............                            Things Ain't What They Used To Be
```

		18 Aug 1946	(P)
		Meadowbrook Gardens Café (bc)	
		Culver City, CA	

DUKE ELLINGTON & HIS ORCHESTRA
SH CA FW HB RN, WDP LB CJ, JHtn JH RP AS HC, DE FG OP SG.

```
...............                            Blue Is The Night
...............                            Rockabye River
...............                            Solid Old Man
...............                            Jack The Bear
...............                            The Suburbanite
...............                            Blue Skies
...............                            Things Ain't What They Used To Be
```

		19 Aug 1946	(P)
		Meadowbrook Gardens Café (bc)	
		Culver City, CA	

DUKE ELLINGTON & HIS ORCHESTRA
TJ SH CA FW HB RN, WDP LB CJ, JHtn JH RP AS HC, DE FG OP SG.

```
...............    Ffr                     9:20 Special
...............    Ffr                     Just Squeeze Me —vRN
```

		22 Aug 1946	(P)
		Meadowbrook Gardens Café (bc)	
		Culver City, CA	

DUKE ELLINGTON & HIS ORCHESTRA
TJ SH CA FW HB RN, WDP LB CJ, JHtn JH RP AS HC, DE FG OP SG.

```
...............                            Indiana
...............                            My Honey's Lovin' Arms —vRN
...............                            Just You, Just Me
```

		24 Aug 1946	(P)
		Meadowbrook Gardens Café (bc)	
		Culver City, CA	

DUKE ELLINGTON & HIS ORCHESTRA
TJ SH CA FW HB RN, WDP LB CJ, JHtn JH RP AS HC, DE FG OP SG, KD AH.

```
                   > DE piano solo.
...............    DET                     Take The "A" Train
...............    DET                     Medley¹
...............    DET                     Background music (w. bond promotion)
                   > OP added.
...............    DET                     Solitude
                   > Entire band.
...............    DET                     Stomp, Look And Listen
...............    DET                     A Gathering In A Clearing
...............    DET                     Cynthia's In Love —vKD
...............    DET                     Bond promotion
...............    DET                     The "C" Jam Blues
...............    DET                     Things Ain't What They Used To Be
...............    DET                     Take The "A" Train
...............    DET                     Rugged Romeo    >>>
```

....	DET	Magenta Haze
....	DET	Bond promotion
....	DET	Jack The Bear
....	DET	The Suburbanite
....	DET	You Don't Love Me No More –vAH
....	DET	Bond promotion
....	DET	Solid Old Man
....	DET	Hollywood Hangover

[1]Including: Mood Indigo; Don't Get Around Much Anymore; Sophisticated Lady.

25 Aug 1946   (S)
NBC Studios (bc)
Hollywood, CA

DUKE ELLINGTON WITH TOMMY DORSEY & HIS ORCHESTRA
DE with Tommy Dorsey & His Orchestra and chorus.

| .... | Joy | Solitude –vChorus |
| .... | Joy | Take The "A" Train |

DUKE ELLINGTON & HIS ORCHESTRA
TJ SH CA FW HB RN, WDP LB CJ, JHtn JH RP AS HC, DE FG OP SG.

Meadowbrook Gardens Café (bc)   (P)
Culver City, CA

....	Magenta Haze
....	Take The "A" Train
....	Rugged Romeo
....	Solid Old Man
....	Hollywood Hangover
....	Things Ain't What They Used To Be

26 Aug 1946   (S)
Hollywood Recording Studio
Hollywood, CA

DUKE ELLINGTON & HIS ORCHESTRA
TJ SH CA FW HB RN, WDP LB CJ, JHtn JH RP AS HC, DE FG OP SG, MC.

....	Vi	D6VB-2113-1	Indiana
....	Vi	D6VB-2114-1	Blue Is The Night
....	Vi	D6VB-2115-1	Lover Man –vMC
....	Vi	D6VB-2115-2	Lover Man –vMC
....	Vi	D6VB-2116-1	Just You, Just Me
....	Vi	D6VB-2117-1	Beale Street Blues

31 Aug 1946   (P)
Lincoln Theater (bc)
Los Angeles, CA

DUKE ELLINGTON & HIS ORCHESTRA
TJ SH CA FW HB RN, WDP LB CJ, JHtn JH RP AS HC, DE FG OP SG, KD MC AH.

....	DET	Take The "A" Train
....	DET	My Honey's Lovin' Arms –vRN
....	DET	Warm Valley
....	DET	Bond promotion
....	DET	Jumpin' Punkins
....	DET	Come Rain Or Come Shine –vKD
....	DET	Swamp Fire
....	DET	Pretty Woman –vAH

> BS piano solo.

| .... | DET | Background music (w. bond promotion) |

> Entire band, DE replaces BS.

....	DET	Moon Mist
....	DET	Take The "A" Train
....	DET	Take The "A" Train
....	DET	Memphis Blues
....	DET	Beale Street Blues
....	DET	St. Louis Blues –vMC

> BS piano solo.

| .... | DET | Background music (w. bond promotion) |

> Entire band, DE added.

| .... | DET | Three Cent Stomp |

> BS omitted.

| .... | DET | Just Squeeze Me –vRN |

> BS piano solo.

| .... | DET | Background music (w. bond promotion) |

> Entire band, DE added.

| .... | DET[1] | Blues On The Double[2]   >>> |

> BS omitted.

.... DET   Things Ain't What They Used To Be

[1]The original release on JSo (78rpm) is incomplete.
[2]"Blues On The Down Beat" on JSo.

				3 Sep 1946 (S)

DUKE ELLINGTON & HIS ORCHESTRA
Hollywood Recording Studio
Hollywood, CA
TJ SH CA FW HB RN, WDP LB CJ, JHtn JH RP AS HC, DE FG OP SG, MC.

....	Vi	D6VB-2126-1	My Honey's Lovin' Arms –vRN
....	Vi	D6VB-2127-1	Memphis Blues
....	Vi	D6VB-2128-1	A Ghost Of A Chance –vMC
....	Vi	D6VB-2129-1	St. Louis Blues –vMC
....	Vi	D6VB-2130-1	Swamp Fire
....	Vi	D6VB-2131-1	Royal Garden Blues
....	Sw	D6VB-2132-1	Esquire Swank
....	Sw	D6VB-2133-1	Midriff

3 Oct 1946 (P)
Aquarium Restaurant (bc)
New York City, NY

DUKE ELLINGTON & HIS ORCHESTRA
TJ SH CA FW HB RN, WDP LB CJ, JHtn JH RP AS HC, DE FG OP SG.

....		Take The "A" Train
....		Jam-A-Ditty
....		Just Squeeze Me –vRN
....		Suddenly It Jumped

5 Oct 1946 (S)
Radio City, Studio 6B (bc)
New York City, NY

DUKE ELLINGTON & HIS ORCHESTRA
TJ SH CA FW HB RN, WDP LB CJ, JHtn JH RP AS HC, DE FG OP SG, KD.

.... DET   Take The "A" Train

> BS replaces DE.

.... DET   Can't Help Loving That Man Of Mine –vKD

> BS piano solo.

.... DET   Background music (w. bond promotion)

> Entire band, DE replaces BS.

....	DET	Just You, Just Me
....	DET	Just Squeeze Me –vRN
....	DET	Things Ain't What They Used To Be

7 Oct 1946 (S)
NBC Studios (bc)
New York City, NY

DUKE ELLINGTON WITH THE PERCY FAITH ORCHESTRA
DE with the Percy Faith Orchestra.

....	UTD	Nobody Was Lookin'[1]
....	UTD	Medley[2]

[1]Part of the future *Deep South Suite*.
[2]Including: I'm Beginning To See The Light; Do Nothin' Till You Hear From Me; Don't Get Around Much Anymore.

11 Oct 1946 (P)
Aquarium Restaurant (bc)
New York City, NY

DUKE ELLINGTON & HIS ORCHESTRA
TJ SH CA FW HB RN, WDP LB CJ, JHtn JH RP AS HC, DE FG OP SG.

....	Ffr	In A Mellotone
....	Ffr	This Is Always

12 Oct 1946 (S)
Radio City (bc)
New York City, NY

DUKE ELLINGTON & HIS ORCHESTRA
TJ SH CA FW HB RN, WDP LB CJ, JHtn JH RP AS HC, DE FG OP SG.

> JCte added.

.... AFR   Somebody Loves Me –vJCte

> JCte omitted.

....	AFR	Blue Skies
....	AFR	Just Squeeze Me –vRN

> JCte added.

....	AFR	September Song –vJCte
....	AFR	Teentimers' Theme

DUKE ELLINGTON & HIS ORCHESTRA
TJ SH FW HB RN, WDP LB CJ, JHtn JH RP AS HC, DE FG OP SG.

23 Oct 1946   (S)
WOR Studio 3
New York City, NY

| .... | Mu | 5765-4 | Diminuendo In Blue |
| .... | Mu | 5766-4 | Magenta Haze |

DUKE ELLINGTON & HIS ORCHESTRA
TJ SH CA FW HB RN, WDP LB CJ, JHtn JH RP AS HC, DE FG OP SG.

25 Oct 1946   (P)
Aquarium Restaurant (bc)
New York City, NY

....	Ffr	A Garden In The Rain
....	Ffr	The Whole World Is Singing My Song
....	Ffr	Jennie
....	Ffr	The Things We Did Last Summer
....	Ffr	Rugged Romeo
....	Ffr	The "C" Jam Blues
....	Ffr	Things Ain't What They Used To Be

DUKE ELLINGTON & HIS ORCHESTRA
TJ SH CA HB RN, WDP LB CJ, JHtn JH RP AS HC, DE FG OP SG, KD MC AH.

10 Nov 1946   (P)
Civic Opera House
Chicago, IL

....	Pr	Overture To A Jam Session
....	Pr	Ring Dem Bells
....		The Mooche
....	Pr	Jumpin' Punkins
....	Pr	Beale Street Blues
....	Pr	Memphis Blues
....	Pr	St. Louis Blues –vMC
....	Pr	The Eighth Veil
....	JHtg	Golden Feather[1]
....	Pr	Air Conditioned Jungle
....	Pr	Golden Cress[2]
....	Pr	Unbooted Character
....	Pr	Sultry Sunset

THE DEEP SOUTH SUITE
....	Pr	- Magnolias Dripping With Molasses
....	Pr	- Hearsay Or Orson Welles[3]
....	Pr	- Nobody Was Lookin'[4]
....	Pr	- Happy-Go-Lucky Local

| .... | Pr | Things Ain't What They Used To Be |

THE BEAUTIFUL INDIANS
....	Pr	- Chaugogagog Maushaugagog Chaubunagungamaug[5]
....	Pr	- Minnehaha –vKD
....	Pr	- Hiawatha

> DjR added.

| .... | Vge | Ride Red Ride[6] |
| .... | Vge | Blues[7] |

> DjR gt solo.

| .... | Pr | Improvisation No. 2 |

> Entire band.

| .... | Vge | Honeysuckle Rose |

> DjR omitted.

....		My Little Brown Book –vAH
....		You Don't Love Me No More –vAH
....		Fat And Forty –vAH
....		I'm Just A Lucky So-And-So –vAH
....	Pr	Medley[8]
....		Just Squeeze Me –vRN
....	Pr	Blue Skies

[1]Dedicated to Leonard Feather.
[2]Dedicated to Cress Courtney.
[3]Originally titled "Hear Say."
[4]DE piano solo; this applies to all future performances of the suite, unless stated otherwise.
[5]*aka* "Good Fishin'"
[6]"Improvisation sur Tiger Rag" on Vge.
[7]"Blues Riff" on Vge.
[8]Including: In A Sentimental Mood; Mood Indigo; I'm Beginning To See The Light; Sophisticated Lady; Caravan; Solitude; I Let A Song Go Out Of My Heart/Don't Get Around Much Anymore.

23 Nov 1946   (P)
Carnegie Hall
New York City, NY

DUKE ELLINGTON & HIS ORCHESTRA
TJ SH CA FW HB RN, WDP LB CJ, JHtn JH RP AS HC, DE FG OP SG.

.... QuD		The Eighth Veil
.... QuD		Golden Feather
.... QuD		Flippant Flurry
.... VD	JDB305	Golden Cress
.... QuD		Unbooted Character
.... VD	JDB326	Sultry Sunset
		THE DEEP SOUTH SUITE
.... VD	JBB327	- Magnolias Dripping With Molasses
.... VD	JB328	- Hearsay Or Orson Welles
.... VD	JBB329	- Nobody Was Lookin'
.... VD	JB330	- Happy-Go-Lucky Local

25 Nov 1946   (S)
WOR Longacre Theater
New York City, NY

DUKE ELLINGTON & HIS ORCHESTRA
TJ SH CA FW HB RN, WDP LB CJ, JHtn JH RP AS HC, DE FG OP SG.

.... Mu	5813-2	Sultry Sunset
.... Mu	5814-2	Happy-Go-Lucky Local, part 2
.... Mu	5815-1	Trumpet-No-End[1]
.... Mu	5816-2	Happy-Go-Lucky Local, part 1

[1]sa "Blue Skies"; the arrangement is by Mary Lou Williams.

5 Dec 1946   (S)
WOR Longacre Theater
New York City, NY

DUKE ELLINGTON & HIS ORCHESTRA
TJ SH FW HB RN, WDP LB CJ, JHtn JH RP AS HC, DE FG OP SG, KD.

.... Mu	5817-1	The Beautiful Indians, part 1 (Hiawatha)
.... Mu	5818-3	Flippant Flurry
.... Mu	5823-1	Golden Feather
.... Mu	5824-3	The Beautiful Indians, part 2 –vKD (Minnehaha)

11 Dec 1946   (S)
WOR Longacre Theater
New York City, NY

DUKE ELLINGTON & HIS ORCHESTRA
TJ SH FW HB RN, WDP LB CJ, JHtn JH RP AS HC, DE FG OP SG.

.... Mu	5845-3	Overture To A Jam Session, part 1
.... Mu	5846-3	Overture To A Jam Session, part 2
.... Mu	5847-1	Jam-A-Ditty[1]

[1]Subtitled "Concerto For Four Jazz Horns."

18 Dec 1946   (S)
WOR Longacre Theater
New York City, NY

DUKE ELLINGTON & HIS ORCHESTRA
TJ SH HB RN, WDP LB CJ, JHtn JH RP AS HC, DE FG OP SG, AH.

.... Mu	5841-2	Tulip Or Turnip –vRN[1]
.... Mu	5842-3	It Shouldn't Happen To A Dream –vAH

[1]aka "Tell Me, Dream Face."

A tape of dubious authenticity is circulating among collectors of a concert at Princeton University from 1946. The title selections almost completely resemble those of the concert at Cornell University, on 19 Apr 1947, although the sequence of titles has been changed around.

7 Jan 1947   (S)
Pathé Studios
New York City, NY

DUKE ELLINGTON & HIS ORCHESTRA
TJ SH CA FW WJ RN, WDP LB CJ, JHtn JH RP AS HC, DE FG OP SG.

.... JSp		Golden Feather
.... De		Golden Cress
.... DE		Flippant Flurry
.... QuD		Jam-A-Ditty
.... QuD		Fugue-A-Ditty
.... De		Happy-Go-Lucky Local, part 1
.... De		Happy-Go-Lucky Local, part 2
.... QuD		Overture To A Jam Session
.... De		Sultry Sunset

The above titles have been recorded originally for Capitol Transcriptions.

2 Feb 1947   (P)
Civic Opera House
Chicago, IL

DUKE ELLINGTON & HIS ORCHESTRA
TJ SH FW EBfd RN, WDP LB CJ, JHtn JH RP AS HC, DE FG OP SG, KD MC.

....		Happy-Go-Lucky Local >>>

....		Beggar's Holiday Medley[1]
....		Award presentation to LB, HC, JH, BS and the orchestra

> BS replaces DE.

....	MJ	Triple Play

> DE replaces BS.

....		Near Miss
		THE BEAUTIFUL INDIANS
....		- Minnehaha –vKD
....		- Hiawatha

[1]Including: Take Love Easy; When I Walk With You –vMC; Tomorrow Mountain; Brown Penny –vKD.

21 Feb 1947 (S)[1]
Howard Theater (bc?)
Washington, DC

DUKE ELLINGTON
DE interviewed by Emerson Parker.

....		Interview

[1]Backstage.

19 Apr 1947 (P)
Bailey Hall, Cornell University
Ithaca, NY

DUKE ELLINGTON & HIS ORCHESTRA
TJ SH FW HB EBfd RN, WDP LB CJ, JHtn JH RP AS HC, DE FG OP EMcC, KD MC AH.

....	Std	Blutopia
....	Std	Overture To A Jam Session
....	Std	The Mooche
....	Std	Diminuendo In Blue and Crescendo In Blue
....		Frustration
....	Std	Rugged Romeo
....		Flippant Flurry
....		Golden Cress
....		Jam-A-Ditty
....	Std	Passion Flower
....	Std	The Blues –vKD

> DE OP EMcC.

....		Dancers In Love

> Entire band.

....	Std	Frankie And Johnny
....		Things Ain't What They Used To Be
....		Award presentation
....		Take The "A" Train
....		Beale Street Blues
....		Memphis Blues
....		St. Louis Blues –vMC
....		Minnehaha –vKD
....		Transblucency –vKD
....		Hiawatha
....		My Little Brown Book –vAH
....		Don't Take Your Love From Me –vAH
....		Summertime –vAH
....	Std	I'm Just A Lucky So-And-So –vAH
....		Flamingo –vAH
....		Medley[1]
....	Std	Just Squeeze Me –vRN
....	Std	Ring Dem Bells –vRN

[1]Including: In A Sentimental Mood; Mood Indigo; I'm Beginning To See The Light; Sophisticated Lady; Caravan; Solitude; I Let A Song Go Out Of My Heart/Don't Get Around Much Anymore.

10 May 1947 (P)
Studios WNEW (bc)
New York City, NY

DUKE ELLINGTON & HIS MEN
TJ RN, LB, JH AS HC, DE OP SG.

....	IAC		The "C" Jam Blues
....	VD	JB485	Sophisticated Lady
....	VD	JB486	I Can't Give You Anything But Love

> DE, CBsn.

....		Cocktails For Two –vCBsn

> Entire band, CBsn omitted.

....	VD	JB486	It Don't Mean A Thing >>>

> DE, BRsn.

....   Doin' The New Lowdown –BRsn tap

> Entire band, BRsn omitted.

.... VD   JB485   On The Sunny Side Of The Street

> RN, BS.

.... Rar   Moon Mist

> BS LSH.

....   Solitude

> Entire band, BS replaces DE.

....   I've Found A New Baby

> JTdn added.

.... IAC   Take The "A" Train

| | | | 19 May 1947 (S) |
| | | | NBC Studios (bc) |

DUKE ELLINGTON WITH THE PERCY FAITH ORCHESTRA
DE with the Percy Faith Orchestra.   New York City, NY

.... AFR   Solitude––Caravan

                                                                        3 Jun 1947 (P)
          Unidentified location (bc?)

DUKE ELLINGTON & HIS ORCHESTRA
SH FW HB WBcb RN, WDP TG LB CJ, JHtn RP AS HC, DE FG OP SG, CC.   Manchester, MA

....   One O'Clock Jump
....   Flamingo –vCC
....   The Mooche

                                                           9 Jun 1947 (S)
                     Pathé Studios

DUKE ELLINGTON & HIS ORCHESTRA
TJ SH FW HB WBcb RN, WDP TG LB CJ, JHtn JH RP AS HC, DE FG OP SG.   New York City, NY

.... ST   Beale Street Blues
.... ST   Memphis Blues
.... De   St. Louis Blues –vRN
.... ST   Swamp Fire
.... Pfm   How High The Moon
.... ST   Blue Lou
.... ST   Who Struck John?
.... ST   Violet Blue[1]
.... ST   Royal Garden Blues
.... ST   Jumpin' Punkins

[1]*aka "Ultra Blue"; sa "Ultra Violet."*

The above titles have been recorded originally for Capitol Transcriptions.

                                                             10 Jun 1947 (S)
                     Pathé Studios

DUKE ELLINGTON & HIS ORCHESTRA
TJ SH FW HB WBcb RN, WDP TG LB CJ, JHtn JH RP AS HC, DE FG OP SG, CC.   New York City, NY

.... De   Frustration
.... De   Blue Is The Night
.... ST   Jump For Joy –vRN
.... ST   Far Away Blues

> BS replaces DE.

.... JSp   Azalea –vCC

> DE replaces BS.

.... JSp   Orchids For Madam –vCC
.... ST   Frisky
.... ST   Park At 106th

The above titles have been recorded originally for Capitol Transcriptions.

                                                      1 Jul 1947 (P)
       El Patio Ballroom, Lakeside Park (bc)

DUKE ELLINGTON & HIS ORCHESTRA
SH FW HB WBcb RN, TG LB CJ, JHtn JH RP AS HC, DE FG OP SG, KD CC.   Denver, CO

.... J&J   Take The "A" Train
.... J&J   Orchids For Madam –vCC
.... J&J   Golden Feather
.... J&J   Flippant Flurry
.... J&J   Jam-A-Ditty   >>>

.... J&J   Passion Flower

                                            THE BEAUTIFUL INDIANS
.... J&J   - Minnehaha –vKD
.... J&J   - Hiawatha

.... J&J   Take The "A" Train

                                                                        4 Jul 1947   (P)
                                                                        El Patio Ballroom, Lakeside Park (bc)
DUKE ELLINGTON & HIS ORCHESTRA   Denver, CO
SH FW HB WBcb RN, TG LB CJ, JHtn JH RP AS HC, DE FG OP SG, KD CC.

.... J&J   Take The "A" Train
.... J&J   Caravan
.... J&J   Brown Penny –vKD
.... J&J   In A Mellotone
.... J&J   The Mooche
.... J&J   Prisoner Of Love –vCC
.... J&J   Happy-Go-Lucky Local

                                                                        9 Jul 1947   (P)
                                                                        El Patio Ballroom, Lakeside Park (bc)
DUKE ELLINGTON & HIS ORCHESTRA   Denver, CO
SH FW HB WBcb RN, TG LB CJ, JHtn JH RP AS HC, DE FG OP SG, CC.

.... J&J   Take The "A" Train
.... J&J   Overture To A Jam Session
.... J&J   It Shouldn't Happen To A Dream –vCC
.... J&J   One O'Clock Jump
.... MJ   Beale Street Blues
.... J&J   St. Louis Blues –vRN
.... J&J   Things Ain't What They Used To Be

                                                                        11 Jul 1947   (P)
                                                                        El Patio Ballroom, Lakeside Park (bc)
DUKE ELLINGTON & HIS ORCHESTRA   Denver, CO
SH FW HB WBcb RN, TG LB CJ, JHtn JH RP AS HC, DE FG OP SG, KD.

.... J&J   Take The "A" Train
.... J&J   How High The Moon
.... UTD   Transblucency –vKD
.... UTD   Jam-A-Ditty

    > BS replaces DE.

.... UTD   A Flower Is A Lovesome Thing

    > DE replaces BS.

.... UTD   Rockin' In Rhythm
.... UTD   Tulip Or Turnip –vRN

                                                                        25 Jul 1947   (P)
                                                                        Ciro's (bc)
DUKE ELLINGTON & HIS ORCHESTRA   Hollywood, CA
SH FW HB WBcb RN, TG LB CJ, JHtn JH RP AS HC, DE FG OP SG, KD CC.

.... Joy   Moon Mist
.... Joy   Prisoner Of Love –vCC
.... Joy   Harlem Air Shaft
.... Joy   Brown Penny –vKD

The closing number "Moon Mist" is a repeat of the opening number and is therefore not listed again.

DUKE ELLINGTON & HIS ORCHESTRA   (bc)
KD CC omitted, otherwise same personnel.

.... Joy   Beale Street Blues
.... Joy   Memphis Blues
.... Joy   St. Louis Blues –vRN
.... Joy   Mood Indigo

The closing number "Harlem Air Shaft" is a repeat of the same title in the earlier broadcast.

                                                                        30 Jul 1947   (P)
                                                                        Ciro's (bc)
DUKE ELLINGTON & HIS ORCHESTRA   Hollywood, CA
SH FW HB WBcb RN, TG LB CJ, JHtn JH RP AS HC, DE FG OP SG, KD.

.... Rar   Take The "A" Train
.... Joy   Happy-Go-Lucky Local

                                            THE BEAUTIFUL INDIANS
.... Joy   - Minnehaha –vKD
.... Joy   - Hiawatha

.... Joy   Warm Valley
.... Joy   Beale Street Blues

<table>
<tr><td>1 Aug 1947</td><td>(P)</td></tr>
</table>

1 Aug 1947 (P)
Ciro's (bc)
Hollywood, CA

DUKE ELLINGTON & HIS ORCHESTRA
SH FW HB WBcb RN, TG LB CJ, JHtn JH RP AS HC, DE FG OP SG, KD CC.

....	Joy	Take The "A" Train
....	Joy	It's Kinda Lonesome Out Tonight –vCC
....	Joy	Caravan
....	Joy	When I Walk With You –vKD
....	Joy	Passion Flower

DUKE ELLINGTON & HIS ORCHESTRA   (bc)
KD CC omitted, otherwise same personnel.

....	AFR	Passion Flower
....	AFR	Tulip Or Turnip –vRN
....	AFR	Stompy Jones

The opening title "Moon Mist" is a repeat of the 25 Jul 1947 broadcast.

5 Aug 1947 (P)
Ciro's (bc)
Hollywood, CA

DUKE ELLINGTON & HIS ORCHESTRA
SH FW HB WBcb RN, TG LB CJ, JHtn JH RP AS HC, DE FG OP SG, KD CC.

....		Squeeze Me
....		Take The "A" Train
....		Royal Garden Blues
....		I Like The Sunrise –vCC[1]
....		Sophisticated Lady
....		Brown Penny –vKD
....		Blue Is The Night[2]

[1]Part of the future *Liberian Suite.*
[2]Announced as "How Blue The Night."

6 Aug 1947 (P)
Ciro's (bc)
Hollywood, CA

DUKE ELLINGTON & HIS ORCHESTRA
SH FW HB WBcb RN, TG LB CJ, JHtn JHRP AS HC, DE FG OP SG, CC.

....		Take The "A" Train
....		Flippant Flurry
....		It's Kinda Lonesome Out Tonight –vCC
....		Hollywood Hangover
....		Tulip Or Turnip –vRN

7 Aug 1947
Ciro's (bc)
Hollywood, CA

DUKE ELLINGTON & HIS ORCHESTRA
SH FW HB WBcb RN, TG LB CJ, JHtn JH RP AS HC, DE FG OP SG, CC.

....		Take The "A" Train
....		Lady Of The Lavender Mist[1]
....		Hy'a Sue[2]
....		Azalea –vCC
....		Caravan

[1]Announced as "Too Weary To Worry."
[2]Announced as "Flirtation."

14 Aug 1947 (S)
Columbia Studios
Hollywood, CA

DUKE ELLINGTON & HIS ORCHESTRA
SH FW HB WBcb RN, TG LB CJ, JHtn JH RP AS HC, DE FG OP SG, CC.

....	UTD	HCO2531[1]	Hy'a Sue
....	UTD	HCO2531	Hy'a Sue (incomplete)
....	Co	HCO2531-1	Hy'a Sue
....	Co	HCO2532-1	Lady Of The Lavender Mist
....		HCO2532	Lady Of The Lavender Mist
....		HCO2532	Lady Of The Lavender Mist
....	UTD	HCO2532-2	Lady Of The Lavender Mist
....	UTD	HCO2533	Women, They'll Get You –vRN[2]
....	Co	HCO2533-1	Women, They'll Get You –vRN

> BS replaces DE.[3]

....	[4]	Change My Ways –vCC[5]
....		Change My Ways –vCC
....	UTD	Change My Ways –vCC

[1]During the recording session the attending recording engineer would call the different takes in sequence, starting with one. However, at the end, only the take selected for release and maybe an alternate take would be registered as takes 1 and 2. This practice applies to all CBS/Co recording sessions.   >>>

[2]*aka* "Women, Women, Women."
[3]BS has not been mentioned on the recording sheet. His presence is based on aural judgment. The same applies to the sessions on 1, 29 Sep; 1, 2, 6 Oct; 10, 11, 20 Nov 1947.
[4]No master number assigned.
[5]Complete: "Maybe I Should Change My Ways"; *aka* "If I Knew Now What I Knew Then."

A tape of dubious authenticity is circulating among collectors of a concert at the Civic Auditorium, Portland, OR, dated to 24 Aug 1947. The title selections are almost identical with those of the concert at the Hollywood Bowl, Los Angeles, CA, on 31 Aug 1947.

			31 Aug 1947 (P)
			Hollywood Bowl

DUKE ELLINGTON & HIS ORCHESTRA
SH FW HB WBcb RN, TG LB CJ, JHtn JH RP AS HC, DE FG OP SG, KD AH.

Los Angeles, CA

....	UJ	Blutopia
....	UJ	Overture To A Jam Session
....	UJ	The Mooche
....	UJ	Jumpin' Punkins
....	UJ	Ring Dem Bells –vRN
....	UJ	Beale Street Blues
....	UJ	Memphis Blues
....	UJ	St. Louis Blues –vRN
....	UJ	Golden Feather
....	UJ	Air Conditioned Jungle
....	UJ	Golden Cress
....	UJ	Diminuendo In Blue
....	UJ	Transblucency –vKD
....	UJ	Crescendo In Blue
		BLACK, BROWN AND BEIGE
....	UJ	- Come Sunday
....	UJ	- Work Song
....	UJ	- The Blues –vKD
....	UJ	- Emancipation Celebration

> DE OP.

| .... | UJ | Dancers In Love |

> Entire band.

....	UJ	Frankie And Johnny
....	AFR	My Little Brown Book –vAH
....	AFR	Summertime –vAH
....	AFR	It Shouldn't Happen To A Dream –vAH
....	AFR	Fat And Forty –vAH
....	AFR	I Got It Bad –vAH
....	UJ	Take The "A" Train
....	UJ	Moon Mist
....	UJ	Jam-A-Ditty
		THE BEAUTIFUL INDIANS
....	UJ	- Minnehaha –vKD
....	UJ	- Hiawatha
....	AFR	Medley[1]

[1]Including: Do Nothin' Till You Hear From Me; In A Sentimental Mood; Mood Indigo; I'm Beginning To See The Light; Sophisticated Lady; Caravan; Solitude; I Let A Song Go Out Of My Heart/Don't Get Around Much Anymore.

		c Aug/Sep 1947 (S)
		Unspecified studio (?bc)[1]

DUKE ELLINGTON
DE talking.

Hollywood, CA

| .... | | Narration |

[1]For the program "Christmas Jubilee" (1947), with Paul Baron & His Orchestra playing *Jingle Bells*. No other original music has been used. The date of broadcast is not known.

			1 Sep 1947 (S)
			Columbia Studios

DUKE ELLINGTON & HIS ORCHESTRA
SH FW HB WBcb RN, TG LB CJ, JHtn JH RP AS HC, DE FG OP SG, AH.

Hollywood, CA

....		HCO2596	It's Monday Every Day –vAH
....	Co	HCO2596-1	It's Monday Every Day –vAH
....	UTD	HCO2597	Golden Cress
....	Co	HCO2597-1	Golden Cress

> BS replaces DE[1]; unidentified fem. vocalist added.

| .... | UTD | HCO2598-1 | Put Yourself In My Place, Baby –v?? |

[1]See footnote for session on 14 Aug 1947.

<u>DUKE ELLINGTON & HIS ORCHESTRA</u>   29 Sep 1947   (S)
SH FW HB WBcb RN, TG LB CJ, JHtn JH RP AS HC, BS¹ FG OP SG, DP.   Columbia Studios
                                                                                                                            Hollywood, CA

.... Co   HCO2598-2   Put Yourself In My Place, Baby –vDP

> DE replaces BS, WH added.

....   HCO2654-1   Cowboy Rhumba –vWH
.... Co   HCO2654-2   Cowboy Rhumba –vWH
....   HCO2655   The Wildest Gal In Town –vDP
....   HCO2655   The Wildest Gal In Town –vDP
....   HCO2655   The Wildest Gal In Town –vDP
.... Co   HCO2655-1   The Wildest Gal In Town –vDP
....   HCO2655-2   The Wildest Gal In Town –vDP
.... UTD   HCO2656   I Fell And Broke My Heart –vWH
.... FDC   HCO2656-1   I Fell And Broke My Heart –vWH
.... UTD   HCO2658   Antidisestablishmentarianismist –vRN²

¹See footnote for session on 14 Aug 1947.
²Complete: "You're Just An Old Antidisestablishmentarianismist." The arrangement is by Gerald Wilson.

<u>DUKE ELLINGTON & HIS ORCHESTRA</u>   30 Sep 1947   (S)
SH FW HB WBcb RN, TG LB CJ, JHtn JH RP AS HC, DE FG OP SG, AH.   Columbia Studios
                                                                                                                            Hollywood, CA

.... VD   HCO2658-1   Antidisestablishmentarianismist –vRN
....   HCO2662   Don't Be So Mean To Baby –vAH¹
.... Co   HCO2662-1   Don't Be So Mean To Baby –vAH

¹Complete: "Don't Be So Mean To Baby, 'Cause Baby's So Good To You."

<u>DUKE ELLINGTON & HIS ORCHESTRA</u>   1 Oct 1947   (S)
SH FW HB WBcb RN, TG LB CJ, JHtn JH RP AS HC, DE FG OP SG, DP.   Columbia Studios
                                                                                                                            Hollywood, CA

.... Co   HCO2663-1   It's Mad, Mad, Mad –vDP
.... UTD   HCO2664   You Gotta Crawl Before You Walk –vRN¹
.... Co   HCO2664-1   You Gotta Crawl Before You Walk –vRN

> BS replaces DE.²

.... UTD   HCO2665   Change My Ways
.... Co   HCO2665-1A   Change My Ways

¹The arrangement is by Gerald Wilson.
²See footnote for session on 14 Aug 1947.

<u>DUKE ELLINGTON & HIS ORCHESTRA</u>   2 Oct 1947   (S)
SH FW HB WBcb RN, TG LB CJ, JHtn JH RP AS HC, DE FG OP SG, KD.   Columbia Studios
                                                                                                                            Hollywood, CA

.... UTD   HCO2666   Kitty –vRN
.... Co   HCO2666-1   Kitty –vRN

> BS replaces DE.¹

....   HCO2667   Brown Penny –vKD
....   HCO2667-1   Brown Penny –vKD
.... Co   HCO2667-2²   Brown Penny –vKD
....   HCO2667-3   Brown Penny –vKD

¹See footnote for session on 14 Aug 1947.
²All commercial releases have been edited to 3:05; the only complete version (4:10) seems to be preserved on the Social Securities Series #34, "The Genius Of Duke."

<u>DUKE ELLINGTON & HIS ORCHESTRA</u>   Oct 1947   (P)
SH FW HB WBcb RN, TG LB CJ, JHtn JH RP AS HC, DE FG OP SG.   Meadowbrook Gardens Café (bc)
                                                                                                                            Culver City, CA

....   Take The "A" Train
....   Lady Of The Lavender Mist
....   Hy'a Sue
....   How Blue The Night
....   I'm Just A Lucky So-And-So

<u>DUKE ELLINGTON & HIS ORCHESTRA</u>   4 Oct 1947   (P)
SH FW HB WBcb RN, TG LB CJ, JHtn JH RP AS HC, DE FG OP SG.   Meadowbrook Gardens Café (bc)
                                                                                                                            Culver City, CA

....   Blue Lou
.... MJ   Hy'a Sue
....   How High The Moon   >>>

			Emancipation Celebration
....			Antidisestablishmentarianismist –vRN
....			It's Kinda Lonesome Out Tonight

5 Oct 1947   **(P)**
Meadowbrook Gardens Café (bc)
Culver City, CA

<u>DUKE ELLINGTON & HIS ORCHESTRA</u>
SH FW HB WBcb RN, TG LB CJ, JHtn JH RP AS HC, DE FG OP SG.

....			Honeysuckle Rose
....			It's Kinda Lonesome Out Tonight

6 Oct 1947   **(S)**
Columbia Studios
Hollywood, CA

<u>DUKE ELLINGTON & HIS ORCHESTRA</u>
SH FW WBcb RN, TG LB CJ, JHtn JH RP AS HC, BS[1] FG OP SG.

....	UTD	HCO2565[2]	Change My Ways
....	Co	HCO2565-2	Change My Ways

> DE replaces BS.

....	UTD	HCO2676	Boogie Bop Blues[3]
....	Co	HCO2676-1	Boogie Bop Blues
....		HCO2677	Sultry Serenade[4] (incomplete)
....		HCO2677	Sultry Serenade (incomplete)
....	UTD	HCO2677	Sultry Serenade (incomplete)
....	UTD	HCO2677	Sultry Serenade
....		HCO2677	Sultry Serenade (incomplete)
....		HCO2677	Sultry Serenade (incomplete)
....		HCO2677	Sultry Serenade (incomplete)
....		HCO2677	Sultry Serenade (incomplete)
....		HCO2677	Sultry Serenade (incomplete)
....		HCO2677	Sultry Serenade (incomplete)
....	Co	HCO2677-1	Sultry Serenade

[1]See footnote for session on 14 Aug 1947.
[2]Remake.
[3]*aka* "Basso Mo Thundo"; "Grand Slam Jam."
[4]Originally titled "Working Eyes"; according to Art Baron, this composition was written by Tyree Glenn, then "borrowed" by DE and retitled. TG repossessed it and renamed it "How Could You Do A Thing Like That To Me?"

10 Nov 1947   **(S)**
Liederkranz Hall
New York City, NY

<u>DUKE ELLINGTON & HIS ORCHESTRA</u>
SH FW HB WBcb RN, TG LB CJ, JHtn JH RP AS HC, DE/BS[1] FG OP SG.

....	UTD	CO38371	Stomp, Look And Listen
....	Co	CO38371-1	Stomp, Look And Listen
....	UTD	CO38372	Air Conditioned Jungle
....		CO38372	Air Conditioned Jungle
....		CO38372	Air Conditioned Jungle
....	Co	CO38372-1	Air Conditioned Jungle
....	VD	CO38372-2	Air Conditioned Jungle[2]
....	Co	CO38373-1	Three Cent Stomp
....	So	CO38373 alt.	Three Cent Stomp

[1]See footnote for session on 14 Aug 1947.
[2]"Discontinued Jungle" on VD.

11 Nov 1947   **(S)**
Liederkranz Hall
New York City, NY

<u>DUKE ELLINGTON & HIS ORCHESTRA</u>
SH FW HB WBcb RN, TG LB CJ, JHtn JH RP AS HC, DE/BS[1] FG OP SG, DP.

....		CO38374	Progressive Gavotte[2]
....	FDC	CO38374	Progressive Gavotte
....	Co	CO38374-1	Progressive Gavotte[3]
....	UTD	CO38374 alt.	Progressive Gavotte
....		CO38375	He Makes Me Believe –vDP[4]
....		CO38375-1	He Makes Me Believe –vDP
....		CO38375	He Makes Me Believe –vDP
....		CO38375	He Makes Me Believe –vDP
....		CO38375	He Makes Me Believe –vDP
....	Co	CO38375-2	He Makes Me Believe –vDP

[1]See footnote for session on 14 Aug 1947.
[2]*aka* "Re Bop Gavotte."
[3]"Ellington Mood" on VD.
[4]Complete: "He Makes Me Believe That He's Mine."

| | | | | 14 Nov 1947 | (S) |
| | | | | Liederkranz Hall | |

DUKE ELLINGTON & HIS ORCHESTRA
SH FW HB WBcb RN, TG LB CJ, JHtn JH RP AS HC, DE FG OP SG, DP.

New York City, NY

....		CO38386	Take Love Easy –vDP
....	UTD	CO38386	Take Love Easy –vDP
....		CO38386	Take Love Easy –vDP
....	Co	CO38386-1	Take Love Easy –vDP
....	Co	CO38387-1	I Can't Believe That You're In Love With Me
....	Co	CO38388-1	How High The Moon
....	UTD	CO38389	Singing In The Rain
....	Co	CO38389-1	Singing In The Rain

18 Nov 1947   (S)
Liederkranz Hall
New York City, NY

DUKE ELLINGTON & HIS ORCHESTRA
SH FW HG WBcb RN, TG LB CJ, JHtn JH RP AS HC, DE FG EB SG, AH.

....		CO38705	Do Nothin' Till You Hear From Me –vAH
....		CO38705	Do Nothin' Till You Hear From Me –vAH
....	Co	CO38705-1	Do Nothin' Till You Hear From Me –vAH

20 Nov 1947   (S)
Liederkranz Hall
New York City, NY

DUKE ELLINGTON & HIS ORCHESTRA
SH FW HB WBcb RN, TG LB CJ, JHtn JH RP AS HC, DE/BS[1] FG OP SG, DP AH.

....		CO38398	Don't Get Around Much Anymore –vAH
....		CO38398	Don't Get Around Much Anymore –vAH
....		CO38398	Don't Get Around Much Anymore –vAH
....	Co	CO38398-1	Don't Get Around Much Anymore –vAH
....		CO38399	Once Upon A Dream –vDP
....	UTD	CO38399	Once Upon A Dream –vDP
....		CO38399	Once Upon A Dream –vDP
....	FDC	CO38399-1	Once Upon A Dream –vDP
....		CO38400	It's Love I'm In –vAH
....	FDC	CO38400-1	It's Love I'm In –vAH

[1]See footnote for session on 14 Aug 1947.

6 Dec 1947   (P)
Unspecified radio studio (bc)
Cincinnati, OH

DUKE ELLINGTON
Piano solo.

| .... | VJC | | Mood Indigo |

7 Dec 1947   (P)
Lookout House (bc)
Covington, KY

DUKE ELLINGTON & HIS ORCHESTRA
SH FW HB WBcb RN, TG LB CJ, JHtn JH RP AS HC, DE FG OP SG, DP.

....			Riff'n' Drill
....			Old Buttermilk Sky –vDP
....			The Mooche

22 Dec 1947   (S)
Liederkranz Hall
New York City, NY

DUKE ELLINGTON & HIS ORCHESTRA
SH FW HB AK RN, TG LB CJ, JHtn JH RP AS HC, DE FG OP JR SG, DP.

....		CO38591	I Could Get A Man –vDP
....		CO38591	I Could Get A Man –vDP
....	Co	CO38591-1	I Could Get A Man –vDP

> RN, TG LB, JHtn JH AS HC, DE OP JR SG, KD.

| .... | Co | CO38592-1 | On A Turquoise Cloud –vKD |

24 Dec 1947   (S)
Liederkranz Hall
New York City, NY

DUKE ELLINGTON & HIS ORCHESTRA
SH FW HB AK RN, TG LB CJ, JHtn JH RP AS HC, DE FG OP JR SG. (AH)[1]

THE LIBERIAN SUITE

....	VD	XCO40788	1 I Like The Sunrise
....	UTD	XCO40789	1 I Like The Sunrise –vAH[1]
....	Co	XCO40789 alt.[2]	1 I Like The Sunrise –vAH[1]
....		XCO40790	2 Dance #1 (rehearsal)
....	Co	XCO40790	2 Dance #1
....	UTD	XCO40790 alt.	2 Dance #1
....	Co	XCO40791	3 Dance #2
....	UTD	XCO40792	4 Dance #3 (incomplete)
....	Co	XCO40792	4 Dance #3
....	Co	XCO40793	5 Dance #4
....	Co	XCO40794	6 Dance #5 >>>

.... Co   XCO40794 alt.   6 Dance #5

[1]AH was not present at this session; his vocal part was overdubbed at a later date.
[2]Identical with VD, except for the overdubbed vocal.

			26 Dec 1947 (P)

DUKE ELLINGTON & HIS ORCHESTRA   26 Dec 1947   (P)
SH FW HB AK RN, TG LB CJ, JHtn JH RP AS HC, DE FG OP JR SG, KD DP AH.   Carnegie Hall
                                                                       New York City, NY

....		The Star Spangled Banner
....		The New Look
....		Blue Serge
....		Midriff
....		Triple Play
....		He Makes Me Believe –vDP
....		Harlem Air Shaft
....		Mella Brava
....		Kickapoo Joy Juice
....		On A Turquoise Cloud –vKD
....		Johnny Hodges Medley[1]
....		Basso Profundo[2]
....		New York City Blues[3]
....		The Clothed Woman

THE LIBERIAN SUITE

....		1 I Like The Sunrise –vAH
....		2 Dance #1
....		3 Dance #2
....		4 Dance #3
....		5 Dance #4
....		6 Dance #5

....		Medley[4]
....		Presentation
....		Stomp, Look And Listen
....		Bakiff
....		Rockin' In Rhythm
....		On The Sunny Side Of The Street
....		It's Monday Every Day –vAH
....		Lover Come Back To Me –vAH
....		Don't Take Your Love From Me –vAH
....		It Don't Mean A Thing –vAH
....		Medley[5]

[1]Including: Wanderlust; Junior Hop; Jeep's Blues; Dooji Wooji; The Jeep Is Jumpin'; The Mood To Be Wooed.
[2]*aka* "Boogie Bop Blues."
[3]*aka* "An Urban Fantasy."
[4]Including: East St. Louis Toodle-Oo; Echoes Of Harlem; Things Ain't What They Used To Be.
[5]Including: Do Nothin' Till You Hear From Me; In A Sentimental Mood; Mood Indigo; I'm Beginning To See The Light;
Sophisticated Lady; Caravan; Solitude; I Let A Song Go Out Of My Heart/Don't Get Around Much Anymore.

In addition to the above, three students from the Julliard School of Music played the BS original "Entrance Of Youth."

DUKE ELLINGTON & HIS ORCHESTRA   27 Dec 1947   (P)
SH FW HB AK RN, TG LB CJ, JHtn JH RP AS HC, DE FG OP JR SG, KD DP AH.   Carnegie Hall
                                                                       New York City, NY

....		The Star Spangled Banner
....	Pre	The New Look
....	Pre	Blue Serge
....		Midriff
....	Pre	Triple Play
....		He Makes Me Believe –vDP
....	Pre	Harlem Air Shaft
....	Pre	Mella Brava
....	Pre	Kickapoo Joy Juice
....	Pre	On A Turquoise Cloud –vKD
....	Pre	Johnny Hodges Medley[1]
....	Pre	Basso Profundo
....	Pre	New York City Blues
....	Pre	The Clothed Woman

THE LIBERIAN SUITE

....	Pre	1 I Like The Sunrise –vAH
....	Pre	2 Dance #1
....	Pre	3 Dance #2
....	Pre	4 Dance #3
....	Pre	5 Dance #4
....	Pre	6 Dance #5 >>>

....	Pre	Medley[2]
....		Stomp, Look And Listen
....	Pre	Bakiff
....		Rockin' In Rhythm
....		On The Sunny Side Of The Street
....		Cotton Tail
....		It's Monday Every Day –vAH
....		Lover Come Back To Me –vAH
....		Don't Take Your Love From Me –vAH
....		It Don't Mean A Thing –vAH
....		Medley[3]
....		Tulip Or Turnip –vRN
....	Pre	Trumpet-No-End

[1]Including: Wanderlust; Junior Hop; Jeep's Blues; Dooji Wooji; The Jeep Is Jumpin'; The Mood To Be Wooed.
[2]Including: East St. Louis Toodle-Oo; Black And Tan Fantasy; Echoes Of Harlem; Things Ain't What They Used To Be.
[3]Including: Do Nothin' Till You Hear From Me; In A Sentimental Mood; Mood Indigo; I'm Beginning To See The Light; Sophisticated Lady; Caravan; Solitude; I Let A Song Go Out Of My Heart/Don't Get Around Much Anymore.

In addition to the above, three students from the Julliard School of Music played the BS original "Entrance Of Youth."

DUKE ELLINGTON & HIS ORCHESTRA
AK, TG LB, JHtn JH HC, DE JR SG.

29 Dec 1947   (P)
Studios WMCA (bc)
New York City, NY

....		Take The "A" Train
....		The "C" Jam Blues

> BS JR, MTrm.

....		September Song –vMTrm

> BS, EBtn.

....		Them There Eyes –vEBtn

> Entire band, DE BRch replace BS SG.

....		Things Ain't What They Used To Be

> BS, VDmn.

....		They Didn't Believe Me –vVDmn

> BS, BWn.

....		I Didn't Know About You –vBWn.

> BS, TP.

....		I Can't Give You Anything But Love –vTP

> BS, DP.

....		He Makes Me Believe –vDP

> Entire band, DE SG replace BS BRch.

....		On The Sunny Side Of The Street
....		Take The "A" Train

Listed above are only those titles DE or his sidemen participated in. The program contains intermittent small talk.

DUKE ELLINGTON & HIS ORCHESTRA
HB AK, LB, JHtn JH AS HC, DE JR SG, DP.

30 Dec 1947   (S)
Liederkranz Hall
New York City, NY

....		CO38670	A Woman And A Man –vDP
....	UTD	CO38670	A Woman And A Man –vDP
....		CO38670	A Woman And A Man –vDP
....	Co	CO38670-1	A Woman And A Man –vDP

> HB, LB, JH HC, DE JR SG.

....	UTD[1]	CO38671	The Clothed Woman
....		CO38671	The Clothed Woman
....	Co	CO38671-1	The Clothed Woman
....	Co	CO38672-1	New York City Blues
....	VD	CO38672-2	New York City Blues

> HC omitted, TG, JHtn AS added.

....	Co	CO119017[2]	Let's Go Blues

[1]The original release on FDC has been edited.
[2]This title was not scheduled for release and therefore not given a master number at the time of recording.

6 Nov 1948[1]   (P)
Union College (bc)
Schenectady, NY

DUKE ELLINGTON & HIS ORCHESTRA
SH FW HB AK RN, TG LB QJ, JHtn JH RP AS BW/HSgr, HC, DE FG WMsl SG, KD AH.

....		Take The "A" Train
....	JSo	You Oughta[2]
....	KoJ	Don't Be So Mean To Baby –vAH
....	KoJ	How You Sound[3]
....	KoJ	On A Turquoise Cloud –vKD
....	KoJ	Don't Blame Me –vKD
....		Just A-Settin' And A-Rockin' –vRN
....		Hy'a Sue

[1]The Union College "Football Holiday" fall prom began on 5 Nov; the broadcast was done past midnight.
[2]Variant spelling "Y'Oughta."
[3]aka "A Sound Thumping."

13 Nov 1948   (P)
Carnegie Hall
New York City, NY

DUKE ELLINGTON & HIS ORCHESTRA
SH FW HB AK RN, TG LB QJ, JHtn JH RP AS BW HC, DE FG WMsl SG, KD AH.

....		The Star Spangled Banner
....	VJC	Three Cent Stomp
....	Car	Lady Of The Lavender Mist
....	VJC	Suddenly It Jumped
....	VJC	Reminiscing In Tempo
....	Car	She Wouldn't Be Moved
....	Car	THE SYMPHOMANIAC
....	Car	- Symphonic Or Bust[1]
....	Car	- How You Sound
....	Car	My Friend
....	Car	Tootin' Through The Roof
....	Car	Creole Love Call –vKD
....	Car	Don't Blame Me –vKD
....	VJC	Paradise[2]
....	VD J676-J677	The Tattooed Bride[3]
....	Car	Manhattan Murals[4]

> BS, KD.

| .... | Car | Lush Life –vKD |

> Entire band, DE replaces BS.

....	Car	Hy'a Sue
....	Car	Fantazm[5]
....	Car	You Oughta
....	Car	Brown Betty
....	Car	Humoresque
....	JP	How High The Moon
....	JP	Cotton Tail
....	VJC	Don't Be So Mean To Baby –vAH
....	VJC	Lover Come Back To Me –vAH
....	VJC	Trees –vAH
....	VJC	It's Monday Every Day –vAH
....	Joy	Medley[6]
....	Car	Limehouse Blues
....	Car	Just A-Settin' And A-Rockin' –vRN
....	Car	Trumpet-No-End
....	Car	Things Ain't What They Used To Be

[1]This title is a derivative of The Eighth Veil.
[2]No resemblance with Paradise (=In A Sentimental Mood) from 30 Apr 1935.
[3]The three movements are "Kitchen Stove," "Omaha," and "Aberdeen."
[4]sa "Take The "A" Train" (extended version).
[5]aka "Fantazzamp"; variant spelling "Fantazzm."
[6]Including: Don't Get Around Much Anymore; Do Nothin' Till You Hear From Me; In A Sentimental Mood; Mood Indigo; I'm Beginning To See The Light; Sophisticated Lady; Caravan; It Don't Mean A Thing; Solitude; I Let A Song Go Out Of My Heart/Don't Get Around Much Anymore.

22 Nov 1948   (P)
Click Restaurant (bc)
Philadelphia, PA

DUKE ELLINGTON & HIS ORCHESTRA
SH FW HB AK RN, TG LB QJ, JHtn JH RP AS BW HC, DE FG WMsl SG, KD AH.

....	Joy	Take The "A" Train
....	Joy	Suddenly It Jumped
....	Joy	It's Monday Every Day –vAH
....	Joy	How High The Moon >>>

.... Joy   On A Turquoise Cloud –vKD
.... Rt   Just A-Settin' And A-Rockin' –vRN
.... Rt   Trumpet-No-End
.... Rt   Hy'a Sue

                                                                                          23 Nov 1948   (P)
        DUKE ELLINGTON & HIS ORCHESTRA   Click Restaurant (bc)
        SH FW HB AK RN, TG LB QJ, JHtn JH RP AS BW HC, DE FG WMsl SG, KD AH.   Philadelphia, PA

.... Rt   Tootin' Through The Roof
....   Creole Love Call –vKD
....   The "C" Jam Blues
.... Rt   Don't Blame Me –vKD
.... Rt   Humoresque
....   Don't Be So Mean To Baby –vAH
....   Hy'a Sue

                                                                                          24 Nov 1948   (P)
        DUKE ELLINGTON & HIS ORCHESTRA   Click Restaurant (bc)
        SH FW HB AK RN, TG LB QJ, JHtn JH RP AS BW HC, DE FG WMsl SG, KD AH.   Philadelphia, PA

.... Rt   Progressive Gavotte
....   Mood Indigo –vKD
....   St. Louis Blues –vRN
.... BBI   It Don't Mean A Thing –vAH
....   Hy'a Sue

                                                                                          26 Nov 1948   (P)
        DUKE ELLINGTON & HIS ORCHESTRA   Click Restaurant (bc)
        SH FW HB AK RN, TG LB QJ, JHtn JH RP AS BW HC, DE FG WMsl SG, KD AH.   Philadelphia, PA

.... Rt   Rockabye River
....   How You Sound
....   Tulip Or Turnip –vRN
.... Rt   He Makes Me Believe –vKD
.... Rt   Trees –vAH

    > DE WMsl SG.

....   Dancers In Love

    > Entire band.

....   Hy'a Sue

                                                                                          27 Nov 1948   (P)
        DUKE ELLINGTON & HIS ORCHESTRA   Click Restaurant (bc)
        SH FW HB AK RN, TG LB QJ, JHtn JH RP AS BW HC, DE FG WMsl SG, KD AH.   Philadelphia, PA

....   Singing In The Rain
.... Rt   Limehouse Blues
....   Interview with DE
.... Rt   Lover Man –vKD
....   Humoresque
.... Rt   S'posin' –vAH
....   Hy'a Sue

                                                                                          Dec 1948   (P)
        DUKE ELLINGTON & HIS ORCHESTRA   Unidentified location (bc)
        SH FW HB AK RN, TG LB QJ, JHtn JH RP AS BW HC, DE FG WMsl SG.   U.S.A.

.... Rt   Take The "A" Train
.... Rt   The "C" Jam Blues
.... Rt   Brown Betty
.... Rt   Trumpet-No-End
.... Rt   Take The "A" Train

                                                                                          10 Dec 1948   (P)
        DUKE ELLINGTON & HIS ORCHESTRA   Cornell University
        SH FW HB AK RN, TG LB QJ, JHtn JH RP AS BW HC, DE FG WMsl SG, KD AH.   Ithaca, NY

.... JHtg   The Star Spangled Banner
.... WRC   Lady Of The Lavender Mist
.... WRC   Suddenly It Jumped
.... DD   Reminiscing In Tempo
.... WRC   She Wouldn't Be Moved
.... WRC   Paradise   >>>

		THE SYMPHOMANIAC
....	DD	- Symphonic Or Bust
....	DD	- How You Sound
....	WCR	Tootin' Through The Roof
....	WCR	Creole Love Call –vKD
....	WCR	Don't Blame Me –vKD
....	DD	Lover Man –vKD
....	WCR	The Tattooed Bride
....	DD	Manhattan Murals
....	DD	Hy'a Sue
....	DD	Fantazm
....	DD	My Friend
....	WRC	You Oughta
....	WCR	Brown Betty
....	WRC	Humoresque
....	WRC	How High The Moon
....	WRC	Don't Be So Mean To Baby –vAH
....	DD	Lover Come Back To Me –vAH
....	DD	Trees –vAH
....	DD	It's Monday Every Day –vAH
....	WRC	Medley[1]
....	WCR	Limehouse Blues
....	WCR	Trumpet-No-End
....	DD	Just A-Settin' And A-Rockin' –vRN

> DE WMsl SG.

> DD   Dancers In Love

[1]Including: Don't Get Around Much Anymore; Do Nothin' Till You Hear From Me; In A Sentimental Mood; Mood Indigo; I'm Beginning To See The Light; Sophisticated Lady; Caravan; It Don't Mean A Thing; I Let A Song Go Out Of My Heart/ Don't Get Around Much Anymore.

DUKE ELLINGTON & HIS ORCHESTRA
SH FW HB AK RN, TG LB QJ, JHtn JH RP AS BW HC, DE FG WMsl SG.

29 Dec 1948   (P)
Apollo Theater (bc)
New York City, NY

....		Cotton Tail

> DE WMsl SG.

....		Dancers In Love

> Entire band.

....		Medley[1]

[1]Including: Just Squeeze Me; Just A-Settin' And A-Rockin'; Lady Of The Lavender Mist; Suddenly It Jumped.

DUKE ELLINGTON & HIS ORCHESTRA
SH FW HB AK RN, TG LB QJ, JHtn JH RP BW HC, DE WMsl SG, KD.

Feb 1949   (P)
Hollywood Empire Hotel (bc)
Hollywood, CA

....	AFR	Hy'a Sue
....	AFR	He Makes Me Believe –vKD
....	AFR	Stomp, Look And Listen
....	ST	Brown Betty
....	MP	St. Louis Blues –vRN
....	MP	Humoresque

DUKE ELLINGTON & HIS ORCHESTRA
SH FW HB AK RN, TG LB QJ, JHtn JH RP BW HC, DE WMsl SG, KD.

6 Feb 1949   (P)
Hollywood Empire Hotel (bc)
Hollywood, CA

....	Ozo	How High The Moon
....	Ozo	Lover Man –vKD
....	Ozo	Rockin' In Rhythm

> BHol with her own group, augmented by members of the Ellington band.

....	Ozo	My Man –vBHol
....	Ozo	Miss Brown To You –vBHol

> BHol and her group omitted, entire band.

....	Ozo	Just Squeeze Me –vRN
....	Ozo	How You Sound
....	Ozo	Things Ain't What They Used To Be

<table>
<tr><td colspan="3"></td><td align="right">9 Feb 1949   (P)</td></tr>
</table>

DUKE ELLINGTON & HIS ORCHESTRA   9 Feb 1949   (P)
SH FW HB AK RN, TG LB QJ, JHtn JH RP BW HC, DE WMsl SG, AH.   Hollywood Empire Hotel (bc)
Hollywood, CA

....	AFR	Take The "A" Train
....	MP	The Tattooed Bride
....	AFR	Rockin' In Rhythm
....	AFR	Do Nothin' Till You Hear From Me
....	AFR	How You Sound

DUKE ELLINGTON & HIS ORCHESTRA   10 Feb 1949   (P)
SH FW HB AK RN, TG LB QJ, JHtn JH RP BW HC, DE WMsl SG.   Hollywood Empire Hotel (bc)
Hollywood, CA

....	Joy	One O'Clock Jump[1]
....	Joy	Solid Old Man
....	Joy	Singing In The Rain
....	Joy	Three Cent Stomp
....	Joy	Tulip Or Turnip –vRN
....	Joy	Take The "A" Train
....	Joy	One O'Clock Jump[1]

[1]Possibly recorded at an earlier date and used as a theme song and close for this broadcast.

DUKE ELLINGTON & HIS ORCHESTRA   Feb 1949   (P)
SH FW HB AK RN, TG LB QJ, JHtn JH RP BW HC, DE WMsl SG, KD AH.   Hollywood Empire Hotel (bc)
Hollywood, CA

....	AFR	The Tattooed Bride
....	AFR	Just Squeeze Me –vRN
....	AFR	Body And Soul –vKD
....	AFR	Do Nothin' Till You Hear From Me –vAH
....	AFR	Rockin' In Rhythm

DUKE ELLINGTON & HIS ORCHESTRA   Feb 1949   (P)
SH FW HB AK RN, TG LB QJ, JHtn JH RP BW HC, DE WMsl SG, AH.   Hollywood Empire Hotel (bc)
Hollywood, CA

....	Stv	Unbooted Character
....	MP	Paradise
....	MP[1]	How You Sound
....	Stv	It's Monday Every Day –vAH
....	Stv	Caravan
....	Stv	Cotton Tail
....	AFR	One O'Clock Jump[2]

[1]Edited version on SR. The first group of four choruses is from 6 Feb 1949.
[2]Possibly recorded at an earlier date and used to close this broadcast.

DUKE ELLINGTON & HIS ORCHESTRA   Feb 1949   (P)
SH FW HB AK RN, TG LB QJ, JHtn JH RP BW HC, DE WMsl SG, AH.   Hollywood Empire Hotel (bc)
Hollywood, CA

....	Ozo	Caravan
....	MP	Brown Betty
....	Ozo	Main Stem
....	Ozo	You Oughta
....	Ozo	Solitude –vAH
....	AFR	Stomp, Look And Listen

DUKE ELLINGTON & HIS ORCHESTRA   Feb 1949   (P)
SH FW HB AK RN, TG LB QJ, JHtn JH RP BW HC, DE WMsl SG.   Hollywood Empire Hotel (bc)
Hollywood, CA

....	Rt	Hy'a Sue
....	Rt	The "C" Jam Blues
....	Rt	Passion Flower
....	Rt	Clementine
....	Rt	Just A-Settin' And A-Rockin' –vRN
....	Stv	One O'Clock Jump

DUKE ELLINGTON & HIS ORCHESTRA   Feb 1949   (P)
SH FW HB AK RN, TG LB QJ, JHtn JH RP BW HC, DE WMsl SG.   Hollywood Empire Hotel (bc)
Hollywood, CA

....		Beale Street Blues
....		Tootin' Through The Roof
....		Harlem Air Shaft
....		Blue Lou >>>

....			Three Cent Stomp
....			The "C" Jam Blues
....			On The Sunny Side Of The Street
....			Cotton Tail
....			Things Ain't What They Used To Be

The above selections are probably a composite of more than one broadcast.

16 Feb 1949   (T)[1]
Universal Studios, Stage 10
Hollywood, CA

DUKE ELLINGTON & HIS ORCHESTRA
SH FW HB AK RN, TG LB QJ, JHtn JH RP BW HC, DE WMsl SG, KD.

....	Az[2]	SM568-2	Take The "A" Train
....	Az	SM569-2	On A Turquoise Cloud –vKD
....	Az	SM570-3	[3]You Oughta –vRN
....	Az	SM571-1	Suddenly It Jumped

> DE WMsl SG.

....	Az	SM572-1	Dancers In Love

> Entire band.

....	Az	SM573	Frankie And Johnny

[1]Music for the movie short "Symphony In Swing."
[2]The Az releases are unedited soundtrack prerecordings.
[3]This item was not included in the film.

Mar 1949   (P)
Private residence
Los Angeles, CA

DUKE ELLINGTON
Piano solo.

....	I'm Afraid Of Loving You Too Much –vDE[1]
....	Lover Man
....	She[2]
....	Harlem
....	Lots O'Fingers
....	Unidentified title 1
....	Unidentified title 2
....	Creole Blues[3]
....	Uno, Dos, Tres
....	Kinda Dukish[4]
....	Lady Of The Lavender Mist
....	Sentimental Journey
....	The Mystery Song
....	The "C" Jam Blues
....	B Sharp Boston[5]

[1]*aka* "Here Goes."
[2]*aka* "Sensuous."
[3]This title is a derivative of *Creole Rhapsody*.
[4]*aka* "Entertainment Industry."
[5]*aka* "Gentleman Jockey."

29 Apr 1949   (P)
CBS Studios (bc)
Hollywood, CA

DUKE ELLINGTON & HIS ORCHESTRA
SH FW HB AK RN, TG LB QJ, JHtn JH RP BW HC, DE WMsl SG, KD.

....	Mood Indigo
....	Take The "A" Train
....	The "C" Jam Blues
....	Sophisticated Lady
....	On A Turquoise Cloud –vKD

> DE WMsl.

....	Pitter Panther Patter

> Entire band.

....	Warm Valley

2 May 1949   (P)
CBS Studios (bc)
New York City, NY

DUKE ELLINGTON WITH ORCHESTRA
DE with a studio orchestra, directed by Raymond Scott.

....	Medley[1]
....	Caravan

[1]Including: Don't Get Around Much Anymore; Mood Indigo; It Don't Mean A Thing.

DUKE ELLINGTON & HIS ORCHESTRA
HB NW DB AK RN, TG LB QJ, JHtn JH RP ChR JF HC, DE WMsl SG, KD LE.

31 Aug 1949   (P)
Click Restaurant (bc)
Philadelphia, PA

....	Rt		Take The "A" Train
....	Rt		St. Louis Blues —vRN
....	Rt		Caravan
....	Rt		The Hucklebuck —vLE
....	Rt		Don't Blame Me —vKD
....	Rt		Change My Ways
....	Rt		Trumpet-No-End
....	Rt		Take The "A" Train

DUKE ELLINGTON & HIS ORCHESTRA
HB NW DB AK RN, TG LB QJ, JHtn JH RP JF HC, DE WMsl SG, KD LE AH.

1 Sep 1949   (S)
Columbia Studios
New York City, NY

....		CO41687	You Of All People —vAH
....		CO41687	You Of All People (incomplete)
....	Co	CO41687-1	You Of All People —vAH
....	UTD	CO41688	Creole Love Call —vKD
....	Co	CO41688-1	Creole Love Call —vKD
....	Co	CO41688-2	Creole Love Call —vKD
....	UTD	CO41689	The Greatest There Is —vLE[1]
....	Co	CO41689	The Greatest There Is —vLE
....	UTD	CO41690	Snibor[2]
....	Co	CO41690	Snibor

[1]Complete: "He's The Greatest There Is."
[2]*sa* "The New Look"; (=Robins).

DUKE ELLINGTON & HIS ORCHESTRA
HB NW DB AK RN, TG LB QJ, JHtn JH RP ChR JF HC, DE WMsl SG, KD LE AH.

2 Sep 1949   (P)
Click Restaurant (bc)
Philadelphia, PA

....	Rt		Creole Love Call —vKD
....	Rt		All Of Me —vLE
....	Rt		Solitude —vAH
....	Rt		Trebop[1]
....	Rt		It Don't Mean A Thing —vAH
....	Rt		Things Ain't What They Used To Be

[1]*sa* "Dance #2" of the *Liberian Suite*. "Tribal" on Rt.

DUKE ELLINGTON & HIS ORCHESTRA
HB NW DB AK RN, TG LB QJ, JHtn JH RP ChR JF HC, DE WMsl SG, KD AH.

3 Sep 1949   (P)
Click Restaurant (bc)
Philadelphia, PA

....	Rar		Take The "A" Train
....	Rar		Singing In The Rain
....	Rar		Mood Indigo —vKD
....	Rar		Caravan
....	Rt		Paradise
....	Rt		S'posin' —vAH
....	Rt		Take The "A" Train

DUKE ELLINGTON WITH ORCHESTRA
DE with a studio orchestra, directed by Alan Roth.

20 Sep 1949   (P)
NBC Studios (tc)
New York City, NY

....		Medley[1]

[1]Including: Don't Get Around Much Anymore; Mood Indigo; I'm Beginning To See The Light; Caravan; It Don't Mean A Thing; Sophisticated Lady.

DUKE ELLINGTON & HIS ORCHESTRA
HB NW DB AK RN, TG LB QJ, JHtn JH RP ChR JF HC, DE WMsl SG, AH.

23 Nov 1949   (P)
Earle Theater (bc)
Philadelphia, PA

....		Jam-A-Ditty
....		You Of All People —vAH

DUKE ELLINGTON & HIS ORCHESTRA
RN, TG, JHtn JH HC, BS WMsl SG, LE AH.

22 Dec 1949   (S)
Columbia Studios
New York City, NY

....		CO42550	The World Is Waiting For The Sunrise —vAH
....		CO42550	The World Is Waiting For The Sunrise —vAH
....	Co	CO42550-1	The World Is Waiting For The Sunrise —vAH >>>

> Unidentified vcl group added, DE replaces BS.

| .... | | CO42551 | Joog Joog –vLE Grp |
| .... | Co | CO42551-1 | Joog Joog –vLE Grp |

> Unidentified vcl group omitted.

| .... | Co | CO42552-1 | Good Woman Blues –vAH[1] |

> BS added.

....	UTD		On The Sunny Side Of The Street (rehearsal)
....	UTD	CO42553	On The Sunny Side Of The Street –vLE
....	Co	CO42553-1	On The Sunny Side Of The Street –vLE

> BS omitted.

| .... | Co | CO42554-1 | B Sharp Boston |
| .... | Co[2] | CO42554 alt. | B Sharp Boston |

[1]*aka* "Duke's Good Girl Blues"; "Good Girl Blues."
[2]The unspecified version on UTD is the alternate take, which was first released on CBS/Co (F) 62993.

DUKE ELLINGTON
Piano solo and vcl.

Late Jan 1950   (S)
DE's hotel room
Detroit, MI

| .... | UTD | I'm Afraid Of Loving You Too Much –vDE |
| .... | UTD | Joog Joog –vDE |

DUKE ELLINGTON & HIS ORCHESTRA
HB NW DB AK RN, TG LB QJ, JHtn JH RP ChR JF HC, DE WMsl SG, KD LE AH.

Late Jan 1950   (P)
Paradise Theater (bc)
Detroit, MI

....	UTD	Take The "A" Train
....	UTD	B Sharp Boston
....	UTD	How High The Moon
....	UTD	DE message on polio
....	UTD	Creole Love Call –vKD
....	UTD	On The Sunny Side Of The Street –vLE
....	UTD	You Of All People –vAH
....	UTD	DE promoting the March of Dimes
....	UTD	Suddenly It Jumped
....	UTD	Take The "A" Train

DUKE ELLINGTON & HIS ORCHESTRA
HB NW DB AK RN, TG LB QJ, JHtn JH RP ChR AMC HC, DE WMsl SG, KD CK AH.

6 Mar 1950   (T)[1]
Universal Studios, Stage 10
Hollywood, CA

....	Az[2]		Things Ain't What They Used To Be
....	Az		[3] Hello, Little Boy (incomplete)
....	Az	M-V-6-1	Hello, Little Boy –vCK
....	Az	M-S-3-3	The History Of Jazz In Three Minutes
....	Az		She Wouldn't Be Moved
....	Az	M-V-7-1	Violet Blue –vKD
....	Az		Take The "A" Train
....	Az	M-V-5-1	[3] You Of All People –vAH

[1]Music for the movie short "Salute To Duke Ellington."
[2]The Az releases are unedited soundtrack prerecordings.
[3]These items were not included in the film.

DUKE ELLINGTON
DE interviewed by person unknown.

7 Apr 1950   (S)
DE's hotel room
Paris, France

| .... | IMV | Interview |

DUKE ELLINGTON
DE interviewed by Loys Chocart.

4 May 1950   (S)
Unidentified location
Lausanne, Switzerland

| .... | | Interview |

DUKE ELLINGTON & HIS ORCHESTRA
HB NW ER AK RN, TK LB QJ, JHtn JH RP DBs AMC HC, DE WMsl SG/BBld, KD CK.

29 May 1950   (P)
Musikhalle (bc)
Hamburg, Germany

....		Suddenly It Jumped
....		The Mooche
....		Ring Dem Bells
....		Paradise >>>

		Air Conditioned Jungle
....		You Oughta
....	MJ	How High The Moon
....		Creole Love Call –vKD
....		On A Turquoise Cloud –vKD
....		Frankie And Johnny

> BS replaces DE.

| .... | | Take The "A" Train |

> DE replaces BS.

....		Rockin' In Rhythm
....		Violet Blue
....		Don't Get Around Much Anymore
....		Hello, Little Boy –vCK
....		Juke Bop Boogie –vCK
....		Mood Indigo
....		St. Louis Blues –vRN
....		Caravan
....		Trumpet-No-End

31 May 1950   (P)
Restaurant Sct. Thomas
Copenhagen, Denmark

DUKE ELLINGTON & FRIENDS
JHtn DBs, BS.

| .... | | Laura |
| .... | | Sophisticated Lady |

> DE piano solo.

| .... | Az | I Can't Get Started |

> JHtn DBs added.

| .... | Az | Body And Soul |
| .... | Az | Blues[1] |

[1] sa "Nix It, Mix It"; "Prelude To A Mood."

6 Jun 1950   (S)
Radio & Photo Shop Hammerschmidt
Arhus, Denmark

DUKE ELLINGTON
Piano solo and vcl.

....	PP	Sophisticated Lady –spoken introduction by DE
....	PP	Mood Indigo –spoken introduction by DE
....		I'm Afraid Of Loving You Too Much –vDE

> IBH added.

| .... | | I Met A Little Miss –vIBH |

18 Jul 1950   (P)
DuMont Studios (tc)
New York City, NY

DUKE ELLINGTON & HIS ORCHESTRA
HB NW ER AF RN, LB QJ, JHtn JH RP AMC HC, DE WMsl SG, MC CK JNtn.

| .... | | Take The "A" Train |
| .... | | Rockin' In Rhythm |

> BBgs HCol TR added.

| .... | | Everybody's Doin' It –vTR, BBgs HCol tap |
| .... | | Take The "A" Train –BBgs HCol tap |

> BBgs HCol TR omitted.

....		Hello, Little Boy –vCK
....		Caravan
....		Take The "A" Train
....		Creole Love Call—The Jeep Is Jumpin'—Creole Love Call –vJNtn
....		On A Turquoise Cloud –vMC CK JNtn
....		Stomp, Look And Listen

13 Sep 1950   (S)
?Apex Studios
New York City, NY

OSCAR PETTIFORD, HIS CELLO AND QUARTET
DE OP LT JJ.

| .... | Mer | M4004 | Untitled Blues |
| .... | Mer | M4005 | Perdido |

> BS added.

| .... | Mer | M4006 | Take The "A" Train |
| .... | Mer | M4007-1 | Oscalypso   >>> |

> BS omitted.

.... Mer   M4008   Blues For Blanton
....   M4009   [Twelve O'Clock Rock¹]

¹Variant spellings "Twelve O'Clock Jump/ ... Bump."

20 Sep 1950   (P)
Apollo Theater (bc)
New York City, NY

DUKE ELLINGTON & HIS ORCHESTRA
HB NW AF RN, LB QJ, JHtn RP AMC HC, DE WMsl SG.

....   Danny Boy
....   Take The "A" Train

21 Sep 1950   (S)
?Apex Studios
New York City, NY

CHUBBY KEMP & HER ALL STARS
Vcl, acc. by RR, JH HC, EDk* OP WMsl MR.

.... UTD   M4010   Mean Old Choo Choo –vCK

THE ELLINGTONIANS WITH AL HIBBLER
RR, JH HC, BS OP WMsl MR, AH.

.... Mer   M4011   White Christmas –vAH

> OP omitted.

.... Mer   M4012   Nobody Knows The Trouble I've Seen –vAH

THE ELLINGTONIANS WITH CHUBBY KEMP
RR, JH HC, EDk* OP WMsl MR, CK.

.... Mer   M4013   Me And My Wig –vCK¹

> BS replaces EDk.

.... Mer   M4014   How Blue Can You Get –vCK

¹sa "A Slip Of The Lip."

CHUBBY KEMP & HER ALL STARS
Vcl, acc. by RR, JH HC, EDk* WMsl MR.

.... Mer   M4015-2   Juke Bop Boogie –vCK¹

¹"Juke Box Boogie" on some releases.

SARA FORDE WITH MERCER ELLINGTON & HIS ORCHESTRA
Vcl, acc. by RR, JH HC, EDk* WMsl MR.

.... Mer   M4016   Set 'Em Up –vSF¹

¹aka "Rack 'Em Back."

THE ELLINGTONIANS
RR, JH HC, EDk* WMsl MR.

.... Mer   M4017   The New Piano Roll Blues

SARA FORDE WITH BILLY STRAYHORN
Vcl, acc. by BS.

.... Mer   M4018   The Man I Love –vSF

*DE used the nom de plume Edward Duke for this session.

3 Oct 1950   (S)
24ᵗʰ St. Studios
New York City, NY

JIMMY McPHAIL WITH THE BILLY STRAYHORN TRIO
Vcl, acc. by DE BS WMsl.

....   M5706   [I Wonder Why –vJMP]
....   M5707   [I'll Remember April –vJMP]
....   M5708   [No Smoking –vJMP]
....   M5709   [Brown Suede –vJMP]

BILLY STRAYHORN TRIO
DE BS WMsl.

.... Mer   M5710   Cotton Tail
.... Mer   M5711   The "C" Jam Blues
.... Mer   M5712   Flamingo
.... Mer   M5713   Bang-Up Blues

                                                                          21 Oct 1950   (S)
    THE ELLINGTONIANS WITH AL HIBBLER   ?Apex Studios
    ME, BCrt HC, BS DBbr WMsl CS, AH.   New York City, NY

.... Mer   M4019   Stormy Weather –vAH

   > DE replaces BS.

.... Mer   M4020   Cherry –vAH

   > BS replaces DE.

.... Mer   M4021   Star Dust –vAH

   > ME omitted, DE replaces BS.

.... Mer   M4022   Honeysuckle Rose –vAH

                                                                          Oct 1950   (S)
    WILD BILL DAVIS & HIS REAL GONE ORGAN   ?Apex Studios
    BD DE JC JJ.   New York City, NY

.... Mer   M4023   Things Ain't What They Used To Be

                                                                          Nov 1950   (S)
    BILLY STRAYHORN TRIO   24th St. Studios
    DE BS JSmn.   New York City, NY

.... Mer   M2479   Tonk
.... Mer   M2480   Johnny Come Lately
.... Mer   M2481   In A Blue Summer Garden
.... Mer   M2482   Great Times

                                                                          19 Nov 1950   (P)
    DUKE ELLINGTON & HIS ORCHESTRA   ABC Studios (tc)
    HB NW AF CA RN, LB QJ, JHtn JH RP PG HC, DE WMsl SG.   New York City, NY

   > BD added.
....   The World Is Waiting For The Sunrise
....   Oh! Lady Be Good

   > BD omitted.

....   St. Louis Blues –vRN
.... JSo   Trumpet-No-End

    Listed above are only those titles of the program DE or his sidemen participated in.

                                                                          20 Nov 1950   (S)
    DUKE ELLINGTON & HIS ORCHESTRA   30th Street Studio
    HB NW AF CA RN, LB QJ, ?ME, JHtn JH RP PG HC, DE WMsl SG, YL[1] AH. New York City, NY

.... Co   CO44662-1   Build That Railroad –vAH[2]
.... Co   CO44663-1   Love You Madly –vYL
.... Co   CO44664-1   Great Times

[1]Vovalist Yvonne Duke assumed the stage name Yvonne Lanauze while singing with the Ellington band.
[2]According to AH, JJ was on drums for this title.

                                                                          18 Dec 1950   (S)
    DUKE ELLINGTON & HIS ORCHESTRA   30th Street Studio
    HB NW AF CA RN, TG LB QJ, JHtn JH RP PG HC, DE BS WMsl SG, YL.   New York City, NY

.... Co   CO44749-1   The Tattooed Bride
.... Co   CO44750-1   Mood Indigo –vYL
.... Co   CO44751-1   Sophisticated Lady –vYL
.... Co   CO44752-1   Solitude

                                                                          26 Dec 1950   (S)
    DUKE ELLINGTON & HIS ORCHESTRA   DuMont Studios (tc)
    HB NW AF CA RN, TG LB QJ, JHtn JH RP PG HC, DE WMsl SG, YL.   New York City, NY

....   Take The "A" Train
....   Ko-Ko
....   Co-Percussional Intricacies

   > HK added.

....   On The Alamo –HK tap
....   The World Is Waiting For The Sunrise –HK tap

   > HK omitted.

....   Tea For Two
....   I Know That you Know
....   Coloratura   >>>

....   > HK added.

....   Perdido –HK tap

....   > HK omitted.

....   Love You Madly –vYL
....   Take The "A" Train
....   Great Times
....   Don't Get Around Much Anymore
....   Mood Indigo

....   > BDvs added.

....   Oh! Lady Be Good –BDvs tap
....   Stompy Jones –BDvs tap

The first nine titles can be found on a soundtrack "Audition" LP (Reeves Soundtrack Corp.).

                                                                        2 Jan 1951   (S)
DUKE ELLINGTON & HIS ORCHESTRA   Unidentified radio studio[1] (bc)
HB NW AF CA RN, LB QJ, JHtn JH RP PG HC, BS WMsl SG, YL AH.   New York City, NY

....   GoJ   Take The "A" Train

....   > DE replaces BS.

....   GoJ   Solitude –vYL
....   GoJ   You Of All People –vAH

....   > OP added.

....   GoJ   Great Times

[1]Live recording for radio transcription.

                                                                        21 Jan 1951   (P)
DUKE ELLINGTON & HIS ORCHESTRA   Metropolitan Opera House
HB NW FW CA RN, LB QJ, JHtn JH RP PG HC, DE WMsl JBjm SG BClk, YL.   New York City, NY

....   Eph   The Mooche
....   Eph   Ring Dem Bells –vRN
....   Eph   Frustration
....   Eph   Coloratura
....   Eph   Rose Of The Rio Grande
....   Eph   Love You Madly –vYL
....   Eph   Take The "A" Train
....   Eph   A TONE PARALLEL TO HARLEM

                                             THE CONTROVERSIAL SUITE
....   RR   - Later[1]
....   RR   - Before My Time

....   VoA   Violet Blue

....   > JHtn RP HC, DE.

....   Eph   Monologue –DE narration[2]

....   > Entire band.

....   Eph   Duet
....   Eph   Threesome
....   RR   Medley[3]
....   VoA   St. Louis Blues –vRN
....   RR   Trumpet-No-End

[1]This title is a derivative of *Tiger Rag.*
[2]*aka "Pretty And The Wolf."*
[3]Including: Don't Get Around Much Anymore; In A Sentimental Mood; Mood Indigo; I'm Beginning To See The Light;
Sophisticated Lady; Caravan; Solitude; I Let A Song Go Out Of My Heart/Don't Get Around Much Anymore.

                                                                        23 Jan 1951   (P)
DUKE ELLINGTON   Studios WFIL (tc)
DE piano and talking, interviewed by Frank Brookhauser.   Philadelphia, PA

....   Az   Interview
....   Az   Medley[1]

[1]Including: Mood Indigo; It Don't Mean A Thing; Sophisticated Lady; In A Sentimental Mood; Solitude; Caravan; I Let
A Song Go Out Of My Heart; Take The "A" Train; I Got It Bad; Don't Get Around Much Anymore; Do Nothin' Till You
Hear From Me.

THE CORONETS
CA, JT, WS PG, BS WMsl LBsn.

			17 Apr 1951 (S)
			?Apex Studios
			New York City, NY

.... Mer   M4029   Cat Walk
.... Mer   M4030-1   Moonlight Fiesta
.... Mer   M4030-2   Moonlight Fiesta
.... Mer   M4031   She
.... Mer   M4032   The Happening

Although DE's name is not mentioned, this session is listed here regardless, since The Coronets can be considered a genuine Ellington Unit.

DUKE ELLINGTON & HIS ORCHESTRA
HB NW AF CA RN, BWmn QJ JT, JHtn WS RP PG HC, DE WMsl LBsn, EL TC.

3 May 1951 (P)
ABC Studios (tc)
New York City, NY

.... Sn   Take The "A" Train[1]
.... Sn   Something To Live For –vTC
.... Sn   Caravan
.... Sn   I Got It Bad –vEL
.... Sn   Do Nothin' Till You Hear From Me –vTC
.... Sn   Threesome

[1]The release on Sn seems to have been edited: Note change of tempo and ambience when PG's solo part begins.

DUKE ELLINGTON & HIS ORCHESTRA
HB NW AF CA RN, BWmn QJ JT, JHtn WS RP PG HC, DE WMsl LBsn.

4 May 1951 (P)
Birdland (bc)
New York City, NY

....   Take The "A" Train
.... Alt   Threesome
.... Alt   Frustration
.... Alt   Sultry Serenade
.... Alt   Sophisticated Lady

DUKE ELLINGTON & HIS ORCHESTRA
HB NW AF CA RN, BWmn QJ JT, JHtn WS RP PG HC, DE WMsl LBsn, AH.

5 May 1951 (P)
Birdland (bc)
New York City, NY

....   Take The "A" Train
.... Alt   Just A-Settin' And A-Rockin' –vRN
.... Alt   Air Conditioned Jungle
.... Alt   Coloratura
.... Alt   Solitude –vAH
.... Alt   Skin Deep
.... Alt   Perdido
....   Take The "A" Train

DUKE ELLINGTON & HIS ORCHESTRA
HB NW AF CA RN, BWmn QJ JT, JHtn WS RP PG HC, DE WMsl LBsn.

10 May 1951 (S)
Columbia Studios
New York City, NY

.... Co   CO45814-1   Fancy Dan
.... Co   CO45815-1   The Hawk Talks
.... Co   CO45816-1   V.I.P.'s Boogie[1, 2]
.... Co   CO45817-1   Jam With Sam[2]

> JHtn ?WS RP HC, DE WMsl LBsn.

.... Co   CO45818-1   Monologue –DE narration

[1]*sa* "Threesome"; V.I.P. stands for Very Important Persons.
[2]"V.I.P.'s Boogie" and "Jam With Sam" began as the third section of the suite "Monolog" [*sic*], "Duet" and "Threesome." However, when the project could not be realized as planned, DE divided the two parts of "Threesome" and renamed them "V.I.P.'s Boogie" and "Jam With Sam."

THE CORONETS
BWmn QJ JT, WS, DE WMsl LBsn.

18 May 1951 (S)
Unspecified studio
Boston, MA

.... Mer   M4033   Swamp Drum
.... Mer   M4034   Sultry Serenade

> BS replaces DE.

.... Mer   M4035   Indian Summer

> DE replaces BS.

.... Mer   M4036   Britt And Butter Blues[1]

[1]Refers to Britt Woodman and Quentin "Butter" Jackson.

DUKE ELLINGTON WITH ORCHESTRA
DE with a studio orchestra and chorus, directed by David Brockman.

| | | | | | 19 May 1951 (P)
CBS Studios (tc)
New York City, NY |

.... Az   Medley[1]
.... Az   I Like The Wild Open Spaces –vChorus

[1]Including: Caravan; Sophisticated Lady; Mood Indigo; It Don't Mean A Thing; I Got It Bad –vChorus; I Let A Song Go Out Of My Heart/Don't Get Around Much Anymore.

DUKE ELLINGTON & HIS ORCHESTRA
HB NW AF CA RN, BWmn QJ JT, JHtn WS RP PG HC, DE WMsl LBsn.

24 May 1951 (S)
Columbia Studios
New York City, NY

.... Co   CO45829-1   Ting-A-Ling[1]
.... Co   CO45830-1   The Eighth Veil
.... Co   CO45831-1   Brown Betty

[1]Dedicated to Ms. Carol Bruce, star of the show *Pal Joey*.

THE CORONETS
JT, WS, DE WMsl LBsn, NO.

1 Jun 1951 (S)
?Apex Studios
New York City, NY

....   M4037   [The Nearness Of You –vNO]
....   M4038   [More Than You Know –vNO]

> BS added.

.... Mer   M4039   Caravan

DUKE ELLINGTON & HIS ORCHESTRA
HB NW CA RN, BWmn QJ JT, JHtn WS RP PG HC, DE WMsl LBsn, NO AH.

5 Jun 1951 (P)
Meadowbrook Inn (bc)
Cedar Grove, NJ

.... VoA   Happy-Go-Lucky Local
....   Love You Madly –vNO
.... VoA   Mood Indigo
.... VoA   Ting-A-Ling
....   Danny Boy –vAH
....   Rockin' In Rhythm

DUKE ELLINGTON & HIS ORCHESTRA
HB NW CA RN, BWmn QJ JT, JHtn WS RP PG HC, DE WMsl LBsn, NO AH.

6 Jun 1951 (P)
Meadowbrook Inn (bc)
Cedar Grove, NJ

.... DJI   Take The "A" Train
.... DJI   The Tattooed Bride[1]
.... Std   Indian Summer
.... DJI   Love You Madly –vNO
.... DJI   Moonlight Fiesta
.... DJI   All Day Long
.... DJI   I Let A Song Go Out Of My Heart –vAH
.... DJI   The Hawk Talks
.... DJI   Take The "A" Train
.... DJI   Gotta Go

[1]"Aberdeen" part only.

DUKE ELLINGTON & HIS ORCHESTRA
HB NW CA RN, BWmn QJ JT, JHtn WS RP PG HC, DE WMsl LBsn, NO AH.

7 Jun 1951 (P)
Meadowbrook Inn (bc)
Cedar Grove, NJ

....   Take The "A" Train
.... Std   Midriff
....   Sophisticated Lady
....   Love You Madly –vNO
....   The Hawk Talks
....   Solitude –vAH
.... Std   All Day Long
.... MJ   Just A-Settin' And A-Rockin' –vRN
....   Gotta Go

DUKE ELLINGTON & HIS ORCHESTRA
HB NW CA RN, BWmn QJ JT, JHtn WS RP PG HC, DE WMsl LBsn, AH.

8 Jun 1951 (P)
Meadowbrook Inn (bc)
Cedar Grove, NJ

.... OTR   Take The "A" Train
.... OTR   How High The Moon
.... OTR   Brown Betty
.... OTR   S'posin' –vAH   >>>

	OTR	Frustration
	OTR	St. Louis Blues –vRN
	OTR	Primpin' For The Prom
	OTR	Swamp Drum
	OTR	Perdido

9 Jun 1951 (P)
NBC Studios (tc)
New York City, NY

DUKE ELLINGTON
Brief appearance on Milton Berle's Damon Runyon Cancer Fund Telethon.

		DE talking

DUKE ELLINGTON & HIS ORCHESTRA
HB NW CA RN, BWmn QJ JT, JHtn WS RP PG HC, DE WMsl LBsn, NO AH.

Meadowbrook Inn (bc) (P)
Cedar Grove, NJ

> DE WMsl LBsn.

	DJI	I Can't Get Started

> Entire band.

	MJ	Primpin' For The Prom
	DJI	Later
	DJI	Unidentified title
	DJI	Take The "A" Train

> DE piano solo.

	DJI	New World A-Comin'

> Entire band.

	OTR	Harlem Air Shaft
	Std	Night Walk[1]
	OTR	Love You Madly –vNO
	OTR	Sultry Sunset
	OTR	Ol' Man River –vAH
	Std	Things Ain't What They Used To Be

[1] sa "Cat Walk."

10 Jun 1951 (P)
Meadowbrook Inn (bc)
Cedar Grove, NJ

DUKE ELLINGTON & HIS ORCHESTRA
HB NW CA RN, BWmn QJ JT, JHtn WS RP PG HC, DE WMsl LBsn, NO AH.

	VoA	Warm Valley
		Flamingo –vAH
	ST	Tea For Two
	VoA	The Eighth Veil
		Love You Madly –vNO
		Blue Lou
		Creole Love Call

11 Jun 1951 (P)
Meadowbrook Inn (bc)
Cedar Grove, NJ

DUKE ELLINGTON & HIS ORCHESTRA
HB NW CA RN, BWmn QJ JT, JHtn WS RP PG HC, DE WMsl LBsn, NO AH.

		Take The "A" Train
		V.I.P.'s Boogie
		Jam With Sam
		Don't Get Around Much Anymore –vAH
		Sultry Serenade
		Duet
		Love You Madly –vNO
		The Hawk Talks
	Std	The Happening
	Std	Gotta Go

5-11 Jun 1951 (P)
Meadowbrook Inn (bc)
Cedar Grove, NJ

DUKE ELLINGTON & HIS ORCHESTRA
HB NW CA RN, BWmn QJ JT, JHtn WS RP PG HC, DE WMsl LBsn.

	VoA	All Day Long
	VoA	Sophisticated Lady
	VoA	The Hawk Talks
	VoA	Midriff
	VoA	Just A-Settin' And A-Rockin' –vRN
	VoA	Caravan

The above is a composite of VoA programs #41, 42, 43 and 44, most probably originating from this engagement at The Meadowbrook Inn.

19 Jun 1951   (S)
?Apex Studios
New York City, NY

THE CORONETS
JT, JHtn WS, DE WMsl LBsn.

.... Mer   M4040   Alternate
.... Mer   M4041   Hoppin' John[1]

> BS replaces DE.

.... Mer   M4042   Jumpin' With Symphony Sid

[1]Misspelled "Noppin' John" on some releases. The theme was used in the future to enhance the extended version of *Perdido*.

23 Jun 1951   (P)
Birdland (bc)
New York City, NY

DUKE ELLINGTON & HIS ORCHESTRA
HB NW CA RN, BWmn QJ JT, JHtn WS RP PG HC, DE WMsl LBsn, AH.

....   Jumpin' With Symphony Sid
....   Take The "A" Train
.... Sn   Fancy Dan
.... Sn   The Hawk Talks
.... Sn   Swamp Drum
.... Sn   Rockin' In Rhythm
....   Happy Birthday
.... Sn   The Tattooed Bride[1]
....   Caravan
....   All Day Long
....   Ol' Man River –vAH
.... Std   Harlem Air Shaft
....   Things Ain't What They Used To Be
....   Take The "A" Train

[1]"Aberdeen" part only.

30 Jun 1951   (P)
CBS Studios (tc)
New York City, NY

DUKE ELLINGTON
DE on the show "Songs for Sale."

....   Panel duties

DUKE ELLINGTON & HIS ORCHESTRA   Birdland (bc)   (P)
HB NW CA RN, BWmn QJ JT, JHtn WS RP PG HC, DE WMsl LBsn, NO AH.

....   Jumpin' With Symphony Sid
....   Take The "A" Train
....   Midriff
.... Std   Warm Valley
....   The Eighth Veil
....   The Hawk Talks
....   Flamingo –vAH
.... Std   Boy Meets Horn
....   How High The Moon
....   Mood Indigo
.... Std   Love You Madly –vNO
....   Fancy Dan
.... Std   Diminuendo In Blue and Crescendo In Blue (w. interval)[1]
.... Std   Take The "A" Train
....   Jumpin' With Symphony Sid

[1]This is the first recording with PG playing the bridge between the two titles, which developed over time into the "Wailing Interval," and put the band in the spotlight at the Newport Jazz Festival 1956.

7 Aug 1951   (S)
30th Street Studio
New York City, NY

DUKE ELLINGTON & HIS ORCHESTRA
HB NW CA RN, BWmn QJ JT, JHtn WS RP PG HC, DE WMsl LBsn.

.... UTD   CO47018   Deep Night
.... Co   CO47018-1   Deep Night
.... UTD   CO47019   Please Be Kind
.... Co   CO47019-1   Please Be Kind

> BS replaces DE.

.... UTD   CO47020   Smada[1]
.... OK   CO47020-1   Smada
....   CO47021 [-1]   Rock Skippin' At The Blue Note (incomplete)
....   CO47021 [-2]   Rock Skippin' At The Blue Note (incomplete)
.... UTD   CO47021 [-3]   Rock Skippin' At The Blue Note
.... Co   CO47021-1   Rock Skippin' At The Blue Note   >>>

> DE replaces BS.

....   CO47022-1   (Don't Take My Love)

[1]*aka* "Rickshaw"; (=Adams). Dedicated to Los Angeles deejay Joe Adams.

19 Aug 1951   (S)
Unidentified radio studio[1] (bc)
New York City, NY

<u>DUKE ELLINGTON & HIS ORCHESTRA</u>
HB FW CA RN, BWmn QJ JT, JHtn WS RP PG HC, DE WMsl LBsn, AH.

.... SoP   Take The "A" Train
.... Plm   Fancy Dan
.... Plm   The Hawk Talks
.... Plm   Ol' Man River –vAH
.... KoJ   The "C" Jam Blues
.... Gth   Caravan
.... Gth   Mood Indigo –DE talking

> BS added.

.... Gth   Ad Lib Blues

> BS omitted.

.... Gth   Tea For Two

> JHtn RP HC, DE.

.... Gth   Monologue –DE narration

> Entire band.

.... Gth   Duet
.... Gth   Threesome
.... Gth   Primpin' For The Prom
.... Gth   Moonlight Fiesta
.... Gth   Sophisticated Lady

[1]Live recordings for radio transcriptions.

p Autumn 1951   (P)
Unidentified TV studio (tc)[1]
U.S.A.

<u>DUKE ELLINGTON</u>
DE, GP.

....   I'm Beginning To See The Light –GP tap

[1]DE on the Benay Venuta show.

15 Nov 1951   (P)
University of Michigan
Ann Arbor, MI

<u>SARAH VAUGHAN WITH DUKE ELLINGTON AND NAT KING COLE</u>
Vcl, acc. by DE and an unidentified orchestra.

....   Mean To Me –vSV
....   Perdido –vSV

> NKC added.

....   Love You Madly –vSV NKC[1]

[1]DE's presence is questionable, however, CA seems to be audible.

7 Dec 1951   (S)
30th Street Studio
New York City, NY

<u>DUKE ELLINGTON & HIS ORCHESTRA</u>
HB FW CT WC RN, BWmn QJ JT, JHtn WS RP PG HC, DE BS WMsl LBsn.

....   [-1]   A TONE PARALLEL TO HARLEM (ending)
....   [-2]   A TONE PARALLEL TO HARLEM (ending)
....   [-3]   A TONE PARALLEL TO HARLEM (ending)
....   [-4]   A TONE PARALLEL TO HARLEM (ending)
....   A TONE PARALLEL TO HARLEM (beginning/rehearsal)
....   A TONE PARALLEL TO HARLEM (beginning/rehearsal)
.... Co   CO50717-1   A TONE PARALLEL TO HARLEM[1]
               CO50717-2   A TONE PARALLEL TO HARLEM (incomplete)
.... UTD CO50717-3   A TONE PARALLEL TO HARLEM

> DV added.

.... UTD CO47263   Bensonality[2]
.... Co   CO47263-1   Bensonality

[1]Edited version on Co.
[2]*aka* "Alavantin' Al"; "The Bend." Dedicated to Chicago deejay Al Benson.

DUKE ELLINGTON & HIS ORCHESTRA
HB CT WC RN, BWmn QJ JT, JHtn WS RP PG HC, DE WMsl LBsn, LO.

11 Dec 1951   (S)
30th Street Studio
New York City, NY

....		CO47267	Blues At Sundown –vLO
....		CO47267	Blues At Sundown (incomplete)
....	UTD	CO47267	Blues At Sundown –vLO
....	Co	CO47267-1	Blues At Sundown –vLO
....		[-1]	Duet (insert 1)
....		[-1]	Duet (insert 1)
....		[-2]	Duet (insert 1)
....		[-3]	Duet (insert 1; incomplete)
....		[-4]	Duet (insert 1; incomplete)
....		[-5]	Duet (insert 1)
....	Co	CO47268-1	Duet
....		[-6]	Duet (insert 1)
....		[-7]	Duet (insert 1; incomplete)
....		[-7]	Duet (insert 1)

THE CONTROVERSIAL SUITE

....		CO47269 [-1]	2 Before My Time (incomplete)
....	UTD	CO47269-2	2 Before My Time
....		CO47269 [-2]	2 Before My Time (incomplete)
....	Co	CO47269-3	2 Before My Time
....		CO47269 [-1]	1 Later (incomplete)
....	UTD	CO47269-2	1 Later
....		CO47269 [-3]	1 Later
....		CO47269 [-4]	1 Later (incomplete)
....		CO47269 [-7]	1 Later (incomplete)
....	Co	CO47269-3	1 Later
....			1 Later (insert 1)
....			1 Later (insert 2)

    > RN omitted, BS replaces DE.

....		CO47270 [-1]	Azalea –vLO (incomplete)
....		CO47270 [-2]	Azalea –vLO (incomplete)
....		CO47270 [-3]	Azalea –vLO
....		CO47270 [-4]	Azalea (incomplete)
....	UTD	CO47270 [-6]	Azalea –vLO

    > DE replaces BS.

....	UTD	CO47271 [-1]	Vagabonds[1]
....		CO47271 [-2]	Vagabonds (incomplete)
....		CO47271 [-3]	Vagabonds
....		CO47271 [-4]	Vagabonds
....		CO47271 [-5]	Vagabonds (incomplete)
....		CO47271 [-6]	Vagabonds (incomplete)
....	FM	CO47271 [-6]	Vagabonds
....		CO47272 [-3]	Something To Live For –vLO
....		CO47272 [-4]	Something To Live For (incomplete)
....	Co	CO47272-1	Something To Live For –vLO

    [1]*aka* "Cuidado"; "Careful."

DUKE ELLINGTON & HIS ORCHESTRA
CT WC CA RN, BWmn QJ JT, JHtn WS RP PG HC, DE WMsl LBsn.

p late 1951   (P)
Unidentified location
U.S.A.

....		Take The "A" Train

DUKE ELLINGTON & HIS ORCHESTRA
CT WC CA RN, BWmn QJ JT, JHtn WS RP PG HC, DE WMsl LBsn, BR JGsm.

5 Jan 1952   (P)
Metropolitan Opera House
New York City, NY

....		The Hawk Talks
....		Frustration
....		Sultry Serenade
....		Sophisticated Lady
....		Perdido
....		I Got It Bad –vBR
....		HARLEM[1]
....		Take The "A" Train
....		V.I.P.'s Boogie
....		Jam With Sam

    > JHtn RP HC, DE.

....		Monologue –DE narration >>>

> Entire band.

....		Blues At Sundown –vJGsm
....		Do Nothin' Till You Hear From Me –vJGsm
....		Once There Lived A Fool –vJGsm
....		Skin Deep
....		Medley[2]
....		Tulip Or Turnip –vRN
....	Std	Basin Street Blues –vRN

[1]sa "A Tone Parallel To Harlem."
[2]Including: Don't Get Around Much Anymore; In A Sentimental Mood; Mood Indigo; I'm Beginning to See The Light; Prelude To A Kiss; It Don't Mean A Thing; Solitude; I Let A Song Go Out Of My Heart/Don't Get Around Much Anymore.

	6 Jan 1952	(S)
	Labor Temple	

DUKE ELLINGTON & HIS ORCHESTRA
CT WC CA RN, BWmn QJ JT, JHtn WS RP PG HC, DE WMsl LBsn.
Minneapolis, MN

....		Take The "A" Train
....	Plm	The Eighth Veil
....	Plm	Duet
....	Plm	Mood Indigo
....	Plm	Rockin' In Rhythm
....		Take The "A" Train

Sister Kenny Foundation recording session; no audience in attendance. The transcriptions were used in radio broadcasts.

	29 Feb 1952	(S)
	Unidentified club	

DUKE ELLINGTON & HIS ORCHESTRA
CT WC CA RN, BWmn QJ JT, JHtn WS RP PG HC, DE WMsl LBsn.
Fresno, CA

....	Co	CO48377-1	Skin Deep

The above was a Mercer recording session. The item was acquired by CBS/Co on 8 Dec 1952 and given a master number.

	14 Mar 1952	(T)[1]
	General Service Studios	

DUKE ELLINGTON & HIS ORCHESTRA
CT WC CA RN, BWmn QJ JT, JHtn WS RP PG HC, DE WMsl LBsn, JGsm.
Balboa Beach, CA

....	Cmy	13001	Caravan
....	Cmy	13002	V.I.P.'s Boogie[2]
....	Cmy[3]	13003	Sophisticated Lady
....	KD[3]	13004	Mood Indigo
....	Cmy	13005	The Hawk Talks
....	KD	13006	The Mooche
....	Cmy[3]	13007	Solitude –vJGsm

[1]Filmed for Snader Transcriptions Corp. Each entry represents an individual movie short. The Snader production numbers are not necessarily indicative of chronology.
[2]This item includes "Jam With Sam."
[3]Most of the commercial releases of these titles have been edited—cut short, or had sections substituted from earlier recordings—which may create the impression that different takes exist. Contrary to both sleeve notes and label, instead of "Mood Indigo," Camay put an edited version of "Sophisticated Lady" on its record.

	22 Mar 1952	(P)
	Crystal Inn	

DUKE ELLINGTON & HIS ORCHESTRA
CT WC CA RN, BWmn QJ JT, JHtn WS RP PG HC, WMsl LBsn, JGsm.
Salem, OR

....	Skt	Deep Purple

> DE added.

....	Fws	Caravan
....		Warm Valley
....		I Let A Song Go Out Of My Heart/Don't Get Around Much Anymore –vRN
....	Sbt	Take The "A" Train
....		Sophisticated Lady
....	Skt	Don't Worry 'Bout Me
....		Perdido
....	Std	The Jeep Is Jumpin'
....	Az	Mood Indigo
....	Fws	How High The Moon

> JHtn RP HC, DE WMsl LBsn.

....		Monologue –DE narration

> Entire band.

....		Duet
....		Skin Deep
....	Sbt	Fancy Dan
....		The Hawk Talks >>>

....	Std	Tenderly
....		Frustration
....	Skt	Tea For Two
....		Solitude –vJGsm
....		Blues At Sundown –vJGsm
....		Do Nothin' Till You Hear From Me –vJGsm
....	Sbt	It Don't Mean A Thing –vRN
....		Take The "A" Train

> JHtn, DE.

| .... | Std | Black Beauty |

> DE WMsl.

| .... | | Dancers In Love |

> Entire band.

....		The Tattooed Bride
....		Flamingo –vJGsm
....	Skt	Trumpet-No-End
....		Take The "A" Train

25 Mar 1952   (P)
Civic Auditorium
Seattle, WA

DUKE ELLINGTON & HIS ORCHESTRA
CT WC CA RN, BWmn QJ JT, JHtn WS RP PG HC, DE WMsl LBsn, BR.

....	Az	The Mooche
....	Az	The Tattooed Bride
....	Vi	Sophisticated Lady
....	Az	Frustration
....	Vi	Sultry Serenade[1]
....	Az	How High The Moon
....	Vi	Perdido
....	Az	I Got It Bad –vBR
....	Vi	Caravan
....	Az	Take The "A" Train
....	Vi	HARLEM
....	Vi	Medley[2]
....	Vi	Skin Deep
....	Vi	The Hawk Talks
....	Vi	Jam With Sam
....	Az	Trumpet-No-End

[1]Reissued on CD under its other title "How Could You Do A Thing Like That To Me?"; see footnote for session on 6 Oct 1947.
[2]Including: Don't Get Around Much Anymore; In A Sentimental Mood; Mood Indigo; I'm Beginning To See The Light; Prelude To A Kiss; It Don't Mean A Thing; Solitude; I Let A Song Go Out Of My Heart/Don't Get Around Much Anymore.

29 Apr 1952   (P)
Armory
Yakima, WA

DUKE ELLINGTON & HIS ORCHESTRA
CT WC CA RN, BWmn QJ JT, JHtn HJsn RP PG HC, WMsl LBsn, BR JGsm.

....		Primpin' For The Prom
....	Std	Johnny Come Lately
....	Std	W.C.[1]
....	Skt	Time On My Hands
....	Std	Margie
....	Sbt	Chelsea Bridge
....		Midriff

(P)

> DE added.

....		Take The "A" Train
....	Sbt	Happy Birthday
....	Std	Ting-A-Ling
....	Sbt	Sophisticated Lady
....	Sbt	The "C" Jam Blues
....	JG	Passion Flower
....	Sbt	Mood Indigo
....	Skt	Caravan
....	Std	Moonlight Fiesta
....	Skt	Love You Madly –vBR
....		I Got It Bad –vBR
....		Take The "A" Train –vBR
....		Deep Purple –vBR
....	Skt	Bensonality
....	Sbt	The Tattooed Bride[2]
....		Just Squeeze Me –vRN
....	Skt	Once There Lived A Fool –vJGsm >>>

	Std		Blues At Sundown –vJGsm
....	Std		Blues At Sundown –vJGsm
....			Do Nothin' Till You Hear From Me –vJGsm
....	Skt		Cotton Tail
....	Std		Felanges[3]
....			V.I.P.'s Boogie
....	Sbt		Solitude –vJGsm
....	Skt		Summertime –vJGsm
....			My Little Brown Book –vJGsm
....	Std		Good Woman Blues –vJGsm
....			The Hawk Talks
....	Skt		Lady Of The Lavender Mist
....	Skt		How High The Moon
....	Skt		On The Sunny Side Of The Street
....			I Love My Lovin' Lover –vBR
....			Fancy Dan
....	Std		One O'Clock Jump
....	Std		Take The "A" Train

[1]Stands for <u>Wi</u>llie <u>C</u>ook.
[2]"Aberdeen" part only.
[3]Actually and correctly "Phalanges."

The origin of this material is still being debated, the alternative being McElroy's Ballroom on 21 Apr 1952. Some sources suggest that WS can be heard on both Margie and Moonlight Fiesta. On the other hand, WS left the band in March after the Seattle concert to be replaced temporarily by PKi. HJsn joined the band on 1 Apr, a fact which precludes the presence of WS also at McElroy's on 21 Apr. We believe that it can be safely assumed that the material originates from the Yakima dance date and have therefore listed it here.

				30 Jun 1952 (S)

DUKE ELLINGTON & HIS ORCHESTRA — 30th Street Studio
CT CA, BWmn QJ, JHtn RP PG HC, DE WMsl LBsn, BR. — New York City, NY

....	UTD	CO47482	I Love My Lovin' Lover –vBR
....	Co	CO47482-1	I Love My Lovin' Lover –vBR

> CT WC CA RN, BWmn QJ JT, JHtn HJsn RP PG HC, DE WMsl LBsn, BR JGsm.

....	Co	CO47483-1	Come On Home –vJGsm
....	Co[1]	CO48343[2]	Take The "A" Train –vBR

[1]Some of the reissues have been edited.
[2]This title was recorded in a private recording session. After CBS/Co acquired the item, it was given this control number. There is no information available regarding the take numbers. The same applies to the following session.

1 Jul 1952 (S)
DUKE ELLINGTON & HIS ORCHESTRA — 30th Studio Studio
CT WC CA RN, BWmn QJ JT, JHtn HJsn RP PG HC, DE WMsl LBsn. — New York City, NY

....	Co	CO48344[1]	The Mooche
....	Co	-2	The Mooche (insert)
....	Co	CO48345[1]	Perdido

[1]See footnote #2 for the previous session.

25 Jul 1952 (S)
DUKE ELLINGTON & JIMMY GRISSOM — Universal Studios
DE, JGsm. — Chicago, IL

....		She (rehearsal)
....		She –vJGsm
....		She –vJGsm
....		Weatherman –vJGsm[1]

> WMsl added.

....		She Didn't Have Much To Say –vJGsm
....		Night Train –vJGsm[2]

> WMsl omitted.

....		She –vJGsm (rehearsal)
....		She –vJGsm
....		She –vJGsm

[1]Complete: "Weatherman, How Does It Look For Tomorrow?"
[2]This title is a derivative of *Happy-Go-Lucky Local.*

The above is a rehearsal session; the music is from Man With Four Sides.

30 Jul 1952 (P)
DUKE ELLINGTON & HIS ORCHESTRA — Blue Note (bc)
CT WC CA RN, BWmn QJ JT, JHtn HJsn RP PG HC, DE WMsl LBsn, BR JGsm. — Chicago, IL

....	ACh		Take The "A" Train >>>

....	ACh	Bensonality	
....	ACh	All Of Me –vBR	
....	ACh	Bakiff	
....	ACh	The Hawk Talks	
....	ACh	Do Nothin' Till You Hear From Me –vJGsm	
....	ACh	V.I.P.'s Boogie	
....	ACh	Jam With Sam	
....	ACh	Just A-Settin' And A-Rockin' –vRN	
....	ACh	Mood Indigo	

2 Aug 1952   (P)
Blue Note (bc)
Chicago, IL

DUKE ELLINGTON & HIS ORCHESTRA
CT WC RN, BWmn QJ JT, JHtn HJsn RP PG HC, DE WMsl LBsn, JGsm.

....		Take The "A" Train
....		Smada
....		Do Nothin' Till You Hear From Me –vJGsm
....		Jam With Sam
....		Just Squeeze Me –vRN
....		Cotton Tail
....		Take The "A" Train

6 Aug 1952   (P)
Blue Note (bc)
Chicago, IL

DUKE ELLINGTON & HIS ORCHESTRA
CT WC CA RN, BWmn QJ JT, JHtn HJsn RP PG HC, DE WMsl LBsn, BR JGsm.

....	Cdy	Take The "A" Train
....	RDs	The Eighth Veil
....	RDs	How High The Moon
....	RDs	Solitude –vJGsm
....	Cdy	Duet
....	Ros	Take The "A" Train –vBR
....	RDs	Caravan
....	RDs	I Let A Song Go Out Of My Heart/Don't Get Around Much Anymore –vRN
....	Cdy	Jam With Sam

13 Aug 1952   (P)
Blue Note (bc)
Chicago, IL

DUKE ELLINGTON & HIS ORCHESTRA
CT WC CA RN, BWmn QJ JT, JHtn HJsn RP PG HC, DE WMsl LBsn, BR JGsm.

....	ACh	Take The "A" Train
....	ACh	Tulip Or Turnip –vRN
....	ACh	Ting-A-Ling
....	ACh	Flamingo –vJGsm
....	ACh	Rockin' In Rhythm
....	ACh	Sophisticated Lady
....	ACh	Take The "A" Train –vBR
....	ACh	Flying Home

Sep 1952[1]   (P)
Ritz Ballroom (bc)
Bridgeport, CT

DUKE ELLINGTON & HIS ORCHESTRA
CT WC CA RN, BWmn QJ JT, JHtn HJsn RP PG HC, DE WMsl LBsn, BR JGsm.

....		Perdido
....		Do Nothin' Till You Hear From Me –vJGsm
....		Take The "A" Train –vBR
....		I Let A Song Go Out Of My Heart/Don't Get Around Much Anymore –vRN
....		Skin Deep

[1]Broadcast on 21 Sep 1952.

19-25 Sep 1952   (P)
Town Casino (bc)
Cleveland, OH

DUKE ELLINGTON & HIS ORCHESTRA
CT WC CA RN, BWmn QJ JT, JHtn HJsn RP PG HC, DE WMsl LBsn.

....	VoA	Ko-Ko
....	VoA	Mood Indigo
....	VoA	V.I.P.'s Boogie
....	VoA	Jam With Sam

27 Sep 1952   (P)
ABC Studios (tc)
New York City, NY

DUKE ELLINGTON
DE piano and talking on the show "Chance of a Lifetime."

....		Interview
....		Mood Indigo –DE talking

> HC, WMsl LBsn added.[1]

....		Caravan—Sophisticated Lady—Caravan >>>

[1]A studio orchestra, directed by Bernie Leighton, joins in briefly toward the end.

				8 Nov 1952	(S)

DUKE ELLINGTON & HIS ORCHESTRA
CT WC CA RN, BWmn QJ JT, JHtn HJsn RP PG HC, DE WMsl LBsn, BR JGsm.

Columbia Studios
New York City, NY

....	UTD	CO48640-1	Blues –vJGsm[1]
....	UTD	CO48641-1	Body And Soul –vBR
....			[The "C" Jam Blues –vBR]

[1]sa "Good Woman Blues."

This was a Mercer recording session. The first two titles were acquired by Co on 8 Dec 1952 and given control numbers.

		14 Nov 1952	(P)

DUKE ELLINGTON & HIS ORCHESTRA
CT WC CA RN, BWmn QJ JT, JHtn HJsn RP PG HC, DE WMsl LBsn, BR JGsm.

Carnegie Hall (bc)
New York City, NY

....	FDC		The Star Spangled Banner
....	FDC		The Mooche
....	FDC		How High The Moon
....	FDC		The Tattooed Bride
....			Take The "A" Train
....	FDC		Lullaby Of Birdland
....	FDC		The Hawk Talks

> JHtn RP HC, DE.

| .... | | Monologue –DE narration |

DUKE ELLINGTON & HIS ORCHESTRA
Same personnel.

....		The Star Spangled Banner
....		The Mooche
....		How High The Moon
....		The Tattooed Bride
....		The Hawk Talks
....		Lullaby Of Birdland

> DG added.

| .... | FDC | Body And Soul |

> DG omitted.

| .... | | Take The "A" Train |

> JHtn RP HC, DE.

| .... | | Monologue –DE narration |

> Entire band.

....		V.I.P.'s Boogie
....		Jam With Sam
....		Skin Deep
....	FDC	Medley[1]

[1]Including: Don't Get Around Much Anymore; In A Sentimental Mood; Mood Indigo; I'm Beginning To See The Light; Sophisticated Lady; Caravan; It Don't Mean A Thing; Solitude; I Let A Song Go Out Of My Heart/Don't Get Around Much Anymore.

		20 Nov 1952	(P)

DUKE ELLINGTON & HIS ORCHESTRA
CT WC CA RN, BWmn QJ JT, JHtn HJsn RP PG HC, DE WMsl LBsn, BR JGsm.

Birdland (bc)
New York City, NY

....	JUn	Take The "A" Train
....	JUn	The Mooche
....	JUn	How High The Moon
....	JUn	The Tattooed Bride[1]
....	JUn	Solitude –vJGsm
....	JUn	Lullaby Of Birdland
....	JUn	Take The "A" Train
....	JUn	Lullaby Of Birdland
....	JUn	Take The "A" Train –vBR
....	JUn	Perdido

> JHtn RP HC, DE.

| .... | JUn | Monologue –DE narration |

> Entire band.

| .... | JUn | Things Ain't What They Used To Be |

[1]"Aberdeen" part only.

22 Nov 1952 (P)
Birdland (bc)
New York City, NY

DUKE ELLINGTON & HIS ORCHESTRA
CT WC RN, BWmn QJ JT, HJsn RP PG HC, DE WMsl LBsn, BR JGsm.

.... Take The "A" Train
.... Smada
.... Rockin' In Rhythm
.... Flamingo –vJGsm
.... Bensonality
.... All Of Me –vBR
.... Bakiff
.... Just A Settin' And A-Rockin' –vRN
.... Jam With Sam

24 Nov 1952[1] (P)
Birdland (bc)
New York City, NY

DUKE ELLINGTON & HIS ORCHESTRA
CT WC RN, BWmn QJ JT, JHtn HJsn RP PG HC, DE WMsl LBsn, BR JGsm.

.... JUn Take The "A" Train
.... JUn Caravan
.... JUn Do Nothin' Till You Hear From Me –vJGsm
.... JUn The "C" Jam Blues
.... JUn Creole Love Call
.... JUn Just Squeeze Me –vRN
.... JUn Take The "A" Train
.... JUn Lullaby Of Birdland

[1]Broadcast on 25 Nov 1952.

26 Nov 1952[1] (P)
Birdland (bc)
New York City, NY

DUKE ELLINGTON & HIS ORCHESTRA
CT WC RN, BWmn QJ JT, JHtn HJsn RP PG HC, DE WMsl LBsn, BR JGsm.

.... Take The "A" Train
.... MJ Warm Valley
.... Harlem Air Shaft
.... Strange Feeling –vJGsm
.... Tulip Or Turnip –vRN
.... I Got It Bad –vBR
.... V.I.P.'s Boogie
.... Jam With Sam

[1]Broadcast on 28 Nov 1952.

Nov 1952 (P)
Birdland (bc)
New York City, NY

DUKE ELLINGTON & HIS ORCHESTRA
CT WC CA RN, BWmn QJ JT, JHtn HJsn RP PG HC, DE WMsl LBsn, JGsm.

.... Lullaby Of Birdland
.... Rock Skippin' At The Blue Note
.... Ko-Ko
.... My Little Brown Book –vJGsm
.... Cotton Tail
.... Smada
.... Honeysuckle Rose
.... Take The "A" Train

Nov 1952 (P)
Birdland (?bc)
New York City, NY

DUKE ELLINGTON & HIS ORCHESTRA
CT WC CA RN, BWmn QJ JT, JHtn HJsn RP PG HC, DE WMsl LBsn.

.... Rock Skippin' At The Blue Note

6 Dec 1952 (S)
BBC Studios (bc)
London, England

DUKE ELLINGTON (& HIS ORCHESTRA)
Broadcast by BBC Radio, with comments by Spike Hughes, Jack Fellon and Malcolm Raymond;
intermittent previously recorded music.

.... Three Aspects of Duke Ellington

Notwithstanding the fact that DE was not present, this broadcast has been included because of the qualification of the panel members and the insight they were able to give the listener into the subject matter.

12 Dec 1952[1] (S)
Apollo Theater (tc)
New York City, NY

DUKE ELLINGTON & HIS ORCHESTRA
CT WC CA RN, BWmn QJ JT, JHtn HJsn RP PG HC, DE WMsl LBsn.

.... The Mooche

> DE omitted, LDon added.

.... What Do You Want Me To Do? –vLDon   >>>

> LDon omitted, C&A added.

....   Untitled tune --C&A tap

> C&A omitted, DE added.

....   The Hawk Talks

[1]This event was broadcast live by MBS, and on 17 Dec 1952 by WMCA.

				22 Dec 1952 (S)
				Columbia Studios
				Chicago, IL

DUKE ELLINGTON & HIS ORCHESTRA
CT WC JCrr JHnt RN, BWmn QJ JT, JHtn HJsn RP PG HC, DE WMsl LBsn, JGsm.

.... Co   CCO5397-1   Primpin' For The Prom
.... Co   CCO5398-1   The Vulture Song --vJGsm[1]
.... Co   CCO5399-1   Follow Me --vJGsm

[1]*aka* "Without You."

22 Dec 1952   (S)
Columbia Studios
Chicago, IL

29 Dec 1952   (P)
Private residence
Winnetka, IL

DUKE ELLINGTON & HIS GROUP
RN, JHtn HC, DE WMsl, JGsm.[1]

.... PP   How High The Moon
.... PP   Do Nothin' Till You Hear From Me --vJGsm
.... PP   Follow Me --vJGsm
.... PP   Solitude --vJGsm
.... PP   Monologue --DE narration
.... PP   Basin Street Blues --vRN

> DE WMsl.

.... PP   Pitter Panther Patter
.... PP   New York City Blues

> Entire band.

.... PP   Sophisticated Lady
.... PP   Tangerine
.... PP   Tea For Two
.... PP   Tenderly

[1]JGsm was also on drums.

31 Dec 1952   (P)
Blue Note (bc)
Chicago, IL

DUKE ELLINGTON & HIS ORCHESTRA
CT WC CA RN, BWmn QJ JT, JHtn HJsn RP PG HC, DE WMsl LBsn.

....   Take The "A" Train
....   I Let A Song Go Out Of My Heart/Don't Get Around Much Anymore
....   Rock Skippin' At The Blue Note
....   Things Ain't What They Used To Be

1 Jan 1953   (P)
Blue Note (bc)
Chicago, IL

DUKE ELLINGTON & HIS ORCHESTRA
CT WC CA RN, BWmn QJ JT, JHtn HJsn RP PG HC, DE WMsl LBsn, BR JGsm.

....   Take The "A" Train
....   Fancy Dan
....   My Little Brown Book --vJGsm
....   Bensonality
....   The Hawk Talks
....   Creole Love Call
....   All Of Me --vBR
....   Smada
....   How High The Moon

30 Jan 1953   (P)
Bandbox (bc)
New York City, NY

DUKE ELLINGTON & HIS ORCHESTRA
CT WC CA RN, BWmn QJ JT, JHtn HJsn RP PG HC, DE CM LBsn, BR JGsm.

....   Take The "A" Train
....   Summertime
....   Come On Home --vJGsm
....   The Hawk Talks
....   Bakiff
....   Take The "A" Train --vBR

> JHtn RP HC, DE.

....   Monologue --DE narration   >>>

> Entire band.

....   Rockin' In Rhythm
....   Smada
....   Take The "A" Train

DUKE ELLINGTON'S QUARTET   1 Feb 1953   (P)
JHtn RP HC, DE.   Bandbox (tc)
                                                                 New York City, NY
....   Take The "A" Train
....   Monologue –DE narration
....   Mood Indigo

DUKE ELLINGTON & HIS ORCHESTRA   2 Feb 1953   (P)
CT WC CA RN, BWmn QJ JT, JHtn HJsn RP PG HC, DE CM LBsn, BR JGsm. Bandbox (bc)
                                                                 New York City, NY
....   Take The "A" Train
....   Caravan
....   Smada
....   Do Nothin' Till You Hear From Me –vJGsm
....   The Mooche
....   How High The Moon
....   Take The "A" Train
....   Caravan
....   Love You Madly –vBR
....   V.I.P.'s Boogie
....   Jam With Sam
....   St. Louis Blues –vRN
....   Things Ain't What They Used To Be

DUKE ELLINGTON & HIS ORCHESTRA   4 Feb 1953   (P)
CT WC CA RN, BWmn QJ JT, JHtn HJsn RP TSct HC, DE OP LBsn, BR JGsm. Bandbox (bc)
                                                                 New York City, NY
....   Take The "A" Train
....   Bensonality
....   September Song –vJGsm
....   Baby, You And Me –vBR[1]
....   Trumpet-No-End
....   Mood Indigo
....   Just A-Settin' And A-Rockin' –vRN
....   Smada

[1]sa "In A Mellotone."

DUKE ELLINGTON'S TRIO   8 Feb 1953   (P)
RN, DE OP.   Bandbox (tc)
                                                                 New York City, NY
....   I Can't Get Started –vRN

DUKE ELLINGTON & HIS ORCHESTRA   9 Feb 1953   (P)
CT WC CA RN, BWmn QJ JT, JHtn HJsn RP TSct HC, DE OP LBsn, BR JGsm. Bandbox (bc)
                                                                 New York City, NY
....   Caravan
....   Happy-Go-Lucky Local
....   Harlem Air Shaft
....   Frustration
....   Sultry Serenade
....   Cotton Tail

> SGtz added.

.... Rt   I Got It Bad

> SGtz omitted.

....   All Of Me –vBR
....   I Can't Get Started –vRN
....   Jam With Sam
....   Vagabonds
....   The Hawk Talks

15 Feb 1953   (P)
NBC Studios (tc)
New York City, NY

<u>PATTI PAGE & DUKE ELLINGTON WITH ORCHESTRA</u>
PPge and DE with the Scott Music Hall orchestra, directed by Carl Hoff.

> DE piano solo.

....   Medley[1]

> Orchestra added.

....   Medley (ctd.)[2]
....   Don't Get Around Much Anymore –vPPge

[1]Including: In A Sentimental Mood; Mood Indigo; Do Nothin' Till You Hear From Me; Solitude.
[2]Including: It Don't Mean A Thing; Sophisticated Lady.

25 Feb 1953   (P)
Apollo Theater (bc)
New York City, NY

<u>DUKE ELLINGTON & HIS ORCHESTRA</u>
CT WC CA RN, BWmn QJ JT, JHtn HJsn RP TSct HC, DE OP LBsn.

....   Take The "A" Train
....   Trumpet-No-End

p Mar 1953   (P)
Unidentified location
U.S.A. or Canada

<u>DUKE ELLINGTON</u>
Piano and vcl.

.... TOM   Ain't Nothin' Nothin' –vDE[1]

[1]Complete: "Ain't Nothin' Nothin', Baby, Without You."

22 Mar 1953   (P)
Unidentified location
Albuquerque, NM

<u>DUKE ELLINGTON & HIS ORCHESTRA</u>
CT WC CA RN, BWmn QJ, JHtn RH RP PG HC, DE WMsl BBld, JGsm.

....   Take The "A" Train
....   All Day Long
....   Stomp, Look And Listen
....   Balcony Serenade
....   Sophisticated Lady
....   Bensonality
....   Perdido
....   Ting-A-Ling
....   Hy'a Sue
....   Blue Lou
....   Happy-Go-Lucky Local
....   Summertime
....   I Let A Song Go Out Of My Heart/Don't Get Around Much Anymore –vRN
....   Sultry Serenade
....   The Hawk Talks
....   Mood Indigo
....   Caravan
....   Cotton Tail
....   The Vulture Song –vJGsm
....   Vagabonds –vJGsm
....   Do Nothin' Till You Hear From Me –vJGsm
....   Ain't Nothin' Nothin' –vJGsm
....   I'm In The Mood For Love –vJGsm ??
....   V.I.P.'s Boogie
....   Jam With Sam
....   Things Ain't What They Used To Be
....   The Tattooed Bride[1]
....   Take The "A" Train
....   Just A-Settin' And A-Rockin' –vRN
....   Flying Home

> OP added.

....   All Of Me
....   Perdido

> OP omitted.

....   Solitude –vJGsm
....   Flamingo –vJGsm
....   She Moved –vJGsm[2]
....   Ring Dem Bells –vRN
....   The Mooche
....   Trumpet-No-End
....   Take The "A" Train   >>>

[1]"Aberdeen" part only.
[2]*sa* "Good Woman Blues"; *aka* "Street Blues."

| | | | 30 Mar 1953 | (P) |

DUKE ELLINGTON & HIS ORCHESTRA
CT WC CA RN, BWmn QJ JT, JHtn RH RP PG HC, DE WMsl BBld, JGsm.
Civic Auditorium
Pasadena, CA

....	GNP	The Tattooed Bride
....	GNP	Diminuendo In Blue and Crescendo In Blue (w. interval)
....	GNP	The Hawk Talks

> JHtn RP HC, DE.

| .... | GNP | Monologue –DE narration |

> Entire band.

....	GNP	St. Louis Blues –vRN
....	GNP	V.I.P.'s Boogie
....	GNP	Jam With Sam
....	GNP	Without A Song –vJGsm
....	GNP	Do Nothin' Till You Hear From Me –vJGsm
....	GNP	Ballin' The Blues –vJGsm[1]

> OP added.

| .... | GNP | Perdido |

> OP omitted.

| .... | GNP | Medley[2] |

[1]*sa* "She Moved."
[2]Including: Don't Get Around Much Anymore; In A Sentimental Mood; Mood Indigo; I'm Beginning To See The Light; Sophisticated Lady; Caravan; It Don't Mean A Thing; Solitude; I Let A Song Go Out Of My Heart/Don't Get Around Much Anymore.

| | | | | 6 Apr 1953 | (S) |

DUKE ELLINGTON & HIS FAMOUS ORCHESTRA
CT WC CA RN, BWmn QJ JT, JHtn RH RP PG HC, DE WMsl BBld, JGsm.
Capitol Studios
Los Angeles, CA

....	Cap	11398-1	Satin Doll
....	Cap	11399-4	Without A Song –vJGsm
....	Cap	11400-7	Cocktails For Two

| | | | | 7 Apr 1953 | (S) |

DUKE ELLINGTON & HIS FAMOUS ORCHESTRA
CT WC CA RN, BWmn QJ JT, JHtn RH RP PG HC, DE WMsl BBld, JGsm.
Capitol Studios
Los Angeles, CA

....	Cap	11414-3	My Old Flame
....	Cap	11415-3	I Can't Give You Anything But Love
....	Cap	11416-3	Ain't Nothin' Nothin', Baby, Without You –vJGsm
....	Cap	11417-5	Stormy Weather
....	Cap	11418-8	Star Dust
....	Cap	11419-6	Three Little Words
....	Cap	11420-5	Orson

| | | | | 9 Apr 1953 | (S) |

DUKE ELLINGTON & HIS FAMOUS ORCHESTRA
CT WC CA RN, BWmn QJ JT, JHtn RH RP PG HC, BS WMsl BBld, JGsm.
Capitol Studios
Los Angeles, CA

| .... | Cap | 11421-6 | Boo-Dah |

> DE replaces BS.

....	Cap	11422-6	Blossom
....	Cap	11423-2	Ballin' The Blues –vJGsm
....	Cap	11424-5	Warm Valley
....	Cap[1]	11406-9	Flamingo
....	Cap	11407-8	Bluejean Beguine[2]
....	Cap	11408-10	Liza

[1]The first two bars have been edited out on all Cap issues.
[2]Dedicated to impresario Gene Norman.

| | | | | 13 Apr 1953 | (S) |

DUKE ELLINGTON WITH RHYTHM ACCOMPANIMENT
DE WMsl BBld.
Capitol Studios
Los Angeles, CA

| .... | Cap | 11431-6 | Who Knows |

> BBld omitted.

| .... | Cap | 11432-1 | Retrospection   >>> |

> BBld added.

....	Cap	11433-4	B Sharp Boston
....	Cap	11434-3	Passion Flower
....	Cap	11435-2	Dancers In Love

> BBld omitted.

| .... | Cap | 11436-1 | Reflections In D |
| .... | Cap | 11437-4 | Melancholia |

> BBld added.

| .... | Cap | 11438-2 | Prelude To A Kiss |

14 Apr 1953   (S)
Capitol Studios
Los Angeles, CA

DUKE ELLINGTON WITH RHYTHM ACCOMPANIMENT
DE WMsl BBld.

....	Cap	11439-2	In A Sentimental Mood
....	Cap	11440-5	Things Ain't What They Used To Be
....	Cap	11441-3	All Too Soon
....	Cap	11442-2	Janet

30 Apr 1953   (P)
McElroy's Ballroom
Portland, OR

DUKE ELLINGTON & HIS ORCHESTRA
CT WC CA RN, BWmn QJ JT, JHtn RH RP PG HC, WMsl BBld, JGsm.

....	Std	Primpin' For The Prom
....	Std	Smada
....	Std	Time On My Hands
....		All Day Long
....	Std	Lullaby Of Birdland
....	Std	Change My Ways
....	Std	Don't Worry 'Bout Me

> DE added.

....	LL	Take The "A" Train
....	Std	Liza
....	Std	Creole Love Call[1]
....	Std	Boo-Dah
....	JG	Stomp, Look And Listen
....	LL	Happy-Go-Lucky Local
....	LL	Summertime
....	JG	Warm Valley
....	JG	Sultry Serenade
....	Std	Hy'a Sue[2]
....	LL	Sophisticated Lady
....	LL	I Let A Song Go Out Of My Heart/Don't Get Around Much Anymore –vRN
....	LL	Just Squeeze Me –vRN
....	LL	Caravan
....	LL	Perdido
....	LL	Without A Song –vJGsm
....	JBd	Do Nothin' Till You Hear From Me –vJGsm
....	Std	Come On Home –vJGsm
....	JBd	Vagabonds –vJGsm
....	LL	Things Ain't What They Used To Be
....	LL	The Hawk Talks
....	LL	The "C" Jam Blues
....	LL	Tenderly
....	LL	All The Things You Are
....		V.I.P.'s Boogie
....		Jam With Sam
....		Once There Lived A Fool –vJGsm
....		Flamingo –vJGsm
....	LL	Solitude –vJGsm
....		I'm Just A Lucky So-And-So –vJGsm
....		Without A Song –vJGsm
....	LL	She Moved –vJGsm
....	LL	She Moved –vJGsm
....	Std	Please Be Kind
....	Std	Happy Birthday
....	LL	Mood Indigo
....	LL	Trumpet-No-End
....	LL	Take The "A" Train

[1]Erroneously as "The Mooche" on Std.
[2]Std runs 7:29, JG only 7:10.

p 23 May 1953   (P)
Unspecified fraternity house
Madison, WI

<u>DUKE ELLINGTON & BILLY STRAYHORN</u>
DE piano solo.

....		Deep Purple[1]
....		Falling Like A Raindrop
....		Sophisticated Lady
....		Mood Indigo

> BS piano solo.

....		Drawing Room Blues
....		You Go To My Head
....		Lush Life

> DE piano solo.

....		Falling Like A Raindrop
....		Janet
....		The Clothed Woman
....		What More Can I Say?[2]

[1]The first few chords were played by another person, probably JHtn, before DE took over.
[2]This title is a derivative of *Never No Lament/Don't Get Around Much Anymore.*

12 Jun 1953   (P)
Blue Note (bc)
Chicago, IL

<u>DUKE ELLINGTON & HIS ORCHESTRA</u>
CT WC CA RN, BWmn QJ JT, JHtn RH RP PG HC, DE WMsl BBld, JGsm.

....	Joy	Take The "A" Train
....	Joy	Smada
....	Joy	Bakiff
....	Joy	Just A-Settin' And A-Rockin' –vRN
....	Joy	Jam With Sam
....	Joy	Flamingo –vJGsm
....	Joy	Do Nothin' Till You Hear From Me –vJGsm
....	Joy	Rockin' In Rhythm
....	AFR	Take The "A" Train

24 Jun 1953   (P)
Blue Note (bc)
Chicago, IL

<u>DUKE ELLINGTON & HIS ORCHESTRA</u>
CT WC CA RN, BWmn QJ JT, JHtn RH RP PG HC, DE WMsl BBld, JGsm.

....	DET	Take The "A" Train
....	DET	Harlem Air Shaft
....	DET	Creole Love Call
....	DET	The "C" Jam Blues
....	DET	Is It A Sin? –vJGsm[1]
....	DET	Just A-Settin' And A-Rockin' –vRN
....	DET	Moonlight Fiesta
....	DET	The Hawk Talks
....	DET	Satin Doll

[1]Complete: "Is It A Sin My Loving You?"

Jun 1953   (P)
Blue Note (bc)
Chicago, IL

<u>DUKE ELLINGTON & HIS ORCHESTRA</u>
CT WC CA RN, BWmn QJ JT, JHtn RH RP PG HC, DE WMsl BBld.

....	AFR	Take The "A" Train
....	AFR	In A Mellotone
....	AFR	Warm Valley
....	AFR	Things Ain't What They Used To Be
....	AFR	St. Louis Blues –vRN
....	AFR	Satin Doll
....	AFR	Blue Moon
....	AFR	Take The "A" Train

27 Jun 1953   (P)
Blue Note (bc)
Chicago, IL

<u>DUKE ELLINGTON & HIS ORCHESTRA</u>
CT WC CA RN, BWmn QJ JT, JHtn RH RP PG HC, DE WMsl BBld, JGsm.

....	Cen	Take The "A" Train
....	Joy	Satin Doll
....	Joy	Bluejean Beguine
....	Joy	Without A Song –vJGsm
....	Cen	Smada
....	Joy	Hy'a Sue
....	Joy	Just Squeeze Me –vRN
....	Cen	Jam With Sam
....	Cen	Take The "A" Train

DUKE ELLINGTON & HIS ORCHESTRA | Jun 1953[1] | (P)
CT WC CA RN, BWmn QJ JT, JHtn RH RP PG HC, DE WMsl BBld, JGsm.

Blue Note (bc)
Chicago, IL

.... DET   Take The "A" Train
.... DET   Caravan
.... DET   I Let A Song Go Out Of My Heart/Don't Get Around Much Anymore –vRN
.... DET   The Hawk Talks
.... DET   Come On Home –vJGsm
.... DET   Flamingo –vJGsm
.... DET   Jump For Joy –vRN
.... DET   Satin Doll
.... DET   Take The "A" Train

[1]Broadcast on 17 Jul 1953.

DUKE ELLINGTON & HIS ORCHESTRA | Jun 1953[1] | (P)
CT WC CA RN, BWmn QJ JT, JHtn RH RP PG HC, DE WMsl BBld, JGsm.

Blue Note (bc)
Chicago, IL

.... DET   Take The "A" Train
.... DET   The Tattooed Bride
.... DET   Ain't Nothin' Nothin' –vJGsm
.... DET   Rock Skippin' At The Blue Note
.... DET   Just Squeeze Me –vRN
.... DET   Ting-A-Ling
.... DET   Satin Doll

[1]Broadcast on 24 Jul 1953.

DUKE ELLINGTON & HIS ORCHESTRA | Jun 1953 | (P)
CT WC CA RN, BWmn QJ JT, JHtn RH RP PG HC, DE WMsl BBld, JGsm.

Blue Note (bc)
Chicago, IL

.... DET   Take The "A" Train
.... DET   Boo-Dah
.... DET   What More Can I Say? –vJGsm
.... DET   Frustration

> CT RN, QJ, RP, DE WMsl BBld.

.... DET   Basin Street Blues –vRN

> Entire band.

.... DET   Duet
.... DET   Ballin' The Blues –vJGsm
.... DET   Satin Doll

[1]Broadcast on 1 Aug 1953.

DUKE ELLINGTON & HIS FAMOUS ORCHESTRA | 30 Jun 1953 | (S)
CT WC CA RN, BWmn QJ JT, JHtn RH RP PG HC, DE WMsl BBld, JGsm.

Universal Studios
Chicago, IL

.... Cap   11620-4   Give Me The Right –vJGsm
.... Cap   11621-5   Is It A Sin? –vJGsm
.... Mo   11622-6   Don't Touch Me –vJGsm

> CT RN, QJ, RP, DE WMsl BBld.

.... UTD   11623-4   Basin Street Blues –vRN

DUKE ELLINGTON & HIS FAMOUS ORCHESTRA | 1 Jul 1953 | (S)
CT WC CA RN, BWmn QJ JT, JHtn RH RP PG HC, DE WMsl BBld, JGsm.

Universal Studios
Chicago, IL

.... Cap   11624-8   Big Drag
.... Mo   11625-10   Hear My Plea –vJGsm
.... UTD   11626-3   Don't Ever Say Goodbye
.... Mo   11627-1   What More Can I Say? –vJGsm

DUKE ELLINGTON & HIS ORCHESTRA | Blue Note (bc) | (P)
Same personnel.

.... DET   Take The "A" Train
.... DET   Bluejean Beguine
.... DET   Boo-Dah
.... DET   Cocktails For Two
.... DET   Ain't Nothin' Nothin' –vJGsm
.... DET   Jump For Joy –vRN
.... DET   Perdido   >>>

| .... | DET | Blue Moon –vJGsm |
| .... | DET | Satin Doll |

12 Jul 1953   (P)
CBS Studios (tc)
New York City, NY

DUKE ELLINGTON
DE on the show "What's My Line?"

| .... | | DE appears as mystery guest |

19 Aug 1953   (P)
Apollo Theater (bc)
New York City, NY

DUKE ELLINGTON & HIS ORCHESTRA
CT WC CA RN, BWmn QJ JT, JHtn RH RP PG HC, DE WMsl BBld, JGsm.

| .... | | Bluejean Beguine |
| .... | | Ballin' The Blues –vJGsm |

23 Aug 1953   (P)
American Legion Park (bc)
Ephrata, PA

DUKE ELLINGTON & HIS ORCHESTRA
CT WC CA RN, BWmn QJ JT, JHtn RH RP PG HC, DE WMsl BBld, JGsm.

....		Take The "A" Train
....		Satin Doll
....		V.I.P.'s Boogie
....		Jam With Sam
....		Give Me The Right –vJGsm
....		Take The "A" Train –vRN
....		Satin Doll

4 Oct 1953   (P)
NIJC Auditorium
Coeur d'Alene, ID

DUKE ELLINGTON & HIS ORCHESTRA
CT WC CA RN, BWmn QJ JT, JHtn RH RP PG HC, DE WMsl BBld.

....	Joy	Take The "A" Train
....	Joy	V.I.P.'s Boogie
....	Joy	Jam With Sam
> BBld.		
....		Drum solo
> Entire band.		
....		The Hawk Talks
....	Joy	Duet
....	Joy	Duet
....	SR	Satin Doll
....	SR	Caravan
....		Medley[1]
....	SR	I Can't Give You Anything But Love

[1]Including: Don't Get Around Much Anymore; In A Sentimental Mood; Mood Indigo; I'm Beginning To See The Light; Sophisticated Lady; Caravan; It Don't Mean A Thing; Solitude; The "C" Jam Blues; I Let A Song Go Out Of My Heart/ Don't Get Around Much Anymore.

Autumn 1953   (P)
Sauls Bridges American Legion Post
Tallahassee, FL

DUKE ELLINGTON & HIS ORCHESTRA
CT WC CA RN, BWmn QJ JT, JHtn RH RP PG HC, DE WMsl DBck, JGsm.

....		The Star Spangled Banner
....		The Mooche
....		How High The Moon
....		Satin Doll
....		The Tattooed Bride
....		Frustration
....		Theme For Trambean
> JHtn RP HC, DE.		
....		Monologue –DE narration
> Entire band.		
....		Bluejean Beguine
....		Take The "A" Train –vRN
....		V.I.P.'s Boogie
....		Jam With Sam
....		Take The "A" Train –vRN
....		Flamingo –vJGsm
....		Teach Me Tonight –vJGsm
....		Do Nothin' Till You Hear From Me –vJGsm
....		Blue Moon –vJGsm
....		Gonna Tan Your Hide >>>

....   Medley[1]
....   Just Squeeze Me –vRN
....   Twelfth Street Rag Mambo

[1]Including: Don't Get Around Much Anymore; In A Sentimental Mood; Mood Indigo; I'm Beginning To See The Light;
Sophisticated Lady; Caravan; It Don't Mean A Thing; Solitude; The "C" Jam Blues; I Let A Song Go Out Of My Heart/
Don't Get Around Much Anymore.

			3 Dec 1953	(S)

DUKE ELLINGTON WITH RHYTHM ACCOMPANIMENT — 3 Dec 1953 (S)
DE WMsl DBck. — Capitol Studios / New York City, NY

.... Cap   20246-9   Kinda Dukish

> RC added.

.... Cap   20247-11   Montevideo[1]

> RC omitted.

.... UTD   20248-6   December Blue[2]

> JGsm added.

.... UTD   20249-2   I'm Just A Lucky So-And-So –vJGsm
.... UTD   20250-7   It Shouldn't Happen To A Dream –vJGsm

[1]Issued under the wrong title of "Night Time" on the original Cap release.
[2]Originally listed as "Title No. 3."

DUKE ELLINGTON & HIS FAMOUS ORCHESTRA — 5 Dec 1953 (S)
CT WC CA RN, BWmn QJ JT, JHtn RH RP PG HC, DE WMsl DBck, JGsm. — Capitol Studios / New York City, NY

.... UTD   20263-7[1]   What More Can I Say? –vJGsm
.... UTD   20264-2   Rockin' In Rhythm
.... UTD   20265-1   Ultra Deluxe[2]
.... UTD   20266-3   Flying Home[3]

[1]Remake.
[2]Although not mentioned on the recording sheet, it is possibly BS at the piano for this title.
[3]The arrangement is by Dick Vance.

DUKE ELLINGTON & HIS RHYTHM WITH BAND — 11 Dec 1953 (P)
DE WMsl DBck, with an unidentified band on the show "Life Begins at Eighty." — DuMont Studios (tc) / New York City, NY

....   Take The "A" Train[1]
....   Interview and panel discussion
....   Medley[2]

[1]Not performed by DE.
[2]Including: Don't Get Around Much Anymore; I Got It Bad; Solitude; Mood Indigo; It Don't Mean A Thing; Sophisticated
Lady; Caravan.

DUKE ELLINGTON'S SEPTET — 13 Dec 1953 (P)
CT RN, QJ, RP, DE WMsl DBck. — NBC Studios (tc) / New York City, NY

....   Basin Street Blues –vRN

DUKE ELLINGTON & HIS QUARTET — 15 Dec 1953 (S)
RN, DE WMsl DBck, JGsm. — Capitol Studios / New York City, NY

.... Mo   20275-7   Chile Bowl[1]
.... Cap   20276-6   Blue Moon –vJGsm

> RN omitted.

.... Mo   20277-1   Oh Well –vJGsm

> RN added.

.... Pck   20278-2   Just A-Settin' And A-Rockin' –vRN

[1]Misspelled in the Capitol ledger and hence on all releases; recté "Chili Bowl."

DUKE ELLINGTON WITH STEVE ALLEN'S ALL STARS — 16 Dec 1953 (P)
ChS, UG, cl, DE SA b dr. — NBC Studios (tc) / New York City, NY

....   Take The "A" Train

> DE SA b dr.

....   It Don't Mean A Thing   >>>

          > UG added.
....   In A Sentimental Mood
          > DE SA.
....   Mood Indigo
          > dr, EGm added.
....   I Let A Song Go Out Of My Heart –vEGm
          > EGm omitted, b added.
....   Caravan
          > cl, SLw added.
....   Don't Get Around Much Anymore –vSLw
          > DE SA b.
....   Sophisticated Lady
          > ChS, dr added.
....   Boy Meets Horn
          > Entire band.
....   The "C" Jam Blues

				Dec 1953	(P)
				Birdland (bc)	
				New York City, NY	

DUKE ELLINGTON & HIS ORCHESTRA
CT WC CA RN, BWmn QJ AC, JHtn RH RP PG HC, DE WMsl DBck, JGsm.

....	AFR		Take The "A" Train
....	AFR		The Mooche
....	AFR		Stomp, Look And Listen
....	AFR		Duet
....	AFR		My Old Flame
....	AFR		What More Can I Say? –vJGsm
....	AFR		How High The Moon
....	AFR		Just Squeeze Me –vRN

				21 Dec 1953	(S)
				Capitol Studios	
				New York City, NY	

DUKE ELLINGTON & HIS FAMOUS ORCHESTRA
CT WC CA RN, BWmn QJ AC, JHtn RH RP PG HC, DE WMsl DBck, JGsm.

....	Cap	20287-5[1]	Ultra Deluxe[2]
....	Cap	20288-5[1]	Flying Home
....	Cap	20289-8[1]	What More Can I Say? –vJGsm
....	UTD	20290-6	Serious Serenade[3]
....	UTD	20291-5[1]	Just A-Settin' And A-Rockin' –vRN
....	Cap	20292-7	Honeysuckle Rose

[1]Remakes.
[2]Although not mentioned on the recording sheet, it is probably BS at the piano for this title.
[3]Complete: "Serious Serenade In B-Flat Minor" *aka* "Gorillas And Peacocks"; "Barisol."

				28 Dec 1953	(S)
				Universal Studios	
				Chicago, IL	

DUKE ELLINGTON & HIS FAMOUS ORCHESTRA
CT WC CA RN, BWmn QJ GJ, JHtn RH RP PG HC, DE WMsl DBck.

....	Mo	12247-10	Night Time
....	Cap	12248-6	Stompin' At The Savoy[1]

[1]The arrangement is by Dick Vance.

				29 Dec 1953	(S)
				Universal Studios	
				Chicago, IL	

DUKE ELLINGTON & HIS FAMOUS ORCHESTRA
CT WC CA RN, BWmn QJ GJ, JHtn RH RP PG HC, DE BS WMsl DBck.

....		12249[1]	Don't Ever Say Goodbye
....	Cap	12249-13	Don't Ever Say Goodbye
....	Cap	12250-2	Black And Tan Fantasy

[1]Remake.

				1 Jan 1954	(S)
				Universal Studios	
				Chicago, IL	

DUKE ELLINGTON & HIS FAMOUS ORCHESTRA
CT WC CA RN, BWmn QJ GJ, JHtn RH RP PG HC, DE WMsl DBck.

....	Cap	12251-12	Frivolous Banta[1]
....	Cap	12252	In The Mood[2] >>>

[1]*aka* "Wendell And Rick."
[2]The arrangement is by Dick Vance.

2 Jan 1954   (S)
Universal Studios
Chicago, IL

DUKE ELLINGTON & HIS FAMOUS ORCHESTRA
CT WC CA RN, BWmn QJ GJ, JHtn RH RP PG HC, DE WMsl DBck.

.... Cap   12253-4   One O'Clock Jump[1]
.... Cap   12254-3   Things Ain't What They Used To Be

[1]The arrangement is by Buck Clayton.

17 Jan 1954   (S)
Universal Studios
Chicago, IL

DUKE ELLINGTON & HIS FAMOUS ORCHESTRA
CT WC CA RN, BWmn QJ GJ, JHtn RH RP PG HC, DE WMsl DBck.

.... Cap   12309-4   Happy-Go-Lucky Local
.... Cap   12310-2[1]   Rockin' In Rhythm

> BS added.

.... Cap   12311-12   Falling Like A Raindrop

[1]Remake.

8 Feb 1954   (P)
Forum
Hamilton, ON

DUKE ELLINGTON & HIS ORCHESTRA
CT WC CA RN, BWmn QJ GJ, JHtn RH RP PG HC, DE WMsl DBck.

.... Rx   Take The "A" Train
.... Rx   The Mooche
.... Rx   How High The Moon
.... Rx   Serious Serenade
.... Rx   Theme For Trambean
.... Rx   Skin Deep
.... Rx   Tenderly
.... Rx   Perdido

> JHtn RP HC, DE.

.... Rx   Monologue –DE narration

> Entire band.

.... Rx   Medley[1]

[1]Including: Don't Get Around Much Anymore; In A Sentimental Mood; Mood Indigo; I'm Beginning To See The Light;
Sophisticated Lady; Caravan; It Don't Mean A Thing; Solitude; The "C" Jam Blues; I Let A Song Go Out Of My Heart/
Don't Get Around Much Anymore.

DUKE ELLINGTON & HIS ORCHESTRA
Same personnel.

.... Rx   Things Ain't What They Used To Be
.... Rx   Satin Doll
.... Rx   Stompin' At The Savoy
.... Rx   I Let A Song Go Out Of My Heart/Don't Get Around Much Anymore
.... Rx   Caravan
.... Rx   Bunny Hop Mambo
.... Rx   Isle Of Capri
.... Rx   The Hawk Talks
.... Rx   All The Things You Are
.... Rx   Duet
.... Rx   Bluejean Beguine
.... Rx   Take The "A" Train –vRN
.... Rx   Warm Valley
.... Rx   Jam With Sam
.... Rx   God Save The Queen

The first set of the above listing originates from a concert, whereas the second set is from a subsequent dance.

13 Apr 1954   (P)
Embassy Auditorium
Los Angeles, CA

DUKE ELLINGTON & HIS ORCHESTRA
CT WC CA RN, BWmn QJ JSrs, JHtn RH RP PG HC, DE WMsl DBck.

.... GNP   Smada
.... GNP   Black And Tan Fantasy
.... GNP   How High The Moon
.... GNP   Skin Deep
.... GNP   Take The "A" Train –vRN
.... GNP   Mood Indigo
.... GNP   Bluejean Beguine   >>>

....	GNP	Serious Serenade
....	GNP	Theme For Trambean
....	GNP	Satin Doll
....	GNP	Stompin' At The Savoy

26 Apr 1954   (S)
Unspecified studio
San Francisco, CA

DUKE ELLINGTON & HIS FAMOUS ORCHESTRA
CT WC CA RN, BWmn QJ JSrs, JHtn RH RP PG HC, DE WMsl DBck.

....	Cap	12579-4	All Day Long

> RC added.

....	Cap	12580-12	Bunny Hop Mambo

> GW added.

....	Cap	12583-9	Isle Of Capri[1]

> GW, RC omitted.

....	Cap	12584-4	The "C" Jam Blues
....	Cap	12585-4	Band Call

[1]The arrangement is by Gerald Wilson.

Master numbers 12581 and 12582 are untraced.

29 Apr 1954   (P)
McElroy's Ballroom
Portland, OR

DUKE ELLINGTON & HIS ORCHESTRA
CT WC CA RN, BWmn QJ JSrs, JHtn RH RP PG HC, WMsl DBck, JGsm.

....		Band warming up
....		Smada
....	JG	Cobb's Tune[1]
....	JG	Coffee And Kisses
....	JG	Easy To Love
....	LL	Johnny Come Lately
....	JG	Change My Ways
....	JG	Primpin' For The Prom

> DE added.

....		Stomp, Look And Listen
....		Cocktails For Two
....	JG	Liza
....	LL	Band Call
....	JBd	Stompin' At The Savoy
....		Take The "A" Train
....	LL	Satin Doll
....	JBd	All The Things You Are
....	LL	Bluejean Beguine
....		I Let A Song Go Out Of My Heart/Don't Get Around Much Anymore –vRN
....	LL	Tulip Or Turnip –vRN
....	LL	Honeysuckle Rose
....	LL	Theme For Trambean
....		Mood Indigo
....		Without A Song –vJGsm
....		Ain't Nothin' Nothin' –vJGsm
....		Solitude –vJGsm
....	LL	Blue Moon –vJGsm
....	LL	V.I.P.'s Boogie
....	LL	Jam With Sam
....		Satin Doll
....		Things Ain't What They Used To Be
....		Caravan
....	LL	Bunny Hop Mambo
....	LL	Isle Of Capri
....		Sophisticated Lady
....	LL	Take The "A" Train –vRN
....		Skin Deep
....		Moon Mist
....		The "C" Jam Blues
....		I Let A Song Go Out Of My Heart/Don't Get Around Much Anymore –vRN
....	LL	Flamingo –vJGsm

> DE WMsl DBck, JGsm.

....	LL	I Got It Bad –vJGsm
....	LL	I'm Just A Lucky So-And-So –vJGsm

> Entire band.

....	LL	Ballin' The Blues –vJGsm >>>

.... LL   Ballin' The Blues —vJGsm
.... LL   Satin Doll

[1] *aka* "Cobb's Theme."

DUKE ELLINGTON & HIS ORCHESTRA CT WC CA RN, BWmn QJ JSrs, JHtn RH RP PG HC, WMsl DBck, JGsm.	**1 May 1954** (P) **Trianon Ballroom** **Seattle, WA**

....   Band warming up
....   Smada
....   Cobb's Tune
....   Coffee And Kisses
....   My Own
....   Johnny Come Lately

> DE added.

....   U.M.M.G.[1]
....   In The Mood
....   Ultra Deluxe
....   All The Things You Are
....   Theme For Trambean
....   Satin Doll
....   Serious Serenade
....   Honeysuckle Rose
....   Bluejean Beguine
....   Take The "A" Train —vRN
....   One O'Clock Jump
....   Mood Indigo
....   Stompin' At The Savoy
....   Star Dust
....   Jump For Joy —vRN
....   Without A Song —vJGsm
....   Give Me The Right —vJGsm
....   Ain't Nothin' Nothin' —vJGsm
....   Do Nothin' Till You Hear From Me —vJGsm
....   Love You Madly —vJGsm
....   Solitude —vJGsm
....   Blue Moon —vJGsm
....   Skin Deep
....   Things Ain't What They Used To Be
....   Caravan
....   Bunny Hop Mambo
....   Is It A Sin? —vJGsm
....   Isle Of Capri
....   What More Can I Say? —vJGsm
....   Jack The Bear
....   Sophisticated Lady
....   Perdido
....   The Mooche
....   I Got It Bad —vJGsm
....   I'm Just A Lucky So-And-So —vJGsm
....   Satin Doll

[1] Stands for <u>U</u>pper <u>M</u>anhattan <u>M</u>edical <u>G</u>roup.

DUKE ELLINGTON & HIS ORCHESTRA CT WC CA RN, BWmn QJ JSrs, JHtn RH RP PG HC, DE WMsl DBck.	**Jun 1954** (P) **Birdland (bc)** **New York City, NY**

.... AFR   Take The "A" Train
.... AFR   Three Little Words
.... AFR   Stompin' At The Savoy
.... AFR   Star Dust
.... AFR   V.I.P's Boogie
.... AFR   Jam With Sam
.... AFR   Take The "A" Train

DUKE ELLINGTON & HIS ORCHESTRA CT WC CA RN, BWmn QJ JSrs, JHtn RH RP PG HC, DE WMsl DBck, JGsm.	**15 Jun 1954** (P) **Birdland (tc)** **New York City, NY**

....   Take The "A" Train
....   Blue Moon —vJGsm

> BS added.

....   The "C" Jam Blues   >>>

> BS omitted.

....   Isle Of Capri

      17 Jun 1954   (S)

DUKE ELLINGTON & HIS FAMOUS ORCHESTRA   Capitol Studios
CT WC CA RN, BWmn QJ JSrs, JHtn RH RP PG HC, DE WMsl DBck.   New York City, NY

.... Cap   20402-1   Gonna Tan Your Hide
.... UTD[1] 20403-4   It Don't Mean A Thing

[1]The original release on Pck has been edited.

      Late Jun 1954   (P)

DUKE ELLINGTON & HIS ORCHESTRA   Mentor Ballroom
CT WC CA RN, BWmn QJ JSrs, JHtn RH RP PG HC, WMsl DBck.   Mentor, MN

....   Easy To Love
....   Cobb's Tune
....   Coffee And Kisses
....   Chelsea Bridge

> DE added.

....   Take The "A" Train
....   Satin Doll
....   Cocktails For Two
....   Liza
....   In The Mood
....   Stormy Weather
....   Mood Indigo
....   All The Things You Are
....   Frivolous Banta
....   Stompin' At The Savoy
....   Star Dust
....   Caravan

      6 Jul 1954   (P)

DUKE ELLINGTON & HIS ORCHESTRA   Civic Auditorium
CT WC CA RN, BWmn QJ JSrs, JHtn RH RP HC, DE WMsl DBck.   Denver, CO

....   The Mooche
....   How High The Moon
....   The Tattooed Bride
....   Frustration
....   Theme For Trambean
....   Happy-Go-Lucky Local
....   Summertime

> JHtn RP HC, DE.

....   Monologue –DE narration

> Entire band.

....   Take The "A" Train –vRN
....   Satin Doll

> PG added.

....   V.I.P.'s Boogie
....   Jam With Sam

      26 Jul 1954   (P)

DUKE ELLINGTON   NBC Studios (tc)
DE on the Art Linkletter show "House Party."   Hollywood, CA

....   Interview

> DE acc. by the Muzzy Marcellini Trio.

....   Medley[1]

[1]Including: Take The "A" Train; Mood Indigo; Sophisticated Lady; Don't Get Around Much Anymore.

      1 Sep 1954   (S)

DUKE ELLINGTON & HIS FAMOUS ORCHESTRA   Capitol Studios
CT WC CA GW RN, BWmn QJ JSrs, JHtn RH RP PG HC, DE WMsl DBck.   Los Angeles, CA

.... Cap   12992-10   Smile[1]

> GW omitted.

.... Cap   12993-13   Tyrolean Tango[2] >>>

      > GW added.

.... Cap   12994-10   If I Give My Heart To You[1]

      > GW omitted.

.... Cap   12995-6[3]   Chile Bowl

      > GW, RC added.

.... Cap   12996-3   Bakiff

[1]The arrangements are by Gerald Wilson.
[2]*aka* "Echo Tango" and as such on all European releases.
[3]Remake.

DUKE ELLINGTON & HIS FAMOUS ORCHESTRA
CT WC CA RN, BWmn QJ JSrs, JHtn RH RP PG HC, DE OP DBck FR, JGsm.

8 Oct 1954   (S)
Universal Studios
Chicago, IL

.... Cap   13090-4   Twelfth Street Rag Mambo

      > FR omitted.

.... Cap   13091-2   September Song –vJGsm

      > FR added.

.... Cap   13092-1   Caravan

DUKE ELLINGTON
DE introduces Stan Getz at the Shrine.

8 Nov 1954   (P)
Shrine
Los Angeles, CA

....   DE talking

DUKE ELLINGTON & HIS ORCHESTRA
CT WC CA RN, BWmn QJ JSrs, JHtn RH RP PG HC, DE PMsn FBlr, JGsm.

13 Nov 1954   (P)
Jantzen Beach
Portland, OR

....   Stompin' At The Savoy
....   Change My Ways
....   Smile
....   Cocktails for Two
....   Time On My Hands
....   Summertime
....   Take The "A" Train –vRN
....   Smada
....   In The Mood
....   If I Give My Heart To You
....   Sophisticated Lady
....   Serious Serenade
....   Perdido
....   Caravan
....   Chile Bowl
....   Mood Indigo
....   Just Squeeze Me –vRN
....   I Let A Song Go Out Of My Heart/Don't Get Around Much Anymore –vRN
....   All The Things You Are
....   Theme For Trambean
....   Satin Doll
....   Jam With Sam

      > DE PMsn FBlr.

....   Do Nothin' Till You Hear From Me
....   Prelude To A Kiss

      > Entire band.

....   Do Nothin' Till You Hear From Me –vJGsm
....   Honeysuckle Rose
....   Isle Of Capri
....   Give Me The Right –vJGsm
....   September Song –vJGsm
....   Love You Madly –vJGsm
....   Creole Love Call

      > JHtn RP HC, DE.

....   Monologue –DE narration

      > Entire band.

....   Mood Indigo

28 Dec 1954   (P)
NBC Studios (tc)
New York City, NY

<u>DUKE ELLINGTON</u>
DE b dr.

....   I'm Beginning To See The Light

> DE piano solo.

....   In A Sentimental Mood

> DE SA with the Skitch Henderson Orchestra.

....   Medley[1]

> DSev added.

....   Boy Meets Horn

> DSev omitted.

....   Sophisticated Lady
....   The "C" Jam Blues

[1]Including: Don't Get Around Much Anymore; Mood Indigo; Caravan; It Don't Mean A Thing; I Let A Song Go Out Of My Heart.

1 Jan 1955   (P)
Basin Street East (bc)
New York City, NY

<u>DUKE ELLINGTON & HIS ORCHESTRA</u>
CT WC CA RN, BWmn QJ JSrs, JHtn RH RP PG HC, DE WMsl LBsn, JGsm.

....   Chile Bowl
....   Twelfth Street Rag Mambo
....   Coquette –vJGsm
....   Mood Indigo
....   Just Squeeze Me –vRN
....   Lullaby Of Birdland
....   Satin Doll
....   Take The "A" Train
....   Chile Bowl

CBS Studios (tc)   (P)
New York City, NY

<u>DUKE ELLINGTON WITH THE DORSEY BROTHERS ORCHESTRA</u>
DE with the Dorsey Brothers Orchestra, featuring TD, JDrs, BRch, JRay.

.... GoJ   Medley[1]
.... GoJ   When The Saints Go Marching In –vJRay

[1]Including: Don't Get Around Much Anymore; In A Sentimental Mood; Mood Indigo; I'm Beginning To See The Light; Sophisticated Lady; Caravan; Solitude; Do Nothin' Till You Hear From Me; I Let A Song Go Out Of My Heart/Don't Get Around Much Anymore.

17 Feb 1955   (P)
Brant Inn (bc)
Burlington, ON

<u>DUKE ELLINGTON & HIS ORCHESTRA</u>
CT WC CA RN, BWmn QJ JSrs, JHtn RH RP PG HC, DE JW DBck.

....   Caravan
....   Mood Indigo
....   Twelfth Street Rag Mambo
....   V.I.P.'s Boogie
....   Jam With Sam
....   Satin Doll

Early Mar 1955   (P)
Academy of Music (bc)
Philadelphia, PA

<u>DUKE ELLINGTON & HIS ORCHESTRA WITH THE PHILADELPHIA SYMPHONY ORCHESTRA</u>
CT WC CA RN, BWmn QJ JSrs, JHtn RH RP PG HC, DE JW DBck, with the Philadelphia Symphony Orchestra, DE conducting.

....   NIGHT CREATURE
....   1st Movement (Blind Bug)
....   2nd Movement (Stalking Monster)
....   3rd Movement (Dazzling Creature)

....   HARLEM
....   New World A-Comin'

9 Mar 1955   (P)
ABC Studios (tc)
New York City, NY

<u>DUKE ELLINGTON</u>
DE as guest on the show "Masquerade Party."

....   DE talking

			16 Mar 1955 (S)

DUKE ELLINGTON & HIS ORCHESTRA WITH THE SYMPHONY OF THE AIR ORCHESTRA   Carnegie Hall
CT WC CA RN, BWmn QJ JSrs, JHtn RH RP PG HC, DE JW DBck, with the Symphony of the   New York City, NY
Air Orchestra, Don Gillis conducting, featuring Don Shirley –p.

.... New World A-Comin' (rehearsal)
.... New World A-Comin' (rehearsal)
.... New World A-Comin' (rehearsal)

The above is a rehearsal session with no audience in attendance.

DUKE ELLINGTON & HIS ORCHESTRA WITH THE SYMPHONY OF THE AIR ORCHESTRA   (P)
Same personnel.

> DE piano and conducting.

                    NIGHT CREATURE
.... MJ   1st Movement (Blind Bug)
.... MJ   2nd Movement (Stalking Monster)
.... MJ   3rd Movement (Dazzling Creature)

> DSh (p) replaces DE, Don Gillis conducting.

.... MJ   New World A-Comin'

> DSh omitted, Don Gillis conducting.

.... MJ   HARLEM

			20 Apr 1955 (P)

DUKE ELLINGTON & HIS ORCHESTRA   National Guard Armory
CT WC CA RN, BWmn QJ JSrs, JHtn RH RP PG HC, DE JW DBck, JGsm.   Washington, DC

.... JG   La Virgen de la Macarena[1]
....   Satin Doll
.... JG   HARLEM
.... JG   Perdido
.... JG   All The Things You Are

> JHtn RP HC, DE.

....   Monologue –DE narration

> Entire band.

.... JG   Take The "A" Train –vRN
....   Flamingo –vJGsm
....   Teach Me Tonight –vJGsm
.... JG   Happy-Go-Lucky Local
....   Medley[2]
.... JG   Just Squeeze Me –vRN
....   Twelfth Street Rag Mambo

[1]The arrangement is by Gerald Wilson.
[2]Including: Don't Get Around Much Anymore; I Got It Bad; In A Sentimental Mood; Mood Indigo; I'm Beginning To See The Light; Sophisticated Lady; Caravan; It Don't Mean A Thing; Solitude; The "C" Jam Blues; I Let A Song Go Out Of My Heart/ Don't Get Around Much Anymore.

			17 May 1955 (S)

DUKE ELLINGTON & HIS FAMOUS ORCHESTRA   Universal Studios
CT WC CA GW RN, BWmn QJ JSrs, JHtn RH RP PG HC, DE JW DBck, JGsm.   Chicago, IL

.... Mo[1]   14094-1   La Virgin de la Macarena

> GW omitted.

.... Mo   14095-2   Harlem Air Shaft
.... Cap   14095-5   Harlem Air Shaft
.... UTD   14096-4   Blues –vJGsm[2, 3]
.... UTD   14097-1   Commercial Time[3, 4]

[1]Edited version on all releases, except for the boxed Mosaic LP/CD set.
[2]*aka* "Look What I've Got For You."
[3]The arrangements are by Rick Henderson.
[4]*aka* "Californio Mello."

			18 May 1955 (S)

DUKE ELLINGTON & HIS FAMOUS ORCHESTRA   Universal Studios
CT WC CA RN, BWmn QJ JSrs, JHtn RH RP PG HC, DE JW DBck.   Chicago, IL

.... Cap   14098-5   Clarinet Melodrama
.... Cap   14099-4   Theme For Trambean   >>>

DUKE ELLINGTON'S SEPTET
CT, BWmn QJ, RP, DE JW DBck, JGsm.

.... Pck   14100-4   Coquette –vJGsm

DUKE ELLINGTON & HIS FAMOUS ORCHESTRA
Same personnel as in first set.

.... Cap   14101-1[1]   Serious Serenade

[1]Remake.

DUKE ELLINGTON'S SEPTET
RN, QJ, RP PG, DE JW DBck.

.... UTD   14304-2   Body And Soul

19 May 1955   (S)
Universal Studios
Chicago, IL

DUKE ELLINGTON'S SEXTET
RN, QJ, RP, DE JW DBck, JGsm.

.... Mo   14102-7   Discontented Blues
.... UTD   14103-10   Once In A Blue[1]
.... Pck   14104-7   Oh! Lady Be Good –vJGsm
.... UTD   14105   So Long –vJGsm[2]
.... Mo   14105-9   So Long –vJGsm

[1]Complete: "Once In A Blue Mood"; sa "December Blue"; "Title No. 3."
[2]This title is a derivative of Blue Moon.

11 Jun 1955   (P)
Jantzen Beach
Portland, OR

DUKE ELLINGTON & HIS ORCHESTRA
CT WC CA RN, BWmn QJ JSrs, JHtn RH RP PG HC, JW DBck, JGsm.

....   Smada
....   Easy To Love
....   Coffee And Kisses
....   Time On My Hands

        > DE added.

....   Take The "A" Train
....   Sophisticated Lady
....   Perdido
....   Black And Tan Fantasy
....   Theme For Trambean
....   Honeysuckle Rose
....   Mood Indigo
....   Caravan
....   Bluejean Beguine
....   The Happy One

        > DE JW DBck.

.... JG   John Sanders' Blues[1]

        > Entire band.

....   All The Things You Are
....   I Let A Song Go Out Of My Heart/Don't Get Around Much Anymore –vRN
....   Satin Doll
.... JG   Body And Soul
....   Flamingo –vJGsm
....   Teach Me Tonight –vJGsm
....   Do Nothin' Till You Hear From Me –vJGsm
....   Look What I've Got For You –vJGsm
....   If I Give My Heart To You
....   Smile
....   Stomp, Look And Listen
....   Blue Cellophane
....   Emancipation Celebration
....   Stompin' At The Savoy
....   Gonna Tan Your Hide
....   Take The "A" Train
....   The Mooche
....   One O'Clock Jump
....   Day In, Day Out –vJGsm
....   I Got It Bad –vJGsm
....   Everything But You –vJGsm
....   Solitude –vJGsm
....   Isle Of Capri   >>>

```
..............          Mambo Jambo
..............          Just Squeeze Me –vRN
..............          Caravan
..............          Jam With Sam
..............          Mood Indigo
```

[1]*sa* "Commercial Time"; "Californio Mello."

		Jun 1955	(S)

DUKE ELLINGTON
DE interviewed by Harvey Peterson.

Unidentified location (bc)
Denver, CO

```
..............          Interview
```

		9 Jul 1955	(P)

DUKE ELLINGTON & HIS ORCHESTRA
CT JSpr CA RN, WSlw QJ JSrs, JHtn RP VDvs JKlp HC, DE JW SWrd.

CBS Studios (tc)
New York City, NY

```
..............          Intro by Paul Whiteman and Fletcher Henderson
..............          Take The "A" Train
..............          Harlem Air Shaft
..............          Sophisticated Lady—I Let A Song Go Out Of My Heart
..............          Jump For Joy –vRN
..............          Jam With Sam
```

		20 Jul 1955	(P)

DUKE ELLINGTON WITH ORCHESTRA
DE, CR FL with a studio orchestra, directed by Jimmy Carroll.

CBS Studios (tc)
New York City, NY

```
..............          Take The "A" Train[1]
..............          Caravan[1]
..............          I Got It Bad –vCR[1]
..............          Don't Get Around Much Anymore –vFL
..............          Solitude –vFL
..............          I'm Just A Lucky So-And-So –vFL
..............          Take The "A" Train
```

[1]There is no audible evidence of DE's presence on these titles.

		26 Jul 1955	(P)

DUKE ELLINGTON WITH STAN KENTON & HIS ORCHESTRA
DE with Stan Kenton & His Orchestra.

CBS Studios (tc)
New York City, NY

```
.............. Df       Take The "A" Train
..............          Monologue –DE narration
```

DUKE ELLINGTON AND YEHUDI MENUHIN
YM, DE.

```
..............          Come Sunday
```

		28 Aug 1955	(S)

DUKE ELLINGTON & HIS QUARTET
DE[1] narration, acc. by LHsn JW, MC JGsm; intermittent conversations.

NBC Studios (bc)
New York City, NY

```
                       MAN WITH FOUR SIDES
..............          - Train Blues –vJGsm[2]
..............          - She –vMC JGsm
..............          - It's Rumor –vJGsm
..............          - Twilight Time –vMC
```

> DE replaces LHsn.

```
..............          - Weatherman –vJGsm
..............          - The Blues –vMC[3]
```

[1]DE on the David Garroway show, with guest Leonard Feather.
[2]*sa* "Night Train."
[3]*sa* "The Blues" from *Black, Brown And Beige*.

		24 Oct 1955	(P)

DUKE ELLINGTON & HIS ORCHESTRA
CT WC CA RN, BWmn QJ JSrs, JHtn JH RP PG HC, DE JW SWrd, JGsm.

Unidentified location
New York City, NY

```
.............. UST      Take The "A" Train
.............. GE       Stomp, Look And Listen
.............. GE       Sophisticated Lady
.............. GE       Do Nothin' Till You Hear From Me –vJGsm
.............. GE       I Got It Bad
.............. GE       The Happy One
.............. UST      Take The "A" Train
```

<u>DUKE ELLINGTON & HIS ORCHESTRA</u>
CT WC CA RN, BWmn QJ JSrs, JHtn JH RP PG HC, DE JW SWrd.

....	The Mooche
....	Harlem Air Shaft
....	Serious Serenade
....	Theme For Trambean
....	La Virgen de la Macarena
....	Happy-Go-Lucky Local

p Nov 1955   (P)
Unidentified location
Midwest, U.S.A.

<u>DUKE ELLINGTON & HIS ORCHESTRA</u>
CT WC CA RN, BWmn QJ JSrs, JHtn JH RP PG HC, DE JW SWrd, JGsm.

....	Take The "A" Train
....	Smada
....	Prelude To A Kiss
....	The "C" Jam Blues
....	Day In, Day Out –vJGsm
....	Take The "A" Train

27 Nov 1955   (P)
Zardi's (bc)
Hollywood, CA

<u>DUKE ELLINGTON & HIS ORCHESTRA</u>
CT WC CA RN, BWmn QJ JSrs, JHtn JH RP PG HC, DE JW SWrd.

....	Boo-Dah
....	Isle Of Capri
....	Orson
....	Hey, Cherie –vRN
....	Things Ain't What They Used To Be

3 Dec 1955   (P)
Zardi's (bc)
Hollywood, CA

<u>DUKE ELLINGTON & HIS ORCHESTRA</u>
CT WC CA RN, BWmn QJ JSrs, JHtn JH RP PG HC, DE JW SWrd, JGsm.

....	Things Ain't What They Used To Be
....	Grievin' –vJGsm
....	Just Scratchin' The Surface[1]
....	V.I.P.'s Boogie
....	Jam With Sam
....	Passion Flower

4 Dec 1955   (P)
Zardi's (bc)
Hollywood, CA

[1] *aka* "New Trends In Music."

<u>DUKE ELLINGTON & HIS ORCHESTRA</u>
CT WC CA RN, BWmn QJ JSrs, JHtn JH RP PG HC, DE JW SWrd.

....	Take The "A" Train
....	Stompin' At The Savoy
....	Black And Tan Fantasy
....	Happy-Go-Lucky Local
....	Serious Serenade
....	Perdido
....	Clarinet Melodrama

13 Dec 1955   (P)
Dodge City Auditorium (bc)
Dodge City, KS

<u>DUKE ELLINGTON & HIS ORCHESTRA</u>
CT WC CA RN, BWmn QJ JSrs, JHtn JH RP PG HC, DE JW SWrd.

....	Boo-Dah
....	Laura
....	Snibor
....	Coffee And Kisses
....	My Funny Valentine

29 Dec 1955   (P)
Blue Note (?bc)
Chicago, IL

<u>DUKE ELLINGTON & HIS ORCHESTRA</u>
CT WC CA RN, BWmn QJ JSrs, JHtn JH RP PG HC, DE JW SWrd, JGsm.

....	Stompin' At The Savoy
....	I Got It Bad
....	Hey, Cherie –vRN
....	Solitude –vJGsm
....	Smada
....	Things Ain't What They Used To Be

31 Dec 1955   (P)
Blue Note (bc)
Chicago, IL

DUKE ELLINGTON
DE interviewed by Leonard Feather.

1955   (S)
Unidentified location (bc?)
U.S.A.

.... Interview

DUKE ELLINGTON & HIS ORCHESTRA
CT WC CA RN, BWmn QJ JSrs, JHtn JH RP PG HC, DE JW SWrd, JGsm.

1 Jan 1956   (P)
Blue Note (bc)
Chicago, IL

.... Rockin' In Rhythm
.... Prelude To A Kiss
.... Do Nothin' Till You Hear From Me –vJGsm
.... Feetbone
.... Things Ain't What They Used To Be

DUKE ELLINGTON & HIS ORCHESTRA
CT WC CA RN, BWmn QJ JSrs, JHtn JH RP PG HC, DE JW SWrd.

3 Jan 1956   (S)
Universal Studios
Chicago, IL

.... Az   56131-1   Feetbone
....   56131-2   Feetbone (incomplete)
....   56131-3   Feetbone

> DE piano solo.

....   Feetbone (rehearsal)

> Entire band.

....   56131-6   Feetbone
....   56131-7   Feetbone (incomplete)
....   56131-8   Feetbone (incomplete)
.... WEA   56131-9   Feetbone
....   Leotard (rehearsal)
....   Leotard (rehearsal)
....   56132   Discontented[1] (rehearsal)
....   56132   Discontented (incomplete)
....   56132   Discontented (incomplete)
....   56132-1   Discontented
.... Az   56132-3   Discontented (incomplete)
.... WEA   56132-4   Discontented

> JH, BS.

.... Az   Carnegie Blues (incomplete)

> RN, JH, BS JW SWrd.

.... Az   Blues Improvisation

> Entire band, DE replaces BS.

.... Az   56133   Just Scratchin' The Surface
....   56133-2   Just Scratchin' The Surface
....   56133-3   Just Scratchin' The Surface (incomplete)
....   56133-4   Just Scratchin' The Surface
....   56133   Just Scratchin' The Surface (incomplete)
.... WEA   56133-5   Just Scratchin' The Surface
....   56134-1   Do Not Disturb
....   56134-2   Do Not Disturb
....   56134-3   Do Not Disturb (incomplete)
....   56134-5   Do Not Disturb (incomplete)
....   56134-7   Do Not Disturb
.... LMR   56134-9   Do Not Disturb
.... Az   56134-10   Do Not Disturb
.... WEA   56134-11   Do Not Disturb
.... Az   56135   Tea For Two
....   56136   Long Time Blues (incomplete)
....   56136   Long Time Blues (incomplete)
....   56136   Long Time Blues (incomplete)
.... Az[2]   56136-1   Long Time Blues

[1] *aka "Trombone Trio."*
[2] *Az has used the full-length, 11-minute version of this title, whereas WEA shortened its release to 8:34.*

From this day onward, Ellington started to make his so-called stockpile recordings. He booked studio time at his own expense and recorded music unimpeded by existing contracts with record companies. He also had some of his concerts recorded privately. In cooperation with Mercer Ellington, who donated the material in the form of studio tapes, Radio Denmark selected the music for 59 of mostly one-hour broadcasts, starting in 1986 and terminating in 1992. Many of these stockpile recordings were subsequently released commercially—some with minor editing—under various labels.

<u>DUKE ELLINGTON & HIS ORCHESTRA</u>
CT WC CA RN, BWmn QJ JSrs, JHtn JH RP PG HC, DE JW SWrd.

....		Take The "A" Train
....		Satin Doll
....		Feetbone
....		Passion Flower

<u>ROSEMARY CLOONEY WITH DUKE ELLINGTON & HIS ORCHESTRA</u>
Vcl,[1] acc. by CT WC CA RN, BWmn QJ JSrs, JHtn JH RP PG HC, DE JW SWrd.

....	Co		Me And You –vRCln
....	Co		Grievin' –vRCln
....	Co	CO55818	I'm Checkin' Out, Go'om-Bye –vRCln

[1]The voice of RCln has been overdubbed for the titles of this session as well as the following two sessions, at Radio Recorders, Hollywood, CA, on 8 and 11 Feb 1956.

<u>ROSEMARY CLOONEY WITH DUKE ELLINGTON & HIS ORCHESTRA</u>
Vcl, acc. by same as above.

....	Co	ZEP37987-3[1]	Blue Rose –vRCln[2]
....			Blue Rose (insert)
....			Blue Rose (insert)
....	Co	CO55819-2	Sophisticated Lady –vRCln
....	Co	ZEP37985-4[1]	Mood Indigo –vRCln

> BS replaces DE.

| .... | Co | CO55591-7 | If You Were In My Place –vRCln |

[1]These are control numbers.
[2]sa "Leotard."

<u>ROSEMARY CLOONEY WITH DUKE ELLINGTON & HIS ORCHESTRA</u>
Vcl, acc. by CT WC CA RN, BWmn QJ JSrs, JHtn JH RP PG HC, DE JW SWrd.

....	Co	ZEP37987-3[1]	I Let A Song Go Out Of My Heart –vRCln
....	Co	ZEP37988-4[1]	It Don't Mean A Thing –vRCln
....	Co	ZEP37986-3[1]	Just A-Settin' And A-Rockin' –vRCln
....	Co	ZEP37958-1[1]	I Got It Bad –vRCln
....	UTD	CO55592-1	Passion Flower
....	Co	CO55592-3	Passion Flower
....	UTD	ZEP37983-2[1]	Hey, Baby
....	Co	ZEP37983-5[1]	Hey, Baby –vRCln

[1]These are control numbers.

<u>DUKE ELLINGTON & HIS ORCHESTRA</u>
CT WC CA RN, BWmn QJ JSrs, JHtn JH RP PG HC, DE JW SWrd.

....		Take The "A" Train
....		Daddy's Blues[1]
....		The "C" Jam Blues
....		Stompin' At The Savoy

[1]sa "Discontented"; "Trombone Trio."

<u>DUKE ELLINGTON & HIS ORCHESTRA</u>
CT WC CA RN, BWmn QJ JSrs, JHtn JH RP PG HC, DE JW SWrd, JGsm.

....	Bth	Creole Love Call
....	Bth	Stompy Jones
....	Bth	Jack The Bear
....	Bth	Ko-Ko
....	Bth	Stomp, Look And Listen
....	Bth[1]	Unbooted Character
....	Bth	East St. Louis Toodle-Oo
....	Bth	The Jeep Is Jumpin'
....	Bth	In A Mellotone
....	Bth	Midriff
....	Bth	Lonesome Lullaby
....	Bth	U.M.M.G.
....	Bth	Blues[2]
....	Bth[3]	Summertime
....	Bth	Laura >>>

....	Bth		I Can't Get Started –vRN
....	Bth		My Funny Valentine
....	Bth		Cotton Tail
....	Bth		Day Dream
....	Bth		Deep Purple
....	Bth		Indian Summer
....	Bth		Everything But You –vJGsm
....	Bth		Frustration

[1]The release on GS has been edited.
[2]*sa* "Ballin' The Blues."
[3]An edited excerpt was included in Bth's three-LP set of *Porgy And Bess*.

18 Mar 1956   (S)
Universal Studios
Chicago, IL

DUKE ELLINGTON & HIS ORCHESTRA
CT WC CA RN, BWmn QJ JSrs, JHtn JH RP PG HC, BS JW SWrd.

....		3054-6[1]	Blue Rose (incomplete)
....		3054-7	Blue Rose (incomplete)
....		3054-8	Blue Rose
....		3054-10	Blue Rose
....		3054-11	Blue Rose
....		3054-12	Blue Rose

> DE replaces BS.

....		3055[1]	Short Sheet Cluster[2] (incomplete)
....	Az	3055	Short Sheet Cluster (incomplete)
....	Az	3055-1	Short Sheet Cluster (incomplete)
....	Az	3055-2	Short Sheet Cluster
....	Az	3055-3	Short Sheet Cluster
....	Az	3055-5	Short Sheet Cluster
....	WEA	3055-7	Short Sheet Cluster
....		3055-8	Short Sheet Cluster
....	Az	3055-10	Short Sheet Cluster
....	Az	3056[1]	Uncontrived (rehearsal)
....	Az	3056	Uncontrived (rehearsal)
....	Az	3056	Uncontrived (incomplete)
....	Az	3056	Uncontrived

[1]These are control numbers.
[2]*aka* "Terry And The Spacemen."

19 Mar 1956   (S)
Universal Studios
Chicago, IL

DUKE ELLINGTON & HIS ORCHESTRA
CT WC CA RN, BWmn QJ JSrs, JHtn JH RP PG HC, DE JW SWrd.

....		56319-1-11[1]	Miss Lucy (incomplete)
....	WEA	56319-1-12	Miss Lucy
....	Az	56319-2-2	Prelude To A Kiss
....	WEA	56319-2-5	Prelude To A Kiss
....	WEA	56319-3-1	March 19th Blues[2]

[1]These are control numbers.
[2]*aka* "22 Cent Stomp."

DUKE ELLINGTON & HIS SEXTET
CT, JSrs, JHtn JH, DE JW SWrd.

....	Ptp	55319-5[1]	Where's The Music?[2]
....	Ptp	55319-6	Rubber Bottom[2]
....	Ptp	55319-7	Way Back Blues[2]
....	Ptp	55319-8	Play The Blues And Go[2]

[1]These are control numbers.
[2]*aka* "Back Where"; "In The Stands"; "Brass Top"; "Go, Blues, Go," respectively.

14 Apr 1956   (P)
Basin Street East (bc)
New York City, NY

DUKE ELLINGTON & HIS ORCHESTRA
CT NW CA PBrb, BWmn QJ JSrs, JHtn JH RP PG HC, DE JW SWrd, JGsm.

....	BSJ		Take The "A" Train
....	Ech		Caravan
....	Ech		Sophisticated Lady
....	BSJ		Kinda Dukish/Rockin' In Rhythm
....	BSJ		Do Nothin' Till You Hear From Me –vJGsm
....	Ech		Stompin' At The Savoy
....	BSJ		Prelude To A Kiss
....	BSJ		Things Ain't What They Used To Be >>>

DUKE ELLINGTON & HIS ORCHESTRA   (bc)
JGsm omitted, otherwise same personnel.

....   Take The "A" Train
....   Saturday Night At Basin Street
....   The Mooche
....   Take The "A" Train

DUKE ELLINGTON & HIS ORCHESTRA   May 1956   (P)
CT WC CA RN, BWmn QJ JSrs, JHtn JH RP PG HC, DE JW SWrd, JGsm.   Flamingo Hotel
                                                           Las Vegas, NV

....   Take The "A" Train
....   V.I.P.'s Boogie
....   Jam With Sam
....   I Got It Bad
....   Flamingo –vJGsm

> JHtn RP HC, DE.

....   Monologue –DE narration

> Entire band.

....   Hey, Cherie –vRN
....   Medley[1]

> DE omitted.

....   Medley[2]

> HSct added.

....   Ebony Rhapsody
....   Les Feuilles Mortes –vHSct[3]
....   St. Louis Blues –vHSct
....   Unidentified title

[1]Including: Don't Get Around Much Anymore; Do Nothin' Till You Hear From Me; In A Sentimental Mood; Mood Indigo; I'm Beginning To See The Light; Sophisticated Lady; Caravan; It Don't Mean A Thing; Solitude; The "C" Jam Blues; I Let A Song Go Out Of My Heart.
[2]Including: The Poor People Of Paris; Mademoiselle de Paris; The Poor People Of Paris; unidentified title; Autumn Leaves.
[3]sa "Autumn Leaves."

DUKE ELLINGTON & HIS ORCHESTRA   2 Jul 1956   (P)
CT WC CA RN, BWmn QJ JSrs, JHtn JH RP PG HC, DE JW SWrd, JGsm.   Hill Auditorium, University of Michigan
                                                           Ann Arbor, MI

....   Black And Tan Fantasy
....   Stompin' At The Savoy
....   Clarinet Melodrama
....   Harlem Air Shaft
....   Sophisticated Lady
....   Theme For Trambean
....   Satin Doll
....   Take The "A" Train
....   La Virgen de la Macarena

> JHtn RP HC, DE.

....   Monologue –DE narration

> Entire band.

....   V.I.P.'s Boogie
....   Jam With Sam
....   The Hawk Talks
....   Prelude To A Kiss
....   Things Ain't What They Used To Be
....   Day In, Day Out –vJGsm
....   Do Nothin' Till You Hear From Me –vJGsm
....   Blue Moon –vJGsm
....   Skin Deep
....   Medley[1]

> DE JW.

....   Dancers In Love

> Entire band.

....   Hey, Cherie –vRN
....   Perdido   >>>

[1]Including: Don't Get Around Much Anymore; Do Nothin' Till You Hear From Me; In A Sentimental Mood, Mood Indigo; I'm Beginning To See The Light; Sophisticated Lady; I Got It Bad; Caravan; It Don't Mean A Thing; Solitude; The "C" Jam Blues; I Let A Song Go Out Of My Heart/Don't Get Around Much Anymore.

7 Jul 1956   (P)
Freebody Park (bc)
Newport, RI

DUKE ELLINGTON & HIS ORCHESTRA
?JMxl WC CA, BWmn QJ JSrs, JH RP PG HC, DE AL SWrd.[1]

....	Co		The Star Spangled Banner
....	Co	BL38263	Black And Tan Fantasy
....	Co		Tea For Two

[1]The band was short of four of its members for the first set, which was ended prematurely for that reason. JMxl claims to have temporarily replaced CT.

DUKE ELLINGTON & HIS ORCHESTRA
?JMxl, AL omitted, CT RN, JHtn, JW, JGsm added, otherwise same personnel.

....	Co	CO56804	Take The "A" Train
			THE NEWPORT FESTIVAL SUITE
....	Co	CO56791	- Festival Junction
....	Co	CO56791	- Blues To Be There[1]
....	Co	CO56791	- Newport Up
....	Co	CO56805	Sophisticated Lady
....	Co		Day In, Day Out –vJGsm
....	Co	CO56806	Diminuendo In Blue and Crescendo In Blue (w. Wailing Interval)
....	Co	CO56807	I Got It Bad
....	Co[2]		Jeep's Blues
....	Co		Tulip Or Turnip –vRN
....	Co	CO56808	Skin Deep
....	Co		Mood Indigo

[1]sa "In A Blue Summer Garden."
[2]Edited version on Co.

The second set started shortly before midnight and extended well into 8 Jul 1956.

9 Jul 1956   (S)
799 Seventh Ave., Studio D
New York City, NY

DUKE ELLINGTON & HIS ORCHESTRA
CT WC CA RN, BWmn QJ JSrs, JHtn JH RP PG HC, DE JW SWrd.

			THE NEWPORT JAZZ FESTIVAL SUITE
....	Co	CO56791[1]	- Festival Junction
....	Co	CO56791	- Blues To Be There
....	Co	CO56791	- Newport Up
....	Co	CO56807[1]	I Got It Bad
....	Co	CO56792	Jeep's Blues[2]

[1]The same master numbers were used for these remakes as for the live recordings done on 7 Jul 1956.
[2]Parts of this studio recording have been used to improve the concert version from 7 Jul 1956.

DUKE ELLINGTON   Unspecified studio (T)[1]
DE piano solo and talking intermittently about his music.

....			Mood Indigo
....			Mood Indigo
....			Caravan
....			Sophisticated Lady
....			Satin Doll

[1]Appearance in the movie short "Time-Life Promo."

10 Jul 1956   (P)
Yale Bowl
New Haven, CT

DUKE ELLINGTON & HIS ORCHESTRA WITH THE NEW HAVEN SYMPHONY ORCHESTRA
CT WC CA RN, BWmn QJ JSrs, JHtn JH RP PG HC, DE JW SWrd, JGsm, with the New Haven
Symphony Orchestra, Frank Brieff conducting.

....			New World A-Comin'
			NIGHT CREATURE
....			1st Movement (Blind Bug)
....			2nd Movement (Stalking Monster)
....			3rd Movement (Dazzling Creature)
....			HARLEM

> JHtn RP HC, DE.

| .... | | | Monologue –DE narration |

> Entire band w. NHSO.

| .... | | | Medley[1]   >>> |

> NHSO omitted.

....   V.I.P.'s Boogie
....   Jam With Sam
....   The Star Spangled Banner

[1]Including: Don't Get Around Much Anymore; In A Sentimental Mood; Mood Indigo; I'm Beginning To See The Light; Sophisticated Lady; Caravan; Just Squeeze Me; Do Nothin' Till You Hear From Me –vJGsm; I Got It Bad; Just Squeeze Me –vRN.

15 Jul 1956   (P)
Berkshire Music Barn
Lenox, MA

DUKE ELLINGTON & HIS ORCHESTRA
CT WC CA RN, BWmn QJ JSrs, JHtn JH RP PG HC, DE JW SWrd, JGsm.

.... QuD   Take The "A" Train
.... QuD   Black And Tan Fantasy
.... QuD   Harlem Air Shaft
.... QuD   Clarinet Melodrama
.... QuD   Theme For Trambean
.... QuD   Sophisticated Lady
.... QuD   Take The "A" Train –vRN
.... QuD   La Virgen de la Macarena

> JHtn RP HC, DE JW SWrd.

.... QuD   Monologue –DE narration

> Entire band.

                     THE NEWPORT JAZZ FESTIVAL SUITE
.... QuD   - Festival Junction
.... QuD   - Blues To Be There
.... QuD   - Newport Up

.... QuD   The Hawk Talks
.... QuD   Prelude To A Kiss
.... QuD   Things Ain't What They Used To Be
.... QuD   I Got It Bad
....   Day In, Day Out –vJGsm
....   Do Nothin' Till You Hear From Me –vJGsm
....   Skin Deep
....   Medley[1]
....   Hey, Cherie –vRN
....   Perdido
....   Mood Indigo

[1]Including: Don't Get Around Much Anymore; In A Sentimental Mood; Mood Indigo; I'm Beginning To See The Light; Sophisticated Lady; Caravan; It Don't Mean A Thing; Solitude; The "C" Jam Blues; I Let A Song Go Out Of My Heart/ Don't Get Around Much Anymore.

18 Jul 1956   (P)
Festival Hall
Stratford, ON

DUKE ELLINGTON & HIS ORCHESTRA
CT WC CA RN, BWmn QJ JSrs, JHtn JH RP PG HC, DE JW SWrd, JGsm.

.... SR   Hark, The Duke's Trumpets[1]
.... SR   Harlem Air Shaft
.... SR   Clarinet Melodrama
.... SR   Theme For Trambean
.... SR   Sophisticated Lady
.... SR   Take The "A" Train –vRN
.... M&A   La Virgen de la Macarena

> JHtn RP HC, DE JW SWrd.

.... M&A   Monologue –DE narration

> Entire band.

.... SR   I Got It Bad
.... M&A   HARLEM

                     THE NEWPORT JAZZ FESTIVAL SUITE
....   - Festival Junction
....   - Blues To Be There
....   - Newport Up

....   Things Ain't What They Used To Be
....   Hey, Cherie –vRN
....   Perdido
....   Day In, Day Out –vJGsm
....   Do Nothin' Till You Hear From Me –vJGsm
....   Blue Moon –vJGsm
....   Medley[2]   >>>

[1]sa "Discontented"; "Trombone Trio"; "Daddy's Blues."
[2]Including: Don't Get Around Much Anymore; In A Sentimental Mood; Mood Indigo; I'm Beginning To See The Light;
Sophisticated Lady; Caravan; It Don't Mean A Thing; Solitude; The "C" Jam Blues; I Let A Song Go Out Of My Heart/
Don't Get Around Much Anymore.

| | | 19 Jul 1956 | (P) |

DUKE ELLINGTON & HIS ORCHESTRA   Brant Inn (bc)
CT WC CA RN, BWmn QJ JSrs, JHtn JH RP PG HC, DE JW SWrd.   Burlington, ON

....   THE NEWPORT JAZZ FESTIVAL SUITE
....   - Festival Junction
....   - Blues To Be There
....   - Newport Up

....   Prelude To A Kiss
....   Mood Indigo

                                                                         21 Jul 1956   (P)
DUKE ELLINGTON & HIS ORCHESTRA   Brant Inn (bc)
CT WC CA RN, BWmn QJ JSrs, JHtn JH RP PG HC, DE JW SWrd, JGsm.   Burlington, ON

....   Take The "A" Train
....   Caravan
....   Sophisticated Lady
....   Flamingo –vJGsm
....   Jam With Sam
....   I Got It Bad
....   Tulip Or Turnip –vRN
....   The E&D Blues[1]
....   Take The "A" Train

[1]sa "Saturday Night At Basin Street." E&D stands for Ella and Duke.

                                                                         Jul 1956[1]   (P)
DUKE ELLINGTON & HIS ORCHESTRA   NBC Studios (tc)
CT WC CA RN, BWmn QJ JSrs, JHtn JH RP PG HC, DE JW SWrd.   New York City, NY

....   Take The "A" Train

[1]This appearance on the "Tonight" show is dated 21 Jul, which seems unlikely on account of the band's engagement
in Burlington, ON at the same date. It is assumed that the show was telecast on 21 Jul, and taped at an earlier date.

                                                                         25 Jul 1956   (P)
DUKE ELLINGTON & HIS ORCHESTRA WITH THE CLEVELAND POPS ORCHESTRA   Severance Hall
CT WC CA RN, BWmn QJ JSrs, JHtn JH RP PG HC, DE JW SWrd, with the Cleveland   Cleveland, OH
Pops Orchestra, Louis Lane conducting.

.... RDB   New World A-Comin'

                          NIGHT CREATURE
.... RDB   1st Movement (Blind Bug)
.... RDB   2nd Movement (Stalking Monster)
.... RDB   3rd Movement (Dazzling Creature)
   > CPO omitted.

....   Skin Deep
   > CPO added.

.... RDB[1]   Medley[2]
   > CPO omitted.

.... SR   V.I.P.'s Boogie
.... SR   Jam With Sam

[1]Incomplete on RDB.
[2]Including: Don't Get Around Much Anymore; Do Nothin' Till You Hear From Me; In A Sentimental Mood; Mood Indigo;
I'm Beginning To See The Light; Sophisticated Lady; Caravan; I Got It Bad; It Don't Mean A Thing; Solitude; The "C"
Jam Blues; I Let A Song Go Out Of My Heart/Don't Get Around Much Anymore.

                                                                         28 Jul 1956   (P)
DUKE ELLINGTON & HIS ORCHESTRA   University Stadium (bc)
CT WC CA RN, BWmn QJ JSrs, JHtn JH RP PG HC, DE JW SWrd, JGsm.   Fairfield, CT

....   The Star Spangled Banner

                          THE NEWPORT JAZZ FESTIVAL SUITE
.... IAC   - Festival Junction
.... IAC   - Blues To Be There
.... IAC   - Newport Up   >>>

> BCtn, JHtn PG, HJo SGrs WP/JW SWrd.

.... IAC[1]   Tea For Two

> WP/JW omitted.

.... QuD   Jazz Festival Blues

> Entire band, BCtn, HJo SGrs omitted.

.... IAC   The Hawk Talks
.... IAC   Sophisticated Lady
.... QuD   Diminuendo In Blue and Crescendo In Blue (w. Wailing Interval)
.... IAC   I Got It Bad
....   Things Ain't What They Used To Be
....   Day In, Day Out –vJGsm
.... IAC   Do Nothin' Till You Hear From Me –vJGsm
.... IAC   Hey, Cherie –vRN
.... IAC   Take The "A" Train –vRN
....   Skin Deep
.... QuD   Ballin' The Blues –vJGsm[2]
....   Mood Indigo

[1]On QuD this title has been edited (1:35); full length on IAC (8:06).
[2]"The Blues Jam" on QuD.

		29 Jul 1956	(S)
DUKE ELLINGTON WITH ORCHESTRA		CBS Studios (bc)	
DE with a studio orchestra, directed by Johnny Green.		New York City, NY	

.... Medley[1]

[1]Including: Don't Get Around Much Anymore; Do Nothin' Till You Hear From Me; In A Sentimental Mood; Mood Indigo; Sophisticated Lady; It Don't Mean A Thing; Solitude.

		1 Aug 1956	(P)
FRANKIE LAINE WITH DUKE ELLINGTON, ORCHESTRA AND CHORUS		CBS Studios (tc)	
DE piano solo.		New York City, NY	

.... Dancers In Love

> FL, studio orchestra and chorus, directed by Russ Case, added.

.... Tomorrow Mountain –vFL Chorus

		7 Aug 1956	(S)
DUKE ELLINGTON & HIS ORCHESTRA		30th Street Studio	
CT WC CA RN, BWmn QJ JSrs, JHtn JH RP PG HC, DE JW SWrd.		New York City, NY	

.... UTD   A-Flat Minor[1] (rehearsal)
.... UTD   A-Flat Minor (rehearsal)
.... Co   CO56565-1   A-Flat Minor
.... UTD   CO56565-3   A-Flat Minor
.... Co   CO56565-6   A-Flat Minor
.... UTD[2]   CO56566-3   Lately[3]
.... Co   CO56566-5   Lately
.... UTD   CO56567-4   Suburban Beauty
.... Co   CO56567-8   Suburban Beauty

[1]Complete: "Tune In A-Flat Minor."
[2]The version issued on UTD is actually take 3 and not take 1, as per liner notes.
[3]Part of the future *Shakespearean Suite* (part 11: "Half The Fun," and as such on UTD); see also sessions on 15, 24 Apr; 3 May 1957.

		26 Aug 1956	(P)
DUKE ELLINGTON & HIS ORCHESTRA		Blue Note (bc)	
CT WC CA RN, BWmn QJ JSrs, JHtn JH RP PG HC, DE JW SWrd.		Chicago, IL	

....   Newport Up
....   I Got It Bad
....   Tulip Or Turnip –vRN
....   Mood Indigo

		2 Sep 1956	(P)
DUKE ELLINGTON & HIS ORCHESTRA		Blue Note (bc)	
CT WC CA RN, BWmn QJ JSrs, JHtn JH RP PG HC, DE JW SWrd.		Chicago, IL	

....   Take The "A" Train
....   Blues To Be There
....   Jam With Sam
....   Things Ain't What They Used To Be

DUKE ELLINGTON & HIS ORCHESTRA
CT WC CA RN, BWmn QJ JSrs, JHtn JH RP PG HC, DE JW SWrd, JGsm.

....		Take The "A" Train
....		Caravan
....		Stompin' At The Savoy
....		V.I.P.'s Boogie
....		Jam With Sam
....		Do Nothin' Till You Hear From Me –vJGsm
....		Tulip Or Turnip –vRN
....		Mood Indigo

DUKE ELLINGTON & HIS ORCHESTRA
CT WC CA RN, BWmn QJ JSrs, JHtn RH RP PG HC, DE JW SWrd, JS MTns.

....			A DRUM IS A WOMAN[1]
....		-1	- Matumbe (incomplete)
....		-2	- Matumbe
....	Co	-3	- Matumbe
....	Co	-4	- Matumbe
....		-2	- Carribee Joe[2] (incomplete)
....		-3	- Carribee Joe –vJS
....		-4	- Carribee Joe –vJS (incomplete)
....		-5	- Carribee Joe (incomplete)
....		-6	- Carribee Joe (incomplete)
....		-7	- Carribee Joe –vJS (incomplete)
....	Co	-8	- Carribee Joe –vJS
....		-9	- Carribee Joe (incomplete)
....		-10	- Carribee Joe –vJS
....		-11	- Carribee Joe (incomplete)
....			- Carribee Joe –vJS
....			- Carribee Joe (incomplete)
....			- Carribee Joe (incomplete)
....	Co		- Carribee Joe -vJS
....	Co		- A Drum Is A Woman (I) –vMTns
....			- A Drum Is A Woman (I) –vMTns
....	Co		- Rhumbop[3]
....			- Rhumbop
> DE (voicetrack).			
....	Co		- Congo Square –DE narration[4]
....	Co	alt.	- Congo Square –DE narration
....			- Carribee Joe –DE narration

[1]See also sessions on 24, 25, 28 Sep; 22, 23 Oct; 6 Dec 1956.
[2]"Carabea Joe" on the recording sheet.
[3]This title is a derivative of *Dance #2/Trebop* from *The Liberian Suite*. The voicetrack for this title was recorded on 22 Oct.
[4]Voicetrack for "Matumbe."

DUKE ELLINGTON & HIS ORCHESTRA
CT WC CA RN, BWmn QJ JSrs, JHtn JH RH RP PG HC, DE BS JW SWrd, JS MTns OB.

....			A DRUM IS A WOMAN (ctd.)[1]
....			- Rhythm Pum-Te-Dum –vJS MTns OB[2]
....			- Rhythm Pum-Te-Dum –vJS MTns OB
....			- Carribee Joe –vJS MTns OB (incomplete)
....			- Carribee Joe –vJS MTns OB (incomplete)
....			- Carribee Joe –vJS MTns OB (incomplete)
....		-1	- Rhythm Pum-Te-Dum –vJS MTns OB (incomplete)
....	Co	-2	- Rhythm Pum-Te-Dum –vJS MTns OB
....			- Rhythm Pum-Te-Dum –vJS MTns OB (incomplete)
....	Co	-3	- Rhythm Pum-Te-Dum –vJS MTns OB
....	Co		- Carribee Joe –vJS MTns OB (incomplete)
....		-1	- What Else Can You Do With A Drum? –vOB[3]
....		-2	- What Else Can You Do With A Drum? –vOB
....		-3	- What Else Can You Do With A Drum? (incomplete)
....		-4	- What Else Can You Do With A Drum? –vOB (incomplete)
....	Co	-5	- What Else Can You Do With A Drum? -vOB
....	Co	-6	- What Else Can You Do With A Drum? –vOB
....		-1	- Carribee Joe
....		-2	- Carribee Joe
....		-3	- Carribee Joe
....		-1	- Matumbe (A) (incomplete)
....		-2	- Matumbe (A) (incomplete) >>>

....		-3	- Matumbe (A) (incomplete)
....		-4	- Matumbe (A) (incomplete)
....		-5	- Matumbe (A) (incomplete)
....		-6	- Matumbe (A) (incomplete)
....	Co	-7	- Matumbe (A) (incomplete)
....		-1	- Matumbe (B) (incomplete)
....		-2	- Matumbe (B) (incomplete)
....		-3	- Matumbe (B) (incomplete)
....		-2	- Matumbe (C) (incomplete)
....		-3	- Matumbe (C) (incomplete)
....		-4	- Matumbe (C) (incomplete)
....	Co	-5	- Matumbe (C) (incomplete)

[1]See also sessions on 17, 25, 28 Sep; 22, 23 Oct; 6 Dec 1956.
[2]*aka* "Rhythm Came From Africa Around."
[3]Originally titled "Calypso."

25 Sep 1956   (S)
30th Street Studio
New York City, NY

DUKE ELLINGTON & HIS ORCHESTRA
CT WC CA RN, BWmn QJ JSrs, JHtn JH RH RP PG HC, DE JW SWrd, JS MTns grp.

			A DRUM IS A WOMAN (ctd.)[1]
....		-1	- Carribee Joe (incomplete)
....		-2	- Carribee Joe (incomplete)
....			- Carribee Joe (incomplete)
....			- Carribee Joe –vJS
....	Co	-2	- Carribee Joe –vJS
....			- Carribee Joe (rehearsal)
....	Co	-3	- Carribee Joe –vJS
....		-1	- A Drum Is A Woman (II) –vMTns[2]
....		-2	- A Drum Is A Woman (II) –vMTns (incomplete)
....		-3	- A Drum Is A Woman (II) (incomplete)
....		-4	- A Drum Is A Woman (II) –vMTns
....		-5	- A Drum Is A Woman (II) (incomplete)
....		-6	- A Drum Is A Woman (II) –vMTns (incomplete)
....		-7	- A Drum Is A Woman (II) –vMTns
....	Co	-8	- A Drum Is A Woman (II) –vMTns
....		-1	- Hey, Buddy Bolden (incomplete)
....		-2	- Hey, Buddy Bolden (incomplete)
....		-3	- Hey, Buddy Bolden –vJS Grp (incomplete)
....		-4	- Hey, Buddy Bolden (incomplete)
....		-5	- Hey, Buddy Bolden (incomplete)
....		-6	- Hey, Buddy Bolden –vJS Grp (incomplete)
....		-7	- Hey, Buddy Bolden (incomplete)
....		-8	- Hey, Buddy Bolden –vJS Grp
....		-9	- Hey, Buddy Bolden (incomplete)
....		-10	- Hey, Buddy Bolden –vJS Grp (incomplete)
....	Co	-11	- Hey, Buddy Bolden –vJS Grp

> DE (voicetrack).

....	Co		- Carribee Joe –DE narration

[1]See also sessions on 17, 24 28 Sep; 22, 23 Oct; 6 Dec 1956.
[2]Designated as "Rabbit's version" on the recording sheet.

28 Sep 1956   (S)
30th Street Studio
New York City, NY

DUKE ELLINGTON & HIS ORCHESTRA
CT WC CA RN, BWmn QJ JSrs, JHtn RH RP PG HC, DE JW SWrd, MTns.

			A DRUM IS A WOMAN (ctd.)[1]
....		-1	- New Orleans (Sunrise) –RP's part
....	Co	-2	- New Orleans (Sunrise) –RP's part
....	Co	-1	- New Orleans (Sunrise) –BWmn's part
....		-2	- New Orleans (Sunrise) –BWmn's part
....		-3	- New Orleans (Sunrise) –BWmn's part
....	Co	-5	- New Orleans (Sunrise) –BWmn's part
....		-9	- New Orleans (Sunrise) –BWmn's part
....		-1	- Rhumbop –CT's part
....		-2	- Rhumbop –CT's part
....		-1	- Rhumbop –JHtn's part
....		-3	- Rhumbop –JHtn's part
....		-4	- Rhumbop –JHtn's part
....		-1	- Hey, Buddy Bolden –CT's part
....	Co	-2	- Hey, Buddy Bolden –CT's part
....		-1	- Zajj's Dream (Carribee Joe interlude)
....		-3	- Zajj's Dream (Carribee Joe interlude)
....		-4	- Zajj's Dream (Carribee Joe interlude) (incomplete) >>>

....		-5	- Zajj's Dream (Carribee Joe interlude)
....		-6	- Zajj's Dream (Carribee Joe interlude)
....		-7	- Zajj's Dream (Carribee Joe interlude)
....		-8	- Zajj's Dream (Carribee Joe interlude)
....		-9	- Zajj's Dream (Carribee Joe interlude)
....		-10	- Zajj's Dream (Carribee Joe interlude)
....		-11	- Zajj's Dream (Carribee Joe interlude)
....	Co	-12	- Zajj's Dream (Carribee Joe interlude)
....		-1	- New Orleans (Parade)
....		-2	- New Orleans (Parade)
....	Co	-3	- New Orleans (Parade)

> MBrc added.

....	-1	The Greatest There Is (incomplete)
....	-3	The Greatest There Is –vMBrc
....	-4	The Greatest There Is –vMBrc

> MBrc omitted.

A DRUM IS A WOMAN (ctd.)[1]

....		-1	- Zajj's Dream (CA's ending)
....	Co	-2	- Zajj's Dream (CA's ending)
....		-1	- Matumbe (PG's stanza)
....	Co	-2	- Matumbe (PG's stanza)
....		-1	- A Drum Is A Woman (II) –vMTns (ending)
....	Co	-2	- A Drum Is A Woman (II) –vMTns (ending)
....		-1	- Trumpet fugue (CT WC CA RN)
....		-2	- Trumpet fugue (CT WC CA RN)

[1]See also sessions on 17, 24 25 Sep; 22, 23 Oct; 6 Dec 1956.

22 Oct 1956   (S)
799 Seventh Ave., Studio A
New York City, NY

DUKE ELLINGTON, JOYA SHERRILL, CAMERO CANDIDO
Varying personnel.

A DRUM IS A WOMAN (ctd.)[1]

> JS (voicetrack)

.... Co	-3	- Rhumbop –vJS

> DE, JS, Cnd. (voicetrack).

.... Co	- Carribee Joe –vJS, Cnd, DE narration

> Chorus (voicetrack).

.... Co	-3	- Dialogue –Chorus

> Cnd.

.... Co	-1	- Bongo sequence (Carribee Joe)

> DE (voicetrack).

.... Co	-1	- New Orleans –DE narration[2]
.... Co	alt.	- New Orleans –DE narration[2]

[1]See also sessions on 17, 24, 25, 28 Sep; 23 Oct; 6 Dec 1956.
[2]Including: New Orleans; Mardi Gras; Congo Square.

23 Oct 1956   (S)
30th Street Studio
New York City, NY

DUKE ELLINGTON & HIS ORCHESTRA
CT WC CA RN, BWmn QJ JSrs, JHtn JH RH RP PG HC, DE JW SWrd.

A DRUM IS A WOMAN (ctd.)[1]

> JH, TS.

.... Co	-2	- Code sequence

> SWrd.

.... Co	-11	- Bass drum solo (Matumbe)

> Entire band.

.... Co	-5	- Ballet Of The Flying Saucers
.... Co	alt.	- Ballet Of The Flying Saucers

> BGmn.

.... Co	- Harp chords (Zajj's Dream)

> LBsn.

.... Co	- Tympany roll (Zajj's Dream)

[1]See also sessions on 17, 24, 25, 28 Sep; 22 Oct; 6 Dec 1956.

DUKE ELLINGTON & HIS ORCHESTRA
CT WC CA RN, BWmn QJ JSrs, JHtn JH RP PG HC, DE JW SWrd.

18 Nov 1956   (P)
Birdland (tc)
New York City, NY

....		Take The "A" Train
....		Medley[1]
....		Presentation
....		It Don't Mean A Thing

[1]Including: Don't Get Around Much Anymore; I Got It Bad; I'm Beginning To See The Light; Sophisticated Lady; Caravan; Mood Indigo.

DUKE ELLINGTON & HIS ORCHESTRA
Same personnel.

(bc)

....		Take The "A" Train
....		Festival Junction
....		Prelude To A Kiss
....		Tulip Or Turnip –vRN
....		Blues To Be There
....		Newport Up

DUKE ELLINGTON & HIS ORCHESTRA
CT WC CA RN, BWmn QJ JSrs, JHtn JH RP PG HC, DE JW SWrd, JGsm.

Nov 1956   (P)
Birdland (bc)
New York City, NY

....		Take The "A" Train
....		Rock City Rock –vGsm
....		Sophisticated Lady
....		Perdido
....		Mood Indigo
....		Solitude –vJGsm
....		Jam With Sam

DUKE ELLINGTON
Piano solo.

22 Nov 1956   (P)
CBS Studios (tc)
New York City, NY

....		Black And Tan Fantasy

> tp, tb, cl, b dr added.

....		Medley[1]

[1]Including: 'Way Down Yonder In New Orleans; It Don't Mean A Thing; Basin Street Blues.

DUKE ELLINGTON
DE interviewed by Dorothy Fuldheim.

23 Nov-2 Dec 1956 (S)
Unspecified studio (tc)
Cleveland, OH

....		Interview

DUKE ELLINGTON & HIS ORCHESTRA
CT WC CA RN, BWmn QJ JSrs, JHtn JH RP PG HC, DE JW SWrd, MTns OB.

6 Dec 1956   (S)
30th Street Studio
New York City, NY

			A DRUM IS A WOMAN (ctd.)[1]
....		CO57013	- You Better Know It (incomplete)
....	Co	CO57013-7	- You Better Know It –vOB
....	UTD	CO57014-1	Café au Lait[2]
....	UTD	CO57014-2	Café au Lait
....	UTD		Café au Lait (rehearsal)
....	UTD		Café au Lait (rehearsal)
....	UTD		Café au Lait (rehearsal)
....	UTD	CO57014-3	Café au Lait
....		CO57014	Café au Lait (incomplete)
....		CO57014-4	Café au Lait (incomplete)
....		CO57014-4	Café au Lait
....		CO57014-5	Café au Lait (incomplete)
....		CO57014-6	Café au Lait (incomplete)
....	Co	CO57014-8	Café au Lait
			A DRUM IS A WOMAN (ctd.)[1]
....	Co	[3]	- Finale –vMTns OB
....	UTD	CO57015-1	Pretty Girl[4]
....	UTD	CO57015-2	Pretty Girl
....	UTD	CO57015-3	Pretty Girl (incomplete)
....	UTD	CO57015-4	Pretty Girl (incomplete)
....	UTD	CO57015-5	Pretty Girl >>>

A DRUM IS A WOMAN (ctd.)[1]

> DE (voicetrack).

.... Co   [3]   - Madam Zajj—Zajj's Dream –DE narration
.... Co   alt.[3]   - Madam Zajj—Zajj's Dream –DE narration

[1]See also session on 17, 24, 25, 28 Sep; 22, 23 Oct 1956.
[2]*aka* "Lucy."
[3]No master numbers assigned.
[4]*sa* "Pretty Little Girl."

                                        A DRUM IS A WOMAN (summation—original release)
          Co   - A Drum Is A Woman
          Co   - Rhythm Pum-Te-Dum –vJS MTns OB
          Co   - What Else Can You Do With A Drum? –vOB
          Co   - New Orleans –DE narration
          Co   - Hey, Buddy Bolden –vJS MTns OB
          Co   - Carribee Joe –vJS
          Co   - Congo Square –DE narration[1]
          Co   - A Drum Is A Woman –vMTns
          Co   - You Better Know It –vOB
          Co   - Madam Zajj –DE narration
          Co   - Ballet Of The Flying Saucers
          Co   - Zajj's Dream –vJS MTns OB, DE narration
          Co   - Rhumbop –vJS
          Co   - Carribee Joe –vJS
          Co   - Finale –vMTns OB

[1]*sa* "Matumbe."

The above summation shows "A Drum Is A Woman" as originally issued on LP. However, two slightly different versions have been released by Co on LP, partly by using different takes and partly by editing the original master tapes and overlaying different tracks for voice and bongo. In the absence of master numbers and in some instances take numbers, and the editing that has been done, it was impossible to determine with accuracy, which parts or snippets were used for either one of the two versions as issued on LP. However, those titles, takes and parts that could be clearly identified have been marked as issued under the respective datelines. The reissue on CBS/Co JCL 951 used a number of alternate takes and made changes to the sequence of titles; Hey, Buddy Bolden has been omitted.

                                                                          8 Dec 1956   (P)
DUKE ELLINGTON & HIS ORCHESTRA   Red Hill Inn (bc)
CT WC CA RN, BWmn QJ JSrs, JHtn JH RP PG HC, DE JW SWrd, JGsm.   Pennsauken, NJ

....   Take The "A" Train
....   Things Ain't What They Used To Be
....   Newport Up
....   Rock City Rock –vJGsm
....   Bluejean Beguine
....   Sophisticated Lady
....   Mood Indigo
....   Blues To Be There

                                                                          9 Dec 1956   (P)
DUKE ELLINGTON & HIS ORCHESTRA   Red Hill Inn (bc)
CT WC CA RN, BWmn QJ JSrs, JHtn JH RP PG HC, DE JW SWrd, JGsm.   Pennsauken, NJ

....   Take The "A" Train
....   Caravan
....   Do Nothin' Till You Hear From Me –vJGsm
....   Newport Up
....   Blues To Be There
....   Tulip Or Turnip –vRN

                                                                          12 Dec 1956   (S)
DUKE ELLINGTON   NBC Studios (bc)
DE interviewed by Dave Garroway.   New York City, NY

....   Interview[1]

[1]Subject: "Man With Four Sides"; the music presented was recorded on 28 Aug 1955.

                                                                          15 Dec 1956   (P)
DUKE ELLINGTON & HIS ORCHESTRA   Red Hill Inn (bc)
CT WC CA RN, BWmn QJ JSrs, JHtn JH RP PG HC, DE JW SWrd.   Pennsauken, NJ

....   Take The "A" Train
....   La Virgen de la Macarena
....   Sophisticated Lady
....   Perdido
....   Take The "A" Train   >>>

....   Take The "A" Train
....   Jeep's Blues

                                                                    18 Dec 1956   (S)
DUKE ELLINGTON & HIS ORCHESTRA   Civic Auditorium (tc)[1]
CT WC CA RN, BWmn QJ JSrs, JHtn JH RP PG HC, DE JW SWrd.   Omaha, NE

....   Congo Square (rehearsal)

> DE interviewed by Dave Garroway.

....   Interview

> Entire band.

....   Medley[2]

[1]The Ellington portion of the program was picked up by NBC in Chicago; there was no audience in attendance at this rehearsal session.
[2]Including: Do Nothin' Till You Hear From Me; In A Sentimental Mood; I Got It Bad; I'm Beginning To See The Light; Sophisticated Lady; Caravan; It Don't Mean A Thing; Solitude; Don't Get Around Much Anymore; Mood Indigo.

                                                                    23 Dec 1956   (P)
DUKE ELLINGTON & HIS ORCHESTRA   Blue Note (bc)
CT WC CA RN, BWmn QJ JSrs, JHtn JH RP PG HC, DE JW SWrd.   Chicago, IL

....   Take The "A" Train
....   Presentation
....   Diminuendo In Blue and Crescendo In Blue (w. Wailing Interval)

                                                                    30 Dec 1956   (P)
DUKE ELLINGTON & HIS ORCHESTRA   Blue Note (bc)
CT WC CA RN, BWmn QJ JSrs, JHtn JH RP PG HC, DE JW SWrd.   Chicago, IL

....   Take The "A" Train
....   Newport Up
....   Jeep's Blues

                                                                    31 Dec 1956   (P)
DUKE ELLINGTON & HIS ORCHESTRA   Blue Note (bc)
CT WC CA RN, BWmn QJ JSrs, JHtn JH RP PG HC, DE JW SWrd.   Chicago, IL

....   Take The "A" Train
....   Trumpet-No-End
....   Sophisticated Lady
....   Caravan
....   Do Nothin' Till You Hear From Me
....   Things Ain't What They Used To Be
....   Mood Indigo

                                                                    1 Jan 1957   (P)
DUKE ELLINGTON & HIS ORCHESTRA   Blue Note (bc)
CT WC CA RN, BWmn QJ JSrs, JHtn JH RP PG HC, DE JW SWrd.   Chicago, IL

....   Take The "A" Train
....   Diminuendo In Blue and Crescendo In Blue (w. Wailing Interval)
....   Jeep's Blues
....   Just Squeeze Me --vRN
....   Mood Indigo

                                                                    6 Jan 1957   (P)
DUKE ELLINGTON & HIS ORCHESTRA   Blue Note (bc)
CT WC CA RN, BWmn QJ JSrs, JHtn JH RP PG HC, DE JW SWrd.   Chicago, IL

....   Take The "A" Train
....   Sophisticated Lady
....   Caravan
....   I Got It Bad
....   Mood Indigo—Solitude

                                                                    10 Jan 1957   (P)
DUKE ELLINGTON & HIS ORCHESTRA   Darby Gym, Grinnell College
CT WC CA RN, BWmn QJ JSrs, JHtn JH RP PG HC, DE JW SWrd.   Grinnell, IA

.... GC   Stompin' At The Savoy
.... GC   Black And Tan Fantasy
.... GC   Newport Up
.... GC   Clarinet Melodrama
.... GC   Perdido
.... GC   Prelude To A Kiss
.... GC   All Of Me   >>>

.... GC   Trumpet-No-End
.... GC   Skin Deep
.... GC   Medley[1]

> JHtn RP HC, DE.

.... GC   Monologue —DE narration

[1]Including: Don't Get Around Much Anymore; Do Nothin' Till You Hear From Me; In A Sentimental Mood; Mood Indigo; I'm Beginning To See The Light; Sophisticated Lady; Caravan; It Don't Mean A Thing; Solitude; The "C" Jam Blues; I Let A Song Go Out Of My Heart/Don't Get Around Much Anymore.

17 Jan 1957	(S)
Universal Studios	
Chicago, IL	

DUKE ELLINGTON & HIS GROUP
CT WC RN, PG, DE JW SWrd.

.... Saj   The Riff
.... Saj   Bluer[1]

> CT WC RN omitted.

.... Saj   I Cover The Waterfront
.... Saj   Wailing Bout[2]

[1]This title is a derivative of *Hey, Buddy Bolden.*
[2]*sa* "Wailing Interval," which has been used as bridge between *Diminuendo In Blue* and *Crescendo In Blue.*

29 Jan 1957	(S)
Universal Studios	
Chicago, IL	

DUKE ELLINGTON & HIS GROUP
WC RN, DE JW SWrd.

.... UTD   Blues à la Willie Cook

> CT, PG added.

.... UTD   Slow Blues Ensemble

> CT, PG, DE JW SWrd.

.... Saj   Circle Of Fourths[1]
.... Saj   Perdido

> CT WC RN, DE JW SWrd.

.... UTD   Three Trumps

> PG, DE JW SWrd.

.... Saj   Deep Blues

[1]Part of the future *Shakespearean Suite.*

Cahn Auditorium, Northwestern University   (P)
Evanston, IL

DUKE ELLINGTON & HIS ORCHESTRA
CT WC CA RN, BWmn QJ JSrs, JHtn JH RP PG HC, DE JW SWrd.

....   Matumbe
....   Stompin' At The Savoy
....   The Mooche
....   Perdido
....   Clarinet Melodrama
....   Theme For Trambean
....   Sophisticated Lady
....   Take The "A" Train —vRN
....   La Virgen de la Macarena

> JHtn RP HC, DE.

....   Pretty And The Wolf —DE narration

> Entire band.

....   V.I.P.'s Boogie—Jam With Sam
....   The Hawk Talks
....   Newport Up
....   Jeep's Blues
....   All Of Me
....   Things Ain't What They Used To Be
....   Prelude To A Kiss
....   Skin Deep
....   Medley[1]

[1]Including: Don't Get Around Much Anymore; Do Nothin' Till You Hear From Me; In A Sentimental Mood; Mood Indigo; I'm Beginning To See The Light; Sophisticated Lady; Caravan; I Got It Bad; Just Squeeze Me —vRN; It Don't Mean A Thing; Solitude; The "C" Jam Blues; I Let A Song Go Out Of My Heart/Don't Get Around Much Anymore.

DUKE ELLINGTON & HIS ORCHESTRA
CT WC CA RN, BWmn QJ JSrs, JHtn JH RP PG HC, DE JW SWrd.

> PG, DE JW SWrd.

.... WEA   1216-2   In A Sentimental Mood

> Entire band.

.... WEA   1216-3   Satin Doll
.... WEA   1216-4   Love You Madly
.... WEA   1216-5   Jump For Joy[1]
.... WEA   1216-6   Moon Mist
.... Saj   1216-6 alt.[2]   Moon Mist
.... Az   1216-7   The "C" Jam Blues
.... Saj   1216-8   Things Ain't What They Used To Be

[1]This version was subtitled "Clary, Box And Bass."
[2]This is a much longer version (6:13) than the one released on WEA (3:24).

DUKE ELLINGTON & HIS ORCHESTRA
CT WC CA RN, BWmn QJ JSrs, JHtn JH RP PG HC, DE JW SWrd.

> JH, DE JW SWrd, vcl group.

.... Saj   1217-1   Something Saxual –vGrp
.... Saj   1217-2   Take The "A" Train –vGrp

> BWmn QJ JSrs, JHtn, DE JW SWrd.

.... Az   1217-3   Jump For Joy

> Entire band, vcl group added.

.... Az   1217-4   Perdido –vGrp

DUKE ELLINGTON & HIS ORCHESTRA
CT WC CA RN, BWmn QJ JSrs, JHtn JH RP PG HC, DE JW SWrd.

....   Take The "A" Train –vRN
....   Take The "A" Train
....   Sophisticated Lady
....   Things Ain't What They Used To Be
....   I Got It Bad
....   Newport Up
....   Matumbe

DUKE ELLINGTON & HIS ORCHESTRA
CT WC CA RN, BWmn QJ JSrs, JHtn JH RP PG HC, DE ASh SWrd, MTns OB.

....   CO57520   West Indian Dance[1]
....   CO57520-1   West Indian Dance
....   CO57520   West Indian Dance (incomplete)
....   CO57520   West Indian Dance (incomplete)
....   CO57520-2   West Indian Dance
....   CO57520-4   West Indian Dance
....   CO57520-6   West Indian Dance
.... Co   CO57520-7   West Indian Dance

> JW replaces ASh.

.... Co   CO57521-7   Pomegranate –vMTns OB[2]
....   Your Love Has Faded –vOB (rehearsal)
....   Your Love Has Faded –vOB (rehearsal)
....   Your Love Has Faded –vOB (rehearsal)
....   Your Love Has Faded –vOB (rehearsal)
....   CO57522-1   Your Love Has Faded –vOB
....   CO57522-2   Your Love Has Faded –vOB (incomplete)
....   CO57522-3   Your Love Has Faded –vOB (incomplete)
....   CO57522-3   Your Love Has Faded –vOB
....   CO57522-4   Your Love Has Faded –vOB (incomplete)

[1]"West Indian Suite" on the recording sheet.
[2]This title is part of A Drum Is A Woman, but has been only included in the telecast on 8 May 1957 under the title "On Credit," with slightly different lyrics.

<u>DUKE ELLINGTON</u>
DE interviewed by Bob McEwen.

9 Mar 1957   (P)
Masonic Hall (bc?)
Washington, DC

....   Interview

<u>DUKE ELLINGTON & HIS ORCHESTRA</u>
CT WC CA RN, BWmn QJ JSrs, JHtn JH RP PG HC, DE JW SWrd, JGsm.

13 Mar 1957   (S)
30th Street Studio
New York City, NY

.... Co   CO57533-8   Cop Out[1]
.... Co   CO57534-3   Rock City Rock –vJGsm
.... Co   CO57535-4   The Sky Fell Down[2]

[1]This title is a derivative of *The Duke's In Bed.*
[2]*sa* "Someone"; "You've Got My Heart": "Blue Again."

<u>DUKE ELLINGTON</u>
DE interviewed by Edward R. Murrow.

15 Mar 1957   (S)
DE's private residence[1] (tc)
New York City, NY

....   Interview

> DE piano solo.

....   Satin Doll

[1]Murrow was filmed sitting in his office at CBS, from where he conducted the interview.

<u>DUKE ELLINGTON & HIS ORCHESTRA</u>
CT WC CA RN, BWmn QJ JSrs, JHtn JH RP PG HC, DE JW SWrd, OB.

20 Mar 1957   (S)
30th Street Studio
New York City, NY

....   CO57522-5   Your Love Has Faded –vOB (incomplete)
....   CO57522-6   Your Love Has Faded –vOB (incomplete)
....   CO57522-6   Your Love Has Faded –vOB
....   CO57522-7   Your Love Has Faded (incomplete)
....   CO57522-8   Your Love Has Faded –vOB
.... UTD   CO57522-9   Your Love Has Faded –vOB
....   CO57562-1   Allah-Bye (incomplete)
.... UTD   CO57562-2   Allah-Bye
....   Allah-Bye (rehearsal)
....   CO57562-3   Allah-Bye (incomplete)
....   CO57562-3   Allah-Bye
....   Allah-Bye (rehearsal)
.... FM   CO57562-4   Allah-Bye
....   Allah-Bye (rehearsal)
.... Co   CO57562-5   Allah-Bye

> DE JW SWrd.

.... UTD   CO57338   Piano Improvisation I
.... Co   CO57338-2   Piano Improvisation I
....   CO57338   Piano Improvisation II (incomplete)
....   Piano Improvisation II (rehearsal)
....   CO57338   Piano Improvisation II (incomplete)
.... Co   CO57338-4   Piano Improvisation II
.... Co   CO57338-5   Piano Improvisation III
....   Piano Improvisation IV[1] (rehearsal)
.... Co   CO57338-6   Piano Improvisation IV

[1]This part is a derivative of *Bitches' Ball.*

<u>DUKE ELLINGTON & HIS ORCHESTRA</u>
CT WC CA RN, BWmn QJ JSrs, JHtn JH RP PG HC, DE JW SWrd, JGsm

3 Apr 1957   (P)
Medinah Temple
Chicago, IL

....   East St. Louis Toodle-Oo
....   Rockin' In Rhythm
....   Mood Indigo
....   It Don't Mean A Thing –vRN
....   Sophisticated Lady

> DE piano solo.

....   In A Sentimental Mood

> Entire band.

....   Solitude –vJGsm
....   Caravan
....   I Let A Song Go Out Of My Heart   >>>

....			Boy Meets Horn
....			Take The "A" Train
....			I Got It Bad
....			Perdido

> DE JW SWrd.

....   Don't Get Around Much Anymore

> Entire band.

....   Do Nothin' Till You Hear From Me –vJGsm
....   I'm Beginning To See The Light
....   Things Ain't What They Used To Be

                                                                          15 Apr 1957   (S)
                                                                          30th Street Studio

DUKE ELLINGTON & HIS ORCHESTRA
CT WC CA RN, BWmn QJ JSrs, JHtn JH RP PG HC, DE JW SWrd.   New York City, NY

                                      SUCH SWEET THUNDER[1, 2]

....	Co	CO57712-6	- Sonnet For Caesar (Sonnet 1)[3]
....	Co	CO57713-4	- Sonnet In Search For A Moor (Sonnet 2)
....		CO57714	- Madness In Great Ones
....	Co	CO57715-2	- Sonnet For Sister Kate (Sonnet 3)
....	Co	CO57715-2 alt.	- Sonnet For Sister Kate

[1]*aka* "The Shakespearean Suite."
[2]See also sessions on 7 Aug 1956, 24 Apr, 3 May 1957.
[3]*aka* "My Love Is As A Fever."

                                                                           20 Apr 1957   (P)
                                                                          Birdland (bc)

DUKE ELLINGTON & HIS ORCHESTRA
CT WC CA RN, BWmn QJ JSrs, JHtn JH RP PG HC, DE JW SWrd, JGsm.   New York City, NY

....	Take The "A" Train
....	Cop Out
....	I Got It Bad
....	Rock City Rock –vJGsm
....	Rock City Rock –vJGsm
....	Sophisticated Lady
....	Caravan

                                                                           21 Apr 1957   (P)
                                                                          Birdland (bc)

DUKE ELLINGTON & HIS ORCHESTRA
CT WC CA RN, BWmn QJ JSrs, JHtn JH RP PG HC, DE JW SWrd, JGsm OB.   New York City, NY

....	Take The "A" Train
....	Things Ain't What They Used To Be
....	Newport Up
....	Mood Indigo
....	Rock City Rock –vJGsm
....	What Else Can You Do With A Drum? –vOB
....	Cop Out
....	Mood Indigo

                                                                            23 Apr 1957   (P)
                                                                         Hickory House (tc)

DUKE ELLINGTON'S QUINTET
JH HC, DE OP MR.   New York City, NY

....	Take The "A" Train
....	Things Ain't What They Used To Be
....	Perdido

DUKE ELLINGTON
DE interviewed by Ben Gross.

....   Interview

                                                                           24 Apr 1957   (S)
                                                                          30th Street Studio

DUKE ELLINGTON & HIS ORCHESTRA
CT WC CA RN, BWmn QJ JSrs, JHtn JH RP PG HC, DE JW SWrd.   New York City, NY

                                      SUCH SWEET THUNDER (ctd.)[1]

....	Co	CO57721-1	- Up And Down, Up And Down (Puck)[2]
....	Co	CO57721-12	- Up And Down, Up And Down
....	Co	CO57722-3	- Such Sweet Thunder (Cleo)
....	Co	CO57723-4	- Lady Mac (Lady Macbeth)
....	Co	CO57723-4 alt.[3]	- Lady Mac

[1]See also sessions on 7 Aug 1956, 15 Apr, 3 May 1957.   >>>

[2]*aka* "I Will Lead Them Up And Down."
[3]This version on CD Co CK 65568 has a longer pause before the closing bar; it is debatable if this is a different take or just a matter of editing.

26 Apr 1957   (S)
Peacock Alley, Waldorf Astoria Hotel (tc)
New York City, NY

DUKE ELLINGTON
DE, piano and talking, interviewed by Jinx Falkenburg, Tex McCrary and Jerry Valburn; intermittent previously recorded music has not been listed.

....	Interview
....	Self Portrait[1]
....	What Else Can You Do With A Drum?
....	Interview (ctd.)
....	Mood Indigo
....	Lady Mac

[1]This title is a derivative of *Stompy Jones.*

Birdland (bc?)   (P)

DUKE ELLINGTON & HIS ORCHESTRA
CT WC CA RN, BWmn QJ JSrs, JHtn JH RP PG HC, DE JW SWrd, OB.

....	Take The "A" Train
....	Cop Out
....	Sophisticated Lady
....	Things Ain't What They Used To Be
....	Take The "A" Train –vRN
....	Mood Indigo
....	What Else Can You Do With A Drum? –vOB
....	Diminuendo In Blue and Wailing Interval

27 Apr 1957   (P)
Birdland (bc)
New York City, NY

DUKE ELLINGTON & HIS ORCHESTRA
CT WC CA RN, BWmn QJ JSrs, JHtn JH RP PG HC, DE JW SWrd, JGsm.

....	Take The "A" Train
....	Rock City Rock –vJGsm
....	Sophisticated Lady
....	Perdido
....	Mood Indigo
....	Solitude –vJGsm
....	Jam With Sam

28 Apr 1957   (P)
Town Hall (bc)
New York City, NY

DUKE ELLINGTON & HIS ORCHESTRA
CT WC CA RN, BWmn QJ JSrs, JHtn JH RP PG HC, DE JW SWrd.

SUCH SWEET THUNDER
....	- Such Sweet Thunder
....	- Sonnet For Caesar
....	- Sonnet To Hank Cinq[1]
....	- Lady Mac
....	- Sonnet In Search For A Moor
....	- The Telecasters
....	- Up And Down, Up And Down
....	- Sonnet For Sister Kate
....	- The Star-Crossed Lovers[2]
....	- Madness In Great Ones
....	- Half The Fun
....	Cop Out

[1]*aka* "Take All My Loves."
[2]*sa* "Pretty Little Girl"; "Pretty Girl."

29 Apr 1957[1]   (S)
Unidentified location
New York City, NY

DUKE ELLINGTON
DE interviewed by Harry Rasky.

| .... | Interview |

[1]Date of broadcast 15 May 1957.

3 May 1957   (S)
30th Street Studio
New York City, NY

DUKE ELLINGTON & HIS ORCHESTRA
CT WC CA RN, BWmn QJ JSrs, JHtn JH RP PG HC, DE JW SWrd.

SUCH SWEET THUNDER (ctd.)[1]
| .... | Co | CO57906-7 | - Sonnet To Hank Cinq (Britt's Sonnet) (w. insert 2) |
| .... | Co | CO57907-4 | - The Telecasters   >>> |

....	Co	CO57907 alt.	- The Telecasters
....	Co	CO57714-4[2]	- Madness In Great Ones (Hamlet)
....	Co	CO57714-4 alt.	- Madness In Great Ones[3]
....	Co	CO57015-1[4]	- The Star-Crossed Lovers
....	Co	CO57015-3[4, 5]	- The Star-Crossed Lovers
....	Co	CO57015-4[4]	- The Star-Crossed Lovers (with insert)
....	Co	CO57908-1[6]	- Circle Of Fourths (Fourths)
....	Co	CO57908-2	- Circle Of Fourths
....	Co	CO57908-4	- Circle Of Fourths

[1]See also sessions on 7 Aug 1956, 15, 24 Apr 1957.
[2]Remake with insert.
[3]CD Co CK 65568 uses an insert at 2:00.
[4]Remakes; see also "Pretty Girl" from session on 6 Dec 1956 (identical master and take numbers!).
[5]Take 1 intro with insert from take 4.
[6]The coda from this take has been edited into take 4 on CD Co CK 65568.

			SUCH SWEET THUNDER (summation—original release)[1]
	Co	CO57722-3	- Such Sweet Thunder
	Co	CO57712-6	- Sonnet For Caesar
	Co	CO57906-7	- Sonnet To Hank Cinq
	Co	CO57723-4	- Lady Mac
	Co	CO57713-4	- Sonnet In Search Of A Moor
	Co	CO57907-4	- The Telecasters
	Co	CO57721-12	- Up And Down, Up And Down
	Co	CO57715-2	- Sonnet For Sister Kate
	Co	CO57015-4	- The Star-Crossed Lovers
	Co	CO57714-4	- Madness In Great Ones
	Co	CO56566-5	- Half The Fun[2]
	Co	CO57908-2	- Circle Of Fourths

[1]For the release on CD some of the alternate takes were used.
[2]This part was recorded on 7 Aug 1956 as "Lately."

8 May 1957[1]   (T)
CBS Studios (tc)
New York City, NY

DUKE ELLINGTON & HIS ORCHESTRA
CT WC CA RN, BWmn QJ JSrs, JHtn JH RP PG HC, BGmn, DE JW SWrd Cnd, JS MTns OB, DE narrating throughout.

		A DRUM IS A WOMAN
....		- A Drum Is A Woman –vMTns
....		- What Else Can You Do With A Drum? –vOB
....		- New Orleans
....		- Hey, Buddy Bolden –vJS MTns OB
....		- Carribee Joe –vJS
....		- A Drum Is A Woman –vMTns
....		- Congo Square
....		- Madam Zajj
....		- A Drum Is A Woman –vMTns
....		- You Better Know It –vOB
....		- Madam Zajj
....		- Zajj's Dream
....		- Rhumbop –vJS
....		- A Drum Is A Woman –vMTns
....		- On Credit –vOB[2]
....		- Carribee Joe

> BGmn added.

| .... | | - Ballet Of The Flying Saucers |

> BGmn omitted.

| .... | | - A Drum Is A Woman –vMTns |
| .... | | - You Better Know It |

[1]Date of telecast.
[2]This title is a derivative of *Pomegranate*.

The material originates to a large degree from the Sep-Dec 1956 recording sessions.

1 Jun 1957   (P)
Sunset Ballroom
Carrolltown, PA

DUKE ELLINGTON & HIS ORCHESTRA
CT WC HB RN, BWmn QJ JSrs, JHtn JH RP PG HC, DE JBjm SWrd, JGsm.

....	Jzy	Stompin' At The Savoy
....	DJ	Sophisticated Lady
....	DJ	Star Dust
....	DJ	Jeep's Blues
....	DJ	All Of Me >>>

....	DJ		Perdido
....	DJ		Mood Indigo
....	DJ		Bass-ment[1]
....			Flamingo –vJGsm
....			Do Nothin' Till You Hear From Me –vJGsm
....	DJ		Take The "A" Train
....	DJ		Take The "A" Train –vRN
....	DJ		Such Sweet Thunder

> HB, QJ, RP, DE JBjm SWrd.

| .... | | | There'll Be Some Changes Made |

> Entire band.

....	DJ		Cop Out
....	DJ		Frustration
....	Az		Take The "A" Train
....	Az		The Hawk Talks
....	Koa		Three Little Words
....	Koa		As Time Goes By
....	Koa		The Happy One
....	Az		Caravan
....	DJ		Diminuendo In Blue and Crescendo In Blue (w. Wailing Interval)
....	Az		Things Ain't What They Used To Be
....	DJ		I Got It Bad
....	DJ		On The Sunny Side Of The Street
....	Az		I Let A Song Go Out Of My Heart/Don't Get Around Much Anymore

[1]*sa* "Discontented"; "Trombone Trio"; "Daddy's Blues"; "Hark, The Duke's Trumpets."

ELLA FITZGERALD WITH DUKE ELLINGTON & HIS ORCHESTRA
Vcl, acc. by CT WC CA, BWmn QJ JSrs, JHtn JH RP FFst HC, BS JW SWrd.

24 Jun 1957   (S)
Fine Studios[1]
New York City, NY

| .... | Vrv | 21033-6 | Day Dream –vEF |

> HB DG RN added, DE replaces BS.

| .... | Vrv | 21034-6 | Take The "A" Train –vEF |

> DG HB/RN omitted, BS replaces DE.

| .... | | 21035 | [Lush Life –vEF] |

[1]At Fifth Avenue; also known as Fine Recording and Fine Sound Inc.

ELLA FITZGERALD WITH DUKE ELLINGTON & HIS ORCHESTRA
Vcl, acc. by CT WC CA HB/RN, BWmn QJ JSrs, JHtn JH RP PG HC, DE JW SWrd.

25 Jun 1957   (S)
Fine Studios
New York City, NY

| .... | Vrv | 21036-6 | Everything But You –vEF |

> BS replaces DE.

| .... | Vrv | 21037-6 | I Got It Bad –vEF |

> DE replaces BS.

| .... | Vrv | 21038-3 | Drop Me Off At Harlem –vEF |

> HB/RN, DE omitted, ME (claves) added.

| .... | Vrv | 21039-3 | Lost In Meditation –vEF |

> ME omitted, HB/RN, DE added.

| .... | Vrv | 21040-4 | I Ain't Got Nothin' But The Blues –vEF |

ELLA FITZGERALD WITH DUKE ELLINGTON & HIS ORCHESTRA
Vcl, acc. by CT WC CA HB/RN, BWmn QJ JSrs, JHtn JH RP FFst HC, BS JW SWrd.

26 Jun 1957   (S)
Fine Studios
New York City, NY

| .... | Vrv | 21049-2 | Clementine –vEF |

> DE replaces BS.

....	Vrv	21050-1	I'm Just A Lucky So-And-So –vEF
....	Vrv	21051-12	I'm Beginning To See The Light –vEF
....	Vrv	21052-2	I Didn't Know About You –vEF
....	Vrv	21053-3	Rockin' In Rhythm –vEF

ELLA FITZGERALD WITH DUKE ELLINGTON & HIS ORCHESTRA
Vcl, acc. by CT WC CA HB/RN, BWmn QJ JSrs, JHtn JH RP PG HC, DE JW SWrd.

27 Jun 1957   (S)
Fine Studios
New York City, NY

| .... | Vrv | 21063-3 | All Too Soon –vEF   >>> |

....	Vrv	21064-8	Caravan –vEF
....	Vrv	21065-7	Bli-Blip –vEF

> BS replaces DE.

....	Vrv		Talking and orchestra noodling
....	Vrv		Chelsea Bridge –vEF (rehearsal)
....	Vrv		Chelsea Bridge –vEF
....	Vrv		Orchestra noodling
....	Vrv		Chelsea Bridge –vEF
....	Vrv		Orchestra noodling
....	Vrv		Chelsea Bridge –vEF (incomplete)
....	Vrv		Chelsea Bridge –vEF (incomplete)
....	Vrv		Chelsea Bridge –vEF (incomplete)
....	Vrv		Chelsea Bridge –vEF (incomplete)
....	Vrv		Orchestra noodling
....	Vrv		Chelsea Bridge –vEF (incomplete)
....	Vrv		Chelsea Bridge (rehearsal)
....	Vrv		Chelsea Bridge –vEF (rehearsal)
....	Vrv	21066-8	Chelsea Bridge –vEF

> DE replaces BS.

....	Vrv	21067-4	Perdido –vEF
....	Vrv	21068-2	The E&D Blues –vEF

DUKE ELLINGTON & HIS ORCHESTRA
CT WC CA HB RN, BWmn HChb JSrs, JHtn JH RP PG HC, DE JW GWrn, JGsm OB.

12 Jul 1957[1]   (P)
Blue Note (bc)
Chicago, IL

....	TOM	Rock City Rock –vJGsm
....	TOM	You Better Know It –vOB
....	TOM	I Got It Bad

[1]Broadcast on 13 Jul 1957.

DUKE ELLINGTON WITH THE BUFFALO PHILHARMONIC ORCHESTRA
DE JW SWrd with the Buffalo Philharmonic Orchestra, Willis Page conducting.

23 Jul 1957   (P)
Kleinhans Music Hall
Buffalo, NY

....	New World A-Comin'
....	Stalking Monster

> BPO omitted.

....	Take The "A" Train
....	Ad Lib Blues

> BPO added.

....	Mood Indigo

DUKE ELLINGTON & HIS ORCHESTRA
CT WC CA HB, BWmn QJ JSrs, JHtn JH RP PG HC, DE JW SWrd, JGsm OB.

27 Jul 1957   (P)
Stony Brook
Long Island, NY

....	Take The "A" Train
....	Black And Tan Fantasy
....	Newport Up
....	Sophisticated Lady
....	What Else Can You Do With A Drum? –vOB
....	You Better Know It –vOB
....	Jeep's Blues
....	All Of Me
....	Rock City Rock –vJGsm
....	La Virgen de la Macarena
....	Skin Deep
....	Medley[1]

[1]Including: Don't Get Around Much Anymore; Do Nothin' Till You Hear From Me –vJGsm; In A Sentimental Mood; Mood Indigo; I'm Beginning To See The Light; Sophisticated Lady; Caravan; I Got It Bad; It Don't Mean A Thing; Solitude –vJGsm; The "C" Jam Blues; I Let A Song Go Out Of My Heart/Don't Get Around Much Anymore.

DUKE ELLINGTON & HIS ORCHESTRA
CT WC CA HB RN, BWmn QJ JSrs, JHtn JH RP PG HC, DE JW SWrd, JGsm OB.

29 Jul 1957   (P)
East River Amphitheater (bc)
New York City, NY

....	The Star Spangled Banner
....	Black And Tan Fantasy
....	Perdido
....	Clarinet Melodrama
....	Theme For Trambean >>>

....   Sophisticated Lady
....   Matumbe
....   Take The "A" Train –vRN
....   Just Squeeze Me –vRN
....   La Virgen de la Macarena
....   What Else Can You Do With A Drum? –vOB
....   You Better Know It –vOB
....   V.I.P.'s Boogie
....   Jam With Sam
....   The Hawk Talks
....   Jeep's Blues
....   All Of Me
....   Flamingo –vJGsm
....   Do Nothin' Till You Hear From Me –vJGsm
....   Rock City Rock –vJGsm
....   Skin Deep
....   Medley[1]

[1]Including: Don't Get Around Much Anymore; Do Nothin' Till You Hear From Me; In A Sentimental Mood; Mood Indigo, I'm Beginning to See The Light; Sophisticated Lady; Caravan; I Got It Bad; It Don't Mean A Thing –vRN; Solitude –vJGsm; The "C" Jam Blues; I Let A Song Go Out Of My Heart/Don't Get Around Much Anymore.

DUKE ELLINGTON & HIS ORCHESTRA   24 Aug 1957   (P)
CT WC CA HB RN, BWmn QJ JSrs, JHtn JH RP PG HC, DE JW SWrd, OB.   Blue Note (bc)
                                                                            Chicago, IL
....   What Else Can You Do With A Drum? –vOB
....   Newport Up
....   Jeep's Blues

DUKE ELLINGTON & HIS ORCHESTRA   Aug 1957   (P)
CT WC CA HB RN, BWmn QJ JSrs, JHtn JH RP PG HC, DE JW SWrd, OB.   Blue Note (bc?)
....   Newport Up
....   Pomegranate –vOB
....   Just Squeeze Me –vRN
....   Things Ain't What They Used To be

DUKE ELLINGTON & HIS ORCHESTRA   31 Aug 1957   (P)
CT WC CA HB RN, BWmn QJ JSrs, JHtn JH RP PG HC, DE JW SWrd, JS OB.   Blue Note (bc)
                                                                            Chicago, IL
....   Take The "A" Train
....   Rhumbop –vJS
....   Pomegranate –vOB
....   Such Sweet Thunder

DUKE ELLINGTON & HIS ORCHESTRA   2 Sep 1957   (S)
CT WC CA HB, BWmn QJ JSrs, JHtn JH RP PG HC, DE JW SWrd.   Universal Studios
                                                                            Chicago, IL
                          A PORTRAIT OF ELLA FITZGERALD
.... Vrv   21380-13   1 Royal Ancestry
....   21381   2 All Heart[1] (incomplete)
....   21381   2 All Heart (incomplete)
....   21381   2 All Heart (incomplete)
....   21381   2 All Heart
.... Vrv   21381-1   2 All Heart
.... Vrv   21381-3   2 All Heart
.... Vrv   21381-6   2 All Heart
.... Vrv   21381-8   2 All Heart
.... Vrv   21381-12   2 All Heart
.... Vrv   21382-7   3 Beyond Category
.... Vrv   21383-4   4 Total Jazz[2]

[1]aka "Entrance Of Youth."
[2]aka "P.O.O. #4" (P.O.E. stands for Portrait Of Ella); sa "Saturday night At Basin Street:; "The E&D Blues."

DUKE ELLINGTON & HIS ORCHESTRA   5 Sep 1957   (P)
CT WC CA HB, BWmn QJ JSrs, JHtn JH RP PG HC, DE JW SWrd.   Festival Theatre (bc)
                                                                            Stratford, ON
                          SUCH SWEET THUNDER
....   - Sonnet For Caesar
....   - Sonnet To Hank Cinq
....   - The Telecasters
....   - Lady Mac   >>>

....			- Circle Of Fourths
....			- Sonnet In Search Of A Moor
....			- Such Sweet Thunder
....			- Sonnet For Sister Kate
....			- Up And Down, Up And Down
....			- The Star-Crossed Lovers
....			- Madness In Great Ones

9 Sep 1957   (S)
30th Street Studio
New York City, NY

DUKE ELLINGTON & HIS ORCHESTRA
CT WC CA HB, BWmn QJ JSrs, JHtn JH RP PG HC, DE JW SWrd, OB.

....	Co	CO59716-1	Commercial Time
....	Co	CO59717	Tenderly
....		CO59718	Autumn Leaves –vOB
....	Co	CO59719-1	Mood Indigo
....	Co	CO59719-2	Mood Indigo
....	Co	CO59719 alt.	Mood Indigo

11 Sep 1957   (P)
CBS Studios (tc)
New York City, NY

VIC DAMONE & DUKE ELLINGTON WITH THE BERT FARBER ORCHESTRA
VDmn and DE with the Bert Farber Orchestra.

....	Take The "A" Train
....	Medley[1]

[1]Including: Mood Indigo; Don't Get Around Much Anymore; Solitude –vVDmn; I'm Beginning To See The Light; Do Nothin'
Till You Hear From Me; I Let A Song Go Out Of My Heart; I Got It Bad –vVDmn; Caravan.

28 Sep 1957   (P)
Storyville Club (bc)
Boston, MA

DUKE ELLINGTON & HIS ORCHESTRA
CT WC CA HB RN, BWmn QJ JSrs, JHtn JH RP PG HC, DE JW SWrd.

....	Take The "A" Train
....	Jeep's Blues
....	Newport Up
....	La Virgen de la Macarena
....	Just Squeeze Me –vRN
....	Diminuendo In Blue and Crescendo In Blue (w. Wailing Interval)

1 Oct 1957   (S)
30th Street Studio
New York City, NY

DUKE ELLINGTON & HIS ORCHESTRA
CT WC CA HB RN, BWmn QJ JSrs, JHtn JH RP PG HC, DE JW SWrd, OB.

....	Co	CO59896-2	Dancing In The Dark
....	Co	CO59897-3	Prelude To A Kiss
....	Co	CO59718-1[1]	Autumn Leaves –vOB

[1]Several edited versions of this title have been released, which leads one to the wrong conclusion that different takes
exist: No vocal, English vocal only, French vocal only. A complete rendition of this title, with vocal both in English and
French, can be found on CBS/Co (US) J-44444 and on CD.

3 Oct 1957   (S)
Fine Studios, Fifth Ave.
New York City, NY

DUKE ELLINGTON & BILLY STRAYHORN
DE and BS, piano and talking.

			A PORTRAIT OF ELLA FITZGERALD
....	Vrv	21557-1	1 Royal Ancestry –BS p, DE voice
....	Vrv	21557-2	1 Royal Ancestry –BS p, DE voice (incomplete)
....	Vrv	21557-3	1 Royal Ancestry –BS p, DE voice
....	Vrv	21557-4	1 Royal Ancestry –BS p, DE voice (incomplete)
....	Vrv	21557-5	1 Royal Ancestry –BS p, DE voice (incomplete)
....	Vrv	21557-6	1 Royal Ancestry –BS p, DE voice
....	Vrv	21557-7	1 Royal Ancestry –BS p, DE voice (incomplete)
....	Vrv	21557-8	1 Royal Ancestry –BS p, DE voice
....	Vrv	21557-1	2 All Heart –BS p, DE voice
....	Vrv	21557-1	3 Beyond Category –BS p, DE voice
....	Vrv	21557-1	4 Total Jazz –DE p, BS voice (incomplete)
....	Vrv	21557-?[1]	4 Total Jazz –DE p, BS voice

[1]Spliced tape.

The above is the voicetrack for the instrumental portion, which was recorded on 2 Sep 1957.

10 Oct 1957   (S)
30th Street Studio
New York City, NY

DUKE ELLINGTON & HIS ORCHESTRA
CT WC CA HB RN, BWmn QJ JSrs, JHtn JH RP PG HC, DE JW SWrd.

....	Co	CO59936-3	Willow Weep For Me
....	Co	CO59936 alt.	Willow Weep For Me
....	Co	CO59937-3	Where Or When >>>

....	Co	CO59937 alt.	Where Or When

> DE JW SWrd.

....	FM	CO59938-1	All The Things You Are
....	Co	CO59938-2	All The Things You Are

> Entire band.

....	Co	CO59939	Night And Day

13 Oct 1957   (P)
NBC Studios (tc)
New York City, NY

DUKE ELLINGTON & HIS ORCHESTRA
CT WC CA HB RN, BWmn QJ JSrs, JHtn JH RP PG HC, DE JW SWrd.

....	Take The "A" Train
....	Such Sweet Thunder
....	The Telecasters
....	Lady Mac
....	Medley[1]

[1]Including: Do Nothin' Till You Hear From Me; I'm Beginning To See The Light; Sophisticated Lady; Caravan; Mood Indigo.

14 Oct 1957   (S)
30th Street Studio
New York City, NY

DUKE ELLINGTON & HIS ORCHESTRA
CT WC HB CA RN, BWmn QJ JSrs, JHtn JH RP PG HC, DE JW SWrd, JGsm.

....	Co	CO59960-3	Solitude –vJGsm
....	Co	CO59961-10	My Heart, My Mind, My Everything –vJGsm[1]

[1]aka "Love (My Everything)."

10 Nov 1957   (P)
Holiday Ballroom
Chicago, IL

DUKE ELLINGTON & HIS ORCHESTRA
CT WC CA HB RN, BWmn QJ JSrs, JHtn JH RP PG HC, DE JW SWrd, JGsm OB.

....	Creole Love Call
....	Deep Purple
....	Bluejean Beguine
....	The Happy One
....	Take The "A" Train
....	Perdido
....	Cop Out
....	Sophisticated Lady
....	What Else Can You Do With A Drum? –vOB
....	You Better Know It –vOB
....	My Funny Valentine
....	Jeep's Blues
....	All Of Me
....	Take The "A" Train –vRN
....	Just Squeeze Me –vRN
....	Skin Deep
....	In The Mood
....	Flamingo –vJGsm
....	Do Nothin' Till You Hear From Me –vJGsm
....	Blue Moon –vJGsm
....	Mambo Jambo
....	Such Sweet Thunder
....	The Star-Crossed Lovers
....	Passion Flower
....	Madness In Great Ones
....	Mood Indigo
....	Madness In Great Ones
....	Diminuendo In Blue and Crescendo In Blue (w. Wailing Interval)
....	Autumn Leaves –vOB
....	Mambo #5
....	Love You Madly –vJGsm
....	Baby, Bye-Bye –vJGsm[1]
....	Caravan
....	Laura
....	Mood Indigo

[1]sa "Ballin' The Blues."

25 Nov 1957[1]   (P)
Studios WGN (tc)
Chicago, IL

DUKE ELLINGTON & HIS ORCHESTRA
CT WC CA HB AF RN, BWmn QJ JSrs, JHtn JH RH RP PG HC, DE JW SWrd, LH JGsm.

....	Joy	Take The "A" Train
....	Joy	Jam With Sam >>>

> DE piano solo.

.... Joy   Soda Fountain Rag

> Entire band.

.... Joy   Such Sweet Thunder
.... Joy   The Telecasters
.... Joy   Lady Mac

                                       THE PERFUME SUITE
.... Joy   - Balcony Serenade
.... Joy   - Strange Feeling –vJGsm
.... Joy   - Coloratura
.... Joy   - Dancers In Love

.... Joy   I'm Beginning To See The Light –vLH
.... Joy   Don't You Know I Care? –vLH
....   Medley[2]
.... Joy   Satin Doll
....   Take The "A" Train

[1]Date of telecast; probably taped at an earlier date since DE had a club date at the "Riviera" in St. Louis, MO, on 25 Nov.
[2]Including: Don't Get Around Much Anymore; Do Nothin' Till You Hear From Me; In A Sentimental Mood; Mood Indigo;
I'm Beginning To See The Light; Sophisticated Lady; Caravan; I Got It Bad; Just Squeeze Me –vRN; It Don't Mean A
Thing –vRN; Solitude; The "C" Jam Blues; I Let A Song Go Out Of My Heart/ Don't Get Around Much Anymore.

			2 Dec 1957	(S)
DUKE ELLINGTON & HIS ORCHESTRA			30th Street Studio	
CT CA AF RN, BWmn QJ JSrs, JHtn JH RH RP PG HC, DE JW SWrd.			New York City, NY	

.... Co   CO59457-8   Slamar In D-Flat

                                       THE PERFUME SUITE
.... Co   CO59458-2   4 Coloratura
.... Co   CO59459-6   1 Under The Balcony

			9 Dec 1957	(S)
DUKE ELLINGTON & HIS ORCHESTRA			30th Street Studio	
CT CA HB AF RN, BWmn QJ JSrs, JHtn JH RP PG HC, DE JW SWrd, JGsm			New York City, NY	

....   CO59457[1]   Slamar In D-Flat
.... Co   CO59486   Together –vJGsm[2]

                                       THE PERFUME SUITE (ctd.)
.... Co   CO59487   2 Strange Feeling –vJGsm[3]
.... Co   CO59487-2   3 Dancers In Love

[1]Remake.
[2]Contrary to what is documented on the recording sheet, the liner notes for CBS/Co 26306 list OP instead of JW.
[3]The liner notes for the LP CBS/Co FC 38028 are misleading by listing MGsn as vocalist.

		30 Dec 1957	(P)
DUKE ELLINGTON & HIS ORCHESTRA		Blue Note (tc)[1]	
CT WC CA HB RN, BWmn QJ JSrs, JHtn JH RP PG HC, DE JW SWrd.		Chicago, IL	

.... KoJ   Ballet Of The Flying Saucers
.... KoJ   Such Sweet Thunder

[1]The above is DE's contribution to the "Timex All Star Jazz Show #1," which was produced in New York.
The Ellington segment was wired in from Chicago.

		31 Dec 1957	(P)
DUKE ELLINGTON & HIS ORCHESTRA		Blue Note (bc)	
CT WC CA HB RN, BWmn QJ JSrs, JHtn JH RP PG HC, DE JW SWrd, JGsm OB.		Chicago, IL	

....   Take The "A" Train

....   Auld Lang Syne   1 Jan 1958
....   Newport Up
....   Together –vJGsm
....   La Virgen de la Macarena
....   You Better Know It –vOB
....   The Star-Crossed Lovers

The above is a continuous performance and has therefore not been separated at the dateline.

		1 Jan 1958	(P)
DUKE ELLINGTON & HIS ORCHESTRA		Blue Note (bc)	
CT WC CA HB RN, BWmn QJ JSrs, JHtn JH RP PG HC, DE JW SWrd.		Chicago, IL	

....   Such Sweet Thunder
....   Diminuendo In Blue and Crescendo In Blue (w. Wailing Interval)
....   Such Sweet Thunder   >>>

DUKE ELLINGTON & HIS ORCHESTRA
OB added, otherwise same personnel.

....		Take The "A" Train
....		The Telecasters
....		Jump For Joy –vRN
....		Bond promotion
....		Passion Flower
....		Newport Up
....		Bond promotion
....		Duke's Place –vOB[1]
....		My Heart, My Mind, My Everything –vOB

[1]This title is a derivative of *The "C" Jam Blues*.

20 Jan 1958   (P)
Keesler AFB
Biloxi, MS

DUKE ELLINGTON & HIS ORCHESTRA
CT CA HB RN, BWmn QJ JSrs, JHtn BGhm RP PG HC, DE JW SWrd, OB.

....		Take The "A" Train
....		Stompin' At The Savoy
....		What Else Can You Do With A Drum? –vOB
....		Autumn Leaves –vOB
....		La Virgen de la Macarena
....		Skin Deep
....		Medley[1]
....		Diminuendo In Blue and Crescendo In Blue (w. Wailing Interval)
....		Take The "A" Train

[1]Including: Don't Get Around Much Anymore; Do Nothin' Till You Hear From Me; In A Sentimental Mood; Mood Indigo; I'm Beginning To See The Light; Sophisticated Lady; Caravan; I Got It Bad; Just Squeeze Me –vRN; It Don't Mean A Thing –vRN; Solitude; The "C" Jam Blues; I Let A Song Go Out Of My Heart/Don't Get Around Much Anymore.

21 Jan 1958   (S)[1]
Municipal Auditorium (bc)
Pensacola, FL

DUKE ELLINGTON
DE interviewed by Ted Cassidy.

....	RDB	Interview

[1]Backstage.

22 Jan 1958   (P)
Keesler AFB
Biloxi, MS

DUKE ELLINGTON & HIS ORCHESTRA
CT CA HB RN, BWmn QJ JSrs, JHtn BGhm RP PG HC, DE JW SWrd, OB.

....		Take The "A" Train
....		Stompin' At The Savoy
....		What Else Can You Do With A Drum? –vOB
....		You Better Know It –vOB
....		La Virgen de la Macarena
....		Skin Deep
....		Medley[1]
....	SR[2]	Diminuendo In Blue and Crescendo In Blue (w. Wailing Interval)
....		Take The "A" Train

[1]Including: Don't Get Around Much Anymore; Do Nothin' Till You Hear From Me –vOB; In A Sentimental Mood; Mood Indigo; I'm Beginning To See The Light; Sophisticated Lady; Caravan; I Got It Bad; Just Squeeze Me –vRN; It Don't Mean A Thing –vRN; Solitude; The "C" Jam Blues; Satin Doll; I Let A Song Go Out Of My Heart/Don't Get Around Much Anymore.
[2]The "Wailing Interval" has been edited out on SR.

4 Feb 1958   (S)
Radio Recorders
Hollywood, CA

DUKE ELLINGTON & HIS ORCHESTRA
CT CA HB RN, BWmn QJ JSrs, JHtn BGhm RP PG HC, DE JW SWrd.

....		RHCO40625-1	Track 360[1] (incomplete)
....			Track 360 (rehearsal)
....		RHCO40625-2	Track 360 (incomplete)
....	Co	RHCO40625-3	Track 360
....		RHCO40625-4	Track 360 (incomplete)
....		RHCO40625-5	Track 360 (incomplete)
....		RHCO40625-6	Track 360 (incomplete)
....			Track 360 (rehearsal)
....		RHCO40625-7	Track 360 (incomplete)
....		RHCO40625-8	Track 360 (incomplete)
....		RHCO40625-9	Track 360 (incomplete)
....		RHCO40625-10	Track 360 (incomplete)
....		RHCO40625-11	Track 360
....		RHCO40625-12	Track 360
....		RHCO40625-13	Track 360 (incomplete) >>>

....		RHCO40625-14	Track 360 (incomplete)
....	FM	RHCO40625-15	Track 360
....	Co	RHCO40625-16^2	Track 360
....	Co	RHCO40626-1	Blues In Orbit^3
			BLACK, BROWN AND BEIGE^4
....	Co	RHCO40627-1	1 Work Song
....	Co	RHCO40627-1	2 Come Sunday
....	Co	RHCO40627-1	3 Light

^{1}aka "Trains (That Pass In The Night)."
^{2}Some issues have been edited by adding the sound of a steam locomotive.
^{3}Originally titled "Tender."
^{4}See also sessions on 5, 11 and 12 Feb 1958.

5 Feb 1958   (S)
Unidentified location
Hollywood, CA

MAHALIA JACKSON & DUKE ELLINGTON
Vcl, acc. by DE.

....			23rd Psalm –vMJ^1
....			23rd Psalm –vMJ (incomplete)
....			23rd Psalm –vMJ (incomplete)
....			23rd Psalm –vMJ
....			Come Sunday –vMJ
....			Come Sunday –vMJ (incomplete)
....			Come Sunday –vMJ

^{1}sa "The Lord Is My Shepherd."

The above is a prerecording rehearsal session.

Radio Recorders   (S)
Hollywood, CA

DUKE ELLINGTON & HIS ORCHESTRA
CT CA HB RN, BWmn QJ JSrs, JHtn BGhm RP PG HC, DE JW SWrd.

			BLACK, BROWN AND BEIGE (ctd.)^1
....	Co	RHCO40633-5	1 Work Song (w. insert take 2)
....	Co	RHCO40634-6^2	2 Come Sunday
....	Co	RHCO40634-7^2	2 Come Sunday

^{1}See also sessions on 4, 11 and 12 Feb 1958.
^{2}The violin solo from take 6 has been edited into take 7.

11 Feb 1958   (S)
Radio Recorders
Hollywood, CA

DUKE ELLINGTON & HIS ORCHESTRA FEATURING MAHALIA JACKSON
CT CA HB RN, BWmn QJ JSrs, JHtn BGhm RP PG HC, DE JW SWrd, MJ.

			BLACK, BROWN AND BEIGE (ctd.)^1
....	Co	RHCO40635-4	4 Come Sunday –vMJ
....	Co	RHCO40635-10	4 Come Sunday –vMJ
....	Co	RHCO40636-1	6 23rd Psalm –vMJ
....	Co	RHCO40636-8	6 23rd Psalm –vMJ (w. insert 1, take 10 and insert 2, take 8)
....		RHCO40649^2	3 Light

^{1}See also sessions on 4, 5 and 12 Feb 1958.
^{2}Remake.

12 Feb 1958   (S)
Radio Recorders
Hollywood, CA

DUKE ELLINGTON & HIS ORCHESTRA
CT CA HB RN, BWmn QJ JSrs, JHtn BGhm RP PG HC, DE JW SWrd.

			BLACK, BROWN AND BEIGE (ctd.)^1
> MJ a cappella.			
....	Co	RHCO40651-1	4 Come Sunday –vMJ
> Entire band, MJ omitted.			
....	Co	RHCO40652-3	5 Come Sunday Interlude
....	Co	RHCO40652-8	5 Come Sunday Interlude
....	Co	RHCO40649-5^2	3 Work Song And Come Sunday^3
....	Co	RHCO40649-6^2	3 Work Song And Come Sunday
....	Co	RHCO40626-2^4	Blues In Orbit
....	Co	RHCO40626-6^4	Blues In Orbit

^{1}See also sessions on 4, 5 and 11 Feb 1958.
^{2}The intro from take 5 has been edited into take 6.
^{3}sa "Light."
^{4}Remakes.

4 Mar 1958   (P)
Travis AFB
Fairfield, CA

DUKE ELLINGTON & HIS ORCHESTRA
CT HB RN, BWmn QJ JSrs, JHtn BGhm RP PG HC, DE JW SWrd, OB.

....		Where Or When
....	JCo	Smada
....	WEA	Dancing In The Dark
....	WEA	Main Stem
....	JCo	Vivi
....	JCo	Frivolous Banta
....	JCo	Willow Weep For Me
....	JCo	Just Scratchin' The Surface
....	WEA	Time On My Hands
....	WEA	Stompy Jones
....	JCo	Blues In Orbit[1]
....	JCo	Discontented
....	WEA	Stompin' At The Savoy
....	Koa	Blues To Be There
....	JCo	Juniflip
....	WEA	Sophisticated Lady
....	Koa	Satin Doll
....	Koa	Sophisticated Lady
....	JCo	Beer Barrel Polka
....		What Else Can You Do With A Drum? –vOB
....		You Better Know It –vOB
....		Do Nothin' Till You Hear From Me –vOB
....	JCo	Caravan
....	WEA	Take The "A" Train
....	Koa	Mood Indigo
....	WEA	All Heart
....	WEA	Where Or When
....	WEA	Just A-Settin' And A-Rockin' –vRN
....	WEA	Take The "A" Train –vRN
....		My Heart, My Mind, My Everything –vOB
....		Together –vOB
....	WEA	One O'Clock Jump
....	Saj	Wailing Interval
....	WEA	The Mooche
....	WEA	Autumn Leaves –vOB
....	Koa	Perdido
....	WEA	Oh! Lady Be Good
....	WEA	Things Ain't What They Used To Be

[1]"Blue Star" on JCo.

5 Mar 1958   (P)
Mather AFB
Sacramento, CA

DUKE ELLINGTON & HIS ORCHESTRA
CT HB RN, BWmn QJ JSrs, JHtn BGhm RP PG HC, DE JW SWrd, OB.

....	UJ	Dancing In The Dark
....	UJ	Where Or When
....	Koa	Frivolous Banta
....		Vivi
....	UJ	Main Stem
....		Time On My Hands
....	Koa	Boo-Dah
....	UJ	Commercial Time
....		My Heart, My Mind, My Everything –vOB
....		Do Nothin' Till You Hear From Me –vOB
....	Koa	The "C" Jam Blues
....	UJ	All Heart
....	Koa	I Let A Song Go Out Of My Heart/Don't Get Around Much Anymore –vRN
....	Saj	Juniflip
....		Tenderly
....		Where Or When
....		Stompin' At The Savoy
....	UJ	Autumn Leaves –vOB
....	UJ	Sophisticated Lady
....	UJ	Suburban Beauty
....	UJ	Caravan
....	UJ	Take The "A" Train
....	UJ	Blues To Be There
....	UJ	Perdido
....	UJ	Just Squeeze Me –vRN
....	Saj	Such Sweet Thunder
....	UJ	The Star-Crossed Lovers >>>

.... UJ   Together –vOB
....   Solitude –vOB
....   Day In, Day Out –vOB
.... UJ   Blue Moon –vOB
.... UJ   Take The "A" Train

20 Mar 1958   (S)
30th Street Studio
New York City, NY

DUKE ELLINGTON & HIS ORCHESTRA
CT WC CA HB RN, BWmn QJ JSrs, JHtn BGhm RP PG HC, DE JW SWrd.

.... Co   CO60573-14   Got A Date With An Angel
.... Co   CO60574-13   Laugh, Clown, Laugh
....   CO60575-1   Spooky Takes A Holiday[1]
....   CO60575-2   Spooky Takes A Holiday (incomplete)
.... Co   CO60575-4   Spooky Takes A Holiday

[1]*aka "Satan Takes A Holiday."*

The titles of this recording session and those on 24, 26, 31 Mar and 1 Apr 1958 have been enhanced with noises and canned applause to simulate the ambiance of a ballroom.

24 Mar 1958   (S)
30th Street Studio
New York City, NY

DUKE ELLINGTON & HIS ORCHESTRA
CT WC CA HB RN, BWmn QJ JSrs, JHtn BGhm RP PG HC, DE JW SWrd.

....   Poor Butterfly (incomplete)
....   CO60592-15   Poor Butterfly (incomplete)
.... Co   CO60592-16   Poor Butterfly
....   CO60593-1   The Peanut Vendor (incomplete)
....   CO60593-2   The Peanut Vendor
....   CO60593-3   The Peanut Vendor
.... Co   CO60593-7   The Peanut Vendor

26 Mar 1958   (S)
30th Street Studio
New York City, NY

DUKE ELLINGTON & HIS ORCHESTRA
CT WC CA HB RN, BWmn QJ JSrs, JHtn BGhm RP PG HC, DE JW SWrd.

.... Co   CO60706-8   Indian Love Call
....   CO60707-2   Medley[1]

[1]Including: Greensleeves; Alice Blue Gown; The Lady In Red.

DUKE ELLINGTON   Radio City, Studio 8H (tc) (P)
DE interviewed by Gilbert Seldes on the program "The Subject Is Jazz."

....   Interview

31 Mar 1958   (S)
30th Street Studio
New York City, NY

DUKE ELLINGTON & HIS ORCHESTRA
CT WC CA HB RN, BWmn QJ JSrs, JHtn JH BGhm RP PG HC, DE JW SWrd.

.... Co   CO60707-9   The Lady In Red
....   CO60748   Alice Blue Gown
.... Co   CO60748-8   Alice Blue Gown
.... Co   CO60749-1   Satin Doll
.... Co   CO60750-8   The Donkey Serenade

1 Apr 1958   (S)
30th Street Studio
New York City, NY

DUKE ELLINGTON & HIS ORCHESTRA
CT WC CA HB RN, BWmn QJ JSrs, JHtn JH RP PG HC, DE JW SWrd, OB.

.... Co   CO60751-10   Who's Afraid Of The Big Bad Wolf?
.... Co   CO60752-6   Gypsy Love Song[1]
....   CO60753   Hand-Me-Down Love –vOB

[1]*aka "Gypsy Sweetheart."*

2 Apr 1958   (S)
30th Street Studio
New York City, NY

DUKE ELLINGTON'S SPACEMEN
CT, BWmn QJ JSrs, JHtn PG, DE JW SWrd.

.... Co   CO60756-3   Midnight Sun
.... Co   CO60757-3   Avalon
.... Co   CO60758-5   Take The "A" Train
.... Co   CO60759-1   Body And Soul
.... Co   CO60759-2   Body And Soul

3 Apr 1958   (S)
30th Street Studio
New York City, NY

DUKE ELLINGTON'S SPACEMEN
CT, BWmn QJ JSrs, JHtn PG, DE JW SWrd.

.... Co   CO60760-2   St. Louis Blues   >>>

....	Co	CO60761-2[1]	Perdido
....	Co	CO60762	Jones[2]
....	Co	CO60762-3	Jones
....	Co	CO60763-9[1]	Early Autumn
....	Co	CO60764-5	Bass-ment
....	Co	CO60765-3[1]	Spacemen[3]

[1]The actual take numbers differ from those on the recording sheet.
[2]aka "Shuffle."
[3]sa "Three Trumps."

24 Apr1958   (S)
30th Street Studio
New York City, NY

DUKE ELLINGTON & HIS ORCHESTRA
CT WC CA HB RN, BWmn QJ JSrs, JHtn JH RP PG HC, DE OP SWrd, OB.

....		CO60753-1[1]	Hand-Me-Down Love –vOB (incomplete)
....		CO60753-2	Hand-Me-Down Love –vOB
....			Duke's Place (rehearsal)
....		CO60901-1	Duke's Place –vOB (incomplete)
....		CO60901-2	Duke's Place –vOB
....			Duke's Place (rehearsal)
....		CO60901-3	Duke's Place –vOB (incomplete)
....		CO60901-4	Duke's Place –vOB
....		CO60901-5	Duke's Place –vOB
....		CO60901-6	Duke's Place (incomplete)
....		CO60901-7	Duke's Place (incomplete)
....		CO60901-8	Duke's Place (incomplete)
....		CO60901-9	Duke's Place –vOB (incomplete)
....		CO60901-11	Duke's Place –vOB
....		CO60901-12	Duke's Place –vOB (incomplete)
....		CO60901-13	Duke's Place –vOB (incomplete)
....		CO60901-14	Duke's Place –vOB
....	Co	CO60901-15	Duke's Place –vOB
....		CO60902-1	Lullaby Of Birdland (incomplete)
....	UTD	CO60902-2	Lullaby Of Birdland
....		CO60902-3	Lullaby Of Birdland (incomplete)
....		CO60902-4	Lullaby Of Birdland (incomplete)
....		CO60902-5	Lullaby Of Birdland (incomplete)
....	FM[2]	CO60902-6	Lullaby Of Birdland
....	FM[2]	CO60902-7	Lullaby Of Birdland

[1]Remake.
[2]FM and Co have spliced the opening intro of take 6 and the balance of take 7 together.

4 Jun 1958[1]   (P)
Studios WBBM (tc)
Chicago, IL

DUKE ELLINGTON'S SEPTET
CT HB, BWmn, JHtn, DE JW SWrd.

....		Perdido
....		Tenderly
....		Blues In The Round

> JHtn, JW.

....		Duet

> Entire band.

....		Jones
....		Take The "A" Train

[1]This program was telecast live by WBBM and aired again by WGN on 18 Jun 1958.

9 Jun 1958[1]   (P)
Blue Note (bc)
Chicago, IL

DUKE ELLINGTON & HIS ORCHESTRA
CT WC CA HB RN, BWmn QJ JSrs, JHtn JH RP PG HC, DE JW SWrd, OB.

....		Madness In Great Ones
....		Duke's Place –vOB
....		Jones

[1]Broadcast on 6 Sep 1958.

24 Jun 1958   (S)
Universal Studios
Chicago, IL

DUKE ELLINGTON & PAUL GONSALVES
PG, DE JW SWrd.

....	DJ	-1	In A Mellotone
....	DJ	-2	In A Mellotone
....	DJ	-1	Happy Reunion[1]
....	DJ	-2	Happy Reunion
....	DJ		Wailing Interval >>>

[1]Originally titled "Reunion."

27 Jun 1958   (S)
Universal Studios
Chicago, IL

DUKE ELLINGTON & HIS ORCHESTRA
CT WC CA HB RN, BWmn QJ JSrs, JHtn JH RP PG HC, BS JW SWrd, LG.

....	-3	I Got It Bad –vLG
....	-4	I Got It Bad –vLG
....		Walkin' And Singin' The Blues –vLG
....	-7	Bill Bailey –vLG[1]
....	-10	Bill Bailey –vLG
....		St. Louis Blues –vLG

[1]Complete: "Won't You Come Home, Bill Bailey?"

3 Jul 1958   (P)
Freebody Park (bc)
Newport, RI

DUKE ELLINGTON & HIS ORCHESTRA
CT CA FW HB RN, BWmn QJ JSrs, JHtn JH RP PG HC, DE JW SWrd, OB.

....	Co	Take The "A" Train
....	Co	Princess Blue[1]
....	Co	Duke's Place –vOB

[1]This title is a derivative of *Symphonic Or Bust.*

DUKE ELLINGTON & HIS ORCHESTRA
LG added, otherwise same personnel.

....	Co	Just Scratchin' The Surface

> PG, DE JW SWrd.

....	Co	Happy Reunion

> Entire band.

....	Co	Juniflip
....	Co	Mr. Gentle And Mr. Cool
....	Co	Jazz Festival Jazz
....	Co	Feetbone
....	Co	Hi Fi Fo Fum
....	Co	I Got It Bad –vLG
....	Co	Bill Bailey –vLG

> GM added.

....	Co	Prima Bara Dubla

> GM omitted.

....	Co	El Gato
....	Co	Multicolored Blue –vOB[1]
....		Come Sunday

> MJ added.

....	Co	Come Sunday –vMJ

> MJ omitted.

....	Co	Take The "A" Train
....	Co	Jones

[1]*aka* "MC Blues"; *sa* "Ultra Violet"; "Ultra Blue"; "Violet Blue."

18 Jul 1958   (P)
Dogwood Hollow, Stony Brook
Long Island, NY

DUKE ELLINGTON & HIS ORCHESTRA
CT CA HB RN, BWmn QJ JSrs, JHtn JH RP PG HC, DE OP SWrd, LG OB.

....	Take The "A" Train
....	Black And Tan Fantasy—Creole Love Call—The Mooche
....	Newport Up
....	Tenderly
....	Perdido
....	Such Sweet Thunder
....	Sophisticated Lady
....	Sonnet To Hank Cinq
....	What Else Can You Do With A Drum? –vOB
....	You Better Know It –vOB
....	Autumn Leaves –vOB
....	Take The "A" Train –vRN
....	Such Sweet Thunder
....	Multicolored Blue –vOB
....	All Of Me
....	St. Louis Blues –vLG >>>

....			Bill Bailey –vLG
....			Walkin' And Singin' The Blues –vLG
....			Hi Fi Fo Fum
....			Medley[1]

[1]Including: Don't Get Around Much Anymore; Do Nothin' Till You Hear From Me –vOB; In A Sentimental Mood; Mood Indigo; I'm Beginning To See The Light; Sophisticated Lady; Caravan; I Got It Bad; Just Squeeze Me –vRN; It Don't Mean A Thing –vRN.

21 Jul 1958 (S)
30th Street Studio
New York City, NY

DUKE ELLINGTON & HIS ORCHESTRA
CT CA HB RN, BWmn QJ JSrs, JHtn JH BGhm RP PG HC, DE JW SWrd, OB.

....	Co	CO61280-5	Jazz Festival Jazz
....	Co	CO61281-3	Princess Blue
....	Co	CO61282-2	El Gato
....	Co	CO61283-3	Multicolored Blue –vOB
....	Co	CO61284-1	Hi Fi Fo Fum
....	Co	CO61285-1	Mr. Gentle And Mr. Cool
....	Co	CO61286-1	Juniflip

> PG, DE JW SWrd.

| .... | Co | CO61287-3 | Happy Reunion |

The above studio recordings have been enhanced by canned applause to simulate the ambience of the concert in Newport on 3 Jul 1958.

31 Jul 1958 (S)
CBC Studios (tc)
Toronto, ON

DUKE ELLINGTON
DE piano solo, interviewed by Bill Herbert.

| .... | | | Princess Blue |
| .... | | | Interview |

DUKE ELLINGTON & HIS QUARTET
JH HC, DE JW SWrd.

....	Vid		I'm Beginning To See The Light
....	Vid		Sophisticated Lady
....	Vid		Caravan
....	Vid		I Got It Bad
....	Vid		I Let A Song Go Out Of My Heart/Don't Get Around Much Anymore

6 Aug 1958 (S)
30th Street Studio
New York City, NY

DUKE ELLINGTON & HIS ORCHESTRA
TJ CA HB RN, BWmn QJ JSrs, JHtn JH RP PG HC, DE JW SWrd, LG OB.

....			CO61389-1	Red Carpet[1] (incomplete)
....			CO61389-2	Red Carpet
....			CO61389-3	Red Carpet (incomplete)
....			CO61389-3	Red Carpet
....	Co	CO61389-5	Red Carpet
....			CO61390-1[2]	Hand-Me-Down Love –vOB
....				Hand-Me-Down Love (rehearsal)
....			CO61390-2	Hand-Me-Down Love –vOB (incomplete)
....			CO61390-2	Hand-Me-Down Love –vOB
....	Co	CO61390-3	Hand-Me-Down Love –vOB
....			CO61390-4	Hand-Me-Down Love –vOB (incomplete)
....			CO61390-5	Hand-Me-Down Love –vOB (incomplete)
....			CO61391-1	Walkin' And Singin' The Blues –vLG (incomplete)
....			CO61391-2	Walkin' And Singin' The Blues –vLG (incomplete)
....			CO61391-3	Walkin' And Singin' The Blues –vLG (incomplete)
....			CO61391-4	Walkin' And Singin' The Blues –vLG
....	Co	CO61391-5	Walkin' And Singin' The Blues –vLG
....	Co	CO61392-1	I Can't Give You Anything But Love –vLG

[1]Part of the future *Toot Suite;* this title is a derivative of *Discontented Blues.*
[2]Remake.

15 Aug 1958 (P)
Sheraton Hotel
French Lick, IN

DUKE ELLINGTON & HIS ORCHESTRA
CT CA HB RN, BWmn QJ JSrs, JHtn JH BGhm RP PG HC, DE JW SWrd, LG OB.

....			Take The "A" Train
....			
....			TOOT SUITE[1]
....	SR		- Red Garter
....			- Red Shoes
....			- Red Carpet
....			- Ready, Go >>>

....		Mr. Gentle And Mr. Cool
....		El Gato
....		Hand-Me-Down Love –vOB
....		Duke's Place –vOB
....	SR	Multicolored Blue –vOB
....		All Of Me
....		St. Louis Blues –vLG
....		Bill Bailey –vLG
....		Walkin' And Singin' The Blues –vLG
....		Hi Fi Fo Fum
....		Medley[2]
....		Diminuendo In Blue and Crescendo In Blue (w. Wailing Interval)
....		Jones

[1]*aka* "The Great South Bay Suite."
[2]Including: Don't Get Around Much Anymore; Do Nothin' Till You Hear From Me –vOB; In A Sentimental Mood; Mood Indigo; I'm Beginning To See The Light; Sophisticated Lady; Caravan; I Got It Bad; Just Squeeze Me –vRN; It Don't Mean A Thing –vRN; Solitude –vLG; I Let A Song Go Out Of My Heart/Don't Get Around Much Anymore.

			p Aug 1958 (S)
DUKE ELLINGTON			Armos Ballroom (bc)
DE interviewed by person unknown.			Cedar Rapids, IA
....		Interview	

			9 Sep 1958 (P)
DUKE ELLINGTON & HIS ORCHESTRA			Edwardian Room, Plaza Hotel
CT CA HB RN, BWmn QJ JSrs, JHtn JH RP PG HC, DE JW SWrd, LG OB.			New York City, NY
....	Co	Take The "A" Train	
		JAZZ FESTIVAL SUITE[1]	
....	Co	- Red Garter	
....	Co	- Red Shoes	
....	Co	- Red Carpet	
....	Co	- Ready, Go	
....		Jones	
> BCtn, MWld JW SWrd, BHol.			
....	Co	When Your Lover Has Gone –vBHol	
....	Co	Don't Explain –vBHol[2]	
....		Easy To Remember –vBHol	
> Entire band, BCtn, MWld, BHol omitted.			
....		Take The "A" Train	
....		What Else Can You Do With A Drum? –vOB	
....		Autumn Leaves –vOB	
....	Co	El Gato	
....	Co	All Of Me	
> JRsh added.			
....	Co	Go Away Blues –vJRsh	
....	Co	Hello, Little Girl –vJRsh	
....	Co	I Love To Hear My Baby Call My Name –vJRsh	
> JRsh omitted.			
....		Hi Fi Fo Fum	
....		Bill Bailey –vLG	
....		Walkin' And Singin' The Blues –vLG	
....	Co	Jones	

[1]*sa* "Toot Suite"; "The Great South Bay Suite."
[2]Complete: "Hush, Don't Explain."

			26 Sep 1958 (S)
JOHNNY RAY WITH DUKE ELLINGTON & HIS ORCHESTRA			30th Street Studio
Vcl, acc. by CT CA HB RN, BWmn QJ JSrs, JHtn JH BGhm RP PG HC, BS JW SWrd.			New York City, NY
....	Co	CO61513	To Know You Is To Love You –vJRay
....	Co	CO61514	The Lonely Ones –vJRay

			7 Oct 1958[1] (S)
DUKE ELLINGTON			Dorchester Hotel (bc)
DE interviewed by Frank Henning.			London, England
....		Interview	

[1]Broadcast on 12 Oct 1958.

DUKE ELLINGTON
Piano solo.

11 Oct 1958   (P)
Private residence
London, England

....   A Single Petal Of A Rose[1]

[1]Part of the future *Queen's Suite.*

DUKE ELLINGTON
DE interviewed by Charles Melville.

Mid-Oct 1958   (S)
Unidentified location (bc?)
London, England

....   Interview

DUKE ELLINGTON
DE interviewed by person unknown; intermittent previously recorded music.

Mid-Oct 1958   (S)
BBC Studios (bc)
London, England

....   Conversation with Music

DUKE ELLINGTON
DE RSfd MMII.

17 Oct 1958   (S)
Empress of Britain, Liverpool Docks
Liverpool, England

.... JUn   Take The "A" Train

DUKE ELLINGTON & HIS ORCHESTRA
CT CA HB RN, BWmn QJ JSrs, JHtn JH RP PG HC, DE JW SWrd, OB.

25 Oct 1958   (P)
Kilburn Gaumont State Theatre
London, England

....	SR	Black And Tan Fantasy—Creole Love Call—The Mooche
....	SR	Newport Up
....	SR	Tenderly
....		Perdido
....		Sophisticated Lady
....	SR	What Else Can You Do With A Drum? –vOB
....	SR	Autumn Leaves –vOB
....	SR	On The Sunny Side Of The Street
....	SR	Things Ain't What They Used To Be
....	SR	El Gato
....	SR	Boo-Dah
....		Hi Fi Fo Fum
....		Medley[1]
....		Diminuendo In Blue and Crescendo In Blue (w. Wailing Interval)
....		Jones

[1]Including: Don't Get Around Much Anymore; Do Nothin' Till You Hear From Me; Don't You Know I Care?; In A Sentimental Mood; Mood Indigo; I'm Beginning To See The Light; Sophisticated Lady; Caravan; I Got It Bad; Just Squeeze Me –vRN; It Don't Mean A Thing –vRN; Satin Doll; Solitude –vOB; I Let A Song Go Out Of My Heart/Don't Get Around Much Anymore.

DUKE ELLINGTON & HIS ORCHESTRA
Same personnel.

....	SR	Take The "A" Train
....	SR	Red Garter
....		Ko-Ko
....	SR	Red Carpet
....		Newport Up
....	SR	My Funny Valentine
....	SR	Juniflip
....	SR	Frustration
....		Kinda Dukish/Rockin' In Rhythm
....		You Better Know It –vOB
....		Hand-Me-Down Love –vOB
....	SR	Summertime
....	SR	Passion Flower
....		All Of Me
....		El Gato
....		Main Stem
....		Hi Fi Fo Fum
....	SR[1]	Medley[2]
....		Cotton Tail
....	SR	Mr. Gentle And Mr. Cool
....	SR	Take The "A" Train –vRN
....	SR	Jones
....	SR	God Save The Queen

[1]Incomplete on SR.
[2]Including: Don't Get Around Much Anymore; Do Nothin' Till You Hear From Me; Don't You Know I Care?; In A Sentimental Mood; Mood Indigo; I'm Beginning To See The Light; Sophisticated Lady; Caravan; I Got It Bad; Just Squeeze Me –vRN; It Don't Mean A Thing –vRN; Satin Doll; Solitude –vOB; I Let A Song Go Out Of My Heart/Don't Get Around Much Anymore.

                                                             26 Oct 1958   (P)

DUKE ELLINGTON & HIS ORCHESTRA   Kilburn Gaumont State Theatre
CT CA HB RN, BWmn QJ JSrs, JHtn JH RP PG HC, DE JW SWrd.   London, England

....		Take The "A" Train
....		Creole Love Call
....		Kinda Dukish/Rockin' In Rhythm
....		Red Garter
....		Ko-Ko
....		Red Carpet
....		Newport Up
....		My Funny Valentine
....		Juniflip

                                                              28 Oct 1958   (P)

DUKE ELLINGTON & HIS ORCHESTRA   Théâtre National Populaire, Palais de Chaillot
CT CA HB RN, BWmn QJ JSrs, JHtn JH RP PG HC, DE JW SWrd, OB.   Paris, France

....		Take The "A" Train
....		Black And Tan Fantasy—Creole Love Call—The Mooche
....		Newport Up
....	Mgn	El Gato
....	Mgn	Stompy Jones
....		Medley[1]
....		Diminuendo In Blue and Crescendo In Blue (w. Wailing Interval)

[1]Including: Don't Get Around Much Anymore; Do Nothin' Till You Hear From Me; Don't You Know I Care?; In A Sentimental Mood; Mood Indigo; I'm Beginning To See The Light; Sophisticated Lady; Caravan; I Got It Bad; Just Squeeze Me –vRN; It Don't Mean A Thing –vRN; Satin Doll; Solitude –vOB; I Let A Song Go Out Of My Heart/Don't Get Around Much Anymore.

DUKE ELLINGTON & HIS ORCHESTRA
OB omitted, otherwise same personnel.

....		Perdido
....		Sophisticated Lady
....		Sonnet To Hank Cinq
....	Mgn	On The Sunny Side Of The Street
....	Mgn	Things Ain't What They Used To Be
....		El Gato
....		V.I.P.'s Boogie
....		Jam With Sam
....	Pab	Diminuendo In Blue and Crescendo In Blue (w. Wailing Interval)

                                                              29 Oct 1958   (P)

DUKE ELLINGTON & HIS ORCHESTRA   L'Alhambra-Maurice Chevalier
CT CA HB RN, BWmn QJ JSrs, JHtn JH RP PG HC, DE JW SWrd.   Paris, France

....	Pab	Take The "A" Train
....	Pab	Black And Tan Fantasy—Creole Love Call—The Mooche
....	Pab	Newport Up
....	Pab	Tenderly
....	Mgn	Juniflip
....	Mgn	Frustration
....	Mgn	Such Sweet Thunder
....	Mgn	Sonnet To Hank Cinq
....	Mgn	Passion Flower
....	Pab	Hi Fi Fo Fum
....	Mgn	Jam With Sam
....	Mgn	Diminuendo In Blue and Crescendo In Blue (w. Wailing Interval)

DUKE ELLINGTON & HIS ORCHESTRA
OB added, otherwise same personnel.

....	Mgn	Take The "A" Train
....	Mgn	Black And Tan Fantasy—Creole Love Call—The Mooche
....	Mgn	Newport Up
....	Mag	Deep Purple
....	Mag	Harlem Air Shaft
....	Mag	Such Sweet Thunder
....	Eu1	Sonnet To Hank Cinq
....	Eu1	Sophisticated Lady
....	Eu1	Kinda Dukish/Rockin' In Rhythm
....	Mag	What Else Can You Do With A Drum? –vOB
....	Eu1	Together –vOB
....	Eu1	Jeep's Blues
....	Mag	All Of Me
....	Mag	Things Ain't What They Used To Be >>>

....	Mag	El Gato
....	Mag	Stompy Jones
....	Mag	Hi Fi Fo Fum[1]
....	Eu1	Medley[2]
....	Eu1	Diminuendo In Blue and Crescendo In Blue (w. Wailing Interval)

[1]Edited on Eu1.
[2]Including: Don't Get Around Much Anymore; Do Nothin' Till You Hear From Me; In A Sentimental Mood; Mood Indigo; I'm Beginning To See The Light; Sophisticated Lady; Caravan; I Got It Bad; Just Squeeze Me –vRN; It Don't Mean A Thing –vRN; Satin Doll; Solitude –vOB; I Let A Song Go Out Of My Heart/Don't Get Around Much Anymore.

2 Nov 1958[1]   (P)
Concertgebouw (tc)
Amsterdam, Netherlands

DUKE ELLINGTON & HIS ORCHESTRA
CT CA HB RN, BWmn QJ JSrs, JHtn JH RP PG HC DE JW SWrd, OB.

....	Az	Take The "A" Train
....	DVD	Black And Tan Fantasy—Creole Love Call—The Mooche
....	Az	Tenderly
....	Az	Perdido
....	Az	Sophisticated Lady
....	DVD	My Funny Valentine
....		Kinda Dukish/Rockin' In Rhythm
....	DVD	Mr. Gentle And Mr. Cool
....	DVD	All Of Me
....		Things Ain't What They Used To Be
....	Az	Hi Fi Fo Fum
....	DVD	Medley[2]
....	Az	Diminuendo In Blue and Crescendo In Blue (w. Wailing Interval)

[1]Telecast on 17 Nov 1958.
[2]Including: Don't Get Around Much Anymore; Do Nothin' Till You Hear From Me; Don't You Know I Care?; In A Sentimental Mood; Mood Indigo; I'm Beginning To See The Light; Sophisticated Lady; Caravan; I Got It Bad; Just Squeeze Me –vRN; It Don't Mean A Thing –vRN; Solitude –vOB; I Let A Song Go Out Of My Heart/Don't Get Around Much Anymore.

4 Nov 1958   (S)
Tennishallen (bc)
Stockholm, Sweden

DUKE ELLINGTON
DE interviewed for the new program "Dagens Eko."

....		Interview

5 Nov 1958   (P)
Njårdhallen
Oslo, Norway

DUKE ELLINGTON & HIS ORCHESTRA
CT CA HB RN, BWmn QJ JSrs, JHtn JH RP PG HC, DE JW SWrd, OB.

....	Az	Take The "A" Train
....	Az	Black And Tan Fantasy—Creole Love Call—The Mooche
....	Az	Newport Up
....	Az	Tenderly
....	Az	Perdido
....	Az	Sophisticated Lady
....	Az	Sonnet To Hank Cinq
....	Az	What Else Can You Do With A Drum? –vOB
....	Az	You Better Know It –vOB
....	Az	Rockin' In Rhythm
....	Az	Jeep's Blues
....	Az	All Of Me
....	Az	El Gato
....	Az	Boo-Dah
....	Az	Hi Fi Fo Fum
....	Az	Medley[1]
....	Az	Take The "A" Train
....	Az	Diminuendo In Blue and Crescendo In Blue (w. Wailing Interval)
....	Az	Jones

[1]Including: Don't Get Around Much Anymore; Do Nothin' Till You Hear From Me; Don't You Know I Care? In A Sentimental Mood; Mood Indigo; I'm Beginning To See The Light; Sophisticated Lady; Caravan; I Got It Bad; Just Squeeze Me –vRN; It Don't Mean A Thing –vRN; Satin Doll; Solitude –vOB; I Let A Song Go Out Of My Heart/Don't Get Around Much Anymore.

Liner notes for CD releases on BL, Bst and JHr suggest that a number of titles originate from a concert in Oslo on this date (5 Nov 1958); the versions of these titles are different from those on Az. Since there is no evidence for a second concert in Oslo, it is assumed that the titles in question are identical with those originally issued on MFC.

6 Nov 1958   (P)
Konserthuset
Gothenburg, Sweden

DUKE ELLINGTON & HIS ORCHESTRA
CT CA HB RN, BWmn QJ JSrs, JHtn JH RP PG HC, DE JW SWrd, OB.

....	Take The "A" Train
....	Black And Tan Fantasy—Creole Love Call—The Mooche
....	Newport Up >>>

....		Sophisticated Lady
....	MFC	Sonnet To Hank Cinq
....		What Else Can You Do With A Drum? –vOB
....		Do Nothin' Till You Hear From Me –vOB
....	MFC	Jeep's Blues
....		El Gato
....		Boo-Dah
....		Boo-Dah
....		Hi Fi Fo Fum
....		Medley[1]
....	MFC	Diminuendo In Blue and Crescendo In Blue (w. Wailing Interval)
....		Jones

[1]Including: Don't Get Around Much Anymore; Do Nothin' Till You Hear From Me; Don't You Know I Care?; In A Sentimental Mood; Mood Indigo; I'm Beginning To See The Light; Sophisticated Lady; Caravan; I Got It Bad; Just Squeeze Me –vRN; It Don't Mean A Thing –vRN; Satin Doll; I Let A Song Go Out Of My Heart/Don't Get Around Much Anymore.

DUKE ELLINGTON & HIS ORCHESTRA
Same personnel.

....	JI	Take The "A" Train
....	JI	Black And Tan Fantasy—Creole Love Call—The Mooche
....		Newport Up
....		My Funny Valentine
....	MFC	Perdido
....	MFC	Sophisticated Lady
....		Sonnet To Hank Cinq
....	JI	What Else Can You Do With A Drum? –vOB
....	JI	You Better Know It –vOB
....	JI	On The Sunny Side Of The Street
....	MFC	Things Ain't What They Used To Be
....	JI	El Gato
....	MJ	Boo-Dah
....	MJ	Boo-Dah
....		Hi Fi Fo Fum
....	MFC[1]	Medley[2]
....		Happy Birthday
....	BSt	Diminuendo In Blue and Crescendo In Blue (w. Wailing Interval)

[1]Incomplete on MFC and all subsequent releases.
[2]Including: Don't Get Around Much Anymore; Do Nothin' Till You Hear From Me; In A Sentimental Mood; Mood Indigo; I'm Beginning To See The Light; Sophisticated Lady; Caravan; I Got It Bad; Just Squeeze Me –vRN; It Don't Mean A Thing –vRN; Satin Doll; Solitude –vOB; I Let A Song Go Out Of My Heart/Don't Get Around Much Anymore.

DUKE ELLINGTON
DE appears on the news program "Actuelt Kvarter."

7 Nov 1958   (S)
K.B. Hallen[1] (tc)
Copenhagen, Denmark

....		Interview

[1]Backstage.

DUKE ELLINGTON & HIS ORCHESTRA
CT CA HB RN, BWmn QJ JSrs, JHtn JH RP PG HC, DE JW SWrd, OB.

K.B. Hallen   (P)

....	Take The "A" Train
....	Newport Up
....	My Funny Valentine
....	Perdido
....	Sophisticated Lady
....	Sonnet To Hank Cinq
....	What Else Can You Do With A Drum? –vOB
....	Rockin' In Rhythm
....	Prelude To A Kiss
....	Things Ain't What They Used To Be
....	El Gato
....	Hi Fi Fo Fum
....	Medley[1]
....	Diminuendo In Blue and Crescendo In Blue (w. Wailing Interval)

[1]Including: I'm Beginning To See The Light; Sophisticated Lady; Caravan; I Got It Bad; Just Squeeze Me –RN; It Don't Mean A Thing –vRN; Satin Doll; Solitude –vOB; I Let A Song Go Out Of My Heart/ Don't Get Around Much Anymore.

DUKE ELLINGTON & HIS ORCHESTRA
CT CA HB RN, BWmn QJ JSrs, JHtn JH RP PG HC, DE JW SWrd, OB.

8 Nov 1958   (P)
Deutschlandhalle
Berlin, Germany

....	Take The "A" Train
....	Black And Tan Fantasy—Creole Love Call—The Mooche
.... >>>	Newport Up

....		Tenderly
....		Perdido
....		Sophisticated Lady
....		Sonnet To Hank Cinq
....		Kinda Dukish/Rockin' In Rhythm
....		What Else Can You Do With A Drum? –vOB
....		You Better Know It –vOB
....		Jeep's Blues
....		All Of Me
....		El Gato
....		Hi Fi Fo Fum
....		Stompy Jones
....		Medley[1]

[1]Including: Don't Get Around Much Anymore; Do Nothin' Till You Hear From Me; In A Sentimental Mood; Mood Indigo; I'm Beginning To See The Light; Sophisticated Lady; Caravan; I Got It Bad; Just Squeeze Me –vRN; It Don't Mean A Thing –vRN; Satin Doll; Solitude –vOB; I Let A Song Go Out Of My Heart/Don't Get Around Much Anymore.

14 Nov 1958   (S)
Unidentified location (bc)
Munich, Germany

DUKE ELLINGTON
DE interviewed about the Shakespearean Suite by person unknown.

....		Interview

DUKE ELLINGTON & HIS ORCHESTRA   Kongreßsaal, Deutsches Museum (P)
CT CA HB RN, BWmn QJ JSrs, JHtn JH RP PG HC, DE JW SWrd, OB.

....	Stv	Take The "A" Train
....	Stv	Black And Tan Fantasy—Creole Love Call—The Mooche
....	Stv	Newport Up
....	Stv	Sophisticated Lady
....	Stv	Sonnet To Hank Cinq
....	Stv	What Else Can You Do With A Drum? –vOB
....	Stv	Do Nothin' Till You Hear From Me –vOB
....	Stv	Jeep's Blues
....	Stv	DE introduces BS
....	Stv	Take The "A" Train
....	Stv	Hi Fi Fo Fum
....	Stv	Medley[1]
....	Stv	Diminuendo In Blue and Wailing Interval

[1]Including: Don't Get Around Much Anymore; Do Nothin' Till You Hear From Me; In A Sentimental Mood; Mood Indigo; I'm Beginning To See The Light; Sophisticated Lady; Caravan; I Got It Bad; Just Squeeze Me –vRN; It Don't Mean A Thing –vRN; Satin Doll; Solitude –vOB; I Let A Song Go Out Of My Heart/Don't Get Around Much Anymore.

16 Nov 1958   (P)
Unidentified location
Basel, Switzerland

DUKE ELLINGTON & HIS ORCHESTRA
CT CA HB RN, BWmn QJ JSrs, JHtn JH RP PG HC, DE JW SWrd, OB.

....		Take The "A" Train
....		Black And Tan Fantasy—Creole Love Call—The Mooche
....		Newport Up
....		Tenderly
....		Perdido
....		Sophisticated Lady
....		Sonnet To Hank Cinq
....		Rockin' In Rhythm
....		What Else Can You Do With A Drum? –vOB
....		You Better Know It –vOB
....		Jeep's Blues
....		All Of Me
....		Things Ain't What They Used To Be
....		El Gato
....		Stompy Jones
....		Medley[1]
....		Diminuendo In Blue and Wailing Interval

[1]Including: Don't Get Around Much Anymore; Do Nothin' Till You Hear From Me; Don't You Know I Care?; In A Sentimental Mood; Mood Indigo; I'm Beginning To See The Light; Sophisticated Lady; Caravan; I Got It Bad; Just Squeeze Me –vRN; It Don't Mean A Thing –vRN; Satin Doll; Solitude –vOB; I Let A Song Go Out Of My Heart/Don't Get Around Much Anymore.

18 Nov 1958   (P)
Teatro Alfieri (tc?)[1]
Turin, Italy

DUKE ELLINGTON & HIS ORCHESTRA
CT CA HB RN, BWmn QJ JSrs, JHtn JH RP PG HC, DE JW SWrd, OB.

....		Take The "A" Train
....		Black And Tan Fantasy—Creole Love Call—The Mooche
....		Newport Up >>>

....		Tenderly
....		Perdido
....		Sonnet To Hank Cinq
....		What Else Can You Do With A Drum? –vOB >>>
....		Do Nothin' Till You Hear From Me –vOB
....		Jeep's Blues
....		All of Me
....		El Gato
....		Stompy Jones
....		Hi Fi Fo Fum
....		Medley[2]
....		Diminuendo In Blue and Crescendo In Blue (w. Wailing Interval)

[1]The concert has been taped for RAI, but was never telecast.
[2]Including: Don't Get Around Much Anymore; Do Nothin' Till You Hear From Me; Don't You Know I Care?; In A Sentimental Mood; Mood Indigo; I'm Beginning To See The Light; Sophisticated Lady; Caravan; I Got It Bad; Just Squeeze Me –vRN; It Don't Mean A Thing –vRN; Satin Doll; Solitude –vOB; I Let A Song Go Out Of My Heart/Don't Get Around Much Anymore.

DUKE ELLINGTON & HIS ORCHESTRA   20 Nov 1958   (P)
CT CA HB RN, BWmn QJ JSrs, JHtn JH RP PG HC, DE JW SWrd, OB.   Salle Pleyel (tc?)
                                                                        Paris, France

....	Mag	Take The "A" Train
....	Mag	Black And Tan Fantasy—Creole Love Call—The Mooche
....	Mag	Harlem Air Shaft
....	Mag	Tenderly
....		Honeysuckle Rose
....	Mag	Jeep's Blues
....	Mag	On The Sunny Side Of The Street
....	Mag	The "C" Jam Blues
....	Mag	Duke's Place –vOB
....	Mag	Kinda Dukish/Rockin' In Rhythm
....	Mag	Such Sweet Thunder
....	Mag	Caravan
....	Mag	Newport Up
....	Mag	Multicolored Blue –vOB
....	Mag	El Gato
....	Mag	Take The "A" Train –vRN
....	Mag	V.I.P.'s Boogie
....	Mag	Jam With Sam
....	Mag	Stompy Jones
....	Mag	Hi Fi Fo Fum
....	Mag	Medley[1]
....	GdJ	The Hawk Talks

[1]Including: Don't Get Around Much Anymore; Do Nothin' Till You Hear From Me; I'm Beginning To See The Light; Sophisticated Lady; Caravan; I Got It Bad; Just Squeeze Me –vRN; It Don't Mean A Thing –vRN; Satin Doll; Solitude –vOB; I Let A Song Go Out Of My Heart/Don't Get Around Much Anymore.

DUKE ELLINGTON   21 Dec 1958   (S)
DE interviewed by Norman Ross.   Studios WBKW (tc)
                                                                        Chicago, IL

....		Interview

DUKE ELLINGTON & HIS ORCHESTRA   Blue Note (bc)   (P)
CT CA HB RN, BWmn QJ JSrs, JHtn JH RP PG HC, DE JW SWrd, OB.

....		Newport Up
....		Sophisticated Lady
....		What Else Can You Do With A Drum? –vOB
....		Perdido
....		Satin Doll
....		Take The "A" Train
....		Things Ain't What They Used To Be

DUKE ELLINGTON & HIS ORCHESTRA   28 Dec 1958   (P)
CT CA HB RN, BWmn QJ JSrs, JHtn JH RP PG HC, DE JW SWrd, LG OB.   Blue Note (bc)
                                                                        Chicago, IL

....		Take The "A" Train
....		Duke's Place –vOB
....		Jam With Sam
....		Medley[1]

[1]Including: Don't Get Around Much Anymore; In A Sentimental Mood; Mood Indigo; I'm Beginning To See The Light; Sophisticated Lady; Caravan; I Got It Bad; Just Squeeze Me –vRN; It Don't Mean A Thing –vRN; Satin Doll; Solitude –vLG; I Let A Song Go Out Of My Heart.

DUKE ELLINGTON   Private residence   (P)
Piano solo.

....   Blues
....   Unidentified title
....   Do Not Disturb
....   I Got It Bad—New World A-Comin'
....   Piano Interlude
....   Unidentified title
....   Piano Interlude
....   Lonesome Lullaby

                                                                 31 Dec 1958   (P)
DUKE ELLINGTON & HIS ORCHESTRA   Blue Note (bc)
CT CA HB RN, BWmn QJ JSrs, JHtn JH RP PG HC, DE JW SWrd, LG OB. Chicago, IL

....   Take The "A" Train
....   El Gato
....   Multicolored Blue –vOB
....   Diminuendo In Blue and Crescendo In Blue (w. Wailing Interval)
....   St. Louis Blues –vLG
....   Walkin' And Singin' The Blues –vLG
....   Jump For Joy

                                                                 1 Jan 1959   (P)
DUKE ELLINGTON & HIS ORCHESTRA   Blue Note (bc)
CT CA HB RN, BWmn QJ JSrs, JHtn JH RP PG HC, DE JW SWrd, LG OB. Chicago, IL

....   Auld Lang Syne
....   Jam With Sam
....   Medley[1]
....   Take The "A" Train

[1]Including: Don't Get Around Much Anymore; Do Nothin' Till You Hear From Me –vOB; In A Sentimental Mood; Mood Indigo; I'm Beginning To See The Light; Sophisticated Lady; Caravan; I Got It Bad; Just Squeeze Me –vRN; It Don't Mean A Thing –vRN; Satin Doll; Solitude –vLG.

                                                                 4 Jan 1959   (P)
DUKE ELLINGTON & HIS ORCHESTRA   Blue Note (bc)
CT CA HB RN, BWmn QJ JSrs, JHtn JH RP PG HC, DE JW SWrd, OB.   Chicago, IL

....   Take The "A" Train
....   Multicolored Blue –vOB
....   El Gato
....   Medley[1]
....   Things Ain't What They Used To Be

[1]Including: Don't Get Around Much Anymore; Do Nothin' Till You Hear From Me –vOB; In A Sentimental Mood; Mood Indigo; I'm Beginning to See The Light; Sophisticated Lady; Caravan; I Got It Bad; Just Squeeze Me –vRN; It Don't Mean A Thing –vRN; Satin Doll.

                                                                 7 Jan 1959   (P)
DUKE ELLINGTON & HIS ORCHESTRA   CBS Studios (tc)
CT CA HB RN, BWmn QJ JSrs, JHtn JH RP PG HC, DE JW GJsn.   New York City, NY

.... SGL   Satin Doll
.... SGL   Take The "A" Train
.... SGL   Rockin' In Rhythm
.... SGL   Just Squeeze Me[1]

> RO added.

.... SGL   I Let A Song Go Out Of My Heart –vRO

> RO omitted.

.... SGL   Sophisticated Lady
.... SGL   Things Ain't What They Used To Be

> LA DG RE, VD, CHwk, MN MHtn JJ GK added.

.... SGL   Perdido

[1]Hardly audible as background music.

The above listing contains only the Ellington portion of the event.

                                                                 Jan 1959   (P)
DUKE ELLINGTON & HIS ORCHESTRA   Unidentified location
CT CA HB RN, BWmn QJ JSrs, JHtn JH RP PG HC, DE JW SWrd, LG Wrs. ?Philadelphia, PA

....   When I Trilly With My Filly –vWrs
....   Medley[1]
....   Caravan   >>>

....   El Gato
....   Jump For Joy –vWrs

[1]Including: Don't Get Around Much Anymore; Do Nothin' Till You Hear From Me; In A Sentimental Mood; Mood Indigo;
I'm Beginning To See The Light; Sophisticated Lady; Just Squeeze Me –vRN; It Don't Mean A Thing –vRN; Solitude;
Things Ain't What They Used To Be; I Got It Bad –vLG; Walkin' And Singin' The Blues –vLG.

                                                                                                    20 Jan-8 Feb 1959 (P)
DUKE ELLINGTON & HIS ORCHESTRA   Copa City Dinner Theater
CT CA HB RN, BWmn QJ JSrs, JHtn JH RP PG HC, DE JW SWrd.   Miami Beach, FL

                           JUMP FOR JOY
....   Overture
   > OD TR MBrs added.
....   Nerves, Nerves, Nerves –vOD TR MBrs
   > OD TR omitted, NM added.
....   The Natives Are Restless Tonight –vNM MBrs
   > Omit all, BMN HCro JRd TR JCrs added.
....   Resigned To Living –vBMN HCro JRd TR JCrs
   > Omit all vcl.
....   Concerto For Klinkers
   > BMN TR added.
....   The Brown-Skin Gal In The Calico Dress –vBMN TR[1]
   > BMN omitted.
....   Presenting Timmie Rogers
   > TR omitted, MBrs added.
....   So The Good Book Says –vMBrs
   > LG NM OD added.
....   Don't Believe Everything You Hear –vLG NM OD MBrs
   > LG OD MBrs omitted, HCro JCrs TR added.
....   Walk It Off –vNM HCro JCrs TR

   > Omit all, BMN JRd added.
....   But –vBMN JRd
   > NM & Her Jazz Men.
....   The Wailer
   > DE & His Orchestra, OD JCrs TR added
....   Strange Intruder –vOD JCrs TR
   > OD JCrs omitted, BMN chorus added.
....   Show 'Em You Got Class –vBMN TR Chorus
   > Chorus omitted.
....   Vignette –vBMN TR
   > TR omitted.
....   Three Shows Nightly –vBMN
   > BMN omitted, LG NM added.
....   I Got It Bad –vLG NM
   > Omit all, HCro JCrs TR added.
....   Made To Order –vHCro JCrs TR
   > BMN LG OD NM JRd MBrs added.
....   When I Trilly With My Filly –vBMN LG OD NM HCro JCrs TR JRd MBrs
   > JHtn RP HC, DE, CCwl BDsn.
....   Pretty And The Wolf –CCwl BDsn narration
   > Entire band, entire cast.
....   Jump For Joy –vEntire Cast   >>>

> Band only.

....   Medley[2]

[1]sa "The Brown-Skin Gal In The Calico Gown."
[2]Including: Don't Get Around Much Anymore; Do Nothin' Till You Hear From Me; In A Sentimental Mood; Mood Indigo;
I'm Beginning To See The Light; Sophisticated Lady; Just Squeeze Me –vRN; It Don't Mean A Thing –vRN; Solitude;
Things Ain't What They Used To Be.

*It appears that one entire show was recorded live for the Columbia label, but nothing has been released as yet. However,
there is a tape circulating among collectors, which contains some of the material listed above.*

			10 Feb 1959 (P)

ELLA FITZGERALD & DUKE ELLINGTON
Vcl, acc. by DE JHII WM GJsn.

NBC Brooklyn Studios (tc)
Brooklyn, NY

....		Satin Doll –vEF	
....		Don't Get Around Much Anymore –vEF	
....		Caravan—Mood Indigo	
....		I'm Just A Lucky So-And-So –vEF	

> GJsn omitted.

| .... | | Caravan | |

> GJsn added.

| .... | | Do Nothin' Till You Hear From Me –vEF | |

> Studio band added.

| .... | | I'm Beginning To See The Light –vEF | |

19 Feb 1959   (S)
30th Street Studio
New York City, NY

DUKE ELLINGTON & HIS ORCHESTRA
CT HB RN, BWmn QJ JSrs, JHtn JH RP PG HC, DE JW SWrd.

		TOOT SUITE	
.... Co	CO62192	1 Red Garter	
.... Co	CO62193	3 Red Carpet	
.... Co	CO62194	4 Ready, Go	

DUKE ELLINGTON & HIS ORCHESTRA
CA AF DG added, otherwise same personnel.

.... Co	CO62195	U.M.M.G.	

> DG omitted.

.... Co	CO62196	All Of Me	
		TOOT SUITE (ctd.)	
.... Co	CO62197	2 Red Shoes	
.... Co	CO62198	Satin Doll	
.... UTD	CO62199	Fillie Trillie[1]	

> DG, JRsh added, JJns replaces DE.

| .... Phi[2] | CO62118 | Hello, Little Girl –vJRsh | |

[1]sa "When I Trilly With My Filly."
[2]All Co releases have been edited in one way or another; only Phi is complete.

20 Feb 1959   (S)
Columbia Studios
New York City, NY

DUKE ELLINGTON'S ALL STARS
HE, JH, DE LS SJ JJ.

.... Vrv	22729-2	St. Louis Blues	
.... Vrv	22730-3	Royal Garden Blues	
.... Vrv	22731-4	Beale Street Blues	
.... Vrv	22732-5	Loveless Love	
.... Vrv	22733-4	Basin Street Blues	

25 Feb 1959   (S)
30th Street Studio
New York City, NY

DUKE ELLINGTON & HIS ORCHESTRA
CT CA HB RN, BWmn QJ JSrs, JHtn JH RP PG HC, DE JW SWrd, plus a group of nine
percussionists.

.... Co	CO62255	Tymperturbably Blue	
.... Co	CO62256[1]	Malletoba Spank[2] >>>	

> Additional percussionists omitted.

THE QUEEN'S SUITE[3]

....	Pab	CO62257	4 Northern Lights
....	Pab	CO62258	3 Le Sucrier Velours[4]
....	Pab	CO62259	2 Lightning Bugs And Frogs[5]

> RN, BWmn QJ JSrs, JH HC, DE JW SWrd.

....	Co	CO62260-3	Villes Ville Is The Place, Man

[1]Two 45rpm sides have been edited from this master and issued as "Spank 1" and "Spank 2," with their own respective master numbers CO62342 and CO62343.
[2]aka "Spank."
[3]See also sessions on 1 and 14 Apr 1959.
[4]sa "Do Not Disturb."
[5]Originally titled "Bugs."

26 Feb 1959   (S)
Columbia Studios
New York City, NY

DUKE ELLINGTON'S ALL STARS
HE, JH, DE LS AHll JJ.

....	Vrv	22734-1	Weary Blues
....	Vrv	22735-9	Squeeze Me
....	Vrv	22736-5	Wabash Blues
....	Vrv	22737-2	Stompy Jones
....	Vrv	22738-11	Goin' Up

Mar 1959   (P)
Unidentified location
U.S.A. or Canada

DUKE ELLINGTON WITH BAND
DE, LG with an unidentified band.

....	Walkin' And Singin' The Blues –vLG

9 Mar 1959[1]   (S)
ABC Studios (tc)
New York City, NY

PATTI PAGE & DUKE ELLINGTON WITH THE VIC SCHOEN ORCHESTRA
PPge and DE with the Vic Schoen Orchestra.

....	Sophisticated Lady

> DE added.

....	Caravan

> DE omitted, PPge added.

....	Mood Indigo –vPPge

> DE added.

....	Don't Get Around Much Anymore –vPPge >>>

> PPge omitted.

.... Rar	Monologue –DE narration

> DE omitted, PPge added.

....	I Got It Bad –vPPge

[1]Date of telecast; filmed at an earlier date.

Since it seems likely that DE was involved in supervising the musical content of this show, the titles for which he did not sit in at the piano have been listed as well.

10 Mar 1959   (S)
Unidentified location[1] (bc)
Hollywood, CA

DUKE ELLINGTON
DE interviewed by Frank Evans.

....	Interview

[1]DE paid a surprise visit to the DEJS in Hollywood, where this exclusive interview was taped; broadcast in Sep 1959.

14 Mar 1959   (P)
Storyville Club (bc)
Boston, MA

DUKE ELLINGTON & HIS ORCHESTRA
CT CA HB RN, BWmn QJ JSrs, JHtn JH RP PG HC, DE JW SWrd, LG OB.

....	Take The "A" Train
....	Caravan
....	Juniflip
....	Medley[1]
....	Things Ain't What They Used To Be

[1]Including: Don't Get Around Much Anymore; Do Nothin' Till You Hear From Me –vOB; I Got It Bad –vLG.

DUKE ELLINGTON & HIS ORCHESTRA
CT CA HB AF RN, BWmn QJ JSrs, JHtn JH RP PG HC, DE JW JJsn, LG.

....		You Don't Love Me No More –vLG
....		Go Away Blues –vLG
....		I Love My Lovin' Lover –vLG
....		My Man Sends Me –vLG[1]

> BS replaces DE.

....		I Wonder Why –vLG

> DE replaces BS.

....		Hello, Little Boy –vLG
....		I Got It Bad –vLG
....		Walkin' And Singin' The Blues –vLG
....	alt.	Walkin' And Singin' The Blues –vLG
....		The Ghost Of Love –vLG
....		My Little Brown Book –vLG

> HB, DE JW JJsn, LG.

....		Solitude –vLG

[1]sa "The Greatest There Is."

DUKE ELLINGTON & HIS ORCHESTRA
CT CA HB RN, BWmn QJ JSrs, JHtn JH RP PG HC, DE JW JJsn.

.... SES		Spoken introduction by DE[1]
.... SES		Fat Mouth

> BS replaces DE.

.... SES		Frou Frou

> DE replaces BS.

.... SES		Lost In The Night
.... SES		Little John's Tune[2]
.... SES		Dankworth Castle[2]
.... SES		Moonstone[2,3]
.... SES		Lullaby For Dreamers
.... SES		Night Stick
.... SES		She Was A Tinkling Thing
.... SES		Jamaica Tomboy[2]
.... SES		Still Water
.... SES		Jet Strip

[1]The spoken introduction has been recorded at another date.
[2]The arrangements for these titles are by JHtn.
[3]sa "W.C."

DUKE ELLINGTON & HIS ORCHESTRA
CT HB RN, BWmn QJ JSrs, JHtn JH RP PG HC, DE JW JJsn.

			THE QUEEN'S SUITE (ctd.)[1]
....	Pab	CO63072	1 Sunset And The Mocking Bird
....	Pab	CO63073	6 Apes And Peacocks

[1]See also sessions on 25 Feb and 14 Apr 1959.

DUKE ELLINGTON & JIMMY WOODE
DE JW.

			THE QUEEN'S SUITE (ctd.)[1]
....	Pab	CO63249	5 A Single Petal Of A Rose

[1]See also sessions on 25 Feb and 1 Apr 1959.

		THE QUEEN'S SUITE (summation)
Pab	CO63072	1 Sunset And The Mocking Bird
Pab	CO62259	2 Lightning Bugs And Frogs
Pab	CO62258	3 Le Sucrier Velours
Pab	CO62257	4 Northern Lights
Pab	CO63249	5 A Single Petal Of A Rose
Pab	CO63073	6 Apes And Peacocks

DUKE ELLINGTON & HIS ORCHESTRA
CT CA HB RN, BWmn QJ JSrs, JHtn JH RP PG HC, DE BS JW JJsn.

....	Co		Polly
....	Co		Merrily Rolling Along[2]
....	Co		Sunswept Sunday (rehearsal)
....	Co		Sunswept Sunday (rehearsal)
....	Co		Sunswept Sunday (rehearsal)
....	Co		Beer Garden (incomplete)

[1]Music for the motion picture "Anatomy Of A Murder."
[2]This title is a derivative of *Polly*.

This is a rehearsal session; no master numbers were given, and none of the above was used in the film.

DUKE ELLINGTON & HIS ORCHESTRA
CT CA HB GW RN, BWmn QJ JSrs, JHtn JH RP PG HC, DE BS JW JJsn.

....	Co	RHCO46258-13	Happy Anatomy
....	Co	RHCO46261-5	Flirtibird
....		RHCO46262	Flirtibird Down
....	Co	RHCO46263-2	Almost Cried[2]
....	Co	RHCO46267-9	Anatomy Of A Murder

[1]Music for the motion picture "Anatomy Of A Murder."
[2]*aka* "Almost Cry."

All of the above and the material recorded in the following sessions has been mixed and edited for the film soundtrack. Master numbers 46259, 46260, 46264 and 46266 cannot be accounted for.

DUKE ELLINGTON & HIS ORCHESTRA
CT CA HJs GW RN, BWmn QJ JSrs, JHtn JH RP PG HC, DE BS JW JJsn.

....	Co	RHCO46267-14[2]	Anatomy Of A Murder
....	Co	RHCO46265-6	Polly
....	Co	RHCO46265-8	Haupê[3] (Polly, pt. 1)

> RN violin solo.

| .... | Co | RHCO46265-8 | Low Key Lightly[3] (Polly, pt. 2) |

> Entire band.

| .... | | RHCO46268 | Polly |

[1]Music for the motion picture "Anatomy Of A Murder."
[2]Remake.
[3]These titles are derivatives of *Polly*.

DUKE ELLINGTON & HIS ORCHESTRA
CT CA HB/HJs GW RN, BWmn QJ JSrs, JHtn JH RP PG HC, DE JW JJsn.

....	Co	-7	Anatomy Of A Murder –DE talking[2]
....	Co	-17	Flirtibird
....	Co	-20	Flirtibird
....	Co	-34	Almost Cried

> RN, QJ, RP, DE JW JJsn.

| .... | Co | -37 | Happy Anatomy |

> Entire band.

....	Co	-40	Hero To Zero[3, 4]
....	Co	-46	Hero To Zero[4]
....	Co	-50	Way Early Subtone
....	Co	-54	Sunswept Sunday
....	Co	-61	Main Title
....	Co	-68	Upper And Outest[5]
....	Co	-77	Anatomy Of A Murder (incl. finale)

> DE piano solo.

| .... | Co | -79 | Low Key Lightly[6] |

> Entire band.

....	Co	-82	Happy Anatomy
....	Co	-84	Grace Valse[3]
....	Co	-87	Midnight Indigo[3] >>>

> P.I. Five (RN, JHtn, DE JW JJsn.)

....	Co	-97	Happy Anatomy (incomplete)
....	Co		Happy Anatomy
....	Co	-103	More Blues (incomplete)

[1]Music for the motion picture "Anatomy Of A Murder."
[2]After the main theme, intermittent talk by DE and snippets of music from the score. The interview part has been issued on a CP promotional record earlier.
[3]These titles are derivatives of *Polly.*
[4]Both titles have been edited together on Co.
[5]*aka* "That's Love."
[6]This piano part was edited to "Low Key Lightly," master #RHCO46265-8.

Jun 1959   (S/T)[1]
DUKE ELLINGTON & HIS ORCHESTRA   Radio Recorders Annex
CT CA HB/HJs GW RN, BWmn JSrs, JHtn JH RP PG HC, DE JW SWrd JJsn.   Hollywood, CA

....	LL	Glory[2]

[1]Music for the motion picture "Anatomy Of A Murder."
[2]*sa* "Anatomy Of A Murder." This title was not used in the film.

21 Jun 1959   (P)
DUKE ELLINGTON & HIS ORCHESTRA   Oakdale Musical Theater
CT CA HB RN, BWmn QJ JSrs, JHtn JH RP PG HC, DE JW JJsn, LG OB.   Wallingford, CT

> JRsh added.

....	On The Sunny Side Of The Street –vJRsh
....	Goin' To Chicago –vJRsh
....	Hello, Little Girl –vJRsh
....	Sent For You Yesterday –vJRsh

> JRsh omitted.

....	Skin Deep
....	Medley[1]
....	I Got It Bad –vLG
....	Walkin' And Singin' The Blues –vLG
....	Diminuendo In Blue and Crescendo In Blue (w. Wailing Interval)

[1]Including: Don't Get Around Much Anymore; Do Nothin' Till You Hear From Me –vOB; In A Sentimental Mood; Mood Indigo; I'm Beginning To See The Light; Sophisticated Lady; Caravan; Just Squeeze Me –vRN; It Don't Mean A Thing –vRN; Solitude; Things Ain't What They Used To Be.

27 Jun 1959   (P)
DUKE ELLINGTON & HIS ORCHESTRA   Playhouse
CT CA HB RN, BWmn QJ JSrs, JHtn JH RP PG HC, DE JW JJsn, LG OB.   Tamiment-In-The-Poconos, PA

....		Take The "A" Train
....		Black And Tan Fantasy—Creole Love Call—The Mooche
....		Perdido
....		Sophisticated Lady
....		Sonnet To Hank Cinq
....		What Else Can You Do With A Drum? –vOB
....		Autumn Leaves –vOB
....		Hand-Me-Down Love –vOB
....		Tenderly
....		V.I.P.'s Boogie
....	SR	Haupê
....	SR	Flirtibird
....		All Of Me
....		Take The "A" Train –vRN
....		Take The "A" Train
....		Skin Deep
....		Medley[1]
....		I Got It Bad –vLG
....		Walkin' And Singin' The Blues –vLG
....		Diminuendo In Blue and Wailing Interval
....		Jones

[1]Including: Don't Get Around Much Anymore; Do Nothin' Till You Hear From Me –vOB; In A Sentimental Mood; Mood Indigo; I'm Beginning To See The Light; Sophisticated Lady; Caravan; Satin Doll; Just Squeeze Me –vRN; It Don't Mean A Thing –vRN; Solitude; Things Ain't What They Used To Be.

28 Jun 1959   (P)
DUKE ELLINGTON WITH THE RAY BLOCH ORCHESTRA   CBS Studios (tc)
DE with the Ray Bloch Orchestra and chorus.   New York City, NY

....	Main Title (from "Anatomy Of A Murder") >>>

```
        > DE b dr.
..............               Happy Anatomy
        > RBO added.
..............               Flirtibird –vChorus
..............               Hero To Zero
..............               Almost Cried
```

DUKE ELLINGTON & HIS ORCHESTRA   4 Jul 1959   (P)
CT CA HB RN, BWmn QJ JSrs, JHtn JH RP PG HC, DE JW SWrd JJsn, LG OB.   Freebody Park
                                                                  Newport, RI

```
.............. Fox             Take The "A" Train

                               IDIOM '59
.............. Em              - Part I (Vapor)
.............. Em              - Part II
.............. Em              - Part III (Jet Strip)

.............. Fox             Anatomy Of A Murder
.............. Fox             Rockin' In Rhythm
.............. Fox             Flirtibird
.............. Fox             Perdido
..............                 Hand-Me-Down Love –vOB
.............. Fox             Cop Out Extension
.............. Fox             Almost Cried
.............. Fox             V.I.P.'s Boogie
.............. Fox             Jam With Sam
.............. Fox             I Got It Bad –vLG
.............. Fox             Walkin' And Singin' The Blues –vLG
.............. Fox             Walkin' And Singin' The Blues –vLG
.............. Fox             St. Louis Blues –vLG
.............. Fox             Bill Bailey –vLG
..............                 Walkin' And Singin' The Blues –vLG

        > CT RN, QJ, RP, DE JW JJsn.

.............. Fox             Basin Street Blues –vRN

        > Entire band.

.............. Fox             Skin Deep
.............. Fox             Launching Pad[1]

        > JRsh added.

.............. Fox             Jimmy's Blues –vJRsh
.............. Fox             Sent For You Yesterday –vJRsh
.............. Fox             Hello, Little Girl –vJRsh
.............. Fox             I Love To Hear My Baby Call My Name –vJRsh
.............. Fox             I Love To Hear My Baby Call My Name –vJRsh
.............. Fox             I Love To Hear My Baby Call My Name –vJRsh
.............. Fox             I Love To Hear My Baby Call My Name[2]

        > JRsh omitted.

.............. Fox             Things Ain't What They Used To Be
.............. Fox             Jones
.............. Fox             Jones
.............. Fox             Take The "A" Train
```

[1]sa "Blues In The Round."
[2]Incomplete on Fox.

DUKE ELLINGTON & HIS ORCHESTRA   8 Aug 1959   (P)
CT CA HB RN, BWmn QJ JSrs, JHtn JH RP PG HC, DE JW SWrd JJsn, LG OB.   Chicago Stadium
                                                                  Chicago, IL

```
.............. AFR             Take The "A" Train
.............. AFR             V.I.P.'s Boogie
.............. AFR             Jam With Sam
.............. AFR             Launching Pad
.............. AFR             Newport Up
.............. AFR             Walkin' And Singin' The Blues –vLG
.............. AFR             Take The "A" Train

                               DUAEL FUEL[1]
.............. AFR             - Part 1
.............. AFR             - Part 2
.............. AFR             - Part 3

.............. AFR             Diminuendo In Blue and Crescendo In Blue (w. Wailing Interval)   >>>
```

....	AFR	Satin Doll
....	AFR	Take The "A" Train

> JRsh added.

....	AFR	Goin' To Chicago –vJRsh
....	AFR	Hello, Little Girl –vJRsh
....	AFR	Sent For You Yesterday –vJRsh
....	AFR	Sent For You Yesterday –vJRsh

> JRsh omitted.

....	AFR	Things Ain't What They Used To Be
....	AFR	El Gato
....	AFR	Hand-Me-Down Love –vOB

[1]*aka* "Dual Filter."

DUKE ELLINGTON & HIS ORCHESTRA
CT CA HB RN, BWmn QJ JSrs, JHtn JH RP PG HC, DE SWrd JJsn.

9 Aug 1959   (P)
Blue Note
Chicago, IL

....	Rlt	The "C" Jam Blues
....	Rlt	Tenderly
....	Rlt	Honeysuckle Rose

> DE BS JJsn.

....	Rlt	Drawing Room Blues—A Hundred Dreams Ago
....	Rlt	Tonk

> Entire band, BS omitted.

....	Vge	All Of Me
....	Vge	Jeep's Blues

> JPte added.

....	Vge	In A Mellotone
....	Vge	Things Ain't What They Used To Be
....	Rlt	Perdido

DUKE ELLINGTON & HIS ORCHESTRA
BS replaces DE, otherwise same personnel.

....	Rlt	Take The "A" Train

> DE replaces BS.

....	Rlt	Newport Up
....	Koa	Polly
....	Koa	Flirtibird
....	Rlt	Pie Eye's Blues[1]
....	Rlt	Almost Cried
		DUAEL FUEL
....	Rlt	- Part 1
....	Rlt	- Part 2
....	Rlt	- Part 3
....	Vge	Sophisticated Lady
....	Vge	Mr. Gentle And Mr. Cool
....	Rlt	El Gato

[1]This title is a derivative of *Flirtibird.*

DUKE ELLINGTON & HIS ORCHESTRA
Same personnel.

....	Rlt	Mood Indigo
....	Rlt	Perdido
....	Rlt	Satin Doll
....	Rlt	"A Disarming Visit" –DE introduces JChr and SK
....	Rlt	Newport Up
....	Rlt	Black And Tan Fantasy—Creole Love Call—The Mooche

> BS added.

....	Vge	Passion Flower

> BS omitted.

....	Vge	On The Sunny Side Of The Street
....	Rlt	El Gato

For contractual reasons the above sets were recorded under the name of Billy Strayhorn. Vogue issued its record as by Johnny Hodges with the Duke Ellington Orchestra.

8 Sep 1959   (S)
30th Street Studio
New York City, NY

DUKE ELLINGTON & HIS ORCHESTRA
CT WC CA HB AF RN, BWmn JSrs, JHtn JH RP PG HC, DE QJ SWrd JJsn.

			DUAEL FUEL
....	Co	CO63502	- Part 1
....	Co	CO63503	- Part 2
....	Co	CO63504	- Part 3[1]

> QJ switches back to tb, JBjm added.

			IDIOM '59
....	Co	CO63505	- Part I (Vapor)

> JW replaces JBjm.

....	Co	CO63506	- Part II
....	Co	CO63507	- Part III (Jet Strip)
....	Co	CO63508	Launching Pad
....	Co	CO63509	Cop Out Extension
....	Co	CO63510	Things Ain't What They Used To Be
....	Co	CO63511	V.I.P.'s Boogie—Jam With Sam
....	Co	CO63512	Perdido[2]

[1]Complete only on CBS/Co CD CK 87044.
[2]Complete only on CBS/Co CD C3K 65841.

20 Sep 1959   (P)
Salle Pleyel
Paris, France

DUKE ELLINGTON & HIS ORCHESTRA
CT CA AF RN, BWmn QJ BWd, JHtn JH RP PG HC, DE JW JJsn, LG.

....	BYG	Black And Tan Fantasy—Creole Love Call—The Mooche
....	BYG	Newport Up
....	BYG	Such Sweet Thunder
....		Kinda Dukish/Rockin' In Rhythm
....		El Gato
....		Jeep's Blues
....	BYG	All Of Me
....	BYG	Skin Deep
....	STJ	Things Ain't What They Used To Be
....	STJ	Juniflip
....	STJ	The "C" Jam Blues
....	STJ	V.I.P.'s Boogie
....	BYG	Medley[1]
....	BYG	Diminuendo In Blue and Crescendo In Blue (w. Wailing Interval)

[1]Including: Don't Get Around Much Anymore; Do Nothin' Till You Hear From Me; In A Sentimental Mood; Mood Indigo; I'm Beginning To See The Light; Sophisticated Lady; Caravan; Satin Doll; Just Squeeze Me –vRN; It Don't Mean A Thing –vRN; Solitude –vLG; I Let A Song Go Out Of My Heart/Don't Get Around Much Anymore.

DUKE ELLINGTON & HIS ORCHESTRA
Same personnel

....		Black And Tan Fantasy—Creole Love Call—The Mooche
....	STJ	Newport Up
....		Such Sweet Thunder
....	BYG	Kinda Dukish/Rockin' In Rhythm
....	BYG	El Gato
....		Jeep's Blues
....		Things Ain't What They Used To Be
....		All Of Me
....		Skin Deep
....		Take The "A" Train
....	BYG	Bill Bailey –vLG
....	BYG	Walkin' And Singin' The Blues –vLG
....	STJ	I Got It Bad –vLG
....	BYG	V.I.P.'s Boogie
....	BYG	Jam With Sam
....	STJ	Medley[1]
....	STJ	Diminuendo In Blue and Crescendo In Blue (w. Wailing Interval)

[1]Including: I'm Beginning To See The Light; Sophisticated Lady; Caravan; Solitude –vLG; Satin Doll; Just Squeeze Me –vRN; It Don't Mean A Thing –vRN; I Let A Song Go Out Of My Heart/Don't Get Around Much Anymore.

26 Sep 1959   (P)
Konserthuset
Stockholm, Sweden

DUKE ELLINGTON & HIS ORCHESTRA
CT CA AF RN, BWmn QJ BWd, JHtn JH RP PG HC, DE JW JJsn, LG.

....	Az	Take The "A" Train
....	Az	Black And Tan Fantasy—Creole Love Call—The Mooche >>>

....	Az	Deep Purple
....		El Gato
....	Az	Jeep's Blues
....	Az	All Of Me
....	Az	V.I.P.'s Boogie
....	Az	Jam With Sam
....		Medley[1]
....	Az	Diminuendo In Blue and Crescendo In Blue (w. Wailing Interval)

[1]Including: Don't Get Around Much Anymore; Do Nothin' Till You Hear From Me; In A Sentimental Mood; Mood Indigo; I'm Beginning To See The Light; Sophisticated Lady; Caravan; Solitude –vLG; Satin Doll; Just Squeeze Me –vRN; It Don't Mean A Thing –vRN; I Let A Song Go Out Of My Heart/Don't Get Around Much Anymore.

<u>DUKE ELLINGTON & HIS ORCHESTRA</u>
Same personnel.

....		Black And Tan Fantasy—Creole Love Call—The Mooche
....	MFC	Such Sweet Thunder
....	MFC	Kinda Dukish/Rockin' In Rhythm
....		El Gato
....	MFC	Passion Flower
....		Things Ain't What They Used To Be
....		All Of Me
....		Happy Anatomy
....	MFC/Az[1]	Medley[2]

[1]Only "Satin Doll" on MFC; "Just Squeeze Me" and "It Don't Mean A Thing" on Az.
[2]Including: Don't Get Around Much Anymore; Do Nothin' Till You Hear From Me; In A Sentimental Mood; Mood Indigo; I'm Beginning To See The Light; Sophisticated Lady; Caravan; Solitude –vLG; Satin Doll; Just Squeeze Me –vRN; It Don't Mean A Thing –vRN; I Let A Song Go Out Of My Heart/Don't Get Around Much Anymore.

	4 Oct 1959 (P)
<u>DUKE ELLINGTON & HIS ORCHESTRA</u>	Sportpalast
CT CA AF RN, BWmn QJ BWd, JHtn JH RP PG HC. DE JW JJsn, LG.	Berlin, Germany

....		Take The "A" Train
....	SwH	Black And Tan Fantasy—Creole Love Call—The Mooche
....	DBD	Newport Up
....	SwH	Such Sweet Thunder
....	SwH	Sonnet To Hank Cinq
....		Happy Anatomy
....	SwH	Kinda Dukish/Rockin' In Rhythm
....	SwH	El Gato
....	SwH	Flirtibird
....	SwH	Things Ain't What They Used To Be
....		All Of Me
....	SwH	V.I.P.'s Boogie
....	SwH	Jam With Sam
....	SwH	St. Louis Blues –vLG
....	SwH	Bill Bailey –vLG
....	SwH	Walkin' And Singin' The Blues –vLG
....	SwH/DBD[1]	Medley[2]

> PG, DE JW JJsn.

....		Happy Reunion

> CT RN, QJ, RP, DE JW JJsn.

....	SwH	Basin Street Blues –vRN

> Entire band.

....	SwH	Skin Deep

[1]Incomplete on SwH and all subsequent releases. DBD includes only the last two titles.
[2]Including: Don't Get Around Much Anymore; Do Nothin' Till You Hear From Me; I Got It Bad; In A Sentimental Mood; Mood Indigo; I'm Beginning To See The Light; Sophisticated Lady; Caravan; Solitude –vLG; Satin Doll; Just Squeeze Me –vRN; It Don't Mean A Thing –vRN; I Let A Song Go Out Of My Heart/Don't Get Around Much Anymore.

	9 Oct 1959 (P)
<u>DUKE ELLINGTON & HIS ORCHESTRA</u>	Kongresshaus (tc)[1]
CT CA AF RN, BWmn QJ BWd, JHtn JH RP PG HC, DE JW JJsn, LG.	Zurich, Switzerland

....		Take The "A" Train
....		Black And Tan Fantasy—Creole Love Call—The Mooche
....		Newport Up
....		Such Sweet Thunder
....		Sonnet To Hank Cinq
....		Kinda Dukish/Rockin' In Rhythm
....		El Gato >>>

....		Passion Flower
....		Things Ain't What They Used To Be
....		All Of Me
....		V.I.P.'s Boogie
....		Jam With Sam
....	Vid[2]	Medley[3]

> PG, DE JW JJsn.

| .... | | Happy Reunion |

> Entire band.

| .... | Vid | Diminuendo In Blue and Wailing Interval |

> CT RN, QJ, RP, DE JW JJsn.

| .... | Vid | Basin Street Blues –vRN |

[1]The event has been recorded for Swiss tv (German and Italian); the date(s) of the telecast(s) are not known.
[2]The video contains only the last three titles of the medley.
[3]Including: Sophisticated Lady; Just Squeeze Me –vRN; It Don't Mean A Thing –vRN; Solitude –vLG; Satin Doll; I Let A Song Go Out Of My Heart/Don't Get Around Much Anymore.

			11 Oct 1959	(P)

DUKE ELLINGTON & HIS ORCHESTRA   Kongreßsaal, Deutsches Museum
CT CA AF RN, BWmn QJ BWd, JHtn JH RP PG HC, DE JW JJsn, LG.   Munich, Germany

....		Black And Tan Fantasy—Creole Love Call—The Mooche
....		Such Sweet Thunder
....		Kinda Dukish/Rockin' In Rhythm
....		Passion Flower
....		Things Ain't What They Used To Be
....		Take The "A" Train
....		Walkin' And Singin' The Blues –vLG
....		Medley[1]
....		Diminuendo In Blue and Wailing Interval

[1]Including: Don't Get Around Much Anymore; Do Nothin' Till You Hear From Me; In A Sentimental Mood; Mood Indigo; I'm Beginning To See The Light; Sophisticated Lady; Caravan; Solitude –vLG; Satin Doll; Just Squeeze Me –vRN; I Let A Song Go Out Of My Heart/Don't Get Around Much Anymore.

			13 Nov 1959[1]	(P)

DUKE ELLINGTON & HIS ORCHESTRA   NBC Studios (tc)
DE at the taping session for the Grammy Awards presentation ceremony.   New York City, NY

| .... | | DE accepting the Grammy Award |

> WC AF EMls RN, BWmn MG BWd. JHtn JH RP PG HC, DE JW JJsn.

| .... | | Anatomy Of A Murder |

[1]Telecast on 27 Nov 1959.

			2 Dec 1959	(S)

DUKE ELLINGTON & HIS AWARD WINNERS   30th Street Studio
RN, BWmn MG BWd, JHtn JH RP PG HC, DE JW JJsn.   New York City, NY

| .... | Co | CO64441-6 | Three J's Blues |

> RN, JHtn RP PG omitted.

| .... | Co | CO64442-2 | Brown Penny |

> Entire band.

....	Co	CO64443-2	Pie Eye's Blues
....	Co	CO64443-4	Pie Eye's Blues
....	Co[1]	CO64444-3	The "C" Jam Blues
....	UTD	CO64445-2	Sentimental Lady
....	Co	CO64446-2	Sweet And Pungent
....	Co	CO64446-3	Sweet And Pungent

[1]Some of the releases have been edited.

			3 Dec 1959	(S)

DUKE ELLINGTON & HIS AWARD WINNERS   30th Street Studio
RN, BWmn MG BWd, JHtn JH RP PG HC, DE BS JW JJsn/SWrd.   New York City, NY

| .... | Co | CO64447-7 | Smada |

> DE omitted.

| .... | Co | CO64448-8 | Blues In Blueprint[1]   >>> |

> DE replaces BS.

	Co	CO64449-4	In A Mellow Tone[2]
....	Co	CO64449-4	In A Mellow Tone[2]
....	Co	CO64450-3	The Swingers Get The Blues, Too[3]
....	Co	CO64551-6	The Swingers Jump[4]
....	Co	CO46551-7	The Swingers Jump

[1]*aka* "T.A.B. Blues."
[2]*sa* "In A Mellotone"; "Baby, You And Me."
[3]*aka* "Those Ever Lovin', Gutbucket, Swingin' Blues"; "Those Swinging Blues."
[4]*aka* "Last Minute Blues."

DUKE ELLINGTON WITH JACK KANE & HIS MUSIC MAKERS   7 Dec 1959   (P)
DE with Jack Kane & His Music Makers.   CBC Studios (tc)
                                                                                   Toronto, ON

....   Take The "A" Train

> DE JW.

....   A Single Petal Of A Rose

> JKMM added.

....   Cotton Tail

> HC added.

....   Sophisticated Lady

> HC omitted.

....   The "C" Jam Blues

> JH added.

....   I Got It Bad

> JH omitted, RN added.

....   It Don't Mean A Thing –vRN

> RN omitted.

....   Take The "A" Train

DUKE ELLINGTON & HIS ORCHESTRA   31 Dec 1959   (P)
WC AF EMls RN, BWmn MG BWd, JHtn JH RP PG HC, DE JW JJsn, OB.   Blue Note (bc)
                                                                   Chicago, IL

....   Take The "A" Train
....   Medley[1]
....   Auld Lang Syne

[1]Including: Don't Get Around Much Anymore; Do Nothin' Till You Hear From Me –vOB; Mood Indigo; I'm Beginning To See The Light; Sophisticated Lady; Caravan; I Got It Bad; Just Squeeze Me –vRN; It Don't Mean A Thing –vRN; Satin Doll.

DUKE ELLINGTON & HIS ORCHESTRA   1 Jan 1960   (P)
WC AF EMls RN, BWmn MG BWd, JHtn JH RP PG HC, DE JW JJsn, LG.   Blue Note (bc)
                                                                   Chicago, IL

....   Take The "A" Train
....   V.I.P.'s Boogie
....   Jam With Sam
....   Walkin' And Singin' The Blues –vLG
....   Things Ain't What They Used To Be
....   Satin Doll

DUKE ELLINGTON   Early 1960[1]   (S)
DE with previously recorded music.   Unidentified studio (bc)
                                                                   New York City, NY

....   Bond promotion –DE talking
....   Bond promotion –DE talking

[1]Date of broadcast.

DUKE ELLINGTON   21 Feb 1960   (S)
DE interviewed by students of the William and Mary College.   William and Mary College (bc)
                                                                   Williamsburg, VA

....   Interview

22 Feb 1960   (P)
Shriver Hall, Johns Hopkins University
Baltimore, MD

DUKE ELLINGTON & HIS ORCHESTRA
WC AF EMls RN, BWmn MG BWd, JHtn JH RP PG HC, DE JW JJsn, LG OB.

....	Take The "A" Train
....	Black And Tan Fantasy—Creole Love Call—The Mooche
....	Newport Up
....	Tenderly
....	Anatomy Of A Murder
....	Happy Anatomy
....	Flirtibird
....	Pie Eye's Blues
....	Such Sweet Thunder
....	Sonnet To Hank Cinq
....	Medley[1]
....	Jones
....	Take The "A" Train
....	V.I.P.'s Boogie
....	Jam With Sam
....	Caravan
....	Jeep's Blues
....	All Of Me
....	Things Ain't What They Used To Be
	DUAEL FUEL
....	- Part 1
....	- Part 2
....	- Part 3
....	St. Louis Blues –vLG
....	Bill Bailey –vLG
....	Hello, Little Boy –vLG
....	Diminuendo In Blue and Wailing Interval
....	Take The "A" Train

[1]Including: Do Nothin' Till You Hear From Me; In A Sentimental Mood; Don't Get Around Much Anymore; Mood Indigo; I'm Beginning To See The Light; Sophisticated Lady; Caravan; I Got it Bad –vLG; Satin Doll; Just Squeeze Me –vRN; It Don't Mean A Thing –vRN.

26 Feb 1960   (P)
Webster Hall, Dartmouth College
Hanover, NH

DUKE ELLINGTON & HIS ORCHESTRA
WC AF EMls RN, BWmn MG BWd, JHtn JH RP PG HC, DE JW JJsn, LG.

....	Black And Tan Fantasy—Creole Love Call—The Mooche
....	Newport Up
....	Tenderly
....	Such Sweet Thunder
....	Sonnet To Hank Cinq
....	Anatomy Of A Murder
....	Happy Anatomy
....	Flirtibird
....	Pie Eye's Blues
....	Prelude To A Kiss
....	All Of Me
....	Things Ain't What They Used To Be
	DUAEL FUEL
....	- Part 1
....	- Part 2
....	- Part 3
....	Jones
....	Take The "A" Train
....	V.I.P.'s Boogie
....	Jam With Sam
....	Caravan –vAF
....	St. Louis Blues –vLG
....	Bill Bailey –vLG
....	Walkin' And Singin' The Blues –vLG
....	Hello, Little Boy –vLG
....	Medley[1]
....	Diminuendo In Blue and Wailing Interval
....	Take The "A" Train

[1]Including: Do Nothin' Till You Hear From Me; In A Sentimental Mood; Don't Get Around Much Anymore; Mood Indigo; I'm Beginning To See The Light; Sophisticated Lady; Caravan; I Got It Bad –vLG; Satin Doll; Just Squeeze Me –vRN; It Don't Mean A Thing –vRN; I Let A Song Go Out Of My Heart/Don't Get Around Much Anymore.

25 Apr 1960   (T)[1]
M-G-M Studios
Culver City, CA

DUKE ELLINGTON & HIS ORCHESTRA
WC AF EMls RN, BWmn BWd JT, JHtn JH RP PG HC, DE BS AB FD.

....		Blues For Asphalt Jungle
....		Dreamy Sort Of Thing[2]
....		Wild Car
....		Cops
....		Robbers

[1]Music for "The Lady And The Lawyer," an episode of the TV series *Asphalt Jungle,* which was aired on 9 Apr 1961. The full score is undoubtedly the result of extensive editing. It could not be ascertained to what degree additional original music by DE other than listed above, has been used.
[2]*aka* "Pretty Girl—Angello Theme."

26 May 1960   (S)
Radio Recorders Annex
Hollywood, CA

DUKE ELLINGTON & HIS ORCHESTRA
WC AF EMls RN, LB BWmn BWd JT, JHtn JH RP PG HC, DE AB SWrd.

....			THE NUTCRACKER SUITE[1]
....		RHCO46653	1 Overture
....	Co	RHCO46653-5	1 Overture
....	Co	RHCO46654-6	5 Entr'acte
....		RHCO46655-8	9 Arabesque Cookie[2] (Arabian Dance)
....			9 Arabesque Cookie (insert)
....		RHCO46656-4	2 Toot Toot Tootie Toot (Dance of the Reed Pipes)

[1]See also sessions on 31 May, and 3, 21 and 22 Jun 1960.
[2]*aka* "Naibara" (=Arabian).

27 May 1960   (P)
Civic Auditorium
Santa Monica, CA

DUKE ELLINGTON & HIS ORCHESTRA
WC AF EMls RN, LB BWmn BWd JT, JHtn JH RP PG HC, DE AB SWrd, LG MGsn.

....	SR	Take The "A" Train—Perdido
....	QuD	Red Carpet
....	QuD	Newport Up
....	QuD	Sophisticated Lady
....	QuD	Matumbe
....	QuD	What Else Can You Do With A Drum –vMGsn
....	QuD	Day In, Day Out –vMGsn
....	QuD	Lost In Loveliness –vMGsn
....	QuD	One More Once –vMGsn[1]
....	QuD	One More Once –vMGsn
....	QuD	Passion Flower
....	QuD	Things Ain't What They Used To Be
....	QuD	All Of Me
....	QuD	I Got It Bad –vLG
....	QuD	Bill Bailey –vLG
....	QuD	Take The "A" Train –vRN
....	QuD	Mood Indigo
....	QuD	Diminuendo In Blue and Crescendo In Blue (w. Wailing Interval)
....	QuD	Jones

[1]This song is often—as is the case here—announced as "One More Time."

31 May 1960   (S)
Radio Recorders Annex
Hollywood, CA

DUKE ELLINGTON & HIS ORCHESTRA
WC AF EMls RN, LB BWmn BWd JT, JHtn JH RP PG HC, DE AB SWrd.

....			THE NUTCRACKER SUITE (ctd.)[1]
....	Co	RHCO46656-6[2]	2 Toot Toot Tootie Toot (Dance of the Reed Pipes)
....	Co	RHCO46662-6	I'm Beginning To See The Light[3]
....	Co	RHCO46663-7	Perdido[4]

[1]See also sessions on 26 May, and 3, 21 and 22 Jun 1960.
[2]Remake.
[3]The arrangement is by Bill Mathieu.
[4]The arrangement for the second half of this version is by Gerald Wilson.

1 Jun 1960   (S)
Radio Recorders Annex
Hollywood, CA

DUKE ELLINGTON & HIS ORCHESTRA
WC AF EMls RN, LB BWmn BWd JT, JHtn JH RP PG HC, DE AB SWrd, MGsn.

....		RHCO46664	Asphalt Jungle
....	Co	RHCO46670	Lost In Loveliness –vMGsn
....		RHCO46671	I'm Just A Lucky So-And-So –vMGsn
....		RHCO46672	One More Once –vMGsn

DUKE ELLINGTON & HIS ORCHESTRA
WC AF EMls RN, LB BWmn BWd JT, JHtn JH RP PG HC, DE AB SWrd, MGsn.

2 Jun 1960   (S)
Radio Recorders Annex
Hollywood, CA

.... Co   RHCO46673-3   It Don't Mean A Thing[1]
.... Co   RHCO46671[2]   I'm Just A Lucky So-And-So –vMGsn
.... Co   RHCO46672[2]   One More Once –vMGsn

[1]The arrangement is by Bill Mathieu.
[2]Remakes.

DUKE ELLINGTON & HIS ORCHESTRA
WC AF EMls RN, LB BWmn BWd JT, JHtn JH RP PG HC, DE AB SWrd.

3 Jun 1960   (S)
Radio Recorders Annex
Hollywood, CA

                                       THE NUTCRACKER SUITE (ctd.)[1]
.... Co   RHCO46674-20   8 Danse Of The Floreadores (Waltz Of The Flowers)
....   RHCO46675-1   4 Sugar Rum Cherry (Dance Of The Sugar-Plum Fairy)
.... Co   RHCO46675-2   4 Sugar Rum Cherry (Dance Of The Sugar-Plum Fairy)

[1]See also sessions on 26 and 31 May, and 21 and 22 Jun 1960.

DUKE ELLINGTON & HIS ORCHESTRA
WC AF EMls RN, LB BWmn BWd, JHtn JH RP PG HC, DE AB SWrd.

20 Jun 1960   (S)
Radio Recorders Annex
Hollywood, CA

.... Co   RHCO46676-4   Lullaby Of Birdland
.... Co   RHCO46676-5   Lullaby Of Birdland

  > BS replaces DE.

.... Co   RHCO46677-5   Dreamy Sort Of Thing

  > DE replaces BS.

.... Co   RHCO46681-1   Kinda Dukish/Rockin' In Rhythm

DUKE ELLINGTON & HIS ORCHESTRA
WC AF EMls RN, LB BWmn BWd, JHtn JH RP PG HC, DE AB SWrd.

21 Jun 1960   (S)
Radio Recorders Annex
Hollywood, CA

                                       THE NUTCRACKER SUITE (ctd.)[1]
.... Co   RHCO46684-5   7 Chinoiserie (Chinese Dance)
....   RHCO46685-?   3 Peanut Brittle Brigade (March)
.... Co   RHCO46685-5   3 Peanut Brittle Brigade (March)
....   RHCO46655-1A[2]   9 Arabesque Cookie (Arabian Dance)

[1]See also sessions on 26 and 31 May, and 3 and 22 Jun 1960.
[2]Remake.

DUKE ELLINGTON & HIS ORCHESTRA
WC AF EMls RN, LB BWmn BWd JT, JHtn JH RP PG HC, DE AB SWrd.

22 Jun 1960   (S)
Radio Recorders Annex
Hollywood, CA

                                       THE NUTCRACKER SUITE (ctd.)[1]
.... Co   RHCO46655-5A[2]   9 Arabesque Cookie (Arabian Dance)
.... Co   RHCO46688-5   6 Volga Vouty (Russian Dance)
.... Co   RHCO46689-4   Main Stem

[1]See also sessions on 25 and 31 May, and 3 and 21 Jun 1960.
[2]Remake.

                                       THE NUTCRACKER SUITE (summation)
           Co   RHCO46653-5   1 Overture
           Co   RHCO46656-6   2 Toot Toot Tootie Toot (Dance of the Reed Pipes)
           Co   RHCO46685-5   3 Peanut Brittle Brigade (March)
           Co   RHCO46675-2   4 Sugar Rum Cherry (Dance Of The Sugar-Plum Fairy)
           Co   RHCO46654-6   5 Entr'acte
           Co   RHCO46688-5   6 Volga Vouty (Russian Dance)
           Co   RHCO46684-5   7 Chinoiserie (Chinese Dance)
           Co   RHCO46674-20   8 Danse Of The Floreadores (Dance Of The Flowers)
           Co   RHCO46655-5A   9 Arabesque Cookie (Arabian Dance)

The alternate takes of parts of The Nutcracker Suite *have not yet been released on CD.*

DUKE ELLINGTON & HIS ORCHESTRA
WC AF EMls RN, LB BWmn BWd, JHtn JH RP PG HC, DE AB SWrd.

26 Jun 1960   (T)[1]
Radio Recorders
Hollywood, CA

....   Peanut Brittle Brigade (fragment)
....   Peanut Brittle Brigade (fragment)
....   Interview[2]   >>>

....   Overture
....   Sugar Rum Cherry (fragment)

[1]Movie short "Playback—Duke Ellington" for the promotion of Columbia records.
[2]DE interviewed by Goddard Lieberson.

DUKE ELLINGTON & HIS ORCHESTRA   28 Jun 1960   (S)
WC AF EMls RN, LB BWmn BWd, JHtn JH RP PG HC, DE AB SWrd.   Radio Recorders, Studio 1
                                       Hollywood, CA

                                    PEER GYNT SUITES #1&2[1]

....	Co	RHCO46705-5	1 Morning Mood
....	Co	RHCO46706-4	5 Anitra's Dance
....	Co	RHCO46707-5	Midriff
....	Co	RHCO46708-1	Take The "A" Train

[1]See also sessions on 29 and 30 Jun 1960.

DUKE ELLINGTON & HIS ORCHESTRA   29 Jun 1960   (S)
WC AF EMls RN, LB BWmn BWd, JHtn JH RP PG HC, DE AB SWrd.   Radio Recorders, Studio 1
                                       Hollywood, CA

                                    PEER GYNT SUITES #1&2 (ctd.)[1]

....	Co	RHCO46709-8	3 Solvejg's Song
....	Co	RHCO46710-7	4 Ase's Death
....	Co	RHCO46711-2	What Am I Here For?

[1]See also sessions on 28 and 30 Jun 1960.

DUKE ELLINGTON & HIS ORCHESTRA   30 Jun 1960   (S)
WC AF EMls GW RN, LB BWmn BWd, JHtn JH RP PG HC, DE AB SWrd.   Radio Recorders, Studio 1
                                        Hollywood, CA

....	Co	RHCO46713-5	The Wailer

                                    PEER GYNT SUITES #1&2 (ctd.)[1]

....	Co	RHCO46714-9	2 In The Hall Of The Mountain King
....	Co	RHCO46715-2	Happy-Go-Lucky Local

[1]See also sessions on 28 and 29 Jun 1960.

                                    PEER GYNT SUITES #1&2 (summation)

Co	RHCO46705-5	1 Morning Mood
Co	RHCO46714-9	2 In The Hall Of The Mountain King
Co	RHCO46709-8	3 Solvejg's Song
Co	RHCO46710-7	4 Ase's Death
Co	RHCO46706-4	5 Anitra's Dance

DUKE ELLINGTON & BILLY STRAYHORN   Jun 1960   (S)
DE and BS talking.   Unidentified location (bc?)
                                         U.S.A.

....   In Conversation

DUKE ELLINGTON & HIS ORCHESTRA   1 Jul 1960   (S)
WC AF EMls RN, LB BWmn BWd, JHtn JH RP PG HC, DE AB SWrd.   Radio Recorders
                                          Hollywood, CA

                                      THE ASPHALT JUNGLE SUITE

....	Co	RHCO46717	1 Wild Car
....	Co	RHCO46718	2 Cops[1]
....	Co	RHCO46719	3 Robbers

[1]sa "Asphalt Jungle (Theme)."

DUKE ELLINGTON   10 Jul 1960   (S)
DE interviewed by Russ Wilson.   ?Studios KJAZ-FM (bc)
                                          San Francisco, CA

....   Interview

DUKE ELLINGTON & BILLY STRAYHORN   11 Jul 1960   (S)
DE AB SWrd.   Studios KQED (tc)
                                          San Francisco, CA

....   Happy-Go-Lucky Local

> DE interviewed by Ralph J. Gleason.

....   Interview   >>>

> BS AB SWrd.

....   Quod Erat Demonstrandum Blues

> DE added.

....   Take The "A" Train

> DE piano solo.

....   A Single Petal Of A Rose (incomplete)

			14 Jul 1960 (S)
			Radio Recorders Annex

DUKE ELLINGTON & HIS SEPTET
RN, LB, JH PG HC, DE AB SWrd.   Hollywood, CA

....	Co	RHCO46703	Everything But You
....	Co	RHCO46704	Black Beauty
....	Co	RHCO46712	All Too Soon
....	Co	RHCO46716	Something To Live for
..............,......	Co	RHCO46720	Mood Indigo

DUKE ELLINGTON & HIS SEPTET
Same personnel.

....	Co	RHCO46725	Creole Blues
....	Co	RHCO46726	Don't You Know I Care?
....	Co	RHCO46727	A Flower Is A Lovesome Thing
....	Co	RHCO46728	Mighty Like The Blues
....	Co	RHCO46729	Tonight I Shall Sleep
....	Co	RHCO46730	Dual Highway[1]
....	Co	RHCO46731	Blues

[1]sa "Something Saxual."

19 Jul 1960 (P)	
Moulin Rouge	

DUKE ELLINGTON & HIS ORCHESTRA   Los Angeles, CA
WC AF EMls RN, LB BWmn BWd, JHtn JH RP PG HC, DE AB SWrd, LG MGsn.

....	Take The "A" Train
....	Stompin' At The Savoy
....	All Of Me
....	What Else Can You Do With A Drum? –vMGsn
....	Lost In Loveliness –vMGsn
....	One More Once –vMGsn
....	Medley[1]
....	Bill Bailey –vLG
....	Walkin' And Singin' The Blues –vLG
....	Jones

[1]Including: Do Nothin' Till You Hear From Me; In A Sentimental Mood; Don't Get Around Much Anymore; Mood Indigo; I'm Beginning To See The Light; Sophisticated Lady; Caravan; Solitude –vLG; Satin Doll; Just Squeeze Me –vRN; It Don't Mean A Thing –vRN; I Let A Song Go Out Of My Heart/Don't Get Around Much Anymore.

21 Jul 1960 (S/T)[1]	
Unspecified studio	

DUKE ELLINGTON & HIS ORCHESTRA/GROUP   Hollywood, CA
MME, PG, DE AB SWrd.

....   Paris Blues

> WC AF EMls RN, LB BWmn BWd, JHtn JH RP PG HC, DE AB SWrd.

....   Big Bash

> MME, BS.

....   Paris Blues

> DE piano solo.

....   Piano Improvisation

> Entire band, MME added, BS replaces DE.

....   Paris Blues

> MME, PG, BS gt AB SWrd, NWn.

....		Sophisticated Lady –vNWn
....	UA	Mood Indigo
....		Sophisticated Lady

[1]Music for the motion picture "Paris Blues."

22 Jul 1960   (P)
Mather AFB
Sacramento, CA

DUKE ELLINGTON & HIS ORCHESTRA
WC AF EMls RN, LB BWmn BWd, JHtn JH RP PG HC, AB SWrd, LG MGsn.

....		Boo-Dah
....		Laura
....	UJ	Star Dust
....		Frivolous Banta

> DE added.

....	RB	Take The "A" Train
....	UJ	Paris Blues
....	UJ	Big Bash
....	UJ	Overture
....	UJ	Tenderly
....	Koa	Such Sweet Thunder
....	RB	Satin Doll
....	UJ	Black And Tan Fantasy—Creole Love Call—The Mooche
....		Day In, Day Out –vMGsn
....		Lost In Loveliness –vMGsn
....	UJ	Take The "A" Train
....		I Let A Song Go Out Of My Heart/Don't Get Around Much Anymore –vRN
....	Koa	Tulip Or Turnip –vRN
....	Koa	All Of Me
....	UJ	Jeep's Blues
....	UJ	Moonglow
....	Koa	Laura
....		St. Louis Blues –vLG
....	Koa	Danse Of The Floreadores

> JHtn RP HC, DE.

....	RB	Monologue –DE narration

> Entire band.

....		Skin Deep
....	RB[1]	Medley[2]
....		Caravan -vAF
....	RB	Diminuendo In Blue and Wailing Interval[3]
....		One More Once –vMGsn
....		One More Once –vMGsn
....		Mood Indigo

[1]Incomplete on RB.
[2]Including: Do Nothin' Till You Hear From Me; I Got It Bad; I'm Just A Lucky So-And-So –vMGsn; Don't Get Around Much Anymore; Mood Indigo; I'm Beginning To See The Light; Solitude –vLG; Sophisticated Lady; Just Squeeze Me –vRN; It Don't Mean A Thing –vRN.
[3]"Diminuendo and Crescendo In Blue" on RB.

28 Jul 1960   (P)
Red Rocks Open Theater
Denver, CO

DUKE ELLINGTON & HIS ORCHESTRA
WC AF EMls RN, LB BWmn BWd, JHtn JH RP PG HC, DE AB SWrd, LG MGsn.

....		Take The "A" Train
....		Black And Tan Fantasy—Creole Love Call—The Mooche
....		Newport Up
....		Flirtibird
....		All Of Me
....		Day In, Day Out –vMGsn
....		Lost In Loveliness –vMGsn
....		One More Once –vMGsn
....		Medley[1]
....		Diminuendo In Blue and Wailing Interval
....		Jones

[1]Including: Do Nothin' Till You Hear From Me; In A Sentimental Mood; I'm Just A Lucky So-And-So; I Got It Bad; Don't Get Around Much Anymore; Mood Indigo; I'm Beginning To See The Light; Sophisticated Lady; Caravan; Solitude –vLG; Satin Doll; Just Squeeze Me –vRN; It Don't Mean A Thing –vRN; I Let A Song Go Out Of My Heart/Don't Get Around Much Anymore.

19 Aug 1960   (P)
State Fairgrounds (bc)
Detroit, MI

DUKE ELLINGTON & HIS ORCHESTRA
WC AF EMls RN, LB BWmn BWd, JHtn JH RP PG HC, DE AB SWrd.

....		Take The "A" Train
....		V.I.P.'s Boogie
....		Jam With Sam
....		Jeep's Blues >>>

....		All Of Me
....		Medley[1]

[1]Including: Do Nothin' Till You Hear From Me; In A Sentimental Mood; I'm Just A Lucky So-And-So; I Got It Bad; Don't Get Around Much Anymore; Mood Indigo; I'm Beginning To See The Light; Sophisticated Lady; Caravan; I Let A Song Go Out Of My Heart/Don't Get Around Much Anymore.

26 Aug 1960   (P)
Connie Mack Stadium
Philadelphia, PA

DUKE ELLINGTON & HIS ORCHESTRA
WC AF EMls RN, LB BWmn BWd, JHtn JH RP PG HC, DE AB SWrd.

....	Rar	Take The "A" Train
....	Rar	Perdido
....	Rar	Congo Square
....	Rar	V.I.P.'s Boogie
....	Rar	Jam With Sam
....	Rar	Medley[1]

[1]Including: Do Nothin' Till You Hear From Me; In A Sentimental Mood.

24 Sep 1960   (P)
Festival Grounds
Monterey, CA

DUKE ELLINGTON & HIS ORCHESTRA
WC AF EMls RN, LB MG BWd, JHtn JH RP PG HC, DE AB SWrd.

....	Sts	Take The "A" Train
....	Sts	Perdido
....	Sts	Overture
....	Sts	Half The Fun
....	Sts	Jeep's Blues
....	Sts	Newport Up
....	Sts	Sophisticated Lady
		SUITE THURSDAY
....	Sts	- Misfit Blues
....	Sts	- Schwiphti
....	Sts	- Zweet Zurzday
....	Sts	- Lay-By[1]
....	Sts	Danse Of The Floreadores
....	Sts	Jam With Sam
....	Sts	Jones

> JRsh added.

....	Sts	On The Sunny Side Of The Street –vJRsh
....	Sts	Goin' To Chicago –vJRsh
....	Sts	Sent For You Yesterday –vJRsh
....	Sts	Sent For You Yesterday –vJRsh
....	Sts	If You Wanna Be My Baby –vJRsh

> JRsh omitted.

....	Sts[2]	Red Carpet

[1]Originally titled "Strad."
[2]Incomplete on Sts.

27 Sep 1960   (P)
Club Neve (bc)
San Francisco, CA

DUKE ELLINGTON & HIS ORCHESTRA
WC AF EMls RN, LB MG BWd, JHtn JH RP PG HC, DE AB SWrd, MGsn.

....	Take The "A" Train
	SUITE THURSDAY
....	- Misfit Blues
....	- Schwiphti
....	- Zweet Zurzday
....	- Lay-By
....	Prelude To A Kiss
....	The "C" Jam Blues
....	Lost In Loveliness –vMGsn
....	One More Once –vMGsn

4 Oct 1960   (P)
Club Neve (bc)
San Francisco, CA

DUKE ELLINGTON & HIS ORCHESTRA
WC AF EMls RN, LB MG BWd, JHtn PH RP PG HC, DE AB SWrd, LG MGsn.

....	Launching Pad
....	Take The "A" Train
....	Red Shoes
....	Red Carpet
....	St. Louis Blues –vLG >>>

....			*Frustration*
....			*One More Once* –vMGsn
....			*Jones*

10 Oct 1960   (S)
Radio Recorders Annex
Hollywood, CA

<u>DUKE ELLINGTON & HIS ORCHESTRA</u>
WC AF EMls RN, LB MG BWd JT, JHtn PH RP PG HC, DE AB SWrd.

SUITE THURSDAY

....	Co	RHCO46797-7	- Misfit Blues
....	Co	RHCO46798-3	- Schwiphti
....	Co	RHCO46799-6	- Zweet Zurzday
....	Co	RHCO46800-3	- Lay-By

Oct 1960   (P)
Southern Illinois University
Carbondale, IL

<u>DUKE ELLINGTON & HIS ORCHESTRA</u>
WC AF EMls RN, LB MG BWd, JHtn PH RP PG HC, DE AB MTrm, MGsn.

....	*One More Once* –vMGsn
....	*Take The "A" Train*

24 Oct 1960   (S)
St. Mary's College, Notre Dame University (bc)
Notre Dame, IN

<u>DUKE ELLINGTON</u>
DE interviewed by Frank Hamilton.

....	*Interview*

p 14-15 Dec 1960   (T)[1]
Barclay Studios
Paris, France

<u>STUDIO BAND/ORCHESTRA</u>
?DE supervising.

> BRso guitar solo.

....	-5	*Guitar Improvisation*
....	-6	*Guitar Improvisation*

> Orchestra

....	*Wild Man Moore* (incomplete)

> LA added.

....	UA	*Wild Man Moore*

> DE/BD.

....	-4	*Piano Improvisation*

> Orchestra, LA added.

....	UA	-6	*Battle Royal*[2]

> LA omitted.

....	-7	*Battle Royal*
....	-10	*Battle Royal*

> BBrs, GL, BS ?JGrl ?MGdr FGpd, JAW.

....	*Sophisticated Lady* –vJAW

> BBrs, GL, BS/ABrd ?MGdr FGpd.

....	UA	*Take The "A" Train*

[1]Music for the motion picture "Paris Blues."
[2]*sa* "Big Bash."

The above is a composite of the recordings made in Paris on or around 14–15 Dec 1960.

Dec 1960[1]   (S)
Unspecified studio (bc)
Paris, France

<u>DUKE ELLINGTON & BILLY STRAYHORN</u>
DE and BS interviewed for a French radio program; intermittent previously recorded music.

....	*Interview*

[1]Taping session; the date of bc is not known.

17 Dec 1960[1]   (P)
Private residence (tc)
Paris, France

<u>DUKE ELLINGTON</u>
Piano solo.

....	*Paris Blues*
....	*Medley*[2]
....	*Take The "A" Train*
....	*Just Scratchin' The Surface* >>>

> JSbl added.

....   Solitude –vJSbl

[1]Telecast on 23 Dec 1960.
[2]Including: Do Nothin' Till You Hear From Me; In A Sentimental Mood; Just Squeeze Me; Prelude To A Kiss; I Let A Song Go Out Of My Heart; Don't Get Around Much Anymore; I Got It Bad; I'm Beginning To See The Light; Sophisticated Lady; Caravan; Mood Indigo.

29+30 Dec 1960   (S)
Théâtre National Populaire, Palais de Chaillot
Paris, France

DUKE ELLINGTON & BILLY STRAYHORN WITH ORCHESTRA
DE and BS with a 16 piece orchestra.

                           TURCARET

....	Az	-1	Ouverture (incomplete)
....	Az	-1	Ouverture

> DE piano solo.

....	Az	-1	Annonce du Spectacle (incomplete)
....	Az	-2	Annonce du Spectacle (incomplete)
....	Az	-3	Annonce du Spectacle

> Orchestra added.

....	Az	-2	Frontin (incomplete)
....	Az	-3	Frontin
....	Az	-1	Lisette (incomplete)
....	Az	-2	Lisette
....	Az	-3	Lisette
....	Az	-1	La Baronne
....	Az	-2	La Baronne (incomplete)
....	Az	-3	La Baronne
....	Az		Turcaret (rehearsal)
....	Az	-1	Turcaret
....	Az	-2	Turcaret
....	Az	-1	Colère de Monsieur Turcaret
....	Az	-1	Le Chevalier (incomplete)
....	Az	-2	Le Chevalier (incomplete)
....	Az	-3	Le Chevalier
....	Az	-4	Le Chevalier (incomplete)
....	Az	-5	Le Chevalier
....	Az	-1	Mathilde
....	Az	-1	Madame Turcaret
....	Az	-2	Madame Turcaret

> DE b dr.

....	Az	-1	Motif de Flamand

No audience in attendance. It is assumed that a contingent from the Ellington orchestra participated in this session.

Dec 1960   (T)[1]
Barclay Studios
Paris, France

DUKE ELLINGTON
DE MGdr FGpd.

....		Sophisticated Lady

> JGrl/JVs added.

....		Paris Blues

[1]Music for the motion picture "Paris Blues."

Early 1961   (S)
Unspecified studio
Paris, France

DUKE ELLINGTON & BILLY STRAYHORN
DE BS.

....		Guitar Amour
....		Guitar Amour

> BS omitted.

....	Stv	Blues
....		Blues

1 Mar 1961   (S)
Radio Recorders Annex
Hollywood, CA

DUKE ELLINGTON & HIS RHYTHM
DE AB SWrd.

....	Co	RHCO70018-2	So*
....	Co	RHCO70019-1	I Can't Get Started
....	Co	RHCO70020-4	Body And Soul >>>

.... Co   RHCO70021-1   Cong-Go*/1
.... Co   RHCO70022-2   Blues For Jerry2

   > SWrd omitted.

.... Co   RHCO70023-1   Fontainebleau Forest*

   > SWrd added.

.... Co   RHCO70024-1   Summertime
.... Co   RHCO70025-2   It's Bad To Be Forgotten*
.... Co   RHCO70026-1   A Hundred Dreams Ago
.... Co   RHCO70027-7   Pleadin' For Love3
.... Co   RHCO70028-2   Springtime In Africa

   *On the recording sheet as "Original #1, 2, 3 and 4" respectively.
   1aka "Improvisation."
   2aka "Blues To Jerry."
   3aka "Searching"; erroneously as "Yearning For Love" on the original release.

| | | | 2 Mar 1961 (S) |
| | | | Radio Recorders Annex |

DUKE ELLINGTON & HIS ORCHESTRA
WC AF EMls RN, LB MG JT, JHtn RP PG HC, DE AB SWrd, MGsn.   Hollywood, CA

.... Co   RHCO70029   Day In, Day Out –vMGsn
.... Co   RHCO70036   Why Was I Born? –vMGsn
.... Co   RHCO70037   Matumbe
.... FM   RHCO70038   Love You Madly –vMGsn
.... FM   RHCO70039   Just A-Settin' And A-Rockin' –vRN

DUKE ELLINGTON & HIS RHYTHM
DE AB SWrd.

.... Co   1   Lotus Blossom

   1No master number assigned.

| | | | 3 Mar 1961 (S) |
| | | | Radio Recorders Annex |

DUKE ELLINGTON & HIS ORCHESTRA
WC AF EMls RN, LB MG JT, JHtn RP PG HC, DE AMK SWrd, MGsn.   Hollywood, CA

.... Co   RHCO70041   Where In The World –vMGsn
....   RHCO70042-2   Tulip Or Turnip –vRN
.... FM   RHCO70042-3   Tulip Or Turnip –vRN
.... Co   RHCO70042-6   Tulip Or Turnip –vRN

   > BS1 replaces DE, AB replaces AMK.

.... Co   RHCO70043   Song from "Moulin Rouge" –vMGsn

   > DE replaces BS.

....   RHCO700442   Harlem Air Shaft
....   RHCO70044   Harlem Air Shaft
....   RHCO70044   Harlem Air Shaft
....   RHCO70044-2   Harlem Air Shaft
.... Co   RHCO70044-6   Harlem Air Shaft

   1BS has not been mentioned on the recording sheet; his presence is based on aural judgement.
   2The various takes include one false start and one breakdown; not listed are two rehearsals. The material could not be auditioned.

| | | | 3 Apr 1961 (S) |
| | | | 24th St., Studio A |

DUKE ELLINGTON WITH LOUIS ARMSTRONG & HIS ALL STARS
LA, TY, BB, DE MHbt DBcl.   New York City, NY

.... Rlt   15969   It Don't Mean A Thing –vLA
.... Rlt   15970   Solitude –vLA
.... Rlt   In A Mellotone (warm up)
.... Rlt   15971-1   In A Mellotone
.... Rlt   15971   In A Mellotone
.... Rlt   15972-1   I'm Beginning To See The Light (incomplete)
.... Rlt   15972-4   I'm Beginning To See The Light (incomplete)
.... Rlt   15972-4   I'm Beginning To See The Light (incomplete)
.... Rlt   15972-5   I'm Beginning To See The Light –vLA
.... Rlt   15972-6   I'm Beginning To See The Light (incomplete)
.... Rlt   15972-7   I'm Beginning To See The Light –vLA (incomplete)
.... Rlt   15972   I'm Beginning To See The Light –vLA
.... Rlt   15973-1   Do Nothin' Till You Hear From Me –vLA (rehearsal)
.... Rlt   15973-2   Do Nothin' Till You Hear From Me –vLA
.... Rlt   15973-3   Do Nothin' Till You Hear From Me (incomplete)
.... Rlt   15973   Do Nothin' Till You Hear From Me –vLA   >>>

....	Rlt	15974-2	Don't Get Around Much Anymore –vLA (incomplete)
....	Rlt	15974-3	Don't Get Around Much Anymore (incomplete)
....	Rlt	15974-4	Don't Get Around Much Anymore (incomplete)
....	Rlt	15974-5	Don't Get Around Much Anymore –vLA
....	Rlt		Don't Get Around Much Anymore (rehearsal)
....	Rlt	15974	Don't Get Around Much Anymore –vLA
....	Rlt	15975-5	Duke's Place –vLA
....	Rlt	15975	Duke's Place –vLA

> TY, BB omitted.

| .... | Rlt | 15976 | I Got It Bad –vLA |

> TY, BB added.

| .... | Rlt | 15977 | Just Squeeze Me –vLA |
| .... | Rlt | 15978 | The Beautiful American |

The take numbers of the titles first released on LP have not been specified. This also applies to the following session.

4 Apr 1961   (S)
24th St., Studio A
New York City, NY

DUKE ELLINGTON WITH LOUIS ARMSTRONG & HIS ALL STARS
LA, TY, BB, DE MHbt DBcl.

....	Rlt	15979-2	Drop Me Off At Harlem –vLA
....	Rlt	15979	Drop Me Off At Harlem –vLA
....	Rlt	15980	Mood Indigo

> TY, BB omitted.

....	Rlt	15981-1	I'm Just A Lucky So-And-So –vLA (incomplete)
....	Rlt	15981-2	I'm Just A Lucky So-And-So –vLA
....	Rlt	15981	I'm Just A Lucky So-And-So –vLA
....	Rlt	15982-8	Azalea (incomplete)
....	Rlt	15982-9	Azalea (incomplete)
....	Rlt	15982-10	Azalea –vLA (incomplete)
....	Rlt	15982-10	Azalea –vLA (incomplete)
....	Rlt	15982	Azalea –vLA

> TY, BB added.

....	Rlt	15983-3	Black And Tan Fantasy (incomplete)
....	Rlt	15983-4[1]	Black And Tan Fantasy
....	Rlt	15983-5	Black And Tan Fantasy (incomplete)
....	Rlt	15983-6[1]	Black And Tan Fantasy
....	Rlt	15984	The Mooche
....	Rlt		Cotton Tail (rehearsal)
....	Rlt	15985	Cotton Tail –vLA

[1]Takes 4 and 6 have been edited together for the release. The unedited version of take 6 can only be found on CD Rlt 7243 5 24548 2 2.

19 Apr 1961[1]   (S)
CBC Studios (tc)
Toronto, ON

DUKE ELLINGTON WITH JACK KANE & HIS MUSIC MAKERS
HC and DE with Jack Kane & His Music Makers, BBab SMph DFks.

....		Take The "A" Train (featuring DE)
....		Love You Madly –vSMph
....		In A Sentimental Mood –DE talking, –vBBab (incomplete)
....		Sophisticated Lady (featuring HC and DE)
....		Satin Doll (featuring DE)
....		Caravan (incomplete)
....		Medley[2]
....		Mood Indigo

[1]Telecast on 24 Apr 1961.
[2]Including: In A Mellotone; I Let A Song Go Out Of My Heart –vSMph; It Don't Mean A Thing; Do Nothin' Till You Hear From Me –vDFks; Don't Get Around Much Anymore –vGrp, Prelude To A Kiss –vBBab; I'm Beginning to See The Light –vSMph DFks (featuring DE).

The entire set has been listed, because it can be assumed that DE was involved in supervising the musical content of the show.

27 Apr 1961   (S)
Unspecified studio (bc)
New York City, NY

DUKE ELLINGTON
DE interviewed by Claus Dahlgren.

| .... | | Interview |

DUKE ELLINGTON & HIS ORCHESTRA
CT WC CA EMls RN, LB BWmn LBlb MME, JHtn JH ON RP PG ACrk HC HSml, DE AB JJsn
SG MR DJ PJJ.

1 May 1961   (S)
Reeves Sound Studios
New York City, NY

....		Paris Blues
....		Big Bash (incomplete)
....		Big Bash

> MME, DE.

| .... | | Paris Blues |

> DE piano solo.

| .... | -1 | Piano Improvisation[1] |
| .... | -3 | Piano Improvisation[1] |

[1]Based on chords of *Paris Blues.*

DUKE ELLINGTON & HIS ORCHESTRA
CT WC CA EMls RN, LB BWmn LBlb MME JT, JHtn JH ON RP PG BClr HC HSml, DE LS AB
JJsn SG MR DJ PJJ.

2+3 May 1961   (T)[1]
Reeves Sound Studios
New York City, NY

....	UA	Nite[2]
....		Nite
....		Paris Blues
....		Paris Blues
....	UA	Paris Blues
....		Paris Blues
....	UA	Autumnal Suite[2]
....		Autumnal Suite
....		Autumnal Suite
....	UA	Bird Jungle[3]
....		Bird Jungle
....	UA	Paris Stairs
....		Paris Stairs

> MME tb solo.

| .... | UA | Paris Blues (theme) |

[1]Music for the motion picture "Paris Blues."
[2]These titles are derivatives of *Paris Blues.*
[3]Variant spelling "Birdie Jungle." This title is a derivative of *Guitar Amour.*

The work on this project started as early as Jul 1960 and was done in part in the U.S.A. and in part in France (see the respective rehearsal/recording sessions).

DUKE ELLINGTON
DE commenting on previously recorded music for the Shakespearean Suite.

14 May 1961   (S)
CBS Studios (tc)
New York City, NY

| .... | | DE talking |

DUKE ELLINGTON & HIS ORCHESTRA
CT WC EMls RN, LB BWmn JT, JHtn JH RP PG HC, DE AB SWrd.

c 25 May 1961   (P)
p Apollo Theater (?bc)
New York City, NY

| .... | | In The Hall Of The Mountain King |
| .... | | Caravan |

I have listened to this "Phantom Session" many times on the radio (AFN-Tehran) in 1962/63. Unfortunately I did not tape it or follow up on it. In about 1970 I was offered an acetate by a reliable source, containing the above music (with location and date given). Again, I missed the opportunity by turning down the deal, because the bulk of the content of the record was of no interest for me, and the asking price was hefty. It was definitely a live broadcast, featuring RN on violin in the "Mountain King," and it was an extended and swinging performance as compared with the studio recording.

DUKE ELLINGTON & HIS ORCHESTRA
CT WC EMls RN, LB BWmn JT, JHtn JH RP PG HC, DE AB ELck OJ.

1 Jun 1961   (S)
30th Street Studio
New York City, NY

....	Az	CO67171-3	Strange Feeling
....		CO67172	Asphalt Jungle (incomplete)
....		CO67172	Asphalt Jungle
....		CO67172	Asphalt Jungle
....		CO67173	Jingle Bells (incomplete)
....		CO67173	Jingle Bells (incomplete)
....		CO67173	Jingle Bells
....		CO67173	Jingle Bells (incomplete)
....		CO67173	Jingle Bells (incomplete) >>>

....   CO67173   Jingle Bells
.... Har   CO67173   Jingle Bells

24 Jun 1961   (P)
Roberts Municipal Stadium
Evansville, IN

DUKE ELLINGTON & HIS ORCHESTRA
WC CA EMls RN, LB LBlb JT, JHtn JH RP PG HC, DE AB SWrd, MGsn.

....   Flirtibird
....   Pie Eye's Blues
....   Paris Blues

                SUITE THURSDAY
....   - Misfit Blues
....   - Schwiphti
....   - Zweet Zurzday
....   - Lay-By

      > DE piano solo.

....   A Single Petal Of A Rose

      > Entire band.

....   Skin Deep
....   Medley[1]
....   Diminuendo In Blue and Wailing Interval

[1]Including: Do Nothin' Till You Hear From Me; In A Sentimental Mood; I'm Just A Lucky So-And-So –vMGsn; I Got It Bad; Don't Get Around Much Anymore; Mood Indigo; I'm Beginning To See The Light; Sophisticated Lady; Caravan; Solitude; Just Squeeze Me –vRN; It Don't Mean A Thing --vRN.

28 Jun 1961   (P)
Public Hall
Cleveland, OH

DUKE ELLINGTON & HIS ORCHESTRA WITH THE CLEVELAND SYMPHONY ORCHESTRA
WC CA EMls RN, LB BWmn JT, JHtn JH RP PG HC, DE AB SWrd, MGsn.

....   Asphalt Jungle Theme
....   Overture
....   Flirtibird
....   Pie Eye's Blues

                SUITE THURSDAY
....   - Misfit Blues
....   - Schwiphti
....   - Zweet Zurzday
....   - Lay-By

    CSO added, Louis Lane conducting.

                NIGHT CREATURE
....   - 1st Movement (Blind Bug)
....   - 2nd Movement (Stalking Monster)
....   - 3rd Movement (Dazzling Creature)

....   HARLEM
....   Medley[1]

[1]Including: Do Nothin' Till You Hear From Me; In A Sentimental Mood; I'm Just A Lucky So-And-So –vMGsn; I Got It Bad; Don't Get Around Much Anymore; Mood Indigo; I'm Beginning To See The Light; Sophisticated Lady; Caravan; Solitude; Just Squeeze Me –vRN; It Don't Mean A Thing –vRN; I Let A Song Go Out Of My Heart/Don't Get Around Much Anymore.

3 Jul 1961   (P)
Freebody Park
Newport, RI

DUKE ELLINGTON & HIS ORCHESTRA
WC CA EMls RN, LB LBlb JT, JHtn JH RP PG HC, DE AB SWrd, MGsn.

....   Take The "A" Train
....   Perdido

                SUITE THURSDAY
....   - Misfit Blues
....   - Schwiphti
....   - Zweet Zurzday
....   - Lay-By

....   Kinda Dukish/Rockin' In Rhythm
....   Passion Flower
....   One More Once –vMGsn
....   Jones

6 Jul 1961   (S)
30th Street Studio
New York City, NY

DUKE ELLINGTON & COUNT BASIE WITH THEIR COMBINED ORCHESTRAS
Composite personnel: WC CA EMls RN, LB LBlb JT, JHtn JH RP PG HC, DE AB SWrd, plus Count Basie & His Orchestra.

.... Co   CO67609-9   Until I Met You[1]   >>>

....	Co	CO67610-2	To You
....	Co	CO67611-2	Wild Man[2]
....	Co[3]	CO67611-6	Wild Man
....	Co	CO67612-4	Battle Royal
....	Co	CO67612-5	Battle Royal
....	Co	CO67612-7	Battle Royal
....	Co	CO67613-6	Segue In C
....		CO67614-1	Take The "A" Train (incomplete)

> BS replaces CBas.

....	Co	CO67614-2	Take The "A" Train (incomplete)
....	Co	CO67614-3	Take The "A" Train

> CBas replaces BS.

....	Co	CO67614-7	Take The "A" Train
....	Co	CO67615-4	BDB[4]
....	Co[5]	CO67615-5	BDB
....	Co	CO67616-2	Jumpin' At The Woodside
....	Co	CO67616-10	Jumpin' At The Woodside
....	Co	CO67617-1	One More Once
....	Co[5]	CO67618-1	Blues In Hoss' Flat[6]

[1]*aka* "Corner Pocket."
[2]*sa* "Wild Man Moore."
[3]Edited on most releases on Co; complete on Phi 847.016 BY and CD Co CK 65571.
[4]Stands for Basie, Duke, Billy.
[5]Original releases have been edited; complete on CD Co CK 65571.
[6]*aka* "Frankie's Place."

DUKE ELLINGTON & HIS ORCHESTRA
CT WC CA EMls RN, LB LBlb CCrs, JHtn JH RP PG HC, DE AB SWrd.

30 Jul 1961   (S)
30th Street Studio
New York City, NY

....		CO67172[1]	Asphalt Jungle Theme, part 1
....	Co	CO67855	Asphalt Jungle Theme, part 2 (version 1)
....	Co	CO67855	Asphalt Jungle Theme, part 2[2] (version 2)

[1]Remake.
[2]*aka* "Asphalt Jungle Twist."

DUKE ELLINGTON & HIS ORCHESTRA
WC CA EMls, LB LBlb CCrs, JHtn JH RP PG HC, DE AB SWrd, MGsn.

Aug 1961   (P)
Sheraton Park Hotel
Washington, DC

....	Asphalt Jungle Theme
....	Happy-Go-Lucky Local
....	Satin Doll
....	Diminuendo In Blue and Wailing Interval
....	Mood Indigo –vMGsn
....	One More Once –vMGsn

DUKE ELLINGTON & HIS GROUP
DE AB SWrd.

11 Aug 1961   (P)
Studios WBBM (tc)
Chicago, IL

....	Take The "A" Train

> JHtn RP HC added.

....	Monologue –DE narration

> DD added.

....	Perdido

DUKE ELLINGTON & HIS ORCHESTRA
WC CA EMls RN, LB LBlb CCrs, JHtn JH RP PG HC, DE AB SWrd, MGsn.

20 Aug 1961   (P)
Holiday Ballroom
Chicago, IL

....	Asphalt Jungle Theme
....	Where Or When
....	Day In, Day Out –vMGsn
....	Why Was I Born? –vMGsn
....	Where In The World –vMGsn
....	Where In The World –vMGsn
....	Do Nothin' Till You Hear From Me –vMGsn
....	Cotton Tail
....	Prelude To A Kiss
....	All Of Me
....	The "C" Jam Blues >>>

....	Jones
....	Do Nothin' Till You Hear From Me –vMGsn
....	One More Once –vMGsn
....	Caravan
....	Amor
....	Autumn Leaves
....	I Let A Song Go Out Of My Heart/Don't Get Around Much Anymore –vRN
....	Mack The Knife –vRN
....	Sophisticated Lady
....	Mood Indigo –vMGsn
....	Diminuendo In Blue and Wailing Interval
....	Happy-Go-Lucky Local
....	On The Sunny Side Of The Street
....	Jeep's Blues
....	Take The "A" Train
....	Stompin' At The Savoy
....	Deep Purple
....	Tenderly
....	Satin Doll
....	Jack The Bear
....	Love You Madly –vMGsn
....	Take The "A" Train

DUKE ELLINGTON & HIS ORCHESTRA   24 Aug 1961   (P)
WC CA EMls RN, LB LBlb CCrs, JHtn JH RP PG HC, DE AB SWrd.   Moon Bowl, Freedomland Park (bc)
                                                                       Bronx, NY

....	Mood Indigo
....	All Of Me
....	I Let A Song Go Out Of My Heart/Don't Get Around Much Anymore –vRN
....	Jones

DUKE ELLINGTON & HIS ORCHESTRA   26 Aug 1961   (P)
WC CA EMls RN, LB LBlb CCrs, JHtn JH RP PG HC, DE AB SWrd, MGsn.   Moon Bowl, Freedomland Park (bc)
                                                                       Bronx, NY

....	Take The "A" Train
....	Asphalt Jungle Twist
....	Satin Doll
....	Rockin' In Rhythm
....	I Let A Song Go Out Of My Heart/Don't Get Around Much Anymore –vRN
....	One More Once –vMGsn
....	One More Once –vMGsn

DUKE ELLINGTON & HIS ORCHESTRA   7 Sep 1961   (P)
WC CA EMls RN, LB LBlb CCrs, JHtn JH RP PG HC, DE AB SWrd, MGsn.   Music Hall
                                                                       Houston, TX

....	Take The "A" Train
....	Black And Tan Fantasy—Creole Love Call—The Mooche
....	Newport Up
....	Tenderly
....	Asphalt Jungle Twist
....	Matumbe
....	Summertime
....	Autumn Leaves
....	Rockin' In Rhythm
....	Passion Flower
....	All Of Me
....	Day In, Day Out –vMGsn
....	Why Was I Born? –vMGsn
....	One More Once –vMGsn
....	Jones
....	Take The "A" Train
....	V.I.P.'s Boogie
....	Jam With Sam
....	Skin Deep
....	Medley[1]
....	Diminuendo In Blue and Wailing Interval
....	Take The "A" Train

[1]Including: In A Sentimental Mood; Don't Get Around Much Anymore; Mood Indigo; I'm Beginning To See The Light;
Sophisticated Lady; Caravan; Do Nothin' Till You Hear From Me –vMGsn; Just Squeeze Me –vRN; It Don't Mean A Thing
–vRN; I Let A Song Go Out Of My Heart/Don't Get Around Much Anymore.

DUKE ELLINGTON & BILLY STRAYHORN
DE and BS interviewed by Paul Werth; intermittent previously recorded music.

....	RDB[2]	Interview
....		Take The "A" Train

Sep 1961[1]   (S)
Studios KBCA (bc)
Los Angeles, CA

[1]Broadcast on 6 Jan 1962.
[2]RDB contains only the DE portion of the interview.

DUKE ELLINGTON & HIS ORCHESTRA
WC CA EMls RN, LB LBlb CCrs, JHtn JH RP PG HC, DE AB SWrd.

19 Sep 1961   (S)
Radio Recorders
Hollywood, CA

THE GIRLS SUITE

....	Co	RHCO70342-1	1 Girls
....	Co	RHCO70343-1	2 Mahalia
....		RHCO70343-2	2 Mahalia
....	Co	RHCO70344-1	3 Peg O'My Heart
....	Co	RHCO70345-1	4 Sweet Adeline
....	Co	RHCO70346-1	5 Juanita
....	Co	RHCO70347-1	6 Sylvia

DUKE ELLINGTON & HIS ORCHESTRA
WC CA EMls RN, LB LBlb CCrs, JHtn JH RP PG HC, DE AB SWrd.

20 Sep 1961   (S)
Radio Recorders
Hollywood, CA

THE GIRLS SUITE (ctd.)

....	Co	RHCO70348-1	7 Lena
....		RHCO70349	8 Dinah
....	Co	RHCO70349-5	8 Dinah
....	Co	RHCO70350-1	9 Clementine
....	Co	RHCO70351-1	10 Diane

DUKE ELLINGTON & HIS ORCHESTRA
WC CA EMls RN, LB LBlb CCrs, JH RP PG HC, DE AB SWrd, MGsn.

23 Sep 1961   (P)
Festival Grounds
Monterey, CA

....	Take The "A" Train
....	Black And Tan Fantasy—Creole Love Call—The Mooche
....	Stompin' At The Savoy
....	In A Sentimental Mood
....	Congo Square
....	Summertime
....	Jam With Sam

SUITE THURSDAY

....	- Misfit Blues
....	- Schwiphti
....	- Zweet Zurzday
....	- Lay-By

....	Rockin' In Rhythm
....	Sophisticated Lady

> JHtn added.

THE GIRLS SUITE

....	- The Girls
....	- Sarah
....	- Lena
....	- Mahalia
....	- Dinah

....	Skin Deep
....	Passion Flower
....	All Of Me
....	Things Ain't What They Used To Be
....	Day In, Day Out –vMGsn
....	Do Nothin' Till You Hear From Me –MGsn
....	One More Once –vMGsn
....	Jones

DUKE ELLINGTON & HIS ORCHESTRA
WC CA EMls RN, LB LBlb CCrs, JHtn JH RP PG HC, DE AB SWrd, MGsn.

11 Oct 1961   (P)
Piccadilly Theater
Chicago, IL

....	Take The "A" Train
....	Black And Tan Fantasy—Creole Love Call—The Mooche
....	Newport Up >>>

....		Overture
....	Az	Asphalt Jungle Twist
....	Az	Matumbe
....		Summertime
....	Az	Flirtibird
....		All Of Me
....		Things Ain't What They Used To Be
....		Warm Valley
....		Jeep's Blues
....		Day In, Day Out –vMGsn
....		Why Was I Born? –vMGsn
....		One More Once –vMGsn
....		Take The "A" Train
....		Skin Deep
....		Medley[1]
....		Satin Doll
....		Diminuendo In Blue and Wailing Interval
....		Lullaby Of Birdland
....		Caravan
....		One More Once –vMGsn
....		Lost In Loveliness –vMGsn
....		Take The "A" Train

[1]Including: In A Sentimental Mood; Solitude –vMGsn; Don't Get Around Much Anymore; Mood Indigo; Sophisticated Lady; Caravan; Do Nothin' Till You Hear From Me –vMGsn; Just Squeeze Me –vRN; It Don't Mean A Thing –vRN; I Let A Song Go Out Of My Heart/Don't Get Around Much Anymore.

DUKE ELLINGTON & HIS ORCHESTRA
WC CA EMls RN, LB LBlb CCrs, JHtn JH RP PG HC, DE AB SWrd.

25 Oct 1961   (S)
30th Street Studio
New York City, NY

....	Co	CO68440-1	Bon Amour[1]
....	RDB	CO68441	Paris Blues, part 1
....	Co	CO68441 alt.	Paris Blues, part 1
....	Co	CO68441	Paris Blues, part 2

[1]aka "Mon Ami"; this title is a derivative of *Bird Jungle*.

DUKE ELLINGTON
DE interviewed by Barry Gray.

15 Nov 1961   (S)
Studios WMCA (bc)
New York City, NY

| .... | Interview |

21 Nov 1961[1]   (S)
30th Street Studio (tc)
New York City, NY

DUKE ELLINGTON & HIS OCTET
CA, LB, JHtn JH RP PG HC, DE AB SWrd; intermittent interviews with Big Wilson.

....	Take The "A" Train
....	Interview
	SUITE THURSDAY
....	- Misfit Blues
....	Interview (ctd.)
....	- Schwiphti (shortened version)
....	- Zweet Zurzday (shortened version)
....	- Lay-By
....	Interview (ctd.)

> Big Wilson AB SWrd.

| .... | WNEW jingle |

> DE added.

| .... | WNEW jingle |

> Entire band, Big Wilson omitted.

....	Twistin' Time
....	Interview (ctd.)
....	Cotton Tail
....	Interview (ctd.)
....	Medley[2]
....	Interview (ctd.)
....	Take The "A" Train
....	Announcement by DE
....	Announcement by DE

[1]Telecast on 8 Dec 1961.
[2]Including: I Got It Bad; Caravan; Mood Indigo; I'm Beginning To See The Light; Sophisticated Lady.

17 Dec 1961   (P)
CBS Studios (tc)
New York City, NY

DUKE ELLINGTON WITH LOUIS ARMSTRONG & HIS ALL STARS
LA, TY, JDbg, DE IMng DBcl.

.... Pkn   Duke's Place –vLA
.... Pkn   In A Mellotone

2 Jan 1962   (S)
30th Street Studio
New York City, NY

DUKE ELLINGTON & HIS ORCHESTRA
HB CA EMls BBry RN, LB LC CCrs, JHtn JH RP PG HC, BS AB SWrd.

.... Co   CO68920   We Speak The Same Language

> DE replaces BS.

.... Co   CO68921   Once Upon A Time
.... Co   CO68922   If I Were You

4 Jan 1962   (P)
Museum of Modern Art
New York City, NY

DUKE ELLINGTON & HIS RHYTHM
DE piano solo.

....   New York City Blues
....   Blue Belles Of Harlem
....   The Clothed Woman
.... DET   Melancholia
.... DET   Janet
.... DET   Reflections In D
.... DET   Nobody Was Lookin'
.... DET   New World A-Comin'

> AB SWrd added.

....   Take The "A" Train

> AB SWrd omitted.

....   Lotus Blossom

> AB SWrd added.

....   Satin Doll
....   A Single Petal Of A Rose
....   Kinda Dukish
....   Medley[1]
....   Dancers In Love

[1]Including: Do Nothin' Till You Hear From Me; Solitude; Don't Get Around Much Anymore; Mood Indigo; Asphalt Jungle Theme; I'm Beginning to See The Light; Sophisticated Lady; Caravan.

5 Jan 1962   (S)
30th Street Studio
New York City, NY

DUKE ELLINGTON & HIS ORCHESTRA
HB CA EMls BBry RN, LB LC CCrs, JHtn JH RP PG HC, DE AB SWrd.

.... Co   CO68957   I Couldn't Have Done It Alone
....   CO68958   I've Just Seen Her

> BS added.

.... Co   CO68959   Night Life

9 Jan 1962   (T)[1]
Pathé Studios
New York City, NY

DUKE ELLINGTON & HIS ORCHESTRA
HB CA EMls BBry RN, LB LC CCrs, JHtn JH RP PG HC, DE AB SWrd.

.... Gdr   Take The "A" Train
.... Gdr   Satin Doll
.... Gdr   Blow By Blow[2]
.... Gdr   Things Ain't What They Used To Be
.... Gdr   V.I.P.'s Boogie
.... Gdr   Jam With Sam
.... Gdr   Kinda Dukish
.... RDB   -1   Goodyear Theme
.... RDB   -2   Goodyear Theme
.... RDB   -1   The Good Years Of Jazz[3]
.... Gdr   alt.   The Good Years Of Jazz

[1]Music for a promotional film for the Goodyear Tyre Company, titled "The Good Years Of Jazz."
[2]sa "Wailing Interval"; "Wailing Bout."
[3]This title is a derivative of One More Once.

Some sources suggest that the musictrack for the film was done on 5 Jan, which would clash with the recording session of the same date.

DUKE ELLINGTON & HIS ORCHESTRA
HB CA EMls BBry RN, LB LC CCrs, JHtn JH RP PG HC, DE BS AB SWrd.

10 Jan 1962   (S)
799 Seventh Ave., Studio A
New York City. NY

| .... | Co | CO69232 | Which Way? |

> BS omitted.

| .... | Co | CO69233 | Our Children |

> DE replaces BS.

| .... | | CO69234-1 | Back To School |

DUKE ELLINGTON & HIS ORCHESTRA
HB CA BBry RN, LB LC CCrs, JHtn JH RP PG HC, BS AB SWrd.

23 Jan 1962   (S)
30th Street Studio
New York City, NY

....		CO69234-2[1]	Back To School (incomplete)
....		CO69234-3	Back To School (incomplete)
....		CO69234-4	Back To School (incomplete)
....		CO69234-5	Back To School (incomplete)
....		CO69234-6	Back To School
....	Co	CO69234-7	Back To School

> DE replaces BS.

....		CO68958-1[1]	I've Just Seen Her
....	Co	CO68958-2	I've Just Seen Her
....		CO69015-1	What A Country (incomplete)
....		CO69015-2	What A Country (incomplete)
....		CO69015-3	What A Country
....		CO69015-4	What A Country
....	Co	CO69015-5	What A Country
....	Co	CO69016	Turkish Coffee

[1]Remakes.

DUKE ELLINGTON & HIS ORCHESTRA
HB CA BBry RN, LB LC CCrs, JHtn JH RP PG HC, BS AB SWrd.

30 Jan 1962   (S)
799 Seventh Ave., Studio A
New York City, NY

....	Co	CO69326-10	Spreak To Me Of Love
....	Co	[1]	Speak To Me Of Love (insert)
....	Co	CO69327-4	Guitar Amour[2]
....		CO69452	Paris Blues
....	Co	CO69452	Paris Blues

[1]The separately recorded insert ending was used for the release of CO69236-10.
[2]sa "Bon Amour"; "Mon Ami."

DUKE ELLINGTON & HIS ORCHESTRA
HB CA HMG RN, LB LC CCrs, JHtn JH RP PG HC, BS AB SWrd.

31 Jan 1962   (S)
799 Seventh Ave., Studio A
New York City, NY

....	Co	CO69332-7	The Petite Waltz
....	Co	CO69333-5	Javapachacha[1]
....	Co	CO69334	Comme çi, comme ça

[1]aka "Apache."

DELLA REESE AND DUKE ELLINGTON & HIS ORCHESTRA
HB CA BBry RN, LB LC CCrs, JHtn JH RP PG HC, DE BS AB SWrd, and DRse acc. by a
studio orchestra, directed by Martin Block.
The vcl titles are accompanied by the studio orchestra, augmented by some of the Ellongtonians, while the instrumental
numbers are played by the Ellington band. Intermittent brief interviews with DE and DRse throughout.

13 Feb 1962   (S)
Bell Sound Studios
New York City, NY

....	JBR		National Guard Song –vDRse
....	JBR		Once In A Lifetime –vDRse
....	JBR		Sophisticated Lady
....	JBR		Chopin's Etude In E –vDRse
....	JBR		Take The "A" Train
....	JBR		Bye-Bye Blackbird –vDRse
....	JBR		Satin Doll
....	JBR		Don't You Know? –vDRse
....	JBR		Things Ain't What They Used To Be
....	JBR		A Foggy Day –vDRse
....	JBR		Mood Indigo
....	JBR		That Reminds Me –vDRse
....	JBR		Taffy Twist
....	JBR		Bill Bailey –vDRse >>>

....	JBR		Do Nothin' Till You Hear From Me
....	JBR		You're Nobody Until Somebody Loves You –vDRse
....	JBR		Jam With Sam

24 Feb 1962   (P)

DUKE ELLINGTON & HIS ORCHESTRA   Armory
HB CA BBry RN, LB LC CCrs, JHtn JH RP PG HC, DE AB SWrd.   Troy, NY

....		Take The "A" Train
....		Someone
....		In A Mellotone
....		Sophisticated Lady
....		Summertime
....		Diminuendo In Blue and Wailing Interval
....		Things Ain't What They Used To Be

27 Feb 1962   (S)

DUKE ELLINGTON & HIS ORCHESTRA   799 Seventh Ave., Studio A
HB BBry RN, LB LC CCrs, JHtn JH RP PG HC, BS AB SWrd.   New York City, NY

....	Co	CO69722	Under Paris Skies[1]
....		CO69723	The River Seine[2]
....	Az	CO69724	Medley[3]

[1]*aka "Sous le Ciel de Paris."*
[2]*aka "La Seine."*
[3]Including: My Heart Sings (En Ecoutant Mon Cœr Chanter); My Man (Mon Homme); No Regrets.

16 Mar 1962   (S)

DUKE ELLINGTON & HIS GROUP   Universal Studios
RN, LB, PG, BS AB SWrd, MGsn.   Chicago, IL

....	RDB	-1[1]	The Blues (incomplete)
....	RDB	-2	The Blues –vMGsn
....	RDB	-3	The Blues –vMGsn
....	RDB	-4	The Blues –vMGsn (incomplete)
....	RDB	-5	The Blues –vMGsn (incomplete)
....	RDB	-6	The Blues –vMGsn

> DE replaces BS.

....	RDB	-7	Do Nothin' Till You Hear From Me –vMGsn
....		-8	Blue Moon (incomplete)
....		-9	Blue Moon –vMGsn
....		-10	Where In The World (incomplete)
....	RDB	-11	Where In The World (rehearsal)
....	RDB	-12	Where In The World –vMGsn (incomplete)
....	RDB	-13	Where In The World –vMGsn
....		-14	One More Twist –vMGsn[2] (incomplete)
....	RDB	-15	One More Twist –vMGsn (incomplete)
....	RDB	-16	One More Twist –vMGsn

[1]These are sequential numbers particular to this session and not to be confused with master or take numbers. This practice will apply to some of the sessions from now on. Lack of consistency may be confusing at times.
[2]*sa "One More Once."*

19 Mar 1962   (S)

DUKE ELLINGTON & HIS GROUP   Universal Studios[1]
RN, LB, PG, DE AB SWrd, MGsn.   Chicago, IL

....		-1	Love You Madly –vMGsn
....		-2	Love You Madly –vMGsn
....		-3	Love You Madly –vMGsn
....	RDB	-4	Love You Madly –vMGsn
....			Solitude (rehearsal)
....		-5	Solitude –vMGsn

> BS replaces DE.

....		-6	There's No One But You –vMGsn (incomplete)
....			There's No One But You –vMGsn (rehearsal0
....		-7	There's No One But You –vMGsn

> DE replaces BS.

....		-8	You Better Know It –vMGsn (incomplete)
....		-9	You Better Know It (incomplete)
....		-10	You Better Know It –vMGsn (incomplete)
....		-11	You Better Know It –vMGsn
....		-12	You Better Know It –vMGsn (incomplete)
....		-13	You Better Know It –vMGsn >>>

[1]A reliable source suggests that this session took place at the A&R Studio in New York; however, the band's travel log places it in Chicago for this date.

				29 Mar 1962 (S)
				A&R Studio
				New York City, NY

DUKE ELLINGTON & HIS GROUP
RN, LB, JHtn JH PG HC, DE AB SWrd, MGsn.

....		-1	I Feel So Good --vMGsn
....		-3	I Feel So Good --vMGsn
....		-4	I Feel So Good --vMGsn
....		-5	I Feel So Good --vMGsn

> BS replaces DE.

....		-1	Paris Blues --vMGsn (incomplete)
....		-2	Paris Blues --vMGsn (incomplete)
....		-3	Paris Blues --vMGsn
....			Paris Blues (incomplete)
....			Paris Blues (incomplete)
....		-4	Paris Blues --vMGsn
....			Paris Blues (incomplete)
....		-6	Paris Blues --vMGsn (incomplete)
....		-7	Paris Blues --vMGsn (incomplete)
....		-8	Paris Blues --vMGsn
....	RDB	-9	Paris Blues --vMGsn (incomplete)
....	RDB	-10	Paris Blues --vMGsn
....		-11	Paris Blues --vMGsn
....		-12	Paris Blues --vMGsn
....	Saj	-13	Paris Blues --vMGsn

> DE replaces BS.

....	Saj		Things Ain't What They Used To Be
....			I Got It Bad (rehearsal)
....	Saj	-2	I Got It Bad

> SG replaces SWrd.

....			Circle Blues[1] (rehearsal)
....		-1	Circle Blues (incomplete)
....	Saj	-2	Circle Blues

[1]aka "Jam On C."

		23 Apr 1962 (P)
		Howard Theater
		Washington, DC

DUKE ELLINGTON & HIS ORCHESTRA
CA RBws BBry RN, LB LC CCrs, JHtn JH RP PG HC, DE AB SWrd, MGsn.

....	Stompin' At The Savoy
....	Paris Blues
....	Things Ain't What They Used To Be
....	All Of Me
....	Jam With Sam
....	Diminuendo In Blue and Wailing Interval
....	Love You Madly --vMGsn
....	Do Nothin' Till You Hear From Me --vMGsn
....	One More Twist --vMGsn

> DE omitted, OM added.

....	St. Louis Blues
....	I'm So Tired Of Being An Angel --vOM
....	Award presentation to DE

> OM omitted, DE, BBgs added.

| .... | Tulip Or Turnip --vBBgs |

> BBgs omitted.

....	Asphalt Jungle Theme
....	Paris Blues
....	Kinda Dukish/Rockin' In Rhythm
....	I Got It Bad
....	Things Ain't What They Used To Be

DUKE ELLINGTON   (S)[1]
DE interviewed by Tony....

| .... | Interview |

[1]Backstage.

DUKE ELLINGTON & HIS ORCHESTRA   24 Apr 1962   (P)
CA RBws BBry RN, LB LC CCrs, JHtn JH RP PG HC, DE AB SWrd, MGsn.   Howard Theater
                                                                       Washington, DC

....   Take The "A" Train
....   Asphalt Jungle Twist
....   Mood Indigo –vMGsn
....   One More Twist –vMGsn

DUKE ELLINGTON & HIS ORCHESTRA   1 May 1962   (S)
CA RBws BBry RN, LB LC CCrs, JHtn JH RP PG HC, DE AB SWrd.   A&R Studio
                                                                       New York City, NY

....	Fan	-1	The "C" Jam Blues
....		-1	Take The "A" Train (incomplete)
....		-2	Take The "A" Train (incomplete)
....		-3	Take The "A" Train (incomplete)
....		-4	Take The "A" Train
....		-5	Take The "A" Train (insert)
....		-6	Take The "A" Train (insert)
....	Fan	-7?	Take The "A" Train
....	Fan		Happy-Go-Lucky Local
....	Fan	-1	Caravan
....		-1	Just A-Settin' And A-Rockin'
....	Fan	-2	Just A-Settin' And A-Rockin'
....	Fan	-2	Jam With Sam
....		-1	Paris Blues
....	Fan	-2	Paris Blues
....		-1	Ready, Go (incomplete)
....	Fan	-2	Ready, Go

DUKE ELLINGTON & HIS ORCHESTRA   1-4 May 1962[1]   (P)
CA RBws BBry RN, LB LC CCrs, JHtn JH RP PG HC, DE AB SWrd.   CBS Studios (tc)
                                                                       New York City, NY

....   Caravan
....   Rockin' In Rhythm

> DE with a studio orchestra, several vocalists and chorus, under the direction of Irwin Costal.

....   Medley[2]

> Entire band; studio orchestra, vocalists and chorus omitted.

....   Take The "A" Train

[1]Taping session; telecast on 8 May 1962.
[2]Including: Sophisticated Lady; Solitude –vMLne; I Got It Bad –vDL; I Let A Song Go Out Of My Heart/Don't Get Around Much Anymore –vRMtn; I'm Beginning To See The Light –vRMtn; Mood Indigo –vChorus; It Don't Mean A Thing –vRMtn, Chorus.

DUKE ELLINGTON & HIS ORCHESTRA   24 May 1962   (S)
CA RBws BBry RN, LB LC CCrs, JHtn JH RP PG HC, DE AB SWrd.   Bell Sound Studios
                                                                       New York City, NY

....	MFC	-1	Smada
....		-1	Flirtibird (incomplete)
....		-2	Flirtibird (incomplete)
....	RDB	-3	Flirtibird
....	Az	-4	Flirtibird
....		-1	What Am I Here For?
....	MFC	-2	What Am I Here For?
....	MFC	-1	Take The "A" Train

DUKE ELLINGTON & HIS ORCHESTRA   25 May 1962   (S)
CA RBws BBry RN, LB LC CCrs, JHtn JH RP PG HC, DE AB SWrd, MGsn   Bell Sound Studios
                                                                       New York City, NY

....		-1	I'm Gonna Go Fishin' (incomplete)
....		-2	I'm Gonna Go Fishin' (incomplete)
....	MFC	-3	I'm Gonna Go Fishin'
....	RDB	-1	Boo-Dah (incomplete)
....	Az	-2	Boo-Dah
....		-3	Boo-Dah (incomplete)
....	MFC	-4	Boo-Dah
....	Az	-1	Black And Tan Fantasy (incomplete)
....	Az	-2	Black And Tan Fantasy

> BS added.

....	MFC	-3	Black And Tan Fantasy >>>

> BS omitted.

.... Az   -1   One More Twist –vMGsn

> DE, MGsn.

....   -1   The Feeling Of Jazz –vMGsn (incomplete)
....   -2   The Feeling Of Jazz –vMGsn (incomplete)
.... Az   -3   The Feeling Of Jazz –vMGsn

DUKE ELLINGTON & HIS ORCHESTRA
CA RBws BBry RN, LB LC CCrs, JHtn JH RP PG HC, DE AB SWrd.

| 28 May 1962 | (S) |
| Bell Sound Studios |
| New York City, NY |

....   -1   Mr. Gentle And Mr. Cool (incomplete)
.... MFC -2   Mr. Gentle And Mr. Cool
....   -1   Perdido (incomplete)
.... Saj   -2   Perdido

> BS replaces DE.

.... Saj   -1   The Sky Fell Down
....   -1   Passion Flower (incomplete)
.... WEA -2   Passion Flower

DUKE ELLINGTON
DE interviewed by Patti Cavern.

| 31 May 1962 | (S) |
| NBC Studios (bc) |
| Washington, DC |

....   Interview

DUKE ELLINGTON & HIS ORCHESTRA WITH THE NATIONAL SYMPHONY ORCHESTRA
CA RBws BBry RN, LB LC CCrs, JHtn JH RP PG HC, DE AB SWrd, with the National Symphony Orchestra, Gunter Schuller conducting.

Constitution Hall   (P)

                               NIGHT CREATURE
.... VoA   - 1st Movement (Blind Bug)
.... VoA   - 2nd Movement (Stalking Monster)
.... VoA   - 3rd Movement (Dazzling Creature)

DUKE ELLINGTON & HIS RHYTHM
DE AB SWrd.

| 2 Jun 1962 | (P) |
| Howard University |
| Washington, DC |

.... SR   Take The "A" Train
.... SR   Satin Doll
.... SR   A Single Petal Of A Rose
....   Kinda Dukish

> MGsn added.

....   The Blues –vMGsn

DUKE ELLINGTON & HIS ORCHESTRA
CA RBws BBry RN, LB LC CCrs, JHtn JH RP PG HC, DE AB SWrd, MGsn.

Coliseum   (P)

.... VoA   Opening remarks by Willis Conover
.... VoA   Take The "A" Train
.... VoA   Kinda Dukish/Rockin' In Rhythm
.... VoA   Passion Flower
.... VoA   Things Ain't What They Used To Be
.... VoA   V.I.P.'s Boogie
.... VoA   Jam With Sam
.... VoA   Just Squeeze Me –vRN
.... VoA   Diminuendo In Blue and Wailing Interval

> BS replaces DE.

.... VoA   Take The "A" Train
.... VoA   Do Nothin' Till You Hear From Me -vMGsn
.... VoA   Why Was I Born? –vMGsn
.... VoA   One More Once –vMGsn
.... VoA   One More Once –vMGsn
.... VoA   Jones

DUKE ELLINGTON & HIS ORCHESTRA
CA RBws BBry RN, LB LC CCrs, JHtn JH RP PG HC, DE AB SWrd, MGsn, ME conducting.

| 3 Jun 1962 | (P) |
| Coliseum |
| Washington, DC |

.... VoA   Take The "A" Train
.... VoA   Perdido
.... VoA   Congo Square   >>>

> BS replaces DE.

.... VoA		The Feeling Of Jazz –vMGsn
.... VoA		The Blues –vMGsn
.... VoA		One More Once –vMGsn

> DE replaces BS.

.... VoA		I Got It Bad
.... VoA		Guitar Amour
.... VoA		Jam With Sam
.... VoA		Take The "A" Train

6 Jun 1962 (S)
Bell Sound Studios
New York City, NY

DUKE ELLINGTON & HIS ORCHESTRA
CA RBws BBry RN, LB LC CCrs, JHtn JH RP PG HC, DE AB SWrd.

....	Az[1]	-1	Taffy Twist
....		-1	Hy'a Sue
....	Az	-2	Hy'a Sue
....		-3	Hy'a Sue (incomplete)
....		-4	Hy'a Sue (incomplete)
....		-1	Cotton Tail (incomplete)
....		-2	Cotton Tail (incomplete)
....		-4	Cotton Tail (incomplete)
....	RDB	-5	Cotton Tail (incomplete)
....	RDB	-6	Cotton Tail (incomplete)
....	WEA	-7	Cotton Tail

> BS replaces DE.

....	-1	Misty
....	-2	Misty

[1]The original release on MFC is incomplete.

17 Jun 1962 (P)
Mineola Playhouse
Mineola, NY

DUKE ELLINGTON & HIS ORCHESTRA
CA RBws BBry RN, LB BCpr CCrs, JHtn JH RP PG HC, DE AB SWrd.

....	Stompin' At The Savoy
....	Tenderly
....	Honeysuckle Rose
....	Tea For Two
....	Matumbe
....	Summertime
....	Jam With Sam
....	Guitar Amour
....	Kinda Dukish/Rockin' In Rhythm
....	I Got It Bad
....	All Of Me
....	Things Ain't What They Used To Be
....	Medley[1]

[1]Including: Solitude; Don't Get Around Much Anymore.

21 Jun 1962 (S)
30th Street Studio
New York City, NY

DUKE ELLINGTON & HIS ORCHESTRA
CA RBws BBry RN, LB BWmn CCrs, JHtn JH RP PG HC, DE AB SWrd.

....	Co	CO75567	Mademoiselle de Paris

> BS replaces DE.

....	Co	CO75568	A Midnight In Paris

> DE replaces BS.

....	Co	CO67173[1]	Jingle Bells

[1]Remake.

26 Jun 1962 (S)
30th Street Studio
New York City, NY

DUKE ELLINGTON & HIS ORCHESTRA
CA RBws BBry RN, LB BCpr CCrs, JHtn JH RP PG HC, DE AB SWrd.

....	Co	CO69723-9[1]	The River Seine

> BS replaces DE.

....	Co	CO75582-10	I Wish You Love[2] >>>

.... > DE replaces BS.
.... Co   CO75949   My Heart Sings[3]

.... > BS added.
.... Co   CO75950-4   No Regrets

[1]Remake.
[2]*aka* "Que Reste T'il de Nos Amour."
[3]*aka* "En Ecoutant Mon Cœr Chanter."

                                                                          3 Jul 1962   (S)
DUKE ELLINGTON & HIS ORCHESTRA   Bell Sound Studios
CA RBws BBry RN, LB BCpr CCrs, JHtn JH RP PG HC, DRiv AB SWrd, JDle.   New York City, NY

....   -1   Drinking Again –vJDle
.... RDB   -2   Drinking Again –vJDle

.... > DE replaces DRiv.
.... MFC   -1   Jump For Joy –vRN
....   -2   I Let A Song Go Out Of My Heart/Don't Get Around Much Anymore –vRN
....   -3   I Let A Song Go Out Of My Heart (incomplete)
.... MFC   -4   I Let A Song Go Out Of My Heart/Don't Get Around Much Anymore –vRN
.... DJ   -2   Mack The Knife –vRN
.... Az   -1   Take The "A" Train –vRN (incomplete)
.... Az   -2   Take The "A" Train –vRN
.... RDB   -1   Slow Rhythm[1] (incomplete)
.... RDB   -2   Slow Rhythm (incomplete)
.... RDB   -3   Slow Rhythm (incomplete)
.... DJ   -4   The Feeling Of Jazz
....   -5   Slow Rhythm
....   -6   Slow Rhythm
....   -7   Slow Rhythm (incomplete)
.... MFC   -8   The Feeling Of Jazz
....   Slow Rhythm (incomplete)
....   Slow Rhythm (incomplete)

[1]*sa* "The Feeling Of Jazz."

                                                                          8 Jul 1962   (P)
DUKE ELLINGTON & HIS ORCHESTRA   Freebody Park
CA RBws BBry RN, LB BCpr CCrs, JHtn JH GHII PG HC, DE AB SWrd.   Newport, RI

.... > DE piano solo.

....   Kinda Dukish

.... > Entire band.
.... ToE   [1] Rockin' In Rhythm
.... ToE   [1] Passion Flower
.... ToE   [1] Things Ain't What They Used To Be
....   Jam With Sam
....   Do Nothin' Till You Hear From Me
....   Hy'a Sue

.... > TMk replaces DE.

....   Monk's Dream
....   Frère Monk

.... > DE replaces TMk.

....   Perdido
....   Guitar Amour
....   Broad Stream[2]
....   Satin Doll

[1]These titles have been included in the documentary "Newport Jazz Festival 1962."
[2]*aka* "U.M.G."; "P.M.G." (=Paul "Mex" Gonsalves).

                                                                          13 Jul 1962   (S)
DUKE ELLINGTON   Unidentified location (bc)
DE interviewed by Jack Harris.   Detroit, MI

....   Interview

.... > DE piano solo.

....   A Single Petal Of A Rose
....   Interview (ctd.)

17 Jul 1962   (S)
Universal Studios
Chicago, IL

<u>MILT GRAYSON</u>
Vcl, acc. by LStd dr, DE supervising.

....		-1	Prelude To A Kiss –vMGsn
....		-2	Prelude To A Kiss –vMGsn
....		-3	Flamingo (incomplete)
....		-3	Flamingo –vMGsn
....		-4	Flamingo –vMGsn
....		-5	Take Love Easy –vMGsn (incomplete)
....		-6	Take Love Easy –vMGsn
....		-7	I Let A Song Go Out Of My Heart –vMGsn (incomplete)
....		-8	I Let A Song Go Out Of My Heart –vMGsn
....		-9	I Let A Song Go Out Of My Heart –vMGsn (incomplete)
....		-10	I Let A Song Go Out Of My Heart (incomplete)
....		-11	I Let A Song Go Out Of My Heart –vMGsn
....		-12	I Let A Song Go Out Of My Heart –vMGsn
....		-13	Do Nothin' Till You Hear From Me (incomplete)
....		-14	Do Nothin' Till You Hear From Me –vMGsn (incomplete)
....		-15	Do Nothin' Till You Hear From Me –vMGsn
....		-16	Goin' Fishin' –vMGsn (incomplete)
....		-17	Goin' Fishin' –vMGsn (incomplete)
....		-18	Goin' Fishin' –vMGsn
....		-19	Goin' Fishin' –vMGsn (incomplete)
....		-20	Goin' Fishin' –vMGsn
....		-21	Solitude –vMGsn
....		-22	Mood Indigo –vMGsn
....			Medley[1]

[1]Including: Prelude To A Kiss –vMGsn; Flamingo –vMGsn; Take Love Easy –vMGsn; I Let A Song Go Out Of My Heart –vMGsn; Do Nothin' Till You Hear From Me –vMGsn; Goin' Fishin' –vMGsn; Solitude –vMGsn; Mood Indigo –vMGsn.

25 Jul 1962   (S)
A&R Studio
New York City, NY

<u>DUKE ELLINGTON & HIS OCTET</u>
BWmn BCpr CCrs, JH PG HC, DE AB SWrd.

....		-1	Blue Too (incomplete)
....		-2	Blue Too (incomplete)
....		-3	Blue Too (incomplete)
....		-4	Blue Too (incomplete)
....	WEA	-5	Blue Too
....		-1	Tune Up
....		-2	Tune Up (incomplete)
....		-3	Tune Up
....	WEA	-4	Tune Up

> BS replaces DE.

....		-1	Take It Slow[1]
....	WEA	-2	Take It Slow

> DE added.

....		-1	Telstar (incomplete)
....		-2	Telstar (incomplete)
....		-3	Telstar
....		-4	Telstar
....		-5	Telstar (incomplete)
....		-6	Telstar
....		-7	Telstar (incomplete
....	WEA	-8	Telstar

> JH HC, BS omitted.

....		-1	Like Late[2] (incomplete)
....		-2	Like Late (incomplete)
....		-3	Like Late (incomplete)
....		-4	Like Late (incomplete)
....		-5	Like Late
....	WEA	-6	Like Late
....		-4	Major
....	WEA	-5	Major
....		-1	Minor (incomplete)
....		-2	Minor (incomplete)
....		-3	Minor (incomplete)
....		-4	Minor
....		-5	Minor
....		-6	Minor
....	WEA	-7	Minor >>>

....		-8	Minor (incomplete)
....			"G" For Groove[3] (incomplete)
....		-1	"G" For Groove (incomplete)
....	WEA	-2	"G" For Groove

[1]*sa* "Self Portrait."
[2]*aka* "Spic And Span."
[3]*aka* "G"; "Groove."

18 Aug 1962   (S)
Rudy Van Gelder Studio
Englewood Cliffs, NJ

DUKE ELLINGTON & COLEMAN HAWKINS
RN, LB, JH CHwk HC, DE AB SWrd.

....	lps	11044	You Dirty Dog
....	lps	11045	Ray Charles' Place
....	lps	11046	Mood Indigo
....	lps	11047	The Jeep Is Jumpin'
....	lps	11048	Self Portrait Of The Bean[1]
....	lps	11049	Limbo Jazz[2]
....		11050	Limbo Blues
....	lps	11051	Wanderlust

> LB, JH HC omitted.

....	lps	11052	Solitude
....	lps	11053	The Recitic[3]

[1]This title is a derivative of *Grievin'.*
[2]*aka* "Imbo"; *sa* "Self Portrait"; "Take It Slow."
[3]*aka* "Backwards."

Aug 1962   (S)
Unspecified studio (bc)
Chicago, IL

DUKE ELLINGTON
DE interviewed by Sid McCoy; intermittent previously recorded music.

....	Interview

12 Sep 1962   (S)
24th St. Studios
New York City, NY

DUKE ELLINGTON & HIS ORCHESTRA
CA CW RBws BBry RN, LB BCpr CCrs, JHtn JH RP PG HC, DE AB SWrd, MGsn.

....		-1	Tootie For Cootie[1] (incomplete)
....		-2	Tootie For Cootie (incomplete)
....	Az	-3	Tootie For Cootie
....		-1	Broad Stream
....		-2	Broad Stream (incomplete)
....		-3	Broad Stream
....		-4	Broad Stream (incomplete)
....	WEA	-5	ESP[2]

> BS replaces DE.

....		-1	To Know You Is To Love You (incomplete)
....		-2	To Know You Is To Love You (incomplete)
....		-3	To Know You Is To Love You –vMGsn
....		-4	To Know You Is To Love You (incomplete)
....		-5	To Know You Is To Love You –vMGsn (incomplete)
....		-6	To Know You Is To Love You –vMGsn (incomplete)
....		-7	To Know You Is To Love You –vMGsn (incomplete)
....		-8	To Know You Is To Love You –vMGsn (incomplete)
....		-9	To Know You Is To Love You –vMGsn (incomplete)
....		-10	To Know You Is To Love You –vMGsn (incomplete)
....		-11	To Know You Is To Love You –vMGsn (incomplete)
....		-12	To Know You Is To Love You (incomplete)
....		-13	To Know You Is To Love You –vMGsn
....		-14	To Know You Is To Love You (incomplete)
....		-14	To Know You Is To Love You (incomplete)
....		-15	To Know You Is To Love You –vMGsn (incomplete)
....	WEA[3]	-16	To Know You Is To Love You –vMGsn

> DE replaces BS.

....	UTD[3]		A Medium Blues[4]

[1]"Tutti For Cootie" on some releases.
[2]*sa* "Broad Stream" (=Extra Special Paul).
[3]The original releases on WEA have been edited; a complete version of "A Medium Blues" can be found on UTD.
[4]*aka* "September 12th Blues," and as such on most commercial releases.

DUKE ELLINGTON & HIS ORCHESTRA | 13 Sep 1962 (S)
CA CW RBws BBry RN, LB BCpr CCrs, JHtn JH RP PG HC, DE AB SWrd, MGsn. | 24th St. Studios
New York City, NY

....		-1	Monk's Dream
....		-2	Monk's Dream (incomplete)
....		-3	Monk's Dream (incomplete)
....		-4	Monk's Dream (incomplete)
....	UTD	-5	Monk's Dream
....	UTD	-1	Frère Monk
....	WEA	-2	New Concerto For Cootie[1]
....		-3	New Concerto For Cootie

> BS added.

| .... | UTD | -1 | Cordon-Bleu |

> BS omitted.

....		-1	The Lonely Ones (incomplete)
....		-2	The Lonely Ones –vMGsn
....	WEA	-3	The Lonely Ones –vMGsn

[1]This title is a derivative of *Concerto For Cootie*.

DUKE ELLINGTON WITH CHARLIE MINGUS AND MAX ROACH | 17 Sep 1962 (S)
DE CM MR. | Sound Makers
New York City, NY

....	SSR	-1	Very Special
....	BN	-6	A Little Max[1]
....			A Little Max
....			A Little Max
....			A Little Max
....	BN	-14	A Little Max
....		-1	Fleurette Africaine
....	SSR	-2	Fleurette Africaine
....	BN	-1	REM Blues[2]
....	BN	-3	REM Blues
....	SSR	-1	Wig Wise
....	BN	-2	Switch Blade
....	BN	-4	Switch Blade
....	SSR	-1	Caravan
....	SSR	-2	Money Jungle
....	BN	-3	Solitude
....	SSR	-4	Solitude
....	SSR	-3	Warm Valley
....	BN	-1	Backward Country Boy Blues (incomplete)
....	BN	-2	Backward Country Boy Blues

[1]aka "Parfait."
[2]Stands for Roach, Ellington, Mingus; this title is a derivative of *Blues For Blanton*.

CAT ANDERSON & HIS ORCHESTRA | 18 Sep 1962 (S)
CA, CCrs, PG, DBag AB SMrt, DE supervising. | A&R Studio
New York City, NY

....	RDB	-4	De-De-Dada-Dum[1]
....	RDB	-3	En Flight
....			Tuesday Blues

[1]aka "De-De-De-Da-Dum"; sa "Organ Grinder's Swing."

DUKE ELLINGTON | 19 Sep 1962 (S)
DE, George T. Simon and Pastor John G. Gensel interviewed by Art Linkletter. | NBC Studios (tc)
New York City, NY

| .... | | | Interview |

> DE piano solo.

| .... | | | Little African Flower[1] |

> CW and studio orchestra, directed by Skitch Henderson added.

| .... | Mon | | Montage Tonight |

[1]sa "Fleurette Africaine." Announced as *Little Flower of Africa*.

DUKE ELLINGTON & HIS ORCHESTRA | 20 Sep 1962 (S)
CA CW RBws RN, LB BCpr CCrs, JHtn JH RP PG HC, DE AB SWrd. | Rudy Van Gelder Studio
Englewood Cliffs, NJ

| .... | 11108 | | Limbo Jazz, part 2 |

	24 Sep 1962	(P)

DUKE ELLINGTON & HIS ORCHESTRA
CA CW RBws RN, LB BCpr CCrs, JHtn JH RP PG HC, DE AB SWrd, JS MGsn.

24 Sep 1962   (P)
Town Hall
New York City, NY

.... Take The "A" Train
.... Asphalt Jungle Theme
.... Black And Tan Fantasy—Creole Love Call—The Mooche
.... Stompin' At The Savoy
.... Tenderly
.... Satin Doll
.... Summertime
.... Guitar Amour
.... Jam With Sam
.... I Got It Bad
.... All Of Me
.... Things Ain't What They Used To Be
.... The Feeling Of Jazz –vJS
.... Take The "A" Train
.... New Concerto For Cootie
.... Tootie For Cootie
.... Show Me –vJS
.... My Heart Belongs To Daddy –vJS
.... Katiusha –vJS
.... I'm Beginning To See The Light –vJS
.... Things Ain't What They Used To Be –vJS
.... Skin Deep
.... Diminuendo In Blue and Wailing Interval
.... One More Once –vJS MGsn
.... Mood Indigo

26 Sep 1962[1]   (S)
Rudy Van Gelder Studio
Englewood Cliffs, NJ

DUKE ELLINGTON & JOHN COLTRANE
JCtr, DE AB SWrd.

.... lps   11114   Stevie[2]

> JCtr, DE AB EJ.

.... lps   11115   In A Sentimental Mood

> JCtr, DE JGsn EJ.

.... lps   11116   Angelica[3]
.... lps   11117   Big Nick[4]

> JCtr, DE AB SWrd.

.... lps   11118   My Little Brown Book
.... lps   11119   The Feeling Of Jazz

> JCtr, DE JGsn EJ.

.... lps   11120   Take The Coltrane

[1]Contradicting the Impulse master ledger, the CD release gives 9 Sep 1962 as date for this recording session.
[2]*aka* "Blues In C Minor."
[3]*aka* "Angelique."
[4]*aka* "Bick Nick."

27 Sep 1962[1]   (P)
ABC Studios (tc)
New York City, NY

EDIE ADAMS AND DUKE ELLINGTON WITH ORCHESTRA
Vcl, acc. by JH HC, DE and a studio orchestra, directed by Peter Matz.

.... Medley[2]
.... Satin Doll –vEA

[1]Telecast on 23 Oct 1962.
[2]Including: I Got It Bad –vEA; I'm Beginning To See The Light –vEA; Sophisticated Lady –vEA; Take The "A" Train.

Listed above is only the Ellington portion of the program.

c 5 Oct 1962   (S)
Unidentified location (bc)
Salt Lake City, UT

DUKE ELLINGTON
DE and Dr. Wm. Fowler interviewed by Paul Smith.

.... Interview

30 Oct 1962   (S)
Studios CKNW (bc)
Vancouver, BC

DUKE ELLINGTON
DE interviewed by Jack Cullen.

.... Vin[1]   Interview

[1]Incomplete On Vin.

DUKE ELLINGTON & BILLY STRAYHORN
DE and BS interviewed by Bob Smith.

....   Interview

[1]The date of broadcast is not known.

8 Nov 1962   (P)
Western Washington State College
Bellingham, WA

DUKE ELLINGTON & HIS ORCHESTRA
CA CW RBws RN, LB BCpr CCrs, JHtn JH RP PG HC, DE EShp SWrd.

....   Take The "A" Train
....   Asphalt Jungle Theme
....   Black And Tan Fantasy—Creole Love Call—The Mooche
....   Perdido
....   Tenderly
....   Honeysuckle Rose
....   New Concerto For Cootie
....   Tootie For Cootie
....   Guitar Amour
....   Summertime

19 Nov 1962   (P)
Cullen Auditorium
Houston, TX

DUKE ELLINGTON & HIS ORCHESTRA
CA CW RBws RN, LB BCpr CCrs, JHtn JH RP HC, DE EShp SWrd, MGsn.

....   Take The "A" Train
....   Black And Tan Fantasy—Creole Love Call—The Mooche
....   Stompin' At The Savoy
....   Tenderly
.... Az   Honeysuckle Rose
.... Az   Anatomy Of A Murder
....   Summertime
....   Guitar Amour
....   I Got It Bad
....   All Of Me
....   Things Ain't What They Used To Be
.... Az   Jam With Sam
....   Medley[1]
....   Jones
....   Take The "A" Train
....   New Concerto For Cootie
....   Tootie For Cootie
....   Skin Deep
....   Diminuendo In Blue and Wailing Interval
....   The Blues –vJGsm
....   One More Once –vJGsm

    > JHtn RP HC, DE.

....   Monologue –DE narration

[1]Including: Satin Doll; Solitude; Don't Get Around Much Anymore; Mood Indigo; I'm Beginning To See The Light;
Sophisticated Lady; Caravan; Do Nothin' Till You Hear From Me –vMGsn; Just Squeeze Me –vRN; It Don't Mean
A Thing –vRN; I Let A Song Go Out Of My Heart/Don't Get Around Much Anymore.

29 Nov 1962   (S)
Universal Studios
Chicago, IL

DUKE ELLINGTON & HIS ORCHESTRA
CA CW RBws RN, LB BCpr CCrs, JHtn JH RP PG HC, DE EShp SWrd.

.... Atc   3220-4   Christopher Columbus
.... Atc   3221-4   Let's Get Together
.... Rpr   3222-6   Goodbye

30 Nov 1962   (S)
Universal Studios
Chicago, IL

DUKE ELLINGTON & HIS ORCHESTRA
CA CW RBws RN, LB BCpr CCrs, JHtn JH RP PG HC, DE EShp SWrd.

.... Atc   3223-5   Chant Of The Weed[1]
.... Rpr   3224 (1708-14) Volupté
.... Atc   3225-3   I'm Getting Sentimental Over You
.... Rpr   3226-2   One O'Clock Jump
....   3227   Afro-Bossa

[1]The arrangement is by Don Redman.

It is possible that the 29 and 30 Nov sessions were indeed one long session that ran past midnight.

DUKE ELLINGTON & HIS GROUP   10 Dec 1962   (P)
fl, DE EShp SWrd, BMo RLay.   NBC Studios (tc)
                                                                    New York City, NY

....   I Got It Bad –vBMo
....   In A Sentimental Mood –vRLay
....   Don't Get Around Much Anymore –vBMo

DUKE ELLINGTON & HIS ORCHESTRA   11 Dec 1962   (S)
CA CW RBws EPtn RN, LB BCpr CCrs, JHtn JH RP PG HC, DE EShp SWrd.   Fine Studios
                                                                    Bayside, NY

.... Rpr   3368   Tuxedo Junction

> BS replaces DE.

.... Atc   3369   Ciribiribin

> DE replaces BS.

.... Atc   3370-10   It's A Lonesome Old Town When You're Not Around

DUKE ELLINGTON WITH ORCHESTRA   NBC Studios (tc)   (P)
DE with the NBC studio orchestra.   New York City, NY

....   Guitar Amour

JOHNNY NASH AND DUKE ELLINGTON WITH ORCHESTRA   12 Dec 1962   (P)
JNsh and DE with the NBC studio orchestra.   NBC Studios (tc)
                                                                    New York City, NY

....   I Surrender, Dear –vJNsh

DUKE ELLINGTON & HIS ORCHESTRA   13 Dec 1962   (S)
CA CW RBws RN, LB BCpr CCrs, JHtn JH RP PG HC, DE EShp SWrd.   Fine Studios
                                                                    Bayside, NY

.... Atc   3381-8   Minnie The Moocher
....   3381-9   Minnie The Moocher
.... Rpr   3382-12   Sentimental Journey

DUKE ELLINGTON WITH ORCHESTRA   NBC Studios (tc)   (P)
BBry and DE with the NBC studio orchestra.   New York City, NY

....   Take The "A" Train

DUKE ELLINGTON & HIS ORCHESTRA   14 Dec 1962   (S)
CA BBry RBws RN, LB BCpr CCrs, JHtn JH RP PG HC, DE EShp SWrd.   Fine Studios
                                                                    Bayside, NY

....   1704-14[1] Silk Lace
....   3375-2[1]   Cherokee
.... Rpr   3388-6   When It's Sleepy-Time Down South
.... Atc   3389-2   For Dancers Only
....   1711-8   The Eighth Veil
....   The Eighth Veil (coda)
.... Rpr   1711-16   The Eighth Veil
....   3226-8[2]   One O'Clock Jump
....   3226-10[2] One O'Clock Jump

[1]Remakes.
[2]Both recordings are in the Smithsonian collection.

DUKE ELLINGTON WITH ORCHESTRA   NBC Studios (tc)   (P)
BBry and DE with the NBC studio orchestra.   New York City, NY

....   Perdido

> DE piano solo.

.... Stv   A Single Petal Of A Rose

DUKE ELLINGTON & HIS ORCHESTRA   20 Dec 1962   (S)
CA CW RBws RN, LB BCpr CCrs, JHtn JH RP PG HC, DE EShp SWrd.   Fine Studios
                                                                    Bayside, NY

....   3383-5   Rhapsody In Blue
....   3383-7   Rhapsody In Blue
.... Rpr   3383-8   Rhapsody In Blue
....   3384-1   Contrasts[1]
.... Atc   3384-2   Contrasts   >>>

....	Rpr	3385-5[2]	Sleep, Sleep, Sleep
....	Rpr	1704-21[3]	Silk Lace
....	Rpr	1710-10	Pyramid

[1]*aka* "Oodles Of Noodles."
[2]In the liner notes for the Mo CD-set the same master and take number has been assigned to *Sleep, Sleep, Sleep; Artistry In Rhythm; Absinthe; Sempre Amoré.*
[3]Remake.

29 Dec 1962   (S)
Fine Studios
Bayside, NY

DUKE ELLINGTON & HIS ORCHESTRA
CA CW RBws RN, LB BCpr CCrs, JHtn JH RP PG HC, DE EShp SWrd.

....	Rpr	3386-5	Don't Get Around Much Anymore
....		3387-3	Auld Lang Syne[1] (incomplete)
....	Atc	3387-3	Auld Lang Syne
....	Atc	3387-7	Auld Lang Syne (insert)
....		1700-3	Purple Gazelle[2]
....		1700-5	Purple Gazelle

[1]*aka* "Candlelight Waltz."
[2]*aka* "Cali"; "Ragtime Cha Cha"; *sa* "Angelica"; "Angelique."

31 Dec 1962   (P)
Empire Room, Waldorf Astoria Hotel (bc)
New York City, NY

DUKE ELLINGTON & HIS ORCHESTRA
CA CW RBws RN, LB BWmn BCpr CCrs, JHtn JH RP PG HC, DE EShp AB SWrd, MGsn.

....	Take The "A" Train
....	Satin Doll
....	Rockin' In Rhythm
....	Sophisticated Lady
....	The Eighth Veil
....	Mood Indigo
....	Tootie For Cootie
....	Do Nothin' Till You Hear From Me –vMGsn
....	Things Ain't What They Used To Be

1 Jan 1963[1]   (P)
Empire Room, Waldorf Astoria Hotel (bc)
New York City, NY

DUKE ELLINGTON & HIS ORCHESTRA
CA CW RBws RN, LB BWmn BCpr CCrs, JHtn JH RP PG HC, DE EShp AB SWrd, MGsn.

....	Take The "A" Train
....	The "C" Jam Blues
....	Silk Lace
....	Love You Madly –vMGsn
....	Take The "A" Train

[1]Broadcast on 16 Apr 1963.

3 Jan 1963   (S)
Fine Studios
Bayside, NY

DUKE ELLINGTON & HIS ORCHESTRA
CA CW RBws RN, LB BCpr CCrs, JHtn JH RP PG HC, DE EShp SWrd.

....	Atc	3377-15	The Midnight Sun Will Never Set
....		3378-8	At The Woodchoppers' Ball
....		3378-9	At The Woodchoppers' Ball
....	Rpr	3378	At The Woodchoppers' Ball

> BS replaces DE.

....		3372-4	Artistry In Rhythm
....		3372-5	Artistry In Rhythm
....		3372-10	Artistry In Rhythm
....	Rpr	3372-11	Artistry In Rhythm

> DE replaces BS.

....		1700[1]	Purple Gazelle
....		3381	Minnie The Moocher

[1]Remake.

4 Jan 1963   (S)
Fine Studios
Bayside, NY

DUKE ELLINGTON & HIS ORCHESTRA
CA CW RBws RN, LB BCpr CCrs, JHtn JH RP PG HC, BS EShp SWrd.

....	Rpr	3371-5	Smoke Rings

> DE replaces BS.

....	Rpr	3373	The Waltz You Saved For Me
....	Atc	3375	Cherokee >>>

.... Rpr   1709-1   Bonga[1]
....   1709   Bonga

[1]*aka* "Empty Town Blues."

DUKE ELLINGTON & HIS ORCHESTRA   5 Jan 1963   (S)
CA CW RBws RN, LB BCpr CCrs, JHtn JH RP PG HC, DE BS EShp SWrd.   Fine Studios
                                                         Bayside, NY

.... Rpr   1699-8   Angû

  > BS omitted.

.... Rpr   1708-6   Afro-Bossa
.... Rpr   1700-16[1]   Purple Gazelle

  > BS replaces DE.

.... Rpr   1701-9   Absinthe[2]

  > DE replaces BS.

.... Rpr   1702-3   Moonbow[3]
.... Rpr   1703-11   Sempre Amoré[4]
....   1707-41   Tigress[5] (incomplete)
....   1707-42   Tigress
....   1707-43   Tigress (incomplete)
.... Rpr   1707-45   Tigress

[1]Remake.
[2]*aka* "Ricard"; "Lament For An Orchid"; "Fluid Jive"; "Water Lily."
[3]*aka* "Call 'Em."
[4]*sa* "Frontin."
[5]*sa* "Telstar."

DUKE ELLINGTON & HIS RHYTHM   8 Jan 1963   (S)
DE EShp SWrd.   Fine Studios
                                                      Bayside, NY

.... DET   1705   Resume #1[1]
.... DET   1712   Resume #2[2, 3]

[1]*aka* "Piano Summation for Afro-Bossa, part 1." Including: Silk Lace; Tigress; Pyramid; Bonga; Sempre Amoré; The Eighth Veil.
[2]*aka* "Piano Summation for Afro-Bossa, part 2." Including: Volupté; Absinthe; Moonbow; Purple Gazelle; Afro-Bossa; Angû.
[3]Aural evidence suggests that BS may also be playing on sections of this set.

DUKE ELLINGTON & JOHN COLTRANE   ?15 Jan 1963   (S)[1]
JCtr, DE; no further information available.   Rudy Van Gelder Studio
                                                  Englewood Cliffs, NJ

....   11295   [In A Sentimental Mood]
....   11296   [My Little Brown Book]

[1]This session is listed in the Impulse master ledger without any further comment. Apparently these titles are remakes of the 26 Sep 1962 session, however, they seem not to have been issued. On the other hand, DE had left the U.S.A. on 9 Jan 1963 to tour Europe, and it is unlikely that he took it upon himself to travel the distance for this recording session.

DUKE ELLINGTON & HIS ORCHESTRA   19 Jan 1963   (P)
CA CW RBws RN, LB BCpr CCrs, JHtn JH RP PG HC, DE EShp SWrd, MGsn.   Free Trade Hall
                                                       Manchester, England

....   Take The "A" Train
....   Bula[1]
....   Kinda Dukish/Rockin' In Rhythm
....   Caliné[2]
....   The Eighth Veil
....   Pyramid
....   Asphalt Jungle Theme
....   Guitar Amour
....   Cop Out
....   Jam With Sam
....   Main Stem
....   New Concerto For Cootie
....   Tootie For Cootie
....   The Star-Crossed Lovers
....   Things Ain't What They Used To Be
....   All Of Me
....   Perdido
....   The Blues –vMGsn
....   Do Nothin' Till You Hear From Me –vMGsn   >>>

> JHtn RP HC, DE.

....   Monologue –DE narration

> Entire band.

....   Take The "A" Train
....   God Save The Queen

[1]*sa* "Afro-Bossa."
[2]Variant spelling "Kaline"; *sa* "Silk Lace."

DUKE ELLINGTON & HIS ORCHESTRA
Same personnel.

....   Take The "A" Train
....   Bula
....   Kinda Dukish/Rockin' In Rhythm
....   Caliné
....   The Eighth Veil
....   Pyramid
....   Asphalt Jungle Theme
....   Guitar Amour
....   Cop Out
....   Jam With Sam
....   Main Stem
....   New Concerto For Cootie
....   Tootie For Cootie
....   The Star-Crossed Lovers
....   Things Ain't What They Used To Be
....   All Of Me
....   Perdido
....   The Blues –vMGsn
....   Do Nothin' Till You Hear From Me –vMGsn
....   One More Once –vMGsn[1]

> JHtn RP HC, DE.

....   Monologue –DE narration

> Entire band.

....   Take The "A" Train
....   God Save The Queen

[1]Announced as "One More Bossa Nova."

There are tapes in circulation which are claimed to have been recorded at the Bristol (18 Jan) and Liverpool (20 Jan) events. In fact, they have been compiled by using material from these Manchester concerts.

21+22 Jan 1963[1]   (P)
Granada Studios (tc)
London, England

DUKE ELLINGTON & HIS ORCHESTRA
CA CW RBws RN, LB BCpr CCrs, JHtn JH RP PG HC, DE EShp SWrd, MGsn

....   Take The "A" Train
.... MM   The "C" Jam Blues
....   The Eighth Veil
....   Rockin' In Rhythm

> BS replaces DE.

.... MJ   Angû

> DE replaces BS.

.... MM   Mood Indigo

> DE piano solo.

.... MM   A Single Petal Of A Rose

> Entire band.

.... MM   Don't Get Around Much Anymore –vMGsn
.... MM   Diminuendo In Blue and Wailing Interval

[1]Telecast on 13 Feb 1963.

Jan 1963   (S)
Fairfield Hall (tc)
Croydon, England

DUKE ELLINGTON
DE interviewed by Sven Lindahl for Swedish TV.[1]

....   Interview

[1]The program contains segments of the concert at Fairfield Hall, Croydon, England, on 25 Jan 1963.

DUKE ELLINGTON
DE interviewed by Jo Joseph.

....   Interview

[1]Broadcast on 16 Apr 1963.

DUKE ELLINGTON
DE interviewed by Timme Rosenkrantz.

....   Interview

DUKE ELLINGTON & HIS ORCHESTRA WITH THE PARIS SYMPHONY ORCHESTRA
CA CW RBws RN, LB BCpr CCrs, JHtn JH RP PG HC, DE EShp SWrd, with the Paris
Symphony Orchestra, Gérard Calvi conducting.

			NIGHT CREATURE
....			- 1st Movement (Blind Bug) (rehearsal)
....			- 1st Movement (Blind Bug) (rehearsal)
....		2433-1	- 1st Movement (Blind Bug)
....		2433 alt.	- 1st Movement (Blind Bug)
....		2435-1	- 3rd Movement (Dazzling Creature) (incomplete)
....		2435-2	- 3rd Movement (Dazzling Creature) (incomplete)
....		2435-3	- 3rd Movement (Dazzling Creature) (incomplete)
....		2435-4	- 3rd Movement (Dazzling Creature) (incomplete)
....		2435-5	- 3rd Movement (Dazzling Creature)
....		2435-6	- 3rd Movement (Dazzling Creature) (incomplete)
....		2435-7	- 3rd Movement (Dazzling Creature) (incomplete)
....		2435-8	- 3rd Movement (Dazzling Creature) (incomplete)
....		2435-9	- 3rd Movement (Dazzling Creature) (incomplete)
....		2435-10	- 3rd Movement (Dazzling Creature) (incomplete)
....		2435-11	- 3rd Movement (Dazzling Creature) (incomplete)
....		2435	- 3rd Movement (Dazzling Creature) (incomplete)
....		2435	- 3rd Movement (Dazzling Creature) (incomplete)
....	Rpr	2435-12	- 3rd Movement (Dazzling Creature)
....	Az	2434-1	- 2nd Movement (Stalking Monster) (incomplete)
....	Az	2434-2	- 2nd Movement (Stalking Monster)
....		2434-3	- 2nd Movement (Stalking Monster)
....		2438-1	HARLEM (incomplete)
....		2438-2	HARLEM (incomplete)
....		2438-3	HARLEM (incomplete)
....		2438-4	HARLEM
....		2438-5	HARLEM (incomplete)
....		2438-6	HARLEM (incomplete)
....		2438-7	HARLEM (incomplete)
....		2438-8	HARLEM (incomplete)
....		2438-9	HARLEM (incomplete)
....		2438-9	HARLEM (incomplete)
....		2438-10	HARLEM (incomplete)
....		2438-11	HARLEM (incomplete)
....		2438-12	HARLEM (incomplete)
....			HARLEM (insert)
....			HARLEM (insert)
....			HARLEM (insert)
....			HARLEM (insert)
....		2438-13	HARLEM (incomplete)
....			HARLEM (insert)
....	Rpr	2438-14	HARLEM

DUKE ELLINGTON & HIS ORCHESTRA
CA CW RBws RN, LB BCpr CCrs, JHtn JH RP PG HC, DE EShp SWrd, MGsn.

....		Take The "A" Train
....		SUITE THURSDAY
....	Atc	- Misfit Blues
....	Atc	- Schwiphti
....	Atc	- Zweet Zurzday
....	Atc	- Lay-By
....	Atc	Bula
....	Atc	Kinda Dukish/Rockin' In Rhythm
....		Caliné >>>

....	Atc	The Eighth Veil
....	Rpr	Pyramid
....	Atc	Asphalt Jungle Theme
....		Guitar Amour
....	Atc	Jam With Sam
....	Atc	Cop Out
....		Stompy Jones
....	Atc	New Concerto For Cootie
....	Atc	Tootie For Cootie
....		Echoes Of Harlem
....	Atc	The Star-Crossed Lovers
....		Things Ain't What They Used To Be
....	Atc	All Of Me
....	Atc	Perdido
....		The Blues −vMGsn
....		Do Nothin' Till You Hear From Me −vMGsn
....		One More Once −vMGsn
....		Take The "A" Train

DUKE ELLINGTON & HIS ORCHESTRA
CA CW RBws RN, LB BCpr CCrs, JHtn JH RP PG HC, DE EShp SWrd, MGsn.

2 Feb 1963   (P)
Théâtre de l'Olympia
Paris, France

....	Az	Take The "A" Train
....	Az	Bula
....	Az	Kinda Dukish/Rockin' In Rhythm
....	Az	The Eighth Veil
....	Az	Pyramid
....	Az	Asphalt Jungle Theme
....	Az	Guitar Amour
....	Az	Cop Out
....	Az	Jam With Sam
....	Az	Stompy Jones
....	Az	Misfit Blues
....	Az	Schwiphti
....	Az	New Concerto For Cootie
....	Az	Tootie For Cootie
....	Az	The Star-Crossed Lovers
....	Az	Things Ain't What They Used To Be
....	Az	Perdido
....	Az	The Blues −vMGsn
....	Az	Do Nothin' Till You Hear From Me −vMGsn
....	Az	One More Once −vMGsn
....	Az	Take The "A" Train

DUKE ELLINGTON & HIS ORCHESTRA
Same personnel.

....		Take The "A" Train
....		Bula
....		Kinda Dukish/Rockin' In Rhythm
....		Caliné
....		The Eighth Veil
....		Pyramid
....		Asphalt Jungle Theme
....		Guitar Amour
....		Cop Out
....		Jam With Sam
....		Take The "A" Train
....	Az	Misfit Blues
....		Schwiphti
....		New Concerto For Cootie
....		Tootie For Cootie
....		Echoes Of Harlem
....		The Star-Crossed Lovers
....		Things Ain't What They Used To Be
....		All Of Me
....		Perdido
....		The Blues −vMGsn
....		Do Nothin' Till You Hear From Me −vMGsn
....		One More Once −vMGsn
....		Just Squeeze Me −vRN
....		Take The "A" Train −vRN
....		Take The "A" Train
....		Take The "A" Train

<table>
<tr><td></td><td colspan="2">DUKE ELLINGTON
DE interviewed by Gun Allroth.</td><td>3 Feb 1963   (S)
Bulltofta Airport (bc)
Malmö, Sweden</td></tr>
</table>

| .... | | Interview |

<table>
<tr><td colspan="3">DUKE ELLINGTON & HIS ORCHESTRA
CA CW RBws RN, LB BCpr CCrs, JHtn JH RP PG HC, DE EShp SWrd, MGsn.</td><td>5 Feb 1963   (P)
Unidentified location
Helsinki, Finland</td></tr>
</table>

....		Take The "A" Train
....		Bula
....		Kinda Dukish/Rockin' In Rhythm
....		Caliné
....		The Eighth Veil
....	Az	Pyramid
....	Az	Asphalt Jungle Theme
....		Guitar Amour
....		Jam With Sam
....		Cop Out
....		New Concerto For Cootie
....		Tootie For Cootie
....	MJ	The Star-Crossed Lovers
....		Things Ain't What They Used To Be
....		Perdido
....		The Blues –vMGsn
....		Do Nothin' Till You Hear From Me –vMGsn
....		One More Once –vMGsn

<table>
<tr><td colspan="3">DUKE ELLINGTON & HIS ORCHESTRA
CA CW RBws RN, LB BCpr CCrs, JHtn JH RP PG HC, DE EShp SWrd, MGsn.</td><td>6 Feb 1963   (P)
Konserthuset
Stockholm, Sweden</td></tr>
</table>

....		Take The "A" Train
....		Bula
....		Kinda Dukish/Rockin' In Rhythm
....		Pyramid
....		Asphalt Jungle Theme
....		Guitar Amour
....		New Concerto For Cootie
....		Tootie For Cootie
....	MFC	The Star-Crossed Lovers
....		Things Ain't What They Used To Be
....	JL	Perdido
....		Do Nothin' Till You Hear From Me –vMGsn
....	MFC	The "C" Jam Blues

<table>
<tr><td colspan="3">DUKE ELLINGTON & HIS ORCHESTRA
CA CW RBws RN, LB BCpr CCrs, JHtn JH RP PG HC, DE EShp SWrd, ABbs.</td><td>7 Feb 1963   (S)
Cirkus Djurgården
Stockholm, Sweden</td></tr>
</table>

....	Az	Take Love Easy –vABbs
....	Az	Take Love Easy –vABbs
....		The Star-Crossed Lovers
....		The Star-Crossed Lovers

The above is a rehearsal session.

<table>
<tr><td colspan="3">DUKE ELLINGTON & HIS ORCHESTRA
MGsn added, otherwise same personnel.</td><td>(tc)[1]   (P)</td></tr>
</table>

....	Vid	Mood Indigo
....	Vid	Take The "A" Train –vABbs
....	Vid	Do Nothin' Till You Hear From Me –vMGsn
....	Vid	The Blues –vMGsn
....	Vid	The Eighth Veil
....	Vid	The Star-Crossed Lovers
....	Vid	Sophisticated Lady
....	Vid	Honeysuckle Rose
....	Az	Take Love Easy –vABbs

> DE EShp SWrd.

| .... | Vid | Dancers In Love |

> Entire band.

....	Vid	I Got It Bad
....	Vid	Guitar Amour
....	Vid	Tootie For Cootie >>>

.... Vid   Come Sunday –vABbs
.... Vid   Bula

[1]Telecast on 6 Apr 1963. The closing *Mood Indigo* is a repeat of the first title.

8 Feb 1963   (S)
Europa Film Studio
Stockholm, Sweden

DUKE ELLINGTON & HIS ORCHESTRA
WITH MEMBERS OF THE STOCKHOLM SYMPHONY ORCHESTRA
CA CW RBws AM RN, LB BCpr CCrs JPsn, JHtn JH RP PG HC, DE EShp SWrd, with 17 members
of the Stockholm Symphony Orchestra.

NIGHT CREATURE
....   2433   - 1st Movement (Blind Bug)
....   2433-3   - 1st Movement (Blind Bug)
....   2433-4   - 1st Movement (Blind Bug)
.... Rpr 2433-5   - 1st Movement (Blind Bug)
....   2434-2   - 2nd Movement (Stalking Monster) (incomplete)
....   2434   - 2nd Movement (Stalking Monster) (incomplete)

> BS added.

....   2434-3   - 2nd Movement (Stalking Monster) (incomplete)

> BS omitted.

....   2434   - 2nd Movement (Stalking Monster) (incomplete)
....   2434   - 2nd Movement (Stalking Monster) (incomplete)
.... Rpr 2434-4   - 2nd Movement (Stalking Monster)
....   2435-1   - 3rd Movement (Dazzling Creature) (incomplete)
....   2435-2   - 3rd Movement (Dazzling Creature) (incomplete)
....   2435-3   - 3rd Movement (Dazzling Creature)
....   2435-4   - 3rd Movement (Dazzling Creature)

> BS added.

....   - 3rd Movement (Dazzling Creature) (rehearsal)

> BS omitted.

....   2435-5   - 3rd Movement (Dazzling Creature)

DUKE ELLINGTON & HIS ORCHESTRA
CA CW RBws RN, LB BCpr CCrs, JHtn JH RP HC, DE EShp SWrd, MGsn.

Falkoner Centret   (P)
Copenhagen, Denmark

....   Take The "A" Train
....   Bula
....   Kinda Dukish/Rockin' In Rhythm
....   Caliné
....   The Eighth Veil
....   Pyramid
....   Asphalt Jungle Theme
....   Guitar Amour
....   Jam With Sam
....   New Concerto For Cootie
....   Tootie For Cootie
....   The Star-Crossed Lovers
....   Things Ain't What They Used To Be
....   All Of Me
....   Perdido
....   The Blues –vMGsn
....   Do Nothin' Till You Hear From Me –vMGsn

DUKE ELLINGTON & HIS ORCHESTRA
PG added, otherwise same personnel.

....   Take The "A" Train
....   Bula
....   Kinda Dukish/Rockin' In Rhythm
....   Caliné
....   The Eighth Veil
....   Pyramid
....   Asphalt Jungle Theme
....   Guitar Amour
....   Jam With Sam
....   New Concerto For Cootie
....   Tootie For Cootie
....   The Star-Crossed Lovers
....   Things Ain't What They Used To Be
....   All Of Me
....   Perdido
....   The Blues –vMGsn
....   Do Nothin' Till You Hear From Me –vMGsn
....   One More Once –vMGsn

DUKE ELLINGTON & HIS ORCHESTRA
CA CW RBws RN, LB BCpr CCrs, JHtn JH RP PG HC, DE EShp SWrd, MGsn.

....   Take The "A" Train
....   Kinda Dukish/Rockin' In Rhythm
....   Caliné
....   New Concerto For Cootie
....   Tootie For Cootie
....   The Star-Crossed Lovers
....   Things Ain't What They Used To Be
....   Perdido
....   The Blues –vMGsn
....   Do Nothin' Till You Hear From Me –vMGsn

DUKE ELLINGTON & HIS ORCHESTRA
MGsn omitted, otherwise same personnel.

....   Take The "A" Train
....   Kinda Dukish/Rockin' In Rhythm

DUKE ELLINGTON & HIS ORCHESTRA
CA CW RBws RN, LB BCpr CCrs, JHtn JH RP PG HC, DE EShp SWrd.

.... MFC   Stompy Jones
.... MFC   Guitar Amour
.... MFC   Pyramid

DUKE ELLINGTON & HIS RHYTHM
DE EShp SWrd.

.... MFC   Dancers In Love

DUKE ELLINGTON & HIS ORCHESTRA
CA CW RBws RN, LB BCpr CCrs, JHtn JH RP PG HC, DE EShp SWrd, MGsn.

....   Take The "A" Train
....   Bula
....   Kinda Dukish/Rockin' In Rhythm
....   Caliné
....   The Eighth Veil
....   Pyramid
....   Asphalt Jungle Theme
....   Guitar Amour
....   Cop Out
....   Jam With Sam
....   Main Stem

                                   SUITE THURSDAY
....   - Misfit Blues
....   - Schwiphti
....   - Zweet Zurzday
....   - Lay-By

....   New Concerto For Cootie
....   Tootie For Cootie
....   The Star-Crossed Lovers
....   Things Ain't What They Used To Be
....   I Got It Bad
....   Jeep's Blues
....   Perdido
....   The Blues –vMGsn
....   Do Nothin' Till You Hear From Me –vMGsn
....   One More Once –vMGsn

DUKE ELLINGTON
DE interviewed by Dan Marshall.

....   Interview

DUKE ELLINGTON & HIS ORCHESTRA
WITH MEMBERS OF THE HAMBURG SYMPHONY ORCHESTRA
CA CW RBws RN, LB BCpr CCrs, JHtn JH RP PG HC, DE EShp SWrd, with members of the
Hamburg Symphony Orchestra.

.... Rpr   2436   Non-Violent Integration[1]   >>>

[1]This title is a derivative of *Grand Slam Jam.*

15 Feb 1963   (P)
Deutschlandhalle (bc)
Berlin, Germany

DUKE ELLINGTON & HIS ORCHESTRA
CA CW RBws RN, LB BCpr CCrs, JHtn JH RP PG HC, DE EShp SWrd, MGsn.

....		Take The "A" Train
....		Bula
....		Kinda Dukish/Rockin' In Rhythm
....		Caliné
....		The Eighth Veil
....		Pyramid
....		Asphalt Jungle Theme
....		HARLEM
....		Stompy Jones
....		New Concerto For Cootie
....		Tootie For Cootie
....		The Star-Crossed Lovers
....		Things Ain't What They Used To Be
....		Perdido
....		The Blues –vMGsn
....		Do Nothin' Till You Hear From Me –vMGsn
....		One More Once –vMGsn
....		Mood Indigo
....		Take The "A" Train

DUKE ELLINGTON   Unidentified location (bc) (S)
DE interviewed by Dieter Pruess.   Berlin, Germany

| .... | | Interview |

19 Feb 1963   (P)
Kongresshaus
Zurich, Switzerland

DUKE ELLINGTON & HIS ORCHESTRA
CA CW RBws RN, LB BCpr CCrs, JHtn JH RP PG HC, DE EShp SWrd, MGsn.

....	JPo	Take The "A" Train
....	JPo	Bula
....	JPo	Caliné
....	JPo	The Eighth Veil
....	JPo	Asphalt Jungle Theme
....	JPo	HARLEM
....	JPo	Guitar Amour
....	JPo	Kinda Dukish/Rockin' In Rhythm

> PG, DE EShp SWrd.

| .... | JPo | Happy Reunion |

> Entire band.

....	JPo	Jam With Sam
....		Take The "A" Train
....		New Concerto For Cootie
....		Tootie For Cootie
....		The Star-Crossed Lovers
....		All Of Me
....		Things Ain't What They Used To Be
....		Perdido
....		The Blues –vMGsn
....		Do Nothin' Till You Hear From Me –vMGsn
....		One More Once –vMGsn
....		Black And Tan Fantasy

21 Feb 1963   (S)
Studio Zanibelli
Milan, Italy

DUKE ELLINGTON & HIS SEXTET[1] WITH THE LA SCALA SYMPHONY ORCHESTRA
DE EShp SWrd, with the La Scala Symphony Orchestra.

....		La Scala, She Too Pretty To Be True[2] (incomplete)
....		La Scala, She Too Pretty To Be True (incomplete)
....	Rpr 2437	La Scala, She Too Pretty To Be True

[1]The contributions of CW, LB, RP PG have been overdubbed; they did not attend the recording session.
[2]Originally titled "La Scala, She Too Pretty Blues"; variant spelling "La Scala, She Too Pretty To Be Blue."

DUKE ELLINGTON & HIS ORCHESTRA   Conservatorio Guiseppe Verdi (tc?) (P)
CA CW RBws RN, LB BCpr CCrs, JHtn JH RP PG HC, DE EShp SWrd, MGsn.

| .... | Pab | Bula |
| .... | Pab | Asphalt Jungle Theme   >>> |

.... Pab		Guitar Amour[1]
.... Pab		Silk Lace
.... MJ		Pyramid
.... Pab		In A Sentimental Mood[2]
.... MJ		Jam With Sam
.... MJ		Take The "A" Train –vEShp
.... Pab		Broad Stream
.... MJ		New Concerto For Cootie
.... MJ		Echoes Of Harlem
.... Pab		The Star-Crossed Lovers
.... MJ		Things Ain't What They Used To Be
.... MJ		All Of Me
.... MJ		The Blues –vMGsn
.... MJ		One More Once –vMGsn
.... MJ		Mood Indigo

[1]Erroneously as "Paris Blues" on Pab.
[2]Erroneously as "I'm Getting Sentimental Over You" on Pab.

22 Feb 1963   (S)
Barclay Studios
Paris, France

DUKE ELLINGTON'S JAZZ VIOLINS
BCpr, RP PG, SGrp SAs RN, DE EShp SWrd.

....	Atc	3523-1	Limbo Jazz

> BS replaces DE.

....	Az	3524-2	Pretty Little One
....	Atc	3524-3	Pretty Little One

> DE added.

....	Az	3525-1	String Along With Strings (incomplete)
....	Az	3525-2	String Along With Strings (incomplete)
....		3525-3	String Along With Strings (incomplete)
....	Atc	3525-4	String Along With Strings

> BS omitted.

....		3526-1	The Feeling Of Jazz (incomplete)
....		3526-3	The Feeling Of Jazz (incomplete)
....		3526-4	The Feeling Of Jazz
....		3526-5	The Feeling Of Jazz
....		3526-6	The Feeling Of Jazz (incomplete)
....	Atc	3526-7	The Feeling Of Jazz

> BCpr, RP PG omitted.

....	Atc	3527-1	Take The "A" Train

> BCpr, RP PG added.

....	Az	3528	Tricky's Lick (rehearsal)
....	Az	3528	Tricky's Lick (incomplete)
....	Az	3528-2	Tricky's Lick (incomplete)
....	Az	3528	Tricky's Lick (incomplete)
....	Az	3528-3	Tricky's Lick
....		3528-5	Tricky's Lick (incomplete)
....		3528	Tricky's Lick (incomplete)
....		3528-6	Tricky's Lick (rehearsal)
....		3528-7	Tricky's Lick (rehearsal)
....	Atc	3528-8	Tricky's Lick
....	Atc	3529	Blues In C

> SGrp, DE EShp SWrd.

....		3530-1	In A Sentimental Mood (incomplete)
....		3530-2	In A Sentimental Mood (incomplete)
....		3530-3	In A Sentimental Mood
....		3530-4	In A Sentimental Mood (incomplete)
....	Atc	3530-5	In A Sentimental Mood

> SGrp omitted, SAs added.

....		3531-1	Don't Get Around Much Anymore (incomplete)
....	Az	3531-3	Don't Get Around Much Anymore (incomplete)
....	Atc	3531-4	Don't Get Around Much Anymore

> SAs omitted, RN added.

....		3532-1	Day Dream (incomplete)
....	Atc	3532-2	Day Dream
....		3532-3	Day Dream (incomplete) >>>

> SGrp SAs added.

....		3533-1	Cotton Tail (incomplete)
....	Az	3533-2	Cotton Tail
....	Atc	3533-3	Cotton Tail

23 Feb 1963   (P)
Théâtre de l'Olympia
Paris, France

DUKE ELLINGTON & HIS ORCHESTRA
CA CW RBws RN, LB BCpr CCrs, JHtn JH RP PG HC, DE EShp SWrd, MGsn.

....	Take The "A" Train
....	HARLEM
....	Black And Tan Fantasy—Creole Love Call—The Mooche
....	Stompin' At The Savoy
....	Caliné
....	The Eighth Veil
....	Pyramid
....	Kinda Dukish/Rockin' In Rhythm

> PG, DE EShp SWrd.

....	Happy Reunion

> Entire band.

....	Broad Stream
....	Take The "A" Train –vEShp
....	Caravan
....	Tootie For Cootie
....	Day Dream
....	Things Ain't What They Used To Be
....	Skin Deep
....	The Blues –vMGsn
....	I'm Just A Lucky So-And-So –vMGsn
....	Mr. Gentle And Mr. Cool

DUKE ELLINGTON & HIS ORCHESTRA
Same personnel.

....		Take The "A" Train
....	Atc	HARLEM
....		Stompin' At The Savoy
....	Rpr	Black And Tan Fantasy—Creole Love Call—The Mooche
....	Atc	Rose Of The Rio Grande
....		Caliné
....		The Eighth Veil
....		Pyramid
....		Kinda Dukish/Rockin' In Rhythm

> PG, DE EShp SWrd.

....	Happy Reunion

> Entire band.

....	Az	Broad Stream
....		Take The "A" Train –vEShp
....	Atc	Happy-Go-Lucky Local
....		New Concerto For Cootie
....		Tootie For Cootie
....	Rpr	Echoes Of Harlem
....		The Star-Crossed Lovers
....	Rpr	Things Ain't What They Used To Be
....	Atc	On The Sunny Side Of The Street
....		Skin Deep
....	Rpr	The Blues –vMGsn
....	Rpr	Do Nothin' Till You Hear From Me –vMGsn
....		One More Once –vMGsn
....		Just Squeeze Me –vRN
....		Diminuendo In Blue and Wailing Interval

24 Feb 1963   (S)
Studio Hoche
Paris, France

BILLY STRAYHORN & BEATRICE BENJAMIN
BS and BBjm; DE supervising.

....		You Don't Know (rehearsal)
....	-1	You Don't Know –vBBjm
....	-2	You Don't Know –vBBjm
....	-3	You Don't Know –vBBjm
....	-1	A Nightingale Sang In Berkeley Square -vBBjm (incomplete)
....	-2	A Nightingale Sang In Berkeley Square –vBBjm >>>

The second rehearsal session of this day took place without DE or BS participating.

BILLY STRAYHORN WITH DOLLAR BRAND AND BEATRICE BENJAMIN
SAs, JGze MNts, BBjm; DE supervising.

....	EN		The Man I Love –vBBjm
....	EN		Soon –vBBjm
....	EN		Lover Man –vBBjm
....	EN		Spring Will Be Late This Year –vBBjm
....	EN		I Could Write A Book –vBBjm
....		-1	Darn That Dream –vBBjm
....	EN	-2	Darn That Dream –vBBjm

> BS replaces JGze.

....			A Nightingale Sang At Berkeley Square –vBBjm (rehearsal)
....	EN	-3	A Nightingale Sang At Berkeley Square –vBBjm
....		-1	Your Love Has Faded –vBBjm
....		-2	Your Love Has Faded –vBBjm
....		-3	Your Love Has Faded –vBBjm (incomplete)
....		-4	Your Love Has Faded –vBBjm (incomplete)
....		-5	Your Love Has Faded –vBBjm
....	EN	-6	Your Love Has Faded –vBBjm
....		-7	Your Love Has Faded –vBBjm

DUKE ELLINGTON & BEATRICE BENJAMIN
DE, BBjm.

| .... | EN | | I Got It Bad –vBBjm |
| .... | Az | | Solitude (rehearsal) |

> SAs (pizzicato) added.

| .... | | | Solitude –vBBjm |
| .... | EN | | Solitude –vBBjm |

ALICE BABS & DUKE ELLINGTON
Vcl, acc. by DE GR ChG, plus four french horns.

28 Feb 1963   (S)
Studio Hoche
Paris, France

....		-1	Azure –vABbs
....	Az	-2	Azure –vABbs (rehearsal)
....		-3	Azure –vABbs (incomplete)
....			Azure –vABbs
....			Azure –vABbs (rehearsal)
....		-4	Azure –vABbs (incomplete)
....		-5	Azure –vABbs (incomplete)
....	Rpr	-6	Azure –vABbs
....	Az	-7	Azure –vABbs (incomplete)
....	Az	-8	Azure –vABbs
....			Satin Doll –vABbs (rehearsal)
....	Az	-1	Satin Doll –vABbs
....	Rpr	-2	Satin Doll –vABbs
....	Az	-1	Untitled Lullaby (incomplete)
....	Az	-2	Untitled Lullaby –vABbs
....	Rpr	-3	Untitled Lullaby –vABbs
....		-1	Things Ain't What They Used To Be (incomplete)
....	Az	-2	Things Ain't What They Used To Be
....		-3	Things Ain't What They Used To Be (incomplete)
....		-4	Things Ain't What They Used To Be –vABbs (incomplete)
....		-5	Things Ain't What They Used To Be –vABbs (incomplete)
....		-6	Things Ain't What They Used To Be (incomplete)
....		-7	Things Ain't What They Used To Be –vABbs (incomplete)
....		-8	Things Ain't What They Used To Be –vABbs (incomplete)
....	Az	-9	Things Ain't What They Used To Be –vABbs
....		-10	Things Ain't What They Used To Be –vABbs (incomplete)
....		-11	Things Ain't What They Used To Be –vABbs (incomplete)
....		-12	Things Ain't What They Used To Be –vABbs (incomplete)
....		-13	Things Ain't What They Used To Be –vABbs (incomplete)
....		-14	Things Ain't What They Used To Be (incomplete)
....		-15	Things Ain't What They Used To Be –vABbs (incomplete)
....		-16	Things Ain't What They Used To Be –vABbs (incomplete)

ALICE BABS & DUKE ELLINGTON
Vcl, acc. by DE GR KC[1].

1 Mar 1963   (S)
Studio Hoche
Paris, France

| .... | Az | -1 | La De Doody Do (incomplete) |
| .... | Az | -2 | La De Doody Do –vABbs (incomplete)   >>> |

....	Az	-3	La De Doody Do (incomplete)
....	Rpr	-4	La De Doody Do –vABbs
....	Rpr	-1	I Didn't Know About You –vABbs
....		-1	Take Love Easy –vABbs
....	Az	-2	Take Love Easy –vABbs
....	Rpr	-3	Take Love Easy –vABbs
....	Az	-1	I'm Beginning To See The Light (incomplete)
....	Az	-2	I'm Beginning To See The Light –vABbs (incomplete)
....		-3	I'm Beginning To See The Light –vABbs
....	Rpr	-4	I'm Beginning To See The Light –vABbs

> PGo JHko GB added.

| .... | Az | -1 | The "C" Jam Blues –vABbs |
| .... | Rpr | -2 | The "C" Jam Blues –vABbs |

> PGo JHko GB, KC omitted, ChG, plus four french horns added.

....		-1	Serenade To Sweden –vABbs
....	Az	-2	Serenade To Sweden –vABbs (incomplete)
....	Az	-3	Serenade To Sweden –vABbs (incomplete)
....	Az	-4	Serenade To Sweden –vABbs
....	Rpr	-5	Serenade To Sweden –vABbs
....	Az	-1	The Boy In My Dreams –vABbs[2] (incomplete)
....	Az	-2	The Boy In My Dreams –vABbs (incomplete)
....	Rpr	-3	The Boy In My Dreams –vABbs
....	Az	-1	Stoona –vABbs (incomplete)
....	Rpr	-2	Stoona –vABbs
....		-1	Come Sunday –vABbs
....	Az	-2	Come Sunday –vABbs
....	Az	-3	Come Sunday –vABbs (incomplete)
....	Rpr	-4	Come Sunday –vABbs
....	Rpr	-1	Babsie –vABbs

> BS replaces DE.

....		-1	Something To Live For –vABbs (incomplete)
....		-2	Something To Live For –vABbs
....	Az	-3	Something To Live For
....		-4	Something To Live For –vABbs
....	Rpr	-5	Something To Live For –vABbs

> DE, ABbs.

| .... | Az | -1 | Strange Visitor –vABbs[3] (incomplete) |

> GR added.

| .... | Az | -2 | Strange Visitor –vABbs (incomplete) |

> BS GR KC, ABbs.

....	Az	-3	Strange Visitor –vABbs (incomplete)
....	Az	-4	Strange Visitor –vABbs (incomplete)
....	Az	-5	Strange Visitor –vABbs (incomplete)
....		-6	Strange Visitor –vABbs (incomplete)

> ABbs piano solo.

| .... | Rpr | -7 | Strange Visitor –vABbs |

[1]Some sources suggest that ChG and/or PGig were on dr for this session.
[2]sa "The Girl In My Dreams."
[3]aka "Baby, Baby, Baby."

31 Mar 1963   (P)
Bolling AFB
Washington, DC

DUKE ELLINGTON & HIS ORCHESTRA
WC CW RBws RN, LB BCpr CCrs, JHtn JH RP PG HC, DE EShp SWrd, MGsn.

....	Sophisticated Lady
....	Jack The Bear
....	Take The "A" Train
....	I Let A Song Go Out Of My Heart/Don't Get Around Much Anymore –vRN
....	Jump For Joy –vRN
....	The Star-Crossed Lovers
....	Things Ain't What They Used To Be
....	All Of Me
....	New Concerto For Cootie
....	Tootie For Cootie

> DE EShp SWrd.

| .... | Volupté   >>> |

> Entire band.

....			Caravan
....			One More Once –vMGsn
....			One More Once –vMGsn

DUKE ELLINGTON & HIS OCTET
RN, JHtn JH RP PG HC, DE EShp SWrd.

....		-1	Got Nobody Now (incomplete)
....		-2	Got Nobody Now (incomplete)
....		-3	Got Nobody Now (incomplete)
....		-4	Got Nobody Now (incomplete)
....		-5	Got Nobody Now (incomplete)
....		-6	Got Nobody Now
....	WEA	-7	Got Nobody Now
....		-1	Jeep's Blues
....		-2	Jeep's Blues (incomplete)
....		-3	Jeep's Blues (incomplete)
....		-4	Jeep's Blues
....		-5	Jeep's Blues
....	WEA	-6	Jeep's Blues
....		-1	M.G.[1]
....		-2	M.G. (incomplete)
....		-3	M.G. (incomplete)
....		-4	M.G. (incomplete)
....		-5	M.G.
....		-6	M.G. (incomplete)
....	WEA	-7	M.G.
....		-1	Killian's Lick[2] (incomplete)
....		-2	Killian's Lick (incomplete)
....		-3	Killian's Lick (incomplete)
....	WEA	-4	Killian's Lick

[1]Stands for Matthew Gee; *sa* "It's Strange To Be Forgotten."
[2]*aka* "Kel[l]un's Lick."

DUKE ELLINGTON & HIS OCTET
RN, JHtn JH RP PG HC, DE EShp SWrd.

....			Blousons Noir (incomplete)
....		-3	Blousons Noir
....	WEA	-4	Blousons Noir
....		-2	Elysée (incomplete)
....		-3	Elysée (incomplete)
....		-5	Elysée (incomplete)
....		-6	Elysée
....	WEA	-7	Elysée
....		-1	Blue Rose
....		-3	Blue Rose (incomplete)
....		-4	Blue Rose (incomplete)
....		-5	Blue Rose
....		-6	Blue Rose
....	WEA	-9	Blue Rose
....		-6	Blousons Noir (incomplete)
....		-7	Blousons Noir (incomplete)
....	Az	-8	Blousons Noir
....			Butter And Oleo (rehearsal)
....	WEA	-1	Butter And Oleo

DUKE ELLINGTON
DE, Pastor John G. Gensel and Father Norman J. O'Connor, interviewed by Nat Henthoff.

| .... | | | Interview |

DUKE ELLINGTON WITH ORCHESTRA
DE with a studio orchestra, directed by Skitch Henderson.

| .... | | | Satin Doll |
| .... | | | Jones |

DUKE ELLINGTON & HIS OCTET
RN, JHtn JH RP PG HC, DE EShp SWrd.

| .... | | | Serenade To Sweden (rehearsal)   >>> |

> DE piano solo.

....   Second Portrait Of The Lion (incomplete)
....   Second Portrait Of The Lion (incomplete)
....   Second Portrait Of The Lion (incomplete)

> EShp SWrd added.

....   Unidentified title (rehearsal)

> Entire band.

....   -4   Stoona (incomplete)
....   WEA   -5   Stoona
....   -1   Serenade To Sweden (incomplete)
....   WEA   -2   Serenade To Sweden
....   -3   Serenade To Sweden
....   -1   Bad Woman[1] (incomplete)
....   Bad Woman (rehearsal)
....   -3   Bad Woman (incomplete)
....   -6   Bad Woman
....   Az   -8   Bad Woman
....   WEA   -10   Bad Woman
....   -1   Harmony In Harlem
....   -2   Harmony In Harlem (incomplete)
....   -3   Harmony In Harlem (incomplete)
....   WEA   -4   Harmony In Harlem

[1]Complete: "Bad Woman, Walk Right In."

17 May 1963[1]   (S)
DUKE ELLINGTON & MERCER ELLINGTON   Unspecified studio (bc)
DE and ME talking over previously recorded music.   New York City, NY

....   Introductory remarks for a VoA broadcast.

[1]Date of broadcast; probably recorded at an earlier date.

25 May 1963   (P)
DUKE ELLINGTON & HIS ORCHESTRA   U.S. Army Installation (bc)
EPtn CW REsn RN, LB BCpr CCrs, JHtn JH RP PG HC, DE EShp SWrd.   Wiesbaden, Germany

....   Take The "A" Train
....   Star Dust
....   Happy-Go-Lucky Local
....   Deep Purple
....   Volupté
....   Diminuendo In Blue and Wailing Interval
....   Medley[1]
....   Perdido

> JHtn RP HC, DE.

....   Monologue –DE narration

> Entire band.

....   Tootie For Cootie

[1]Including: Solitude; Don't Get Around Much Anymore; Mood Indigo; I'm Beginning To See The Light; Sophisticated Lady; Caravan; Do Nothin' Till You Hear From Me; I Got It Bad; Just Squeeze Me –vRN; I Let A Song Go Out Of My Heart/Don't Get Around Much Anymore.

26 May 1963   (P)
DUKE ELLINGTON & HIS ORCHESTRA   7th Army Dining and Dancing Center (bc)
EPtn CW REsn RN, LB BCpr CCrs, JHtn JH RP PG HC, DE EShp SWrd.   Stuttgart, Germany

....   Take The "A" Train
....   Afro-Bossa
....   Silk Lace
....   Satin Doll
....   Boo-Dah
....   Jeep's Blues
....   Happy-Go-Lucky Local

31 May 1963   (P)
DUKE ELLINGTON   Arlanda Airport (bc)
No particulars available.   Stockholm, Sweden

....   Interview

4 Jun 1963   (P)
Grona Lund
Stockholm, Sweden

DUKE ELLINGTON & HIS ORCHESTRA
EPtn CW REsn RN, LB BCpr CCrs, JHtn JH RP PG HC, DE EShp SWrd.

....   Take The "A" Train
....   Afro-Bossa
....   Perdido
....   Medley[1]

[1]Including: Satin Doll; Solitude; Don't Get Around Much Anymore; Mood Indigo; I'm Beginning To See The Light;
Sophisticated Lady; Caravan; Do Nothin' Till You Hear From Me; I Got It Bad; Just Squeeze Me –vRN; It Don't Mean
A Thing –vRN; I Let A Song Go Out Of My Heart/Don't Get Around Much Anymore.

5 Jun 1963   (P)
Grona Lund
Stockholm, Sweden

DUKE ELLINGTON & HIS ORCHESTRA
EPtn CW REsn RN, LB BCpr CCrs, JHtn JH RP PG HC, DE EShp SWrd.

....   Take The "A" Train
....   Afro-Bossa
....   Perdido
....   Medley[1]
....   Take The "A" Train

[1]Including: Satin Doll; Solitude; Don't Get Around Much Anymore; Mood Indigo; I'm Beginning To See The Light;
Sophisticated Lady; Caravan; Do Nothin' Till You Hear From Me; I Got It Bad; Just Squeeze Me –vRN; It Don't Mean
A Thing –vRN; I Let A Song Go Out Of My Heart/Don't Get Around Much Anymore.

6 Jun 1963   (P)
Grona Lund
Stockholm, Sweden

DUKE ELLINGTON & HIS ORCHESTRA
EPtn CW REsn RN, LB BCpr CCrs, JHtn JH RP PG HC, DE EShp SWrd.

....   Take The "A" Train
....   Afro-Bossa
....   Perdido
....   Medley[1]
....   Satin Doll

[1]Including: Satin Doll; Solitude; Don't Get Around Much Anymore; Mood Indigo; I'm Beginning To See The Light;
Sophisticated Lady; Caravan; Do Nothin' Till You Hear From Me; I Got It Bad; Just Squeeze Me –vRN; It Don't Mean
A Thing –vRN; I Let A Song Go Out Of My Heart/Don't Get Around Much Anymore.

7 Jun 1963   (P)
Grona Lund
Stockholm, Sweden

DUKE ELLINGTON & HIS ORCHESTRA
EPtn CW REsn RN, LB BCpr CCrs, JHtn JH RP PG HC, DE EShp SWrd.

....   Take The "A" Train
....   Afro-Bossa
....   Perdido
....   Medley[1]
....   Take The "A" Train

[1]Including: Satin Doll; Solitude; Don't Get Around Much Anymore; Mood Indigo; I'm Beginning To See The Light;
Sophisticated Lady; Caravan; Do Nothin' Till You Hear From Me; I Got It Bad; Just Squeeze Me –vRN; It Don't Mean
A Thing –vRN; I Let A Song Go Out Of My Heart/Don't Get Around Much Anymore.

8 Jun 1963   (P)
Grona Lund
Stockholm, Sweden

DUKE ELLINGTON & HIS ORCHESTRA
EPtn CW REsn RN, LB BCpr CCrs, JHtn JH RP PG HC, DE EShp SWrd.

....   Take The "A" Train
....   Afro-Bossa
....   Perdido
....   Medley[1]
....   Take The "A" Train

[1] Including: Satin Doll; Solitude; Don't Get Around Much Anymore; Mood Indigo; I'm Beginning To See The Light;
Sophisticated Lady; Caravan; Do Nothin' Till You Hear From Me; I Got It Bad; Just Squeeze Me –vRN; It Don't Mean
A Thing –vRN; I Let A Song Go Out Of My Heart/Don't Get Around Much Anymore.

Danse In   (P)

DUKE ELLINGTON & HIS ORCHESTRA
DE omitted, otherwise same personnel.

....   Boo-Dah
....   Laura
....   Main Stem

> DE added.

.... Az   Take The "A" Train   >>>

....	Az	SUITE THURSDAY
....	Az	- Misfit Blues
....	Az	- Schwiphti
....	Az	- Zweet Zurzday
....	Az	- Lay-By
....	Az	Deep Purple
....	Az	Silk Lace
....	Az	New Concerto For Cootie
....	Az	Tootie For Cootie
....	Az	The Star-Crossed Lovers
....	Az	Things Ain't What They Used To Be

> DE EShp SWrd.

....	Az	Interlude

> JH added.

....	Az	I Didn't Know About You

> Entire band.

....	Az	All Of Me
....	Az	Jeep's Blues
....	Az	Rose Of The Rio Grande
....	Az	Black And Tan Fantasy
....	Az	Kinda Dukish/Rockin' In Rhythm
....	Az	In A Sentimental Mood
....	Az	Mr. Gentle And Mr. Cool
....	Az	Lullaby Of Birdland
....	Az	Mood Indigo—Sophisticated Lady
....	Az	I Let A Song Go Out Of My Heart/Don't Get Around Much Anymore –vRN
....	Az	One More Once –vRN
....	Az	One More Once –vRN

9 Jun 1963   (P)
Grona Lund
Stockholm, Sweden

DUKE ELLINGTON & HIS ORCHESTRA
EPtn CW REsn RN, LB BCpr CCrs, JHtn JH RP PG HC, DE EShp SWrd.

....	Az	Take The "A" Train
....	Az	Afro-Bossa
....	Az	Perdido
....	Az	Medley[1]
....	Az	Take The "A" Train

[1]Including: Satin Doll; Solitude; Don't Get Around Much Anymore; Mood Indigo; I'm Beginning To See The Light; Sophisticated Lady; Caravan; Do Nothin' Till You Hear From Me; I Got It Bad; Just Squeeze Me –vRN; It Don't Mean A Thing –vRN; I Let A Song Go Out Of My Heart/Don't Get Around Much Anymore.

DUKE ELLINGTON & HIS ORCHESTRA
Same personnel.

....	Take The "A" Train
....	Afro-Bossa
....	Perdido
....	Medley[1]
....	Take The "A" Train

[1]Including: Satin Doll; Solitude; Don't Get Around Much Anymore; Mood Indigo; I'm Beginning To See The Light; Sophisticated Lady; Caravan; Do Nothin' Till You Hear From Me; I Got It Bad; Just Squeeze Me –vRN; It Don't Mean A Thing –vRN; I Let A Song Go Out Of My Heart/Don't Get Around Much Anymore.

19 Jun 1963   (P)
Admiralen Danse Hall (bc)
Malmö, Sweden

DUKE ELLINGTON & HIS ORCHESTRA
EPtn CW REsn RN, LB BCpr CCrs, JHtn JH RP PG HC, DE EShp SWrd.

....		Take The "A" Train
....		The "C" Jam Blues
....		Volupté
....		Kinda Dukish/Rockin' In Rhythm
....	Az	For He's A Jolly Good Fellow
....		Jeep's Blues
....		Perdido
....		I Let A Song Go Out Of My Heart/Don't Get Around Much Anymore –vRN

1963   (P)
Unidentified location (bc?)
U.S.A.

DUKE ELLINGTON & HIS ORCHESTRA
CA CW REsn RN, LB BCpr CCrs, JHtn JH RP PG HC, DE EShp SWrd.

....	Satin Doll—Sophisticated Lady

			4 Jul 1963	(P)
			NBC Studios (tc)	
			New York City, NY	

DUKE ELLINGTON WITH ORCHESTRA
DE with a studio orchestra, directed by Skitch Henderson.

.... Volupté
.... Conversation
.... Action In Alexandria

The above is the Ellington portion of this event.

6 Jul 1963	(P)	
Freebody Park		
Newport, RI		

DUKE ELLINGTON & HIS ORCHESTRA
CA CW REsn RN, LB BCpr CCrs, JHtn JH RP PG HC, DE EShp SWrd.

.... Take The "A" Train
.... Afro-Bossa
.... The Eighth Veil
.... Kinda Dukish/Rockin' In Rhythm
.... Silk Lace
.... Lullaby Of Birdland
.... Az Black And Tan Fantasy—Creole Love Call—The Mooche
.... Guitar Amour
.... Tootie For Cootie
.... I Got It Bad
.... Things Ain't What They Used To Be
.... Diminuendo In Blue and Wailing Interval

18 Jul 1963	(S)	
A&R Studio		
New York City, NY		

DUKE ELLINGTON & HIS ORCHESTRA
CA CW REsn RN, LB BCpr CCrs, JHtn JH RP PG HC, DE EShp SWrd.

.... -1 Action In Alexandria
.... -2 Action In Alexandria (incomplete)
.... -3 Action In Alexandria
.... Action In Alexandria (rehearsal)
.... WEA -4 Action In Alexandria
.... -5[1] Action In Alexandria
.... -6[1] Action In Alexandria
.... Az -7[1] Action In Alexandria
.... -1 TAJM[2] (incomplete)
.... -3 TAJM
.... -4 TAJM (incomplete)
.... -5 TAJM
.... -6 TAJM (incomplete)
.... WEA -7 TAJM
.... -1 Elf
.... -2 Elf
.... -3 Elf (incomplete)
.... WEA -4 Elf[3]
.... WEA -1 July 18th Blues

[1]The version as per takes 5 thru 7 is different from that of the previous takes.
[2]*sa* "For He's A Jolly Good Fellow."
[3]"Isfahan" on WEA; part of the future *Far East Suite.*

CBS Studios (tc)[1]	(P)	

DUKE ELLINGTON
DE on the Keefe Brasselle show.

> DE piano solo.

.... Banquet Scene[2]—Caravan

> Studio orchestra, directed by Charles Sanford, added.

.... Satin Doll

[1]Taping session; telecast on 20 Aug 1963.
[2]Part of the music for *Timon Of Athens.*

Jul/Aug 1963	(S)	
Studios WENR (bc)		
Chicago, IL		

DUKE ELLINGTON
DE interviewed by David Wayne.

.... Interview

12 Aug 1963	(P)	
Music Circus		
Lambertville, NJ		

CAB CALLOWAY WITH THE DUKE ELLINGTON ORCHESTRA
Vcl and directing, with CA CW REsn RN, LB BCpr CCrs, JHtn JH RP PG HC, EShp SWrd.

.... Az Nova Exotique[1]
.... Az The Eighth Veil   >>>

> BS added.

....	Az	Silk Lace
....	Az	Lullaby Of Birdland
....	Az	Guitar Amour
....	Az	Tootie For Cootie
....	Az	I Got It Bad
....	Az	Things Ain't What They Used To Be
....	Az	Things Ain't What They Used To Be
....	Az	Medley[2]
....		Get Happy –vCCwy
....		Our Day Will Come –vCCwy
....		I Want To Be Around –vCCwy
....	Az	St. James Infirmary –vCCwy
....		Let's Rock The Boat –vCCwy
....		Minnie The Moocher –vCCwy
....		Take The "A" Train

[1]sa "Afro-Bossa"; "Bula."
[2]Including: Sophisticated Lady; Caravan; Do Nothin' Till You Hear From Me; Just Squeeze Me –vRN; It Don't Mean A Thing –vRN; I Let A Song Go Out Of My Heart/Don't Get Around Much Anymore.

DE was unable to attend this concert because of other commitments; instead, BS sat in at the piano and Cab Calloway emceed. Although this constitutes a borderline case, I believe that under the circumstances this event should qualify as a genuine Ellington recording.

		20 Aug 1963 (S)
STUDIO ORCHESTRA		Universal Studios
BBry ZH NWrd RN, BWmn JSrs BWd, RP RPwl HAsh PC BFrm, BS JBjm LBsn JA, JS JMP		Chicago, IL
JGsm IBS, DE directing.		

MY PEOPLE[1]

....		-1	Ain't But The One –vJMP IBS (incomplete)
....		-2	Ain't But The One –vJMP IBS
....		-4	Ain't But The One –vJMP IBS (incomplete)
....	Con	-5	Ain't But The One –vJMP IBS
....		-6	Will You Be There?—99% Won't Do –vIBS (incomplete)
....		-7	Will You Be There?—99% Won't Do –vIBS (incomplete)
....		-8	Will You Be There?—99% Won't Do –vIBS
....		-9	Blues At Sundown (incomplete)
....		-10	Blues At Sundown –vJGsm (incomplete)
....		-13	Blues At Sundown –vJGsm
....	Con	-14	Blues At Sundown –vJGsm
....		-15	Come Sunday –vIBS (incomplete)
....		-16	Come Sunday (incomplete)
....		-17	Come Sunday –vIBS (incomplete)
....		-18	Come Sunday (incomplete)
....		-19	Come Sunday –vIBS
....		-20	Come Sunday –vIBS
....		-21	Come Sunday –vIBS
....	Con	-22	Come Sunday –vIBS
....		-23	The Blues –vJS (incomplete)
....		-24	The Blues –vJS (incomplete)
....	Az	-25	The Blues –vJS
....		-26	The Blues –vJS (incomplete)
....		-27	The Blues –vJS (incomplete)
....			The Blues –vJS (rehearsal)
....		-28	The Blues –vJS
....		-29	The Blues –vJS
....		-31	The Blues –vJS (incomplete)
....		-32	The Blues –vJS (incomplete)
....	Con	-33	The Blues –vJS
....		-35	King Fit The Battle Of Alabam' –vIBS (incomplete)
....		-36	King Fit The Battle Of Alabam' –vIBS (incomplete)
....		-38	King Fit The Battle Of Alabam' –vIBS (incomplete)
....		-39	King Fit The Battle Of Alabam' –vIBS (incomplete)
....	Az	-40	King Fit The Battle Of Alabam' –vIBS
....	Con	-42	King Fit The Battle Of Alabam –vIBS
....		-44	David Danced Before The Lord –vIBS[2] (incomplete)
....		-47	David Danced Before The Lord –vIBS (incomplete)
....		-48	David Danced Before The Lord –vIBS (incomplete)

> BBgs[3] added.

....	Con	-49	David Danced Before The Lord –vIBS, BBgs tap

> BBgs omitted.

....		-50	Montage[4] (incomplete) >>>

....	Con	-51	Montage
....			My Mother, My Father[5] (rehearsal)
....	Az	-53[6]	My Mother, My Father –vJS (incomplete)
....	Az	-53	My Mother, My Father –vJS (incomplete)
....		-54	My Mother, My Father (incomplete)
....		-56	My Mother, My Father –vJS (incomplete)
....		-57	My Mother, My Father –vJS (incomplete)
....		-58	My Mother, My Father –vJS
....		-59	A Jungle Triangle (incomplete)
....		-60	A Jungle Triangle (incomplete)
....	MFC	-62	A Jungle Triangle
....		-63	Strange Feeling –vJGsm (incomplete)
....		-65	Strange Feeling –vJGsm
....		-66	Strange Feeling (incomplete)
....		-67	Strange Feeling –vJGsm (incomplete)
....		-68	Strange Feeling –vJGsm
....		-69	Strange Feeling (incomplete)
....		-70	Strange Feeling
....	Con	-71	Montage (intro)
....		-73	Montage (intercut)
....		-74	Montage (intercut)
....		-75	Strange Feeling –vJGsm (incomplete)
....	Az	-77	Strange Feeling –vJGsm
....		-78	The Blues (incomplete)
....		-79	The Blues
....		-80	Montage (insert)
....		-82	Montage (insert)
....		-83	Montage (insert)
....		-84	Montage (insert)
....		-85	My People –BBgs narration
....		-86	My People –BBgs narration

> BWd, HAsh, JJns JBjm LBsn, JGsm.

....		-87	Workin' Blues –vJGsm
....	Az	-88	Piano Blues Overture[7]
....		-89	Workin' Blues –vJGsm (incomplete)
....		-90	Workin' Blues –vJGsm
....	Con	-91	Workin' Blues –vJGsm
....	Az	-92[6]	Jail Blues –vJGsm
....	Con	✓-93	Jail Blues –vJGsm

[1]See also sessions on 21 and 27 Aug 1963.
[2]sa "Come Sunday" from *Black, Brown and Beige.*
[3]BBgs' tap dancing was overdubbed at a later date.
[4]sa "Light" from *Black, Brown and Beige.*
[5]Complete: "My Mother, My Father And Love"; subtitled "My Heritage."
[6]Voicetrack only.
[7]sa "Working Blues."

21 Aug 1963   (S)
Universal Studios
Chicago, IL

STUDIO ORCHESTRA
BBry ZH NWrd RN, BWmn JSrs BWd, RP RPwl HAsh PC BFrm, BS JBjm LBsn JA, JS JMP IBS, DE voice and directing.

			MY PEOPLE (ctd.)[1]
....		-1	After Bird Jungle (incomplete)
....		-2	After Bird Jungle
....	Az	-3	After Bird Jungle
....	Az	-4	After Bird Jungle
....		-5	My Mother, My Father –vJMP (incomplete)
....		-6	My Mother, My Father –vJMP
....		-7	My Mother, My Father –vJMP (incomplete)
....	Con	-8	My Mother, My Father –vJMP
....		-9	Purple People –JS narration (incomplete)
....		-10	Purple People –JS narration (incomplete)
....	RDB	-12	Purple People –JS narration
....		-13	Will You Be There? –vIBS
....	Con	-14	Will You Be There?—99% Won't Do –vIBS
....	Az	-15	What Color Is Virtue? (incomplete)
....	Az	-16	What Color Is Virtue? –vJS (incomplete)
....	Con	-18	What Color Is Virtue? –vJS IBS
....			What Color Is Virtue? (ending)
....			What Color Is Virtue? –vJS IBS
....			What Color Is Virtue? –vIBS (incomplete)
....			What Color Is Virtue? –vIBS (incomplete)
....			What Color Is Virtue? –vIBS (incomplete) >>>

....			What Color Is Virtue? –vIBS (coda)
....	Con		What Color Is Virtue? –vIBS (coda)
....			Come Sunday –vJMP IBS (incomplete)
....		-19	Come Sunday –vJMP IBS

> DE, IBS.

....	Con	-20	My People –DE narration, vIBS
....		-21	My People –vIBS (insert)

> Entire band, JJns replaces BS.

....	Az	-22	King Fit The Battle Of Alabam' (incomplete)
....	Az	-23	King Fit The Battle Of Alabam'
....	Az	-24	King Fit The Battle Of Alabam'

> BS replaces JJns.

....	Az	My Mother, My Father -vJMP

[1]See also sessions on 20 and 27 Aug 1963.

25 Aug 1963   (P)
Arie Crown Theater, McCormick Place
Chicago, IL

PERFORMING ORCHESTRA
BBry ZH NWrd RN, BWmn JSrs BWd, RP RPwl HAsh PC BFrm, BS JBjm LBsn JA,
JS LG RLNG JMP BBgs IBS.

		MY PEOPLE
....		Come Sunday –vJMP IBS
....		Will You Be There?—99% Won't Do –vIBS
....		Ain't But The One –vJMP IBS
....		David Danced Before The Lord –vIBS, BBgs tap
....		My Mother, My Father –JS narration
....	RDB	Guitar Amour
....		After Bird Jungle
....		My Mother, My Father –vJS
....		Montage
....		Will You Be There? –vIBS
....		My People –BBgs narration
....		The Blues –vJS
....		Blues At Sundown –vLG JS
....		Walkin' And Singin' The Blues –vLG
....		Workin' Blues –vLG
....		My Man Sends Me –vLG
....		Jail Blues –vLG
....		I Love My Lovin' Lover –vLG
....	RDB	A Jungle Triangle
....		King Fit The Battle Of Alabam' –vIBS
....		King Fit The Battle Of Alabam'
....	RDB	Purple People –RLNG narration
....	RDB	What Color Is Virtue? –vJS IBS

26 Aug 1963   (P)
State Fairground
Detroit, MI

DUKE ELLINGTON & HIS ORCHESTRA
CA CW REsn WC TJo, LB BCpr CCrs, JHtn JH HJsn PG HC, DE EShp SWrd.

....	Az	Take The "A" Train
....	Az	Afro-Bossa
....	Az	The Eighth Veil
....	Az	Stompin' At The Savoy
....	Az	Silk Lace
....	Az	Lullaby Of Birdland
....	Az	Medley[1]

> DWtn added.

....	Ros	Do Nothin' Till You Hear From Me –vDWtn
....	Az	Salty Papa Blues –vDWtn

> DWtn omitted.

....		Skin Deep
....	MJ	Jeep's Blues
....	Az	Jam With Sam

[1]Including: Satin Doll; Solitude; Don't Get Around Much Anymore; Mood Indigo; I'm Beginning To See The Light;
Sophisticated Lady; Caravan; Do Nothin' Till You Hear From Me; I Let A Song Go Out Of My Heart/Don't Get
Around Much Anymore.

27 Aug 1963   (S)
Universal Studios
Chicago, IL

STUDIO ORCHESTRA
BBry ZH NWrd RN, BWmn JSrs CCrs, RP RPwl HAsh PC BFrm, BS JJns JBjm LBsn JA,
LG JGsm, DE directing.

			MY PEOPLE (ctd.)[1]
....		-1	Purple People –segments 1-3
....			Purple People –segment 3 (intercut)
....			Purple People –segment 3 (intercut)
....		-2	Purple People –segments 1+2 (incomplete)
....		-3	Purple People –segments 1+2
....			Purple People –segment 3 (rehearsal)
....			Purple People –segment 3 (rehearsal)
....	RDB	-3	Purple People –segments 1-3
....		-4	Purple People –segment 1
....		-5	Purple People
....		-6	Purple People
....		-8	Walkin' And Singin' The Blues –vLG (incomplete)
....	Az	-9	Walkin' And Singin' The Blues –vLG
....		-10	Walkin' And Singin' The Blues –vLG
....		-12	My Man Sends Me –vLG (incomplete)
....		-13	My Man Sends Me –vLG (incomplete)
....	Con	-14	My Man Sends Me –vLG
....		-15	I Love My Lovin' Lover –vLG (incomplete)
....		-16	I Love My Lovin' Lover –vLG
....		-18	I Love My Lovin' Lover (incomplete)
....	Az	-19	I Love My Lovin' Lover –vLG
....	Con	-20	I Love My Lovin' Lover –vLG
....		-21	My Mother, My Father –vJGsm
....		-22	My Mother, My Father –vJGsm (incomplete)
....		-24	My Mother, My Father –vJGsm (incomplete)
....		-25	My Mother, My Father –vJGsm (incomplete)
....		-28	My Mother, My Father –vJGsm
....		-29	My Mother, My Father –vLG (incomplete)
....		-30	My Mother, My Father –vLG
....		-32	My Mother, My Father –vLG (incomplete)
....		-34	My Mother, My Father –vLG
....	RDB	-35	The Blues –vLG
....		-36	The Blues –vLG (incomplete)
....	RDB	-36	The Blues –vLG (coda)

[1]See also sessions on 20 and 21 Aug 1963.

9 Sep 1963   (P)
Damascus Fair
Damascus, Syria

DUKE ELLINGTON & HIS ORCHESTRA
CA CW REsn RN, LB BCpr CCrs, JHtn JH RP PG HC, DE EShp SWrd.

....	Take The "A" Train
....	Afro-Bossa
....	The Eighth Veil
....	Rockin' In Rhythm
....	Silk Lace
....	Lullaby Of Birdland
....	Black And Tan Fantasy—Creole Love Call—The Mooche
....	Skin Deep
....	Medley[1]
....	Take The "A" Train
....	V.I.P.'s Boogie
....	Jam With Sam
....	I Got It Bad
....	Things Ain't What They Used To Be
....	New Concerto For Cootie
....	Tootie For Cootie
....	Diminuendo In Blue and Wailing Interval

[1]Including: Satin Doll; Solitude; Don't Get Around Much Anymore; Mood Indigo; I'm Beginning To See The Light;
Sophisticated Lady; Caravan; Do Nothin' Till You Hear From Me; Just Squeeze Me –vRN; It Don't Mean A Thing –vRN;
I Let A Song Go Out Of My Heart/Don't Get Around Much Anymore.

11 Sep 1963   (P)
Damascus Fair
Damascus, Syria

DUKE ELLINGTON & HIS ORCHESTRA
CA CW REsn RN, LB BCpr CCrs, JHtn JH RP PG HC, DE EShp SWrd.

....	Take The "A" Train
....	Afro-Bossa
....	The Eighth Veil
....	Black And Tan Fantasy—Creole Love Call—The Mooche >>>

....	Lullaby Of Birdland
....	Stompin' At The Savoy
....	Silk Lace
....	Jam With Sam
....	Medley[1]
....	Take The "A" Train
....	Skin Deep
....	I Got It Bad
....	Things Ain't What They Used To Be
....	All Of Me
....	Tootie For Cootie
....	Diminuendo In Blue and Wailing Interval
....	Take The "A" Train

[1]Including: Satin Doll; Solitude; Don't Get Around Much Anymore; Mood Indigo; I'm Beginning To See The Light; Sophisticated Lady; Caravan; Do Nothin' Till You Hear From Me; Just Squeeze Me –vRN; It Don't Mean A Thing –vRN; I Let A Song Go Out Of My Heart/Don't Get Around Much Anymore.

DUKE ELLINGTON & HIS ORCHESTRA
CA CW REsn, LB BCpr CCrs, JHtn JH RP PG HC, DE EShp SWrd.

13 Sep 1963 (P)
Unidentified location
Amman, Jordan

....	Take The "A" Train
....	Afro-Bossa
....	The Eighth Veil
....	Rockin' In Rhythm
....	Silk Lace
....	Lullaby Of Birdland
....	I Got It Bad
....	Things Ain't What They Used To Be
....	Jam With Sam
....	Medley[1]
....	Take The "A" Train –vEShp
....	Skin Deep

[1]Including: Satin Doll; Solitude; Don't Get Around Much Anymore; Mood Indigo; I'm Beginning To See The Light; Sophisticated Lady; Caravan; Do Nothin' Till You Hear From Me; I Let A Song Go Out Of My Heart/Don't Get Around Much Anymore.

DUKE ELLINGTON & HIS ORCHESTRA
CA CW REsn, LB BCpr CCrs, JHtn JH RP PG HC, DE EShp SWrd.

24 Sep 1963
Vigyan Bhavan
New Delhi, India

....	DE talks about Jazz
....	The "C" Jam Blues
....	Black And Tan Fantasy—Creole Love Call—The Mooche
....	Perdido

DUKE ELLINGTON & HIS ORCHESTRA
CA CW REsn PBk, LB BCpr CCrs, JHtn JH RP PG HC, DE EShp SWrd.

26 Sep 1963 (P)
Delhi University
New Delhi, India

....	Medley[1]
....	Diminuendo In Blue and Wailing Interval
....	Jones

[1]Including: Satin Doll; Solitude; Don't Get Around Much Anymore; Mood Indigo; I'm Beginning To See The Light; Sophisticated Lady; Caravan; Do Nothin' Till You Hear From Me; I Let A Song Go Out Of My Heart/Don't Get Around Much Anymore.

DUKE ELLINGTON & HIS ORCHESTRA
CA CW REsn PBk, LB BCpr CCrs, JHtn JH RP PG HC, BS EShp SWrd.

10 Oct 1963 (P)
Rang Bhavan
Bombay, India

....	Take The "A" Train
....	Afro-Bossa
....	Stompin' At The Savoy
....	Lullaby At Birdland
....	Silk Lace
....	Tootie For Cootie
....	I Got It Bad
....	Things Ain't What They Used To Be
....	All Of Me
....	The Eighth Veil
....	Jam With Sam
....	The "C" Jam Blues
....	Skin Deep

> DE replaces BS.

....	Take The "A" Train >>>

....   Medley[1]

> BS replaces DE.

....   Diminuendo In Blue and Wailing Interval
....   Take The "A" Train -vEShp
....   One More Once —vEShp
....   Take The "A" Train

[1]Including: Satin Doll; Solitude; Don't Get Around Much Anymore; Mood Indigo; I'm Beginning To See The Light;
Sophisticated Lady; Caravan; Do Nothin' Till You Hear From Me; I Let A Song Go Out Of My Heart/Don't Get Around
Much Anymore.

                                                                         p 11 Oct 1963   (P)
DUKE ELLINGTON & HIS ORCHESTRA   Unidentified location (tc)[1]
CA CW REsn PBk, LB BCpr CCrs, JHtn JH RP PG HC, DE/BS[2] EShp SWrd.   Bombay, India

....   All Of Me
....   Tootie For Cootie
....   One More Once —vEShp

[1]French telecast "La Légende du Duke." The program contains excerpts from the above titles.
[2]DE was taken ill from 24 Sep to 8 Oct. He makes a brief appearance on stage, but cannot be seen at the piano. Since
JHtn is seen directing the band, the presence of BS is questionable.

                                                                         12 Oct 1963   (P)
DUKE ELLINGTON & HIS ORCHESTRA   Shri Shanmukhananda Sabha
CA CW REsn PBk, LB BCpr CCrs, JHtn JH RP PG HC, DE EShp SWrd.   Bombay, India

....   DE talks about Jazz

> PG, DE EShp SWrd.

....   In A Sentimental Mood

> Entire band.

....   In A Mellotone
....   Jeep's Blues
....   Harmony In Harlem
....   Tea For Two
....   Honeysuckle Rose
....   Black And Tan Fantasy—Creole Love Call—The Mooche
....   Guitar Amour
....   Tootie For Cootie
....   Duke's Place —vEShp
....   Take The "A" Train

                                                                         Oct 1963   (P)
DUKE ELLINGTON   Private residence
Piano solo.   Mumbay (Bombay), India

....   My Mother, My Father And Love
....   Take The "A" Train
....   Satin Doll

                                                                         24 Oct 1963   (P)
DUKE ELLINGTON & HIS ORCHESTRA   Perideniya University
CA REsn HJns, LB BCpr CCrs, JHtn JH RP PG HC, DE EShp SWrd.   Kandy, Sri Lanka (Ceylon)

....   Take The "A" Train
....   Afro-Bossa
....   Silk Lace
....   Perdido
....   Guitar Amour
....   Kinda Dukish/Rockin' In Rhythm
....   The Eighth Veil
....   Jam With Sam
....   Skin Deep
....   Medley[1]
....   Diminuendo In Blue and Wailing Interval

> BS piano solo.

.... MJ   A Flower Is A Lovesome Thing

> Entire band, BS replaces DE.

.... MJ   Take The "A" Train —vEShp
....   One More Once —vEShp
....   Take The "A" Train

[1]Including: Satin Doll; Solitude; Don't Get Around Much Anymore; Mood Indigo; I'm Beginning To See The Light;
Sophisticated Lady; Caravan; Do Nothin' Till You Hear From Me; I Let A Song Go Out Of My Heart/Don't Get Around
Much Anymore.

DUKE ELLINGTON & HIS ORCHESTRA

3 Nov 1963   (P)
Hotel Metropole
Karachi, Pakistan

CA CW REsn HJns, LB BCpr CCrs, JHtn JH RP PG HC, DE EShp SWrd.

....		Take The "A" Train
....		Afro-Bossa
....		Silk Lace
....		Honeysuckle Rose
....		Perdido
....		Guitar Amour
....		Stompin' At The Savoy
....		New Concerto For Cootie
....		Tootie For Cootie
....		Kinda Dukish/Rockin' In Rhythm
....		I Got It Bad
....		Things Ain't What They Used To Be
....		All Of Me
....		Skin Deep
....		Medley[1]
....		Diminuendo In Blue and Wailing Interval

> BS EShp.

....   All Heart

> Entire band, BS replaces DE.

....   Take The "A" Train –vEShp
....   One More Once –vEShp
....   Jones

[1]Including: Satin Doll; Solitude; Don't Get Around Much Anymore; Mood Indigo; I'm Beginning To See The Light; Sophisticated Lady; Caravan; Do Nothin' Till You Hear From Me; I Let A Song Go Out Of My Heart/Don't Get Around Much Anymore.

DUKE ELLINGTON & HIS ORCHESTRA

Nov 1963   (P)
Unidentified location[1] (tc)[2]
Pakistan or Lebanon

CA CW REsn HJns, LB BCpr CCrs, JHtn JH RP PG HC, DE EShp SWrd.

....   Medley[3]
....   Afro-Bossa
....   Guitar Amour
....   Wailing Interval

> BS piano solo.

....   Lush Life

> Entire band, DE replaces BS.

....   Take The "A" Train

[1]This event originates either from Karachi (1 Nov 1963), or Beirut (20 Nov 1963).
[2]French telecast "La Légende du Duke." The program contains excerpts from the above titles.
[3]Including: Satin Doll; Solitude.

DUKE ELLINGTON

Dec 1963   (S)
Unidentified location (bc)
New York City, NY

DE interviewed by Fred Robbins.

....   Interview

DUKE ELLINGTON & HIS QUARTET

9 Jan 1964   (S)
NBC Studios (tc)
New York City, NY

JH HC, DE EShp SWrd.

....		Interview[1]
....	Egm	Satin Doll
....		Interview (ctd.)
....	Egm	Passion Flower
....		Interview (ctd.)
....	Egm	Take The "A" Train –vEShp
....	Egm	Sophisticated Lady

[1]Intermittent interviews with Hugh Downs.

DUKE ELLINGTON & HIS ORCHESTRA

14 Jan 1964   (P)
Basin Street East (bc)
New York City, NY

CA CW REsn HJns, LB BCpr CCrs, JHtn JH RP PG HC, DE EShp SWrd.

....	JBR	Take The "A" Train
....	JBR	Afro-Bossa
....		Silk Lace >>>

	JBR	Kinda Dukish/Rockin' In Rhythm[1]
	> DE EShp SWrd.	
		A Single Petal Of A Rose
	> Entire band.	
	Az	Tootie For Cootie
	> BS EShp SWrd.	
	MJ	Lush Life –vBS
	> Entire band.	
	MJ	Passion Flower
	> DE replaces BS.	
	M&A	Award presentation
	Az	Jam With Sam
	Az	Jam With Sam
	Az	Sophisticated Lady
	Az	Satin Doll
	M&A	Rose Of The Rio Grande
	M&A	Diminuendo In Blue and Wailing Interval
	JBR	East St. Louis Toodle-Oo

[1]"New Rockin' In Rhythm" on JBR.

DUKE ELLINGTON
DE interviewed by Humphrey Lyttelton and Max Jones.

15 Feb 1964   (S)
BBC Studios (bc)
London, England

		Interview

DUKE ELLINGTON & HIS ORCHESTRA
CA CW REsn HJns, LB BCpr CCrs, JHtn JH RP TH HC, DE EShp SWrd.

Royal Festival Hall (P)

	The Mooche
	Perdido
	IMPRESSIONS FROM THE FAR EAST[1]
	- Amad
	- Agra
	- Bluebird Of Delhi[2]
	- Depk
	The Opener[3]
	The Opener
	HARLEM

[1]Parts of the future *Far East Suite.*
[2]*aka* "Mynah.'
[3]The arrangement is by Herbie Jones.

DUKE ELLINGTON & HIS ORCHESTRA
CA CW REsn HJns, LB BCpr CCrs, JHtn JH RP PG HC, DE EShp SWrd,

16 Feb 1964   (P)
Hammersmith Odeon
London, England

	Take The "A" Train
	Black And Tan Fantasy—Creole Love Call—The Mooche
	Perdido
	IMPRESSIONS FROM THE FAR EAST
	- Amad
	- Agra
	- Bluebird Of Delhi
	- Depk
	The Opener
> PG, DE EShp SWrd.	
	Happy Reunion
> Entire band.	
	HARLEM

DUKE ELLINGTON
DE interviewed by Michael Brown about the Beatles.

18 Feb 1964   (S)
Unidentified location (bc)
Bristol, England

	RDB	Interview

19 Feb 1964   (P)
Fairfield Hall
Croydon, England

DUKE ELLINGTON & HIS ORCHESTRA
CA CW REsn HJns, LB BCpr CCrs, JHtn JH RP PG HC, DE EShp SWrd.

....	Take The "A" Train
....	Black And Tan Fantasy—Creole Love Call—The Mooche
....	Perdido
	IMPRESSIONS FROM THE FAR EAST
....	- Amad
....	- Agra
....	- Bluebird Of Delhi
....	- Depk
....	The Opener

> PG, DE EShp SWrd.

....	Happy Reunion

> Entire band.

....	Blow By Blow
....	HARLEM
....	Take The "A" Train
....	Caravan
....	Tootie For Cootie
....	Isfahan[1]
....	Things Ain't What They Used To Be
....	Banquet Scene
....	Skillipoop[2]
....	The Prowling Cat[3]
....	Kinda Dukish/Rockin' In Rhythm
....	Take The "A" Train –vEShp

> JHtn RP HC, DE.

....	Monologue –DE narration

> Entire band.

....	God Save The Queen

[1]sa "Elf"; part of the future *Far East Suite*.
[2]sa "A Jungle Triangle" and part of the music for *Timon Of Athens. Skillepooping* or *skill-a-pooping*—the exact spelling is not documented—is an American colloquialism for "making what you are doing looking better than what you are supposed to be doing." However, since *Skillipoop* is the generally accepted spelling of this title, this book will abide by it.
[3]The arrangement is by Herbie Jones.

DUKE ELLINGTON & HIS ORCHESTRA
Same personnel.

....	Take The "A" Train
....	Black And Tan Fantasy—Creole Love Call—The Mooche
....	Perdido
	IMPRESSIONS FROM THE FAR EAST
....	- Amad
....	- Agra
....	- Bluebird Of Delhi
....	- Depk
....	The Opener

> PG, DE EShp SWrd.

....	Happy Reunion

> Entire band.

....	Blow By Blow
....	HARLEM
....	Take The "A" Train
....	Caravan
....	Tootie For Cootie
....	Isfahan
....	Things Ain't What They Used To Be
....	Banquet Scene
....	Skillipoop
....	The Prowling Cat
....	Kinda Dukish/Rockin' In Rhythm
....	Take The "A" Train –vEShp

> JHtn RP HC, DE.

....	Monologue –DE narration >>>

```
            > Entire band.
..............                              God Save The Queen
```

20 Feb 1964[1]   (P)
BBC Theatre (tc)
London, England

DUKE ELLINGTON & HIS ORCHESTRA
CA CW REsn HJns, LB BCpr CCrs, JHtn JH RP PG HC, DE EShp SWrd.

```
..............  Az                Take The "A" Train[2]
..............  Az                Perdido[2]
..............  Az                Comments by DE[2]
..............  MM                Take The "A" Train
..............  MM                Perdido
..............  MM                Caravan
..............  MM                Isfahan
..............  MM                The Opener
..............  MM                HARLEM
..............  DVD               Take The "A" Train –vEShp
..............                    Banquet Scene
..............                    Skillipoop

            > DE piano solo.

..............  DVD               Little African Flower

            > Entire band.

..............  MM                Kinda Dukish/Rockin' In Rhythm
```

[1]Taping session; telecast on 21 Apr 1964.
[2]Because of technical problems these items had to be rerecorded.

21 Feb 1964   (P)
BBC Theatre (tc?)[1]
London, England

DUKE ELLINGTON & HIS ORCHESTRA
CA CW REsn HJns, LB BCpr CCrs, JHtn JH RP PG HC, DE EShp SWrd.

```
..............                    Take The "A" Train
..............                    Honeysuckle Rose
..............                    Afro-Bossa
..............                    The Star-Crossed Lovers
..............                    Tootie For Cootie
..............                    Cotton Tail
..............                    In A Sentimental Mood
..............                    Jam With Sam
..............                    Medley[2]

            > DE EShp SWrd.

..............                    Dancers In Love

            > Entire band.

..............                    Take The "A" Train
```

[1]Taping session; we have no evidence that this program was ever aired. The original tape has been reused and its original content was consequently lost.
[2]Including: Satin Doll; Solitude; Don't Get Around Much Anymore; Mood Indigo; I'm Beginning To See The Light; Sophisticated Lady; Caravan; Do Nothin' Till You Hear From Me; I Got It Bad; Just Squeeze Me –vEShp, I Let A Song Go Out Of My Heart/Don't Get Around Much Anymore.

29 Feb 1964   (P)
Free Trade Hall
Manchester, England

DUKE ELLINGTON & HIS ORCHESTRA
CA CW REsn HJns, LB BCpr CCrs, JHtn JH RP PG HC, DE EShp SWrd.

```
..............                    Take The "A" Train
..............                    Black And Tan Fantasy—Creole Love Call—The Mooche
..............                    Perdido

..............                    IMPRESSIONS FROM THE FAR EAST
..............                    - Amad
..............                    - Agra
..............                    - Bluebird Of Delhi
..............                    - Depk

..............                    The Opener

            > PG, DE EShp SWrd.

..............                    Happy Reunion

            > Entire band.

..............                    Blow By Blow
..............                    HARLEM
```

DUKE ELLINGTON & HIS ORCHESTRA
CA CW REsn HJns, LB BCpr CCrs, JHtn JH RP PG HC, DE EShp SWrd.

1 Mar 1964   (P)
New Victoria Theatre
London, England

....	Stompy Jones
....	Caravan
....	Tootie For Cootie
....	Isfahan
....	Things Ain't What They Used To Be
....	Banquet Scene
....	Skillipoop
....	Kinda Dukish/Rockin' In Rhythm
....	Take The "A" Train –vEShp

> JHtn RP HC, DE.

....	Monologue –DE narration

DUKE ELLINGTON & HIS ORCHESTRA
Same personnel.

....	Take The "A" Train
....	Black And Tan Fantasy—Creole Love Call—The Mooche
....	Perdido
	IMPRESSIONS FROM THE FAR EAST
....	- Amad
....	- Agra
....	- Bluebird Of Delhi
....	- Depk
....	The Opener

> PG, DE EShp SWrd.

....	Happy Reunion

> Entire band.

....	Blow By Blow
....	HARLEM
....	Stompy Jones
....	Caravan
....	Isfahan
....	Things Ain't What They Used To Be
....	Skillipoop
....	Kinda Dukish/Rockin' In Rhythm
....	Take The "A" Train –vEShp

> JHtn RP HC, DE.

....	Monologue –DE narration

> Entire band.

....	God Save The Queen

DUKE ELLINGTON & HIS ORCHESTRA
CA CW REsn HJns, LB BCpr CCrs, JHtn JH RP PG HC, DE EShp SWrd.

2 Mar 1964   (P)
?Liederhalle
Stuttgart, Germany

....	Take The "A" Train
....	Black And Tan Fantasy—Creole Love Call—The Mooche
....	Perdido
	IMPRESSIONS FROM THE FAR EAST
....	- Amad
....	- Agra
....	- Bluebird Of Delhi
....	- Depk
....	The Opener

> PG. DE EShp SWrd.

....	Happy Reunion

> Entire band.

....	Blow By Blow
....	HARLEM
....	Stompy Jones
....	Caravan
....	Tootie For Cootie
....	Isfahan
....	Things Ain't What They Used To Be >>>

....   Banquet Scene
....   Skillipoop
....   Kinda Dukish/Rockin' In Rhythm
....   Take The "A" Train –vEShp
....   The "C" Jam Blues
....   Cotton Tail
....   Satin Doll

9 Mar 1964   (P)
Konserthuset
Stockholm, Sweden

DUKE ELLINGTON & HIS ORCHESTRA
CA CW REsn HJns, LB BCpr CCrs, JHtn JH RP PG HC, DE JW SWrd.

....   Take The "A" Train
....   Creole Love Call—The Mooche
....   Perdido

                     IMPRESSIONS FROM THE FAR EAST
....   - Amad
....   - Agra
....   - Bluebird Of Delhi
....   - Depk

....   The Opener

> PG, DE JW SWrd.

....   Happy Reunion

DUKE ELLINGTON & HIS ORCHESTRA
Same personnel.

....   Take The "A" Train
....   Black And Tan Fantasy—Creole Love Call—The Mooche
....   Perdido

                     IMPRESSIONS FROM THE FAR EAST
....   - Amad
....   - Agra
....   - Bluebird Of Delhi
....   - Depk

.... Pab   The Opener

> PG, DE JW SWrd.

.... Pab   Happy Reunion

> Entire band.

.... Pab   Blow By Blow
.... Pab   HARLEM
.... Pab   Caravan
....   Isfahan
.... Pab   Tootie For Cootie
.... Pab   Things Ain't What They Used To Be
.... Pab   All Of Me
.... Pab   The Prowling Cat
.... Pab   Satin Doll

10 Mar 1964   (P)
Kulturhuset
Helsinki, Finland

DUKE ELLINGTON & HIS ORCHESTRA
CA CW REsn HJns, LB BCpr CCrs, JHtn JH RP PG HC, DE JW SWrd EVal.

....   Take The "A" Train
....   Black And Tan Fantasy—Creole Love Call—The Mooche
....   Perdido

                     IMPRESSIONS FROM THE FAR EAST
....   - Amad
....   - Agra
....   - Bluebird Of Delhi
....   - Depk

....   The Opener

> PG, DE JW SWrd.

....   Happy Reunion

> Entire band.

....   HARLEM
....   Caravan

11 Mar 1964   (P)
Konserthuset
Gothenburg, Sweden

<u>DUKE ELLINGTON & HIS ORCHESTRA</u>
CA CW REsn HJns, LB BCpr CCrs, JHtn JH RP PG HC, DE JW SWrd.

....		Take The "A" Train
....		Black And Tan Fantasy—Creole Love Call—The Mooche
....		Perdido
		IMPRESSIONS FROM THE FAR EAST
....		- Amad
....	MFC	- Agra
....		- Bluebird Of Delhi
....		- Depk
....		The Opener

> PG, DE JW SWrd.

....	MFC	Happy Reunion

> Entire band.

....		Blow By Blow
....		HARLEM
....	MFC	Caravan
....	MFC	Isfahan
....		The Prowling Cat
....		Kinda Dukish/Rockin' In Rhythm
....		Jones

13 Mar 1964   (P)
Tivoli's Koncertsal
Copenhagen, Denmark

<u>DUKE ELLINGTON & HIS ORCHESTRA</u>
CA CW REsn HJns, LB BCpr CCrs, JHtn JH RP PG HC, DE JW SWrd.

....		Take The "A" Train
....		Black And Tan Fantasy—Creole Love Call—The Mooche
....		Perdido
		IMPRESSIONS FROM THE FAR EAST
....		- Amad
....		- Agra
....		- Bluebird Of Delhi
....		- Depk
....		The Opener

> PG, DE JW SWrd.

....		Happy Reunion

> Entire band.

....		Blow By Blow
....		HARLEM
....		Stompy Jones
....		The Prowling Cat
....		Isfahan
....		Things Ain't What They Used To Be
....		Banquet Scene
....		Skillipoop
....		Kinda Dukish/Rockin' In Rhythm
....		Satin Doll
....		Jones

<u>DUKE ELLINGTON & HIS ORCHESTRA</u>
Same personnel.

....		Take The "A" Train
....		Black And Tan Fantasy—Creole Love Call—The Mooche
....		Perdido
		IMPRESSIONS FROM THE FAR EAST
....		- Amad
....		- Agra
....		- Bluebird Of Delhi
....		- Depk
....		The Opener

> PG, DE JW SWrd.

....		Happy Reunion

> Entire band.

....		Blow By Blow >>>

....	HARLEM
....	Stompy Jones
....	The Prowling Cat
....	Tootie For Cootie
....	Isfahan
....	Things Ain't What They Used To Be
....	Banquet Scene
....	Skillipoop
....	Kinda Dukish/Rockin' In Rhythm
....	Satin Doll
....	The "C" Jam Blues
....	Jones

15 Mar 1964   (P)
Sportpalast
Berlin, Germany

DUKE ELLINGTON & HIS ORCHESTRA
CA CW REsn HJns, LB BCpr CCrs, JHtn JH RP PG HC, DE JW SWrd.

....	Take The "A" Train
....	Black And Tan Fantasy—Creole Love Call—The Mooche
....	Perdido
	IMPRESSIONS FROM THE FAR EAST
....	- Amad
....	- Agra
....	- Bluebird Of Delhi
....	- Depk
....	The Opener
....	The Opener

> PG, DE JW SWrd.

....	Happy Reunion

> Entire band.

....	Blow By Blow
....	HARLEM
....	Stompy Jones
....	Caravan
....	Tootie For Cootie
....	Isfahan
....	Things Ain't What They Used To Be
....	Banquet Scene
....	Skillipoop
....	The Prowling Cat
....	Kinda Dukish/Rockin' In Rhythm
....	Satin Doll
....	The "C" Jam Blues
....	Jam With Sam
....	Jones

20 Mar 1964   (P)
Théâtre des Champs Elysées
Paris, France

DUKE ELLINGTON & HIS ORCHESTRA
CA CW REsn HJns, LB BCpr CCrs, JHtn JH RP PG HC, DE JW SWrd.

....	Take The "A" Train
....	Black And Tan Fantasy—Creole Love Call—The Mooche
....	Perdido
	IMPRESSIONS FROM THE FAR EAST
....	- Amad
....	- Agra
....	- Bluebird Of Delhi
....	- Depk
....	The Opener

> PG, DE JW SWrd.

....	Happy Reunion

> Entire band.

....	Blow By Blow
....	HARLEM
....	Harmony In Harlem
....	Stompy Jones
....	Caravan
....	Tootie For Cootie
....	Isfahan
....	Things Ain't What They Used To Be >>>

....		Banquet Scene
....		Skillipoop
....		Satin Doll
....		The Prowling Cat

DUKE ELLINGTON
Interviewed by Line Renaud.

21 Mar 1964   (S)
Radio Monte Carlo (bc)
Paris, France

.... Interview

DUKE ELLINGTON
Piano solo.

ORTF Studios (tc)   (P)

....		Take The "A" Train
....		Fleurette Africaine

DUKE ELLINGTON & HIS ORCHESTRA
CA CW REsn HJns, LB BCpr CCrs, JHtn JH RP PG HC, DE GR SWrd.

Théâtre des Champs Elysées (P)

....		Black And Tan Fantasy—Creole Love Call—The Mooche
		IMPRESSIONS FROM THE FAR EAST
....		- Amad
....		- Agra
....		- Bluebird Of Delhi
....		- Depk
....		The Opener

> PG, DE GR SWrd.

....		Happy Reunion

> Entire band.

....		Blow By Blow
....	RTE	Caravan
....		The Jeep Is Jumpin'
....		Things Ain't What They Used To Be
....		Skillipoop
....		The Prowling Cat
....		Kinda Dukish/Rockin' In Rhythm
....		Satin Doll
....		Sophisticated Lady
....		Happy-Go-Lucky Local
....		Take The "A" Train

DUKE ELLINGTON & HIS JAZZ GROUP
REsn, LB, JH PG HC, DE GR SWrd.

22 Mar 1964[1]   (P)
Teatro Ariston (tc)
San Remo, Italy

....	Car	Take The "A" Train
....	Car	The "C" Jam Blues
....	Car	On The Sunny Side Of The Street

> DE GR SWrd.

....	Car	Caravan

> Entire band.

....	Car	I Got It Bad
....	Car	Solitude
....	Car	Kinda Dukish/Rockin' In Rhythm
....	Car	Sophisticated Lady
....	Car	I Let A Song Go Out Of My Heart/Don't Get Around Much Anymore

[1]Filmed for telecast; it is not known if and when the program was aired.

DUKE ELLINGTON & HIS ORCHESTRA
CA CW REsn HJns, LB BCpr CCrs, JHtn JH RP PG HC, DE MH SWrd.

29 Mar 1964   (P)
Carnegie Hall
New York City, NY

....	JU	Take The "A" Train
....	JU	Black And Tan Fantasy—Creole Love Call—The Mooche
....	JU	Perdido
		IMPRESSIONS FROM THE FAR EAST
....	JU	- Amad
....	JU	- Agra
....	JU	- Bluebird Of Delhi
....	JU	- Depk >>>

.... JU		The Opener
	> PG, DE MH SWrd.	
.... JU		Happy Reunion
	> Entire band.	
.... JU		Blow By Blow
.... JU		HARLEM
.... JU		Stompy Jones
.... JU		Take The "A" Train
.... JU		Caravan
.... JU		Tootie For Cootie
.... JU		Isfahan
.... JU		Things Ain't What They Used To Be
.... JU		Banquet Scene
.... JU		Skillipoop
.... JU		The Prowling Cat
.... JU		Kinda Dukish/Rockin' In Rhythm
.... JU		Satin Doll
	> JHtn RP HC, DE.	
.... JU		Monologue –DE narration
	> Entire band.	
.... JU		Jam With Sam
.... JU		Jones

5-8 Apr 1964[1]   (P)
Conrad Hilton Hotel
Chicago, IL

DUKE ELLINGTON & HIS ORCHESTRA
DE MH JBH.

....		Medley[2]
....		Take The "A" Train
....		A Single Petal Of A Rose
....		Satin Doll
	> LB added.	
....		Rose Of The Rio Grande
....		Do Nothin' Till You Hear From Me
	> LB omitted, JH added.	
....		I Got It Bad
....		On The Sunny Side Of The Street
....		Passion Flower
	> LB added.	
....		Things Ain't What They Used To Be
....		The Drum And The Blues

[1]This is the first of two nights when DE performed at a convention; the exact dates are not known.
[2]Including: Solitude; Don't Get Around Much Anymore; Mood Indigo; I'm Beginning To See The Light; Sophisticated Lady; Caravan.

5-8 Apr 1964[1]   (P)
Conrad Hilton Hotel
Chicago, IL

DUKE ELLINGTON & HIS GROUP
DE MH SWrd.

....		Take The "A" Train
....		A Single Petal Of A Rose
....		Satin Doll
	> HC added.	
....		Sophisticated Lady
....		I Let A Song Go Out Of The Heart
	> HC omitted, JHtn added.	
....		Tenderly
....		Honeysuckle Rose
	> CW, JHtn PG HC, DE MH SWrd.	
....		Mood Indigo
....		Solitude
....		Fat Mouth
....		Caravan
....		Tootie For Cootie >>>

> PG, DE MH SWrd.

....   Body And Soul

> CW, JHtn HC added.

....   Blow By Blow

> DE MH SWrd.

....   Dancers In Love

> CW HJns, JHtn PG HC added.

....   Jones

> HJns, JH, DE MH SWrd.

....   It Shouldn't Happen To A Dream
....   The Jeep Is Jumpin'
....   I Got It Bad

> LB added.

....   Things Ain't What They Used To Be

> DE MH SWrd.

....   Dancers In Love
....   Mood Indigo

[1]This is the second of two nights when DE performed at a convention; the exact dates are not known.

				15 Apr 1964[1] (S)

DUKE ELLINGTON & HIS ORCHESTRA   Fine Studios[1]
CA CW REsn HJns, LB BCpr CCrs, JHtn JH RP PG HC, DE MH SWrd.   New York City, NY

....		5018	Hello Dolly
....	Rpr	5017	Call Me Irresponsible
....	Rpr	5022	The Second Time Around
....	Rpr	5023	Never On Sunday
....	Rpr	5025	Blowing In The Wind

[1]At the Great Northern Hotel, 58th Street; applies also to the sessions on 16, 27 April and 19 May 1964.

16 Apr 1964   (S)
DUKE ELLINGTON & HIS ORCHESTRA   Fine Studios
CA CW REsn HJns, LB BCpr CCrs, JHtn JH RP PG HC, DE MH SWrd.   New York City, NY

....	Rpr	5018	Fly Me To The Moon
....	Rpr	5019	So Little Time[1]
....		5020	Danke Schoen
....	Rpr	5021	More
....	Rpr	5026	Stranger On The Shore
....			Maria

[1]aka "The Peking Theme."

20 Apr 1964[1]   (P)
DUKE ELLINGTON & HIS ORCHESTRA   Le Jazz Hot Room, Casa Loma Club (tc)
CA CW REsn HJns, LB BCpr CCrs, JHtn JH RP PG HC, DE MH SWrd.   Montréal, QC

....	DVD	Boo-Dah
....	DVD	Take The "A" Train
....	DVD	Afro-Bossa
....	DVD	Perdido
....	DVD	Never On Sunday

> PG, DE MH SWrd.

....	DVD	Happy Reunion

> Entire band.

....	DVD	Blow By Blow
....	DVD	Caravan
....	DVD	Banquet Scene
....	DVD	Things Ain't What They Used To Be
....	DVD	Skillipoop
....	DVD	The Prowling Cat
....	DVD	Medley[2]
....	DVD	Take The "A" Train

[1]Telecast on 17 Sep 1964.
[2]Including: Satin Doll; Solitude; Don't Get Around Much Anymore; Mood Indigo; I'm Beginning To See The Light; Sophisticated Lady; It Don't Mean A Thing; Do Nothin' Till You Hear From Me; I Let A Song Go Out Of My Heart/ Don't Get Around Much Anymore.

				21 Apr 1964 (S)

DUKE ELLINGTON
DE interviewed by Kate Vita Marson.

21 Apr 1964   (S)
p Casa Loma Club (bc)
Montréal, PQ

....   Interview

DUKE ELLINGTON & HIS ORCHESTRA
CA CW REsn HJns, LB BCpr CCrs, JHtn JH RP PG HC, DE MH SWrd.

27 Apr 1964   (S)
Fine Studios
New York City, NY

.... Rpr   5016[1]   Hello Dolly
.... Rpr   5020[1]   Danke Schoen
.... Rpr   5024   I Left My Heart In San Francisco
....   Maria

> BS replaces DE.

....   Take Five

[1]Remakes.

DUKE ELLINGTON & HIS ORCHESTRA
CA CW REsn HJns, LB BCpr CCrs, JHtn JH RP PG HC, DE MH SWrd.

29 Apr 1964[1]   (P)
Metromedia Studios (tc)
New York City, NY

.... MdJ   Take The "A" Train
.... MdJ   Black And Tan Fantasy—Creole Love Call—The Mooche
.... MdJ   The Opener
.... MdJ   HARLEM
.... MdJ   Metromedia Blues
.... MdJ   Jam With Sam
.... MdJ   Passion Flower
.... MdJ   Things Ain't What They Used To Be
.... MdJ   Kinda Dukish/Rockin' In Rhythm
.... MdJ   Take The "A" Train

[1]Taping session; telecast on 2 Sep 1964.

DUKE ELLINGTON & HIS ORCHESTRA
CA CW REsn HJns, LB BCpr CCrs, JHtn JH RP PG HC, DE MH SWrd.

14 May 1964   (P)
Madison Square Garden (tc)
New York City, NY

....   Things Ain't What They Used To Be

DUKE ELLINGTON & HIS ORCHESTRA
CA CW REsn HJns, LB BCpr CCrs, JHtn JH RP PG HC, DE PMsn SWrd.

19 May 1964   (S)
Fine Studios
New York City, NY

.... Rpr   5093   People
.... Rpr   5094   The Good Life
.... Rpr   5095   Charade
.... RDB   5096-2   I Can't Stop Loving You
.... Rpr   5096 alt.   I Can't Stop Loving You

DUKE ELLINGTON & HIS RHYTHM AND FRIENDS
DE.

20 May 1964   (P)
Wollman Auditorium, Columbia University
New York City, NY

....   Presentation to DE and reply

> DE piano solo.

.... Fox   New York City Blues—Melancholia—Reflections In D
.... Fox   Little African Flower
.... Fox   Bird Of Paradise
.... Fox   A Single Petal Of A Rose
.... Fox   New World A-Comin'

> PMsn SWrd added.

.... Fox   Take The "A" Train
.... Fox   Satin Doll
.... MM   Caravan
....   Banquet Scene
.... Fox   Skillipoop

> DE recital.

.... MM   Recital –DE talking

> DE PMsn SWrd.

.... Fox+MM[1]   Medley[2]   >>>

> WLS piano solo.

.... MM   Carolina Shout

> DE BS.

.... MM   Tonk

> BS piano solo.

....   Lush Life –vBS

> BS PMsn SWrd, DE.

.... MM   Things Ain't What They Used To Be –DE talking

[1]Both releases (LP and CD) are incomplete, but together they give a complete rendition of the medley.
[2]Including: Solitude; Don't Get Around Much Anymore; Mood Indigo; I Got It Bad; Sophisticated Lady; Just Squeeze Me; In A Sentimental Mood; Do Nothin' Till You Hear From Me; It Don't Mean A Thing; Mood Indigo; Happy-Go-Lucky Local; The E&D Blues; The "C" Jam Blues; Stevie.

<table>
<tr><td></td><td>24 May 1964   (P)</td></tr>
<tr><td><u>DUKE ELLINGTON & HIS ORCHESTRA</u></td><td>CBS Studios (tc)</td></tr>
<tr><td>CA CW REsn HJns, LB BCpr CCrs, JHtn JH RP PG HC, DE PMsn SWrd.</td><td>New York City, NY</td></tr>
</table>

....   Satin Doll
....   Things Ain't What They Used To Be
....   Jam With Sam
....   Take The "A" Train

<table>
<tr><td></td><td>26 May 1964[1]   (P)</td></tr>
<tr><td><u>DUKE ELLINGTON & HIS ORCHESTRA WITH ELLA FITZGERALD & TERI THORNTON</u></td><td>NBC Studios (tc)</td></tr>
<tr><td>CA CW REsn HJns, LB BCpr CCrs, JHtn JH RP PG HC, DE PMsn SWrd.</td><td>New York City, NY</td></tr>
</table>

....   Take The "A" Train
....   Afro-Bossa

> EF added.

....   I'm Beginning To See The Light –vEF
....   Satin Doll –vEF

> EF omitted.

....   Happy-Go-Lucky Local
....   Satin Doll
....   Midriff

> BS PMsn SWrd, TTh.

....   Sophisticated Lady –vTTh

> Entire band, DE replaces BS.

....   Bluebird Of Delhi

> BS replaces DE, TTh added.

....   I Let A Song Go Out Of My Heart –vTTh

> BS PMsn, TTh.

....   I Got It Bad –vTTh

> DE interviewed by Hugh Downs.

....   Interview

> Entire band, DE replaces BS.

....   The "C" Jam Blues
....   Black And Tan Fantasy—Creole Love Call—The Mooche
....   Take The "A" Train

> TTh added.

....   Mood Indigo –vTTh

> TTh omitted.

....   Take The "A" Train
....   Things Ain't What They Used To Be
....   Interview (ctd.)

> DE BS.

....   Tonk

[1]Taping session; telecast on 5 Nov 1964.

DUKE ELLINGTON & HIS ORCHESTRA   31 May 1964   (P)
CA CW NWrd HJns, LB BCpr CCrs, JHtn JH RP PG HC, PMsn SWrd.   Holiday Ballroom
                                                                                         Chicago, IL

| .... | | The Second Time Around |
| .... | | I Left My Heart In San Francisco |

> DE added.

....		Hello Dolly
....		Hello Dolly
....	DJ	Mood Indigo
....	DJ	Satin Doll
....	DJ	Do Nothin' Till You Hear From Me
....	DJ	Silk Lace

> DE PMsn SWrd.

| .... | | Dance #3 (from the *Liberian Suite*) |

> Entire band.

....	DJ	I Got It Bad
....	DJ	Isfahan
....	DJ	Banquet Scene
....	DJ	Skillipoop
....	DJ	Tootie For Cootie
....	DJ	Summertime
....	DJ	The "C" Jam Blues
....	DJ	Happy-Go-Lucky Local
....	DJ	Things Ain't What They Used To Be
....		Things Ain't What They Used To Be
....	DJ	Guitar Amour
....		Danke Schoen
....		Cotton Tail
....	DJ	Stompin' At The Savoy
....	DJ	Jeep's Blues
....	DJ	I Can't Stop Lovin' You
....	DJ	Diminuendo In Blue and Wailing Interval
....	DJ	Satin Doll

DUKE ELLINGTON & HIS ORCHESTRA   12 Jun 1964   (P)
CA CW NWrd HJns, LB BCpr CCrs, JHtn JH RP PG HC, DE PMsn SWrd.   Disneyland (tc)
                                                                                         Anaheim, CA

....		Take The "A" Train
....		Take The "A" Train
....		Satin Doll
....		Things Ain't What They Used To Be
....		V.I.P.'s Boogie
....		Jam With Sam
....		Satin Doll

DUKE ELLINGTON   Jun 1964   (S)
No particulars available.   Unspecified studio (tc)
                                                                                         Los Angeles, CA

| .... | | Interview |

DUKE ELLINGTON & HIS ORCHESTRA   24 Jun 1964   (P)
CA CW NWrd HJns, LB BCpr CCrs, JHtn JH RP PG HC, DE PMsn SWrd.   Daiichi Kaikan
                                                                                         Kyoto, Japan

....		Take The "A" Train
....		Black And Tan Fantasy—Creole Love Call—The Mooche
		IMPRESSIONS FROM THE FAR EAST
....		- Amad
....		- Agra
....		- Bluebird Of Delhi
....		- Depk
....		The Opener

> PG, DE PMsn SWrd.

| .... | | Happy Reunion |

> Entire band.

| .... | | Blow By Blow |
| .... | | HARLEM   >>> |

DUKE ELLINGTON & HIS ORCHESTRA   (tc)[1]
Same personnel.

....   Take The "A" Train
....   Depk
....   Black And Tan Fantasy—Creole Love Call—The Mooche

> DE piano solo.

....   Nagoya

> Entire band.

....   I Got It Bad
....   Amad
....   HARLEM
....   Medley[2]
....   Things Ain't What They Used To Be

[1]The concert was filmed and edited excerpts telecast by CBS in the U.S. on 20 Oct 1964, under the title of "The Duke Swings Through Japan."
[2]Including: Satin Doll; Solitude; Mood Indigo; Sophisticated Lady.

26 Jun 1964   (P)
Koseinenkin Kaikan
Tokyo, Japan

DUKE ELLINGTON & HIS ORCHESTRA
CA CW NWrd HJns, LB BCpr CCrs, JHtn JH RP PG HC, DE PMsn SWrd.

....   Take The "A" Train
....   Smada
....   Black And Tan Fantasy—Creole Love Call—The Mooche

                     IMPRESSIONS FROM THE FAR EAST
....   - Amad
....   - Agra
....   - Bluebird Of Delhi
....   - Depk

....   The Opener

> PG, DE PMsn SWrd.

....   Happy Reunion

> Entire band.

....   Blow By Blow

Jun 1964   (S)
Unidentified location (bc/tc)
Japan

DUKE ELLINGTON
DE interviewed by person unknown; the program contains previously recorded music.

.... RDB   Interview

28 Jun 1964   (P)
NHK Television Hall (tc)
Tokyo, Japan

DUKE ELLINGTON & HIS ORCHESTRA
CA CW NWrd HJns, LB BCpr CCrs, JHtn JH RP PG HC, DE PMsn SWrd.

....   Black And Tan Fantasy—Creole Love Call—The Mooche
....   I Got It Bad
....   Perdido
....   Medley[1]
....   HARLEM
....   Things Ain't What They Used To Be

[1]Including: Satin Doll; Solitude; Don't Get Around Much Anymore; Mood Indigo; I'm Beginning To See The Light; Sophisticated Lady; Caravan; Do Nothin' Till You Hear From Me; I Let A Song Go Out Of My Heart/Don't Get Around Much Anymore.

29 Jun 1964   (S)
Golden Akasa Night Club (bc)
Tokyo, Japan

DUKE ELLINGTON—BILLY STRAYHORN—HARRY CARNEY
DE, BS, HC interviewed by person unknown.

....   Interview

1 Jul 1964   (S)
Tokyo Sound Records[1]
Tokyo, Japan

DUKE ELLINGTON
Piano solo.

.... Stv   Nagoya
.... Stv   Unidentified title
.... Stv   Little African Flower

[1]Some sources suggest that DE played these titles on the stage of the Koseinenkin Hall after a concert.

		3 Jul 1964[1] (P)
		TBS Studios (tc)
		Tokyo, Japan

DUKE ELLINGTON & HIS ORCHESTRA
CA CW NWrd HJns, LB BCpr CCrs, JHtn JH RP PG HC, DE PMsn SWrd.

....	Take The "A" Train
....	Satin Doll
....	Caravan
....	Jam With Sam
....	Black And Tan Fantasy—Creole Love Call—The Mooche
....	Rockin' In Rhythm
....	Rockin' In Rhythm
....	Passion Flower
....	Happy-Go-Lucky Local
....	Things Ain't What They Used To Be

[1]Taping session; telecast on 11 Jul 1964.

		Jul 1964 (P)
		Marine Ballroom, Steel Pier (bc)
		Atlantic City, NJ

DUKE ELLINGTON & HIS ORCHESTRA
CA CW NWrd HJns, LB BCpr CCrs, JHtn JH GHbt RP PG HC, DE PMsn SWrd.

....	Joy	Take The "A" Train
....	Joy	Things Ain't What They Used To Be
....	Joy	More
....	Joy	Never On Sunday
....	Joy	Stranger On The Shore
....	Joy	Tootie For Cootie
....	Joy	Satin Doll
....	Joy	Happy-Go-Lucky Local[1]
....	Joy	Take The "A" Train

[1]"Night Train" on Joy.

DUKE ELLINGTON & HIS ORCHESTRA
Same personnel.   (bc)

....		Take The "A" Train
....	Joy	Afro-Bossa
....	Joy	Call Me Irresponsible
....	Joy	Hello Dolly
....	Joy	Danke Schoen
....		The Second Time Around
....		Jam With Sam
....		Satin Doll
....		I Left My Heart In San Francisco

		8 Aug 1964 (P)
		Moon Bowl, Freedomland Park
		Bronx, NY

DUKE ELLINGTON & HIS ORCHESTRA
CA CW NWrd HJns, LB BCpr CCrs, JHtn JH RP PG HC, DE PMsn SWrd.

....	Afro-Bossa
....	Fly Me To The Moon
....	Hello Dolly
....	The Opener
....	I Got It Bad
....	Things Ain't What They Used To Be
....	Happy-Go-Lucky Local
....	Satin Doll

		17 Aug 1964 (P)
		Basin Street East (bc)
		New York City, NY

DUKE ELLINGTON & HIS ORCHESTRA
CA CW NWrd HJns, LB BCpr CCrs, JHtn JH RP PG HC, DE PMsn SWrd.

....	Take The "A" Train
....	Afro-Bossa
....	Kinda Dukish/Rockin' In Rhythm
....	Call Me Irresponsible
....	Hello Dolly
....	Never On Sunday
....	The Second Time Around
....	Things Ain't What They Used To Be
....	Satin Doll
....	East St. Louis Toodle-Oo
....	The Prowling Cat
....	Stranger On The Shore
....	Take The "A" Train

26 Aug 1964   (S)
Unspecified studio
New York City, NY

DUKE ELLINGTON & HIS ORCHESTRA
CA CW NWrd HJns, LB BCpr CCrs, JHtn JH GHbt RP PG HC, DE JL SWrd.

....			Spon (rehearsal)
....			Spon (rehearsal)
....			Spon (rehearsal)
....			Spon (rehearsal)
....			Spon (rehearsal)
....			Spon (rehearsal)
....			Spon (rehearsal)
....			Spon (rehearsal)
....			Spon (rehearsal)
....	RDB		Spon (rehearsal)
....	RDB		Spon (rehearsal)
....	RDB		Spon (rehearsal)
....	RDB		Spon (rehearsal)
> DE JL SWrd.			
....	RDB	-1	Spon (incomplete)
....			Spon (incomplete)
....	RDB	-2	Spon (incomplete)
....		-1[1]	Volupté
> Entire band.			
....		-1	Iglo[2] (ending)
....		-1[1]	Iglo
....		-2	Iglo (incomplete)
....		-3[1]	Iglo
....		-4[1]	Iglo
....			Shuffelody[3] (rehearsal)
....			Shuffelody (rehearsal)
....			Shuffelody (rehearsal)
....			Shuffelody (rehearsal)
....		-1	Shuffelody (incomplete)
....		-2[1]	Shuffelody
....			Shuffelody (ending)
....			Shuffelody (ending/incomplete)
> DE JL SWrd.			
....			Shuffelody (rehearsal)
> Entire band.			
....			Soul Train (rehearsal)
....			Soul Train (rehearsal)
....			Soul Train (rehearsal)
....			Soul Train (rehearsal)
....			Soul Train (rehearsal)
....			Soul Train (rehearsal)
....			Soul Train (rehearsal)
....			Soul Train (rehearsal)
....			Soul Train (rehearsal)
....			Soul Train (rehearsal)
....		-1[1]	Soul Train
....			Soul Train (incomplete)
....		-2	Soul Train (incomplete)
....		-2	Soul Train (incomplete)
....		-3[1]	Soul Train
....		-4	Soul Train
....			Shuffelody (rehearsal)
....		-5[1]	Shuffelody
....		-6	Shuffelody
....	RDB	-3[1]	Spon (in progress)
....		-4	Spon
....	RDB	-5[1]	Spon
....			Iglo (rehearsal)
....			Iglo (rehearsal)

[1] These takes have been used for the promotional film "Astrofreight" (*aka* "Cargo By Air"). The recordings were heavily edited for the soundtrack. For that reason only the unedited versions as broadcast by RDB are mentioned. A synopsis of the record release can be found below.
[2] *aka* "Iglo Blue"; "Igoo."
[3] "Shufflelady" or "Shuffelady" in all publications. This title is actually a contraction of the words *shuffle* and *melody*. The sound engineer who called it *Shuffle Lady* missed the finer point.

SUITE FOR SWINGING[1] (summation)

ER	-1/-3	- Iglo
ER	-2	- Shuffelody
ER	-1	- Volupté
ER	-1/-3	- Soul Train
ER	-4	- Iglo
ER	-3/-5	- Spon
ER	-5	- Shuffelody

[1]The release contains the heavily edited soundtrack, with some additional minor editing.

		2 Sep 1964[1] (S)
		CBC Studios (bc+tc)
		Toronto, ON

DUKE ELLINGTON & HIS RHYTHM
DE JL SWrd, intermittent interviews with Byng Whitteker.

....	Rar	Soda Fountain Rag
....	Rar	What's You Gonna Do When The Bed Breaks Down?
....	Rar	My Heritage –DE narration[2]
....		East St. Louis Toodle-Oo
....	Rar[3]	My People –DE narration
....		Piano improvisation
....	Vid	Sophisticated Lady
....		Medley[4]
....		Happy-Go-Lucky Local
....		I'm Beginning To See The Light
....		Isfahan
....	Rar	Take The "A" Train

[1]Taping session. Broadcast in part on 26 Dec 1967; telecast in part on 3 Mar 1965.
[2]*sa* "My Mother, My Father."
[3]The release has been edited and only the first portion is from this session; the remainder originates from 5 Sep 1964.
[4]Including: Don't You Know I Care?; Prelude To A Kiss; Someone; Do Nothin' Till You Hear From Me; I'm Just A Lucky So-And-So.

		5 Sep 1964[1] (S)
		CBC Studios (tc)
		Toronto, ON

DUKE ELLINGTON & HIS ORCHESTRA
CA CW NWrd HJns, LB BCpr CCrs, JHtn JH RP PG HC, DE JL SWrd, JS.

....	Rar	Happy-Go-Lucky Local
> DE.		
....	Rar[2]	My People –DE narration; other participants.
> Entire band.		
....	Rar	The Blues –vJS[3]
....	Rar	Kinda Dukish/Rockin' In Rhythm
		IMPRESSIONS FROM THE FAR EAST
....	Rar	- Bluebird Of delhi
....	Rar	- Agra
....	Rar	- Amad
....	Rar	My Mother, My Father –vJS
> BBgs, added.		
....	Rar	David Danced Before The Lord –vJS, BBgs tap
> BBgs, omitted.		
....	Rar	Banquet Scene
> FSt added.		
....	Rar	Skillipoop
> FSt omitted.		
....	Rar	Jam With Sam
> DE.		
....	Rar	Recital –DE talking

[1]Taping session; telecast on 3 Mar 1965.
[2]The release has been edited and only the second portion is from this session; the remainder originates from 2 Sep 1964.
[3]"The Blues Ain't" on Rar.

		6, 8, 9 Sep 1964 (S)
		Universal Studios
		Chicago, IL

DUKE ELLINGTON & HIS ORCHESTRA
CA CW NWrd HJns, LB BCpr CCrs, JHtn JH RP PG/EJsn HC, DE JL SWrd.

....	Rpr	2948	A Spoonful Of Sugar
....	Rpr	2949	Stay Awake >>>

....	Rpr	2950	Feed The Birds
....	Rpr	2951	Supercalifragilisticexpialidocious
....	Rpr	2952	Let's Go Fly A Kite
....	Rpr	2953	Chim Chim Cheree
....	Rpr	2954	Sister Suffragette
....	Rpr	2955	The Perfect Nanny
....	Rpr	2956	I Love To Laugh
....	Rpr	2957	The Life I Lead
....	Rpr	2958	Step In Time
....	Rpr	2959	Jolly Holiday

The titles are adaptions from the motion picture "Mary Poppins."

11 Sep 1964   (S)[1]
Cullen Auditorium (bc)
Houston, TX

DUKE ELLINGTON
DE interviewed by Ed Case.

....   Interview

[1]Backstage.

30 Sep 1964   (P)
City College Auditorium
Long Beach, CA

DUKE ELLINGTON & HIS ORCHESTRA
CA CW NWrd HJns, LB BCpr CCrs, JHtn JH RP PG HC, DE JL SWrd.

....   Take The "A" Train
....   Black And Tan Fantasy—Creole Love Call—The Mooche

                          IMPRESSIONS FROM THE FAR EAST
....   - Amad
....   - Agra
....   - Bluebird Of Delhi
....   - Depk

....   The Opener
....   In A Sentimental Mood
....   Blow By Blow
....   Medley[1]
....   The "C" Jam Blues
....   Never On Sunday
....   I Left My Heart In San Francisco
....   Take The "A" Train
....   Take The "A" Train
....   Tootie For Cootie
....   Skillipoop
....   The Prowling Cat
....   Kinda Dukish/Rockin' In Rhythm

> JHtn RP HC, DE.

....   Monologue –DE narration

> Entire band.

....   Fly Me To The Moon
....   Happy-Go-Lucky Local
....   Things Ain't What They Used To Be

[1]Including: Satin Doll; Solitude; Don't Get Around Much Anymore; Mood Indigo; I'm Beginning To See The Light; Sophisticated Lady; Caravan; Do Nothin' Till You Hear From Me; I Let A Song Go Out Of My Heart/Don't Get Around Much Anymore.

DUKE ELLINGTON   (bc)   (S)[1]
DE interviewed by Irving L. Jacobs.

....   Interview

[1]Backstage.

17 Nov 1964   (P)
Westinghouse Studios (tc)
Hollywood, CA

DUKE ELLINGTON
DE on the Regis Philbin show.

....   No particulars available

13 Dec 1964   (P)
Bolling AFB
Washington, DC

DUKE ELLINGTON & HIS ORCHESTRA
CA CW NWrd HJns, LB BCpr CCrs, JHtn JH RP PG HC, JL JBH.

....   Autumn Leaves

> DE added.

....   Take The "A" Train   >>>

....	Afro-Bossa	
....	Caravan	
....	Summertime	
....	Sophisticated Lady	
....	I Left My Heart In San Francisco	
....	Do Nothin' Till You Hear From Me	
....	Never On Sunday	
....	I Let A Song Go Out Of My Heart/Don't Get Around Much Anymore	
....	I Got It Bad	
....	Things Ain't What They Used To Be	

> JMP added.

....	Solitude –vJMP
....	Love You Madly –vJMP

> JMP omitted.

....	Mood Indigo
....	Happy-Go-Lucky Local

> DE JL JBH.

....	The "C" Jam Blues

> Entire band.

....	Call Me Irresponsible
....	Satin Doll
....	A Spoonful Of Sugar
....	Black And Tan Fantasy
....	Fly Me To The Moon
....	In A Mellotone
....	The Second Time Around
....	Danke Schoen
....	Mademoiselle de Paris
....	Warm Valley
....	On The Sunny Side Of The Street
....	Two Pros
....	The Mooche
....	Kinda Dukish/Rockin' In Rhythm

DUKE ELLINGTON & HIS ORCHESTRA   31 Dec 1964   (P)
CA CW NWrd HJns, LB BCpr CCrs, JHtn JH RP PG HC, DE JL SWrd.   Basin Street East (bc)
                                                                    New York City, NY

....	Take The "A" Train
....	Afro-Bossa
....	Silk Lace
....	Jam With Sam
....	Passion Flower
....	Fly Me To The Moon
....	Diminuendo In Blue and Wailing Interval
....	Satin Doll

DUKE ELLINGTON & HIS ORCHESTRA   (bc)
Same personnel.

....	The "C" Jam Blues
....	I Got It Bad
....	Things Ain't What They Used To Be
....	Things Ain't What They Used To Be

DUKE ELLINGTON & HIS ORCHESTRA WITH ETHEL ENNIS   5 Jan 1965[1]   (P)
CA CW NWrd HJns, LB BCpr CCrs, JHtn JH RP PG HC, DE JL SWrd.   NBC Studios (tc)
                                                                   New York City, NY

....	Medley[2]

> DE piano solo.

....	Dancers In Love

> Entire band, EEns added.

....	Love You Madly –vEEns

> EEns omitted.

....	Mood Indigo

[1]Taping session; telecast on 6 Jan 1965.
[2]Including: Satin Doll; Sophisticated Lady; Don't Get Around Much Anymore; I Got It Bad; I'm Beginning To See The Light.

<table>
<tr><td></td><td></td><td></td><td></td><td>12 Jan 1965[1]   (T/P)[2]</td></tr>
</table>

DUKE ELLINGTON & HIS ORCHESTRA   Universal Studios (tc)
CA CW HJns ME, LB BCpr CCrs, JHtn JH RP PG HC, DE JL SWrd.   Chicago, IL

....	Aff	Take The "A" Train
....	Aff	Rockin' In Rhythm
....	Aff	Step In Time
....	Aff	Supercalifragilisticexpialidocious
....	Aff	Tootie For Cootie
....	Aff	Medley[3]
....	DVD	Jam With Sam
....		Take The "A" Train

[1]Taping session; telecast on 23 Jan 1965.
[2]Soundtrack for the telecast "The Big Bands—Duke Ellington & His Orchestra. #1."
[3]Including: Caravan; I Got It Bad; Don't Get Around Much Anymore; Mood Indigo; I'm Beginning To See The Light;
Sophisticated Lady; Do Nothin' Till You Hear From Me.

DUKE ELLINGTON & HIS ORCHESTRA   (tc)[1]   (T/P)[2]
Same personnel.

....	Aff	Take The "A" Train
....	Aff	Afro-Bossa
....	Aff	Satin Doll
....	Aff	The Prowling Cat
....	Aff	Never On Sunday
....	Aff	Cotton Tail
....	Aff	Fly Me To The Moon
....	Aff	Banquet Scene
....	Aff	Skillipoop
....		Things Ain't What They Used To Be

[1]Taping session; telecast on 6 Mar 1965.
[2]Soundtrack for the telecast "The Big Bands—Duke Ellington & His Orchestra. #2."

19 Jan 1965   (S)

DUKE ELLINGTON & HIS ORCHESTRA   Fine Studios[1]
CA CW HJns ME RN, LB BCpr CCrs, JHtn JH RP PG HC, DE JL SWrd.   New York City, NY

....	Rpr	5097	Moon River
....	Rpr	5098	All My Lovin'
....	Rpr	5099	Days Of Wine And Roses
....	Rpr	5100	Satin Doll

[1]At the Great Northern Hotel, 58th Avenue; applies also to session on 21 Jan 1965.

21 Jan 1965   (S)
Fine Studios

DUKE ELLINGTON & HIS ORCHESTRA   New York City, NY
CA CW HJns RN, LB BCpr CCrs, JHtn JH RP PG HC, DE JL SWrd.

....	Rpr	5101	Red Roses For A Blue Lady
....		5102	I Want To Hold Your Hand
....	Rpr	5102-8	I Want To Hold Your Hand
....	RDB	5102-9	I Want To Hold Your Hand
....	Rpr	5103	A Beautiful Romance
....		5103 alt.	A Beautiful Romance
....	Rpr	5104-9	Ellington '66
....		5104 alt.	Ellington '66

26 Jan 1965   (S)
Unidentified location (bc)

DUKE ELLINGTON   Paris, France
Piano solo.

| .... | Nagoya |

29 Jan 1965   (P)
Théâtre des Champs Elysées (bc)[1]

DUKE ELLINGTON & HIS ORCHESTRA   Paris, France
CA CW HJns ME RN, LB BCpr CCrs, JHtn JH RP PG HC, DE JL SWrd.

....	LL	Midriff
....	RTE	Happy-Go-Lucky Local
....		BLACK, BROWN AND BEIGE
....		- Work Song
....		- Come Sunday
....	RTE	Take The "A" Train
....	RTE	Kinda Dukish/Rockin' In Rhythm[2]
....	RTE	Jam With Sam
....	RTE	The "C" Jam Blues >>>

[1]Excerpts of this and possibly the following concert have been broadcast by EUROPE 1.
[2]Only "Rockin' In Rhythm" on RTE.

30 Jan 1965   (P)
Théâtre des Champs Elysées (bc?)
Paris, France

<u>DUKE ELLINGTON & HIS ORCHESTRA</u>
CA CW HJns ME RN, LB BCpr CCrs, JHtn JH RP PG HC, DE JL SWrd.

....	Mad	Take The "A" Train
....	Mad	Midriff
....	Mad	Afro-Bossa
....		AD LIB ON NIPPON
....	Mad	- Part 1 (Fugi)[1]
....	Mad	- Part 2 (Igoo)[2]
....	Mad	- Part 3 (Nagoya)[3]
....	Mad	- Part 4 (Tokyo)
....		The Opener
....		Chelsea Bridge
....		Blow By Blow
....		BLACK, BROWN AND BEIGE
....	Mad	- Work Song
....	Mad	- Come Sunday
....	Mad	- Light
....	JC	Take The "A" Train
....	JC	Satin Doll—Sophisticated Lady
....	JC	Meow
....	JC	Meow
....	JC	I Got It Bad
....	JC	Harmony In Harlem
....	JC	Things Ain't What They Used To Be
....	JC	Perdido
....	JC	Tootie For Cootie
....	JC	Carolina Shout/Rockin' In Rhythm
....	Az	Jump For Joy –vRN
....	Az	He Huffed 'n' He Puffed –vRN[4]
....	JC	Take The "A" Train

[1]DE b dr; this applies to all future performances, unless stated otherwise.
[2]This title is a derivative of *Iglo* from the *Suite for Swinging.*
[3]DE piano solo; this applies to all future performances, unless stated otherwise.
[4]*aka* "Blow Those Blues Away."

<u>DUKE ELLINGTON & HIS ORCHESTRA</u>
Same personnel.

....	RTE	Boo-Dah
....	RTE	Afro-Bossa
....		AD LIB ON NIPPON
....	RTE	- Part 1 (Fugi)
....	RTE	- Part 2 (Igoo)
....	RTE	- Part 3 (Nagoya)
....	RTE	- Part 4 (Tokyo)
....	RTE	The Opener
....	RTE	Chelsea Bridge
....	LL	Happy-Go-Lucky Local
....		BLACK, BROWN AND BEIGE
....	RTE	- Work Song
....	RTE	- Come Sunday
....	RTE	- Light
....	RTE	Satin Doll
....	RTE	Sophisticated Lady
....	RTE	Meow
....	RTE	Meow
....	RTE	Passion Flower
....	RTE	Things Ain't What They Used To Be
....	RTE	Jeep's Blues
....	RTE	Perdido
....	RTE	Tootie For Cootie
....	RTE	East St. Louis Toodle-Oo
....	Az	Soda Fountain Rag/Rockin' In Rhythm
....	RTE	Just Squeeze Me –vRN
....	RTE	Just A-Settin' And A-Rockin' –vRN

DUKE ELLINGTON & HIS ORCHESTRA
CA CW HJns ME RN, LB BCpr CCrs, JHtn JH RP PG HC, DE JL SWrd.

....	Vid	Take The "A" Train
....	Vid	Midriff
....	Vid	Afro-Bossa

AD LIB ON NIPPON

....	Vid	- Part 1 (Fugi)
....	Vid	- Part 2 (Igoo)
....	Vid	- Part 3 (Nagoya)
....	Vid	- Part 4 (Tokyo)

....	Vid	The Opener
....	Vid	Chelsea Bridge
....	Vid	Blow By Blow

BLACK, BROWN AND BEIGE

....	Vid	- Work Song
....	Vid	- Come Sunday
....	Vid	- Light

....	Vid	Take The "A" Train
....	Vid	Satin Doll—Sophisticated Lady
....	Vid	Meow
....	Vid	Meow
....	Vid	Passion Flower
....	Vid	Things Ain't What They Used To Be
....	Vid	Jeep's Blues
....	Vid	Perdido
....	Vid	Tootie For Cootie
....	Vid	Kinda Dukish/Rockin' In Rhythm

> BS replaces DE.

| .... | Vid | Take The "A" Train |

> DE replaces BS.

| .... | Vid | He Huffed 'n' He Puffed –vRN |

> CW, RP, JGze JL SWrd, BBjm.

| .... | | Solitude –vBBjm |

> Entire band, DE replaces BS, BBjm omitted.

| .... | | Jam With Sam |
| .... | | Take The "A" Train |

> DE JL.

| .... | | Dancers In Love |

[1]The date of telecast is not known.

DUKE ELLINGTON
DE interviewed by Per Møller-Hansen.

| .... | | Interview |

[1]Probably backstage.

DUKE ELLINGTON & HIS ORCHESTRA
CA CW HJns ME RN, LB BCpr CCrs, JHtn JH RP PG HC, DE JL SWrd.

....		Take The "A" Train
....		Afro-Bossa
....		The Opener
....		Chelsea Bridge

BLACK, BROWN AND BEIGE

....		- Work Song
....		- Come Sunday
....		- Light

....		Passion Flower
....		Things Ain't What They Used To Be
....		Tootie For Cootie
....		Take The "A" Train

3 Feb 1965   (P)
Philharmonie
Berlin, Germany

DUKE ELLINGTON & HIS ORCHESTRA
CA CW HJns ME RN, LB BCpr CCrs, JHtn JH RP PG HC, DE JL SWrd.

....		Take The "A" Train
....	Pab	Midriff
....		The Opener
....		Afro-Bossa
		AD LIB ON NIPPON
....	Pab	- Part 1 (Fugi)
....	Pab	- Part 2 (Igoo)
....	Pab	- Part 3 (Nagoya)
....	Pab	- Part 4 (Tokyo)
....	Pab	Chelsea Bridge
....	Pab	Happy-Go-Lucky Local
....		Satin Doll—Sophisticated Lady
....		Meow
....		Passion Flower
....		Harmony In Harlem
....		Things Ain't What They Used To Be
....		Perdido
....		Tootie For Cootie
....	Az	Kinda Dukish/Rockin' In Rhythm
....	Az	The "C" Jam Blues
....	Az	The Nearness Of You
....	Az	Blues

9 Feb 1965   (P)
Liederhalle
Stuttgart, Germany

DUKE ELLINGTON & HIS ORCHESTRA
CA CW HJns ME RN, LB BCpr CCrs, JHtn JH RP PG HC, DE JL SWrd.

....	Midriff
....	Afro-Bossa
	AD LIB ON NIPPON
....	- Part 1 (Fugi)
....	- Part 2 (Igoo)
....	- Part 3 (Nagoya)
....	- Part 4 (Tokyo)
....	The Opener
....	Chelsea Bridge
....	Blow By Blow
	BLACK, BROWN AND BEIGE
....	- Work Song
....	- Come Sunday
....	- Light
....	Stompy Jones
....	Satin Doll—Sophisticated Lady
....	Meow
....	Meow
....	Passion Flower
....	Things Ain't What They Used To Be
....	Harmony In Harlem
....	Jeep's Blues
....	Perdido
....	Tootie For Cootie
....	Kinda Dukish/Rockin' In Rhythm
....	Take The "A" Train --vRN
....	Just A-Settin' And A-Rockin' --vRN
....	The "C" Jam Blues
....	Jam With Sam
....	Take The "A" Train

10 Feb 1965   (P)
Private residence
Villingen, Germany

DUKE ELLINGTON & HIS RHYTHM
DE JL SWrd.

....	MPS	Take The "A" Train
....	MPS	Prelude To A Kiss

12 Feb 1965   (P)
Unidentified location
Munich, Germany

DUKE ELLINGTON & HIS ORCHESTRA
CA CW HJns ME RN, LB BCpr CCrs, JHtn JH RP PG HC, DE JL SWrd.

....	Midriff >>>

....   Afro-Bossa

                                                     AD LIB ON NIPPON
....   - Part 1 (Fugi)
....   - Part 2 (Igoo)
....   - Part 3 (Nagoya)
....   - Part 4 (Tokyo)

....   The Opener
....   Chelsea Bridge
....   Blow By Blow

                                                     BLACK, BROWN AND BEIGE
....   - Work Song
....   - Come Sunday
....   - Light

....   Take The "A" Train
....   Satin Doll—Sophisticated Lady
....   Meow
....   Passion Flower
....   Prelude To A Kiss
....   Harmony In Harlem
....   Tootie For Cootie
....   Unidentified title/Rockin' In Rhythm
....   Black And Tan Fantasy
....   Tell Me, It's The Truth[1]
....   Jam With Sam

[1]aka "The Truth."

DUKE ELLINGTON   Unidentified location (bc) (S)[1]
DE interviewed by Pat Patrick.   Munich, Germany

....   Interview

[1]Presumably backstage.

                                                                           13 Feb 1965   (P)
                                                                           Royal Festival Hall
DUKE ELLINGTON & HIS ORCHESTRA   London, England
CA CW HJns ME RN, LB BCpr CCrs, JHtn JH RP PG HC, DE JL SWrd.

....   Take The "A" Train
....   Afro-Bossa

                                                     AD LIB ON NIPPON
....   - Part 1 (Fugi)
....   - Part 2 (Igoo)
....   - Part 3 (Nagoya)
....   - Part 4 (Tokyo)

....   The Opener
....   Chelsea Bridge

                                                     BLACK, BROWN AND BEIGE
....   - Work Song
....   - Come Sunday
....   - Light

....   Take The "A" Train
....   Satin Doll—Sophisticated Lady
....   Tootie For Cootie
....   Prelude To A Kiss
....   Harmony In Harlem
....   Meow
....   Unidentified title/Rockin' In Rhythm
....   The "C" Jam Blues
....   Take The "A" Train –vRN
....   Just A-Settin' And A-Rockin' –vRN
....   Jam With Sam
....   God Save The Queen

DUKE ELLINGTON & HIS ORCHESTRA
Same personnel.

....   Take The "A" Train
....   Midriff
....   Afro-Bossa

                                                     AD LIB ON NIPPON
....   - Part 1 (Fugi)
....   - Part 2 (Igoo)   >>>

....	- Part 3 (Nagoya)
....	- Part 4 (Tokyo)
....	The Opener
....	Chelsea Bridge
....	Blow By Blow
	BLACK, BROWN AND BEIGE
....	- Work Song
....	- Come Sunday
....	- Light
....	Stompy Jones
....	Satin Doll—Sophisticated Lady
....	Tootie For Cootie
....	Prelude To A Kiss
....	Harmony In Harlem
....	Jeep's Blues
....	Meow
....	Meow
....	Carolina Shout/Rockin' In Rhythm
....	The "C" Jam Blues
....	Take The "A" Train -vRN
....	Just A-Settin' And A-Rockin' –vRN
....	Jam With Sam
....	God Save The Queen

DUKE ELLINGTON & HIS ORCHESTRA

14 Feb 1965   (P)
Hammersmith Odeon
London, England

CA CW HJns ME RN, LB BCpr CCrs, JHtn JH RP PG HC, DE JL SWrd.

....	Take The "A" Train
....	Midriff
....	Afro-Bossa
	AD LIB ON NIPPON
....	- Part 1 (Fugi)
....	- Part 2 (Igoo)
....	- Part 3 (Nagoya)
....	- Part 4 (Tokyo)
....	The Opener
....	Chelsea Bridge
....	Blow By Blow
	BLACK, BROWN AND BEIGE
....	- Work Song
....	- Come Sunday
....	- Light
....	Stompy Jones
....	Satin Doll—Sophisticated Lady
....	Tootie For Cootie
....	Prelude To A Kiss
....	Harmony In Harlem
....	Meow
....	Unidentified title/Rockin' In Rhythm
....	The "C" Jam Blues
....	Take The "A" Train –vRN
....	God Save The Queen

DUKE ELLINGTON & HIS ORCHESTRA
Same personnel.

....	Take The "A" Train
....	Midriff
....	Afro-Bossa
	AD LIB ON NIPPON
....	- Part 1 (Fugi)
....	- Part 2 (Igoo)
....	- Part 3 (Nagoya)
....	- Part 4 (Tokyo)
....	The Opener
....	Chelsea Bridge
....	Blow By Blow
	BLACK, BROWN AND BEIGE
....	- Work Song
....	- Come Sunday >>>

....		- Light
....		Stompy Jones
....		Tootie For Cootie
....		Satin Doll—Sophisticated Lady
....		Prelude To A Kiss
....		Harmony In Harlem
....		Jeep's Blues
....		Meow
....		Meow
....		Skin Deep
....		Kinda Dukish/Rockin' In Rhythm
....		The "C" Jam Blues
....		Take The "A" Train –vRN
....		Just A-Settin' And A-Rockin' –vRN

16 Feb 1965   (S)
BBC Studios
London, England

DUKE ELLINGTON & HIS ORCHESTRA
CA CW HJns ME RN, LB BCpr CCrs, JHtn JH RP PG HC, DE JL SWrd.

....		Igoo
....		The Opener
	> CW tp solo.	
....		'Round About Midnight
	> Entire band.	
....		Chelsea Bridge
....		Mood Indigo[1]
....		Mood Indigo
....		Mood Indigo
....		Mood Indigo
....		Mood Indigo
....		Mood Indigo
....		Mood Indigo
....		Mood Indigo
....		Mood Indigo
....		Mood Indigo
....		Mood Indigo
....		Mood Indigo
....		Mood Indigo
....		The Prowling Cat (incomplete)
....		The Prowling Cat
....		Tell Me, It's The Truth
....		The Prowling Cat (incomplete)
....		Tell Me, It's The Truth
	> CW omitted.	
....		Passion Flower
....		Jump For Joy (incomplete)
....		Jump For Joy (incomplete)
	> DE piano solo.	
....		Jump For Joy—Bird Of Paradise—Band Call
	> Entire band.	
....		Jump For Joy
....		Mood Indigo (incomplete)
	> DE piano solo.	
....		Nagoya
	> LB tb solo.	
....		When You're Smiling
	> DE piano solo.	
....		Fugi
	> Entire band.	
....		Take The "A" Train
....		Midriff
....		Afro-Bossa
....		Fugi
....		Igoo
....		Nagoya >>>

....	Tokyo
....	The Opener
....	Chelsea Bridge
....	Mood Indigo
....	The Prowling Cat
....	Passion Flower
....	Jump For Joy
....	Take The "A" Train (incomplete)
....	Take The "A" Train

[1]Of the fourteen "takes" of *Mood Indigo,* six were only 4 bars or less. More details are not available, since the tape could not be auditioned.

The above is a rehearsal session.

DUKE ELLINGTON & HIS ORCHESTRA   BBC Studios (tc)[1]   (P)
Same personnel.

....	Opening remarks by DE
....	Take The "A" Train
....	Midriff
....	Afro-Bossa
....	Comments by DE
....	The Opener
	AD LIB ON NIPPON
....	- Part 1 (Fugi)
....	- Part 2 (Igoo)
....	- Part 3 (Nagoya)
....	- Part 4 (Tokyo)
....	Chelsea Bridge (comments by DE over music)
....	Mood Indigo (comments by DE over music)
....	The Prowling Cat
....	Passion Flower
....	Jump For Joy –vRN
....	Take The "A" Train

[1]The above program "The Duke In Europe #1" was telecast on 27 Mar 1965.

                                                                        18 Feb 1965[1]   (P)
DUKE ELLINGTON & HIS ORCHESTRA   BBC Studios (tc)
CA HJns ME RN, LB BCpr CCrs, JHtn JH RP PG HC, DE JL SWrd.   London, England

....	Take The "A" Train
	BLACK, BROWN AND BEIGE
....	Work Song
....	Come Sunday
....	Montage

> BS replaces DE.

....	Dig Not The Distortion[2]

> DE replaces BS.

....	Tell Me, It's The Truth

> DE piano solo.

....	Le Sucrier Velours

> Entire band.

....	Happy-Go-Lucky Local
....	Take The "A" Train -vRN
....	Satin Doll

[1]The above program "The Duke In Europe #2" was telecast on 10 Apr 1965.
[2]*sa* "Taffy Twist."

                                                                        23 Feb 1965   (P)
DUKE ELLINGTON & HIS ORCHESTRA   City Hall
CA CW HJns ME RN, LB BCpr CCrs, JHtn JH RP PG HC, DE JL SWrd.   Newcastle, England

....	Take The "A" Train

                                                                        27 Feb 1965   (P)
DUKE ELLINGTON & HIS ORCHESTRA   Free Trade Hall
CA CW HJns ME RN, LB BCpr CCrs, JHtn JH RP PG HC, DE JL SWrd.   Manchester, England

....	Midriff
....	Afro-Bossa >>>

	AD LIB ON NIPPON
....	- Part 1 (Fugi)
....	- Part 2 (Igoo)
....	- Part 3 (Nagoya)
....	- Part 4 (Tokyo)
....	The Opener
....	Chelsea Bridge
....	Blow By Blow
	BLACK, BROWN AND BEIGE
....	- Work Song
....	- Come Sunday
....	- Light
....	Take The "A" Train
....	Satin Doll—Sophisticated Lady
....	Tootie For Cootie
....	Prelude To A Kiss
....	Harmony In Harlem
....	Meow
....	Kinda Dukish/Rockin' In Rhythm
....	Black And Tan Fantasy
....	Take The "A" Train --vRN
....	God Save The Queen

DUKE ELLINGTON & HIS ORCHESTRA
Same personnel.

	Midriff
....	Afro-Bossa
	AD LIB ON NIPPON
....	- Part 1 (Fugi)
....	- Part 2 (Igoo)
....	- Part 3 (Nagoya)
....	- Part 4 (Tokyo)
....	The Opener
....	Chelsea Bridge
	BLACK, BROWN AND BEIGE
....	- Work Song
....	- Come Sunday
....	- Light
....	Take The "A" Train
....	Satin Doll—Sophisticated Lady
....	Tootie For Cootie
....	Passion Flower
....	Harmony In Harlem
....	Pass-Out Blues
....	Meow
....	Meow
....	Kinda Dukish/Rockin' In Rhythm
....	Tell Me, It's The Truth
....	Take The "A" Train --vRN
....	Jam With Sam
....	God Save The Queen

28 Feb 1965   (P)
New Victoria Theatre
London, England.

DUKE ELLINGTON & HIS ORCHESTRA
CA CW HJns ME RN, LB BCpr CCrs, JHtn JH RP PG HC, DE JL SWrd.

	Midriff
....	Afro-Bossa
	AD LIB ON NIPPON
....	- Part 1 (Fugi)
....	- Part 2 (Igoo)
....	- Part 3 (Nagoya)
....	- Part 4 (Tokyo)
....	The Opener
....	Chelsea Bridge
....	Blow By Blow
	BLACK, BROWN AND BEIGE
....	- Work Song
....	- Come Sunday
....	- Light >>>

....		Take The "A" Train
....		Satin Doll—Sophisticated Lady
....		Tootie For Cootie
....		I Got It Bad
....		Harmony In Harlem
....		Meow
....		Kinda Dukish/Rockin' In Rhythm
....		Mood Indigo
....		Take The "A" Train –vRN
....		God Save The Queen

DUKE ELLINGTON & HIS ORCHESTRA
Same personnel.

....		Afro-Bossa
		AD LIB ON NIPPON
....		- Part 1 (Fugi)
....		- Part 2 (Igoo)
....		- Part 3 (Nagoya)
....		- Part 4 (Tokyo)
....		The Opener
....		Chelsea Bridge
....		Blow By Blow
		BLACK, BROWN AND BEIGE
....		- Work Song
....		- Come Sunday
....		- Light
....		Take The "A" Train
....		Satin Doll—Sophisticated Lady
....		Tootie For Cootie
....		Passion Flower
....		Harmony In Harlem
....		Pass-Out Blues
....		Meow
....		Kinda Dukish/Rockin' In Rhythm
....		Tell Me, It's The Truth
....		Harlem Air Shaft
....		Take The "A" Train –vRN
....		Jam With Sam
....		God Save The Queen

Feb 1965   (S)
BBC Studios (tc)
London, England

DUKE ELLINGTON
DE interviewed by Michael Dean.

....		Interview

> DE piano solo.

....		Sophisticated Lady—Satin Doll

3 Mar 1965[1]   (S)
Unidentified location (bc)
New York City, NY

DUKE ELLINGTON
DE interviewed by Henry F. Whiston; intermittent previously recorded music.

....		Interview

[1]Broadcast on 20 Apr 1965.

4 Mar 1965   (S)
Fine Studios[1]
New York City, NY

DUKE ELLINGTON & HIS ORCHESTRA
CA CW HJns RN, LB BCpr CCrs, JHtn JH RP PG HC, DE JL SWrd.

			AD LIB ON NIPPON
....		-1	- Part 2 (Igoo) (incomplete)
....			- Part 2 (Igoo) (incomplete)
....		-2	- Part 2 (Igoo)
....		-2	- Part 3 (Nagoya)
....		-2	- Part 4 (Tokyo)
....	Saj	-3	- Part 1 (Fugi)
....	Saj	-3	- Part 2 (Igoo)
....	Saj	-3	- Part 3 (Nagoya)
....	Saj	-3	- Part 4 (Tokyo)
....	Rpr	3393-1	Chelsea Bridge

			BLACK, BROWN AND BEIGE[2]
....			- Come Sunday (incomplete)
....	Saj	-2	- Come Sunday
....	Saj	-1	- Work Song
....		-1	- Montage (incomplete)
....		-2	- Montage (incomplete)
....	Saj	-3	- Montage
....	Rpr	3396-1	The Opener
....	RDB	3397	Fade Up (incomplete)[3]
....	Rpr	3397-9	Fade Up
> BS JL SWrd.			
....	RDB	-1	Unidentified title
....	RDB	-2	Unidentified title

[1]At the Great Northern Hotel, 58th Street; applies also to sessions on 17 Mar and 14 Apr 1965.
[2]See also sessions on 31 Mar and 18 May 1965.
[3]sa "Tootie For Cootie."

7 Mar 1965 (P)
CBS Studios (tc)
New York City, NY

ELLA FITZGERALD WITH DUKE ELLINGTON & HIS ORCHESTRA
Vcl, acc. by CA CW HJns RN, LB BCpr CCrs, JHtn JH RP PG HC, DE JL SWrd.

....		It Don't Mean A Thing –vEF
....		The Opener
....		Medley[1]

[1]Including: Do Nothin' Till You Hear From Me –vEF; I'm Beginning To See The Light –vEF; I Got It Bad –vEF; Don't Get Around Much Anymore –vEF; Mood Indigo –vEF; Cotton Tail –vEF.

17 Mar 1965 (S)
Fine Studios
New York City, NY

DUKE ELLINGTON & HIS ORCHESTRA
CA HMG HJns RN, LB BCpr CCrs, JHtn JH RP PG HC, DE JL SWrd.

....		-1	[1] Depk
....		-3	Depk
....		-4	Depk (incomplete)
....		-5	Depk
....		-1	[1] Isfahan
....		-2	Isfahan
....		-1	The Prowling Cat
....		-2	The Prowling Cat
....	Rpr	3382-1	[2] Jungle Kitty[3]
....		3382-2	Jungle Kitty (insert/incomplete)
....		3382-3	Jungle Kitty (insert/incomplete)
....		3382-4	Jungle Kitty (insert/incomplete)
....		3382-5	Jungle Kitty (insert)
....		3382	Jungle Kitty (insert/incomplete)
....	Rpr	3382-8[4]	Jungle Kitty (insert)
....		-1	Counter Theme[5]
....		-2	Counter Theme (incomplete)
....	Saj	-3	Counter Theme
....		-2	Pass-Out Blues (incomplete)
....		-3	Pass-Out Blues (incomplete)
....	RDB	-4	Pass-Out Blues
....		-1	Skillipoop (incomplete)
....	Saj	-3	Skillipoop
....	Rpr	3374-1	Things Ain't What They Used To Be
....	RDB	-1	[1] Amad
....		-2	Amad (incomplete)
....		-3	Amad (incomplete)
....		-4	Amad
> JHtn RP HC, DE.			
....		-1	Monologue –DE narration (incomplete)
....	RDB	-1	Monologue –DE narration
....		-2	Monologue –DE narration (incomplete)

[1]Parts of the future Far East Suite.
[2]Parts of The Virgin Islands Suite; see also footnote for the 14 Apr session.
[3]sa "Meow."
[4]Insert was used for the Rpr release.
[5]sa "Banquet Scene."

31 Mar 1965   (S)
Universal Studios
Chicago, IL

DUKE ELLINGTON & HIS ORCHESTRA
CA CW HJns RN, LB BCpr CCrs, JHtn JH RP PG HC, DE JL SWrd.

                                   BLACK, BROWN AND BEIGE (ctd.)[1]
.... Saj   - West Indian Dance
.... Saj   - Y.G.O.[2]
.... MM   -20   The Prowling Cat
.... RDB   -21   The "C" Jam Blues
....   [3] Amad
....   [3] Agra
....   [3] Bluebird Of Delhi
....   [3] Isfahan

[1]See also sessions on 1 Mar and 18 May 1965.
[2]*aka* "Youth"; *sa* "Emancipation Celebration"; "Graceful Awkwardness"; "Creamy Brown."
[3]Parts of the future *Far East Suite*.

Apr 1965[1]   (P)
Studios KYW (tc)
Philadelphia, PA

DUKE ELLINGTON & HIS ORCHESTRA
CA CW HJns RN, LB BCpr CCrs, JHtn JH RP PG HC, DE JL SWrd.

> JS acc. by members of the Ellington orchestra and/or studio band.

....   Everybody Loves My Baby –vJS
....   JS interviewed by Mike Douglas
....   Katiusha –vJS
....   The Thrill Is Gone –vJS

> Entire band.

....   Take The "A" Train
....   The Opener
....   Tootie For Cootie
....   Satin Doll

> MDgs added.

....   Solitude –vMDgs

> MDgs omitted, JS added.

....   Just Squeeze Me –vJS

> JS omitted.

....   Take The "A" Train

[1]Taping session; telecast on 16 Apr 1965.

14 Apr 1965   (S)
Fine Studios
New York City, NY

DUKE ELLINGTON & HIS ORCHESTRA
CA CW HJns RWls RN, LB BCpr CCrs, JHtn JH RP PG HC, DE JL SWrd.

....   -1   Rod la Rocque (incomplete)
....   -2   Rod la Rocque
....   -3   Rod la Rocque
.... Saj   -4   Rod la Rocque
.... RDB   -1   Obmil[1]
.... RDB   -2   Obmil
.... RDB   3376-2   [2] Island Virgin
.... Rpr   3376-3   Island Virgin
....   3379-1   [2] Virgin Jungle
.... Rpr   3379-2   Virgin Jungle
.... Rpr   3379-4   Virgin Jungle (coda insert)
....   3380-1   [2] Fiddler On The Diddle[3]
.... Rpr   3380-2   Fiddler On The Diddle
....   3395-1   Mysterious Chick[4] (incomplete)
....   3395-2   Mysterious Chick
....   3395-3   Mysterious Chick (incomplete)
.... Rpr   3395-4   Mysterious Chick
....   3396-1   The Barefoot Stomper[5] (incomplete)
....   3396-3   The Barefoot Stomper (incomplete)
....   3396   The Barefoot Stomper (incomplete)
....   3396-4   The Barefoot Stomper (incomplete)
....   3396   The Barefoot Stomper (incomplete)
.... RDB   3396-5   The Barefoot Stomper
....   3396-6   The Barefoot Stomper (incomplete)
....   3396-7   The Barefoot Stomper
.... Rpr   3396-8   The Barefoot Stomper
....   -1   That Scene   >>>

.... Saj   -2   That Scene[6]

    > DE JL SWrd.

.... Saj   3324-1   Rhythm Section Blues[7]

    > Entire band.

.... RDB   3324-2   Blues[7]
.... Rpr   3324-3   Big Fat Alice's Blues[7]
.... RDB   -1   Limbo Jazz (incomplete)
.... RDB   -2   Limbo Jazz

[1]*sa* "Self Portrait"; "Take It Slow"; "Limbo Jazz"; "Imbo"; (=Limbo).
[2]These titles, plus "Jungle Kitty" —see session on 17 Mar 1965—have been released as "The Virgin Islands Suite."
[3]*aka* "Volta."
[4]*aka* "Love."
[5]*aka* "Skip."
[6]"Love" on Saj.
[7]Same tune, different titles.

DUKE ELLINGTON
DE interviewed by Mike Wallace.

7 May 1965   (S)
CBS Studios (tc)
New York City, NY

....   Interview

DUKE ELLINGTON & HIS ORCHESTRA
CA CW HJns PSo RN, LB BCpr CCrs, JHtn JH RP PG HC, DE JL SWrd.

18 May 1965   (S)
Universal Studios
Chicago, IL

                      BLACK, BROWN AND BEIGE (ctd.)[1]
                      Beige No. 2
.... Az   -4   - A View From Central Park[2]
.... Saj   -12   - Sirens' Rock Waltz[3]
....   -13   - Interlude[4]
.... Saj   -19   - Interlude
.... Saj   -25   - Sugar Hill Penthouse

.... DJ   -29   New Mood Indigo

[1]See also sessions on 1 and 31 Mar 1965.
[2]As "Introduction" on Az.
[3]*aka* "Jazz Waltz"; "Cy Runs Rock Waltz" [*sic*] on Saj.
[4]*sa* "Sirens' Rock Waltz"; "Jazz Waltz."

DUKE ELLINGTON & HIS ORCHESTRA
CA CW HJns PSo RN, LB BCpr CCrs, JHtn JH RP PG HC, DE JL SWrd.

20 May 1965   (S)
Universal Studios
Chicago, IL

.... LL   Cool Rock
.... LL   P.S. 170
.... LL   The Twitch
.... LL   Hi, Jane
.... LL   Hi, June

    > RN, JHtn, DE JL SWrd.

.... LL   That's Love[1]

[1]*sa* "Upper And Outest"; "Anatomy Of A Murder" on LL.

DUKE ELLINGTON
No particulars available.

28 May 1965   (S)
South Campus Fieldhouse (bc?)
Waukesha, WI

....   Interview

DUKE ELLINGTON
DE interviewed by Willis Conover; intermittent previously recorded music.

4 Jun 1965   (S)
Unspecified studio (bc)
Washington, DC

.... Vta   Interview

DUKE ELLINGTON & HIS ORCHESTRA
CA CW HJns ME RN, LB BCpr CCrs, JHtn JH RP PG HC, DE JL SWrd.

14 Jun 1965   (P)
The White House
Washington, DC

....   Take The "A" Train

                      IMPRESSIONS FROM THE FAR EAST
....   - Amad
....   - Agra   >>>

....   - Bluebird Of Delhi

                   BLACK, BROWN AND BEIGE
....   - Work Song
....   - Come Sunday
....   - Light
....   Satin Doll
....   Medley[1]

[1]Including: Solitude; I Got It Bad; Don't Get Around Much Anymore; Mood Indigo; I'm Beginning To See The Light; Sophisticated Lady; Caravan.

                                                                 20 Jun 1965   (P)

JAZZ PIANO WORKSHOP   Civic Arena
BTlr DE EH.   Pittsburgh, PA

....   Bb   Father's Day Greetings –talking

    > DE piano solo.

....   Vi   TPA5-3353   Second Portrait Of The Lion

    > DE EH LGls BRly.

....   Vi   TPA5-3356   House Of Lords[1]

    > EH omitted.

....   Bb   TPA5-3362   Take The "A" Train

[1]*aka* "Early Duke."

                                                                29 Jun 1965   (S)

BILLY STRAYHORN'S GROUP   RCA Studios
CT, BWbr, BS WMsl DBly, DE supervising.   New York City, NY

....   RB   -6   U.M.M.G.

    > DE added.

....   RB   -7   Boo-Dah

    > DE omitted.

....   Az   -3   Passion Flower
....   RB   -3   Take The "A" Train

    > BS WMsl DBly.

....   -5   Day Dream

    > Entire group.

....   RB   -5   Just A-Settin' And A-Rockin'

                                                                 2 Jul 1965   (S)

BILLY STRAYHORN'S GROUP   RCA Studios
CT WRff, BWbr, BS WMsl DBly, OB, DE supervising.   New York City, NY

....   -1   Raincheck (incomplete)
....   RB   -2   Raincheck
....   -1   Chelsea Bridge (incomplete)
....   -2   Chelsea Bridge
....   -2   Chelsea Bridge (incomplete)
....   RB   -4   Chelsea Bridge
....   -1   Multicolored Blue –vOB (incomplete)
....   -2   Multicolored Blue –vOB (incomplete)
....   RB   -4   Multicolored Blue –vOB

    > DE added.

....   RDB   -1   Pig Sty (incomplete)
....   RB   -2   Pig Sty[1]
....   RB   -1   Oink

    > DE omitted.

....   Your Love Has Faded (rehearsal)
....   -1   Your Love Has Faded –vOB (incomplete)
....   RB   -3   Your Love Has Faded –vOB
....   -4   Your Love Has Faded (insert)
....   -5   Your Love Has Faded (insert)
....   -1   Love Came –vOB
....   RB   -2   Love Came –vOB
....   RB   -1   A Flower Is A Lovesome Thing –vOB   >>>

....		-1	Love Has Passed Me By –vOB (incomplete)
....		-2	Love Has Passed Me By –vOB (incomplete)
....	RB	-3	Love Has Passed Me By –vOB
....			Something To Live For –vOB
....		-4	Something To Live For –vOB (incomplete)
....	RB	-4	Something To Live For –vOB

[1]"Pick Side" [*sic*] on RB.

9 Jul 1965 (P)
NBC Studios (tc)
New York City, NY[1]

DUKE ELLINGTON & HIS ORCHESTRA
CA CW HJns ME, LB BCpr CCrs, JHtn JH RP PG HC, DE JL JBH, intermittent interviews with the host of the Today show.

....	Never On Sunday
....	Red Roses For A Blue Lady
....	Cool Rock
....	Satin Doll
....	Sophisticated Lady
....	Things Ain't What They Used To Be

> CA, PG, DE JL JBH.

....	Misty

[1]Part of the event originates from the Sheraton Hotel in Philadelphia, PA.

10 Jul 1965 (P)
Enzio Pinza Theater, Stamford Nature Museum
Rock Rimmon, CT

DUKE ELLINGTON & HIS ORCHESTRA
CA CW HJns ME, LB BCpr CCrs, JHtn JH RP PG HC, DE JL SWrd.

....	Take The "A" Train
....	Award presentation to Benny Goodman

> BG added.

....	Let's Dance
....	The Nature Museum Blues

> BG omitted.

....	Fade Up[1]
....	I Got It Bad
....	Things Ain't What They Used To Be
....	Day Dream
....	The Prowling Cat
....	Medley[2]

> DE JL SWrd.

....	A Single Petal Of A Rose

> Entire band.

....	Never On Sunday
....	Red Roses For A Blue Lady
....	Jam With Sam
....	Things Ain't What They Used To Be

[1]Announced as "Fade Out."
[2]Including: Satin Doll; Solitude; Don't Get Around Much Anymore; Mood Indigo; I'm Beginning To See The Light; Sophisticated Lady; Caravan; Do Nothin' Till You Hear From Me; I Let A Song Go Out Of My Heart; Don't Get Around Much Anymore.

28 Jul 1965 (S)
Tanglewood Music Center
Lenox, MA

DUKE ELLINGTON WITH THE BOSTON POPS ORCHESTRA
DE JL LBsn, with the Boston Pops Orchestra, Arthur Fiedler conducting.

....	Bb	-1	The Mooche
....	Bb	-1	The Mooche
....	Bb	-2	Love Scene
....	Bb	-4	Love Scene
....	Bb	-1	I'm Beginning To See The Light
....	Bb	-1	Do Nothin' Till You Hear From Me
....	Bb	-1	Satin Doll
....	Bb	-3	Satin Doll

The above is a rehearsal session.

DUKE ELLINGTON WITH THE BOSTON POPS ORCHESTRA (P)
Same personnel.

....	Vi	SRA5-5803	Caravan	>>>

....	Vi	SRA5-5803	Mood Indigo
....	Vi	SRA5-5803	The Mooche
....	Vi	SRA5-5803	I Let A Song Go Out Of My Heart
....	Vi	SRA5-5803	I'm Beginning To See The Light
....	Vi	SRA5-5804	Do Nothin' Till You Hear From Me
....	Vi	SRA5-5804	Sophisticated Lady

> DE omitted.

....	Vi	SRA5-5804	Timon Of Athens March[1]

> DE added.

....	Vi	SRA5-5804	Solitude
....	Vi	SRA5-5804	I Got It Bad
....	Vi	SRA5-5804	Satin Doll
....	Vi		Love Scene

> DE piano solo.

....	Vi		A Single Petal Of A Rose

[1]Part of *Timon Of Athens*.

DUKE ELLINGTON WITH THE NEW YORK PHILHARMONIC ORCHESTRA
DE with the New York Philharmonic Orchestra, Lucas Foss conducting.

31 Jul 1965   (P)
Philharmonic Hall, Lincoln Center
New York City, NY

....   New World A-Comin'

> JL LBsn added, DE conducting.

THE GOLDEN BROOM AND THE GREEN APPLE
....   - Stanza 1 (The Golden Broom)
....   - Stanza 2 (The Green Apple)
....   - Stanza 3 (The Handsome Traffic Policeman)

> JL LBsn omitted.

....   Preamble For A Solemn Occasion –DE recital

DUKE ELLINGTON
Award presentation.

2 Aug 1965   (P)
City Hall Park (tc)
New York City, NY

....   Acceptance speech by DE

DUKE ELLINGTON
DE with Joey Bishop and Skitch Henderson.

ABC Studios (tc)

....   Conversation

> DE piano solo.

....   A Single Petal Of A Rose

DUKE ELLINGTON
DE interviewed by Jim Gossa.

16 Aug 1965   (S)
Unidentified location (bc)
Los Angeles, CA

....   Interview

DUKE ELLINGTON & HIS ORCHESTRA
CA CW HJns ME, LB BCpr CCrs, JHtn JH RP PG HC, DE JL LBsn.

25 Aug 1965[1]   (P)
Basin Street West (tc)
San Francisco, CA

....	Vid[2]	Take The "A" Train
		IMPRESSIONS FROM THE FAR EAST
....		- Amad
....		- Agra
....	Vid	- Bluebird Of Delhi
....	Vid	The Opener
....		Isfahan
....		Things Ain't What They Used To Be
....	Vid	Kinda Dukish/Rockin' In Rhythm
....	Vid	Chelsea Bridge
....		Skin Deep
....	Vid	Jeep's Blues
....	Vid	Cotton Tail
....		Things Ain't What They Used To Be

[1]Excerpts were telecast on 14 Jun 1967.
[2]This title has been edited on Vid; the middle part is from 18 Sep 1965.

26 Aug 1965[1]   (P)
Basin Street West (tc)
San Francisco, CA

<u>DUKE ELLINGTON & HIS ORCHESTRA</u>
CA CW HJns ME, LB BCpr CCrs, JHtn JH RP PG HC, DE JL LBsn.

....	Vid	AD LIB ON NIPPON
....	Vid	- Part 1 (Fugi)
....		- Part 2 (Igoo)
....		- Part 3 (Nagoya)
		- Part 4 (Tokyo)

> JHtn RP HC, DE.

....   Monologue –DE narration

> DE piano solo.

.... Az   Medley[2]

> Entire band.

....   Take The "A" Train

....   IMPRESSIONS FROM THE FAR EAST
....   - Amad
....   - Agra
....   - Bluebird Of Delhi

....   The Prowling Cat
....   Isfahan
.... Vid   Medley[3]
....   Take The "A" Train

[1]Excerpts were telecast on 14 Jun 1967.
[2]Including: Meditation; Azalea; A Hundred Dreams From Now; Azalea; As Time Goes By; Take The "A" Train.
[3]Including: Satin Doll*; Solitude*; Don't Get Around Much Anymore; Mood Indigo*; I'm Beginning To See The Light; Sophisticated Lady*; Caravan; Do Nothin' Till You Hear From Me; In A Sentimental Mood; I Let A Song Go Out Of My Heart/Don't Get Around Much Anymore. (*Only these titles are on Vid.)

30 Aug 1965   (S)
Coast Recorders
San Francisco, CA

<u>DUKE ELLINGTON & HIS ORCHESTRA</u>
CA NA ASm ME, LB BCpr CCrs, JHtn JH RP PG HC, DE JL LBsn.

....		-1	When I'm Feelin' Kinda Blue[1] (incomplete)
....		-2	When I'm Feelin' Kinda Blue
....			When I'm Feelin' Kinda Blue (rehearsal)
....		-3	When I'm Feelin' Kinda Blue (incomplete)
....		-4	When I'm Feelin' Kinda Blue (incomplete)
....	Saj	-5	When I'm Feelin' Kinda Blue
....	RDB	-6	When I'm Feelin' Kinda Blue
....		-1	El Viti[2] (incomplete)
....		-2	El Viti
....		-3	El Viti (incomplete)
....	Saj	-4	El Viti
....			El Viti (incomplete)
....			El Viti (incomplete)
....		-1	Countdown
....		-2	Countdown (incomplete)
....		-3	Countdown
....	Saj	-4	Countdown
....		-1	El Busto[3] (incomplete)
....		-2	El Busto (incomplete)
....		-3	El Busto (incomplete)
....		-4	El Busto (incomplete)
....		-5	El Busto (incomplete)
....		-6	El Busto
....		-7	El Busto
....	MM	-8	Trombone Buster[4]

[1]*aka* "Feelin' Kinda Blue."
[2]*aka* "El Matador."
[3]The arrangement is by Herbie Jones.
[4]*sa* "El Busto."

16 Sep 1965[1]   (P)
Grace Cathedral (tc)
San Francisco, CA

<u>DUKE ELLINGTON & HIS ORCHESTRA</u>
CA CW HJns ME, LB BCpr CCrs, JHtn JH RP PG HC, DE JL LBsn, EMrw JMP TWtk JHck HMC GCC BBgs.

....   CONCERT OF SACRED MUSIC
.... RDB   Overture (to "Back, Brown And Beige")
.... Vid   Come Sunday –vHMC   >>>

....	Vid	Montage

> GCC a cappella.

....		Come Sunday –vGCC
....		Do You Call that Religion? –vGCC
....		My Lord, What A Morning –vGCC
....		Every Time I Feel The Spirit –vGCC
....		Swing Low, Sweet Chariot –vGCC

> Entire band.

| .... | RDB | Tell Me, It's The Truth –vEMrw |

> GCC a cappella.

....		We Shall Walk This Lonesome Road –vGCC[2] (incomplete)
....		We Shall Walk This Lonesome Road –vGCC (incomplete)
....	RDB	We Shall Walk This Lonesome Road –vGCC
....	RDB	Only Joyful –vGCC

> JHck HMC a cappella.

| .... | Sts | In The Beginning God –vJHck HMC[3] |
| .... | Sts | Will You Be There? –vTWtk HMC |

> Entire band.

| .... | Sts | 99% Won't Do –vJHck HMC |
| .... | Sts | Ain't But The One –vJHck HMC |

> DE piano solo.

| .... | Sts | New World A-Comin' |

> Entire band.

....	Sts	In The Beginning God –vJHck
....	Sts	My Mother, My Father –vJMP[4]
....	Sts	The Lord's Prayer –vEMrw
....	Sts	Come Sunday –vEMrw
....	Sts	David Danced Before The Lord –vJHck HMC, BBgs tap

> TWtk a cappella.

| .... | Sts | The Preacher's Song –vTWtk[5] |

[1]Excerpts were broadcast on 16 Jun 1967.
[2]"Purvis à la Jazz Hot" as per program notes (Richard I. Purvis was the director of the GCC).
[3]*aka* "Pacabe."
[4]"Heritage" on Sts.
[5]"The Lord's Prayer II" on Sts; different melody, using the same lyrics as for *The Lord's Prayer*.

DUKE ELLINGTON & HIS ORCHESTRA   18 Sep 1965[1]   (P)
CA CW HJns ME, LB BCpr CCrs, JHtn JH RP PG HC, DE JL LBsn, EMrw BBgs.   Festival Grounds (tc)
                                                                 Monterey, CA

....	Vid[2]	Take The "A" Train
		AD LIB ON NIPPON
....	GdJ	- Part 1 (Fugi)
....	GdJ	- Part 2 (Igoo)
....	GdJ	- Part 3 (Nagoya)
....	GdJ	- Part 4 (Tokyo)
....	GdJ	Chelsea Bridge
....	GdJ	Olds[3]
....		El Viti
....		El Busto
....		When I'm Feelin' Kinda Blue
....		Things Ain't What They Used To Be
....		Things Ain't What They Used To Be
....		Harmony In Harlem
....		Skin Deep
....		Tell Me, It's The Truth –vEMrw
....		Come Sunday –vEMrw
....		The Lord's Prayer –vEMrw
....		Tulip Or Turnip –vBBgs
....		David Danced Before The Lord –vBBgs tap
....		The Apple Jack –vBBgs[4]
....		Satin Doll—Sophisticated Lady
....		Tootie For Cootie

> DG CT RS added.

| .... | | Kinda Dukish/Rockin' In Rhythm   >>> |

[1]Excerpts were telecast on 16 Jun 1967.
[2]The middle part was edited into the version of this title from 25 Aug 1965.
[3]*aka* "El Pide"; this title is a derivative of *In the Beginning God.*
[4]*sa* "Honeysuckle Rose."

20 Sep 1965[1]   (S)
Coast Recorders (tc)
San Francisco, CA

<u>DUKE ELLINGTON & HIS ORCHESTRA</u>
CA CW HJns ME, LB BCpr CCrs, JHtn JH RP PG HC, DE JL LBsn.

....			In The Beginning God (incomplete)
....			In The Beginning God (incomplete)
....	Vid		In The Beginning God
....			In The Beginning God (rehearsals)
....			In The Beginning God (incomplete)
....			In The Beginning God (incomplete)
....	Az[2]		In The Beginning God
....	Az	-1	Olds II[3] (incomplete)
....	Az	-2	Olds II
....	Az	-3	Olds II

[1]Excerpts were telecast on 14 Jun 1967.
[2]Incomplete on Az.
[3]*sa* "In The Beginning God."

<u>DUKE ELLINGTON</u>
DE interviewed by Ralph Gleason.

Fairmont Hotel   (S)

| .... | | Interview |

> DE piano solo.

....		Interlude
....		Tone Poem[1]
....	Vid	Sugar Hill Penthouse
....	Vid	Unidentified title

> BS added.

| .... | | Love Came –DE recital |

[1]Including: Blue Too; Take It Slow; Tune Up.

Late Sep 1965   (S)
Unidentified location (bc)
Vancouver, BC

<u>DUKE ELLINGTON</u>
DE interviewed by Bob Smith.

| .... | | Interview |

Autumn 1965   (S)
p Narwood Productions
New York City, NY

<u>DUKE ELLINGTON</u>
Comments on the Tanglewood LP.

| .... | Vi | DE talking |

17-20 Oct 1965   (S)
United Recorders
Los Angeles, CA

<u>ELLA FITZGERALD WITH DUKE ELLINGTON & HIS ORCHESTRA</u>
Vcl, acc. by CA CW HJns ME, LB BCpr CCrs, JHtn JH RP PG HC, DE JL LBsn.

....		65KV5533-1-2	Imagine My Frustration –vEF[1]
....	Vrv	65KV5533-1-4	Imagine My Frustration –vEF
....		65KV5533-1-5	Imagine My Frustration –vEF
....	Vrv	65KV5533-2-3	What Am I Here For? –vEF
....	Az	65KV5533-3	Duke's Place –vEF
....	Vrv	65KV5533-3-2	Duke's Place –vEF
....	Vrv	65KV5533-4	Azure –vEF

> JJns replaces DE.

| .... | Vrv | 65KV5533-5 | I Like The Sunrise –vEF |

> DE added.

| .... | Vrv | 65KV5533-6 | Cotton Tail –vEF |

> DE omitted.

....	Vrv	65KV5533-7	Something To Live For –vEF
....	Vrv	65KV5533-8	A Flower Is A Lovesome Thing –vEF
....		65KV5533-9-1	Passion Flower –vEF
....	Vrv	65KV5533-9-2	Passion Flower –vEF
....		65KV5533-10	The Brown-Skin Gal –vEF
....	Vrv	65KV5533-10 alt.	The Brown-Skin Gal –vEF

[1]*sa* "When I'm Feelin' Kinda Blue"; "Feelin' Kinda Blue."

			24 Oct 1965 (P)

DUKE ELLINGTON & HIS ORCHESTRA   24 Oct 1965   (P)
CA CW HJns ME, LB BCpr CCrs, JHtn JH RP PG HC, DE JL LBsn.   CBS Studios (tc)
                                                                               Los Angeles, CA

.... Rar   The Opener[1]
....   Medley[2]

[1]"Flashback From The Future" on Rar.
[2]Including: Concerto For Cootie; Don't Get Around Much Anymore; Caravan; Satin Doll.

DUKE ELLINGTON & HIS ORCHESTRA   31 Oct 1965   (P)
CA HJns ME, LB BCpr CCrs, JHtn JH RP PG HC, DE JL LBsn.   Frost Amphitheater, Stanford University
                                                                               Palo Alto, CA

....   Take The "A" Train

                                           AD LIB ON NIPPON
....   - Part 1 (Fugi)
....   - Part 2 (Igoo)
....   - Part 3 (Nagoya)
....   - Part 4 (Tokyo)

....   Chelsea Bridge
....   Blow By Blow
....   El Viti
....   The Opener
....   Passion Flower
....   Things Ain't What They Used To Be
....   Things Ain't What They Used To Be
....   Medley[1]
....   Things Ain't What They Used To Be

[1]Including: Satin Doll; Solitude; In A Sentimental Mood; Don't Get Around Much Anymore; Mood Indigo; I'm Beginning To
See The Light; Sophisticated Lady; Caravan; Do Nothin' Till You Hear From Me; I Let A Song Go Out Of My Heart/Don't
Get Around Much Anymore.

DUKE ELLINGTON & HIS ORCHESTRA WITH DINAH SHORE   5 Dec 1965   (P)
CA CW HJns ME, LB BCpr CCrs, JHtn JH RP PG HC, DE JL LBsn.   NBC Studios (tc)
                                                                               New York City, NY

.... DVD   Stormy Weather
.... DVD   Between The Devil And The Deep Blue Sea

      > DShe added.

.... DVD   Blues In The Night –vDShe

DUKE ELLINGTON   10 Dec 1965   (S)
DE interviewed by Jim Fawcett   Unidentified location (bc)
                                                                               New York City, NY

....   Interview

DUKE ELLINGTON   Dec 1965[1]   (S)
DE piano and talking, interviewed by Ruggero Orlando.   DE's residence and Tempo Music (tc)
                                                                               New York City, NY

....   Interview
....   Take The "A" Train
....   In The Beginning God

[1]Telecast in Italy on 1 Apr 1966.

DUKE ELLINGTON & HIS ORCHESTRA   Mid Dec 1965   (T/S)[1]
CA CW HJns ME, LB BCpr CCrs, JHtn JH RP PG HC, DE JL LBsn.   CBS Studios/Savoy Ballroom (tc)[2]
                                                                               New York City, NY

....   Mood Indigo
....   Rockin' In Rhythm

[1]Taping session; telecast on 21 Feb 1966.
[2]Ellington portion of the TV special "The Strolling Twenties."

DUKE ELLINGTON & HIS ORCHESTRA   26 Dec 1965   (P)
CA CW HJns ME, LB QJ BCpr CCrs, JHtn JH RP PG HC, DE BS JL JMK LBsn,   Fifth Avenue Presbyterian Church (tc)
LHrn EMrw BPtr JMP TWtk HMC MZC FPC, BBgs.   New York City, NY

                                           SACRED CONCERT
....   Speech and Prayer
....   Come Sunday
....   Recital by Miss Carroll Gensel   >>>

```
                > HMC a cappella.
...............                                Come Sunday –vHMC
...............                                I Cried Then I Cried –vHMC
...............                                Swing Low, Sweet Chariot –vHMC
                > Entire band.
...............                                Tell Me, It's The Truth
............... Vi                             Tell Me, It's The Truth –vEMrw
                > MZC a cappella.
...............                                Praise Ye The Lord –vMZC
                > Entire band.
...............                                In The Beginning God –vBPtr HMC
                > BS, LHrn.
............... Vi                             Christmas Surprise –vLHrn
                > DE piano solo.
............... Vi                             New World A-Comin'
                > JMP HMC a cappella.
...............                                Will You Be There? –vJMP HMC
                > Entire band.
............... Vi                             99% Won't Do –vJMP HMC
...............                                Ain't But The One –vJMP HMC
...............                                Come Sunday –vEMrw
...............                                The Lord's Prayer –vEMrw
                > FPC a cappella.
...............                                O Magnify The Lord In Me –vFPC
                > Entire band.
...............                                David Danced Before The Lord –vHMC, BBgs tap
                > TWtk a cappella.
...............                                The Preacher's Song –vTWtk
                > DE, HMC.
...............                                In The Beginning God –vHMC
```

DUKE ELLINGTON & HIS ORCHESTRA
Same personnel.

```
                                               SACRED CONCERT
...............                                Speech and Prayer
............... Vi         TPA5-3237           Come Sunday
                > HMC a cappella.
...............                                Come Sunday –vHMC
...............                                I Cried Then I Cried –vHMC
...............                                Swing Low, Sweet Chariot –vHMC
                > BS, LHrn.
............... Vi                             Christmas Surprise –vLHrn
                > MZC a cappella.
...............                                Praise Ye The Lord –vMZC
                > Entire band.
...............           TPA5-3235            Tell Me, It's The Truth –vEMrw
............... Vi        TPA5-3233            In The Beginning God –vBPtr HMC
...............                                Recital by Miss Carroll Gensel
                > DE piano solo.
............... Vi                             New World A-Comin'
                > JMP HMC a cappella.
............... Vi        TPA5-3239            Will You Be There? –vJMP HMC
                > Entire band.
...............                                99% Won't Do –vJMP HMC
............... Vi        TPA5-3238            Ain't But The One –vJMP HMC
...............                                My Mother, My Father –DE narration, -vJMP     >>>
```

> FPC a cappella.

....   O Magnify The Lord In Me –vFPC

> Entire band.

.... Vi   TPA5-3234   Come Sunday –vEMrw
.... Vi   TPA5-3236   The Lord's Prayer –vEMrw
.... Vi   David Danced Before The Lord –vHMC, BBgs tap

> TWtk a cappella.

....   The Preacher's Song –vTWtk

> DE HMC.

....   In The Beginning God –vHMC

	31 Dec 1965 (P)

DUKE ELLINGTON & HIS ORCHESTRA   Memorial Auditorium (bc)
CA CW HJns ME, LB BCpr CCrs, JHtn JH RP PH HC, DE JL LBsn.   Worcester, MA

....   Take The "A" Train
....   Satin Doll
....   Soul Call[1]
....   Azure
....   Things Ain't What They Used To Be
....   Sophisticated Lady

[1]sa "Countdown."

31 Dec 1965

16 Jan 1966   (P)

DUKE ELLINGTON   CBS Studios (tc)
DE on the show "Look Up and Live."   New York City, NY

....   Interview and discussion

19+20 Jan 1966   (T)[1]

DUKE ELLINGTON & HIS ORCHESTRA   United Recorders, Studio A[2]
Collective personnel: CA CW CCnd APor RT, MBrn HBo MME KS, JHtn JH BSh BClt PG HC,   Los Angeles, CA
DE CG JL LBsn, plus a studio orchestra.

....   Mama Bahama
....   She Walks Well

> Studio orchestra added.

....   The First Dive

> Studio orchestra omitted.

....   She Walks Well

[1]Music for the motion picture "Assault On A Queen."
[2]Soundtrack only; the filming took place at Paramount Studios Scoring Stage.

*The above titles are prerecordings which were later overdubbed, supplemented and in part replaced with selections
recorded by a studio orchestra for the movie soundtrack.*

23 Jan 1966   (P)

DUKE ELLINGTON & HIS ORCHESTRA WITH MARIE COLE   CBS Studios (tc)
CA CW HJns ME, LB BCpr CCrs, JHtn JH RP PG HC, DE JL SMsh.   New York City, NY

....   Medley[1]

> MCle added.

....   There Will Never Be Another You –vMCle

> MCle omitted.

....   Satin Doll

[1]Including: Things Ain't What They Used To Be; I Got It Bad; Cotton Tail; Jam With Sam.

28 Jan 1966   (P)

DUKE ELLINGTON & HIS ORCHESTRA WITH ELLA FITZGERALD   Jahrhunderthalle (bc)
CA CW HJns ME, LB BCpr CCrs, JHtn JH RP PG HC, DE JL EJ SMsh.   Frankfurt, Germany

....   Black And Tan Fantasy—Creole Love Call—The Mooche
....   Stompy Jones
....   The Opener
....   Chelsea Bridge

                                    AD LIB ON NIPPON
....   - Part 1 (Fugi)
....   - Part 2 (Igoo)   >>>

....		- Part 3 (Nagoya)
....		- Part 4 (Tokyo)
....		Sophisticated Lady
....		Kinda Dukish/Rockin' In Rhythm
....		Passion Flower
....	Az	Things Ain't What They Used To Be
....	Az	Wings And Things
....		Jam With Sam

> DE JL EJ SMsh omitted, JJns JCft GJsn, EF added.

....	Satin Doll –vEF
....	Wives And Lovers –vEF
....	Something To Live For –vEF
....	Let's Do It –vEF
....	Sweet Georgia Brown –vEF

> DE replaces JJns.

....	Cotton Tail –vEF
....	Duke's Place –vEF

DE shared the bill for this European tour and some subsequent events with EF and her trio. For a portion of each concert EF was accompanied by the full Ellington contingent, sometimes with DE at the piano. On many occasions, some of the Ellingtonians played along with the trio. To be consistent, these recordings have been included as well.

DUKE ELLINGTON   (bc)   (S)[1]
DE interviewed by person unknown.

....	Interview

[1]Backstage.

	29 Jan 1966 (P)
	Salle Pleyel
	Paris, France

DUKE ELLINGTON & HIS ORCHESTRA
CA CW HJns ME, LB BCpr CCrs, JHtn JH RP PG HC, DE JL EJ SMsh.

....	La Plus Belle Africaine[1]
....	Take The "A" Train
....	Passion Flower
....	Things Ain't What They Used To Be
....	Wings And Things
....	Wings And Things
....	Jam With Sam

[1]Adapted from some of the material for the unproduced musical *Saturday Laughter*.

DUKE ELLINGTON & HIS ORCHESTRA
Same personnel.

....	Take The "A" Train
....	Black And Tan Fantasy—Creole Love Call—The Mooche
....	Soul Call
....	Chelsea Bridge
....	El Viti
....	The Opener
....	La Plus Belle Africaine
....	El Busto
....	Passion Flower
....	Things Ain't What They Used To Be
....	Wings And Things
....	Sophisticated Lady
....	Jam With Sam

> DE JL EJ SMsh omitted, JJns JCft GJsn, EF added.

....	Satin Doll –vEF
....	Wives And Lovers –vEF
....	Something To Live For –vEF
....	Let's Do It –vEF

> DE replaces JJns.

....	Duke's Place –vEF
....	Cotton Tail –vEF
....	Imagine My Frustration –vEF

	30 Jan 1966 (P)
	Teatro Lirico
	Milan, Italy

DUKE ELLINGTON & HIS ORCHESTRA WITH ELLA FITZGERALD
CA CW HJns ME, LB BCpr CCrs, JHtn JH RP PG HC, DE JL EJ SMsh.

....	JBS	Take The "A" Train >>>

.... JBS	Black And Tan Fantasy—Creole Love Call—The Mooche	
.... JBS	Soul Call	
.... JBS	Chelsea Bridge	
.... JBS	El Viti	
.... JBS	The Opener	
.... JBS	Sophisticated Lady	
.... JBS	Take The "A" Train	
.... JBS	Passion Flower	
.... JBS	Things Ain't What They Used To Be	
.... JBS	Wings And Things	
.... JBS	Jam With Sam	

> JL EJ SMsh omitted, JCft GJsn, EF added.

.... JBS   Cotton Tail –vEF

VITTORIO GASSMAN & DUKE ELLINGTON   (tc)   (S)[1]
Vittorio Gassman, acc. by DE.

.... Az   Hamlet's Monologue –VGmn reciting

ELLA FITZGERALD AND DUKE ELLINGTON   (tc)   (S)[1]
EF, acc. by DE.

....   I'm Just A Lucky So-And-So –vEF

[1]Backstage.

		2 Feb 1966 (P)
DUKE ELLINGTON & HIS ORCHESTRA CA CW HJns ME, LB BCpr CCrs, JHtn JH RP PG HC, DE JL SWrd.		Unidentified location Basel, Switzerland.

....   The Mooche
....   What Am I Here For?
....   Soul Call

> PG, DE JL SWrd.

....   Happy Reunion

> Entire band.

....   The Opener
....   Kinda Dukish/Rockin' In Rhythm
....   El Viti
....   Mood Indigo
....   Tootie For Cootie
....   Passion Flower
....   Things Ain't What They Used To Be
....   Magenta Haze
....   Wings And Things
....   Satin Doll—Sophisticated Lady
....   Jam With Sam

		6 Feb 1966 (P)
DUKE ELLINGTON & HIS ORCHESTRA WITH ELLA FITZGERALD CA CW HJns ME, LB BCpr CCrs, JHtn JH RP PG HC, DE JL SWrd.		Falkoner Teatret Copenhagen, Denmark

....   Black And Tan Fantasy—Creole Love Call—The Mooche
....   Soul Call
....   Chelsea Bridge
....   West Indian Pancake[1]
....   El Viti
....   The Opener
....   La Plus Belle Africaine
....   Magenta Haze
....   Things Ain't What They Used To Be
....   Wings And Things

> JL SWrd omitted, JCft GJsn, EF added.

....   Cotton Tail –vEF
....   Imagine My Frustration –vEF

[1]aka "Cool West Indian Summer."

DUKE ELLINGTON & HIS ORCHESTRA
Same personnel.

....   Take The "A" Train
....   What Am I Here For?   >>>

```
                          > PG, DE JL SWrd.
..............                         Happy Reunion
                          > Entire band.
..............                         West Indian Pancake
..............                         Soul Call
..............                         El Viti
..............                         The Opener
..............                         La Plus Belle Africaine
..............                         Kinda Dukish/Rockin' In Rhythm
..............                         Magenta Haze
..............                         Things Ain't What They Used To Be
..............                         Wings And Things
..............                         Things Ain't What They Used To Be
                          > DE piano solo.
..............                         Dancers In Love
```

7 Feb 1966 (P)
Konserthuset
Stockholm, Sweden

DUKE ELLINGON & HIS ORCHESTRA
CA CW HJns ME, LB BCpr CCrs, JHtn JH RP PG HC, DE JL SWrd.

```
.............. MFC         El Viti
.............. MFC         La Plus Belle Africaine
.............. MFC         Magenta Haze
```

DUKE ELLINGTON & HIS ORCHESTRA WITH ELLA FITZGERALD
Same personnel.

```
..............             Take The "A" Train
..............             Black And Tan Fantasy—Creole Love Call—The Mooche
..............             Soul Call
..............             West Indian Pancake
..............             El Viti
..............             The Opener
..............             La Plus Belle Africaine
.............. Az          Veldt Amor
..............             Magenta Haze
..............             Things Ain't What They Used To Be
               > JL SWrd omitted, JCft GJsn, EF added.
.............. Az          Cotton Tail –vEF
..............             Imagine My Frustration –vEF
```

8 Feb 1966 (S)
Circus, Djurgården (tc?)*
Stockholm, Sweden

DUKE ELLINGTON & HIS ORCHESTRA
CA CW HJns ME, LB BCpr CCrs, JHtn JH RP PG HC, DE JL SWrd.

```
               > DE piano solo.
..............             Looking Glass¹
..............             Looking Glass
               > JL added.
..............             The Queen's Guard (incomplete)
.............. Az          The Queen's Guard
..............             Serenade To Sweden²
..............             Serenade To Sweden (incomplete)
               > Entire band.
..............             Orchestra warming up
..............             Take The "A" Train
..............             West Indian Pancake
..............             Rockin' In Rhythm (incomplete)
..............             Rockin' In Rhythm
..............             La Plus Belle Africaine (incomplete)
```

¹This title is a derivative of *I Don't Mind*.
²Some band members cutting in with a few notes.

The above is a rehearsal session.

DUKE ELLINGTON & HIS ORCHESTRA WITH ELLA FITZGERALD (tc?)* (P)
Same personnel.

```
..............             Take The "A" Train
..............             West Indian Pancake
..............             Rockin' In Rhythm    >>>
```

....	Az	La Plus Belle Africaine
....	Az	The Opener

> DE JL SWrd omitted, JJns JCft GJsn, EF added.

....	Pab	Wives And Lovers –vEF
....		Sweet Georgia Brown –vEF
....	Pab	Só Danço Samba –vEF
....		Medley[1]

> DE replaces JJns.

....	Pab	Imagine My Frustration –vEF

> JJns added.

....	Pab	Duke's Place –vEF

[1]Including: How High The Moon –vEF; It's Been A Hard Day's Night –vEF; Smoke Gets In Your Eyes –vEF.

DUKE ELLINGTON & HIS ORCHESTRA WITH ELLA FITZGERALD   (tc?)*
Same personnel.

....		Take The "A" Train
....		Black And Tan Fantasy
....	Az	Soul Call
....	Az	Wings And Things
....		Jam With Sam

> DE JL SWrd omitted, JJns JCft GJsn, EF added.

....	Pab	Satin Doll –vEF
....	Pab	Something To Live For –vEF
....		Wives And Lovers –vEF
....		Só Danço Samba –vEF
....	Pab	Let's Do It –vEF
....	Pab	Lover Man –vEF

> DE replaces JJns.

....	Pab[1]	Cotton Tail –vEF

> JJns piano solo.

....		Serenade To Sweden

[1]Edited version on Pab.

*The band was filmed by Swedish TV for two 40-minute programs; titles and dates of the telecasts are not known.

DUKE ELLINGTON & HIS ORCHESTRA
CA CW HJns ME, LB BCpr CCrs, JHtn JH RP PG HC, DE JL SWrd.

11 Feb 1966   (P)
Salle Pleyel
Paris, France

....		Black And Tan Fantasy—Creole Love Call—The Mooche
....		Soul Call
....		West Indian Pancake
....		El Viti
....		The Opener
....		La Plus Belle Africaine
....		Magenta Haze
....		Things Ain't What They Used To Be
....		Wings And Things

DUKE ELLINGTON & HIS ORCHESTRA WITH ELLA FITZGERALD
Same personnel.

....		Take The "A" Train
....		Black And Tan Fantasy—Creole Love Call—The Mooche
....		Soul Call
....		West Indian Pancake
....		El Viti
....		The Opener
....		La Plus Belle Africaine
....		Veldt Amor
....		Magenta Haze
....		Things Ain't What They Used To Be
....		Wings And Things
....		Jam With Sam

> JL SWrd omitted, JCft GJsn, EF added.

....		Cotton Tail –vEF
....		Imagine My Frustration –vEF

12 Feb 1966 (P)
Royal Festival Hall
London, England

DUKE ELLINGTON & HIS ORCHESTRA WITH ELLA FITZGERALD
CA CW HJns ME, LB BCpr CCrs, JHtn JH RP PG HC, DE JL SWrd.

....	Take The "A" Train
....	Black And Tan Fantasy—Creole Love Call—The Mooche
....	Soul Call
....	West Indian Pancake
....	El Viti
....	Veldt Amor
....	The Opener
....	La Plus Belle Africaine
....	Kinda Dukish/Rockin' In Rhythm
....	Magenta Haze
....	Things Ain't What They Used To Be

> JL SWrd omitted, JCft GJsn, EF added.

....	Cotton Tail –vEF
....	Imagine My Frustration –vEF

13 Feb 1966 (P)
Hammersmith Odeon
London, England

DUKE ELLINGTON & HIS ORCHESTRA WITH ELLA FITZGERALD
CA HJns ME, LB BCpr CCrs, JHtn JH RP PG HC, DE JL SWrd.

....	Take The "A" Train
....	Black And Tan Fantasy—Creole Love Call—The Mooche
....	Soul Call
....	West Indian Pancake
....	El Viti
....	Veldt Amor
....	The Opener
....	La Plus Belle Africaine
....	El Busto
....	Magenta Haze
....	Things Ain't What They Used To Be

> JL SWrd omitted, JCft GJsn, EF added.

....	Cotton Tail –vEF
....	Imagine My Frustration –vEF

DUKE ELLINGTON & HIS ORCHESTRA WITH ELLA FITZGERALD
Same personnel.

....	Take The "A" Train
....	Black And Tan Fantasy—Creole Love Call—The Mooche
....	Soul Call
....	West Indian Pancake
....	Veldt Amor
....	El Viti
....	The Opener
....	La Plus Belle Africaine
....	El Busto
....	Magenta Haze
....	Things Ain't What They Used To Be

> JL SWrd omitted, JCft HJsn, EF added.

....	Cotton Tail –vEF
....	Imagine My Frustration –vEF

14 Feb 1966 (P)
Cliffs Pavilion
Southend-On-Sea, England

DUKE ELLINGTON & HIS ORCHESTRA
CA HJns ME, LB BCpr CCrs, JHtn JH RP PG HC, DE JL SWrd.

....	Take The "A" Train
....	Black And Tan Fantasy—Creole Love Call—The Mooche
....	Soul Call
....	Chelsea Bridge
....	West Indian Pancake
....	El Viti
....	Veldt Amor
....	The Opener
....	La Plus Belle Africaine
....	Kinda Dukish/Rockin' In Rhythm
....	Take The "A" Train
....	Take The "A" Train
....	El Busto
....	Magenta Haze >>>

....		Things Ain't What They Used To Be
....		Wings And Things
....		Medley[1]

[1]Including: Satin Doll; Solitude; Don't Get Around Much Anymore; Mood Indigo; I'm Beginning To See The Light; Sophisticated Lady; Caravan.

DUKE ELLINGTON & HIS ORCHESTRA
Same personnel.

....		Take The "A" Train
....		Black And Tan Fantasy—Creole Love Call—The Mooche
....		Soul Call
....		Chelsea Bridge
....		West Indian Pancake
....		El Viti
....		Veldt Amor
....		The Opener
....		La Plus Belle Africaine
....		Kinda Dukish/Rockin' In Rhythm
....		Take The "A" Train
....		Take The "A" Train
....		El Busto
....		Magenta Haze
....		Things Ain't What They Used To Be
....		Wings And Things
....		I Let A Song Go Out Of My Heart/Don't Get Around Much Anymore
....		Jam With Sam
....		Satin Doll

17 Feb 1966   (P)
University Of Liverpool
Liverpool, England

DUKE ELLINGTON & HIS ORCHESTRA
CA HJns ME, LB BCpr CCrs, JHtn JH RP PG HC, DE JL SWrd.

....		Take The "A" Train
....		Black And Tan Fantasy—Creole Love Call—The Mooche
....		Soul Call
....		Chelsea Bridge
....		West Indian Pancake
....		El Viti
....		Veldt Amor
....		The Opener
....		La Plus Belle Africaine

> DE piano solo.

....		Carolina Shout

> Entire band.

....		Come Sunday
....		Montage
....		Magenta Haze
....		Things Ain't What They Used To Be
....		Wings And Things
....		Medley[1]
....		Things Ain't What They Used To Be
....		God Save The Queem

[1]Including: Satin Doll; Solitude; Don't Get Around Much Anymore; Mood Indigo; I'm Beginning To See The Light; Sophisticated Lady; Caravan; Do Nothin' Till You Hear From Me.

19 Feb 1966   (P)
Free Trade Hall
Manchester, England

DUKE ELLINGTON & HIS ORCHESTRA WITH ELLA FITZGERALD
CA CW HJns ME, LB BCpr CCrs, JHtn JH RP PG HC, DE JL SWrd.

....		Take The "A" Train
....	Az	Main Stem
....		Soul Call
....		West Indian Pancake
....		El Viti
....		Veldt Amor
....		The Opener
....		La Plus Belle Africaine

> DE piano solo.

....		Carolina Shout

> Entire band.

....		Magenta Haze >>>

....   Things Ain't What They Used To Be
....   Wings And Things

> JL SWrd omitted, JCft GJsn, EF added.

....   Cotton Tail –vEF

> EF omitted.

....   God Save The Queen.

DUKE ELLINGTON & HIS ORCHESTRA WITH ELLA FITZGERALD
Same personnel.

....   Main Stem
....   Soul Call
....   West Indian Pancake
....   El Viti
....   Veldt Amor
....   The Opener
....   La Plus Belle Africaine
....   Rockin' In Rhythm
....   Magenta Haze
....   Things Ain't What They Used To Be
....   Wings And Things
....   Jam With Sam

> JL SWrd omitted, JCft GJsn, EF.

....   Cotton Tail –vEF
....   Imagine My Frustration –vEF

> EF omitted.

....   God Save The Queen

20 Feb 1966[1]   (S)
Unspecified studio (tc)
London, England

DUKE ELLINGTON
DE interviewed by Derek Jewell; intermittent previously recorded music.

....   Interview

[1]Telecast on 3 Mar 1966.

DUKE ELLINGTON & HIS ORCHESTRA
CA CW HJns ME, LB BCpr CCrs, JHtn JH RP PG HC, DE JL SWrd.

Hammersmith Odeon (P)

....   Stompy Jones
....   Take The "A" Train
....   Black And Tan Fantasy
....   Soul Call
....   West Indian Pancake
....   El Viti
....   Veldt Amor
....   The Opener
....   La Plus Belle Africaine
....   Rockin' In Rhythm
....   Magenta Haze
....   Things Ain't What They Used To Be
....   Wings And Things

DUKE ELLINGTON & HIS ORCHESTRA
Same personnel.

....   Stompy Jones
....   Soul Call
....   West Indian Pancake
....   El Viti
....   Veldt Amor
....   The Opener
....   La Plus Belle Africaine

> DE piano solo.

....   Carolina Shout

> Entire band.

....   Magenta Haze
....   Things Ain't What They Used To Be
....   Wings And Things
....   Jam With Sam

	21 Feb 1966	(P)
	Coventry Cathedral	
	Coventry, England	

<u>**DUKE ELLINGTON**</u>
Piano solo.

....   Tingling Is A Happiness[1] (rehearsal)

[1]This title is a derivative of *Kinda Dukish*.

<u>**DUKE ELLINGTON & HIS ORCHESTRA**</u>   (tc)[1]   (P)
CA CW HJns ME, LB BCpr CCrs, JHtn JH RP PG HC, DE JL SWrd, GWbb CAS.

                  SACRED CONCERT

> DE piano solo.

....   New World A-Comin'

> Entire band.

....   Come Sunday
....   Montage
.... Az   Come Easter
.... Az   Tell Me, It's The Truth
....   In The Beginning God –vGWbb CAS
.... Az   West Indian Pancake
.... Az   La Plus Belle Africaine

[1]Telecast on 10 Apr 1966.

	22 Feb 1966[1]	(P)
	Théâtre Americain (tc)	
	Brussels, Belgium	

<u>**DUKE ELLINGTON & HIS ORCHESTRA WITH ELLA FITZGERALD**</u>
CA CW HJns ME, LB BCpr CCrs, JHtn JH RP PG HC, DE JL SWrd.

....   Take The "A" Train
....   Black And Tan Fantasy—Creole Love Call—The Mooche
....   Soul Call
....   West Indian Pancake
....   El Viti
....   The Opener
....   Things Ain't What They Used To Be
....   Wings And Things
....   Sophisticated Lady
....   Take The "A" Train
....   Things Ain't What They Used To Be

> JL SWrd omitted, JCft HJsn, EF added.

....   Cotton Tail –vEF
....   Imagine My Frustration –vEF

[1]Telecast on 3 May 1966.

	24 Feb 1966	(P)
	Estudios de TVE (tc)[1]	
	Prado del Rey, Spain	

<u>**DUKE ELLINGTON & HIS ORCHESTRA WITH ELLA FITZGERALD**</u>
CA CW HJns ME, LB BCpr CCrs, JHtn JH RP PG HC, DE JL SWrd.

....   Take The "A" Train
....   Sophisticated Lady
....   The Opener
....   Wings And Things
....   Things Ain't What They Used To Be
....   Soul Call
....   West Indian Pancake
....   Veldt Amor
....   Perdido

> JL SWrd omitted, JCft GJsn, EF added.

....   Imagine My Frustration –vEF
....   Duke's Place –vEF
....   Cotton Tail –vEF

[1]This event was taped under the title "Noches del Sabado" and telecast in France by M6 in 1984 or later.

	25 Feb 1966	(P)
	Chateau de Goutelas	
	Goutelas-en-Forez, France	

<u>**DUKE ELLINGTON**</u>
Piano solo.

.... Pdt   New World A-Comin'[1]
.... Pdt   Medley[2]

[1]"Symphonie Pour Un Monde Meilleur" on Pdt.
[2]Including: It Don't Mean A Thing; Satin Doll; Solitude; I Got It Bad; Don't Get Around Much Anymore; Mood Indigo; I'm Beginning To See The Light; Sophisticated Lady; Caravan.

DUKE ELLINGTON
DE interviewed by Helen McNamara.

....   Interview

15 Mar 1966   (S)
O'Keefe Centre (bc)
Toronto, ON

DUKE ELLINGTON
DE interviewed by person unknown.

....   Interview

23 Mar 1966   (S)
Devine's Million Dollar Ballroom (bc)
Milwaukee, WI

DUKE ELLINGTON & HIS ORCHESTRA
CA CW HJns ME, LB BCpr CCrs, JHtn JH RP PG JRsn, DE JL SWrd.

29 Mar 1966   (S)
RCA Studios
New York City, NY

....	Az	-1	Take The "A" Train (incomplete)
....		-2	Take The "A" Train (incomplete)
....	Az	-3	Take The "A" Train
....		-1	West Indian Pancake (incomplete)
....	DJ	-2	West Indian Pancake

> HC replaces JRsn.

....	Stv	-1	El Viti
....		-2	El Viti (insert)
....	Stv	-3	El Viti (insert)
....		-1	Veldt Amor (incomplete)
....	DJ	-3	Veldt Amor
....		-1	La Plus Belle Africaine
....	RDB	-1	Wings And Things
....	DJ	-2	Wings And Things

DUKE ELLINGTON & HIS ORCHESTRA
CA CW HJns ME, LB BCpr CCrs, JHtn JH RP PG HC, DE JL SWrd.

9 Apr 1966   (P)
Théâtre Daniel Sorano
Dakar, Sénégal

....	Take The "A" Train
....	Black And Tan Fantasy—Creole Love Call—The Mooche
....	Soul Call
....	West Indian Pancake
....	El Viti
....	The Opener
....	La Plus Belle Africaine
....	El Busto
....	Medley[1]
....	Things Ain't What They Used To Be

> DE piano solo.

....	Dancers In Love

> Entire band.

....	Jam With Sam

[1]Including: Satin Doll; Solitude; Just Squeeze Me; I Got It Bad; Don't Get Around Much Anymore; Mood Indigo; I'm Beginning To See The Light; Sophisticated Lady; Caravan; Do Nothin' Till You Hear From Me; I Let A Song Go Out Of My Heart/Don't Get Around Much Anymore.

DUKE ELLINGTON & HIS ORCHESTRA
CA CW HJns ME, BCpr CCrs, JHtn JH RP PG HC, DE JL SWrd.

Apr 1966   (P)
Unidentified location
Dakar, Sénégal

....	The Opener
....	I'm Beginning To See The Light—Sophisticated Lady

DUKE ELLINGTON & SAM WOODYARD
DE; Don De Michael moderating.

13 Apr 1966   (P)
Wilson Music Hall, University of Cincinnati
Cincinnati, OH

.... RDB	Master Class

> DE SWrd.

....	A Single Petal Of A Rose
....	Le Sucrier Velours
....	Satin Doll
....	Sophisticated Lady
....	Nobody Was Lookin'
....	Medley[1]
....	Take The "A" Train >>>

....   Mood Indigo
....   Dancers In Love

[1]Including: Don't Get Around Much Anymore; Ellington '66; Don't Get Around Much Anymore; Ellington '66.

                                                                                          16 Apr 1966   (P)
DUKE ELLINGTON WITH THE CINCINNATI SYMPHONY ORCHESTRA   Wilson Music Hall, University of Cincinnati
DE with the Cincinnati Symphony Orchestra, Erich Kunzel conducting.   Cincinnati, OH

....   DE speech
....   New World A-Comin'

> DE piano solo.

....   Prelude To A Kiss—In A Sentimental Mood
....   A Single Petal Of A Rose
....   DE talks about "The Queen's Suite"

> JBjm SWrd added.

....   Medley[1]
....   Satin Doll
....   La Plus Belle Africaine
....   Take The "A" Train

> dr added.

....   Tea For Two

> dr omitted, cl added.

....   Body And Soul

> cl omitted, tp added.

....   Blues

> cl added.

....   Things Ain't What They Used To Be

> tp, cl omitted.

....   Dancers In Love

[1]Including: I Got It Bad; Just Squeeze Me; Don't Get Around Much Anymore; Mood Indigo; I'm Beginning To See The
Light; Sophisticated Lady; Caravan; It Don't Mean A Thing; Solitude; I Let A Song Go Out Of My Heart/Don't Get Around
Much Anymore.

                                                                                          24 Apr 1966   (P)
DUKE ELLINGTON & HIS ORCHESTRA   Bolling AFB
CA CW HJns ME, LB BCpr CCrs, JHtn JH RP PG HC, DE JL SWrd, JNtn JMP.   Washington, DC

....   Take The "A" Train
....   Happy Birthday
....   Mood Indigo
....   Bill Bailey –vJNtn
....   Azure
....   Sophisticated Lady

> DE, JNtn.

....   Sophisticated Lady –vJNtn

> Entire band.

....   Fly Me To The Moon –vJNtn
....   Fly Me To The Moon

> DE JL SWrd.

....   Beautiful Woman Walks Well[1]

> Entire band.

....   The Opener
....   Satin Doll –vJMP

> DE JL SWrd, JMP.

....   Solitude –vJMP

> Entire band.

....   Things Ain't What They Used To Be
....   Love You Madly –vJMP
....   Workin' Blues –vJMP
....   Diminuendo In Blue and Wailing Interval
....   Passion Flower
....   Things Ain't What They Used To Be   >>>

....		Happy Birthday
....		Wings And Things

> RP, DE JL SWrd.

....		Rose Room

> Entire band.

....		Tenderly
....		Tootie For Cootie
....		Afro-Bossa

> LB, DE JL SWrd.

....		My Little Brown Book

>Entire band.

....		Satin Doll

[1]*aka* "She Walks Well."

26 Apr 1966[1]   (P)
Unidentified location (tc)
?Brooklyn, NY

DUKE ELLINGTON & HIS ORCHESTRA WITH TONY BENNETT
CA CW HJns ME, LB BCpr CCrs, JHtn JH RP PG HC, DE JL SWrd.

....		Take The "A" Train
....		Satin Doll

> TBnt added.

....		Don't Get Around Much Anymore –vTBnt

[1]Taping session; telecast on 16 May 1966.

9 May 1966   (S)
Hollywood Studio B
Hollywood, CA

DUKE ELLINGTON & HIS ORCHESTRA
CA CW HJns ME, LB BCpr CCrs, JHtn JH RP PG HC, DE JL SWrd.

....	Vi[1]	TPA3-3927-3	Take The "A" Train
....	Vi	TPA3-3928-5	The Mooche
....	Vi	TPA3-3929-1	I Got It Bad
....	Vi	TPA3-3930	Do Nothin' Till You Hear From Me
....	Vi	TPA3-3931-3	Caravan

[1]On some of the releases, 14 bars of the piano introduction have been edited out.

10 May 1966   (S)
Hollywood Studio B
Hollywood, CA

DUKE ELLINGTON & HIS ORCHESTRA
CA CW HJns ME, LB BCpr CCrs, JHtn JH RP PG HC, DE JL SWrd.

....	Vi	TPA3-3932-4	Black And Tan Fantasy
....	Vi	TPA3-3933-7	Sophisticated Lady
....	Vi	TPA3-3934-5	The Twitch
....	Vi	TPA3-3935-3	Creole Love Call

11 May 1966   (S)
Hollywood Studio B
Hollywood, CA

DUKE ELLINGTON & HIS ORCHESTRA
CA WBsb HJns ME, LB BCpr CCrs, JHtn JH RP PG HC, DE JL SWrd.

....	Vi	TPA3-3936-2	Wings And Things
....	Vi	TPA3-3966-3	Solitude
....	Vi	TPA3-3930-9[1]	Do Nothin' Till You Hear From Me
....	Vi	TPA3-3937-8	Perdido
....	Vi	TPA3-3938-3	Mood Indigo

[1]Remake.

13 May 1966   (P)
Satin Doll Yotsura
Tokyo, Japan

DUKE ELLINGTON
DE MHa MTo.

....		Caravan
....		Take The "A" Train

14 May 1966[1]   (P)
TBS Studios (tc)
Tokyo, Japan

DUKE ELLINGTON & HIS ORCHESTRA
CA CW HJns ME, LB BCpr CCrs, JHtn JH RP PG HC, DE JL SWrd.

....		Take The "A" Train
....	Az	Perdido
....	Az	Interview with DE[2]
....	Az	Soul Call
....	Az	El Viti >>>

....	Mood Indigo
....	Caravan
....	Satin Doll
....	Take The "A" Train

[1]The date of telecast is not known.
[2]On stage.

20 May 1966   (P)
Kyoto Kaikan (tc)
Kyoto, Japan

DUKE ELLINGTON & HIS ORCHESTRA
CA CW HJns ME, LB BCpr CCrs, JHtn JH RP PG HC, DE JL SWrd.

....	Take The "A" Train
....	Black And Tan Fantasy—Creole Love Call—The Mooche
....	Soul Call
....	West Indian Pancake
....	El Viti
....	The Opener
	AD LIB ON NIPPON
....	- Part 1 (Fugi)
....	- Part 2 (Igoo)
....	- Part 3 (Kyoto)
....	- Part 4 (Tokyo)
....	Medley[1]
....	Take The "A" Train
....	Take The "A" Train
....	Tootie For Cootie
....	Skin Deep
....	Passion Flower
....	Things Ain't What They Used To Be
....	Wings And Things
....	I Got It Bad
....	Kinda Dukish/Rockin' In Rhythm
....	Satin Doll
....	Never On Sunday

[1]Including: Satin Doll; Solitude; In A Sentimental Mood; Don't Get Around Much Anymore; Mood Indigo; I'm Beginning To See The Light; Sophisticated Lady; Caravan; Do Nothin' Till You Hear From Me; I Let A Song Go Out Of My Heart/Don't Get Around Much Anymore.

30 May 1966   (S)
KDKA Studios
Pittsburgh, PA

DUKE ELLINGTON
Piano solo.

....	Commercial Jingles –DE talking[1]

[1]Music for the Duquesne Company's "Duke" beer commercial.

2 Jun 1966   (P)
Golden West Ballroom
Norwalk, CA

DUKE ELLINGTON & HIS ORCHESTRA
CA CW HJns ME, LB BCpr CCrs, JHtn JH RP PG HC, JL SWrd.

....	Boo-Dah
....	Laura
....	Smada
....	Star Dust
....	In A Mellotone

> DE added.

....	Take The "A" Train
....	More
....	Stranger On The Shore
....	Call Me Irresponsible
....	Days Of Wine And Roses
....	Azure
....	Perdido

> LB, DE JL SWrd.

....	Flamingo

> Entire band.

....	Diminuendo In Blue and Wailing Interval
....	Mood Indigo
....	I Got It Bad
....	On The Sunny Side Of The Street
....	Things Ain't What They Used To Be
....	Wings And Things >>>

....		Ellington '66
....		Passion Flower
....		All Of Me
....		Summertime
....		Jam With Sam
....		Chelsea Bridge
....		What Am I Here For?
....		Caravan
....		I Let A Song Go Out Of My Heart/Don't Get Around Much Anymore
....		The "C" Jam Blues
....		The "C" Jam Blues
....		Sophisticated Lady
....		Satin Doll
....		Skin Deep

> DE JL.

....	Harlem Air Shaft—It's Freedom

> Entire band, JRss added.

....	Ad Lib Blues

> JRss omitted.

....	Ginza Blues
....	The Birth Of The Blues
....	Take The "A" Train
....	Tootie For Cootie
....	Things Ain't What They Used To Be

26 Jun 1966[1]   (P)
NBC Studios (tc)
Hollywood, CA

DUKE ELLINGTON WITH ORCHESTRA
DE with a studio orchestra, directed by Les Brown.

....	Medley[2]

> DMtn and the ASrs added.

....	Medley –vDMtn ASrs[3]

[1]Taping session; telecast on 29 Sep 1966.
[2]Including: Do Nothin' Till You Hear From Me; Don't Get Around Much Anymore; Mood Indigo; Caravan; Satin Doll.
[3]Including: It Don't Mean A Thing; Hold Tight; Hubba, Hubba, Hubba; The Music Goes 'Round And Around; Swingin' Down The Lane. DE plays 8 bars between the fourth and fifth selections.

2 Jul 1966   (S)
Unidentified location (bc)
Milwaukee, WI

DUKE ELLINGTON
Interviewed by Bob Knudsen.

....	Interview

3 Jul 1966   (P)
Freebody Park
Newport, RI

DUKE ELLINGTON & HIS ORCHESTRA WITH ELLA FITZGERALD
CA CW HJns ME, LB BCpr CCrs, JHtn JH RP PG HC, DE JL SWrd.

....	GdJ	Take The "A" Train
....	GdJ	Black And Tan Fantasy—Creole Love Call—The Mooche
....	GdJ	Soul Call
....	GdJ	West Indian Pancake
....	GdJ	El Viti
....	GdJ	The Opener
....		La Plus Belle Africaine
....		Kinda Dukish/Rockin' In Rhythm
....	GdJ	I Got It Bad
....	GdJ	Things Ain't What They Used To Be
....	GdJ	Wings And Things
....	GdJ	Jam With Sam
....		Things Ain't What They Used To Be

> JL SWrd omitted, JHgh ET, EF added.

....	Cotton Tail –vEF
....	Imagine My Frustration –vEF

4 Jul 1966   (P)
Carter Barron Amphitheater
Washington, DC

DUKE ELLINGTON & HIS ORCHESTRA WITH ELLA FITZGERALD
CA CW HJns ME, LB BCpr CCrs, JHtn JH RP PG HC, DE JL SWrd.

....	Take The "A" Train
....	Black And Tan Fantasy—Creole Love Call—The Mooche
....	Soul Call >>>

....	West Indian Pancake
....	Blow By Blow
....	El Viti
....	The Opener
....	La Plus Belle Africaine
....	Take The "A" Train
....	I Got It Bad
....	Things Ain't What They Used To Be
....	Wings And Things
....	Medley[1]
....	Things Ain't What They Used To Be

> JL SWrd omitted, JHgh ET, EF added.

....	Cotton Tail -vEF
....	Imagine My Frustration --vEF

[1]Including: Solitude; Don't Get Around Much Anymore; Mood Indigo; I'm Beginning To See The Light; Sophisticated Lady; Caravan; Do Nothin' Till You Hear From Me; I Let A Song Go Out Of My Heart/Don't Get Around Much Anymore.

6 Jul 1966   (P)
Carter Barron Amphitheater
Washington, DC

DUKE ELLINGTON & HIS ORCHESTRA WITH ELLA FITZGERALD
CA CW HJns ME, LB BCpr CCrs, JHtn JH RP PG HC, DE JL SWrd.

....	Take The "A" Train
....	Soul Call
....	West Indian Pancake
....	El Viti
....	The Opener
....	I Got It Bad
....	Things Ain't What They Used To Be
....	Wings And Things
....	Medley[1]
....	Things Ain't What They Used To Be

> JL SWrd omitted, JHgh ET, EF added.

....	Cotton Tail --vEF
....	Imagine My Frustration --vEF

> EF omitted.

....	Take The "A" Train

[1]Including: Solitude; Don't Get Around Much Anymore; Sophisticated Lady; Caravan; Do Nothin' Till You Hear From Me; I Let A Song Go Out Of My Heart/Don't Get Around Much Anymore.

8 Jul 1966   (P)
Carter Barron Amphitheater
Washington, DC

DUKE ELLINGTON & HIS ORCHESTRA WITH ELLA FITZGERALD
CA CW HJns ME, LB BCpr CCrs, JHtn JH RP PG HC, DE JL SWrd.

....	Take The "A" Train
....	Soul Call
....	West Indian Pancake
....	El Viti
....	The Opener
....	La Plus Belle Africaine
....	Take The "A" Train
....	I Got It Bad
....	Things Ain't What They Used To Be
....	Medley[1]
....	Things Ain't What They Used To Be

> JL SWrd omitted, JHgh ET, EF added.

....	Cotton Tail --vEF
....	Imagine My Frustration --vEF

[1]Including: Solitude; Don't Get Around Much Anymore; Mood Indigo; I'm Beginning To See The Light; Sophisticated Lady; Caravan; Do Nothin' Till You Hear From Me; I Let A Song Go Out Of My Heart/Don't Get Around Much Anymore.

10 Jul 1966   (P)
Carter Barron Amphitheater
Washington, DC

DUKE ELLINGTON & HIS ORCHESTRA WITH ELLA FITZGERALD
CA CW HJns ME, LB BCpr CCrs, JHtn JH RP PG HC, DE JL SWrd.

....	Take The "A" Train
....	Soul Call
....	West Indian Pancake
....	El Viti
....	The Opener
....	La Plus Belle Africaine >>>

....		Take The "A" Train
....		I Got It Bad
....		Things Ain't What They Used To Be
....		Medley[1]
....		Things Ain't What They Used To Be

> JL SWrd, JHgh ET, EF added.

....		Cotton Tail –vEF
....		Imagine My Frustration –vEF

[1]Including: Solitude; Don't Get Around Much Anymore; Mood Indigo; I'm Beginning To See The Light; Sophisticated Lady; Caravan; Do Nothin' Till You Hear From Me; I Let A Song Go Out Of My Heart/Don't Get Around Much Anymore.

15 Jul 1966   (P)
Lewisohn Stadium
New York City, NY

DUKE ELLINGTON & HIS ORCHESTRA
CA CW HJns ME, LB BCpr CCrs, JHtn JH RP PG HC, DE JL SWrd.

....		Take The "A" Train
....		Black And Tan Fantasy—Creole Love Call—The Mooche
....		Soul Call
....		West Indian Pancake
....		El Viti
....		The Opener
....		La Plus Belle Africaine
....		Take The "A" Train
....		I Got It Bad
....		Things Ain't What They Used To Be
....		Wings And Things
....		Rockin' In Rhythm
....		Medley[1]
....		Things Ain't What They Used To Be

[1]Including: Satin Doll; Solitude; In A Sentimental Mood; Don't Get Around Much Anymore; Mood Indigo; I'm Beginning To See The Light; Sophisticated Lady; Caravan; Do Nothin' Till You Hear From Me; I Let A Song Go Out Of My Heart/Don't Get Around Much Anymore.

18 Jul 1966   (S)
24th St., Studio A
New York City, NY

DUKE ELLINGTON & HIS RHYTHM
DE JL SWrd.

....	RDB		The Shepherd[1] (incomplete)
....	IA[2]		The Shepherd (w. spoken introduction by Jack Benny and DE.)
....	Fan	-2	The Shepherd
....	Fan	-3	The Shepherd
....			Don Juan –vDE (rehearsal)
....	RDB		Don Juan –vDE (rehearsal)
....	Fan		Don Juan
....	Fan		Sam Woodyard's Blues[2]
....	Fan	-3	Tap Dancer's Blues
....	Fan		Slow Blues
....			Looking Glass (incomplete)
....			Looking Glass (incomplete)
....			Looking Glass (incomplete)
....	Fan		Looking Glass

> JL SWrd omitted.

....	RDB	-1	Tingling Is A Happiness
....	IA[3]	alt.	Tingling Is A Happiness (w. spoken introduction by DE.)
....	RDB		DE –spoken promotion for Field Enterprises (incomplete)
....	RDB		DE –spoken promotion for Field Enterprises (incomplete)
....	IA[3]		DE –spoken promotion for Field Enterprises
....	IA[3]		DE –spoken introduction to "Dancers In Love."
....	RDB[3]		Dancers In Love
....		-2	Dancers In Love
....	IA[3,4]	alt.	Dancers In Love (w. spoken introduction by DE.)

[1]Complete: "The Shepherd Who Watches Over The Night Flock"; aka "The Blues Is Waiting."
[2]aka "6:40 Blues."
[3]Souvenir record for the International Achievement Conference of Field Enterprises Educational Corporation.
[4]It is not known which of the takes have been used by RDB and IA respectively.

26 Jul 1966   (S)
Unidentified location (tc)
Juan-les-Pins, France

DUKE ELLINGTON
DE interviewed about the forthcoming Jazz Festival in Antibes.

....		Interview >>>

DUKE ELLINGTON & HIS ORCHESTRA   Square Frank Jay Gould (P)
CA CW HJns ME, LB BCpr CCrs, JHtn JH RP PG HC, JL SWrd.

.... STJ   Smada

        > DE added.

.... STJ   Take The "A" Train
.... STJ   Black And Tan Fantasy—Creole Love Call—The Mooche
.... STJ   Soul Call
.... STJ   West Indian Pancake
.... STJ   El Viti
.... STJ   The Opener
.... STJ   La Plus Belle Africaine
.... STJ   Azure
.... STJ   Take The "A" Train
.... STJ   Satin Doll
.... Vrv   Diminuendo In Blue and Blow By Blow
                                       Take The "A" Train
.... STJ   Caravan
.... Vrv   Rose Of The Rio Grande
.... MJ   Tootie For Cootie
.... Vrv   Skin Deep
.... Mn   Passion Flower
.... Mn   Things Ain't What They Used To Be
.... Mn   Wings And Things
.... Vrv   The Star-Crossed Lovers
.... Vrv   Such Sweet Thunder
.... Vrv   Madness In Great Ones
.... MR   Kinda Dukish/Rockin' In Rhythm
.... Vrv   Things Ain't What They Used To Be

                                                                 27 Jul 1966   (P)
DUKE ELLINGTON   Fondation Maeght
Piano solo.   Saint Paul de Vence, France

.... Az   Tingling Is A Happiness

        > JL SWrd added.

.... Pab   The Shepherd
.... Pab   alt.   The Shepherd
.... Pab   Kinda Dukish

DUKE ELLINGTON & HIS ORCHESTRA WITH ELLA FITZGERALD   Square Frank Jay Gould (tc) (P)
CA CW HJns ME, LB BCpr CCrs, JHtn JH RP PG HC, DE JL SWrd.   Juan-les-Pins

.... Vrv   Main Stem
.... Vrv   Black And Tan Fantasy—Creole Love Call—The Mooche
....   Soul Call
.... Vrv   West Indian Pancake
.... Vrv   El Viti
.... Vrv   The Opener
.... MR   La Plus Belle Africaine
.... MR   Azure

        > DE JL SWrd omitted, JJns JHgh GTt, EF added.

.... Vrv   Let's Do It –vEF
.... Vrv   Satin Doll –vEF

        > DE replaces JJns.

.... Vrv   Cotton Tail –vEF

DUKE ELLINGTON & HIS ORCHESTRA
Same personnel.

.... MR   Take The "A" Train
.... Vrv   Take The "A" Train
.... Vrv   Take The "A" Train
.... MR   Such Sweet Thunder
.... MR   Half The Fun
.... MR   Madness In Great Ones
.... MR   The Star-Crossed Lovers
.... Vrv   I Got It Bad
.... Vrv   Things Ain't What They Used To Be
.... Vrv   Wings And Things
.... MR   Kinda Dukish/Rockin' In Rhythm
.... MR   Chelsea Bridge   >>>

....	Vrv	Skin Deep
....	Mad	Sophisticated Lady
....	Vrv	Jam With Sam
....	Vrv	Things Ain't What They Used To Be

28 Jul 1966   (S)
Unidentified location (tc)[1]
Juan-les-Pins, France

DUKE ELLINGTON & HIS ORCHESTRA
CA CW HJns ME, LB BCpr CCrs, JHtn JH RP PG HC, DE JL SWrd.

....		The Old Circus Train Turn-Around Blues (incomplete)
....		The Old Circus Train Turn-Around Blues (incomplete)
....		The Old Circus Train Turn-Around Blues (incomplete)
....	Vrv	The Old Circus Train Turn-Around Blues (incomplete)
....	Vrv	The Old Circus Train Turn-Around Blues (incomplete)
....	Vrv	The Old Circus Train Turn-Around Blues (incomplete)

> JJns relaces DE.

....	Vrv	The Old Circus Train Turn-Around Blues (incomplete)

> DE replaces JJns.

....	Vrv	The Old Circus Train Turn-Around Blues (incomplete

> JJns replaces DE.

....	Vrv	The Old Circus Train Turn-Around Blues (incomplete

> DE replaces JJns.

....	Vrv	The Old Circus Train Turn-Around Blues (incomplete)
....	Vrv	The Old Circus Train Turn-Around Blues (chord)

> JJns replaces DE.

....	Vrv	Blue Fuse No. 2 (incomplete)
....	Vrv	Blue Fuse No. 1 (incomplete)
....	Vrv	Blue Fuse No. 1 (incomplete)
....	Vrv	Blue Fuse No. 1 (incomplete)
....	Vrv	Blue Fuse No. 1 (incomplete)

> DE replaces JJns.

....	Vrv	The Shepherd (incomplete)
....	Vrv	The Shepherd

> JJns added.

....	Vrv	The Old Circus Train Turn-Around Blues
....	Vrv	The Old Circus Train Turn-Around Blues

[1]Part of this session was telecast.

The above is a rehearsal session and includes intermittent talk.

DUKE ELLINGTON & HIS ORCHESTRA WITH ELLA FITZGERALD
Same personnel.

Square Frank Jay Gould (tc) (P)

....		In A Mellotone
....		Main Stem
....		Black And Tan Fantasy—Creole Love Call—The Mooche
....	Vrv	Soul Call
....	Vrv	West Indian Pancake
....	Vrv	El Viti
....	Vrv	The Opener
....	Vrv	La Plus Belle Africaine
....	Vrv	Take The "A" Train
....	Vrv	Trombonio Bustoso Issimo[1]
....	Az	Such Sweet Thunder
....	Az	Half The Fun
....	Az	Madness In Great Ones
....	Vrv	The Star-Crossed Lovers
....	Vrv	Prelude To A Kiss
....	Vrv	Things Ain't What They Used To Be
....	Vrv	The Old Circus Train Turn-Around Blues
....		Skin Deep
....		Things Ain't What They Used To Be

> DE JL SWrd omitted, JJns JHgh GTt, EF added.

....	Vrv	Thou Swell –vEF
....	Vrv	Satin Doll –vEF
....	Vrv	Wives And Lovers –vEF
....	Vrv	Something To Live For –vEF
....	Vrv	Let's Do It –vEF >>>

....   Sweet Georgia Brown –vEF
.... Vrv   Mack The Knife –vEF

> DE replaces JJns.

....   Cotton Tail –vEF
....   Imagine My Frustration –vEF

[1]*sa* "El Busto"; "Trombone Buster."

29 Jul 1966   (P)
Square Frank Jay Gould
Juan-les-Pins, France

DUKE ELLINGTON & HIS ORCHESTRA WITH ELLA FITZGERALD
CA CW HJns ME, LB BCpr CCrs, JHtn JH RP PG HC, DE JL SWrd.

....   Take The "A" Train
.... Vrv   Black And Tan Fantasy—Creole Love Call—The Mooche
.... Vrv   Soul Call
.... Vrv   West Indian Pancake
.... Vrv   El Viti
....   The Opener
.... Vrv   La Plus Belle Africaine
.... Vrv   Such Sweet Thunder
.... Vrv   Half The Fun
.... Vrv   Madness In Great Ones
.... Vrv   The Star-Crossed Lovers
.... Az   Things Ain't What They Used To Be
.... Vrv   Wings And Things
.... Vrv   Things Ain't What They Used To Be

> DE JL SWrd omitted, JJns JHgh GTt, EF added.

.... Vrv   Who?—Though Swell –vEF
.... Vrv   Satin Doll –vEF
.... Vrv   Wives And Lovers –vEF
.... Vrv   Something To Live For –vEF
.... Vrv   Mack The Knife –vEF

> DE replaces JJns.

.... Vrv   Cotton Tail –vEF

DUKE ELLINGTON & HIS ORCHESTRA
RN, BW added, otherwise same personnel.

....   In A Mellotone

> CW omitted.

.... Vrv   The Trip[1]
....   Motel
....   Jive Jam
.... Vrv   Jive Jam
.... Vrv   All Too Soon
....   Motel

> JJns added.

.... Vrv   The Old Circus Train Turn-Around Blues

> JJns omitted.

....   Take The "A" Train

> JH omitted, EF added.

.... Vrv   It Don't Mean A Thing –vEF RN

> RN, LB CCrs, PG, DE JL SWrd, EF.

.... Vrv   Just Squeeze Me –vEF RN

[1]*aka* "High Passage."

15 Aug 1966   (P)
Wollman Memorial Skating Rink, Central Park
New York City, NY

DUKE ELLINGTON & HIS ORCHESTRA
CA CW HJns ME, LB BCpr CCrs, JHtn JH RP PG HC, DE JL SWrd.

....   Take The "A" Train
....   Satin Doll
....   Soul Call
....   West Indian Pancake
....   El Viti
....   The Opener
....   Medley[1]
....   Take The "A" Train
....   I Got It Bad   >>>

....   Things Ain't What They Used To Be
....   Things Ain't What They Used To Be

[1]Including: Solitude; Don't Get Around Much Anymore; Mood Indigo; I'm Beginning To See The Light; Sophisticated Lady; Caravan; Do Nothin' Till You Hear From Me; I Let A Song Go Out Of My Heart/Don't Get Around Much Anymore.

			18 Aug 1966	(S)

DUKE ELLINGTON & HIS ORCHESTRA
CA CW HJns ME, LB BCpr CCrs, JHtn JH RP PG HC, DE JL SWrd.   RCA Studios / New York City, NY

.... WEA   HARLEM
....   HARLEM (incomplete)

> JJns added.

....   -1   Mellow Ditty
....   -2   Mellow Ditty
....   -3   Mellow Ditty
.... Az   -4   Mellow Ditty
....   -1   The Old Circus Train[1] (incomplete)
....   -2   The Old Circus Train (incomplete)
....   -3   The Old Circus Train (incomplete)
....   -4   The Old Circus Train (incomplete)
.... Az   -5   The Old Circus Train
.... Stv   The Tin Soldier (rehearsal)

[1]sa "The Old Circus Train Turn-Around Blues."

			25 Aug 1966	(P)

DUKE ELLINGTON & HIS ORCHESTRA WITH THE LOS ANGELES SYMPHONY ORCHESTRA   Hollywood Bowl
CA CW HJns ME, LB BCpr CCrs, JHtn JH RP PG HC, DE JL SWrd, with the Los Angeles   Los Angeles, CA
Symphony Orchestra, William Kraft conducting.

> LASO.

....   The Star Spangled Banner

> DE JL SWrd added.

....   New World A-Comin'

> DE piano solo.

....   Prelude To A Kiss—In A Sentimental Mood—Prelude To A Kiss
....   A Single Petal Of A Rose

> LASO added.

                               THE GOLDEN BROOM AND THE GREEN APPLE
....   - Stanza 1 (The Golden Broom)
....   - Stanza 2 (The Green Apple)
....   - Stanza 3 (The Handsome Traffic Policeman)

> LASO omitted, entire band added.

....   Black And Tan Fantasy—Creole Love Call—The Mooche
....   Soul Call
....   West Indian Pancake
....   El Viti
....   The Opener
....   La Plus Belle Africaine
....   I Got It Bad
....   Things Ain't What They Used To Be
....   HARLEM
....   Medley[1]
....   Satin Doll
....   Take The "A" Train

[1]Including: Do Nothin' Till You Hear From Me; Don't Get Around Much Anymore; Mood Indigo; I'm Beginning To See The Light; Sophisticated Lady; Caravan; It Don't Mean A Thing; Solitude; I Let A Song Go Out Of My Heart/Don't Get Around Much Anymore.

			p 2 Sep 1966	(S)

DUKE ELLINGTON
Piano solo.   Unidentified location / New York City, NY

.... CS   Just One Big Question

			18 Sep 1966[1]	(P)

DUKE ELLINGTON & HIS ORCHESTRA   Festival Grounds (bc)
CA CW HJns ME, LB BCpr CCrs, JHtn JH RP PG HC, DE JL SWrd, TWtk BBgs.   Monterey, CA

....   Take The "A" Train
....   Black And Tan Fantasy—Creole Love Call—The Mooche
....   Soul Call   >>>

....		West Indian Pancake
....		El Viti
....		The Opener
....		La Plus Belle Africaine
....		The Old Circus Train
....		Kinda Dukish/Rockin' In Rhythm
....		David Danced Before The Lord –vTWtk, BBgs tap
....		Honeysuckle Rose –BBgs tap
....		I Got It Bad
....		Things Ain't What They Used To Be
....		Wings And Things
....		Things Ain't What They Used To Be

[1]Broadcast on 18 Dec 1966.

DUKE ELLINGTON & HIS ORCHESTRA WITH ELLA FITZGERALD   23 Sep 1966   (P)
CA CW HJns ME, LB BCpr CCrs, JHtn JH RP PG HC, JJns JHgh ET, EF.   Greek Theater
                                                               Los Angeles, CA

....	Sts	Sweet Georgia Brown –vEF
....	Sts	St. Louis Blues –vEF
....	Sts	Mack The Knife –vEF

> DE replaces JJns, EF omitted, BBgs added.

....	Sts	Tap Dancer's Blues –BBgs tap
....	Sts	Tap Dancer's Blues –BBgs tap

> BBgs omitted, EF added.

....	Sts	Cotton Tail –vEF

> EF omitted.

....	Sts	Things Ain't What They Used To Be

DUKE ELLINGTON & HIS ORCHESTRA WITH ELLA FITZGERALD   24 Sep 1966   (P)
CA CW HJns ME, LB BCpr CCrs, JHtn JH RP PG HC, DE JL SWrd.   Greek Theater
                                                               Los Angeles, CA

....	Sts	Take The "A" Train
....	Sts	Take The "A" Train
....	Sts	Soul Call
....	Sts	In A Sentimental Mood
....	Sts	The Prowling Cat
....	Sts	La Plus Belle Africaine
....	Sts	The Old Circus Train

> BBgs added.

....		Tulip Or Turnip –vBBgs
....		David Danced Before The Lord –BBgs tap
....		Honeysuckle Rose –BBgs tap

> BBgs omitted.

....		I Got It Bad
....		Things Ain't What They Used To Be

> JHtn RP HC, DE.

....		Monologue –DE narration

> Entire band.

....		Things Ain't What They Used To Be

> DE JL SWrd omitted, JJns JHgh ET, EF added.

....		I'm Just A Lucky So-And-So –vEF
....		The Moment Of Truth –vEF
....		Satin Doll –vEF
....	Co	These Boots Are Made For Walkin' –vEF
....		These Boots Are Made For Walkin' –vEF
....		Something To Live For –vEF
....		Let's Do It –vEF
....		Sweet Georgia Brown –vEF
....		Baby, Bye-Bye –vEF
....		Mack The Knife –vEF

> DE replaces JJns, EF omitted, BBgs added.

....		Tap Dancer's Blues –BBgs tap

> BBgs omitted, EF added.

....		Cotton Tail –vEF

23 Oct 1966   (P)
CBS Studios (tc)
New York City, NY

<u>DUKE ELLINGTON & HIS ORCHESTRA</u>
CA CW HJns ME, LB BCpr CCrs, JHtn JH RP PG HC, DE JL SWrd.

....   In The Beginning God

> BBgs, choir added.

....   David Danced Before The Lord –vChoir, BBgs tap

> BBgs, choir omitted.

....   Satin Doll (aborted)

28 Oct 1966   (P)
Westbury Music Fair
Westbury, NY

<u>DUKE ELLINGTON & HIS ORCHESTRA WITH ELLA FITZGERALD</u>
CA CW HJns ME, LB BCpr CCrs, JHtn JH RP PG HC, DE JL SWrd, BBgs.

....   Take The "A" Train
....   Black And Tan Fantasy—Creole Love Call—The Mooche
....   Soul Call
....   West Indian Pancake
....   El Viti
....   The Opener
....   La Plus Belle Africaine
....   Take The "A" Train
....   I Got It Bad
....   Things Ain't What They Used To Be
....   Wings And Things
....   Tulip Or Turnip –vBBgs
....   David Danced Before The Lord –BBgs tap
....   Honeysuckle Rose –BBgs tap

> JHtn RP HC, DE.

....   Monologue –DE narration

> Entire band.

....   Things Ain't What They Used To Be

> JL SWrd omitted, JHgh ET, EF added.

....   Cotton Tail –vEF

2 Nov 1966[1]   (T)[2]
Unspecified studio (tc)
New York City, NY[3]

<u>BARBARA McNAIR WITH THE DUKE ELLINGTON TRIO</u>
DE JL SWrd.

....   The "C" Jam Blues
....   Take The "A" Train
....   Dancers In Love

> DE, BMN, house orchestra and chorus.

....   Medley[4]

[1]Taping session of (Celanese) Center Stage; this syndicated program was telecast throughout the U.S. in early Mar 1967.
[2]DE portion of the show.
[3]According to some sources, this show was produced in Los Angeles, which seems unlikely on account of DE's busy schedule on the east coast at the time.
[4]Including: Solitude –vBMN; I'm Beginning To See The Light –vBMN; Mood Indigo –vBMN; Do Nothin' Till You Hear From Me –vBMN; Satin Doll –vChorus; I Got It Bad –vBMN Chorus; Don't Get Around Much Anymore –vBMN Chorus; Sophisticated Lady –vBMN Chorus.

3 Nov 1966   (P)
Studios WOR (bc)
New York City, NY

<u>DUKE ELLINGTON</u>
DE, among other guests, interviewed by Jack O'Brien.

....   Interview

4+5 Nov 1966[1]   (T)
Dade County Auditorium (tc)
Miami Beach, FL

<u>DUKE ELLINGTON & HIS ORCHESTRA</u>
CA CW HJns ME, LB BCpr CCrs, JHtn JH RP PG HC, DE JL SWrd.

....   Satin Doll
....   Take The "A" Train
....   Jam With Sam
....   Things Ain't What They Used To Be

[1]Taping session for the Jackie Gleason show; telecast on 26 Nov 1966.

16 Nov 1966   (P)
Civic Theater
San Diego, CA

<u>DUKE ELLINGTON & HIS ORCHESTRA</u>
CA CW HJns ME, LB BCpr CCrs, JHtn JH RP PG HC, DE JL, TWtk.

....	Take The "A" Train
....	Black And Tan Fantasy---Creole Love Call---The Mooche
....	Harmony In Harlem
....	I Got It Bad
....	Things Ain't What They Used To Be
....	Wings And Things

> LPts added.

....	Medley[1]
....	La Plus Belle Africaine
....	Take The "A" Train
....	Soul Call
....	In The Beginning God --vTWtk.
....	West Indian Pancake
....	El Viti
....	Kinda Dukish/Rockin' In Rhythm

> DE piano solo.

....	Dancers In Love

> JHtn RP HC, DE.

....	Monologue --DE narration

> Entire band.

....	Jam With Sam
....	Things Ain't What They Used To Be

[1]Including: Satin Doll; Solitude; In A Sentimental Mood; Don't Get Around Much Anymore; Mood Indigo; I'm Beginning To See The Light; Sophisticated Lady; Caravan; Do Nothin' Till You Hear From Me; Don't You Know I Care?; I'm Just A Lucky So-And-So; I Let A Song Go Out Of My Heart/Don't Get Around Much Anymore.

<u>DUKE ELLINGTON & HIS ORCHESTRA WITH THE SAN DIEGO SYMPHONY ORCHESTRA</u>
San Diego Symphony Orchestra added, otherwise same personnel.

....	HARLEM
....	Medley[1]
....	Satin Doll
....	Take The "A" Train

[1]Including: Do Nothin' Till You Hear From Me; Don't Get Around Much Anymore; Mood Indigo; I'm Beginning To See The Light; Sophisticated Lady; Caravan; It Don't Mean A Thing; Solitude; I Let A Song Go Out Of My Heart/Don't Get Around Much Anymore.

19 Nov 1966   (P)
Royce Hall
Westwood, CA

<u>DUKE ELLINGTON & HIS ORCHESTRA</u>
CA CW HJns ME, LB BCpr CCrs, JHtn JH RP PG HC, DE JL SWrd, EMrw TWtk.

....	Take The "A" Train
....	Black And Tan Fantasy---Creole Love Call---The Mooche
....	Soul Call
....	West Indian Pancake
....	El Viti
....	The Opener
....	La Plus Belle Africaine
....	Medley[1]
....	Take The "A" Train
....	Take The "A" Train
....	Passion Flower
....	Things Ain't What They Used To Be
....	In The Beginning God --vTWtk
....	Kinda Dukish/Rockin' In Rhythm
....	Never On Sunday
....	Red Roses For A Blue Lady
....	The Lord's Prayer --vEMrw
....	Jam With Sam
....	Things Ain't What They Used To Be

[1]Including: Satin Doll; Solitude; In A Sentimental Mood; Don't Get Around Much Anymore; Mood Indigo; I'm Beginning To See The Light; Sophisticated Lady; Caravan; Do Nothin' Till You Hear From Me; I Let A Song Go Out Of My Heart/ Don't Get Around Much Anymore.

21 Nov 1966   (P)
DUKE ELLINGTON & HIS ORCHESTRA   Mark Twain Riverboat (bc)
CA CW HJns ME, LB BCpr CCrs, JHtn JH RP PG HC, DE JL SWrd.   New York City, NY

....   Take The "A" Train
....   The Old Circus Train
....   Sophisticated Lady
....   Satin Doll
....   Fade Up
....   Mood Indigo
....   The Opener
....   Passion Flower
....   Things Ain't What They Used To Be
....   Wings And Things
        > JBsh SHsn added.

....   Jam With Sam
        > JBsh SHsn omitted.

....   Satin Doll

25 Nov 1966   (P)
DUKE ELLINGTON & HIS ORCHESTRA   Mark Twain Riverboat (tc)
CA CW HJns ME, LB BCpr CCrs, JHtn JH RP PG HC, DE JL SWrd.   New York City, NY

....   Take The "A" Train
....   Satin Doll
....   Fade Up
....   Trombonio Bustoso Issimo
....   I Let A Song Go Out Of My Heart/Don't Get Around Much Anymore
....   Mood Indigo
....   Things Ain't What They Used To Be
....   David Danced Before The Lord

29 Nov 1966   (P)
DUKE ELLINGTON & HIS ORCHESTRA   Mark Twain Riverboat (bc)
CA CW HJns ME, LB BCpr CCrs, JHtn JH RP PG HC, DE JL SWrd.   New York City, NY

....   Take The "A" Train
....   Mellow Ditty
....   DE interviewed by Johnny Carson
....   Mount Harissa[1]

[1]Originally titled "Nob Hill"; part of the future *Far East Suite.*

Early Dec 1966   (P)
DUKE ELLINGTON & HIS ORCHESTRA   Mark Twain Riverboat (bc)
CA CW HJns ME, LB BCpr CCrs, JHtn JH RP PG HC, DE JL RJo.   New York City, NY

....   Take The "A" Train
....   Satin Doll
....   Mood Indigo
....   Do Nothin' Till You Hear From Me
....   I Let A Song Go Out Of Heart/Don't Get Around Much Anymore
....   Things Ain't What They Used To Be
....   The Birth Of The Blues
....   Sophisticated Lady
....   The Old Circus Train
....   Caravan

5 Dec 1966   (P)
DUKE ELLINGTON & HIS ORCHESTRA   Constitution Hall
CA CW HJns ME, LB BCpr CCrs, JHtn JH RP PG HC, DE JL RJo, EMrw TWtk JMP BBgs VHC.   Washington, DC

                        CONCERT OF SACRED MUSIC

        > VHC a cappella.

....   Come Sunday –vVHC
        > Entire band.

....   Come Sunday
....   Montage
....   My Mother, My Father –vJMP
....   Soul Call
....   Tell Me, It's The Truth –vEMrw
....   In The Beginning God –vTWtk VHC
        > DE piano solo.

....   New World A-Comin'   >>>

> DE, JMP VHC.

....   Will You Be There? –vJMP VHC

> Entire band.

....   99% Won't Do –vJMP VHC
....   Ain't But The One –vJMP VHC
....   Come Sunday –vEMrw
....   The Lord's Prayer –vEMrw

> BBgs added.

....   David Danced Before The Lord –vVHC, BBgs tap

> TWtk a cappella.

....   The Preacher's Song –vTWtk

> Entire band.

....   In The Beginning God –vVHC

17 Dec 1966   (P)
Lyric Theater
Baltimore, MD

DUKE ELLINGTON WITH THE BALTIMORE SYMPHONY ORCHESTRA
DE JL RJo, TWtk, with the Baltimore Symphony Orchestra, Elyakum Shapiro conducting.

....   New World A-Comin'

> DE piano solo.

....   Medley[1]
....   A Single Petal Of A Rose

> JL RJo, BSO added.

                           THE GOLDEN BROOM AND THE GREEN APPLE
....   - Stanza 1 (The Golden Broom)
....   - Stanza 2 (The Green Apple)
....   - Stanza 3 (The Handsome Traffic Policeman)
....   Medley[2]

> DE JL RJo.

                           AD LIB ON NIPPON
....   - Part 1 (Fugi)
....   - Part 2 (Igoo)
....   - Part 3 (Nagoya)
....   - Part 4 (Tokyo)

> BSO added.

....   Satin Doll

> BSO omitted.

....   Take The "A" Train
....   In The Beginning God –vTWtk
....   Things Ain't What They Used To Be

[1]Including: Prelude To A Kiss; In A Sentimental Mood; Don't You Know I Care?; Prelude To A Kiss.
[2]Including: I Got It Bad; Do Nothin' Till You Hear From Me; Don't Get Around Much Anymore; Mood Indigo; I'm Beginning To See The Light; Sophisticated Lady; Caravan; It Don't Mean A Thing; Solitude; I Let A Song Go Out Of My Heart/Don't Get Around Much Anymore.

19 Dec 1966   (S)
24th St., Studio A
New York City, NY

DUKE ELLINGTON & HIS ORCHESTRA
CA CW HJns ME, LB BCpr CCrs, JHtn JH RP PG HC, DE JL RJo.

                           THE FAR EAST SUITE[1]
.... Bb   TPA1-9147-4   - Tourist Point Of View
.... Bb   TPA1-9147-5   - Tourist Point Of View
.... Vi   TPA1-9147-7   - Tourist Point Of View
.... Vi   TPA1-9148-3   - Amad
.... Bb   TPA1-9148-5   - Amad
.... Bb   TPA1-9148-7   - Amad

[1]See also sessions on 20 and 21 Dec 1966.

20 Dec 1966   (S)
24th St., Studio A
New York City, NY

DUKE ELLINGTON & HIS ORCHESTRA
CA CW HJns ME, LB BCpr CCrs, JHtn JH RP PG HC, DE JL RJo.

                           THE FAR EAST SUITE (ctd.)[1]
.... Vi   TPA1-9149-3   - Agra
....   TPA1-9150   - Bluebird Of Delhi   >>>

	Vi	TPA1-9151-2[2]	- Ad Lib On Nippon, parts 1-4
		TPA1-9151-3	- Ad Lib On Nippon (incomplete)
	Vi	TPA1-9151-4[2]	- Ad Lib On Nippon, parts 1-4
	Vi	TPA1-9152-1	- Isfahan
	Bb	TPA1-9152-2	- Isfahan

[1]See also sessions on 19 and 21 Dec 1966.
[2]Both takes have been edited together for the original release on Vi and have also been reissued that way. Due to variants in the editing and a longer JHtn segment, both Vi LPM-3792 and the centennial edition run a bit longer than the original release. Also, the first four bars of part 4 (Tokyo) differ between the versions as released on Victor and Bluebird.

21 Dec 1966   (S)
24th St., Studio A
New York City, NY

DUKE ELLINGTON & HIS ORCHESTRA
CA CW HJns ME, LB BCpr CCrs, JHtn JH RP PG HC, DE JL RJo.

THE FAR EAST SUITE (ctd.)[1]

	Bb	TPA1-9150-8	- Bluebird Of Delhi
	Bb	TPA1-9150-9	- Bluebird Of Delhi
	Vi	TPA1-9150-12	- Bluebird Of Delhi
		TPA1-9153-11	- Depk
		TPA1-9153-13	- Depk
	Bb	TPA1-9153-15	- Depk
	Vi	TPA1-9153-17	- Depk
	Bb	TPA1-9154-4	- Mount Harissa
	Vi	TPA1-9154-5	- Mount Harissa
	Vi	TPA1-9155-2	- Blue Pepper[2]

[1]See also sessions on 19 and 20 Dec 1966.
[2]aka "Far East Of The Blues."

THE FAR EAST SUITE (summation—original release)[1]

Vi	TPA1-9147-7	- Tourist Point Of View
Vi	TPA1-9150-12	- Bluebird Of Delhi
Vi	TPA1-9152-1	- Isfahan
Vi	TPA1-9153-17	- Depk
Vi	TPA1-9154-5	- Mount Harissa
Vi	TPA1-9155-2	- Blue Pepper
Vi	TPA1-9149-3	- Agra
Vi	TPA1-9148-3	- Amad
Vi	TPA1-9151-2/4	- Ad Lib On Nippon

[1]For the CD releases some alternate takes were used.

28 Dec 1966   (S)
24th St., Studio B
New York City, NY

DUKE ELLINGTON
Piano solo.

	Az		Meditation[1] (incomplete)
	Az		Meditation (incomplete)
	Stv	-1	Meditation
	Az		Unidentified title (fragment)
	Az		Beautiful Woman Walks Well
	Az		Ad-Libbing

[1]sa "Just One Big Question."

DUKE ELLINGTON & HIS SEPTET
CA CW, JH PG HC, DE JL RJo.

			I'm Beginning To See The Light (incomplete)
		-1	I'm Beginning To See The Light
			I'm Beginning To See The Light (incomplete)
			I'm Beginning To See The Light (incomplete)
			I'm Beginning To See The Light (incomplete)
	RDB	-2	I'm Beginning To See The Light (incomplete)
	RDB	-3	I'm Beginning To See The Light
			I'm Beginning To See The Light (insert)
			I'm Beginning To See The Light (insert)
	RDB	-1	Draggin' Blues (incomplete)
	RDB	-2	Draggin' Blues (incomplete)
	RDB	-3	Draggin' Blues (incomplete)
	RDB	-4	Draggin' Blues
	Saj	-5	Draggin' Blues
			Now It Ain't, Ain't It? (incomplete)
			Now It Ain't, Ain't It? (incomplete)
			Now It Ain't, Ain't It?
			Now It Ain't, Ain't It? (incomplete)
		-1	Now It Ain't, Ain't It? (incomplete)
		-2	Now It Ain't, Ain't It? (incomplete) >>>

....			Now It Ain't, Ain't It? (rehearsal)
....		-3	Now It Ain't, Ain't It? (incomplete)
....	Saj	-4[1]	Now It Ain't, Ain't It?
....	RDB		Cotton Head (rehearsal)
....	RDB		Cotton Head (rehearsal)
....	Saj	-2[1]	Cotton Head[2]
....			The Last Go-Round (incomplete)
....		-1	The Last Go-Round (incomplete)
....		-2	The Last Go-Round (incomplete)
....	Saj	-3	The Last Go-Round
....			Blues

[1]Minor editing was performed on these titles for their release on Saj.
[2]"Cottontail" [sic] on Saj.

DUKE ELLINGTON & HIS ORCHESTRA
CA CW HJns ME, LB BCpr BPwl, JHtn JH RP PG HC, DE JL RJo, TWtk.

29 Dec 1966   (S)
24th St., Studio B
New York City, NY

....	RDB	-1	I'm Just A Lucky So-And-So –vTWtk (incomplete)[1]
....		-2	I'm Just A Lucky So-And-So –vTWtk
....		-3	I'm Just A Lucky So-And-So –vTWtk
....	RDB	-4	I'm Just A Lucky So-And-So –vTWtk
....		-5	I'm Just A Lucky So-And-So
....		-2	Blues At Sundown –vTWtk (incomplete)
....		-3	Blues At Sundown –vtWtk
....		-4	Blues At Sundown –vTWtk
....		-6	Blues At Sundown –vTWtk
....		-7	Blues At Sundown –vTWtk (incomplete)
....	RDB	-8	Blues At Sundown –vTWtk
....		-9	Blues At Sundown –vTWtk
....		-1	The Lonely Ones –vTWtk (incomplete)
....		-2	The Lonely Ones –vTWtk (incomplete)
....		-3	The Lonely Ones –vTWtk
....	RDB	-4	The Lonely Ones –vTWtk

[1]The arrangement is by Melba Liston.

DUKE ELLINGTON & HIS ORCHESTRA
CA CW HJns ME, LB BCpr CCrs, JHtn JH RP PG HC, MLst JL RJo, TWtk, DE supervising.

7 Jan 1967   (S)
24th St., Studio B
New York City, NY

....			Rhythm section test
....		-1	I'm Just A Lucky So-And-So –vTWtk
....		-2	I'm Just A Lucky So-And-So –vTWtk
....		-3	I'm Just A Lucky So-And-So –vTWtk (incomplete)
....		-4	I'm Just A Lucky So-And-So
....		-1	The Lonely Ones –vTWtk (incomplete)
....		-2	The Lonely Ones –vTWtk

> MLst JL RJo, TWtk.

....			Angels Are Watchin' Over Me –vTWtk (rehearsal)
....		-1	Angels Are Watchin' Over Me –vTWtk

> Entire band.

....		-1	Jump For Joy –vTWtk (incomplete)
....		-2	Jump For Joy
....		-3	Jump For Joy –vTWtk (incomplete)
....		-4	Jump For Joy –vTWtk (incomplete)
....		-5	Jump For Joy
....		-6	Jump For Joy –vTWtk
....	RDB	-7	Jump For Joy –vTWtk
....			Jump For Joy (rehearsal)
....	RDB	-9	Jump For Joy (incomplete)
....	RDB	-10	Jump For Joy –vTWtk
....	RDB	-1	I Like The Sunrise
....	RDB	-2	I Like The Sunrise –vTWtk (incomplete)
....	RDB	-3	I Like The Sunrise –vTWtk (incomplete)
....	RDB	-4	I Like The Sunrise –vTWtk (incomplete)
....	RDB	-5	I Like The Sunrise –vTWtk (incomplete)
....		-8	I Like The Sunrise –vTWtk
....	RDB	-9	I Like The Sunrise –vTWtk
....			I Like The Sunrise –vTWtk
....		-11	I Like The Sunrise –vTWtk (incomplete)
....		-12	I Like The Sunrise –vTWtk (incomplete)
....		-13	I Like The Sunrise –vTWtk (incomplete) >>>

....	-14	I Like The Sunrise –vTWtk
....	-1	Rocks In My Bed (incomplete)
....	-3	Rocks In My Bed –vTWtk (incomplete)
....		Rocks In My Bed –vTWtk
....	-5	Rocks In My Bed –vTWtk (incomplete)
....	-6	Rocks In My Bed –vTWtk
....	-1	Don't You Know I Care? –vTWtk (incomplete)
....		Don't You Know I Care? (rehearsal)
....	-2	Don't You Know I Care? –vTWtk (incomplete)
....	-3	Don't You Know I Care? –vTWtk
....	-1	The Brown-Skin Gal –vTWtk (incomplete)
....	-3	The Brown-Skin Gal –vTWtk
....	-4	The Brown-Skin Gal –vTWtk
....		The Brown-Skin Gal –vTWtk (rehearsal)
....	-5	The Brown-Skin Gal –vTWtk
....	-6	The Brown-Skin Gal –vTWtk
....		Patti's Blues

The arrangements for the above session are by Melba Liston.

DUKE ELLINGTON & HIS ORCHESTRA
CA CW HJns ME, LB BCpr CCrs, JHtn JH RP PG HC, MLst JL RJo, TWtk, DE supervising.

9 Jan 1967   (S)
RCA Studios, Webster Hall
New York City, NY

> MLst JL RJo, TWtk.

....	-1	To Know You Is To Love You –vTWtk
....	-2	To Know You Is To Love You –vTWtk
....		Why Am I Treated So Bad? –vTWtk
....		Wade In The Water –vTWtk (rehearsal)
....	-1	Wade In The Water –vTWtk

> Entire band.

....		Everything But You
....	-1	Everything But You –vTWtk (incomplete)
....	-2	Everything But You –vTWtk (incomplete)
....	-3	Everything But You –vTWtk (incomplete)
....	-4	Everything But You –vTWtk (incomplete)
....	-6	Everything But You –vTWtk
....	-7	Everything But You –vTWtk (incomplete)
....	-8	Everything But You –vTWtk
....	-1	Time's A-Wastin' (incomplete)
....	-2	Time's A-Wastin' –vTWtk (incomplete)
....	-3	Time's A-Wastin' –vTWtk
....	-4	Time's A-Wastin' (incomplete)
....	-5	Time's A-Wastin' –vTWtk

> MLst, TWtk.

....	-1	I'm Afraid –vTWtk[1] (rehearsal)
....	-2	I'm Afraid –vTWtk (incomplete)
....		I'm Afraid –vTWtk (rehearsal)
....		I'm Afraid –vTWtk

[1] *sa* "I'm Afraid Of Loving You Too Much"; "Here Goes."

DUKE ELLINGTON & HIS ORCHESTRA
CA MJsn OV, LB BCpr CCrs, JHtn JH RP PG HC , DE JL RJo.

14 Jan 1967   (S)
Studio Zanibelli
Milan, Italy

....		Rue Bleue[1] (incomplete)
....		Rue Bleue (incomplete)
....		Rue Bleue (incomplete)
....		Rue Bleue (incomplete)
....		Rue Bleue (incomplete)
....		Rue Bleue (incomplete)
....		Rue Bleue (incomplete)
....		Rue Bleue
....		Rue Bleue (incomplete)
....		Rue Bleue (incomplete)
....		Rue Bleue (incomplete)
....		Rue Bleue (incomplete)
....		Rue Bleue
....		Rue Bleue (incomplete)
....		Rue Bleue (incomplete)
....		Rue Bleue
....		Rue Bleue >>>

> CW HJns added.

....	Beautiful Woman Walks Well (incomplete)
....	Beautiful Woman Walks Well (incomplete)
....	Beautiful Woman Walks Well (incomplete)
....	Beautiful Woman Walks Well (incomplete)
....	Beautiful Woman Walks Well (incomplete)
....	Beautiful Woman Walks Well (incomplete)
....	Beautiful Woman Walks Well (incomplete)
....	Beautiful Woman Walks Well (incomplete)
....	Beautiful Woman Walks Well (incomplete)
....	Beautiful Woman Walks Well (incomplete)
....	Beautiful Woman Walks Well (incomplete)
....	Beautiful Woman Walks Well
....	Beautiful Woman Walks Well (incomplete)
....	Beautiful Woman Walks Well (incomplete)
....	Beautiful Woman Walks Well (incomplete)
....	Beautiful Woman Walks Well (incomplete)
....	Beautiful Woman Walks Well (incomplete)
....	Beautiful Woman Walks Well
....	Wild Onions[2] (incomplete)
....	Wild Onions (incomplete)
....	Wild Onions (incomplete)
....	Wild Onions (incomplete)
....	Wild Onions (incomplete)
....	Wild Onions (incomplete)
....	Wild Onions (incomplete)
....	Wild Onions (incomplete)
....	Wild Onions (incomplete)
....	Wild Onions (incomplete)
....	Wild Onions (incomplete)
....	Wild Onions (incomplete)
....	Wild Onions (incomplete)
....	Wild Onions (incomplete)
....	Wild Onions (incomplete)
....	Wild Onions (incomplete)
....	Wild Onions (short version)
....	Wild Onions (incomplete)
....	Wild Onions (incomplete)
....	Wild Onions

> JH omitted.

....	Wild Onions (incomplete)
....	Johnny Come Lately
....	Johnny Come Lately (incomplete)
....	Girdle Hurdle (incomplete)
....	Girdle Hurdle (incomplete)
....	The Shepherd
....	The Shepherd (incomplete)
....	The Shepherd (incomplete)
....	The Shepherd (incomplete)
....	The Shepherd (incomplete)
....	The Shepherd (incomplete)
....	The Shepherd (incomplete)
....	The Shepherd (incomplete)
....	The Shepherd
....	Swamp Goo (incomplete)
....	Swamp Goo (incomplete)
....	Swamp Goo (incomplete)
....	Swamp Goo
....	Swamp Goo (incomplete)
....	Swamp Goo (incomplete)
....	Swamp Goo (incomplete)
....	Swamp Goo (incomplete)
....	Up Jump (incomplete)
....	A Chromatic Love Affair (incomplete)
....	Up Jump[3] (incomplete)
....	Up Jump (rehearsal)
....	Up Jump (rehearsal)
....	Up Jump
....	Blessings On The Night (incomplete)
....	Blessings On The Night
....	Blessings On The Night (incomplete)
....	Blessings On The Night >>>

....	Blessings On The Night (incomplete)
....	Rue Bleue (incomplete)
....	Rue Bleue
....	Rue Bleue (incomplete)
....	Rue Bleue (incomplete)
....	Rue Bleue
....	Wild Onions (incomplete)
....	Wild Onions (incomplete)
....	Wild Onions
....	Wild Onions (incomplete)
....	Wild Onions
....	Swamp Goo/Action In Alexandria (incomplete)
....	Swamp Goo
....	Mara Gold (incomplete)
....	Mara Gold
....	Mara Gold (rehearsal)
....	A Chromatic Love Affair
....	A Chromatic Love Affair
....	A Chromatic Love Affair (incomplete)
....	A Chromatic Love Affair (rehearsal)
....	A Chromatic Love Affair (incomplete)
....	A Chromatic Love Affair (incomplete)
....	A Chromatic Love Affair
....	A Chromatic Love Affair (rehearsal)

[1]*aka* "Blue Blood."
[2]*sa* "For Jammers Only."
[3]This title is a derivative of *Wailing Bout.*

The above is a rehearsal session.

15 Jan 1967   (P)
Teatro Lirico
Milan, Italy

DUKE ELLINGTON & HIS ORCHESTRA WITH ELLA FITZGERALD
HJns MJsn OV, LB BCpr CCrs, JHtn JH RP, JJns BCrs RJo.

....	The "C" Jam Blues
....	Perdido

> DE replaces JJns, HC added.

....	Take The "A" Train

> JH, DE BCrs RJo.

....	Sentimental Lady

> Entire band.

....	All Of Me
....	Harmony In Harlem

> CA added.

....	Swamp Goo

> JL replaces BCrs.

....	Blessings On The Night

> CW, PG added.

....	Mount Harissa
....	Wild Onions
....	Rue Bleue
....	Mara Gold
....	The Shepherd
....	Harlem Air Shaft
....	Things Ain't What They Used To Be

> JL RJo omitted, BCrs SWrd, EF added.

....	Cotton Tail –vEF

DE shared the bill for this European tour and some subsequent events with EF and her trio. For a portion of each concert EF was accompanied by the full Ellington contingent, sometimes with DE at the piano. On many occasions, some of the Ellingtonians played along with the trio. To be consistent, these recordings have been included as well.

DUKE ELLINGTON & HIS ORCHESTRA
CA CW HJns MJsn OV, LB BCpr CCrs, JHtn JH RP PG HC, DE JL RJo.

....	Take The "A" Train
....	The Shepherd
....	Harlem Air Shaft
....	Blessings On The Night
....	Johnny Come Lately >>>

....	Mount Harissa
....	Up Jump
....	Swamp Goo
....	Wild Onions
....	The Birth Of The Blues
....	Rue Bleue
....	Mara Gold
....	Beautiful Woman Walks Well
....	All Of Me
....	Harmony In Harlem
....	The Star-Crossed Lovers
....	Things Ain't What They Used To Be
....	Things Ain't What They Used To Be

DUKE ELLINGTON & NORMAN GRANZ   (bc?)   (S)[1]
DE and Norman Granz interviewed by Lilian Terry.

....   Interview

                                                            22 Jan 1967*   (P)

DUKE ELLINGTON & HIS ORCHESTRA WITH ELLA FITZGERALD   Falkoner Teatret (tc)
CA CW HJns MJsn ME, LB BCpr CCrs, JHtn JH RP PG HC, DE JL RJo.   Copenhagen, Denmark

....	Open Ears
....	Johnny Come Lately
....	Swamp Goo
....	Take The "A" Train
....	The Shepherd
....	Raincheck
....	A Chromatic Love Affair
....	Mount Harissa
....	Up Jump
....	Rue Bleue
....	Wild Onions

> JH, DE JL RJo.

....	Sentimental Lady

> Entire band.

....	Harmony In Harlem
....	Drag
....	Things Ain't What They Used To Be

> JL RJo omitted, BCrs SWrd, EF added.

....	Cotton Tail –vEF

DUKE ELLINGTON & HIS ORCHESTRA WITH ELLA FITZGERALD   (tc)*
Same personnel.

....	Take The "A" Train
....	The Shepherd
....	Raincheck
....	Kinda Dukish/Rockin' In Rhythm
....	A Chromatic Love Affair
....	Swamp Goo
....	Mount Harissa
....	Up Jump
....	Rue Bleue
....	Wild Onions
....	Beautiful Woman Walks Well
....	Harmony In Harlem
....	Things Ain't What They Used To Be
....	Things Ain't What They Used To Be

> JL RJo omitted, BCrs SWrd, EF added.

....	Cotton Tail -vEF

*Selections from both concerts were telecast on 7 Mar 1967.

                                                         23 Jan 1967[1]   (P)

DUKE ELLINGTON & HIS RHYTHM/SEPTET   TV Byen Studios (tc)
DE JL RJo.   Copenhagen, Denmark

....	Vid	Le Sucrier Velours
....	Vid	Lotus Blossom
....	Az	Second Portrait Of The Lion >>>

....	Vid	Meditation
....	Az	On The Fringe Of The Jungle
....	Az	Mood Indigo
....	Az	Take The "A" Train

> CA, LB, JH PG HC added.

....	Vid	Take The "A" Train

> JH, DE JL RJo.

....	Vid	Passion Flower

> Entire band.

....	Vid	The Jeep Is Jumpin'
....	Vid	Sophisticated Lady
....	Vid	Tippin' And Whisperin'

> PG, DE JL RJo.

....	Vid	Happy Reunion

> Entire band.

....	Vid	Satin Doll
....	Vid	Jam With Sam
....	Vid	Things Ain't What They Used To Be

[1]Taping session; telecast on 7 Mar 1967.

DUKE ELLINGTON & HIS ORCHESTRA WITH ELLA FITZGERALD
CA CW HJns MJsn ME, LB BCpr CCrs, JHtn JH RP PG HC, DE JL RJo.

24 Jan 1967   (P)
Konserthuset (bc)*
Stockholm, Sweden

....		Johnny Come Lately
....		Swamp Goo
....		Up Jump
....		The Shepherd
....		Kinda Dukish/Rockin' In Rhythm
....		Rue Bleue
....		A Chromatic Love Affair
....		Wild Onions

> JH, DE JL RJo.

....		Sentimental Lady

> Entire band.

....		The Jeep Is Jumpin'
....		Things Ain't What They Used To Be
....		Mara Gold
....		Things Ain't What They Used To Be

> JL RJo omitted, BCrs SWrd, EF added.

....		Cotton Tail –vEF

DUKE ELLINGTON & HIS ORCHESTRA
Same personnel.

(bc)*

....		Stompy Jones
....		Swamp Goo
....		Up Jump
....		The Shepherd
....		Wild Onions

> JH, DE JL RJo.

....	MFC	Sentimental Lady

> Entire band.

....		Drag

*Selections from both concerts were broadcast by SR.

DUKE ELLINGTON & HIS ORCHESTRA
CA CW HJns MJsn ME, LB BCpr CCrs, JHtn JH RP PG HC, DE JL RJo.

25 Jan 1967   (P)
Njårdhallen (tc)[1]
Oslo, Norway

....		Take The "A" Train
....		Rue Bleue
....		Wild Onions
....		Mara Gold
....		Beautiful Woman Walks Well >>>

....   The Jeep Is Jumpin'
....   I Got It Bad
....   Things Ain't What They Used To Be

[1]Taped for telecast; however, we have no confirmation if the program has ever been aired.

DUKE ELLINGTON & HIS ORCHESTRA   (bc)
TWtk added, otherwise same personnel.

....   Take The "A" Train
....   Johnny Come Lately
....   Swamp Goo
....   Up Jump
....   The Shepherd
....   A Chromatic Love Affair
....   Kinda Dukish/Rockin' In Rhythm
....   La Plus Belle Africaine
....   Wild Onions
....   I Got It Bad
....   Things Ain't What They Used To Be
....   In The Beginning God –vTWtk.

DUKE ELLINGTON   Downtown Key Club (P)
DE attending a dinner party.

....   Dr. Fred Lange-Nilsen addresses DE
....   DE replies

                                                      28 Jan 1967   (P)

DUKE ELLINGTON & HIS ORCHESTRA WITH ELLA FITZGERALD   De Doelen
CA CW HJns MJsn ME, LB BCpr CCrs, JHtn JH RP PG HC, DE JL RJo.   Rotterdam, Netherlands

.... MJ   Take The "A" Train
.... MJ   Johnny Come Lately
.... MJ   Swamp Goo
.... MJ   Up Jump
.... MJ   The Shepherd
.... MJ   Take The "A" Train
.... MJ   A Chromatic Love Affair
.... MJ   Rue Bleue
.... MJ   Wild Onions
.... MJ   Mara Gold
.... MJ   Beautiful Woman Walks Well
....   Things Ain't What They Used To Be
....   Things Ain't What They Used To Be

> JL RJo omitted, BCrs SWrd, EF added.

.... MJ   Cotton Tail –vEF

                                                      31 Jan 1967   (P)

DUKE ELLINGTON & HIS ORCHESTRA   Salle Pleyel
CA CW HJns MJsn ME, LB BCpr CCrs, JHtn JH RP PG HC. DE JL RJo.   Paris, France

....   The Shepherd
....   Mara Gold
.... Az   Beautiful Woman Walks Well
.... Az   Drag
....   I Got It Bad
....   Things Ain't What They Used To Be
....   Satin Doll

DUKE ELLINGTON & HIS ORCHESTRA WITH ELLA FITZGERALD   (bc)
Same personnel.

....   Take The "A" Train
....   Johnny Come Lately
....   Chelsea Bridge
....   Swamp Goo
....   Salomé
....   Rue Bleue
....   Mara Gold
....   The Shepherd
....   Take The "A" Train
....   Beautiful Woman Walks Well
....   Drag
....   I Got It Bad
....   Things Ain't What They Used To Be
....   Things Ain't What They Used To Be   >>>

> JL RJo omitted, BCrs SWrd, EF added.

....   Cotton Tail –vEF

                                                                          1 Feb 1967   (S)
DUKE ELLINGTON   DE's hotel room
DE talking about the Fondation Maeght.   Paris, France

.... Vid   DE talking[1]

[1]These comments were used in the film/video "Duke and Ella at the Cote d'Azur."

DUKE ELLINGTON & HIS ORCHESTRA   Salle Pleyel (bc)   (P)
CA CW HJns MJsn ME, LB BCpr CCrs, JHtn JH RP PG HC, DE JL RJo.

....   Up Jump
....   Beautiful Woman Walks Well
....   Drag
....   I Got It Bad
....   Things Ain't What They Used To Be

It is suspected that the above is not a genuine recording of the 1st concert.

DUKE ELLINGTON & HIS ORCHESTRA WITH ELLA FITZGERALD   (bc)
Same personnel.

....   Up Jump
....   The Shepherd
....   A Chromatic Love Affair
....   Mara Gold
....   Drag

> DE JL RJo omitted, JJns BCrs SWrd, EF added.

....   The Moment Of Truth –vEF
....   Don't Be That Way –vEF
....   You've Changed –vEF
....   How Long Has This Been Going On? –vEF

> DE replaces JJns.

....   Cotton Tail –vEF
....   Duke's Place –vEF
....   Imagine My Frustration –vEF

                                                                          5 Feb 1967   (P)
DUKE ELLINGTON & HIS ORCHESTRA   Guild Hall
CA CW HJns ME, LB BCpr CCrs, JHtn JH RP PG HC, DE JL RJo.   Portsmouth, England

....   Take The "A" Train
....   Harlem Air Shaft
....   Drop Me Off At Harlem
....   Swamp Goo
....   Mount Harissa
....   Up Jump
....   Rue Bleue
....   A Chromatic Love Affair
....   Salomé
....   Wild Onions
....   La Plus Belle Africaine

> DE JL RJo.

....   Second Portrait Of The Lion

> Entire band.

....   Take The "A" Train
....   The Shepherd
....   Tootie For Cootie
....   Mara Gold
....   Beautiful Woman Walks Well
....   Drag
....   I Got It Bad
....   Things Ain't What They Used To Be
....   Things Ain't What They Used To Be

DUKE ELLINGTON & HIS ORCHESTRA
Same personnel.

....   Take The "A" Train
....   Johnny Come Lately
....   Swamp Goo   >>>

. . . .	Mount Harissa
. . . .	Up Jump
. . . .	Rue Bleue
. . . .	A Chromatic Love Affair
. . . .	Salomé
. . . .	Wild Onions
. . . .	La Plus Belle Africaine

> DE JL RJo.

| . . . . | Second Portrait Of The Lion |

> Entire band.

. . . .	Take The "A" Train
. . . .	Take The "A" Train
. . . .	The Shepherd
. . . .	Tootie For Cootie
. . . .	Mara Gold
. . . .	Beautiful Woman Walks Well
. . . .	Drag
. . . .	I Got It Bad
. . . .	Things Ain't What They Used To Be
. . . .	Things Ain't What They Used To Be

DUKE ELLINGTON & HIS ORCHESTRA WITH ELLA FITZGERALD
CA CW HJns ME, LB BCpr CCrs, JHtn JH RP PG HC, DE JL RJo.

10 Feb 1967   (P)
Free Trade Hall
Manchester, England

. . . .	Take The "A" Train
. . . .	Johnny Come Lately
. . . .	Swamp Goo
. . . .	Mount Harissa
. . . .	Up Jump
. . . .	Rue Bleue
. . . .	A Chromatic Love Affair
. . . .	Salomé
. . . .	Wild Onions
. . . .	Take The "A" Train
. . . .	The Shepherd
. . . .	Mara Gold
. . . .	Beautiful Woman Walks Well
. . . .	I Got It Bad
. . . .	Drag
. . . .	Things Ain't What They Used To Be

> JL RJo omitted, BCrs SWrd, EF added.

| . . . . | Cotton Tail –vEF |
| . . . . | Take The "A" Train |

DUKE ELLINGTON & HIS ORCHESTRA WITH ELLA FITZGERALD
CA CW HJns ME, LB BCpr CCrs, JHtn JH RP PG HC, DE JL RJo.

11 Feb 1967   (P)
Royal Festival Hall
London, England

. . . .	Open Ears
. . . .	Johnny Come Lately
. . . .	Swamp Goo
. . . .	Mount Harissa
. . . .	Up Jump
. . . .	Rue Bleue
. . . .	A Chromatic Love Affair
. . . .	Salomé
. . . .	Wild Onions
. . . .	Take The "A" Train
. . . .	The Shepherd
. . . .	Mara Gold
. . . .	Beautiful Woman Walks Well
. . . .	I Got It Bad

> JL RJo omitted, BCrs SWrd, EF added.

| . . . . | Cotton Tail –vEF |
| . . . . | |

DUKE ELLINGTON & HIS ORCHESTRA
CA CW HJns ME, LB BCpr CCrs, JHtn JH RP PG HC, DE JL RJo.

12 Feb 1967   (P)
Hammersmith Odeon
London, England

. . . .	Johnny Come Lately
. . . .	Swamp Goo
. . . .	Mount Harissa

13 Feb 1967   (P)
Philharmonic Hall
Liverpool, England

<u>DUKE ELLINGTON & HIS ORCHESTRA</u>
CA CW HJns ME, LB BCpr CCrs, JHtn JH RP PG HC, DE JL RJo.

..........,.........	Johnny Come Lately
....	Mount Harissa
....	La Plus Belle Africaine
....	The Shepherd
....	Tootie For Cootie
....	Beautiful Woman Walks Well
....	I Got It Bad
....	Things Ain't What They Used To Be
....	Drag

p 18 Feb 1967   (S)
Dorchester Hotel (tc)
London, England

<u>DUKE ELLINGTON</u>
DE interviewed by Michael Dean.

....	Interview

19 Feb 1967   (P)
Royal Albert Hall (tc)
London, England

<u>DUKE ELLINGTON & HIS ORCHESTRA WITH THE LONDON PHILHARMONIC ORCHESTRA</u>
CA CW HJns ME, LB BCpr CCrs, JHtn JH RP PG HC, DE JL RJo, with the London Philharmonic Orchestra, John Pritchard conducting.

....	Opening remarks by John Dankworth

> DE JL RJo, LPO.

....	[1] New World A-Comin'

> DE piano solo.

....	A Single Petal Of A Rose

> JL RJo, LPO added.

	THE GOLDEN BROOM AND THE GREEN APPLE
....	- Stanza 1 (The Golden Broom)
....	- Stanza 2 (The Green Apple)
....	- Stanza 3 (The Handsome Traffic Policeman)

> LPO omitted, entire band added.

....	[1] Take The "A" Train
....	The Shepherd
....	Up Jump
....	[1] I Got It Bad
....	[1] Things Ain't What They Used To Be

> LPO added.

....	[1] HARLEM
....	[1] Medley[2]

> DE acc. by the LPO.

....	Satin Doll

> LPO omitted, entire band added.

....	Mara Gold
....	Things Ain't What They Used To Be

[1]Telecast on 20 Feb 1967.
[2]Including: Do Nothin' Till You Hear From Me; In A Sentimental Mood; Don't Get Around Much Anymore; Mood Indigo; I'm Beginning to See The Light; Sophisticated Lady, Caravan; It Don't Mean A Thing; Solitude; I Let A Song Go Out Of My Heart/Don't Get Around Much Anymore.

p Feb 1967[1]   (S)
BBC Studios (tc)
London, England

<u>DUKE ELLINGTON</u>
DE on the program "Be My Guest."

....	Interview

[1]Telecast on 10 Jan 1968.

22 Feb 1967   (P)
Teatro Sistina
Rome, Italy

<u>DUKE ELLINGTON & HIS ORCHESTRA</u>
CA CW HJns ME, LB BCpr CCrs, JHtn JH RP PG HC, DE JL RJo.

....	JU	Johnny Come Lately
....		Swamp Goo
....		Mount Harissa
....		Up Jump
....		Rue Bleue >>>

....		A Chromatic Love Affair
....		Salomé
....		Wild Onions
....		La Plus Belle Africaine

> DE JL RJo.

....		Second Portrait Of The Lion

> Entire band.

....		Take The "A" Train
....		Take The "A" Train
....		The Shepherd
....		Tootie For Cootie
....		Mara Gold
....	JU	The Star-Crossed Lovers
....	JU	Things Ain't What They Used To Be
....	JU	Drag
....	JU	Things Ain't What They Used To Be
....		Jam With Sam

DUKE ELLINGTON & HIS ORCHESTRA
Same personnel.

....	JU	Take The "A" Train
....	JU	The Twitch
....	JU	Swamp Goo
....	JU	Mount Harissa
....	JU	Up Jump
....	JU	Rue Bleue
....	JU	A Chromatic Love Affair
....	JU	Salomé
....	JU	Wild Onions
....		La Plus Belle Africaine

> DE JL RJo.

....	JU	Second Portrait Of The Lion

> Entire band.

....	JU	Stompy Jones
....	JU	Take The "A" Train
....	JU	Take The "A" Train
....	JU	The Shepherd
....	JU	Tootie For Cootie
....	JU	Mara Gold
....	JU	The Star-Crossed Lovers
....	JU	Harmony In Harlem

> JH, DE JL RJo.

....	JU	Magenta Haze

> Entire band.

....	JU	Drag
....	JU	Kinda Dukish/Rockin' In Rhythm

24 Feb 1967   (P)
Teatro Metastasio
Prato, Italy

DUKE ELLINGTON & HIS ORCHESTRA
CA CW HJns ME, LB BCpr CCrs, JHtn JH RP PG HC, DE JL RJo.

....	Wild Onions
....	La Plus Belle Africaine
....	Medley[1]
....	Take The "A" Train
....	The Shepherd
....	Tootie For Cootie
....	Mara Gold
....	Beautiful Woman Walks Well
....	Harmony In Harlem
....	Prelude To A Kiss
....	Things Ain't What They Used To Be
....	Drag
....	Kinda Dukish/Rockin' In Rhythm

[1]Including: Satin Doll; Solitude; In A Sentimental Mood; Don't Get Around Much Anymore; Mood Indigo.

DUKE ELLINGTON & HIS ORCHESTRA
Same personnel.

....	Take The "A" Train >>>

.... Johnny Come Lately
.... Swamp Goo
.... Mount Harissa
.... Up Jump
.... Rue Bleue
.... A Chromatic Love Affair
.... Salomé
.... Days Of Wine And Roses
.... Wild Onions
.... La Plus Belle Africaine
.... What Am I Here For?
.... Take The "A" Train
.... The Shepherd
.... Tootie For Cootie
.... Mara Gold
.... Beautiful Woman Walks Well
.... Harmony In Harlem
.... Things Ain't What They Used To Be
.... Drag
.... Medley[1]

[1]Including: Satin Doll; Don't Get Around Much Anymore; Mood Indigo; I'm Beginning To See The Light; Sophisticated Lady; Caravan; Do Nothin' Till You Hear From Me; I Let A Song Go Out Of My Heart/Don't Get Around Much Anymore.

DUKE ELLINGTON & HIS ORCHESTRA   25 Feb 1967   (S)
CA CW HJns ME, LB BCpr CCrs, JHtn JH RP PG HC, DE JL RJo.   Studio Zambelli
                                                           Milan, Italy

.... Girdle Hurdle (incomplete)
.... Girdle Hurdle (incomplete)
.... Girdle Hurdle (incomplete)
.... Girdle Hurdle (incomplete)
.... Girdle Hurdle (incomplete)
.... Girdle Hurdle (incomplete)
.... Girdle Hurdle (incomplete)
.... Girdle Hurdle (incomplete)
.... Girdle Hurdle

> JH, DE.

.... Blood Count[1] (incomplete)
.... Blood Count (incomplete)
.... Blood Count (incomplete)
.... Blood Count (incomplete)

> Entire band.

.... Blood Count (incomplete)
.... Blood Count
.... Blood Count
.... Blood Count (incomplete)
.... Blood Count (incomplete)
.... Blood Count (incomplete)
.... Blood Count (incomplete)
.... Blood Count
.... Blood Count (incomplete)
.... Traffic Jam[2] (incomplete)
.... Traffic Jam (incomplete)
.... Traffic Jam (incomplete)
.... Traffic Jam (incomplete)
.... Traffic Jam (incomplete)
.... Traffic Jam (incomplete)
.... Traffic Jam (incomplete)
.... Traffic Jam (incomplete)
.... Traffic Jam (incomplete)
.... Traffic Jam (incomplete)
.... Traffic Jam (incomplete)
.... Traffic Jam (incomplete)
.... Traffic Jam (incomplete)
.... Traffic Jam
.... Traffic Jam (incomplete)
.... Traffic Jam (incomplete)
.... Traffic Jam (incomplete)
.... Traffic Jam (incomplete)
.... Traffic Jam (incomplete)
.... Traffic Jam (incomplete)
.... Traffic Jam (incomplete)
.... Traffic Jam   >>>

....	Traffic Jam
....	Traffic Jam
....	Eggo[3,4] (incomplete)
....	Eggo (incomplete)
....	Eggo (incomplete)
....	Eggo
....	Eggo (incomplete)
....	Eggo (incomplete)
....	Eggo (incomplete)
....	Eggo (incomplete)
....	Eggo (incomplete)
....	Eggo (incomplete)
....	Eggo (incomplete)
....	Eggo (incomplete)
....	Eggo
....	Eggo
....	Eggo
....	The Little Purple Flower[4,5] (incomplete)
....	The Little Purple Flower (incomplete)
....	The Little Purple Flower (incomplete)
....	The Little Purple Flower (incomplete)
....	The Little Purple Flower (incomplete)
....	The Little Purple Flower (incomplete)

> DE piano solo.

....	Handful Of Keys (incomplete)
....	Carolina Shout
....	Meditation (incomplete)

> PG added.

....	A Single Petal of A Rose

[1]*aka* "Freakish Light"; "Blue Cloud."
[2]*aka* "A Fire-And-Brimstone Sermonette."
[3]*sa* "On The Fringe Of The Jungle."
[4]Sometimes referred to as *The Psychodelic Suite.*
[5]*aka* "F.L."

The above is a rehearsal session.

DUKE ELLINGTON & HIS ORCHESTRA
CA CW HJns ME, LB BCpr CCrs, JHtn JH RP PG HC, DE JL RJo.

28 Feb 1967   (P)
Unidentified location (bc)
Düsseldorf, Germany

....	Mount Harissa
....	Up Jump
....	Rue Bleue
....	A Chromatic Love Affair
....	Salomé
....	The Little Purple Flower
....	Wild Onions
....	La Plus Belle Africaine
....	Days Of Wine And Roses

> DE JL RJo.

....	Second Portrait Of the Lion

> Entire band.

....	Take The "A" Train
....	Girdle Hurdle
....	Take The "A" Train
....	The Shepherd
....	Tootie For Cootie
....	Traffic Jam
....	Blood Count[1]
....	Things Ain't What They Used To Be
....	Drag
....	Kinda Dukish/Rockin' In Rhythm
....	Medley[2]

[1]Announced as *Freakish Light.*
[2]Including: Satin Doll; Solitude; In A Sentimental Mood; Don't Get Around Much Anymore; Mood Indigo; I'm Beginning To See The Light; Sophisticated Lady; Caravan; Do Nothin' Till You Hear From Me; I Got It Bad; I Let A Song Go Out Of My Heart/Don't Get Around Much Anymore.

Feb/Mar 1967   (P)
Unidentified location
Europe

DUKE ELLINGTON & HIS ORCHESTRA
CA CW HJns ME, LB BCpr CCrs, JHtn JH RP PG HC, DE JL RJo.

.... Johnny Come Lately
.... Swamp Goo
.... Mount Harissa
.... Up Jump
.... Rue Bleue
.... A Chromatic Love Affair
.... Salomé
.... Wild Onions
.... Take The "A" Train
.... The Shepherd

2 Mar 1967   (P)
Unidentified location (bc)
Berlin, Germany

DUKE ELLINGTON
DE interviewed for the program "Weekend World."

.... Interview

DUKE ELLINGTON & HIS ORCHESTRA   Philharmonie   (P)
CA CW HJns ME, LB BCpr CCrs, JHtn JH RP PG HC, DE JL RJo.

.... Take The "A" Train
.... Take The "A" Train
.... Up Jump
.... The Shepherd
.... Tootie For Cootie
.... La Plus Belle Africaine

> EMrw added.

.... Come Sunday –vEMrw
.... The Lord's Prayer -vEMrw

> EMrw omitted.

.... Johnny Come Lately
.... Take The "A" Train

6 Mar 1967   (P)
Liederhalle
Stuttgart, Germany

DUKE ELLINGTON & HIS ORCHESTRA
CA CW HJns ME, LB BCpr CCrs, JHtn JH RP PG HC, DE JL RJo.

.... Take The "A" Train
.... Johnny Come Lately
.... JBR Swamp Goo
.... Mount Harissa
.... JBR Up Jump
.... JBR Rue Bleue
.... Girdle Hurdle
.... JBR A Chromatic Love Affair
.... Salomé
.... JBR Wild Onions
.... La Plus Belle Africaine
.... Take The "A" Train
.... JBR Take The "A" Train
.... The Little Purple Flower
.... Eggo
.... The Shepherd
.... JBR Tootie For Cootie
.... Traffic Jam
.... JBR Blood Count
.... Things Ain't What They Used To Be
.... JBR Drag
.... Medley[1]

[1]Including: Satin Doll; Solitude; In A Sentimental Mood; Don't Get Around Much Anymore; Mood Indigo; I'm Beginning To
See The Light; Sophisticated Lady; Caravan; Do Nothin' Till You Hear From Me; I Got It Bad; I Let A Song Go Out Of My
Heart/Don't Get Around Much Anymore.

10 Mar 1967   (S)
Unspecified studio
Paris, France

DUKE ELLINGTON
Piano solo.

.... Stv Meditation
.... Stv T.G.T.T.[1]
.... Stv The Little Purple Flower

[1]Stands for "Too Good To Title."   >>>

DUKE ELLINGTON & HIS ORCHESTRA   Théâtre des Champs Elysées (P)
CA CW HJns ME, LB BCpr CCrs, JHtn JH RP PG HC, DE JL RJo.

....	Az	A Chromatic Love Affair
....	Az	Salomé
....	Az	Eggo
....	Az	Wild Onions
....	Az	HARLEM
....		Take The "A" Train
....		The Little Purple Flower
....		Take The "A" Train
....		The Shepherd
....		Tootie For Cootie
....		Traffic Jam
....	Pab	Blood Count
....	Pab	Harmony In Harlem
....	Pab	Things Ain't What They Used To Be
....	Pab	Drag

> DE JL RJo.

....   Second Portrait Of The Lion

> Entire band.

.... Pab   Rockin' In Rhythm

DUKE ELLINGTON & HIS ORCHESTRA   11 Mar 1967   (P)
                                                                       Hotel Statler Hilton
CA CW HJns ME, LB BCpr CCrs, JHtn JH RP PG HC, DE JL RJo, JMP.   Washington, DC

....	Rondolet[1]
....	Days Of Wine And Roses
....	Rue Bleue
....	Mount Harissa
....	Sophisticated Lady
....	Satin Doll
....	Do Nothin' Till You Hear From Me
....	The Little Purple Flower
....	Eggo
....	Always

> DE piano solo.

....   Le Sucrier Velour—T.G.T.T.

> Entire band.

....	Serenade To Sweden—Black And Tan Fantasy
....	Azure
....	I Got It Bad
....	Things Ain't What They Used To Be
....	Solitude
....	Solitude –vJMP
....	Love You Madly –vJMP
....	Warm Valley
....	Drag
....	Sophisticated Lady
....	Hello Dolly
....	Salomé
....	Mood Indigo
....	Tootie For Cootie
....	Take The "A" Train
....	On The Sunny Side Of The Street
....	Days Of Wine And Roses
....	Things Ain't What They Used To Be
....	Things Ain't What They Used To Be

DE piano solo.
....   Mood Indigo—Sophisticated Lady—Satin Doll

[1]aka "Rondolette"; sa "Slamar In D-Flat."

DUKE ELLINGTON & HIS SEPTET   15 Mar 1967   (S)
                                                                       24th St., Studio B
CA, LB, JH PG HC, DE JL RJo.   New York City, NY

....	Az	The Intimacy Of The Blues (rehearsal)
....	Fan -1	The Intimacy Of The Blues
....		The Intimacy Of The Blues (incomplete)
....		The Intimacy Of The Blues (incomplete)
....	Az -2	The Intimacy Of The Blues >>>

....			Tell Me 'Bout My Baby[1] (#3) (incomplete)
....			Tell Me 'Bout My Baby (incomplete)
....		-1	Tell Me 'Bout My Baby
....	Az	-2	Tell Me 'Bout my Baby
....	Fan	-3	Tell Me 'Bout My Baby
....	Az	-4	Tell Me 'Bout My Baby
....	RDB		Kentucky Avenue, A.C.[2] (#5) (incomplete)
....	RDB		Kentucky Avenue, A.C. (incomplete)
....	Fan	-1	Kentucky Avenue, A.C.
....	Az	-2	Kentucky Avenue, A.C. (incomplete)
....	Az	-3	Kentucky Avenue, A.C. (incomplete)
....			Near North (#4) (incomplete)
....		-1	Near North
....	Fan	-2	Near North
....			Soul Country[3] (#6) (rehearsal)
....	Az		Soul Country (incomplete)
....	Az		Soul Country (incomplete)
....	RDB		Soul Country (incomplete)
....	RDB	-1	Soul Country
....	RDB		Soul Country (incomplete)
....	RDB		Soul Country (incomplete)
....	Az		Soul Country (incomplete)
....	Fan	-2	Soul Country
....	Az	-3	Soul Country
....	Az	-4	Soul Country
....	Az		Soul Country
....	RDB		Soul Country (incomplete)
....	Az	-5	Soul Country
....	RDB	-6	Soul Country
....		-1	Out South (#?) (incomplete)
....	Fan	-2	Out South

[1]aka "I Don't Want Nobody But You."
[2]aka "Nati."
[3]aka "Lucy."

The above sequence—with the exception of "The Intimacy Of The Blues"—is referred to as "The Combo Suite" on Fan. No such claim could be found elsewhere. Originally, numbers instead of titles have been assigned to the parts.

			23 Mar 1967 (S)
DUKE ELLINGTON & HIS ORCHESTRA			RCA Studios
CA CW HJns ME, LB BCpr CCrs, JHtn JH RP PG HC, DE JL RJo JA.			New York City, NY

			THE JAYWALKER
....	Stv	-1	Traffic Cop
....	Stv	-1	Untitled Blues
....	Stv	-1	Polizia
....	Az	-1	The Queen (incomplete)
....		-2	The Queen (incomplete)
....	Az	-3	The Queen
....			The Queen (incomplete)
....			The Queen (incomplete)
....			The Queen
....			The B.O. Of Traffic[1] (incomplete)
....			The B.O. Of Traffic
....	Stv	-3	The B.O. Of Traffic
....			Mac[2] (rehearsal)
....		-1	Mac (incomplete)
....	Az	-2	Mac (incomplete)
....	Az	-3	Mac
....	Stv	-5	Mac
....	Stv		Traffic Extension[3]
....			Star
....	Stv	-1	Star
....	Stv	-1	Cross Climax
....		-2	Cross Climax (incomplete)
....		-3	Cross Climax
....		-1	Mac A&B (incomplete)
....		-2	Mac A&B
....			Mac A&B (incomplete)
....			Mac A&B (incomplete)
....		-1[4]	Mac A&B
....		-2/-3[4]	Mac A&B (rhythm)
....		-1	Mac A
....		-1	Mac C
....		-1	Mac B >>>

....		-1	Mac C (incomplete)
....		-2	Mac C
....			The B.O. Man[5] (rehearsal)
....			The B.O. Man (incomplete)
....			The B.O. Man (incomplete)
....	Stv	-1	The B.O. Man
....			Letter B In Reverse
....			Letter B In Reverse (incomplete)
....			Letter B In Reverse (incomplete)
....			Letter B In Reverse (incomplete)
....			Letter B In Reverse (incomplete)

[1]B.O. stands for <u>B</u>ody <u>O</u>dor.
[2]*sa* "T.G.T.T."
[3]*sa* "Traffic Jam"; *aka* "Kixx."
[4]This version is different from that of the previous takes.
[5]This title is a derivative of *The B.O. Of Traffic.*

26 Mar 1967   (P)
Carnegie Hall
New York City, NY

DUKE ELLINGTON & HIS ORCHESTRA
CA CW HJns ME, LB BCpr CCrs, JHtn JH RP PG HC, DE JL RJo.

....		Rue Bleue
....		Salomé
....		A Chromatic Love Affair
....	Pab	Blood Count

DUKE ELLINGTON & HIS ORCHESTRA WITH ELLA FITZGERALD
Same personnel.

....	Pab	Swamp Goo
....	Pab	Girdle Hurdle
....	Pab	The Shepherd
....	Pab	Rue Bleue
....	Pab	Mount Harissa
....	Pab	Rockin' In Rhythm

> ZS added.

| .... | Pab | Very Tenor |

> ZS omitted.

....	Pab	Tootie For Cootie
....	Pab	Up Jump
....	Pab	Things Ain't What They Used To Be
....	Pab	Things Ain't What They Used To Be

> DE JL RJo omitted, JJns BCrs SWrd, EF added.

....	Pab	Don't Be That Way –vEF
....	Pab	You've Changed –vEF
....	Pab	Let's Do It –vEF
....	Pab	On The Sunny Side Of The Street –vEF

> DE replaces JJns.

| .... | Pab | Cotton Tail –vEF |

2 Apr 1967   (P)
Place des Arts (bc)
Montréal, QC

DUKE ELLINGTON & HIS ORCHESTRA
CA CW HJns ME, LB BCpr CCrs, JHtn JH RP PG HC, DE JL BDhm.

....		Take The "A" Train
....		Swamp Goo
....		Girdle Hurdle
....		Rue Bleue
....		A Chromatic Love Affair
....		Salomé
....		Things Ain't What They Used To Be

DUKE ELLINGTON   (S)[1]
DE interviewed by Martin Braunstein.

| .... | RDB | Interview |

[1]Backstage.

4 Apr 1967   (S)
24th St., Studio A
New York City, NY

DUKE ELLINGTON & HIS ORCHESTRA
CA CW HJns ME, LB BCpr CCrs, JHtn JH RP PG HC, DE JL BDhm JA.

| .... | Az | Traffic Extension (incomplete)   >>> |

....	Stv	-1	Traffic Extension
....			Eggo (incomplete)
....		-2	Eggo
....		-3	Eggo (incomplete)
....		-4	Eggo (incomplete)
....	RDB	-6	Eggo (incomplete)
....			Eggo (incomplete)
....	Az	-7	Eggo (incomplete)
....	Stv	-7	Eggo
....		-1	I'm Hip, Too (incomplete)
....		-2	I'm Hip, Too
....		-3	I'm Hip, Too
....	Stv	-4	I'm Hip, Too
....		-2	Amta (incomplete)
....	Stv	-3	Amta
....	Stv	-1	Warr[1]
....			The Little Purple Flower (rehearsal)[2]
....		-1	The Little Purple Flower
....			The Little Purple Flower (rehearsal)
....		-2	The Little Purple Flower (incomplete)
....			The Little Purple Flower (rehearsal)
....		-4	The Little Purple Flower (incomplete)
....	Az	-5	The Little Purple Flower
....	Stv	-6	The Little Purple Flower

[1]*sa* "Traffic Extension." (?=[R]raw.)
[2]*aka* "F.L."

	14 Apr 1967 (P)
DUKE ELLINGTON & HIS ORCHESTRA	Civic Opera House
CA CW HJns ME, LB BCpr CCrs, JHtn JH RP PG HC, DE JL BDhm.	Chicago, IL

....	Take The "A" Train
....	Swamp Goo
....	Girdle Hurdle
....	The Shepherd
....	Up Jump
....	A Chromatic Love Affair
....	Things Ain't What They Used To Be

> OPsn added.

....	Take The "A" Train

	25 Apr 1967[1] (S)
DUKE ELLINGTON & HIS ORCHESTRA	Veterans Memorial Auditorium (tc)
CA CW HJns ME, LB BCpr CCrs, JHtn JH RP PG HC, DE JL BDhm, SCC.	Columbus, OH

....	David Danced Before The Lord –vSCC
....	David Danced Before The Lord –vSCC

[1]Telecast on 13 Oct 1967.

The above is a rehearsal session.

DUKE ELLINGTON & HIS ORCHESTRA	(tc)[1] (P)
TWtk added, otherwise same personnel.	

....	In The Beginning God –vTWtk

[1]Telecast on 13 Oct 1967.

	Apr 1967 (P)
DUKE ELLINGTON	Unidentified location
Piano solo.	U.S.A. or Canada

....	Soda Fountain Rag

	Apr 1967[1] (S)
DUKE ELLINGTON	Unidentified location (tc)
Piano solo.	*p* Baltimore, MD
....	Salute To Morgan State
....	Salute To Morgan State

[1]Telecast on 13 Oct 1967.

The above is a rehearsal session.

DUKE ELLINGTON & HIS RHYTHM   *p* Apr 1967   (S)
DE JL BDhm.   Unidentified location
                                                              U.S.A.
....   Satin Doll
    > DE piano solo.
....   A Chromatic Love Affair
    > fem. vcl added.
....   I Got It Bad –vcl
    > fem. vcl omitted.
....   My Mother, My Father And Love
    > JL, fem. vcl added.
....   Solitude –vcl

DUKE ELLINGTON & HIS RHYTHM   1 May 1967[1]   (P)
DE JL BDhm.   Murphy Fine Arts Center, Morgan State College (tc)
                                                              Baltimore, MD
....   Take The "A" Train
....   Salute To Morgan State
    > BDhm omitted.
....   Jones
....   Medley[2]
....   Things Ain't What They Used To Be
    > BDhm added.
....   Dancers In Love
....   Take The "A" Train
[1]Excerpts have been telecast on 13 Oct 1967.
[2]Including: I Got It Bad; Caravan; Do Nothin' Till You Hear From Me; I Let A Song Go Out Of My Heart/Don't Get Around
Much Anymore.

DUKE ELLINGTON   1 Jun 1967   (S)
DE talking.   Unidentified location (bc)
                                                              Reno, NV
....   Reading of the eulogy about Billy Srayhorn.

DUKE ELLINGTON   12 Jun 1967   (P)
No particulars available.   Yale University
                                                              New Haven, CT
....   Medley[1]
[1]Including: Do Nothin' Till You Hear From Me; Sophisticated Lady; I Got It Bad.

DUKE ELLINGTON   *p* 12 Jun 1967[1]   (S)
DE interviewed by Frank Knight.   Crystal Lake Ballroom (bc)
                                                              Ellington, CT
....   Interview
[1]Broadcast on 14 Jun 1967.

DUKE ELLINGTON & HIS ORCHESTRA   23 Jun 1967   (S)
CA CW HJns ME, LB BCpr CCrs, JHtn JH RP PG HC, DE JL CClb.   RCA Hollywood Studios
                                                              Hollywood, CA
....   Rondolet (rehearsal)
....   Rondolet (rehearsal)
....   Rondolet (rehearsal)
....   Rondolet (rehearsal)
....   Take The "A" Train (rehearsal)
....   Swamp Goo (incomplete)
....   U3KM6687-1   Swamp Goo (incomplete)
....   U3KM6687-2   Swamp Goo
....   U3KM6687-3   Swamp Goo (incomplete)
....   U3KM6687-4   Swamp Goo (incomplete)
.... Az   U3KM6687-5   Swamp Goo
.... MM   U3KM6687-6   Swamp Goo
.... Az   Girdle Hurdle (rehearsal)
....   Girdle Hurdle (incomplete)
....   Girdle Hurdle (incomplete)   >>>

....			Girdle Hurdle (incomplete)	
....			Girdle Hurdle (incomplete)	
....			Girdle Hurdle (incomplete)	
....	MM	U3KM6688-1	Girdle Hurdle	
....		U3KM6689-1	The Shepherd	
....	Stv	U3KM6689-2	The Shepherd	
....			Up Jump	
....			Up Jump	
....			Up Jump	
....		U3KM6690-1	Up Jump	
....		U3KM6690-2	Up Jump	
....	Stv	U3KM6690-4	Up Jump	
....		U3KM6691-1	Rue Bleue	
....	Stv	U3KM6691-2	Rue Bleue	
....	Stv	U3KM6692-1	A Chromatic Love Affair	
....	Stv	U3KM6693-1	Salomé	
....	Stv	U3KM6694-1	Blood Count	

27 Jun 1967   (P)
The White House
Washington, DC

DUKE ELLINGTON & STAN GETZ WITH THE NORTH TEXAS STATE UNIVERSITY LAB BAND
DE and Stan Getz with the North Texas State University Lab Band.

....	Take The "A" Train

29 Jun 1967   (P)
ABC Studios (tc)
Los Angeles, CA

DUKE ELLINGTON
DE interviewed by Joey Bishop.

....	Interview

> DE with a studio orchestra, directed by Johnny Mann.

....	Take The "A" Train
....	Satin Doll

1 Jul 1967   (P)
Hollywood Bowl
Los Angeles, CA

DUKE ELLINGTON & HIS ORCHESTRA
CA CW HJns ME, LB BCpr CCrs, JHtn JH RP PG HC, DE JL CClb.

....	Pab	Swamp Goo
....	Pab	Girdle Hurdle
....	Pab	The Shepherd
....	Pab	Rue Bleue
....	Pab	Salomé
....	Pab	A Chromatic Love Affair

> CT added.

....	Pab	Wild Onions

> CT omitted, OPsn added.

....	Pab	Take The "A" Train

> OPsn omitted, BCrt added.

....	Pab	Satin Doll

> BCrt omitted.

....	Pab	Tootie For Cootie
....	Pab	Up Jump

> BCrt added.

....	Pab	Prelude To A Kiss

> BCrt omitted.

....	Pab	Mood Indigo—I Got It Bad

> JL CClb omitted, BCrs SWrd, EF added.

....	Pab	Cotton Tail –vEF

Early Jul 1967   (P)
Carter Barron Amphitheater
Washington, DC

DUKE ELLINGTON & HIS ORCHESTRA
CA CW HJns ME, LB BCpr CCrs, JHtn JH RP PG HC, DE BCrs CClb.

....	Take The "A" Train
....	Swamp Goo
....	Girdle Hurdle
....	Things Ain't What They Used To Be
....	Take The "A" Train
....	The Shepherd >>>

....   Mount Harissa
....   Up Jump
....   Salomé
....   Things Ain't What They Used To Be
....   Medley[1]
....   Jam With Sam

> JHtn RP HC, DE.

....   Monologue –DE narration

> Entire band.

....   Take The "A" Train

[1]Including: Satin Doll; Solitude; Don't Get Around Much Anymore; Mood Indigo; I'm Beginning To See The Light;
Sophisticated Lady; Caravan; Do Nothin' Till You Hear From Me; I Got It Bad; I Let A Song Go Out Of My Heart/
Don't Get Around Much Anymore.

                                                                        Early Jul 1967   (P)
DUKE ELLINGTON & HIS ORCHESTRA   Carter Barron Amphitheater
CA CW HJns ME, LB BCpr CCrs, JHtn JH RP PG HC, DE JL CClb.   Washington, DC

....   Take The "A" Train
....   Swamp Goo
....   Girdle Hurdle
....   Take The "A" Train
....   Mount Harissa
....   Salomé
....   Passion Flower
....   Things Ain't What They Used To Be
....   Medley[1]
....   Things Ain't What They Used To Be

[1]Including: Satin Doll; Solitude; Don't Get Around Much Anymore; Mood Indigo; I'm Beginning To See The Light;
Sophisticated Lady; Caravan; Do Nothin' Till You Hear From Me; I Let A Song Go Out Of My Heart/Don't Get Around
Much Anymore.

                                                                        Early Jul 1967   (P)
DUKE ELLINGTON & HIS ORCHESTRA   Carter Barron Amphitheater
CA CW HJns ME, LB BCpr CCrs, JHtn JH RP PG HC, DE JL CClb.   Washington, DC

....   Take The "A" Train
....   Swamp Goo
....   Girdle Hurdle
....   The Shepherd
....   Mount Harissa
....   Salomé
....   Passion Flower
....   Things Ain't What They Used To Be
....   Medley[1]
....   Things Ain't What They Used To Be

[1]Including: Satin Doll; Solitude; Don't Get Around Much Anymore; Mood Indigo; I'm Beginning To See The Light:
Sophisticated Lady; Caravan; Do Nothin' Till You Hear From Me; I Let A Song Go Out Of My Heart/Don't Get Around
Much Anymore.

                                                                        Early Jul 1967   (P)
DUKE ELLINGTON & HIS ORCHESTRA   Carter Barron Amphitheater
CA CW HJns ME, LB BCpr CCrs, JHtn JH RP PG HC, DE JL CClb.   Washington, DC

....   Take The "A" Train
....   Swamp Goo
....   Girdle Hurdle
....   The Shepherd
....   Mount Harissa
....   Salomé

                                                                        Early Jul 1967   (P)
DUKE ELLINGTON & HIS ORCHESTRA   Carter Barron Amphitheater
CA CW HJns ME, LB BCpr CCrs, JHtn JH RP PG HC, DE JL CClb.   Washington, DC

....   Take The "A" Train
....   Swamp Goo
....   Girdle Hurdle
....   Take The "A" Train
....   Up Jump
....   Salomé
....   I Got It Bad
....   Things Ain't What They Used To Be   >>>

.... Medley[1]
.... Things Ain't What They Used To Be

[1]Including: Satin Doll; Don't Get Around Much Anymore; Mood Indigo; I'm Beginning To See The Light; Sophisticated Lady; Caravan; Do Nothin' Till You Hear From Me; I Let A Song Go Out Of My Heart/Don't Get Around Much Anymore.

Early Jul 1967   (P)
Carter Barron Amphitheater
Washington, DC

DUKE ELLINGTON & HIS ORCHESTRA
CA CW HJns ME, LB BCpr CCrs, JHtn JH RP PG HC, DE JL CClb.

.... Take The "A" Train
.... Swamp Goo
.... Girdle Hurdle
.... The Shepherd
.... Mount Harissa
.... Salomé
.... Passion Flower
.... Things Ain't What They Used To Be
.... Medley[1]
.... Things Ain't What They Used To Be

[1]Including: Satin Doll; Solitude; Don't Get Around Much Anymore; Mood Indigo; I'm Beginning To See The Light; Sophisticated Lady; Caravan; Do Nothin' Till You Hear From Me; I Let A Song Go Out Of My Heart/Don't Get Around Much Anymore.

9 Jul 1967   (P)
Carter Barron Amphitheater
Washington, DC

DUKE ELLINGTON & HIS ORCHESTRA
CA CW HJns ME, LB BCpr CCrs, JHtn JH RP PG HC, DE JL CClb.

.... Take The "A" Train
.... Swamp Goo
.... Girdle Hurdle
.... The Shepherd
.... Mount Harissa
.... Up Jump
.... Salomé
.... Passion Flower
.... Things Ain't What They Used To Be
.... Medley[1]
.... Things Ain't What They Used To Be

[1]Including: Satin Doll; Solitude; Don't Get Around Much Anymore; Mood Indigo; I'm Beginning To See The Light; Sophisticated Lady; Caravan; Do Nothin' Till You Hear From Me; I Got It Bad; I Let A Song Go Out Of My Heart/ Don't Get Around Much Anymore.

11 Jul 1967   (S)
24th Street Studios
New York City, NY

DUKE ELLINGTON & HIS ORCHESTRA
CA CW HJns ME, LB BCpr CCrs, JHtn JH RP PG HC, DE JL SL.

....			Rondolet (incomplete)
....			Rondolet (rehearsal)
....		-1	Rondolet
....		-2	Rondolet
....		-3	Rondolet
....	Saj	-4	Rondolet
....	Saj	-5	Mich[1]
....			Lady (incomplete)
....			Lady (incomplete)
....		-6	Lady (incomplete)
....	Saj	-6	Lady
....	Az	-7	Lele[2] (incomplete)
....	Stv	-7	Lele

[1]aka "Tropical Delight."
[2]aka "Night Sweet"; "Lili."

21 Jul 1967   (P)
Ravinia Festival
Highland Park, IL

DUKE ELLINGTON & HIS ORCHESTRA
CA CW HJns ME, LB BCpr CCrs, JHtn JH RP PG HC, DE JL SL.

.... Things Ain't What They Used To Be
.... Wings And Things
.... In The Beginning God

22 Jul 1967   (P)
Private residence
Chicago, IL

DUKE ELLINGTON & HIS ORCHESTRA
CA CW HJns ME, LB BCpr CCrs, JHtn JH RP PG HC, DE JL SL.

.... Take The "A" Train   >>>

....			Jeep's Blues
....			I Got It Bad
....			Azure
....			Mood Indigo
....			Satin Doll
....			Tenderly
....			Diminuendo In Blue and Wailing Interval
....			The Jeep Is Jumpin'
....			Things Ain't What They Used To Be
....			I Can't Get Started—Eggo
....			Stompin' At The Savoy
....			Rondolet
....			The Shadow Of Your Smile

24 Jul 1967   (S)
Hallmark Recording Studios
Toronto, ON

DUKE ELLINGTON WITH THE RON COLLIER ORCHESTRA
DE with the Ron Collier Orchestra.

....	De	12641	Aurora Borealis
....	De	12642	Nameless Hour
....	Att[1]	12642 alt.[2]	Nameless Hour

[1]Originally released on *Radio Canada International,* a non-commercial label.
[2]Another "alternate take," which is apparently the result of a different mixing process, can be found on a 13-LP set titled "Music Canada."

The arrangements for the above titles and those of the following session are by Ron Collier.

25 Jul 1967   (S)
Hallmark Recording Studios
Toronto, ON

DUKE ELLINGTON WITH THE RON COLLIER ORCHESTRA
DE with the Ron Collier Orchestra.

....	De	12643	Collage No. 3
....	De	12644	Fair Wind
....	De	12645	Silent Night, Lonely Night
....	De	12646	Song And Dance

26 Jul 1967[1]   (P)
Gilmore Bros. Auto Park (tc)
Kalamazoo, MI

DUKE ELLINGTON & HIS ORCHESTRA
CA CW HJns ME, LB BCpr CCrs, JHtn JH RP PG HC, DE JL SL, TWtk choir.

....		Take The "A" Train
....		Medley[2]
....		Traffic Jam
....		In The Beginning God --vTWtk Choir
....		David Danced Before The Lord

[1]Telecast (minus the medley) on 13 Dec 1967.
[2]Including: Satin Doll; Solitude; Don't Get Around Much Anymore; Mood Indigo; Caravan; Do Nothin' Till You Hear From Me; I Let A Song Go Out Of My Heart/Don't Get Around Much Anymore.

29 Jul 1967   (P)
Cedar Point Ballroom (bc)
Sandusky, OH

DUKE ELLINGTON & HIS ORCHESTRA
CA CW HJns ME, LB BCpr CCrs, JHtn JH RP PG HC, DE JL SL.

....		Take The "A" Train
....		Eggo
....		Caravan
....		I Got It Bad
....		Satin Doll
....		Things Ain't What They Used To Be

2 Aug 1967   (P)
Rainbow Grill[1] (bc)
New York City, NY

DUKE ELLINGTON'S OCTET
CA, LB, JH PG HC, DE JL SL.

> DE piano solo.

....		Salute To Morgan State

> Entire band.

....		Take The "A" Train
....	JSo[2]	Take The "A" Train
....		Satin Doll
....	JSo[2]	Mood Indigo
....	JSo	Acht O'Clock Rock[3]
....	JSo	I Got It Bad
....	JSo	Things Ain't What They Used To Be >>>

[1]Radio City Building, at the Rockefeller Center.
[2]Edited releases, containing only a portion from this session; the remainders originate from other Rainbow Grill dates.
[3]sa "Mich"; "Tropical Delight." Due to DE's pronounciation of the German word "Acht" (=eight), the wrong spelling "Ocht" is generally used; on the recording sheet for the session on 15 Nov 1967 the title has been spelled correctly "Acht."

In order to secure a five-week engagement at the Rainbow Grill, starting on 31 Jul 1967, DE had to lay-off half the band for the duration, since he was paid for the octet only. The same applies to the band's future engagements at this venue.

			3 Aug 1967	(P)
			Rainbow Grill (bc)	
			New York City, NY	

DUKE ELLINGTON'S OCTET
CA, LB, JH PG HC, DE JL SL.

....		Prelude To A Kiss
....		Take The "A" Train
....	UJ	Satin Doll
....	UJ	Mood Indigo
....	UJ	Take The "A" Train
....	UJ	Passion Flower
....	UJ	Things Ain't What They Used To Be
....	UJ	Tricky's Lick
....	UJ	Sophisticated Lady
....	UJ	First Bass[1]

[1]sa "Kentucky Avenue, A.C."; "Nati."

		7 Aug 1967[1]	(P)
		CBS Studios (tc)	
		New York City, NY	

DUKE ELLINGTON & HIS RHYTHM
DE interviewed by Merv Griffin.

| .... | Interview |

> DE JL SL.

| .... | Medley[2] |

> MGfn APry JWS added.

| .... | Medley[3] |

[1]Telecast on 14 Aug 1967.
[2]Including: Take The "A" Train; Sophisticated Lady; Satin Doll.
[3]Including: Mood Indigo –vMGfn; Don't Get Around Much Anymore –vAPry; Solitude –vJWS; I Got It Bad –APry; I Let A Song Go Out Of My Heart –vMGfn/Don't Get Around Much Anymore –vAPry.

		10 Aug 1967	(S)
		NBC Studios (tc)	
		New York City, NY	

DUKE ELLINGTON & HIS RHYTHM
DE JL SL.

| .... | Satin Doll |

> DE interviewed by Barbara Walters.

| .... | Interview |

> DE JL SL.

| .... | Take The "A" Train |

> SL omitted.

| .... | Come Sunday |

> SL added.

| .... | Rock The Clock |
| .... | Mount Harissa |

DUKE ELLINGTON'S OCTET
CA , LB, JH PG HC, DE JL SL.   Rainbow Grill (bc)   (P)

> DE piano solo.

| .... | Meditation |

> JL SL added.

....	The Shepherd
....	I Can't Get Started
....	Fly Me To The Moon

> Entire band.

....	Mame
....	Take The "A" Train
....	One O'Clock Jump
....	Take The "A" Train
....	Take The "A" Train >>>

. . . .		Satin Doll
. . . .	JSo	Black And Tan Fantasy
. . . .		Acht O'Clock Rock
. . . .		Passion Flower
. . . .		Tricky's Lick
. . . .	JSo	In A Sentimental Mood
. . . .	JSo	I Let A Song Go Out Of My Heart/Don't Get Around Much Anymore

14 Aug 1967   (P)
Rainbow Grill (bc)
New York City, NY

DUKE ELLINGTON'S OCTET
CA, LB, JH PG HC, DE JL SL.

. . . .		Take The "A" Train
. . . .		Satin Doll
. . . .	UJ	The Intimacy Of The Blues
. . . .	UJ	Solitude
. . . .	UJ	Day Dream
. . . .	UJ	Caravan
. . . .		Take The "A" Train

17 Aug 1967   (P)
Raibow Grill (bc)
New York City, NY

DUKE ELLINGTON'S OCTET
CA, LB JH PG HC, DE JL SL.

> DE piano solo.

| . . . . | MR | Heaven |
| . . . . | MR | Le Sucrier Velours |

> PG, JL SL added.

| . . . . | MR | In A Sentimental Mood |

> Entire band.

. . . .	Az	Azure
. . . .	MR	I'm Beginning To See The Light
. . . .	MR	Rock The Clock
. . . .	MR	Take The "A" Train
. . . .	MR	Satin Doll
. . . .	MR[1]	Sophisticated Lady
. . . .	JSo	Take The "A" Train
. . . .	JSo	Passion Flower
. . . .	JSo	Perdido
. . . .	MR[1]	Solitude
. . . .	MR	Things Ain't What They Used To Be
. . . .	MR	Acht O'Clock Rock

[1]The original releases on JSo have been edited and contain each only a portion from this session; the remainders originate from other Rainbow Grill dates. Unedited versions were first issued on MR.

DUKE ELLINGTON   (bc)   (S)
DE interviewed by Henry F. Whiston.

| . . . . | Az[1] | Interview |

[1]Excerpt on Az.

21 Aug 1967   (P)
Rainbow Grill (bc)
New York City, NY

DUKE ELLINGTON'S OCTET
CA, LB, JH PG HC, DE JL SL.

. . . .		Take The "A" Train
. . . .		Satin Doll
. . . .	JSo	The Intimacy Of The Blues
. . . .		Caravan
. . . .	JSo[1]	Acht O'Clock Rock
. . . .	JSo	Mood Indigo

> DE JL SL.

| . . . . | Az | It's Freedom |

[1]Edited release containing only a portion from this session; the remainder originates from another Rainbow Grill date.

24 Aug 1967   (P)
Rainbow Grill (bc)
New York City, NY

DUKE ELLINGTON'S OCTET
CA, LB, JH PG HC, DE JL SL.

> DE JL SL.

| . . . . | | Heaven |
| . . . . | | Salute To Morgan State   >>> |

....		Salute To Morgan State
> JH added.		
....		Sentimental Lady
> Entire band.		
....		First Bass
....		The Jeep Is Jumpin'
....		I Let A Song Go Out Of My Heart/Don't Get Around Much Anymore
....		Mame
> DE JL SL.		
....		I Can't Get Started.
> Entire band.		
....		Take The "A" Train
....		Satin Doll
....		Take The "A" Train
.... JSo[1]		Mood Indigo—Do Nothin' Till You Hear From Me
....		Things Ain't What They Used To Be
.... JSo		Lady Baby[2]
....		Acht O'Clock Rock
.... JSo		Tricky's Lick

[1]Edited release; the first half of "Do Nothin' …" originates from another Rainbow Grill date. The original "Mood Indigo" portion has not been released as yet.
[2]sa "Lady."

28 Aug 1967   (S)
24th St., Studio A
New York City, NY

DUKE ELLINGTON & HIS ORCHESTRA
CA CW CT HJns ME, LB BCpr CCrs, JHtn JH RP PG HC, DE AB SWrd.

....			Boo-Dah (incomplete)
....			Boo-Dah (incomplete)
....			Boo-Dah
....			Boo-Dah (incomplete)
....			Boo-Dah (incomplete)
....			Boo-Dah
....			Boo-Dah (incomplete)
....			Boo-Dah (incomplete)
....		UPA1-8528-1	Boo-Dah
....			Boo-Dah (incomplete)
....			Boo-Dah (incomplete)
....			Boo-Dah (incomplete)
....			Boo-Dah (incomplete)
....	Vi	UPA1-8528-2	Boo-Dah
....			U.M.M.G. (incomplete)
....		UPA1-8529-1	U.M.M.G. (incomplete)
....		UPA1-8529-2	U.M.M.G.
....			Band Call (incomplete)
....		UPA1-8529-3	U.M.M.G. (incomplete)
....			U.M.M.G. (incomplete)
....			U.M.M.G. (incomplete)
....			U.M.M.G. (incomplete)
....			U.M.M.G. (incomplete)
....			U.M.M.G. (incomplete)
....	Vi	UPA1-8529-4	U.M.M.G.
....			U.M.M.G. (incomplete)
....			U.M.M.G. (incomplete)
....			U.M.M.G. (incomplete)
....			U.M.M.G. (incomplete)
....			U.M.M.G. (incomplete)
> CT omitted.			
....			Blood Count (incomplete)
....		UPA1-8530-1	Blood Count
....			Blood Count (incomplete)
....			Blood Count (incomplete)
....		UPA1-8530-3	Blood Count
....	Vi	UPA1-8530-4	Blood Count
> CT added.			
....			Smada (incomplete)
....			Smada (incomplete)
....			Smada (incomplete)
....		UPA1-8531-1	Smada >>>

....			Smada (incomplete)
....			Smada (incomplete)
....		UPA1-8531-2	Smada
....	Vi	UPA1-8531-3	Smada
....	Bb	UPA1-8531-4	Smada

30 Aug 1967   (S)
24th St., Studio A
New York City, NY

DUKE ELLINGTON & HIS ORCHESTRA
CA CW HJns ME, LB BCpr JSrs CCrs, JHtn JH RP PG HC, DE AB SWrd.

....			Rock Skippin' At The Blue Note (incomplete)
....			Rock Skippin' At The Blue Note (incomplete)
....			Rock Skippin' At The Blue Note (incomplete)
....			Rock Skippin' At The Blue Note (incomplete)
....			Rock Skippin' At The Blue Note (incomplete)
....		UPA1-8532-1	Rock Skippin' At The Blue Note
....			Rock Skippin' At The Blue Note (incomplete)
....			Rock Skippin' At The Blue Note (incomplete)
....			Rock Skippin' At The Blue Note (incomplete)
....			Rock Skippin' At The Blue Note (incomplete)
....			Rock Skippin' At The Blue Note (incomplete)
....			Rock Skippin' At The Blue Note (incomplete)
....			Rock Skippin' At The Blue Note (incomplete)
....			Rock Skippin' At The Blue Note (incomplete)
....			Rock Skippin' At The Blue Note (incomplete)
....		UPA1-8532-2	Rock Skippin' At The Blue Note
....		UPA1-8532-3	Rock Skippin' At The Blue Note (incomplete)
....	Vi	UPA1-8532-4[1]	Rock Skippin' At The Blue Note
....	Vi	UPA1-8532-5[1]	Rock Skippin' At The Blue Note
....	Vi	UPA1-8533-4	Raincheck
....	Vi	UPA1-8533-6	Raincheck
....	RDB	UPA1-8534-1	Midriff
....	Bb	UPA1-8534-2	Midriff
....	Bb	UPA1-8535-2	My Little Brown Book
....		UPA1-8536	Snibor

> DE piano solo.

....	Vi	test[2]	Lotus Blossom

[1]Both the original release and the centennial edition use an edited version: The piano intro from take 4 and the main portion of take 5 have been spliced together. All others use the unaltered take 5.
[2]No master number assigned.

DUKE ELLINGTON'S OCTET   Rainbow Grill (bc)   (P)
CA, LB, JH PG HC, DE AB SL.

....		Take The "A" Train
....		Satin Doll
....	JSo[1]	Lady Baby
....		Caravan
....		I Got It Bad
....		Take The "A" Train
....		Acht O'Clock Rock
....		Things Ain't What They Used To Be

[1]Edited release containing only a portion from this session; the remainder originates from another Rainbow Grill date.

31 Aug 1967   (P)
Rainbow Grill (bc)
New York City, NY

DUKE ELLINGTON'S OCTET
CA, LB, JH PG HC, DE AB SL.

....		Unidentified title
....		I Don't Want Nobody At All

> DE AB SL.

....		I Can't Get Started

> Entire band.

....		Mame
....	JSo[1]	Do Nothin' Till You Hear From Me
....		On The Sunny Side Of The Street
....		My Little Brown Book

> DE piano solo.

....		In A Sentimental Mood

> Entire band.

....		Take The "A" Train >>>

....		Satin Doll	
....	JSo[1]	Lady Baby	
....		Tricky's Lick	
....		Passion Flower	
....		Things Ain't What They Used To Be	
....		Mood Indigo	
....	JSo[1]	Acht O'Clock Rock	
....	JSo[1]	Sophisticated Lady	

[1]Edited releases containing only a portion from this session; the remainders originate from other Rainbow Grill dates.

DUKE ELLINGTON & HIS ORCHESTRA
CA CW HJns ME, LB BCpr CCrs, JHtn JH RP PG HC, DE AB SWrd.

1 Sep 1967   (S)
24th St., Studio A
New York City, NY

....	Vi	UPA1-8536-7[1]	Snibor
....	Vi	UPA1-8537-6	After All
....	Vi	UPA1-8538-4	All Day Long

> HC, DE AB.

....	Bb	UPA1-8539-1	Lotus Blossom
....		UPA-18539-2	Lotus Blossom (incomplete)
....		UPA1-8539-3	Lotus Blossom (incomplete)
....		UPA1-8539-4	Lotus Blossom
....		UPA1-8539-5	Lotus Blossom

[1]Remake.

DUKE ELLINGTON & HIS ORCHESTRA
CA CW HJns ME, LB BCpr CCrs, JHtn JH RP PG HC, DE AB SL, CCsn.

16 Sep 1967   (P)
Hempstead Town's Merrick Road Park Ballroom
Merrick, Long Island, NY

....	Satin Doll
....	Take The "A" Train
....	Do Nothin' Till You Hear From Me
....	Acht O'Clock Rock
....	I Got It Bad
....	Things Ain't What They Used To Be
....	Wings And Things
....	Solitude
....	Caravan
....	Honeysuckle Rose
....	The Shepherd
....	Mount Harissa
....	Up Jump
....	Mood Indigo
....	Hello Dolly —vCCsn
....	Take The "A" Train
....	Perdido
....	Salomé
....	The Opener
....	Sophisticated Lady
....	El Busto
....	Come Sunday
....	Montage
....	Things Ain't What They Used To Be

DUKE ELLINGTON & HIS ORCHESTRA
CA CW HJns ME, LB BCpr CCrs, JHtn JH RP PG HC, DE BY SWrd.

3 Oct 1967   (S)
Unspecified studio
San Francisco, CA

	Variations On A Commercial Theme[1]
.... UTD	Variation #1
.... MHS	Variation #2
.... UTD	Variation #3
.... UTD	Variation #4
.... MHS	Variation #5
.... UTD	Variation #6
.... UTD	Variation #7

[1]"Duke Ellington's Hot Shoppes Themes" produced as musical background both in radio and televison commercials for Marriott/Hot Shoppes Inc.

DUKE ELLINGTON & HIS ORCHESTRA
CA CW HJns ME, LB BCpr CCrs, JHtn JH RP PG HC, DE BY SWrd.

7 Oct 1967   (P)
Orange County Fair Grounds Stadium
Costa Mesa, CA

....	Take The "A" Train >>>

....		Soul Call
....		Swamp Goo
....		Girdle Hurdle
....		The Shepherd
....		Take The "A" Train
....		Mount Harissa
....		Up Jump
....		La Plus Belle Africaine
....		Rue Bleue
....		Salomé
....		Jam With Sam
....		I Got It Bad
....		Things Ain't What They Used To Be
....		Drag
....		Acht O'Clock Rock
....		Satin Doll

13 Oct 1967[1]   (T)
Various locations
U.S.A.

DUKE ELLINGTON

Telecast "On The Road With Duke Ellington." Comments and interviews with music by Duke Ellington & His Orchestra, chosen from previously recorded material with varying personnel. In the following only the music has been listed, with date of origin where known.

....	RDB	Introductory remarks
....	RDB	Medley: Do Nothin' Till You Hear From Me; Sophisticated Lady; I Got It Bad (edited) (Yale, 12 Jun 67)
....	RDB	Take The "A" Train (beginning) (Kalamazoo, 26 Jul 67)
....	RDB	Mood Indigo
....	RDB	Happy Birthday –vTWtk
....	RDB	Take The "A" Train (ending)
....	RDB	Satin Doll—Solitude (edited)
....	RDB	Salute To Morgan State (fragment) (Apr 67)
....	RDB	Salute To Morgan State (Apr 67)
....	RDB	Salute To Morgan State (Apr 67)
....	RDB	Salute To Morgan State (fragments) (Apr 67)
....	RDB	Salute To Morgan State (edited) (Morgan State, 1 May 67)
....	RDB	Rondolet (RCA Studio, 11 Jul 67)
....	RDB	Rondolet (fragment) (RCA Studio, 11 Jul 1967)
....	RDB	Rondolet (fragment) (RCA Studio, 11 Jul 67)
....	RDB	Rondolet (RCA Studio, 11 Jul 67)
....	RDB	Rondolet (ending) (RCA Studio, 11 Jul 67)
....	RDB	Take The "A" Train (ending) (Kalamazoo, 26 Jul 67)
....	RDB	Traffic Jam (Kalamazoo, 26 Jul 67)
....	RDB	Soda Fountain Rag (Apr 67)
....	RDB	Salute To Morgan State (fragment) (Morgan State, 1 May 67)
....	RDB	Things Ain't What They Used To Be (Morgan State, 1 May 67)
....	RDB	Take The "A" Train (fragment) (soundtrack, 8 Oct 42)
....	RDB	Take The "A" Train (Morgan State, 1 May 67)
....	RDB	Take The "A" Train (edited) (St. Peter's, NYC, 5 Jun 67)
....	RDB	Unidentified title
....	RDB	David Danced Before The Lord (in progress) (Columbus, 25 Apr 67)
....	RDB	In The Beginning God (edited) (Columbus, 25 Apr 67)
....	RDB	Don't Get Around Much Anymore
....	RDB	Medley: Caravan; Do Nothin' Till You Hear From Me; I Let A Song Go Out Of My Heart/ Don't Get Around Much Anymore.
....	RDB	Igoo

> Footage added in 1974.

....	RDB	Take The "A" Train (edited) (Morgan State, 1 May 67)
....	RDB	I Got It Bad (Morgan State, 1 May 67)

[1]Date of telecast; the filming was done earlier in the year.

Upon cross-checking, the reader will notice that some of the recording dates given above are not listed in this book. The reason is that no information other than the title is at hand. For those items with no recording date mentioned, the origins could not be determined as yet.

18 Oct 1967   (P)
Civic Auditorium
Santa Monica, CA

DUKE ELLINGTON & HIS ORCHESTRA

CA CW HJns ME, LB BCpr CCrs, JHtn JH RP PG HC, DE BY SWrd.

....	Take The "A" Train
....	Girdle Hurdle
....	Swamp Goo
....	Salomé
....	I Got It Bad
....	Things Ain't What They Used To Be >>>

....		Acht O'Clock Rock
....		Medley[1]
....		Things Ain't What They Used To Be

[1]Including: Satin Doll; Solitude; Don't Get Around Much Anymore; Mood Indigo; I'm Beginning To See The Light; Sophisticated Lady; Caravan; Do Nothin' Till You Hear From Me; I Let A Song Go Out Of My Heart/Don't Get Around Much Anymore.

15 Nov 1967   (S)
Coast Recorders
San Francisco, CA

DUKE ELLINGTON & HIS ORCHESTRA
CA CW HJns ME, LB BCpr CCrs, JHtn JH RP PG HC, DE JCmn SL.

....	Vi[1]	WPA5-0917	Day Dream
....	Vi[1]		Day Dream (insert)
....	Vi	WPA5-0918	The Intimacy Of The Blues
....	Vi	WPA5-0919	Charpoy[2]
....	Vi	WPA5-0920	Acht O'Clock Rock

[1]Both the original release (RCA PD89565) and the centennial edition use a coda taken from an insert; CD Bb 6287-2 is different and perhaps the original unedited version.
[2]*aka* "Anal Renrut" (=Lana Turner); originally titled "Francesca."

Nov 1967   (S)
Unidentified location
Los Angeles, CA

DUKE ELLINGTON
No particulars available.

....		Interview

5 Dec 1967   (P)
DJ's (bc)
Seattle, WA

DUKE ELLINGTON & HIS ORCHESTRA
CA CW HJns ME, LB BCpr CCrs, JHtn JH RP PG HC, DE JCmn SWrd.

....	Az	The "C" Jam Blues
....	RDB	Mount Harissa
....	Az	Take The "A" Train
....	RDB	Satin Doll
....		Medley[1]
....	RDB	Jam With Sam
....	Az	The Shepherd
....	Az	Drag
....	Az	Take The "A" Train

[1]Including: Satin Doll; I Got It Bad; Solitude; Don't Get Around Much Anymore; Mood Indigo; I'm Beginning To See The Light, Sophisticated Lady; Caravan; Do Nothin' Till You Hear From Me; It Don't Mean A Thing –vTWtk.

11 Dec 1967   (S)
Western Recorders
Los Angeles, CA

FRANK SINATRA WITH DUKE ELLINGTON & HIS ORCHESTRA
Vcl, acc. by CA CW HJns APor ME, LB BCpr CCrs, JHtn JH RP PG HC, DE JCmn WMlr.

....	Rpr	K6319	All I Need Is The Girl –vFS
....	Rpr	K6320	Yellow Days –vFS
....	Rpr	K6321	Indian Summer –vFS
....	Rpr	K6322	Come Back To Me –vFS

The arrangements for the above titles and those of the following session are by Billy May.

12 Dec 1967   (S)
Western Recorders
Los Angeles, CA

FRANK SINATRA WITH DUKE ELLINGTON & HIS ORCHESTRA
Vcl, acc. by CA CW HJns APor ME, LB BCpr CCrs, JHtn JH RP PG HC, DE JCmn WMlr.

....	Rpr	K6323	Poor Butterfly –vFS
....	Rpr	K6324	Sunny –vFS

> JJns replaces DE.

....	Rpr	K6325	I Like The Sunrise –vFS

> DE replaces JJns.

....	Rpr	K6326	Follow Me –vFS

1967   (P)
p private residence
Cincinnati, OH

DUKE ELLINGTON
Piano solo, fem vcl.

....	Az	A Chromatic Love Affair[1]
....		I Got It Bad –vcl[2]
....		My Heritage
....		Solitude –vcl[2]

[1]*aka* "Apollo Hall."
[2]*p* PPge or AFcs.

DUKE ELLINGTON & HIS ORCHESTRA
CA CW HJns ME, LB BCpr CCrs, JHtn JH RP PG HC, DE JCmn SWrd.

13 Jan 1968   (P)
NBC Studios (tc)
New York City, NY

....	Don't Get Around Much Anymore
....	Do Nothin' Till You Hear From Me
....	Black And Tan Fantasy—Creole Love Call—The Mooche
....	Things Ain't What They Used To Be
....	Azure
....	Harmony In Harlem
....	Satin Doll
....	The Blues
....	Interview[1]
....	Take The "A" Train
....	Interview (ctd.)
....	Cotton Tail
....	Comments on DE

[1]DE interviewed by the host of the Today show.

DUKE ELLINGTON & HIS ORCHESTRA
CA CW HJns ME, LB BCpr CCrs, JHtn JH RP PG HC, DE JCmn SWrd.

14 Jan 1968   (P)
CBS Studios (tc)
New York City, NY

....	Acht O'Clock Rock

> DE BGrc with studio orchestra.

....	Medley[1]

[1]Including: Don't Get Around Much Anymore; Just Squeeze Me; Do Nothin' Till You Hear From Me; Mood Indigo; Caravan; Satin Doll –vBGrc.

DUKE ELLINGTON WITH ORCHESTRA
DE interviewed by Johnny Carson and with a studio orchestra, directed by Skitch Henderson.

17 Jan 1968   (P)
NBC Studios (tc)
New York City, NY

....	Rockin' In Rhythm
....	Interview
....	Satin Doll

DUKE ELLINGTON & HIS ORCHESTRA
CA CW HJns ME, LB BCpr BGrn CCrs, JHtn JH RP PG HC, DE JCmn SWrd SL, ABbs choir.

19 Jan 1968   (S)
Cathedral of St. John The Divine
New York City, NY

....	Heaven –vABbs
....	Something About Believing –vChoir

The above is a rehearsal session.

DUKE ELLINGTON & HIS ORCHESTRA
AWtn, DGrd TT RG TWtk JMP MZC StHi StHu MotC, GHdr added, otherwise same personnel.

(bc+tc[1])   (P)

	THE SECOND SACRED CONCERT
....	Fanfare
....	Greetings by Bishop Donegan

> AWtn organ solo.

....	Praise Him In The Sound Of The Trumpet

> Entire band.

....	Praise God
....	99% Won't Do –vJMP MZC
....	Supreme Being –vChoir
....	Something About Believing –vChoir
....	Almighty God –vABbs Choir[2]
....	Heaven –vABbs
....	It's Freedom –vABbs DGrd TT RG TWtk JMP Choir
....	Don't Get Down On Your Knees –vTWtk

> TWtk Choir a cappella.

....	Father Forgive –vTWtk Choir

> Entire band.

....	Don't Get Down On Your Knees –vTWtk

> DE JCmn.

....	Meditation

> Entire band.

....	The Shepherd >>>

....						The Biggest And Busiest Intersection[3]

> Choir a cappella.

....						There's A Great Camp Meeting In The Promised Land –vChoir

> DE, ABbs.

....						T.G.T.T. –vABbs

> Entire band.

....						Praise God And Dance –vABbs, HHdr tap

> TWtk a cappella.

....						The Preacher's Song –vTWtk

[1]Telecast on 19 Jun 1968.
[2]*aka* "God Has His Angels."
[3]*sa* "Warr."

20 Jan 1968			(P)
DUKE ELLINGTON & HIS ORCHESTRA				St. Mark's Episcopal Church
CA CW HJns ME, LB BCpr BGrn CCrs, JHtn JH RP PG HC, DE JCmn SWrd SL, ABbs DGrd		New Canaan, CT
PPt TWtk JMP StMa.

THE SECOND SACRED CONCERT
....		Praise God
....		99% Won't Do –vJMP StMa
....		Supreme Being –vStMa
....		Something About Believing –vStMa
....		Almighty God –vABbs StMa
....		Heaven –vABbs
....		It's Freedom –vABbs DGrd PPt TWtk JMP StMa

> DE JCmn.

....		Meditation

> Entire band.

....		The Shepherd
....		The Biggest And Busiest Intersection
....		Don't Get Down On Your Knees –vTWtk

> TWtk a cappella.

....		Father Forgive –vTWtk

> Entire band.

....		Don't Get Down On Your Knees –vTWtk

> DE, ABbs.

....		T.G.T.T. –vABbs

> Entire band.

....		Praise God And Dance –vABbs

22 Jan 1968			(S)
Fine Studios[1]
DUKE ELLINGTON & HIS ORCHESTRA				New York City, NY
CA CW HJns ME, LB BCpr BGrn CCrs, JHtn JH RP PG HC, DE JCmn SWrd SL, ABbs DGrd
TT RG TWtk MZC StHi StHu.

THE SECOND SACRED CONCERT[2]
.... Fan		Almighty God –vABbs
.... Fan		Heaven –vABbs
.... Fan		It's Freedom –vABbs DGrd TT RG TWtk Choir

> DE, ABbs.

.... Fan		T.G.T.T. –vABbs

> Entire band.

.... Fan		Praise God And Dance –vABbs Choir

[1]At the Great Northern Hotel, 58th Street; this also applies to the sessions on 31 Jan, 19 and 20 Feb 1968.
[2]See also sessions on 31 Jan, 19 and 20 Feb 1968.

23 Jan 1968			(P)
Choate School
DUKE ELLINGTON & HIS ORCHESTRA				Wallingford, CT
CA CW HJns ME, LB BCpr CCrs, JHtn JH RP PG HC, DE JCmn SWrd, DGrd TT RG TWtk.

THE SECOND SACRED CONCERT
....		Introduction spoken by DE >>>

....   Supreme Being –TWtk recital
....   It's Freedom –vDGrd TT RG TWtk
....   Praise God
....   Something About Believing –vDGrd TT RG TWtk
....   Heaven
....   Don't Go Down On Your Knees –vTWtk
....   Almighty God –vDGrd TT RG TWtk
....   The Biggest And Busiest Intersection

25 Jan 1968   (P)
NCO Club, Fort Meade
Glen Burnie, MD

DUKE ELLINGTON & HIS ORCHESTRA
CA CW HJns ME, LB BCpr CCrs, JHtn JH RP PG HC, JCmn SWrd, TT.

....   Laura

> PG, DE JCmn SWrd.

....   Unidentified title

> Entire band, DE added.

....   Take The "A" Train
....   Caravan
....   Satin Doll
....   Autumn Leaves
....   Swamp Goo
....   Girdle Hurdle
....   I'm Beginning To See The Light
....   Sophisticated Lady
....   Mood Indigo
....   Mount Harissa
....   Up Jump
....   Jeep's Blues
....   Unidentified title
....   Willow Weep For Me –vTT
....   Misty –vTT
....   Stormy Monday Blues –vTT
....   Happy Birthday
....   Caravan
....   Put-Tin
....   Warm Valley
....   I Got It Bad –vTT
....   It Don't Mean A Thing –vTT
....   It Don't Mean A Thing
....   Summertime
....   The Biggest And Busiest Intersection

> DE JCmn SWrd.

....   Kinda Dukish

> Entire band.

....   Satin Doll

26 Jan 1968   (P)
Woolsey Hall, Yale University
New Haven, CT

DUKE ELLINGTON & HIS ORCHESTRA
CA CW HJns ME, LB BCpr CCrs, JHtn JH RP PG HC, DE JCmn SWrd, TT TWtk.

....   Take The "A" Train
.... Fan   Swamp Goo
....   Girdle Hurdle
.... Fan   Put-Tin
.... Fan   Take The "A" Train
.... Fan   A Chromatic Love Affair
.... Fan   Up Jump
....   La Plus Belle Africaine
.... Fan   Salomé
.... Fan   The Little Purple Flower
.... Fan   Eggo[1]
....   HARLEM

> DE JCmn SWrd.

.... Fan   Boola Boola

> Entire band.

.... Fan   Warm Valley
.... Fan   Drag
....   It Don't Mean A Thing –vTWtk
....   Willow Weep For Me –vTT   >>>

....   Misty –vTT
....   Medley[2]

[1]Erroneously as "The Little Purple Flower, part 2" on Fan.
[2]No particulars available.

27 Jan 1968   (P)
Eastwind Club
Baltimore, MD

DUKE ELLINGTON & HIS ORCHESTRA
CA HJns ME, LB BCpr CCrs, JHtn JH RP PG HC, JCmn SWrd.

....   Boo-Dah
....   Laura
....   Smada
....   Stranger On The Shore
....   The "C" Jam Blues

> DE added.

....   Take The "A" Train
....   Satin Doll
....   I'm Beginning To See The Light
....   Happy Birthday
....   I Let A Song Go Out Of My Heart/Don't Get Around Much Anymore
....   Drag
....   Happy Birthday
....   Caravan
....   Jeep's Blues
....   I Got It Bad
....   Things Ain't What They Used To Be
....   Put-Tin

30 January 1968   (P)
Officers Club, Fort Meade
Glen Burnie, MD

DUKE ELLINGTON & HIS ORCHESTRA
CA CW HJns ME, LB BCpr CCrs, JHtn JH RP PG HC, JCmn SWrd, TT TWtk.

....   The "C" Jam Blues
....   Perdido

> DE added.

....   Take The "A" Train
....   Satin Doll
....   I Let A Song Go Out Of My Heart/Don't Get Around Much Anymore

> DE JCmn SWrd.

....   Salute To Morgan State

> Entire band.

....   In A Sentimental Mood
....   Creole Love Call
....   Autumn Leaves
....   Eggo
....   Azure
....   Happy Birthday
....   I'm Beginning To See The Light
....   Mood Indigo
....   Tootie For Cootie
....   I Got It Bad
....   Drag
....   Jam With Sam
....   The "C" Jam Blues
....   Sophisticated Lady
....   Do Nothin' Till You Hear From Me
....   Put-Tin
....   Prelude To A Kiss
....   Things Ain't What They Used To Be
....   Acht O'Clock Rock
....   Willow Weep For Me –vTT
....   Misty –vTT
....   Stormy Monday Blues –vTT
....   The Old Circus Train
....   I'm Just A Lucky So-And-So –vTWtk
....   It Don't Mean A Thing –vTWtk
....   Bill Bailey –vTWtk

> DE piano solo.

....   Neenah   >>>

> Entire band.

....   Diminuendo In Blue and Wailing Interval

> DE piano solo.

....   A Single Petal Of A Rose

> Entire Band.

....   My Melancholy Baby
....   Isfahan

31 Jan, 19+20 Feb 1968 (S)
Fine Studios
New York City, NY

DUKE ELLINGTON & HIS ORCHESTRA
CA CW HJns ME, LB BCpr BGrn CCrs, JHtn JH RP PG HC, DE JCmn SWrd SL, DGrd TT RG
TWtk CCS FPS.

                          THE SECOND SACRED CONCERT (ctd.)[1]
.... Fan   Praise God
.... Fan   Supreme Being –vChoir
....   It's Freedom –vDGrd TT RG TWtk
.... Fan   Something About Believing –vChoir
....   Don't Get Down On Your Knees –vTWtk
....   Don't Get Down On Your Knees –vTWtk
.... Fan   Don't Get Down On Your Knees –vTWtk

> TWtk Choir a cappella.

.... Fan   Father Forgive –vTWtk Choir

> DE JCmn.

.... Fan   Meditation

> Entire band.

.... Fan   The Shepherd
.... Fan   The Biggest And Busiest Intersection

[1]See also session on 22 Jan 1968; sessions on 28 Feb and 22 Apr were dubbing sessions.

The above is a summary of recording sessions for which we lack sufficient documentation. It is assumed that versions 1 and 2 of "Don't Get Down … " as well as "It's Freedom" were recorded on 31 Jan. It is also likely that the choral selections were done on 5 Feb and overdubbed. From that it can be concluded that the remainder originates from the 19 and 20 Feb sessions.

28 Feb 1968   (S)
24th St., Studio A
New York City, NY

DUKE ELLINGTON
DE piano solo.

.... Bb   Spoken introduction by WLS and George Wein.
.... Bb   Sweet Fat And That[1]
.... Bb   Satin Doll
.... Bb   Carolina Shout

[1]*sa* "It's Freedom."

DUKE ELLINGTON & TONY BENNETT WITH ORCHESTRA   NBC Studios (tc)   (P)
DE, TBnt with a studio orchestra.

....   Medley[1]

> DE piano solo.

....   Meditation

> DE interviewed by Steve Allen.

....   Interview

> DE, TBnt with orchestra.

....   Making That Love Scene –vTBnt[2]
....   It Don't Mean A Thing –vTBnt

> TBnt omitted, SA added.

....   Satin Doll

[1]Including: Don't Get Around Much Anymore; Just Squeeze Me; Do Nothin' Till You Hear From Me; Mood Indigo; Caravan; Satin Doll –vTBnt.
[2]*sa* "That Scene."

1 Mar 1968   (P)
Chaminade High School
Mineola, NY

DUKE ELLINGTON & HIS ORCHESTRA
CA CW HJns ME, LB BCpr CCrs, JHtn JH RP PG HC, DE JCmn SWrd, TT TWtk.

....   Take The "A" Train   >>>

....	Black And Tan Fantasy—Creole Love Call—The Mooche
....	Take The "A" Train
....	Mount Harissa
....	Up Jump
....	La Plus Belle Africaine
....	Girdle Hurdle
....	Medley[1]
....	Satin Doll
....	Take The "A" Train
....	The Biggest And Busiest Intersection
....	Misty –vTT
....	Salomé
....	Passion Flower
....	Things Ain't What They Used To Be
....	Jam With Sam
....	Satin Doll

[1]Including: Solitude; In A Sentimental Mood; Don't Get Around Much Anymore; Mood Indigo; I'm Beginning To SeeThe Light; Sophisticated Lady; Caravan; Do Nothin' Till You Hear From Me; It Don't Mean A Thing –vTWtk; I Got It Bad –vTT; I Let A Song Go Out Of My Heart/Don't Get Around Much Anymore.

4 Apr 1968 (S)
Unidentified location (bc)
New York City, NY

DUKE ELLINGTON
No particulars available.

....   Interview

8-11 Apr 1968* (P)
NBC Studios (tc)
Burbank, CA

ELLA FITZGERALD WITH THE DUKE ELLINGTON ORCHESTRA
Vcl, acc. by CA CW HJns ME, LB BCpr CCrs, JHtn JH RP PG HC, JJns KBts LBsn, strings, tim, hrp.

....	DVD	People –vEF
....	DVD	Just One Of Those Things –vEF
....	DVD	Street Of Dreams –vEF
....	DVD	I Can't Stop Loving You –vEF
....	DVD	Summertime –vEF

DUKE ELLINGTON & HIS ORCHESTRA
DE JCmn RJo replace JJns KBts LBsn, omit strings, tim, hrp.

....	DVD	Satin Doll
....	DVD	Things Ain't What They Used To Be
....	DVD	Take The "A" Train

ELLA FITZGERALD WITH THE DUKE ELLINGTON ORCHESTRA
JJns KBts LBsn replace DE JCmn RJo.

....	DVD	Loch Lomond –vEF

> strings, tim, hrp added.

....	DVD	A Foggy Day –vEF

ELLA FITZGERALD WITH DUKE ELLINGTON
Vcl, acc. by DE KBts LBsn.

....	DVD	Don't Get Around Much Anymore –vEF

> KBts LBsn omitted.

....	DVD	Lush Life –vEF[1]

> KBts LBsn added.

....	DVD	Oh! Lady Be Good –vEF

[1]Although DE can be seen sitting behind the keyboard, it is doubtful that it is he who can be heard playing; this show was—at least in part—played back.

ELLA FITZGERALD WITH THE DUKE ELLINGTON ORCHESTRA
Vcl, acc. by the entire band, JJns replaces DE, KBts LBsn omitted, DE directing.

....	DVD	Sweet Georgia Brown –vEF
....	DVD	Lover Man –vEF
....	DVD	Mack The Knife –vEF

> KBts LBsn replace JCmn RJo, DE omitted.

....	DVD	People –vEF

*Taping session; telecast on 15 Jul 1968.

12 Apr 1968   (P)
Grace Cathedral
San Francisco, CA

<u>DUKE ELLINGTON</u>
DE talking.

....   Press Conference

<u>DUKE ELLINGTON WITH ORCHESTRA</u>   ABC Studios (tc)[1]   (P)
DE with a studio orchestra, directed by Johnny Mann.   Los Angeles, CA

....   Medley[2]

> DE interviewed by Joey Bishop.

....   Interview

> DE piano solo.

....   Meditation
....   Sophisticated Lady

[1]Taping session; telecast on 15 Apr 1968.
[2]Including: Mood Indigo; Things Ain't What they Used To Be; Take The "A" Train; Satin Doll.

17 Apr 1968   (P)
El Caballero Country Club
Los Angeles, CA

<u>DUKE ELLINGTON & HIS ORCHESTRA</u>
pp CA CW HJns ME, LB BCpr CCrs, JHtn JH RP PG HC, DE JCmn RJo, TT TWtk.

> DE piano solo.

....   Salute To Morgan State
....   I Can't Get Started

> Entire band.

....   I Let A Song Go Out Of My Heart/Don't Get Around Much Anymore

> JJns replaces DE.

....   Satin Doll
....   I Left My Heart In San Francisco

> DE replaces JJns.

....   The Twitch
....   Mood Indigo
....   Fly Me To The Moon
....   Satin Doll

> DE piano solo.

....   Dance No. 3 (from the Liberian Suite)

> Entire band, CT added.

....   Stompin' At The Savoy
....   Blue Belles Of Harlem
....   Meditation
....   New World A-Comin'
....   New York City Blues

> DE and JJns.

....   Squeeze Me

> Entire band, CT added.

....   Drag
....   Prelude To A Kiss
....   Things Ain't What They Used To Be (incomplete—end of tape)
....   I'm Beginning to See The Light
....   Satin Doll
....   Happy Birthday

> JJns replaces DE, MLgn JWls added.

....   I Got It Bad –vMLgn
....   Tenderly –vMLgn
....   Every Day I Have The Blues –vJWls
....   Jump For Joy –vJWls

> MLgn JWls omitted.

....   Paper Doll
....   Shine On Harvest Moon –vcl by chorus of guests
....   Unidentified title

> DE replaces JJns.

....   Misty –vTT
....   Come Sunday –vTWtk   >>>

> JHtn RP HC, DE.

....   Monologue –DE narration

> Entire band.

....   Sophisticated Lady

> BCrt added.

....   Body And Soul

> BCrt omitted.

....   It Don't Mean A Thing –vTT TWtk
....   Things Ain't What They Used To Be

> JJns replaces DE, JWls added.

....   Blues Medley –vTT TWtl J Wls[1]

> DE replaces JJns, JWls omitted.

....   Satin Doll
....   Tootie For Cootie
....   Me And You –vTT
....   Willow Weep For Me –vTT (?BCrt –tp, ON –ts added.)
....   Take The "A" Train (incomplete—end of tape)
....   Solitude
....   Happy-Go-Lucky Local
....   I Got It Bad
....   Acht O'Clock Rock
....   Satin Doll

[1]Including: Stormy Monday and others.

The above is based on second-hand information about a tape recording of a noisy private birthday party. Date, location, personnel as well as song titles should be correct. Since the tape could not be auditioned, any particulars given should be taken cum granum salis.

19 Apr 1968   (P)
DUKE ELLINGTON & HIS ORCHESTRA   Convention Center
CA CW HJns ME, LB BCpr CCrs, JHtn JH RP PG HC, DE JCmn RJo.   Anaheim, CA

....   Take The "A" Train
....   Take The "A" Train
....   Satin Doll
....   Come Off The Veldt[1]
....   I Got It Bad
....   Acht O'Clock Rock
....   Medley[2]
....   Things Ain't What They Used To Be

[1]This title is a derivative of *Traffic Jam.*
[2]Including: Satin Doll; Solitude; In A Sentimental Mood; Don't Get Around Much Anymore; Mood Indigo; I'm Beginning To See The Light; Sophisticated Lady; Caravan.

25 Apr 1968   (P)
DUKE ELLINGTON & HIS ORCHESTRA   Dane County Exposition Center
CA CW HJns ME, LB BCpr CCrs, JHtn JH RP PG HC, JLnd JCmn RJo.   Madison, Wi

....   Satin Doll

> DE replaces JLnd.

....   Take The "A" Train
....   Take The "A" Train
....   Take The "A" Train
....   Satin Doll
....   Come Off The Veldt
....   Salomé
....   I Got It Bad
....   Acht O'Clock Rock
....   Medley[1]
....   Things Ain't What They Used To Be

[1]Including: Satin Doll; Solitude; In A Sentimental Mood; Don't Get Around Much Anymore; Mood Indigo; I'm Beginning To See The Light; Sophisticated Lady; Caravan.

TONY BENNETT WITH THE DUKE ELLINGTON ORCHESTRA
Vcl, acc. by the same as above, JLnd replaces DE.

....   Making That Love Scene –vTBnt
....   Fool Of Fools –vTBnt
....   Don't Get Around Much Anymore –vTBnt   >>>

....	On The Sunny Side Of The Street –vTBnt
....	I'm Just A Lucky So-And-So –vTBnt
....	Solitude –vTBnt
....	Broadway –vTBnt
....	I Left My Heart In San Francisco –vTBnt
....	I Wanna Be Around –vTBnt
....	If I Ruled The World –vTBnt
....	Keep Smiling At Trouble –vTBnt
....	Yesterday I Heard The Rain –vTBnt
....	Always –vTBnt
....	The Moment Of Truth –vTBnt
....	The Shadow Of Your Smile –vTBnt
....	It Don't Mean A Thing –vTBnt
....	Once In My Life –vTBnt
....	It Don't Mean A Thing –vTBnt

7 May 1968   (P)

DUKE ELLINGTON & HIS ORCHESTRA
CA CW HJns ME, LB BCpr CCrs, JHtn JH RP PG HC, DE JCmn RJo, DGrd TT RG TWtk CCC.

Milwaukee Auditorium
Milwaukee, WI

	THE SECOND SACRED CONCERT
....	Praise God
....	I Will Praise Thee O Lord –vCCC
....	Supreme Being –vCCC
....	Something About Believing –vCCC
....	Almighty God –vCCC
....	The Shepherd
....	Heaven –vTT
....	It's Freedom –vDGrd TT GR TWtk CCC
....	The Biggest And Busiest Intersection
....	Don't Get Down On Your Knees –vTWtk

> TWtk CCC a cappella.

....	Father Forgive –vTWtk CCC

> Entire band.

....	Don't Get Down On Your Knees –vTWtk

> DE JCmn.

....	Meditation

> Entire band.

....	Praise God And Dance –vDGrd

May 1968   (P)
Studios KYW (tc)
Philadelphia, PA

DUKE ELLINGTON & HIS RHYTHM
DE JCmn RJo.

....	Satin Doll
....	Sophisticated Lady

> DE interviewed by Mike Douglas.

....	Interview

> DE JCmn RJo.

....	Take The "A" Train

> DE piano solo.

....	Meditation

20 May-29 Jun 1968 (P)
Private party[1]
Woodbridge, NJ

DUKE ELLINGTON & HIS GROUP
CA, LB, JH PG HC, DE JCmn RJo, TT TWtk.

> DE JCmn.

....	TTC	Meditation

> Entire group.

....	TTC	Satin Doll
....	TTC	Take The "A" Train
....	TTC	Body And Soul
....	TTC	Mood Indigo
....	TTC	Contrapuntal Riposte[2]
....	TTC	Me And You –vTT
....	TTC	Passion Flower
....	TTC	I'm Beginning To See The Light >>>

.... TTC   It Don't Mean A Thing –vTT TWtk
.... TTC   Acht O'Clock Rock
.... TTC   Satin Doll

[1]Issued on TTC as the *Famed Fieldcup Concert*. In fact, this event was hosted by the Fieldcrest Company, and took place most probably during the band's engagement at the Rainbow Grill.
[2]This title is a derivative of *Killian's Lick*.

24 May 1968   (P)
Rainbow Grill
New York City, NY

DUKE ELLINGTON'S OCTET
CA, LB, JH PG HC, DE JCmn RJo.

> DE piano solo.

....   Meditation
....   A Single Petal Of A Rose

> Entire band.

....   Caravan
....   Do Nothin' Till You Hear From Me
....   Body And Soul
....   Satin Doll
....   Come Off The Veldt
....   Acht O'Clock Rock
....   I Got It Bad
....   Things Ain't What They Used To Be
....   I'm Beginning To See The Light
....   Take The "A" Train
....   Sophisticated Lady
....   Alice Blue Gown
....   Kiki
....   I Let A Song Go Out Of My Heart/Don't Get Around Much Anymore
....   Mood Indigo—Serenade To Sweden
....   Happy Birthday
....   Satin Doll

Spring/summer 1968 (S)
Unidentified location
U.S.A. or Canada

DUKE ELLINGTON
DE interviewed by person unknown.

....   Interview

> DE RJo.

....   In The Beginning God

> RJo omitted.

....   It's Freedom
....   Medley[1]

[1]Including: I Got It Bad; I'm Beginning To See The Light; Mood Indigo; Don't Get Around Much Anymore; Caravan; Sophisticated Lady; Solitude; It Don't Mean A Thing; Satin Doll; I Let A Song Go Out Of My Heart.

8 Jun 1968[1]   (S)
Unspecified studio (tc)
New York City, NY

DUKE ELLINGTON & HIS MEN
DE JCmn.

....   Meditation

> DE interviewed by Father Norman O'Connor.

....   Interview

> JH, DE JCmn.

....   Passion Flower

> DE piano solo.

....   Lotus Blossom

[1]Telecast on 9 Jun 1968.

11 Jun 1968   (P)
Bryant Park
New York City, NY

DUKE ELLINGTON & HIS TRIO
DE JCmn RJo, TWtk.

....   Take The "A" Train
....   Satin Doll
....   In A Mellotone
....   Solitude –vTWtk
....   It Don't Mean A Thing –vTWtk

13 Jun 1968   (P)
Rainbow Grill (tc)
New York City, NY

DUKE ELLINGTON'S OCTET
CA, LB, JH PG HC, DE JCmn RJo.

> DE piano solo.

....   Interlude

> Entire band.

....   Take The "A" Train
....   Things Ain't What They Used To Be
....   Sophisticated Lady
....   I'm Beginning To See The Light
....   Mood Indigo
....   Black And Tan Fantasy
....   Take The "A" Train
....   Prelude To A Kiss
....   Solitude
....   It Don't Mean A Thing

> DE JCmn.

....   Meditation

> Entire band.

....   Satin Doll

> DE interviewed by Hugh Downs.

....   Interview

> DE piano solo.

....   Lotus Blossom

DUKE ELLINGTON'S OCTET   (tc)
Same personnel.

....   Take The "A" Train

> DE interviewed by Merv Griffin.

....   Interview

> DE JCmn RJo.

....   Sophisticated Lady
....   Satin Doll

Mid-Jun 1968[1]   (P)
CBS Studios (tc)
New York City, NY

DUKE ELLINGTON'S OCTET
CA, LB, JH PG HC, DE JCmn RJo.

....   Take The "A" Train
....   Mood Indigo
....   Satin Doll
....   Conversation between DE and Father Norman J. O'Connor
....   Things Ain't What They Used To Be
....   Things Ain't What They Used To Be
....   Take The "A" Train

[1]Taping session; telecast on 28 Jul 1968.

23 Jun 1968   (P)
Crescent Avenue Presbyterian Church
Plainfield, NJ

DUKE ELLINGTON & HIS ORCHESTRA
CA CW HJns ME, LB BCpr CCrs, JHtn JH RP PG HC, DE JCmn RJo, DGrd TT RG TWtk choir.

....   THE SECOND SACRED CONCERT
....   Supreme Being —vChoir
....   Something About Believing —vDGrd RG TWtk Choir
....   Almighty God —vDGrd Choir
....   The Shepherd
....   Heaven —vTT
....   It's Freedom —vDGrd TT RG TWtk Choir

1 Jul 1968   (P)
Music Circus
Lambertville, NJ

DUKE ELLINGTON & HIS ORCHESTRA
CA CW HJns ME, LB BCpr CCrs, JHtn JH RP PG HC, DE JCmn RJo, TT TWtk.

....   Take The "A" Train
....   Satin Doll
....   Come Off The Veldt   >>>

....	Kinda Dukish/Rockin' In Rhythm
....	Passion Flower
....	Things Ain't What They Used To Be
....	Blues With Bridge[1]
....	Me And You –vTT
....	Solitude –vTWtk
....	It Don't Mean A Thing –vTT TWtk
....	Acht O'Clock Rock

> JHtn RP HC, DE.

....	Monologue –DE narration

> Entire band.

....	Satin Doll

[1]aka "Something Else"; "A Little Jive"; "Burg."

5 Jul 1968 (P)
Freebody Park
Newport, RI

DUKE ELLINGTON & HIS ORCHESTRA
CA CW HJns MJsn ME, LB BCpr CCrs, RP JH PG HAsh HC, DE JCmn RJo DWsn.

....	Take The "A" Train
....	Take The "A" Train
....	Sophisticated Lady
....	The Biggest And Busiest Intersection
....	Swamp Goo
....	Up Jump
....	Salomé
....	Passion Flower
....	Things Ain't What They Used To Be
....	Satin Doll

6 Jul 1968 (P)
Freebody Park
Newport, RI

DUKE ELLINGTON & HIS ORCHESTRA
CA CW HJns ME, LB BCpr CCrs, RP JH PG HAsh HC, DE JCmn RJo.

....	Take The "A" Train
....	Black And Tan Fantasy—Creole Love Call—The Mooche
....	Take The "A" Train
....	La Plus Belle Africaine/Come Off The Veldt
....	Kinda Dukish/Rockin' In Rhythm
....	Body And Soul
....	Salomé
....	The Star-Crossed Lovers
....	Things Ain't What They Used To Be
....	Satin Doll

7 Jul 1968 (P)
Festival Theatre
Stratford, ON

DUKE ELLINGTON & HIS ORCHESTRA
CA CW HJns ME, LB BCpr CCrs, RP JH PG HAsh HC, DE JCmn RJo, NL TWtk SUC.

	THE SECOND SACRED CONCERT
....	Don't Get Down On Your Knees –vTWtk

> TWtk SUC a cappella.

....	Father Forgive –vTWtk SUC

> Entire band.

....	Don't Get Down On Your Knees –vTWtk
....	Praise God And Dance –vNL SUC

> TWtk a cappella.

....	The Preacher's Song –vTWtk

DUKE ELLINGTON (S)[1]
Interviewed by person unknown.

....	Interview

[1]Backstage.

10 Jul 1968 (P)
Unidentified location
Oak Brook, IL

DUKE ELLINGTON & HIS ORCHESTRA
CA CW HJns ME, LB BCpr CCrs, RP JH PG HAsh HC, DE JCmn RJo, TT TWtk.

....	Take The "A" Train
....	Black And Tan Fantasy—Creole Love Call—The Mooche
....	Take The "A" Train >>>

....	Soul Call
....	Mount Harissa
....	Up Jump
....	Satin Doll
....	Salomé
....	Medley[1]
....	Things Ain't What They Used To Be
....	Me And You –vTT
....	Solitude –vTWtk
....	It Don't Mean A Thing –vTT TWtk
....	Acht O'Clock Rock
....	Satin Doll

[1]Including: I Got It Bad; Don't Get Around Much Anymore; Mood indigo; I'm Beginning To See The Light; Sophisticated Lady; Caravan.

11 Jul 1968   (P)
Historyland
Hayward, WI

DUKE ELLINGTON & HIS ORCHESTRA
CA CW HJns ME, LB BCpr CCrs, RP JH PG HAsh HC, JCmn RJo, TT.

....	The "C" Jam Blues
....	Laura
....	Boo-Dah

> DE added.

....	Contrapuntal Riposte
....	Take The "A" Train
....	Tootie For Cootie
....	Satin Doll
....	Soul Call
....	Salomé
....	Do Nothin' Till You Hear From Me
....	I'm Beginning To See The Light
....	Passion Flower
....	Things Ain't What They Used To Be
....	Just A Little Jive
....	Sophisticated Lady
....	Satin Doll
....	Take The "A" Train
....	Take The "A" Train
....	Kinda Dukish/Rockin' In Rhythm
....	Satin Doll –vTT
....	Stormy Monday Blues –vTT
....	Satin Doll

14 Jul 1968   (P)
Woodland Hills Park
Cleveland, OH

DUKE ELLINGTON & HIS ORCHESTRA
CA CW HJns ME, LB BCpr CCrs, RP JH PG HAsh HC, DE JCmn RJo.

....	Take The "A" Train
....	Satin Doll
....	Mount Harissa
....	Up Jump
....	La Plus Belle Africaine
....	Sophisticated Lady
....	Salomé

3 Aug 1968   (P)
Hollywood Bowl
Los Angeles, CA

DUKE ELLINGTON WITH THE LOS ANGELES SYMPHONY ORCHESTRA
DE JCmn RJo, with the Los Angeles Symphony Orchestra.

....	The Star Spangled Banner
	THE GOLDEN BROOM AND THE GREEN APPLE
....	- Stanza 1 (The Golden Broom)
....	- Stanza 2 (The Green Apple)
....	- Stanza 3 (The Handsome Traffic Policeman)

> JH added.

....	Passion Flower
....	Things Ain't What They Used To Be
....	Medley[1]

> JH omitted.

....	Come Off The Veldt
....	Take The "A" Train
....	Satin Doll >>>

....   Satin Doll

[1]Including: Do Nothin' Till You Hear From Me; Mood Indigo; I'm Beginning To See The Light; Sophisticated Lady;
Caravan; It Don't Mean A Thing; Solitude; Don't Get Around Much Anymore; I Got It Bad; I Let A Song Go Out Of
My Heart/Don't Get Around Much Anymore.

19 Aug 1968   (P)
Steel Pier
DUKE ELLINGTON & HIS ORCHESTRA
CA CW HJns ME, LB BCpr CCrs, RP JH PG HAsh HC, DE JCmn RJo, TT TWtk.   Atlantic City, NJ

....   Sophisticated Lady
....   Caravan
....   Satin Doll
....   Satin Doll
....   Sunny
....   Take The "A" Train
....   Tootie For Cootie
....   I Got It Bad
....   In A Mellotone
....   Main Stem
....   Kinda Dukish/Rockin' In Rhythm
....   Mood Indigo
....   Mount Harissa
....   Up Jump
....   Sunny –vTT
....   Solitude –vTWtk
....   Stormy Monday Blues –vTT
....   The Old Circus Train
....   Satin Doll
....   Jeep's Blues

> JH, DE JCmn RJo.

....   Hodges' Blues

> Entire band.

....   Take The "A" Train

> LB, DE JCmn RJo.

....   Serenade To Sweden

> Entire band.

....   Swamp Goo
....   Acht O'Clock Rock
....   Diminuendo In Blue and Wailing Interval
....   Do Nothin' Till You Hear From Me
....   I Let A Song Go Out Of My Heart/Don't Get Around Much Anymore
....   Ashby's Blues
....   Come Off The Veldt
....   Satin Doll

26 Aug 1968   (P)
High School Stadium
DUKE ELLINGTON & HIS ORCHESTRA
CA CW HJns ME, LB BCpr CCrs, RP JH PG HAsh HC, DE JCmn RJo, TT TWtk.   Woodbridge, NJ

....   Take The "A" Train
....   Soul Call
....   Swamp Goo
....   Take The "A" Train
....   Satin Doll   (S)
....   Come Off The Veldt
....   Oclupaca[1]
....   Salomé
....   I Got It Bad
....   Things Ain't What They Used To Be
....   Sunny –vTT
....   Solitude –vTWtk
....   It Don't Mean A Thing –vTT TWtk
....   Medley[2]

[1]Part of the future *Latin American Suite*.
[2]Including: Do Nothin' Till You Hear from Me; Don't Get Around Much Anymore; Mood Indigo; I'm Beginning To See The
Light; Sophisticated Lady.

2 Sep 1968   (P)
Teatro Municipal (tc)
DUKE ELLINGTON & HIS ORCHESTRA
CA CW HJns WC ME, LB BCpr CCrs, RP JH PG HAsh HC, DE JCmn RJo, TT.   São Paulo, Brazil

.... DC   Medley[1]   >>>

.... DC   Satin Doll
.... DC   Come Off The Veldt
.... DC   Passion Flower
.... DC   Things Ain't What They Used To Be
.... DC   Sunny –vTT

　　　> DE JCmn.

.... DC   Meditation

　　　> Entire band.

.... DC   The "C" Jam Blues
.... DC   Satin Doll

[1]Including: Satin Doll; Do Nothin' Till You Hear From Me; In A Sentimental Mood; Don't Get Around Much Anymore; Mood Indigo; I'm Beginning To See The Light; Sophisticated Lady; Caravan.

DUKE ELLINGTON & HIS ORCHESTRA   5 Sep 1968   (P)
CA CW HJns WC ME, LB BCpr CCrs, RP JH PG HAsh HC, DE JCmn RJo, TT TWtk.   Teatro Gran Rex
                                                                Buenos Aires, Argentina

....   Take The "A" Train
....   Black And Tan Fantasy—Creole Love Call—The Mooche
....   Soul Call
....   Take The "A" Train
....   Mount Harissa
....   Up Jump
....   La Plus Belle Africaine
....   Come Off The Veldt
....   Medley[1]
....   Take The "A" Train
....   B.P. Blues[2]
....   Salomé
....   Passion Flower
....   Things Ain't What They Used To Be
....   Wings And Things
....   I Got It Bad
....   Sunny –vTT
....   Solitude –vTWtk
....   It Don't Mean A Thing –vTT TWtk
....   Every Day I Have The Blues –vTT TWtk
....   Acht O'Clock Rock

　　　> DE JCmn.

....   Meditation

[1]Including: Satin Doll; Do Nothin' Till You Hear From Me; In A Sentimental Mood.
[2]Stands for Black Power.

DUKE ELLINGTON & HIS ORCHESTRA   9 Sep 1968   (P)
CA CW HJns WC ME, LB BCpr CCrs, RP JH PG HAsh HC, DE JCmn RJo, TT TWtk.   Sala del Gran Roche
                                                                La Plata, Argentina

....   Sunny –vTT
....   Solitude –vTWtk

DUKE ELLINGTON & HIS ORCHESTRA   10 Sep 1968   (P)
CA CW HJns WC ME, LB BCpr CCrs, RP JH PG HAsh HC, DE JCmn RJo.   Teatro Gran Rex
                                                                Buenos Aires, Argentina

....   Kinda Dukish/Rockin' In Rhythm
....   Tootie For Cootie
....   Take The "A" Train
....   Chelsea Bridge
....   Cotton Tail

DUKE ELLINGTON & HIS ORCHESTRA   11 Sep 1968   (P)
CA CW HJns WC ME, LB BCpr CCrs, RP JH PG HAsh HC, DE JCmn RJo, TT TWtk.   S.O.D.R.E. Auditorium
                                                                Montevideo, Uruguay

....   Take The "A" Train
....   Black And Tan Fantasy—Creole Love Call—The Mooche
....   Soul Call
....   Take The "A" Train
....   Mount Harissa
....   Up Jump
....   La Plus Belle Africaine
....   Salomé
....   The Birth Of The Blues   >>>

....	Medley[1]
....	Take The "A" Train
....	Kinda Dukish/Rockin' In Rhythm
....	Come Off The Veldt
....	Passion Flower
....	Things Ain't What They Used To Be
....	I Got It Bad
....	Drag
....	Sunny –vTT
....	Solitude –vTWtk
....	It Don't Mean A Thing –vTT TWtk
....	Be Cool And Groovy For Me –vTT TWtk[2]
....	Acht O'Clock Rock

> HAsh, DE JCmn RJo.

....	I Can't Get Started

> Entire band.

....	B.P. Blues
....	Jam With Sam

> DE JCmn.

....	Meditation

> Entire band.

....	Chico Cuadradino[3]

[1]Including: Satin Doll; In A Sentimental Mood; Do Nothin' Till You Hear From Me; Just Squeeze Me; Don't Get Around Much Anymore; Mood Indigo; I'm Beginning To See The Light; Sophisticated Lady; Caravan.
[2]sa "Put-Tin."
[3]Part of the future *Latin American Suite*.

                                                                              12 Sep 1968   (P)
DUKE ELLINGTON & HIS ORCHESTRA   Teatro Gran Rex
CA CW HJns WC ME, LB BCpr CCrs, RP JH PG HAsh HC, DE JCmn RJo.   Buenos Aires, Argentina

....	The "C" Jam Blues
....	Kinda Dukish/Rockin' In Rhythm

> PG, DE JCmn RJo.

....	Happy Reunion

> Entire band.

....	Girdle Hurdle
....	The Shepherd
....	Take The "A" Train
....	The Mooche
....	Soul Call
....	La Plus Belle Africaine
....	Summertime
....	Summertime
....	The Prowling Cat
....	Basin Street Blues
....	Come Off The Veldt
....	Prelude To A Kiss
....	Drag
....	Jeep's Blues
....	Things Ain't What They Used To Be
....	All Of Me
....	Acht O'Clock Rock

> HAsh, DE JCmn RJo.

....	I Can't Get Started

> Entire band.

....	B.P. Blues
....	Jam With Sam

> DE piano solo.

....	The Sleeping Lady And The Giant Who Watches Over Her[1]

> Entire band.

....	How High The Moon

[1]Part of the future *Latin American Suite*.

15 Sep 1968   (P)
Teatro Gran Rex
Buenos Aires, Argentina

DUKE ELLINGTON & HIS ORCHESTRA
CA CW JHns WC ME, LB BCpr CCrs, RP PG HAsh HC, DE JCmn RJo.

> PG, DE JCmn RJo.

....   Happy Reunion

> Entire band.

....   Cotton Tail
....   How High The Moon
....   Tootie For Cootie
....   Mood Indigo
....   Come Off The Veldt
....   HARLEM
....   The "C" Jam Blues
....   The Birth Of The Blues
....   Basin Street Blues
....   Things Ain't What They Used To Be
....   B.P. Blues

> DE JCmn RJo.

....   Latin American Sunshine[1]

[1]Part of the future *Latin American Suite.*

19 Sep 1968   (P)
Marine Stadium
Miami, FL

DUKE ELLINGTON & HIS ORCHESTRA
CA CW HJns WC ME, LB BCpr CCrs, RP JH PG HAsh HC, DE JCmn RJo.

....   Take The "A" Train
....   Black And Tan Fantasy—Creole Love Call—The Mooche
....   Soul Call
....   Take The "A" Train
....   Mount Harissa
....   Up Jump
....   Satin Doll
....   Salomé
....   The Biggest And Busiest Intersection
....   Prelude To A Kiss
....   Things Ain't What They Used To Be
....   Medley[1]

[1]Including: In A Sentimental Mood; I Let A Song Go Out Of My Heart; Do Nothin' Till You Hear From Me; Just Squeeze Me; Don't Get Around Much Anymore; Mood Indigo; I Got It Bad; I'm Beginning To See The Light; Sophisticated Lady; Caravan.

23-29 Sep 1968 (P/T[1])
Various locations
Mexico

DUKE ELLINGTON & HIS ORCHESTRA
CA CW HJns WC ME, LB BCpr CCrs, RP JH PG HAsh HC, DE JCmn RJo.

....   Happy-Go-Lucky Local

                                       THE LATIN AMERICAN SUITE[2]
.... AV   - Chico Cuadradino
.... AV   - Latin American Sunshine[3]
....   - The Sleeping Lady And The Giant Who Watches Over Her
....   - Oclupaca
.... AV   Take The "A" Train
....   Mood Indigo—I Got It Bad
.... AV   Satin Doll
.... AV   Come Off The Veldt
....   Things Ain't What They Used To Be

> DE piano solo.

....   A Single Petal Of The Rose

[1]Documentary "The Mexican Suite"; probably filmed in Puebla (23 Sep) and Tequesquitengo (24 Sep).
[2]Presented as "Mexicantipation."
[3]Presented as "Mexican Sunshine."

23-29 Sep 1968 (P/T[1])
Various locations
Mexico

DUKE ELLINGTON & HIS ORCHESTRA
CA CW HJns WC ME, LB BCpr CCrs, RP JH PG HAsh HC, DE JCmn/JRo RJo, TT.

.... Trg   Satin Doll
.... Trg   Black And Tan Fantasy—Creole Love Call—The Mooche
.... Trg   Happy-Go-Lucky Local   >>>

THE LATIN AMERICAN SUITE

....	Trg	- Chico Cuadradino
....	Trg	- Latin American Sunshine
....	Trg	- The Sleeping Lady And The Giant Who Watches Over Her
....	Trg	- Oclupaca
....	Trg	It Don't Mean A Thing —vTT
....	Trg	I Got It Bad
....	Trg	Things Ain't What They Used To Be
....	Trg	Mood Indigo
....	Trg	Take The "A" Train
....	Trg	Sophisticated Lady
....	Trg	Do Nothin' Till You Hear From Me

[1]Documentary "Memories Of The Duke"; including footage from Guadalajara (26 Sep) and Mexico City (29 Sep), with intermittent comments by CW and RP. The Trg release contains the music portion only, plus a second *Mood Indigo* (Snader telesc. #13004). The closing *"A" Train* is a repeat of the opening track and has therefore not been listed here.

2 Oct 1968　　(P)
Music Hall
Cleveland, OH

DUKE ELLINGTON & HIS ORCHESTRA
CA CW HJns WC ME, LB BCpr CCrs, RP JH PG HAsh HC, DE JCmn RJo, TT TWtk.

....	Take The "A" Train
....	Soul Call
....	Satin Doll
....	Take The "A" Train
....	Mount Harissa
....	I Got It Bad
....	Things Ain't What They Used To Be
....	Medley[1]
....	Acht O'Clock Rock

[1]Including: Do Nothin' Till You Hear From Me; Just Squeeze Me; Don't Get Around Much Anymore; Mood Indigo; I'm Beginning To See The Light; Solitude —vTWTk, It Don't Mean A Thing —vTT TWtk; Be Cool And Groovy For Me —vTT TWtk; Sophisticated Lady; Caravan.

14 Oct 1968　　(P)
Flagship Dinner Theater
Union, NJ

DUKE ELLINGTON & HIS ORCHESTRA
CA HJns WC ME, LB BCpr CCrs, RP JH PG HAsh HC, DE JCmn RJo, TT TWtk.

....	Boo-Dah
....	Black And Tan Fantasy—Creole Love Call—The Mooche
....	Soul Call
....	Mount Harissa
....	Up Jump
....	Take The "A" Train
....	Warm Valley
....	Things Ain't What They Used To Be
....	I Let A Song Go Out Of My Heart/Don't Get Around Much Anymore
....	I Got It Bad
....	Drag
....	Sophisticated Lady
....	Salomé
....	Satin Doll
....	Sunny —vTT
....	Solitude —vTWtk
....	It Don't Mean A Thing —vTT TWtk
....	Be Cool And Groovy For Me —vTT TWtk
....	Acht O'Clock Rock
....	Satin Doll

DUKE ELLINGTON & HIS ORCHESTRA
TWtk omitted, otherwise same personnel.

....	The "C" Jam Blues
....	Caravan
....	Do Nothin' Till You Hear From Me
....	Latin American Sunshine
....	Azure
....	I'm Beginning To See The Light
> HAsh, DE JCmn RJo.	
....	I Can't Get Started
> Entire band.	
....	B.P. Blues
....	Willow Weep For Me —vTT
....	Misty —vTT　　>>>

....	Stormy Monday Blues –vTT
....	Prelude To A Kiss
....	All Of Me
....	On The Sunny Side Of The Street
....	Oclupaca
....	Satin Doll
....	The Sleeping Lady And The Giant Who Watches Over Her
....	U.M.M.G.
....	The Peanut Vendor
....	Take The "A" Train

*At about this time DE started practicing his "delayed entrance" more regularly, i.e. he was not present for the opening
number, usually "The "C" Jam Blues" or "Take The "A" Train" or "Boo-Dah" in this case. He would enter the stage only
during the final chords of the tune without playing one note. We will consider him as being present regardless.*

	26 Oct 1968 (P)
	Benjamin Franklin Junior High School
	New Castle, PA

DUKE ELLINGTON & HIS ORCHESTRA
CA CW HJns WC ME, LB BCpr CCrs, RP JH PG HAsh HC, DE JCmn RJo, TT TWtk.

....	Take The "A" Train
....	Black And Tan Fantasy—Creole Love Call—The Mooche
....	Soul Call
....	Take The "A" Train
....	Mount Harissa
....	Up Jump
....	Satin Doll
....	Salomé
....	The Birth Of The Blues
....	Medley[1]
....	Take The "A" Train
....	The Biggest And Busiest Intersection
....	Prelude To A Kiss
....	Things Ain't What They Used To Be
....	I Got It Bad
....	Sunny –vTT
....	Misty –vTT
....	Stormy Monday Blues –vTT TWtk
....	Satin Doll

> HAsh, DE JCmn RJo.

....	I Can't Get Started

> Entire band.

....	Jam With Sam
....	Things Ain't What They Used To Be

[1]Including: I Let A Song Go Out Of My Heart; In A Sentimental Mood; Do Nothin' Till You Hear From Me; Just Squeeze Me.

	5 Nov 1968 (S)
	National Recording Studios[1]
	New York City, NY

DUKE ELLINGTON & HIS ORCHESTRA
CA CW WC ME, LB BCpr CCrs, RP JH PG HAsh HC, DE JCmn RJo.

		THE LATIN AMERICAN SUITE
....	Fan	1 Oclupaca
....	Fan	2 Chico Cuadradino
....	Fan	3 Eque[2]
....	Fan	5 The Sleeping Lady And The Giant Who Watches Over Her
....	Fan	6 Latin American Sunshine
....	Fan	7 Brasilliance

[1]At Fifth Avenue and 59th Street.
[2]Stands for "Equator."

Part 4 of the suite—"Tina"—has been recorded only on 7 Jan 1970.

	6 Nov 1968 (S/T*)
	National Recording Studios, Edison Hall
	New York City, NY

DUKE ELLINGTON & HIS ORCHESTRA
WC, CCrs, RP JH PG HAsh HC, DE JCmn RJo.

> DE JCmn RJo.

....	Az	-1	Race[1]
....	Az	-2	Race (incomplete)

> DE piano solo.

....	Az	-3	Race (incomplete)

> Entire band.

....	Az[2]	-4	Race >>>

....		-5	Race (incomplete)
....		-6	Race (incomplete)
....		-8	Race
....		-9	Race (incomplete)
....		-10	Opening Titles[3] (incomplete)
....			Opening Titles (incomplete)
....		-11	Opening Titles (incomplete)
....			Opening Titles (incomplete)
....		-13	Opening Titles (incomplete)
....	Az[2]	-14	Opening Titles (incomplete)
....		-15	Race (intro)
....		-16	Race (intro)
....		-17	Race (intro)
....		-19	Race (intro)
....		-20	Race (intro)
....			Pastel (incomplete)
....			Pastel (incomplete)
....			Pastel (incomplete)
....			Pastel (incomplete)
....			Pastel (incomplete)
....		-21	Pastel (incomplete)
....		-22	Pastel (incomplete)
....		-24	Pastel
....		-25	Pastel
....		-26	Pastel
....			Pastel (incomplete)
....			Pastel (incomplete)

[1]*sa* "Kiki."
[2]The original releases on WEA have been edited; the only complete versions can be found on Az.
[3]*aka* "A.C."

DUKE ELLINGTON & HIS ORCHESTRA
Same personnel.

....		-1	Race
....		-3	Race (incomplete)
....	Az	-4	Race (incomplete)
....	WEA	-5	Race (incomplete)
....		-6	Racing[1]
....	WEA	-7	Racing
....		-9	Pastel (incomplete)
....		-10	Pastel (incomplete)
....		-12	Pastel (incomplete)
....		-14	Pastel
....		-15	Pastel (incomplete)
....	RDB	-16	Pastel

> DE piano solo.

....	WEA	-17	Trump[2]

> Entire band.

....			Prat[3]
....		-21	Prat
....	Az	-23	Prat
....		-25	Sonnet (incomplete)
....		-26	Sonnet
....		-27	Sonnet
....		-28	Sonnet
....		-30	Sonnet

> DE piano solo.

....	WEA	-31	Piano Pastel

> Entire band.

....		-32	Sonnet
....	WEA	-33	Sonnet
....		-35	Promenade[4]
....		-37	Promenade
....	WEA	-38	Promenade
....	Az	-42	Pastel
....		-43	Race
....	Az	-46	Race
....	Az[5]	-49	Opening Titles
....		-50	Sonnet
....		-51	Sonnet >>>

....	Az	-52	Sonnet (incomplete)
....	Az	-53	Sonnet
....	Az	-55	Race
....	Az	-56	Race
....	WEA	-59	Drawings
....	Az	-60	Improvisations[6]
....	Az	-61	Improvisations
....	WEA	-62	Improvisations

[1]*sa* "Race."
[2]*sa* "Anticipation And Hesitation."
[3]=Tarp.
[4]*aka* "Red Circle."
[5]The original release on WEA has been edited; the only complete version can be found on Az.
[6]*aka* "Marcia Regina"; *sa* "The Queen's Guard."
*Music for the documentary "Racing World"; see also sessions on 23 Nov and 3 Dec 1968.

9 Nov 1968   (P)
National Guard Armory
Washington, DC

DUKE ELLINGTON & HIS ORCHESTRA
CA CW WC ME, LB BCpr CCrs, RP JH PG HAsh HC, DE JCmn RJo, TT TWtk.

....	The "C" Jam Blues
....	Laura
....	Take The "A" Train
....	Soul Call
....	Take The "A" Train
....	Mount Harissa
....	Up Jump
....	Satin Doll
....	Salomé
....	Medley[1]
....	Take The "A" Train
....	Tootie For Cootie
....	The Biggest And Busiest Intersection
....	I Got It Bad
....	Things Ain't What They Used To Be
....	Sunny –vTT
....	I'm Just A Lucky So-And-So –vTWtk
....	Stormy Monday Blues –vTT TWtk
....	Satin Doll

[1]Including: I Let A Song Go Out Of My Heart; In A Sentimental Mood; Do Nothin' Till You Hear From Me; Just Squeeze Me; Don't Get Around Much Anymore; Mood Indigo; I'm Beginning To See The Light; Solitude –vTWtk; It Don't Mean A Thing –vTT; Be Cool And Groovy For Me –vTT TWtk; Sophisticated Lady.

23 Nov 1968   (S/T[1])
National Recording Studios, Edison Hall
New York City, NY

DUKE ELLINGTON & HIS GROUP
WC, LB, JH PG HAsh HC, DE JCmn RJo.

> HAsh HC, DE JCmn RJo.

....	RDB[2]		[3]	Race
....	RDB			Race
....				Race
....				Race
....				Race
....				Race
....				Race
....	RDB	-1		Race

> PG added.

....	Az	-2	Race

> DE piano solo.

....	-3	Meditation

> HAsh, DE JCmn RJo.

....		-4	I Can't Get Started
....	Saj	-5	I Can't Get Started
....	Az		I Can't Get Started (incomplete)
....	Az		I Can't Get Started (incomplete)
....	Az		I Can't Get Started (incomplete)

> Entire band.

....	Blues[4]
....	Blues
....	Blues (incomplete) >>>

....		-9	Blues (incomplete)
....		-11	Blues
....			Blues (incomplete)
....			Blues
....		-13	Blues (incomplete)
....			Blues (incomplete)
....		-14	Blues
....			Just A Little Jive[5] (incomplete)
....			Just A Little Jive (incomplete)
....			Just A Little Jive (incomplete)
....		-15	Just A Little Jive (incomplete)
....	Az	-16	Just A Little Jive (incomplete)
....	Az	-17	Just A Little Jive
....			Country[6] (incomplete)
....	RDB		Country (incomplete)
....			Country (incomplete)
....	RDB	-19	Country

[1]Music for the documentary "Racing World"; see also sessions on 6 Nov and 3 Dec 1968.
[2]It is not certain which one of the takes of "Race" has been broadcast by Radio Denmark.
[3]This title was cut for the documentary "Racing World."
[4]aka "Nati"; sa "First Bass"; "Kentucky Avenue, A.C."
[5]sa "Blues With Bridge"; "Jive"; "Burg"; "Something Else."
[6]aka "Riverboat."

25 Nov 1968   (S)
Julie's Mansion Restaurant (bc)[1]
Toronto, ON

DUKE ELLINGTON & FRIENDS
DE, Ron Collier, John Norris, ?Louis Applebaum, interviewed by Ted O'Reilly.

....	Att		Interview

[1]Broadcast on 29 Nov 1968.

29 Nov 1968   (S)
National Recording Studios, Edison Hall
New York City, NY

DUKE ELLINGTON & HIS GROUP
WC, BCpr, RP JH PG HAsh HC, DE JCmn RJo.

> DE piano solo.

....		-2	Meditation (incomplete)
....		-3	Meditation (incomplete)
....		-4	Meditation (incomplete)
....		-6	Meditation (incomplete)

> WC, RP JH PG HAsh, JCmn RJo added.

....		-7	Waiting For You[1]
....	Saj	-8	Waiting For You

> BCpr, HC added.

....	Saj	-9	Knuf[2]
....	Saj	-12	Gigl[3]

> DE JCmn.

....	Saj	-14	Meditation

> JH, RJo added.

....	Saj	-15	Sophisticated Lady

> Entire band.

....	Saj	-16	Just Squeeze Me

> PG, DE JCmn RJo.

....	Saj	-19	In A Sentimental Mood

> Entire band.

....	Saj	-20	Mood Indigo
....		-22	Reva
....	Saj	-24	I Let A Song Go Out Of My Heart/Don't Get Around Much Anymore
....	RDB	-25	Reva (incomplete)
....		-26	Reva
....	Saj	-28	Reva
....	Saj	-29	The "C" Jam Blues
....	RDB	-30	Caravan

[1]aka "Just Blues."
[2]=Funk.
[3]Part of the future ballet suite *The River*.

3 Dec 1968   (S/T[1])

DUKE ELLINGTON & HIS ORCHESTRA   National Recording Studios, Edison Hall
CA CW WC ME, LB BCpr CCrs, RP JH PG HAsh HC, DE JCmn RJo, (TT TWtk).   New York City, NY

.... Az   Copa II
.... WEA   Daily Double[2]

[1]Music for the documentary "Racing World"; see also sessions on 6 and 23 Nov 1968.
[2]sa "Race."

                                        THE DEGAS SUITE[1] (summation)
         WEA   -14/-49   - Opening Titles
         WEA   -4   - Race
         WEA   -7   - Racing
         WEA   -17   - Trump[2]
         WEA   -62   - Improvisations
         WEA   - Daily Double
         WEA   -59   - Drawings
         WEA   -31   - Piano Pastel
         WEA   -38   - Promenade
         WEA   -33   - Sonnet
         WEA   -5   - Race

[1]Released—partly edited—under this title on WEA; aka "Impressionists At The Race Track." (The sequence of songs on
the record differs both from label and liner notes.)
[2]"Piano Pastel" on WEA.

.... Saj   Elos[1]
.... Saj   Be Cool And Groovy For Me –vTT[2]
....   Be Cool And Groovy For Me –vTWtk[2]
....   Be Cool And Groovy For Me –vTT TWtk[2]

         > SWsp added.

....   Be Cool And Groovy For Me –vSWsp

         > SWsp omitted.

.... RDB   Ortseam[3]

[1]aka "Elous" (=Soul[e]).
[2]The vocals have been overdubbed: TT on 4 Dec 1968; TT+TWtk on 14 Jul 1969; TWtk on 18 Sep 1969.
[3]=Maestro.

5 Dec 1968   (P)

DUKE ELLINGTON & HIS RHYTHM   Studios KYW (tc)
DE JCmn RJo.   Philadelphia, PA

....   I'm Beginning To See The Light
         > RJo omitted.

....   Meditation
         > DE interviewed by Mike Douglas.

....   Interview
         > Trio.

....   La Plus Belle Africaine
         > Studio ochestra added.

....   Satin Doll

Dec 1968[1]   (P)

DUKE ELLINGTON & HIS RHYTHM   Studios KYW (tc)
DE JCmn RJo.   Philadelphia, PA

....   Salute To Morgan State
....   Sophisticated Lady

         > DE interviewed by Mike Douglas.

....   Interview
         > Trio.

....   Caravan.

[1]Telecast on 29 Dec 1968.

6 Dec 1968   (P)

DUKE ELLINGTON & HIS ORCHESTRA   Academy of Music
CA CW WC ME, LB BCpr CCrs, RP JH PG HAsh HC, DE JCmn RJo, TT TWtk.   Philadelphia, PA

....   Take The "A" Train   >>>

....	Soul Call
....	Take The "A" Train
....	I Got It Bad
....	Things Ain't What They Used To Be
....	The Birth of The Blues
....	La Plus Bell Africaine—Come Off The Veldt
....	Medley[1]
....	Jam With Sam
....	Stormy Monday Blues –vTT TWtk
....	Happy Birthday
....	Satin Doll

[1]Including: Satin Doll; In A Sentimental Mood; Do Nothin' Till You Hear From Me; Just Squeeze Me; Don't Get Around Much Anymore; Mood Indigo; I'm Beginning To See The Light; Solitude –vTWtk; It Don't Mean A Thing –vTT; Be Cool And Groovy For Me –vTT TWtk; Sophisticated Lady; Caravan.

Dec 1968[1]   (S)
Unidentified location (tc)
New York City, NY

DUKE ELLINGTON
DE interviewed by John Dankworth.

....   Interview

[1]Telecast on 31 May 1969.

27 Dec 1968   (P)
United Methodist Church

DUKE ELLINGTON & HIS ORCHESTRA
CA CW WC ME, LB BCpr CCrs, RP JH PG HAsh HC, DE JCmn RJo, DGrd NL BPmr TWtk choir.   San Diego, CA

	THE SECOND SACRED CONCERT
....	Praise God
....	Supreme Being -vChoir
....	Something About Believing –vChoir
....	Almighty God –vDGrd Choir
....	The Shepherd
....	Heaven –vDGrd
....	It's Freedom –vDGrd NL BPmr TWtk Choir

> DE JCmn.

....	Meditation

> Entire band.

....	The Biggest And Busiest Intersection
....	T.G.T.T. –vNL
....	Don't Get Down On Your Knees –vTWtk

> TWtk Choir a cappella.

....	Father Forgive –vTWtk Choir

> Entire band.

....	Don't Get Down On Your Knees –vTWtk
....	Praise God And Dance –vNL Choir

> TWtk a cappella.

....	The Preacher's Song –vTWtk

31 Dec 1968   (P)
Astro Hall (bc)
Houston, TX

DUKE ELLINGTON & HIS ORCHESTRA
CA CW WC ME, LB BCpr CCrs, RP JH PG HAsh HC, DE JCmn RJo, TT TWtk.

....	Take The "A" Train
....	Satin Doll

....	Auld Lang Syne	1 Jan 1969
....	Be Cool And Groovy For Me –vTT TWtk	
....	Prelude To A Kiss	
....	Things Ain't What They Used To Be	
....	Jam With Sam	
....	Mood Indigo –vTT TWtk	

The above is a continuous performance and has therefore not been separated at the dateline.

2 Jan 1969   (P)
ABC Studios (tc)
Los Angeles, CA

DUKE ELLINGTON WITH BAND
DE HEls RBrn FC.

....	C.E.B. Blues[1]

> DE interviewed by Joey Bishop.

....	Interview >>>

> DE with band.

....   The "C" Jam Blues
....   Interview (ctd.)
....   Love You Madly

[1]Stands for Capp, Ellis, Brown.

DUKE ELLINGTON & HIS ORCHESTRA   5 Jan 1969
CA CW WC ME, LB BCpr CCrs, RP JH PG HAsh HC, DE JCmn RJo, TT TWtk.   Disneyland
                                                           Anaheim, CA

....   Take The "A" Train
....   Take The "A" Train
....   Prelude To A Kiss
....   Things Ain't What They Used To Be
....   The Birth Of The Blues
....   Come Off The Veldt
....   Medley[1]

[1]Including: Satin Doll; In A Sentimental Mood; Do Nothin' Till You Hear From Me; Just Squeeze Me –vTT; Don't Get Around Much Anymore; Mood Indigo –vTT; I'm Beginning To See The Light; Solitude –vTT TWtk; It Don't Mean A Thing –vTT TWtk, Be Cool And Groovy For Me –vTT TWtk; Sophisticated Lady; Caravan.

DUKE ELLINGTON & HIS ORCHESTRA   20 Jan 1969   (P)
CA CW WC ME RN ??, LB BCpr CCrs, RP JH PG HAsh HC, DE JCmn RJo, TT SWsp TWtk ??.   Smithsonian Institution
                                                           Washington, DC

....   Hail To The Chief
....   Satin Doll
....   Prelude To A Kiss
....   Drag
....   It Don't Mean A Thing
....   Take The "A" Train
....   Things Ain't What They Used To Be
....   Caravan
....   Sophisticated Lady
....   Just Squeeze Me
....   Solitude –vTT TWtk
....   It Don't Mean A Thing –vTT TWtk
....   Be Cool And Groovy For Me –vTT TWtk
....   Acht O'Clock Rock
....   Satin Doll –vSWsp ??
....   Mood Indigo
....   I Let A Song Go Out Of My Heart/Don't Get Around Much Anymore
....   Drag
....   I Can't Get Started
....   B.P. Blues –vSWsp
....   Tootie For Cootie
....   Satin Doll

DUKE ELLINGTON & HIS ORCHESTRA   25 Jan 1969   (S)
CA CW WC ME, LB BCpr CCrs, RP JH PG HAsh HC, DE JCmn RJo.   Pfister Hotel
                                                           Milwaukee, WI

....   HARLEM
....   HARLEM
....   HARLEM
....   HARLEM
....   HARLEM
....   HARLEM
....   HARLEM
....   HARLEM

The above is a rehearsal session.

DUKE ELLINGTON & HIS ORCHESTRA   18 Feb 1969   (P)
CA CW WC ME, LB BCpr CCrs, RP JH PG HAsh HC, DE JCmn RJo, TT TWtk.   Coliseum
                                                         St. Petersburg, FL

....   Take The "A" Train
....   Black And Tan Fantasy—Creole Love Call—The Mooche
....   Soul Call
....   Mount Harissa
....   Up Jump
....   The Birth Of The Blues
....   Salomé
....   Medley[1]
....   Take The "A" Train   >>>

....		Come Off The Veldt
....		Prelude To A Kiss
....		Things Ain't What They Used To Be
....		I Got It Bad
....		Drag
....		All Of Me

> BCpr, DE JCmn RJo.

....   The Nearness Of You

> Entire band.

....   Stormy Monday Blues –vTT TWtk
....   Satin Doll

[1]Including: Satin Doll; In A Sentimental Mood; I Let A Song Go Out Of My Heart; Do Nothin' Till You Hear From Me; Just Squeeze Me; Don't Get Around Much Anymore; Mood Indigo; I'm Beginning To See The Light; Solitude –vTT TWtk; It Don't Mean A Thing –vTT TWtk; Be Cool And Groovy For Me –vTT TWtk; Sophisticated Lady; Caravan.

                                                        25 Feb 1969   (S)

DUKE ELLINGTON & HIS ORCHESTRA   National Recording Studios
CA CW WC ME, LB BCpr CCrs, RP JH PG HAsh HC, DE JCmn RJo, JS OB.   New York City, NY

....   Woman –vOB
....   Something About Believing –vJS

                                                        Mar 1969   (P)

DUKE ELLINGTON & HIS ORCHESTRA   Casbah Lounge, Sahara Hotel
CA CW WC ME, LB BCpr CCrs, RP JH PG HAsh HC, DE JCmn RJo, SWsp.   Las Vegas, NV

....   The "C" Jam Blues

> DE piano solo.

....   Kinda Dukish

> Entire band.

....   Satin Doll
....   Take The "A" Train
....   Walkin' And Singin' The Blues –vSWsp
....   Creole Love Call
....   I Got It Bad

                                                        Mar 1969[1]   (S)

DUKE ELLINGTON   Sahara Hotel (tc)
DE interviewed by Boy Edgar.   Las Vegas, NV

....   Interview

> DE piano solo.

....   Moon Maiden
....   Delta Derenade
....   Black Beauty

[1]Taped for Dutch TV during the band's engagement at the Sahara Hotel, in the time from 4-29 Mar 1969. The date of the telecast is not known.

                                                        9 Mar 1969   (P)

DUKE ELLINGTON WITH THE CALIFORNIA YOUTH SYMPHONY ORCHESTRA   Stanford University
DE with the California Youth Symphony Orchestra, Aaron Sten conducting.   Palo Alto, CA

.... RDB   The Mooche
....   Mood Indigo
....   Sophisticated Lady
....   Solitude
....   Alcibiades[1]

                          THE GOLDEN BROOM AND THE GREEN APPLE[2]
....   - Stanza 1 (The Golden Broom)
....   - Stanza 2 (The Green Apple)
....   - Stanza 3 (The Handsome Traffic Policeman)

....   Take The "A" Train
....   Things Ain't What They Used To Be

> TWtk added.

....   Medley[3]

> TWtk omitted.

....   Satin Doll
....   Caravan
....   The "C" Jam Blues   >>>

[1]*sa* "Timon Of Athens March"; part of the music for *Timon Of Athens*.
[2]DE conducting.
[3]Including: Don't You Know I Care?; In A Sentimental Mood; Prelude To A Kiss; Do Nothin' Till You Hear From Me; Don't Get Around Much Anymore; I Got It Bad; I'm Beginning To See The Light; Jump For Joy; I Like The Sunrise –vTWtk; It Don't Mean A Thing –vTWtk; Be Cool And Groovy For Me –vTWtk; I Let A Song Go Out Of My Heart/Don't Get Around Much Anymore.

                                                                1-5 Apr 1969[1]   (S)
DUKE ELLINGTON, MERCER ELLINGTON, CAT ANDERSON, STANLEY DANCE   Unidentified location(s) (tc)
DE, ME, CA and Stanley Dance interviewed for Radio Denmark on the occasion of DE's   New York City, NY
forthcoming 70th birthday.

....   Interviews[2]

[1]Telecast in Denmark on 29 Apr 1969.
[2]The above consists of a series of five interviews, conducted in the time from 1 to 5 Apr 1969.

                                                                3 Apr 1969   (S)
DUKE ELLINGTON & HIS ORCHESTRA   National Recording Studios
CA CW WC ME, LB BCpr CCrs, RP JH PG HAsh HC, DE PK RJo, SWsp.   New York City, NY

....   -1   Walkin' And Singin' The Blues –vSWsp
....   -3   Walkin' And Singin' The Blues –vSWsp
....   -4   The Blues –vSWsp (incomplete)
....   -5   The Blues –vSWsp (incomplete)
....   -6   The Blues –vSWsp (incomplete)
....   -7   The Blues –vSWsp (incomplete)
....   -8   The Blues –vSWsp
....   The Blues (rehearsal)
....   -10   The Blues –vSWsp
.... Az   -11   Kinda Dukish/Rockin' In Rhythm

                                                                4 Apr 1969   (S)
DUKE ELLINGTON & HIS ORCHESTRA   National Recording Studios
CA CW WC ME, LB BCpr CCrs, RP JH PG HAsh HC, DE PK RJo, SWsp.   New York City, NY

....   -2   I Love My Lovin' Lover –vSWsp
....   -3   I Love My Lovin' Lover –vSWsp

> DE piano solo.

....   Kinda Dukish
....   Kinda Dukish

> Entire band.

....   -4   Kinda Dukish/Rockin' In Rhythm

> JJns replaces DE.

.... RDB   -5   I Love My Lovin' Lover –vSWsp
....   I Love My Lovin' Lover (incomplete)
....   I Love My Lovin' Lover (incomplete)
....   -7   Walkin' And Singin' The Blues –vSWsp

> DE replaces JJns.

....   -10   The Blues (incomplete)
....   -11   The Blues –vSWsp (incomplete)
....   -13   The Blues –vSWsp (incomplete)
....   -14   The Blues (incomplete)
.... RDB   Happy Birthday
....   -18   The Blues –vSWsp
....   You Don't Love Me No More –vSWsp (incomplete)
....   -19   You Don't Love Me No More –vSWsp
....   -20   You Don't Love Me No More –vSWsp
....   -21   You Don't Love Me No More (incomplete)
....   -22   You Don't Love Me No More –vSWsp[1]

[1]The vocal for this item has been overdubbed on 18 Apr 1969.

                                                                6 Apr 1969   (P)
TONY BENNETT WITH DUKE ELLINGTON & HIS ORCHESTRA   CBS Studios (tc)
Vcl, acc. by CA CW WC ME, LB BCpr CCrs, RP JH PG HAsh HC, DE PK RJo.   New York City, NY

....   Rockin' In Rhythm
....   Making That Love Scene –vTBnt

> DE PK RJo, TBnt.

....   Solitude –TBnt

> Entire band.

....   What The World Needs Now –vTBnt[1]   >>>

....   People –vTBnt

[1]Complete: "What The World Needs Now Is Love Sweet Love."

                                                                        25 Apr 1969   (T)[1]
DUKE ELLINGTON & HIS ORCHESTRA   National Recording Studios, Edison Hall
CW WC, BGrn BPwl, RP PG HAsh HC, DE PK RJo.   New York City, NY

.... RDB   -1   What Good Am I Without You?
.... RDB   -2   What Good Am I Without You?
.... RDB   -4   What Good Am I Without You?
.... RDB   -5   What Good Am I Without You?
.... RDB   -8   What Good Am I Without You? (insert)
.... RDB   -10   What Good Am I Without You?
.... RDB   -11   What Good Am I Without You?
.... RDB   -14   Hullucinations
.... RDB   -15   Hallucinations

      > DE PK RJo.

....   -17   Neo-Creole[2]
....   -18   Neo-Creole
.... Az   -19   Neo-Creole

      > Entire band.

.... RDB   -21   Wanderlust
.... Pab[3] -22   Wanderlust
....   -23   What Good Am I Without You?
....   What Good Am I Without You?
....   What Good Am I Without You?
....   What Good Am I Without You?
....   -24   Background music
....   -27   Background music
.... RDB   -28   Background music
.... RDB   -30   Background music
....   -31   Background music

[1]Music for the motion picture "Change Of Mind"; see also sessions on 23 and 26 May 1969.
[2]aka "Neo-Creo"; this title is a derivative of *Creole Rhapsody*.
[3]Recording dates and personnel as per sleeve notes for Pab 2310-815, are incorrect for all titles, except for "Bateau."

                                                                        26 Apr 1969[1]   (S)
DUKE ELLINGTON   Unidentified location(s) (tc)
DE piano and talking.   New York City, NY

....   Solitude
....   Interview (segmented)
....   "To Duke with Love"[2]

[1]Date of Swedish telecast; taped probably in early April 1969.
[2]A celebration of Duke Ellington: Interviews with DE, ABbs, ME, WLS and TW, with intermittent previously recorded music.

                                                                        29 Apr 1969   (P)
DUKE ELLINGTON   The White House (tc)
DE at the White House on the occasion of his 70th birthday.   Washington, DC

.... Vid   Introduction (using previously recorded material)
.... Vid   A Tribute to Duke Ellington (performed by a host of invited fellow musicians)
.... Vid   DE speech

      > DE piano solo.

.... Vid   Pat
.... Vid   Presentation by President Richard M. Nixon
.... Vid   Happy Birthday

A portion of this event was edited for the short documentary "Duke Ellington at the White House."

                                                                        16 May 1969   (P)
DUKE ELLINGTON & HIS ORCHESTRA   Senior High School
CA CW WC ME, LB BCpr CCrs, RP NTrn PG HAsh HC, DE CPrt RJo, SWsp.   Oil City, PA

....   Take The "A" Train
....   Kinda Dukish/Rockin' In Rhythm
....   The Blues –vSWsp
....   The Birth Of The Blues
....   St. Louis Blues
....   The Biggest And Busiest Intersection
....   Acht O'Clock Rock
....   Things Ain't What They Used To Be   >>>

> DE CPrt.

....   Meditation

23 May 1969   (T)[1]
National Recording Studios, Edison Hall
New York City, NY

DUKE ELLINGTON & HIS ORCHESTRA
CA CW WC JO, LB BCpr CCrs, RP JH NTrn PG HAsh HC, DE PK VG RJo.

....		-1	Change Of Mind "A"
....	Az	-4	Change Of Mind "A"
....		-1	Change Of Mind "A"
....		-2	Change Of Mind "A"
....	Az	-3	Change Of Mind "A"
....		-1	Change Of Mind "A"
....		-2	Change Of Mind "A"
....		-3	Change Of Mind "A"

> NTrn, PK.

....		-1	Change Of Mind "A"
....		-2	Change Of Mind "A"
....		-3	Change Of Mind "A"
....	Az	-4	Change Of mind "A"

> WC.

....		-1	Change Of Mind "A"

> PK added.

....		-2	Change Of Mind "A"
....	Az	-3	Change Of Mind "A"
....		-5	Change Of Mind "A"

> WC.

....			Change Of Mind "A"
....			Change Of Mind "A"

> HC, PK.

....	Az		Change Of Mind "A"

> Entire band.

....		-1	Change Of Mind "B"
....	Az	-3	Change Of Mind "B"
....		-1	Change Of Mind "B"
....	Az	-2	Change Of Mind "B"
....		-1	Change Of Mind "B"
....		-1	Change Of Mind "B"
....		-2	Change Of Mind "B"
....	Az		Change Of Mind "B"
....		-2	Change Of Mind "B"
....	Az		Change Of Mind "B"
....	Az	-3	Change Of Mind "B"
....		-1	Change Of Mind "B"
....		-2	Change Of Mind "B"
....		-3	Change Of Mind "B"
....	Az	-4	Change Of Mind "B"
....		-1	Change Of Mind "C"
....		-2	Change Of Mind "C"

> NTrn HC, PK.

....		-1	Change Of Mind "C"
....		-2	Change Of Mind "C"
....		-3	Change Of Mind "C"

> Entire band.

....			Background music
....			Background music
....		-1	Background music
....		-2	Background music
....		-3	Background music

> NTrn.

....		-1	Background music
....		-2	Background music
....		-3	Background music

> Entire band.

....		-1	Background music >>>

....		-2	Background music
....		-3	Background music
....		-4	Background music

> DE piano solo.

....	Az	-2	Change Of Mind "C"
....	Az	-3	Change Of Mind "C"

> Entire band.

....		Black Butterfly
....		Background music
....		What Good Am I Without You?
....		Background music
....		Black Butterfly

> DE piano solo.

....		Black Butterfly
....		Black Butterfly

> Entire band.

....		-1	Wanderlust
....		-5	Wanderlust
....		-6	Wanderlust
....		-1	Change Of Mind "D"
....		-2	Change Of Mind "D"
....		-3	Change Of Mind "D"
....	Az	-4	Change Of Mind "D"

[1]Music for the motion picture "Change Of Mind"; see also sessions on 25 Apr and 26 May 1969.

26 May 1969   (T)[1]
National Recording Studios, Edison Hall
New York City, NY

DUKE ELLINGTON & HIS ORCHESTRA
CA CW WC JO, LB BCpr CCrs, RP JH NTrn PG HAsh HC, DE PK VG RJo.

....	-36	Background music
....	-37	Background music
....	-38	Background music

> HC, PK.

....	-39	Background music
....	-40	Background music
....	-41	Background music
....	-42	Background music

> DE piano solo.

....	-43	Black Butterfly
....	-44	Black Butterfly
....	-46	Black Butterfly
....	-47	Black Butterfly

> WC, PK.

....	-50	Background music
....	-51	Background music
....	-52	Background music

> Entire band.

....	-55	Background music
....	-56	Background music
....	-58	High Passage
....	-59	High Passage
....	-60	High Passage
....	-61	Background music
....	-62	Background music
....	-66	Change Of Mind "A"
....	-67	Change Of Mind "A"
....	-69	Change Of Mind "A"
....	-70	Background music
....	-75	Background music

> CW, DE PK.

....	-76	Echoes Of Harlem
....	-77	Echoes Of Harlem
....	-78	Echoes Of Harlem

> Entire band.

....	-81	Echoes Of Harlem >>>

> DE PK.

....	-88	Echoes Of Harlem
....	-89	Echoes Of Harlem
....	-91	Echoes Of Harlem
....	-92	Echoes Of Harlem
....	-98	Neo-Creole
....	-99	Neo-Creole
....	-100	Neo-Creole
....	-101	Background music
....	-102	Background music

> Entire band.

....	-109	Echoes Of Harlem
....	-110	Echoes Of Harlem
....	-111	Echoes Of Harlem

> DE PK.

....		Echoes Of Harlem

> DE piano solo.

....	-112	Change Of Mind "E"

> DE PK.

....	-113	Background music

> Entire band.

....	-119	Neo-Creole
....	-121	Neo-Creole
....	-122	Neo-Creole
....		Neo-Creole
....	-124	Background music
....	-125	Background music
....	-126	Background music
....	-132	Neo-Creole
....	-133	Neo-Creole
....	-134	Neo-Creole
....	-135	Neo-Creole
....	-136	What Good Am I Without You?/Neo-Creole
....	-137	What Good Am I Without You?/Neo-Creole
....	-138	What Good Am I Without You?/Neo-Creole
....	-139	What Good Am I Without You?/Neo-Creole
....	-142	What Good Am I Without You?/Neo-Creole
....	-143	What Good Am I Without You?/Neo-Creole
....	-145	What Good Am I Without You?/Neo-Creole
....	-146	What Good Am I Without You?/Neo-Creole
....	-148	Black Butterfly
....	-149	Black Butterfly

> DE PK RJo.

....	Pab	Edward The First[2]

[1]Music for the motion picture "Change Of Mind"; see also sessions on 25 Apr and 23 May 1969.
[2]sa "What Good Am I Without You?"

30 May 1969   (P)
Naval Academy
Annapolis, MD

DUKE ELLINGTON & HIS ORCHESTRA
CA CW WC ME, LB BCpr CCrs, RP JH NTrn PG HAsh HC, DE PK RJo, SWsp TWtk.

....	Satin Doll
....	Mood Indigo
....	Caravan
....	Sophisticated Lady
....	The Birth Of The Blues
....	I Got It Bad
....	Things Ain't What They Used To Be
....	Making That Love Scene –vTWtk
....	You Don't Love Me No More –vSWsp
....	Acht O'Clock Rock
....	Satin Doll

DUKE ELLINGTON & HIS ORCHESTRA
Same personnel.

....	The "C" Jam Blues

> HAsh, DE PK RJo.

....	I Can't Get Started >>>

> Entire band.

....		B.P. Blues
....		The Biggest And Busiest Intersection
....		Solitude –vSWsp TWtk
....		It Don't Mean A Thing –vSWsp TWtk
....		Be Cool And Groovy For Me –vSWsp TWtk
....		Satin Doll
....		Take The "A" Train
....		Drag
....		I Let A Song Go Out Of My Heart/Don't Get Around Much Anymore
....		I'm Just A Lucky So-And-So –vTWtk
....		Walkin' And Singin' The Blues –vSWsp
....		I Love My Lovin' Lover –vSWsp
....		Tootie For Cootie
....		Neo-Creole
....		I Left My Heart In San Francisco
....		Red Roses For A Blue Lady
....		Kinda Dukish/Rockin' In Rhythm
....		La Plus Belle Africaine
....		Take The "A" Train
....		Star Dust
....		Satin Doll

9 Jun 1969   (S)
ρ Queen's College (bc)
Georgetown, Guiana

DUKE ELLINGTON
No particulars available.

.... RDB   Interview

In Jun 1969 the band went on a brief tour to the Caribbean.

19 Jun 1969   (P)
Studios KYW (tc)
Philadelphia, PA

DUKE ELLINGTON & HIS RHYTHM
DE PK RJo.

....   La Plus Belle Africaine

> DE interviewed by Mike Douglas.

....   Interview

> DE PK RJo, DDW MDgs.

....   Medley[1]

[1]Including: Take The "A" Train; Satin Doll –vDDW; I'm Beginning To See The Light –vMDgs; Sophisticated Lady; Don't Get Around Much Anymore –vDDW; I Let A Song Go Out Of My Heart –MDgs; Mood Indigo.

20 Jun 1969   (S)
National Recording Studios, Edison Hall
New York City, NY

DUKE ELLINGTON & HIS ORCHESTRA
MJsn CW WC ME, LB BGrn CCrs, RP JH NTrn PG HAsh HC, DE PK VG RJo.

....		-1	Neo-Creole
....		-2	Neo-Creole
....		-3	Neo-Creole (incomplete)
....	Pab	-4	Neo-Creole
....		-6	Black Butterfly
....			Black Butterfly (incomplete)
....		-7	Black Butterfly
....	Pab	-8	Black Butterfly
....		-9	HARLEM

Items 1 thru 8 are titles from the motion picture "Change Of Mind." The above versions are different from those used for the movie soundtrack. See also sessions on 23 Apr, 23 and 26 May 1969.

21 Jun 1969   (P)
Blossom Music Center
Cuyahoga Falls, OH

DUKE ELLINGTON & HIS ORCHESTRA WITH THE CLEVELAND SYMPHONY ORCHESTRA
pp MJsn CW WC ME, LB BGrn CCrs, RP JH NTrn PG HAsh HC, DE PK RJo, with the Cleveland Symphony Orchestra, Michael Cherry conducting.

.... Az   Opening remarks by DE

> CSO, PK RJo, DE conducting.

                        THE GOLDEN BROOM AND THE GREEN APPLE

....	Az	- *Stanza 1 (The Golden Broom)*
....	Az	- *Stanza 2 (The Green Apple)*
....	Az	- *Stanza 3 (The Handsome Traffic Policeman)*

.... Az   Introductory remarks by DE   >>>

> Entire band added.

.... Az   HARLEM
.... Az   Take The "A" Train

23 Jun 1969   (P)
DUKE ELLINGTON & HIS ORCHESTRA   Conrad Hilton Hotel
MJsn CW WC ME, LB BGrn CCrs, RP JH NTrn PG HAsh HC, DE PK RJo.   Chicago, IL

....   Take The "A" Train
....   Black And Tan Fantasy—Creole Love Call—The Mooche
....   Soul Call
....   Mount Harissa
....   Take The "A" Train

29 Jun 1969   (P)
DUKE ELLINGTON & HIS ORCHESTRA   Marine Stadium
MJsn CW WC ME, LB BGrn CCrs, RP JH NTrn PG HAsh HC, DE PK RJo, SWsp DDW TWtk.   Miami, FL

....   Soul Call
....   Up Jump
....   Take The "A" Train
....   La Plus Belle Africaine
....   Come Off The Veldt
....   Passion Flower
....   Things Ain't What They Used To Be
....   Medley[1]

[1]Including: Do Nothin' Till You Hear From Me; Just Squeeze Me; Don't Get Around Much Anymore; Mood Indigo; I'm Beginning To See The Light; Solitude –vSWsp TWtk; It Don't Mean A Thing –vDDW TWtk; Be Cool And Groovy For Me –vDDW TWtk; Sophisticated Lady; Satin Doll.

2 Jul 1969   (P)
DUKE ELLINGTON WITH THE RON COLLIER ORCHESTRA   Ford Auditorium
DE with the Ron Collier Orchestra; featuring FSt and EAm.   Detroit, MI

....   Song And Dance
....   Satin Doll
....   Nameless Hour

> DE b dr.

....   Take The "A" Train

> Entire band.

....   Aurora Borealis

Listed above is only the Ellington portion of the event.

14 Jul 1969   (S)
DUKE ELLINGTON   National Recording Studios
Celeste solo.   New York City, NY

.... Pab   Moon Maiden –vDE

15 Jul 1969[1]   (S)
DUKE ELLINGTON & HIS RHYTHM   ABC Studios (tc)
DE ACht PK RJo.   New York City, NY

....   Moon Maiden

> DE piano solo.

....   Anticipation And Hesitation

> Entire group, TWtk added.

....   In The Beginning God –vTWtk

[1]Taping session; telecast on 20 Jul 1969.

21 Jul 1969   (P)
DUKE ELLINGTON & HIS ORCHESTRA   Steel Pier
MJsn CW WC ME, LB BGrn CCrs, RP JH NTrn PG HAsh HC, PK RJo, DHff TWtk.   Atlantic City, NJ

....   Boo-Dah
....   Laura
....   Soul Call

> DE added.

....   Satin Doll
....   Take The "A" Train
....   Tootie For Cootie   >>>

....		Mood Indigo
....		I Let A Song Go Out Of My Heart/Don't Get Around Much Anymore
....		Honeysuckle Rose
....		The Star-Crossed Lovers
....		Things Ain't What They Used To Be
....		Wings And Things
....		Solitude –vDHff TWtk
....		It Don't Mean A Thing
....		On The Sunny Side Of The Street
....		Come Off The Veldt
....		Satin Doll

DUKE ELLINGTON & HIS ORCHESTRA
DHff omitted, SWsp added, otherwise same personnel.

....		I Want To Blow Now –vBGrn
....		The "C" Jam Blues
....		Satin Doll
....		Take The "A" Train

> HAsh, DE PK RJo.

....		I Can't Get Started

> Entire band.

....		B.P. Blues
....		Rockin' In Rhythm
....		Half The Fun
....		Things Ain't What They Used To Be
....		Making That Love Scene –vTWtk
....		You Don't Love Me No More –vSWsp
....		Walkin' And Singin' The Blues –vSWsp
....		In A Sentimental Mood
....		I Let A Song Go Out Of My Hear/Don't Get Around Much Anymore
....		Delta Serenade
....		Latin American Sunshine
....		Caravan

24 Jul 1969   (S)
Studios WNEW (tc)
New York City, NY

DUKE ELLINGTON & WILLIE "THE LION" SMITH
DE and WLS interviewed by David Frost.

....		Interview

12 Aug 1969   (S)
National Recording Studios
New York City, NY

DUKE ELLINGTON & HIS ORCHESTRA
WC, LB, RP JH PG HAsh HC, DE BD PK RJo, LRls.

....	-2	Have You Seen The Circus? –vLRls (incomplete)
....		Have You Seen The Circus? –vLRls (incomplete)
....	-3	Have You Seen The Circus? –vLRls (incomplete)
....	-5	Have You Seen The Circus? –vLRls (incomplete)
....	-6	Have You Seen The Circus? –vLRls
....	-8	Have You Seen The Circus? –vLRls
....	-10	Moon Maiden –vLRls (incomplete)
....	-11	Moon Maiden (incomplete)
....	-12	Moon Maiden –vLRls
....	-14	Moon Maiden –vLRls
....	-15	Moon Maiden –vLRls (incomplete)
....	-16	Moon Maiden –vLRls

22 Aug 1969   (P)
ABC Studios (tc)
New York City, NY

DUKE ELLINGTON WITH ORCHESTRA
DE with a studio orchestra, directed by Bobby Rosengarden.

....		Medley[1]

> DE interviewed by Dick Cavett.

....		Interview

> DE with orchestra.

....		Satin Doll
....		The "C" Jam Blues

[1]Including: Mood Indigo; I Let A Song Go Out Of My Heart; It Don't Mean A Thing; What Am I Here For?; Ring Dem Bells.

DUKE ELLINGTON & HIS ORCHESTRA
WC, LB, RP JH PG HAsh HC, DE PK RJo, LRls.

29 Aug 1969   (S)
National Recording Studios
New York City, NY

....		-1	Baby, You're Too Much –vLRls (incomplete)
....		-3	Baby, You're Too Much –vLRls (incomplete)
....		-4	Baby, You're Too Much (incomplete)
....		-6	Baby, You're Too Much –vLRls
....		-7	Baby, You're Too Much –vLRls
....		-8	Baby, You're Too Much –vLRls
....		-10	Baby, You're Too Much –vLRls (incomplete)
....		-11	Baby, You're Too Much –vLRls
....			Layin' On Mellow (incomplete)
....			Layin' On Mellow (incomplete)
....		-12	Layin' On Mellow
....		-13	Layin' On Mellow (incomplete)
....	Pab	-14	Layin' On Mellow
....		-15	The Lonely Ones –vLRls
....		-16	The Lonely Ones –vLRls
....		-17	The Lonely Ones –vLRls

DUKE ELLINGTON & HIS ORCHESTRA
CA CW WC LMch, LB BGrn CCrs, RP JH NTrn PG HAsh HC, DE PK RJo, TWtk.

31 Aug 1969   (P)
Constitution Hall
Washington, DC

....	Black And Tan Fantasy—Creole Love Call—The Mooche
....	Soul Call
....	Mount Harissa
....	Up Jump
....	La Plus Belle Africaine
....	Come Off The Veldt
....	Satin Doll
....	The Birth Of The Blues
....	Medley[1]
....	HARLEM
....	Take The "A" Train
....	Passion Flower
....	Things Ain't What They Used To Be
....	I Got It Bad
....	Layin' On Mellow
....	Acht O'Clock Rock
....	Acht O'Clock Rock
....	Satin Doll

> DE piano solo.

....	A Single Petal Of A Rose

[1]Including: In A Sentimental Mood; Do Nothin' Till You Hear From Me; Just Squeeze Me; Don't Get Around Much Anymore; Mood Indigo; I'm Beginning To See The Light; Making That Love Scene –vTWtk; Solitude –vTWtk; It Don't Mean A Thing –vTWtk; Come Sunday –vTWtk; Be Cool And Groovy For Me –vTWtk; Sophisticated Lady; Caravan.

DUKE ELLINGTON & HIS ORCHESTRA
CA CW WC LMch, LB BGrn CCrs, RP JH NTrn PG HAsh HC, LHsn PK RJo SL.

2 Sep 1969   (S)
RCA Studio C
New York City, NY

....	Bb	XR1S-9501-1	La Dolce Vita

> BD VG added.

....	RD	XR1S-9501-2	La Dolce Vita

> VG omitted, JP replaces BGrn.

....	RD	XR1S-9501-5	The Spanish Flea

The arrangements for the above titles are by Luther Henderson.

DUKE ELLINGTON & HIS ORCHESTRA
CA CW WC LMch ME, LB JP CCrs, RP JH NTrn PG HAsh HC, DE PK VG RJo.

3 Sep 1969   (S)
RCA Studio C
New York City, NY

....	Bb	XR1S-9501-5	Alfie[1]
....	RD	XR1S-9501-4/8	A Day In The Life Of A Fool[2,3]
....	Bb	XR1S-9501-2	A Taste Of Honey[3]
....	RD	XR1S-9501-4	A Taste Of Honey
....	Bb	XR1S-9501-2	Summer Samba[1]
....	RD	XR1S-9501-6	Summer Samba

> VG omitted.

....	RD	XR1S-9501-4/7	Misty[4] >>>

> VG added.

....	Bb	XR1S-9501-4	One Note Samba[4]
....	RD	XR1S-9501-5	One Note Samba
....	Bb	XR1S-9501-1	Soon It's Gonna Rain[1]

> BD replaces DE.

....	Bb	XR1S-9501-3	Soon It's Gonna Rain
....	Bb	XR1S-9501-4	Soon It's Gonna Rain

[1]The arrangements are by Wild Bill Davis.
[2]Originally titled "Mañha de Carnaval."
[3]The arrangements are by Ron Collier.
[4]The arrangements are by Luther Henderson.

4 Sep 1969 (S)
RCA Studio C
New York City, NY

<u>DUKE ELLINGTON & HIS ORCHESTRA</u>
CA CW WC LMch ME, LB BGrn JP CCrs, RP JH NTrn PG HAsh HC, BD PK RJo.

....	Bb	XR1S-9501-5[1]	Soon It's Gonna Rain[1]
....	RD	XR1S-9501-4/8[1]	Alfie[2]

> JP, BD omitted, DE VG added.

....	RD	XR1S-9501-2	Mr. Lucky[2]

> BD added.

....	Bb	XR1S-9501-5	Mr. Lucky
....	Bb	XR1S-9501-1	Walking Happy[2] (incomplete)
....	Bb	XR1S-9501-2	Walking Happy (incomplete)
....	Bb	XR1S-9501-3	Walking Happy (incomplete)
....	Bb[3]	XR1S-9501-4	Walking Happy
....	Bb	XR1S-9501-6	Walking Happy
....	RD	XR1S-9501-7	Walking Happy
....	Bb	XR1S-9501-5	Moon Maiden –vDE
....	RD	XR1S-9501-5	Moon Maiden

[1]Remakes.
[2]The arrangements are by Wild Bill Davis.
[3]Excerpt on Bb.

10 Sep 1969 (S)
RCA Studios
New York City, NY

<u>DUKE ELLINGTON & TONY WATKINS</u>
DE, TWtk.

....		-1	To Know You Is To Love You –vTWtk
....		-2	To Know You Is To Love You (incomplete)
....		-3	To Know You Is To Love You –vTWtk
....		-4	To Know You Is To Love You –vTWtk (incomplete)
....	MM	-5	To Know You Is To Love You –vTWtk
....		-6	To Know You Is To Love You –vTWtk

> RJo added.

....			Pretty People's Plea –vTWtk
....			Tell Me, It's The Truth –vTWtk

> RJo omitted.

....		-7	To Know You Is To Love You –vTWtk (incomplete)
....		-8	To Know You Is To Love You (incomplete)
....		-9	To Know You Is To Love You –vTWtk
....		-10	To Know You Is To Love You –vTWtk

18 Sep 1969 (P)
Sherman House
Chicago, IL

<u>DUKE ELLINGTON & HIS ORCHESTRA</u>
CA CW WC ME, LB BGrn CCrs, RP JH PG HAsh HC, DE BD VG RJo.

....		Main Stem
....		Work Song
....		Caravan—Black Beauty—West Indian Dance
....		Take The "A" Train

27 Sep 1969 (P)
Montview Boulevard Presbyterian Church
Denver, CO

<u>DUKE ELLINGTON & HIS ORCHESTRA</u>
CA CW WC ME, LB BGrn CCrs, RP JH PG HAsh HC, DE BD VG RJo, DGrd NL RG TWtk choir.

....		THE SECOND SACRED CONCERT
....		Praise God
....		Supreme Being –vChoir
....		Something About Believing –vDGrd RG TWtk Choir >>>

....   Almighty God –vDGrd Choir
....   The Shepherd
....   Heaven –vDGrd
....   It's Freedom –vDGrd NL RG TWtk Choir
> DE VG.

....   Meditation
> Entire band.

....   The Biggest And Busiest Intersection
> DE, NL.

....   T.G.T.T. –vNL
> Entire band.

....   Don't Get Down On Your Knees –vTWtk
> TWtk Choir a cappella.

....   Father Forgive –vTWtk Choir
> Entire band.

....   Don't Get Down On Your Knees –vTWtk
....   Praise God And Dance –vNL Choir
> TWtk a cappella.

....   The Preacher's Song –vTWtk
> Entire band.

....   In The Beginning God –vChoir

DUKE ELLINGTON & HIS ORCHESTRA
Same personnel.

                                    THE SECOND SACRED CONCERT
....   Praise God
....   Supreme Being –vChoir
....   Something About Believing –vDGrd RG TWtk Choir
....   Almighty God –vDGrd Choir
....   The Shepherd
....   Heaven –vDGrd
....   It's Freedom –vDGrd NL RG TWtk Choir
> DE VG.

....   Meditation
> Entire band.

....   The Biggest And Busiest Intersection
> DE, NL.

....   T.G.T.T. –vNL
> Entire band.

....   Don't Get Down On Your Knees –vTWtk
> TWtk Choir a cappella.

....   Father Forgive –vTWtk Choir
> Entire band.

....   Don't Get Down On Your Knees –vTWtk
....   Praise God And Dance –vNL Choir
> TWtk a cappella.

....   The Preacher's Song –vTWtk
> Entire band.

....   In The Beginning God –vChoir

29 Sep 1969   (P)
Zellerbach Auditorium, University of California
Berkeley, CA

DUKE ELLINGTON & HIS ORCHESTRA
CA CW WC ME, LB BGm CCrs, RP JH PG HAsh HC, DE BD VG RJo.
....   The Clown –DE narration

28 Oct 1969   (P)
Teatro Lirico
Milan, Italy

DUKE ELLINGTON & HIS ORCHESTRA
CA CW OV ME, LB CCrs, RP JH NTrn[1] HAsh HC, DE BD VG RJo, TWtk.

....   Take The "A" Train   >>>

....		Kinda Dukish/Rockin' In Rhythm
....		4:30 Blues
....		Take The "A" Train
....		B.P. Blues
....		Up Jump[2]
....		El Gato
....		The Birth Of The Blues
....		Passion Flower
....		Things Ain't What They Used To Be
....		Layin' On Mellow
....		Summer Samba
....		April In Paris
....		April In Paris
....		Come Off The Veldt

        > PG added.

....		Satin Doll
....		Making That Love Scene –vTWtk
....		It Don't Mean A Thing –vTWtk
....		Be Cool And Groovy For Me –vTWtk
....		Sophisticated Lady
....		Diminuendo In Blue and In Triplicate[3]
....		Satin Doll

[1]During this European tour NTrn was also playing tb parts and filling the place of BGrn on many occasions.
[2]Often announced as "Tenor Saxophonic Calisthenics" during this European tour.
[3]This title is a derivative of *Wailing Interval*.

30 Oct 1969   (P)
Lucerna Hall (tc?)[1]
Prague, Czechia (Czechoslovakia)

DUKE ELLINGTON & HIS ORCHESTRA
CA CW ME, LB CCrs, RP JH NTrn PG HAsh HC, DE BD VG RJo, TWtk.

....		Take The "A" Train
....		Black And Tan Fantasy—Creole Love Call—The Mooche
....		Up Jump
....		Take The "A" Train
....		La Plus Belle Africaine
....		Come Off The Veldt
....		Medley[2]
....		Satin Doll
....		April In Paris
....		April In Paris
....	Az	Moon Maiden
....		El Gato
....		Passion Flower
....		Things Ain't What They Used To Be
....		I Got It Bad
....		Drag
....		Kinda Dukish/Rockin' In Rhythm
....		Diminuendo In Blue and In Triplicate
....		The "C" Jam Blues
....		Satin Doll

[1]The concert was filmed, but has not been aired as yet.
[2]Including: Do Nothin' Till You Hear From Me; Just Squeeze Me; I Let A Song Go Out Of My Heart; Don't Get Around Much Anymore; Mood Indigo; I'm Beginning To See The Light; Solitude –vTWtk; It Don't Mean A Thing –vTWtk; Be Cool And Groovy For Me –vTWtk; Sophisticated Lady.

31 Oct 1969   (P)
Stadthalle
Vienna, Austria

DUKE ELLINGTON & HIS ORCHESTRA
CA CW ME, LB CCrs, RP JH NTrn PG HAsh HC, DE BD VG RJo, TWtk.

....		Take The "A" Train
....		4:30 Blues
....		Take The "A" Train
....		Up Jump
....		La Plus Belle Africaine
....		Come Off The Veldt
....		El Gato
....		Black Butterfly
....		Drag
....		Satin Doll
....		Satin Doll
....		The Blues –vTWtk
....		It Don't Mean A Thing –vTWtk
....		Satin Doll >>>

DUKE ELLINGTON   (S)[1]
DE interviewed by Fatty George.

....   Interview

[1]Backstage.

DUKE ELLINGTON & HIS ORCHESTRA   1 Nov 1969   (P)
CA CW ME, LB CCrs, RP JH NTrn PG HAsh HC, DE VG RJo.   Salle Pleyel
                                                                           Paris, France
....   Kinda Dukish/Rockin' In Rhythm
.... JMY   Black And Tan Fantasy
.... JMY   Caravan
.... JMY   Up Jump
.... JMY   Take The "A" Train
.... JMY   Honeysuckle Rose
.... JMY   B.P. Blues
.... JMY   Perdido
.... JMY   El Gato
.... JMY   Black Butterfly
.... JMY   Things Ain't What They Used To Be
.... JMY   Satin Doll
.... JMY   Sophisticated Lady
....   The "C" Jam Blues

DUKE ELLINGTON & HIS ORCHESTRA
AJck HJon, FGn, TWtk added, otherwise same personnel.

.... BYG   Take The "A" Train
....   Kinda Dukish/Rockin' In Rhythm
....   Black And Tan Fantasy
.... BYG   B.P. Blues
.... BYG   Take The "A" Train
.... BYG   Up Jump
....   La Plus Belle Africaine
.... BYG   Come Off The Veldt
.... BYG   Black Butterfly
.... BYG   Things Ain't What They Used To Be
.... BYG   El Gato
.... BYG   Satin Doll
.... BYG   Making That Love Scene –vTWtk
.... BYG   Solitude –vTWtk
.... BYG   It Don't Mean A Thing –vTWtk
.... BYG   Be Cool and Groovy For Me –vTWtk

   > DBs added.

.... BYG   Diminuendo In Blue and In Triplicate

   > DBs omitted.

.... BYG   Satin Doll

   > AShp added.

.... GdJ   The "C" Jam Blues

   > AShp omitted.

.... BJz   Sophisticated Lady
.... BJz   Honeysuckle Rose
....   Take The "A" Train

DUKE ELLINGTON & HIS ORCHESTRA   2 Nov 1969[1]   (P)
CA CW HJon ME, LB CCrs, RP JH NTrn PG HAsh HC, DE BD VG RJo, TWtk.   Tivoli's Koncertsal (tc)
                                                                           Copenhagen, Denmark
.... Vid   The "C" Jam Blues
.... Vid   Kinda Dukish/Rockin' In Rhythm
.... Vid   4:30 Blues
.... Vid   Take The "A" Train
.... Vid   Up Jump
.... Vid   La Plus Belle Africaine
.... Vid   Come Off The Veldt
.... Vid   El Gato
.... Vid   Black Butterfly
.... Vid   Things Ain't What They Used To Be
.... Vid   Drag
....   Summer Samba
.... Vid   Satin Doll   >>>

> DE, TWtk.

.... Vid   Come Sunday –vTWtk

> Entire band.

.... Vid   It Don't Mean A Thing –vTWtk
.... Vid   Be Cool And Grovy For Me –vTWtk
.... Vid   Diminuendo In Blue and In Triplicate
.... Vid   Satin Doll

> DE VG RJo.

.... Vid   Black Swan

[1]The date of telecast is not known.

DUKE ELLINGTON & HIS ORCHESTRA   3 Nov 1969   (P)
CA CW HJon ME, LB CCrs, RP JH NTrn PG HAsh HC, DE VG RJo, TWtk. Unidentified location
                           Bergen, Norway

....   Take The "A" Train
....   Cotton Tail
....   Up Jump
....   La Plus Belle Africaine
....   Come Off The Veldt
....   El Gato
....   Don't Get Around Much Anymore
....   Solitude –vTWtk
....   It Don't Mean A Thing –vTWtk
....   Be Cool And Groovy For Me –vTWtk
....   Acht O'Clock Rock

DUKE ELLINGTON & HIS ORCHESTRA   4 Nov 1969   (P)
CA CW AJck ME, LB CCrs, RP JH NTrn PG HAsh HC, DE BD VG RJo, TWtk. Kongresshallen
                           Stockholm, Sweden

....   The "C" Jam Blues
....   Kinda Dukish/Rockin' In Rhythm

> LB, DE VG RJo.

.... MFC   Serenade To Sweden

> Entire band.

....   Take The "A" Train
....   Up Jump
....   El Gato
....   Black Butterfly
....   Things Ain't What They Used To Be
....   Don't Get Around Much Anymore
....   Medley[1]
....   Sophisticated Lady
....   It Don't Mean A Thing[2]
....   Come Off The Veldt
....   Satin Doll
....   Satin Doll

[1]Including: Caravan; Mood Indigo; I'm Beginning To See The Light; Solitude –vTWtk; It Don't Mean A Thing –vTWtk.
[2]Announced as "The African Loudspeaker," featuring VG.

DUKE ELLINGTON & HIS ORCHESTRA
Same personnel.

....   The "C" Jam Blues
....   Fife

> HAsh, DE VG RJo.

....   I Can't Get Started

> Entire band.

....   B.P. Blues

> LB, DE VG RJo.

....   Serenade To Sweden

> Entire band.

....   Take The "A" Train
....   Up Jump
....   La Plus Belle Africaine
....   Come Off The Veldt >>>

....	MFC	Black Butterfly
....		Things Ain't What They Used To Be
....		El Gato
....		Don't Get Around Much Anymore
....		Medley[1]
....		Satin Doll
....		Kinda Dukish/Rockin' In Rhythm

[1]Including: Caravan; Mood Indigo; I'm Beginning To See The Light; Solitude –vTWtk; It Don't Mean A Thing –vTWtk; Be Cool And Groovy For Me –vTWtk.

5 Nov 1969   (S)
Gustav Vasa Kyrkan
Stockholm, Sweden

DUKE ELLINGTON & HIS ORCHESTRA
CA CW REsn AJck ME, LB CCrs GMbg, RP JH NTrn PG HAsh HC, DE BD VG RJo, ABbs SRC.

....		T.G.T.T. –vABbs
....		Praise God And Dance (opening theme)
....		Praise God And Dance (opening theme)
....		Supreme Being
....		The Biggest And Busiest Intersection
....		T.G.T.T.
....		T.G.T.T.
....		T.G.T.T. –vABbs
....		In The Beginning God –vSRC

The above is a rehearsal session with no audience in attendance.

6 Nov 1969[1]   (P)
Gustav Vasa Kyrkan (tc)
Stockholm, Sweden

DUKE ELLINGTON & HIS ORCHESTRA
CA CW REsn AJck ME, LB CCrs GMbg, RP JH NTrn PG HAsh HC, DE BD VG RJo, ABbs TWtk SRC.

		THE SECOND SACRED CONCERT
....		Praise God
....		Supreme Being –vSRC
....		Something About Believing –vSRC
....		Almighty God –vABbs SRC
....		The Shepherd
....	MJ	Heaven –vABbs
....		It's Freedom –vABbs TWtk SRC
	> DE VG.	
....		Meditation
	> Entire band.	
....		The Biggest And Busiest Intersection
....		Don't Get Down On Your Knees –vTWtk
	> TWtk SRC a cappella.	
....		Father Forgive –vTWtk SRC
	> Entire band.	
....		Don't Get Down On Your Knees –vTWtk
	> DE, ABbs.	
....		T.G.T.T. –vABbs
	> Entire band, cga added.	
....		Praise God And Dance –vABbs SRC

[1]The concert was filmed by Sverige Radio under the working title "Praise God And Dance"; the date of telecast is not known.

7 Nov 1969   (P)
De Doelen
Rotterdam, Netherlands

DUKE ELLINGTON & HIS ORCHESTRA
CA CW NW BBal ME, LB CCrs, RP JH NTrn PG HAsh HC, DE BD VG RJo, TWtk.

....		Take The "A" Train
....		Kinda Dukish/Rockin' In Rhythm
....		Take The "A" Train
....		Up Jump
....		La Plus Belle Africaine
....		Come Off The Veldt
....		El Gato
....	Az	Black Butterfly
....		Things Ain't What They Used To Be
....		Don't Get Around Much Anymore
....		Medley[1] >>>

		April In Paris
		R.T.M.[2]
		Diminuendo In Blue and In Triplicate
		Satin Doll

[1]Including: Caravan; I'm Beginning To See The Light; Solitude –vTWtk; It Don't Mean A Thing –vTWtk; Be Cool And Groovy For Me –vTWtk; Sophisticated Lady.
[2]Stands for Rufus, Turney, Malcolm; aka "Rhythmal Roof."

DUKE ELLINGTON & HIS ORCHESTRA
Same personnel.

		Take The "A" Train
		The "C" Jam Blues
		Kinda Dukish/Rockin' In Rhythm
		Take The "A" Train
		Up Jump
		La Plus Belle Africaine
		Come Off The Veldt
		El Gato
		Black Butterfly
		Things Ain't What They Used To Be
		Don't Get Around Much Anymore
		Medley[1]
		Making That Love Scene –vTWtk
		It Don't Mean A Thing –vTWtk
		Be Cool And Groovy For Me –vTWtk
	Az	Satin Doll
	Az	Satin Doll
	Az	R.T.M.
		In Triplicate
		Satin Doll

> DE BD VG RJo.

		Black Swan
	Az	The Lake[2]
		Satin Doll
	Az	Just Squeeze Me

[1]Including: Caravan; Mood Indigo; Sophisticated Lady.
[2]Part of the future ballet suite The River.

DUKE ELLINGTON & HIS ORCHESTRA
CA CW NW BBal ME, LB APsn CCrs, RP JH NTrn PG HAsh HC, DE BD VG RJo, TWtk.

8 Nov 1969[1]   (P)
Philharmonie (tc)
Berlin, Germany

		Take The "A" Train
		Kinda Dukish/Rockin' In Rhythm
	Vid	Take The "A" Train
		Up Jump
	Vid	La Plus Belle Africaine
		Come Off The Veldt
		El Gato
	Vid	Black Butterfly
	Vid	Things Ain't What They Used To Be
	JDr	Don't Get Around Much Anymore
	Vid[2]	Medley[3]
	Vid	April In Paris
	Vid	Satin Doll
		R.T.M.
		Diminuendo In Blue and In Triplicate

> DE VG RJo.

| | | Black Swan |

> BBal added.

| | | I Can't Get Started |

> NTrn, BD added.

| | | The "C" Jam Blues |

[1]The date of telecast is not known.
[2]Incomplete on Vid.
[3]Including: Caravan; Mood Indigo; Sophisticated Lady; I'm Beginning To See The Light; Solitude –vTWtk; It Don't Mean A Thing –vTWtk.

9 Nov 1969   (P)
Stadsteatern
Malmö, Sweden

DUKE ELLINGTON & HIS ORCHESTRA
CA CW NW BBal ME, LB APsn CCrs, RP JH NTrn PG HAsh HC, DE BD VG RJo, TWtk.

....   The "C" Jam Blues
....   Kinda Dukish/Rockin' In Rhythm
....   4:30 Blues
....   Serenade To Sweden
....   Fife
....   Take The "A" Train
....   Up Jump
....   La Plus Belle Africaine
....   Come Off The Veldt
....   Medley[1]
....   Take The "A" Train
....   Jump For Joy
....   Satin Doll
....   Black Butterfly
....   Things Ain't What They Used To Be
....   Diminuendo In Blue and Wailing Interval

[1]Including: Don't You Know I Care?; Do Nothin' Till You Hear From Me; Just Squeeze Me; Don't Get Around Much Anymore; Mood Indigo; I'm Beginning To See The Light; The Blues –vTWtk; It Don't Mean A Thing –vTWtk; Sophisticated Lady; Caravan.

DUKE ELLINGTON & HIS ORCHESTRA
Same personnel.

....   The "C" Jam Blues
....   Kinda Dukish/Rockin' In Rhythm
....   4:30 Blues
....   Serenade To Sweden
....   Take The "A" Train
....   Mount Harissa
....   Up Jump
....   La Plus Belle Africaine
....   Come Off The Veldt
....   Medley[1]

[1]Including: Don't You Know I Care?; Do Nothin' Till You Hear From Me; Just Squeeze Me; Don't Get Around Much Anymore; Mood Indigo; I'm Beginning To See The Light; The Blues –vTWtk; Come Sunday –vTWtk; Don't Get Down On Your Knees –vTWtk; Solitude; I Let A Song Go Out Of My Heart; Sophisticated Lady; Caravan.

10 Nov 1969   (P)
Opernhaus
Cologne, Germany

DUKE ELLINGTON & HIS ORCHESTRA
CA CW NW BBal ME, LB APsn CCrs, RP JH NTrn PG HAsh HC, DE BD VG RJo.

....   The "C" Jam Blues
.... WW   Kinda Dukish/Rockin' In Rhythm
.... WW   4:30 Blues
.... WW   Take The "A" Train
.... WW   Up Jump[1]
.... WW   Satin Doll
.... WW   April In Paris
.... WW   April In Paris
.... WW   El Gato
....   Black Butterfly
....   Things Ain't What They Used To Be
.... WW   Don't Get Around Much Anymore
.... WW[2]   Medley[3]
.... WW   Diminuendo In Blue and In Triplicate

[1]Announced as "Jam With Paul."
[2]Only "Mood Indigo" on WW.
[3]Including: Caravan; Mood Indigo; I'm Beginning To See The Light; Sophisticated Lady.

DUKE ELLINGTON & HIS ORCHESTRA
Same personnel.

....   Take The "A" Train
....   The Biggest And Busiest Intersection[1]
....   B.P. Blues
....   Fife
.... WW   Passion Flower
.... WW   Drag[2]

[1]Called up as "Kixx."
[2]Announced as "Jive Stomp."

12 Nov 1969   (P)
Teatro Massimo
Pescara, Italy

<u>DUKE ELLINGTON & HIS ORCHESTRA</u>
CA CW NW BBal ME, LB CCrs, RP JH NTrn PG HAsh HC, DE BD VG RJo, TWtk.

....	Take The "A" Train
....	Kinda Dukish/Rockin' In Rhythm
....	4:30 Blues
....	B.P. Blues
....	Fife
....	Take The "A" Train
....	Fly Me To The Moon
....	Up Jump
....	La Plus Belle Africaine
....	Come Off The Veldt
....	Medley[1]
....	Organ Rag
....	Satin Doll
....	R.T.M.
....	El Gato
....	The Star-Crossed Lovers
....	Things Ain't What They Used To Be
....	Black Butterfly
....	Drag
....	Diminuendo In Blue and In Triplicate
....	The "C" Jam Blues

> NTrn, DE BD VG RJo.

....	Black Swan
....	April In Paris
....	Blue Turney

> DE VG.

....	Meditation

> DE BD.

....	East St. Louis Toodle-Oo

[1]Including: Don't You Know I Care?; Do Nothin' Till You Hear From Me; Just Squeeze Me; Don't Get Around Much Anymore; Mood Indigo; I'm Beginning To See The Light; The Blues –vTWtk; Solitude –vTWtk; It Don't Mean A Thing –vTWtk; Be Cool And Groovy For Me –vTWtk.

13 Nov 1969   (P)
Palazzo dello Sport
Bologna, Italy

<u>DUKE ELLINGTON & HIS ORCHESTRA</u>
CA CW NW BBal ME, LB CCrs, RP JH NTrn PG HAsh HC, DE BD VG RJo, TWtk.

....	The "C" Jam Blues
....	Kinda Dukish/Rockin' In Rhythm
....	Take The "A" Train
....	Up Jump
....	El Gato
....	Black Butterfly
....	Things Ain't What They Used To Be
....	Layin' On Mellow
....	Satin Doll
....	R.T.M.
....	Medley[1]
....	Diminuendo In Blue and In Triplicate
....	Satin Doll

[1]Including: Don't You Know I Care?; In A Sentimental Mood; Prelude To A Kiss; I Let A Song Go Out of My Heart; Do Nothin' Till You Hear From Me; Just Squeeze Me; Don't Get Around Much Anymore; Mood Indigo; I'm Beginning To See The Light; The Blues –vTWtk; Solitude –vTWtk; It Don't Mean A Thing –vTWtk; Be Cool And Groovy For Me –TWtk; Sophisticated Lady; Caravan.

15 Nov 1969   (P)
Théâtre de Beaulieu
Lausanne, Switzerland

<u>DUKE ELLINGTON & HIS ORCHESTRA</u>
CA CW NW BBal ME, LB APsn CCrs, RP JH NTrn PG HAsh HC, DE BD VG RJo, TWtk.

....	Come Sunday –vTWtk
....	Don't Get Down On Your Knees –vTWtk
....	Satin Doll
....	R.T.M.
....	El Gato
....	Black Butterfly
....	Things Ain't What They Used To Be
....	Fife >>>

> NTrn, DE BD VG RJo.

....   Black Swan
....   April In Paris
....   April In Paris

DUKE ELLINGTON & HIS ORCHESTRA   Victoria Halle   (P)
Same personnel.   Geneva, Switzerland

....   The "C" Jam Blues
....   Kinda Dukish/Rockin' In Rhythm
....   4:30 Blues
....   Take The "A" Train
....   Up Jump
....   La Plus Belle Africaine
....   Come Off The Veldt
....   Medley[1]
....   Take The "A" Train
....   Satin Doll
....   R.T.M.
....   El Gato
....   Black Butterfly
....   Things Ain't What They Used To Be
....   I Got It Bad
....   Diminuendo In Blue and In Triplicate

> DE VG.

....   Meditation

> Entire band.

....   Fife

> NTrn, DE BD VG RJo.

....   Black Swan

[1]Including: Don't You Know I Care?; In a Sentimental Mood; Prelude To A Kiss; I Let A Song Go Out Of My Heart; Do Nothin' Till You Hear From Me; Just Squeeze Me; Jig Walk; Don't Get Around Much Anymore; Mood Indigo; I'm Beginning To See The Light; The Blues –vTWtk; Solitude –vTWtk; It Don't Mean A Thing –vTWtk; Be Cool And Groovy For Me –vTWtk; Sophisticated Lady; Caravan.

                                                            16 Nov 1969   (S)
DUKE ELLINGTON & HIS ORCHESTRA   Eglise Saint Sulpice
CA CW NW REsn ME, LB APsn CCrs, RP JH NTrn PG HAsh HC, DE BD VG RJo,   Paris, France
ABbs TWtk SSrs.

....   Praise God
....   Something About Believing –vSSrs
....   Supreme Being –vSSrs
....   It's Freedom –vABbs TWtk SSrs
....   Almighty God
....   Almighty God –vABbs SSrs
....   Don't Get Down On Your Knees
....   Father Forgive –vSSrs
....   Praise God And Dance –vABbs

The above is a rehearsal session with no audience in attendance.

DUKE ELLINGTON & HIS ORCHESTRA   (tc)[1]   (P)
Same personnel.

                                        THE SECOND SACRED CONCERT
....   Praise God
....   Supreme Being –vSSrs
....   Something About Believing –vSSrs
....   Almighty God –vABbs SSrs
....   The Shepherd
....   Heaven –vABbs
....   It's Freedom –vABbs TWtk SSrs
....   The Biggest And Busiest Intersection

> DE VG.

....   Meditation

> Entire band.

....   Don't Get Down On Your Knees –vTWtk

> TWtk SSrs a cappella.

....   Father Forgive –vTWtk SSrs   >>>

> Entire band.

.... Don't Get Down On Your Knees –vTWtk

> DE, ABbs.

.... T.G.T.T. –vABbs

> Entire band.

.... Praise God And Dance –vABbs SSrs

> TWtk a cappella.

.... The Preacher's Song –vTWtk

> Entire band.

.... In The Beginning God –vABbs TWtk SSrs

[1]The date of telecast is not known.

17 Nov 1969 (P)
Théâtre de la Cité
Lyon, France

DUKE ELLINGTON & HIS ORCHESTRA
CA CW REsn ME, LB APsn CCrs, RP JH NTrn PG HAsh HC, DE BD VG RJo, TWtk.

.... Medley[1]
.... Take The "A" Train
.... Satin Doll
.... R.T.M.
.... El Gato
.... Black Butterfly

> JH, DE BD VG RJo.

.... I Got It Bad

> Entire band.

.... Drag
.... Fife
.... Perdido

> DE VG.

.... Meditation

[1]Including: Just Squeeze Me; Don't Get Around Much Anymore; Mood Indigo; I'm Beginning To See The Light; The Blues –vTWtk; Solitude –vTWtk; It Don't Mean A Thing –vTWtk; Be Cool And Groovy For Me –vTWtk; Sophisticated Lady; Caravan.

20 Nov 1969 (P)
L'Alcazar (tc)
Paris, France

DUKE ELLINGTON & HIS ORCHESTRA
CA CW REsn ME, LB APsn CCrs, RP JH NTrn PG HAsh HC, DE BD VG RJo.

.... STJ Kinda Dukish/Rockin' In Rhythm
.... STJ Take The "A" Train
.... STJ A Day In The Life Of A Fool
.... STJ Things Ain't What They Used To Be
.... STJ Summer Samba[1]
.... STJ Satin Doll
.... STJ Wild Bill Blues[2]
.... STJ El Gato
.... STJ Sophisticated Lady
.... Vid Satin Doll
.... Vid Happy Birthday
.... Vid Fife
.... STJ In A Sentimental Mood
.... STJ B.P. Blues
.... STJ Diminuendo In Blue and In Triplicate
.... STJ Satin Doll

[1]Announced as "Orpheo Negro."
[2]aka "Improvisation sur les Blues"; sa "R.T.M."; "Rhythmal Roof."

24 Nov 1969 (P)
Basilica de Santa Maria del Mar (tc)
Barcelona, Spain

DUKE ELLINGTON & HIS ORCHESTRA
CA CW REsn ME, LB MBG CCrs, RP JH NTrn PG HAsh HC, DE BD VG RJo, ABbs TWtk SJC.

.... THE SECOND SACRED CONCERT
Praise God
.... Supreme Being –vSJC
.... Something About Believing –vSJC
.... Almighty God –vABbs SJC
.... The Shepherd
.... Heaven –vABbs
.... It's Freedom –vABbs TWtk SJC   >>>

> DE VG.

....   Meditation

> Entire band.

....   The Biggest And Busiest Intersection
....   Don't Get Down On Your Knees --vTWtk

> TWtk SJC a cappella.

....   Father Forgive --vTWtk SJC

> Entire band.

....   Don't Get Down On Your Knees --vTWtk

> DE, ABbs.

....   T.G.T.T. --vABbs

> Entire band.

....   Praise God And Dance --vABbs SJC

> TWtk a cappella.

....   The Preacher's Song --vTWtk

> Entire band.

....   In The Beginning God --vABbs TWtk SJC

		25 Nov 1969 (P)

DUKE ELLINGTON & HIS ORCHESTRA
CA CW REsn ME, LB CCrs, RP JH NTrn PG HAsh HC, DE BD VG RJo.

25 Nov 1969   (P)
Colston Hall
Bristol, England

....   4:30 Blues
....   The "C" Jam Blues
....   Take The "A" Train
....   Azure-Te
....   Satin Doll
....   Medley[1]

[1]Including: Don't You Know I Care?; In A Sentimental Mood; Prelude To A Kiss; I Let A Song Go Out Of My Heart; Do Nothin' Till You Hear From Me; Just Squeeze Me; Don't Get Around Much Anymore; Mood Indigo; I'm Beginning To See The Light.

DUKE ELLINGTON & HIS ORCHESTRA
TWtk added, otherwise same personnel.

....   The "C" Jam Blues
....   Kinda Dukish/Rockin' In Rhythm
....   B.P. Blues
....   Take The "A" Train
....   Tootie For Cootie
....   Up Jump
....   4:30 Blues
....   El Gato
....   Black Butterfly
....   Things Ain't What They Used To Be
....   Layin' On Mellow
.... SSR   Satin Doll
....   Medley[1]
....   In Triplicate
....   Perdido
....   Fife

> DE VG.

....   Meditation

> BD RJo added.

....   Black Swan

[1]Including: Mood Indigo; I'm Beginning To See The Light; The Blues --vTWtk; It Don't Mean A Thing --vTWtk; Sophisticated Lady; Caravan.

26 Nov 1969   (P)

DUKE ELLINGTON & HIS ORCHESTRA
CA CW REsn ME, LB CCrs, RP JH NTrn PG HAsh HC, DE BD VG RJo.

26 Nov 1969   (P)
Free Trade Hall
Manchester, England

.... SSR   Kinda Dukish/Rockin' In Rhythm
.... SSR   B.P. Blues
.... SSR   Take The "A" Train
.... SSR   Tootie For Cootie   >>>

....	SSR	4:30 Blues
....	SSR	El Gato
....	SSR	Black Butterfly
....	SSR	Things Ain't What They Used To Be
....	SSR	Layin' On Mellow
....	SSR	Azure-Te
....	SSR[1]	Medley[2]
....	SSR	In Triplicate
....	SSR	Perdido
....	SSR	Fife

> NTrn, DE BD VG RJo.

....	SSR	Black Swan

> Entire band.

....	SSR	Satin Doll

[1]Incomplete on SSR (LP as well as CD); however, due to different content/omissions, LP and CD together give a complete rendition of the medley.
[2]Including: Don't You Know I Care?; In A Sentimental Mood; Prelude To A Kiss; I'm Just A Lucky So-And-So; I Let A Song Go Out Of My Heart; Do Nothin' Till You Hear From Me; Just Squeeze Me; Don't Get Around Much Anymore; Mood Indigo; Sophisticated Lady; Caravan.

DUKE ELLINGTON & HIS ORCHESTRA
CA CW REsn ME, LB CCrs, RP JH NTrn PG HAsh HC, DE BD VG RJo, TWtk.

29 Nov 1969   (P)
Hammersmith Odeon
London, England

....	The "C" Jam Blues
....	Boo-Dah
....	Unidentified title
....	Smada
....	Tippytoeing Through The Jungle Garden
....	Kinda Dukish
....	Take The "A" Train
....	Up Jump
....	Rose Room
....	El Gato
....	Black Butterfly
....	Things Ain't What They Used To Be
....	Take The "A" Train
....	Fife
....	Come Off The Veldt
....	Medley[1]
....	In Triplicate
....	Perdido
....	R.T.M.

> DE VG.

....	Meditation

> Entire band.

....	April In Paris
....	April In Paris

> DE BD VG RJo.

....	Black Swan

[1]Including: Don't You Know I Care?; In A Sentimental Mood; Prelude To A Kiss; I Let A Song Go Out Of My Heart; Do Nothin' Till You Hear From Me; Just Squeeze Me; Don't Get Around Much Anymore; Mood Indigo; I'm Beginning To See The Light; The Blues –vTWtk; It Don't Mean A Thing –vTWtk; I Got It Bad; Be Cool And Groovy For Me –vTWtk; Sophisticated Lady; Caravan.

DUKE ELLINGTON & HIS ORCHESTRA
CA CW REsn ME, LB CCrs, RP JH NTrn PG HAsh HC, DE BD VG RJo, TWtk.

30 Nov 1969   (P)
Winter Gardens
Bournemouth, England

....	The "C" Jam Blues
....	Kinda Dukish/Rockin' In Rhythm
....	Take The "A" Train
....	Up Jump
....	What Am I Here For?
....	El Gato
....	Black Butterfly
....	Tippytoeing Through The Jungle Garden
....	Come Off The Veldt
....	Medley[1]

[1]Including: Don't You Know I Care?; In A Sentimental Mood; Prelude To A Kiss; The Brown-Skin Gal; I Let A Song   >>>

Out Of My Heart; Do Nothin' Till You Hear From Me; Just Squeeze Me; Don't Get Around Much Anymore; Mood Indigo;
I'm Beginning To See The Light; The Blues –vTWtk; It Don't Mean A Thing –vTWtk; Sophisticated Lady; Caravan.

DUKE ELLINGTON & HIS ORCHESTRA
Same personnel.

....	The "C" Jam Blues
....	4:30 Blues
....	El Gato
....	Black Butterfly
....	Things Ain't What They Used To Be
....	Azure-Te
....	Satin Doll
....	The Biggest And Busiest Intersection
....	Medley[1]
....	In Triplicate

[1]Including: Don't You Know I Care?; In A Sentimental Mood; Prelude To A Kiss; The Brown-Skin Gal; Do Nothin' Till You
Hear From Me; Just Squeeze Me; Don't Get Around Much Anymore; Mood Indigo; I'm Beginning To See The Light; The
Blues –vTWtk; It Don't Mean A Thing –vTWtk; I Got It Bad; Be Cool And Groovy For Me –vTWtk; Sophisticated Lady;
Caravan.

p Nov 1969[1]   (S)
Unidentified location (?tc)
Europe

DUKE ELLINGTON
Piano solo.

....	The Sleeping Lady And The Giant Who Watches Over Her

[1]The date of the telecast is not known.

15-17 Dec 1969[1]   (P)
TV City (tc)
Hollywood, CA

DUKE ELLINGTON & HIS ORCHESTRA
CA CW WC ME, LB BWd CCrs, RP JH NTrn PG HAsh HC, DE BD VG PK RJo.

....	Satin Doll
....	I Got It Bad
....	Take The "A" Train

[1]Taping session; telecast on 13 Jan 1970.

31 Dec 1969   (P)
Caesar's Palace
Las Vegas, NV

DUKE ELLINGTON & HIS ORCHESTRA
CA CW WC JMlm ME, LB BWd CCrs, RP JH NTrn PG HAsh HC, DE BD VG PK RJo.

....	Black Beauty
....	Star Dust
....	Misty
....	The Spanish Flea
....	Happy Birthday
....	Satin Doll
....	Happy Birthday
....	I Can't Give You Anything But Love
....	Things Ain't What They Used To Be

1 Jan 1970   (P)
Caesar's Palace
Las Vegas, NV

DUKE ELLINGTON & HIS ORCHESTRA
CA CW WC JMlm ME, LB BWd CCrs, RP JH NTrn PG HAsh HC, DE BD VG PK RJo.

....	Take The "A" Train
....	Satin Doll
....	Things Ain't What They Used To Be
....	I Got It Bad
....	In Triplicate
....	Mood Indigo
....	Sophisticated Lady

7 Jan 1970   (S)
United Recording Studios
Las Vegas, NV

DUKE ELLINGTON & HIS GROUP
WC, LB, PG, DE BD VG PK RJo.

....	Az -4	The Kissing Mist

> DE omitted.

....	Fan	Tippytoeing Through The Jungle Garden

> DE added.

....	Fan -1	Noon Mooning

> DE BD PK RJo.

....	-3	Black Swan >>>

> BD omitted, PG, VG added.

....	Fan		Rocochet[1]

> DE VG PK RJo.

....	Fan		Never Stop Remembering Bill
....	Fan		Duck Amok

THE LATIN AMERICAN SUITE (ctd.)[2]

....	Fan	-1	4 Tina[3]

> PK omitted.

....	Fan	-2	Fat Mess

[1]"Rockochet" on Fan; also "Ricochet" in some publications.
[2]The other parts of the suite have been recorded on 5 Nov 1968.
[3]Stands for "Argentina."

10 Jan 1970   (P)
Koseinenkin Kaikan
Tokyo, Japan

DUKE ELLINGTON & HIS ORCHESTRA
CA CW ME, JP CCrs, RP JH NTrn HAsh HC, DE BD YA RJo, TWtk.

....	The "C" Jam Blues
....	Take The "A" Train
....	Tootie For Cootie
....	Fife
....	B.P. Blues
....	Up Jump
....	La Plus Belle Africaine
....	Come Off The Veldt
....	Medley[1]
....	Take The "A" Train
....	Azure-Te
....	Salomé
....	Black Butterfly
....	Things Ain't What They Used To Be
....	I Got It Bad
....	Satin Doll
....	In Duplicate[2]

> DE BD YA RJo.

....	Black Swan
....	April In Paris
....	April In Paris

> DE YA.

....	Meditation

[1]Including: In A Sentimental Mood; Prelude To A Kiss; I Let A Song Go Out Of My Heart: Do Nothin' Till You Hear From Me; Just Squeeze Me; Don't Get Around Much Anymore; Mood Indigo; I'm Beginning To See The Light; Solitude –vTWtk; Be Cool And Groovy For Me –vTWtk; It Don't Mean A Thing –vTWtk, Sophisticated Lady; Caravan.
[2]This title is a derivative of *Wailing Interval.*

DUKE ELLINGTON & HIS ORCHESTRA
Same personnel.

....	The "C" Jam Blues
....	Take The "A" Train
....	Tootie For Cootie
....	4:30 Blues
....	Fife
....	B.P. Blues
....	Up Jump
....	La Plus Belle Africaine
....	Come Off The Veldt
....	Medley[1]
....	Soon It's Gonna Rain
....	Summer Samba
....	The Birth Of The Blues
....	Black Butterfly
....	Things Ain't What They Used To Be
....	I Got It Bad
....	Satin Doll
....	In Duplicate
....	April In Paris
....	April In Paris

> DE BD YA RJo.

....	Black Swan >>>

> DE YA.

....   Meditation

[1]Including: Don't You Know I Care?; In A Sentimental Mood; Do Nothin' Till You Hear From Me; Prelude To A Kiss; Just Squeeze Me; Don't Get Around Much Anymore; Mood Indigo; I'm Beginning To See The Light; Solitude –vTWtk; It Don't Mean A Thing –vTWtk; Be Cool And Groovy For Me –vTWtk; Sophisticated Lady; Caravan.

                                                                                          14 Jan 1970   (P)
DUKE ELLINGTON & HIS ORCHESTRA   Unidentified location (tc)
CA CW JMlm ME, JP BWd CCrs, RP JH NTrn HAsh HC, DE BD JBjm RJo.   Tokyo, Japan

....   Black Butterfly
....   Satin Doll
....   Medley[1]

[1]Including: Don't You Know I Care?; In A Sentimental Mood; Prelude To A Kiss; Do Nothin' Till You Hear From Me; Don't Get Around Much Anymore; Mood Indigo; I'm Beginning To See The Light; Sophisticated Lady; Caravan.

                                                                                          15 Jan 1970   (P)
DUKE ELLINGTON & HIS ORCHESTRA   Koseinenkin Kaikan
CA CW JMlm ME, JP BWd CCrs, RP JH NTrn HAsh HC, DE BD JBjm RJo.   Osaka, Japan

....   The "C" Jam Blues
....   B.P. Blues
....   Up Jump
....   4:30 Blues
....   Fife
....   Passion Flower
....   Soon It's Gonna Rain
....   Medley[1]
....   In Duplicate
....   April In Paris
....   April In Paris

> DE BD JBjm RJo.

....   Black Swan

> DE JBjm.

....   Meditation

[1]Including: Don't You Know I Care?; In A Sentimental Mood; Prelude To A Kiss; Jump For Joy; The Brown-Skin Gal; Do Nothin' Till You Hear From Me; I Let A Song Go Out Of My Heart; Just Squeeze Me; Don't Get Around Much Anymore; Mood Indigo; I'm Beginning To See The Light; Solitude; Caravan; Sophisticated Lady; Satin Doll.

DUKE ELLINGTON & HIS ORCHESTRA
TWtk added, otherwise same personnel.

....   The "C" Jam Blues
....   Take The "A" Train
....   B.P. Blues
....   Up Jump
....   4:30 Blues
....   HARLEM
....   Medley[1]
....   Soon It's Gonna Rain
....   Summer Samba
....   The Birth Of The Blues
....   Black Butterfly
....   Things Ain't What They Used To Be
....   Drag
....   I Got It Bad
....   Making That Scene –vTWtk[2]
....   Solitude –vTWtk
....   Satin Doll

[1]Including: Don't You Know I Care?; Do Nothin' Till You Hear From Me; I Let A Song Go Out Of My Heart; Just Squeeze Me; Don't Get Around Much Anymore; Mood Indigo; I'm Beginning to See The Light; Sophisticated Lady; Caravan.
[2]sa "That Scene"; "Making That Love Scene."

                                                                                          Jan 1970   (S)
DUKE ELLINGTON   Unidentified location
No particulars available.   Japan

....   Interview

                                                                                          5 Feb 1970   (P)
DUKE ELLINGTON & HIS ORCHESTRA   Festival Hall
CA CW JMlm ME, JP BWd CCrs, RP JH NTrn HAsh HC, DE BD JBjm RJo, TWtk.   Melbourne, Australia

....   Take The "A" Train   >>>

....	La Plus Belle Africaine
....	Medley[1]
....	The Birth Of The Blues
....	Black Butterfly
....	Making That Scene –vTWtk
....	It Don't Mean A Thing –vTWtk
....	I Got It Bad
....	In Duplicate
....	April In Paris
....	April In Paris
....	Basin Street Blues
....	Acht O'Clock Rock

[1]Including: Don't You Know I Care; In A Sentimental Mood; Prelude To A Kiss; Do Nothin' Till You Hear From Me; Don't Get Around Much Anymore; Mood Indigo; I'm Beginning To See The Light; Sophisticated Lady; Caravan.

6 Feb 1970[1]   (T/P)

DUKE ELLINGTON & HIS ORCHESTRA   ABC Studio Theatre (tc)
CA CW JMlm ME, JP BWd CCrs, RP JH NTrn HAsh HC, DE BD JBjm RJo, TWtk.   Sydney, Australia

....	The "C" Jam Blues
....	Kinda Dukish/Rockin' In Rhythm
....	Black Butterfly
....	Things Ain't What They Used To Be
....	Take The "A" Train
....	Crescendo In Blue
....	La Plus Belle Africaine
....	Come Off The Veldt
....	Medley[2]
....	The Birth Of The Blues
....	Satin Doll
....	Satin Doll

[1]The band was filmed for the ABC-TV special "Duke Ellington In Australia"; telecast in the U.S. on 11 Mar 1970.
[2]Including: Do Nothin' Till You Hear From Me; Don't Get Around Much Anymore; Mood Indigo; I'm Beginning To See The Light; Solitude –vTWtk; It Don't Mean A Thing –vTWtk; I Got It Bad; Be Cool And Groovy For Me –vTWtk; Sophisticated Lady.

DUKE ELLINGTON   Unidentified location (bc) (S)
DE interviewed by Anne Jefferson and Ellis Blaine.

....	Interview

7 Feb 1970   (P)

DUKE ELLINGTON & HIS ORCHESTRA   Municipal Stadium
CA CW JMlm ME, JP BWd CCrs, RP JH NTrn HAsh HC, DE BD JBjm RJo, TWtk.   Sydney, Australia

....	The 'C" Jam Blues
....	Kinda Dukish/Rockin' In Rhythm
....	B.P. Blues
....	Up Jump
....	Take The "A" Train
....	HARLEM
....	La Plus Belle Africaine
....	Come Off The Veldt
....	Medley[1]
....	R.T.M.
....	The Birth Of The Blues
....	Passion Flower
....	Things Ain't What They Used To Be
....	Making That Scene –vTWtk
....	Solitude –vTWtk
....	It Don't Mean A Thing –vTWtk
....	I Got It Bad
....	Be Cool And Groovy For Me –vTWtk
....	Satin Doll
....	In Duplicate
....	April In Paris
....	April In Paris
....	April In Paris

> DE JBjm.

....	Meditation

> *Entire band.*

....	Satin Doll

[1]Including: I Let A Song Go Out Of My Heart; Don't You Know I Care?; In A Sentimental Mood; Prelude To A Kiss;   >>>

Do Nothin' Till You Hear From Me; Don't Get Around Much Anymore; Mood Indigo; I'm Beginning to See The Light; Sophisticated Lady; Caravan.

Some sources suggest that the above concert dates to 6 Feb 1970 and that both events were played back-to-back at the Municipal Stadium.

			8 Feb 1970	(T)

DUKE ELLINGTON & HIS ORCHESTRA
CA CW JMlm ME, JP BWd CCrs, RP JH NTrn HAsh HC, DE BD JBjm RJo.

Unidentified studio
Sydney, Australia

....	-1	Craven Filter Song
....	-2	Craven Filter Song

Music for a cigarette commercial.

9 Feb 1970   (P)
Town Hall (bc)[1]
Wellington, New Zealand

DUKE ELLINGTON & HIS ORCHESTRA
CA CW JMlm ME, JP BWd CCrs, RP JH NTrn HAsh HC, DE BD JBjm RJo, TWtk.

....	La Plus Belle Africaine
....	Come Off The Veldt
....	Medley[2]
....	In Duplicate

[1]There were two delayed broadcasts, dates are not known.
[2]Including: Love You Madly; Don't You Know I Care?; In A Sentimental Mood; Prelude To A Kiss; Do Nothin' Till You Hear From Me; Don't Get Around Much Anymore; Mood Indigo; I'm Beginning To See The Light; Solitude –vTWtk; It Don't Mean A Thing –vTWtk; I Got It Bad; Be Cool And Groovy For Me –vTWtk; Sophisticated Lady; Caravan.

DUKE ELLINGTON
DE interviewed by Brian Edwards.

Unidentidied location (tc) (S)

| .... | Interview |

DUKE ELLINGTON & HIS ORCHESTRA
Same personnel.

Town Hall (bc)[1]   (P)

....	The "C" Jam Blues
....	Take The "A" Train
....	Passion Flower
....	Things Ain't What They Used To Be
....	The Birth Of The Blues
....	HARLEM
....	La Plus Belle Africaine
....	Come Off The Veldt
....	Medley[2]
....	In Duplicate
....	Satin Doll

> DE JBjm.

| .... | Meditation |

> Entire band.

....	April In Paris
....	April In Paris
....	Fife
....	Acht O'Clock Rock
....	Satin Doll

[1]There were two delayed broadcasts. Dates are not known.
[2]Including: Do Nothin' Till You Hear From Me; Don't Get Around Much Anymore; Mood Indigo; I'm Beginning To See The Light; Solitude –vTWtk; It Don't Mean A Thing –vTWtk; I Got It Bad; Be Cool And Groovy For Me –vTWtk; Sophisticated Lady; Caravan.

10 Feb 1970   (P)
Town Hall
Auckland, New Zealand

DUKE ELLINGTON & HIS ORCHESTRA
CA CW JMlm ME, JP BWd CCrs, RP JH NTrn HAsh HC, DE BD JBjm RJo.

....	The "C" Jam Blues
....	Take The "A" Train
....	Black Butterfly
....	Things Ain't What They Used To Be
....	The Birth Of The Blues
....	HARLEM
....	La Plus Belle Africaine
....	Come Off The Veldt

DUKE ELLINGTON & HIS ORCHESTRA
TWtk added, otherwise same personnel.

(bc)

| .... | The "C" Jam Blues   >>> |

....		Take The "A" Train
....		Passion Flower
....		Things Ain't What They Used To Be
....		The Birth Of The Blues
....		La Plus Belle Africaine
....		Come Off The Veldt
....		Satin Doll

> DE JBjm.

....		Meditation

> Entire band.

....		April In Paris
....		Fife
....		Acht O'Clock Rock
....		Satin Doll
....		Medley[1]
....		In Duplicate

[1]Including: Do Nothin' Till You Hear From Me; Don't Get Around Much Anymore; Mood Indigo; I'm Beginning To See The Light; Solitude –vTWtk; It Don't Mean A Thing –vTWtk; I Got It Bad; Be Cool and Groovy For Me –vTWtk; Sophisticated Lady; Caravan.

22 Feb 1970[1]   (P)

DUKE ELLINGTON & HIS ORCHESTRA   CBS Studios (tc)
CA CW WC ME, JP BWd CCrs, RP JH NTrn PG HC, DE BD TGrs VG RJo.   New York City, NY

....		Medley[2]

[1]Taping session; telecast on 1 Mar 1970.
[2]Including: She Loves You; All My Loving; Eleanor Rigby; She's Leaving Home; Norwegian Wood; A Ticket to Ride.

23 Feb 1970   (P)

DUKE ELLINGTON & HIS ORCHESTRA WITH LOUIS ARMSTRONG AND RAY CHARLES   Madison Square Garden
CA CW WC ME, JP BWd CCrs, RP JH NTrn PG HAsh, RCh BD JBjm RJo, TWtk.   New York City, NY

....		Satin Doll
....		Satin Doll

> LA added.

....		Hello Dolly –vLA

> LA, RCh omitted, DE added.

....		Kinda Dukish Rockin' In Rhythm
....		Take The "A" Train
....		Things Ain't What They Used To Be
....		Be Cool And Groovy For Me –vTWtk

> JRsh added.

....		Goin' To Chicago –vJRsh

9 Mar 1970   (S)

DUKE ELLINGTON & HIS ORCHESTRA   National Recording Studios
CA CW WC ME, JP BWd CCrs, RP JH NTrn PG HAsh HC, DE BD JBjm RJo.   New York City, NY

			THE RIVER[1]
....		-1	4 Grap[2] (incomplete)
....		-2	4 Grap (incomplete)
....		-3	4 Grap (incomplete)
....		-4	4 Grap
....			4 Grap (incomplete)
....		-5	4 Grap
....		-6	3 The Meander[3]
....	Az	-7	3 The Meander
....		-8	4 Grap (incomplete)
....			4 Grap (incomplete)
....	Az	-9	4 Grap
....		-10	4 Grap
....			4 Grap (incomplete)
....		-11	4 Grap (incomplete)
....		-12	4 Grap (incomplete)
....		-14	4 Grap
....		-15	4 Grap (incomplete)
....	RDB	-16	4 Grap
....		-17	8 Riba[4] (incomplete)
....		-18	8 Riba
....	Az	-19	8 Riba
....		-20	HARLEM (incomplete) >>>

....		HARLEM (incomplete)
....		HARLEM (incomplete)
....		HARLEM (incomplete)
....	-21	HARLEM (incomplete)
....	-22	HARLEM (incomplete)

[1]See also sessions on 11, 25 May; 3, 8, 15 Jun 1970.
[2]Stands for Giggling Rapids; *aka* "Big Bubble Coming"; *sa* "Gigl."
[3]*aka* "Romantic Encounter."
[4]*aka* "Main Stream"; *sa* "Taffy Twist."

14 Mar 1970   (P)
National Presbyterian Church
Washington, DC

DUKE ELLINGTON & HIS ORCHESTRA
CA CW WC ME, JP BWd CCrs, RP JH NTrn PG HAsh HC, DE BD JBjm RJo, DGrd NL
TWtk choir.

		THE SECOND SACRED CONCERT
....		Praise God
....		Supreme Being –vChoir
....		Something About Believing –vChoir
....		Almighty God –vDGrd Choir
....		The Shepherd
....		Heaven –vDGrd
....		It's Freedom –vDGrd NL TWtk Choir

> DE JBjm.

| .... | | Meditation |

> Entire band.

| .... | | The Biggest And Busiest Intersection |

> DE, NL.

| .... | | T.G.T.T. –vNL |

> Entire band.

| .... | | Don't Get Down On Your Knees –vTWtk |

> TWtk Choir a cappella.

| .... | | Father Forgive –vTWtk |

> Entire band.

| .... | | Don't Get Down On Your Knees –vTWtk |
| .... | | Praise God And Dance –vNL Choir |

> TWtk a cappella.

| .... | | The Preacher's Song –vTWtk |

> Entire band.

| .... | | In The Beginning God –vChoir |

15 Mar 1970   (P)
National Prebyterian Church
Washington, DC

DUKE ELLINGTON & HIS ORCHESTRA
CA CW WC ME, JP BWd CCrs, RP JH NTrn PG HAsh HC, DE BD JBjm RJo; DGrd NL
TWtk choir.

| | | THE SECOND SACRED CONCERT |

> BD organ solo.

| .... | | Heaven—Something About Believing—Azure—Something About Believing |

> DE JBjm.

| .... | | Meditation |

> Entire band.

....		Praise God
....		Supreme Being –vChoir
....		Something About Believing –vChoir
....		Almighty God –vDGrd Choir
....		The Shepherd
....		Heaven –vDGrd
....		It's Freedom –vDGrd NL TWtk Choir
....		The Biggest And Busiest Intersection

> DE, NL.

| .... | | T.G.T.T. –vNL |

> Entire band.

| .... | | Don't Get Down On Your Knees –vTWtk   >>> |

> TWtk Choir a cappella.

....   Father Forgive –vTWtk Choir

> Entire band.

....   Don't Get Down On Your Knees –vTWtk
....   Praise God And Dance –vNL Choir

> TWtk a cappella.

....   The Preacher's Song –vTWtk

> Entire band.

....   In The Beginning God –vChoir

DUKE ELLINGTON
DE interviewed by Alex Reynolds.

16 Mar 1970 (S)
Royal York Hotel (bc)
Toronto, ON

....   Interview

DUKE ELLINGTON
DE interviewed by Ted O'Reilly.

17 Mar 1970 (S)
Royal York Hotel (bc)
Toronto, ON

....   Interview

DUKE ELLINGTON
DE on the program "Front Page Challenge."

Mar 1970 (S)
CBC Studio (tc)
Toronto, ON

....   DE talking

DUKE ELLINGTON & HIS ORCHESTRA
CA CW FSt ME, JP BWd CCrs, RP JH NTrn PG HAsh HC, DE BD JBjm RJo, TWtk.

24 Mar 1970 (S)
Revolution Sound Studios
Toronto, ON

.... RDB   Orgasm
....   Don't Get Down On Your Knees –vTWtk

> DE JBjm.

....   Meditation

> Entire band.

....   The Shepherd
....   The Biggest And Busiest Intersection

DUKE ELLINGTON & HIS ORCHESTRA
CA CW ME, JP BWd CCrs, RP JH NTrn PG HAsh HC, DE BD RRd RJo.

25 Mar 1970 (P)
High Chaparral
Chicago, IL

....   The "C" Jam Blues
....   Kinda Dukish/Rockin' In Rhythm
....   Mount Harissa
....   Up Jump
....   Take The "A" Train

> HAsh, DE RRd RJo.

....   I Can't Get Started

> Entire band.

....   The Birth Of The Blues
....   Passion Flower
....   Things Ain't What They Used To Be
....   Summer Samba

> PG, DE RRd RJo.

....   Happy Reunion

> Entire band.

....   Diminuendo In Blue and In Triplicate
....   Soon It's Gonna Rain
....   Kinda Dukish/Rockin' In Rhythm
....   A Day In The Life Of A Fool
....   Jeep's Blues

> DE BD RRd RJo.

....   Jack The Bear   >>>

> Entire band.

....	Take The "A" Train
....	What Am I Here For?
....	The "C" Jam Blues
....	Squaty Roo

30 Mar 1970 (S)
Unidentified location (tc)
Saskatoon, SK

DUKE ELLINGTON
No particulars available.

.... Interview

2 Apr 1970 (P)
The Cave Theatre Restaurant
Vancouver, BC

DUKE ELLINGTON & HIS ORCHESTRA
CA CW AR ME, JP BWd CCrs, RP JH NTrn PG HAsh HC, DE BD JBjm RJo, TWtk.

....	TOM	The "C" Jam Blues
....	TOM	Kinda Dukish/Rockin' In Rhythm
....	TOM	4:30 Blues
....	TOM	Fife
....	TOM	B.P. Blues
....	TOM	Take The "A" Train
....	TOM	Up Jump
....	TOM	The Birth Of The Blues
....	TOM	Passion Flower
....	TOM	Things Ain't What They Used To Be
....	TOM	Come Off The Veldt
....	TOM	Medley[1]

[1]Including: Don't You Know I Care?; In A Sentimental Mood; Prelude To A Kiss; Do Nothin' Till You Hear From Me; Don't Get Around Much Anymore; Mood Indigo; I'm Beginning To See The Light; Solitude; It Don't Mean A Thing --vTWtk; I Got It Bad; Be Cool And Groovy For Me --vTWtk; Sophisticated Lady; Caravan.

DUKE ELLINGTON & HIS ORCHESTRA
TWtk omitted, otherwise same personnel.

....	TOM	Happy Birthday
....	TOM	Take The "A" Train

> HAsh, DE JBjm RJo.

....	TOM	I Can't Get Started

> Entire band.

....	TOM	Don't Be Cool[1]
....	TOM	April In Paris
....	TOM	April In Paris
....	TOM	April In Paris
....	TOM	April In Paris
....	TOM	Come Off The Veldt

[1]DE introduced BD by his nickname "Stone Soul Jones"; hence the misunderstood title "Stomp Soul Jump" on TOM.

8 Apr 1970 (S)
Studios CBUT (tc)
Vancouver, BC

DUKE ELLINGTON
DE on the program "In The Round."

.... Interview by Bob Smith

> DE JBjm RJo with a small studio band, directed by Doug Barker.

.... Satin Doll

> DE JBjm.

.... Meditation

19 Apr 1970 (P)
Grosmont Junior College
El Cajon, CA

DUKE ELLINGTON & HIS ORCHESTRA
CA CW FSt ME, JP BWd CCrs, RP JH NTrn PG HAsh HC, DE BD JBjm RJo, TWtk.

....	The "C" Jam Blues
....	Soon It's Gonna Rain
....	Kinda Dukish/Rockin' In Rhythm

> HAsh, DE JBjm RJo.

....	I Can't Get Started

> Entire band.

....	Fife
....	Up Jump
....	Take The "A" Train >>>

....	La Plus Belle Africaine
....	Come Off The Veldt
....	Medley[1]
....	R.T.M.
....	Passion Flower
....	Things Ain't What They Used To Be
....	The Birth Of The Blues
....	April In Paris
....	April In Paris
....	April In Paris
....	Making That Scene —vTWtk
....	Solitude —vTWtk
....	It Don't Mean A Thing —vTWtk
....	I Got It Bad
....	Be Cool And Groovy For Me —vTWtk
....	Satin Doll
....	Satin Doll

[1]Including: In A Sentimental Mood; Do Nothin' Till You Hear From Me; Don't Get Around Much Anymore; Mood Indigo; I'm Beginning To See The Light; Sophisticated Lady; Caravan.

	Apr 1970[1] (S)
DUKE ELLINGTON WITH ORCHESTRA	TV City (tc)
DE JBjm RJo with a studio orchestra, directed by either Jack Elliot or Allyn Ferguson.	Hollywood, CA

> DE JBjm RJo.

| .... | Sophisticated Lady |
| .... | Caravan |

> Studio orchestra added.

| .... | Don't Get Around Much Anymore |
| .... | Take The "A" Train |

> DE piano solo.

| .... | Mood Indigo |

> JBjm RJo, studio orchestra added.

| .... | It Don't Mean A Thing |

[1]Taping session; telecast on 30 Jul 1970.

	23 Apr 1970 (P)
DUKE ELLINGTON & HIS ORCHESTRA	Al Hirt's Club
CA CW FSt ME, JP BWd CCrs, RP JH NTrn PG HAsh HC, DE BD JBjm RJo, TWtk.	New Orleans, LA

....	Rockin' In Rhythm
....	Take The "A" Train
....	Passion Flower
....	Things Ain't What They Used To Be
....	The Birth Of The Blues
....	April In Paris
....	April In Paris
....	Medley[1]
....	Making That Scene —vTWtk
....	Be Cool And Groovy For Me —vTWtk
....	Satin Doll

[1]Including: Do Nothin' Till You Hear From Me; Don't Get Around Much Anymore; Mood Indigo; I'm Beginning To See The Light; Solitude; It Don't Mean A Thing; I Got It Bad; Caravan.

DUKE ELLINGTON	(tc)	(S)[1]
DE interviewed by Bill Wilson.		

| .... | Interview |

[1]At Al Hirt's Club.

DUKE ELLINGTON & HIS ORCHESTRA	(P)
TWtk omitted, otherwise same personnel.	

| .... | The "C" Jam Blues |
| .... | Take The "A" Train |

	THE NEW ORLEANS SUITE
....	- Thanks For The Beautiful Land On The Delta
....	- Aristocracy à la Jean Lafitte
....	- Second Line
....	- Bourbon Street Jingling Jollies
....	- Blues For New Orleans >>>

....			Passion Flower
....			Things Ain't What They Used To Be
....			Satin Doll

                                                       27 Apr 1970   **(S)**
                                                       National Recording Studios[1]

DUKE ELLINGTON & HIS ORCHESTRA   New York City, NY
AR CW FSt MJsn, JP BWd MTlr, RP JH NTrn PG HAsh HC, DE JBjm RJo.

THE NEW ORLEANS SUITE[2]

....		-1	4 Line[3] (incomplete)
....		-2	4 Line (incomplete)
....		-3	4 Line (incomplete)
....		-4	4 Line
....		-5	4 Line (incomplete)
....	Atc	-6	4 Second Line
....		-7	2 Orle[4] (incomplete)
....			2 Orle (incomplete)
....		-9	2 Orle (incomplete)
....		-12	2 Orle
....		-14	2 Orle (incomplete)
....		-15	2 Orle (incomplete)
....		-16	2 Orle (incomplete)
....	Atc	-18	2 Bourbon Street Jingling Jollies

      > ME replaces MJsn.

....		-20	5 Aris[5]
....	Atc	-21	5 Aristocracy à la Jean Lafitte
....		-22	5 Aris
....		-33	3 Upth[6] (incomplete)
....		-34	3 Upth (incomplete)
....		-35	3 Upth
....	Atc	-36	3 Thanks For The Beautiful Land On The Delta

      > BD added.

....		-39	1 Newe[7] (incomplete)
....		-40	1 Newe (incomplete)
....	Atc	-41	1 Blues For New Orleans
....			Rext[8] (incomplete)
....	Az	-42	Rext

[1]The editing was done at Atlantic Recording Studios, NYC.
[2]See also sessions on 13 and 25 May 1970.
[3]*sa* "Second Line."
[4]*sa* "Bourbon Street Jingling Jollies."
[5]*sa* "Aristocracy à la Jean Lafitte."
[6]*sa* "Thanks For The Beautiful Land On The Delta."
[7]*sa* "Blues For New Orleans."
[8]This title is not part of the suite.

                                                       3 May 1970   **(S)**
                                                       CBC Studios (tc)

DUKE ELLINGTON WITH BAND   Toronto, ON
DE with the Don Thompson Quartet.

....		Take The "A" Train

DE interviewed by Danny Finkleman.

....		Interview

                                                       11 May 1970   **(S)**
                                                       National Recording Studios

DUKE ELLINGTON   New York City, NY
Piano solo.

THE RIVER (ctd.)[1]

.... Az		- The Spring (incomplete)
.... Az		- The Spring

      > JBjm added

.... Stv		- The Spring[2]

      > JBjm omitted.

.... Stv		- The Run[3]—The Meander—The Run
.... Stv		- The Giggling Rapids[4]
.... Az		- The Lake (incomplete)
.... Stv		- The Lake
.... Az		- The Meander
.... Stv		- Stud[5] >>>

¹See also sessions on 9 Mar; 25 May; 3, 8, 15 Jun 1970.
²*sa* "The Queen's Guard"; "Marcia Regina"; "Improvisation"; *aka* "Marche Run."
³Overdubbing by DE of the previous take.
⁴*sa* "Gigl"; "Grap"; "Big Bubble Coming."
⁵Stands for <u>Students</u>. As "The Neo-Hip Hot-Cool Kiddies Community" on Stv.

13 May 1970   (S)
National Recording Studios¹
New York City, NY

DUKE ELLINGTON & HIS ORCHESTRA
CA CW FSt ME, JP BWd CCrs, RP NTrn PG HAsh HC, DE JBjm RJo.

			THE NEW ORLEANS SUITE (ctd.)²
....		-2	- Portrait Of Wellman Braud (incomplete)
....		-3	- Portrait Of Wellman Braud
....		-4	- Portrait Of Wellman Braud
....		-6	- Portrait Of Wellman Braud (incomplete)
....			- Portrait Of Wellman Braud (incomplete)
....	Atc	-7	- Portrait Of Wellman Braud
....		-8	- Portrait Of Sidney Bechet³ (incomplete)
....		-9	- Portrait Of Sidney Bechet (incomplete)
....		-10	- Portrait Of Sidney Bechet (incomplete)
....		-11	- Portrait Of Sidney Bechet
....		-12	- Portrait Of Sidney Bechet (incomplete)
....		-14	- Portrait Of Sidney Bechet (incomplete)
....		-15	- Portrait Of Sidney Bechet
....		-16	- Portrait Of Sidney Bechet (incomplete)
....		-17	- Portrait Of Sidney Bechet
....	Atc	-19	- Portrait Of Sidney Bechet
....		-20	- Portrait Of Louis Armstrong⁴ (incomplete)
....		-21	- Portrait Of Louis Armstrong (incomplete)
....	Atc	-22⁵	- Portrait Of Louis Armstrong
....			- Portrait Of Louis Armstrong (incomplete)
....	Atc	-23⁵	- Portrait Of Louis Armstrong
....		-26	- Portrait Of Mahalia Jackson⁶ (incomplete)
....	Atc	-28	- Portrait Of Mahalia Jackson

¹The editing was done at Atlantic Recording Studios, NYC.
²See also sessions on 27 Apr and 25 May 1970.
³*aka* "Gula."
⁴*aka* "Looie."
⁵Takes 22 and 23 have been edited together for the release on Atc.
⁶*aka* "Maha"; "Mala"; this title is a derivative of *Mahalia* from *The Girls Suite*.

19 May 1970¹   (P)
Studios WNEW (tc)
New York City, NY

DUKE ELLINGTON
DE interviewed by Orson Welles (sitting in for David Frost).

....		Interview

> DE JBjm RJo.

....		Satin Doll
....		Take The "A" Train

¹Taping session; telecast on 8 Jun 1970.

25 May 1970   (S)
Universal Studios
Chicago, IL

DUKE ELLINGTON & HIS ORCHESTRA
CA CW FSt ME, JP BWd CCrs, RP NTrn PG HAsh HC, DE JBjm RJo.

			THE NEW ORLEANS SUITE (ctd.)¹
....		-1	- Oo-Ee²
....		-2	- Oo-Ee (incomplete)
....		-3	- Oo-Ee
....		-4	- Oo-Ee
....		-5	- Oo-Ee (incomplete)
....		-6	- Oo-Ee
			THE RIVER (ctd.)³
....			2 The Run (incomplete)
....		-7	2 The Run
....		-9	2 The Run (incomplete)
....		-10	2 The Run (incomplete)
....		-11	2 The Run
....		-12	2 The Run
....		-13	2 The Run (incomplete)
....		-14	2 The Run
....		-15	2 The Run
....	WEA	-16	2 The Run
....		-17	3 The Meander >>>

....		-19	3 The Meander (incomplete)
....	WEA	-20	3 The Meander
....	WEA	-21	5 The Lake
....			4 Grap (incomplete)
....		-22	4 Grap
....	WEA	-23	4 The Giggling Rapids

> DE JBjm.

| .... | WEA | -24 | 1/12 The Spring |

[1]See also sessions on 27 Apr and 13 May 1970.
[2]*sa* "Portrait of Louis Armstrong"; "Looie."
[3]See also sessions on 9 Mar; 11 May; 3, 8, 15 Jun 1970.

		THE NEW ORLEANS SUITE (summation)
Atc	-41	1 Blues For New Orleans
Atc	-18	2 Bourbon Street Jingling Jollies
Atc	-22/-23	- Portrait Of Louis Armstrong
Atc	-36	3 Thanks For The Beautiful Land On The Delta
Atc	-7	- Portrait Of Wellman Braud
Atc	-6	4 Second Line
Atc	-19	- Portrait Of Sidney Bechet
Atc	-21	5 Aristocracy à la Jean Lafitte
Atc	-28	- Portrait Of Mahalia Jackson

28 May 1970   (S)

DUKE ELLINGTON WITH THE CINCINNATI SYMPHONY ORCHESTRA   Wilson Music Hall, University of Cincinnati
DE with the Cincinnati Symphony Orchestra, Erich Kunzel conducting.   Cincinnati, OH

| .... | De | New World A-Comin' |
| .... | De | HARLEM |

		THE GOLDEN BROOM AND THE GREEN APPLE
....	De	- Stanza 1 (The Golden Broom)
....	De	- Stanza 2 (The Green Apple)
....	De	- Stanza 3 (The Handsome Traffic Policeman)

No audience in attendance.

May/Jun 1970   (S)

DUKE ELLINGTON   Unspecified studio
DE talking about his Decca recordings.   New York City, NY

| .... | De | DE talking |

3 Jun 1970   (S)

DUKE ELLINGTON & HIS ORCHESTRA   National Recording Studios
CA CW FSt AR, JP BWd CCrs, RP NTrn PG HAsh HC, DE JBjm RJo.   New York City, NY

			THE RIVER (ctd.)[1]
....	WEA	-1	10 The Village Of The Virgins[2]

> EJns WR DFtz added.

....			7 Vortex (incomplete)
....			7 Vortex (incomplete)
....			7 Vortex (incomplete)
....			7 Vortex (incomplete)
....			7 Vortex (incomplete)
....			7 Vortex (incomplete)
....			7 Vortex (incomplete)
....			7 Vortex (incomplete)
....			7 Vortex (incomplete)
....			7 Vortex
....			7 Vortex (incomplete)
....		-3	7 Vortex (incomplete)
....		-4	7 Vortex (incomplete)
....		-5	7 Vortex (incomplete)
....			7 Vortex (incomplete)
....		-6	7 Vortex (incomplete)
....		-7	7 Vortex (incomplete)
....		-8	7 Vortex (incomplete)
....	WEA	-9	7 The Whirlpool[3]

> EJns WR DFtz omitted.

....		-2	4 Grap (incomplete)
....		-3	4 Grap
....		-5	4 Grap >>>

....		-6	4 Grap (incomplete)
....		-8	4 Grap (incomplete)
....		-9	4 Grap (incomplete)
....	Az	-10	4 Grap
....		-1	9 Stud
....		-2	9 Stud (incomplete)
....		-3	9 Stud
....		-4	9 Stud
....		-6	9 Stud (incomplete)
....		-8	9 Stud
....		-9	9 Stud
....		-10	9 Stud
....	Az	-11	9 Stud
....		-12	9 Stud (incomplete)
....		-13	9 Stud (incomplete)
....	WEA	-14	9 The Neo-Hip Hot-Cool Kiddies Community[4]
....		-1	8 Riba (incomplete)
....	WEA	-2	8 The River[5]

[1]See also sessions on 9 Mar; 11, 25 May; 8, 15 Jun 1970.
[2]*aka* "Vivi"; not identical with same title from 1956.
[3]*sa* "Vortex."
[4]*sa* "Stud."
[5]*sa* "Riba"; "Taffy Twist"; "Main Stream."

DUKE ELLINGTON   Half-Note Club   (T)[1]
DE interviewed by Louis Panassié

....	Interview

[1]This interview became part of the documentary "L'aventure du Jazz" (Jazz Odyssey); see also session on 3 Jul 1972.

8 Jun 1970   (S)
National Recording Studios
New York City, NY

DUKE ELLINGTON & HIS ORCHESTRA
CA CW FSt DB, CHth BWd CCrs, RP NTrn PG HAsh HC, DE JBjm RJo.

> EJns WR DFtz added.

			THE RIVER (ctd.)[1]
....			6 The Falls
....		-1	6 The Falls
....		-2	6 The Falls
....		-3	6 The Falls
....		-4	6 The Falls
....		-5	6 The Falls (incomplete)
....		-6	6 The Falls (incomplete)
....	WEA	-7	6 The Falls
....		-8	6 The Falls
....		-9	6 The Falls

> EJns WR DFtz omitted.

....	Az	-10	Flute[2]
....		-11	Flute (incomplete)

[1]See also sessions on 9 Mar; 11, 25 May; 3, 15 Jun 1970.
[2]This title is not a part of the suite.

15 Jun 1970   (S)
National Recording Studios
New York City, NY

DUKE ELLINGTON & HIS ORCHESTRA
CA CW FSt ME, JP BWd CCrs, RP NTrn PG HAsh HC, DE JBjm RJo.

			THE RIVER (ctd.)[1]
....		-1	11 The Mother, Her Majesty The Sea
....		-5	11 The Mother, Her Majesty The Sea (incomplete)
....	WEA	-7	11 The Mother, Her Majesty The Sea

> RP NTrn HC, DE JBjm RJo.

....	Az	-8	12 Soft[2]

> Entire band.

....		-9	4 Grap (incomplete)
....		-10	4 Grap
....		-11	4 Grap
....		-14	4 Grap (incomplete)
....		-15	4 Grap
....		-16	4 Grap (incomplete)
....		-17	4 Grap
....		-18	4 Grap >>>

		-19	4 Grap
....	Az	-20	4 Grap
....	Az	-24	Hard[3] (incomplete)
....	Az	-24	Hard

> BD added.

....			Mixt[4] (incomplete)
....		-25	Mixt (incomplete)
....	Az	-26	Mixt

> CA, HAsh, DE JBjm RJo.

....	Az	-27	All Too Soon (incomplete)
....	Az	-28	All Too Soon
....	Fan	-29	All Too Soon

> Entire band, BD added.

....		-30	Hard Way (incomplete)
....		-31	Hard Way (incomplete)
....		-33	Hard Way
....		-34	Hard Way (incomplete)
....		-35	Hard Way (incomplete)
....		-36	Hard Way
....			Some Summer Fun[5] (incomplete)
....	Pab	-38	Some Summer Fun
....	Pab	-40	Mendoza[6]

> NTrn PG, DE BD JBjm RJo.

....	RDB	-41	Just A-Settin' And A-Rockin'
....	RDB	-42	Just A-Settin' And A-Rockin' (incomplete)
....	Fan	-42	Just A-Settin' And A-Rockin'

[1]See also sessions on 9 Mar; 11, 25 May; 3, 8 Jun 1970.
[2]*sa* "The Spring."
[3]Part of the future *Afro-Eurasian Eclipse,* then renamed "Hard Way"; as "Mendoza" on Az.
[4]*aka* "Ballad."
[5]*sa* "Orgasm."
[6]*sa* "Hard Way"; *aka* "Foreign Blues." The unissued "East East Of East" is a derivative of *Mendoza.*

		THE RIVER (summation)
WEA	-24	1 The Spring
WEA	-16	2 The Run
WEA	-20	3 The Meander
WEA	-23	4 The Giggling Rapids
WEA	-21	5 The Lake
WEA	-7	6 The Falls
WEA	-9	7 The Whirlpool
WEA	-2	8 The River
WEA	-14	9 The Neo-Hip Hot-Cool Kiddies Community
WEA	-1	10 The Village Of The Virgins
WEA	-7	11 The Mother, Her Majesty The Sea
WEA	-24 (alt.?)	12 The Spring

20 Jun 1970   (P)
Dahlgren Hall, U.S. Naval Academy
Annapolis, MD

DUKE ELLINGTON & HIS ORCHESTRA
CA CW FSt ME, JP BWd CCrs, RP NTrn PG HAsh HC, DE BD JBjm RJo, TWtk.

....	The "C" Jam Blues
....	Kinda Dukish/Rockin' In Rhythm
....	Thanks For The Beautiful Land On The Delta
....	Bourbon Street Jingling Jollies
....	Portrait Of Louis Armstrong
....	Take The "A" Train
....	Portrait Of Sidney Bechet
....	In Triplicate
....	Medley[1]
....	R.T.M.
....	4:30 Blues
....	Fife
....	Blues For New Orleans
....	April In Paris
....	April In Paris
....	Come Off The Veldt
....	April In Paris
....	The Birth Of The Blues
....	The Mooche
....	Making That Scene –vTWtk >>>

....		Solitude –vTWtk
....		It Don't Mean A Thing –vTWtk
....		I Got It Bad
....		Be Cool And Groovy For Me –vTWtk
....		Satin Doll

[1]Including: In A Sentimental Mood; Just Squeeze Me; Do Nothin' Till You Hear From Me; Don't Get Around Much Anymore; Mood Indigo; I'm Beginning To See The Light; Sophisticated Lady, Caravan.

Jun 1970   (S)
Unspecified Studio
Glenville, IL

DUKE ELLINGTON
Piano solo.

....		Satin Doll

Music for a Zenith commercial.

28 Jun 1970   (P)
RAI Exhibition Centre
Amsterdam, Netherlands

DUKE ELLINGTON & HIS ORCHESTRA
CA CW FSt ME, MTlr BWd CCrs, RP NTrn PG HAsh HC, DE BD JBjm RJo, TWtk.

....		The "C" Jam Blues
....		Summer Samba
....		R.T.M.
....		Soon It's Gonna Rain
....		Kinda Dukish/Rockin' In Rhythm
....		Perdido
....		I Can't Get Started
		THE NEW ORLEANS SUITE
....		- Thanks For The Beautiful Land On The Delta
....		- Bourbon Street Jingling Jollies
....		- Fife
....		- Aristocracy à la Jean Lafitte
....		- Second Line
....		- Portrait Of Sidney Bechet
....		Wailing Interval
....		Take The "A" Train
....		Medley[1]
....		Alfie
....		Creole Love Call
....		The Birth Of The Blues
....		St. Louis Blues
....		Orgasm
....		April In Paris
....		April In Paris
....		Come Off The Veldt
....		April In Paris
....		Making That Scene –vTWtk
....		Solitude –vTWtk
....		It Don't Mean A Thing –vTWtk
....		I Got It Bad
....		Be Cool And Groovy For Me –vTWtk
....		Satin Doll
....		Satin Doll
....		Things Ain't What They Used To Be

[1]Including: Do Nothin' Till You Hear From Me; Don't Get Around Much Anymore; Mood Indigo; I'm Beginning To See The Light; Sophisticated Lady; Caravan.

2 Jul 1970[1]   (S)
ORTF Studios (tc)
Paris, France

DUKE ELLINGTON
Piano and intermittent talk.

....	TJC	Fleurette Africaine
....	TJC	Carolina Shout
....	TJC	Take The "A" Train
....	TJC	Black Beauty
....	TJC	Warm Valley
....	TJC	Things Ain't What They Used To Be
....	TJC	Paris Blues
....	TJC	New World A-Comin'
....	TJC	Paris Blues
....	TJC	Paris Blues
....	TJC	Come Sunday
....	TJC	Lotus Blossom
....	Mad	Satin Doll
....	Mad	Dancers In Love >>>

[1]Taping session; telecast on 7 Aug 1973. The date of the original telecast of excerpts is not known.

3 Jul 1970   (P)
DUKE ELLINGTON & HIS ORCHESTRA   Casino
CA CW FSt NW ME, MTlr BWd CCrs, RP NTrn PG HAsh HC, DE BD JBjm RJo, TWtk.   Montreux, Switzerland

....   The "C" Jam Blues
....   Summer Samba

                        THE NEW ORLEANS SUITE
....   - Second Line
....   - Bourbon Street Jingling Jollies
....   - Aristocracy à la Jean Lafitte
....   - Blues For New Orleans

....   Kinda Dukish/Rockin' In Rhythm
....   Take The "A" Train
....   La Plus Belle Africaine

        > PG, DE JBjm RJo.

....   Body And Soul   (P)

      ➤ Entire band.

....   Medley[1]
....   R.T.M.
....   Hard Way
....   The Birth Of The Blues
....   April In Paris
....   April In Paris
....   Come Off The Veldt
....   April In Paris
....   Making That Scene –vTWtk
....   It Don't Mean A Thing –vTWtk
....   I Got It Bad
....   Be Cool And Groovy For Me –vTWtk
....   Satin Doll
....   Satin Doll

[1]Including: In A Sentimental Mood; Just Squeeze Me; Do Nothin' Till You Hear From Me; Don't Get Around Much
Anymore; Mood Indigo; I'm Beginning To See The Light; Sophisticated Lady; Caravan.

4 Jul 1970   (S)
DUKE ELLINGTON WITH BAND   ORTF Studios (tc)
BCmn, GL, ABrd MBkr MGdr DHmr, CF GBrt.   Paris, France

....   It Don't Mean A Thing

        > DE and GBrt.

....   Conversation

      ➤ DE piano solo.

.... Mad   Meditation
.... Mad   Soda Fountain Rag
.... Mad   Le Sucrier Velours—Somebody Cares

        > MGdr DHmr added.

.... Mad   Caravan

        > Entire band.

.... Mad   Take The "A" Train –vCF

        > ABrd replaces DE.

....   Satin Doll

        > DE MBkr MGdr DHmr.

.... Mad   The Mooche

        > DE DHmr.

.... Mad   The Lake

        > DE piano solo.

.... Mad   Heaven

        > DE and BCmn.

....   Conversation

        > Entire band.

.... Mad   The "C" Jam Blues   >>>

> DE MBkr MGdr DHmr.

.... Mad   Medley[1]

> DE MBkr.

.... Mad   Monologue –DE narration

> Entire band, DE omitted.

....   St. Germaine des Pres –vGBrt

> DE added.

.... Mad   Woman, Girl, Child, Baby –vCF DE

[1]Including: Sophisticated Lady; I Let A Song Go Out Of My Heart; Don't Get Around Much Anymore; Mood Indigo.

DUKE ELLINGTON & HIS ORCHESTRA   Unidentified location (P)
CA CW FSt NW ME, MTlr BWd CCrs, RP NTrn PG HAsh HC, DE BD JBjm RJo.   Provins, France

....   The "C" Jam Blues

                                       THE NEW ORLEANS SUITE
....   - Aristocracy à la Jean Lafitte
....   - Second Line
....   - Bourbon Street Jingling Jollies
....   - Thanks For The Beautiful Land On The Delta
....   - Portrait Of Louis Armstrong
....   - Blues For New Orleans

....   Take The "A" Train
....   April In Paris
....   April In Paris
....   La Plus Belle Africaine
....   Satin Doll
....   Kinda Dukish/Rockin' In Rhythm
....   The Birth Of The Blues
....   St. Louis Blues

---

8 Jul 1970   (P)
DUKE ELLINGTON & HIS ORCHESTRA   Liseberg Konsert Hall
CA CW FSt NW ME, MTlr BWd CCrs, RP NTrn PG HAsh HC, DE BD JBjm RJo, TWtk.   Gothenburg, Sweden

....   The "C" Jam Blues
....   Summer Samba
....   Kinda Dukish/Rockin' In Rhythm

                                     THE NEW ORLEANS SUITE
....   - Second Line
....   - Bourbon Street Jingling Jollies
....   - Aristocracy à la Jean Lafitte
....   - Thanks For The Beautiful Land On The Delta
....   - Portrait Of Louis Armstrong

....   Take The "A" Train
....   In A Sentimental Mood
....   Wailing Interval
....   Medley[1]
....   The Birth Of The Blues
....   St. Louis Blues
....   April In Paris
....   April In Paris
....   Come Off The Veldt
....   Solitude –vTWtk
....   It Don't Mean A Thing –vTWtk
....   Be Cool And Groovy For Me –vTWtk
....   Satin Doll
....   Satin Doll
....   Things Ain't What They Used To Be

> DE BD JBjm RJo.

....   Black Swan

[1]Including: Do Nothin' Till You Hear From Me; Don't Get Around Much Anymore; Mood Indigo; I'm Beginning To See The Light; Sophisticated Lady; Caravan.

DUKE ELLINGTON & HIS ORCHESTRA
TWtk omitted, otherwise same personnel.

....   The "C" Jam Blues
....   Summer Samba
....   Kinda Dukish/Rockin' In Rhythm   >>>

THE NEW ORLEANS SUITE
.... - Second Line
.... - Bourbon Street Jingling Jollies
.... - Aristocracy à la Jean Lafitte
.... - Thanks For The Beautiful Land On The Delta
.... - Portrait Of Louis Armstrong

.... Take The "A" Train
.... In A Sentimental Mood
.... Up Jump
.... Medley[1]

[1]Including: Do Nothin' Till You Hear From Me; Just Squeeze Me; Don't Get Around Much Anymore.

DUKE ELLINGTON & HIS ORCHESTRA   9 Jul 1970   (S)
CA CW FSt NW ME, MTlr BWd CCrs, RP NTrn PG HAsh HC, DE BD JBjm RJo.   Rhenus Studio 7
                                                                     Cologne, Germany

.... RDB   -1   Alerado[1]
              -3   Alerado
.... RDB   -4   Alerado
              -1   Afrique[2]
.... RDB   -2   Afrique

[1]Short for Alexandre Rado; often misspelled "Alredado."
[2]Part of the future Afro-Eurasian Eclipse.

DUKE ELLINGTON & HIS ORCHESTRA   14 Jul 1970   (P)
CA CW FSt NW ME, MTlr BWd CCrs, RP NTrn PG HAsh HC, DE BD JBjm RJo.   Unidentified location
                                                                     Belgrade, Serbia (Yugoslavia)

.... The "C" Jam Blues

THE NEW ORLEANS SUITE
.... - Second Line
.... - Bourbon Street Jingling Jollies
.... - Aristocracy à la Jean Lafitte
.... - Thanks For The Beautiful Land On The Delta
.... - Portrait Of Louis Armstrong

.... Take The "A" Train
.... La Plus Belle Africaine
.... 4:30 Blues
.... Fife
.... Spacemen
.... Up Jump
.... Summer Samba
.... Black Butterfly
.... Things Ain't What They Used To Be
.... I Got It Bad
.... Satin Doll

DUKE ELLINGTON & HIS ORCHESTRA   17 Jul 1970   (P)
CA CW FSt NW ME, MTlr BWd CCrs, RP NTrn PG HAsh HC, DE BD JBjm RJo, TWtk.   Stadio della Favorita
                                                                     Palermo, Italy

.... The "C" Jam Blues
.... Kinda Dukish/Rockin' In Rhythm

THE NEW ORLEANS SUITE
.... - Second Line
.... - Bourbon Street Jingling Jollies
.... - Aristocracy à la Jean Lafitte
.... - Thanks For The Beautiful Land On The Delta

.... Take The "A" Train
.... Diminuendo In Blue and Wailing Interval
.... Medley[1]
.... The Birth Of The Blues
.... April In Paris
.... April In Paris
.... Come Off The Veldt
.... April In Paris
.... Making That Scene –vTWtk
.... Solitude –vTWtk
.... It Don't Mean A Thing –vTWtk
.... I Got It Bad
.... Be Cool And Groovy For Me –vTWtk
.... Satin Doll
.... Things Ain't What They Used To Be   >>>

....	In Triplicate	
....	Perdido	

> DE BD JBjm RJo.

....	Black Swan	

[1]Including: Mood Indigo; Sophisticated Lady; Caravan.

18 Jul 1970   (P)
Piper Music Hall
Rome, Italy

DUKE ELLINGTON & HIS ORCHESTRA
CA CW FSt NW ME, MTlr BWd CCrs, RP NTrn PG HAsh HC, DE BD JBjm RJo, TWtk.

	THE NEW ORLEANS SUITE
....	- Second Line
....	- Bourbon Street Jingling Jollies
....	- Aristocracy à la Jean Lafitte
....	- Thanks For The Beautiful Land On The Delta
....	Take The "A" Train
....	Up Jump
....	Medley[1]
....	R.T.M.
....	The Birth Of The Blues
....	April In Paris
....	April In Paris
....	Making That Scene –vTWtk
....	Solitude –vTWtk
....	It Don't Mean A Thing –vTWtk
....	Be Cool And Groovy For Me –vTWtk
....	Satin Doll
....	Things Ain't What They Used To Be

[1]Including: Do Nothin' Till You Hear From Me; Don't Get Around Much Anymore; Mood Indigo; I'm Beginning To See The Light; Sophisticated Lady; Caravan.

DUKE ELLINGTON & HIS ORCHESTRA
Same personnel.

....	The "C" Jam Blues
....	Take The "A" Train
....	Kinda Dukish/Rockin' In Rhythm
	THE NEW ORLEANS SUITE
....	- Second Line
....	- Bourbon Street Jingling Jollies
....	- Aristocracy à la Jean Lafitte
....	- Thanks For The Beautiful Land On The Delta
....	- Portrait Of Louis Armstrong
....	Take The "A" Train
....	In A Sentimental Mood
....	Up Jump
....	Medley[1]
....	R.T.M.
....	The Birth Of The Blues
....	St. Louis Blues
....	April In Paris
....	April In Paris
....	Come Off The Veldt
....	April In Paris
....	Making That Scene –vTWtk
....	Solitude –vTWtk
....	I Got It Bad
....	Be Cool And Groovy For Me –vTWtk
....	Satin Doll
....	In Triplicate
....	Things Ain't What They Used To Be
....	Love You Madly

[1]Including: Do Nothin' Till You Hear From Me; Don't Get Around Much Anymore; Mood Indigo; I'm Beginning To See The Light; Sophisticated Lady; Caravan.

19 Jul 1970   (P)
Parco delle Naiadi
Pescara, Italy

DUKE ELLINGTON & HIS ORCHESTRA
CA CW FSt NW ME, MTlr BWd CCrs, RP NTrn PG HAsh HC, DE BD JBjm RJo, TWtk.

....	The "C" Jam Blues
....	Take The "A" Train
....	Kinda Dukish/Rockin' In Rhythm >>>

THE NEW ORLEANS SUITE
.... - Second Line
.... - Bourbon Street Jingling Jollies
.... - Aristocracy à la Jean Lafitte
.... - Thanks For The Beautiful Land On The Delta
.... - Portrait Of Louis Armstrong

.... Take The "A" Train
.... In A Sentimental Mood
.... Up Jump
.... Medley[1]
.... R.T.M.
.... The Birth Of The Blues
.... St. Louis Blues
.... April In Paris
.... April In Paris
.... Come Off The Veldt
.... April In Paris
.... Making That Scene –vTWtk
.... Solitude –vTWtk
.... It Don't Mean A Thing –vTWtk
.... Be Cool And Groovy For Me –vTWtk
.... Satin Doll
.... Things Ain't What They Used To Be

[1]Including: Do Nothin' Till You Hear From Me; Don't Get Around Much Anymore; Mood Indigo; I'm Beginning To See The Light; Sophisticated Lady; Caravan.

20 Jul 1970[1]   (P)
DUKE ELLINGTON & HIS ORCHESTRA   La Bussola (tc)
CA CW FSt NW ME, MTlr BWd CCrs, RP NTrn PG HAsh HC, DE BD JBjm RJo.   Forte del Mari, Italy

.... Take The "A" Train
.... Kinda Dukish/Rockin' In Rhythm

THE NEW ORLEANS SUITE
.... - Second Line
.... - Bourbon Street Jingling Jollies
.... - Aristocracy à la Jean Lafitte
.... - Thanks For The Beautiful Land On The Delta
.... - Portrait Of Louis Armstrong

.... Medley[2]
.... The Birth Of The Blues
.... Things Ain't What They Used To Be

[1]Telecast in Italy on 27 Apr 1971.
[2]Including: Don't You Know I Care?; Prelude To A Kiss; Do Nothin' Till You Hear From Me; Don't Get Around Much Anymore; Mood Indigo; Caravan.

21 Jul 1970   (P)
DUKE ELLINGTON & HIS ORCHESTRA   Teatro dei Parchi
CA CW FSt NW ME, MTlr BWd CCrs, RP NTrn PG HAsh HC, DE BD JBjm RJo, TWtk.   Nervi, Italy

.... The "C" Jam Blues
.... Kinda Dukish/Rockin' In Rhythm

THE NEW ORLEANS SUITE
.... - Second Line
.... - Bourbon Street Jingling Jollies
.... - Aristocracy à la Jean Lafitte
.... - Thanks For The Beautiful Land On The Delta
.... - Portrait Of Louis Armstrong

.... Take The "A" Train
.... In A Sentimental Mood
.... Up Jump
.... Medley[1]
.... The Birth Of The Blues
.... St. Louis Blues
.... April In Paris
.... April In Paris
.... Come Off The Veldt
.... April In Paris
.... Making That Scene –vTWtk
.... Solitude –vTWtk
.... It Don't Mean A Thing –vTWtk
.... Be Cool And Groovy For Me –vTWtk   >>>

....		Satin Doll
....		In Triplicate
....		Perdido
....		David Danced Before The Lord
....		Things Ain't What They Used To Be

> DE BD JBjm RJo.

.... Black Swan

> PG added.

.... I Got It Bad

> PG omitted.

.... Alerado

[1]Including: Do Nothin' Till You Hear From Me; Don't Get Around Much Anymore; Mood Indigo; I'm Beginning To See The Light; Sophisticated Lady; Caravan.

22 Jul 1970   (P)
Teatro Romano
Verona, Italy

DUKE ELLINGTON & HIS ORCHESTRA
CA CW FSt NW ME, MTlr BWd CCrs, RP NTrn PG HAsh HC, DE BD JBjm RJo, TWtk.

.... The "C" Jam Blues
.... Summer Samba
.... Kinda Dukish/Rockin' In Rhythm

THE NEW ORLEANS SUITE
.... - Second Line
.... - Bourbon Street Jingling Jollies
.... - Aristocracy à la Jean Lafitte
.... - Thanks For The Beautiful Land On The Delta

.... Take The "A" Train
.... In A Sentimental Mood
.... In Triplicate
.... The Birth Of The Blues
.... April In Paris
.... April In Paris
.... Come Off The Veldt
.... April In Paris
.... Things Ain't What They Used To Be
.... R.T.M.
.... Medley[1]
.... Satin Doll
.... Perdido
.... Afrique
.... The Specific Split[2]

> NTrn, DE BD JBjm RJo.

.... Black Swan

[1]Including: Prelude To A Kiss; Do Nothin' Till You Hear From Me; Don't Get Around Much Anymore; Mood Indigo; I'm Beginning To See The Light; Solitude –vTWtk; It Don't Mean A Thing –vTWtk; I Got It Bad; Be Cool And Groovy For Me –vTWtk; Sophisticated Lady; Caravan.
[2]Some sources suggest the title to be "The Pacific Split"; documentation for either title could not be found.

23 Jul 1970   (S)
Studio Fontana
Milan, Italy

DUKE ELLINGTON & HIS ORCHESTRA
CA CW FSt NW ME, MTlr BWd CCrs, RP NTrn PG HAsh HC, DE BD JBjm RJo.

....	Az	-2	Maiera
....	MM	alt.	Maiera

THE NEW ORLEANS SUITE
.... MM - Portrait Of Louis Armstrong
.... MM - Thanks For The Beautiful Land On The Delta
.... LIt - Second Line
.... MM - Bourbon Street Jingling Jollies

24 Jul 1970   (P)
Palazzo dello Sport
Turin, Italy

DUKE ELLINGTON & HIS ORCHESTRA
CA CW FSt NW ME, MTlr BWd CCrs, RP NTrn PG HAsh HC, DE BD JBjm RJo, TWtk.

.... The "C" Jam Blues
.... Summer Samba
.... Kinda Dukish/Rockin' In Rhythm

THE NEW ORLEANS SUITE
.... - Second Line   >>>

....   - Bourbon Street Jingling Jollies
....   - Aristocracy à la Jean Lafitte
....   - Thanks For The Beautiful Land On The Delta
....   - Portrait Of Louis Armstrong

....   In A Sentimental Mood
....   Up Jump
....   Medley[1]
....   R.T.M.
....   Alfie
....   The Birth Of The Blues
....   St. Louis Blues
....   April In Paris
....   April In Paris
....   Come Off The Veldt
....   April In Paris
....   Making That Scene –vTWtk
....   Solitude –vTWtk
....   It Don't Mean A Thing –vTWtk
....   I Got It Bad
....   Be Cool And Groovy For me –vTWtk
....   Satin Doll
....   Afrique
....   Take The "A" Train
....   Happy Birthday
....   Maiera
....   The Specific Split

> MTlr, NTrn, DE BD JBjm RJo.

....   Things Ain't What They Used To Be

[1]Including: Do Nothin' Till You Hear From Me; Don't Get Around Much Anymore; Mood Indigo; I'm Beginning To See The Light; Sophisticated Lady; Caravan.

DUKE ELLINGTON & HIS ORCHESTRA   25 Jul 1970   (P)
CA CW FSt NW ME, MTlr BWd CCrs, RP NTrn PG HAsh HC, DE BD JBjm RJo, TWtk.   Théâtre Antique
                                                                     Orange, France

....   The "C" Jam Blues
....   Kinda Dukish/Rockin' In Rhythm

....   THE NEW ORLEANS SUITE
....   - Second Line
....   - Bourbon Street Jingling Jollies
....   - Aristocracy à la Jean Lafitte
....   - Thanks For The Beautiful Land On The Delta
....   - Portrait Of Louis Armstrong

....   Take The "A" Train
....   Portrait Of Sidney Bechet
....   Up Jump
....   Medley[1]

> DE BD JBjm RJo.

....   Black Swan

> Entire band.

....   R.T.M.
....   Salomé
....   St. Louis Blues
....   April In Paris
....   April In Paris
....   Come Off The Veldt
....   April In Paris
....   Making That Scene –vTWtk
....   Solitude –vTWtk
....   It Don't Mean A Thing –vTWtk
....   I Got It Bad
....   Be Cool And Groovy For Me –vTWtk
....   Satin Doll
....   Things Ain't What They Used To Be
....   Maiera
....   The Specific Split

> DE JBjm RJo.

....   Portrait Of Wellman Braud   >>>

[1]Including: Prelude To A Kiss; Do Nothin' Till You Hear From Me; Don't Get Around Much Anymore; Mood Indigo; I'm Beginning To See The Light; Sophisticated Lady, Caravan.

	26 Jul 1970	(P)
DUKE ELLINGTON & HIS ORCHESTRA	Théâtre Antique	
CA CW FSt NW ME, MTlr BWd CCrs, RP NTrn PG HAsh HC, DE BD JBjm RJo, DGrd TWtk	Orange, France	
SJC, BLau.		

THE SECOND SACRED CONCERT

> BD organ solo.
....   Organ Prelude

> Entire band.
....   Praise God

> SJC a cappella.
....   Let My People Go –vSJC

> Entire band.
....   Supreme Being –vSJC
....   Something About Believing –vDGrd TWtk SJC
....   Almighty God –vDGrd SJC
....   The Shepherd
....   Heaven –vDGrd SJC
....   It's Freedom –vDGrd TWtk SJC
....   The Biggest And Busiest Intersection

> DE JBjm.
....   Meditation

> Entire band.
....   Don't Get Down On Your Knees –vTWtk

> TWtk SJC a cappella.
....   Father Forgive –vTWtk SJC

> Entire band.
....   Don't Get Down On Your Knees –vTWtk
....   David Danced Before The Lord –vSJC, BLau tap

> DE JBjm RJo, TWtk.
....   Come Sunday –vTWtk

> Entire band.
....   Praise God And Dance –vDGrd SJC

> TWtk a cappella.
....   The Preacher's Song –vTWtk

> Entire band.
....   In The Beginning God –vSJC

DUKE ELLINGTON	Orange (bc)	(S)
DE on Radio France Culture.		

....   Interview

	28 Jul 1970	(P)
DUKE ELLINGTON & HIS ORCHESTRA	La Citadelle	
CA CW FSt NW ME, MTlr BWd CCrs, RP NTrn PG HAsh HC, DE BD JBjm RJo, TWtk.	Saint Tropez, France	

....   The "C" Jam Blues
....   Kinda Dukish/Rockin' In Rhythm

        THE NEW ORLEANS SUITE
....   - Second Line
....   - Bourbon Street Jingling Jollies
....   - Aristocracy à la Jean Lafitte
....   - Thanks For The Beautiful Land On The Delta
....   - Portrait Of Louis Armstrong

....   Take The "A" Train
....   Portrait Of Sidney Bechet
....   Up Jump
....   Medley[1]
....   R.T.M.
....   The Birth Of The Blues   >>>

....	St. Louis Blues
....	April In Paris
....	April In Paris
....	Come Off The Veldt
....	April In Paris
....	Making That Scene –vTWtk
....	Solitude –vTWtk
....	It Don't Mean A Thing –vTWtk
....	I Got It Bad
....	Be Cool And Groovy For Me –vTWtk
....	Satin Doll
....	In Triplicate
....	Afrique
....	Maiera

> DE, TWtk.

.... My Mother, My Father –vTWtk

> Entire band.

.... Things Ain't What They Used To Be

[1]Including: Do Nothin' Till You Hear From Me; Don't Get Around Much Anymore; Mood Indigo; I'm Beginning To See The Light; Sophisticated Lady; Caravan.

DUKE ELLINGTON & HIS ORCHESTRA
CA CW FSt NW ME, MTlr BWd CCrs, RP NTrn PG HAsh HC, DE BD JBjm RJo.

1 Aug 1970 (P)
Kursaal
Ostende, Belgium

....	The "C" Jam Blues
....	Summer Samba
....	Kinda Dukish/Rockin' In Rhythm
	THE NEW ORLEANS SUITE
....	- Second Line
....	- Bourbon Street Jingling Jollies
....	- Aristocracy à la Jean Lafitte
....	- Thanks For The Beautiful Land On The Delta
....	- Portrait Of Louis Armstrong
....	Take The "A" Train
....	In A Sentimental Mood
....	Up Jump
....	Medley[1]

[1]Including: Do Nothin' Till You Hear From Me … *Break of tape.*

DUKE ELLINGTON
DE interviewed by Merv Griffin.

6 Aug 1970 (P)
Metromedia Studios (tc)
New York City, NY

.... Interview

> BBry, DE JBjm, MGfn with a studio orchestra, directed by Mort Lindsay.

.... I'm Beginning To See The Light –vMGfn

> DE, MGfn

.... Interview (ctd.)

DUKE ELLINGTON
DE talking.

Aug 1970 (P)
Rainbow Grill
New York City, NY

.... A message to a friend (Boy Edgar)

> DE piano solo.

.... Solitude

DUKE ELLINGTON & HIS GROUP
CA, BWd, RP NTrn PG HAsh HC, DE JBjm RJo.

8 Aug 1970 (P)
Rainbow Grill (bc)
New York City, NY

.... Take The "A" Train
.... Caravan

> PG, DE JBjm RJo.

.... *In A Sentimental Mood*

> Entire group.

.... *In Triplicate*   >>>

....   Medley[1]
....   Take The "A" Train

[1]Including: Do Nothin' Till You Hear From Me; Don't Get Around Much Anymore; Mood Indigo.

9 Aug 1970   (P)
Miami Beach Auditorium
Miami Beach, FL

DUKE ELLINGTON WITH THE MIAMI BEACH SYMPHONY ORCHESTRA
DE JBjm RJo with the Miami Beach Symphony Orchestra, Barnett Breeskin conducting.

....   New World A-Comin'

     THE GOLDEN BROOM AND THE GREEN APPLE
....   - Stanza 1 (The Golden Broom)
....   - Stanza 2 (The Green Apple)
....   - Stanza 3 (The Handsome Traffic Policeman)
....   Medley[1]
....   Take The "A" Train

> MBSO omitted.

....   La Plus Belle Africaine

> MBSO added.

....   Come Off The Veldt
....   Satin Doll
....   Things Ain't What They Used To Be

[1]Including: Do Nothin' Till You Hear From Me; Prelude To A Kiss; Don't Get Around Much Anymore; Mood Indigo; I'm Beginning To See The Light; Sophisticated Lady; Caravan; It Don't Mean A Thing –vTWtk; My Mother, My Father –vTWtk; Be Cool And Groovy For Me –vTWtk; Solitude; I Let A Song Go Out Of My Heart.

10 Aug 1970   (P)
ABC Studios (tc)
New York City, NY

DUKE ELLINGTON WITH ORCHESTRA
DE with a studio band, directed by Bobby Rosengarden.

....   Medley[1]

> DE interviewed by Dick Cavett.

....   Interview

[1]Including: Mood Indigo; I Let A Song Go Out Of My Heart; It Don't Mean A Thing; Solitude; Rockin' In Rhythm.

15 Aug 1970   (P)
Rainbow Grill (bc)
New York City, NY

DUKE ELLINGTON & HIS GROUP
CA, BWd, RP NTrn PG HAsh HC, DE JBjm RJo.

     THE NEW ORLEANS SUITE
....   - Second Line
....   - Bourbon Street Jingling Jollies
....   - Aristocracy à la Jean Lafitte
....   - Thanks For The Beautiful Land On The Delta

22 Aug 1970   (P)
Rainbow Grill (bc)
New York City, NY

DUKE ELLINGTON & HIS GROUP
CA, MTlr BWd, RP NTrn PG HAsh HC, DE JBjm RJo.

....   Take The "A" Train
....   Black And Tan Fantasy—Creole Love Call—The Mooche
....   Fife
....   Satin Doll
....   Things Ain't What They Used To Be

29 Aug 1970   (P)
Rainbow Grill (bc)
New York City, NY

DUKE ELLINGTON & HIS GROUP
CA, MTlr BWd, RP NTrn PG HAsh HC, DE JBjm RJo.

....   Take The "A" Train
....   Second Line
....   Thanks For The Beautiful Land On The Delta
....   Sophisticated Lady
....   Deep Forest[1]
....   Things Ain't What They Used To Be

[1]sa "Afrique."

Aug 1970   (P)
Rainbow Grill
New York City, NY

DUKE ELLINGTON & HIS GROUP
CA, MTlr BWd, RP NTrn PG HAsh HC, DE JBjm RJo.

     THE NEW ORLEANS SUITE
....   - Second Line   >>>

....	- Bourbon Street Jingling Jollies	
....	- Aristocracy à la Jean Lafitte	
....	- Thanks For The Beautiful Land On The Delta	
....	Take The "A" Train	

30 Aug 1970[1]   (P)
Unspecified studio (tc)
New York City, NY

DUKE ELLINGTON & JOYA SHERRILL
DE piano and talking, JS vcl and talking.

.... My Mother, My Father –vJS
.... The Three Bears –DE narration

[1]Taping session; telecast on 20 Sep 1970.

Aug/Sep 1970[1]   (P)
Royal York Hotel (tc)
Toronto, ON

DUKE ELLINGTON WITH ORCHESTRA
DE and RJo with a studio orchestra.

.... DVD   Satin Doll

> LRls added.

.... DVD   Sophisticated Lady –vLRls

[1]Taping session; telecast on 14 Feb 1971.

10 Sep 1970   (P)
Disneyland
Anaheim, CA

DUKE ELLINGTON & HIS ORCHESTRA
CA CW MJsn ME, MTlr BWd CCrs, RP NTrn PG HAsh Hc, DE JBjm RJo.

.... The "C" Jam Blues
.... Take The "A" Train
.... Tootie For Cootie
.... Solitude
.... Mood Indigo
.... Happy Birthday
.... Hard Way
.... Satin Doll

12 Sep 1970   (P)
Disneyland
Anaheim, CA

DUKE ELLINGTON & HIS ORCHESTRA
CA CW MJsn ME, MTlr BWd CCrs, RP NTrn PG HAsh HC, DE JBjm RJo.

.... The "C" Jam Blues
.... Mood Indigo
.... Sophisticated Lady
.... Second Line
.... Aristocracy à la Jean Lafitte
.... Bourbon Street Jingling Jollies
.... Things Ain't What They Used To Be
.... Deep Forest
.... Satin Doll
.... Tang[1]
.... Diminuendo In Blue and Wailing Interval
.... I Got It Bad
.... Gong[1]
.... Hard Way
.... Hard Way
.... Take The "A" Train
.... Cotton Tail
.... Tang
.... Satin Doll

[1]Parts of the future *Afro-Eurasian Eclipse*.

18 Sep 1970   (P)
Monterey County Fairgrounds
Monterey, CA

DUKE ELLINGTON & HIS ORCHESTRA
CA CW MJsn ME, MTlr BWd CCrs, RP NTrn PG HAsh HC, DE BD JBjm RJo, TWtk.

.... R.T.M.
.... The "C" Jam Blues

THE AFRO-EURASIAN ECLIPSE
.... - Gong
.... - Chinoiserie[1]
.... - Tang[2]
.... - True[3]
.... - Big Luv
.... - Deep Forest
.... - Hard Way   >>>

> WH added.

....   I Got It Bad

> JWls added.

....   Don't Get Around Much Anymore –vJWls
....   Every Day –vJWls[4]

> WH, JWls omitted.

....   El Gato
....   April In Paris
....   April In Paris
....   Come Off The Veldt
....   April In Paris
....   Take The "A" Train
....   Making That Scene –vTWtk

> DE JBjm RJo, TWtk.

....   My Mother, My Father –vTWtk

> Entire band.

....   Be Cool And Groovy For Me –vTWtk
....   Satin Doll
....   Things Ain't What They Used To Be

[1] *aka* "Schn."
[2] Announced as "Django, Django."
[3] *sa* "Tell Me, It's The Truth."
[4] Complete: "Every Day I Have The Blues."

20 Sep 1970   (P)
Monterey County Fairgrounds
Monterey, CA

<u>DUKE ELLINGTON & DIZZY GILLESPIE</u>
DG, DE.

....   Monologue –DE narration
....   Take The "A" Train

25 Sep 1970   (P)
War Memorial Auditorium
Nashville, TN

<u>DUKE ELLINGTON & HIS ORCHESTRA WITH THE NASHVILLE SYMPHONY ORCHESTRA</u>
CA CW MJsn ME, MTlr BWd CCrs, RP NTrn PG HAsh HC, DE BD JBjm RJo, with the
Nashville Symphony Orchestra, Thor Johnson conducting.

> DE JBjm RJo, NSO.

....   THE GOLDEN BROOM AND THE GREEN APPLE
....   - Stanza 1 (The Golden Broom)
....   - Stanza 2 (The Green Apple)
....   - Stanza 3 (The Handsome Traffic Policeman)

> NSO omitted, entire band added.

....   Chinoiserie

> NSO added.

....   Take The "A" Train

> NSO omitted.

....   Bourbon Street Jingling Jollies

> NSO added.

....   Things Ain't What They Used To Be

> NSO omitted.

....   Acht O'Clock Rock

> NSO added.

....   Medley[1]

> NSO omitted.

....   Second Line
....   Take The "A" Train

> NSO added.

....   Take The "A" Train

> NSO omitted.

....   April In Paris
....   April In Paris
....   Come Off The Veldt   >>>

....   April In Paris

> NSO added.

....   Satin Doll

[1]Including: Prelude To A Kiss; Do Nothin' Till You Hear From Me; Don't Get Around Much Anymore; Mood Indigo; I'm Beginning To See The Light; Sophisticated Lady; Caravan; It Don't Mean A Thing; Solitude; I Let A Song Go Out Of My Heart.

                                                                                  2 Oct 1970   (P)
DUKE ELLINGTON & HIS ORCHESTRA   Constitution Hall
CA CW MJsn ME, MTlr BWd CCrs, RP NTrn PG HAsh HC, DE BD JBjm RJo, TWtk   Washington, DC

....   The "C" Jam Blues
....   Second Line
....   Portrait Of Louis Armstrong
....   Take The "A" Train
....   Creole Love Call
....   Chinoiserie
....   Bourbon Street Jingling Jollies
....   Hard Way
....   Deep Forest
....   Medley[1]
....   R.T.M.
....   El Gato
....   The Birth Of The Blues
....   April In Paris
....   April In Paris
....   Come Off The Veldt
....   April In Paris
....   Making That Scene –vTWtk
....   Solitude –vTWtk
....   It Don't Mean A Thing –vTWtk
....   My Mother, My Father –vTWtk
....   Be Cool And Groovy For Me –vTWtk
....   Satin Doll

> PG, DE JBjm RJo.

....   In A Sentimental Mood

> Entire band.

....   Diminuendo In Blue and Wailing Interval
....   Things Ain't What They Used To Be
....   Satin Doll
....   Acht O'Clock Rock
....   I Got It Bad

[1]Including: Don't You Know I Care?; Prelude To A Kiss; Do Nothin' Till You Hear From Me; Don't Get Around Much Anymore; Mood Indigo; I'm Beginning To See The Light; Sophisticated Lady; Caravan.

                                                                                  24 Oct 1970[1]   (P)
                                                                                  Unidentified location (bc)
DUKE ELLINGTON & HIS ORCHESTRA
CA CW MJsn ME, MTlr BWd CCrs, RP NTrn PG HAsh HC, DE BD JBjm RJo, TWtk.   New York City, NY

....   The "C" Jam Blues
....   Kinda Dukish/Rockin' In Rhythm
....   Bourbon Street Jingling Jollies
....   Chinoiserie
....   Take The "A" Train
....   Medley[2]
....   Making That Scene –vTWtk
....   Be Cool And Groovy For Me –vTWtk
....   Satin Doll
....   Things Ain't What They Used To Be

[1]Taping session; broadcast on 10 Dec 1970 (United Nations Day).
[2]Including: Do Nothin' Till You Hear From Me; Don't Get Around Much Anymore; Mood Indigo; I'm Beginning To See The Light; Sophisticated Lady.

                                                                                  12 Nov 1970   (S)
                                                                                  Unidentified location (bc)
DUKE ELLINGTON
DE and Howard Roberts, interviewed by Scott Ellsworth; intermittent previously recorded music.   Los Angeles, CA

....   Interview

DUKE ELLINGTON & HIS ORCHESTRA
CA CW MJsn ME, MTlr BWd CCrs, RP NTrn PG HAsh HC, DE JBjm RJo.

Late 1970   (S)
Unidentified location
U.S.A.

....   Tastycake Jingle –DE talking

Music for a Tastycake *commercial.*

DUKE ELLINGTON & HIS ORCHESTRA
CA CW MJsn AR, MTlr BWd CCrs, RP NTrn PG HAsh HC, DE BD JBjm RJo.

9 Dec 1970   (S)
National Recording Studios
New York City, NY

....	-1	R.T.M.
.... RDB	-2	R.T.M.
....	-3	Sophisticated Lady
.... MM	-4	Sans Snyphelle
....	-5	I Got It Bad (incomplete)
.... Pab	-7	I Got It Bad
.... Pab	-9	Bateau
....	-10	Big Luv
....	-11	Big Luv
.... RDB	-12	Big Luv

DUKE ELLINGTON & HIS ORCHESTRA
CA CW MJsn ME, MTlr BWd CCrs, RP NTrn PG HAsh HC, DE BD JBjm RJo JJ, KMrs.

11 Dec 1970   (S)
National Recording Studios
New York City, NY

....		Naidni Remmus[1] (incomplete)
....		Naidni Remmus (incomplete)
....		Naidni Remmus (incomplete)
....		Naidni Remmus (incomplete)
....	-1	Naidni Remmus
.... MM	-2	Naidni Remmus
....	-3	Hard[2] (incomplete)
....	-4	Hard (incomplete)
....	-5	Hard
.... RDB	-6	Hard
....	-7	Mercy, Mercy, Mercy
....	-8	I Got It Bad (incomplete)
....	-9	I Got It Bad
....		I Got It Bad (rehearsal)
....	-10	I Got It Bad (incomplete)
.... RDB	-11	I Got It Bad
....		Sophisticated Lady
.... Pab	-16	Sophisticated Lady
....	-17	I'm Afraid –vKMrs (incomplete)
....	-18	I'm Afraid –vKMrs
....	-19	I Got It Bad –vKMrs

[1]Variant spelling "Naidni Remus" (=Indian Summer).
[2]*sa* "Hard Way"; not identical with "Hard" from 15 Jun 1970.

DUKE ELLINGTON & HIS ORCHESTRA
CA CW MJsn ME, MTlr BWd CCrs, RP NTrn PG HAsh HC, DE BD JBjm RJo, BGrd.

22 Dec 1970   (S)
Universal Studios
Chicago, IL

....	It's The Talk Of The Town
....	I Got It Bad –vBGrd
....	Don't Get Around Much Anymore

DUKE ELLINGTON & HIS ORCHESTRA
CA CW MJsn ME, MTlr BWd CCrs, RP NT PG HAsh HC, DE ?BD JBjm RJo.

Late Dec 1970   (P)
Unidentified location
Las Vegas, NV

.... NTR	Take The "A" Train
.... NTR	Creole Love Call

DUKE ELLINGTON & HIS ORCHESTRA
CA CW MJsn ME, MTlr BWd CCrs, RP NTrn PG HAsh HC, DE BD JBjm RJo, BGrd.

31 Dec 1970   (P)
Caesar's Palace (bc)
Las Vegas, NV

....	Take The "A" Train
....	Mood Indigo—Sophisticated Lady
....	I'm Beginning To See The Light
....	I Got It Bad –vBGrd

5 Jan 1971   (P)
DUKE ELLINGTON & HIS ORCHESTRA WITH ELLA FITZGERALD   Coconut Grove, Ambassador Hotel
CA CW MJsn ME, MTlr BWd CCrs, RP NTrn PG HAsh HC, DE BD JBjm RJo, TWtk.   Los Angeles, CA

....		Take The "A" Train
....		Kinda Dukish/Rockin' In Rhythm
....		Bourbon Street Jingling Jollies
....		Chinoiserie
....		Take The "A" Train
....		April In Paris
....		April In Paris
....		Come Off The Veldt
....		Medley[1]
....		Making That Scene –vTWtk
....		Be Cool And Groovy For Me –vTWtk
....		Satin Doll
....		Things Ain't What They Used To Be

> JBjm RJo omitted, FdR ET, EF added.

....		Cotton Tail –vEF TWtk

[1]Including: Do Nothin' Till You Hear From Me; Don't Get Around Much Anymore; Mood Indigo; I'm Beginning To See The Light; Sophisticated Lady.

1 Feb 1971   (S)
DUKE ELLINGTON & HIS ORCHESTRA   National Recording Studios
CW MJsn EPtn ME, MTlr BWd CCrs, RP NTrn PG HAsh HC, DE BD JBjm RJo.   New York City, NY

....	Pab	-2	Love Is Just Around The Corner
....			Love Is Just Around The Corner (insert coda)
....		-5	Love Is Just Around The Corner (insert coda)

DUKE ELLINGTON & HIS RHYTHM
DE JBjm RJo.

....	Pab	-6	Edward The Second

DUKE ELLINGTON & HIS ORCHESTRA
NB[1] TWtk added, otherwise same personnel.

....	Az	-11	Rocks In My Bed –vNB
....		-15	One More Time For The People –vNB TWtk[2] (incomplete)
....			One More Time For The People –vNB TWtk
....		-18	One More Time For The People –vNB TWtk

[1]Vocalist Bobbie Gordon (BGrd) assumed the stage name "Nell Brookshire" at some point in time after having joined the Ellington band and will be listed under that name from here on.
[2]sa "One More Once"; "One More Twist"; "There's A Place."

2 Feb 1971   (S)
DUKE ELLINGTON & HIS QUARTET   National Recording Studios
NTrn HC, DE JBjm RJo.   New York City, NY

....	Pab	Intimate Interlude

DUKE ELLINGTON WITH GROUP   Studios KYW (tc)   (P)
Unidentified group (p b gt dr).   Philadelphia, PA

....		Take The "A" Train

> DE interviewed by Mike Douglas.

....		Interview

> DE gt b dr.

....		Jump For Joy

> NB added.

....		I Got It Bad –vNB
....		Interview (ctd.)

3 Feb 1971   (S)
DUKE ELLINGTON & HIS ORCHESTRA   National Recording Studios
CW MJsn EPtn ME, MTlr BWd CCrs, RP NTrn PG HAsh HC, DE BD JBjm RJo, NB TWtk.   New York City, NY

....		-31	I Don't Want Nobody At All –vNB
....	RDB	-37	Love You Madly –vNB
....		-38	Looking For My Man –vNB
....	RDB	-39	Looking For My Man –vNB
....	Pab	-41	Dick[1] >>>

.... Stv   -45   Peke
....   -47   One More Time For The People –vNB TWtk

[1]Actually "Hick"; also, incorrectly, "Nick" in some publications.

DUKE ELLINGTON & HIS ORCHESTRA
CW MJsn EPtn ME, MTlr BWd CCrs, RP NTrn PG HAsh HC, DE BD JBjm RJo.

.... RDB   -1   Freddy The Freeloader[1] (incomplete)
.... RDB   -2   Freddy The Freeloader

                                    THE AFRO-EURASIAN ECLIPSE[2]
.... RDB   -4   - Gong (incomplete)
.... RDB   -4   - Gong (incomplete)
.... RDB   -5   - Gong (incomplete)
.... RDB   -6   - Gong (incomplete)
.... RDB   -7   - Gong (incomplete)
.... RDB   -8   - Gong (incomplete)
....   -9   - Gong (incomplete)
....   -10   - Gong (incomplete)
....   -11   - Gong (incomplete)
....   - Gong (incomplete)
....   -12   - Gong
....   -13   - Gong (incomplete)
....   -14   - Gong (incomplete)
.... RDB   -15   - Gong
.... RDB   -16   - Chinoiserie
.... RDB   -17   - Tang (incomplete)
.... RDB   -18   - Tang (incomplete)
.... RDB   -19   - Tang (incomplete)
.... RDB   -19   - Tang (incomplete)
.... RDB   -20   - Tang

        > DE BD JBjm RJo.

.... Stv   -21   Riddle
.... Stv   -22   Unidentified title 1

        > Entire band.

                                    THE AFRO-EURASIAN ECLIPSE (cdt.)
....   - Didjeridoo[3] (incomplete)
....   - Didjeridoo (incomplete)
....   -24   - Didjeridoo
....   -25   - Didjeridoo (incomplete)
....   - Didjeridoo (incomplete)
....   -26   - Didjeridoo (incomplete)
....   -27   - Didjeridoo
....   -28   - True (incomplete)
....   -29   - True (incomplete)
....   -31   - True
....   - True (incomplete)
....   - True
....   -32   - True

....   -34   Unidentified title 2 (incomplete)
....   -36   Unidentified title 2 (incomplete)
.... RDB   -38   Unidentified title 2

[1]Announced by Radio Denmark as a Miles Davis composition, based on information received from Mercer Ellington; to be taken *cum grano salis*.
[2]See also sessions on 17 Feb and 13 May 1971.
[3]*aka* "Didj."

DUKE ELLINGTON & HIS ORCHESTRA
CW MJsn EPtn ME, MTlr BWd CCrs, RP NTrn PG HAsh HC, BD JBjm RJo, NB TWtk.

....   The "C" Jam Blues
....   Alfie
....   Love Is Just Around The Corner
....   I Can't Get Started

        > DE added.

....   B.P. Blues
....   Perdido
....   Hard Way
....   Things Ain't What They Used To Be
....   Summer Samba   >>>

....		Happy Birthday
....		Happy Birthday
....		Happy Birthday
....		Happy Birthday
....		I Can't Give You Anything But Love
....		One Note Samba
....		Bei Mir Bist Du Schoen
....		Happy Birthday
....		A Day In The Life Of A Fool
....		Satin Doll
....		I Got It Bad –vNB
....		Everybody Wants To Know –vNB[1]
....		Do Nothin' Till You Hear From Me –vNB

> DE BD JBjm RJo.

| .... | | Black Swan |

> Entire band.

....		Take The "A" Train
....		Sophisticated Lady
....		Making That Scene –vTWtk
....		Solitude –vTWtk
....		I Don't Want Nobody At All –vTWtk

> DE BD JBjm RJo, TWtk.

| .... | | My Mother, My Father –vTWtk |

> Entire band.

....		Be Cool And Groovy For Me –vTWtk
....		April In Paris
....		April In Paris
....		Come Off The Veldt
....		April In Paris
....		One More Time For The People –vNB TWtk
....		One More Time For The People –vNB TWtk
....		Mood Indigo
....		Love You Madly –vNB
....		Love You Madly –vNB
....		Rocks In My Bed –vNB

> BD JBjm RJo.

| .... | | Misty |

> Entire band.

....		Azure-Te
....		I'm Beginning To See The Light
....		Big Luv
....		Tang
....		Diminuendo In Blue and Wailing Interval
....		Satin Doll

[1]Complete: "Everybody Wants To Know Why I Sing The Blues."

17 Feb 1971   (S)
National Recording Studios
New York City, NY

DUKE ELLINGTON & HIS ORCHESTRA
CW MJsn EPtn ME, MTlr BWd CCrs, RP NTrn PG HAsh HC, DE BD JBjm RJo.

THE AFRO-EURASIAN ECLIPSE (ctd.)[1]

....		-1	- Gong (incomplete)
....		-2	- Gong (incomplete)
....		-3	- Gong (incomplete)
....		-4	- Gong (incomplete)
....		-5	- Gong (incomplete)
....		-6	- Gong (incomplete)
....		-7	- Gong (incomplete)
....	Fan	-8	- Gong
....		-9	- Tang (incomplete)
....	RDB	-10	- Tang (incomplete)
....	RDB	-12	- Tang
....	Fan[2]		- Tang
....		-15	- Didjeridoo
....	Fan[3]	-16	- Didjeridoo
....	Fan[3]	-17	- Didjeridoo (incomplete)
....		-18	- True
....		-19	- True
....	Fan	-20	- True >>>

....		-21	- Chinoiserie
....	Fan[2]		- Chinoiserie
....	Fan[2]		- Afrique
....		-24	- Hard Way[4]
....	Fan[2]		- Hard Way
....		-25	There's A Place –vNB TWtk[5]
....		-26	There's A Place (incomplete)
....		-27	There's A Place –vNB TWtk (incomplete)
....		-28	There's A Place –vNB TWtk (incomplete)
....	Az	-30	There's A Place –vNB TWtk
....			There's A Place –vNB TWtk

[1]See also sessions on 11 Feb and 13 May 1971.
[2]The takes used by Fan for some of the releases remain unspecified.
[3]Takes 16 and 17 have been edited together for release on Fan.
[4]sa "Hard"; no resemblance with "Hard Way." These two titles got mixed up sometimes.
[5]aka "There's A Place Somewhere"; sa "One More Once"; "One More Twist"; "One More Time For The People."

THE AFRO-EURASIAN ECLIPSE[1] (summation)

Fan		1	Chinoiserie
Fan	-16/-17	2	Didjeridoo
Fan		3	Afrique
Fan	-9	[2] 4	Acht O'Clock Rock
Fan	-8	5	Gong
Fan		6	Tang
Fan	-20	7	True
Fan		8	Hard Way

[1]Remixed 1975 at Fantasy Studios, Berkeley, CA, under the supervision of Mercer Ellington.
[2]Recorded on 13 May 1971.

DUKE ELLINGTON WITH BAND   ABC Studios (tc)   (P)
DE with a studio band, directed by Bobby Rosengarden.

....	In A Mellotone

> DE interviewed by Dick Cavett.

....	Interview

> DE with studio band, CW and NB added.

....	I Got It Bad –vNB CW

22 Feb 1971   (P)
Left Bank
Baltimore, MD

DUKE ELLINGTON WITH JOHN LAMB & TONY WATKINS
DE JL, TWtk.

....	Take The "A" Train
....	Unidentified title 1
....	Lotus Blossom
....	Sophisticated Lady
....	Unidentified title 2
....	Satin Doll
....	Dancers In Love
....	Mood Indigo
....	I'm Beginning To See The Light
....	Flamingo
....	Kinda Dukish
....	Jeep's Blues
....	Caravan
....	East St. Louis Toodle–Oo
....	Carolina Shout
....	Misty
....	Solitude –vTWtk
....	It Don't Mean A Thing –vTWtk
....	My Mother, My Father –vTWtk
....	I Don't Want Nobody At All –vTWtk
....	Monologue –DE narration

Due to a holdup in traffic the band was late and arrived only in time for the second set.

DUKE ELLINGTON & HIS ORCHESTRA
CW MJsn EPtn ME, MTlr BWd CCrs, RP NTrn PG HAsh HC, BD JBjm RJo, NB TWtk.

....	The "C" Jam Blues
....	I Can't Get Started
....	B.P. Blues
....	Perdido >>>

> DE added.

....		Kinda Dukish/Rockin' In Rhythm
....		In A Sentimental Mood
....		Wailing Interval
....		Creole Love Call
....		Take The "A" Train
....		Chinoiserie
....		Bourbon Street Jingling Jollies
....		I Got It Bad –vNB
....		I'm Just A Lucky So-And-So—Things Ain't What They Used To Be
....		I'm Just A Lucky So-And-So –vTWtk
....		One More Time For The People –vNB TWtk
....		One More Time For The People –vNB TWtk
....		Sophisticated Lady
....		I Let A Song Go Out Of My Heart/Don't Get Around Much Anymore
....		Satin Doll
....		Be Cool And Groovy For Me –vTWtk
....		Layin' On Mellow
....		Azure-Te
....		April In Paris
....		April In Paris
....		Come Off The Veldt
....		April In Paris
....		Do Nothin' Till You Hear From Me –vNB
....		Love You Madly –vNB
....		Rocks In My Bed –vNB
....		I Don't Want Nobody At All –vNB TWtk
....		Hold Me, Baby –vNB TWtk
....		Satin Doll

23 Feb 1971   (S)
National Recording Studios
New York City, NY

DUKE ELLINGTON & HIS ORCHESTRA
CW MJsn EPtn ME, MTlr BWd CCrs, RP NTrn PG HAsh HC, DE BD JBjm RJo, NB TWtk.

....		-1	Checkered Hat
....		-2	Checkered Hat (incomplete)
....		-3	Checkered Hat (incomplete)
....		-4	Checkered Hat (incomplete)
....		-5	Checkered Hat (incomplete)
....		-6	Checkered Hat
....		-7	Checkered Hat (incomplete)
....		-9	Checkered Hat (incomplete)
....	Stv	-10	Checkered Hat
....		-11	There's A Place –vNB TWtk
....		-12	There's A Place –vNB TWtk
....		-14	There's A Place –vNB TWtk (incomplete)
....	Stv	-15	There's A Place –vNB TWtk

> DE BD JBjm RJo.

....	Stv	-16	Blues
....	Stv		Blues

26 Feb 1971   (P)
St. John Hospital
Milwaukee, WI

DUKE ELLINGTON & HIS ORCHESTRA
CW MJsn EPtn RN, MTlr BWd CCrs, RP NTrn PG HAsh HC, DE BD JBjm RJo, NB TWtk.

....		The "C" Jam Blues
....		Kinda Dukish/Rockin' In Rhythm
....		Creole Love Call
....		Perdido

> DE JBjm.

....		Meditation

> Entire band.

....		Chinoiserie
....		Bourbon Street Jingling Jollies
....		Take The "A" Train
....		In A Sentimental Mood
....		Up Jump
....		Medley¹
....		I Got It Bad –vNB CW
....		Everybody Wants To Know –vNB
....		R.T.M.
....		April In Paris >>>

....	April In Paris
....	Come Off The Veldt
....	April In Paris
....	Making That Scene –vTWtk
....	Solitude –vTWtk
....	It Don't Mean A Thing –vTWtk

> DE JBjm RJo, TWtk.

| .... | My Mother, My Father –vTWtk |

> Entire band.

....	Be Cool And Groovy For Me –vTWtk
....	Satin Doll
....	Things Ain't What They Used To Be
....	In Triplicate
....	One More Time For The People –vNB TWtk
....	Satin Doll

[1]Including: Don't You Know I Care?; Prelude To A Kiss; Do Nothin' Till You Hear From Me; Don't Get Around Much Anymore; Mood Indigo; Caravan; I'm Beginning To See The Light –vDE; Sophisticated Lady.

		27 Feb 1971 (P)

DUKE ELLINGTON & HIS ORCHESTRA
CW MJsn EPtn ME, MTlr BWd CCrs, RP NTrn PG HAsh HC, DE BD JBjm RJo, DGrd.

St. Paul's Anglican Church
Toronto, ON

| .... | Almighty God –vDGrd |
| .... | The Biggest And Busiest Intersection |

2 Mar 1971 (S)
Four Seasons Hotel (tc)

DUKE ELLINGTON
DE interviewed by Elwood Glover.

Toronto, ON

| .... | Interview |

Early Mar 1971 (P)
Beverly Hills Motel (tc)

DUKE ELLINGTON & HIS ORCHESTRA
CW MJsn EPtn ME, MTlr BWd CCrs, RP NTrn PG HAsh HC, DE BD JBjm RJo.

Downsview, ON

| .... | April In Paris |
| .... | Do Nothin' Till You Hear From Me |

5 Mar 1971[1] (S)
Beverly Hills Motel (tc)

DUKE ELLINGTON
Interviewed by person unknown.

Downsview, ON

| .... | DE talking about his life and music |

[1]The date of telecast is not known.

16 Mar 1971 (P)
Hollywood Palladium (tc)

DUKE ELLINGTON
Grammy Award presentation.

Los Angeles, CA

| .... | Acceptance speech by DE |

23 Mar 1971[1] (P)
Unidentified location (tc)

DUKE ELLINGTON
DE on the show "And Beautiful Too"; no particulars available.

U.S.A.

| .... | Take The "A" Train |

[1]Date of telecast; probably recorded at an earlier date.

12 Apr 1971 (P)
Terrace Ballroom

DUKE ELLINGTON & HIS ORCHESTRA
CW MJsn EPtn ME, MTlr BWd CCrs, HAsh NTrn TGfn PG HC, DE BD JBjm RJo, NB.

Newark, NJ

....	Kinda Dukish/Rockin' In Rhythm
....	Creole Love Call
....	Azure-Te
....	Big Luv
....	Hard Way
....	Take The "A" Train
....	I Let A Song Go Out Of My Heart/Don't Get Around Much Anymore
....	Tea For Two
....	A Day In The Life Of A Fool
....	Summer Samba
....	R.T.M.
....	Satin Doll
....	April In Paris >>>

....   April In Paris
....   Come Off The Veldt
....   April In Paris
....   I Got It Bad –vNB CW
....   Things Ain't What They Used To Be

                                                                                  16 Apr 1971   (P)
DUKE ELLINGTON & HIS ORCHESTRA   Philharmonic Hall, Lincoln Center
CW MJsn EPtn ME, MTlr BWd CCrs, HAsh NTrn TGfn PG HC, DE BD JBjm RJo, NB TWtk.   New York City, NY

....   The "C" Jam Blues
....   Kinda Dukish/Rockin' In Rhythm
....   Creole Love Call
....   Chinoiserie
....   Bourbon Street Jingling Jollies
....   Take The "A" Train
....   The Shepherd
....   In A Sentimental Mood

                          THE GOUTELAS SUITE
....   - Goutelas
....   - Get-With-Itness[1]
....   - Something[2]
....   - Having At It
....   - Fanfare

....   One More Time For The People –vNB TWtk
....   One More Time For The People –vNB TWtk
....   April In Paris
....   April In Paris
....   Come Off The Veldt
....   I Got It Bad –vNB
....   Medley[3]
....   Satin Doll
....   In Triplicate
....   Caravan

[1]aka "Le Brûlot."
[2]aka "Brot" (=Brothers); "Gout" (=Goutelas).
[3]Including: Do Nothin' Till You Hear From Me; Don't Get Around Much Anymore; Mood Indigo.

                                                                                  20 Apr 1971   (P)
DUKE ELLINGTON & HIS ORCHESTRA   The Blue Room, Shoreham Hotel
CW MJsn EPtn ME, MTlr BWd CCrs, HAsh NTrn HMn PG HC, DE BD JBjm RJo, NB TWtk.   Washington, DC

....   The "C" Jam Blues
....   Kinda Dukish/Rockin' In Rhythm
....   Creole Love Call
....   Chinoiserie
....   Bourbon Street Jingling Jollies
....   Take The "A" Train
....   In A Sentimental Mood
....   I Got It Bad –vNB CW
....   April In Paris
....   April In Paris
....   Come Off The Veldt
....   Medley[1]
....   Making That Scene –vTWtk
....   Solitude –vTWtk
....   It Don't Mean A Thing –vTWtk
....   Be Cool And Groovy For Me –vTWtk
....   Satin Doll

[1]Including: Do Nothin' Till You Hear From Me; Don't Get Around Much Anymore; Mood Indigo; I'm Beginning To See The
Light; Sophisticated Lady.

                                                                                  24 Apr 1971   (P)
DUKE ELLINGTON & HIS ORCHESTRA   The Blue Room, Shoreham Hotel
CW MJsn EPtn ME, MTlr BWd CCrs, HAsh NTrn HMn PG HC, DE BD JBjm RJo, NB TWtk.   Washington, DC

....   Pretty Girl
....   Perdido
....   Big Luv
....   I Can't Get Started
....   April In Paris
....   April In Paris
....   Come Off The Veldt
....   April In Paris   >>>

....		Rocks In My Bed –vNB
....		The Blues –vTWtk
....		I Don't Want Nobody At All –vTWtk
....		Do Nothin' Till You Hear From Me –vNB
....		It Don't Mean A Thing –vTWtk
....		One More Time For The People –vNB TWtk
....		Sophisticated Lady
....		Things Ain't What They Used To Be
....		In Triplicate
....		Mood Indigo
....		I'm Beginning To See The Light
....		Caravan
....		Be Cool And Groovy For Me –vTWtk
....		Black Butterfly
....		Satin Doll
....		In A Sentimental Mood
....		Satin Doll

27 Apr 1971 (S)
DUKE ELLINGTON & HIS ORCHESTRA — National Recording Studios
CW MJsn EPtn ME, MTlr BWd CCrs, HAsh NTrn HMn PG HC, DE JBjm RJo. — New York City, NY

THE GOUTELAS SUITE

....		-1	5 Having At It (incomplete)
....		-3	5 Having At It (incomplete)
....		-4	5 Having At It
....	Pab	-5	5 Having At It
....		-6	2 Goutelas (incomplete)
....		-7	2 Goutelas
....		-8	2 Goutelas
....		-9	2 Goutelas (incomplete)
....		-11	2 Goutelas
....	Pab[1]	-12	2 Goutelas
....		-14	3 Get-With-Itness
....		-15	3 Get-With-Itness
....	Pab	-16	3 Get-With-Itness
....		-18	4 Something
....	Pab	-19	4 Something
....		-22	4 Something (incomplete)
....		-23	4 Something
....		-24	4 Something (incomplete)
....		-25	4 Something (incomplete)
....		-26	4 Something
....	RDB	-27	1+6 Fanfare
....	Pab	-28	1+6 Fanfare

[1]It is assumed that two of the various takes of "Goutelas" have been edited together for the release on Pab, one of which is take 12, the other one could not be determined with certainty as yet.

28 Apr 1971 (S)
DUKE ELLINGTON & HIS ORCHESTRA — National Recording Studios
CW MJsn EPtn ME, MTlr BWd CCrs, HAsh NTrn HMn PG HC, DE JBjm RJo, TWtk. — New York City, NY

....		-29	Hick[1]
....		-30	Hick (incomplete)
....	Stv	-31	Hick
....		-32	Grap (incomplete)
....	Stv	-33	Grap
....	Stv	-34	Something

> BD replaces DE.

....	Stv	-35	Making That Scene –vTWtk

[1]This title is a derivative of *New York, New York;* no similarity with "Dick"/"Hick" from 3 Feb 1971.

DUKE ELLINGTON & AARON BRIDGERS — Unspecified studio (S)
DE and ABrd on two pianos.

....	Guitar Amour
....	Guitar Amour
....	Blues
....	Blues

The above titles are listed under the given date. If, however, the second pianist is indeed Billy Strayhorn, as suggested by some sources, the recording would fall into a time prior to May 1967, and probably even as far back as 1963, when "Guitar Amour" was a "hot" item.

6 May 1971   (S)
National Recording Studios
New York City, NY

DUKE ELLINGTON & HIS ORCHESTRA
CW MJsn EPtn RWls, MTlr BWd CCrs, HAsh NTrn BPsn PG HC, DE JBjm RJo, TWtk.

....	Pab	-36	Symphonette[1]
....		-37	Pretty Girl
....		-38	The Blues (incomplete)
....		-39	The Blues (incomplete)
....		-40	The Blues –vTWtk
....		-42	The Blues –vTWtk
....		-44	The Blues –vTWtk (incomplete)
....		-45	The Blues –vTWtk
....	Saj	-46	The Blues –vTWtk

> BD replaces DE.

....		-47	Dreaming By The Fire[2]
....		-48	Dreaming By The Fire (incomplete)
....		-50	Dreaming By The Fire

> DE replaces BD.

....		-51	Rick's Blues[3]
....		-52	Rick's Blues (incomplete)
....		-53	Rick's Blues

[1]This title is a derivative of *Sugar Hill Penthouse.*
[2]*aka* "Fire."
[3]*aka* "Pat Your Feet."

10 May 1971   (P)
Constitution Hall
Washington, DC

DUKE ELLINGTON & HIS ORCHESTRA
CW MJsn EPtn ME, MTlr BWd CCrs, HAsh NTrn BPsn PG HC, DE BD JBjm RJo, NB TWtk.

....	The "C" Jam Blues
....	Kinda Dukish/Rockin' In Rhythm
....	Creole Love Call
....	Chinoiserie
....	Bourbon Street Jingling Jollies
....	Take The "A" Train
....	Things Ain't What They Used To Be
....	April In Paris
....	April In Paris
....	Come Off The Veldt
....	One More Time For The People –vNB
....	One More Time For The People –vNB TWtk

> DBs added.

| .... | In Quadruplicate[1] |

> DBs, BD.

| .... | Orgasm |

> Entire band, DBs omitted.

| .... | Satin Doll |

[1]This title is a derivative of *Wailing Interval.*

13 May 1971   (S)
National Recording Studios
New York City, NY

DUKE ELLINGTON & HIS ORCHESTRA
CW MJsn EPtn ME, MTlr BWd CCrs, HAsh NTrn BPsn PG HC, DE BD JBjm RJo, NB.

....	RDB	-1	Lover Man –vNB (incomplete)
....	RDB	-1	Lover Man –vNB
....	RDB	-2	Lover Man –vNB (incomplete)
....		-3	Lover Man (incomplete)
....		-5	Lover Man (incomplete)
....	Stv	-6[1]	Lover Man –vNB
....	Stv	-7[1]	Lover Man –vNB (incomplete)
....			Lover Man –vNB (insert)
....	RDB	-8	Acht O'Clock Rock (incomplete)
....	Fan	-9	Acht O'Clock Rock[2]
....	RDB	-10	Charpoy
....	Stv	-11	Perdido
....	MM	-12	Charpoy

[1]Both takes were spliced together for the version released on Stv.
[2]Part of the *Afro-Eurasian Suite;* see also sessions on 11 and 17 Feb 1971.

22 May 1971   (P)

DUKE ELLINGTON   Berklee College, New England Life Hall's Charter Room
DE talking.   Boston, MA

....   Acceptance speech for an Honorary Doctorate of Music.

> DE piano solo.

.... Az   Take The "A" Train—Satin Doll
.... Az   Baby, You Can't Miss –vDE Crowd
.... Az   Sophisticated Lady—Baby, You Can't Miss
.... Az   Honeysuckle Rose

> NB added.

.... Az   Love You Madly –vNB

> NB omitted, TWtk added.

.... Az   Come Sunday –vTWtk[1]

[1]TWtk sings in Hebrew.

May/Jun 1971   (P)

DUKE ELLINGTON & HIS ORCHESTRA   Unidentified location
CW MJsn EPtn ME, MTlr BWd CCrs, HAsh NTrn BPsn PG HC, DE BD JBjm RJo. U.S.A.

....   Big Luv
....   Perdido

14 Jun 1971   (T)[1]

DUKE ELINGTON WITH THE UWIS BRASS BAND AND CHOIR   Humanities Building, University of Wisconsin
DE piano solo.   Madison, WI

....   New World A-Comin'

> UWIS Choir.

....   Praise To Thee My Alma Mater –vChoir

> UWIS Brass Band.

....   It Don't Mean A Thing

> DE piano solo.

....   Black And Tan Fantasy
....   Take The "A" Train
....   Satin Doll

[1]The above titles have been included in the documentary "The Good Old Days Are Tomorrow"; additional footage was filmed on 21 Jul 1972.

16 Jun 1971   (P)

DUKE ELLINGTON & HIS ORCHESTRA   Madison Square Garden
CW MJsn EPtn ME RN, MTlr BWd CCrs, HAsh NTrn BPsn PG HC, DE JBjm RJo, NB TWtk. New York City, NY

....   Take The "A" Train
....   Kinda Dukish/Rockin' In Rhythm
....   Medley[1]
....   Take The "A" Train
....   One More Time For The People –vNB TWtk
....   One More Time For The People –vNB TWtk
....   Satin Doll

[1]Including: Do Nothin' Till You Hear From Me; Don't Get Around Much Anymore; Mood Indigo; I'm Beginning To See The Light; Sophisticated Lady; Love You Madly –vNB; Solitude –vTWtk.

18 Jun 1971   (P)

DUKE ELLINGTON & HIS ORCHESTRA   Steak Pit
CW MJsn EPtn ME, MTlr BWd CCrs, HAsh NTrn BPsn PG HC, BD JBjm RJo, NB. Paramus, NJ

....   Love Is Just Around The Corner
....   Perdido

> DE added.

....   Mood Indigo
....   How High The Moon
....   A Day In The Life Of A Fool
....   Summer Samba
....   I Can't Get Started
....   Acht O'Clock Rock
....   A Mural From Two Perspectives
....   Jig Walk
....   The Spanish Flea   >>>

. . . .	Satin Doll
. . . .	Mambo Italiano
. . . .	I Let A Song Go Out Of My Heart/Don't Get Around Much Anymore
. . . .	Something To Live For
. . . .	Big Luv
. . . .	Happy Birthday
. . . .	Kinda Dukish/Rockin' In Rhythm
. . . .	Creole Love Call
. . . .	I Can't Give You Anything But Love
. . . .	Chinoiserie
. . . .	Bourbon Street Jingling Jollies
. . . .	Take The "A" Train
. . . .	Echoes Of Harlem
. . . .	April In Paris
. . . .	In A Sentimental Mood
. . . .	Love You Madly –vNB
. . . .	I Got It Bad –vNB CW
. . . .	Everybody Wants To Know –vNB
. . . .	April In Paris
. . . .	Come Off The Veldt
. . . .	R.T.M.
. . . .	B.P. Blues

> BD piano solo.

. . . .	Star Dust

> Entire band.

. . . .	Tiger Rag
. . . .	I'm Beginning To See The Light
. . . .	Things Ain't What They Used To Be

                                                                                                    22 Jun 1971   (P)
DUKE ELLINGTON & HIS ORCHESTRA   Edinboro State College
CW MJsn EPtn ME, MTlr BWd CCrs, RP NTrn HAsh HC, DE BD JBjm RJo, NB TWtk.   Edinboro, PA

. . . .	The "C" Jam Blues
. . . .	Kinda Dukish/Rockin' In Rhythm
. . . .	Creole Love Call
. . . .	Perdido
. . . .	Chinoiserie
. . . .	Bourbon Street Jingling Jollies
. . . .	Take The "A" Train
. . . .	Medley[1]
. . . .	Satin Doll
. . . .	Big Luv
. . . .	April In Paris
. . . .	April In Paris
. . . .	Come Off The Veldt
. . . .	Solitude –vTWtk

[1]Including: Do Nothin' Till You Hear From Me; Don't Get Around Much Anymore; Mood Indigo; I'm Beginning To See The Light; Love You Madly –vNB; I Got It Bad –vNB; Sophisticated Lady.

                                                                                                    24 Jun 1971   (P)
DUKE ELLINGTON & HIS ORCHESTRA   Wollman Memorial Skating Rink, Central Park
CW MJsn EPtn ME, MTlr BWd CCrs, RP NTrn PG HAsh HC, DE BD JBjm RJo, NB TWtk.   New York City, NY

. . . .	Take The "A" Train
. . . .	Take The "A" Train
. . . .	Creole Love Call
. . . .	Chinoiserie
. . . .	Bourbon Street Jingling Jollies
. . . .	Sophisticated Lady
. . . .	April In Paris
. . . .	April In Paris
. . . .	Come Off The Veldt
. . . .	Lover Man –vNB
. . . .	Making That Scene –vTWtk
. . . .	One More Time For The People –vNB TWtk
. . . .	One More Time For The People –vNB TWtk
. . . .	Satin Doll

28 Jun 1971   (S)
National Recording Studios
New York City, NY

DUKE ELLINGTON & HIS ORCHESTRA
CW MJsn RWls ME, MTlr BWd CCrs, RP NTrn BPsn PG HAsh HC, DE BD JBjm RJo.

			TOGO BRAVA—BRAVA TOGO[1]
....			1 M'kis[2] (incomplete)
....	Stv	-1	1 M'kis
....	RDB		2 Tego[3] (incomplete)
....		-2	2 Tego
....			2 Tego (incomplete)
....			2 Tego (incomplete)
....	Stv	-3	2 Tego
....		-4	3 Yoyo[4] (incomplete)
....		-5	3 Yoyo (incomplete)
....	RDB	-6	3 Yoyo (incomplete)
....	Stv	-7	3 Yoyo

[1]See also session on 29 Jun 1971.
[2]*aka* "Mris."
[3]This title is a derivative of *Limbo Jazz.*
[4]*aka* "Togo."

29 Jun 1971   (S)
National Recording Studios
New York City, NY

DUKE ELLINGTON & HIS ORCHESTRA
CW MJsn RWls ME, MTlr BWd CCrs, RP NTrn BPsn PG HAsh HC, DE BD JBjm RJo.

....		-10	Goof
....	Pab	-11	Goof
			TOGO BRAVA—BRAVA TOGO (ctd.)[1]
....	Stv	-12	4 Too-Kee
....	Stv	-17	5 Buss
....	RDB		6 Soso[2] (incomplete)
....	Stv	-22	6 Soso
....	Pab	-25	Eulb[3]
....	Pab	-31	Tenz
			TOGO BRAVA—BRAVA TOGO (ctd.)
....		-32	7 Toto[4]
....	Stv	-34	7 Toto

[1]See also session on 28 Jun 1971.
[2]*sa* "Afrique"; "Deep Forest."
[3]=Blue.
[4]This title is a derivative of *Afrique.*

			TOGO BRAVA—BRAVA TOGO (summation)
Stv	-1		1 M'kis
Stv	-3		2 Tego
Stv	-7		3 Yoyo
Stv	-12		4 Too-Kee
Stv	-17		5 Buss
Stv	-22		6 Soso
Stv	-34		7 Toto

2 Jul 1971   (P)
Freebody Park
Newport, RI

DUKE ELLINGTON & HIS ORCHESTRA
CW MJsn EPtn ME RN, MTlr BWd CCrs, RP NTrn PG HAsh HC, DE BD JBjm RJo, TWtk.

....	Naturellement[1]
....	Take The "A" Train
....	I Don't Want Nobody At All –vTWtk

[1]*sa* "Yoyo"; "Togo."

14 Jul 1971   (P)
Ravinia Festival
Highland Park, IL

DUKE ELLINGTON & HIS ORCHESTRA
CW MJsn EPtn ME, MTlr BWd CCrs, NTrn PG HAsh HC, DE JBjm RJo, NB TWtk.

....	The "C" Jam Blues
....	Kinda Dukish/Rockin' In Rhythm
....	Black Beauty—Creole Love Call
....	Perdido
	TOGO BRAVA—BRAVA TOGO
....	- Soul Soothing Beach[1]
....	- Naturellement
....	- Amour, Amour[2]
....	- Right On Togo[3]
....	Chinoiserie >>>

....   Bourbon Street Jingling Jollies

[1]*sa* "M'kis"; "Mris."
[2]*sa* "Too-Kee."
[3]*sa* "Buss."

                                                                              16 Jul 1971   (P)
DUKE ELLINGTON & HIS ORCHESTRA   Baldwin Pavilion, Oakland University
CW MJsn EPtn ME, MTlr BWd CCrs, NTrn PG HAsh HC, DE JBjm RJo, NB TWtk.   Rochester, MI

....   Take The "A" Train
....   Kinda Dukish/Rockin' In Rhythm
....   Medley[1]
....   Love You Madly –vNB
....   Solitude –vTWtk
....   Take The "A" Train
....   Satin Doll

[1]Particulars not available.

                                                                              21 Jul 1971   (P)
DUKE ELLINGTON & HIS ORCHESTRA   High Chaparral
CW MJsn EPtn ME, MTlr BWd CCrs, RP NTrn PG HAsh HC, DE BD JBjm RJo.   Chicago, IL

....   The "C" Jam Blues
....   Kinda Dukish/Rockin' In Rhythm
....   How High The Moon

                                             THE GOUTELAS SUITE
....   - Goutelas
....   - Get-With-Itness
....   - Something
....   - Having At It

....   4:30 Blues
....   Chinoiserie
....   Diminuendo In Blue and Wailing Interval

                                             TOGO BRAVA—BRAVA TOGO
....   - Soul Soothing Beach
....   - Naturellement
....   - Amour, Amour
....   - Right On Togo

....   The Gal From Joe's
....   Take The "A" Train
....   Happy Birthday
....   Naturellement

                                                                              27 Jul 1971   (P)
DUKE ELLINGTON & HIS ORCHESTRA   Golden Dome Ballroom, Steel Pier
CW MJsn JCl EPtn ME, MTlr BWd CCrs, RP NTrn PG HAsh HC, BD JBjm RJo, NB TWtk. Atlantic City, NJ

....   The "C" Jam Blues
....   Alfie
     > DE added.

....   Kinda Dukish/Rockin' In Rhythm
....   Creole Love Call
....   Perdido
....   Soul Soothing Beach
....   Naturellement
....   Take The "A" Train
....   I Got It Bad –vNB CW
....   Satin Doll
....   Be Cool And Groovy For Me –vTWtk
....   One More Time For The People –vNB TWtk
....   One More Time For The People –vNB TWtk
....   Things Ain't What They Used To Be
....   R.T.M.
....   In Triplicate
....   Medley[1]
....   Making That Scene –vTWtk
....   Lover Man –vNB
....   I Don't Want Nobody At All –vTWtk
....   Everybody Wants To Know –vNB
....   Acht O'Clock Rock
....   Acht O'Clock Rock
....   Azure-Te   >>>

....	April In Paris
....	April In Paris
....	Come Off The Veldt
....	April In Paris
....	I Got It Bad —vNB CW
....	Love You Madly —vNB
....	Right On Togo
....	Solitude —vTWtk
....	Solitude

> BD JBjm RJo, DE.

....	Monologue —DE narration

> Entire band.

....	Solitude —vTWtk
....	It Don't Mean A Thing —vTWtk
....	My Mother, My Father —vTWtk
....	Be Cool And Groovy For Me —vTWtk
....	One More Time For The People —vNB TWtk
....	One More Time For The People —vNB TWtk
....	Satin Doll
....	Blue Skies
....	Things Ain't What They Used To Be

[1]Including: Don't Get Around Much Anymore; Mood Indigo; I'm Beginning To See The Light; Sophisticated Lady.

DUKE ELLINGTON & HIS GROUP   4 Aug 1971   (P)
MJsn, MTlr, RP NTrn HAsh HC, DE RJo, NB TWtk.   Rainbow Grill (bc)
                                                   New York City, NY

> DE piano solo.

....	Meditation

> Entire group.

....	Take The "A" Train
....	Creole Love Call
....	Chinoiserie
....	Bourbon Street Jingling Jollies
....	Medley[1]
....	Come Off The Veldt
....	Making That Scene —vTWtk
....	My Mother, My Father —vTWtk
....	It Don't Mean A Thing —vTWtk
....	Solitude —vTWtk
....	I Got It Bad —vNB MJsn
....	Everybody Wants To Know —vNB
....	One More Time For The People —vNB TWtk
....	One More Time For The People —vNB

[1]Including: Don't Get Around Much Anymore; Mood Indigo; I'm Beginning To See The Light; Sophisticated Lady; Caravan.

DUKE ELLINGTON & HIS GROUP   14 Aug 1971   (P)
MJsn, MTlr BWd, RP NTrn HAsh HC, DE AHll RJo.   Rainbow Grill (bc)
                                                   New York City, NY

....	Take The "A" Train
....	Creole Love Call
....	Chinoiserie
....	Medley[1]

[1]Including: Prelude To A Kiss; I Let A Song Go Out Of My Heart; Don't Get Around Much Anymore; Mood Indigo.

DUKE ELLINGTON & HIS GROUP   21 Aug 1971   (P)
MJsn, MTlr BWd, RP NTrn HAsh HC, DE AHll RJo.   Rainbow Grill (bc)
                                                   New York City, NY

....	Medley[1]
....	Stompin' At The Savoy
....	Serenade To Sweden
....	The "C" Jam Blues

[1]Including: Prelude To A Kiss; I Let A Song Go Out Of My Heart; Don't Get Around Much Anymore; Mood Indigo; I'm Beginning To See The Light; Jump For Joy; Sophisticated Lady.

DUKE ELLINGTON WITH ORCHESTRA   23 Aug 1971   (P)
DE with a studio orchestra, directed by Tommy Newsom.   NBC Studios (tc)
                                                   New York City, NY

....	Satin Doll >>>

> DE interviewed by Joey Bishop.

....   Interview

                                                                    24 Aug 1971   (P)
DUKE ELLINGTON & HIS QUARTET   NBC Studios (tc)
BWd, HC, DE AHll RJo.   New York City, NY

....   It Don't Mean A Thing
....   Medley[1]

> DE interviewed by Hugh Downs.

....   Interview

[1]Including: Caravan; Prelude To A Kiss; I Let A Song Go Out Of My Heart; Don't Get Around Much Anymore; Mood Indigo; I'm Beginning To See The Light; Sophisticated Lady; Satin Doll.

                                                                    28 Aug 1971   (P)
DUKE ELLINGTON & HIS GROUP   Rainbow Grill (bc)
MJsn, MTlr BWd, RP NTrn HAsh HC, DE AHll RJo.   New York City, NY

....   Things Ain't What They Used To Be
....   Take The "A" Train
....   Happy Birthday
....   I Can't Give You Anything But Love
....   Chinoiserie
....   Bourbon Street Jingling Jollies

                                                                    9 Oct 1971   (P)
DUKE ELLINGTON & HIS ORCHESTRA   Estradny Teatr
CW MJsn JCl EPtn ME, MTlr BWd CCrs, RP NTrn HMn PG HAsh HC, DE JBjm RJo, NB TWtk.   Moscow, Russia (USSR)

....   HARLEM
....   Perdido
....   Satin Doll
....   Things Ain't What They Used To Be
....   In Triplicate
....   La Plus Belle Africaine
....   Aristocracy à la Jean Lafitte
....   The Blues –vTWtk
....   How High The Moon
....   Medley[1]
....   I Can't Get Started

[1]Including: I Got It Bad –vNB CW; Everybody Wants To Know –vNB; Sophisticated Lady.

                                                                    10 Oct 1971   (S)
DUKE ELLINGTON   Unidentified location
DE interviewed by person unknown,   Moscow, Russia

....   Interview

                                                                    11 Oct 1971   (P)
DUKE ELLINGTON & HIS ORCHESTRA   Dvorets Sporta
CW MJsn JCl EPtn ME, MTlr BWd CCrs, RP NTrn HMn PG HAsh HC, DE JBjm RJo, NB TWtk.   Moscow, Russia

....   The "C" Jam Blues
....   Black And Tan Fantasy––Creole Love Call––The Mooche
....   Kinda Dukish/Rockin' In Rhythm

> PG, DE JBjm RJo.

....   Happy Reunion

> Entire band.

....   Take The "A" Train
....   Fife
....   Chinoiserie
....   HARLEM
....   Perdido
....   Take The "A" Train
....   Satin Doll
....   Things Ain't What They Used To Be
....   In Triplicate
....   La Plus Belle Africaine
....   Come Off The Veldt
....   Medley[1]
....   You Are Beautiful
....   Addi[2]
....   You Are Beautiful   >>>

....   How High The Moon
....   Soul Flute[3]
....   Aristocracy à la Jean Lafitte

          > DE JBjm.

....   Lotus Blossom

          > Entire band.

....   The Specific Split

[1]Including: Caravan; Do Nothin' Till You Hear From Me; I Let A Song Go Out Of My Heart; Don't Get Around Much
Anymore; Mood Indigo; Solitude –vTWtk; It Don't Mean A Thing –vTWtk; I Got It Bad –vNB CW; Everybody Wants
To Know –vNB; Sophisticated Lady; Caravan.
[2]aka "Serenade To The Bird"; "The Jungle."
[3]aka "Flute Amé."

| | | Oct 1971 | (P) |

DUKE ELLINGTON & HIS ORCHESTRA
CW MJsn JCl EPtn ME, MTlr BWd CCrs, RP NTrn HMn PG HAsh HC, DE JBjm RJo.

Oct 1971   (P)
Unidentified location
Moscow, Russia

....   Mood Indigo
....   Sophisticated Lady
....   Caravan

The above is presumed to be part of a medley.

DUKE ELLINGTON & HIS ORCHESTRA
CW MJsn JCl EPtn ME, MTlr BWd CCrs, RP NTrn HMn PG HAsh HC, DE JBjm RJo.

14 Oct 1971   (P)
Jazzhus "Tagskægget"
Århus, Denmark

....   Addi
....   U.M.M.G.
....   How High The Moon
....   Second Line

          > PG, DE JBjm RJo.

....   Happy Reunion

          > Entire band.

....   Up Jump
....   La Plus Belle Africaine
....   Aristocracy à la Jean Lafitte
....   Old Folks
....   Bourbon Street Jingling Jollies
....   Soul Flute
....   Take The "A" Train

DUKE ELLINGTON & HIS ORCHESTRA
CW MJsn JCl EPtn ME, MTlr BWd CCrs, RP NTrn HMn PG HAsh HC, DE JBjm RJo, NB TWtk.

18 Oct 1971   (P)
Cinéma le Colisée
Roubaix, France

....   The "C" Jam Blues
....   Black And Tan Fantasy—Creole Love Call—The Mooche
....   Kinda Dukish/Rockin' In Rhythm

          > PG, DE JBjm RJo.

....   Happy Reunion

          > Entire band.

....   Having At It
....   Take The "A" Train
....   Fife
....   Chinoiserie
....   I Can't Get Started
....   HARLEM
....   Satin Doll
....   Perdido
....   Addi[1]
....   Medley[2]

[1]Announced as "Tego."
[2]Including: I Let A Song Go Out Of My Heart; Don't Get Around Much Anymore; Mood Indigo; I'm Beginning To See The
Light; Solitude –vTWtk; It Don't Mean A Thing –vTWtk; I Got It Bad –vNB CW; Everybody Wants To Know –vNB CW;
Sophisticated Lady.

DUKE ELLINGTON   19 Oct 1971   (P)
DE talking.   Unidentified location
                                                                       Southport, England
....   Press conference

DUKE ELLINGTON & HIS ORCHESTRA   Floral Hall   (P)
CW MJsn JCI EPtn ME, MTlr BWd CCrs, RP NTrn HMn PG HAsh HC, DE JBjm RJo, NB TWtk.

....   The "C" Jam Blues
....   Black And Tan Fantasy—Creole Love Call—The Mooche
....   Kinda Dukish/Rockin' In Rhythm

> PG, DE JBjm RJo.

....   Happy Reunion

> Entire band.

....   Take The "A" Train
....   Fife
....   Chinoiserie
....   I Can't Get Started
....   HARLEM
....   Perdido

                        TOGO BRAVA—BRAVA TOGO
....   - Soul Soothing Beach
....   - Naturellement
....   - Amour, Amour
....   - Right On Togo

....   Come Off The Veldt
....   Medley[1]
....   Satin Doll
....   Things Ain't What They Used To Be
....   Aristocracy à la Jean Lafitte
....   Addi
....   How High The Moon

> DE JBjm.

....   Lotus Blossom

[1]Including: I Let A Song Go Out Of My Heart; Don't Get Around Much Anymore; Mood Indigo; I'm Beginning To See The Light; Solitude –vTWtk; It Don't Mean A Thing –vTWtk; I Got It Bad –vNB CW; Everybody Wants To Know –vNB CW; Sophisticated Lady; Caravan.

DUKE ELLINGTON & HIS ORCHESTRA
Same personnel.

....   The "C" Jam Blues
....   Black And Tan Fantasy—Creole Love Call—The Mooche
....   Kinda Dukish/Rockin' In Rhythm

> PG, DE JBjm RJo.

....   Happy Reunion

> Entire band.

....   Take The "A" Train
....   Fife
....   Chinoiserie
....   I Can't Get Started
....   HARLEM
....   Satin Doll
....   Things Ain't What They Used To Be
....   Perdido
....   Come Off The Veldt
....   Medley[1]
....   Aristocracy à la Jean Lafitte
....   Addi

> DE JBjm.

....   Lotus Blossom

[1]Including: Prelude To A Kiss; In A Sentimental Mood; I Let A Song Go Out Of My Heart; Don't Get Around Much Anymore; Mood Indigo; I'm Beginning To See The Light; Solitude –vTWtk; It Don't Mean A Thing –vTWtk; I Got It Bad –vNB CW; Everybody Wants To Know –vNB; Sophisticated Lady; Caravan.

DUKE ELLINGTON & HIS ORCHESTRA   20 Oct 1971   (P)
CW MJsn JCl EPtn ME, MTlr BWd CCrs, RP NTrn HMn PG HAsh HC, DE JBjm RJo, NB TWtk.   Winter Gardens
                                                                                      Bournemouth, England

....	The "C" Jam Blues
....	Black And Tan Fantasy—Creole Love Call—The Mooche
....	Kinda Dukish
> PG, DE JBjm RJo.	
....	Happy Reunion
> Entire band.	
....	Take The "A" Train
....	Fife
....	Chinoiserie
....	HARLEM
....	Perdido
....	Addi
....	Come Off The Veldt
....	Medley[1]
....	Aristocracy à la Jean Lafitte
> DE JBjm.	
....	Lotus Blossom
> Entire band.	
....	How High The Moon
> NTrn, DE JBjm RJo.	
....	Soul Flute

[1]Including: Jig Walk; I Let A Song Go Out Of My Heart; Don't Get Around Much Anymore; Mood Indigo; Solitude –TWtk; It Don't Mean A Thing –vTWtk; I Got It Bad –vNB CW; Everybody Wants To Know –vNB CW; Sophisticated Lady; Caravan.

DUKE ELLINGTON & HIS ORCHESTRA
Same personnel.

....	The "C" Jam Blues
....	Black And Tan Fantasy
> PG, DE JBjm RJo.	
....	Happy Reunion
> Entire band.	
....	Take The "A" Train
....	Fife
....	Chinoiserie
....	I Can't Get Started
....	La Plus Belle Africaine
....	Come Off The Veldt
....	Satin Doll
....	Perdido
....	Things Ain't What They Used To Be
....	In Triplicate
....	Medley[1]
....	Aristocracy à la Jean Lafitte
....	Addi
....	How High The Moon
....	Hello Dolly –vMJsn
> DE JBjm.	
....	A Single Petal Of A Rose
> Entire band.	
....	One More Time For The People –vNB TWtk
....	One More Time For The People –vNB TWtk
> DE JBjm.	
....	Lotus Blossom

[1]Including: In A Sentimental Mood; Prelude To A Kiss; Do Nothin' Till You Hear From Me; I Let A Song Go Out Of My Heart; Don't Get Around Much Anymore; Mood Indigo; I'm Beginning To See The Light; Solitude –vTWtk; It Don't Mean A Thing –vTWtk; I Got It Bad –vNB; Everybody Wants To Know –vNB; Sophisticated Lady; Caravan.

21 Oct 1971*   (P)
Hammersmith Odeon (tc)
London, England

DUKE ELLINGTON & HIS ORCHESTRA
CW MJsn JCI EPtn ME, MTlr BWd CCrs, RP NTrn HMn PG HAsh HC, DE JBjm RJo, NB TWtk.

....   The "C" Jam Blues
....   R.T.M.
....   Black And Tan Fantasy—Creole Love Call—The Mooche
....   Kinda Dukish/Rockin' In Rhythm

> PG, DE JBjm RJo.

....   Happy Reunion

> Entire band.

....   Take The "A" Train
....   Fife
....   Chinoiserie
....   HARLEM
....   Perdido
....   Things Ain't What They Used To Be
....   In Triplicate
....   Come Off The Veldt
....   Medley[1]
....   Aristocracy à la Jean Lafitte
....   Addi

[1]Including: In A Sentimental Mood; Prelude To A Kiss; I Let A Song Go Out Of My Heart; Don't Get Around Much Anymore; Mood Indigo; I'm Beginning To See The Light; Solitude –vTWtk; It Don't Mean A Thing –vTWtk; I Got It Bad –vNB CW; Everybody Wants To Know –vNB CW; Sophisticated Lady; Caravan.

DUKE ELLINGTON   (tc)*   (S)[1]
DE interviewed by Stanley Dance.

....   Interview

[1]Backstage.

DUKE ELLINGTON & HIS ORCHESTRA   (tc)*
Same personnel.

....   The "C" Jam Blues
....   Black And Tan Fantasy—Creole Love Call—The Mooche
....   Kinda Dukish/Rockin' In Rhythm

> PG, DE JBjm RJo.

....   Happy Reunion

> Entire band.

....   Take The "A" Train
....   Bourbon Street Jingling Jollies
....   Chinoiserie
....   I Can't Get Started
....   HARLEM
....   Perdido
....   Things Ain't What They Used To Be
....   In Triplicate
....   Satin Doll
....   Come Off The Veldt
....   Medley[1]
....   Aristocracy à la Jean Lafitte
....   Addi
....   Hello Dolly –vMJsn
....   One More Time For The People –vNB TWtk

> DE JBjm.

....   Lotus Blossom

[1]Including: In A Sentimental Mood; Prelude To A Kiss; Don't You Know I Care?; I Let A Song Go Out Of My Heart; Don't Get Around Much Anymore; Mood Indigo; I'm Beginning To See The Light; Solitude –vTWtk; It Don't Mean A Thing –vTWtk; I Got It Bad –vNB CW; Everybody Wants To Know –vNB CW; Sophisticated Lady; Caravan.
*Selections from both concerts were telecast on 14 Nov 1971; the interview was telecast on 9 Feb 1972.

22 Oct 1971   (P)
Colston Hall
Bristol, England

DUKE ELLINGTON & HIS ORCHESTRA
CW MJsn JCI EPtn ME, MTlr BWd CCrs, RP NTrn HMn PG HAsh HC, DE JBjm RJo.

> PG, DE JBjm RJo.

.... UA   Happy Reunion   >>>

> Entire band.

.... UA   Soul Flute

                                     TOGO BRAVA—BRAVA TOGO
.... UA   - Soul Soothing Beach
.... UA   - Naturellement
.... UA   - Amour, Amour
.... UA   - Right On Togo

.... UA   La Plus Belle Africaine
.... UA   In A Mellotone[1]
.... UA   Addi

> DE JBjm.

.... UA   Lotus Blossom

[1]"In A Mellow Tone" on UA LP UXS-92

DUKE ELLINGTON & HIS ORCHESTRA   24 Oct 1971   (P)
CW MJsn JCl EPtn ME, MTlr BWd CCrs, RP NTrn HMn PG HAsh HC, DE JBjm RJo, NB TWtk.   Birmingham Theatre
                                                                      Birmingham, England.

.... UA   The "C" Jam Blues
....   Kinda Dukish/Rockin' In Rhythm
....   Checkered Hat
....   Checkered Hat
....   Hard Way
....   Take The "A" Train
....   Azure
....   Goof
....   In A Sentimental Mood
.... UA   Cotton Tail
....   La Plus Belle Africaine
....   Perdido
....   Satin Doll
....   Things Ain't What They Used To Be
....   Chinoiserie
....   Come Off The Veldt
.... UA[1]   Medley[2]

> DE JBjm.

....   Lotus Blossom

[1]Only "I Got It Bad" on UA.
[2]Including: I Let A Song Go Out Of My Heart; Don't Get Around Much Anymore; Mood Indigo; I'm Beginning To See The
Light; Solitude –vTWtk; I Got It Bad –vNB CW; Everybody Wants To Know –vNB CW; Sophisticated Lady; One More Time
For The People –vNB TWtk; One More Time For The People –vNB TWtk.

DUKE ELLINGTON & HIS ORCHESTRA
Same personnel.

.... Az   Perdido
.... Az   Black Beauty
.... Az   The "C" Jam Blues
.... UA   Checkered Hat
.... Az   Hard Way
.... Az   Take The "A" Train
.... Az   Azure
....   Cotton Tail
.... Az   La Plus Belle Africaine
.... Az   Come Off The Veldt
....   Medley[1]
....   Goof
....   Addi
....   How High The Moon
....   All Too Soon
....   One More Time For The People –vNB TWtk
....   One More Time For The People –vNB TWtk

> DE piano solo.

.... UA   Melancholia[2]

> Entire band.

....   In Triplicate
....   Things Ain't What They Used To Be
....   Satin Doll   >>>

> DE JBjm RJo.

....   Black Swan

[1]Including: Prelude To A Kiss; Don't You Know I Care?; The Brown-Skin Gal; Jump For Joy; I Let A Song Go Out Of My Heart; Don't Get Around Much Anymore; Mood Indigo; I'm Beginning To See The Light; Solitude –vTWtk; It Don't Mean A Thing –vTWtk; I Got It Bad.
[2]Erroneously as "Goof" on UA LP UXS-92.

DUKE ELLINGTON & HIS ORCHESTRA   25 Oct 1971   (P)
CW MJsn JCl EPtn ME, MTlr BWd CCrs, RP NTrn HMn PG HAsh HC, DE JBjm RJo.   Palais des Beaux Arts
                                                                Brussels, Belgium

....   The "C" Jam Blues
....   R.T.M.
....   Kinda Dukish/Rockin' In Rhythm

> PG, DE JBjm RJo.

....   Happy Reunion

> Entire band.

....   Having At It
....   Take The "A" Train
....   Fife
....   Perdido
....   Things Ain't What They Used To Be
....   Satin Doll
....   Goof
....   Addi
....   Afrique

DUKE ELLINGTON & HIS ORCHESTRA   27 Oct 1971   (P)
CW MJsn JCl EPtn ME, MTlr BWd CCrs, RP NTrn HMn PG HAsh HC, DE JBjm RJo, NB TWtk.   L'Alhambra
                                                                Bordeaux, France

....   The "C" Jam Blues
....   Black And Tan Fantasy—Creole Love Call—The Mooche
....   Kinda Dukish/Rockin' In Rhythm

                                         THE GOUTELAS SUITE
....   - Goutelas
....   - Get-With-Itness
....   - Something
....   - Having At It

....   Take The "A" Train
....   Chinoiserie

                                         TOGO BRAVA—BRAVA TOGO
....   - Soul Soothing Beach
....   - Naturellement
....   - Amour, Amour
....   - Right On Togo

....   Perdido
....   Satin Doll
....   Jeep's Blues
....   Things Ain't What They Used To Be
....   Afrique
....   Medley[1]
....   Goof
....   Addi
....   Hello Dolly –vMJsn
....   One More Time For The People –vNB TWtk

> DE JBjm.

....   Lotus Blossom

[1]Including: Prelude To A Kiss; I Let A Song Go Out Of My Heart; Don't Get Around Much Anymore; Mood Indigo; I'm Beginning To See The Light; Solitude –vTWtk; It Don't Mean A Thing –vTWtk; I Got It Bad –vNB CW; Everybody Wants To Know –vNB CW; Sophisticated Lady; Caravan.

DUKE ELLINGTON & HIS ORCHESTRA
Same personnel.

....   The "C" Jam Blues
....   Black And Tan Fantasy—Creole Love Call—The Mooche
....   Kinda Dukish/Rockin' In Rhythm

> PG, DE JBjm RJo.

....   Happy Reunion   >>>

> Entire band.

....		Take The "A" Train
....		Fife
....		Chinoiserie
....		I Can't Get Started
....		HARLEM
....		Perdido
....		Satin Doll
....		Things Ain't What They Used To Be
....		In Triplicate
....		La Plus Belle Africaine
....		Come Off The Veldt
....		Medley[1]
....		Goof
....		Addi
....		Hello Dolly –vMJsn
....		One More Time For The People –vNB TWtk

> DE JBjm.

....		Lotus Blossom

[1]Including: In A Sentimental Mood; I Let A Song Go Out Of My Heart; Don't Get Around Much Anymore; Mood Indigo; I'm Beginning To See The Light; Solitude –vTWtk; I Got It Bad –vNB CW; Everybody Wants To Know –vNB CW; Sophisticated Lady; Caravan.

28 Oct 1971   (P)

DUKE ELLINGTON & HIS ORCHESTRA   Théâtre National Populaire, Palais Challiot
CW MJsn JCl EPtn ME, MTlr BWd CCrs, RP NTrn HMn PG HAsh HC, DE JBjm RJo, NB TWtk.   Paris, France

....	Mad	The "C" Jam Blues
....	Mad	Black And Tan Fantasy—Creole Love Call—The Mooche
....	Mad	Kinda Dukish/Rockin' In Rhythm

> PG, DE JBjm RJo.

....	Mad	Happy Reunion

> Entire band.

....	Mad	Take The "A" Train
....	Mad	Chinoiserie
		TOGO BRAVA—BRAVA TOGO
....	Mad	- Soul Soothing Beach
....	Mad	- Naturellement
....	Mad	- Amour, Amour
....	Mad	- Right On Togo
....		La Plus Belle Africaine
....	Mad	Come Off The Veldt
....		Medley[1]
....		Goof
....		Addi

> RFo added.

....		Satin Doll

> RFo omitted.

....		Things Ain't What They Used To Be

> DE JBjm.

....		Lotus Blossom

(P)

[1]Including: I Let A Song Go Out Of My Heart; In A Sentimental Mood; Prelude To A Kiss; Don't Get Around Much Anymore; Mood Indigo; I'm Beginning To See The Light; Solitude –vTWtk; It Don't Mean A Thing –vTWtk; I Got It Bad –vNB CW; Everybody Wants To Know –vNB; Sophisticated Lady; Caravan.

DUKE ELLINGTON & HIS ORCHESTRA
Same personnel.

....		The "C" Jam Blues
....		Black And Tan Fantasy—Creole Love Call—The Mooche
....		Kinda Dukish/Rockin' In Rhythm

> PG, DE JBjm RJo.

....		Happy Reunion

> Entire band.

....		Take The "A" Train
....	Mad	Fife >>>

....	Mad	Chinoiserie
....	Az	I Can't Get Started
		THE GOUTELAS SUITE
....	Az	- Get-With-Itness
....	Az	- Something
....	Az	- Having At It
....		La Plus Belle Africaine
....		Come Off The Veldt
....	Az[1]	Medley[2]
....	Az	Goof
....	Az	Addi
....	Az	In Triplicate
....		Hello Dolly --vMJsn
....		One More Time For The People --vNB TWtk

> RFo added.

....	Az	Satin Doll

> RFo omitted.

....	Az	Things Ain't What They Used To Be

> DE JBjm.

....	Az	Lotus Blossom

[1]Only "I Got It Bad" on Az.
[2]Including: Prelude To A Kiss; I Let A Song Go Out Of My Heart; Don't Get Around Much Anymore; Mood Indigo; I'm Beginning To See The Light; Solitude --vTWtk; It Don't Mean A Thing --vTWtk; I Got It Bad --vNB CW; Everybody Wants To Know --vNB; Sophisticated Lady; Caravan.

	29 Oct 1971 (P)
DUKE ELLINGTON & HIS ORCHESTRA	De Doelen
CW MJsn JCI EPtn ME, MTlr BWd CCrs, RP NTrn HMn PG HAsh HC, DE JBjm RJo, NB TWtk.	Rotterdam, Netherlands

....		The "C" Jam Blues
....		Kinda Dukish/Rockin' In Rhythm

> PG, DE JBjm RJo.

....		Happy Reunion

> Entire band.

....	Az	Get-With-Itness
....		Take The "A" Train
....		Fife
....		Chinoiserie
....		HARLEM
....		La Plus Belle Africaine
....		Come Off The Veldt
....	Az[1]	Medley[2]
....		Perdido
....		Goof
....		Addi
....		One More Time For The People --vNB TWtk
....		In Triplicate
....		Satin Doll

[1]Only "I Got It Bad" on Az.
[2]Including: Prelude To A Kiss; In A Sentimental Mood; I Let A Song Go Out Of My Heart; Don't Get Around Much Anymore; Mood Indigo; I'm Beginning To See The Light; Solitude --vTWtk; It Don't Mean A Thing --vTWtk; I Got It Bad --vNB CW; Everybody Wants To Know --vNB; Sophisticated Lady; Caravan.

	30 Oct 1971 (P)
DUKE ELLINGTON & HIS ORCHESTRA	Sali Kongresovej
CW MJsn JCI EPtn ME, MTlr BWd CCrs, RP NTrn HMn PG HAsh HC, DE JBjm RJo, NB.	Warsaw, Poland

....	Pj	La Plus Belle Africaine
....	Pj	Medley[1]
....	Pj	Satin Doll
....	Pj	Goof
....	Pj	Addi[2]
....	Pj	Things Ain't What They Used To Be
....	Pj	Hello Dolly --vMJsn

> DE JBjm.

....	Pj	Lotus Blossom

[1]Including: I'm Beginning To See The Light; Everybody Wants To Know --vNB[3]; Sophisticated Lady; Caravan.   >>>

[2]"Duke's Tune" on Pj.
[3]"I Got The Blues" on Pj.

1 Nov 1971[1]   (P)
Erkel Theatre (?tc)
Budapest, Hungary

DUKE ELLINGTON & HIS ORCHESTRA
CW MJsn JCl EPtn ME, MTlr BWd CCrs, RP NTrn HMn PG HAsh HC, DE JBjm RJo, NB TWtk.

Concert (tape extant)

[1]It is not known, if and when the program has been aired.

3 Nov 1971   (P)
Palasport
Bologna, Italy

DUKE ELLINGTON & HIS ORCHESTRA
CW MJsn JCl EPtn ME, MTlr BWd CCrs, RP NTrn HMn PG HAsh HC, DE JBjm RJo, NB TWtk.

.... Black And Tan Fantasy—Creole Love Call—The Mooche
.... Kinda Dukish/Rockin' In Rhythm

> PG, DE JBjm RJo.

.... DVD Happy Reunion

> Entire band.

.... DVD Take The "A" Train
.... Fife
.... Chinoiserie
.... HARLEM
.... Satin Doll
.... Things Ain't What They Used To Be
.... Come Off The Veldt
.... Medley[1]
.... Goof
.... How High The Moon
.... Addi
.... Hello Dolly –vMJsn
.... DVD In Triplicate
.... One More Time For The People –vNB TWtk

[1]Including: I Let A Song Go Out Of My Heart; Do Nothin' Till You Hear From Me; Don't Get Around Much Anymore; Mood Indigo; I'm Beginning To See The Light; Solitude –vTWtk; It Don't Mean A Thing –vTWtk; I Got It Bad –vNB CW; Everybody Wants To Know –vNB CW; Sophisticated Lady; Caravan.

4 Nov 1971[1]   (P)
Sala Paltalui (?tc)
Bucharest, Romania

DUKE ELLINGTON & HIS ORCHESTRA
CW MJsn JCl EPtn ME, MTlr BWd, RP NTrn HMn PG HAsh HC, DE JBjm RJo, NB TWtk.

Two concerts (tapes extant)

[1]It is not known, if and when the program has been aired.

5 Nov 1971[1]   (P)
Philharmonie (tc)
Berlin, Germany

DUKE ELLINGTON & HIS ORCHESTRA
CW MJsn JCl EPtn ME, MTlr BWd CCrs, RP NTrn HMn PG HAsh HC, DE JBjm RJo, NB TWtk.

.... Az The "C" Jam Blues
.... Az Kinda Dukish/Rockin' In Rhythm

> PG, DE JBjm RJo.

.... JDr Happy Reunion

> Entire band.

.... JDr Take The "A" Train
.... Az Fife
.... Az Aristocracy à la Jean Lafitte
.... Az I Can't Get Started

> Kid Thomas & the Preservation Hall Jazz Band, augmented by members of the Ellington orchestra.

.... Bugle Call Rag
.... Darktown Strutters' Ball –vABk

> Kid Thomas & the Preservation Hall Jazz Band omitted.

.... Az Satin Doll
.... Az Thing Ain't What They Used To Be
.... JDr In Triplicate
.... Addi
.... Medley[2]
.... Come Off The Veldt
.... Come Off The Veldt

[1]The date of telecast is not known.   >>>

[2]Including: Don't Get Around Much Anymore; Mood Indigo; I'm Beginning To See The Light; Solitude –vTWtk; I Got It Bad –vNB; Sophisticated Lady; Caravan.

DUKE ELLINGTON & HIS ORCHESTRA   7 Nov 1971*   (P)
CW MJsn JCl EPtn ME, MTlr BWd CCrs, RP NTrn HMn BW HAsh HC, DE JBjm RJo, NB TWtk.   Tivoli's Koncertsal (?tc)
                                                                  Copenhagen, Denmark

.... Vid   The "C" Jam Blues

  > PG replaces BW.

.... Vid   Kinda Dukish/Rockin' In Rhythm

  > BW added.

.... Vid   All Too Soon
.... Vid   Cotton Tail

  > BW omitted.

.... Vid   Take The "A" Train
.... Vid   Fife
.... Vid   Satin Doll
.... Vid   Chinoiserie

  > BW added.

.... Vid   In Quadruplicate

  > BW omitted.

.... Vid   Come Off The Veldt
.... Vid   Medley[1]
.... Vid   Goof
....   Addi
....   One More Time For The People –vNB TWtk   (P)

[1]Including: Prelude To A Kiss; Do Nothin' Till You Hear From Me; I Let A Song Go Out Of My Heart; Don't Get Around Much Anymore; Mood Indigo; I'm Beginning To See The Light; Solitude –vTWtk; Love You Madly –vNB; Sophisticated Lady; Caravan.

DUKE ELLINGTON & HIS ORCHESTRA   (?tc)
PG added, otherwise same personnel.

.... Vid   The "C" Jam Blues

  > BW omitted.

.... Vid   Kinda Dukish/Rockin' In Rhythm

  > PG, DE JBjm RJo.

.... Vid   Happy Reunion

  > Entire band, BW added.

.... Vid   Cotton Tail

  > BW, DE JBjm RJo.

.... Vid   I Got It Bad

  > Entire band, BW omitted.

.... Vid   Take The "A" Train
.... Vid   Fife
.... Vid   Chinoiserie
.... Vid   Satin Doll
.... Vid   Things Ain't What They Used To Be

  > BW added.

.... Vid   In Quadruplicate[1]
.... Vid   Come Off The Veldt

  > BW omitted.

.... Vid   Medley[2]
.... Vid   Hello Dolly –vMJsn
.... Vid   One More Time For The People –vNB TWtk.

[1]Announced as "The Quadrupedisticalissimists In Blue."
[2]Including: Prelude To A Kiss; Do Nothin' Till You Hear From Me; In A Sentimental Mood; I Let A Song Go Out Of My Heart; Don't Get Around Much Anymore; Mood Indigo; I'm Beginning To See The Light; Solitude –vTWtk; Love You Madly –vNB; Sophisticated Lady; Caravan.

*Filmed for telecast; it is not known, if and when the program has been aired.

8 Nov 1971   (P)
Chateau Neuf Konsertsal
Oslo, Norway

<u>DUKE ELLINGTON & HIS ORCHESTRA</u>
CW MJsn JCI EPtn ME, MTlr BWd CCrs, RP NTrn HMn PG HAsh HC, DE JBjm RJo.

....   Kinda Dukish/Rockin' In Rhythm
....   Black And Tan Fantasy—Creole Love Call—The Mooche
....   Take The "A" Train

> PG, DE JBjm RJo.

....   Happy Reunion

> Entire band.

....   Fife
....   Chinoiserie
....   I Can't Get Started
....   HARLEM
....   Satin Doll
....   Medley[1]

[1]Including: Sophisticated Lady; Caravan.

9 Nov 1971   (P)
Universitetsaulan
Uppsala, Sweden

<u>DUKE ELLINGTON & HIS ORCHESTRA</u>
CW MJsn JCI EPtn ME, MTlr BWd CCrs, RP NTrn HMn PG HAsh HC, DE JBjm RJo, NB TWtk.

....   The "C" Jam Blues
....   Kinda Dukish/Rockin' In Rhythm

> PG, DE JBjm RJo.

....   Happy Reunion

> Entire band.

....   Take The "A" Train
....   Satin Doll
....   Fife
....   Chinoiserie
....   HARLEM
....   Medley[1]
....   Things Ain't What They Used To Be

[1]Including: Prelude To A Kiss; Do Nothin' Till You Hear From Me; In A Sentimental Mood; I Let A Song Go Out Of My Heart; Don't Get Around Much Anymore; Mood Indigo; I'm Beginning To See The Light; Solitude –vTWtk; Love You Madly –vNB; Sophisticated Lady; Caravan.

<u>DUKE ELLINGTON</u>   (bc)   (S)[1]
DE interviewed by person unknown.

....   Interview

[1]Backstage.

<u>DUKE ELLINGTON & HIS ORCHESTRA</u>   (P)
Same personnel.

.... RDB   The "C" Jam Blues
.... RDB   Kinda Dukish/Rockin' In Rhythm

> PG, DE JBjm RJo.

.... RDB   Happy Reunion

> Entire band.

.... RDB   Take The "A" Train
.... RDB   Fife
....   Satin Doll
.... MFC   Chinoiserie
.... RDB   HARLEM
.... Az[1]   Medley[2]
.... RDB   Things Ain't What They Used To Be
.... RDB   Hello Dolly –vMJsn
.... RDB   One More Time For The People –vNB TWtk

> DE JBjm.

.... RDB   Lotus Blossom

> RJo added.

....   Black Swan

[1]Only "I Got It Bad" on Az.   >>>

[2]Including: Prelude To A Kiss; Do Nothin' Till You Hear From Me; In A Sentimental Mood; Don't You Know I Care?; The Brown-Skin Gal; I Let A Song Go Out Of My Heart; Don't Get Around Much Anymore; Mood Indigo; I'm Beginning To See The Light; Solitude –vTWtk; It Don't Mean A Thing –vTWtk; I Got It Bad –vNB CW; Sophisticated Lady; Caravan.

		10 Nov 1971[1]	(S)
DUKE ELLINGTON		Savoy Hotel (tc)	
DE interviewed by Per Møller-Hansen.		Malmö, Sweden	

.... Interview

[1]Telecast in Sweden on 3 Nov 1972.

DUKE ELLINGTON & HIS ORCHESTRA   Stadsteatern   (P)
CW MJsn JCl EPtn REsn ME, MTlr BWd APsn CCrs, RP NTrn HMn BW PG HAsh HC, DE JBjm RJo, NB TWtk.

.... The "C" Jam Blues
.... Kinda Dukish/Rockin' In Rhythm
.... I Can't Get Started
.... Unidentified title
.... Soul Flute
.... How High The Moon

> PG, DE JBjm RJo.

.... Happy Reunion

> Entire band.

.... Perdido

> LJnf added.

.... I Let A Song Go Out Of My Heart –vLJnf

> LJnf omitted.

.... HARLEM
.... Medley[1]
.... Goof
.... Addi
.... Satin Doll
.... Things Ain't What They Used To Be
.... Take The "A" Train
.... In Quadruplicate

[1]Including: Prelude To A Kiss; In A Sentimental Mood; Don't Get Around Much Anymore; Mood Indigo; I'm Beginning To See The Light; Carolina Shout; Solitude –vTWtk; I Got It Bad –vNB CW; Sophisticated Lady; Caravan.

		11 Nov 1971	(P)
DUKE ELLINGTON & HIS ORCHESTRA		Kongreßsaal, Deutsches Museum	
CW MJsn JCl EPtn ME, MTlr BWd CCrs, RP NTrn HMn PG HAsh HC, DE JBjm RJo, NB TWtk.		Munich, Germany	

.... The "C" Jam Blues
.... Black And Tan Fantasy—Creole Love Call—The Mooche
.... Kinda Dukish/Rockin' In Rhythm

> PG, DE JBjm RJo.

.... Happy Reunion

> Entire band.

.... Take The "A" Train
.... Fife
.... Chinoiserie
.... I Can't Get Started
.... HARLEM
.... Perdido
.... Satin Doll
.... Things Ain't What They Used To Be
.... In Triplicate
.... La Plus Belle Africaine
.... Come Off The Veldt
.... Medley[1]
.... Goof
.... Addi
.... Hello Dolly –vMJsn
.... One More Time For The People –vNB TWtk

> DE JBjm.

.... Lotus Blossom

[1]Including: Prelude To A Kiss; Do Nothin' Till You Hear From Me; In A Sentimental Mood; I Let A Song Go Out Of My Heart; Don't Get Around Much Anymore; Mood Indigo; I'm Beginning To See The Light; Solitude –vTWtk; It Don't Mean A Thing –vTWtk; I Got It Bad –vNB CW; Everybody Wants To Know –vNB; Sophisticated Lady; Caravan.

14 Nov 1971[1]   (P)

Palau de la Musica Catalana (tc)

Barcelona, Spain

DUKE ELLINGTON & HIS ORCHESTRA
MJsn JCl EPtn ME, MTlr BWd CCrs, RP NTrn HMn PG HAsh HC, DE JBjm RJo.

....	The "C" Jam Blues
....	Goof
....	Kinda Dukish/Rockin' In Rhythm

> PG, DE JBjm RJo.

....	Happy Reunion

> Entire band.

....	Cotton Tail
....	Take The "A" Train
....	Fife
....	Chinoiserie
....	All Too Soon
....	HARLEM

[1]The date of telecast is not known.

DUKE ELLINGTON & HIS ORCHESTRA   (P)
NB TWtk added, otherwise same personnel.

....	Perdido

> RFo added..

....	Satin Doll

> RFo omitted.

....	Things Ain't What They Used To Be
....	In Triplicate
....	La Plus Belle Africaine
....	Come Off The Veldt
....	Medley[1]

[1]Including: Prelude To A Kiss; Do Nothin' Till You Hear From Me; In A Sentimental Mood; I Let A Song Go Out Of My Heart; Don't Get Around Much Anymore; Mood Indigo; I'm Beginning To See The Light; Solitude –vTWtk; It Don't Mean A Thing –vTWtk; I Got It Bad –vNB; I Don't Know What Kind Of Blues I Got –vNB; Everybody Wants To Know –vNB; Sophisticated Lady; Caravan.

16 Nov 1971   (P)

Maracanazhinho

Rio de Janeiro, Brazil

DUKE ELLINGTON & HIS ORCHESTRA
CW MJsn JCl EPtn HJns ME, MTlr BWd CCrs, RP NTrn HMn PG HAsh HC, DE JBjm RJo.

....	The "C" Jam Blues

> PG, DE JBjm RJo.

....	Happy Reunion

> Entire band.

....	Take The "A" Train
....	Chinoiserie

22 Nov 1971   (P)

Teatro Gran Rex

Buenos Aires, Argentina

DUKE ELLINGTON & HIS ORCHESTRA
CW MJsn JCl EPtn HJns ME, MTlr BWd CCrs, RP NTrn HMn PG HAsh HC, DE JBjm RJo, NB TWtk.

....	The "C" Jam Blues
....	Black And Tan Fantasy—Creole Love Call—The Mooche
....	Kinda Dukish/Rockin' In Rhythm

> PG, DE JBjm RJo.

....	Happy Reunion

> Entire band.

....	Take The "A" Train
....	Fife
....	Chinoiserie
....	HARLEM
....	Perdido
....	Satin Doll
....	Things Ain't What They Used To Be
....	In Triplicate
....	La Plus Belle Africaine
....	One More Time For The People –vNB TWtk >>>

TOGO BRAVA—BRAVA TOGO
.... - Naturellement
.... - Amour, Amour
.... - Right On Togo
> NTrn, DE JBjm RJo.

.... Black Swan
> Entire band.

.... Soul Flute
> DE JBjm.

.... Lotus Blossom

24 Nov 1971   (P)
Teatro Metro

DUKE ELLINGTON & HIS ORCHESTRA   Buenos Aires, Argentina
CW MJsn JCI EPtn HJns ME, MTlr BWd CCrs, RP NTrn HMn PG HAsh HC, DE JBjm RJo, NB.

.... The "C" Jam Blues
.... Black And Tan Fantasy—Creole Love Call—The Mooche
.... Kinda Dukish/Rockin' In Rhythm
.... Take The "A" Train
.... Fife
.... Satin Doll
.... Goof
.... In Triplicate
.... Medley[1]
.... Things Ain't What They Used To Be

[1]Including: Everybody Wants To Know –vNB; Sophisticated Lady; Caravan.

25 Nov 1971   (P)
Estadio Pacifico

DUKE ELLINGTON & HIS ORCHESTRA   Mendoza, Argentina
CW MJsn JCI EPtn HJns ME, MTlr BWd CCrs, RP NTrn HMn PG HAsh HC, DE JBjm RJo,
NB TWtk.

.... The "C" Jam Blues
.... Black And Tan Fantasy—Creole Love Call—The Mooche
.... Kinda Dukish/Rockin' In Rhythm
> PG, DE JBjm RJo.

.... Happy Reunion
> Entire band.

.... Take The "A" Train
.... Fife
.... Chinoiserie
.... HARLEM
.... Perdido
.... Satin Doll
.... Goof
.... In Triplicate
.... La Plus Belle Africaine
.... Come Off The Veldt
.... Medley[1]
.... Blue Moon
.... Things Ain't What They Used To Be
.... How High The Moon
.... Addi
.... Hello Dolly –vMJsn
.... One More Time For The People –vNB TWtk

[1]Including: Prelude To A Kiss; Do Nothin' Till You Hear From Me; In A Sentimental Mood; Don't You Know I Care?; I Let
A Song Go Out Of My Heart; Don't Get Around Much Anymore; Mood Indigo; I'm Beginning To See The Light; Solitude
–vTWtk; It Don't Mean A Thing –vTWtk; I Got It Bad –vNB TWtk; Everybody Wants To Know –vNB; Sophisticated Lady;
Caravan.

26 Nov 1971   (P)
Teatro Caupolican

DUKE ELLINGTON & HIS ORCHESTRA   Santiago, Chile
MJsn JCI EPtn HJns ME, MTlr BWd CCrs, RP NTrn HMn PG HAsh HC, DE JBjm RJo, NB TWtk.

.... Az[1]   The "C" Jam Blues
.... Az   Black And Tan Fantasy—Creole Love Call—The Mooche
.... Az   Kinda Dukish/Rockin' In Rhythm
> PG, DE JBjm RJo.

.... Az   Happy Reunion   >>>

> Entire band.

....	Az	Take The "A" Train
....	Az	Fife
....	Az	Soul Flute
....		I Can't Get Started
....		HARLEM
....	Az[2]	Perdido
....	Az	Satin Doll
....	Az	Things Ain't What They Used To Be
....	Az	In Triplicate
....	Az[2]	La Plus Belle Africaine
....		Come Off The Veldt
....		Medley[3]
....		Goof
....	Az	How High The Moon
....	Az	Addi
....		Hello Dolly –vMJsn
....		One More Time For The People –vNB TWtk

> DE JBjm.

....	Az	Lotus Blossom

[1]Only "Creole Love Call" and The "Mooche" on Az.
[2]Incomplete on Az.
[3]Including: Prelude To A Kiss; Do Nothin' Till You Hear From Me; In A Sentimental Mood; Don't You Know I Care?; I Let A Song Go Out Of My Heart; Don't Get Around Much Anymore; Mood Indigo; I'm Beginning To See The Light; Solitude –vTWtk; It Don't Mean A Thing –vTWtk; I Got It Bad –vNB; I Don't Know What Kind Of Blues I Got –vNB; Everybody Wants To Know –vNB; Sophisticated Lady; Caravan.

		11 Dec 1971 (P)
DUKE ELLINGTON & HIS ORCHESTRA		Aragon Ballroom
CW MJsn JCl EPtn HJns ME, MTlr BWd CCrs, RP NTrn HMn PG HAsh HC, DE JBjm RJo.		Chicago, IL

....		Caravan
....		You Are Beautiful
....		Kinda Dukish/Rockin' In Rhythm
....		Checkered Hat

	14 Dec 1971 (S)
DUKE ELLINGTON	Unidentified location (bc)
DE interviewed by Pat Collins.	New York City, NY

....	Interview

DUKE ELLINGTON & HIS GROUP	Rainbow Grill (bc) (P)
MJsn, RP NTrn HMn PG HAsh HC, DE JBjm RJo.	

> DE piano solo.

....	Meditation

> Entire group.

....	Take The "A" Train
....	Creole Love Call
....	Kinda Dukish/Rockin' In Rhythm
....	In A Sentimental Mood

	Dec 1971 (P)[1]
DUKE ELLINGTON & HIS GROUP	Rainbow Grill (tc)
MJsn, MTlr, RP NTrn HAsh HC, DE PK RJo, NB.	New York City, NY

> DE piano solo.

....	Unidentified title (conclusion)

> Entire group.

....	Take The "A" Train (incomplete)
....	Creole Love Call
....	Mood Indigo (incomplete)
....	Chinoiserie (in progress)
....	Bourbon Street Jingling Jollies
....	Love You Madly –vNB

[1]The event was taped by ABC; ultimately only a short clip was used for a news telecast.

	1 Jan 1972 (P)
DUKE ELLINGTON & HIS GROUP	Rainbow Grill (bc)
MJsn, RP NTrn HMn PG HAsh HC, DE JBjm RJo, NB TWtk.	New York City, NY

....	Auld Lang Syne –vNB TWtk >>>

....	One More Time For The People –vNB TWtk
....	Mood Indigo
....	Things Ain't What They Used To Be
....	Sophisticated Lady
....	Take The "A" Train
....	Satin Doll

5 Jan 1972   (S)
Unidentified location (bc?)
Tokyo, Japan

DUKE ELLINGTON
DE interviewed by Ed McKean.

| .... | Interview |

6 Jan 1972   (P)
Koseinenkin Kaikan
Tokyo, Japan

DUKE ELLINGTON & HIS ORCHESTRA
CW MJsn JCl ME, MTlr BWd CCrs, RP NTrn HMn PG HAsh HC, DE JBjm RJo, NB TWtk.

....	The "C" Jam Blues
....	Black And Tan Fantasy—Creole Love Call—The Mooche
....	Kinda Dukish/Rockin' In Rhythm

> PG, DE JBjm RJo.

| .... | Happy Reunion |

> Entire band.

....	Take The "A" Train
....	Chinoiserie
....	Fife
....	HARLEM
....	Perdido
....	Satin Doll

	TOGO BRAVA—BRAVA TOGO
.... SR	- Soul Soothing Beach
....	- Naturellement
....	- Amour, Amour
....	- Right On Togo

....	La Plus Belle Africaine
....	Come Off The Veldt
....	Medley[1]
....	Goof
....	Things Ain't What They Used To Be
....	In Triplicate
....	Addi
....	One More Time For The People –vNB TWtk
....	Hello Dolly –vMJsn

> DE JBjm.

| .... | Lotus Blossom |

[1]Including: Prelude To A Kiss; Do Nothin' Till You Hear From Me; I Let A Song Go Out Of My Heart; Don't Get Around Much Anymore; Mood Indigo; I'm Beginning To See The Light; Solitude –vTWtk; Heaven –vTWtk; It Don't Mean A Thing –vTWtk; I Got It Bad –vNB CW; I Don't Know What Kind Of Blues I Got –vNB; Everybody Wants To Know –vNB; Sophisticated Lady; Caravan.

DUKE ELLINGTON & HIS ORCHESTRA
Same personnel.

....	The "C" Jam Blues
....	Black And Tan Fantasy—Creole Love Call—The Mooche
....	Kinda Dukish/Rockin' In Rhythm

> PG, DE JBjm RJo.

| .... | Happy Reunion |

> Entire band.

....	Take The "A" Train
....	Fife
....	Chinoiserie
....	Satin Doll
....	HARLEM
....	Perdido

	TOGO BRAVA—BRAVA TOGO
....	- Soul Soothing Beach
....	- Naturellement
....	- Amour, Amour
....	- Right On Togo >>>

		La Plus Belle Africaine
....		Come Off The Veldt
....		Medley[1]
....		Goof
....		Things Ain't What They Used To Be
....		In Triplicate
....		Addi
....		Hello Dolly –vMJsn
....		One More Time For The People –vNB TWtk

> DE JBjm.

| .... | | Lotus Blossom |

[1]Including: Prelude To A Kiss; Do Nothin' Till You Hear From Me; Mellow Ditty; I Let A Song Go Out Of My Heart; Don't Get Around Much Anymore; Mood indigo; I'm Beginning To See The Light; Solitude –vTWtk; It Don't Mean A Thing –vTWtk; I Got It Bad –NB CW; Everybody Wants To Know –vNB CW; Sophisticated Lady; Caravan.

7 Jan 1972   (S)
NHK Studios (tc)
Tokyo, Japan

DUKE ELLINGTON & HIS ORCHESTRA
CW MJsn JCl ME, MTlr BWd CCrs, RP NTrn HMn PG HAsh HC, DE JBjm RJo.

....		Take The "A" Train
....		Kinda Dukish/Rockin' In Rhythm
....		Sophisticated Lady—Caravan
....	RDB	Interview with DE[1]

> Unidentified vcl group added.

| .... | | Satin Doll –vGrp |

> DE JBjm.

| .... | | Meditation |

> Entire band.

....		The "C" Jam Blues
....	RDB	Interview (ctd.)[1]
....		Perdido

[1]Onstage.

8 Jan 1972   (P)
Koseinenkin Kaikan
Tokyo, Japan

DUKE ELLINGTON & HIS ORCHESTRA
CW MJsn JCl ME, MTlr BWd CCrs, RP NTrn HMn PG HAsh HC, DE JBjm RJo, NB TWtk.

| .... | | The "C" Jam Blues |
| .... | | Kinda Dukish/Rockin' In Rhythm |

> PG, DE JBjm RJo.

| .... | | Happy Reunion |

> Entire band.

....		Take The "A" Train
....		Fife
....		Chinoiserie
....		Satin Doll
....		HARLEM
....		Perdido
....		Addi
....		In Triplicate
....		La Plus Belle Africaine
....		Come Off The Veldt
....		Medley[1]
....		One More Time For The People –vNB TWtk

> DE JBjm.

| .... | | Lotus Blossom |

[1]Including: Prelude To A Kiss; Do Nothin' Till You Hear From Me; In A Sentimental Mood; I Let A Song Go Out Of My Heart; Don't Get Around Much Anymore; Mood Indigo; I'm Beginning To See The Light; Solitude –vTWtk; It Don't Mean A Thing –vTWtk; I Got It Bad –vNB CW; Everybody Wants To Know –vNB CW; Sophisticated Lady; Caravan.

10 Jan 1972   (P)
Festival Hall
Osaka, Japan

DUKE ELLINGTON & HIS ORCHESTRA
CW MJsn JCl ME, MTlr BWd CCrs, RP NTrn HMn PG HAsh HC, DE JBjm RJo, NB TWtk.

....		The "C" Jam Blues
....		Perdido
....		Black And Tan Fantasy—Creole Love Call—The Mooche
....		Kinda Dukish/Rockin' In Rhythm >>>

> PG, DE JBjm RJo.

....   Happy Reunion

> Entire band.

....   Take The "A" Train
....   Fife
....   Chinoiserie
....   HARLEM
....   Things Ain't What They Used To Be
....   How High The Moon
....   Addi
....   In Triplicate
....   La Plus Belle Africaine
....   Come Off The Veldt
....   Medley[1]
....   Satin Doll
....   Hallo Dolly –vMJsn
....   One More Time For The People –vNB TWtk

> DE JBjm.

....   Lotus Blossom

[1]Including: Prelude To A Kiss; Do Nothin' Till You Hear From Me; In A Sentimental Mood; I Let A Song Go Out Of My Heart; Don't Get Around Much Anymore; Mood Indigo; I'm Beginning To See The Light; Solitude –vTWtk; I Got It Bad –vNB CW; Everybody Wants To Know –vNB; Sophisticated Lady; Caravan.

DUKE ELLINGTON & HIS ORCHESTRA   *p* Jan 1972   **(P)**
CW MJsn JCl ME, MTlr BWd CCrs, RP NTrn HMn PG HAsh HC, DE JBjm RJo.   Unidentified location
                                                                                       p Japan
....   Black And Tan Fantasy—Creole Love Call—The Mooche
....   Kinda Dukish/Rockin' In Rhythm

> PG, DE JBjm RJo.

....   Happy Reunion

> Entire band.

....   Take The "A" Train
....   Fife
....   Chinoiserie
....   HARLEM

DUKE ELLINGTON & HIS ORCHESTRA   16 Jan 1972   **(P)**
CW MJsn JCl ME, MTlr BWd CCrs, RP NTrn HMn PG HAsh HC, DE JBjm RJo, NB TWtk.   Fukuoka Denki Hall
                                                                                       Fukuoka, Japan
....   The "C" Jam Blues
....   Black And Tan Fantasy—Creole Love Call—The Mooche
....   Kinda Dukish/Rockin' In Rhythm

> PG, DE JBjm RJo.

....   Happy Reunion

> Entire band.

....   Cotton Tail
....   Take The "A" Train
....   Fife
....   Chinoiserie
....   HARLEM
....   Perdido
....   Satin Doll
....   Goof
....   Things Ain't What They Used To Be
....   In Triplicate
....   La Plus Belle Africaine
....   Come Off The Veldt
....   Medley[1]
....   Addi
....   Hello Dolly –vMJsn
....   One More Time For The People –vNB TWtk

[1]Including: Prelude To A Kiss; Do Nothin' Till You Hear From Me; I Let A Song Go Out Of My Heart; Don't Get Around Much Anymore; Mood Indigo; I'm Beginning To See The Light; Solitude –vTWtk; It Don't Mean A Thing –vTWtk; I Got It Bad –vNB CW; Everybody Wants To Know –vNB CW; Sophisticated Lady; Caravan.

DUKE ELLINGTON & HIS ORCHESTRA
CW MJsn JCI ME, MTlr BWd CCrs, RP NTrn HMn PG HAsh HC, DE JBjm RJo, NB TWtk.

.... The "C" Jam Blues
.... Black And Tan Fantasy—Creole Love Call—The Mooche
.... Kinda Dukish/Rockin' In Rhythm

> PG, DE JBjm RJo.

.... Happy Reunion

> Entire band.

.... Take The "A" Train
.... Fife
.... Chinoiserie
.... HARLEM
.... Perdido
.... Satin Doll
.... Goof
.... Things Ain't What They Used To Be
.... In Triplicate
.... La Plus Belle Africaine
.... Come Off The Veldt
.... Medley[1]
.... Addi

[1]Including: Prelude To A Kiss; Do Nothin' Till You Hear From Me; In A Sentimental Mood; I Let A Song Go Out Of My Heart; Don't Get Around Much Anymore; Mood Indigo; I'm Beginning To See The Light; Solitude –vTWtk; It Don't Mean A Thing –vTWtk; I Got It Bad –vNB CW; Everybody Wants To Know –vNB CW; Sophisticated Lady; Caravan.

DUKE ELLINGTON & HIS ORCHESTRA
CW MJsn JCI ME, MTlr BWd CCrs, RP NTrn HMn PG HAsh HC, DE JBjm RJo, NB TWtk.

.... The "C" Jam Blues
.... Black And Tan Fantasy—Creole Love Call—The Mooche
.... Kinda Dukish/Rockin' In Rhythm

> PG, DE JBjm RJo.

.... Happy Reunion

> Entire band.

.... Take The "A" Train
.... Fife
.... Chinoiserie
.... HARLEM
.... Perdido
.... Satin Doll
.... Goof
.... Things Ain't What They Used To Be
.... In Triplicate
.... La Plus Belle Africaine
.... Come Off The Veldt
.... Medley[1]
.... Addi
.... Hello Dolly –vMJsn
.... One More Time For The People –vNB TWtk

[1]Including: Prelude To A Kiss; Do Nothin' Till You Hear From Me; In A Sentimental Mood; I Let A Song Go Out Of My Heart; Don't Get Around Much Anymore; Mood Indigo; I'm Beginning To See The Light; Solitude –vTWtk; It Don't Mean A Thing –vTWtk; I Got It Bad –vNB CW; Everybody Wants To Know –vNB CW; Sophisticated Lady; Caravan.

DUKE ELLINGTON & HIS ORCHESTRA
CW MJsn JCI ME, MTlr BWd CCrs, RP NTrn HMn PG HAsh HC, DE JBjm RJo, NB TWtk.

.... The "C" Jam Blues
.... Creole Love Call
.... Perdido
.... Second Line
.... Aristocracy à la Jean Lafitte
.... Fife

TOGO BRAVA—BRAVA TOGO
.... - Soul Soothing Beach
.... - Naturellement
.... - Amour, Amour
.... - Right On Togo   >>>

....   Satin Doll
....   In A Sentimental Mood
....   Take The "A" Train
....   Chinoiserie
....   I Can't Get Started
....   HARLEM
....   Take The "A" Train
....   Goof
....   Cotton Tail
....   Things Ain't What They Used To Be
....   Kinda Dukish/Rockin' In Rhythm
....   The Blues –vTWtk
            > DE, TWtk.

....   Heaven –vTWtk
            > Entire band.

....   In The Beginning God –vTWtk
....   Solitude –vTWtk
....   It Don't Mean A Thing –vTWtk
....   Addi
....   Come Off The Veldt
....   Medley[1]
....   Hello Dolly –vMJsn
....   One More Time For The People –vNB TWtk
            > DE JBjm.

....   Lotus Blossom

            [1]Including: Do Nothin' Till You Hear From Me; I Let A Song Go Out Of My Heart; Don't Get Around Much Anymore;
            Mood Indigo; I'm Beginning To See The Light; I Don't Know What Kind Of Blues I Got –vNB; I Got It Bad –vNB CW;
            Everybody Wants To Know –vNB; Sophisticated Lady; Caravan.

                                                                                                   15 Feb 1972   (P)
            DUKE ELLINGTON & HIS ORCHESTRA   H.I.C. Arena
            CW MJsn JCI ME, MTlr BWd CCrs, RP NTrn HMn PG HAsh HC, DE JBjm RJo.   Honolulu, HI

....   The "C" Jam Blues
....   Take The "A" Train
....   Creole Love Call
....   Kinda Dukish/Rockin' In Rhythm
....   In A Sentimental Mood
....   Take The "A" Train
....   Fife
....   Chinoiserie
....   Perdido
....   Satin Doll
....   Sophisticated Lady
....   Things Ain't What They Used To Be
....   In Triplicate
....   Come Off The Veldt

                                                                                                   18 Feb 1972   (P)
            DUKE ELLINGTON & HIS ORCHESTRA   p Queen Elizabeth Theatre
            CW MJsn JCI ME, MTlr BWd CCrs, RP NTrn HMn PG HAsh HC, DE JBjm RJo.   Vancouver, BC

....   The "C" Jam Blues
....   Creole Love Call
....   Take The "A" Train
....   Chinoiserie
....   Satin Doll
....   Things Ain't What They Used To Be
....   Come Off The Veldt
....   Sophisticated Lady

                                                                                                   21 Feb 1972   (P)
            DUKE ELLINGTON & HIS ORCHESTRA   Hoyt Hotel
            CW MJsn JCI ME, MTlr BWd CCrs, RP NTrn HMn PG HAsh HC, JBjm RJo.   Portland, OR

....   Perdido
....   Laura
....   Love Is Just Around The Corner
            > DE added.

....   Black And Tan Fantasy—Creole Love Call—The Mooche
....   Azure   >>>

....	Kinda Dukish/Rockin' In Rhythm
....	In A Sentimental Mood
....	Cotton Tail
....	Pitter Panther Patter
....	Take The "A" Train
....	Fife
....	Soul Flute
....	Chinoiserie
....	I Can't Get Started
....	Satin Doll
....	Come Off The Veldt
....	Medley[1]
....	Things Ain't What They Used To Be

[1]Including: Prelude To A Kiss; Do Nothin' Till You Hear From Me; I Let A Song Go Out Of My Heart; Don't Get Around Much Anymore; Mood Indigo; I'm Beginning To See The Light; Solitude; Sophisticated Lady; Caravan.

DUKE ELLINGTON & HIS ORCHESTRA
DE omitted, otherwise same personnel.

....	The "C" Jam Blues
....	Soon It's Gonna Rain
....	Perdido
....	Love Is Just Around The Corner

> DE added.

....	Things Ain't What They Used To Be
....	Goof
....	Kinda Dukish/Rockin' In Rhythm
....	Addi
....	Diminuendo In Blue and Wailing Interval
....	4:30 Blues
....	Take The "A" Train
	TOGO BRAVA—BRAVA TOGO
....	- Soul Soothing Beach
....	- Naturellement
....	- Amour, Amour
....	- Right On Togo
....	Satin Doll
....	In Triplicate

                                                                          25 Feb 1972   (P)
DUKE ELLINGTON & HIS ORCHESTRA   Zellerbach Auditorium, University of California
CW MJsn JCl ME, MTlr BWd CCrs, RP NTrn HMn HAsh HC, DE JBjm RJo, TWtk.   Berkeley, CA

....	The "C" Jam Blues
....	Creole Love Call
....	Kinda Dukish/Rockin' In Rhythm

> DE JBjm.

....	Lotus Blossom

> Entire band.

....	Take The "A" Train
....	Fife
	TOGO BRAVA—BRAVA TOGO
....	- Soul Soothing Beach
....	- Naturellement
....	- Amour, Amour
....	- Right On Togo
....	Satin Doll
....	Satin Doll
....	Take The "A" Train
....	Perdido
....	Chinoiserie
....	I Can't Get Started
....	Goof
....	Things Ain't What They Used To Be
....	In Duplicate
....	La Plus Belle Africaine
....	Come Off The Veldt
....	Medley[1]
....	Hello Dolly –vMJsn

> HC, DE JBjm RJo.

....   Monologue –DE narration

[1]Including: Prelude To A Kiss; Do Nothin' Till You Hear From Me; I Let A Song Go Out Of My Heart; Don't Get Around Much Anymore; Mood Indigo; I'm Beginning To See The Light; Solitude –vTWtk; Heaven –vTWtk; In The Beginning God –vTWtk; One More Time For The People –vTWtk.

<table>
<tr><td></td><td></td><td>10 Apr 1972   (P)</td></tr>
</table>

DUKE ELLINGTON & HIS RHYTHM   Whitney Museum of American Art
DE JBjm RJo.   New York City, NY

....   Opening remarks by DE

> DE piano solo.

.... lps   Medley[1]
.... lps   Meditation
.... lps   A Mural From Two Perspectives[2]
.... lps   Sophisticated Lady—Solitude
.... lps   Soda Fountain Rag
.... lps   New World A-Comin'

> JBjm RJo added.

.... lps   Amour, Amour
.... lps   Soul Soothing Beach

> RJo omitted.

.... lps   Lotus Blossom

> RJo added.

.... Az   Take The "A" Train

> RJo omitted.

.... lps   Flamingo
.... lps   Le Sucrier Velours
.... Az   A Single Petal Of A Rose

> RJo added.

.... MP   Night Pastor[3]
.... lps   The "C" Jam Blues
.... lps   Mood Indigo
.... lps   I'm Beginning To See The Light –vDE
.... lps   Dancers In Love
.... Az   La Plus Belle Africaine
.... lps   Come Off The Veldt
.... lps   Satin Doll

[1]Including: Black And Tan Fantasy; Prelude To A Kiss; Do Nothin' Till You Hear From Me; Caravan.
[2]Sometimes referred to as "A Blue Mural From Two Perspectives."
[3]sa "The Shepherd (Who Watches Over The Nightflock)"; "The Blues Is Waiting."

Some sources suggest that titles 1-7 originate from an event at the Krannert Center, University of Illinois, Champaign-Urbana, IL, on 5 May 1972.

DUKE ELLINGTON   (S)[1]
DE interviewed by Sid Paul.

....   Interview

[1]Backstage.

<table>
<tr><td></td><td></td><td>14 Apr 1972   (P)</td></tr>
</table>

DUKE ELLINGTON & HIS ORCHESTRA   Covered Wagon Inn
CW MJsn HMG ME, VP CCrs, RP NTrn HMn PG HAsh HC, JBjm RJo, TWtk.   Wayne, PA

....   The "C" Jam Blues
....   Love Is Just Around The Corner
....   Perdido

> DE JBjm RJo.

....   Dancers In Love

> Entire band, DE added.

....   In A Sentimental Mood
....   Diminuendo In Blue and Wailing Interval
....   Mood Indigo
....   Star Dust
....   How High The Moon   >>>

....   Addi
....   Satin Doll
....   Sophisticated Lady
....   Prelude To A Kiss—I Didn't Know About You
....   Black And Tan Fantasy—Creole Love Call—The Mooche
....   Happy Birthday
....   Let Me Call You Sweetheart—My Buddy
....   My Buddy
....   Making That Scene –vTWtk
....   Solitude –vTWtk
....   Solitude –vTWtk
....   I Got It Bad –vTWtk
....   Be Cool And Groovy For Me –vTWtk

        > DE, TWtk.

....   Heaven –vTWtk

        > Entire band.

....   Love you Madly –vTWtk
....   Take The "A" Train
....   I Can't Get Started
....   One More Time For The People –vTWtk
....   In A Mellotone
....   Things Ain't What They Used To Be
....   Hello Dolly –vMJsn
....   The Biggest And Busiest Intersection
....   Caravan—Don't Get Around Much Anymore

19 Apr 1972   **(P)**
Timbers Restaurant
Newtown Square, PA

<u>DUKE ELLINGTON & HIS ORCHESTRA</u>
CW MJsn JCl ME, VP CCrs, RP NTrn HMn PG HAsh HC, DE JBjm dr.

....   I'm Beginning To See The Light
....   In A Sentimental Mood
....   Goof
....   How High The Moon
....   Mood Indigo
....   Ain't Misbehavin'
....   Blueberry Hill –vMJsn
....   Hello Dolly –vMJsn

        > RJo replaces dr.

....   Satin Doll
....   Things Ain't What They Used To Be
....   Soon It's Gonna Rain
....   Laura
....   Rose Of The Rio Grande
....   Diminuendo In Blue and Wailing Interval
....   Happy Birthday
....   Take The "A" Train
....   Black And Tan Fantasy
....   Hard
....   I Can't Give You Anything But Love
....   Let Me Call You Sweetheart

        > DE JBjm RJo.

....   Autumn Leaves

        > Entire band.

....   Soul Flute

        > DE JBjm.

....   Lotus Blossom

        > Entire band.

....   Solitude
....   I Let A Song Go Out Of My Heart/Don't Get Around Much Anymore
....   Addi
....   Caravan
....   Take The "A" Train

23 Apr 1972   **(P)**
Left Bank
Baltimore, MD

<u>DUKE ELLINGTON & HIS ORCHESTRA</u>
CW MJsn JCl ME, VP CCrs, RP NTrn HMn PG HAsh HC, DE JBjm RJo.

....   Love Is Just Around The Corner   >>>

....   Kinda Dukish/Rockin' In Rhythm
....   Goof
....   How High The Moon

                              TOGO BRAVA—BRAVA TOGO
....   - Soul Soothing Beach
....   - Naturellement
....   - Amour, Amour
....   - Right On Togo

          > DE piano solo.

....   Flamingo

          > Entire band.

....   You Are Beautiful
....   Addi
....   HARLEM
....   La Plus Belle Africaine
....   Come Off The Veldt
....   Caravan
....   One O'Clock Jump
....   In Triplicate

                                             28 Apr 1972   (P)
DUKE ELLINGTON & HIS ORCHESTRA   T.G. Williams High School Auditorium
CW MJsn JCl ME, VP CCrs, RP NTrn HMn PG HAsh HC, DE JBjm RJo.   Alexandria, VA

....   The "C" Jam Blues
....   Take The "A" Train
....   Creole Love Call
....   Perdido
....   Kinda Dukish/Rockin' In Rhythm

                              TOGO BRAVA—BRAVA TOGO
....   - Soul Soothing Beach
....   - Naturellement
....   - Amour, Amour
....   - Right On Togo

....   In A Sentimental Mood
....   Take The "A" Train
....   Fife
....   Chinoiserie
....   HARLEM
....   Things Ain't What They Used To Be
....   Happy Birthday
....   Goof
....   Satin Doll
....   In Triplicate
....   La Plus Belle Africaine
....   Medley[1]
....   Addi
....   Hello Dolly –vMJsn
....   One More Time For The People

          > DE JBjm.

....   Lotus Blossom

[1]Including: It Don't Mean A Thing; Prelude To A Kiss; Do Nothin' Till You Hear From Me; I Let A Song Go Out Of My Heart; Solitude; Don't Get Around Much Anymore; Mood Indigo; I'm Beginning To See The Light; Sophisticated Lady; Caravan.

                                             9 May 1972   (P)
DUKE ELLINGTON & HIS ORCHESTRA   Ramada Inn Southwest
CW MJsn JCl ME, VP CCrs, RP NTrn HMn PG HAsh HC, JBjm RJo, TWtk.   Fenton, MO

....   The "C" Jam Blues
....   Love Is Just Around The Corner
....   Perdido
....   Laura

          > DE added.

....   Kinda Dukish/Rockin' In Rhythm
....   Ceole Love Call
....   Take The "A" Train
....   Fife
....   Chinoiserie
....   Satin Doll   >>>

....		Come Off The Veldt
....		Medley[1]
....		Hello Dolly –vMJsn
....		One More Time For The People –vTWtk

[1]Including: Prelude To A Kiss; Do Nothin' Till You Hear From Me; I Let A Song Go Out Of My Heart; Don't Get Around Much Anymore; Mood Indigo; Sophisticated Lady.

DUKE ELLINGTON & HIS ORCHESTRA
DE added, otherwise same personnel.

....		Things Ain't What They Used To Be
....		Goof
....		Soon It's Gonna Rain
....		I Let A Song Go Out Of My Heart/Don't Get Around Much Anymore
....		Kinda Dukish/Rockin' In Rhythm
....		Addi
....		How High The Moon
....		Satin Doll
....		Take The "A" Train
....		In A Sentimental Mood
....		In Triplicate
....		Mood Indigo
....		I'm Beginning To See The Light—Sophisticated Lady
....		Making That Scene –vTWtk
....		Rocks In My Bed –vTWtk
....		Love You Madly –vTWtk
....		It Don't Mean a Thing –vTWtk
....		Blueberry Hill –vMJsn
....		One More Time For The People –vTWtk
....		Satin Doll

14 May 1972   (S)
Unidentified location (?bc)
U.S.A.

DUKE ELLINGTON
DE interviewed by Jim Bolen.

....		Interview

> DE JBjm RJo.

....		Solitude
....		Warm Valley

12 Jun 1972   (S)
National Recording Studios
New York City, NY

DUKE ELLINGTON & HIS ORCHESTRA
CW MJsn JCl ME, VP TG CCrs, RP NTrn HMn PG HAsh HC, DE JBjm RJo, TWtk.

....	RDB	-1	Don't You Know I Care?
....	LL	alt.	Don't You Know I Care?
....			Mood Indigo (incomplete)
....			Mood Indigo (incomplete)
....	Az	-1	Mood Indigo
....	RDB	-2	Mood Indigo (incomplete)
....	RDB	-3	Mood Indigo
....		-1	Blem
....		-2	Blem
....			Blem (insert)
....	Pab		Blem
....			It Don't Mean A Thing (incomplete)
....			It Don't Mean A Thing –vTWtk (incomplete)
....			It Don't Mean A Thing –vTWtk (incomplete)
....			It Don't Mean A Thing –vTWtk
....	LL		Chinoiserie

22 Jun 1972   (S)
Toronto Sound Studios
Toronto, ON

DUKE ELLINGTON & HIS ORCHESTRA
CW MJsn JCl ME[1], VP CCrs, RP NTrn HMn PG HAsh HC, DE JBjm RJo.

....	LL		Satin Doll
....	LL		Hello Dolly –vMJsn

> NTrn, JBjm RJo.

....	LL		Alone Together

> Entire band.

....	Az	-3	Vancouver Lights
....	LL		Relaxin'[2]
....	LL		Things Ain't What They Used To Be >>>

....		New York, New York[3]
....		Untitled original
....		Untitled original

[1]According to one source, the Canadian trumpet player Arnie Chycosti replaced ME on some of the titles.
[2]Erroneously as "Vancouver Lights" on LL.
[3]*aka* "New York Is A Summer Festival"; the piece is not identical with the Frank Sinatra hit.

		23 Jun 1972	(P)
DUKE ELLINGTON & HIS ORCHESTRA		O'Keefe Centre	
CW MJsn JCl ME, VP TG CCrs, RP NTrn HMn PG HAsh HC, DE JBjm RJo, TWtk.		Toronto, ON	

.... Az	The "C" Jam Blues	
.... Az	Kinda Dukish/Rockin' In Rhtyhm	
.... Az	Goof	
	TOGO BRAVA—BRAVA TOGO	
.... Az	- Soul Soothing Beach	
.... Az	- Right On Togo	
.... Az	- Amour, Amour	
.... Az	- Naturellement	
.... Az	In A Sentimental Mood	
.... Az	Up Jump	
.... Az	Fife	
.... Az	Take The "A" Train	
.... Az	Chinoiserie	
.... Az	HARLEM	
.... Az	Perdido	
.... Az	Satin Doll	
.... Az	La Plus Belle Africaine	
.... Az	Come Off The Veldt	
.... Az[1]	Medley[2]	
....	Making That Scene –vTWtk	

> DE, TWtk.

....	Heaven –vTWtk	

> Entire band.

....	Love You Madly –vTWtk	
....	I Got It Bad –vTWtk	
....	Caravan	
....	Addi	
....	Hello Dolly –vMJsn	
....	One More Time For The People –vTWtk	

> DE JBjm.

.... Az	Lotus Blossom	

[1]Only "Mood Indigo" on Az.
[2]Including: Prelude To A Kiss; Do Nothin' Till You Hear From Me; I Let A Song Go Out Of My Heart; Don't Get Around Much Anymore; Mood Indigo; I'm Beginning To See The Light; Sophisticated Lady.

		3 Jul 1972	(T)[1]
DUKE ELLINGTON & HIS ORCHESTRA		Bell Studios	
CW MJsn JCl ME, VP TG CCrs, RP NTrn HMn PG HAsh HC, DE JBjm RJo.		New York City, NY	

....	Satin Doll	
....	Kinda Dukish/Rockin' In Rhythm	
....	Chinoiserie	
....	Take The "A" Train	

[1]Music for the documentary "L'aventure du Jazz" (A Jazz Odyssey); see also interview on 3 Jun 1970.

		8 Jul 1972[1]	(P)
DUKE ELLINGTON & HIS ORCHESTRA		Carnegie Hall (tc)	
CW MJsn JCl ME, VP TG CCrs, RP NTrn HMn PG HAsh HC, DE JBjm RJo, AMo TWtk.		New York City, NY	

....	The "C" Jam Blues	
....	Things Ain't What They Used To Be	
....	Kinda Dukish/Rockin' In Rhythm	
	TOGO BRAVA—BRAVA TOGO	
....	- Soul Soothing Beach	
....	- Right On Togo	
....	- Amour, Amour	
....	- Naturellement	

> PG, DE JBjm RJo.

.... LSR	Happy Reunion >>>	

> Entire band.

.... LSR   Take The "A" Train
.... LSR   Ac-Ac
.... LSR   La Plus Belle Africaine
....   East St. Louis Toodle-Oo

> DE SG.

....   Soda Fountain Rag

> Entire band, SG omitted.

.... LSR   HARLEM
.... LSR   Satin Doll
.... LSR   Hello Dolly –vMJsn

> BB added.

.... LSR   Rose Room

> BB, DE omitted, BSht added.

....   Me And You –vBSht
....   It Don't Mean A Thing –vBSht
....   I Got It Bad –vBSht

> BSht omitted, BB, DE, BFmr added.

.... Az   St. Louis Blues –vBFmr

> BB, BFmr omitted.

....   I'm Beginning To See The Light –vAMo

> ARly added.

....   Mood Indigo –vARly
....   Blem –vARly

> BFmr added.

....   One More Time For The People –vAMo BFmr ARly TWtk.

[1]The date of telecast is not known.

17 Jul 1972   (S)
University of Wisconsin
Madison, WI

DUKE ELLINGTON
DE and Dr. James Latimer.

....   Conversation

> DE piano solo.

....   Improvisations and excerpts

DUKE ELLINGTON WITH CHOIR
DE with choir.

....   It's Freedom –vChoir
....   It's Freedom –vChoir
....   It's Freedom –vChoir
....   It's Freedom –vChoir
....   It's Freedom –vChoir
....   It's Freedom –vChoir
....   It's Freedom –vChoir

The above is a rehearsal session.

18 Jul 1972   (P)
Camp Randall Stadium
Madison, WI

DUKE ELLINGTON & HIS ORCHESTRA
CW MJsn JCl ME, VP TG CCrs, RP NTrn HMn PG HAsh HC, DE JBjm RJo, AMo TWtk.

....   Perdido
....   Take The "A" Train
....   Kinda Dukish/Rockin' In Rhythm
....   Creole Love Call
....   Goof
....   In A Sentimental Mood

          TOGO BRAVA—BRAVA TOGO
....   - Soul Soothing Beach
....   - Right On Togo
....   - Amour, Amour
....   - Naturellement

....   Take The "A" Train
....   Fife >>>

....	Chinoiserie
....	La Plus Belle Africaine
....	I'm Beginning To See The Light –vAMo
....	Ac-Ac
....	Satin Doll
....	Hello Dolly –vMJsn
....	Making That Love Scene –vTWtk
....	Solitude –vTWtk
....	I Got It Bad –vTWtk
....	Love You Madly –vTWtk
....	Come Off The Veldt
....	Medley[1]
....	One More Time For The People –vAMo TWtk
....	Things Ain't What They Used To Be

[1]Including: Prelude To A Kiss; Do Nothin' Till You Hear From Me; I Let A Song Go Out Of My Heart; Don't Get Around Much Anymore; Mood Indigo; It Don't Mean A Thing –vTWtk; Sophisticated Lady.

19 Jul 1972   (P)
Wisconsin Union Theater
Madison, WI

<u>DUKE ELLINGTON & HIS ORCHESTRA</u>
CW MJsn JCI ME, VP TG CCrs, RP NTrn HMn PG HAsh HC, DE JBjm RJo, DGrd PHoy RG TWtk choir.

....	THE SECOND SACRED CONCERT
....	Praise God
....	Supreme Being –vChoir
....	Something About Believing –vDGrd RG TWtk Choir
....	Almighty God –vDGrd Choir
....	The Shepherd
....	Heaven –vDGrd Choir
....	It's Freedom –vDGrd PHoy RG TWtk Choir
> DE JBjm.	
....	Meditation
> Entire band.	
....	The Biggest And Busiest Intersection
> DE, PHoy.	
....	T.G.T.T. –vPHoy
> Entire band.	
....	Don't Get Down On Your Knees –vTWtk
> TWtk Choir a cappella.	
....	Father Forgive –vTWtk Choir
> Entire band.	
....	Don't Get Down On Your Knees –vTWtk
....	Praise God And Dance –vPHoy TWtk Choir
> TWtk a cappella.	
....	The Preacher's Song –vTWtk
> Entire band.	
....	In The Beginning God –vChoir

20 Jul 1972   (P)
Mills Hall, University of Wisconsin
Madison, WI

<u>DUKE ELLINGTON, DICK "TWO TON" BAKER, BROOKS KERR</u>
DE talking.

....	Master Class
> BKrr piano solo.	
....	Take The "A" Train
....	Relaxin'
....	I'm All Out Of Breath
....	Carolina Shout
> DE piano solo.	
....	Soda Fountain Rag (incomplete)
> BKrr piano solo.	
....	Soda Fountain Rag
> TTB piano solo.	
....	I'm Afraid >>>

....   I'm Afraid –vTTB DE
....   Dancers In Love

    > DE piano solo.

....   The Anticipation[1]

[1]Part of the future *Uwis Suite.*

The above and next day's master class have been taped and edited for the documentary "Duke Ellington and Friends."

DUKE ELLINGTON & HIS ORCHESTRA   Performing Arts Center (P)
CW MJsn JCI ME, VP TG CCrs, RP NTrn HMn PG HAsh HC, DE JBjm RJo.   Milwaukee, WI

....   The "C" Jam Blues
....   Kinda Dukish/Rockin' In Rhythm
....   Creole Love Call
....   Goof

....   **TOGO BRAVA—BRAVA TOGO**
....   - Soul Soothing Beach
....   - Right On Togo
....   - Amour, Amour
....   - Naturellement

....   Take The "A" Train
....   Fife
....   Satin Doll
....   Chinoiserie
....   Things Ain't What They Used To Be
....   HARLEM
....   Perdido

                                                       21 Jul 1972   (S)
DUKE ELLINGTON   Studios WHA (tc)
Taping session with DE.   Madison, WI

....   An Inner View with Duke Ellington

DUKE ELLINGTON & PAUL GONSALVES   Mills Hall, University of Wisconsin (P)
DE talking.

....   Master Class

    > DE piano solo.

....   Unidentified title
....   A Mural From Two Perspectives
....   Le Sucrier Velours

    > PG added.

....   Happy Reunion

The above and the previous day's master class have been taped and edited for the documentary "Duke Ellington and Friends."

DUKE ELLINGTON & HIS ORCHESTRA   Wisconsin Union Theater (P)
CW MJsn JCI ME, VP TG CCrs, RP NTrn HMn PG HAsh HC, DE JBjm RJo, AMo TWtk.

....   The "C" Jam Blues

....   THE GOUTELAS SUITE
....   [1] - Goutelas
....   [1] - Get-With-Itness
....   - Something
....   - Having At It

    > PG, DE JBjm RJo.

....   Happy Reunion

    > Entire band.

....   How High The Moon
....   Ac-Ac

    > DE piano solo.

....   Le Sucrier Velours
....   A Single Petal Of A Rose

    > Entire band.

....   Take The "A" Train
....   Soul Flute
....   Chinoiserie   >>>

....		I Can't Get Started
		THE UWIS SUITE[2]
....		- The Anticipation
....	Az	- Loco Madi[3]
....	Az	- Uwis
....	Az	- Klop[4]
....		Perdido
....		Kiss
....		Medley[5]
....		Hello Dolly –vMJsn
....		One More Time For The People –vAMo TWtk
....		[1] Things Ain't What They Used To Be

[1]These titles have been included in the documentary "The Good Old Days Are Tomorrow"; additional footage originates from 14 Jun 1971.
[2]UWIS stands for University of Wisconsin.
[3]Short for Madison Locomotive (Locomotion?); aka "Tran" (=Tra[i]n?).
[4]=Polk[a].
[5]Including: Prelude To A Kiss; Do Nothin' Till You Hear From Me; I Let A Song Go Out Of A Heart; I'm Beginning To See The Light –vAMo; Blem –vAMo; Don't Get Around Much Anymore; Mood Indigo; Jump For Joy; Come Sunday –TWtk; In The Beginning God –vTWtk; Sophisticated Lady; Caravan.

DUKE ELLINGTON & HIS ORCHESTRA
MJsn JCl ME, VP TG CCrs, RP NTrn HMn PG HAsh HC, DE JBjm RJo, AMo TWtk.

30 Jul 1972   (P)
Brandywine Raceway
Wilmington, DE

....	Take The "A" Train
....	In Quadruplicate
....	I Got It Bad –vTWtk
....	Blem –vAMo
....	Satin Doll

DUKE ELLINGTON & HIS GROUP
MJsn, RP NTrn HMn PG HAsh HC, DE JBjm RJo, AMo.

2 Aug 1972   (S)
MediaSound Studios
New York City, NY

....	RDB		New York, New York (incomplete)
....	RDB		New York, New York (incomplete)
....	RDB		New York, New York (incomplete)
....	RDB	-1	New York, New York –vAMo
....		-2	New York, New York –vAMo
....		-3	New York, New York –vAMo (incomplete)
....		-4	New York, New York –vAMo
....			New York, New York (rehearsal)

> JA added.

....		-5	New York, New York –vAMo
....			New York, New York –vAMo (coda insert rehearsal)
....			New York, New York -vAMo (coda insert)
....			New York, New York –vAMo (coda insert)
....			I'm Beginning To See The Light –vAMo
....			I Got It Bad –vAMo
....	MM		Woods[1]

[1]aka "Not A Portrait Of Count Basie"; this title is a derivative of Solitude.

DUKE ELLINGTON & HIS GROUP
MJsn RP NTrn HMn PG HAsh HC, DE JBjm JA RJo, AMo TWtk.

Aug 1972   (P)
Rainbow Grill (bc)
New York City, NY

....	Take The "A" Train
....	New York, New York –vAMo
....	Blem –vAMo
....	Mood Indigo
....	Sophisticated Lady
....	Things Ain't What They Used To Be
....	Solitude –vTWtk
....	One More Time For The People –vAMo TWtk
....	Satin Doll—New York, New York –vAMo TWtk DE

DUKE ELLINGTON WITH ANITA MOORE & TONY WATKINS
DE, AMo TWtk.

25 Aug 1972   (S)
MediaSound Studios
New York City, NY

....	Az		I'm Afraid Of Loving You Too Much (incomplete)
....	Az	-1	The Anticipation
....	Az		Le Sucrier Velours (incomplete) >>>

....	Az	-2	Le Sucrier Velours
....			Lotus Blossom
....	Az		A Mural From Two Perspectives
....	Az		I'm Afraid Of Loving You Too Much –vAMo
....			I Didn't Know About You
....			I Didn't Know About You –vAMo (incomplete)
....	Az	-3	I Didn't Know About You (incomplete)
....	Az	-4	I Didn't Know About You –vAMo

> JA added.

....			Loco Madi (incomplete)

> JA omitted.

....	Az	-6	Lotus Blossom
....	Az		New World A-Comin'
....	Az		Le Sucrier Velours
....	Az		Melancholia
....			A Single Petal Of A Rose

> JA added.

....	Az		The Blues[1] (rehearsal)

> JA omitted.

....	Az		The Blues –vTWtk[2]
....			My Mother, My Father –vTWtk
....			My Mother, My Father (rehearsal)
....			The Blues (rehearsal)
....	Az	-9	Come Sunday –vTWtk
....		-10	My Mother, My Father –vTWtk
....	Az		A Mural From Two Perspectives
....	Az		My Little Brown Book (rehearsal)

[1]Although not clearly identifiable, it is assumed that this brief piano fragment is an attempt on "The Blues."
[2]The second chorus of the vocal is performed in Hebrew.

27 Aug 1972   (P)
Lakeside Theater
East Meadow, NY

DUKE ELLINGTON & HIS ORCHESTRA
CW MJsn JCI ME, VP CCrs, RP HMn PG HAsh HC, DE JBjm RJo, AMo.

....	Take The "A" Train
....	Azure
....	Satin Doll
....	The Piano Player[1]—I Can't Give You Anything But Love
....	Just Squeeze Me
....	Soul Flute
....	Perdido
....	Mood Indigo
....	The "C" Jam Blues
....	Perdido
....	Love Is Just Around The Corner
....	Don't You Know I Care?
....	I Let A Song Go Out Of My Heart –vAMo
....	The Lonely Ones –vAMo
....	Acht O'Clock Rock
....	Acht O'Clock Rock

[1]*sa* "Woods"; "Not A Portrait Of Count Basie."

31 Aug 1972   (P)
Steel Pier
Atlantic City, NJ

DUKE ELLINGTON & HIS ORCHESTRA
CW MJsn JCI ME, VP BWd CCrs, RP NTrn HMn PG HAsh HC, DE JBjm RJo, AMo TWtk.

....	The "C" Jam Blues
....	Kinda Dukish/Rockin' In Rhythm
....	In A Sentimental Mood
....	How High The Moon
....	Soul Flute
....	Take The "A" Train
....	New York, New York –vAMo
....	I Got It Bad –vAMo
....	Blem –vAMo
....	Satin Doll
....	Come Off The Veldt
....	Things Ain't What They Used To Be
....	Hello Dolly
....	Medley[1] >>>

....			Making That Scene –vTWtk
....			Mood Indigo –vTWtk
....			One More Time For The People –vAMo TWtk
....			Satin Doll

[1]Including: Don't Get Around Much Anymore; Mood Indigo; I'm Beginning To See The Light; I Let A Song Go Out Of My Heart; Sophisticated Lady.

DUKE ELLINGTON & HIS ORCHESTRA
Same personnel.

....			Perdido
....			Kinda Dukish/Rockin' In Rhythm
....			Goof
....			Soul Soothing Beach
....			Naturellement
....			Take The "A" Train
....			Satin Doll
....			Come Off The Veldt
....			New York, New York –vAMo
....			I Didn't Know About You –vAMo
....			Blem –vAMo

> PG, DE JBjm RJo.

| .... | | | Happy Reunion |

> Entire band.

....			Hello Dolly –vMJsn
....			Sophisticated Lady
....			It Don't Mean A Thing –vTWtk
....			Do Nothin' Till You Hear From Me –vTWtk
....			Mood Indigo –vTWtk
....			Be Cool And Groovy For Me –vTWtk
....			One More Time For The People –vAMo TWtk
....			Things Ain't What They Used To Be

5 Sep 1972   (S)
MediaSound Studios
New York City, NY

DUKE ELLINGTON & HIS GROUP
MJsn, RP NTrn HMn PG HAsh HC, DE JBjm RJo, AMo.

....		-1	New York, New York (incomplete)
....	Az	-2	New York, New York (incomplete)
....	Az	-3	New York, New York (incomplete)
....	Az	-4	New York, New York –vAMo
....			I Got It Bad (incomplete)
....			I Got It Bad (incomplete)
....	RDB	-5	I Got It Bad –vAMo
....		-6	I Didn't Know About You –vAMo (incomplete)
....		-7	I Didn't Know About You –vAMo
....		-8	I Let A Song Go Out Of My Heart (incomplete)
....		-9	I Let A Song Go Out Of My Heart –vAMo (incomplete)
....			I Let A Song Go Out Of My Heart (incomplete)
....	RDB	-10	I Let A Song Go Out Of My Heart –vAMo
....			I Let A Song Go Out Of My Heart (rehearsal)
....	RDB	-11	I Let A Song Go Out Of My Heart (incomplete)
....	RDB		I Let A Song Go Out Of My Heart (rehearsal)
....	RDB	-12	I Let A Song Go Out Of My Heart –vAMo
....		-13	I Let A Song Go Out Of My Heart –vAMo
....		-14	I'm Afraid –vAMo (incomplete)
....		-15	I'm Afraid –vAMo (incomplete)
....		-16	I'm Afraid –vAMo (coda)

> DE JBjm RJo, AMo.

| .... | RDB | -17 | Misty –vAMo |

> Entire group.

....		-18	I'm Afraid –vAMo (coda)
....			I'm Afraid –vAMo (coda/incomplete)
....			I'm Afraid –vAMo (coda/incomplete)
....			I'm Afraid (coda)
....			I'm Afraid (coda/rehearsal)
....			I'm Afraid (coda/rehearsal)
....		-22	I'm Afraid –vAMo
....		-24	The Lonely Ones (incomplete)
....		-25	The Lonely Ones –vAMo
....			New York, New York –vAMo

21 Sep 1972 (P)
College Fieldhouse, Carthage College
Kenosha, WI

<u>DUKE ELLINGTON & HIS ORCHESTRA</u>
CW MJsn JCl ME, VP CCrs, RP NTrn PG HAsh HC, DE JBjm RJo, TWtk.

....		The "C" Jam Blues
....		Kinda Dukish/Rockin' In Rhythm
....		Creole Love Call
....		Goof
....		Soul Flute
....		Take The "A" Train
....		Chinoiserie

TOGO BRAVA—BRAVA TOGO
....		- Soul Soothing Beach
....		- Right On Togo
....		- Amour, Amour
....		- Naturellement

....		Perdido
....		Satin Doll
....		In Duplicate
....		La Plus Belle Africaine
....		Ac-Ac
....		Come Off The Veldt
....		Medley[1]
....		Making That Scene –vTWtk
....		Do Nothin' Till You Hear From Me –vTWtk
....		Solitude –vTWtk
....		One More Time For The People –vTWtk

> DE, TWtk.

.... Heaven –vTWtk

> Entire band.

.... Things Ain't What They Used To Be

[1]Including: Don't Get Around Much Anymore; Mood Indigo; I'm Beginning To See The Light; Sophisticated Lady.

One source suggests that this event took place in Racine, WI, which is unlikely because the band's itinerary clearly documents its presence at Carthage College on this date. An alternative date and place for the above recording are 16 Sep 1972 at the Willowbrook Ballroom in Willow Springs, IL, where the band in fact did play a dance date on that day. However, the choice of titles and their sequence led us to believe that the recorded event was rather a concert performance than a dance date.

1 Oct 1972[1] (S)
Unidentified location (tc)
U.S.A.

<u>DUKE ELLINGTON</u>
DE on the TV program "Jazz: The American Art Form."

.... DE talking

[1]Date of telecast; probably taped at an earlier date.

5 Oct 1972 (S)
MediaSound Studios
New York City, NY

<u>DUKE ELLINGTON & HIS ORCHESTRA</u>
CW MJsn JCl ME, VP BWd CCrs, RP NTrn HMn RA HAsh HC, DE JBjm RJo.

....	Az	-1	Chinoiserie
....		-1	Ac-Ac (incomplete)
....	Az	-2	Ac-Ac
....			Ac-Ac (insert)
....		-3	Kiss

THE UWIS SUITE
....	RDB	-1	3 Uwis (incomplete)
....	RDB		3 Uwis (rehearsal)
....	RDB	-4	3 Uwis (incomplete)
....		-5	3 Uwis (incomplete)
....		-6	3 Uwis (incomplete)
....	Pab	-7	3 Uwis
....			3 Uwis (insert/incomplete)
....			3 Uwis (insert/incomplete)
....			3 Uwis (insert/incomplete)
....			3 Uwis (insert)
....		-8	4 Klop
....		-9	4 Klop (incomplete)
....		-10	4 Klop
....	RDB	-11	4 Klop
....	Pab	-12	4 Klop >>>

> WF added.

.... RDB   2 Loco Madi (incomplete)
.... Pab[1]   -1   2 Loco Madi

[1]The complete version as broadcast by Radio Denmark runs for 9:25. Pab (J) VIJC-5143 and the reissue on Pab (US)
CD PA 2310-762-2 run for 9:07. The first releases on Pab (both LP and CD) fade after 6:07.

The first part of the suite—The Anticipation—was never recorded in a studio by the orchestra.

                                                                                          13 Oct 1972   (P)
DUKE ELLINGTON & HIS ORCHESTRA   Civic Auditorium
CW MJsn JCl ME, VP CCrs, RP NTrn HMn RA HAsh HC, DE JBjm RJo.   Knoxville, TN

....   The "C" Jam Blues
....   Kinda Dukish/Rockin' In Rhythm
....   Creole Love Call
....   Goof
....   Caravan
....   Fife
....   Take The "A" Train
....   Chinoiserie

                                 TOGO BRAVA—BRAVA TOGO
....   - Soul Soothing Beach
....   - Right On Togo
....   - Amour, Amour
....   - Naturellement

                                                                                          17 Oct 1972   (P)
DUKE ELLINGTON & HIS ORCHESTRA   Bucks County Community College
CW MJsn JCl ME, VP CCrs, RP NTrn HMn RA HAsh HC, DE JBjm RJo, TWtk.   Newtown, PA

....   The "C" Jam Blues
....   Take The "A" Train
....   Kinda Dukish/Rockin' In Rhythm
....   Creole Love Call
....   Goof
....   Caravan
....   Take The "A" Train
....   Fife
....   Chinoiserie

                                 TOGO BRAVA—BRAVA TOGO
....   - Soul Soothing Beach
....   - Right On Togo
....   - Amour, Amour
....   - Naturellement

....   Perdido
....   Satin Doll
....   In Duplicate
....   La Plus Belle Africaine
....   Ac-Ac
....   Come Off The Veldt
....   Hello Dolly –vMJsn
....   Medley[1]
....   Making That Scene –vTWtk
....   Do Nothin' Till You Hear From Me –vTWtk
....   Solitude –vTWtk
....   One More Time For The People –vTWtk
....   In The Beginning God –vTWtk

> DE JBjm RJo.

....   Dancers In Love

> Entire band.

....   Things Ain't What They Used To Be
....   Blueberry Hill –vMJsn

> MJsn, VP, RP, DE JBjm RJo.

....   Tiger Rag

> DE JBjm.

....   Lotus Blossom

[1]Including: Don't Get Around Much Anymore; Mood Indigo; I'm Beginning To See The Light; Sophisticated Lady.

22+23 Oct 1972[1]   (P)
Lincoln Center (tc)
New York City, NY

DUKE ELLINGTON & HIS ORCHESTRA
CW MJsn JCI ME, VP TG CCrs, RP NTrn HMn RA HAsh HC, DE JBjm RJo.

....	Tx	The "C" Jam Blues
....	Tx	Into Each Life Some Jazz Must Fall –DE recital
....	Tx	It Don't Mean A Thing

DUKE ELLINGTON WITH COUNT BASIE & HIS ORCHESTRA
DE, BG, DSev with Count Basie & His Orchestra.

| .... | Tx | One O'Clock Jump |

[1]Taping session; telecast on 29 Nov 1972.

27 Oct 1972   (P)
Memorial Auditorium
Worcester, MA

DUKE ELLINGTON & HIS ORCHESTRA WITH THE DETROIT SYMPHONY ORCHESTRA
CW MJsn JCI ME, VP CCrs, RP NTrn HMn RA HAsh HC, DE JBjm RJo, TWtk with the
Detroit Symphony Orchestra, Sixten Ehrling conducting.

....		Things Ain't What They Used To Be
....		Fife
....		Take The "A" Train
....		HARLEM

> DSO omitted.

....		Chinoiserie
....		Hello Dolly –vMJsn
....		Medley[1]
....		Making That Scene –vTWtk
....		Solitude –vTWtk

> DSO added.

....		Satin Doll
....		One More Time For The People –vTWtk
....		Satin Doll

[1]Including: Don't Get Around Much Anymore; Mood Indigo; I'm Beginning To See The Light; Sophisticated Lady.

Nov 1972   (P)
Hilton Hotel (tc)
Las Vegas, NV

DUKE ELLINGTON
DE as guest on the show "This is Your Life, Peggy Lee."

| .... | | Interview |

5 Dec 1972   (S)
United Recording Studios
Las Vegas, NV

DUKE ELLINGTON & RAY BROWN
DE RBwn.

....	Pab	Do Nothin' Till You Hear From Me
....	Pab	Pitter Panther Patter
....	Pab	Things Ain't What They Used To Be
....	Pab	Sophisticated Lady
....		Body And Soul
....	Pab	See See Rider[1]
....		FRAGMENTED SUITE FOR PIANO AND BASS
....	Pab	- First Movement
....	Pab	- Second Movement[2]
....		- Third Movement[3] (incomplete)
....	Pab	- Third Movement
....	Pab	- Fourth Movement

[1]aka "C.C. Rider"; this recording is in fact "Mr. J.B. Blues."
[2]This title is a derivative of Mr. J.B. Blues.
[3]sa "Pleadin' For Love"; "Yearning."

17 Dec 1972   (P)
Left Bank
Baltimore, MD

DUKE ELLINGTON & HIS ORCHESTRA
CW MJsn JCI ME, VP CCrs, RP NTrn HMn PG HAsh HC, JBjm RJo, m vcl.

....		The "C" Jam Blues
....		Perdido
....		Soon It's Gonna Rain

> DE added.

....		Soul Flute
....		How High The Moon
....		In A Sentimental Mood
....		Kinda Dukish/Rockin' In Rhythm >>>

....	Caravan
....	Don't You Know I Care?
....	I'm Just A Lucky So-And-So –vcl
....	Hello, Little Girl –vcl
	TOGO BRAVA—BRAVA TOGO
....	- Soul Soothing Beach
....	- Right On Togo
....	- Amour, Amour
....	- Naturellement
....	La Plus Belle Africaine
....	Ac-Ac
....	Take The "A" Train
....	Summer Samba

DUKE ELLINGTON & HIS ORCHESTRA
TWtk replaces m vcl, otherwise same personnel.

....	Satin Doll
....	Come Off The Veldt
....	Hello Dolly –vMJsn
....	Mack The Knife –vMJsn
....	Things Ain't What They Used To Be
....	Love You Madly –vTWtk
....	Do Nothin' Till You Hear From Me –vTWtk
....	Solitude –vTWtk
....	I Don't Want Nobody At All –vTWtk
....	One More Time For The People –vTWtk
....	Medley[1]
....	Diminuendo In Blue and Wailing Interval

> PG, DE JBjm RJo.

| .... | Happy Reunion |

> PG omitted.

| .... | What Am I Here For? |

> Entire band.

| .... | The Piano Player |
| .... | It Don't Mean A Thing –vTWtk |

> DE, TWtk.

| .... | My Mother, My Father –vTWtk |

> Entire band.

....	Making That Scene –vTWtk
....	I Let A Song Go Out Of My Heart/Don't Get Around Much Anymore
....	Satin Doll

[1]Including: Don't Get Around Much Anymore; Mood Indigo; I'm Beginning To See The Light; Sophisticated Lady.

DUKE ELLINGTON & HIS GROUP   31 Dec 1972   (P)
MJsn, VP, RP NTrn HMn PG HAsh HC, DE JBjm RJo.   Rainbow Grill (tc)
                                                                     New York City, NY

....	Take The "A" Train
....	Caravan
....	The "C" Jam Blues
....	Don't You Know I Care?
....	Soul Flute
....	In A Sentimental Mood

DUKE ELLINGTON WITH MICHEL LEGRAND & STEPHANE GRAPPELLI   3 Jan 1973[1]   (S)
DE MLgd PMlt GWz.   ORTF Studios (tc)
                                                                     Paris, France

....	Solitude
....	Les Parapluies de Cherbourg
....	Caravan –vMLgd
....	The "C" Jam Blues

[1]Taping session; telecast on 6 Jun 1973.

DUKE ELLINGTON & STEPHANE GRAPPELLI   4 Jan 1973[1]   (S)
SGrp, DE.   ORTF Studios (tc)
                                                                     Paris, France

| .... Mad | Medley[2]   >>> |

[1]Taping session; telecast on 27 Mar 1973.
[2]Including: Solitude; I Let A Song Go Out Of My Heart; Don't Get Around Much Anymore.

5 Jan 1973[1]   (P)
BBC Studios (tc)
London, England

DUKE ELLINGTON
DE interviewed by Michael Parkinson, with intermittent previously recorded music.

....   RDB   Interview

> DE piano solo.

....   Lotus Blossom

> org vib gt b dr added.

....   Satin Doll

[1]Taping session; telecast on 24 Feb 1973.

Some sources date this event to 13 Jan or 15 Feb respectively. Either date can hardly be correct in view of the fact that DE was back in the United States by that time.

7 Jan 1973[1]   (P)
Caesar's Palace (tc)
Las Vegas, NV

DUKE ELLINGTON & HIS RHYTHM WITH ORCHESTRA
Presentation of the "Entertainer of the Year" award.

....   Award presentation and acceptance speech by DE

> DE JBjm RJo with a studio orchestra.

....   Satin Doll

[1]Taping session; telecast on 23 Jan 1973.

8 Jan 1973   (S)
M-G-M Studios
Fairfax, CA

DUKE'S BIG FOUR
DE JPs RBwn LBsn.

....   -1   Cotton Tail
....   Pab   -2   Cotton Tail
....   Pab   Blues[1]
....   Pab   The Hawk Talks
....   Pab   Prelude To A Kiss
....   Pab   Love You Madly
....   Pab   Just Squeeze Me
....   Pab   Everything But You
....   Caravan

[1]This title is a derivative of *Carnegie Blues.*

10+11 Jan 1973[1] (P/T)
New Shubert Theater (tc)
Los Angeles, CA

DUKE ELLINGTON WITH ALL STAR ORCHESTRA
DE with a host of musicians, among them both current and past band members and associates, such as CA BBry ER SY CW, JCld MME TG BWmn, HC PG RP MRoy, KB RBwn RClr LBsn.

....   Medley[2]
....   Love You Madly –vRFck AFkn PL SV.
....   Love You Madly –DE monologue and finger snapping routine
....   Take The "A" Train

[1]Taping session; telecast on 11 Feb 1973.
[2]Including: Mood Indigo; Sophisticated Lady, Satin Doll; I'm Beginning To See The Light; Do Nothin' Till You Hear From Me; Things Ain't What They Used To Be.

The above is the final segment of the telecast "Duke Ellington—We Love You Madly" in which DE himself appears. The event was filmed in front of a live audience.

30 Jan 1973   (P)
Persian Room, Marco Polo Hotel
Miami Beach, FL

DUKE ELLINGTON & HIS ORCHESTRA
CW MJsn JCl ME, VP, RP NTrn HMn PG HAsh HC, DE JBjm RJo, TWtk.

....   Caravan
....   The "C" Jam Blues
....   How High The Moon
....   Fife
....   Satin Doll
....   Take The "A" Train
....   Mood Indigo
....   Chinoiserie
....   Hello Dolly –vMJsn
....   Sophisticated Lady
....   Making That Scene –vTWtk
....   Do Nothin' Till You Hear From Me –vTWtk   >>>

....   Solitude –vTWtk
....   One More Time For The People –vTWtk
....   Things Ain't What They Used To Be

DUKE ELLINGTON & HIS ORCHESTRA
Same personnel.

....   Caravan
....   Satin Doll
....   Kinda Dukish/Rockin' In Rhythm
....   Creole Love Call
....   Don't You Know I Care?
....   How High The Moon
....   In A Sentimental Mood
....   Take The "A" Train
....   Fife
....   Soul Flute

> HAsh, DE JBjm RJo.

....   I Can't Get Started

> Entire band.

....   Hello Dolly –vMJsn
....   Mack The Knife –vMJsn
....   Medley[1]
....   Making That Scene –vTWtk
....   I Got It Bad –vTWtk
....   I Don't Want Nobody At All –vTWtk
....   One More Time For The People –vTWtk
....   Things Ain't What They Used To Be

[1]Including: Don't Get Around Much Anymore; Mood Indigo; I'm Beginning To See The Light; Sophisticated Lady.

DUKE ELLINGTON & HIS ORCHESTRA
CW MJsn JCl ME, VP CCrs, RP NTrn HMn PG HAsh HC, DE JBjm RJo, TWtk.

31 Jan 1973   (P)
Persian Room, Marco Polo Hotel
Miami Beach, FL

....   Caravan
....   The "C" Jam Blues
....   Don't Get Around Much Anymore
....   Mood Indigo
....   Satin Doll
....   How High The Moon
....   In A Sentimental Mood
....   Take The "A" Train
....   Fife
....   Chinoiserie
....   Hello Dolly –vMJsn
....   Mack The Knife –vMJsn
....   Blueberry Hill –vMJsn
....   Sophisticated Lady
....   Making That Scene –vTWtk
....   Do Nothin' Till You Hear From Me –vTWtk
....   Solitude –vTWtk
....   One More Time For The People –vTWtk
....   Things Ain't What They Used To Be

DUKE ELLINGTON & HIS ORCHESTRA
Same personnel.

....   Caravan
....   The "C" Jam Blues
....   Don't Get Around Much Anymore
....   Mood Indigo
....   Satin Doll
....   How High The Moon
....   In A Sentimental Mood
....   Take The "A" Train
....   Don't You Know I Care?
....   Fife
....   Chinoiserie

> HAsh, DE JBjm RJo.

....   I Can't Get Started

> Entire band.

....   Hello Dolly –vMJsn   >>>

....   Mack The Knife –vMJsn
....   Sophisticated Lady
....   All Of Me
....   Making That Scene –vTWtk
....   I Got It Bad –vTWtk
....   I Don't Want Nobody At All –vTWtk
....   One More Time For The People –vTWtk
....   Things Ain't What They Used To Be

1 Feb 1973   (P)

DUKE ELLINGTON & HIS ORCHESTRA   Persian Room, Marco Polo Hotel
CW MJsn JCl ME, VP CCrs, RP NTrn HMn PG HAsh HC, DE JBjm RJo, TWtk.   Miami Beach, FL

....   Caravan
....   The "C" Jam Blues
....   Don't Get Around Much Anymore
....   Mood Indigo
....   Satin Doll
....   Kinda Dukish/Rockin' In Rhythm
....   In A Sentimental Mood
....   How High The Moon
....   Take The "A" Train
....   Chinoiserie

> HAsh, DE JBjm RJo.

....   I Can't Get Started

> Entire band.

....   Hello Dolly –vMJsn
....   Sophisticated Lady
....   Making That Scene –vTWtk
....   Do Nothin' Till You Hear From Me –vTWtk
....   Solitude –vTWtk
....   One More Time For The People –vTWtk
....   Things Ain't What They Used To Be

DUKE ELLINGTON & HIS ORCHESTRA
Same personnel.

....   Caravan
....   The "C" Jam Blues
....   Mood Indigo
....   Satin Doll
....   How High The Moon
....   Don't You Know I Care?
....   Fife
....   Take The "A" Train
....   In A Sentimental Mood
....   Body And Soul
....   Things Ain't What They Used To Be
....   Hello Dolly –vMJsn
....   Medley[1]
....   Making That Scene –vTWtk
....   Do Nothin' Till You Hear From Me –vTWtk
....   One More Time For The People –vTWtk
....   Things Ain't What They Used To Be

[1]Including: Don't Get Around Much Anymore; I Let A Song Go Out Of My Heart; I Got It Bad; I'm Beginning To See The Light; Sophisticated Lady.

During this set, NTrn quit and walked off the bandstand.

2 Feb 1973   (P)

DUKE ELLINGTON & HIS ORCHESTRA   Persian Room, Marco Polo Hotel
CW MJsn JCl ME, VP CCrs, RP HMn PG HAsh HC, DE JBjm RJo, TWtk.   Miami Beach, FL

....   Caravan
....   The "C" Jam Blues
....   Mood Indigo
....   Satin Doll
....   How High The Moon
....   In A Sentimental Mood
....   Take The "A" Train
....   Don't You Know I Care?
....   In Triplicate
....   Creole Love Call
....   Chinoiserie   >>>

....	Hello Dolly –vMJsn
....	Mack The Knife –vMJsn
....	Medley[1]
....	Making That Scene –vTWtk
....	Do Nothin' Till You Hear From Me –vTWtk
....	Solitude –vTWtk
....	One More Time For The People –vTWtk
....	Things Ain't What They Used To Be

[1]Including: Don't Get Around Much Anymore; I Let A Song Go Out Of My Heart; Don't Get Around Much Anymore; I Got It Bad; I'm Beginning To See The Light; Sophisticated Lady.

DUKE ELLINGTON & HIS ORCHESTRA
Same personnel.

....	Caravan
....	The "C" Jam Blues
....	Mood Indigo
....	Kinda Dukish/Rockin' In Rhythm
....	Satin Doll
....	How High The Moon
....	In A Sentimental Mood
....	Take The "A" Train

> PG, DE JBjm RJo.

....	Blue Prelude

> Entire band.

....	Chinoiserie
....	Ac-Ac
....	Come Off The Veldt
....	Hello Dolly –vMJsn
....	Mack The Knife –vMJsn
....	Medley[1]
....	Making That Scene –vTWtk
....	Do Nothin' Till You Hear From Me –vTWtk
....	Solitude –vTWtk
....	One More Time For The People –vTWtk
....	Things Ain't What They Used To Be

[1]Including: Don't Get Around Much Anymore; I Let A Song Go Out Of My Heart; I Got It Bad; I'm Beginning To See The Light; Sophisticated Lady.

3 Feb 1973   (P)
Persian Room, Marco Polo Hotel
Miami Beach, FL

DUKE ELLINGTON & HIS ORCHESTRA
CW MJsn JCI ME, VP CCrs, RP HMn PG HAsh HC, DE JBjm RJo, TWtk.

....	Caravan
....	The "C" Jam Blues
....	Mood Indigo
....	Satin Doll
....	How High The Moon
....	In A Sentimental Mood
....	Take The "A" Train
....	Don't You Know I Care?
....	Kinda Dukish/Rockin' In Rhythm
....	Creole Love Call
....	Chinoiserie
....	Hello Dolly –vMJsn
....	Mack The Knife –vMJsn
....	Medley[1]
....	Making That Scene –vTWtk
....	Do Nothin' Till You Hear From Me –vTWtk
....	Solitude –vTWtk
....	One More Time For The People –vTWtk
....	In The Beginning God –vTWtk
....	Things Ain't What They Used To Be

[1]Including: Don't Get Around Much Anymore; I Let A Song Go Out Of My Heart; Don't Get Around Much Anymore; I Got It Bad; I'm Beginning To See The Light; Sophisticated Lady.

DUKE ELLINGTON & HIS ORCHESTRA
Same personnel.

....	Caravan
....	Happy-Go-Lucky Local
....	The "C" Jam Blues
....	Mood Indigo >>>

> DE JBjm RJo.

....   Carolina Shout

> Entire band.

....   Satin Doll
....   How High The Moon
....   In A Sentimental Mood
....   Soul Flute
....   Mood Indigo—I'm Beginning To See The Light
....   Take The "A" Train
....   Jeep's Blues
....   Chinoiserie

> HAsh, DE JBjm RJo.

....   I Can't Get Started

> Entire band.

....   Hello Dolly –vMJsn
....   Mack The Knife –vMJsn
....   Sophisticated Lady
....   Making That Scene –vTWtk
....   Do Nothin' Till You Hear From Me –vTWtk
....   Love You Madly –vTWtk
....   Solitude –vTWtk
....   Mood Indigo –vTWtk
....   One More Time For The People –vTWtk
....   Things Ain't What They Used To Be

4 Feb 1973   **(S)**
Criteria Sound Studios
Miami, FL

DUKE ELLINGTON & HIS ORCHESTRA
CW MJsn JCI ME, VP CCrs, RP HMn PG HAsh HC, DE JBjm RJo, TWtk.

....   One More Time For The People –vTWtk
....   Mood Indigo
....   Trombone Buster
....   Evil Woman Blues –vTWtk

DUKE ELLINGTON & HIS ORCHESTRA
Same personnel.

Persian Room, Marco Polo Hotel   **(P)**
Miami Beach, FL

....   Caravan
....   The "C" Jam Blues
....   Mood Indigo
....   Satin Doll
....   How High The Moon
....   In A Sentimental Mood
....   Soul Flute
....   Take The "A" Train

> DE JBjm.

....   Pitter Panther Patter

> HC, DE JBjm RJo.

....   Prelude To A Kiss

> Entire band.

....   Chinoiserie
....   Hello Dolly –vMJsn
....   Mack The Knife –vMJsn`
....   Medley[1]
....   Making That Scene –vTWtk
....   Do Nothin' Till You Hear From Me –vTWtk
....   Solitude –vTWtk
....   I Don't Want Nobody At All –vTWtk
....   One More Time For The People –vTWtk

[1]Including: Don't Get Around Much Anymore; I Got It Bad; I'm Beginning To See The Light; Sophisticated Lady.

8 Feb 1973   **(S)**
Unidentified location (bc)
Montego Bay, Jamaica

DUKE ELLINGTON
DE interviewed by ... Ford.

....   Interview

DUKE ELLINGTON   Mar 1973   (S)
DE interviewed by Phil McKellar.   Royal York Hotel (bc)
                                                                                           Toronto, ON

....   Interview

DUKE ELLINGTON   Mar 1973   (S)
DE interviewed by Lorraine Thomson.   ?Royal York Hotel (bc)
                                                                                           Toronto, ON

....   Interview

DUKE ELLINGTON & HIS ORCHESTRA   10 Apr 1973   (P)
BBry MJsn JCI ME, VP MME[1] CCrs, RP HMn PG HAsh HC, DE JBjm RJo SWrd, TWtk.   Paramount Theater
                                                                                           Seattle, WA
....   The "C" Jam Blues
....   Kinda Dukish/Rockin' In Rhythm
....   Creole Love Call
....   Caravan
....   How High The Moon
....   In A Sentimental Mood
....   Take The "A" Train

                                             TOGO BRAVA—BRAVA TOGO
....   - Soul Soothing Beach
....   - Right On Togo
....   - Amour, Amour
....   - Naturellement

....   La Plus Belle Africaine
....   Things Ain't What They Used To Be
....   Satin Doll
....   In Triplicate
....   Chinoiserie
....   Medley[2]
....   Making That Scene –vTWtk
....   Do Nothin' Till You Hear From Me –vTWtk
....   Mood Indigo –vTWtk
....   One More Time For The People –vTWtk
....   Things Ain't What They Used To Be

[1]MME is doubling on alto during his engagement with the band.
[2]Including: Prelude To A Kiss; Don't Get Around Much Anymore; Mood Indigo; I'm Beginning To See The Light;
Sophisticated Lady.

DUKE ELLINGTON & HIS ORCHESTRA   12 Apr 1973   (P)
BBry MJsn JCI ME, VP MME CCrs, RP HMn PG HAsh HC, DE JBjm RJo SWrd.   Queen Elizabeth Theatre
                                                                                           Vancouver, BC
....   The "C" Jam Blues
....   Kinda Dukish/Rockin' In Rhythm
....   Creole Love Call
....   Caravan
....   How High The Moon
....   In A Sentimental Mood
....   Take The "A" Train

                                             TOGO BRAVA—BRAVA TOGO
....   - Soul Soothing Beach
....   - Right On Togo
....   - Amour, Amour
....   - Naturellement

....   La Plus Belle Africaine
....   Perdido
....   Satin Doll
....   In Duplicate
....   Chinoiserie
....   Hello Dolly –vMJsn
....   Medley[1]
....   Making That Scene –vTWtk
....   Do Nothin' Till You Hear From Me –vTWtk
....   Solitude –vTWtk
....   Mood Indigo –vTWtk
....   One More Time For The People –vTWtk
....   Things Ain't What They Used To Be
....   Heaven –vTWtk
....   The Biggest And Busiest Intersection   >>>

> DE JBjm.

....   Lotus Blossom

[1]Including: Prelude To A Kiss; Don't Get Around Much Anymore; Mood Indigo; I'm Beginning To See The Light; Sophisticated Lady.

13 Apr 1973   (P)
DUKE ELLINGTON & HIS ORCHESTRA   Great American Music Hall
BBry MJsn JCI ME, VP MME CCrs, RP HMn PG HAsh HC, DE JBjm RJo SWrd.   San Francisco, CA

....   The "C" Jam Blues
....   Don't You Know I Care?
....   Goof
....   Satin Doll
....   Kinda Dukish/Rockin' In Rhythm
....   In A Sentimental Mood
....   Caravan
....   In Duplicate

> MME, DE JBjm RJo.

....   Warm Valley

> Entire band.

....   Take The "A" Train

20 Apr 1973   (P)
DUKE ELLINGTON & HIS ORCHESTRA   Disneyland
CW MJsn JCI ME MMG, VP MME CCrs, RP HMn PG HAsh HC, DE JBjm RJo SWrd, AMo TWtk.   Anaheim, CA

....   The "C" Jam Blues
....   Kinda Dukish/Rockin' In Rhythm
....   4:30 Blues
....   Satin Doll
....   Caravan
....   How High The Moon
....   In A Sentimental Mood
....   Take The "A" Train
....   New York, New York –vAMo
....   I Got It Bad –vAMo
....   Blem –vAMo[1]
....   Things Ain't What They Used To Be
....   Hello Dolly –vMJsn

> DE piano solo.

....   Sophisticated Lady

> Entire band.

....   Romantic Season[2]
....   Satin Doll
....   Soso
....   Soso

> RPly added.

....   Soso

> RPly omitted.

....   One More Time For The People –vAMo TWtk
....   Satin Doll

[1]Announced as "The Scat Song."
[2]This title is a derivative of *Besa Me Mucho.*

30 Apr 1973   (P)
DUKE ELLINGTON & HIS ORCHESTRA   Methodist Church
CW MJsn JCI ME, VP MME CCrs, RP HMn HAsh HC, DE JBjm RJo, DGrd PHoy RG TWtk choir.   Dallas, TX

....   THE SECOND SACRED CONCERT
....   Praise God
....   Supreme Being –vChoir
....   Something About Believing –vDGrd RG TWtk Choir
....   Almighty God –vDGrd Choir
....   The Shepherd
....   Heaven –vDGrd Choir

> DE JBjm.

....   Meditation   >>>

> Entire band.

....   The Biggest And Busiest Intersection

> DE, PHoy.

....   T.G.T.T. –vPHoy

> Entire band.

....   Don't Get Down On Your Knees –vTWtk

> TWtk Choir a cappella.

....   Father Forgive –vTWtk Choir

> Entire band.

....   Don't Get Down On Your Knees –vTWtk
....   Praise God And Dance –vPHoy TWtk Choir

> TWtk a cappella.

....   The Preacher's Song –vTWtk

1 May 1973   (P)
Ryman Auditorium
Nashville, TN

DUKE ELLINGTON & HIS ORCHESTRA
CW MJsn JCl ME, VP MME CCrs, RP HMn HAsh HC, DE JBjm RJo SWrd, TWtk.

....   The "C" Jam Blues
....   Kinda Dukish/Rockin' In Rhythm
....   Creole Love Call
....   Caravan
....   How High The Moon
....   Soul Soothing Beach
....   Take The "A" Train
....   La Plus Belle Africaine
....   Perdido
....   Romantic Season
....   Chinoiserie
....   Hello Dolly –vMJsn
....   Medley[1]
....   Making That Scene –vTWtk
....   Do Nothin' Till You Hear From Me –vTWtk
....   Solitude –vTWtk
....   One More Time For The People –vTWtk
....   Things Ain't What They Used To Be
....   Come Off The Veldt
....   In The Beginning God –vTWtk

> DE JBjm.

....   Lotus Blossom

[1]Including: Prelude To A Kiss; Don't Get Around Much Anymore; Mood Indigo; I'm Beginning To See The Light;
Sophisticated Lady.

11 May 1973   (P)
Eagles Ballroom
Kenosha, WI

DUKE ELLINGTON & HIS ORCHESTRA
CW MJsn JCl ME, VP JChm CCrs, RP PG HAsh HC, JBjm RJo SWrd, AMo TWtk.

....   The "C" Jam Blues
....   Laura
....   Love Is Just Around The Corner

> DE added.

....   Azure
....   Romantic Season
....   I'm Beginning To See The Light
....   Things Ain't What They Used To Be
....   Soso
....   Mood Indigo
....   Romantic Season
....   Take The "A" Train
....   New York, New York –vDE
....   Satin Doll

> DE JBjm.

....   Interlude

> Entire band.

....   The Piano Player   >>>

> DE JBjm RJo.		
....		I Let A Song Go Out Of My Heart
> Entire band.		
....		New York, New York –vAMo
....		I Got It Bad –vAMo
....		I Let A Song Go Out Of My Heart –vAMo
....		I Didn't Know About You –vAMo
....		Blem
....		Hello Dolly –vMJsn
....		Mack The Knife –vMJsn
....		Sophisticated Lady
....		Love You Madly –vTWtk
....		Do Nothin' Till You Hear From Me –vTWtk
....		Solitude –vTWtk
....		One More Time For The People –vAMo TWtk
....		One More Time For The People –vAMo TWtk
> DE piano solo.		
....		Newport Up
> Entire band.		
....		One O'Clock Jump
....	SR	Jeep's Blues
....		Don't Get Around Much Anymore/I Let A Song Go Out Of My Heart/Don't Get Around Much Anymore
....		Take The "A" Train
....		Satin Doll
....		Mood Indigo
....		Perdido
....		One More Time For The People –vAMo TWtk
....		Satin Doll

25 May 1973[1]   (P)
Centennial Hall (bc)
Winnipeg, MB

DUKE ELLINGTON & HIS ORCHESTRA
CW MJsn JCl ME, VP MME CCrs, RP DHrs PG HAsh HC, DE JBjm RJo.

....	LSR	The "C" Jam Blues
....		Kinda Dukish/Rockin' In Rhythm
....	LSR	Creole Love Call
....	LSR	Caravan
....	LSR	How High The Moon
....		Take The "A" Train
....		TOGO BRAVA—BRAVA TOGO
....		- Soul Soothing Beach
....		- Right On Togo
....		- Amour, Amour
....		- Naturellement
....	SR	La Plus Belle Africaine
....	LSR	Perdido
....		Satin Doll
....	LSR	Chinoiserie
....		Hello Dolly –vMJsn
....		Medley[2]
....		In Triplicate
> DE JBjm.		
....		Lotus Blossom
> MJsn, VP, RP, DE JBjm RJo.		
....		**Tiger Rag**
> Entire band.		
....		Satin Doll

[1]Broadcast on 2 May 1999.
[2]Including: Don't Get Around Much Anymore; Mood Indigo; I'm Beginning To See The Light; Sophisticated Lady; Satin Doll.

2 Jul 1973   (S)
Private residence
New York City, NY

DUKE ELLINGTON
Piano solo.

....	There's Something About Me –vDE

<u>ALICE BABS WITH DUKE ELLINGTON & HIS ORCHESTRA</u>
Vcl, acc. by MJsn WC BLH JCl ME, VP ABrn CCrs, RP HMn PM/PG HAsh HC, DE WF JBjm
JA QW.

3 Jul 1973   (S)
MediaSound Studios
New York City, NY

....	Pho	Far Away Star –vABbs
....	Pho	Serenade To Sweden –vABbs
....	Pho	Spacemen –vABbs
....	Pho	Jeep's Blues –vABbs

<u>DUKE ELLINGTON</u>
DE receiving the Légion d'Honneur.

8 Jul 1973   (P)
French Consulate (tc)
New York City, NY

....   Presentation

DE and the French Ambassador at one piano.

....   Mood Indigo

DE piano solo.

....   Yanie[1]

[1]This title—dedicated to the wife of the ambassador—is a derivative of *The Shepherd*.

<u>DUKE ELLINGTON & HIS ORCHESTRA</u>
MJsn BLH JCl ME, VP MME CCrs, RP HMn PG HAsh HC, DE JBjm RJo.

11 Jul 1973   (P)
First National Bank Plaza
Chicago, IL

....	Caravan
....	In Duplicate
....	In A Sentimental Mood
....	Take The "A" Train
....	Satin Doll

<u>DUKE ELLINGTON & HIS ORCHESTRA</u>
MJsn BLH JCl ME, VP MME CCrs, RP HMn PG HAsh HC, DE JBjm RJo, AMo TWtk.

16 Juil 1973   (P)
Old Orchard Shopping Center
Skokie, IL

....	Take The "A" Train
....	Kinda Dukish/Rockin' In Rhythm
....	In A Sentimental Mood
....	Caravan
....	In Duplicate
....	I'm Beginning To See The Light –vAMo
....	I Got It Bad –vAMo
....	Blem –vAMo
....	Hello Dolly –vMJsn
....	Sophisticated Lady
....	Making That Scene –vTWtk

<u>DUKE ELLINGTON & HIS ORCHESTRA</u>
MJsn BLH JCl ME, VP MME CCrs, RP HMn PG HAsh HC, DE JBjm RJo, TWtk.

21 Jul 1973   (P)
Rainbow Gardens, Waldameer Park
Erie, PA

....	The "C" Jam Blues
....	U.M.M.G.
....	Don't You Know I Care?
....	Perdido
....	Kinda Dukish/Rockin' In Rhythm
....	Creole Love Call
....	Caravan
....	How High The Moon
....	I Let A Song Go Out Of My Hearyt/Don't Get Around Much Anymore
....	Soso
....	Somebody Cares
....	I'll Never Forget Him
....	Take The "A" Train
....	Things Ain't What They Used To Be
....	Soul Flute
....	Spacemen

> RP, DE JBjm RJo.

....   Ring Dem Bells

> MJsn, VP added.

....   Tiger Rag
....   St. Louis Blues   >>>

> Entire band

.... Satin Doll
.... In A Sentimental Mood
.... In A Mellotone
.... Mood Indigo
.... Addi
.... Sophisticated Lady
.... Basin Street Blues –vMJsn

> DE JBjm RJo, TWtk.

.... Medley[1]

> Entire band.

.... Misty

[1]Including: Creole Blues; A Mural From Two Perspectives; Solitude –vTWtk; Prelude To A Kiss; Azure; Ring Dem Bells; Lost In Meditation; unidentified title; Ring Dem Bells; Band Call; New World A-Comin'; Band Call.

<table>
<tr><td></td><td>31 Jul 1973</td><td>(P)</td></tr>
<tr><td>DUKE ELLINGTON & HIS ORCHESTRA</td><td>Robin Hood Dell</td><td></td></tr>
<tr><td>MJsn BLH JCI ME, VP MME CCrs, RP HMn PG HAsh HC, DE JBjm QW JA, AMo TWtk.</td><td>Philadelphia, PA</td><td></td></tr>
</table>

.... The "C" Jam Blues
.... Take The "A" Train
.... Kinda Dukish/Rockin' In Rhythm
.... Creole Love Call
.... Soso
.... Spacemen
.... In A Sentimental Mood
.... Satin Doll
.... Caravan—Prelude To A Kiss—In Duplicate
.... New York, New York –vAMo
.... I Got It Bad –vAMo
.... I'm Beginning To See The Light –vAMo
.... Blem –vAMo

> DE, AMo.

.... I'm Afraid –vAMo

> Entire band.

.... On A Clear Day –vAMo

TOGO BRAVA—BRAVA TOGO
.... - Soul Soothing Beach
.... - Right On Togo
.... - Amour, Amour

.... Come Off The Veldt
.... La Plus Belle Africaine
.... Perdido
.... Take The "A" Train
.... Chinoiserie
.... Things Ain't What They Used To Be
.... Basin Street Blues –vMJsn
.... Hello Dolly –vMJsn
.... Sophisticated Lady
.... Making That Scene –vTWtk
.... Do Nothin' Till You Hear From Me –vTWtk
.... Mood Indigo –vTWtk
.... One More Time For The People –vAMo TWtk
.... One More Time For The People –vAMo TWtk
.... Satin Doll

<table>
<tr><td></td><td>3 Aug 1973</td><td>(P)</td></tr>
<tr><td>DUKE ELLINGTON & HIS ORCHESTRA</td><td>Stokesay Castle</td><td></td></tr>
<tr><td>MJsn BLH JCI ME MMG, VP MME CCrs, RP HMn PG HAsh HC, JBjm QW JA, AMo TWtk.</td><td>Reading PA</td><td></td></tr>
</table>

.... The "C" Jam Blues
.... Don't You Know I Care?
.... Perdido
.... Star Dust
.... I'll Never Forget Him
.... Take The "A" Train

> DE added.

.... Satin Doll
.... The Brotherhood   >>>

....	Romantic Season

> DE piano solo.

....	Prelude To A Kiss

> Entire band.

....	Someone
....	Mood Indigo
....	How High The Moon
....	Acht O'Clock Rock

> HC, DE JBjm QW.

....	Black Butterfly

> Entire band.

....	Things Ain't What They Used To Be
....	I'm Beginning To See The Light —vAMo
....	I Got It Bad —vAMo
....	Blem —vAMo
....	Soul Soothing Beach
....	In Duplicate
....	In A Sentimental Mood
....	Soso
....	Spacemen
....	Happy Birthday
....	Somebody Cares
....	Love Is Just Around The Corner
....	Indian Summer
....	Basin Street Blues —vMJsn
....	Hello Dolly —vMJsn
....	Mood Indigo
....	One More Time For The People —vAMo TWtk
....	Satin Doll

DUKE ELLINGTON & HIS ORCHESTRA   6 Aug 1973   (P)
MJsn BLH JCl ME MMG, VP MME CCrs, RP HMn PG HAsh HC, DE JBjm QW JA, AMo.   NBC Studios (tc)
                                                          New York City, NY

....	Take The "A" Train
....	Soso
....	Spacemen
....	Mood Indigo

> DE interviewed by Frank McGhee.

....	Interview

> Entire band.

....	Things Ain't What They Used To Be
....	Medley[1]
....	New York, New York —vAMo
....	New York, New York —vAMo

[1]Including: Satin Doll; Somebody Cares; Caravan; Sophisticated Lady.

DUKE ELLINGTON & HIS GROUP   11 Aug 1973   (P)
MJsn MMG, RP HMn PG HAsh HC, ?JBr, DE WF JBjm QW JA, AMo TWtk.   Rainbow Grill (bc)
                                                          New York City, NY

....	Take The "A" Train
....	New York, New York —vAMo
....	Blem —vAMo
....	Mood Indigo—Sophisticated Lady
....	Things Ain't What They Used To Be
....	Solitude —vTWtk
....	One More Time For The People —vAMo TWtk
....	Satin Doll
....	New York, New York —vAMo

DUKE ELLINGTON & HIS GROUP   Aug 1973   (P)
MJsn MMG, RP HMn PG HAsh HC, DE WF JBjm QW JA, AMo TWtk.   Rainbow Grill (bc)
                                                          New York City, NY

....	Caravan
....	Creole Love Call
....	In Triplicate
....	Serenade To Sweden
....	Things Ain't What They Used To Be >>>

....	Sophisticated Lady
....	One More Time For The People –vAMo TWtk
....	Satin Doll

25 Aug 1973   (P)
Sheraton Park Hotel
Washington, DC

DUKE ELLINGTON & HIS ORCHESTRA
MJsn BLH JCl ME MMG, VP ABrn CCrs, RP HMn PG HAsh HC, DE WF JBjm QW, AMo TWtk.

....	Take The "A" Train
....	The Piano Player
....	How High The Moon
....	Somebody Cares
....	All Too Soon
....	The Brotherhood
....	Mood Indigo
....	4:30 Blues
....	Take The "A" Train
....	In A Sentimental Mood
....	Diminuendo In Blue and Wailing Interval
....	Romantic Season
....	Spacemen
....	Happy Birthday
....	There's A Lull In My Life
....	Goof
....	Star Dust
....	Things Ain't What They Used To Be
....	Caravan
....	In Duplicate
....	New York, New York –vAMo
....	I Got It Bad –vAMo
....	Blem –vAMo
....	Sophisticated Lady
....	Basin Street Blues –vMJsn
....	Hello Dolly –vMJsn

> MJsn, VP, RP, DE JBjm QW.

....	Tiger Rag

> Entire band.

....	Love You Madly –vTWtk
....	Do Nothin' Till You Hear From Me –vTWtk
....	I Don't Want Nobody At All –vTWtk
....	Solitude –vTWtk
....	One More Time For The People –vAMo TWtk
....	One More Time For The People –vAMo TWtk
....	Perdido
....	St. Louis Blues
....	I'm Beginning To See The Light –vAMo
....	I Didn't Know About You –vAMo
....	Every Day –vAMo
....	Mood Indigo
....	Things Ain't What They Used To Be

4 Sep 1973   (S)
44th/45th St. Studios
New York City, NY

TERESA BREWER WITH DUKE ELLINGTON & HIS ORCHESTRA
Vcl, acc. by MJsn BLH JCl RN, VP ABrn CCrs, RP NTrn HMn HAsh HC, DE JBjm QW.

....	FD	Don't Get Around Much Anymore –vTBrw
....	FD	Satin Doll –vTBrw
....	FD	I Got It Bad –vTBrw
....	FD	It's Kinda Lonesome Out Tonight –vTBrw

5 Sep 1973   (S)
44th/45th St. Studios
New York City, NY

TERESA BREWER WITH DUKE ELLINGTON & HIS ORCHESTRA
Vcl, acc. by MJsn BLH JCl RN, VP ABrn CCrs TG, RP NTrn HMn HAsh HC, DE JBjm QW.

....	FD	I'm Beginning To See The Light –vTBrw
....	FD	I Ain't Got Nothin' But The Blues –vTBrw

> ME JNn ER JO JNm, BBgs added.

....	FD	I've Got To Be A Rug Cutter –vTBrw BBgs
....	FD	It Don't Mean A Thing –vTBrw BBgs

6 Sep 1973   (S)
44th/45th St. Studios
New York City, NY

TERESA BREWER WITH DUKE ELLINGTON & HIS ORCHESTRA
Vcl, acc. by DE JBck HBsh PPdy, BBgs.

....	FD	Tulip Or Turnip –vTBrw BBgs >>>

```
..............  > BBgs omitted, TG, RP HC added.
..............  FD                       Mood Indigo –vTBrw
..............  > JMtm added.
..............  FD                       Poco Mucho –vTBrw
```

p Sep 1973[1]   (S)
Unidentified location (bc)
U.S.A.

DUKE ELLINGTON
DE piano and talking, interviewed by Willis Conover; intermittent previously recorded music.

```
..............                          Interview
..............                          Romantic Season
..............                          Interview (ctd.)
..............                          Volupté
..............                          Interview (ctd.)
```

[1]Taping session; the date of broadcast is not known.

20 Sep 1973   (P)
Covered Wagon Inn
Wayne, PA

DUKE ELLINGTON & HIS ORCHESTRA
MJsn BLH JCl ME RN, VP ABrn CCrs, RP HMn PG HAsh HC, JBjm QW, AMo TWtk JBr.

```
..............                          Love Is Just Around The Corner
..............                          Star Dust
..............  > DE added.
..............                          Goof
..............                          The Brotherhood
..............                          Creole Love Call
..............  > DE piano solo.
..............                          Is God A Three-Letter Word For Love?
..............  > PG, DE JBjm QW.
..............                          Happy Reunion
..............  > Entire band.
..............                          Spacemen
..............                          Don't You Know I Care?
..............                          The Lady Is A Tramp
..............                          I Can't Get Started
..............                          Satin Doll –vJBr
..............                          Romantic Season
..............                          Take The "A" Train –vRN
..............                          Just A-Settin' And A-Rockin' –vRN
..............                          New York, New York –vAMo
..............                          I Got It Bad –vAMo
..............                          I'm Beginning To See The Light –vAMo
..............                          Blem –vAMo
..............                          On The Sunny Side Of The Street –vRN
..............                          Happy Birthday
..............                          Happy Birthday
..............                          Over The Waves
..............                          Mood Indigo
..............                          Basin Street Blues –vMJsn
..............                          Mack The Knife –vMJsn
..............                          Sophisticated Lady
..............                          Love You Madly –vTWtk
..............                          Do Nothin' Till You Hear From Me –vTWtk
..............                          Solitude –vTWtk
..............                          One More Time For The People –vAMo TWtk
..............                          One More Time For The People –vAMo TWtk
..............                          Prelude To A Kiss
..............                          Take The "A" Train –vRN
..............                          Diminuendo In Blue and Wailing Interval
..............                          Blue Moon –vJBr
..............                          All Too Soon
..............                          The Biggest And Busiest Intersection
..............  > DE piano solo.
..............                          Is God A Three-Letter Word For Love?
..............  > RN, DE JBjm QW.
..............                          Echoes Of Harlem
..............  > Entire band.
..............                          Take The "A" Train    >>>
```

....   Satin Doll

                                                                                              3 Oct 1973   (P)
DUKE ELLINGTON & HIS ORCHESTRA   Kennedy Center of the Performing Arts
MJsn BLH JCl ME, VP ABrn CCrs, RP HMn HAsh HC, DE JBjm QW JA, AMo TWtk.   Washington, DC

....   The "C" Jam Blues
....   Kinda Dukish/Rockin' In Rhythm
....   Creole Love Call
....   Spacemen
....   In A Sentimental Mood
....   Caravan
....   How High The Moon

                                                  TOGO BRAVA—BRAVA TOGO
....   - Soul Soothing Beach
....   - Right On Togo
....   - Amour, Amour

....   Chinoiserie
....   La Plus Belle Africaine
....   Soso
....   Satin Doll
....   In Duplicate
....   New York, New York –vAMo
....   I Got It Bad –vAMo
....   Blem –vAMo
....   Take The "A" Train
....   Basin Street Blues –vMJsn
....   Hello Dolly –vMJsn
....   Medley[1]
....   Love You Madly –vTWtk
....   Do Nothin' Till You Hear From Me –vTWtk
....   Solitude –vTWtk
....   One More Time For The People –vAMo TWtk
....   I'm Beginning To See The Light –vAMo
....   In The Beginning God –vTWtk
....   Things Ain't What They Used To Be

        > DE JBjm.

....   Lotus Blossom

        > Entire band.

....   Satin Doll

[1]Including: Don't Get Around Much Anymore; Mood Indigo; I'm Beginning To See The Light; Sophisticated Lady.

                                                                                              24 Oct 1973   (S)
DUKE ELLINGTON & HIS ORCHESTRA   Westminster Abbey
MJsn BLH JCl ME, VP ABrn CCrs, RP HMn PM HAsh HC, DE JBjm QW, ABbs AMo TWtk.   London, England

.... RDB   Tell Me, It's The Truth –vAMo TWtk
.... RDB   Somebody Cares –vABbs AMo TWtk

        The above is a rehearsal session.

DUKE ELLINGTON & HIS ORCHESTRA   (P)
RG JAC added, otherwise same personnel.

                                                  THE THIRD SACRED CONCERT
.... Vi   DPE6-1198   Introductory remarks by Sir Colin Crowe
.... Vi   DPE6-3140   Introductory remarks by DE

        > DE piano solo.

.... Vi   DPE6-1199   The Lord's Prayer

        > Entire band.

.... Vi   DPE6-3141   My Love –vABbs
.... Vi   DPE6-1200   Is God A Three-Letter Word For Love? –vABbs JAC, part 1
.... Vi   DPE6-3145   Is God A Three-Letter Word For Love? –vTWtk JAC, part 2
.... Vi   DPE6-3101   The Brotherhood –vJAC
.... Vi   DPE6-3102   Hallelujah -vJAC
.... Vi   DPE6-3103   Every Man Prays In His Own Language –vABbs JAC
....   Tell Me, It's The Truth –vAMo TWtk
....   Somebody Cares –vAMo TWtk
.... Vi   DPE6-3104   Ain't Nobody Nowhere Nothin' Without God -vTWtk
.... Vi   DPE6-3105   The Majesty Of God –vABbs JAC
.... RDB   Praise God And Dance –vABbs AMo RG TWtk JAC   >>>

> TWtk a cappella.

....   The Preacher's Song –vTWtk

> Entire band.

.... RDB   In The Beginning God –vTWtk
....   Preamble of the Charter of the United Nations
....   Prayer

<table>
<tr><td></td><td></td><td>25 Oct 1973</td><td>(P)</td></tr>
<tr><td></td><td></td><td>Stadsteatern</td><td></td></tr>
<tr><td></td><td></td><td>Malmö, Sweden</td><td></td></tr>
</table>

DUKE ELLINGTON & HIS ORCHESTRA
MJsn BLH JCI REsn ME, VP ABrn APsn CCrs, RP HMn PM HAsh HC, DE JBjm QW,
ABbs, AMo TWtk.

.... Cpr   Kinda Dukish/Rockin' In Rhythm
.... Cpr   Creole Love Call
.... Cpr   Caravan
.... Cpr   In Duplicate
.... Cpr   Take The "A" Train
.... RDB   New York, New York –vAMo
.... RDB   I Got It Bad –vAMo
....   Blem –vAMo
....   Chinoiserie
....   Basin Street Blues –vMJsn
....   Medley[1]
....   Love You Madly –vTWtk
.... Cpr   Satin Doll

> DE JBjm QW, ABbs.

.... Cpr   Serenade To Sweden –vABbs

> Entire band.

.... Cpr   Checkered Hat –vABbs
.... Cpr   Spacemen –vABbs
.... Cpr   Jeep's Blues –vABbs

> NLbg JBjm, ABbs.

.... Cpr   There Is Something About Me –vABbs

> Entire band, NLbg omitted.

.... Cpr   Somebody Cares –vABbs AMo TWtk
.... Cpr   I'm Beginning To See The Light

> NLbg GWn, ABbs AMo TWtk.

.... Cpr   Take The "A" Train –vABbs AMo TWtk

> ABrn APsn, DE.

.... Cpr   St. Louis Blues

> MJsn REsn, VP APsn, DE JBjm QW.

.... Cpr   Tiger Rag

[1]Including: Don't Get Around Much Anymore; Mood Indigo; I'm Beginning To See The Light; Sophisticated Lady.

The above selections are believed to be excerpts from two concerts.

<table>
<tr><td></td><td></td><td>28 Oct 1973[1]</td><td>(P)</td></tr>
<tr><td></td><td></td><td>Konserthuset (tc)</td><td></td></tr>
<tr><td></td><td></td><td>Stockholm, Sweden</td><td></td></tr>
</table>

DUKE ELLINGTON & HIS ORCHESTRA
MJsn BLH JCI ME, VP ABrn APsn CCrs, RP HMn PM HAsh HC, DE JBjm QW, AMo TWtk.

....   The "C" Jam Blues
....   Take The "A" Train
....   Kinda Dukish/Rockin' In Rhythm
....   Creole Love Call
....   Satin Doll
....   Spacemen
.... Az   Tea For Two
....   Caravan
....   How High The Moon
....   In Duplicate
....   La Plus Belle Africaine
....   Come Off The Veldt
....   Take The "A" Train
....   New York, New York –vAMo
....   I Got It Bad –vAMo
....   Blem –vAMo
....   Chinoiserie   >>>

....		Basin Street Blues –vMJsn
....		Hello Dolly –vMJsn
....		Medley[2]
....		Love You Madly –vTWtk
....		Do Nothin' Till You Hear From Me –vTWtk

> DE, TWtk.

....		My Mother, My Father –vTWtk

> Entire band.

....		One More Time For The People –vAMo TWtk
....		Things Ain't What They Used To Be
....		Soso

> DE JBjm.

....		Lotus Blossom

[1]Taped by Swedish TV; the date of telecast is not known.
[2]Including: Don't Get Around Much Anymore; Mood Indigo; I'm Beginning To See The Light; Sophisticated Lady.

Oct/Nov 1973   (S)
Unidentified location (bc)
Germany

DUKE ELLINGTON
DE interviewed by Chaplain Bill Percy.

....		Interview

2 Nov 1973   (P)
Philharmonie (bc)
Berlin, Germany

DUKE ELLINGTON & HIS OCTET
MJsn, RP PG HAsh HC, DE JBjm QW, TWtk.

> DE JBjm.

....	Az	Meditation

> QW added.

....	Az	Mecuria The Lion[1]

> Entire band.

....	Az	Take The "A" Train
....	JDr	Mood Indigo

> DE JBjm QW.

....	Az	Band Call

> Entire band.

....	Az	Blow By Blow

> DE JBjm QW.

....	JDr	Pitter Panther Patter

> Entire band.

....	Az	Sophisticated Lady
....	Az	Basin Street Blues –vMJsn
....	JDr	Mack The Knife –vMJsn
....	Az	Things Ain't What They Used To Be
....		Do Nothin' Till You Hear From Me –vTWtk

> DE JBjm QW, TWtk.

....		Come Sunday –vTWtk[2]

[1]Spelling variant "Metcuria The Lion."
[2]At this point DE terminated the concert on account of the unruly behavior of the audience, which expressed its dissatisfaction with TWtk's vocal performance.

3 Nov 1973   (P)
Stadthalle
Vienna, Austria

DUKE ELLINGTON & HIS ORCHESTRA
MJsn BLH JCl ME, VP ABrn CCrs, RP HMn PM PG HAsh HC, DE JBjm QW, AMo TWtk.

....		Take The "A" Train
....		Kinda Dukish/Rockin' In Rhythm
....		Creole Love Call
....		Satin Doll
....		Spacemen
....		In A Sentimental Mood
....		Caravan
....		How High The Moon
....		New York, New York –vAMo
....		I Got It Bad –vAMo >>>

....   Blem –vAMo
....   I'm Beginning To See The Light –vAMo
....   Chinoiserie
....   Basin Street Blues –vMJsn
....   In Duplicate
....   Medley[1]
....   Love You Madly –vTWtk
....   One More Time For The People –vAMo TWtk
....   Take The "A" Train

[1]Including: Don't Get Around Much Anymore; Mood Indigo; It Don't Mean A Thing; Sophisticated Lady.

5 Nov 1973   (P)
DUKE ELLINGTON & HIS ORCHESTRA   Kongreßsaal, Deutsches Museum
MJsn BLH JCl ME, VP ABrn CCrs, RP HMn PM PG HAsh HC, DE JBjm QW, AMo TWtk.   Munich, Germany

....   The "C" Jam Blues
....   Kinda Dukish/Rockin' In Rhythm
....   Creole Love Call
....   Satin Doll
....   Spacemen
....   In A Sentimental Mood
....   Caravan
....   How High The Moon

                     TOGO BRAVA—BRAVA TOGO
....   - Soul Soothing Beach
....   - Right On Togo
....   - Amour, Amour

                     Chinoiserie
....   I Can't Get Started
....   Take The "A" Train
....   La Plus Belle Africaine
....   Mecuria The Lion
....   Tea For Two
....   In Duplicate
....   New York, New York –vAMo
....   I Got It Bad –vAMo
....   Blem –vAMo
....   Basin Street Blues –vMJsn
....   Hello Dolly –vMJsn
....   Medley[1]
....   Love You Madly –vTWtk
....   Do Nothin' Till You Hear From Me –vTWtk
....   One More Time For The People –vAMo TWtk
....   Things Ain't What They Used To Be
....   Soso
....   Somebody Cares –vAMo TWtk

> MJsn, VP, RP, DE JBjm QW.

....   Tiger Rag

> DE JBjm.

....   Lotus Blossom

> Entire band.

....   The Brotherhood
....   Mood Indigo

[1]Including: Don't Get Around Much Anymore; Mood Indigo; I'm Beginning To See The Light; Sophisticated Lady.

7 Nov 1973   (P)
DUKE ELLINGTON & HIS ORCHESTRA   Unidentified location (tc)
MJsn BLH JCl ME, VP ABrn CCrs, RP HMn PM PG HAsh HC, DE JBjm QW, AMo TWtk.   Ljubljana, Serbia (Yugoslavia)

....   New York, New York –vAMo
....   I Got It Bad –vAMo
....   Blem –vAMo
....   Misty –vAMo
....   I'm Beginning To See The Light –vAMo
....   Basin Street Blues –vMJsn
....   Hello Dolly –vMJsn
....   Soso
....   Medley[1]
....   Love You Madly –vTWtk
....   Do Nothin' Till You Hear From Me –vTWtk
....   One More Time For The People –vAMo TWtk   >>>

....   Somebody Cares –vAMo TWtk
....   Things Ain't What They Used To Be

> MJsn, VP, RP, DE JBjm QW.

....   Tiger Rag

> DE JBjm.

....   Lotus Blossom

[1]Including: Don't Get Around Much Anymore; Mood Indigo; It Don't Mean A Thing; Sophisticated Lady.

                                                                                        8 Nov 1973   (P)
DUKE ELLINGTON & HIS ORCHESTRA   Palasport
MJsn BLH JCl ME, VP ABrn CCrs, RP HMn PM PG HAsh HC, DE JBjm QW, AMo TWtk.   Bologna, Italy

....   Kinda Dukish/Rockin' In Rhythm
....   Creole Love Call
....   Satin Doll
....   Spacemen
....   In A Sentimental Mood
....   Caravan
....   In Duplicate
....   New York, New York –vAMo
....   I Got It Bad –vAMo
....   Blem –vAMo
....   Chinoiserie
....   Basin Street Blues –vMJsn
....   Hello Dolly –vMJsn
....   Medley[1]
....   Love You Madly –vTWtk
....   Do Nothin' Till You Hear From Me –vTWtk
....   One More Time For The People –vAMo TWtk
....   Things Ain't What They Used To Be

[1]Including: Don't Get Around Much Anymore; Mood Indigo; I'm Beginning To See The Light; Sophisticated Lady.

                                                                                        11 Nov 1973[1]   (P)
DUKE ELLINGTON & HIS ORCHESTRA   Basilica de Santa Maria del Mar (tc)
MJsn BLH JCl ME, VP ABrn CCrs, RP HMn PM PG HAsh HC, DE JBjm QW,   Barcelona, Spain
ABbs AMo RG TWtk.

                                        THE THIRD SACRED CONCERT
....   Somebody Cares
....   Praise God

> DE JBjm QW.

....   Hallelujah

> Entire band.

....   Heaven –vTWtk
....   Supreme Being –vRG
....   The Majesty Of God –vABbs
....   Is God A Three-Letter Word For Love? –vABbs
....   My Love –vABbs
....   The Shepherd
....   Tell Me, It's The Truth –vAMo TWtk
....   Somebody Cares –vABbs AMo TWtk
....   Every Man Prays In His Own Language –vABbs
....   Ain't Nobody Nowhere Nothin' Without God –vTWtk
....   Praise God And Dance –vABbs AMo RG TWtk

> TWtk a cappella.

....   The Preachers' Song –vTWtk

[1]The date of telecast is not known.

                                                                                        14 Nov 1973   (P)
DUKE ELLINGTON & HIS ORCHESTRA   Palais des Sports
MJsn BLH JCl ME, VP ABrn CCrs, RP HMn PM PG HAsh HC, DE JBjm QW, AMo TWtk.   Paris, Fance

....   Perdido
....   Kinda Dukish/Rockin' In Rhythm
....   Creole Love Call
....   Spacemen
....   In A Sentimental Mood
....   Caravan
....   How High The Moon
....   New York, New York –vAMo   >>>

....	I Got It Bad –vAMo
....	Blem –vAMo
....	Chinoiserie
....	Basin Street Blues –vMJsn
....	Hello Dolly –vMJsn
....	Medley[1]
....	Things Ain't What They Used To Be
....	Soso
....	Somebody Cares –vAMo TWtk

> RFo added.

....	Take The "A" Train

> DE RFo omitted, CBlg added.

....	Take The "A" Train

> DE JBjm.

....	Lotus Blossom

[1]Including: Don't Get Around Much Anymore; Mood Indigo; I'm Beginning To See The Light; Sophisticated Lady.

16 Nov 1973 (P)
Palais des Beaux Arts
Brussels, Belgium

DUKE ELLINGTON & HIS ORCHESTRA
MJsn BLH JCl ME, VP ABrn CCrs, RP HMn PM PG HAsh HC, DE JBjm QW, AMo TWtk.

....	The "C" Jam Blues
....	Take The "A" Train
....	Creole Love Call
....	Caravan
....	In Duplicate
....	New York, New York –vAMo
....	Blem –vAMo
....	Chinoiserie
....	Mecuria The Lion
....	Medley[1]
....	Somebody Cares –vAMo TWtk

> RFo added.

....	Az	Take The "A" Train

> CBlg replaces RFo.

....	Az	Take The "A" Train

> CBlg omitted.

....	Az	Take The "A" Train

[1]Including: Don't Get Around Much Anymore; Mood Indigo; I'm Beginning To See The Light; Sophisticated Lady.

18 Nov 1973 (P)
De Doelen
Rotterdam, Netherlands

DUKE ELLINGTON & HIS ORCHESTRA
MJsn BLH JCl ME, VP ABrn CCrs, RP HMn PM PG HAsh HC, DE JBjm QW, AMo TWtk.

....	The "C" Jam Blues
....	Perdido
....	Take The "A" Train
....	Creole Love Call
....	Spacemen
....	In A Sentimental Mood
....	Caravan
....	How High The Moon
....	In Duplicate
....	New York, New York –vAMo
....	I Got It Bad –vAMo
....	Blem –vAMo
....	Chinoiserie
....	Mecuria The Lion

> RFo added.

....	Satin Doll

> RFo omitted.

....	Basin Street Blues –vMJsn
....	Hello Dolly –vMJsn
....	Medley[1]
....	Love You Madly –vTWtk
....	Do Nothin' Till You Hear From Me –vTWtk
....	One More Time For The People –vAMo TWtk >>>

....   Things Ain't What They Used To Be
....   Soso
....   Somebody Cared –vAMo TWtk

[1]Including: Don't Get Around Much Anymore; Mood Indigo; I'm Beginning To See The Light; Sophisticated Lady.

26 Nov 1973   (P)
Palladium
DUKE ELLINGTON & HIS ORCHESTRA   London, England
MJsn BLH JCl ME, VP ABrn CCrs, RP HMn PM HAsh HC, DE JBjm QW, AMo TWtk.

....   Take The "A" Train
....   Satin Doll
....   Basin Street Blues –vMJsn
....   Medley[1]
....   Things Ain't What They Used To Be

[1]Including: Don't Get Around Much Anymore; Mood Indigo; I'm Beginning To See The Light; I Got It Bad –vAMo; One More Time For The People –vAMo TWtk.

30 Nov 1973   (P)
Guildhall
DUKE ELLLINGTON & HIS ORCHESTRA   Preston, England
MJsn BLH JCl ME, VP ABrn CCrs, RP HMn PM HAsh HC, DE JBjm QW, AMo TWtk.

....   The "C" Jam Blues
....   Perdido
....   Kinda Dukish/Rockin' In Rhythm
....   Creole Love Call
....   Satin Doll
....   Spacemen
....   Caravan
....   How High The Moon
....   Soul Soothing Beach
....   Chinoiserie
....   I Can't Get Started
....   New York, New York –vAMo
....   I Got It Bad –vAMo
....   Blem –vAMo
....   Basin Street Blues –vMJsn
....   Hello Dolly –vMJsn
....   Medley[1]
....   Things Ain't What They Used To Be
....   Somebody Cares –vAMo TWtk
....   Soso

> DE JBjm QW.

....   Pitter Panther Patter

> Entire band.

....   In Triplicate
....   Take The "A" Train
....   Mecuria The Lion

> DE JBjm.

....   Lotus Blossom

[1]Including: Don't Get Around Much Anymore; Mood Indigo; I'm Beginning To See The Light; It Don't Mean A Thing; Sophisticated Lady.

1 Dec 1973   (P)
Congress Theatre
DUKE ELLINGTON & HIS ORCHESTRA   Eastbourne, England
MJsn BLH JCl ME, VP ABrn CCrs, RP HMn PM HAsh HC, DE JBjm QW, AMo TWtk.

....   The "C" Jam Blues
.... RDB   Perdido

> DE JBjm.

.... Vi   DPE6-2131   The Piano Player

> Entire band.

....   Kinda Dukish/Rockin' In Rhythm
....   Creole Love Call
....   Satin Doll
....   Spacemen
.... Vi   DPE6-2133   Don't You Know I Care?
.... RDB   How High The Moon
.... RDB   I'm Beginning To See The Light –vAMo
.... RDB   I Didn't Know About You –vAMo
.... RDB   Blem –vAMo   >>>

....	Vi	DPE6-2134	Chinoiserie
....	Vi	DPE6-2134	I Can't Get Started
....	Vi	DPE6-2138	Basin Street Blues –vMJsn
....			Hello Dolly –vMJsn
....			Medley[1]
....			Love You Madly –vTWtk
....			Solitude –vTWtk
....			One More Time For The People –vAMo TWtk
....			Things Ain't What They Used To Be
....	Vi	DPE6-2140	Soso[2]
....			I Got It Bad –vAMo
....			It Don't Mean A Thing –vTWtk
....			In Duplicate

> DE JBjm.

| .... | Vi | DPE6-2141 | Meditation |

> MJsn, VP, RP, DE JBjm QW.

| .... | | | Tiger Rag |

> Entire band.

| .... | Vi | [3] | Mecuria The Lion |

> DE JBjm QW.

| .... | RDB | | Pitter Panther Patter |

[1]Including: Don't Get Around Much Anymore; Mood Indigo; Don Juan; Sophisticated Lady.
[2]Mistitled as "Woods" on the original release.
[3]No master number assigned.

DUKE ELLINGTON & HIS ORCHESTRA
Same personnel.

| .... | RDB | | The "C" Jam Blues |

> DE piano solo.

| .... | | | The Piano Player |

> Entire band.

....			Kinda Dukish/Rockin' In Rhythm
....	Vi	DPE6-2132	Creole Love Call
....	RDB		Satin Doll
....			Spacemen
....	Az		Don't You Know I Care?
....			Caravan
....	Vi	DPE6-2137	How High The Moon
....	Vi	DPE6-2135	New York, New York –vAMo
....			I Didn't Know About You –vAMo
....	RDB		I'm Beginning To See The Light –vAMo
....	RDB		Blem –vAMo
....	RDB		Chinoiserie
....	RDB		I Can't Get Started
....	RDB		Basin Street Blues –vMJsn
....	RDB		Hello Dolly –vMJsn
....			Medley[1]
....			Love You Madly –vTWtk
....			Solitude –vTWtk
....			One More Time For The People –vAMo TWtk
....			Things Ain't What They Used To Be
....	RDB		Soso[2]
....			My Mother, My Father –vTWtk
....			It Don't Mean A Thing –vTWtk
....			I Got It Bad –vAMo
....	RDB		Every Day –vAMo
....	RDB		Take The "A" Train
....			In Duplicate

> DE JBjm QW.

| .... | Vi | DPE6-2136 | Pitter Panther Patter |

> MJsn, VP, RP, DE JBjm QW.

| .... | Vi | DPE6-2139 | Tiger Rag |

[1]Including: Don't Get Around Much Anymore; Mood Indigo; Where In The World; Sophisticated Lady.
[2]Announced as "Woods" by RDB.

DUKE ELLINGTON & HIS ORCHESTRA
MJsn BLH JCI ME, VP ABrn CCrs, RP HMn PM PG HAsh HC, DE JBjm QW, AMo.

....	The "C" Jam Blues
....	Take The "A" Train
....	Kinda Dukish/Rockin' In Rhythm
....	Creole Love Call
....	Satin Doll
....	Spacemen
....	Caravan
....	How High The Moon
....	Soul Soothing Beach
....	Chinoiserie
....	I Can't Get Started
....	Things Ain't What They Used To Be
....	New York, New York –vAMo
....	I Got It Bad –vAMo
....	Blem –vAMo
....	Basin Street Blues –vMJsn
....	Hello Dolly –vMJsn
....	Medley[1]

> RFo replaces DE.

| .... | Take The "A" Train |

> DE replaces RFo.

| .... | Somebody Cares |

> PG, DE JBjm QW.

| .... | Happy Reunion |

> MJsn, VP, RP, DE JBjm QW.

| .... | Tiger Rag |

> DE JBjm QW.

| .... | Pitter Panther Patter |

> Entire band.

| .... | In Triplicate |
| .... | Mecuria The Lion |

> DE JBjm.

| .... | Lotus Blossom |

[1]Including: Don't Get Around Much Anymore; Mood Indigo; I'm Beginning To See The Light; Sophisticated Lady.

DUKE ELLINGTON & HIS ORCHESTRA
MJsn BLH JCI ME, VP ABrn CCrs, RP HMn PM PG HAsh HC, DE JBjm QW, AMo.

....	Take The "A" Train
....	Kinda Dukish/Rockin' In Rhythm
....	Creole Love Call
....	Satin Doll
....	I Can't Get Started
....	New York, New York –vAMo
....	I Got It Bad –vAMo
....	Medley[2]
....	Soul Soothing Beach
....	Chinoiserie

> DE JBjm.

| .... | Lotus Blossom |

[1]Taping session; the date of telecast is not known.
[2]Including: Don't Get Around Much Anymore; Mood Indigo; I'm Beginning To See The Light; It Don't Mean A Thing; Sophisticated Lady.

DUKE ELLINGTON & HIS ORCHESTRA
MJsn BLH JCI ME RN, VP ABrn CCrs, RP HMn PM PG HAsh HC, DE JBjm QW, AMo TWtk.

....	The "C" Jam Blues
....	Take The "A" Train
....	Creole Love Call
....	Satin Doll >>>

....	Spacemen
....	In A Sentimental Mood
....	Caravan
....	In Duplicate
....	New York, New York –vAMo
....	I Got It Bad –vAMo
....	Blem –vAMo
....	Chinoiserie
....	Basin Street Blues –vMJsn
....	Sophisticated Lady
....	Love You Madly –vTWtk
....	One More Time For The People –vAMo TWtk
....	Things Ain't What They Used To Be
....	Perdido

                                                                                    1 Jan 1974   (P)
DUKE ELLINGTON & HIS GROUP   Rainbow Grill (bc)
MJsn, RP HMn PM PG HAsh HC, DE JBjm QW, AMo TWtk.   New York, NY

....	Take The "A" Train
....	I'm Beginning To See The Light
....	Satin Doll
....	Medley[1]
....	Sophisticated Lady
....	Caravan
....	Things Ain't What They Used To Be
....	I'm Just A Lucky So-And-So –vTWtk
....	One More Time For The People –vAMo TWtk
....	New York, New York

[1]Including: Solitude; Mood Indigo; I Got It Bad –vAMo; I Let A Song Go Out Of My Heart; Don't Get Around Much Anymore.

                                                                                    16 Jan 1974   (P)
DUKE ELLINGTON   University of Michigan
DE talking.   Ann Arbor, MI

....	Press conference

                                                                                    10 Feb 1974   (P)
DUKE ELLINGTON & HIS ORCHESTRA   Georgetown University
CW MJsn BLH JCl ME, VP ABrn CCrs, RP HMn PM HAsh HC, DE JBrd WF QW, AMo TWtk.   Washington, DC

....	The "C" Jam Blues
....	Take The "A" Train
....	Kinda Dukish/Rockin' In Rhythm
....	Creole Love Call
....	Spacemen
....	Caravan
....	How High The Moon
....	Soul Soothing Beach
....	Chinoiserie
....	Take The "A" Train
....	New York, New York –vAMo
....	I Got It Bad –vAMo
....	Blem –vAMo
....	Basin Street Blues –vMJsn
....	Sophisticated lady
....	Do Nothin' Till You Hear From Me –vTWtk
....	Solitude –vTWtk
....	One More Time For The People –vAMo TWtk
....	Things Ain't What They Used To Be
....	Satin Doll
....	Satin Doll
....	Mecuria The Lion

> DE WF.

....	Lotus Blossom

DUKE ELLINGTON & HIS ORCHESTRA
PG added, otherwise same personnel.

....	The "C" Jam Blues
....	Take The "A" Train
....	In A Sentimental Mood
....	Spacemen
....	Caravan >>>

....	How High The Moon
....	Soul Soothing Beach
....	Chinoiserie
....	New York, New York –vAMo
....	I Got It Bad –vAMo
....	Blem –vAMo
....	Misty –vAMo
....	Basin Street Blues –vMJsn
....	Sophisticated Lady
....	Do Nothin' Till You Hear From Me –vTWtk
....	Solitude –vTWtk
....	One More Time For The People –vAMo TWtk
....	Things Ain't What They Used To Be
....	Somebody Cares –vAMo TWtk
....	Tell Me, It's The Truth –vAMo TWtk

> MJsn, VP, RP, DE WF QW.

....	Tiger Rag

> Entire band.

....	Satin Doll
....	Mood Indigo

5 Mar 1974   (P)
Dade County Auditorium
Miami Beach, FL

DUKE ELLINGTON & HIS ORCHESTRA
CW MJsn BLH JCI ME, VP ABrn CCrs, RP HMn PM PG HAsh GM, DE WF QW, AMo TWtk.

....	The "C" Jam Blues
....	Take The "A" Train
....	Kinda Dukish/Rockin' In Rhythm
....	Creole Love Call
....	Spacemen
....	In A Sentimental Mood
....	Caravan
....	How High The Moon
	TOGO BRAVA—BRAVA TOGO
....	- Soul Soothing Beach
....	- Right On Togo
....	- Amour, Amour
....	Chinoiserie
....	I Can't Get Started
....	Take The "A" Train
....	La Plus Belle Africaine
....	Perdido
....	Satin Doll
....	In Duplicate
....	New York, New York –vAMo
....	I Didn't Know About You –vAMo
....	Blem –vAMo
....	Basin Street Blues –vMJsn
....	Medley[1]
....	Mood Indigo –vTWtk
....	Do Nothin' Till You Hear From Me –vTWtk
....	Solitude –vTWtk
....	One More Time For The People –vAMo TWtk
....	Things Ain't What They Used To Be
....	Soso
....	Mecuria The Lion

> DE WF.

....	Lotus Blossom

[1]Including: Don't Get Around Much Anymore; Mood Indigo; I'm Beginning To See The Light; Sophisticated Lady.

8 Mar 1974   (P)
Van Wezel Performing Arts Center
Sarasota, FL

DUKE ELLINGTON & HIS ORCHESTRA
CW MJsn BLH JCI ME, VP ABrn CCrs, RP HMn PM PG HAsh, DE WF JL QW, AMo TWtk.

....	The "C" Jam Blues
....	Kinda Dukish/Rockin' In Rhythm
....	Creole Love Call
....	Spacemen
....	In A Sentimental Mood
....	Caravan
....	How High The Moon >>>

		TOGO BRAVA—BRAVA TOGO
. . . .		- Soul Soothing Beach
. . . .		- Right On Togo
. . . .		- Amour, Amour
. . . .		Chinoiserie
. . . .		La Plus Belle Africaine

> DE piano solo.

. . . .	Interlude

> Entire band.

. . . .	Take The "A" Train
. . . .	Satin Doll
. . . .	In Duplicate
. . . .	New York, New York –vAMo
. . . .	I'm Beginning To See The Light –vAMo
. . . .	I Got It Bad –vAMo
. . . .	Blem –vAMo
. . . .	Basin Street Blues –vMJsn
. . . .	Hello Dolly –vMJsn
. . . .	Medley[1]
. . . .	Mood Indigo –vTWtk
. . . .	Do Nothin' Till You Hear From Me –vTWtk
. . . .	Solitude –vTWtk
. . . .	One More Time For The People –vAMo TWtk
. . . .	Things Ain't What They Used To Be
. . . .	Mecuria The Lion

[1]Including: Don't Get Around Much Anymore; Mood Indigo; It Don't Mean A Thing; Sophisticated Lady.

		20 Mar 1974 (P)
DUKE ELLINGTON & HIS ORCHESTRA		Central Ballroom, Northern Illinois University
Probably the same personnel as on 8 Mar 1974.		De Kalb, IL

Concert (tape is said to exist)

The following titles are taken from contemporary reviews of the concert:

. . . .	Take The "A" Train
. . . .	Parts of the "Togo Brava—Brava Togo Suite"
. . . .	Parts of the "Afro-Eurasian Eclipse"
. . . .	Mood Indigo –vTWtk
. . . .	Somebody Cares –vAMo
. . . .	Sophisticated Lady

> DE piano solo.

. . . .	Lotus Blossom

This was DE's last recorded public performance. The last concert, however, was held at the Sturgis-Young Auditorium in Sturgis, MI, on 22 Mar 1974, where the band played two sets. No recording of this event has surfaced as yet, and it is assumed that none exists.

The Ellingtonians

EVA TAYLOR
Vcl, acc. by TMrs, *Cl, SB,* CWls, ALmx.

.... OK   72028-C   Old Fashioned Love –vETlr ALmx
.... OK   72029-B   Open Your Heart –ETlr ALmx

GEORGE McCLENNON'S JAZZ DEVILS
TMrs, *Cl,* GMC BFlr, CWls BChr dr.

.... OK   72512-B   Box Of Blues
.... OK   72513-B   Dark Alley Blues

EVA TAYLOR WITH CLARENCE WILLIAMS' HARMONIZERS
Vcl, acc. by TMrs, *Cl,* ?LTio, CWls.

.... OK   72531-B   When You're Tired Of Me –vETlr
.... OK   72532-A   Ghost Of The Blues –vETlr

SARA MARTIN WITH CLARENCE WILLIAMS' HARMONIZERS
Vcl, acc. by TMrs, *Cl,* ?EE, CWls ?BChr.

.... OK   72592-B   He's Never Gonna Throw Me Down –vSMtn

SIPPIE WALLACE WITH CLARENCE WILLIAMS' HARMONIZERS
Vcl, acc. by TMrs, *Cl,* ?EE, CWls BChr.

.... OK   72606-B   Sud Bustin' Blues –vSWlc
.... OK   72607-B   Wicked Monday Morning Blues –vSWlc

LAURA SMITH WITH CLARENCE WILLIAMS' HARMONIZERS
Vcl, acc. by TMrs, *Cl,* EE, CWls BChr.

.... OK   72719-B   Texas Moaner Blues –vLSm
.... OK   72720-B   I'm Gonna Get Myself A Real Man –vLSm
.... OK   72721-B   Has Anybody Seen My Man? –vLSm

MARGARET JOHNSON WITH CLARENCE WILLIAMS' HARMONIZERS
Vcl, acc. by TMrs, *Cl,* ?EE, CWls BChr.

.... OK   72789-B   I Love You Daddy, But You Don't Mean Me No Good –vMJo
.... OK   72790-B   Nobody Knows The Way I Feel This Mornin' –vMJo
.... OK   72791-B   Absent Minded Blues –vMJo

ROSA HENDERSON
Vcl, acc. by ?BM, ?JFrz, LHpr/ARay.

.... Ban   5651-3   Deep River Blues –vRHsn
.... Ban   5652-3   The Basement Blues –vRHsn

KITTY BROWN
Vcl, acc. by ?BM, BFlr, ?EDwl.

.... Ban   5654-3   I Wanna Jazz Some More –vKBwn

> BFlr omitted, BHgs added.

.... Ban   5655-3   Keep On Going –vKBwn BHgs
.... Ban   5656-3   One Of These Days –vKBwn BHgs

JOSIE MILES WITH THE KANSAS CITY FIVE
Vcl, acc. by BM/JDn, JFrz, BFlr, LHpr/ARay ?ES.

.... Ed   9761   Temper'mental Daddy –vJMls
.... Ed   9762   Sweet Man Joe –vJMls

				c 2 Oct 1924 (S)
				New York City, NY

TEXAS BLUES DESTROYERS
BM, ARay.

| .... | Ajx | 31686 | Lenox Avenue Shuffle |
| .... | Ajx | [1] | Down In The Mouth Blues |

[1]The master number could not be traced.

c 5 Oct 1924   (S)
New York City, NY

TEXAS BLUES DESTROYERS
BM, ARay.

| .... | Pth | 105588 | Down In The Mouth Blues |
| .... | Pth | 105589 | Lenox Avenue Shuffle |

7 Oct 1924   (S)
New York City, NY

TEXAS BLUES DESTROYERS
BM, ARay.

| .... | Vo | 13832 | Lenox Avenue Shuffle |
| .... | Vo | 13834 | Down In The Mouth Blues |

17 Oct 1924   (S)
New York City, NY

CLARENCE WILLIAMS' BLUE FIVE
LA, *Cl*, SB, CWls BChr.

| .... | OK | 72914-B | Texas Moaner Blues |

VIRGINIA LISTON WITH CLARENCE WILLIAMS' BLUE FIVE
Vcl, acc. by same as above.

| .... | OK | 72915-B | Early In The Morning –vVL |
| .... | OK | 72916-B | You've Got The Right Key, But The Wrong Keyhole –vVL |

Late Oct 1924   (S)
New York City, NY

KANSAS CITY FIVE
BM, JFrz, BFlr, LHpr ES.

| .... | Pth | 105643 | Get Yourself A Monkey Man (And Make Him Strut His Stuff) |
| .... | Pth | 105644 | Louisville Blues |

28 Oct 1924   (S)
New York City, NY

ROSA HENDERSON WITH THE KANSAS CITY FIVE
Vcl, acc. by *BM*, JFrz, BFlr, LHpr ES.

| .... | Ed | 9812 | Don't Advertise Your Man –vRHsn |

HELEN GROSS WITH THE KANSAS CITY FIVE
Vcl, acc. by same as above.

| .... | Doc | 9813 | Undertaker's Blues –vHGrs |

c 29/30 Oct 1924   (S)
New York City, NY

JULIA MOODY
Vcl, acc. by *BM*, BFlr, LHpr.

| .... | Ban | 5694-2 | Mad Mama's Blues –vJMdy |

ALBERTA PERKINS WITH THE JAZZ CASPER
Vcl, acc. by *BM*, LHpr ES JDs, BHgs.

....	Ban	5695-1	Who Calls You Sweet Mama Now? –vAPns BHgs
....	Ban	5695-2	Who Calls You Sweet Mama Now? –vAPns BHgs
....	Ban	5695-3	Who Calls You Sweet Mama Now? –vAPns BHgs
> JDs omitted.			
....	Ban	5696-1	Sweet Mandy –vAPns BHgs
....	Ban	5696-2	Sweet Mandy –vAPns BHgs

c Oct 1924   (S)
New York City, NY

JOSIE MILES WITH THE CHOO CHOO JAZZERS
Vcl, acc. by *BM*, JFrz, BFlr, CPry/LHpr ES.

....	Ajx	31703	Won't Somebody Help Me Find My Lovin' Man? –vJMls
....	Ajx	31705	South Bound Blues –vJMls
....	Ajx	[1]	Sweet Man Joe

[1]The master number could not be traced.

				c 3 Nov 1924 (S)
				New York City, NY

JULIA MOODY
Vcl, acc. by *BM,* LHpr ES.

| .... | Ban | 5700-1 | Broken, Busted, Can't Be Trusted –vJMdy |
| .... | Ban | 5701-1 | Don't Forget, You'll Regret –vJMdy |

21 Nov 1924 (S)
New York City, NY

VIOLA McCOY WITH THE KANSAS CITY FIVE
Vcl, acc. by *BM,* JFrz, BFlr, LHpr ES.

| .... | Ed | 9860 | Memphis Bound –vVMC |

ROSA HENDERSON WITH THE KANSAS CITY FIVE
Vcl, acc. by same as above.

| .... | Ed | 9861 | Undertaker's Blues –vRHsn |

JOSIE MILES WITH THE KANSAS CITY FIVE
Vcl, acc. by same as above.

| .... | Ed | 9862 | Mad Mama's Blues –vJMls |

c 24 Nov 1924 (S)
New York City, NY

CLEMENTINE SMITH WITH THE KANSAS CITY FIVE
Vcl, acc. by *BM/*LM, BFlr, LHpr ES.

| .... | Re | 5740-5 | Everybody Loves My Baby –vCSm |

JOSIE MILES WITH THE JAZZ CASPER
Vcl, acc. by *BM/*LM, LHpr ES, BHgs.

| .... | Ban | 5741-1 | Let's Agree To Disagree –vJMls BHgs |
| .... | Ban | 5741-2 | Let's Agree To Disagree –vJMls BHgs |

CLEMENTINE SMITH WITH THE KANSAS CITY FIVE
Vcl, acc. by *BM/*LM, BFlr, LHpr ES.

| .... | Ban | 5742-1 | I'm Done, Done, Done With You –vCSm |

Nov 1924 (S)
New York City, NY

MONETTE MOORE
Vcl, acc. by *BM,* JFrz, BFlr, LHpr.

| .... | Ajx | 31706 | Bullet Wound Blues –vMMre |

Nov 1924 (S)
New York City, NY

KANSAS CITY FIVE
BM, JFrz, BFlr, LHpr ES.

....	Ajx	31709	Believe Me, Hot Mama
....	Ajx	31711	St. Louis Blues
....	Ajx	31713	Louisville Blues
....	Ajx	31715	Temper'mental Papa

Nov 1924 (S)
New York City, NY

JOSIE MILES WITH THE CHOO CHOO JAZZERS
Vcl, acc. by *BM,* BFlr, ?LHpr, BHgs.

| .... | Ajx | 31725 | I'm Done, Done, Done With You –vJMls BHgs |

> BFlr, BHgs omitted.

| .... | Ajx | 31727 | A To Z Blues –vJMls |

Nov 1924 (S)
New York City, NY

MONETTE MOORE
Vcl, acc. by *BM,* JFrz, BFlr, LHpr.

| .... | Ajx | 31729 | The Bye-Bye Blues –vMMre |
| .... | Ajx | 31730 | Weeping Willow Blues –vMMre |

c 2 Dec 1924 (S)
New York City, NY

SIX BLACK DIAMONDS
BM LM, JFrz, BFlr, LHpr ES.

....	Ban	5758-1	Those Panama Mamas
....	Ban	5758-2	Those Panama Mamas
....	Ban	5758-3	Those Panama Mamas >>>

CLEMENTINE SMITH WITH THE KANSAS CITY FIVE
Vcl, acc. by same as above.

| .... | Ban | 5759-2 | Nobody Knows What A Red Head Mama Can Do –vCSm |
| .... | Ban | 5760-2 | Big Bad Bill Is Sweet William Now –vCSm |

c 15 Dec 1924 (S)
New York City, NY

NETTIE POTTER
Vcl, acc. by *BM*/LM, JFrz, LHpr.

| .... | Ban | 5786-1 | A Good Man Is Hard To Find –vNPtr |

> JFrz omitted, BFlr added.

| .... | Ban | 5787-1 | Blind Man Blues –vNPtr |

BOOKER'S JAZZ BAND
BM, JFrz, BFlr CBk, LHpr ES.

....	Dom	5788-2	Hot Sax
....	IAC	5789-1	West Texas Blues
....	Dom	5789-2	West Texas Blues

17 Dec 1924 (S)
New York City, NY

CLARENCE WILLIAMS' BLUE FIVE
LA, *Cl*, SB, CWls BChr, ETlr.

| .... | OK | 73026-B | Mandy, Make Up Your Mind –vETlr |
| .... | OK | 73027-B | I'm A Little Blackbird, Looking For A Bluebird –vETlr |

22 Dec 1924 (S)
New York City, NY

JOSEPHINE BEATTY WITH THE RED ONION JAZZ BABIES
Vcl, acc. by LA, *Cl*, SB, LArm BChr, CTd.

....	Gnt	9246	Nobody Knows The Way I Feel Dis Mornin' –vJBty
....	Gnt	9247-A	Early Every Morn' –vJBty
....	Gnt	9248-A	Cake-Walking Babies From Home –vJBty CTd

8 Jan 1925 (S)
New York City, NY

MARGARET JOHNSON WITH CLARENCE WILLIAMS' BLUE FIVE
Vcl, acc. by *BM*, AT, SB, CWls BChr.

| .... | OK | 73081-A | Who Will Chop Your Suey When I'm Gone? –vMJo |
| .... | OK | 73082-B | Done Made A Fool Out Of Me –vMJo |

CLARENCE WILLIAMS' BLUE FIVE
LA, *Cl*, SB, CWls BChr, ETlr.

| .... | OK | 73083-A | Cake-Walking Babies From Home –vETlr |
| .... | OK | 73084-B | Pickin' On Your Baby –vETlr |

c 18 Feb 1925 (S)
New York City, NY

JOSIE MILES
Vcl, acc. by *BM*/TMrs, BFlr, LHpr.

| .... | Ban | 5861-2 | Ghost Walkin' Blues –vJMls |

> BFlr omitted, JFrz added.

| .... | Ban | 5862-2 | Can't Be Trusted Blues –vJMls |

4 Mar 1925 (S)
New York City, NY

CLARENCE WILLIAMS' BLUE FIVE
LA, *Cl*, BBly SB DR, CWls BChr, ETlr.

| .... | OK | 73204-A | Cast Away –vETlr |
| .... | OK | 73205-A | Papa De-Da-Da –vETlr |

c Mar 1925 (S)
New York City, NY

MONETTE MOORE WITH THE CHOO CHOO JAZZERS
Vcl, acc. by *BM*, LHpr.

| .... | Ajx | 31847 | Undertaker's Blues –vMMre |

6 Oct 1925 (S)
New York City, NY

CLARENCE WILLIAMS' BLUE FIVE
LA, *Cl*, BBly DR, CWls BChr, ETlr.

| .... | OK | 73686-B | Just Wait 'Til You See My Baby Do The Charleston –vETlr |
| .... | OK | 73687-B | Livin' High Sometimes –vETlr |

8 Oct 1925 (S)
New York City, NY

CLARENCE WILLIAMS' BLUE FIVE
LA, *Cl*, BBly DR, CWls BChr, ETlr

.... OK 73694-B Coal Cart Blues –vETlr

> DR omitted.

.... OK 73695-B Santa Claus Blues –vETlr

26 Oct 1925 (S)
New York City, NY

CLARENCE WILLIAMS' BLUE FIVE
LA, *Cl*, DR CHwk, CWls BChr, ETlr.

.... OK 73738-A Squeeze Me –vETlr
.... OK 73739-B You Can't Shush Katie –vETlr

17 Nov 1925 (S)
New York City, NY

SARA MARTIN
Vcl, acc. by *BM*, RCks, ?PhWe.

.... OK 73759-B Forget Me Not Blues –vSMtn
.... OK 73760-A Nobody Knows And Nobody Cares Blues –vSMtn
.... OK 73761-B Give Me Just A Little Of Your Time –vSMtn

23 Nov 1925 (S)
New York City, NY

SARA MARTIN WITH CLARENCE WILLIAMS' BLUE FIVE
Vcl, acc. by ct, ?*Cl*, as, CWls ?BChr.

.... OK 73773-B I'm Gonna Hoodoo You –vSMtn CWls
.... OK 73774-B Your Going Ain't Giving Me The Blues –vSMtn
.... OK 73775-B What More Can A Monkey Woman Do? –vSMtn

c 11 Dec 1925 (S)
New York City, NY

ALBERTA HUNTER WITH PERRY BRADFORD'S MEAN FOUR
Vcl, acc. by *BM*, CGrn, DR, PB.

.... OK 73830-B Your Jelly Roll Is Good –vAHtr
.... OK 73831-B Take That Thing Away –vAHtr

4 Jan 1926 (S)
New York City, NY

CLARENCE WILLIAMS' STOMPERS
JSth, *Cl*, DR CHwk, CWls LHrs/BChr CSC.

.... OK 73893-B Spanish Shawl
.... OK 73894-B Dinah

c 22 Jan 1926 (S)
New York City, NY

CLARENCE WILLIAMS' BLUE FIVE
BM, ?*Cl*, OH/DR, CWls ?LHrs CSC, ETlr.

.... OK 73957-A I've Found A New Baby –vETlr
.... OK 73958-B I've Found A New Baby –vETlr
.... OK 73959-B Pile Of Logs And Stone –vETlr

c 23 Mar 1926 (S)
New York City, NY

BUDDY CHRISTIAN'S CREOLE FIVE
ct, *Cl*, BFlr, LHpr/MJck BChr dr, LV.

.... OK 74057-A Sunset Blues –vLV
.... OK 74058-A Texas Mule Stomp –vLV
.... OK 74059-A Sugar House Stomp

25 Mar 1926 (S)
New York City, NY

SARA MARTIN WITH CLARENCE WILLIAMS' BLUE FIVE
Vcl, acc. by ?*BM*, tb, OH/DR, CWls bj ?CSC.

.... OK 74072-A Brother Ben –vSMtn
.... OK 74073-A The Prisoner's Blues –vSMtn
.... OK 74074-B Careless Man Blues –vSMtn
.... OK 74075-A How Could I Be Blue? –vSMtn

7 Apr 1926 (S)
New York City, NY

CLARENCE WILLIAMS' STOMPERS
TMrs *BM*, JN, DR, CWls LHrs/BChr bb.

.... OK 74090-B Jackass Blues
.... OK 74091-B What's The Matter Now?

				2 Nov 1926	(S)
				New York City, NY	

NEW ORLEANS BLUE FIVE
TMrs, *JN,* BFlr, MJck BChr, HBxt.

.... Vi 36895-1 My Baby Doesn't Squawk
.... Vi 36896-1 The King Of The Zulus –vHBxt TMrs JN
.... Vi 36897-1 South Rampart Street Blues

		12 Nov 1926	(S)
		New York City, NY	

THOMAS MORRIS & HIS SEVEN HOT BABIES
TMrs, *JN,* EE, MJck/PhWe BChr WB dr.

.... CC 36925-1 Blues From The Everglades
.... Vi 36925-2 Blues From The Everglades
.... CC 36926-1 P.D.Q. Blues
.... Vi 36926-3 P.D.Q. Blues

		17 Nov 1926	(S)
		New York City, NY	

SIX HOT BABIES
TMrs, *JN,* BFlr, NS ?FWlr ?BLcn.

....   36775-1/-2/-3/-4 [All God's Chillun Got Wings]

		24 Nov 1926	(S)
		New York City, NY	

THOMAS MORRIS & HIS SEVEN HOT BABIES
TMrs, *JN,* BFlr, MJck/PhWe BChr WB dr.

.... Vi 36962-3 The Mess
.... Vi 36963-2 The Chinch

		c 29 Nov 1926	(S)
		New York City, NY	

VIOLA McCOY
Vcl, acc. by *LM,* CJck.

.... Cam 2219-C I'm Savin' It All For You –vVMC
.... Cam 2220-B Papa, If You Can't Do Better –vVMC

		c 28 Dec 1926	(S)
		New York City, NY	

VIOLA McCOY
Vcl, acc. by *LM,* CJck.

.... Cam 2261-C Git Goin" –vVMC
.... Cam 2262-B Someday You'll Come Back To Me –vVMC

		15 Mar 1927	(S)
		New York City, NY	

ORIGINAL JAZZ HOUNDS
LM, JFrz, BFlr, JPJ bj bb dr, PB.

.... Co 143657-2 All That I Had Is Gone –vPB
.... Co 143658-3 Lucy Long –vPB

		18 Mar 1927	(S)
		New York City, NY	

LIZZIE MILES
Vcl, acc. by *LM,* LHpr.

.... OK 80644-B Slow Up, Papa –vLMls
.... OK 80845-A Grievin' Mama Blues –vLMls

		19 Mar 1927	(S)
		New York City, NY	

MARTHA COPELAND
Vcl, acc. by *LM,* LHpr.

.... Co 143689-1 Soul And Body –vMCld
.... Co 143690-3 Sorrow Valley Blues –vMCld

		6 May 1927	(S)
		New York City, NY	

BUTTERBEANS & SUSIE WITH EDDIE HEYWOOD'S JAZZ TRIO
Vcl, acc. by *LM,* EHd.

.... OK 81063-B You're A No-'Count Triflin' Man –vB&S
.... OK 81065-A Gonna Make You Sorry (For Everything You Do) –vB&S

		2 Sep 1927	(S)
		New York City, NY	

JOHNSON'S JAZZERS
LM, JPJ, PB.

.... Co 144621-2 Skiddle-De-Scow –vPB
.... Co 144622-2 Can I Get It Now? –vPB

                                                                        23 Sep 1927   (S)
                                                                        New York City, NY

CLARENCE WILLIMAS' BLUE SEVEN
LM, Cl, BBly ?AHrs, CWls LHrs CSC.

.... OK   81472-A   Baby, Won't You Please Come Home?
.... OK   81473-A   Close Fit Blues

                                                                        26 Jul 1928   (S)
                                                                        New York City, NY

ROY EVANS
Vcl, acc. by AW, JPJ.

.... Co   146811-2   So Sorry –vREvs
.... Co   146812-3   Syncopated Yodelin' Man –vREvs

                                                                        28 Aug 1928   (S)
                                                                        New York City, NY

MARTHA COPELAND
Vcl, acc. by BM, JCJ.

.... Co   146923-2   Mama's Well Has Done Gone Dry –vMCld
.... Co   146924-3   I Ain't Your Hen, Mr. Fly Rooster –vMCld

                                                                        10 Sep 1928   (S)
                                                                        New York City, NY

KING OLIVER & HIS DIXIE SYNCOPATORS
KO EAsn, JCH, OS BB, LR WJsn BMre PBbn.

.... Vo   E28185-A/-B   Speakeasy Blues
.... Vo   E28186-A/-B   Aunt Hagar's Blues

                                                                        12 Sep 1928   (S)
                                                                        New York City, NY

KING OLIVER & HIS DIXIE SYNCOPATORS
KO EAsn, JCH, OS BB, LR WJsn BMre PBbn.

.... Vo   E28203-A/-B   I'm Watchin' The Clock

                                                                        19 Oct 1928   (S)
                                                                        New York City, NY

GULF COAST SEVEN
BM, ?CGrn, GBsh ts, ?JPJ bj dr, PB.

.... Co   147151-1   Daylight Savin' Blues
.... Co   147152-1   Georgia's Always On My Mind –vPB

                                                                        30 Jan 1929   (S)
                                                                        New York City, NY

MUSICAL STEVEDORES
FJ LM, HH, CGrs CHms, CJck ES BHks.

.... Co   147899-3   Happy Rhythm
.... Co   147900-3   Honeycomb Harmony

                                                                        23 May 1929   (S)
                                                                        New York City, NY

IRVING MILLS & HIS MODERNISTS
BMr ?MMos, TD, TPti ?HC JPts, NBr NGch, JCS CKrs HGdm DO, IM.

.... Vi   53435-3   At The Prom –vIM

                                                                        30 Sep 1929   (S)
                                                                        New York City, NY

FATS WALLER & HIS BUDDIES
HRA, JTdn, AN OH LBin, FWlr ECdn AMgn GK, FWrs.

.... Vi   56727-2   Looking Good But Feeling Bad –vFWrs
.... Vi   56728-1   I Need Someone Like You –vFWrs

                                                                        2 Dec 1929   (S)
                                                                        New York City, NY

WILTON CRAWLEY & HIS ORCHESTRA
2tp, tb, WCrl JH, JRM LR bj PFst ?SG.

.... Vi   57565-2   You Oughta See My Gal
.... Vi   57566-1   Futuristic Blues
.... Vi   57567-2   Keep Your Business To Yourself
.... Vi   57568-1   She's Got What I Need

                                                                        17 Dec 1929   (S)
                                                                        New York City, NY

JELLY-ROLL MORTON TRIO
BB, JRM ZStn.

.... Vi   57784-1   Smilin' The Blues Away
.... Vi   57785-1   Turtle Twist
.... Vi   57786-1   My Little Dixie Home
.... Vi   57787-2   That's Like It Ought To Be

| | | | | Early 1932 | (T)[1] |
| | | | | New York City, NY | |

ELMER SNOWDEN & HIS SMALL'S PARADISE ORCHESTRA
RHln RE LD, DW GWtn, *OH* AS WCvr, DK DFbr ES SCtl, MSct.

....	IAC		Bugle Call Rag
....	IAC		Tiger Rag
....	IAC		Stop The Sun, Stop The Moon –vMSct
....	IAC		Concentratin' On You

[1]From the motion picture "Smash Your Baggage."

| | | | | 4 Mar 1935 | (S) |
| | | | | New York City, NY | |

BOB HOWARD & HIS ORCHESTRA
Vcl, acc. by *RS, BB* BCrt, TW CHdy EJms CCle.

....	De	39390-A	Stay Out Of Love –vBHrd
....	De	39391-A	I'll Never Change –vBHrd
....	De	39392-A	Where Were You In The Night Of June The Third? –vBHrd
....	De	39392-B	Where Were You In The Night Of June The Third? –vBHrd
....	De	39393-A	Breakin' The Ice –vBHrd

| | | | | 7 Mar 1935 | (S) |
| | | | | New York City, NY | |

BOB HOWARD & HIS ORCHESTRA
Vcl, acc. by ?*RS,* RP BCrt, TW CHdy BT CCle.

....	De	39518-A	Corinne Corinna –vBHrd
....	De	39519-A	Ev'ry Day –vBHrd
....	De	39520-A	A Porter's Love Song (To A Chambermaid) –vBHrd
....	De	39521-A	I Can't Dance (I Got Ants In My Pants) –vBHrd

| | | | | 3 Dec 1935 | (S) |
| | | | | New York City, NY | |

TEDDY WILSON & HIS ORCHESTRA
DClk, TMac *JH,* TW DBbr GMcr CCle, BHol.

....	Br	B18316-1	These 'n That 'n Those –vBHol
....	Br	B18317-1	Sugar Plum
....	Br	B18318-1	You Let Me Down –vBHol
....	Br	B18319-1	Spreadin' Rhythm Around –vBHol

| | | | | 6 Dec 1935 | (S) |
| | | | | New York City, NY | |

MILDRED BAILEY & HER ALLEY CATS
Vcl, acc. by BBgn, *JH,* TW GMcr.

....	De	60201-A	Willow Tree –vMBly
....	De	60202-A	Honeysuckle Rose –vMBly
....	De	60203-A	Squeeze Me –vMBly
....	De	60204-A	Down-Hearted Blues –vMBly

| | | | | 30 Jun 1936 | (S) |
| | | | | New York City, NY | |

TEDDY WILSON & HIS ORCHESTRA
JJo, *JH HC,* TW LLuc JKrb CCle, BHol.

....	Br	B19495-2	It's Like Reaching For The Moon –vBHol
....	Br	B19496-2	These Foolish Things –vBHol
....	Br	B19497-2	Why Do I Lie To Myself About You?
....	Br	B19498-2	I Cried For You –vBHol
....	Br	B19499-2	Guess Who –vBHol

| | | | | 9 Nov 1936 | (S) |
| | | | | New York City, NY | |

MILDRED BAILEY & HER ORCHESTRA
Vcl, acc. by ZE, AShw *JH* FLwe, TW DBbr JKrb CCle.

| .... | Vo | 20218-1 | It's Love I'm After –vMBly |

| | | | | 25 Mar 1937 | (S) |
| | | | | New York City, NY | |

THE GOTHAM STOMPERS
CW, SWls, *BB JH HC,* TF BA *BT* ChW, *IA.*

....	Vri	M301-1	My Honey's Lovin' Arms –vIA
....	Vri	M302-1	Didn't Anyone Ever Tell You? –vIA
....	Mrt	M302-2	Didn't Anyone Ever Tell You? –vIA
....	Vri	M303-1	Alabamy Home
....	Vri	M304-1	Where Are You? –vIA

| | | | | 31 Mar 1937 | (S) |
| | | | | New York City, NY | |

TEDDY WILSON & HIS ORCHESTRA
CW, *JH HC,* TW ARs JKrb CCle, BHol.

| .... | Br | B20911-3 | Carelessly –vBHol |
| .... | Br | B20912-1 | How Could You? –vBHol   >>> |

| .... | Br | B20913-1 | Moanin' Low –vBHol |
| .... | Br | B20914-1 | Fine And Dandy –vBHol |

14 Apr 1937   (S)
New York City, NY

LIONEL HAMPTON & HIS ORCHESTRA
CW, LB, MMzw *JH,* LHpt JSty ARs JKrb CCle.

....	Vi	07792-1	Buzzin' Around With The Bee –vLHpt
....	Vi	07793-1	Whoa Babe –vLHpt
....	Vi	07794-1	Stompology

23 Apr 1937   (S)
New York City, NY

TEDDY WILSON & HIS ORCHESTRA
HJms, BBly *JH,* TW ARs JKrb CCle, HWrd.

....	Br	B21034-1	There's A Lull In My Life –vHWrd
....	Br	B21035-2	It's Swell Of You –vHWrd
....	Br	B21036-2	How Am I To Know? –vHWrd
....	Br	B21037-1	I'm Coming, Virginia

26 Apr 1937   (S)
New York City, NY

LIONEL HAMPTON & HIS ORCHESTRA
BBly *JH,* LHpt JSty ARs JKrb CCle.

....	Vi	07864-1	On The Sunny Side Of The Street –vLHpt
....	Vi	07865-1	Rhythm, Rhythm
....	Vi	07867-1	I Know That You Know

11 May 1937   (S)
New York City, NY

TEDDY WILSON & HIS ORCHESTRA
BCtn, BBly *JH* LY, TW ARs ABst CCle, BHol.

....	KJ	B21117-1	Sun Showers –vBHol
....	Br	B21117-2	Sun Showers –vBHol
....	KJ	B21118-1	Yours And Mine –vBHol
....	Br	B21118-2	Yours And Mine –vBHol
....	Br	B21119-1	I'll Get By –vBHol
....	Co	B21119-2	I'll Get By –vBHol
....	Br	B21120-1	Mean To Me –vBHol
....	Co	B21120-2	Mean To Me –vBHol

16 Jan 1938   (P)
Carnegie Hall
New York City, NY

ALL STAR BAND
CW, JH HC, JSty HGdm GK.

| .... | Co | | Blue Reverie |

> HJms BCtn, VB, BG *JH* LY *HC,* CBas FGrn WP GK.

| .... | Co | | Honeysuckle Rose[1] |

[1] Portions of the JH and HC solos have been edited out on all releases on LP.

18 Jan 1938   (S)
New York City, NY

LIONEL HAMPTON & HIS ORCHESTRA
CW, JH ESpn, LHpt JSty ARs *BT SG.*

....	Vi	018335-1	You're My Ideal –vLHpt
....	Vi	018336-2	The Sun Will Shine Tonight –vLHpt
....	Vi	018337-1	Ring Dem Bells –vLHpt
....	Vi	018338-1	Don't Be That Way

27 Apr 1938   (S)
New York City, NY

HARRY JAMES & HIS ORCHESTRA
HJms ZE, VB, DM ARln *HC,* JSty TTge DT.

....	Br	B22808-2	Out Of Nowhere
....	Br	B22809-1	Wrap Your Troubles In Dreams
....	Br	B22810-1	Lullaby In Rhythm
....	Br	B22811-1	Little White Lies

29 Apr 1938   (S)
New York City, NY

TEDDY WILSON & HIS ORCHESTRA
BHck, PWR *JH,* TW ARs AHll JBws, NWn.

....	Mrt	B22822-1	If I Were You –vNWn
....	Br	B22822-2	If I Were You –vNWn
....	Br	B22823-1	You Go To My Head –vNWn
....	Br	B22824-1	I'll Dream Tonight –vNWn
....	Mrt	B22824-2	I'll Dream Tonight –vNWn >>>

.... Br   B22825-2   Jungle Love

TIMME ROSENKRANTZ & HIS BARRELHOUSE BARONS   27 May 1938   (S)
RS BHik, TG, RW RP DBs, BKle BF WP JJ, IC.   New York City, NY

.... Vi   023502-1   A Wee Bit Of Swing
.... Vi   023503-1   Is This To Be My Souvenir? –vIC
.... Vi   023304-1   When Day Is Done –vIC
.... Vi   023505-1   The Song Is Ended.

THE ELLINGTONIANS   25 Jun 1938   (P)
CW, JT, BB HC, DBmn BT SG.   CBS Studios
                                                                       New York City, NY

.... JP   Frolic Sam

REX STEWART & HIS FEETWARMERS   5 Apr 1939   (S)
RS, BB, DjR BT.   Paris, France

.... Sw   OSW-63-1   Montmartre[1]
.... Sw   OSW-64-1   Low Cotton
.... Sw   OSW-65-1   Finesse[2]
.... Sw   OSW-66-1   I Know That You Know
.... Sw   OSW-67-1   Solid Rock[3]

[1] *aka "Django's Jump."*
[2] *"Night Wind" on some releases.*
[3] *sa "Solid Old Man."*

FRANKIE "HALF-PINT" JAXON   19 May 1939   (S)
Vcl, acc. by BB, LArm WB SCtl.   New York City, NY

.... De   65607-A   Don't Pan Me –vHPJ
.... De   65608-A   Callin' Corinne –vHPJ
.... De   65609-A   You Can't Put That Monkey On My Back –HPJ
.... De   65610-A   Fan It Boogie Woogie –vHPJ

LIONEL HAMPTON & HIS ORCHESTRA   13 Jun 1939   (S)
RS, LB, HC, LHpt CHrt BT SG.   New York City, NY

.... Vi   037630-1   Memories Of You
.... Vi   037631-1   The Jumpin' Jive –vLHpt
.... Vi   037632-1   Twelfth Street Rag

TRIXIE SMITH   14 Jun 1939   (S)
Vcl, acc. by ?HRA, BB, p gt b ?SCtl.   New York City, NY

.... De   65815-A   No Good Man –vTSth

REX STEWART'S BIG SEVEN   23 Jul 1939   (S)
RS, LB, BB, BKle BF WB DT.   New York City, NY

.... HRS   76396-B   Cherry
.... HRS   76397-AA   Solid Rock
.... HRS   76398-AA   Bugle Call Rag
.... HRS   76399-AA   Diga Diga Doo

SIDNEY BECHET & HIS NEW ORLEANS FOOTWARMERS   6 Sep 1940   (S)
RS, SB, EM JLds BDds, HJ.   Chicago, IL

.... Vi   053432-1   Blue For You, Johnny –vHJ
.... Vi   053432-2   Blue For You, Johnny –vHJ
.... Vi   053433-1   Ain't Misbehavin'
.... Vi   053433-2   Ain't Misbehavin'
.... Vi   053434-1   Save It, Pretty Mama
.... Vi   053435-1   Stompy Jones

JACK TEAGARDEN'S BIG EIGHT   15 Dec 1940   (S)
RS, JTdn, BB BW, BKle BF BT DT.   New York City, NY

.... HRS   3414   St. James Infirmary –vJTdn
.... HRS   3415   The World Is Waiting For The Sunrise   >>>

....	HRS	3416	Big Eight Blues
....	HRS	3417	Shine

27 Mar 1941   (S)
New York City, NY

BENNY GOODMAN & HIS ORCHESTRA
Big band, featuring *CW*.

....	Co	30071-1	Fiesta In Blue

The above title has been selected because of its Ellington Mood.

BEN WEBSTER QUARTET/QUINTET
RN, BW (ts, cl, p), *FG JB SG*.

p Oct 1941   (S)
Unspecified studio, CA

....	Fab		I Never Knew
....	Fab		The Sheik Of Araby
....	Fab		I Can't Believe That You're In Love With Me

> JB omitted.

....	Fab		A♭ Swing
....	Fab		E♭ Swing
....	Fab		Swingin' In 4
....	Fab		Memories Of You

4 Apr 1942   (S)
Hollywood, CA

SLIM GAILLARD & HIS FLAT FOOT FLOOGIE BOYS
BW, JRws SGld SSt LW.

....	Co	H-788-1	Palm Springs Jump –vSGld LW
....	Mrt	H-789-1	Ra Da Da Da –vSGld LW
....	Mrt	H-790-1	Groove Juice Special –vSGld LW
....	Co	H-791-1	It's My Day Now –vSGld LW

p 5 Sep 1943   (P)
Unidentified location U.S.A.

BAND
Small band, featuring *BB* and *JH*.

....	Tpl		Black And Tan Blues
....	Tpl		Whispering Grass

6 Jan 1944   (S)
New York City, NY

COOTIE WILLIAMS SEXTET
CW, EVsn ED, BPl NK VPn.

....	Hit	GR351	Echoes Of Harlem

COOTIE WILLIAMS & HIS ORCHESTRA
Big band, featuring *CW*.

....	Maj	GR356	Things Ain't What They Used To Be

25 Jan 1944   (S)
New York City, NY

LARRY ADLER WITH JOHN KIRBY & HIS ORCHESTRA
Hca, acc. by *RS, BBly* as, *DLW JKrb* dr.

....	De	71699	Blues In The Night
....	De	71700	Star Dust

27 Jan 1944   (S)
New York City, NY

LARRY ADLER WITH JOHN KIRBY & HIS ORCHESTRA
Hca, acc. by *RS, BBly,* as, *DLW JKrb* dr.

....	De	71709	Creole Love Call
....	De	71710	Begin The Beguine

2 Feb 1944   (S)
New York City, NY

LARRY ADLER WITH JOHN KIRBY & HIS ORCHESTRA
Hca, acc. by *RS, BBly* as, *DLW JKrb* dr.

....	De	71725	That Old Black Magic
....	De	71726	St. Louis Blues
....	De	71727	Hand To Mouth Boogie
....	De	71728	As Time Goes By

25 Mar 1944   (S)
New York City, NY

BEN WEBSTER QUARTET
BW, MM JSms SCtl.

....	Sn	170	Perdido

| | | | | 5 Apr 1944 (S) |
| | | | | New York City, NY |

WOODY HERMAN & HIS ORCHESTRA
Big band, featuring *RN, JT, JH.*

| .... | De | 71940 | Perdido |
| .... | De | 71941 | I Didn't Know About You |

| | | | | 14 Apr 1944 (S) |
| | | | | New York City, NY |

HERBIE FIELDS BAND
TJ, HF, JMgn LWre RRsn SCtl.

| .... | Sig | T19002 | These Foolish Things |
| .... | Sig | 1951 | You Can Depend On Me |

| | | | | 26 Apr 1944 (S) |
| | | | | New York City, NY |

EARL HINES SEXTET
RN, JH FP, EH ACas SCtl, BR.

....	Apo	R1006	Blues On My Weary Mind –vBR
....	Apo	R1007	I Love My Lovin' Lover –vBR[1]
....	Apo	R1008	Trouble, Trouble –vBR
....	Apo	R1009	Design For Jivin'
....	Apo	R1010	I'll Get By –vBR
....	Apo	R1011	Life With Fatha

[1]*aka* "Lovin' Lover"; "Ever Lovin' Lover."

| | | | | 2 May 1944 (S) |
| | | | | New York City, NY |

EDDIE HEYWOOD & HIS ORCHESTRA
RN, ASs DBs, EHwd JSms SMn.

....	Sig	rht-1	How High The Moon
....	Sig	rht-2	Sarcastic Lady
....	Sig	rht-3	Them There Eyes
....	Sig	rht-4	Penthouse Serenade[1]

[1]*aka* "When We're Alone."

| | | | | 5 May 1944 (S) |
| | | | | New York City, NY |

EDMOND HALL'S SWINGTET
BMtn, EHll *HC,* DFre EBkd *JR* SCtl.

....	BN	BN973-3	It's Been So Long
....	Mo	BN973 alt.	It's Been So Long
....	BN	BN974-1	I Can't Believe That You're In Love With Me
....	Mo	BN974 alt.	I Can't Believe That You're In Love With Me
....	BN	BN975-1	Big City Blues
....	BN	BN976-1	Steamin' And Beamin'

| | | | | 16 May 1944 (S) |
| | | | | New York City, NY |

SONNY GREER & HIS REXTET
RS, LB, JHtn HC, MM TWlt OP *SG.*

....	Apo	R1012	Sleepy Baboon
....	Apo	R1013	Kansas City Caboose
....	QuD	R1013 alt.	Kansas City Caboose
....	Apo	R1014	Ration Stomp
....	Apo	R1015	Helena's Dream
....	QuD	R1015 alt.	Helena's Dream

| | | | | 23 May 1944 (S) |
| | | | | New York City, NY |

UNA MAE CARLISLE
Piano and vcl, acc. by *RN,* BJsn, SAln BRbn SWsn.

....	Bcn	[1]	'Tain't Yours –vUMC
....	Bcn		Without You, Baby –vUMC
....	Bcn		I'm A Good, Good Woman –vUMC
....	Bcn		Ain't Nothin' Much –vUM

[1]The master numbers for the above session could not be traced.

| | | | | 24 May 1944 (S) |
| | | | | New York City, NY |

COLEMAN HAWKINS & HIS SAX ENSEMBLE
TSm CHwk DBs *HC,* JGrn AL SCtl.

....	Mry	HL29-1	On The Sunny Side Of The Street
....	Kn	HL29-2	On The Sunny Side Of The Street
....	Kn	HL30-1	Three Little Words
....	Kn	HL31-1	Battle Of The Saxes[1]
....	Mry	HL32-1	Louise >>>

.... Kn   HL32-2   Louise

¹*sa* "Chinatown, My Chinatown."

25 May 1944	(S)
New York City, NY	

UNA MAE CARLISLE
Piano and vcl, acc. by *RN*, BJsn, SAln BRbn SWsn.

.... Bcn   ¹   I Like It 'Cause I Love It –vUMC
.... Bcn   You Gotta Take Your Time –vUMC
.... JD   He's The Best Little Yankee To Me –vUMC
.... JD   I Speak So Much About You –vUMC

¹The master numbers for the above session could not be traced.

26 May 1944	(S)
New York City, NY	

EDDIE HEYWOOD TRIO
JH, EHwd SMn.

.... Sig   bob1   Flamingo
.... Sig   bob2   On The Sunny Side Of The Street
.... Sig   bob3   Time On My Hands
.... Sig   bob4   Night And Day

30 May 1944	(S)
New York City, NY	

BENNY MORTON TROMBONE CHOIR
BMtn VD BHrs *CJ*, JGrn AHll SCtl.

.... Kn   HL37-1   Where Or When
.... Kn   HL37-3   Where Or When
.... Em   HL38-1   Liza
.... Kn   HL38-2   Liza
.... Kn   HL39-5   Once In A While
.... Kn   HL40-2   Sliphorn Outing¹

¹*sa* "Avalon."

5 Jun 1944	(S)
New York City, NY	

REX STEWART & HIS ORCHESTRA
RS, LB, TSm HC, JGrn BF SW CCle.

.... Mry   RX1-1   The Little Goose
.... Kn   RX1-2   The Little Goose
.... Mry   RX2-1   I'm True To You¹
.... Kn   RX2-2   I'm True To You
.... Kn   RX3-1   Zaza
.... Mry   RX4-1   Swamp Mist
.... Kn   RX4-2   Swamp Mist

¹This title is a derivative of *It Don't Mean A Thing.*

1 Aug 1944	(S)
New York City, NY	

BILLY TAYLOR & HIS ORCHESTRA
EBry, VB, *JH HC*, JGrn BF BT CCle.

.... Kn   CC1-3   Passin' Me By
.... Mry   CC2-2   Carney-Val In Rhythm
.... Kn   CC2-3   Carney-Val In Rhythm
.... Mry   CC3-1   Sam Pan
.... Mry   CC3-4   Sam Pan
.... Mry   CC4-1   Night Wind¹
.... Kn   CC4-2   Night Wind

¹*sa* "Finesse."

29 Dec 1944	(S)
New York City, NY	

BARNEY BIGARD & HIS ORCHESTRA
JTms, *BB*, CWn SCtl.

.... Slm   ¹   Rose Room
.... Slm   A Lull At Dawn
.... Slm   Blues In Barney's Flat

¹The master numbers for the above session could not be traced.

The above titles have been selected because of their Ellington Mood.

1944	(T)¹
U.S.A.	

ALL STAR BAND
Featuring: *RS*, SGld.

.... Vid   Jam Session   >>>

[1]From the motion picture "Helzapoppin'."

REX STEWART'S BIG EIGHT   26 Jan 1945   (S)
RS, LB, AS HC, EHwd UL JR KP, JS.   Los Angeles, CA

.... Cap   560   'Tain't Like That –vJS
.... Cap   561   Dutch Treat
.... Cap   562   Rexercise
.... Pau   563   Blue Jay –vJS
.... Mo   563 alt.   Blue Jay –vJS

BARNEY BIGARD & HIS ORCHESTRA   5 Feb 1945   (S)
JTms, BB, JGrn BT CCle.   New York City, NY

.... Kn   HL82-1   Rose Room
.... Mry   HL83-2   Bojangles

The above titles have been selected because of their Ellington Mood.

SONNY GREER & THE DUKE'S MEN   24 Feb 1945   (S)
TJ, BB OH, DBks FG RClr SG.   Los Angeles, CA

.... Cap   581   Mood Indigo
.... Mo   581 alt.   Mood Indigo
.... Cap   582   Bug In A Rug
.... Cap   583   The Mooche
.... Cap   583 alt.   The Mooche
.... Cap   584   Kandy Lamb

COOTIE WILLIAMS & HIS ORCHESTRA   26 Feb 1945   (S)
Big band, featuring *CW.*   New York City, NY

.... Hit   T501   I'm Beginning To See The Light –vTWrn

COOTIE WILLIAMS & HIS ORCHESTRA   19 Jul 1945   (S)
Big band, featuring *CW.*   New York City, NY

.... Cap   681   Everything But You

REX STEWART & HIS ORCHESTRA   30 Jul 1945   (S)
RS, TG, EBst CSct, DRiv BF JR JHrd.   New York City, NY

.... Pa   182-A   Big Chief Pawnee
.... Pa   182-B   Three Horn Parley
.... Pa   183-A   Dreamer's Blues
.... Pa   183-B   Shady Side Of The Street

TIMME ROSENKRANTZ & HIS BARONS   22 Aug 1945   (S)
OH JBwl CV HC, RNrv JJns JLvy SPwl.   New York City, NY

.... Ctl   W3344-1   Bouncy
.... Rem   W3344-2   Bouncy
.... Ctl   W3345   Blues At Dawn
.... Rem   [1]   Timme Time

[1]The master number could not be traced.

BRICK FLEAGLE & HIS ORCHESTRA
Big band, featuring *RS.*

.... IAC   ZZ4817-1   Cherry
.... IAC   ZZ4817-2   Do You Ever Think Of Me?
.... IAC   ZZ4817-3   Just You, Just Me
.... IAC   ZZ4817-4   I Cried For You
.... IAC   ZZ4818-1   I'm True To You
.... IAC   ZZ4818-2   Same Old Sheaves
.... IAC   ZZ4818-3   Double Dog House
.... IAC   ZZ4818-4   Dreamer's Blues
.... IAC   ZZ4819-1   Someday, Sweetheart
.... IAC   ZZ4819-2   Pastiche
.... IAC   ZZ4819-3   Wrap Your Troubles In Dreams

			5 Oct 1945 (S)
			New York City, NY

COUSIN JOE WITH LEONARD FEATHER'S HIPTET
Vcl, acc. by DV, *AS HC*, LF JShl LT JHrd.

....	Adn	[1]	Post War Future Blues –vCJoe
....	Adn		Larceny Hearted Woman –vCJoe
....	Adn		Just Another Woman –vCJoe
....	Adn		My Love Comes Tumblin' Down –vCJoe

[1]The master numbers for the above session could not be traced.

			15 Oct 1945 (S)
			New York City, NY

WILLIE BRYANT & THE TAB SMITH SEPTET
Vcl, acc. by *TJ*, TSm JHks, LF CWn BBwn WJn.

....	Apo	R1034	Blues Around The Clock –vWBrt, part 1
....	Apo	R1035	Blues Around The Clock –vWBrt, part 2
....	Apo	R1035 alt.	Blues Around The Clock –vWBrt, part 2
....	Apo	R1036	It's Over Because We're Through –vWBrt
....	Apo	R1037	Amateur Night In Harlem –vWBrt

			Oct 1945 (S)
			New York City, NY

LAUREL WATSON
Vcl, acc. by *TJ*, TSm HS, LF CWn JBwn.

| .... | Apo | R1039 | Kangaroo Blues –vLWsn |
| .... | Apo | R1041 | Honey In A Hurry –vLWsn |

			5 Nov 1945 (S)
			New York City, NY

SANDY WILLIAMS' BIG EIGHT
JTms, SWls, *JH HC*, JJns BF SW SMn.

....	HRS	1009	Mountain Air
....	HRS	1010	Sumpin' Jumpin' 'Round Here
....	HRS	1011	After Hours On Dream Street
....	HRS	1012	Chili Con Carney

			14+15 Nov 1945 (S)
			New York City, NY

DWIGHT "GATEMOUTH" MOORE
Vcl, acc. by DV, *JHtn* BJsn *HC*, SBkn AHll JHrd.

....	Ntl	NSC81	Did You Ever Love A Woman? –vDGM
....	Ntl	NCS82	I'm Going Way Back Home –vDGM
....	Ntl	NSC83	Isabel –vDGM
....	SJ	alt.	Isabel –vDGM
....	Ntl	NSC85	Walking My Blues Away –vDGM
....	Ntl	NSC86	Bum Dee Dah Ra Dee –vDGM
....	Ntl	NSC88	They Can't Do This To Me –DGM
....	SJ	alt.	They Can't Do This To Me –vDGM
....	SJ		I Put Her Out –vDGM
....	SJ	alt.	I Put Her Out –vDGM

			Nov 1945 (S)
			New York City, NY

JIMMY HAMILTON & THE DUKE'S MEN
RN, HChb, *JHtn OH HC*, JJns *OP* SCtl.

....	JS	BN268-1	Old Uncle Bud
....	BN	BN269-1	Blues For Clarinet
....	BN	BN270-1	Slapstick
....	BN	BN271-1	Blues In My Music Room

			1945 (S)
			New York City, NY

SAVANNAH CHURCHILL WITH AL KILLIAN & HIS ORCHESTRA
Vcl, acc. by AK, TY, ASs BJsn *HC*, MN JSmn GJns.

| .... | Man | [1] | Too Blue To Cry –vSChl |
| .... | Man | | I Can't Get Enough Of You –vSChl |

[1]The master numbers for the above session could not be traced.

			p 1945 (S)
			Unidentified location
			U.S.A.

ROBERTA LEE
Vcl, acc. by D'Artega & His Orchestra, featuring *RS*.

....	Sna	[1]	Moanin' Low –vRLee
....	Sna		You Don't Learn That In School –vRLee
....	Sna		My Man –vRLee
....	Sna		I Left My Sugar In Salt Lake City –vRLee

[1]The master numbers for the above session could not be traced.

JOHNNY BOTHWELL'S SWINGTET   1945/1946   (S)
RN, JBwl AE HC, EFkl JJst SMn.   New York City, NY

.... Sig   SRC145   Dear Max
.... Sig   SRC152   Chelsea Bridge

JIMMY JONES' BIG EIGHT   10 Jan 1946   (S)
JTms, LB, OH TN HC, JJns BT SMn.   New York City, NY

.... HRS   1021-2   Old Juice On The Loose
.... HRS   1022-2   Departure From Dixie
.... HRS   1023-1   A Woman's Got The Right To Change Her Mind
.... HRS   1024-2   Muddy Miss

METRONOME ALL STARS   15 Jan 1946   (S)
HE CW RS PCnd NH SBrm, TD WBrd BHrs JCH, BDF JH HF FP GA HC, TW TGrs BBr ChJ DT.   New York City, NY

.... Vi   D6VC5026-1   Look Out

COOTIE WILLIAMS & HIS ORCHESTRA   29 Jan 1946   (S)
Big band, featuring *CW.*   New York City, NY

.... Cap   909   Echoes Of Harlem

HARRY CARNEY'S BIG EIGHT   18 Mar 1946   (S)
JTms, LB, OH TN HC, JJns BT JCfd.   New York City, NY

.... HRS   1029   Minor Mirage
.... HRS   1030   Jamaica Rumble
.... HRS   1031   Shadowy Sands
.... Mo   1031 alt.   Shadowy Sands
.... HRS   1032   Candy Cane

MERCER ELLINGTON OCTET WITH JACQUES BUTLER
ME JBlr, LB, AS HC, LF MO BPtn HJck.

.... Adn   LGF1001   She's Got The Blues For Sale –vJBlr
.... Adn   LGF1002   The Willies
.... Adn   LGF1003   Messy Bessie
.... Adn   LGF1004   Ditty à la Dizzy

AL HIBBLER WITH THE HARRY CARNEY ALL STARS   *p* Jul/Aug 1946   (S)
Vcl, acc. by *TJ HB, RP JMV HC, LWC RHtn RClr HWst.*   Los Angeles, CA

.... Adn   [1]   Fat And Forty –vAH
.... Adn   I Surrender, Dear –vAH

[1]The master numbers for the above session could not be traced.

AL HIBBLER WITH THE HARRY CARNEY ALL STARS   *p* Jul/Aug 1946   (S)
Vcl, acc. by *TJ HB, RP JMV HC, LWC RHtn RClr HWst.*   Los Angeles, CA

.... Adn   RR-2700-5   Don't Take Your Love From Me –vAH
.... Adn   RR-2701-2   I Got It Bad –vAH
.... Adn   [1]   How Long –vAH
.... Adn   S'posin' –vAH

[1]The master numbers for the last two titles could not be traced.

RUSSELL PROCOPE'S BIG SIX   Autumn 1946   (S)
HB, RP JHee, BKle JSms DBst.   New York City, NY

.... HRS   1060   Bottle It
.... HRS   1061   Denzil's Best
.... HRS   1062   Right Foot, Then Left Foot
.... HRS   1063   Four Wheel Drive

ESQUIRE ALL-AMERICAN AWARD WINNERS   12 Dec 1946   (S)
ChS BCtn, JJJ, CHwk HC, TW JC ChJ SWsn.   New York City, NY

.... Vi   D6VB3369-1   Indiana Winter   >>>

> BCtn omitted.

.... Vi   D6VB3370-1   Indian Summer

> BCtn added.

.... Vi   D6VB3371-1   Blow Me Down
.... Vi   D6VB3372-1   Buckin' The Blues

CHUBBY JACKSON & HIS JACKSONVILLE SEVEN
BCtn omitted, otherwise same personnel.

.... Vi   D6VB3373-1   Dixieland Stomp

17 Dec 1946   (S)
New York City, NY

METRONOME ALL STARS
ChS, *LB, JH* CHwk *HC*, NKC BAhn ESaf BRch, JChr FS.

.... Co   37177-1   Sweet Lorraine –vFS
.... Co   37177-2   Sweet Lorraine –vFS
.... Co   37178-1   Nat Meets June –vJChr NKC
.... Co   37178-2   Nat Meets June –vJChr NKC

Early/mid-1947   (P)
Unidentified location
U.S.A.

BILLY STRAYHORN & THE ELLINGTONIANS
HB RN, JHtn RP, BS FG OP.

.... Az   Double Ruff

Jun 1947   (S)
New York City, NY

JOHNNY HODGES & THE ELLINGTONIANS
TJ, LB, JH AS, BS OP WDP.

.... Vge   M1009   A Flower Is A Lovesome Thing
.... Vge   M1010   Frisky
.... Vge   M1011   Long Horn Blues
.... Vge   M1012   Far Away Blues
.... Vge   M1013   Who Struck John?
.... Vge   M1014   It Could Happen To A Dream
.... Vge   M1015   June's Jumpin'
.... Vge   M1016   Violet Blue

c Mid-1947   (S)
New York City, NY

AL HIBBLER WITH THE HARRY CARNEY ALL STARS
Vcl, acc. by *RN, JHtn AS HC, BS* JR FJck.

.... Snr   EB1001   Fat And Forty –vAH
.... Snr   EB1002   Solitude –vAH
.... Snr   EB1003   My Little Brown Book –vAH
.... Snr   EB1004   Feather Roll Blues

c Mid-1947   (S)
Hollywood, CA

BILLY STRAYHORN
Piano solo.

.... Vrv   ¹   Halfway To Dawn
.... Vrv   Tailspin
.... Vrv   Halfway To Dawn

¹The master numbers for the above session could not be traced.

1947   (S)
New York City, NY

AL HIBBLER WITH MERCER ELLINGTON & HIS ORCHESTRA
Vcl, acc. by WSct DB KDhm BRoy, ClR CJon, JFds MLn AMC HRch, LHsn JBjm HJck.

.... Snr   SU-1018   My Eva Lovin' Baby –vAH
.... Snr   SU-1019   Summertime –vAH

27 Sep 1947¹   (S)
Vancouver, BC

IVIE ANDERSON
IA interviewed by Bill Hill.

....   Interview

¹Radio station CKMD. One source suggests that this interview was done in Oct 1948.

c Autumn 1947   (S)
Detroit, MI

AL HIBBLER & HIS ORCHESTRA
Vcl, acc. by TJ, *JH AS HC, BS OP* SG.

.... Mir   SU-2029   Trees –vAH
.... Mir   SU-2030   Lover Come Back To Me –vAH   >>>

.... Snr   SU-2031   Tonight I Shall Sleep –vAH

c Autumn 1947	(S)
New York City, NY	

JOHNNY HODGES & THE ELLINGTONIANS
HB, JH AS HC, BS OP SG.

.... Vge   M2032   Searsy's Blues
.... Vge   M2033   A Little Taste
.... Vge   M2034   Let The Zoomers Drool
.... Vge   M2035   Charlotte Russe

c Autumn 1947   (S)
New York City, NY

THE ELLINGTON GANG
LB, JH HC, JJns BT BS.

.... Wax   133   Key Largo

JOHNNY HODGES TRIO
JH, ?BS BT.

.... Wax   134   You're Driving Me Crazy

HARRY CARNEY ALL STARS
LB, JH HC, JJns BT BS.

.... Wax   135   Why Was I Born?
.... Wax   136   Triple Play

5 Dec 1947   (S)
Cincinnati, OH

IVORY JOE HUNTER
HB, TG, RP, IJH OP SG.

.... Kg   5292   Don't Know –vIJH
.... Kg   5293   I Like It –vIJH
.... Kg   5294   False Friend Blues –vIJH
.... Kg   5285   Don't Fall In Love With Me –vIJH
.... Kg   5296   Send Me, Pretty Mama –vIJH
.... Kg   5297   What Did You Do To Me? –vIJH
.... Kg   5298   Stop Rockin' That Train –vIJH
.... Kg   5299   Siesta With Sonny –vIJH

1 Jul 1948   (S)
London, England

RAY NANCE & THE ELLINGTONIANS[1]
RN, BRd* LRx* GGwn* RPts.*

.... Esq   58   Moon Mist
.... Esq   59   Sometimes I'm Happy
.... Esq   60   I Can't Give You Anything But Love
.... Esq   61   Blues For Duke

[1]Actually the *Ray Ellington Quartet* (no relation).
*The real names of the musicians are Dick Katz (p), Lauderic Caton (gt), Coleridge Good (b), Ray Ellington (dr), who were using pseudonyms for this session to protect their identity for commercial reasons.

1948/1949   (S)
Chicago, IL

AL HIBBLER & THE ELLINGTONIANS
Vcl, acc. by RN, TG, BW, BS JR FJck

.... Snr   SU-2132   Ghost Of Love –vAH
.... Snr   SU-2134   Hey, Baby –vAH
.... Chs   SU-2135   It Don't Mean A Thing –vAH

1948/1949   (S)
Chicago, IL

AL HIBBLER & HIS ORCHESTRA
Vcl, acc. by RN, TG, BW, BS JR FJck.

.... Chs   SU-2140   What Will I Tell My Heart? –vAH
.... Snr   SU-2141   Poor Butterfly –vAH
.... Snr   SU-2142   I Love You –vAH
.... Snr   SU-2143   By The River Ste. Marie –vAH

28 Feb 1949   (S)
Los Angeles, CA

IVORY JOE HUNTER
HB RN, TG, RP, IJH WMsl SG.

.... Kg   5683   Waiting In Vain –vIJH
.... Kg   5684   It's You, Just You –vIJH
.... Kg   5685   That's The Gal For Me –vIJH
.... Kg   5686   Changing Blues –vIJH
.... Kg   5687   Guess Who –vIJH   >>>

.... Kg   5688   Too Late –vIJH

			Spring 1949 (S)
			New York City, NY

HARRY CARNEY ALL STARS
HC, BS FG OP SG, plus strings.

.... Mry   2077-1   Sono
.... Vrv   2077 alt.   Sono[1]
.... Mry   2078-6   Frustration

[1]CD Vrv 314.521.661-2 contains the above titles, but gives master nos. 5001-2, 5001-4, and 5002 as probable.

12 May 1949	(S)
New York City, NY	

TYREE GLENN ALL STARS
TG, JHtn JH HC, BS JD WMsl SG.

.... Aby   G669   Sultry Serenade
.... Aby   G670   Dusty Serenade

15 Jul 1949	(S)
Cincinnati, OH	

IVORY JOE HUNTER
HB, TG, JH RP, IJH WMsl SG.

.... Kg   5752   Please, Don't Cry Anymore –vIJH
.... Kg   5753   I Got Your Water On –vIJH
.... Kg   5754   I Quit My Pretty Mama –vIJH
.... Kg   5755   Lying Woman Blues –vIJH
.... Kg   5756   I Have No Reason To Complain –vIJH

16 Aug 1949	(S)
Cincinnati, OH	

IVORY JOE HUNTER
pp HB, TG, JH RP, IJH WMsl SG.

.... Kg   5765   Jealous Heart –vIJH

18 Aug 1949	(S)
New York City, NY	

CAB CALLOWAY & HIS CAB JIVERS
Vcl, acc. by *JJo, TG, HJsn ST, DRiv MHtn PF.*

.... Bb   DBA2285   Rooming House Boogie –vCCwy
.... Bb   DBA2286   I Beeped When I Shoulda Bopped –vCCwy

18 Sep 1949	(S)
New York City, NY	

RUTH BROWN WITH BUDD JOHNSON'S ORCHESTRA
Vcl, acc. by *HB, TG,* VBB BJsn EC, EWtn LGkn RHns.

.... Atc   A290   Love Me, Baby –vRBwn
.... Atc   A291-1   I'll Get Along –vRBwn
.... Atc   A291-2   I'll Get Along –vRBwn
.... Atc   S292   Happiness Is Just A Thing Called Joe –vRBwn
.... Atc   A293   Rockin' Blues –vRBwn

11 Feb 1950	(S)
New York City, NY	

CHUBBY KEMP & HER ALL STARS
Vcl, acc. by *JHtn JH HC, BS WMsl SG.*

.... Mer   M4000   Hello, Little Boy –vCK
.... Mer   M4001   The Greatest There Is –vCK
....   M4002   [Don't You Know I Care? –vCK]
....   M4003   [I Got It Bad –vCK]

14 Apr 1950	(S)
Paris, France	

HAROLD BAKER ENSEMBLE
HB, QJ, JH DBs, RFo WMsl BBld.

.... Sw   OSW671   St. Germain Des Pres

JOHNNY HODGES & HIS ORCHESTRA
Same personnel.

.... Sw   OSW672   Good To The Last Drop
.... Sw   OSW673   I Only Wish I Knew
.... Sw   OSW674   We Fooled You

15 Apr 1950	(S)
Paris, France	

JOHNNY HODGES & HIS ORCHESTRA
HB, QJ, JHtn JH DBs, RFo WMsl SG.

.... Vge   V3054   Jump, That's All
.... Vge   V3055   Last Leg Blues
.... Vge   V3056   Last Leg Blues   >>>

....	Vge	V3057	Nix It, Mix It[1]
....	Vge	V3058	Time On My Hands
....	MJR	V3058 alt.	Time On My Hands

[1]*aka* "Prelude To A Mood."

NELSON WILLIAMS & HIS ORCHESTRA
NW HB AK ER RN, ASms WMsl BBld.

....	Md	5201-1	Big Al
....	Vge	5201-2	Big Al
....	Md	5202	Five Horn Groove II
....	Md	5203	Five Horn Groove III
....	Md	5204	Five Horn Groove IV
....	Md	5205	Five Horn Groove I
....	Md	5206-1	Chumpa Leezy[1]
....	Vge	5206-2	Chumpa Leezy

[1]Phonetic spelling of *Champs Elysées.*

The alternate takes of the above titles have been edited and pieced together for the reissue on LP JLg JL94. In the process, some of the music has fallen by the wayside.

	19 Apr 1950 (S)
	New York City, NY

AL HIBBLER
Vcl, acc. by Billy Kyle's Orchestra.

....	Atc	A406	Dedicated To You –vAH
....	Atc	A408	Danny Boy –vAH
....	Atc	A409	If I Knew You Were There –vAH
....	Atc	A410	Song Of The Wanderer –vAH

Master #A407 could not be traced.

	20 Apr 1950 (S)
	Paris, France

JOHNNY HODGES & HIS ORCHESTRA
HB, QJ, JHtn JH, RFo WMsl BBld.

....	Vge	V3066	Run About
....	Vge	V3067	Wishing And Waiting
....	Vge	V3068	Get That Geet
....	Vge	V3069	That's Grant
....	Vge	V3070	Skip It

	1 Jun 1950 (S)
	Copenhagen, Denmark

JOHNNY HODGES & HIS ORCHESTRA
HB, QJ, JHtn JH, OF ChJn BBld, *CK.*

....	Ton	3723	Mellow Mood
....	Ton	3724	How I Wish I Was Around –vCK
....	Ton	3725	I Met A Guy –vCK
....	Ton	3726	Tea For Two

	20 Jun 1950 (S)
	Paris, France

JOHNNY HODGES & HIS ORCHESTRA
HB, QJ, JH, RFo WMsl BBld.

....	Vge	V4015	Perdido
....	Vge	V4016	In The Shade Of The Old Apple Tree
....	Vge	V4017	Mood Indigo
....	Vge	V4018	Sweet Lorraine
....	Vge	V4019	Bean Bag Boogie[1]
....	Vge	V4020	Hop, Skip And Jump

[1]*aka* "Rendez-vous At The Hot Club."

	25 Oct 1950 (S)
	New York City, NY

AL HIBBLER
Vcl, acc. by Billy Taylor's Orchestra, including *TG.*

....	Atc	A527	The Blues Came Falling Down –vAH
....	Atc	A528	Old Folks –vAH
....	Atc	A529	I'm Traveling Light –vAH

	1950 or Oct 1951 (P)
	Hotel Kenmore
	Boston, MA

JOHNNY HODGES & FRIENDS
Small band, featuring *HB, LB, JH AS, LL.*

....	Egm		Nothin' Shakin' But The Bacon
....	Egm		Let's Have A Little Taste
....	Egm		The Sheik Of Araby >>>

....	Egm		Very Well, Thank You
....	Egm		Coffee Time
....	Egm		Tea For Two
....	Egm		Sophisticated Lady
....	Egm		How High The Moon
....	Egm		Things Ain't What They Used To Be

> LL piano solo.

....	Egm		I Cover The Waterfront

> Entire band.

....	Egm		Bewitched, Bothered And Bewildered
....	Egm		Man With A Horn
....	Egm		Very Well, Thank You
....	Egm		The Rabbit's Jump[1]
....	Egm		On The Sunny Side Of The Street
....	Egm		The Jeep Is Jumpin'
....	Egm		Castle Rock

[1]*aka* "You Blew Out The Flame In My Heart."

The above is a selective compilation from three half-hour broadcasts.

15 Jan 1951	(S)
New York City, NY	

JOHNNY HODGES & HIS ORCHESTRA
NW, LB, JH AS, LL AMK *SG.*

....	Clf	C477-2	The Rabbit's Jump
....	Clf	C478-3	Something To Pat Your Foot To
....	Clf	C479-1	Blue Fantasia
....	Clf	C480-2	My Reward

28 Feb 1951	(S)
New York City, NY	

JOHNNY HODGES & HIS ORCHESTRA
EBry, LB, JH AS, LL LT *SG.*

....	Ngr	511-1	Good Queen Bess
....	Clf	512-3	Jeep's Blues
....	Ngr	513-2	Solitude
....	Ngr	514-1	The Jeep Is Jumpin'
....	Vrv	514 alt.	The Jeep Is Jumpin'

3 Mar 1951	(S)
New York City, NY	

JOHNNY HODGES & HIS ORCHESTRA
EBry, LB, JH AS, LL LT *SG.*

....	Clf	515-3	Castle Rock
....	Vrv	516-3	Sophisticated Lady
....	Vrv	517-1	Globe Trotter
....	Vrv	518-2	A Gentle Breeze

27 Jun 1951	(S)
New York City, NY	

AL HIBBLER
Vcl, acc. by Jimmy Mundy's Orchestra, including *PG.*

....	Atc	A613	Now I Lay Me Down To Dream –vAH
....	Atc	A614	This Is Always –vAH
....	Atc	A615	I Won't Tell A Soul I Love You –vAH

19 Jul 1951	(S)
p New York City, NY	

AL HIBBLER & THE ELLINGTONIANS
Vcl, acc. by *JT, JHtn WS, BS WMsl LBsn.*

....	Mer	[1]	Trees –vAH
....	Mer		Summertime –vAH
....	Mer		Ol' Man River –vAH
....	Mer		On A Slow Boat To China –vAH

[1]The master numbers for the above session could not be traced.

21 Sep 1951	(S)
New York City, NY	

AL SEARS & HIS ORCHESTRA
EBry, LB, JH AS, LL LT JMsl.

....	Kg	K8056	Baltimore Bounce
....	Kg	K8061	Now Ride "D" Train
....	Kg	K8062	Azores
....	Kg	K8063	Groove Station
....	Kg	K8064	Marshall Plan >>>

	Kg	K8065	Berry Well
....	Kg	K8066	Steady Eddie
....	Kg	K8067	Nell Don't Wear No Button-Up Shoes

13 Jan 1952   (S)
New York City, NY

JOHNNY HODGES & HIS ORCHESTRA
EBry, *LB, JH AS,* LL LT JMsl.

....	Clf	656-3	Sideways
....	Clf	657-1	A Pound Of Blues
....	Clf	658-3	Wham
....	Clf	659-3	Who's Excited?

17 Jan 1952   (S)
New York City, NY

JOHNNY HODGES & HIS ORCHESTRA
EBry, *LB, JH AS,* LL LT JMsl.

....	Clf	660-2	Sweeping The Blues Away
....	Ngr	661-2	Day Dream
....	Ngr	662-1	Standing Room Only
....	Clf	663-4	Below The Azores

26 Jan 1952   (S)
New York City, NY

JOHNNY HODGES & HIS ORCHESTRA
EBry, *LB, JH AS,* LL BRnd SG.

....	Clf	670-4	Tenderly
....	Ngr	671-5	Sweet Georgia Brown
....	Clf	672-3	Duke's Blues
....	Clf	673-6	Tea For Two

Feb 1952   (S)
Los Angeles, CA

LOUIE BELLSON & THE JUST JAZZ ALL STARS
CT JGrs, JT, WS WGry *HC,* BS WMsl LBsn.

....	Cap	9939	The Jeep Is Jumpin'
....	Cap	9940	Passion Flower
....	Cap	9941	Johnny Come Lately
....	Cap	9942	Sticks
....	Cap	9943	Punkin
....	Cap	9944	Eyes
....	Cap	9945	Rainbow
....	Cap	9946	Shadows

1 Apr 1952   (S)
Los Angeles, CA

JOHNNY HODGES & HIS ORCHESTRA
EBry, *LB, JH AS,* TBrn RBrn JHrd.

....	Mry	779-1	What's I'm Gotchere
....	Clf	779-2	What's I'm Gotchere

AL HIBBLER WITH JOHNNY HODGES & HIS ORCHESTRA
Vcl, acc. by same as above, plus ChS, as.

....	Clf	780-2	Please –vAH
....	Clf	781-3	Believe It, Beloved –vAH
....	Clf	782-3	There Is No Greater Love –vAH[1]
....	Clf	783-5	It Must Be True –vAH

[1]*sa* "No Greater Love."

Jun 1952
Los Angeles, CA

ALL STAR BAND
ChS, *JH* BCrt ChP *BW* FP, OPsn BK RBrn JHrd.

....	Clf	802-2	Jam Blues
....	Clf	803-3	What Is This Thing Called Love?
....	Clf	804-2	Ballad Medley[1]
....	Clf	805-2	Funky Blues

[1]Including: All The Things You Are; The Nearness Of You; Dearly Beloved; I'll Get By; Everything Happens To Me; The Man I Love; What's New?; Someone To Watch Over Me; Isn't It Romantic.

17 Jul 1952   (S)
San Francisco, CA

AL HIBBLER WITH JOHNNY HODGES & HIS ORCHESTRA
Vcl, acc. by EBry, *LB, JH* FP, LL TBrn RClr JHrd.

....	Ngr	799-4	This Is My Night To Love –vAH >>>

JOHNNY HODGES & HIS ORCHESTRA
AH omitted, otherwise same personnel.

....	Ngr	800-1		I Got It Bad
....	Ngr	801-8		Nothin' Yet

22 Jul 1952 (S)
Los Angeles, CA

JOHNNY HODGES & HIS ORCHESTRA
EBry, LB, JH BW, TBrn RClr JHrd.

....	Clf	806-2		Rosanne
....	Mry	806-6		Rosanne

AL HIBBLER WITH JOHNNY HODGES & HIS ORCHESTRA
Vcl, acc. by same as above.

....	Ngr	607-9		This Love Of Mine –vAH

JOHNNY HODGES & HIS ORCHESTRA
AH omitted, otherwise same personnel.

....	Ngr	608-5		Hodge Podge
....	Clf	809-1		Jappa

11 Dec 1952 (S)
New York City, NY

JOHNNY HODGES & HIS ORCHESTRA
EBry, LB, JH BW RW, TBrn BRnd AWkr.

....	Clf	952-1		Thru For The Night
....	Clf	953-3		Come Sunday
....	Clf	954-1		The Sheik Of Araby
....	Clf	955-7		Latino

Dec 1952 (P)
Apollo Theater
New York City, NY

JOHNNY HODGES & HIS ORCHESTRA
EBry, LB, JH ts, TBrn BRnd AWkr.

....	Sn			Wham

1952 (S)
Chicago, IL

DINAH WASHINGTON
Vcl, acc. by Jimmy Cobb's Orchestra, featuring CT, RP PG.

....	Mry	9247		My Song –vDWtn
....	Mry	9248		Half As Much –vDWtn
....	Mry	9249		I Cried For You –vDWtn
....	Mry	9250		Gambler's Blues

15 Jan 1953 (S)
Detroit, MI

JIMMY HAMILTON WITH THE EMITT SLAY TRIO
JHtn, BWht ESly LJck.

....	PVS	1188-2		All Too Soon
....	PVS	1189-2		Ellington Theft
....	Sts	1190-1		Big 50[1]
....	Sts	1191-3		Rockaway Special

[1]aka "Texas Special."

17 Mar 1953 (S)
Unidentified location
U.S.A.

DINAH WASHINGTON
Vcl, acc. by CT, GChp, RH ED PQu, JDvs JMce KBts ET.

....	Mry	10242		Short John –vDWtn
....	Mry	10243		Old Man's Darling –vDWtn
....	Em	10244		Love For Sale –vDWtn
....	Mry	10245		Our Love Is Here To Stay -vDWtn

c Apr 1953 (S)
Los Angeles, CA

GERALD WILSON & HIS ORCHESTRA
Big band, featuring CT, BWmn, PG.

....	Frl	F1141		Mambo Mexicano I
....	Frl	F1142		Mambo Mexicano II
....	Frl	F1143		Algerian Fantasy I
....	Frl	F1144		Algerian Fantasy II

c Apr 1953 (S)
Los Angeles, CA

GERALD WILSON & HIS ORCHESTRA
Big band, featuring CT, BWmn, PG.

....	Kg	F1146		Lotus Land I >>>

....	Kg	F1147	Lotus Land II
....	Kg	F1148	Theme
....	Kg	F1149	Since We Said Goodbye

c Apr 1953 (S)
Los Angeles, CA

GERALD WILSON & HIS ORCHESTRA
Big band, featuring *CT, BWmn, PG.*

....	Kg	F1156	Romance
....	Kg	F1157	Bull Fighter
....	Kg	F1158	Black Rose

21 May 1953 (S)
New York City, NY

BEN WEBSTER QUINTET
BW, OPsn BK RBrn JHrd.

| .... | Met | [1] | Cotton Tail |

[1]The master number could not be traced.

This title was selected because of its Ellington Mood.

17 Jun 1953 (S)
New York City, NY

DINAH WASHINGTON
Vcl, acc. by *CT,* GChp, *RH* ED PQu, JDvs KBts ET.

| .... | Em | 9870 | Am I Blue? –vDWtn |
| .... | Em | 9871 | Pennies From Heaven –vDWtn |

30 Jun 1953 (S)
Chicago, IL

JIMMY HAMILTON'S JAZZ ENSEMBLE
CT CA, JHtn HJsn MKE, ?EWrn, DRse. Otherwise unidentified personnel drawn from the bands of Duke Ellington and Red Saunders.

....	PVS	1347-6	Blue And Orange Birds And Bells –vDRse
....	Dk	1348-6	There Will Never Be Another You –vDRse
....	PVS	1349	Love Comes But Once
....	Dk	1350-5	Yes, Indeed –vDRse
....	PVS	1350-6	Yes, Indeed –vDRse
....	PVS	1351	Blues In Your Flat
....	Dk	[1]	The Tattoed Bride[2]

[1]The master number could not be traced.
[2]"Aberdeen" part only.

The titles with Della Reese were issued as *Della Reese with Jimmy Hamilton Orchestra.*

2 Sep 1953 (S)
New York City, NY

ALL STAR BAND
RE DG, *JH* IJ FP *BW,* LHpt OPsn RBrn BRch.

....	Clf	[1]	The "C" Jam Blues
....	Clf	10530	Blue Lou
....	Clf	10531	Just You, Just Me
....	Clf	[1]	Ballad Medley[2]

> DG, *BW* omitted.

| .... | Clf | [1] | Jammin' At Clef |
| .... | Clf | [1] | Rose Room |

[1]The master numbers of this session could not be traced.
[2]Including: Tenderly; I've Got The World On A String; What's New?; I Got It Bad; Don't Blame Me; Imagination; Someone To Watch Over Me, Body And Soul; She's Funny That Way.

27 Sep 1953 (S)
New York City, NY

JOHNNY HODGES & HIS ORCHESTRA
EBry, *LB, JH* ACrk, LL RBrn JHrd.

....	Ngr	1316-6	Easy Going Bounce
....	Ngr	1317-1	Indiana
....	Ngr	1318-4	Johnny's Blues

8 Dec 1953 (S)
New York City, NY

BEN WEBSTER & HIS ORCHESTRA
RE, BCrt *BW,* OPsn HEls RBrn ASt.

| .... | Met | [1] | Don't Get Around Much Anymore |

[1]The master number could not be traced.

This title has been selected because of its Ellington Mood.

After the introduction of the LP it became increasingly difficult to trace the master numbers for individual titles, because they were not put on the stamp or mentioned in the liner notes, but kept in recording ledgers of the record companies. In some cases the numbering system was changed completely. It is therefore that from here on no explanation will be given for missing numbers.

| | | | | 6 Feb 1954 | (S) |
| | | | | New York City, NY | |

PAUL GONSALVES ALL STARS
CT, PKi *PG*, JMce ChJ GMlr.

....	Em	10358	Don't Blame Me
....	Em	10359	It Don't Mean A Thing
....	Wi		Everything Happens To Me
....	Wi		Take Nine

| | | | 9 Apr 1954 | (S) |
| | | | New York City, NY | |

JOHNNY HODGES & HIS ORCHESTRA
HB, LB, JH BW, LL LT OJsn.

....	Clf	1545-4	In A Mellotone
....	Ngr	1546-2	I Let A Song Go Out Of My Heart
....	Ngr	1547-1	Don't Get Around Much Anymore

| | | | 28 May 1954 | (S) |
| | | | New York City, NY | |

BEN WEBSTER WITH STRINGS
Big band, featuring *BW, BS* LBsn.

....	Ngr	1721	Our Love Is Here To Stay
....	Ngr	1722	It Happens To Be Me
....	Ngr	1723	All Too Soon
....	Ngr	1724	Chelsea Bridge
....	Ngr		Almost Like Being In Love

| | | | 2 Jun 1954 | (S) |
| | | | New York City, NY | |

"CATS"
CT, UG, LTho, HSvr TFlw PHth KC.

| .... | MGM | | The Man I Love |

> "Chicks" (tp, hp, vib gt b dr) added.

....	MGM		Mamblues
....	MGM		Cat Meets Chick
....	MGM		Anything You Can Do

| | | | 15 Jun 1954 | (S) |
| | | | New York City, NY | |

DINAH WASHINGTON
Vcl, acc. by *CT*, GChp, *RH* ED, JDvs JMce KBts ET.

....	Em	10618	I Let A Song Go Out Of My Heart –vDWtn
....	Em	10619	A Foggy Day –vDWtn
....	Em	10620	Bye-Bye Blues –vDWtn
....	Em	10621	Blue Skies –vDWtn

| | | | 5 Aug 1954 | (S) |
| | | | New York City, NY | |

JOHNNY HODGES & HIS ORCHESTRA
HB, LB, JH JCtr, CCbs JWlm *LBsn.*

....	Ngr	1860-1	Burgundy Walk
....	Ngr	1861-1	On The Sunny Side Of The Street
....	Ngr	1862-1	Sweet As Bear Meat
....	Ngr	1863-1	Used To Be Duke

> *JHtn* replaces JCtr, *HC* added.

| .... | Ngr | 1864-3 | Warm Valley |
| .... | Ngr | 1865-1 | Madam Butterfly |

> JCtr replaces *JHtn, HC* omitted.

| .... | Ngr | 1866-1 | All Of Me |
| .... | Ngr | 1867-1 | Skokian |

> *JHtn* replaces JCtr, *HC* added.

| .... | Ngr | 1868-1 | Medley[1] |

[1]Including: Sweet Lorraine; Time On My Hands; Smoke Gets In Your Eyes; Autumn In New York; Poor Butterfly; All Of Me.

		Summer 1954	(P)
		Unidentified location	
		U.S.A.	

JOHNNY HODGES & HIS ORCHESTRA
Small band, featuring *HB, LB, JH* JCtr.

| .... | Egm | | Sideways   >>> |

....	Egm		Castle Rock
....	Egm		In A Mellotone
....	Egm		I've Got A Mind To Ramble –vcl
....	Egm		Don't Cry, Baby –vcl
....	Egm		Globe Trotter
....	Egm		Don't Blame Me

14 Aug 1954   (S)
Los Angeles, CA

DINAH WASHINGTON
Vcl, acc. by *CT* CBrn MF, HGlr HLd, RPI JMce KBts GMrw MR.

....	Em	10900	[1] What Is This Thing Called Love?
....	Em	10901	I've Got You Under My Skin –vDWtn
....	Em	10902	No More –vDWtn
....	Em	10903	[1] Move
....	Em	10904	Darn That Dream –vDWtn
....	Em	10905	[1] You Go To My Head
....	Em	10906	[1] It Might As Well Be Spring
....	Em	10907	Lover Come Back To Me –vDWtn
....	Em	10908	Ballad Medley[2]
....	Em	10909	[1] Ballad Medley[3]

[1] These titles have been issued by Em as "Jam Session."
[2] Including: Alone Together; Summertime; Come Rain Or Come Shine –vDWtn.
[3] Including: My Funny Valentine; Don't Worry 'Bout Me; Bess You Is My Woman.

c Oct 1954   (S)
New York City, NY

JIMMY HAMILTON'S JAZZ ENSEMBLE
ER, *JHtn* LTho, EK SGrs OP OJsn.

....	Ur		Salute To Charlie Parker
....	Ur		Mood Indigo
....	Ur		Easy To Love
....	Ur		Prelude To A Mood[1]

[1] sa "Blues" (31 May 1950); "Nix It, Mix It."

c Oct 1954   (S)
New York City, NY

LUCKY THOMPSON & HIS ORCHESTRA
JHtn LTho, BTlr OP OJsn.

....	Ur		Tune For Tex
....	Ur		Where Or When
....	Ur		Kamman's A-Comin'
....	Ur		Ever So Easy
....	Ur		Mr. E-Z

c Oct 1954   (S)
New York City, NY

JIMMY HAMILTON'S JAZZ ENSEMBLE
CT, JHtn, BGbs SGrs OP OJsn.

....	Ur		I Get A Kick Out Of You
....	Ur		Blues In My Music Room
....	Ur		I Can't Give You Anything But Love
....	Ur		Chuckles
....	Ur		Bohemia After Dark
....	Ur		Blues For Clarinet
....	Ur		Solitude
....	Ur		What Am I Here For?

c Dec 1954   (S)
New York City, NY

CLARK TERRY SEPTET
CT, JCld, CPn, HSvr *WMsl* ABky.

| .... | | -1/-2 | [Money In The Bank] |

14 Dec 1954   (S)
New York City, NY

HARRY CARNEY'S BIG EIGHT
RN TM, *JHtn HC,* LL BBr *WMsl* LBsn.

....	Clf	2126	Moonlight On The Ganges
....	Clf	2127	We're In Love Again
....	Clf		I Got It Bad
....	Clf		A Ghost Of A Chance
....	Clf		Take The "A" Train
....	Clf		It Had To Be You
....	Clf		Chalmeu
....	Clf		Fantasy

				15 Dec 1954 (S) New York City, NY

BEN WEBSTER WITH RALPH BURNS' ORCHESTRA
Big band, featuring *BW, WMsl* LBsn.

....	Ngr	2134	Do Nothin' Till You Hear From Me
....	Ngr	2135	Prelude To A Kiss
....	Ngr	2136	Willow Weep For Me
....	Ngr	2137	Come Rain Or Come Shine

17 Dec 1954 (S)
New York City, NY

OSCAR PETTIFORD & HIS ORCHESTRA
CT JWld, JCld, DS *JHtn* DBnk, EK OP OJsn.

....	Bth	Jack The Bear
....	Bth	Tamalpais
....	Bth	Chuckles
....	Bth	Mood Indigo
....	Bth	Time On My Hands
....	Bth	Swing Until The Girls Come Home

3 Jan 1955 (S)
New York City, NY

CLARK TERRY SEPTET
CT, JCld, CPn, HSvr *WMsl* OP ABky.

....	Em	11094	Double Play
....	Em	11095	Slow Boat
....	Em	11096	Swahili
....	Em	11097	Co-Op

4 Jan 1955 (S)
New York City, NY

CLARK TERRY SEPTET
CT, JCld, CPn, HSvr *WMsl* OP ABky.

....	Em	11098	The Countess
....	Em	11099	Chuckles
....	Em	11100	Tuma
....	Em	11101	Kitten

7 Jan 1955 (S)
New York City, NY

JOHNY HODGES & HIS ORCHESTRA
HB, *LB, JH* ACrk, LL JWlm LBsn.

....	Ngr	2149-3	Rose Room
....	Ngr	2150-4	Blues For Basie
....	Ngr	2151-1	Mood Indigo
....	Ngr	2152	Squaty Roo
....	Ngr	2153	Perdido

Early 1955 (S)
New York City, NY

REX STEWART & HIS ORCHESTRA
RS, LB, HJsn DBnk, HJo MHtn OJsn.

....	GA	Boy Meets Horn
....	GA	Take The "A" Train
....	GA	Solitude
....	GA	Mood Indigo
....	GA	Don't Get Around Much Anymore
....	GA	I Let A Song Go Out Of My Heart

Early 1955 (S)
New York City, NY

REX STEWART & HIS ORCHESTRA
RS, TG, CHwk, CHks BBr ASh CCle.

| .... | GA | Perdido |
| .... | GA | Caravan |

15 Mar 1955 (S)
New York City, NY

DINAH WASHINGTON
Vcl, acc. by *CT*, JCld, PQu CPn, WK BGbr KBts JCbb.

....	Em	11401	I Could Write A Book –vDWtn
....	Em	11402	Make The Man Love Me –vDWtn
....	Em	11403	Blue Gardenia –vDWtn
....	Em	11404	You Don't Know What Love Is –vDWtn

17 Mar 1955 (S)
New York City, NY

DINAH WASHINGTON
Vcl, acc. by *CT,* JCld, PQu CPn, WK BGbr KBts, JCbb.

| .... | Em | 11405 | My Old Flame –vDWtn   >>> |

....	Em	11406	Easy Living –vDWtn
....	Em	11407	I Get A Kick Out Of You –vDWtn
....	Em	11408	This Can't Be Love –vDWtn
....	Em	11409	A Cottage For Sale
....	Mry	11410	I Did Die –vDWtn
....	Mry		If I Had You –vDWtn

8/9 Jul 1955   (S)
New York City, NY

MILES DAVIS QUINTET
MD, *BWmn,* TChs CM EJ.

....	Dbt		Nature Boy
....	Dbt		Alone Together
....	Dbt		There's No You
....	Dbt		Easy Living

8 Sep 1955   (S)
New York City, NY

JOHNNY HODGES & HIS ORCHESTRA
CT, LB, JHtn JH HC, BS JW SG.

....	Ngr	2500-4	Honey Bunny
....	Ngr	2501-2	Passion[1]
....	Ngr	2502-2	Pretty Little Girl
....	Ngr	2503-1	No Use Kickin'
....	Ngr	2504-2	Medley[2]
....	Ngr	2505-1	Scufflin'

[1]*sa* "A Flower Is A Lovesome Thing."
[2]Including: Whispering; Tenderly; Don't Take Your Love From Me; Prelude To A Kiss; But Not For Me; Polka Dots and Moonbeams; Passion Flower.

11 Jan 1956   (S)
New York City, NY

JOHNNY HODGES & HIS ORCHESTRA
RN, LB, JHtn JH HC, BS JW SWrd.

....	Ngr	2638-5	Hi'Ya
....	Ngr	2639-1	Snibor
....	Ngr	2640-4	I'm Gonna Sit Right Down And Write Myself A Letter
....	Ngr	2641-1	Texas Blues

12 Jan 1956   (S)
New York City, NY

JOHNNY HODGES & HIS ORCHESTRA
CT WC CA RN, BWmn QJ JSrs, JHtn JH RP PG HC, BS JW SWrd.

....	Ngr	2642-3	The Happy One
....	Ngr	2643-3	Night Walk
....	Ngr	2644-3	You Got It Coming
....	Ngr	2645-6	Duke's Jam

Mar 1956   (S)
New York City, NY

LAWRENCE BROWN ALL STARS
ER PS, LB, ACrk AChn DBnk, HJo WMsl JJ.

....	Clf		Blues For Duke

Mar 1956   (S)
New York City, NY

LAWRENCE BROWN ALL STARS
LB, ST, LL LT LBsn.

....	Clf		Caravan
....	Clf		Rose Of The Rio Grande

1 Sep 1956   (S)
New York City, NY

JOHNNY HODGES & THE DUKE'S MEN
CT RN, QJ, JHtn JH HC, BS JW SWrd.

....	Vrv	2972-6	A-Oddie-Oobie
....	Vrv	2973-3	Meet Mr. Rabbit
....	Vrv	2974-4	The Duke's In Bed
....	Vrv	2875-4	Just Squeeze Me
....	Vrv	2976-3	Ballad For The Very Tired And Sad Lotus Eaters
....	Vrv	2977-3	Confab With Rab
....	Vrv	2978-3	It Had To Be You
....	Vrv	2979-1	Black And Tan Fantasy
....	Vrv	2980-5	Take The "A" Train

21 Sep 1956   (S)
Los Angeles, CA

NAT KING COLE & HIS TRIO
JT, NKC JC ChH LYng.

.... Cap   15920   Caravan

In the time from Oct 1956 and throughout 1957 and while he was a member of the Ellington band, Clark Terry made numerous recordings with the studio big band accompanying Dinah Washington and soloed on quite a few of them. The titles were originally released on the Mercury/EmArcy labels. However, it would go beyond the scope of this book to list these titles, many of which fall into the pop category.

c Dec 1956   (S)
New York City, NY

JIMMY HAMILTON'S JAZZ ENSEMBLE
JHtn, KK SGrs *JW SWrd.*

.... Ur   Blues For A Princess
.... Ur   Easy Living
.... Ur   Rose Room
.... Ur   Tea For Two

11 Dec 1956   (S)
New York City, NY

TONY SCOTT & HIS ORCHESTRA
Big band, featuring *CT.*

.... Vi   G2JB9813   Moonlight Cocktail
.... Vi   G2JB9814   I Surrender, Dear
.... Vi   G2JB9815   Under A Blanket Of Snow
.... Vi   G2JB9816   I'll Remember April

13 Dec 1956   (S)
New York City, NY

TONY SCOTT & HIS ORCHESTRA
Big band, featuring *CT.*

.... Vi   G2JB9817   I Found A Million Dollar Baby
.... Vi   G2JB9818   Skylark
.... Vi   G2JB9819   Finger Poppin' Blues

1956   (S)
New York City, NY

MAXINE SULLIVAN
Vcl, acc. by ChS, BBly *RP,* BKle AB SPwl.

.... Prd   Rose Room –vMSvn
.... Prd   Molly Malone –vMSvn
.... Prd   If I Had A Ribbon Bow –vMSvn
.... Prd   Flow Gently, Sweet Rhythm –vMSvn
.... Prd   Windy –MSvn

6 Mar 1957   (S)
New York City, NY

JACKIE CAIN & ROY KRAL
Vcl, acc. by *CT* AFmr BGlw, UG, PhWs JRsn AO, RK MHtn OJsn

.... ABC   Whisper Not –vJCn RK
.... ABC   I'm Forever Blowing Bubbles –vJCn RK
.... ABC   Look Around –vJCn RK
.... ABC   Stopping The Clock –vJCn RK
.... ABC   So You've Had A Change Of Heart –vJCn RK
.... ABC   Honey Dip –vJCn RK
.... ABC   Say Cheese –vJCn RK
.... ABC   Aura –vJCn RK
.... ABC   Darn That Dream –vJCn RK
.... ABC   Walkin' –vJCn RK

17 Apr 1957   (S)
New York City, NY

CLARK TERRY QUINTET
CT, JGfn, WK PChs PJJ.

.... Riv   That Old Black Magic
.... Riv   Star Dust
.... Riv   Cruising
.... Riv   Digits
.... Riv   Boomerang
.... Riv   Donna Lee
.... Riv   Boardwalk
.... Riv   Serenade To A Bus Seat

30 Apr 1957   (S)
New York City, NY

REX STEWART & COOTIE WILLIAMS
CW RS, LB JCH, CHwk BFmn, HJo BBr MHtn GJsn.

.... Jt   I'm Beginning To See The Light   >>>

.... Jt   Do Nothin' Till You Hear From Me

                                                                                            26 Jun 1957   (S)
JOHNNY HODGES & THE ELLINGTON MEN   New York City, NY
CT RN, BWmn QJ JSrs, JHtn JH RP PG HC, BS JW SWrd.

.... Vrv   21041-2   Gone And Crazy
.... Vrv   21042-3   Segdoh[1]
.... Vrv   21043-1   Little Rabbit Blues
.... Vrv   21044-3   Johnny Come Lately

[1]=Hodges.

ALL STAR BAND
DG, SGtz PG CHwk, WK WMsl JHrd.

.... Vrv   Dizzy Atmosphere
.... Vrv   Ballad Medley[1]
.... Vrv   The Way You Look Tonight
.... Vrv   Ballad Medley[2]

[1]Including: I'm Through With Love; Without A Word Of Warning; Sweet Lorraine; Love Walked In; September Song.
[2]Including: On The Alamo; Stompin' At The Savoy; This Time The Dream's On Me; Time After Time; Gone With The Wind.

                                                                                            26 Jul 1957   (S)
CLARK TERRY ALL STARS   Chicago, IL
CT, MS, WJns RBnd JW SWrd.

.... Arg   Caravan
.... Arg   Candy
.... Arg   Clark's Expeditions
.... Arg   Trumpet Mouthpiece Blues
.... Arg   Phalanges
.... Arg   Blues For Daddy-O
.... Arg   Basin Street Blues
.... Arg   Daylight Express
.... Arg   Taking A Chance On Love

                                                                                            29 Jul 1957   (S)
CLARK TERRY ALL STARS   New York City, NY
CT, QJ, JH, BS JW SWrd.

.... Riv   Come Sunday

   > LHsn, MBrc added.

.... Riv   In A Sentimental Mood –vMBrc

                                                                                            6 Aug 1957   (S)
PAUL GONSALVES ALL STARS   Chicago, IL
CT, PG, WJns JW SWrd.
.... Arg   Festival
.... Arg   Clark's Bars
.... Arg   Daddy-O's Patio
.... Arg   Blues
.... Arg   Impeccable
.... Arg   Paul's Idea
.... Arg   That Bach
.... Arg   Mili-Terry
.... Arg   Funky
.... Chs   The Girl I Call Baby

                                                                                            2 Sep 1957   (S)
JIMMY WOODE ALL STARS   Chicago, IL
CT, MS PKi PG, RLws JW SWrd.

.... Arg   Falmouth Recollection
.... Arg   The Way You Look Tonight
.... Arg   Foody For President
.... Arg   The Man From Potter's Crossing
.... Arg   Dance Of The Reluctant Drag
.... Arg   Empathy for Ruth

                                                                                            3 Sep 1957   (S)
JOHNNY HODGES & THE ELLINGTON MEN   New York City, NY
CT WC CA HB RN, BWmn QJ JSrs, JHtn JH RP PG HC, BS JW SWrd.

.... Vrv   21384-7   Don't Call Me, I'll Call You
.... Vrv   21385-4   An Ordinary Thing
.... Vrv   21386-1   Waiting For Duke   >>>

.... Vrv   21387-3   Dust Bowl

    > *CT HB RN, QJ, JHtn JH RP HC, BS JW SWrd.*

.... Vrv   21388-3   Viscount[1]
.... Vrv   21389-3   Bouquet Of Roses
.... Vrv   21390-2   Digits
.... Vrv   21391-2   Early Morning Rock

    [1]*sa* "Starting With You I'm Through."

6 Sep 1957   (S)
New York City, NY

CLARK TERRY ALL STARS
CT, QJ BWmn TG[1], JH PG, JW SWrd.

.... Riv   The "C" Jam Blues
.... Riv   Just Squeeze Me
.... Riv   Mood Indigo

    > *JH* omitted.

.... Riv   Cotton Tail
.... Riv   Take The "A" Train
.... Riv   In A Mellotone

    [1]*TG* doubling on vib.

22 Oct 1957   (S)
New York City, NY

COUNT BASIE ALL STARS
Big band, featuring *HC.*

.... Co   CO59926   Dickie's Dream
.... Co   CO59927   I Left My Baby –vJRsh

c Nov 1957   (S)
New York City, NY

TONY SCOTT QUINTET
CT, JKpr, TSct, BEvs MHtn PMtn.

.... Sco   Tenderly

    > *HGms* replaces *MHtn.*

.... Ctn   I Can't Get Started
.... Ctn   Body And Soul

17 Nov 1957   (S)
Chicago, IL

BILLY TAYLOR & HIS ORCHESTRA
CT WC, BWmn, JH PG HC, BTlr EMay ET.

.... Arg   Buddy's Beat
.... Arg   Theodora
.... Arg   Mood For Mendes
.... Arg   Daddy-O
.... Arg   Cu-Blu
.... Arg   Day Dreaming
.... Arg   Can You Tell By Looking At Me?
.... Arg   Tune For Tex

30 Dec 1957   (S)
Chicago, IL

DINAH WASHINGTON WITH EDDIE CHAMBLEE'S ORCHESTRA
Vcl, acc. by *CT, QJ, EChb GE, JCrg REdm JSlr.*

.... Em   16709   Trombone Butter –vDWtn
.... Em   16710   Send Me To The 'Lectric Chair –vDWtn
.... Em   16711   Careless Love –vDWtn

5 Mar 1958   (S)
New York City, NY

COOTIE WILLIAMS & HIS ORCHESTRA
Big band, featuring *CW.*

.... Vi   J2JB1906   Caravan
.... Vi   J2JB1908   New Concerto For Cootie

5 Apr 1958   (S)
New York City, NY

JOHNNY HODGES & HIS ORCHESTRA
RE, VD, JH BW, BS JW SWrd.

.... Vrv   22154   Blues A-Plenty
.... Vrv   22155-3   Cool Your Motor

    > *JH, BS JW SWrd.*

.... Vrv   22156   Gone With The Wind   >>>

> Entire band.

.... Vrv   22157-2   Honey Hill

> JH, BS JW SWrd.

.... Vrv   22158   I Didn't Know About You
.... Vrv   22159   Satin Doll

> Entire band.

.... Vrv   22160   Reelin' And Rockin'
.... Vrv   22160 alt.   Reelin' And Rockin'

> JH, BS JW SWrd.

.... Vrv   22161   Don't Take Your Love From Me
.... Vrv   22161 alt.   Don't Take Your Love From Me (incomplete)

> Entire band.

.... Vrv   22162   Saturday Afternoon Blues

CLARK TERRY ALL STARS   7 May 1958   (S)
CT, TMnk SJ PJJ.   New York City, NY

.... Riv   Let's Cool One
.... Riv   Flueg'lin' The Blues

CLARK TERRY ALL STARS   12 May 1958   (S)
CT, JJns SJ PJJ.   New York City, NY

.... Riv   In Orbit
.... Riv   One Foot In The Gutter
.... Riv   Trust In Me
.... Riv   Pea-Eye
.... Riv   Moonlight Fiesta
.... Riv   Argentia
.... Riv   Buck's Business
.... Riv   Very Near Blues

REX STEWART & THE ELLINGTON ALUMNI ALL STARS   4 Jul 1958   (P)
CW RS, TG, HJsn BW, BS OP SG.   Freebody Park
                                                                   Newport, RI

....   East St. Louis Toodle-Oo
....   Rockin' In Rhythm
....   Concerto For Cootie
.... Co   The "C" Jam Blues
....   Boy Meets Horn

> BW, BS OP SG.

.... Co   Chelsea Bridge

> Entire band.

....   La Grande Romp
....   In A Sentimental Mood
....   Perdido
....   The Jeep Is Jumpin'

BEN WEBSTER & BILLY STRAYHORN
BW, BS OP SG.

.... Co   Chelsea Bridge

MERCER ELLINGTON & HIS ORCHESTRA   14 Jul 1958   (S)
CT CA HB, BWmn QJ JSrs, JHtn JH RP BW HC, BS SBst WMsl JMsl.   New York City, NY

.... Cor   105297   Steppin' Into Swing Society
.... Cor   105298   Black Butterfly
.... Cor   105299   Got My Foot In The Door

MERCER ELLINGTON & HIS ORCHESTRA   17 Jul 1958   (S)
CT CA HB, BWmn QJ JSrs, JHtn JH RP BW HC, JJns CL GD DBly.   New York City, NY

.... Cor   105300   Indelible
.... Cor   105301   Ruint   >>>

....	Cor	105302	Frolic Sam
....	Cor	105303	Be Patient

22 Jul 1958   (S)
New York City, NY

MERCER ELLINGTON & HIS ORCHESTRA
CT CA HB, BWmn QJ JSrs, JHtn JH RP BW HC, JJns SBst WMsl DBly.

....	Cor	105304	If You Were In My Place
....	Cor	105305	The Gal From Joe's
....	Cor	105306	Afternoon Moon
....	Cor	105307	Broadway Babe
....	Cor	105308	Yearning For Love

14 Aug 1958   (S)
New York City, NY

JOHNNY HODGES & THE ELLINGTONIANS
RE, LB, JH BW, BS WMsl JJ.

....	Vrv	25000-4	Just A Memory
....	Vrv	25001-5	Let's Fall In Love
....	Vrv	25002-1	Big Shoe
....	Vrv	25003-3	Ruint
....	Vrv	25004-5	Bend One
....	Vrv	25005-6	You Need To Rock

23 Aug 1958   (S)
New York City, NY

CAT ANDERSON & HIS ORCHESTRA
CA CT, RCpd RJns, HChb JCld FRhk, EWm JF EWlk SShb, JJns GD PF.

....	Em	17680	You're The Cream In My Coffee
....	Em	17681	Don't Get Around Much Anymore
....	Em	17682	Cat's In The Alley
....	Em	17683	The Birth Of The Blues

24 Aug 1958   (S)
New York City, NY

CAT ANDERSON & HIS ORCHESTRA
CA ER RCpd RJns, HChb JCld FRhk, EWrn JF EWlk SShb, JJns GD PF.

....	Em	17684	Bluejean Beguine
....	Em	17685	My Adorable D
....	Em	17686	Little Man
....	Em	17687	June Bug
....	Em	17688	Neenah

10 Sep 1958   (S)
New York City, NY

HAROLD BAKER & HIS QUARTET
HB, JJns KB ET.

....	Kg	K7241	Rosetta
....	Kg	K7242	Close Your Eyes
....	Kg	K7243	Them There Eyes
....	Kg	K7244	Love Me Or Leave Me
....	Kg	K7245	The World Is Waiting For The Sunrise
....	Kg	K7246	In A Little Spanish Town
....	Kg	K7247	'S Wonderful
....	Kg	K7248	If I Had You
....	Kg	K7249	Marie
....	Kg	K7250	Cherry
....	Kg	K7251	After You've Gone

JOHNNY HODGES & HIS ORCHESTRA
RE RN, LB, JHtn JH BW, BS JW SWrd.

....	Vrv		MHR[1]
....	Vrv		Broadway Babe
....	Vrv		Three And Six
....	Vrv		Not So Dukish
....	Vrv		Central Park Swing
....	Vrv		Preacher Blues
....	Vrv		Jeep Bounced Back

> *JH, BS JW SWrd.*

....	Vrv		The Last Time I Saw Paris

[1]Stands for <u>M</u>ercer, <u>H</u>odges, <u>R</u>oy.

30 Oct 1958   (S)
Paris, France

CAT ANDERSON SEXTET
CA, QJ, RP, GArv JW SWrd.

....	Co		Concerto For Cootie >>>

....	Co	Black And Tan Fantasy
....	Co	You're The Cream In My Coffee
....	Co	Blues For Lawrence
....	Co	Ain't Misbehavin'

3 Nov 1958   (S)
New York City, NY

EUGENIE BAIRD & THE DUKE'S BOYS
Vcl, acc. by *TJ, TG, BW,* DRiv *WMsl* JMsl.

....	Dsn	Well, Well –vEBrd
....	Dsn	Lush Life –vEBrd
....	Dsn	Everything But You –vEBrd
....	Dsn	In A Sentimental Mood –vEBrd
....	Dsn	I'm Beginning To See The Light –vEBrd
....	Dsn	Something To Live For –vEBrd

5 Nov 1958   (P)
Private home
Oslo, Norway

PAUL GONSALVES & FINN ENGER
PG, FE PI AStr KOH.

....	SoJ	Body And Soul

11 Nov 1958   (S)
New York City, NY

EUGENIE BAIRD & THE DUKE'S BOYS
Vcl, acc. by *TJ,* CIR, HAsh, DRiv SBst *WMsl* JMsl.

....	Dsn	Solitude –vEBrd
....	Dsn	Pass Me By –vEBrd
....	Dsn	I Let A Song Go Out Of My Heart –vEBrd
....	Dsn	Mood Indigo –vEBrd

13 Nov 1958   (S)
Munich, Germany

THE C JAM ALL STARS
CT, PG, CD *JW SWrd.*

....	Bmn	Evad[1]
....	Bmn	Diminuendo In Blue and Crescendo In Blue
....	Bmn	I Cover The Waterfront
....	Bmn	It Don't Mean A Thing
....	Bmn	Autobahn
....	Bmn	Willow Weep For Me
....	Bmn	Hildegard
....	Bmn	Ocean Motion
....	Bmn	Jivin' With Fritz
....	Vi	The "C" Jam Blues

[1]=Dave.

18 Nov 1958   (S)
Stuttgart, Germany

JOHNNY HODGES WITH THE STUTTGART LIGHT ORCHESTRA
JH with the Stuttgart Light Orchestra, Wolfram Röhrig conducting.

....	Vrv	Our Love Is Here To Stay
....	Vrv	Nice Work If You Can Get It
....	Vrv	'S Wonderful
....	Vrv	Summertime
....	Vrv	Soon
....	Vrv	But Not For Me
....	Vrv	Somebody Loves Me
....	Vrv	They Can't Take That Away From Me
....	Vrv	Someone To Watch Over Me
....	Vrv	They All Laughed
....	Vrv	The Man I Love
....	Vrv	Oh! Lady Be Good

28 Jan 1959   (P)
Unidentified location
Paris, France

COOTIE WILLIAMS & HIS ORCHESTRA
Small band, featuring *CW.*

....	De	Echoes Of Harlem

31 Jan 1959   (P)
Unidentified location
Paris, France

COOTIE WILLIAMS & HIS ORCHESTRA
Small band, featuring *CW.*

....	De	Night Train
....	De	Mood Indigo

COOTIE WILLIAMS & HIS ORCHESTRA
Small band, featuring *CW*.

11 Feb 1959   (P)
Unidentified location
Paris, France

.... De   Perdido

24/26 Feb 1959   (S)
New York City, NY

CLARK TERRY ALL STARS
CT, DBut, JJns SJ ATlr.

.... Riv   127
.... Riv   Swingin' Chemise
.... Riv   Mili-Terry
.... Riv   My Heart Belongs To Daddy
.... Riv   Blues For Etta
.... Riv   Top 'n' Bottom
.... Riv   My Sunday Kind Of Love
.... Riv   Mardi Gras Waltz

16 Mar 1959   (S)
New York City, NY

MERCER ELLINGTON & HIS ORCHESTRA
CT CA HB, BWmn QJ JSrs, JHtn JH RP HAsh *HC*, JJns *WMsl* GJsn.

.... Cor   Black And Tan Fantasy
.... Cor   Maroon
.... Cor   Blue Serge
.... Cor   Golden Cress
.... Cor   Mood Indigo
.... Cor   Azure

18 Mar 1959   (S)
New York City, NY

MERCER ELLINGTON & HIS ORCHESTRA
CT CA HB, BWmn QJ JSrs, JHtn JH[1] RP HAsh *HC*, JJns LS *WMsl* GJsn.

.... Cor   Coral Rock
.... Cor   Cherry Pink
.... Cor   Dawn Of A Greenhorn
.... Cor   Aqua Tonic
.... Cor   The Moon Was Yellow
.... Cor   Little White Lies

[1]For contractual reasons, JH is listed as *Alto Jazz Great* on the original release.

7 Apr 1959   (S)
New York City, NY

JOHNNY HODGES & HIS ORCHESTRA
HB, QJ JSrs, JHtn JH BW, JJns LS RBrn JJ.

.... Vrv   [1] First Klass[2]
.... Vrv   [1] Second Klass
.... Vrv   [1] Straight Back
.... Vrv   [1] Steerage
.... Vrv   [1] Third Klass

[1]These titles are alleged to be parts of the *Atlantic Suite*, which was never recorded by DE. Also the fact that JH claims composer credits for these titles makes the assumption of a suite even more questionable. See also the following session.
[2]*aka* "C'mon Home."

8 Apr 1959   (S)
New York City, NY

JOHNNY HODGES & HIS ORCHESTRA
HB, QJ JSrs, JHtn JH BW, JJns LS RBrn JJ.

.... Vrv   Meet The Frog
.... Vrv   [1] Night Life
.... Vrv   My Melancholy Baby
.... Vrv   Lotus Blossom[2]
.... Vrv   [?1] Free For All

[1]See footnote for the previous session.
[2]*sa* "Charlotte Russe."

14 Apr 1959   (S)
New York City, NY

BILLY STRAYHORN SEPTET
HB, QJ, JH RP, BS AHll OJ.

.... Fst   Cue's Blue Now
.... Fst   Gone With The Wind
.... Fst   Cherry
.... Fst   Watch For Cue
.... Fst   You Brought A New Kind Of Love To Me   >>>

               > QJ, RP omitted.

.... Fst   When I Dream Of You

               > QJ, RP added.

.... Fst   Rose Room

19 May 1959   **(S)**
New York City, NY

AL HALL QUARTET
HB, HEds AHII OJ.

.... Co   Should I?
.... Co   Honeysuckle Rose
.... Co   St. Louis Kid
.... Co   I Didn't Know What Time It Was

ALL STAR BAND
CT, JJJ, *BW*, HJo KB GD JJ.

     > GCh REst SGrp added for the following title only:[1]

.... Co   CO63351   Misty

     > RGrn GCh REst BGar RRss MSII SGrp added for the following title only:[1]

.... Co   CO63352   International Blues

     > RGrn GCh REst BGar added for the following title only:[1]

.... Co   CO63353   Cotton Tail

     > SGrp added for the following title only:[1]

.... Co   CO63354   Nuages

     > GCh APsn REst RRss added for the following title only:[1]

.... Co   CO63355   In A Mellotone

     > GCh REst RRss MSII added for the following title only:[1]

.... Co   CO63356   Big Ben's Blues

[1]The contributions from the added musicians from London, Paris and Stockholm, have been overdubbed at a later date.

27+28 May 1959   **(S)**
New York City, NY

QUINCY JONES & HIS ORCHESTRA
Big band, featuring *QJ, SWrd.*

.... Mry   18643   Happy Faces
.... Mry   18644   Along Came Betty
.... Mry   18645   I Remember Clifford
.... Mry   18646   Whisper Not
.... Mry   18647   The Gypsy
.... Mry   18648   Tickle Toe

Summer 1959   **(S)**
New York City, NY

COOTIE WILLIAMS & HIS ORCHESTRA
Small band, featuring *CW.*

.... Wwk   It Don't Mean A Thing
.... Wwk   Don't Get Around Much Anymore
.... Wwk   There's No You
.... Wwk   Caravan
.... Wwk   I Got It Bad
.... Wwk   Do Nothin' Till You Hear From Me
.... Wwk   Drop Me Off At Harlem

Oct 1959   **(S)**
Paris, France

CLARK TERRY ALL STARS
CT, PG, RFo *JW* GTH.[1]

.... De   Satin Doll
.... De   The Lonely Ones
.... De   Pannonica
.... De   alt.   Pannonica
.... De   Serenade To A Bus Seat
.... De   Clark's Bars
.... De   Blues For The Champ Of Champs
.... De   Pea-Eye
.... De   Circeo
.... De   Daniel's Blues
.... De   Mean To Me

[1]Some sources suggest that SWrd was on drums.

14 Oct 1959   (S)
New York City, NY

HAROLD BAKER SEXTET[1]
HB, VD, JF, JGn FSkt OJ.

....	Cdn		I Got Nothing But You
....	Cdn		Give The Lady What She Wants Most
....	Cdn		Bedroom Eyes

[1]Cdn as by *Mainstream Sextet.*

18 Nov 1959   (S)
New York City, NY

EMMETT BERRY SEXTET
EBry, DW, *PG,* SHll MHtn PF.

....	Co		Miss Criss
....	Co		Slow Man, Slow
....	Co		Three Alarm
....	Co		Baby, Won't You Please Come Home?
....			[Pee Gee]

1 Dec 1959   (S)
New York City, NY

ANDY GIBSON & HIS ORCHESTRA
EBry JNm *WC,* DW VD ERsn, GDrs HJsn *PG* LJks, JJns MHtn JCfd.

| .... | Cdn | K3JB6345 | Blueprint |

Late 1959   (S)
New York City, NY

CAT ANDERSON & THE ELLINGTON ALL STARS
CA, QJ, RPwl, *RN,* LL *JW SWrd.*

....	Wyn		Mexican Bandit[1]
....	Wyn		Chelsea Bridge
....	Wyn		Lovelinessence
....	Wyn		A Flower Is A Lovesome Thing

> BJsn replaces RPwl.

....	Wyn		Accentuate
....	Wyn		Summertime
....	Wyn		Like Dig
....	Wyn		Between Some Place, Goin' No Place

[1]*sa* "La Virgen de la Macarena."

11 Jan 1960   (S)
New York City, NY

ERNIE WILKINS & HIS ORCHESTRA
Big band, featuring *PG.*

....	Ev		Broadway
....	Ev		The Surrey With The Fringe On Top
....	Ev		Falling In Love With You
....	Ev		The Continental
....	Ev		Makin' Whoopee
....	Ev		Stompin' At The Savoy
....	Ev		You're Driving Me Crazy
....	Ev		All Of You

29 Feb 1960   (S)
New York City, NY

PAUL GONSALVES & JOHNNY HODGES
RN, JH *PG,* JJns AHll OJ.

| .... | Vi | L3JB1721 | It's Something That You Ought To Know |

> *BWd* added.

| .... | Vi | L3JB1722 | Chocataw |

> *BWd* omitted.

| .... | Vi | L3JB1723 | The Line-Up |

> *BWd* added.

| .... | Vi | L3JB1724 | Way Way Back |

> *PG,* JJns AHll OJ.

| .... | Vi | L3JB1725 | Daydreams[1] |

> Entire band.

| .... | Vi | L3JB1726 | I'm Beginning To See The Light |

> *BWd* added.

| .... | Vi | L3JB1727 | D.A. Blues   >>> |

[1]*sa* "Day Dream."

			Jul 1960	(S)
			Los Angeles, CA	

GERRY MULLIGAN – JOHNNY HODGES QUINTET
JH GM, CWsn BCk MLws.

....	Vrv	Bunny	
	> GM omitted.		
....	Vrv	What's The Rush	
	> GM added.		
....	Vrv	Back Beat	
....	Vrv	What's It All About?	
....	Vrv	18 Carrots For Rabbit	
....	Vrv	Shady Side Of The Street	

			15 Jul 1960	(S)
			Los Angeles, CA	

JO STAFFORD
Vcl, acc. by *RN* DF CCnd, *LB, JH BW HC,* RFrn JRws BGbs JMdn MLws.

....	Co	Just Squeeze Me –vJStd
....	Co	The Folks Who Live On The Hill –vJStd
....	Co	Day Dream –vJStd

			Mid-Jul 1960	(S)
			Los Angeles, CA	

JIMMY HAMILTON & HIS ORCHESTRA
JAnd, *BWmn BWd,* JHtn PG DWls, JRws AB SWrd.

....	Ev	The Blue Room
....	Ev	I've Got The World On A String
....	Ev	Do Nothin' Till You Hear From Me
....	Ev	Tempo de Brazilia
....	Ev	The Nearness Of You
....	Ev	Ain't She Sweet?
....	Ev	I Didn't Know About You
....	Ev	Taj Mahal
....	Ev	In A Sentimental Mood
....	Ev	After You've Gone

			p Mid-1960	(S)
			Columbus, OH	

JOHNNY HODGES WITH THE AL WASLON TRIO
JH, AWas JSch EKnl.

....	Stv	Perdido
....	Stv	Jeep's Blues
....	Stv	All Of Me
....	Stv	The "C" Jam Blues
....	Stv	I Got It Bad

			29 Jul 1960	(S)
			New York City, NY	

JOHN LEWIS' ALL STARS
HP, *PG,* JLws JHll GD CKay.

| .... | Atc | Body And Soul |

			1 Aug 1960	(S)
			Los Angeles, CA	

JO STAFFORD
Vcl, acc. by *RN* DF CCnd, *LB, JH BW HC,* RFrn JRws BGbs JMdn MLws.

....	Co	For You –vJStd
....	Co	S'posin' –vJStd
....	Co	You'd Be So Nice To Come Home To –vJStd
....	Co	What Can I Say –vJStd
....	Co	I've Got The World On A String –vJStd

			10 Aug 1960	(S)
			Los Angeles, CA	

JO STAFFORD
Vcl, acc. by *RN* DF CCnd, *LB, JH BW HC,* RFrn JRws BGbs JMdn MLws.

....	Co	Midnight Sun –vJStd
....	Co	I Didn't Know About You –vJStd
....	Co	I Dream Of You –vJStd
....	Co	Imagination –vJStd

			22 Aug 1960	(S)
			New York City, NY	

BUDD JOHNSON & HIS FOUR BRASS GIANTS
NA HE *CT RN,* BJsn, TFgn JBjm HL.

| .... | Riv | All My Love   >>> |

....	Riv	Blue Lou
....	Riv	Don't Blame Me
....	Riv	I'll Get By

6 Sep 1960   (S)
New York City, NY

BUDD JOHNSON & HIS FOUR BRASS GIANTS
NA HE *CT RN*, BJsn, JJns JBjm HL.

....	Riv	Driftwood
....	Riv	Trinity River Bottom
....	Riv	Blues For Lester
....	Riv	The Message

8 Sep 1960   (S)
New York City, NY

JOHNNY HODGES & HIS ORCHESTRA
HB *RN*, LB *BWd*, JHtn JH HAsh, JJns *AB SWrd*.

....	Vrv	Br'Rabbit
....	Vrv	Starting With You (I'm Through)
....	Vrv	The Hare
....	Vrv	The Things You Miss
....	Vrv	I Told You So
....	Vrv	Wiggle Awhile
....	Vrv	Get Ready
....	Vrv	Peaches[1]
....	Vrv	Hygiene

[1]Complete: "The Peaches Are Better Down The Road."

16 Sep 1960   (S)
Boston, MA

HARRY CARNEY & THE DUKE'S MEN
WC *EMls RN*, BWd, PG HC, RGth *AB SWrd*.

....	Co	Rock Me Gently
....	Co	Mabulaba
....	Co	Jeepers Creepers
....	Co	Tree Of Hope

17 Sep 1960   (S)
Boston, MA

HARRY CARNEY & THE DUKE'S MEN
WC *AF RN*, BWd, PG HC, RGth *AB SWrd*.

....	Co	Blues For Blokes
....	Co	Hand-Me-Down Love
....	Co	Five O'Clock Drag
....	Co	Baby Blue

22 Nov 1960   (S)
The Jazz Cellar
San Francisco, CA

JOHNNY HODGES & HIS ORCHESTRA
JH BW, LLvy HEls WM GJsn.

....	Mo	Ben's Ears
....	Mo	Ben's Web
....	Mo	Don't Kid Yourself (*aka* "Side Door")
....	Mo	Blues'll Blow Your Fuse
....	Mo	I Can't Believe That You're In Love With Me
....	Mo	Dual Highway
....	Stv	Cambridge Blues (*aka* "Shorty Gull")
....	Stv	Brute's Roots (*aka* "Ifida")
....	Stv	Rabbit Pie (*aka* "Big Smack")
....	Stv	One For The Duke (*aka* "I'd Be There")
....	Stv	Walking The Frog (*aka* "Just Another Day")
....	Stv	Bouncing With Ben (*aka* "Lollagin' Now")

Nov/Dec 1960   (T)[1]
Paris, France

STUDIO BAND
BBrs, GL, *BS/ABrd MGdr FGlp*.

....		Take The "A" Train
....		Unidentified title
....	UA	Mood Indigo

[1]Music for the motion picture "Paris Blues," recorded at Barclay Studios.

8+9 Dec 1960   (S)
New York City, NY

JOHNNY HODGES & HIS ORCHESTRA
LB, JH, JJns *AB SG*.

....	MGM	Am I Blue? >>>

....	MGM	Something To Remember You By
....	MGM	Once In A While
....	MGM	Do Nothin' Till You Hear From Me
....	MGM	More Than You Know
....	MGM	Memories Of You
....	MGM	The Very Thought Of You
....	MGM	When Your Lover Has Gone
....	MGM	A Blues Serenade
....	MGM	Night And Day
....	MGM	Lover Come Back To Me
....	MGM	I Gotta Right To Sing The Blues
....	MGM	Two Sleepy People

The above titles have been presented in the form of medleys, however, it seemed appropriate to list them individually.

13 Dec 1960   (S)
New York City, NY

BOOTY WOOD ALL STARS
HB, *BWd, CP[1] PG,* RRR *AB* OJ.

....	Co	Hang On There
....	Co	New Cambridge Blues
....	Co	Easin' On Down Piccadilly
....	Co	Ohso

> *BWd* DW VD, *CP[1] PG,* SCT *AB* OJ.

....	Co	Sunday
....	Co	Snowstorm
....	Co	Blues In Bones
....	Co	Our Delight

[1]For contractual reasons JH is listed as *Cue Porter* on the original release.

20 Dec 1960   (S)
New York City, NY

PAUL GONSALVES ALL STARS
NA, *PG,* WK SJ JCbb.

....	Jld	Hard Groove

> NA omitted.

....	Jld	I Surrender, Dear
....	Jld	I Cover The Waterfront
....	Jld	Walkin'

> NA added.

....	Jld	Yesterdays
....	Jld	J. And B. Blues
....	Jld	Low Gravy
....	Jld	Gettin' Together

CT and BWmn recorded with future band vocalist Teri Thornton 12 titles in two sessions on 23 Dec 1960 and 10 Jan 1961. Notwithstanding that both musicians rejoined the Ellington band for three studio sessions in May and Jun 1961, they have in fact left the band prior to the TTh sessions and have consequently lost their status as active "Ellingtonians."

5 Jan 1961   (S)
New York City, NY

PAUL GONSALVES & HAROLD ASHBY
HAsh, *PG,*[1] SCT *AB* JJ.

....	Co	Swallowing the Blues
....	Co	Out Of Nowhere
....	Co	The Midnight Sun Will Never Set
....	Co	London Broil

> *RN* added.

....	Co	Just Squeeze Me
....	Co	Jeep's Blues
....	Co	Blue Skies
....	Co	You Can Depend On Me

[1]PG doubles on gt in this session.

Jan 1961   (S)
Paris, France

BILLY STRAYHORN
BS, Paris Blue Notes (vcl group).

....	WRC	Lush Life –vPBN

> MGdr added, PBN omitted.

....	WRC	Just A-Settin' And A-Rockin'
....	WRC	Passion Flower >>>

> MGdr omitted, Paris String Quartet added.

.... WRC   Take The "A" Train

> BS piano solo.

.... WRC   Strange Feeling

> MGdr, PBN added.

.... WRC   Day Dream –vPBN

> BS piano solo.

.... Cap   Chelsea Bridge

> MGdr PBN added.

.... WRC   Multicolored Blue –vPBN

> PBN omitted.

.... WRC   Something To Live For

> PSQ added.

.... WRC   A Flower Is A Lovesome Thing

                                           31 Jan 1961   (S)

JOHNNY HODGES & HIS ORCHESTRA   Los Angeles, CA
RN, LB, JH BW, ERch JMdn MLws.

.... Mo   Exactly Like You
.... Mo   I'm Beginning To See The Light
.... Mo   Val's Lament
.... Mo   Tipsy Joe
.... Mo   Waiting For The Champagne

                                           21 Feb 1961   (S)

JOHNNY HODGES & HIS ORCHESTRA   Los Angeles, CA
RN, LB, JH JF, ERch RFrn LVgr MLws.

.... Mo   Sweet Cookie
.... Mo   Frog Hop
.... Mo   Zag Zig
.... Mo   Dag Knows
.... Mo   Twice Daily
.... Mo   John Smith
.... Mo   Romeo
.... Mo   Black Sapphire

                                         14 Mar 1961   (P)

THE DUKE ELLINGTON ALL STARS DIRECTED BY JOHNNY HODGES[1]   Unidentified location
RN, LB, JH HC, AWms AB SWrd.   Stockholm, Sweden

.... Ari   Things Ain't What They Used To Be
.... Ari   The "C" Jam Blues
.... Ari   The Jeep Is Jumpin'
.... Ari   Good Queen Bess
.... Ari   I'll Get By
.... Ari   I Let A Song Go Out Of My Heart/Don't Get Around Much Anymore
.... Ari   Just Squeeze Me –vRN
.... Ari   Take The "A" Train
.... Ari   On The Sunny Side Of The Street
.... Ari   Stompy Jones
.... Ari   Do Nothin' Till You Hear From Me
.... Ari   I Got It Bad
.... Ari   Things Ain't What They Used To Be

[1]Ari as by *Johnny Hodges & the Ellingtonians.*

                                         21 Mar 1961   (S)

JIMMY HAMILTON ALL STARS   New York City, NY
CT, BWmn, JHtn, TFgn WMsl MLws.

.... Svl   2937   Nits And Wits
.... Svl   2938   Gone With The Blues
.... Svl   2939   Mr. Good Blues
.... Svl   2940   Peanut Head
.... Svl   2941   Stupid But Not Crazy
.... Svl   2942   Two For One

THE DUKE ELLINGTON ALL STARS DIRCTED BY JOHNNY HODGES[1]
RN, LB, JH HC, AWms AB SWrd.

22 Mar 1961   (P)
Sportpalast
Berlin, Germany

....	Rar		Take The "A" Train
....	Rar		In The Kitchen[2]
....	Rar		The "C" Jam Blues
....	Rar		Mood Indigo
....	Rar		Solitude
....	Rar		Satin Doll
....	Rar		You Go To My Head
....	Rar		I Got It Bad
....	Rar		Rockin' In Rhythm
....	Pab		Autumn Leaves
....	Pab		Stompy Jones
....	Pab		The Jeep Is Jumpin'
....	Pab		Good Queen Bess
....	Pab		Things Ain't What They Used To Be
....	Pab		I'll Get By
....	Pab		I Let A Song Go Out Of My Heart/Don't Get Around Much Anymore
....	Pab		Just Squeeze Me
....	Pab		Do Nothin' Till You Hear From Me
....	Pab		Rose Of The Rio Grande
....	Pab		All Of Me
....	Pab		On The Sunny Side Of The Street
....	Pab		Blue Moon
....	Pab		Perdido

[1]Pab as by *Johnny Hodges & The Ellington Giants;* Rar as by *Johnny Hodges & The Harry Carney Sextet.*
[2]*aka* "Berlin Thing."

NAT PIERCE ORCHESTRA
Big band, featuring CT, *PG.*

23+24 Mar 1961   (S)
New York City, NY

....	ZIM		Pretty Little Girl
....	Zim		Melancholy Baby
....	ZIM		Black Jack
....	ZIM		Soulville
....	ZIM		Sister Sadie
....	ZIM		The Ballad Of Jazz Street

JIMMY HAMILTON ALL STARS
JHtn, TFgn WMsl EWls.

4 Apr 1961   (S)
New York City, NY

....	Svl	2961	Baby, Won't You Please Come Home?
....	Svl	2962	Town Tavern Rag
....	Svl	2963	Pan Fried
....	Svl	2964	Definite Difference
....	Svl	2965	Route 9W
....	Svl	2966	Lullaby Of The Leaves
....	Svl	2967	No Greater Love
....	Svl	2968	Dancing On The Ceiling

PRESTIGE BLUES SWINGERS
JNn, JCH, *JHtn* CHwk, CHks TGrs *WMsl* BEsh.

14 Apr 1961   (S)
New York City, NY

....	Svl	2977	Jammin' In Swingville
....	Svl	2978	Spring Swing
....	Svl	2979	Love Me Or Leave Me
....	Svl	2980	Cool Sunrise

JOHNNY HODGES & WILD BILL DAVIS
JH, BD LS SJ LHs.

23/24 Aug 1961   (S)
New York City, NY

....	Vrv		Why Are You Blue?
....	Vrv		It Shouldn't Happen To A Dream
....	Vrv		And Then Some
....	Vrv		I Wonder Why
....	Vrv		Azure-Te
....	Vrv		Blue Hodge
....	Vrv		Hodge Podge
....	Vrv		Knuckles
....	Vrv		Stand By Blues
....	Vrv		No Greater Love

		11 Dec 1961 (S)
		New York City, NY

JOHNNY HODGES WITH BILLY STRAYHORN & THE ORCHESTRA
HB CA EMls RN, LB QJ *CCrs, JHtn JH RP PG HC, JJns AB SWrd, BS* arrangements and conducting.

....	Vrv	Don't Get Around Much Anymore
....	Vrv	The Gal From Joe's
....	Vrv	Jeep's Blues
....	Vrv	I Got It Bad
....	Vrv	Juice A-Plenty
....	Vrv	Day Dream
....	Vrv	Your Love Has Faded
....	Vrv	Star Dust

12 Dec 1961 (S)
New York City, NY

JOHNNY HODGES WITH BILLY STRAYHORN & HIS ORCHESTRA
HB CA EMls BBry HMG, *LB* QJ *CCrs, JHtn JH RP PG HC, JJns AB SWrd, BS* arrangements and conducting.

....	Vrv	Azure
....	Vrv	I'm Just A Lucky So-And-So
....	Vrv	Tailor Made Blues

4 Apr 1962 (S)
New York City, NY

COOTIE WILLIAMS & HIS ORCHESTRA
Small band, featuring *CW.*

....	Mdv	Concerto For Cootie
....	Mdv	Night Train

1 May 1962 (S)
New York City, NY

WILD BILL DAVIS ALL STARS
LS *PG,* BD JPtn CN.

....	Co	112143	On A Little Street In Singapore
....	Co	112144	Manhattan
....	Co	112145	African Waltz
....	Co	112146	Midnight In Moscow

15 Aug 1962 (P)
Village Gate
New York City, NY

COLEMAN HAWKINS SEXTET
RE, *JH* CHwk, TFgn MH ELck.

....	Vrv	Satin Doll
....	Vrv	Perdido
....	Vrv	The Rabbit In Jazz

15+18 Aug 1962 (S)
New York City, NY

JOHNNY HODGES WITH ORCHESTRA
JH, BL GD OJsn with an orchestra, directed by Oliver Nelson.

....	Vrv	Eleventh Hour Theme
....	Vrv	I Didn't Know About You
....	Vrv	Warm Valley
....	Vrv	Love Song
....	Vrv	Don't Blame Me
....	Vrv	Something To Live For
....	Vrv	In A Sentimental Mood
....	Vrv	You Blew Out The Flame In My Heart
....	Vrv	Solitude
....	Vrv	Satin Doll
....	Vrv	Prelude To A Kiss
> RN added.		
....	Vrv	Guitar Amour

c Sep 1962 (P)
Unidentified location
U.S.A.

THE ELLINGTON ALL STARS
Small band, featuring HB, *LB, JH* JCtr.

....	ST	In A Mellotone
....	ST	Rab 'n' Trane

Jan 1963 (S)
London, England

PAUL GONSALVES ALL STARS
PG, PSm KN RSt.

....	Vo	I Should Care
....	Vo	Boom Jackie, Boom Chick
....	Vo	If I Should Loose You
....	Vo	Poor Butterfly >>>

| .... | Vo | | Blue P.G. |
| .... | Vo | | Taboo |

> JSh added.

| .... | Vo | | Village Blues |
| .... | Vo | | You Are So Beautiful |

7 Feb 1963   (S)
Stockholm, Sweden

LAWRENCE BROWN
LB interviewed by Leif Anderson.

| .... | Az | | Interview |

15 Mar 1963   (S)
New York City, NY

JOHNNY HODGES ALL STARS
JH, RJck KB *WMsl* BDon.

| .... | Vrv | | Tangerine |
| .... | Vrv | | I Let A Song Go Out Of My Heart |

17 Mar 1963   (S)
New York City, NY

JOHNNY HODGES ALL STARS
JH, RJck KB JLsb BDon.

| .... | Vrv | | Creole Love Call |

20 May 1963   (S)
Englewood Cliffs, NJ

PAUL GONSALVES ALL STARS
PG, DH HJo KB GD RHns MA

....		11494	[Cleo's Blues]
....		11495	[Action In Alexandria]
....		11496	[Anthony And Cleopatra Theme]

21 May 1963   (S)
Englewood Cliffs, NJ

PAUL GONSALVES ALL STARS
PG, DH HJo KB GD RHns MA.

....	lps	11505	Cleo's Blues
....	lps	11506	Anthony And Cleopatra Theme
....	lps	11507	Caesar And Cleopatra Theme
....	lps	11508	Bluz For Liz

> DH omitted.

....	lps	11509	Cleopatra's Lament
....	lps	11510	Action In Alexandria
....	lps	11511	Cleo's Asp

> DH added.

| .... | lps | 11512 | Second Chance |

7 Jun 1963   (S)
Stockholm, Sweden

PAUL GONSALVES & FRIENDS
Small band, featuring *PG.*

| .... | | | [I Cover The Waterfront] |

10 Jun 1963   (S)
Stockholm, Sweden

PAUL GONSALVES SEXTET
REsn RN, PG, OF JW SWrd.

| .... | JCo | | Robin's Nest |
| .... | JCo | | Angel Eyes |

> RN omitted.

| .... | JCo | | Blues |

> REsn omitted.

| .... | JCo | | Blue And Sentimental |

> RN added.

| .... | JCo | | Mr. Gentle And Mr. Cool |
| .... | JCo | | I Can't Get Started –vRN |

> REsn added.

| .... | JCo | | Just Friends |

c Jun 1963   (S)
London, England

PAUL GONSALVES ALL STARS
JDch LCdn, KChr, TH *PG* JSh, STcy LBsh RSt.

.... Co		Tupa
.... Co		Amber Mood
.... Co		Just Friends
.... Co		Pedro's Walk
.... Co		Baby Blue
.... Co		Souraya
.... Co		Mini Minor

3 Sep 1963   (S)
New York City, NY

JOHNNY HODGES & WILD BILL DAVIS
JWld, *JH*, BD HJo KB MHtn OJsn.

.... Vrv		Sandy's Gone
.... Vrv		Wonderful, Wonderful
.... Vrv		Blue Velvet
.... Vrv		Deep Purple
.... Vrv		Since
.... Vrv		So Much In Love
.... Vrv		Candy's Theme

4 Sep 1963   (S)
New York City, NY

JOHNNY HODGES & WILD BILL DAVIS
JWld, *JH*, BD KB OJsn/EShy.

.... Vrv		Jones
.... Vrv		I Cried For You
.... Vrv		Love You Madly
.... Vrv		Little John, Little John
.... Vrv		Stolen Sweets
.... Vrv		A&R Blues[1]
.... Vrv		Lost In Meditation

[1]A&R refers either to the studio (A&R Studios) or to the supervisor of the session.

PAUL GONSALVES ALL STARS
REsn, PG, WBsp EShp OJsn.
Englewood Cliffs, NJ

.... Ips	11704	Impulsive

> *RN, JH* added.

.... Ips	11705	Duke's Place

> *REsn RN, JH* omitted.

.... Ips	11706	Body And Soul

> *REsn RN, JH* added.

.... Ips	11707	Things Ain't What They Used To Be

> *JH* omitted.

.... Ips	11708	Tell It The Way It Is

> *JH* added.

.... Ips	11709	Rapscallion In Rab's Canyon

5 Sep 1963   (S)
New York City, NY

JOHNNY HODGES WITH THE CLAUS OGERMANN ORCHESTRA
JH with the Claus Ogermann Orchestra, including JNn, BD KB MLws.

.... Vrv		Monkey Shack
.... Vrv		Scarlet O'Hara
.... Vrv		The Caretaker's Theme
.... Vrv		Again
.... Vrv		Follow Me

PAUL GONSALVES & SONNY STITT
SStt, *PG*, HJo MHtn OJns.
Englewood Cliffs, NJ

.... Ips		Salt And Pepper
.... Ips		S'posin'
.... Ips		Theme from "The Lord Of The Flies"
.... Ips		Perdido
.... Ips		Star Dust

				1963	(S)
				New York City, NY	

JOHNNY HODGES & HIS ORCHESTRA
JH, LSch BGbr GD DBly.

....	Vrv		Mama Knows
....	Vrv		I'm In Another World
....	Vrv		Dreary Days
....	Vrv		I Can't Believe That You're In Love With Me
....	Vrv		B.A. Blues[1]
....	Vrv		Wanderlust
....	Vrv		All Too Soon
....	Vrv		Somebody Loves Me
....	Vrv		Away From You

[1]B.A. stands for <u>B</u>uenos <u>A</u>ires.

		6 Feb 1964	(S)
		New York City, NY	

JOHNNY HODGES ALL STARS
CA REsn RN, BWmn BCpr, JHtn JH RP PG HC, JJns EShp GTt.

....	Vrv	90052	I Let A Song Go Out Of My Heart/Don't Get Around Much Anymore
....	Vrv	90053	Main Stem
....	Vrv	90054	The Jeep Is Jumpin'
....	Vrv	90055	Open Mike

CA RN, JH PG, JJns EShp GTt.

....	lps	90056	Everybody Knows
....	lps	90057	A Flower Is A Lovesome Thing
....	lps	90058	Papa Knows
....	lps	90059	310 Blues

		11 Mar 1964	(S)
		Englewood Cliffs, NJ	

BEN WEBSTER
BW, HJo RD OJsn.

| .... | lps | 90060 | A Single Petal Of A Rose |
| .... | lps | 90064 | In A Mellotone |

		13 Mar 1964	(S)
		Englewood Cliffs, NJ	

CLARK TERRY'S HAPPY HORNS
CT, PhWs BW, RKwy MHtn WPks.

....	lps	90067	Rockin' In Rhythm
....	lps	90067 alt.	Rockin' In Rhythm
....	lps	90073	Ellington Rides Again[1]
....	lps	90074	Do Nothin' Till You Hear From Me
....	lps	90074 alt.	Do Nothin' Till You Hear From Me

[1]Including: Don't Get Around Much Anymore; Perdido; I'm Beginning To See The Light.

		20 Mar 1964	(S)
		Paris, France	

CAT ANDERSON & THE ELLINGTON ALL STARS
CA, BCpr, RP PG, JTrn RL SWrd.

....	Co		The "C" Jam Blues
....	Co		A Chat With Cat
....	Co		Don't Get Around Much Anymore
....	Co		Muskrat Ramble

> BCpr, RP PG omitted, CBlg replaces JTrn.

| .... | Co | | Confessin' |

> BCpr, RP PG added.

| .... | Co | | A Gathering In A Clearing |
| .... | Co | | For Jammers Only |

		25 Mar 1964	(S)
		Englewood Cliffs, NJ	

BEN WEBSTER
No particulars available.

| .... | | 90080 | [A Single Petal Of A Rose] |

		28 Apr 1964	(S)
		New York City, NY	

JOHNNY HODGES & WILD BILL DAVIS
JH, BD MLow RD OJsn.

....	Vrv		Blues O'Mighty
....	Vrv		Things Ain't What They Used To Be
....	Vrv		Wisteria >>>

.... Vrv   Satin Doll

                                                                    30 Apr 1964   (S)
                                                                    New York City, NY

        JOHNNY HODGES & WILD BILL DAVIS
        JH, BD MLow RD OJsn.

.... Vrv   Mud Pie
.... Vrv   Fiddler's Fancy

                                                                    27 Aug 1964   (S)
                                                                    New York City, NY

        JOHNNY HODGES & THE ELLINGTONIANS
        CA, LB, JH RP HC, VF BCtl *SWrd.*

.... Onx   The Jeep Is Jumpin'
.... Onx   Good Queen Bess
.... Onx   Dooji Wooji
.... Onx   Jeep's Blues

                                                                    5 Nov 1964   (S)
                                                                    New York City, NY

        EARL HINES QUARTET
        RN, EH *AB* JCfd.

.... Vi   RPA1-7408   The Hour Of Parting
.... Bb   RPA1-7408 alt.   The Hour Of Parting
.... Vi   RPA1-7409   It's A Pity To Say Goodnight
.... Bb   RPA1-7409 alt.   It's A Pity To Say Goodnight
.... Vi   RPA1-7410   But Not For Me
.... Vi   RPA1-7411   Man With A Horn
.... Vi   RPA1-7412   Come Sunday
.... Bb   RPA1-7412 alt.   Come Sunday

                                                                    6 Jan 1965   (S)
                                                                    New York City, NY

        JOHNNY HODGES & WILD BILL DAVIS
        LB, JH, BD GGrn BCrs GTt.

.... Vrv   Joe's Blues

> BBsh replaces BCrs.

.... Vrv   Harmony In Harlem

> BCrs replaces BBsh, GGrn omitted.

.... Vrv   Warm Valley

> LB omitted, GGrn added.

.... Vrv   Solitude

> BBsh replaces BCrs, GGrn omitted, LB added.

.... Vrv   I'll Walk Alone

> GGrn added.

.... Vrv   Wild Bill Blues
.... Vrv   Somebody Loves Me
.... Vrv   Clementine

                                                                    7 Jan 1965   (S)
                                                                    New York City, NY

        WILD BILL DAVIS & JOHNNY HODGES
        JH, BD DTho MLow MHtn OJsn.

.... Vi   SPA1-1801   On The Sunny Side Of The Street

> DTho omitted.

.... Vi   SPA1-1802   The Jeep Is Jumpin'

> DTho added.

.... Vi   SPA1-1803   I'm Beginning To See The Light
.... Vi   SPA1-1804   Li'l Darlin'

> DTho omitted.

.... Vi   SPA1-1805   Sophisticated Lady

> DTho added.

.... Vi   SPA1-1806   No One

> GD replaces MHtn.

.... Vi   SPA1-1807   Con-Soul And Sax

> DTho omitted.

.... Vi   SPA1-1808   Drop Me Off At Harlem   >>>

| .... | Vi | SPA1-1809 | On Green Dolphin Street |
| .... | Vi | SPA1-1810 | Johnny Come Lately |

12 Jan 1965 (S)
Chicago, IL

JOYA SHERRILL
Vcl, acc. by *CW, JH,* EHpr *JL SWrd.*

.... Vrv Mood Indigo –vJS
> *CW* omitted.
.... Vrv Prelude To A Kiss –vJS
> *JH* omitted, *CW, PG* added.
.... Vrv Sophisticated Lady –vJS
> *PG* omitted.
.... Vrv Kissing Bug –vJS
> *CW* omitted.
.... Vrv In A Sentimental Mood –vJS
> *CW, JH PG* added.
.... Vrv Duke's Place –vJS
.... Vrv Things Ain't What They Used To Be –vJS
> *JH PG* omitted.
.... Vrv Just Squeeze Me –vJS

20 Jan 1965 (S)
New York City, NY

JOYA SHERRILL
Vcl, acc. by *RN, BS JL* SShd.

.... Vrv I'm Beginning To See The Light –vJS
.... Vrv I'm Just A Lucky So-And-So –vJS
.... Vrv Day Dream –vJS
.... Vrv A Flower Is A Lovesome Thing –vJS

22 Jan 1965 (S)
New York City, NY

MERCER ELLINGTON & HIS ORCHESTRA
RN, LB, JH PG HC, GBr *JL SWrd,* JMP.

.... Jo Cunga –vRN
.... Jo In A Valley Of Dreams –vJMP
.... Jo Undertow –vJMP
.... Jo Take A Giant Step –vRN

25 Jan 1965 (S)
Toronto, ON

JOHNNY HODGES
Interviewed by person unknown.

.... Interview

29 Jan 1965 (S)
Paris, France

CAT ANDERSON & THE ELLINGTON ALL STARS
CA, BCpr CCrs, PG, CBlg CBlr *SWrd.*

.... Phi Looka Here
.... Phi Dede Dada
.... Phi Trombone Butter
> PDtr, CGst, GB added.
.... Phi Clementine
> PDtr, CGst, GB omitted.
.... Phi Hello Dolly

30 Jan 1965 (S)
Paris, France

CAT ANDERSON & THE ELLINGTON ALL STARS
CA, BCpr CCrs, PG, CBlg CBlr *SWrd.*

.... Phi Just In Time
.... Phi The Twins
.... Phi Waltz Accent
.... Phi Paul's
.... Phi Something For Lester

Feb 1965   (S)
London, England

PAUL GONSALVES ALL STARS
TCoe PG TH RSct JSh, TShn *JL* RSt.

....	WRC	Royal Flush
....	WRC	Change Of Setting
....	WRC	Tubby's Theme
....	WRC	Deb's Delight
....	WRC	Don't Fall Off The Bridge

> *RN* added.

....	WRC	Child's Fancy
....	WRC	Min's And Madge's Blues
....	WRC	Speedy Gonsalves

8 Mar 1965   (S)
Englewood Cliffs, NJ

LAWRENCE BROWN ALL STARS
CA RN, LB BCpr, HAsh *JH RP HC,* JJns RD GJsn.

....	lps	90290	Sassy Cue
....	lps	90291	Ruint
....	lps	90292	Do Nothin' Till You Hear From Me

> JBH replaces GJsn.

| .... | lps | 90293 | Mood Indigo |

> GJsn replaces JBH.

| .... | lps | 90294 | Good Queen Bess |

> JBH replaces GJsn.

| .... | | 90295 | [Ballade] |
| .... | lps | 90296 | Little Brother |

> GJsn replaces JBH.

| .... | lps | 90297 | Jeep's Blues |
| .... | lps | 90298 | Stompy Jones |

27 Jul 1965   (S)
New York City, NY

JOHNNY HODGES & WILD BILL DAVIS
LB, JH, BD GGrn BDxn.

....	Vrv	Wings And Things[1]
....	Vrv	Spotted Dog
....	Vrv	Casanova
....	Vrv	Dow De Dow Dow Dow
....	Vrv	Peg O'My Heart

> BD omitted.

| .... | Vrv | Imbo[2] |
| .... | Vrv | Take The "A" Train |

> *LB,* GGrn omitted.

| .... | Vrv | The Nearness Of You |

[1]This title is a derivative of *Things Ain't What They Used To Be.*
[2]sa "Self Portrait"; "Take It Slow"; "Obmil"; "Limbo Jazz."

14 Aug 1965   (S)
p Los Angeles, CA

BILLY STRAYHORN
Piano solo.

| .... | RB | Love Came |
| .... | RB | Baby Clementine |

Late Sep 1965   (S)
Vancouver, BC

HARRY CARNEY
Interviewed by person unknown.

| .... | | Interview |

Dec 1965[1]   (S)
New York City, NY

BILLY STRAYHORN—CAT ANDERSON—LOUIE BELLSON
BS. CA, LBsn interviewed by Ruggero Orlando.

| .... | | Interviews |

[1]Telecast in Italy on 1 Apr 1966.

| | | | 20 Dec 1965 | (S) |
| | | | Los Angeles, CA | |

JOHNNY HODGES WITH THE LAWRENCE WELK ORCHESTRA
JH with the Lawrence Welk Orchestra.

....	Dbt	Misty
....	Dbt	Fantastic, That's You
....	Dbt	In A Sentimental Mood
....	Dbt	Canadian Sunset
....	Dbt	Someone To Watch Over Me
....	Dbt	I'm Beginning To See The Light

| | | | 21 Dec 1965 | (S) |
| | | | Los Angeles, CA | |

JOHNNY HODGES WITH THE LAWRENCE WELK ORCHESTRA
JH with the Lawrence Welk Orchestra.

....	Dbt	Haunting Melody
....	Dbt	Blue Velvet
....	Dbt	When My Baby Smiles At Me
....	Dbt	Sophisticated Lady
....	Dbt	Star Dust
....	Dbt	I Can't Get Started

| | | | 27 Dec 1965 | (S) |
| | | | New York City, NY | |

JOHNNY HODGES & WILD BILL DAVIS
LB, JHtn JH, BD *BBtl BBsh HL.*

| .... | Vrv | Pyramid |
| .... | Vrv | Feelin' Kinda Blue[1] |

> BD omitted.

| .... | Vrv | At Dawn |

> BBtl omitted, BD added, JBH replaces HL.

| .... | Vrv | The Brown-Skin Gal |

[1]*sa* "When I'm Feelin' Kinda Blue"; "Imagine My Frustration."

| | | | 5 Jan 1966 | (S) |
| | | | New York City, NY | |

MERCER ELLINGTON SEPTET
RN, JH PG HC, CCor *AB LBsn.*

....	DJ		Portrait Of Pea[1]
....	Az	alt.	Portrait Of Pea
....	DJ		In The Alley
....	DJ		Sassy
....	DJ		Ugh[2]

[1]"Portrait For Pea" on DJ.
[2]*aka* "Windows."

| | | | 10 Jan 1966 | (S) |
| | | | New York City, NY | |

EARL HINES & THE ELLINGTONIANS
CA RN, LB BCpr, JHtn JH RP PG HAsh, EH RD SG.

| .... | lps | 90457 | Cotton Tail |

> JBH replaces *SG.*

| .... | | 90458 | [At Dawn] |

> CT BBry added, SG replaces JBH.

| .... | | 90459 | [Rockin' In Rhythm] |

> EJ replaces *SG.*

| .... | lps | 90460 | Once Upon A Time |

| | | | 11 Jan 1966 | (S) |
| | | | New York City, NY | |

EARL HINES & THE ELLINGTONIANS
CA, LB, PWR *JHtn PG, EH AB EJ.*

| .... | lps | 90461 | The Blues In My Flat –vRN |
| .... | lps | 90462 | You Can Depend On Me |

> *JHtn, EH AB EJ.*

| .... | lps | 90463 | Fantastic, That's You |

> *CA RN, LB,* PWR *JHtn JH PG HAsh, EH AB SG.*

| .... | lps | 90464 | Black And Tan Fantasy |

> *RN* omitted.

| .... | lps | 90465 | Hash Brown |

14 Jan 1966   (S)
New York City, NY

EARL HINES & JOHNNY HODGES
JH, EH KB RD JMsl.

....	Vrv	Caution Blues[1]
....	Vrv	Stride Right
....	Vrv	Rosetta
....	Vrv	Perdido
....	Vrv	Fantastic, That's You
....	Vrv	Tale Of The Fox
....	Vrv	I'm Beginning To See The Light
....	Vrv	The "C" Jam Blues
....	Vrv	Tippin' In

[1]*sa* "Blues In Thirds."

17 Jan 1966   (S)
New York City, NY

JOHNNY HODGES & WILD BILL DAVIS
LB, JHtn JH, BD BBtl BBsh JMsl.

....	Vrv	Blues For Madeleine

> JHtn omitted.

....	Vrv	Nonchalance

> JHtn added.

....	Vrv	Rabbit Out Of The Hat
....	Vrv	Hash Brown

> JHtn omitted.

....	Vrv	Stormy Weather

10+11 Aug 1966   (P)
Grace's Little Belmont
Atlantic City, NJ

JOHNNY HODGES & WILD BILL DAVIS
LB, JH BBrn, BD D.Tho BDhm.

....	Vi	TPA5-5417	In A Mellotone
....	Vi	TPA5-5418	L.B. Blues[1]
....	Vi	TPA5-5419	Good Queen Bess
....	Vi	TPA5-5420	Belle Of The Belmont
....	Vi	TPA5-5421	I'll Always Love You
....	Vi	TPA5-5422	Taffy
....	Vi	TPA5-5423	Rockville
....	Vi	TPA5-5424	It Don't Mean A Thing
....	Vi	TPA5-5425	It's Only A Paper Moon

[1]L.B. stands for Lawrence Brown.

15 Aug 1966   (S)
New York City, NY

JOHNNY HODGES & HIS ORCHESTRA
SY ER, TStd, JHtn JH FWss JRsn JAsh, HJo KB BCrs GTt.

....	Vrv	101.020	Blue Notes
....	Vrv	101.021	Say It Again

19 Aug 1966   (S)
New York City, NY

JOHNNY HODGES & HIS ORCHESTRA
SY ER, TStd, JHtn JH FWss JRsn JAsh, HJo JV EG BCrs GTt.

....	Vrv	101.022	L.B. Blues
....	Vrv	101.023	I Can't Believe That You're In Love With Me
....	Vrv	101.024	Broad Walk

Sep 1966   (P)
Greek Theater
Los Angeles, CA

ELLA FITZGERALD & HER ORCHESTRA
Vcl, acc. by CA CW HJns ME, LB BCpr CCrs, JHtn JH RP PG HC, JJns JHgh ET.

....	Sal	The Moment Of Truth –vEF
....	Sal	These Boots Are Made For Walkin' –vEF

> vcl, acc. by *CA*, JJns JHgh ET.

....	Sal	Star Dust –vEF
....	Sal	I'm Just A Lucky So-And-So –vEF

24 Oct 1966   (S)
New York City, NY

JOHNNY HODGES & HIS ORCHESTRA
SY ER, TStd, JHtn JH FWss DBnk, HJo JV GD BTt.

....	Vrv	101.441	Midnight Sun[1] >>>

.... > BLcs added.

.... Vrv   101.442   Rent City

.... > BLcs omitted.

.... Vrv   101.443   Sometimes I'm Happy

.... > BLcs added.

.... Vrv   101.444   Sneakin' Up On You

[1]"The Midnight Sun Will Never Set" [*sic*] on Vrv.

HARRY CARNEY & MERCER ELLINGTON   22 Dec 1966   (S)
HC and *ME* interviewed by Henry F. Whiston.   New York City, NY

.... Az[1]   Interview

[1]Not complete on Az (contains only the HC portion of the interview).

JOHNNY HODGES ALL STARS   9 Jan 1967   (S)
RN, BCpr, JH PG, JJns/HJo TGrs MHtn GJsn.   New York City, NY

.... Bb   UPA1-3625   Monkey On A Limb
.... Vi   UPA1-3626   The Nearness Of You
.... Vi   UPA1-3627   Take 'Em Off, Take 'Em Off, part 1
.... Vi   UPA1-3628   Take 'Em Off, Take 'Em Off, part 2

.... > *JH*, TGrs.

.... Vi   UPA1-3629   A Tiny Bit Of Blues

JOHNNY HODGES ALL STARS   10 Jan 1967   (S)
CA, LB, JHtn JH, JJns BBry LS *AB* RJo.   New York City, NY

.... Vi   UPA1-3630   Wild Onions[1]
.... Vi   UPA1-3631   On The Way Up

.... > *JH*, JJns BBry LS *AB*.

.... Vi   UPA1-3632   The Very Thought Of You

.... > Entire band.

.... Vi   UPA1-3633   Figurine

.... > *JH*, LS *AB* RJo.

.... Vi   UPA1-3634   Sir John

.... > RE, BPwl, *JH HC*, JJns NP BBtl JBjm OJ.

.... Bb   UPA1-3635   Big Boy Blues
.... Vi   UPA1-3636   The "C" Jam Blues
.... Vi   UPA1-3640   Fur Piece

[1]*sa* "For Jammers Only."

The missing master numbers are unaccounted for.

PAUL GONSALVES QUARTET   *c* Jan 1967   (S)
PG, JJns BCrs AHth.   Stockholm, Sweden

.... Stv   In A Mellotone
.... Stv   Ballad Medley[1]
.... Stv   You Go To My Head
.... Stv   St. Louis Blues

[1]Including: I Cover The Waterfront; Willow Weep For Me; Gone With The Wind.

ALL STAR BAND   26 Mar 1967   (P)
JH BCrt CHwk, OPsn SJ LHs.   Carnegie Hall
                                                                                   New York City, NY

.... Pab   The "C" Jam Blues

ALL STAR BAND   1 Jul 1967   (P)
CT, BCrt PG ZS, OPsn SJ BDhm.   Hollywood Bowl
                                                                                   Los Angeles, CA

.... Pab   Now's The Time
.... Pab   Wee
.... Pab   Ballad Medley[1]   >>>

[1]Including: Memories Of You; Misty; I Can't Get Started.

T-BONE WALKER
Vcl, acc. by CT, JH PG, OPsn SJ BDhm.

....	Pab		Woman, You Must Be Crazy –vTBW
....	Pab		Stormy Monday –vTBW

17 Aug 1967   (S)
New York City, NY

JOHNNY HODGES & HIS ORCHESTRA
SY ER BBry, TStd, JHtn JH FWss JRsn DBnk, HJo EBkd MHtn GTt.

....	Vrv	103.367	Eydee-Dee Dee
....	Vrv	103.368	A Blues Serenade[1]
....	Vrv	103.369	You've Changed

[1]"Serenade In Blue" [*sic*] on Vrv.

18 Aug 1967   (S)
New York City, NY

JOHNNY HODGES & HIS ORCHESTRA
SY ER BBry, TStd, JHtn JH FWss JRsn DBnk, HJo CL MHtn GTt.

....	Vrv	103.370	The Wonder Of You
....	Vrv	103.371	Heel Kickin'
....	Vrv	103.372	Some Fun

21 Aug 1967   (S)
New York City, NY

JOHNNY HODGES & HIS ORCHESTRA
SY ER BBry, TStd, JHtn JH FWss JRsn DBnk, HJo BLcs EBkd MHtn GTt.

....	Vrv	103.373	Everytime She Walks
....	Vrv	103.374	Wisteria
....	Vrv	103.375	Don't Sleep In The Subway

14 Nov 1967   (S)
San Francisco, CA

JOHNNY HODGES & EARL HINES
CA, BCpr, JHtn JH, EH JCmn SWrd.

....	Vrv	104.010	Mean To Me
....	Vrv	104.011	Night Train To Memphis
....	Vrv	104.012	Doll Valley
....	Vrv	104.013	Can A Moose Crochet?
....	Vrv	104.014	One Night In Trinidad

15 Nov 1967   (S)
San Francisco, CA

JOHNNY HODGES & EARL HINES
CA, BCpr, JHtn JH, EH JCmn SWrd.

....	Vrv	104.015	Bustin' With Buster
....	Vrv	104.016	Do It Yourself
....	Vrv	104.017	Over The Rainbow
....	Vrv	104.018	Open Ears
....	Vrv	104.019	The Cannery Walk

17 Sep 1968   (S)
Buenos Aires, Argentina

PAUL GONSALVES WITH WILLIE COOK AND ENRIQUE VILLEGAS
WC, PG, EV ARms ECsl.

....	Trv		Perdido
....	Trv		Recorro los Muelles (I Cover The Waterfront)
....	Trv		Blues para Buenos Aires
....	Trv		St. Louis Blues
....	Trv		Medley[1]
....	Trv		Simplemente Amigos (Just Friends)
....	Trv		No Puedo Empezar (I Can't Get Started)

[1]Including: Lo que el Viento se Llevo (Gone With The Wind); Tiernamente (Tenderly); Ramona.

Dec 1968   (S)
New York City, NY

JOHNNY HODGES & HIS BAND
JH, WG JPdr RCtr FWts.

....	Vrv	105.883	Cue Time
....	Vrv	105.884	Moonflower
....	Vrv	105.885	Touch Love[1]
....	Vrv	105.888	Jeep Bounced Back
....	Vrv	105.889	Rio Segundo
....	Vrv	105.890	Rippin' And Runnin'
....	Vrv	105.891	Tell Everybody's Children

[1]*aka* "Love Island."   >>>

The missing master numbers are unaccounted for.

28/29 Dec 1968   (S)
Upper Marlboro, MD

HAROLD ASHBY & HIS GROUP
HAsh, JHs KBts JCbb.

....	Mnm	Reminiscing
....	Mnm	Stampash
....	Mnm	Lotus Blossom
....	Mnm	Forever
....	Mnm	Tasty
....	Mnm	Just For You
....	Mnm	Neat
....	Mnm	The Intimacy Of The Blues
....	Mnm	Sultry Serenade
....	Mnm	Sweet Nuthins

17 Nov 1969   (S)
Paris, France

PAUL GONSALVES ALL STARS
PDtr, *CCrs* DBrl MCcs LFts CGst, *NTrn PG* GB, GGbs RGlz TMtn.

....	BSt	Darn That Dream

> XCh, FGn added.

....	BSt	Jumpin' At The Woodside

17+19 Mar 1970   (S)
New York City, NY

JOHNNY HODGES WITH OLIVER NELSON & HIS ORCHESTRA
JH with Oliver Nelson & His Orchestra, featuring ER SY, QJ, EH HJo GTt, LThs.

....	FD	Empty Ballroom Blues
....	FD	Duke's Place –vLThs
....	FD	Echoes Of Harlem
....	FD	Disillusion Blues –vLThs
....	FD	Yearning
....	FD	Welcome To New York –vLThs
....	FD	Black, Brown And Beautiful
....	FD	Rockin' In Rhythm
....	FD	Creole Love Call
....	FD	It's Glory

p 17/19 Mar 1970   (S)
New York City, NY

JOHNNY HODGES WITH OLIVER NELSON & HIS ORCHESTRA
JH with Oliver Nelson & His Orchestra.

....		Three Shades Of Blue
....		Medley[1]

[1]Including: The Mooche; Clarinet Lament; Echoes Of Harlem.

6 Jul 1970   (S)
Paris, France

PAUL GONSALVES ALL STARS
CA, *NTrn PG*, PWrd[1] JBjm ATlr.

....	BSt	Midnight Stroll
....	BSt	I Cover The Waterfront
....	BSt	Walkin'
....	BSt	Alerado

> *NTrn PG* omitted.

....	Riv	St. Louis Blues

> *NTrn PG* added.

....	Riv	Moon Love
....	Riv	Blues For Marilee
....	Riv	Sugar Loaf

[1]BD used the pseudonym *Prince Woodyard* for this session.

19 Jul 1970   (P)
Tortuga Club
Pescara, Italy

PAUL GONSALVES ALL STARS
CA, *PG*, GArv JSam CSds.

....	PS	Just Friends

28 Aug 1970   (S)
New York City, NY

RAY NANCE & PAUL GONSALVES
RN, PG, RFo AHll OJ.

....	BL	Lotus Blossom >>>

....	BL	Just A-Settin' And A-Rockin' –vRN	
....	BL	Hy'a Sue	
....	BL	I'm In The Market For You	
....	BL	Tea For Two	

3 Sep 1970   (S)
New York City, NY

RAY NANCE & PAUL GONSALVES
RN, NTrn PG, HJo AHII OJ.

.... BL   B.P. Blues

    > *RN,* HJo AHII OJ.

.... BL   Don't Blame Me

    > *PG,* HJo AHII OJ.

.... BL   I Cover The Waterfront

    > *NTrn,* HJo AHII OJ.

.... BL   Angel Eyes

    > Entire band.

.... BL   Stompy Jones

15 Dec 1970   (S)
New York City, NY

EARL HINES & PAUL GONSALVES
PG, EH AHII JJ.

....	BL	What Am I Here For?
....	BL	I Got It Bad
....	BL	Moten Swing
....	BL	Over The Rainbow
....	BL	It Don't Mean A Thing

20 Jul 1970   (P)
University of Wisconsin

HAROLD ASHBY & PAUL GONSALVES
HAsh and *PG* talking.

....   Clinic

24 Aug 1973   (S)
New York City, NY

PAUL GONSALVES & ROY ELDRIDGE
RE, *PG,* CSms SJ ELck.

....	Fan	5400 North
....	Fan	I Cover The Waterfront
....	Fan	The "C" Jam Blues
....	Fan	Body And Soul
....	Fan	Somebody Loves Me –vRE
....	Fan	Satin Doll

_____

The *italicized* initials refer to the *Ellingtonians.*

Index of Titles

>Hy'a Sue ... 22nov48; 23nov48; 24nov48; 27nov48; 10dec48; feb49; feb49;
...22mar53; 30mar53; 27jun53; (4)jun62; 8jul62; *28aug70*
HYDE PARK –aka "Every Tub" 13jul33; 16may36
HYGIENE *8sep60*
(A) HYMN OF SORROW –from "Symphony In Black" c.17-24oct34

I AIN'T GOT NOTHIN' BUT THE BLUES .... 1dec44; 19dec44; (6)3jan45;
...3mar45; 25mar45; 6apr45; 7apr45; 22apr45; 4may45; 12may45; 26may45;
...9jun45; 18aug45; 24sep45; 6oct45; oct/nov45; 10nov45; 20jan46; 25jun57;
...5sep73
I AIN'T YOUR HEN, MR. FLY ROOSTER *28aug28*
I AM ANGRY –from "Saturday Laughter"
I AM BUBBLED –from "Beggar's Holiday"
I BEEPED WHEN I SHOULDA BOPPED *18aug49*
I CAN'T BEGIN TO TELL YOU 17nov45; 24nov45; 3dec45
I CAN'T BELIEVE THAT YOU'RE IN LOVE WITH ME .... (2)8mar37;
...*p.oct41*, (2)*5may45*; 17jan45; 8sep45; 28sep45; 8oct45; 27oct45;
...27apr46; 17jul46; 14nov46, 22nov60; *1963*; *19aug66*
I CAN'T DANCE *7may35*
I CAN'T GET ENOUGH OF YOU *1945*
I CAN'T GET STARTED 4may46; 31may50; 9jun51; 8feb53; 9feb53;
...7-8feb56; 1mar61; 10jun63; 21dec65; 22jul67; 10aug67; 24aug67; 31aug67;
...17apr68; 11sep68; 12sep68; *17sep68*; 14oct68; 26oct68; (5)23nov68;
...20jan69; 30may69; 21jul69; 4nov69; 8nov69; 25mar70; 2apr70; 19apt70;
...28jun70; 14feb71; 22feb71; 24apr71; 18jun71; 9oct71; 18oct71; 19oct71;
...19oct71; 20oct71; 21oct71; 21oct71; 28oct71; 5nov71; 8nov71; 10nov71;
...11nov71; 26nov71; 11feb72; 21feb72; 25feb72; 14apr72; 21jul72; 30jan73;
...31jan73; 1feb73; 3feb73; 20sep73; 5nov73; 30nov73; 1dec73; 1dec73;
...2dec73; 3dec73; 5dec73
I CAN'T GIVE YOU ANYTHING BUT LOVE 30oct28; 10nov28;
...(2)22dec32; 26oct37; 10may47; 29dec47; 1jul48; 7apr53; 4oct53; c.oct54;
...6aug58; 31dec69; 14feb71; 18jun71; 28aug71; 19apr72; 27aug72
I CAN'T PUT MY ARMS AROUND A MEMORY
I CAN'T REALIZE YOU LOVE ME 8jan31
I CAN'T STOP LOVING YOU .... (2)19may64; 31may64; 8-11apr68
I COULD GET A MAN –from "Satin Doll" .... (3)22dec47
I COULDN'T HAVE DONE IT ALONE 5jan62
I COULD WRITE A BOOK *15mar55*; 24feb63
I COVER THE WATERFRONT 17jan45; *1950/oct51*; 17jan57; *13nov58*;
...*20dec60*; *17sep68*; 6jul70; 3sep70; 24aug73
I CRIED FOR YOU *30jun36*; *22aug45*; *1952*; 4sep63
I CRIED THEN I CRIED 26dec65; 26dec65
I'D BE THERE –aka "One For The Duke" qv
I'D DO IT ALL OVER AGAIN 23sep45; 4oct45; 20oct45; 24oct45; 29oct45
I DID DIE *17mar55*
I DIDN'T KNOW ABOUT YOU .... *5apr44*; 1dec44; 19dec44; (4)2jan45;
...15jan45; 23jan45; 25mar45; 6apr45; 11apr45; 22apr45; 29apr45; 29dec45;
...26jun45; *5apr58*; *mid.jul60*; 10aug60; 15+18aug62; 1mar63; 8jun63;
...14apr72; (4)25aug72; 31aug72; (2)5sep72; 11may73; 25aug73; 1dec73;
...5mar74
I DIDN'T KNOW WHAT TIME IT WAS *19may59*
IDIOM '59 (I-III) 4jul59; 8sep59
I DO IT 1dec26
I DONE CAUGHT YOU BLUES 30oct28
I DON'T CARE –from "Man With Four Sides"
I DON'T KNOW WHAT KIND OF BLUES I GOT .... (2)2dec41; 6jun43;
...28aug43
I DON'T KNOW WHY I LOVE YOU SO .... (2)20jan36
I DON'T MIND (I) .... (2)26feb42; 7may42; 26jul42; 12may45; 7jul45; 25aug45
I DON'T MIND (II) –aka "All Too Soon" qv; "Slow Tune"
I DON'T WANT ANYBODY AT ALL 4apr43; may43; 7sep43; 9nov43
I DON'T WANT NOBODY AT ALL 31aug67; 3feb71; 14feb71; 22feb71;
...24apr71; 2jul71; 27jul71; 17dec72; 30jan73; 31jan73; 4feb73; 26aug73
I DON'T WANT NOBODY BUT YOU –aka "Tell Me 'Bout My Baby" qv
I DON'T WANT TO SET THE WORLD ON FIRE 3dec41
I DON'T WANT TO WALK WITHOUT YOU, BABY 7may42; 29aug42
I DREAM OF YOU *10aug60*
IF A BODY –from "Satin Doll"
IF DREAMS COME TRUE 24mar38; 1may38; 15may38
I FEEL SO GOOD .... (4)29mar62
I FELL AND BROKE MY HEART .... (2)*29sep47*
IFIDA –aka "Broot's Roots" qv
IF I GIVE MY HEART TO YOU 1sep54; 13nov54; 11jun55
IF I HAD A RIBBON BOW 1958
IF I HAD YOU *17mar55*; 10sep58

IF I LOVED YOU 8sep45; 20oct45; 24nov45
IF I KNEW NOW WHAT I KNEW THEN –aka "Change My Ways" qv; from
..."Pousse-Café"
IF I KNEW YOU WERE THERE *19apr50*
IF I RULED THE WORLD 25apr68
IF I SHOULD LOOSE YOU *jan63*
IF I THOUGHT YOU CARED –aka "Imagination" .... (2)19jan38
IF I WAS JEHOVAH –from "Shout Up A Morning"
IF I WERE YOU .... (2)*29apr38*; 2jan62
I FOUND A MILLION DOLLAR BABY *13dec56*
IF YOU ARE BUT A DREAM ... 21apr45; 26apr45; 19may45; 14jul45; 6oct45;
...3nov45
IF YOU CAN'T HOLD THE MAN YOU LOVE 30mar26; 10jan27
IF YOU'RE EVER IN MY ARMS AGAIN .... (2)16jun37
IF YOU WANNA BE MY BABY 24sep60
IF YOU WERE IN MY PLACE –from "Cotton Club Parade Of 1938"
...(2)24feb38; 24mar38; 28mar38; 22may38; 23jan56; *22jul58*
I GET A KICK OUT OF YOU 15jan45; 23jan45; c.oct54; *17mar55*
I GET LONELY FOR A PLAYTHING –from "Saturday Laughter"
I GIVE YOU MY WORD *sep/oct40*
IGLO –aka "Iglo Blue"; "Igoo" qv; from "Suite For Swinging" .... (7)26aug64
IGLO BLUE –aka "Iglo" qv; "Igoo" qv; from "Suite For Swinging"
IGOO –aka "Iglo" qv; "Iglo Blue"; from Suite For Swinging"; "Ad Lib For
...Nippon," part 2 ... 30jan65; 30jan65; 31jan65; 3feb65; 9feb65; 12feb65;
...13feb65; 13feb65; 14feb65; 14feb65; 16feb65; 16feb65; 16feb65; 27feb65;
...27feb65; 28feb65; 28feb65; (3)4mar65; 26aug65; 18sep65; 31oct65;
...28jan66; 17dec66; (13oct67)
I GOT A STEADY JOB –from "H.M.S. Times Square"
I GOT IT BAD –from "Jump For Joy" .... (2)26jun41; lt.nov41; 5may45;
...17sep45; 13oct45; *p.jul/aug46*; 3aug46; 31aug47; *11feb50*; 3may51;
...5jan52; 25mar52; 29apr52; *17jul52*; 26nov52; 9feb53; 29apr54; 1may54;
...*14dec54*; 11jun55; 20jul55; 24oct55; 31dec55; 27jan56; may56; 7jul56;
...9jul56; 15jul56; 18jul56; 21jul56; 28jul56; 26aug56; 6jan57; 2mar57; 3apr57;
...20apr57; 1jun57; 25jun57; 12jul57; (2)27jun58; 3jul58; 31jul58; 28dec58;
...20jan-8feb59; 9mar59; 24mar59; 21jun59; 27jun59; 4jul59; *sum.59*;
...20sep59; 7dec59; 27may60; *p.mid.60*; 14mar61; *22mar61*; 3apr61;
...*11dec61*; (2)29mar62; 23apr62; 3jun62; 17jun62; 24sep62; 19nov62;
...10dec62; 7feb63; 12feb63; 6jul63; 12aug63; 9sep63; 11sep63; 13sep63;
...10oct63; 3nov63; 22mar64; 5-8apr64; 5-8apr64; 26may64; 31may64;
...24jun64; 28jun64; 13dec64; 31dec64; 30jan65; 28feb65; 10jul65; 28jul65;
...9may66; 20may66; 2jun66; 3jul66; 4jul66; 6jul66; 8jul66; 10jul66; 15jul66;
...27jul66; 15aug66; 25aug66; 18sep66; 24sep66; 28oct66; 16nov66; 25jan67;
...25jan67; 31jan57; 31jan67; 1feb67; 5feb67; 5feb67; 10feb67; 11feb67;
...13feb67; 19feb67; 11mar67; p.apr67; 1jul67; ear.jul67; 22jul67; 29jul67;
...2aug67; 30aug67; 16sep67; 7oct67; 18oct67; 1967; 25jan68; 27jan68;
...30jan68; 19apr68; 25apr68; 24may68; 19aug68; 26aug68; 5sep68;
...17apr68; 17apr68; 11sep68; 23-29sep68; 2oct68; 14oct68; 28oct68;
...9nov68; 6dec68; 18feb69; mar69; 30may69; 31aug69; 30oct69; 17nov69;
...15-17dec69; 1jan70; 10jan70; 10jan70; 15jan70; 5feb70; 19apr70; 20jun70;
...28jun70; 3jul70; 14jul70; 17jul70; 18jul70; 21jul70; 24jul70; 25jul70; 28jul70;
...12sep70; 18sep70; 2oct70; (2)9dec70; (5)11dec70; *15dec70*; 22dec70;
...31dec70; 2feb71; 14feb71; 17feb71; 22feb71; 26feb71; 12apr71; 16apr71;
...20apr71; 18jun71; 27jul71; 4aug71; 7nov71; 14apr72; 23jun72; 8jul72;
...18jul72; 30jul72; 2aug72; 31aug72; (3)5sep72; 30jan73; 31jan73; 20apr73;
...11may73; 16jul73; 31jul73; 3aug73; 25aug73; 4sep73; 20sep73; 3oct73;
...25oct73; 28oct73; 3nov73; 5nov73; 7nov73; 8nov73; 14nov73; 18nov73;
...30nov73; 1dec73; 1dec73; 2dec73; 3dec73; 7dec73; 10feb74; 8mar74
I GOT NOTHIN' BUT YOU 14nov59
I GOTTA RIGHT TO SING THE BLUES .... 8+9dec60
I GOT THE BLUES [sic] –see "Everybody Wants To Know"
I GOT YOUR WATER ON *15jul49*
I HAVE FAITH 20jun43
I HAVE GIVEN MY LOVE
I HAVE NO REASON TO COMPLAIN *15jul49*
I HEAR A RHAPSODY 15jan41
I KNOW THAT YOU KNOW 26apr37; 5apr39; 26dec50
I KNOW WHAT YOU DO 15oct39
I LEFT MY BABY 22oct57
I LEFT MY HEART IN SAN FRANCISCO 27apr64; 31may64; jul64;
...30sep64; 13dec64; 17apr68; 25apr68; 30may69
I LEFT MY SUGAR IN SALT LAKE CITY 6jul43; *p.1945*
I LET A SONG GO OUT OF MY HEART .... (2)3mar38; 28mar38; 8may38;
...6oct38; 20sep39; (2)15may45; jul45; 6jun51; 22mar52; 6aug52; sep52;
...31dec52; 22mar53; 30apr53; jun53; 16dec53; 8frb54; *9apr54*; 29apr54;
...29apr54; *15jun54*; 13nov54; *ear.55*; 11jun55; 9jul55; 27jan56; *3apr57*;   >>>

Song titles with no entry date can be assumed to have not been recorded by Duke Ellington. They were listed regardless, in order to give a complete account of Ellington as a composer as well.

The *italicized* entries refer to "The Ellingtonians" section.

Index of Musicians

The instruments listed are only those the musicians played in performing the music contained in this book.

General Index

Cities and Venues

Not included in the above index are the studios of the record companies as well as the independent studios (such as National Recording Studios in New York City and Universal Studios in Chicago) where Ellington rented studio time to make his own recordings.

On the Air

The following information is based on the file cards of the various radio stations, the files of Jerry Valburn and other sources.

ABC (American Broadcasting Company), also often referred to as "The Blue Network," NYC, with flagship station WJZ. ABC network stations and affiliates: Albany NY: WROW; Chicago IL: WENR; Detroit MI: WJR; Los Angeles CA: KABC, TBC; Philadelphia PA: WSL; Reading PA: WEEU; San Francisco CA: KGO.

CBS (Columbia Broadcasting System), NYC, with flagship station WABC, later WCBS. CBS network stations and affiliates: Albany NY: WROW; Boston MA: WEEI; Chicago IL: WBBM; Knoxville TN: WNOX; Lost Angeles CA: KNX; Madison WI: WKOW; Philadelphia PA: WCAU ; San Francisco CA: KCBS, KFRC; St. Louis MO: KMOX; Washington DC: WTOP, later WJSV.

MBS (Mutual Broadcasting System), NYC, with flagship station WOR, and affiliate station WIP in Philadelphia PA.

Mutual—Don Lee (Los Angeles CA). Separate MBS network operation on the west coast, with affiliated stations KHC (Culver City).

NBC (National Broadcasting System), NYC, maintained until 1942 two separate networks, the "Red" (WEAF), and the "Blue" (WJZ). NBC network stations and affiliates: Chicago IL: WENR (Blue), WMAQ (Red); Cleveland OH: WTAM (Red); Detroit MI: WTMJ (Blue), WWJ; Hollywood CA: KECA (Blue), KFI (Red); Houston TX: KXYZ (Blue); Milwaukee WI: WTMJ (Red); Philadelphia PA: KYW; San Francisco CA: KGO (Red), KNBC (Blue), KPO (Blue); Schenectady NY: WGY; St. Louis MO: KSD; Washington DC: WMAL (Blue), WRC (Red).

Independent radio stations: Boston MA: WCOP, WGHB; Charlotte NC: WBTV; Chicago IL: WBKW, WCFL, WGN; Cincinnati OH: WLWT; Cleveland OH: WEWS; Detroit MI: WJR; Dodge City KS: KENO; Hartford CT: WTYC; Hollywood CA: KMPC, KPAS; Los Angeles CA: KFAC, KTTV; Moorhead MN: KVOX; New York City NY: WABD, WHN, WINS, WMCA, WMGM, WNEW, WNYC, WPIX, WRVR, Niagara Falls NY: WHLD; Pasadena CA: KPAS; Philadelphia PA: WBWS, WDAS, WFIL; Pittsburgh PA: WWSW; San Francisco CA: KHIP, KQED, KTTV; South Bend IN: WSND.

5nov25 WHN Kentucky Club, NYC.
13jan26 WHN Kentucky Club, NYC.
19mar28 CBS Cotton Club, NYC.
30apr28 WHN Cotton Club, NYC.
24oct29 NBC R.K.O. "Theatre of the Air," NYC.
1929 CBS Cotton Club, NYC.
17apr30 CBS International Program to Australia.
30apr30 CBS Cotton Club, NYC.
24oct30 NBS Amos 'n' Andy, Chicago IL. (The Ellington portion was most
...likely transmitted from the Cotton Club.)
10mar32 KHJ Impromptu program, Los Angeles CA.
11apr32* WTIC Publix Allyn Theatre, Hartford CT.
28apr32 CBS Gold Dust Corporation Show, NYC.
2may33 NBC (Blue) Cotton Club, NYC.
4may33 NBC (Red) Cotton Club, NYC (12:00M-12:30A).
5may33 NBC (Blue) Cotton Club, NYC (12:00M).
11may33 NBC (Red) Cotton Club, NYC (12:15-12:30A).
12may33 NBC (Blue) Cotton Club, NYC (12:00M).
18may33 NBC (Red) Cotton Club, NYC (12:15-12:30A).
19may33 NBC (Blue) Cotton Club, NYC (12:00M).
25may33 NBC (Red) Cotton Club, NYC (12:15-12:30A).
26may33 NBC (Red) Cotton Club, NYC (12:00M).
27may33 CBS (remote) Around Town, Capitol Theatre, NYC.
29may33 NBC (Red) Cotton Club, NYC (11:30P).
30may33 NBC (Red) Cotton Club, NYC (12:00M).
14jun33 BBC DE & His American Dance Orchestra, p. London, England.
11jul33 CBS Gold Dust Corporation Show, NYC.
19mar34 KFI MJB Coffee Hour "Demi-Tasse Revue," NBC Studios,
...Hollywood CA (7:30-8:00P).
26mar34 KFI MJB Coffee Hour "Demi-Tasse Revue," NBC Studios,
...Hollywood CA (7:30-8:00P).
2apr34 KFI MJB Coffee Hour "Demi-Tasse Revue," NBC Studios,
...Hollywood CA (7:30-8:00P).
5apr34 KFAC Sebastian's Cotton Club, Culver City CA.
6apr34 KFAC Sebastian's Cotton Club, Culver City CA.
7apr34 KFAC Sebastian's Cotton Club, Culver City CA.
8apr34 KFAC Sebastian's Cotton Club, Culver City CA.
9apr34 KFI MJB Coffee Hour "Demi-Tasse Revue," NBC Studios,
...Hollywood CA (7:30-8:00P).
9apr34 KFAC Sebastian's Cotton Club, Culver City CA.
10apr34 KFAC Sebastian's Cotton Club, Culver City CA.
11apr34 KFAC Sebastian's Cotton Club, Culver City CA.

12apr34 KFAC Sebastian's Cotton Club, Culver City CA.
13apr34 KFAC Sebastian's Cotton Club, Culver City CA.
14apr34 KFAC Sebastian's Cotton Club, Culver City CA.
15apr34 KFAC Sebastian's Cotton Club, Culver City CA.
16apr34 KFI MJB Coffee Hour "Demi-Tasse Revue," NBC Studios,
...Hollywood CA.
16apr34 KFAC Sebastian's Cotton Club, Culver City CA.
17apr34 KFAC Sebastian's Cotton Club, Culver City CA.
18apr34 KFAC Sebastian's Cotton Club, Culver City CA.
23apr34 KFI MJB Coffee Hour "Demi-Tasse Revue," San Francisco CA
...(7:30-8:00P).
30apr34 KFI MJB Coffee Hour "Demi-Tasse Revue," NBC Studios,
...Hollywood CA (6:30-7:00P).
7may34 KFI MJB Coffee Hour "Demi-Tasse Revue," NBC Studios,
...Hollywood CA (7:30-8:00P).
14may34 KFI MJB Coffee Hour "Demi-Tasse Revue," NBC Studios,
...Hollywood CA (7:30-8:00P).
19aug34 NBC Hall of Fame, NBC Studios, Chicago IL.
12nov34 WJSV Community Chest Drive, Studios WJSV, Washington DC
...(11:00P-12:00M).
13dec34 WMCA Apollo Theatre, NYC.
15jul35 KTAT Sylvan Club, Ft. Worth TX.
16jul35 KTAT Sylvan Club, Ft. Worth TX.
17jul35 KTAT Sylvan Club, Ft. Worth TX.
18jul35 KTAT Sylvan Club, Ft. Worth TX.
18jul35 KXYZ Aragon Ballroom, Houston TX (11:00P) (questionable).
19jul35 KTAT Sylvan Club, Ft. Worth TX.
20jul35 KTAT Sylvan Club, Ft. Worth TX.
21jul35 KTAT Sylvan Club, Ft. Worth TX.
9oct35 WMCA Apollo Theatre, NYC.
4nov35 WWSW Savoy Ballroom, Pittsburgh PA (10:00P).
30nov35 WCOP Rhythm News, DE interviewed by Lee Emerson, Roseland
...State Ballroom, Boston MA (3:15P).
31dec35 CBS Bal Tabarin, Hotel Sherman, Chicago IL.
19feb36 WMCA Apollo Theatre, NYC.
8may36* WENR (NBC Blue) Congress Hotel, Chicago IL (11:00-11:30P).
9may36 WENR (NBC Blue) Congress Hotel, Chicago IL (11:00-11:30P).
14may36 WMAQ (NBC Red) Congress Hotel, Chicago IL (11:00-11:30P).
16may36* WENR (NBC Blue) Congress Hotel, Chicago IL (11:00-11:30P).
21may36 WMAQ (NBC Red) Congress Hotel, Chicago IL (11:00-11:30P).
23may36* WENR (NBC Blue) Congress Hotel, Chicago IL (11:00-11:30P).
28may36 WMAQ (NBC Red) Congress Hotel, Chicago IL (11:00-11:30P).

2aug36 WEAF+WTAM Palace Theatre, Cleveland OH (11:00P).
12sep36 CBS Saturday Night Swing Club, CBS Studios, NYC (8:00P).
16sep36 WMCA Apollo Theatre, NYC.
8jan37 KHJ Parade of Bands, Sebastian's Cotton Club, Culver City CA
...(11:30P-12:00M).
12jan37 KHJ Swing Concert, Sebastian's Cotton Club, Culver City CA.
23dec36-18jan37 KFAC/KHJ Sebastian's Cotton Club, Culver City CA; in
...addition to the above listings the band apparently was regularly broadcast
...locally.
1jan37 WDR Sebastian's Cotton Club, Culver City CA (2:45A).
8mar37 CBS Major Bowes Amateur Hour, Capitol Theatre, NYC.
13mar37 CBS Saturday Night Swing Club, CBS Studios, NYC (7:00-7:30P).
18mar37* MBS Cotton Club, NYC (11:30P-12:00M).
20mar37 MBS Cotton Club, NYC (11:15-11:30P).
22mar37 MBS Cotton Club, NYC (11:30P-12:00M).
27mar37 WINS Matinée Frolic, Studios WINS, NYC.
27mar37 MBS Cotton Club, NYC (11:15-11:30P).
28mar37 MBS Cotton Club, NYC (11:30P-12:00M).
31mar37 MBS Cotton Club, NYC (11:30P-12:00M).
3apr37 MBS Cotton Club, NYC (11:15P-12:00M).
10apr37 MBS Cotton Club, NYC (11:30P-12:00M).
15apr37 MBS Cotton Club, NYC (11:15-11:30P).
21apr37 MBS Cotton Club, NYC (11:30P-12:00M).
24apr37 MBS Cotton Club, NYC (11:15-11:30P).
25apr37 MBS Cotton Club, NYC (11:30P-12:00M).
1may37 MBS Cotton Club, NYC.
4may37 MBS Cotton Club, NYC.
8may37* CBS Saturday Night Swing Club, CBS Studios, NYC (7:00P).
8may37 MBS Cotton Club, NYC.
9may37 MBS Cotton Club, NYC.
11may37 MBS Cotton Club, NYC.
16may37 MBS Cotton Club, NYC.
17may37 MBS Cotton Club, NYC.
18may37 MBS Cotton Club, NYC.
21may37 CBS Shortwave radio bc to England.
23may37 MBS Cotton Club, NYC.
30may37 MBS Cotton Club, NYC.
30may37 MBS Midnight Benefit Show, Apollo Theatre, NYC.
31may37 MBS Cotton Club, NYC.
12jun37* CBS Saturday Night Swing Club, CBS Studios, NYC (12:00M-
...1:30A).
17mar-15jun37 MBS Cotton Club, NYC; in addition to the above listings
...there might have been more of the thirty-minute broadcasts within the time
...span.
23jun37 WMCA Apollo Theatre, NYC.
3jul37 CBS Saturday Night Swing Club, CBS Studios, NYC.
29sep37 WMCA Apollo Theatre, NYC.
12nov37 WNOX Chilhowee Park, Knoxville TN (5:30P).
12nov37 WNOX Chilhowee Park, Knoxville TN (10:30P).
16jan38 WNEW Sunday Swing Session, NYC.
22jan38 CBS Saturday Night Swing Club, CBS Studios, NYC (7:00-7:30P).
26jan38 WMCA Apollo Theatre, NYC.
26feb38 CBS Saturday Night Swing Club, CBS Studios, NYC (4:00P).
27feb38 CBS Major Bowes Amateur Hour, CBS Studios or Capitol Theatre,
...NYC.
8mar38 WMCA Harlem Review (?Revue), NYC.
10mar38 CBS Cotton Club, NYC (11:05-11:30P).
13mar38 CBS Cotton Club, NYC (11:30P-12:00M).
17mar38 CBS Cotton Club, NYC (11:05-11:30P).
20mar38 CBS Cotton Club, NYC (11:30P-12:00M).
24mar38* CBS Cotton Club, NYC (11:05-11:30P).
27mar38 CBS Cotton Club, NYC (11:30P-12:00M).
31mar38 CBS Cotton Club, NYC (11:05-11:30P).
3apr38 CBS Cotton Club, NYC (11:30P-12:00M).
7apr38 CBS Cotton Club, NYC (11:05-11:30P).
10apr38 CBS Cotton Club, NYC (11:35P-12:00M).
14apr38 CBS Cotton Club, NYC (11:15-11:30P).
14apr38 CBS Cotton Club, NYC (11:30P-12:00M).
17apr38* CBS Cotton Club, NYC (11:30P-12:00M).
21apr38 CBS Cotton Club, NYC (11:05-11:30P).
24apr38* CBS Cotton Club, NYC (11:30P-12:00M).
28apr38 NBC Glass Container "Steinie Bottle Boys," NYC.
28apr38 CBS Cotton Club, NYC (11:05-11:30P).
29apr38* CBS America Dances, Cotton Club, NYC (9:30-10:00P);
...shortwaved to England for BBC.

30apr38 CBS Saturday Night Swing Club, CBS Studios, NYC.
1may38* CBS Cotton Club, NYC (11:05-11:30P).
5may38* CBS Cotton Club, NYC (11:05-11:30P).
8may38 WMCA All Negro Variety Show, Academy of Music, Brooklyn NY.
8may38* CBS Cotton Club, NYC (11:05-11:30P).
12may38 CBS Cotton Club, NYC (11:05-11:30P).
15may38* CBS Cotton Club, NYC (11:05-11:30P).
19may38 CBS Cotton Club, NYC (11:05-11:30P).
22may38* CBS Cotton Club, NYC (11:05-11:30P).
26may38 CBS Cotton Club, NYC (11:05-11:30P).
29may38 WNEW Randalls Island Stadium, NYC.
29may38* CBS Cotton Club, NYC (11:05-11:30P).
2jun38 CBS Cotton Club, NYC (11:05-11:30P).
5jun38 CBS Cotton Club, NYC (11:05-11:30P).
16jun38 WMCA Apollo Theatre, NYC.
16jun38 CBS Cotton Club, NYC (11:05-11:30P).
18jun38 WMCA Rhode Island Auditorium, Providence RI (9:30P).
25jun38 CBS Saturday Night Swing Club, CBS Studios, NYC.
14sep38 WINS DE interviewed by Rosalyn Sherman, Studios WINS, NYC.
5oct38 WMCA Apollo Theatre, NYC.
6oct38* CBS America Dances, Apollo Theatre, NYC (9:30-10:00P);
...shortwaved to England for BBC.
21dec38* WNEW Make Believe Ballroom Swing Session, Studios WNEW,
...NYC.
11feb39 CBS Saturday Night Swing Club, NYC.
11feb39 CBS NAACP Dance, 389th Regiment Armory, NYC.
22feb39 WMCA Apollo Theatre, NYC.
15mar39* CBS America Dances, CBS Studios, NYC (7:02-7:30P);
...shortwaved to England for BBC.
29apr39* SR DE interviewed by Manne Berggren for Dagens Eko, Grand
...Hotel, Stockholm, Sweden.
29apr39* SR Konserthuset, Stockholm, Sweden.
28may39* NBC (Red) President's Birthday Ball (prerecorded 30jan39?).
24jul39 NBC (Blue) Ritz-Carlton Hotel, Boston MA (10:30-11:00P).
26jul39* NBC (Blue) Ritz-Carlton Hotel, Boston MA (12:05-12:30A).
26jul39 NBC (Blue) Ritz-Carlton Hotel, Boston MA (7:45-8:00P).
27jul39 NBC (Blue) Ritz-Carlton Hotel, Boston MA (7:30-8'00P).
29jul39 NBC (Blue) Ritz-Carlton Hotel, Boston MA (8:00-8:30P).
31jul39 NBC (Blue) Ritz-Carlton Hotel, Boston MA (10;30-11:00P).
1aug39 NBC Salute to Station KKCA Los Angeles CA; bc from Boston MA.
2aug39 NBC (Blue) Ritz-Carlton Hotel, Boston MA (12:00M-12:30A).
9aug39 NBC (Blue) Ritz-Carlton Hotel, Boston MA (12:00M-12:30A).
16aug39 NBC (Blue) Ritz-Carlton Hotel, Boston MA (12:00M-12:30A).
20sep39* NBC (Red) Bristol-Meyers "Georgie Jessel's Celebrity Hour,
...NBC Studios, NYC.
20sep39 WMCA Apollo Theatre, NYC.
28oct39 CBS Sustaining pickup from the Coronado Hotel, St. Louis MO
...(12:30-1:00A).
2nov39* CBS Corona Hotel, St. Louis MO.
9nov39 CBS Lullaby by Duke Ellington (record #1657).
11nov39 CBS Unidentified location/bc (12:30-1:00A).
24nov39* CBS Young Man with a Band, Merchandise Mart, Chicago IL
...(9:30P).
31dec39 WBBM Meet The Band, Chicago IL (12:30-1:00P).
8jan40* NBC (Blue) Southland Café, Boston MA.
9jan40* NBC (Blue) Southland Café, Boston MA (12:00M-12:20A).
12jan40* NBC (Blue) Southland Café, Boston MA (12:00M-12:30A).
16jan40 NBC (Blue) Southland Café, Boston MA (12:00M-12:30A).
19jan40 NBC (Blue) Southland Café, Boston MA (12:00M-12:30A).
26feb40 NBC Quaker Oats "Quaker Party," NYC.
16mar40 KXOK Tune Town, St. Louis MO (10:30-11:45).
1-14apr40 KIRO Show Box , Seattle WA (Mondays; Wednesdays, Fridays
...(10:45-11:15P).
17apr40 KEW Uptown Ballroom, Portland OR (10:30P).
6may40 KLO White City Ballroom, Ogden UT (9:00P).
12may40 WOW Chermot Ballroom, Omaha NE (11:00P).
12jun40* CBS America Dances, CBS Studios, NYC (produced for BBC);
...prerecorded on 10jun40.
12jun40* MBS Radio Newsreel, NYC.
12jun40 WMCA Apollo Theatre, NYC.
26jul40* NBC (Red) Eastwood Gardens, Detroit MI (12:30-1:00A).
29jul40* NBC (Red) Eastwood Gardens, Detroit MI (12:30-1:00A).
31jul40* NBC (Blue) Eastwood Gardens, Detroit MI (12:30-1:00A).
26-31jul40 WWJ Eastwood Gardens, Detroit MI; in addition to the above
...listings the band was regularly broadcast locally (11:30P-12:00M).

17aug40* NBC   Canobie Lake Park, Salem NH.
5sep40 WGN   In Chicago Tonight, Studios WGN, Chicago IL.
6sep40* WENR (NBC Blue) Hotel Sherman, Chicago IL (11:05-11:30P).
7sep40* WMAQ (NBC Red) Hotel Sherman, Chicago IL (11:05-11:30P).
9sep40 WGN   Your Music I.Q., Studios WGN, Chicago IL.
10sep40* WENR/WMAQ (NBC Blue or Red)   Hotel Sherman, Chicago IL
...(11:30-11:57P).
11sep40 WENR (NBC Blue)   Hotel Sherman, Chicago IL (11:04-11:30P).
12sep40* WMAQ (NBC Red) Hotel Sherman, Chicago IL (12:20-12:57A).
13sep40* WENR (NBC Blue) Hotel Sherman, Chicago IL (11:10-11:30P).
14sep40 WMAQ (NBC Red) Hotel Sherman, Chicago IL (11:05-11:30P).
18sep40* WENR/WMAQ (NBC Blue or Red)   Hotel Sherman, Chicago IL
...(12:20-12:57A).
18sep40 WENR (NBC Blue) Hotel Sherman, Chicago IL (11:05-11:30P).
19sep40 WMAQ (NBC Red) Hotel Sherman, Chicago IL (12:30-12:57A).
20sep40* WENR (NBC Blue) Hotel Sherman, Chicago IL (11:05-11:30P).
25sep40* WENR (NBC Blue) Hotel Sherman, Chicago IL (11:05-11:30P).
26sep40* WMAQ (NBC Red) Hotel Sherman, Chicago IL (12:30-12:57A).
27sep40* WWBM (CBS) Pickup Hotel Sherman, Chicago IL.
27sep40* WENR (NBC Blue) Hotel Sherman, Chicago IL (11:05-11:30P).
28sep40* WMAQ (NBC Red) Hotel Sherman, Chicago IL (11:05-11:30P).
30sep40* WENR (NBC Blue) Hotel Sherman, Chicago IL (11:05-11:30P).
4oct40* WENR (NBC Blue) Hotel Sherman, Chicago IL (11:05-11:30P).
5oct40* WMAQ (NBC Red) Hotel Sherman, Chicago IL (11:05-11:30P).
7oct40 WENR (NBC Blue) Hotel Sherman, Chicago IL (11:05-11:30P).
11oct40* WMAQ (NBC Red) Hotel Sherman, Chicago IL (11:05-11:30P).
12oct40* WMAQ (NBC Red) Hotel Sherman, Chicago IL (11:05-11:30P).
7nov40* KVOX (Moorhead MN) Crystal Ballroom, Fargo ND.
18nov40 NBC   p. Regal Theatre, Chicago IL.
18dec40 WMCA   Apollo Theatre, NYC.
30dec40 KROD   Liberty Hall, El Paso TX (11:00P).
3jan41 KHJ   The Lamplighter, Studios KHJ, Los Angeles CA (4:45-5:00P).
16jan41* NBC   Kraft Music Hall, NBC Studios, Hollywood CA.
28jan41* KHJ   Radio Newsreel, DE interviewed by Doug Hatton at Casa
...Mañana, Culver City CA.
9feb41 KMPC   We Too, Sing America, Studios KMPC, Hollywood CA.
9feb41 KHJ   Casa Mañana, Culver City CA.
11feb41* KHJ   Casa Mañana, Culver City CA.
13feb41* KHJ   Casa Mañana, Culver City CA.
14feb41* KHJ   Casa Mañana, Culver City CA.
15feb41 KHJ   Casa Mañana, Culver City CA (11:30P).
16feb41* KHJ   Casa Mañana, Culver City CA (10:00P).
17feb41 KHJ   Casa Mañana, Culver City CA.
18feb41 KHJ   Casa Mañana, Culver City CA (9:30P).
18feb41 KHJ   Casa Mañana, Culver City CA (11:00P).
19feb41 KHJ   Casa Mañana, Culver City CA.
20feb41* KHJ   Casa Mañana, Culver City CA (11:30P).
30mar41* CBS   Tribute to the National Urban League, CBS Studios,
...Hollywood CA.
29may41* NBC   Kraft Music Hall, NBC Studios, Hollywood CA.
may/jun41* KHJ   Trianon Ballroom, Southgate CA.
2jun41 KHJ   Trianon Ballroom, Southgate CA.
2jun41 NBC (Blue)   Chamber Music Society of Lower Basin Street, NYC;
...prerecorded.
9jun41* KHJ   Salute to Canada Lee, Studios KHJ, Los Angeles CA.
9jun41 KHJ   Trianon Ballroom, Southgate CA.
12jun41* KHJ   Trianon Ballroom, Southgate CA.
16jun41* KHJ   Trianon Ballroom, Southgate CA.
29jun41 KNX/KFWB/KGFJ   Mammoth Hollywood Bowl Show, Los Angeles
...CA (7:30-9:00P).
jun/jul41* KHJ   Trianon Ballroom, Southgate CA.
4jul41 KHJ   The Lamplighter, Studios KHJ, Los Angeles CA (4:45-5:00P).
5jul41 KHJ   Trianon Ballroom, Southgate CA.
29jul41 CBS   USO Benefit, unidentified location, CA.
25aug41* CBS   All Star Program #13 "Jubilee," CBS Studios, Hollywood
...CA (9:00-10:00P).
1sep41* NBC   Salute to Labor, NBC Studios, Hollywood CA.
9oct41* NBC   Kraft Music Hall, Hollywood CA (6:00-7:00P).
30jan42 NBC   President's Diamond Jubilee Birthday Celebration.
apr/may42* KHJ   Trianon Ballroom, Southgate CA.
2may42* KHJ   Trianon Ballroom, Southgate CA.
p.may42* KHJ   Trianon Ballroom, Southgate CA.
7may42* KHJ   Trianon Ballroom, Southgate CA.
2apr-12may42 KHJ   Trianon Ballroom, Southgate CA; in addition to the
above listings, acetates and/or broadcasts may exist.

6jun42 CJOR   Kelly's on Seymour, Vancouver BC.
29jun42* WABC   Hollywood Bowl, Los Angeles CA.
10jul42 KHJ   El Patio Ballroom, Lakeside Park, Denver CO.
11jul42 KHJ   El Patio Ballroom, Lakeside Park, Denver CO.
12jul42 KHJ   El Patio Ballroom, Lakeside Park, Denver CO.
13jul42 KHJ   El Patio Ballroom, Lakeside Park, Denver CO.
14jul42* CBS/KLZ El Patio Ballroom, Lakeside Park, Denver CO.
15jul42* CBS/?KLZ El Patio Ballroom, Lakeside Park, Denver CO.
19jul42* WENR   Hotel Sherman, Chicago IL.
21jul42* NBC (Red) Hotel Sherman, Chicago IL.
22jul42* NBC (Red) Hotel Sherman, Chicago IL.
24jul42* WENR   Hotel Sherman, Chicago IL.
26jul42* WENR   Hotel Sherman, Chicago IL.
27jul42* NBC (Red) Hotel Sherman, Chicago IL.
28jul42 WCFL   Treasury Corner, Studios WCFL, Chicago IL.
28jul42* ABC   Hotel Sherman, Chicago IL.
7aug42* ABC   Hotel Sherman, Chicago IL.
8aug42* ABC   Hotel Sherman, Chicago IL.
11aug42* ABC   Hotel Sherman, Chicago IL.
13aug42* NBC (Blue) Hotel Sherman, Chicago IL (11:15-11:30P).
aug42* ABC   Hotel Sherman, Chicago IL; in addition to the above
...broadcasts we have one unidentified program falling into this time span.
29aug42* ABC   Palace Theatre, Cleveland OH.
24sep42 KPAS   The Lamplighter, Studios KHJ, Los Angeles CA.
26sep42 KFOX   Long Beach Auditorium, Long Beach CA (9:00-9:15P).
26sep42 KFOX   Long Beach Auditorium, Long Beach CA (10:00-10:30P).
9oct42* AFRS   El Capitan Theatre, Los Angeles CA.
19nov42* ABC   Victory Parade of Coca Cola Spotlight Bands #52, Fort Dix,
...Trenton NJ (9:30P).
17dec42 WEEI   Biltmore Hotel, Providence RI (12:30-1:00A).
17dec42 CBS (remote through WEEI) Rhode Island Pickup   Rhode Island
...State College Junior Prom (12:30-1:00A).
25dec42 NBC (Blue)   Coca Cola "Uncle Sam's Christmas Tree,"
...unidentified location, p. an army installation in or around Detroit MI.
21jan43 NBC   RCA "Music You Want," NYC.
6mar43 CBS   Negro Press Special Edition, presented by the National
...Negro Publication Association, NYC (2:30-3:30P).
27mar43* CBS   Unidentified broadcast from either Boston MA or Pittsburgh
...PA; p. prerecorded.
1apr43 MBS   Hurricane Club, NYC (10:45-11:00P).
3apr43* MBS   Hurricane Club, NYC.
4apr43* MBS   Hurricane Club, NYC.
apr43* MBS   Hurricane Club, NYC.
7apr43* MBS   Hurricane Club, NYC.
apr43* MBS   Hurricane Club, NYC.
15apr43 MBX   Hurricane Club, NYC (10:45-11:00P).
20apr43* MBS   Hurricane Club, NYC.
21apr43* CBS   Schenley "Cresta Blanca Carnival," CBS Studios, Radio
...City, NYC (10:30-11:00P).
24apr43* MBS   Hurricane Club, NYC.
25apr43* MBS   Hurricane Club, NYC.
1may43* NBC   WEAF War Bond Drive, Radio City, NYC.
2may43* ABC   Chamber Music Society of Lower Basin Street, Studios
...WJZ, NYC.
may43* MBS   Hurricane Club, NYC.
23may43* MBS   Hurricane Club, NYC.
lt.may43* MBS   Hurricane Club, NYC.
28may43* MBS   Hurricane Club, NYC.
29may43* WNEW   News Through a Woman's Eyes; DE interviewed by
...Kathy Craven, Studios WNEW, NYC.
30may43* AFRS   Fitch Bandwagon, NBC Studios, NYC.
6jun43* MBS   Pastel Period, Hurricane Club, NYC.
7jun43* MBS   Hurricane Club, NYC.
jun43* ? (Treasury bc)   Treasury Star Parade #231, Studio Tx recording,
...NYC.
jun43* ? (Treasury bc)   Treasury Star Parade #232, Studio Tx recording,
...NYC.
jun43* ? (Treasury bc)   Treasury Star Parade #233, Studio Tx recording,
...NYC.
11jun43 MBS   Hurricane Club, NYC.
13jun43 MBS   Pastel Period, Hurricane Club, NYC.
18jun43* MBS   Hurricane Club, NYC.
19jun43* NBC   Colgate-Palmolive-Peet Co. "Million Dollar Band," NYC
...(10:00-10:30P)..
20jun43* MBS   Pastel Period, Hurricane Club, NYC.

23jun43* MBS Hurricane Club, NYC.
25jun43* CBS Broadway Band Box, CBS Studios, NYC (11:15P-12:00M).
27jun43* MBS Pastel Period, Huricane Club, NYC.
30jun43* CBS Hurricane Club, NYC.
30jun43 MBS Hurricane Club, NYC.
3jul43 MBS Hurricane Club, NYC.
4jul43 MBS Pastel Period, Hurricane Club, NYC
6jul43* WMCA Pabst Blue Ribbon "Jumpin' Jive," Studios WMCA, NYC.
8jul43* MBS Hurricane Club, NYC.
11jul43* BBC DE interviewed by Alistair Cooke, BBC Studios, NYC;
...shortwaved to England.
11jul43* NBC Pastel Period, Hurricane Club, NYC.
13jul43 MBS Hurricane Club, NYC.
14jul43* MBS Hurricane Club, NYC.
18jul43 MBS Pastel Period, Hurricane Club, NYC.
25jul43 MBS Pastel Period, Hurricane Club, NYC.
2aug43 MBS Hurricane Club, NYC.
3aug43* MBS Hurricane Club, NYC.
9aug43* WHN Hurricane Club, NYC.
14aug43 CBS Hurricane Club, NYC (7:30-8:00P).
14aug43* MBS Hurricane Club, NYC.
19aug43 MBS Hurricane Club, NYC.
21aug43* CBS Hurricane Club, NYC (12:05-12:30A).
21aug43 MBS Hurricane Club, NYC.
24aug43* WHN Hurricane Club, NYC.
26aug43* WHN Hurricane Club, NYC.
27aug43 MBS Hurricane Club, NYC.
28aug43* CBS Hurricane Club, NYC.
28aug43 MBS Hurricane Club, NYC.
29aug43* Hurricane Club, NYC.
aug/sep43* CBS Hurricane Club, NYC.
1sep43* MBS Hurricane Club, NYC.
3sep43* WHN Hurricane Club, NYC.
4sep43 CBS Hurricane Club, NYC (12:05-13:30A).
5sep43* ABC Chamber Music Society of Lower Basin Street, ABC Studios,
...NYC; date of bc is not known.
5sep43* NBC Pastel Period, Hurricane Club, NYC; date of bc is not known.
7sep43* CBS Hurricane Club, NYC.
7sep43* WHN Hurricane Club, NYC (8:00-8:30P).
9sep43* WHN Hurricane Club, NYC.
10sep43* WHN Hurricane Club, NYC.
11sep43* CBS Hurricane Club, NYC (12:05-1:30A).
11sep43 WEAF "Battle of New York" (Bronx portion), NY (1:30-4:00P).
11sep43 MBS Hurricane Club, NYC.
12sep43* MBS Hurricane Club, NYC.
12sep43* CBS Hurricane Club, NYC (11:15-11:30P).
15sep43 MBS Hurricane Club, NYC.
17sep43* MBS Hurricane Club, NYC.
19sep43 CBS Night Clubs for Victory, NYC (12:05-12:30A).
sep43* CBS Hurricane Club, NYC.
sep43* CBS Hurricane Club, NYC.
23sep43* WHN Hurricane Club, NYC.
11nov43* ? War Department voice recording, NYC.
27nov43* ABC Victory Parade of Spotlight Bands #372, Memorial
...Auditorium, Buffalo NY (9:30P).
9dec43* ABC Victory Parade of Spotlight Bands #381, Langley Field ...AFB,
Hampton VA (9:30P); prerecorded 8dec43.
31dec43 CBS (through WBBM) Hotel Stevens, Chicago IL (1:00-1:15A).
1jan44 CBS (through WBBM) Hotel Stevens, Chicago IL (12:30-1:00A).
5jan44 CBS (through WBBM) Hotel Stevens, Chicago IL (12:30-1:00A).
28feb44 CBS Negro News Week Program, Dayton OH (11:30A-12:00N).
30mar44 MBS Hurricane Club, NYC (12:00M-12:30A).
1apr44* MBS Hurricane Club, NYC (11:30-11:45P).
2apr44* MBS Hurricane Club, NYC.
7apr44* MBS Hurricane Club, NYC.
8apr44* MBS Hurricane Club, NYC.
9apr44* MBS Hurricane Club, NYC.
13apr44* MBS Hurricane Club, NYC (12:00M-12:30A).
15apr44 MBS Hurricane Club, NYC (11:30-11:45P).
16apr44* ABC Philco "Hall of Fame," Studios WJZ, NYC (6:00-7:00P).
20apr44* MBS Hurricane Club, NYC.
21apr44* MBS Hurricane Club, NYC (1:30-2:00A).
22apr44* MBS Hurricane Club, NYC (11:30-11:45P).
27apr44* CBS Hurricane Club, NYC (7:30-8:00P).
27apr44* MBS Hurricane Club, NYC.

28apr44* MBS Hurricane Club, NYC (1:30-2:00A).
29apr44 MBS Hurricane Club, NYC (11:30-11:45P).
2may44 MBS Hurricane Club, NYC.
5may44 CBS Hurricane Club, NYC (7:30-8:00P).
5may44* MBS Hurricane Club, NYC (11:30P-12:00M).
6may44* MBS Hurricane Club, NYC (11:30-11:45P).
7may44* MBS Hurricane Club, NYC.
8may44 NBC Atlantic Spotlight, NYC.
9may44* MBS Hurricane Club, NYC (11:30-11:45P).
12may44* MBS Hurricane Club, NYC (11:30P-12:00M).
13may44 MBS Hurricane Club, NYC (11:30-11:45P).
20may44* MBS Hurricane Club, NYC (11:30-11:45P).
21may44* MBS Hurricane Club, NYC.
24may44* MBS Hurricane Club, NYC.
24may44* CBS Hurricane Club, NYC (7:30-8:00P).
26may44* MBS Hurricane Club, NYC.
27may44* CBS Hurricane Club, NYC (7:30-8:00P).
28may44* MBS Hurricane Club, NYC.
31may44* MBS Hurricane Club, NYC (12:00M-12:15A).
1jun44* CBS Hurricane Club, NYC (12:05-12:30A).
1jun44 MBS Hurricane Club, NYC.
2jun44* CBS Hurricane Club, NYC (7:30-8:00P).
2jun44 MBS Hurricane Club, NYC.
3jun44* MBS Hurricane Club, NYC.
4Jun44* MBS Hurricane Club, NYC.
5jun44 MBS Hurricane Club, NYC.
6jun44* MBS Hurricane Club, NYC.
8jul44* ABC Coca Cola "Victory Parade of Spotlight Bands" #564, Naval
...Training Center, Bainbridge MD (9:30P).
2aug44* CBS Mildred Bailey Show, CBS Studios, NYC (9:30-10:00P).
6oct44 NBC Colgate-Palmolive-Peet Co. "Bill Stern Show," NBC Studios,
...NYC.
10oct44 NBC DE interviewed by Bill Stern, Chicago IL.
23oct44 WTMJ "Rumpus Room," DE interviewed by Willie Maddox, p.
...Milwaukee WI.
29nov44* WMCA Apollo Theatre, NYC.
17dec44* NBC Music America Loves Best, NBC Studios, NYC (7:30P).
31dec44 CBS (remote through WEEI) Unidentified bc (11:45P-12:00M).
17jan45* ABC Esquire Jazz Concert, Philharmonic Auditorium, Los
...Angeles CA.
18jan45* NBC Kraft Music Hall, NBC Studios, Hollywood CA.
23jan45* AFRS Jubilee #117, Orpheum Auditorium, Los Angeles CA.
3mar45* KHJ Casa Mañana, Culver City CA.
14mar45 CBS P. Lorillard Co. "Which Is Which," unidentified location; p.
...prerecorded.
19mar45* KPAS Billy Berg's Vine Street Supper Club, Hollywood CA.
25mar45* NBC (Blue) Civic Opera House, Chicago IL (10:30-11:00P).
6apr45* CBS 400 Restaurant, NYC (7:15-7:30P).
6apr45* MBS 400 Restaurant, NYC.
7apr45* ABC Date with the Duke, 400 Restaurant, NYC.
8apr45 CBS 400 Restaurant, NYC (11:15-11:30P).
11apr45* MBS 400 Restaurant, NYC.
14apr45* ABC Tribute to FDR, 400 Restaurant, NYC.
15apr45* Margaret Whiting Show, Radio City, NYC.
19apr45 MBS 400 Restaurant, NYC.
21apr45* ABC Date with the Duke, 400 Restaurant, NYC.
22apr45* MBS Dick Brown Show, Studios WOR, NYC.
22apr45* CBS 400 Restaurant, NYC (11:15-11:30P).
24apr45* MBS 400 Restaurant, NYC.
26apr45* MBS 400 Restaurant, NYC.
27apr45* CBS 400 Restaurant, NYC.
28apr45 NBC RCA "Music America Loves Best," NBC Studios, NYC.
28apr45* ABC Date with the Duke, 400 Restaurant, NYC.
29apr45* NBC RCA Show with Tommy Dorsey, NBC Studios, NYC
29apr45* CBS 400 Restaurant, NYC (7:15-7:30P).
1may45 MBS 400 Restaurant, NYC.
3may45 MBS 400 Restaurant, NYC.
4may45* MBS 400 Restaurant, NYC.
5may45* ABC Date with the Duke, Adams Theatre, Newark NJ.
12may45* ABC Date with the Duke, Studio 6B, Radio City, NYC.
19may45* ABC Date with the Duke, Paradise Theatre, Detroit MI.
26may45* ABC Date with the Duke, Regal Theatre, Chicago IL.
26may45* AFRS Jubilee #117; prerecorded 15jan45 in Hollywood CA.
2jun45* ABC Date with the Duke, Percy Jones Hospital Center, Battle
...Creek MI.

9jun45* ABC Date with the Duke, Paramount Theatre, Toledo OH.
16jun45* ABC Date with the Duke, Franklin Gardens, Evansville IN.
23jun45* ABC Date with the Duke, Palace Theatre, Akron OH.
27jun45* MBS Victory Parade of Spotlight Bands #863, U.S. Coast Guard
...Training Center, Atlantic City NY.
30jun45* ABC Date with The Duke, Apollo Theatre, NYC.
Jul45* ? Apollo Theatre, NYC.
7jul45* ABC Date with the Duke, Studio 6B, Radio City, NYC.
14jul45* ABC Date with the Duke, RKO Theatre, Boston MA.
21jul45* ABC Date with the Duke, Fieldston Ballroom, Marshfield MA.
28jul45* ABC Date with the Duke, State Theatre, Hartford CT.
4aug45* ABC Date with the Duke, Studio 6B, Radio City, NYC.
11aug45* ABC Date with the Duke, Studio 6B, Radio City, NYC.
18aug45* ABC Date with the Duke, Studio 6B, Radio City, NYC.
25aug45* ABC Date with the Duke, Fieldston Ballroom, Marshfield MA.
29aug45* BBC BBC Studios, NYC.
1sep45* ABC Date with the Duke, Earle Theatre, Philadelphia PA.
7sep45 CBS Kate Smith Sings, CBC Studios, NYC (8:30P).
8sep45* ABC Date with the Duke, Studio 6B, Radio City, NYC.
12sep45* NBC (remote) Club Zanzibar, NYC.
15sep45* ABC Date with the Duke, Studio 6B, Radio City, NYC.
16sep45* MBS Club Zanzibar, NYC.
17sep45* NBC Club Zanzibar, NYC.
20sep45* MBS Club Zanzibar, NYC.
22sep45* ABC Date with the Duke, Studio 6B, Radio City, NYC.
23sep45* NBC RCA "Music America Loves Best," NBC Studios, NYC.
23sep45* MBS Club Zanzibar, NYC.
24sep45* MBS Club Zanzibar, NYC.
26sep45* MBS Club Zanzibar, NYC.
28sep45* MBS Club Zanzibar, NYC.
1oct45* NBC Club Zanzibar, NYC.
4oct45* MBS Club Zanzibar, NYC.
6oct45* ABC Date with the Duke, Studio 6B, Radio City, NYC.
10oct45* MBS Club Zanzibar, NYC.
13oct45* ABC Date with the Duke, Studio 6B, Radio City, NYC.
oct45* MBS Club Zanzibar, NYC.
15oct45* ? Club Zanzibar, NYC.
18oct45* MBS Club Zanzibar, NYC.
20oct45* ABC Date with the Duke, Studio 6B, Radio City, NYC.
21oct45* MBS ONS #763, Club Zanzibar, NYC; prerecorded 21sep45.
23oct45 NBC Philip Morris "Johnny Presents," NYC.
24oct45* MBS ONS #764, Club Zanzibar, NYC, prerecorded 7oct45.
24oct45* NBC Club Zanzibar, NYC.
27oct45* ABC Date with the Duke, Radio City, NYC.
28oct45* NBC ONS #786, Club Zanzibar , NYC.
29oct45* NBC Club Zanzibar, NYC.
oct/nov45* AFRS Magic Carpet, Club Zanzibar, NYC.
3nov45* ABC Date with the Duke, Studio 6B, Radio City, NYC.
3nov45 MBS Club Zanzibar, NYC.
5nov45 NBC Club Zanzibar, NYC.
10nov45* ABC Date with the Duke, Studio 6B, Radio City, NYC.
11nov45 MBS Club Zanzibar, NYC.
17nov45* ABC Date with the Duke, Studio 6B, Radio City, NYC.
18nov45* MBS ONS #800, Club Zanzibar, NYC; prerecorded 18sep45.
19nov45 MBS Club Zanzibar, NYC.
nov45* NBC Club Zanzibar, NYC.
23nov45 MBS Club Zanzibar, NYC.
24nov45* ABC Date with the Duke, Studio 6B, Radio City, NYC.
25nov45* NBC RCA "Music America Loves Best," NBS Studios, NYC.
28nov45* MBS Club Zanzibar, NYC.
lt.nov45* AFRS Magic Carpet, Club Zanzibar, NYC.
3dec45* NBC (remote) Club Zanzibar, NYC.
6dec45 CBS Newspaper Guild Praogram "Orchestra Leader Winner,"
...Madison Square Garden, NYC (11:30P-12:00M).
28dec45* BBC Kings of Jazz, World Studios, NYC; prerecorded 3aug45.
29dec45* CBC Queensway Ballroom, Toronto ON.
16jan46* ABC Esquire All American Jazz Concert, Ritz Theatre, NYC.
20jan46* ABC Down Beat Awards Concert, Civic Opera House, Chicago
...IL.
16mar46* NBC/WEAF Teentimers' Club, Radio City, NYC (11:30A).
18mar46 NBC Carnation "Contented Hour," NBC Studios, NYC.
3apr46 WMCA Apollo Theatre, NYC.
13apr46* Date with the Duke, Studios KABC, San Antonio TX.
20apr46 NBC Leaf Gum "Tin Pan Alley of the Air," DE interviewed by Holly
...Wright, Washington DC (4:30P).

20apr45* ABC Date with the Duke, Howard Theatre, Washington DC.
27apr46* ABC Date with the Duke, Municipal Auditorium, Worcester MA.
4may46* ABC Date with the Duke, Dartmouth College, Hanover NH.
18may46* ABC Date with the Duke, Radio City, NYC.
25may46* ABC Date with the Duke, Radio City, NYC.
1jun46* ABC Date with the Duke, Paramount Theatre, NYC.
8jun46* ABC Date with the Duke, Studios WEEU, Reading PA.
6jul46* ABC Million Dollar Theatre, Los Angeles CA.
...There were no broadcasts on either the 13 or 20 July, because ABC was
...unable to set up broadcasting facilities. On the 13th the band was in
...Sacramento, CA and on the 20th in Vallejo, CA.
27jul46* ABC Orpheum Theatre, San Diego CA.
9aug46* ABC Golden Gate Theatre, San Francisco CA; prerecorded
...3aug46.
aug46* AFRS Magic Carpet #437, Meadowbrook Gardens Café, Culver
...City CA.
16aug46* ABC Meadowbrooks Garden Café, Culver City CA.
17aug46* ABC Date with the Duke, Meadowbrook Gardens Café, Culver
...City CA.
18aug46* ABC Meadowbrook Gardens Café, Culver City CA.
19aug46* ABC Meadowbrook Gardens Café, Culver City CA.
22aug46* ABC Meadowbrook Gardens Café, Culver City CA.
24aug46* ABC Meadowbrook Gardens Café, Culver City CA.
25aug46* NBC Standard Brands "Tommy Dorsey Show," NBC Studios,
...Hollywood CA.
25aug46* ABC Meadowbrook Gardens Café, Culver City CA.
31aug46* ABC Date with the Duke, Lincoln Theatre, Los Angeles CA.
3oct46 CBC Aquarium Restaurant, NYC (7:30-8:00P).
3oct46* MBS Aquarium Restaurant, NYC.
4oct46* CBS Aquarium Restaurant, NYC.
5oct46* ABC Treasury Show #47, Studio 6B, Radio City, NYC.
7oct46* NBC Carnation "Contented Hour," NBC Studios, NYC.
11oct46 ? "Guest in the Nest," NYC.
11oct46* MBS Aquarium Restaurant, NYC.
12oct46 NBC/WEAF Teentimers' Club, Radio City, NYC.
24oct46 CBS Aquarium Restaurant, NYC (7:30-8:00P).
25oct46 CBS Aquarium Restaurant, NYC (12:30-1:00A).
25oct46 CBS Jack Smith Program, CBS Studios, NYC (7:15-7:30P).
25oct46* MBS Aquarium Restaurant, NYC.
26oct46 CBS Vaughn Monroe Show (7:30-8:00P).
22nov46 CBS Longiness-Wittnauer "Thanksgiving Festival" (5:00-6:00P).
2feb47 ? Down Beat Awards Presentation, Civic Opera House, Chicago IL
(10:00-10:30P).
19feb47 WMCA Apollo Theatre, NYC.
21apr47 CBS Jack Smith Program, CBS Studios, NYC.
10may47* WNEW Saturday Night Swing Session, Studios WNEW, NYC.
19may47* NBC Carnation "Contented Hour," NBC Studios, NYC.
1jul47* CBS El Patio Ballroom, Lakeside Park, Denver CO.
4jul47* CBS El Patio Ballroom, Lakeside Park, Denver CO.
8jul47 CBS El Patio Ballroom, Lakeside Park, Denver CO.
9jul47* CBS El Patio Ballroom, Lakeside Park, Denver CO.
11jul47* CBS El Patio Ballroom, Lakeside Park, Denver CO.
25jul47* CBS Ciro's, Hollywood CA.
25jul47* NBC Ciro's, Hollywood CA.
29jul47 CBS Ciro's, Hollywood CA.
30jul47* CBS Ciro's, Hollywood CA.
1aug47* CBS Ciro's, Hollywood CA.
1aug47* NBC Ciro's, Hollywood CA.
5aug47* ABC Ciro's, Hollywood CA.
6aug47* ABC Ciro's, Hollywood CA.
7aug47* ABC Ciro's, Hollywood CA.
25jul-8aug47 NBC Ciro's, Hollywood CA; several of the broadcasts listed
...above were transcribed by AFRS into its "Spotlight Bands" series.
c.aug/sep47* ? DE w. Paul Baron on "Christmas Jubilee"; unspecified
...studio, Hollywood CA. Recording session.
oct47* ABC Meadowbrook Gardens Café, Culver City CA.
4oct47* KHJ Meadowbrook Gardens Café, Culver City CA.
5oct47* KHJ Meadowbrook Gardens Café, Culver City CA.
24nov47 MBS Point Lookout, Covington KY.
6dec47* NBC Wildroot Company "King Cole Trio Time," Cincinnati OH.
7dec47* MBS Point Lookout, Covington, KY.
29dec47* WMCA Paradise Wine "Dial the Duke," Studios WMCA, NYC
...(12:00M-1:00A).
7apr48 WMCA Apollo Theatre, NYC.
6nov48* NBC "Football Holiday" fall prom, Union College, Schenectady, NY.

22nov48 KYW (remote) Click Restaurant, Philadelphia PA.
22nov48* WCAU   Click Restaurant, Philadelphia PA.
23nov48* KYW   Click Restaurant, Philadelphia PA.
24nov48* KYW   Click Restaurant, Philadelphia PA.
25nov48 KYW   Click Restaurant, Philadelphia PA.
26nov48 KYW   Click Restaurant, Philadelphia PA.
26nov48* WCAU   Click Restaurant, Philadelphia PA.
27nov48 KYW (remote) Click Restaurant, Philadelphia PA.
27nov48* WCAU   Click Restaurant, Philadelphia PA.
dec48* AFRS   Here's to Veterans, unidentified location, U.S.A.
29dec48* WMCA   Apollo Theatre, NYC.
jan49 KQW   Anniversary of Bob Goerner's Curfew Club, San Francisco CA.
feb49* AFRS   Hollywood Empire Hotel, Hollywood CA.
6feb49* AFRS   Just Jazz #47&83, Hollywood Empire Hotel, Hollywood CA.
9feb49* KABC   Hollywood Empire Hotel, Hollywood CA.
10feb49* KABC   Hollywood Empire Hotel, Hollywood CA.
feb49* AFRS   Jubilee #356, Hollywood Empire Hotel, Hollywood CA.
feb49* AFRS   Jubilee #361, Hollywood Empire Hotel, Hollywood CA.
feb49* AFRS   Just Jazz #39&60, Hollywood Empire Hotel, Hollywood CA.
feb49* AFRS   Just Jazz #46, Hollywood Empire Hotel, Hollywood CA.
feb49* ?   Hollywood Empire Hotel, Hollywood CA.
29apr49* CBS tc   Adventures in Jazz, CBS Studios, Hollywood CA (8:00-
...8:30P).
2may49* CBS   Herb Shriner Show, CBS Studios, NYC (5:45-6:00P).
jun49 WKOW   Program hosted by Pat Hernon, Madison WI; unconfirmed.
10jul49 NBC tc   Garroway at Large, NBC Studios, Chicago IL.
26aug49 WDAS   The Bon Bon Show, Studios WDAS, Philadelphia PA
...(11:30P-12:30A).
31aug49* KYW   Click Restaurant, Philadelphia PA.
2sep49* KYW   Click Restaurant, Philadelphia PA.
3sep49* AFRS   Click Restaurant, Philadelphia PA.
20sep49* NBC tc   Milton Berle Show, NBC Studios, NYC.
2oct49 CBS tc   This is Show Business, CBS Studios, NYC (7:30-8:00P).
23nov49* ?   Earle Theatre, Philadelphia PA.
30nov49 WMCA   Apollo Theatre, NYC.
lt.jan50* WJR   Paradise Theatre, Detroit MI.
p.jun50*   BFN/NWDR   Musikhalle, Hamburg, Germany; prerecorded
...29may50.
18jul50* WABD tc   Cavalcade of Bands, DuMont TV, NYC (9:00-10:00P).
20sep50* WMCA   Apollo Theatre, NYC.
19nov50* ABC tc   Show Time U.S.A., ABC Studios, NYC.
26dec50* WABD tc   Cavalcade of Bands, DuMont Studios, NYC.
2jan51* Radio transcription recording session, unidentified radio studio, NYC.
23jan51* WFIL tc   Frank Brookhauser Show, Studios WFIL, Philadelphia
...PA.
2may51 MBS   Birdland, NYC.
3may51* ABC tc   Kreisler Bandstand, ABC Studios, NYC (8:00-9:30P).
4may51* MBS   Birdland, NYC.
5may51* MBS   Birdland, NYC.
19may51* CBS tc   Ken Murray Show, CBS Studios, NYC (8:30-9:00P).
5jun51* MBS   Meadowbrook Inn, Cedar Grove NJ.
6jun51* MBS   Meadowbrook Inn, Cedar Grove NJ.
7jun51* MBS   Meadowbrook Inn, Cedar Grove NJ.
8jun51* MBS   Meadowbrook Inn, Cedar Grove NJ.
9jun51* NBC tc   Milton Berle's Damon Runyon Cancer Fund Telethon, NBC
...Studios, NYC.
9jun51* MBS   Meadowbrook Inn, Cedar Grove NJ.
10jun51* MBS   Meadowbrook Inn, Cedar Grove NJ.
10jun51 WNEW   Starting on this date, Duke Ellington hosted for two
...months the station's program for classical music, which aired Sunday
...afternoon from 3:00 to 4:00P.
11jun51* MBS   Meadowbrook Inn, Cedar Grove NJ.
5-11jun51* MBS   Meadowbrook Inn, Cedar Grove NJ.
23jun51* ABC   Birdland, NYC.
23jun51 MBS   Birdland, NYC.
jun51 WROW   Robbins Nest, DE interviewed by Fred Robbins, ...?ABC/NBC
Studios, NYC or Studios WROW, Albany NY.
30jun51* CBS   Songs for Sale, CBS Studios, NYC (10:00-11:00P).
30jun51* NBC   Birdland, NYC.
19aug51* USAAF   "Stars on Parade" #575; unidentified radio studio, NYC.
p.aut51* ? tc   Benay Venuta Show, unidentified location, U.S.A.
9jul52 WMCA   Apollo Theatre, NYC.
30jul52* NBC (remote) Parade of Bands, Blue Note, Chicago IL.
2aug52* NBC   Blue Note, Chicago IL.
6aug52* NBC   Parade of Bands, Blue Note, Chicago IL.

13aug52* NBC   Blue Note, Chicago IL.
16sep52* NBC (remote) Unidentified location/bc, U.S.A.
21sep52* NBC   Bob Snyder Show, Ritz Ballroom, Bridgeport CT; pretaped
...sep52.
19-25sep52* Voice of America   Town Casino, Cleveland OH.
27sep52* ABC tc   Chance of a Lifetime, ABC Studios, NYC (8:30-9:00P).
15oct52 NBC   Armour & Co. "Dial Dave Garroway," NBC Studios, NYC.
25oct52 CBS   Steve Allen Show, CBS Studios, NYC (9:30-10:30P)
27oct52 WNEW   Recording Session, Studios WNEW, NYC.
14nov52* NBC   Carnegie Hall, NYC.
20nov52* NBC   Duke Ellington Silver Anniversary Jubilee, Birdland, NYC.
22nov52* NBC   Stars in Jazz, Birdland, NYC.
23nov52 NBC   Stars in Jazz, Birdland, NYC.
24nov52 NBC   Birdland, NYC.
25nov52* NBC   Duke Ellington Silver Anniversary Jubilee, Birdland, NYC;
...pretaped 24nov52.
28nov52* NBC   Birdland, NYC; pretaped 26nov52.
nov52* NBC   Birdland, NYC.
nov52* ?   Birdland, NYC.
6dec52* BBC   Three Aspects of Duke Ellington, BBC Studios, London,
...England.
12dec52* MBS tc   Midnight Benefit Show, host Willie Bryant, Apollo Theatre,
...NYC.
17dec52* WMCA   Apollo Theatre, NYC; pretaped 12dec52.
31dec52* NBC (remote) Blue Note, Chicago IL.
1jan53* NBC   Blue Note, Chicago IL.
30jan53* WMGM   Bandbox, NYC.
1feb53* ? tc   Bandbox, NYC.
2feb53* WMGM   Bandbox, NYC.
4feb53* WMGM   Bandbox, NYC.
8feb53* WABD tc   Bandbox, NYC.
9feb53* WMGM   Bandbox, NYC.
15feb53* NBC tc   Patti Page Show, NBC Studios, NYC (8:30-9:00P).
25feb53* WMCA   Apollo Theatre, NYC.
12jun53* NBC   Music for Moderns, Blue Note, Chicago IL.
24jun53* NBC   Parade of Bands, Blue Note, Chicago IL.
jun53* AFRS   One Night Stand #3365, Blue Note, Chicago IL.
27jun53* NBC   Blue Note, Chicago IL.
28jun53 NBC   Music for Moderns, Blue Note, Chicago IL.
1jul53* NBC   Parade of Bands, Blue Note, Chicago IL.
12jul53* CBS   What's My Line?, CBS Studios, NYC (10:30-11:00P).
17jul53* NBC   Parade of Bands, Blue Note, Chicago IL; pretaped jun53.
24jul53* NBC   Parade of Bands, Blue Note, Chicago IL; pretaped jun53.
1aug53* NBC   Parade of Bands, Blue Note, Chicago IL; pretaped jun53.
19aug53* WMCA   Apollo Theatre, NYC.
23aug53* NBC   Parade of All Star Bands, American Legion Park, Ephrata
...PA.
11dec53* WABD   Life Begins at 80, DuMont Studios, NYC (9:00-9:30P).
11dec53 NBC   Presenting Duke Ellington, Birdland, NYC.
13dec53* NBC tc   Jerry Lester Show, NBC Studios, NYC.
16dec53* NBC tc   Steve Allen Show, NBC Studios, NYC (11:20P-...12:00M).
18dec53 NBC   Presenting Duke Ellington, Birdland, NYC.
dec53* AFRS   One Night Stand #3557, Blue Note, Chicago IL.
p.lt.dec53 NBC   Presenting Duke Ellington, Birdland, NYC.
25apr54 NBC   Sunday with Dave Garroway, NBC Studios, NYC.
jun54* AFRS   Birdland, NYC.
15jun54* NBC tc   Tonight Show, Birdland, NYC.
24jun54 NBC   All Star Parade of Bands; unidentified location, U.S.A.
26jul54* NBC tc   Art Linkletter Show, NBC Studios, Hollywood CA.
31jul54 NBC   All Star Parade of Bands; unidentified location, U.S.A.
28dec54* NBC tc   Tonight Show, NBC Studios, NYC (11:30P-1:00A).
31dec54* NBC   Basin Street East, NYC.
1jan55* CBS   Stage Show, CBS Studios, NYC.
17feb55* CBC   Brant Inn, Burlington ON.
ear.mar55* NBC   Academy of Music, Philadelphia PA.
9mar55* ABC tc   Masquerade Party, ABC Studios, NYC.
9jul55* CBS tc   America's Greatest Bands, CBS Studios, NYC (8:00-
...9:00P).
9jul55 NBC   Bob Haymes Show, ABC Studios, NYC.
20jul55* CBS tc   Frankie Laine Show, CBS Studios, NYC (8:00-9:00P).
26jul55* CBS tc   Music '55, CBS Studios, NYC.
28aug55* NBC   Monitor, Dave Garroway show, NBC Studios, NYC.
28sep55 WMCA   Apollo Theatre, NYC.
6nov55* KENO   Unidentified bc, Dodge City KS.
27nov55* NBC   Zardi's, Hollywood CA.

3dec55* NBC Zardi's, Hollywood CA.
4dec55* NBC Zardi's, Hollywood CA.
11dec55 NBC Monitor, Zardi's, Hollywood CA.
13dec55* KENO Auditorium, Dodge City KS.
31dec55* NBC Blue Note, Chicago IL.
1jan56* CBS Blue Note, Chicago IL.
11jan56 NBC Monitor, Café Society, NYC.
22jan56* NBC Monitor, Café Society, NYC.
28jan56* NBC Monitor, Café Society, NYC.
16feb56 WNYC Adventures in Jazz, Studios WNYC, NYC.
14apr56 NBC Monitor; unidentified taped interview.
14apr56* CBS Basin Street East, NYC.
14apr56* NBC Monitor, Basin Street East, NYC.
3jun56 NBC Monitor; unidentified taped interview.
13jun56 KRON tc Bob Scobey Show "Jazz Session," San Francisco CA.
7jul56 MBS MBS Bandstand U.S.A., Freebody Park, Newport RI.
7jul56* CBS Newport Jazz Festival, Freebody Park, Newport RI.
19jul56* CBC Brant Inn, Burlington ON.
21jul56* CBC Brant Inn, Burlington ON.
21jul56* NBC tc Tonight Show, NBC Studios, NYC; pretaped or remote.
28jul56* NBC (remote) Monitor, University Stadium, Fairfield CT.
29jul56* CBS Woolworth Hour, CBS Studios, NYC.
1aug56* CBS tc Frankie Laine Time, CBS Studios, NYC.
26aug56* NBC Monitor, Blue Note, Chicago IL.
1sep56* NBC Monitor, Blue Note, Chicago IL.
2sep56* NBC Monitor, Blue Note, Chicago IL.
9sep56 NBC Monitor, Blue Note, Chicago IL.
16sep56* WHLD Town Casino, Buffalo NY.
23sep56 NBC Monitor, Blue Note, Chicago IL.
8nov56 NBC Birdland, NYC.
18nov56* NBC tc Steve Allen Show, Birdland, NYC (8:00-9:00P).
18nov56* CBS Birdland, NYC.
nov56* MBS MBS Bandstand U.S.A., Birdland, NYC.
22nov56* CBS tc Longiness-Wittnauer "Thanksgiving Festival," CBS
...Studios, NYC (5:00-6:00P).
22nov-2dec56* WEWS tc DE interviewed by Dorothy Fuldheim,
...Philadelphia PA .
8dec56* MBS MBS Bandstand U.S.A., Red Hill Inn, Pennsauken NJ.
9dec56* MBS MBS Bandstand U.S.A., Red Hill Inn, Pennsauken NJ.
12dec56* NBC Monitor "Man with Four Sides," NBC Studios, NYC.
15dec56* MBS MBS Bandstand U.S.A., Red Hill Inn, Pennsauken NJ.
18dec56* NBC tc Wide Wide World, Civic Auditorium Omaha NE; pickup by
...NBC Studios, Chicago IL.
22dec56 MBS MBS Bandstand U.S.A., Red Hill Inn, Pennsauken NJ.
23dec56* NBC Monitor, Blue Note, Chicago IL.
30dec56* NBC Monitor, Blue Note, Chicago IL.
31dec56* CBS New Year's Eve All Star Parade of Bands; Blue Note,
...Chicago IL.
1jan57* NBC Blue Note, Chicago IL (1:45-2:00A).
6jan57* NBC Monitor, Blue Note, Chicago IL.
2mar57* WNAC MBS Bandstand U.S.A., Storyville Club, Boston MA.
15mar57* CBS tc Person to Person, CBS Studios and Ellington's private
...residence, NYC.
20apr57* MBS MBS Bandstand U.S.A., Birdland, NYC.
21apr57* MBS MBS Bandstand U.S.A., Birdland, NYC.
21apr57* CBS Birdland, NYC.
23apr57* NBC tc America After Dark, Hickory House, NYC.
26apr57* NBC tc Close-Up, Waldorf Hotel, NYC.
27apr57* MBS MBS Bandstand U.S.A., Birdland, NYC.
28apr57* ? Town Hall, NYC.
8may57* CBS tc U.S. Steel Hour, "A Drum is a Woman," CBS Studios,
...NYC (10:00-11:00P); portions have been pretaped sep-oct56.
9may57 NBC Nightline; pretaped.
15may57* CBS DE interviewed by Harry Rasky, NYC, pretaped 29apr57.
13jul57* NBC Monitor, Blue Note, Chicago IL; pretaped 12jul57.
18jul57 NBC Nightline (pretaped interview).
29jul57* WNYC Evenings by the River, East River Amphitheatre, NYC.
29jul57 NBC Monitor, Blue Note, Chicago IL; pretaped earlier in the month.
24aug57* NBC Monitor, Blue Note, Chicago IL.
31aug57* NBC Monitor, Blue Note, Chicago IL.
sep57* KRAM DE interviewed by Frank Evans, Los Angeles CA; pretaped.
5sep57* CBC Festival Theatre, Stratford ON.
11sep57* CBS tc Vic Damone Show, CBS Studios, NYC (8:00-9:00P).
sep57 MBS MBS Bandstand U.S.A., Storyville Club, Boston MA.
28sep57* MBS MBS Bandstand U.S.A., Storyville Club, Boston MA.

13oct57* NBC tc Standard Oil 75th Anniversary, NBC Studios, NYC ...(9:30-
10:30P).
25nov57 WGN tc Hour of Music, Chicago IL (8:30-9:30P); p. pretaped.
30dec57* NBC tc Timex "All Star Jazz Show #1," Ellington segment from
...the Blue Note, Chicago IL.
31dec57* NBC New Year's Eve All Star Parade of Bands, Blue Note,
...Chicago IL.
1jan58* WBBM Blue Note, Chicago IL (1:45-2:00A).
21jan58* WCOA-FM DE interviewed by Ted Cassidy, Municipal
...Auditorium, Pensacola FL.
9feb58 NBC Monitor, pretaped interview; unidentified location.
26mar58* NBC tc The Subject is Jazz—What is Jazz?, DE interviewed by
...Gilbert Seldes, Radio City, NYC (6:00-6:30P).
4jun58* CBS tc Jazz in the Round, Studios WBBM, Chicago IL (6:30-
...7:00P).
9jun58* WBBM Blue Note, Chicago IL.
18jun58* WGN tc Jazz in the Round; repeat of the 4jun58 tc.
3jul58* CBS Newport Jazz Festival, Freebody Park, Newport RI (8:00-
...9:00P).
22jul58* CBS This is New York, NYC (9:30-10:00P).
31jul58* CBC tc DE interviewed by Bill Herbert, CBC Studios, Toronto ON.
p.aug58* KCRC Interview, Armos Ballroom, Cedar Rapids IA.
12oct58* BBC Monitor, DE interviewed by Frank Henning, Dorchester
...Hotel, London, England; pretaped 7oct58.
mid-oct58* BBC Conversation with Music, interview; BBC Studios, London,
...England.
4nov58* SR DE interviewed for Dagens Eko, Stockholm, Sweden.
7nov58* TV Byen tc Actuel Kvarter, Copenhagen, Denmark.
14nov58* ? DE interviewed about the Shakespearean Suite, Munich,
...Germany.
17nov58* AVRO tc Concertgebouw, Amsterdam, Netherlands.
20nov58* ORTF tc Salle Pleyel, Paris, France.
3dec58 NBC Blue Note, Chicago IL.
21dec58* WBKW tc V.I.P. Interview, with Norman Ross, Studios WBKW,
...Chicago IL.
21dec58* CBS Blue Note, Chicago IL.
28dec58* CBS Blue Note, Chicago IL.
31dec58* CBS Blue Note, Chicago IL.
1jan59* NBC Blue Note, Chicago IL.
4jan59* CBS Blue Note, Chicago IL.
7jan59* CBS tc Timex "All Star Jazz Show #4—The Golden Age of Jazz,"
...CBS Studios, NYC (8:00-9:00P).
10feb59* NBC tc Bell Telephone Hour, NBC Brooklyn Studios, Brooklyn
...NY.
9mar59* ABC tc Patti Page Show, ABC Studios, NYC; pretaped
13mar59 WGBH tc DE interviewed by Fr. Norman J. O'Connor, Boston
...MA.
14mar59* MBS MBS Bandstand U.S.A., Storyville Club, Boston MA.
6may59 WGBH tc Dateline Boston, "Jazz Scene," pretaped mar59.
28jun59* CBS tc Ed Sullivan Show, CBS Studios, NYC (8:00-9:00P).
sep59* KRAM DE interviewed by Frank Evans, Los Angeles CA, ...pretaped
10mar59.
9oct59* SRG tc Kongresshaus, Zurich, Switzerland; the date of tc is not
...known.
27nov59* NBC tc Sunday Showcase "Grammy Awards Presentation,"
...Hollywood CA; pretaped 13nov59 at NBC Studios, NYC.
7dec59* CBC tc Jack Kane Hour, CBC Studios, Toronto ON.
31dec59* NBC Blue Note, Chicago IL (10:30P).
1jan60* CBS Blue Note, Chicago IL.
ear.1960* ? Cancer Crusade, unidentified studio, U.S.A.
21feb60* WBCI Interview, William and Mary College, Williamsburg VA.
10jul60* KJAZ-FM Jazz Audition, DE interviewed by Russ Wilson, San
...Francisco CA (8:00P).
11jul60* KQED tc Jazz Casual, Studios KQED, San Francisco CA.
19aug60* CBS Detroit Jazz Festival, State Fairgrounds, Detroit MI.
27sep60* KHIP Club Neve, San Francisco CA.
4oct60* KHIP Club Neve, San Francisco CA.
24oct60* WSND Interview, St. Mary's College, South Bend IN.
21nov60 NBC Today Show, NBC Studios, NYC; p. pretaped.
dec60* ? DE&BS interviewed for French radio, Paris, France; the date of
...bc is not known.
23dec60* ORTF tc DE solo piano, Paris, France; prerecorded 17dec60.
25dec60 ORTF tc Jean Gablon Show, Paris, France.
17feb61* NBC Here's Hollywood, DE interviewed on the set of Paris ...Blues,
Paris, France; pretaped.

18feb61 KTTV tc Arthritis and Rheumatism Telethon, San Francisco CA;
...the DE portion was pretaped in Las Vegas NV.
9apr61* Syndicated tc The Lady and the Lawyer (Asphalt Jungle), MGM
...Studios, Culver City CA; pretaped 25apr60.
24apr61* CBC tc Jack Kane Hour, CBC Studios, Toronto ON; pretaped
...19apr61.
27apr61* ? tc Look Up and Live; CBS Studios, NYC.
c.25may61* ? Apollo Theatre, NYC.
11aug61* WBBM tc Policemen's Benefit Association Telethon, Studios
...WBBM, Chicago IL.
24aug61* Radio Free Europe Moonbowl, Freedomland Park, Bronx NY.
26aug61* NBC Moonbowl, Freedomland Park, Bronx NY.
15nov61* WMCA Barry Gray Show, Studios WMCA, NYC.
21nov61 NBC tc Today Show, NBC Studios NYC.
25nov61 ABC tc Box 20/20, ABC Studios, NYC.
8dec61* WNEW tc Big Wilson's "Music Spectacular," CBS 30th St, Studios,
...NYC; pretaped 21nov61.
17dec61* CBS tc Ed Sullivan Show, CBS Studios, NYC (8:00-9:00P).
6jan62* KBCA DE interviewed by Paul Werth, Studios KBCA, Los Angeles
...CA; pretaped sep61.
10feb62 ABC Music for Dancing, ABC Studios, NYC (8:30-9:20P).
8may62* CBS tc Gary Moore Show, CBS Studios, NYC (10:00-11:00P);
...pretaped 1-4may62.
24may62 CBS tc Ed Sullivan Show, CBS Studios, NYC.
31may62* NBC Patti Cavern Show, NBC Studios, Washington DC (8:30P).
28jun62 KABC Program hosted by George and Betty Shriner, NYC;
...unconfirmed.
13jul62* ? DE interviewed by Jack Harris, Detroit MI.
aug62* ? Sid McCoy Show, Chicago IL.
19sep62* NBC tc Tonight Show, NBC Studios, NYC.
c.5oct62* ? DE and Dr. Wm. Fowler interviewed by Paul Smith, Salt Lake
...City UT.
23oct62* ABC tc Eadie Adams Show, Hollywood CA; pretaped at ABC
...Studios, NYC on 27sep62.
30oct62* CKNW DE interviewed by Jack Cullen, Studios CKNW,
...Vancouver BC.
1nov62* CBC DE and BA interviewed by Bob Smith, Georgian Towers
...Hotel; Vancouver BC; date of bc is not known.
10dec62* NBC tc Merv Griffin Show, NBC Studios, NYC (2:00-3:00P).
11dec62* NBC tc Merv Griffin Show, NBC Studios, NYC (2:00-3:00P).
12dec62* NBC tc Merv Griffin Show, NBC Studios, NYC (2:00-3:00P).
13dec62* NBC tc Merv Griffin Show, NBC Studios, NYC (2:00-3:00P).
14dec62* NBC tc Merv Griffin Show, NBC Studios, NYC (2:00-3:00P).
18dec62* NBC tc Merv Griffin Show, NBC Studios, NYC (2:00-3:00P).
31dec62* ABC Waldorf-Astoria, NYC.
1jan63* CBS Waldorf-Astoria, NYC.
jan63* SR tc DE interviewed for Aktuellt Apropå, BBC Studios, London,
...England.
28jan63 Granada tc "Scene at 6:30," London, England.
3feb63* SR DE interviewed by Gun Allroth, Bulltofta Airport, Malmö,
...Sweden.
11feb63* AFN DE interviewed by Dan Marshall, Munich, Germany.
12feb63* SDR Liederhalle, Stuttgart, Germany.
13feb63* Granada tc Duke Ellington & His Famous Orchestra, Granada
...Studios, London, England; pretaped 21+22jan63.
15feb63* AFN Deutschlandhalle, Berlin, Germany.
15feb63* Radio Bremen DE interviewed by Dieter Bøer, Berlin, Germany.
21feb63* R.A.I. tc Conservatorio G. Verdi, Milan, Italy; the date of tc is not
...known.
6apr63* SR Circus Djurgaarden, Stockholm, Sweden; pretaped 7feb63.
16apr63* BBC DE interviewed by Jo Joseph, London, England; pretaped
...in jan63.
28apr63* WINS "Two Worlds of Jazz," DE interviewed by Nat Henthoff,
...with Pastor John G. Gensel and Fr. Norman O'Connor, Studios WINS,
...NYC (11:00P-12:00M).
13may63* NBC tc Tonight Show, NBC Studios, NYC
17may63* Voice of Liberty Sempre Amore, NYC; p. pretaped.
25may63* AFN U.S. Army Installation, Wiesbaden, Germany.
26may63* AFN 7th Army Dining and Dancing Center, Stuttgart, Germany.
31may63* SR Interview, Arlanda Airport, Stockholm, Sweden.
19jun63* SR Admiralen Dans Hall, Malmö, Sweden.
4jul63* NBC tc Tonight Show, NBC Studios, NYC.
15jul63 WEWS tc Festival Five "Duke Ellington at Karamu," Karamu
...House, Cleveland OH. Filming session, date of tc scheduled for feb64; no
...evidence was available that the program was ever aired.

jul/aug63* WENR DE interviewed by David Wayne, Studios WENR,
...Chicago IL.
20aug63* CBS tc Keefe Brasselle Show, CBS Studios, NYC; pretaped
...18jul63 (10:00-11:00P).
5nov63 live tc Tehran Hilton, Tehran, Iran.
14nov63 ? tc Concert, Baghdad, Iraq; date of tc is not known.
dec63* ? tc DE interviewed by Fred Robbins, NYC.
9jan64* NBC tc Today Show, NBC Studios, NYC (7:00-9:00A).
14jan64* WNEW Basin Street East, NYC.
15feb64* BBC Interview with Humphrey Lyttelton and Max Jones, BBC
..Studios, London, England.
18feb64* BBC Interview, Bristol, England.
21feb64* BBC tc "Most in Music," BBC Theatre, London, England. Taping
...session; the date of the original tc is not known, re-tc 4aug66 by WNEW.
21mar64* Radio Monte Carlo DE interviewed by Henri Renaud, Paris,
...France.
21mar64* ORTF tc Jacques Dieval Show, ORTF Studios, Paris, France.
22mar64* RAI tc Teatro Ariston, San Remo, Italy; the date of tc is not known.
20apr64* CBC DE interviewed by Kate Vita Marson, Montréal, PQ.
21apr64* BBC tc "Jazz 625," BBC Theatre, London, England (11:00P);
...pretaped 20feb64.
14may64* Indep. tc Madison Square Garden, NYC.
24may64* CBS tc Ed Sullivan Show, CBS Studios, NYC (8:00-9:00P).
12jun64* KTTV tc Colgate-Palmolive-Peet Co., Disneyland, Anaheim CA.
28jun64* NHK tc Television Hall, Tokyo, Japan.
Jun64* ? tc/bc Interview, Tokyo, Japan.
29jun64* AF Far East Network DE, BS, HC interviewed, Golden Akasa
...Night Club, Tokyo, Japan.
11jul64* TBS tc Taping session, TBS Studios, Tokyo, Japan; pretaped
...3jul64.
jul64* AFRS One Night Stand #6208, Marine Ballroom, Steel Pier, Atlantic
City NJ.
Jul64* AFRS One Night Stand #6212, Marine Ballroom, Steel Pier, Atlantic
...City NJ.
20jul64* KTLA tc Interview, Los Angeles CA; pretaped jun64.
23jul64 CBS Steel Pier, Atlantic City NJ.
17aug64* WNEW Basin Street East, NYC.
2sep64* WNEW tc Robert Herridge Show "Duke Ellington—A Portrait in
...Music," Metromedia Studios, NYC (9:00P); pretaped 28+29apr64.
11sep64* ? DE interviewed by Ed Case, Cullen Auditorium, Houston TX.
17sep64* CBC tc Casa Loma Club, Montréal PQ; prerecorded 20apr64.
30sep64* ? DE interviewed by Irving L. Jacobs, City College, Long Beach
...CA.
5nov64 ABC tc Tennessee Ernie Ford Show, Los Angeles CA.
5nov64* NBC tc Today Show "Salute to Duke Ellington," NBC Studios,
...NYC (7:00-9:00P); pretaped 26may64.
9nov64* CBC tc "Take 30," Toronto ON.
17nov64* Syndicated tc Regis Philbin Show, Westinghouse Studios,
...Hollywood CA.
20dec64* CBS tc The 20th Century "Duke Ellington Swings Through Japan"
...(6:00-6:30P); pretaped in Kyoto, Japan on 24jun64.I64.
31dec64* CBS Basin Street East, NYC (9:o5-9:30P).
31dec64* NBC Basin Street East, NYC.
6jan65* NBC tc Bell Telephone Hour, NBC Studios, NYC (10:00-11:00P);
...pretaped 5jan65.
23jan65* WGN tc The Big Bands: Duke Ellington & His Orchestra #1,
...Universal Studios, Chicago IL; pretaped 12jan65.
26jan65* RTF Jazz sur Scène, Paris, France.
29jan65* EUROPE I Thèâtre des Champs Elysées, Paris, France.
31jan65* DR tc Falkoner Centret, Copenhagen, Denmark; the date of tc is
...not known.
31jan65* DR bc DE interviewed by Per Møller Hansen for "Jazz Aktuelt,"
...Kopenhagen, Denmark.
feb65* BBC tc DE interviewed by Michael Dean, London, England.
12feb65* ? DE interviewed by Pat Patrick, Munich, Germany.
3mar65* CBC tc Festival—The Duke, CBC Studios, Toronto ON (9:30-
...10:30P); pretaped 2+5sep64.
3mar65* CBC DE interviewed by Harry Whiston, NYC.
6mar65* WGN tc The Big Bands: Duke Ellington & His Orchestra #2,
...Universal Studios, Chicago IL; pretaped 12jan65.
7mar65* CBS tc Ed Sullivan Show, CBS Studios, NYC (8:00-9:00P).
27mar65* BBC Compilation "The Duke in Europe" #1, London, England;
...pretaped feb65.
10apr65* BBC tc Compilation "The Duke in Europe" #2, London, England;
...pretaped feb65.

16apr65* KYW tc Mike Douglas Show, Studios KYW, Philadelphia PA;
...pretaped in apr65.
20apr65* CBC DE interviewed by Henry Whiston, NYC; pretaped 3mar65.
7may65* CBS tc Mike Wallace at Large, interview w. DE, CBS Studios, NYC
...(4:35-5:00P).
4jun65* VoA DE interviewed by Willis Conover, Washington DC.
9jul65* NBC tc Today Show, NBC Studios, NYC.
2aug65* WPIX tc Award presentation, City Hall Park, NYC.
2aug65* ABC tc Joey Bishop Show, ABC Studios, NYC.
16aug65* ? DE interviewed by Jim Gossa, Los Angeles CA.
lt.sep65* CBC DE interviewed by Bob Smith, Vancouver BC.
24oct65* CBS tc Ed Sullivan Show, CBS Studios, NYC (8:00-9:00P).
5dec65* NBC tc Bell Telephone Hour, NBC Studios, NYC (5:30P).
10dec65* CBS DE interviewed by Jim Fawcett, NYC.
26dec65* CBS tc In the Beginning God, 5th Ave. Presbyterian Church, NYC.
26dec65* WRVR tc Concert of Sacred Music, 5th Ave. Presbyterian
...Church, NYC.
31dec65* NBC Dollars for Scholars, War Memorial Auditorium, Worcester
...MA (10:00-P-2:00A).
16jan66* CBS tc Look Up and Live: In the Beginning God (10:00-11:00P).
23jan66* CBS tc Ed Sullivan Show, CBS Studios, NYC (8:00-9:00P).
28jan66* AFN Jahrhunderthalle, Frankfurt, Germany.
28jan66* AFN DE interview, Frankfurt, Germany.
30jan66* RAI tc VGmn, EF, DE, Milan, Italy.
8feb66* SR tc Circus Djurgaarden, Stockholm, Sweden; the date of tc is
...not known.
21feb66* CBS tc The Strolling Twenties, CBS Studios/Savoy Ballroom,
...NYC (10:00-11:00P); pretaped mid.dec65.
24feb66* TVE tc Estudios de TVE, Prado del Rey, Spain; the date of tc is
...not known.
27feb66 ABC American Music—From Folk to Jazz and Pop. Compiled at
...ABC Studios, NYC.
3mar66* ITV tc Tempo: Meet The Duke. DE interviewed by Derek Jewell,
...London, England; pretaped 20feb66.
15mar66* CKFH-FM DE interviewed by Helen McNamara, Toronto ON.
23mar66* ? DE interview, Devine's Ballroom, Milwaukee WI.
1apr66* RAI tc DE interviewed by Ruggero Orlando, NYC; pretaped in
...dec65.
10apr65* ITV tc Sacred Concert, Coventry Cathedral, Coventry, England;
...pretaped 21feb66.
2may66* ? tc Théâtre Americain, Brussels, Belgium (11:15P); pretaped
...22feb66.
14may66* TBS tc Concert, Tokyo, Japan; the date of tc is not known.
16may66* NBC tc Grammy Awards Show, Brooklyn, NY; pretaped 26apr66.
20may66* TBS tc Concert, Kyoto Kaikan, Kyoto, Japan.
19jun66 CBS tc Ed Sullivan Show, CBS Studios, NYC (8:00-9:00P).
2jul66* WTMJ DE interviewed by Bob Knudsen, Milwaukee WI.
26jul66* ? tc DE interview, Juan-les-Pins, France.
27jul66* ORTF tc Concert, Juan-les-Pins, France.
28jul66* ORTF tc Concert, Juan-les-Pins, France.
28jul66* ORTF tc Concert, Juan-les-Pins, France.
4aug66 WNEW tc The Most in Music; taped by BBC London 21feb64.
29sep66* NBC tc Dean Martin Show, NBC Studios, Hollywood CA (10:00-
...11:00P); pretaped 26jun66.
23oct66* CBS tc Ed Sullivan Show, CBS Studios, NYC (8:00-9:00P).
3nov66* WOR Jack O'Brian Show, NYC.
21nov66* WNEW Mark Twain Riverboat, NYC (11:30P-12:15A).
25nov66* CBS Mark Twain Riverboat, NYC.
26nov66* CBS tc Jackie Gleason Show (7:30-8:00P); pretaped in Miami
...Beach FL on 4+5nov66.
lt.nov66 CBS Mark Twain Riverboat, NYC.
29nov66* NBC tc Tonight Show, Mark Twain Riverboat, NYC.
p.nov66 NBC tc Andy Williams Show, Hollywood CA.
ear.dec66* CBS Mark Twain Riverboat, NYC.
8dec66 CBS tc The World of Religion, (3:35-4:00P).
18dec66* Voice of America Monterey Jazz Festival, Monterey CA;
...pretaped 18sep66.
24jan67* SR Konserthuset, Stockholm, Sweden.
25jan67* NKR tc 1st concert, Njårdhallen, Oslo, Norway. Filmed for tc; no
...evidence that the program was ever aired.
25jan67* NKR 2nd concert, Njårdhallen, Oslo, Norway.
31jan67* ORTF Salle Pleyel, Paris, France.
1feb67* ORTF Salle Pleyel, Paris, France.
p.18feb67* BBC tc DE interviewed by Michael Dean, Dorchester Hotel,
...London, England.

20feb67* BBC tc Royal Albert Hall, London, England; pretaped 19feb67.
28feb67* WDR Concert, Düsseldorf, Germany.
2mar67* AFN Weekend World, DE interview, Berlin, Germany.
ear.mar67* Syndicated tc Celanese Center Stage "Barbara McNair Show,"
...NYC; pretaped 2nov66.
7mar67* TV Byen tc Jazz in Concert, Copenhagen, Denmark; pretaped
...22+23jan67.
2apr67* ? DE interviewed by Martin Braunstein, Place des Arts, Montréal
...PQ.
1jun67* WRBR DE's eulogy about Billy Strayhorn, Reno NV.
5jun67 WRVR Billy Strayhorn's funeral, St. Peters Lutheran Church, NYC.
14jun67* WCCC DE interviewed by Frank Knight, Crystal Lake Ballroom,
...Ellington CT; p. pretaped 12jun67.
14jun67* KQED Documentary "Love You Madly," excerpts were filmed in
...San Francisco on 25+26aug65 and 20sep65.
16jun67* KQED tc Concert of Sacred Music, Grace Cathedral, San
...Francisco CA, pretaped 16+18sep65.
29jun67* ABC tc Joey Bishop Show, Los Angeles CA.
29jul67* MBS Cedar Point Ballroom, Sandusky OH.
2aug67* CBS Rainbow Grill, NYC.
3aug67* CBS Rainbow Grill, NYC.
10aug67* NBC tc Today Show, NBC Studios, NYC; p. pretaped.
10aug67* CBS Rainbow Grill, NYC.
14aug67* CBS Rainbow Grill, NYC.
14aug67* CBS tc Merv Griffin Show, CBS Studios, NYC; pretaped 7aug67
...for Westinghouse.
17aug67* CBS Rainbow Grill, NYC.
17aug67* CBC DE interviewed by Henry Whiston, NYC.
21aug67* CBS Rainbow Grill, NYC.
24aug67* CBS Rainbow Grill, NYC.
30aug67* CBS Rainbow Grill, NYC.
31aug67* CBS Rainbow Grill, NYC.
13oct67* NBC tc Bell Telephone Hour "On the Road with Duke Ellington,"
...documentary, filmed 25apr67, apr67, 1may67, 12jun67, mid.67.
5dec67* King-FM DJ's Seattle WA.
13dec67* MBS tc Gilmore Bros. Autopark, Kalamazoo MI; pretaped 25jul67.
26dec67* CBC DE interviewed by Byng Whitteker, CBC Studios, Toronto
...ON; pretaped 2sep64.
10jan68* BBC tc Be My Guest, BBC Studios, London, England; pretaped
...p.feb67.
11jan68 ABC tc Dick Cavett Show, ABC Studios, NYC.
13jan68* NBC tc Today Show, NBC Studuios, NYC.
14jan68* CBS tc Ed Sullivan Show, CBS Studios, NYC.
17jan68* NBC tc Tonight Show, NBC Studios, NYC.
19jan68* WRVR tc Second Sacred Concert, Cathedral of St. John the
...Divine, NYC.
28feb68* NBC tc Tonight Show, NBC Studios, NYC.
4apr68* ? DE interview, unidentified location, NYC.
12apr68 KABC Celebrity Promo, Hollywood CA.
15apr68* ABC tc Joey Bishop Show, ABC Studios, Los Angeles CA;
...pretaped 12apr68.
may68* KYW tc Mike Douglas Show, Studios KYW, Philadelphia PA.
9jun68* WCBS tc A Contemporary Memorial, w. Fr. Norman O'Connor,
...NYC; pretaped 8jun68.
11jun68 ABC tc Dick Cavett Show, ABC Studios, NYC (9:30A).
13jun68* NBC tc Today Show, Rainbow Grill, NYC.
13jun68* WNEW tc Merv Griffin Show, Rainbow Grill, NYC.
19jun68* CBS tc Something About Believing, Cathedral of St. John the
...Divine, NYC; pretaped 19jan68.
15jul68* NBC tc Ella Fitzgerald Show, NBC Studios, Burbank CA;
...pretaped 8-11apr68.
27jul68 NBC tc Tonight Show, NBC Studios, NYC.
28jul68* CBS tc Dial "M" for Music, CBS Studios, NYC; pretaped
...mid.jun68.
8aug68 WOR tc Sound of Youth, Studios WOR, NYC; pretaped 6aug68.
2sep68* ? tc Teatro Municipal, São Paulo, Brazil.
29nov68* CJRT-FM DE and guests, interviewed by Ted O'Reilly, Toronto
...ON; pretaped 25nov68.
5dec68* KYW tc Mike Douglas Show, Studios KYW, Philadelphia PA.
29dec68* KYW tc Mike Douglas Show, Studios KYW, Philadelphia PA.
31dec68* NBC Astrodome, Houston TX.
2jan69* ABC tc Joey Bishop Show, ABC Studios, Los Angeles CA.
6feb69 ? Tom Hallick Show, Sanford FL.
18feb69 KYW Mike Douglas Show, Cypress Gardens FL.
feb69 WLWT Vivienne Della Chiesa Show, Cincinnati OH.

mar69* Dutch TV Sahara Hotel, Las Vegas NV; date of tc is not known.
6apr69* CBS tc Ed Sullivan Show, CBS Studios, NYC.
22apr69 WCAU tc Soul Scene, Philadelphia PA.
26apr69* SR tc 70th Birthday Special: A Celebration of Duke Ellington,
...Stockholm, Sweden.
27apr69* ABC Orchids to the Duke, NYC.
29apr69* NET tc Duke Ellington at the White House, Washington DC.
29apr69* TV Byen tc Birthday Special, Copenhagen, Denmark; includes
...interviews taped in NYC on 1-5sep69.
1may69 CBC Take 30, p. CBC Studios, Toronto ON (no particulars
...available).
31may69* BBC tc DE interviewed by John Dankworth, unidentified
...location, NYC; pretaped dec68.
9jun69* ? DE interview, p. Queen's College, Georgetown, Guiana.
19jun69* KYW tc Mike Douglas Show, Studios KYW, Philadelphia PA.
20jul69* ABC tc Apollo Moon Flight, ABC Studios, NYC; pretaped 15jul69.
24jul69* WNEW tc David Frost Show, Studios WNEW, NYC.
22aug69* ABC tc Dick Cavett Show, ABC Studios, NYC.
30oct69* ? tc Lucerna Hall, Prague, Czechoslovakia; date of tc is not
...known.
2nov69* TV Byen tc Tivoli's Koncertsal, Copenhagen, Denmark; date of tc is
...not known.
6nov69* SR tc Praise God and Dance, Gustav Vasa Kyrkan, Stockholm,
...Sweden; date of tc is not known.
8nov69* ARD tc Philharmonie, Berlin, Germany; date of tc is not known.
16nov69* ORTF tc Second Sacred Concert, Eglise St. Sulpice, Paris,
...France.
20nov69* ORTF tc L'Alcazar, Paris, France.
24nov69* TVE tc Seond Sacred Concert, Basilica Santa Maria del Mar,
...Barcelona, Spain.
p.nov69* ? tc DE, solo piano, unidentified location, Europe.
13jan70* CBS tc Red Skelton Show, TV City, Hollywood CA (8:30-9:30P);
...pretaped 15-17dec69.
13jan70 NBC tc Today Show; pretaped 15dec69.
14jan70* NHK tc Short concert, Tokyo, Japan.
6feb70* ABC DE interviewed by Anne Jefferson and Ellis Blaine, Sydney,
...Australia.
9feb70* NTBC tc DE interviewed by Brian Edwards, Wellington, New
...Zealand.
9feb70* ? Concert, Town Hall, Wellington, New Zealand; two delayed
...broadcasts; dates are not known.
10feb70* ? Concert, Town Hall, Auckland, New Zealand; date of bc is not
...known.
1mar70* CBS tc Ed Sullivan Show, CBS Studios, NYC; pretaped 22feb70.
11mar70* ABC tc Duke Ellington Special, Sydney, Australia; pretaped
...6feb70.
16mar70* CKPC-FM DE interviewed by Alex Reynolds, Royal York Hotel,
...Toronto ON.
17mar70* CJRT-FM DE interviewed by Ted O'Reilly, Royal York Hotel,
...Toronto ON.
mar70* CBC tc Front Page Challenge, CBC Studios, Toronto ON.
30mar70* CJUS-FM DE interview, Saskatoon, SK.
8apr70* CBC tc In the Round, Studios CBUT, Vancouver BC (2:00P).
23apr70* WWL tc DE interviewed by Bill Wilson, Al Hirt's Club, New
...Orleans LA.
3may70* CBC tc The Morning After, CBC Studios, Toronto ON.
8jun70* WNEW tc David Frost Show, NYC; pretaped 19may70,
2jul70* ORTF tc Unidentified program, ORTF Studios, Paris, France. The
...date of the original tc is not known; ?retelevised 7aug73.
26jul70* Radio France Culture, DE interview, Orange, France.
30jul70* CBS tc The Happy Days, TV City, Los Angeles CA; pretaped
...apr70.
6aug70* WNEW tc Merv Griffin Show, Metromedia Studios, NYC
...(syndicated Westinghouse production).
8aug70* NBC Rainbow Grill, NYC.
10aug70* ABC tc Dick Cavett Show, ABC Studios, NYC.
15aug70* CBS Rainbow Grill, NYC.
22aug70* CBS Rainbow Grill, NYC.
29aug70* CBS Rainbow Grill, NYC.
aug70 NBC tc Today Show, NBC Studios, NYC.
20sep70* WPIX tc Time for Joya, NYC; pretaped 30aug70.
12nov70* KFI DE interviewed by Scott Ellsworth, Los Angeles CA.
10dec70* ? United Nations Day; pretaped 24oct70.
31dec70* NBC Caesar's Palace, Las Vegas NV.
2feb71* KYW tc Mike Douglas Show, Studios KYW, Philadelphia PA.

14feb71* WCBS tc Lou Rawls Show, Royal York Hotel, Toronto ON;
...pretaped aug/sep70.
17feb71* ABC tc Dick Cavett Show, ABC Studios, NYC.
2mar71* CBC tc DE interviewed by Elwood Glover, Four Seasons Hotel,
...Toronto ON (12:00N).
ear.mar71* CBC tc Unidentified program, Beverly Hills Motel, Downsview
...ON.
5mar71* CBC tc DE talking about his life and music, Beverly Hills Motel,
...Downsview ON; date of tc is not known.
16mar71* ABC tc Grammy Awards Presentation, Hollywood Palladium, Los
...Angeles CA.
23mar71* ? tc "And Beautiful Too," unidentified location; p. pretaped.
27apr71* RAI tc La Bussola, Forte del Marmi, Italy; pretaped 20jul70.
1jul71 WABC tc Joe Franklin Show, ABC Studios, NYC (10:00A).
4aug71* CBS Rainbow Grill, NYC.
14aug71* CBS Rainbow Grill, NYC.
21aug71* CBS Rainbow Grill, NYC.
23aug71* NBC tc Tonight Show, NBC Studios, NYC.
24aug71* NBC tc Today Show, NBC Studios, NYC.
28aug71* CBS Rainbow Grill, NYC.
1nov71* ? tc Erkel Theatre, Budapest, Hungary; date of tc is not known.
4nov71* ? tc Sala Paltalui, Bucharest, Romania; date of tc is not known.
5nov71* RIAS tc Philharmonie, Berlin, Germany; date of tc is not known.
7nov71* DR tc Two concerts, Copenhagen, Denmark; date of tc is not
...known.
9nov71* SR DE interview, Uppsala, Sweden.
14nov71* BBC tc Omnibus, Hammersmith Odeon, London, England;
...pretaped 21oct71.
14nov71* TVE tc Palau de la Musica Catalana, Barcelona, Spain; date of
...tc is not known.
14dec71* NBC DE interviewed by Pat Collins, NYC.
14dec71* CBS Rainbow Grill, NYC.
dec71* ABC tc Rainbow Grill, NYC.
1jan72* CBS Rainbow Grill, NYC.
7jan72* NHK tc Duke Ellington & His Orchestra, NHK Studios, Tokyo,
...Japan.
9feb72* BBC Conversation with the Duke, DE interviewed by Stanley
...Dance, London, England; pretaped 21oct71.
14may72* ? DE interviewed by Jim Bolen; unidentified location, U.S.A.
8jul72* ABC tc Newport in New York Jazz Festival, Carnegie Hall; taping of
...rehearsal for newscast.
21jul72* WHA/WMVS tc An Inner View with Duke Ellington, Studios WHA,
...Madison WI.
aug72* NBC Monitor, Rainbow Grill, NYC.
1oct72* ABC tc Jazz: The American Art Form, unidentified location, U.S.A.
...(6:00-7:00P); p. pretaped.
3nov72* RD tc DE interview, Malmö, Sweden; pretaped 10nov71.
9nov72 WJR Focus Show, DE interviewed by J.P. McCarthy, Detroit MI.
12nov72 WBTV Lester Strong Show, Charlotte NC (10:30P).
29nov72* NBC tc Timex All Star Swing Festival, Lincoln Center, NYC;
...pretaped 22+23oct72.
nov72* Syndicated tc This is Your Life, Peggy Lee. Hilton Hotel, Las Vegas
...NV.
31dec72* NBC tc Rainbow Grill, NYC.
23jan73* NBC tc Entertainer of the Year Award, Caesar's Palace, Las
...Vegas NV; pretaped 7jan73.
8feb73* ? DE interview, Montego Bay, Jamaica.
11feb73* CBS tc Duke Ellington—We Love You Madly! New Shubert
...Theatre, Los Angeles CA; pretaped 10+11jan73.
24feb73* NBC tc Mike Parkinson Show, BBC Studios, London, England;
...pretaped 5jan73.
mar73* ? DE interviewed by Phil McKellar, Royal York Hotel, Toronto ON.
mar73* CBC DE interviewed by Lorraine Thomson, ?Royal York Hotel,
...Toronto ON.
27mar73* ORTF tc Stephane Grapelli's Birthday Special, ORTF Studios,
...Paris, France; pretaped 4jan73.
6jun73* ORTF tc Michel Legrand Show, ORTF Studios, Paris, France;
...pretaped 3jan73.
8jul73* ? tc Unidentified news program, French Consulate, NYC.
6aug73* NBC tc Today Show, NBC Studios, NYC.
7aug73* ORTF tc Bienvenue à Duke Ellington, ORTF Studios, Paris,
...France; pretaped 4jul70.
11aug73* NBC Rainbow Grill, NYC.
aug73* SR Rainbow Grill, NYC.
p.sep73* Voice of America DE interviewed by Willis Conover, NYC.

28oct73* SR tc Konserthuset, Stockholm, Sweden; date of tc is not known.
oct/nov73* AFN DE interviewed by Chaplain Bill Percy, Berlin, Germany.
2nov73* RIAS Philharmonie, Berlin, Germany.
7nov73* LJ-RTV tc Concert, Ljubljana, Jugoslavia.
11nov73* TVE tc Sacred Concert, Basilica de la Santa del Mar, Barcelona,
...Spain; date of tc is not known.

3dec73* BBC tc Lime Grove Studios, London, England. Taping session;
...date of tc is not known.
1jan74* NBC Rainbow Grill, NYC.
2may99* CBC Centennial Hall, Winnipeg MB; pretaped 25may73.

Entries marked with an asterisk (*) can be found in the *Chronological Section.*

Addenda

DUKE ELLINGTON & HIS ORCHESTRA
WJ RS RN, JN LB JT, BB JH OH BW HC, DE FG JB SG.

....	Clementine
....	Madame Will Drop Her Shawl
....	Jumpin' Punkins

Feb 1941 (P)
Casa Mañana (bc)
Culver City, CA

DUKE ELLINGTON & HIS ORCHESTRA
WJ RS RN, JN LB JT, BB JH OH BW HC, DE FG JB SG.

....	Unidentified title
....	Blue Serge
....	Are You Sticking?
....	Take The "A" Train
....	A Flower Is A Lovesome Thing

Feb 1941 (P)
Casa Mañana (bc)
Culver City, CA

3 Mar 1951 (S)

JOHNNY HODGES & HIS ORCHESTRA

> *BS JMsl replace LL SG.*

....	517-1	Globe Trotter

> *LL SG replace BS JMsl.*

26 Jan 1952 (S)

JOHNNY HODGES & HIS ORCHESTRA

The information for this session was taken from the liner notes for Verve LP's 2356011 and 2304 448. According to the reissue on Classics CD 1389 this session took place in San Francisco on 25 Mar 1952, which seems unlikely on account of the proximity of the master numbers to those of the session on 17 Jan 1952.

28 Jul 1965

Footnote: *Master nos. SRA5-5804 and -5805 were assigned to all individual selections, SRRM-5805 and -5806 to the monaural LP, and SRRM-58-7 and -5808 to the stereo LP. The final selections have no assigned master numbers. LP RCA SP-33 394 and the 3-CD set on Bb 9026-63953-2 include approximately twenty minutes of prerecorded "interviews," in which DE introduces seven of the above selections, see session autumn 1965.*

20 Sep 1965 (S)

Billy Strayhorn's piano part for "Love Came" was prerecorded on 14 Aug 1965.

5 Dec 1965 (S)

The Ellington portion for the telecast of the Bell Telephone Hour was probably prerecorded on 9 Nov 1965.

28 Jul 1966 (P)

ELLA FITZGERALD & THE JIMMY JONES TRIO
Vcl, acc. by JJns JHgh GTt, BCpr (claves), CCrs (maracas).

....	Vrv	Só Danço Samba –vEF

> BCpr, CCrs omitted, CW/CA added.

....	Vrv	Lullaby Of Birdland

First concert: Insert between Let's Do It *and* Sweet Georgia Brown.

Ella Fitzgerald and her combos performed together with the Ellington band on many occasions. Titles which were accompanied by the entire Ellington band—sans Duke—or a small contingent of Ellingtonians are included in the book. Titles performed by EF and her combo exclusively have been left out. Although these performances were always an important part of any concert, they have no place in a book dedicated to the music of Duke Ellington.

29 Jul 1966 (P)

ELLA FITZGERALD & THE ELLINGTON ORCHESTRA
Vcl, acc. by JJns JHgh GTt, and the Ellington orchestra.

....	Vrv	Let's Do It –vEF
....	Vrv	Sweet Georgia Brown –vEF

> Ellington orchestra omitted, add BCpr (claves), CCrs (maracas).

....	Vrv	Só Danço Samba –vEF

First concert: Insert between Mack The Knife *and* Cotton Tail.

<u>DUKE ELLINGTON & HIS ORCHESTRA</u>
CA CW HJns ME, LB BCpr CCrs, JHtn JH RP PG HC, DE JL SWrd, EMrw TWtk JMP Choir tap.

15 Nov 1966 (P)
Temple Emmanuel
Beverly Hills, CA

SACRED CONCERT

> Choir a cappella.

.... Come Sunday –vChoir

> Entire band.

.... Come Sunday
.... Light
.... My Mother, My Father –vJMP
.... Soul Call

> Choir a cappella.

.... I Cried Then I Cried –vChoir
.... Swing Low, Sweet Chariot –vChoir
.... I Feel Like A Motherless Child –vChoir

> Entire band.

.... Tell Me, It's The Truth –vEMrw
.... In The Beginning God –vTWtk Choir
.... New World A-Comin'
.... Will You Be There? –vChoir
.... 99% Won't Do –vJMP Choir
.... Ain't But The One –vJMP Choir
.... Come Sunday –vEMrw
.... The Lord's Prayer –vEMrw
.... Come Sunday –vTWtk
.... David Danced Before The Lord –vChoir, tap

23 Jan 1967 (P)

Le Sucrier Velours, Lotus Blossom and *Meditation* are piano solos. Add RJo for *Second Portrait Of The Lion,* and JL for the other titles of the first set.

1 Feb 1967 (P)

Disregard the 1st concert on 1 Feb 1967. The material originates from the 2nd concert of 31 Jan 1967 and the 2nd concert of 1 Feb 1967. The first concert seems to have gone unrecorded.

10 Feb 1967 (P)

<u>ELLA FITZGERALD & THE ELLINGTON ORCHESTRA</u>
Vcl, acc. by JJns BCrs SWrd, and the Ellington orchestra.

.... The Moment Of Truth –vEF
.... Don't Be That Way –vEF
.... You've Changed –vEF
.... Let's Do It –vEF
.... On The Sunny Side Of The Street –vEF
.... These Boots Are Made For Walkin' –vEF
.... Só Danço Samba –vEF
.... Mack The Knife –vEF

Insert between Things Ain't What They Used To Be *and* Cotton Tail.

26 Mar 1967 (P)

<u>ELLA FITZGERALD & THE ELLINGTON ORCHESTRA</u>
Vcl, acc. by JJns BCrs SWrd, and the Ellington orchestra.

.... Pab Don't Be that Way –vEF
.... Pab You've Changed –vEF
.... Pab Let's Do It –vEF
.... Pab On The Sunny Side Of The Street –vEF

> Only a small contingent of the Ellington orchestra added.

.... Pab Between The Devil And The Deep Blue Sea –vEF

Insert between On The Sunny Side Of The Street *and* Cotton Tail.

Apr-Jun 1969

The motion picture *Change of Mind* for which Duke Ellington wrote and made the soundtrack recordings, is now available on DVD.

24 Jul 1969   (S)

Add to this session, after the interview with David Frost:

DE BTlr WLS, b, dr.

.... Vid   Perdido

Nov 1969   (P)
Unidentified location
Rotterdam, Netherlands

DUKE ELLINGTON & HIS ORCHESTRA
DE BD VG RJo
.... The Lake[1]

[1]Premiere of this part of the future ballet suite *The River,* played as an encore. This seems to be the only surviving part of a concert, which took place prior to the fully recorded concert on 7 Nov 1969, possibly the first concert of the same day.

15 Nov 1970   (P)
Temple Emmanuel
Beverly Hills, CA

DUKE ELLINGTON & HIS ORCHESTRA
CA CW MJsn ME, MTlr BWd CCrs, RP NTrn PG HAsh HC, DE BD JBjm RJo, TWtk ?fem HMC.
SECOND SACRED CONCERT

> DE JBjm.

....   Meditation

> Entire band.

....   Come Sunday –vTWtk
....   The Biggest And Busiest Intersection
....   T.G.T.T. –vfem
....   Don't Get Down On Your Knees –vTWtk

> TWtk HMC a cappella.

....   Father Forgive –vTWtk HMC

> Entire band.

....   Don't Get Down On Your Knees –vTWtk
....   Praise God And Dance –vfem HMC

20 Jan 1972   (P)
Cultural Center
Manila, Philippines

DUKE ELLINGTON WITH THE NATIONAL PHILHARMONIC ORCHESTRA
No particulars available.

....   Blind Bug
....   Stalking Monster
....   Medley[1]

[1]Including: Don't Get Around Much Anymore; Mood Indigo; I'm Beginning to See The Light; Sophisticated Lady; Caravan.

17 Dec 1972   (P)

DUKE ELLINGTON

During the intermission between *Summer Samba* and *Satin Doll,* a brief ceremony took place to bestow on Duke Ellington the honorary citizenship of the city of Baltimore.

ADDITIONAL TITLE VARIANTS AND ALTERNATES

(The) Back Room Romp	- *aka* "The Back Room Stomp."
Drummer's Delight	- *aka* "Jump Barney Jump."
Have A Heart	- Originally titled "What A Man."
Hodge Podge	- Originally titled "Stomp."
Indigo Echoes	- Originally titled "Indigo Echo."
(The) Jeep Is Jumpin'	- The metal part shows two alternate titles: "Krum Elbow"; "Hop, Skip And Jump."
Jeep's Blues	- Originally titled "Johnny's Blues."
Jubilesta	- *aka* "Hey Child."
Just Another Dream	- *aka* "Comme Çi."
Moonlight Fiesta	- *aka* "Swingalero."
Pelican Drag	- *aka* "The Gasser Blues."
Pigeons And Peppers	- *aka* "Piggins & Peppers."
Rexatious	- *aka* "Rexations."
Savoy Strut	- *aka* "Anything You Want."
Sexxitta	- alternate spelling "Sexxita."
That Bach	- *aka* "Phat Bach"; "That Back"; no reliable documentation available.